Sub-State Governance through Territorial Autonomy

Markku Suksi

Sub-State Governance through Territorial Autonomy

A Comparative Study in Constitutional Law of Powers, Procedures and Institutions

Springer

Professor Markku Suksi
Abo Akademi University
Department of Law
Gezeliusgatan 2
20500 Åbo
Finland
msuksi@abo.fi

ISBN 978-3-642-20047-2 e-ISBN 978-3-642-20048-9
DOI 10.1007/978-3-642-20048-9
Springer Heidelberg Dordrecht London New York

Library of Congress Control Number: 2011933721

Cover design: SPi Publisher Services

Printed on acid-free paper

Springer is part of Springer Science+Business Media (www.springer.com)

"Sovereignty, like the atom, can be split."
(Trías Monge 1997, p. 170)

"In modern times, sovereignty is divisible."
(S.M.Z. v. Machano Khamis Ali & 17 Others, Court of Appeal of Tanzania, 2000)

Foreword

Territorial autonomy is an important constitutional phenomenon, but because the sub-state entities that can be identified as territorial autonomies are relatively small, the phenomenon is often overlooked in systematic presentations of constitutional law. This is not to say that treatises of national constitutional law would completely lack information about territorial autonomies, but the internal functioning of sub-state entities, in particular, is not known to a wider audience. Yet at the same time, each sub-state entity operates on the basis of its own constitutional law in the broad sense of the term, whatever the normative nature of that constitutional law might be. Therefore, the inner normative lives of territorial autonomies deserve to be opened up for a systematic review, which is comprehensive and comparative in nature so as to point out similarities and differences between the various sub-state existences.

The similarities may be fewer than the differences, but what is striking in this context is that each of the autonomies included in this inquiry are by and large constructed along common elements, those of the distribution of powers, participation, the executive power, and foreign relations. Incidentally, these elements seem to hold the answer to what it means to be autonomous, that is, what it means not to be an independent state and not a symmetrical part of the governmental structure of the state, but autonomous. Although territorial autonomy may be unknown to the regular constitutional scholar or practitioner, I am convinced that the information contained in this inquiry will be useful for anybody interested in this constitutional phenomenon. At the same time, the inquiry will be interesting and useful for those who deal with sub-state issues, such as law-makers, politicians and civil servants of sub-state entities and of such states in which they exist, because the detailed information and analysis contained in this inquiry may function as a point of reference when, for instance, the development of an existing sub-state entity is planned or when the creation of a new territorial autonomy is on the drawing board. A further purpose of this inquiry is to simply recognize this particular institutional mode of organization.

Autonomy has been on my research agenda since the mid-1990s, and after a number of articles and books about specific issues related to the concept of autonomy, the time was ripe for collecting some of the research strands into a more comprehensive volume. The opportunity to do so was provided by the Academy of Finland, which granted me funding as a so-called Senior Researcher. Obviously, I am very grateful for the grant, which was placed at the Fletcher School of Law and Diplomacy of Tufts University in Massachusetts, USA. At the same time, I am very grateful to my own university, Åbo Akademi University, for the leave of absence during the academic year of 2008–2009, and to Fletcher School for receiving me as a Senior Researcher/Research Professor during that year.

At Fletcher, I wish to thank Professor Hurst Hannum for his kind and collegial support, and Dean Peter Uvin and his academic staff for hosting me in the most pleasant environment. In addition, the Fletcher staff with Celia C., Celia M., Ben, Sandi, Fran and John at the administration and Jeff, Ellen, Miriam, Mariesmith, and Paula at the Library, as well as Giuliana and Linda at the cafeteria and Jane and Lois at the International Centre, deserve warm thanks for all the help and attention, as well as Mr. Risto Vilkko of the Academy of Finland. I also benefited tremendously from the co-operation between Fletcher and the Law School of Harvard University, which gave me access to the excellent collections of Harvard Law Library. I also wish to thank Professor Yash Ghai for his empowering autonomy research and his inspiring example.

During my research, I had the benefit of discussing autonomy-related issues with a great number of persons, around 70 individuals in Puerto Rico, Aceh, Hong Kong, Scotland, Zanzibar and the Åland Islands. They helped me with materials, they functioned as interlocutors concerning particular issues, and they assisted me in all possible ways during my research. It is not possible to mention all of them or to explain what each of them did for my project, but I trust that they will understand how crucial their role was when they see the final product.

In addition, I had the benefit of discussing the various autonomy arrangements with a number of persons and receiving their learned comments, namely Mr. Albeniz Couret-Fuentes, LL.M. (Fletcher), for Puerto Rico, Professor Chris Himsworth for Scotland, Professor Mawardi Ismail for Aceh, Assistant Professor Kelley Loper for Hong Kong, and Mr. Mohamed Hamad, LL.M. (Oslo), for Zanzibar. It should be understood that none of these persons are responsible for any of the faults or omissions that may be attributed to my text, and none of them is responsible for any formulations in the text. However, I am sure that my research would have gone in the wrong direction if it were not for the critical comments of these persons. Obviously, I am solely responsible for what I have written in this inquiry and for how I have analyzed the different sub-state entities, but at the same time, I am deeply grateful to these persons.

At my home base, the Department of Law of Åbo Akademi University in Finland, I wish to thank everybody from this community, and in particular Professor Elina Pirjatanniemi and Ms. Kati Frostell, Lic.Pol.Sc., for their support. I am also grateful to Mrs. Jody Merelle, Mr. Henno Parks and Ms. Darcy Hurford for linguistic editing. Finally, I wish to thank Springer Verlag for accepting my inquiry for publication and Kluwer Law International for giving the permission to use portions of my article on 'Sub-national issues: Local government reform, re-districting, and the Åland Islands in the European Union', published originally in European Public Law 13, pp. 390–404.

The information in the text is good for Puerto Rico as of June 2009, for Hong Kong as of August 2009, for Aceh as of October 2009, for Scotland as of April 2010, for Zanzibar as of October 2010, and for the Åland Islands as of November 2010. Some additions of fact, such as election results, may have taken place after these points of time. The structure of the book is such that it is possible to acquire an overview over the topic of territorial autonomy by means of reading the sections at the end of the different chapters entitled "Reflections" and the concluding chapter. These overviews are based on the more detailed interpretations of the thematic sections. The reader who is interested in a particular autonomy of those included in this study is requested to follow the structure of the book through the various thematic chapters, where each of the six sub-state entities are featured.

I dedicate this book to my family.

In Åbo, Finland, on a beautiful day during the Christmas week of 2010.

Markku Suksi

Contents

List of Abbreviations

AMM	Aceh Monitoring Mission
AMS	Additional Member System
APBA	Aceh income and expenditure budget
APBK	Income and expenditure budget of a *Kapubaten* (district) in Aceh
APEC	Asia-Pacific Economic Community
ASEAN	Association of Southeast Asian Nations
ASP	Afro-Shirazi Party
CALRE	Conférence des assemblées legislatives régionales
CCM	Chama Cha Mapinduzi
CCPR	Covenant on Civil and Political Rights
CE	Chief Executive of Hong Kong
CEDAW	Covenant on the Elimination of Discrimination against Women
CFA	Court of Final Appeal of Hong Kong
CMI	Crisis Management Initiative
CPG	Central People's Government
CSIF	Constituent States in Federations
CUF	Civil United Front
DPD	Regional Representative Council of Indonesia
DPP	Director of Public Prosecution of Zanzibar
DPR	House of Representatives of Indonesia
DPRA	House of Representatives of Aceh
DPRD	Representative bodies of lower administrative levels in Aceh
DPRK	House of representatives of *Kapubaten* (district) in Aceh
EAEC	European Atomic Energy Community
EC	European Community
ECHR	European Convention on Human Rights
ECJ	European Court of Justice
ECSC	European Coal and Steel Community
ECT	European Community Treaty
ECtHR	European Court of Human Rights

EEA	European Economic Area
EEZ	Exclusive Economic Zone
EU	European Union
ExCo	Executive Council of Hong Kong
FC	Functional Constituency in Hong Kong
FPTP	First-Past-The-Post Election
GAM	Gerakan Acheh Merdeka
GATT	General Agreement on Tariffs and Trade
GDP	Gross Domestic Product
HDu	Opinion of the Supreme Court of Finland
HKSAR	Hong Kong Special Administrative Region
ICJ	International Court of Justice
IMO	International Maritime Organisation
IOM	International Organization for Migration
JKU	Economic development force of Zanzibar
JMC	Joint Ministerial Committee
KIP	Aceh election committee
KMKM	Special force for the prevention of smuggling in Zanzibar
KPU	National Elections Commission of Indonesia
LCM	Legislative Consent Motion
LegCo	Legislative Council of Hong Kong
LoGA	Law on the Governing of Aceh
MEP	Member of European Parliament
MMP	Mixed Majority-Proportional Election
MoU	Memorandum of Understanding
MP	Member of Parliament
MPR	People's Consultative Assembly in Indonesia
MPU	Clerics' Deliberation Council
MSP	Member of Scottish Parliament
NAD	Nanggroe Aceh Darussalam
NGO	Non-Governmental Organization
NPC	National People's Congress of China
NPCSC	Standing Committee of the National People's Congress of China
NPP	New Progressive Party
OIC	Organisation of Islamic Conference
PA	Partai Aceh
PCIJ	Permanent Court of International Justice
PDP	Popular Democratic Party
PIP	Puerto Rican Independence Party
PRC	People's Republic of China
RGZ	Revolutionary Government of Zanzibar
SAC	Supreme Administrative Court of Finland
SAR	Special Administrative Region
SMZ	Serikali ya Mapinduzi Zanzibar (Revolutionary Government of Zanzibar)

SNP	Scottish National Party
SNTV	Single Non-Transferable Vote
SoÅ	Statutes of the Åland Islands
SoF	Statutes of Finland
STV	Single Transferable Vote
TANU	Tanganyika African National Union
TEU	Treaty on European Union
TFEU	Treaty on the Functioning of the European Union
UDHR	Universal Declaration of Human Rights
UK	United Kingdom
UN	United Nations
UNDP	United Nations Development Programme
USA	United States of America
VAT	Value Added Tax
WTO	World Trade Organization
ZEC	Zanzibar Electoral Commission
ZNP	Zanzibar Nationalist Party
ZPPP	Zanzibar and Pemba People's Party

List of Figures

List of Tables

List of Cases and Other Interpretations

African Commission on Human and Peoples' Rights

Katangese Peoples' Congress v. Zaire, African Comm. Hum. & Peoples' Rights, Comm. No. 75/92 (not dated), pp. 29–30.

Kevin Mgwanga Gunme et al. v. Cameroon, African Comm. Hum. & Peoples' Rights, Comm. No. 266/03, p. 30.

Court of Appeal of Tanzania

Haji v Nungu and Another, Court of Appeal of Tanzania, [1987] LRC (Const) of 27 September 1986, pp. 206, 346, 349.

Seif Sharif Hamad v. S.M.Z., Court of Appeal of Tanzania, [1998] T.L.R. of 24 February 1993, pp. 194, 205, 208, 349, 351, 643.

S.M.Z. v. Machano Khamis Ali & 17 Others, Court of Appeal of Tanzania at Zanzibar, Criminal Application No. 8 of 2000 on 3 April 2000, pp. 192, 199, 202, 212, 347, 348, 351, 579, 642, 643, 673.

Court of Final Appeal of Hong Kong

Ng Ka Ling and Others v Director of Immigration (1999) 2 HKCFAR 4, p. 231.

Ng Ka Ling & Others v Director of Immigration (No 2) [1999] 1 HKLRD 577, pp. 232, 291.

Hong Kong Special Administrative Region v Ng Kung Siu (1999) 2 HKCFAR 442, pp. 230, 231, 287.

Director of Immigration v Chong Fung Yuen [2001] 2 HKLRD 533, pp. 291, 292.

Gurung Kesh Bahadur v Director of Immigration [2002] 2 HKLRD 775, pp. 230, 231.

Shum Kwok Sher v HKSAR [2002] 2 HKLRD 793, p. 564.

A Solicitor v Law Society of Hong Kong (SJ, intervening) [2004] 1 HKLRD 214, p. 231.

Leung Kwok Hung & Others v HKSAR [2005] 3 HKLRD 164, pp. 230, 231.

C v Director of Immigration, [2008] HKCU 256, p. 614.

Kong Yunming v The Director of Social Welfare [2009] 4 HKLRD 382, p. 231.

European Court of Justice

Case C-42/02 *Diana Elisabeth Lindman*, Judgment (Fifth Chamber) of13 November 2003 (preliminary ruling referred by the Administrative Court of the Åland Islands), p. 600.

C-88/03 *Portuguese Republic* v *Commission of the European Communities*, European Court of Justice (Grand Chamber), Judgment of 6 September 2006, pp. 4, 10.

C-292/03 *Commission of the European Communities* v *Republic of Finland*, Judgment (Fourth Chamber) of 8 July 2004 (the so-called *End-of-life vehicles* case), p. 600.

C-344/03 *Commission of the European Communities* v *Republic of Finland*, Judgment (Second Chamber) of 15 December 2005 (the so-called *Spring hunting* decision), pp. 599, 600.

C-327/04 *Commission of the European Communities* v *Republic of Finland*, Judgment (Fifth Chamber) of 24 February 2005 (the so-called *Equal treatment* case), p. 599.

C-107/05 *Commission of the European Communities* v *Republic of Finland*, Judgment (Fifth Chamber) of12 January 2006 (the so-called *Greenhouse gases* case), p. 599.

C-343/05 *Commission of the European Communities* v *Republic of Finland*, Judgment (Fourth Chamber) of 18 May 2006 (the so-called *Oral tobacco* case), pp. 599, 601–602.

C-152/06 *Commission of the European Communities* v *Republic of Finland*, Judgment (Fourth Chamber) of 26 October 2006 (the so-called *Hazardous electrical equipment* case), p. 599.

C-154/06 *Commission of the European Communities* v *Republic of Finland*, Judgment (Fourth Chamber) of 26 October 2006 (the so-called *Waste electrical equipment* case), p. 599.

C-159/06 *Commission of the European Communities* v *Republic of Finland*, Judgment (Sixth Chamber) of 26 October 2006 (the so-called *Assessment of environmental effects* case), p. 599.

C-428/06 to C-434/06 (joined cases), *Unión General de Trabajadores de La Rioja (UGT-Rioja) and Others* v *Juntas Generales del Territorio Histórico de Vizcaya and Others*, European Court of Justice, (Third Chamber), Judgment of 11 September 2008, pp. 4, 10.

C-428/07 *Mark Horvath* v *Secretary of State for Environment, Food and Rural Affairs*, Judgment of the European Court of Justice (Grand Chamber) of 16 July 2009 (preliminary ruling), p. 10.

European Court of Human Rights

Belgian Linguistics (case "*Relating to Certain Aspects of the Laws on the Use of Languages in Education in Belgium*" *v. Belgium* (merits), application no 1474/62; 1677/62; 1691/62; 1769/63; 1994/63; 2126/64, Judgment of 23 July 1968, Ser. A, No. 6, pp. 153, 519.

Mathieu-Mohin and Clerfayt v. Belgium, Judgment of 2 March 1987, Publications of the European Court of Human Rights, Series A, No. 113, p. 16.

Féderacion Nacionalista Canaria v. Spain, Decision of 7 June 2001, Reports of Judgments and Decisions 1999-VI, p. 16

Santoro v. Italy, Judgment of 1 July 2004, Application No. 36681/96, p. 16

Py v. France, ECtHR, Judgment of 11 January 2005, p. 397

Ekholm v. Finland, Judgment of 24 July 2007, p. 605

European Commission of Human Rights

Timke v. Germany, Decision of 11 September 1985, 82 DR 158, p. 16

High Court of Justiciary

Logan and Other v. Procurator Fiscal, [2008] HCJAC 61, pp. 331, 332.

High Court of Zanzibar

S.M.Z. v. Machano Khamis Ali & 17 Others (High Court of Zanzibar, Session Case No. 17 of 1999), pp. 348, 349, 642.

Seif Sharif Hamad v. S.M.Z., 28 August 1992, criminal sessions case No. 1 of 1991, pp. 194, 205.

International Court of Justice

Accordance with International Law of the Unilateral Declaration of Independence in respect of Kosovo, Advisory Opinion, I.C.J., 22 July 2010, p. 4

Western Sahara, Advisory Opinion, I.C.J. Reports 1975, p. 275

Judicial Committee of the Privy Council

David Shields Montgomery and Andrew Alexander Marshall Coulter v. Her Majesty's Advocate and The Advocate General for Scotland, Judicial Committee of the Privy Council, 19 October 2000, p. 525

Karl Anderson, Alexander Reid and Brian Doherty v. The Scottish Ministers and Advocate General for Scotland, DRA Nos. 9, 10 and 11 of 2000, Judicial Committee of the Privy Council, 15 October 2001, p. 330

Patrick Anthony Flynn, Peter Mitchell Meek, John Gary Nicol and Peter McMurray v. Her Majesty's Advocate, Judicial Committee of the Privy Council, 18 March 2004, p. 330

DS v. Her Majesty's Advocate (Appeal No. 12 of 2006), Judicial Committee of the Privy Council, 22 May 2007, p. 331

David Spiers, Procurator Fiscal v. Kevin Gerald Ruddy (Scotland) and Her Majesty's Advocate General for Scotland, Judicial Committee of the Privy Council, 12 December 2007, pp. 328, 331, 337, 525.

Outer House of the Court of Session

Axa General Insurance Limited and Others v. Scottish Government, [2010] CSOH 2, of 8 January 2010, pp. 326, 327.

Permanent Court of International Justice

Interpretation of the Statute of Memel Territory. Judgment of 11 August 1932, PCIJ, Series A./B.–Fasc. No. 50, pp. 7, 9, 10, 11, 13, 40, 46, 48–80, 81, 142, 277, 499, 511, 570, 575, 607, 609, 610, 619, 620, 622, 626, 632, 638.

Lighthouses of Crete and Samos. Judgment of 8 October 1937, PCIJ, Series A./B.–Fasc. No. 71, p. 47

Standing Committee of the National People's Congress of China

Interpretation of 26 June 1999 by the Standing Committee of the National People's Congress of Articles 22(4) and 24(2)(3) of the Basic Law of the Hong Kong Special Administrative Region of the People's Republic of China, pp. 232, 490.

Interpretation of 6 April 2004 of the NPCSC of art. 7 of Annex I and art. III of Annex II to the Basic Law concerning amendments to the method of selection of the Chief Executive, pp. 228, 480, 491, 493.

Interpretation of 27 April 2005 of the NPCSC of Paragraph 2, Article 53 of the Basic Law of the Hong Kong Special Administrative Region of the People's

Supreme Administrative Court of Finland

Supreme Court of Finland

Supreme Court of Puerto Rico

Supreme Court of the United Kingdom

Supreme Court of the United States

Balzac v. Porto Rico, 258 U.S. 298, 314 (1922), pp. 175, 177, 179.

Puerto Rico v. Shell Co., 302 U.S. 253 (1937), pp. 183, 373, 377.

Calero-Toledo v. Pearson Yacht Leasing Co., 416 U.S. 663 (1974), pp. 175, 375.

Examining Board of Engineers, Architects and Surveyors v. Flores de Otero, 426 U.S. 572 (1976), pp. 175, 373, 374.

Califano v. Torres, 435 U. S. 1 (1978), pp. 175, 377.

Torres v. Puerto Rico, 442 U.S. 465 (1979), pp. 175, 383, 578.

Harris v. Rosario, 446 US 651 (1980) (per curiam), pp. 377, 379.

Posadas de Puerto Rico Associates v. Tourism Co. of P. R., 478 U.S. 328 (1986), p. 175.

Puerto Rico Department of Consumer Affairs v. Isla Petroleum, 485 U.S. 495 (1988), p. 377.

New York v. the United States, 505 U.S. 144 (1992), pp. 379, 572.

El Vocero de Puerto Rico v. Puerto Rico, 508 U.S. 147 (1993), p. 383

Prinz v. United States, 521 U.S. 898 (1997), p. 572.

Small v. United States, 544 U.S. 385 (2005), p. 175.

Other UK Courts

Thoburn v. Sunderland City Council, [2002] EWHC 195 (Admin), p. 650.

Jackson and others (appellants) v. Her Majesty's Attorney General (Respondent), [2005] UKHL 56, [2006], p. 650.

Other US Federal and State Courts

Mora v. Mejias, 206 F. 2d 377, 387 (1st Cir. 1953), p. 375.

Santo v. State, 2 Iowa 164 (1855), p. 178.

Moreno Rios v. United States, 256 F.2d 68, 71 (1st Cir. 1958), pp. 373, 375, 376, 578.

Americana of Puerto Rico, Inc. v. Kaplus, 368 F.2d 431, 435 (3rd Cir. 1966), pp. 373, 374, 375, 577.

Caribtow Corporation v. Occupational Safety and Health Review Commission, 493 F.2d 1064 (1st Cir. 1974), p. 376

Cordova & Simonpietri Insurance Agency Inc. v. Chase Manhattan Bank N.A., 649 F.2d 36 (1981), pp. 184, 373.

United States v. Steele, 685 F. 2d 793, 805 n.7 (3d Cir. 1982), p. 374.

Ramirez v. Puerto Rico Fire Service, 715 F.2d 694, 697 (1st Cir. 1983), p. 374.

United States v. López Andino, 831 F.2d 1164 (1st Circuit, 1987), pp. 184, 378.

United States v. Rafael Sanchez and Luis Sanchez, 992 F.2d 1143 (1993), pp. 182, 183, 378.

Alberto O. Lozada Colon v. U.S. Department of State, 2 F.Supp.2d 43 (D.D.C., 23 April 1998), p. 177.

U.S.I. Properties Corp. v. M.D. Constr. Co., 230 F. 3d 489 (1st Cir. 2000), p. 373

United States v. Acosta-Martinez, 252 F.3d 13, 18 (1st Cir. 2001), pp. 373, 374, 375, 376, 380.

Igartóa de la Rosa v. United States, 417 F.3d 145 (1st Circuit, 3 August 2005), p. 447.

Rosselló-Gonzáales v. The Puerto Rico Electoral Commission, United States Court of Appeals for the 1st Circuit, 04-2611, 28 January 2005 (joined cases), p. 455.

United States v. Marco Laboy-Torres, 3rd Circuit, 29 January 2009, pp. 174, 175, 373, 374.

UN Human Rights Committee

Istvan Matyus v. Slovakia, U.N. Human Rights Committee, Comm. 923/2000, U.N. Doc. CCPR/C/75/D/923/2000, p. 407

Gillot v. France, UN Human Rights Committee, Comm. 932/2000, UN Doc. CCPR/C/75/D/932/2000, p. 397

Chapter 1
Introduction

1.1 Identifying the Sub-State

The way in which to accommodate the interests of a group with those of an entire nation has confounded constitutionalists, constitution-makers, minority rights advocates and also international lawyers for a long time.[1] National government is not necessarily the best or the only level of government where the accommodation of group interests can take place. At the national level, group interests may become overridden by the needs and concerns of the majority, while the capacity at local government level to respond to the needs of the group may be limited, especially in terms of the powers required to bring about the accommodation between the group and the national entity.

Between the national level and the local level, there is a further level of governance, the sub-national level, which holds the potential for the creation of a multitude of different organizational options for taking into account groups of different kinds in the context of entire states or nations. These organizational options include federalism with its "intermediate" state-level entities, normally distributed over the entire sovereign territory, and also a variety of different territorial autonomy arrangements. While there exists a certain theoretical understanding of federalism, there does not seem to be any coherent theory about autonomy. Yet at the same time, both federal solutions and autonomy arrangements are used to accomplish the same thing, to bring about the creation of public authority of a devolved nature for territorially circumscribed entities at the sub-state level. The public authority referred to here is normally the power to make laws, that is, the legislative power or the law-making competence, managed through institutions of self-government.

The above references to 'minority' and 'minorities' does not mean that the sub-national forms of organization would be created solely to address the needs of

[1] For an international perspective to autonomy, see Suksi (2011).

M. Suksi, *Sub-State Governance through Territorial Autonomy*,
DOI 10.1007/978-3-642-20048-9_1, © Springer-Verlag Berlin Heidelberg 2011

minorities that can be described as national or ethnic, linguistic, cultural or religious minorities. Sub-state organization may have aims other than minority protection, such as the general organization of the state,[2] although the consequence of such organization may be the protection of a group that exists in a particular territory of the state. It is nonetheless evident that even the creation of a federation is often necessitated by the wish to take into consideration the varying needs, demands and wishes of different parts of the country, so as to make it easier for the political groups of those parts of the country to join together in a federation for the management of their joint affairs, while at the same time taking care of their own affairs in constituent states at the sub-state level. Therefore, although identity issues are important, once the determination has been made that the recognition of different identities should take on the form of territorial autonomy,[3] the following step is to address constitutional questions about how that identity should manifest itself institutionally and what the mechanisms of governance are that should be created for the self-government of the distinct identity thus bound to a particular territory.[4]

In Europe, the majority of the territorial autonomies exist in states that identify themselves as unitary states. In such states, autonomy arrangements break up the symmetrical constitutional fabric of the state by creating, in most cases, a singular entity vested with particular powers. If states that include one or several

[2]See, e.g., Wheare (1964), p. 38 f., who makes the interesting observation that community of language, race, religion or nationality have not been held to constitute likely essential prerequisites of the desire for union in the federal form. Instead, as he points out on p. 43, the importance of previous models for the creation of federal governments should be recognized. Provided that all situations are unique in one way or another, this may also be relevant to the creation of autonomy solutions. See also Elazar (1987), pp. 232–238, 248, accounting for federal and for some autonomy arrangements that have various minority protection functions. However, in the context of territorial autonomy, Lapidoth (1997), p. 25, is of the opinion that in the majority of cases the resort to autonomy is caused by ethnic tensions, although she admits that other circumstances, such as economic reasons and the internationalization of the issue, may call for the establishment of autonomy.

[3]See, e.g., Wilson and Stapleton (2006a, b). See also Watts (2008), p. xvi, according to whom "explicit recognition of multiple identities and loyalties, and an overarching sense of shared purposes and objectives" are important for federal systems to operate effectively. While this appears correct concerning federations, with regard to autonomy arrangements at sub-state level, however, it is not unusual that there is no overarching sense of shared purposes and objectives. Instead, the opposite may prevail.

[4]As Watts (2008), p. 5, puts it: "The desire for smaller, self-governing political units has arisen from the desire to make governments more responsive to the individual citizen and to give expression to primary group attachments – linguistic and cultural ties, religious connections, historical traditions and social practices – which provide the distinctive basis for a community's sense of identity and yearning for self-determination." See also Watts (2008), p. 165. The maintenance of regional distinctiveness is something that can be done within federal forms of organisation, but even more so by way of using singular autonomy arrangements. In fact, identity preservation appears to be an important factor explaining the creation of autonomies. For a collection of narratives on countries with sub-state entities, see Elazar (1994).

autonomous entities are counted together with the number of federal states,[5] the result at least in Europe is that the "regular" text-book example of state, the entirely monolithic unitary state, finds itself in a minority and is no longer the prime example of a state. Today, the majority of the European states are not based on the model of the clear-cut and symmetrical unitary state.[6] There is therefore no justification for proposing that the creation of an autonomy arrangement or a federal solution for a state is just a stage towards unitary government,[7] quite the contrary; it seems as if the unitary state were undergoing an evolution by way of transfer of its sovereignty and sovereign functions both downward to the sub-state level[8] and upward to the supra-national and international level.[9] As concluded by Elazar, "[t]he existence of more than one government over the same territory is becoming an increasingly common phenomenon", which is a development that "reflects the growing twentieth-century reality of limitations on state sovereignty".[10] This point is sustained by Lapidoth, who writes that sovereignty is not indivisible: "two or more authorities may have either limited or relative, differential or functional sovereignty over certain areas, groups or resources."[11]

Sub-state governance takes place in the context of internal self-determination, a concept which has a connection to the general notion of self-determination as

[5]However, autonomous entities can also exist in federal states. When the symmetrical federal organization is complemented with a singular entity that remains outside of the regular federal organization, it is possible to call that singular entity autonomous. Such is the case, e.g., with Puerto Rico in the US, Jammu and Kashmir in India and Nunavut in Canada.

[6]See also Watts (2008), p. 1, who makes the point that around 25 countries encompassing over 40% of the world's population exhibit the fundamental characteristics of a functioning federation, and p. 4 f.: "There are at present, among the 192 politically sovereign states recognized by the United Nations, 25 that are functioning federations in their character, claim to be federations or exhibit the major characteristics of federations. They contain about two billion people, or 40 percent of the world population, and they encompass 510 constituent or federated units." Hence there are plenty of sub-state forms of governance. For a similar point, see Elazar (1987), pp. 6, 8 f, 226, 259, and Hannum (1996), p. 454 f. On p. 9, Elazar concludes that "although the ideology of the nation-state – a single state embracing a single nation – remains strong, the nation-state itself is rare". On the issue of the nation-state, see also Hannum (1996), pp. 6–10, 23–26, and Kymlicka (2007), p. 61, according to whom in that ideology, the state is implicitly (and sometimes explicitly) seen as the possession of a dominant national group, which used the state to privilege its identity, language, history, culture, literature, myths, religion, and so on, and which defined the state as the expression of its nationhood".

[7]The prognosis of the demise of the federal systems was reported by Wheare (1964), pp. 238, 242, 244, but not really accepted by him, and it was also reported by, e.g., Elazar (1987), pp. 149, 154–157, and not accepted by him (although Elazar seemed to think that Wheare supported such a negative prognosis concerning federations).

[8]For an argument in this vein, see Benedikter (2007), p. 2.

[9]See also Watts (2008), pp. 4 and 7 and Watts (2008), p. 1, who makes the observation that there is a paradigm shift going on "from a world of sovereign nation-states to a world of diminished state sovereignty and increased inter-state linkages of a constitutionally federal character".

[10]Elazar (1987), p. 225.

[11]Lapidoth (1997), p. 46.

a quality of the capacity of a sovereign state to exercise its own and independent legislative powers by way of which the population organized as a state makes decisions about political status and freely pursue economic, social and cultural development.[12] In so far as a part of the entire population can be identified as a people, it may be granted law-making powers, and such power often takes on the form of territorial autonomy.

It may be increasingly difficult to argue in favor of the principle of integrity of national territories and the principle of non-interference in the sovereign matters of a State after the international involvement in and the recent recognition of the controlled independence of Kosovo (whatever that may mean) and after the Russian invasion in the Georgian territories of South-Ossetia and Abchasia. However, the argument in defense of the international order and the United Nations, which goes on to hold that the number of independent States claiming full sovereignty should not be inflated to prevent the international order from becoming unmanageable with numbers of independent States counted perhaps in the thousands, is still at this juncture to be regarded as sound.[13] Therefore, even in the long term, organizational solutions to claims of groups will be sought at the sub-state level.[14] In fact,

[12]The quality of possessing legislative powers in the context of self-determining colonial states as opposed to their colonial possessions is poignantly articulated in Rivera Ramos (2007), p. 193: "While European societies regarded themselves as self-determining subjects (they gave themselves their own law), this quality was denied those subjected to colonial rule." See also Rivera Ramos (2007), p. 230, where he concludes that "[i]n the modern tradition, manifested politically in the ideals of the French and American Revolutions and expressed philosophically by the Kantian notion of moral autonomy, self-determination has principally referred to the capacity of the subject to give himself or herself his or her own norms. This is, in sum, what is meant by the concept of 'self-government'." "In this regard, self-determination extends well beyond the act of choosing among different political status alternatives [in a colonial situation –MS]. It refers to the capacity or, normatively, to the right to continuously adopt, or participate in the production of, the norms that regulate the subject's own life, whether conceived as an individual or as a collective subject. Colonialism entails a denial of this self-governing capacity."

[13]However, the International Court of Justice (ICJ) held in its Advisory Opinion of 22 July 2010 on the *Accordance with International Law of the Unilateral Declaration of Independence in respect of Kosovo* that there is no prohibition in general international law that bars a declaration of independence, nor was the declaration made by Kosovo in violation of S.C.Res. 1244/1999 or the Constitutional Framework developed on the basis of that resolution.

[14]Terminologically, the term 'sub-state' will in this inquiry be preferred to the term 'sub-national', because the research carried out is more focused on institutions, procedures and competences of the intermediate layer of state organisation than on the issue of nationality or ethnicity. A similar use of the term 'sub-state' is found in, e.g., Spiliopoulou Åkermark (1998), Kymlicka (2007) and in Domínguez García (2009). Within European Union (EU) law, the term 'infra-state' is used in some cases of the European Court of Justice, such as C-88/03 *Portuguese Republic* v *Commission of the European Communities*, European Court of Justice (Grand Chamber), Judgment of 6 September 2006 (e.g., paras. 55, 58) and joined cases C-428/06 to C-434/06, *Unión General de Trabajadores de La Rioja (UGT-Rioja) and Others* v *Juntas Generales del Territorio Histórico de Vizcaya and Others*, European Court of Justice, (Third Chamber), Judgment of 11 September 2008 (e.g., paras. 45, 95). The use of the term 'infra-state' would also be possible in our inquiry, but it is perhaps more natural in the EU context to note the position of such entities not only to Member States, but also to the EU as a supra-state entity that places itself between the State level and traditional inter-governmental organisations.

international and national law supports the maintenance of the territorial integrity of sovereign States in spite of the fact that some deviations from that principle have occurred during the first decade of the twenty-first century.[15]

It is more likely than not that internal conflicts between groups will continue to occur for one reason or another. At such moments of conflict, whether violent or non-violent, one inevitable issue to be addressed is the way in which to resolve the conflict and institutionalize the resolution.[16] If organizational solutions are needed, sub-state forms of governance may be involved. Recognizing that there exist no ready-made models that can be slotted into place when needed, it is, however, important to have access to information concerning different sub-state governance arrangements that are already in place so that the most appropriate solution can be created for the country in which the conflict or other need to address group issues is present. The point is that the most salient features of a self-government arrangement should be available in such situations in a form that can support an analytical understanding and discussion of the alternatives of self-government that may be pursued in a conflict situation.[17]

---

[15]See also Lapidoth (1997), p. 47, and Ghai (2000b), p. 16, who says that "[i]t is not surprising that the international community, comprising states, is reluctant to see the dismemberment of states; autonomy seems a suitable compromise". In the British context, Wilson and Stapleton (2006a, b), p. 3, conclude from a sociological point of view that theoretically, "the notion of separate parliaments/assemblies might be expected to intensify feelings of (ethno-)national distinctiveness and/or nationalism, which could ultimately lead to a disintegration of the Union. On the other hand, devolution could work to bolster the Union by providing a space within which different political aspirations can be articulated". Lapidoth (1997), p. 41, makes the point that the central government usually wishes to prevent the regional entity from acquiring sovereignty, apparently a share in the internal sovereignty of the state by means of significant law-making powers, fearing that this will lead to full independence and secession, while the regional group strives for (internal) sovereignty either because of a hidden (or not-so-hidden) wish to eventually gain full independence or to assert its distinct national independence.

[16]See, e.g., Hannum and Babbitt (2006), Benedikter (2009).

[17]For a similar point of view, see Watts (2008), p. 189. See also Wheare (1964), p. 244 f., who concludes in the context of federalism that "[o]ne of the most urgent problems in the world to-day is to preserve diversities either where they are worth preserving for themselves, or where they cannot be eradicated even if they are not desirable, and at the same time to introduce such a measure of unity as will prevent clashes and facilitate co-operation", and Pilkington (2002), p. 15, according to whom "the principal reason for power to be devolved is the need for a unitary state to find the means of evading any threat to its integrity that might be posed by nationalism and separatism; particularly the sort of separatism that is backed by violent action". As pointed out by Ghai (2000b), p. 1, "[o]ne of the most sought after, and resisted, devices for conflict management is autonomy". For a review of theory and examples concerning the use of sub-state arrangements from a conflict resolution point of view, see Weller and Wolff 2005, which contains several cases included in our study, such as the Åland Islands, the Indonesian and Chinese autonomy arrangements, and a continuation of that project from the point of view of asymmetry and conflict-resolution point of view in Weller and Nobbs (2010), which contains analysis of Zanzibar, Hong Kong and Scotland that also are included in our study. See also Navaratna-Bandara (1995), and Sisk (1997), pp. 70–71, where granting of autonomy and creating confederal arrangements are

Having said this, it should also be stated that there is no need to jump straight to sub-state governance in the form of federalism or autonomy arrangements. Instead, it is submitted at the outset that there are a multitude of other mechanisms that may be better suited for resolving a practical problem than sub-state governance of a territorial kind. The observance of general human rights as well as the granting of minority rights guaranteed on an individual basis, functional autonomy and non-territorial cultural autonomy are examples of options which either alone or as two or several of them together may be used to cater for the interests of a group without there being any need to turn to the heaviest mode of organization, that of sub-state governance in territorial entities.[18]

If federalism and especially autonomy are terms with varying and sometimes unclear content, the same is true also for the term 'self-government'. Self-government entails a power to make decisions by a 'self', but how such decisions are to be made is often not clearly spelled out. It is probably possible to agree on at least some features of self-government, such as elections to the highest decision-making body and the existence of an executive for the implementation of the decisions of the central body of self-government, but also other features, such as the mechanism of accountability of the executive body, the relationship of the self-governing entity to the central government of the country, and so forth.

1.2 Identifying Governance and Research Issues

The above references to federalism, autonomy and self-government in the context of the sub-state level have already indicated the approximate area of governance, but the term needs to be broken down in more detail in order to operationalize its contents. From the point of view of law or norms, the intention here is to identify a number of elements which primarily deal with the internal self-governance of entities that are described as states in federations or autonomy arrangements in unitary states. Hence the aim is not to try to specify the concept of good governance, which is rooted in a general development and political science discourse, although

presented as a category of the consociational practices involving territorial divisions of power. See also Hall (1979), for relatively early analyses from a social sciences point of view.

[18]See, e.g., Lapidoth (1997), p. 204, and Buchanan (2006), p. 95, where he holds that "if the case for autonomy is based on the fact that the minority group is oppressed, it would be a mistake to *begin* by promoting autonomy. Instead, the presumption should be that more must be done to protect minorities by respecting their individual rights, including the right to religion, to wear their distinctive cultural dress, and to engage in their cultural rituals and ceremonies, as well as freedom from discrimination and exclusion." A similar point is made in Weller (2010b), p. 306. On the different forms of autonomy, see, e.g., the special edition on the forms of autonomy of the International Journal on Minority and Group Rights 15(2008), edited by André Légaré and Markku Suksi.

many of the elements of good governance (inclusiveness, transparency, etc.) may be relevant for our legally rooted definitions of governance.[19]

The point of departure for our inquiry is constructed on the basis of a legal case that deals with autonomy, the *Interpretation of the Statute of Memel* case, which was resolved by the Permanent Court of International Justice (PCIJ) in 1932.[20] The autonomous territory of Memel, which was part of the Republic of Lithuania between the First and the Second World War, disappeared in the *Maelstrom* of the War. In spite of this, the *Memel* case itself is of relevance, because it raised and – it can be argued – continues to raise legally relevant issues about the internal self-government of an autonomous entity, indeed of any sub-state entity. These issues include the definition of the legislative and administrative powers of the sub-state entity, elections to and dissolution of the highest representative organ, accountability of the executive body of the sub-state entity before the representative body and before national authorities, the relationship of the sub-state entity to the exercise of the foreign powers, and the actual execution of the executive powers of the sub-state entity. In so far as is possible, the inquiry will, in all these contexts, try to indicate in which ways the sub-state entity and the national government interact with each other when the issues that need to be resolved require contacts of some kind.

On the basis of the *Memel* case, it is proposed that these elements, in a somewhat modified form, constitute the so-called *tertium comparationis* for this inquiry, that is, the normative framework that directs our attention towards certain features of existing sub-state arrangements and helps us focus on the most salient features.[21] The modifications that follow are at least to some extent based on a wish to make the terminology used in this inquiry compatible with the terminology of human rights, in so far that it is possible to highlight a connection to human rights.

As concerns the first element, the definition of the legislative and administrative powers of the sub-national entity, a distinction is made between the law-making powers proper held by the legislative body on the one hand and the administrative or regulatory powers held by the executive power on the other. The latter will be commented upon below, but as concerns the former, legislative powers are defined here as the adoption of the law in the formal sense, not in the material sense. Therefore, legislative powers referred to in this context contain those legislative enactments of general application by the sub-state entity that are exclusive in relation to the legislative powers of the national parliament or central legislative body. These powers may be fashioned either as enumerated or residual for either of the law-making bodies.[22] One of the main issues in this inquiry is thus: how are the

---

[19]On good governance, see, e.g., Suksi (2002b), pp. 203–227.

[20]Judgment of 11 August 1932, PCIJ, Series A./B.-Fasc. No. 50, p. 294.

[21]For a similar creation of elements of comparison, but not against the background of the *Memel* case, see Domínguez García (2009), p. 419.

[22]Courts and the judicial powers are not covered to any greater extent, because strictly speaking, they are not a part of governance, although they may have to resolve issues that are caused by

normative powers of the sub-state entities defined and fashioned? In addition, how is competence control between the sub-state entities and the state organized?

As concerns the second element, elections to and dissolution of the representative body in the sub-national entity, we are interested in looking at different forms of participation in the sub-state entities.[23] Primarily, our focus will be on the regular forms of participation in such entities, as identified in art. 25 of the UN Covenant on Civil and Political Rights, namely elections and referendums, although the concept of participation in this provision is very broad. In this respect, it is also interesting to look into the ways in which the population of the sub-national entity is linked to the participatory mechanisms at the national level by means of, e.g., elections and referendums. In this context of participation, it is relevant to inquire into the electoral system, the party structure, and the nature of the referendums and to illustrate these concepts with practical examples.[24] In which ways do individuals living in sub-state entities participate in political life both at the state and the sub-state level, both according to norms and in practice? What is the relationship between participation at the sub-state level and general norms that define participation?

The third element reviewed here is the executive of the sub-state entities, that is, the role and functioning of the governmental organ at the sub-state level. Normally, one main role of such executive bodies would be the implementation of legislative decisions, but an executive body may also have powers of its own and some discretion of its own. In its operations, a sub-state executive body can be expected to be subjected to different forms of accountability, primarily in relation to the

---

governance. Case examples relevant for sub-state governance, however, are used to the extent such cases exist. As concerns the distinctiveness of ethnically based autonomies, Ghai (2000b), p. 11, is of the opinion that the "division of powers is likely to be more focused on cultural matters, like education, religion and arts, and the normal tensions of federalism, like fiscal redistribution or regional influence, take on an ethnic dimension and aggravate them. Distinctions between the private and public spheres may be less sharp than in other types of federations."

[23] As pointed out in Töpperwien (2004), p. 41, from the perspective of minorities, "[t]he new trend toward the self-consciousness of groups can be at least partly explained by the difficulties and legitimacy crises encountered in transition processes that give heightened attractiveness to ethnic and cultural arguments and by the phenomenon normally called globalization or "glocalization" that increases the relevance of the local level and therefore of local groups as well". She continues on p. 42 by stating that more often than not, "these groups want to be recognized as equally state-constituting parts of the population and not as minorities", something that can sometimes be satisfied by autonomy. She also makes the point on p. 46 that participation rights can be foreseen in every governmental institution, that is, within the legislative, executive and judicial branches of government, on every governmental level, that is, on the central government level, sub-state level and local government level. On glocalization, see also Watts (2008), p. 5 f.

[24] When analysing the distinctiveness of ethnically based autonomies, Ghai (2000b), p. 11, makes the observation that the "party structure may be different as there may be no great connection between national parties and regional parties". He also points out on p. 19 that the "question of the role of referenda or plebiscites on autonomy – on which there seems to be no standard practice – is relevant here".

legislature of the sub-state entity,[25] but perhaps also to some extent in relation to the national government. As concerns the practical implementation of sub-state legislation in individual cases, matters that fall into this category include, for instance, appeals procedures for the legal rights of the individual. However, the main question in this context is the following: how is horizontal and vertical accountability organized in connection to the executive of the sub-state entity? More specifically, what is the role of parliamentary accountability, on the one hand, and presidential forms of government, on the other, in the context of sub-state governance?

The fourth element considered here is the relationship of the sub-state entity with the international arena. Normally, a practical connection to international affairs follows from the fact that the legislative powers exercised by the sub-state legislature are touched upon by international treaties entered into by central government. In such situations, it may be essential that the sub-state entity can participate in and affect the treaty negotiations, because the implementation of international commitments of the entire State is also the international responsibility of the State in the autonomous area. However, the needs of a sub-state entity to conduct foreign relations may be even more extensive, and include diplomatic relations of some sort. What is the position of the sub-state entity in the international affairs of the State? What kind of exceptions to their sovereignty are States prepared to accept on behalf of the sub-state entities and what are the problematic areas?

The four elements identified on the basis of the *Memel* case are positioned in the context of conflict resolution and self-determination. What are the particular circumstances leading up to the creation of sub-state autonomies? What is the relevance of conflict resolution in each of the cases reviewed in this inquiry, and how are they affected by the different considerations of self-determination? Because the sub-state level of organization contains different types of entities, it may be difficult to distinguish between the various organizational options. Therefore, with a view to the various elements, it is possible to ask what the difference is between territorial autonomies, on the one hand, and other forms of sub-state organization, such as federalism and decentralization, on the other? Moreover, once a general description of territorial autonomy has been developed, it is important to inquire into the legal and also political nature of the sub-state entities included in this study with a view to establishing how autonomous the entities actually are. What are the similarities and differences between the sub-state entities included in this study, and how do the varying characteristics relate the entities to each other? Is there a core group of territorial autonomies proper and, in addition to them, cases which approach other forms of institutional solutions that can be distinguished from the core of territorial autonomies? What kinds of differences are there in the degree of autonomy of the sub-state entities specifically studied in this inquiry (the Åland Islands, Scotland, Puerto Rico, Hong Kong, Aceh and Zanzibar, as well as the historical example of the Memel Territory)? Although the number of cases is

[25]See also Watts (2008), pp. 24, 27, discussing the models of the executive powers in the constituent states of federations.

limited, it should be possible to extend the general results to such sub-state entities that are not specifically studied here.

It is legitimate to ask whether other sets of criteria exist according to which the point of departure or the *tertium comparationis* for our inquiry could be constructed than the *Memel* case? One possible candidate could be found from the ambit of EU law, where the European Court of Justice (ECJ) has developed a set of criteria for the purposes of determining whether tax decisions made by sub-state entities are selective, in which case they are forbidden under the state aid rules, or non-selective, in which case they are permissible. In a first case, C-88/03 *Portuguese Republic* v *Commission of the European Communities*,[26] the Court found that the Autonomous Region of the Azores was not autonomous enough to qualify for a non-selective and thus permissible state aid scheme. The Court pointed out that "in order that a decision taken in such circumstances can be regarded as having been adopted in the exercise of sufficiently autonomous powers, that decision must, first of all, have been taken by a regional or local authority which has, from a constitutional point of view, a political and administrative status separate from that of the central government. Next, it must have been adopted without the central government being able to directly intervene as regards its content. Finally, the financial consequences of a reduction of the national tax rate for undertakings in the region must not be offset by aid or subsidies from other regions or central government".[27] This set of criteria was refined in a subsequent case (joined cases C-428/06 to C-434/06, *Unión General de Trabajadores de La Rioja (UGT-Rioja) and Others* v *Juntas Generales del Territorio Histórico de Vizcaya and Others*),[28] involving a preliminary ruling to a Spanish court. In this case, the ECJ held that the three criteria comprise of institutional,[29]

[26]European Court of Justice (Grand Chamber), Judgment of 6 September 2006 (action for annulment).

[27]At para. 67. This definition of sufficient autonomy was based on the Opinion of Advocate General Geelhoed, delivered for the resolution of the case on 20 October 2005. In para. 54 of this Opinion, the Advocate General meant by a "truly autonomous" entity one which is institutionally, procedurally and economically autonomous. It seems on the basis of the case that the Azores fulfilled the institutional and procedural criteria, but failed to meet the economic criterion, because Azores did not have "control of both revenue and expenditure", as the matter is defined in joined cases C-428/06 to C-434/06, *Unión General de Trabajadores de La Rioja (UGT-Rioja) and Others* v *Juntas Generales del Territorio Histórico de Vizcaya and Others*, *infra*, note 28, at para. 67.

[28]European Court of Justice (Third Chamber), Judgment of 11 September 2008 (preliminary ruling).

[29]Para. 87: "In that regard, it is apparent from an examination of the Constitution, the Statute of Autonomy and the Economic Agreement that infra-State bodies such as the Historical Territories and the Autonomous Community of the Basque Country, since they have a political and administrative status which is distinct from that of central government, satisfy the institutional autonomy criterion." See also the case of C-428/07 *Mark Horvath* v *Secretary of State for Environment, Food and Rural Affairs*, Judgment of the European Court of Justice (Grand Chamber) of 16 July 2009 (preliminary ruling), in which the ECJ concluded that "[w]here the constitutional system of a Member State provides that devolved administrations are to have legislative competence, the mere

procedural,[30] and economic autonomy,[31] and it concluded that these were to be applied by the relevant national court in the determination of whether the criteria were fulfilled in the Spanish case. It seems on the basis of EU law that the state aid rules distinguish between sub-state entities which are sufficiently autonomous for the purposes of non-selective tax schemes, on the one hand, and not sufficiently autonomous, on the other.

This EU law definition of autonomy is, however, not necessarily a general one for the purposes of all areas of EU law, but could differ in another other area of EU law. At the same time, this EU law definition is geographically limited to the European Union, while the phenomenon of autonomy is a global one. Finally, the definition of sufficient autonomy is a very restrictive one, capable of excluding many such sub-state entities from the core category of sufficient autonomy that are normally considered to be autonomies. Therefore, the *Memel* elements are still to be preferred, in particular as there is a certain overlap between the *Memel* case and the EU law definition of sufficient autonomy, namely in respect of institutional and procedural autonomy (and also in respect of financial and economic autonomy). The EU law definition of sufficient autonomy in the area of state aid rules is, however, important in directing our attention at least to some extent towards the issue of funding of the sub-state entity. The issue of funding is clearly important in this context, although in this inquiry the funding issue is not considered separately, but as a part of the general features that relate to sub-state entities or as a part of the issue of distribution of powers between the national level and the sub-state entity (typically taxation powers), or both.

The crucial issue and the point of departure for the consideration of the position of sub-state entities is thus the possession of law-making powers, and from that consideration, a number of interesting situations relating to the exercise of public powers emerge. Governance is thus here understood as the exercise of public powers within the above-mentioned four elements that can be identified in the *Memel* case against the background of its normative basis. The aim is hence not only to study and compare the black letter law related to the constitutional law of the sub-state entities, but also to try to present the issues from the point of view of

adoption by those administrations of different standards for good agricultural and environmental condition under Article 5 of and Annex IV to Regulation No 1782/2003 does not constitute discrimination contrary to Community law". In the case, certain restrictive provisions were in force in England, but not in Scotland, Wales or Northern Ireland. For an introduction into the constitutional law of the EU, see Rosas and Armati (2010), and pp. 91–96, in particular.

[30]Para. 95: "As is apparent from paragraph 67 of *Portugal* v *Commission*, in order to be adopted in the exercise of powers which are sufficiently autonomous, a decision of an infra-State authority must have been taken without the central government being able directly to intervene as regards its content."

[31]Para. 123: "As is apparent from paragraph 67 of *Portugal* v *Commission*, one condition for an infra-state body to enjoy economic and financial autonomy is that the financial consequences of a reduction of the national tax rate for undertakings in the region must not be offset by aid or subsidies from other regions or central government."

their practical functioning. The objectives of this study are therefore both theoretical and practical: at the same time as we try to define the concept of autonomy and render it some theoretical clarity, it should also be possible to use this study as a guideline in practical situations of, for instance, conflict resolution, when different governance solutions are worked out.

1.3 Method and Materials

The methodological starting point of this research is comparative law, more specifically comparative constitutional law,[32] but in a way which also takes note of such administrative law which may be necessary in the context of governance. In addition, the methodological frames are not only those of law,[33] but an attempt at a certain multi-disciplinarity can probably be discerned on the basis of the inclusion of information that may be of a more politological orientation.[34]

As concerns the comparative method, the underlying idea is to try to carry out a so-called structural comparison, where certain structural elements common to the cases to be compared are studied. At the same time, however, the more traditional

---

[32]When studying formally federal systems, Elazar (1987), pp. 178–179, makes the point that many of the constituent units of other political systems using arrangements that are somewhat similar to federations also have constitutions worthy of investigation, listing, *inter alia*, following as examples of particular interest because of their vitality or historical character: Zanzibar in Tanzania, Puerto Rico in USA, five special regions in Italy, Azores in Portugal, autonomous communities in Spain, Jersey, Guernsey and the Isle of Man as well as Scotland and Wales in the UK and the Åland Islands in Finland. For a comparison of sub-state entities in Portugal, Spain and Italy in a manner similar to ours, see Domínguez García (2009), pp. 419–433.

[33]As concluded by Watts (2008), p. 20, "a merely legalistic study of constitutions will not adequately explain political patterns within federal systems", and this conclusion is relevant also with respect to autonomy arrangements.

[34]The points made by Watts (2008), p. 2, in justifying comparisons concerning federations are relevant also for comparing autonomy arrangements: "Indeed, many problems are common to virtually all federations [and autonomies –MS]. Comparisons may therefore help us in several ways. They may help to identify options that might otherwise be overlooked. They may allow us to foresee more clearly the consequences of particular arrangements advocated. Through identifying similarities and differences they may draw attention to certain features of our own arrangements whose significance might otherwise be underestimated. Furthermore, comparisons may suggest both positive and negative lessons; we can learn not only from the successes but also from the difficulties or failures of other federations [or autonomies] and of the mechanisms and processes they have employed to deal with problems." See also Watts (2008), pp. 189–192. A similar point is made in Blindenbacher and Saunders (2005), p. 4: "Although the circumstances in each federation [and autonomy – MS] are different, many of the problems they face are common to all. The experiences of other federations [and autonomies – MS] allow us to foresee more clearly the likely consequences of various arrangements. Learning comes not only from the successes but also from the difficulties of other federations [and autonomies – MS]." For a summary of conceptual issues related to sub-state organisation from a political science point of view, see Navaratna-Bandara (1995), pp. 20–22, 30–34.

way of carrying out comparative studies, that of functional comparisons, is not set aside. Instead, the structural comparison is, from time to time, returned to the basic question concerning the functionality of the rules that are being compared so as not to lose the focus of the study.[35]

For comparative studies, it is important to identify a so-called *tertium comparationis*, that is, a common framework within which the comparison of legal rules takes place. While the *tertium comparationis* could be constructed entirely on the basis of theoretical notions or some other indicators, this study extracts the terminology needed for the comparison from a legal case, the above-mentioned *Memel* case. The four different elements or areas of comparison identified on the basis of the *Memel* case constitute the platforms that direct our focus to such areas of sub-state governance that are essential for any understanding of how sub-state entities work. Therefore, the first substantive chapter of this study is devoted to an analysis of the *Memel* case and of the Statute of Memel, although the case and the statute are of historical interest only: as explained above, the autonomous territory of Memel ceased to exist before the Second World War. At the same time as questions can be raised concerning the continued validity of the *Memel* case, the example of Memel is nonetheless interesting as a starting point. From a methodological point of view, the Memel example is "frozen" due to the fact that it does not exist anymore, and as a consequence, the normative starting point of the comparison is no longer evolving in any direction.

After the identification of the elements and an analysis of the *Memel* case, the different elements are opened up for discussion in the order presented above. The comparison (and the discussion of the elements) will be carried out in respect of a number of sub-state entities, one of which displays a relationship with a federal structure of government, while others are clearly situated in the constitutional setting of a unitary state. Even in cases where sub-state entities are embedded in a more federal-like structure of government, the aim has been to choose such entities for our study which will display some asymmetrical relationship with the federal arrangement, somewhat similar to the asymmetry introduced by a singular autonomous entity in a unitary state. The reason for the choice of some asymmetrical federated entities is that federalism is already relatively well researched and analyzed, which means that we do not have to devote very much space to an analysis of "regular" federalism. What is more interesting from our perspective is federalism that displays certain asymmetrical features, because such asymmetries constitute "exceptions" or additions to the ordinary symmetrical federations.[36]

Therefore, the core group of sub-state entities included in this study consists of the following: the Åland Islands in Finland, Scotland in the United Kingdom, Puerto Rico in the United States, Zanzibar in Tanzania, Hong Kong in China and

---

[35]Following Elazar (1987), p. 67, it should be recognized that structural approaches have certain limitations, because they may mask the real power relationships surrounding the object of study.

[36]See also Weller and Nobbs (2010), who approach asymmetric autonomy from the point of view of the settlement of ethnic conflicts.

Aceh in Indonesia. These entities, chosen from four different continents, will be studied along each of the elements identified above. By using the example of Memel as a yardstick of some sort and as a given "constant" of a legal definition of territorial autonomy, the intention on the one hand is to provide indications as to how close to or how far away from the historical Memel example these current sub-state entities are in terms of their governance and thus also to indicate how the sub-state entities differ from each other. The other intention is to demonstrate the similarities that exist between sub-state entities (arriving at the same time at conclusion as to differences between them). While this core group of entities is studied along each of the elements, extraneous examples will also be brought in on specific issues, such as Northern Ireland in the United Kingdom, the Faroe Islands and Greenland in Denmark, the Spanish autonomous communities, the Azores and Madeira in Portugal, Gagauzia in Moldova, etc. Such examples, either the ones mentioned or others not mentioned here, all extraneous to the core study, will not be given a full review or consideration within the study, but are instead presented for their special features in relevant places.

However, the number of autonomous territories is far greater than indicated by the above account.[37] Because it is not possible to cover all autonomous territories at a level of sufficient detail, this study relies on a selection of core cases that will in themselves illustrate the various issues related to sub-state governance, complemented by some extraneous illustrations from other autonomous entities.

The positioning of this core group of autonomies may also be illustrated in relation to other territorial jurisdictions that often are called autonomies but which perhaps are not defined with reference to their exclusive law-making powers. When comparing the different autonomy situations, it becomes apparent that the powers granted to autonomies are not of a similar character in terms of extension or substance. The powers do not deal with same material fields, but vary instead from case to case according to the specificities of the aims to be achieved. The creation of the various autonomy arrangements does not, moreover, follow any

[37] At least the following autonomies can be identified: Nakhichevan in Azerbaidzhan, different territories in China labelled as autonomous, among them Hong Kong and Macau, Faroe Islands and Greenland in Denmark, the Åland Islands in Finland, French Polynesia in France, South Ossetia, Abkhasia and Adjara in Georgia (although the position of South Ossetia and Abkhasia is unclear following the Russian recognition of their independence), Mount Athos in Greece (not clearly an autonomy in terms of this study), Aceh, Papua and West Papua in Indonesia, the six traditional autonomous regions, including Trentino-Alto Adige or South Tyrol, in Italy, Rodriguez in Mauritius, Gagauzia in Moldova, North Atlantic Autonomous Region and South Atlantic Autonomous Region in Nicaragua, Azad State of Jammu and Kashmir in Pakistan, Bougainville in Papua New Guinea, Muslim Mindanao in the Philippines, Azores and Madeira in Portugal, various autonomous territories in the Russian Federation, Kosovo (subject to change due to the limited independence in 2008) and Vojvodina in Serbia, Zanzibar in Tanzania, and Northern Ireland and Scotland in the United Kingdom and the Crown Dependencies of Guernsey, Jersey and the Isle of Man. The list could be expanded by including territories which are referred to as autonomies but which do not have law-making powers.

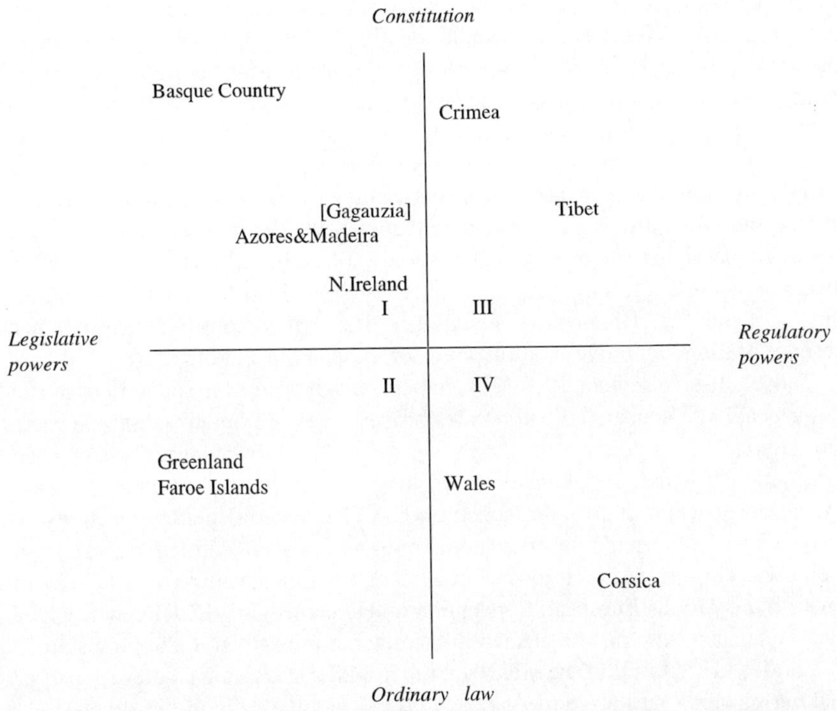

Fig. 1.1 Various autonomy positions I[38]

general pattern and does not display, in all instances, clear features of minority protection. Furthermore, among the national constitutions, it seems that only the Spanish Constitution in its art. 2 sets down autonomy as a constitutional right. The variation in the creation of the autonomies is particularly interesting in respect of the norm-hierarchical level at which any given autonomy is established. The combined (but highly approximate) variation in the powers of a number of autonomies and the norm-hierarchical level of their generic legislation can be illustrated in the following way (see Fig. 1.1 above).

It is possible to conclude on the basis of the chart summarising some key features of certain European autonomies and also autonomies elsewhere in the world that legislative powers and regulatory or administrative competence have,[39] in many

[38]It should be noted that the chart, developed originally as early as the mid-1990s, is of a "work-in-progress" nature, subject to continuous amendment on the basis of information that specify the relative positions of the different autonomy entities in the chart. See, e.g., Suksi (1998a, b), p. 169. As pointed out in Protsyk (2010), p. 232, the de facto position of Gagauzia is far less autonomous than its de jure position.

[39]Exclusive legislative powers are here defined as law-making powers that are of the same normative order as an Act of Parliament, that is, law in the formal sense, while regulatory powers

states, been granted or devolved to so-called sub-national entities. At least a greater part, if not all, of these entities can be identified as autonomies. The competences devolved are, however, not of the same nature and do not normally concern the same substantive areas. Instead, it seems that the competences vary from case to case with a view to the needs that a specific case displays. The creation of individual autonomy arrangements does not perhaps follow any general pattern, and each and every autonomy arrangement is not created in order to establish a minority protection arrangement. It is also important to note that only the Spanish constitution creates a constitutional right to autonomy for territorial entities. In addition, one should also be aware of the difficulties involved in characterising the British sub-national entities in this chart (see Fig. 1.1 above). The absence of a written constitution results in the absence of more definitive fixation points of these entities in the chart.

Those self-governmental arrangements that can be placed in section I of the table can probably be considered autonomies proper. They are organized on the basis of the national constitutions of their respective "mother-countries", and special jurisdictions involving exclusive law-making powers have been created for them against the background of the constitutions. The material fields of activity they possess vary between the different autonomies, but they are entitled to make laws of their own. This brings the European areas clearly within the ambit of Article 3 of the First Protocol to the European Convention on Human Rights (ECHR), which means that the legislatures must be elected in the manner prescribed in the provision.[40]

Entities in section II of the table lack the formal constitutional delegation of law-making powers, but they nevertheless make their own laws in the spheres determined for them in ordinary legislation. From a purely formal point of view they are

---

are decision-making powers of an administrative nature. It may be difficult to determine where the first one transgresses over to the other. However, at least one middle-point can be indicated, namely law in the sense that a norm is sufficiently strong to be used by a court of law as an independent legal basis for a court judgment, such as a conviction in a criminal case. If such is the case, the decision-making powers are not merely administrative in nature, but of a norm-making nature that produces law of a procedurally applicable nature that can exist as an independent basis for making decisions concerning the rights and duties of individuals. Such procedurally applicable law, however, is not necessarily a consequence of exclusive law-making powers, defined in a constitutionally relevant document so as to protect the norm-making powers from being encroached by the national lawmaker. See also Domínguez García (2009), p. 425, who thinks in a similar vein: "Legislative power is the 'hard core' of political autonomy precisely because it allows *autonomy* to be expressed *politically*. The approval of general norms that direct public activity and citizens' lives in a concrete direction (but that could be another) entails the participation of the sub-state entity in a power with a state nature (legislative power) and with a connection to the holder of sovereignty, the people. Conversely, sub-state entities framed in an administrative decentralisation can only carry out state *functions*, since the delegate nature of their activity does not make them participants in any *power* with a connection to the holder of sovereignty."

[40]See, e.g., *Timke v. Germany*, Decision of 11 September 1985, 82 DR 158, by the European Commission of Human Rights and the following cases decided by the European Court of Human Rights: *Santoro v. Italy*, Judgment of 1 July 2004, Application No. 36681/96, *Féderacion Nacionalista Canaria v. Spain*, Decision of 7 June 2001, Reports of Judgments and Decisions 1999-VI, and *Mathieu-Mohin and Clerfayt v. Belgium*, Judgment of 2 March 1987, Publications of the European Court of Human Rights, Series A, No. 113.

not in the category of autonomies in section I, but the powers they exercise and the elevation of their status by way of non-statutory constitutional conventions or by way of customary constitutional law make them, for all practical purposes, autonomies.

Although the entities that can be placed in section III have a certain constitutional basis, their powers are of a non-legislative kind, limited to regulatory or administrative jurisdiction and subordinated to the ordinary legislative powers of the national lawmaker of the country in which they exist. Here the use of the term "autonomy" could be misleading. Section IV represents cases which probably should not be considered autonomies, but rather as regions with self-government of an administrative nature. On the basis of these normative features of a formal nature, it is possible to focus our study mainly on autonomy arrangements which at the outset can be placed in section I of our above chart without, however, excluding any of the other forms of sub-state organisation.

The point of departure is the constitution of the country in question and the autonomy statute(s) of the sub-state entity in question. As a consequence, the study is clearly situated in the area of constitutional law and requires that the relevant legislation is retrieved, including international agreements that may regulate the position of the autonomous entity. At the same time, however, case law that may exist concerning the way in which governance is carried out in the autonomous entity is of relevance, together with any available *travaux preparatoires* of such relevant legislation. In addition, learned writings, such as academic monographs, articles and other pieces, are used to establish the interpretations. Hence the sources of law, arguably presented here in an order of descending legal value, constitute the main sources for this inquiry. It has, however, also been necessary to carry out interviews with key persons to corroborate the interpretations made.

The seven sub-state entities analyzed in this study (the Memel Territory, Puerto Rico, Scotland, the Åland Islands, Hong Kong, Aceh and Zanzibar) might be understood as territorial autonomies. However, the question is how these entities are positioned in the chart and whether all of them can and should, after analyzing them, *inter alia*, in terms of the dimensions of the table, be denoted as territorial autonomies proper. Tentatively, the Åland Islands and Zanzibar could be found in the upper part of section I of the chart, while Hong Kong might be found in the lower part of section I, although relatively far to the left due to the wide legislative powers the entity has. Scotland is likely to be placed in section II. Puerto Rico is in the lower part of the chart, somewhere between sections II and IV, while the approximate position of Aceh is in section IV. The historical starting point of this study, the Memel Territory, should be placed in section I of the chart table.

1.4 Previous Research

Sub-state governance has not been the object of very much academic interest so far, and there is still a need for basic research in the area. Until the end of the 1980s, interest towards sub-state governance was perhaps mainly restricted to those examples of sub-state governance that could be identified as federal arrangements. In 1990, Hurst Hannum published his seminal work entitled *Autonomy, Sovereignty and Self-Determination: the Accommodation of Conflicting Rights*, which opened up the sub-state topic from an international law, human rights law and minority rights perspective. The research work for this piece started in the 1980s, but its publication coincided with major changes in world politics and the collapse of the socialist state structures, the events of which ended the inhibiting effect on constitutional reforms which characterized the frozen landscape of state organization during the Cold War era. Suddenly, minorities became aware of their own existence and of their freedom to voice their demands, including enhanced minority protection by means of, for instance, autonomy arrangements and even independence.

The intention in the current study is not to duplicate Hannum's valuable research, but to approach sub-state issues from a more constitutional and domestic perspective by using the method of comparative law at the same time as this study aims to take a step away from the area of a case study-based presentation of different arrangements to a thematically organized analysis of different arrangements of governance so as to avoid overlap. Certainly, some of the territories included in our study are the same as in the research of Hannum (Hong Kong, the Åland Islands, and Memel), but all of the "old" or then existing autonomies were not included in his research (such as Puerto Rico and Zanzibar) at the same time as new autonomies have emerged (such as Scotland and Aceh). It should also be recognized that Hannum's research contains, on top of the international law perspective, a certain governance perspective,[41] although it is perhaps not the main focus of his research and not systematically expounded in all the cases he reviews. Therefore, at the same time as the importance of Hannum's research is underlined, our study is more focused on certain elements of governance in a systematic and cross-cutting way.[42]

In Ruth Lapidoth's *Autonomy – Flexible Solutions to Ethnic Conflicts* from 1997, the focus is somewhat more on the intra-state constitutional arrangements for autonomies, although the main point of the book is on the different ways to accommodate ethnic differences. In addition to case studies, some of historical interest (*inter alia*, the Memel Territory, autonomies in the Soviet Union and Eritrea), some still currently existing (*inter alia*, the Åland Islands, South Tyrol, the Faroe Islands, Puerto Rico and Greenland), her study also contains dimensions that help in establishing distinctions between autonomy, on the one hand, and federalism and decentralization on the other. Lapidoth is working towards distinguishing autonomy arrangements from federal arrangements, but does not develop

---

[41]See, e.g., Hannum (1996), pp. 130–141, 269–275, 320–322, 371–372, 376–378, 380–382, 385–388, 391–393, 396–399, 402–403, 409–411, 435–438, 466–468.

[42]For a collection of materials, primarily autonomy statutes, which facilitate a comparative constitutional law approach to issues of sub-state governance, see Hannum (1993). A number of the sub-state solutions dealt with in our research (the Memel Territory, the Åland Islands, Eritrea) are also featured in Hannum's collection of documents.

a full-blown juxtaposition between federalism and autonomy arrangements. From the combination of the theoretical distinctions and the case studies, a more practical orientation of her work is derived in the form of issues that should be considered when autonomy is proposed for the resolution of ethnic conflicts. The range of issues is somewhat broader than in the present study, but they contain the institutions of the regime of autonomy, the division of powers (that is, specific areas such as security, foreign relations, economic matters, water and energy, communication and transportation, protection of the environment, matters of culture, social matters, the legal system, powers in financial matters, residual powers), the question of sovereignty, the protection of human rights, participation in the public life of the state, the power to amend the autonomy arrangements, citizenship, preservation of the special character of the area, financing the autonomous entity, dispute settlement, supervision by the center). Although Lapidoth is mainly studying territorial forms of autonomy, she broadens her focus to also include non-territorial and personal forms of autonomy, which are themes not dealt with in our study. She recognizes that minority protection does not necessarily have to involve the creation of territorial autonomy, but that situations of ethnic conflict can also be resolved through arrangements that involve less than territorial autonomy. Again, the purpose of the present study is not to duplicate her research, but to deepen the analysis with more focus on some issues.

The more legally oriented research in autonomy arrangements continued in the 1990s, *inter alia*, by the volume entitled *Autonomy: Applications and Implications*, edited by Markku Suksi. The volume takes conscious steps away from the case-study method towards a study of autonomy from a more general or conceptual point of view. At the same time autonomy is not only defined as territorial autonomy, but understood as a concept that also encompasses other forms of autonomy, such as non-territorial cultural autonomy. The various forms of autonomy are subjected to analysis from the point of view of, *inter alia*, the applicability of the European Convention on Human Rights and international legal remedies on various autonomies, but the issue of autonomy is also studied from a comparative perspective and from the perspective of how the three European organizations, the European Union, the Council of Europe and the Organization of Security and Co-operation in Europe recognize autonomy as a form of institutional organization. A somewhat similar, albeit a more conceptual approach from an explicit minority protection and conflict prevention perspective is present in the volume *Autonomy and Ethnicity*, edited by Yash Ghai, and in the volume *Beyond One-Dimensional State: an Emerging Right to Autonomy?*, edited by Zelim A. Skurbaty.

More recently, research into governance of sub-state entities has been increasing. In an edited volume entitled *Federalism, Subnational Constitutions and Minority Rights* by Tarr, Williams and Marko,[43] the focus is once again more on the protection of minorities than on the mechanisms of governance in sub-state entities, although a number of the chapters in this edited volume make reference to, for instance, the relationship between the executive and the legislative bodies in

[43] Tarr et al. (2004).

sub-state entities.[44] The remark is correctly made that the "federal and state constitutions should be evaluated together, as an interconnected whole", because the "quantity and quality of constitutional interdependence expands and contracts together with subnational constitutional space",[45] and that "[m]uch less common is the view from the subnational, bottom, or peripheral polities – indeed, subnational constitutions have been, and generally remain, low-visibility constitutions",[46] which, of course, is not necessarily the case in respect of the autonomy statutes or constitutional documents of territorial autonomies. At the same time, the contributors conclude – very much in line with our inquiry – that "relatively little research has been undertaken addressing this question",[47] and that there remains relatively little cross-national research on subnational constitutions and on the subnational constitutional space.[48] However, the contributors feel that a variety of possible explanations may be suggested as to why sub-state constitutions look as they do, such as the era in which the sub-state constitutions have been written, the level of ease involved in adopting and amending the sub-state constitution, regional differences reflecting distinctive political or legal traditions and the copying of constitutional provisions from or modeling them on those of other component units within the federal system.[49]

The contributors to the volume raise a number of questions concerning the sub-state constitutions.[50] Although the questions are mainly formulated for the purposes

[44]See, e.g., Tarr et al. (2004), p. 93, Ruiz Vieytez (2004), p. 143 f.

[45]Williams and Tarr (2004), p. 4.

[46]Williams and Tarr (2004), p. 5.

[47]Williams and Tarr (2004), p. 12.

[48]Williams and Tarr (2004), p. 13.

[49]Williams and Tarr (2004), pp. 12–13.

[50]Williams and Tarr (2004), p. 5: "What range of discretion (space) is available to the component units in a federal system in designing their constitutional arrangements, and to what extent have the subnational units occupied the constitutional space permitted them?" Williams and Tarr (2004), p. 13–14: "First, what is the theoretical function of subnational constitutions? Do they limit residual governmental power, or grant enumerated powers? Are there records of the debates on adoption, amendment, and revision of such constitutions? Is there anything in the national constitution that mandates certain provisions or matters be contained in the state constitutions? What is the role of popular sovereignty or constituent power in the process of adopting, amending, and revising the subnational constitution, and does constituent power (initiative, referendum, approval of borrowing, etc.) come into play in the operation of governmental systems under the subnational constitutions? Second, how similar are the subnational constitutions to each other? Is there evidence that provisions in some constitutions have been modelled from others, either within the country or from outside? What have been the processes of evolution of subnational constitutions over the years, both within the subnational polity and, more generally, within each federal system.? Are governmental institutions, rights protections, distribution of powers, and other matters different from or similar to those contained in the national constitution? Is there a standard set of matters and issues – a checklist – that should be dealt with in any subnational constitution? Which governmental institutions provide authoritative interpretation of the subnational constitutions? Is there a subnational judiciary that interprets the subnational constitution, and, if so, can such interpretations be reviewed by the national judiciary? Were there important

of analyses of federal arrangements, many of them are of direct relevance for autonomous territories and their internal self-government. The contributors conclude that these "questions are best addressed from a unit-by-unit, subnational vantage point rather than from the national, top, or center view".[51] Such a method would reveal, *inter alia*, whether or not there exists any sub-state constitution (autonomy statute, charter of self-government, etc.) which is independent from the constitution of the state itself. This is precisely the perspective adopted in our inquiry. When approaching the sub-state constitutions from the sub-state perspective, the analysis requires, according to the contributors, "first and essentially legal assessment of the amount of subnational constitutional space, competency, or autonomy that the component units are allotted within the federal system".[52] Once the scope of the sub-state constitutional space is determined, "the question arises as to how a federal system polices the outer limits of subnational constitution-making space allotted to component units",[53] something that often takes place by means of constitutional courts for the enforcement of attempts by sub-state entities "to over-utilize or expand their subconstitutional space" (as in the Russian Federation, Austria and the United States and Italy),[54] while other systems may use different mechanisms of consultation or negotiation (as in Spain).[55] The contributors think that the "really interesting inquiry is explaining the reasons for the differences among subnational constitutions – that is, why subnational units have made more or less use of the constitutional space available to them".[56]

---

proposals put forward during consideration of subnational constitutions that were not adopted and, if so, were they adopted later? Third, what are the politics of subnational constitutional change? Is the constitution frequently amended or revised, as a normal part of the component unit's politics, or are constitutional politics outside the scope of "normal politics"? Fourth, how have the federal system's origins as integrative (leaving subnational constitutional space) or as devolutionary (creating subnational constitutional space) affected such issues as whether the component units' constitutions primarily limit or grant power? Have pre-existing subnational constitutions served as models or provided experience for drafting the national constitution or for other, more recently admitted or created component units?"

[51] Williams and Tarr (2004), p. 5.

[52] Williams and Tarr (2004), p. 6.

[53] Williams and Tarr (2004), p. 7.

[54] Williams and Tarr (2004), p. 8.

[55] Williams and Tarr (2004), p. 10.

[56] See Williams and Tarr (2004), pp. 8, 9, 11, 15: "One way to minimize conflict between national and subnational constitutions is for the national constitution to give the national government some control over the content of subnational constitutions at the time they are being created." "In the United States, for example, once a state is admitted, Congress no longer has authority over the content of its constitution, even if subsequent constitutional changes introduce departures from the principles that governed it initially. In contrast, South Africa has established a continuing judicial scrutiny of constitutions and constitutional changes before they take effect." "[U]nder the so-called Supremacy Clause of the U.S. Constitution, national law is superior to state law, so that in cases of conflict, valid national enactments – be they constitutional provisions, statutes, or administrative regulations – prevail over state constitutional provisions. This, of course, limits subnational constitutional space. This has led state constitution-makers to seek to avoid such

The contributors suggest that the subnational units they are reviewing in the federal context more often under-utilize their constitution-making competency than they over-utilize it. "If correct, this tentative finding about the tendency of subnational units to underutilize even legally available subnational constitutional space within federal systems has important implications. The development or reawakening of political awareness and regional identity among previously politically powerless and unorganized peoples in various countries has increased the urgency of finding mechanisms for according these peoples recognition and opportunities for self-government. The creation of separate countries for these peoples is typically not an option. Neither is secession; the Ethiopian national constitution is the only one recognizing a right of secession by subnational units. However, these groups may find greater opportunities for political success at the subnational rather than the national level in federal systems, and the allocation of power to subnational units, including the power to determine their own constitutional arrangements, might provide a form of self-determination that can serve as an alternative to illegal movements for secession."[57]

In his review *The World's Working Regional Autonomies: an Introduction and Comparative Analysis*, Thomas Benedikter approaches territorial autonomies from the point of conflict resolution, primarily in a minority rights as well as a self-determination context. The research issues presented in the introduction indicate clearly that the work is in the area of social sciences, not law, and in the main bulk of the inquiry, each of the altogether 25 different autonomy arrangements introduced as case studies raise a multitude of different perspectives. The case studies are selected from among a total of 60 autonomous entities, and it appears that Benedikter's definition of autonomy is in practice overlapping with our definition of territorial autonomy, at least as regards the entities included in his study, because such entities as the Spanish autonomies and also Aceh are included among the autonomies he is studying. At the same time he makes the point that regional autonomy should not be confused with federalism. In fact, all the seven autonomous territories included in our study are also part of his study. According to Benedikter, genuine autonomy systems can be classified with reference to five criteria: democracy, a minimum of legislative and executive powers, stability and rule of law, *de jure* and *de facto* autonomy (applied autonomy), and equality of civil rights and general citizenship rights (with exceptions). In principle, it would be possible to think that his methodology is inductive, leading to generalizations on the basis of

conflicts, even if that has meant forgoing provisions they would have wished to adopt." "The constitution of the Russian Federation, for example, authorizes the president of the Federation to suspend the acts of subnational executives if he believes them to be in violation of the federal law or human rights. The Justice Ministry also has the power to revoke regional laws that are in violation of the Federation Constitution and, as of early 1998, it had used that power to revoke nearly 2000 regional laws." Concerning the latitude for the sub-state entities in federations to determine the internal features of sub-state entities, see also Tarr (2005), p. 8 f.

[57]Williams and Tarr (2004), p. 15. However, the Constitution of Saint Kitts and Nevis also recognises the possibility of secession.

the case studies, but the language which he uses in his inquiry even prior to the case studies is quite prescriptive or normative, proposing different best practices, perhaps from a deductive point of view.

The study of Benedikter is very comprehensive, but does not necessarily go into great depth. It gives a good overall picture of how territorial autonomies tend to be organized, and it has an affinity to our inquiry because it not only identifies a number of similar elements as used in our inquiry but it also carries out a functional study of the autonomies along these elements in the final chapter of the book. The functional study is not very long, but it proceeds along such elements as political representation, the scope of the autonomy, entrenchment and revision mechanisms, financial regulations and forms of control of the economic resources, provisions for regional citizenship, international relations, language rights and protection of ethnic identity and minority rights, consociational structures of internal power-sharing, and settlement of disputes. Consequently, although the research itself is not of a legal nature, the comparison carried out along functional elements comes close to the research issues of our inquiry. Benedikter's study is very interesting from our point of view and certainly a step in the direction of an organic theory of political autonomy, which he feels is a project that should be undertaken.[58] It is submitted here that our inquiry will hopefully be another step in that direction.

As a piece of research which is more oriented towards federalism as a form of organization, *Comparing Federal Systems* by Ronald L. Watts nonetheless contains dimensions which makes it possible to explore the interface between federalism, on the one hand, and autonomy, on the other, at the same time as he finds explanations for the emergence of federations (by "coming together" and by "devolution").[59] Watts uses a relatively flexible notion of federalism that involves two (or even more) "levels of government thus combining elements of shared-rule (collaborative partnership) through a common government and regional self-rule (constituent unit autonomy) for the governments of the constituent units".[60] The resulting spectrum of organizational options range from quasi-federations and federations to confederations and beyond in a way which does not establish sharp border-lines between the categories but make it possible to move in a smooth manner from one category to another. In that spectrum, following Elazar,[61] he also includes a category which he calls federacies, meaning "political arrangements where a smaller unit or units are linked to a larger polity, but the smaller unit or units retain considerable autonomy, have a minimum role in the government of the larger one, and the relationship can be dissolved only by mutual agreement".[62] In the category of federacies, he places the Faroe Islands and Greenland in Denmark, the Åland

[58] Benedikter (2007), p. 4.

[59] Watts (2008), pp. 63–70.

[60] Watts 2008, p. 8. See also Watts 2008, p. 191.

[61] Watts (2008), pp. 8, 10. Watts makes the point that Elazar actually has coined the term 'federacy'. See also Elazar (1987), pp. 54–57, 60.

[62] Watts (2008), p. 10.

Islands in Finland, Jammu and Kashmir in India, Azores and Madeira in Portugal, Guernsey, Jersey and the Isle of Man in the United Kingdom as well as the Northern Marianas and Puerto Rico in the United States.[63]

While Watts does not include these singular entities of unitary states in his actual comparison of federations, it is interesting that he nonetheless wants to assign a descriptive term to them which implies an affinity to federal forms of organization. However, with the possible exception of Jammu and Kashmir, which has a particular position in the federation of India, and Puerto Rico, which has a non-federal relationship to the United States of America, these entities are normally considered autonomies proper in unitary states. In addition, Watts moves the autonomies of Spain from this group of autonomies proper and places the Kingdom of Spain as a state among federations,[64] although Spanish authors tend to disagree on this.[65] Both determinations of Watts may be problematic, because they create the feeling that the category of federations (or federal-type forms of state organization) is being inflated with cases so as to facilitate a clearer case concerning federations.[66] The consequence of expanding the coverage of the research Watts is carrying out in the direction of autonomy arrangements is perhaps no greater clarity in the end. In our research, the aim is to design characteristics that are at least marginally more stringent so as to facilitate categorizations, while at the same time recognizing the existence of the phenomenon on a gliding scale when analyzing different organizational arrangements at the sub-state level. The research of Watts is, however, highly interesting from the point of view of autonomy arrangements as a form of sub-state organization, because he deals from a comparative perspective with similar issues as does our research. Those issues include the constituent units, the distribution of competence, asymmetrical forms of sub-state organization, mechanisms of representation, constitutional supremacy, degrees of decentralization and centralization, and finances. Therefore, in some sense, the research of Watts concerning federal systems could be regarded as parallel to our research concerning autonomy as a form of sub-state governance.

Approaching sub-state governance from the perspective of multiculturalism, Will Kymlicka presents arguments for minority protection from a philosophical point of view, adopting a liberal perspective in his *Multicultural Odysseys – Navigating the New International Politics of Diversity*.[67] The argument is not

[63]Watts (2008), p. 17.

[64]Watts (2008), pp. 4, 8, 10, 13, 17, 18, 21, 25, 27, 41–42. On pp. 41–42, Watts places Spain among emergent federations, and on pp. 4 and 42, Watts concludes that Spain has, in practice, increasingly become a federation in all but name.

[65]See, e.g., Ruiz Vieytez (2004), p. 135 f.: "The Spanish model should not be confused with a federal system, given the existence of a single Constitutional Law and Sovereignty covering the whole of the country."

[66]However, such a broad notion of federal arrangements is not an invention of Watts, but was the approach of Elazar already in the 1980s.

[67]See Kymlicka (2007), *passim*.

limited to sub-state governance of the institutional kind as explored in our research, but different autonomy solutions constitute an important part of the argument, because they can be seen as vehicle for countering the ideology of the nation-state. However, at the same time, there may exist a risk that a sub-state entity behaves in a nationalistic and non-liberal manner towards the minorities that perhaps exist within its boundaries, thereby countering the liberal multiculturalism displayed at the state level.[68] Kymlicka holds that such a risk is not evident in the Western applications of sub-state governance[69] and that they may start to amount to a minority protection standard that can be labeled internal autonomy or internal self-determination as an extension of the people's general right to self-determination.[70] Kymlicka concludes that "multilingual multination federalism gives a very high level of public recognition to the minority's culture, at least at the regional level" in situations where there is a wish to remedy earlier exclusions of the minority's language from public space and public institutions.[71] Although sub-state governance as a model of minority protection and conflict resolution is not directly mandated by any of the binding sets of international norms,[72] inter-governmental organizations have regularly advocated the use of sub-state governance for such purposes, because there seems to exist evidence about its beneficial effects.[73] From our perspective, it is more important that multination federalism, as Kymlicka occasionally calls sub-state governance, also involves a "substantial redistribution of political power, and hence increased opportunities for effective political participation by national minorities" as well as "redistribution of economic opportunities".[74] With a view to Abchasia and South Ossetia in Georgia, Transdnistria in Moldova, Nagorno-Karabakh in Azerbaijan, the cantons in Bosnia, the offer of autonomy to Kosovo in Serbia (which is now passé) and Northern Cyprus in

[68]Kymlicka (2007), p. 182, offering as examples Abchasia in Georgia, Slavonia in Croatia and Kosovo in Serbia. However, Kymlicka (2007), p. 239, also makes the point that groups of persons circumscribed by reference to an ethnically or linguistically determined ideology are not internally homogeneous. According to Kymlicka (2007), p. 254, such situations dramatically increase risks associated with adopting territorial autonomy: "There are fewer guarantees that minorities who receive autonomy will exercise their powers in a way that respects human rights. They may instead use their powers to create islands of local tyranny, establishing authoritarian regimes based on religious fundamentalism or ethnic intolerance. This can be a threat to the human rights of individuals both inside and outside the minority group."

[69]Kymlicka (2007), p. 146.

[70]Kymlicka (2007), p. 205 f.

[71]Kymlicka (2007), p. 141.

[72]The situation has changed somewhat after the adoption of the United Nations Declaration on the Rights of Indigenous Peoples (GA Res. 61/295 on 13 September 2007).

[73]Kymlicka (2007), pp. 233–246, 292. See also Buchanan (2006), pp. 92–92, who clarifies what it means to say that the international legal order should support intrastate autonomy and seeks to answer the question of what the conditions are under which the international community should involve itself in the creation, maintenance, or restoration of intrastate autonomy regimes.

[74]Kymlicka (2007), p. 141.

Cyprus, Kymlicka holds that the states have "lost control over territory to rebellious minorities" and that the states "have been willing to discuss various models of autonomy or federalism, when that was seen as the only alternative to accepting secession".[75] At the same time, the effective participation of minorities has emerged as a result.[76] Autonomy is for him an effective tool for protecting minorities against the clear and present danger that a dominant majority will use its control of the state to assimilate or exclude minorities.[77]

In *Asymmetric Autonomy and the Settlement of Ethnic Conflicts*, edited by Marc Weller and Katherine Nobbs,[78] a number of issues are raised that are touched upon also in our inquiry. Firstly, the piece identifies the category of mono-dimensional settlement as one where "autonomy is simply granted without much consideration of governance within the newly autonomous units, of its relations with the center, or of the way the remaining powers of the center are to be exercised with respect to the unit".[79] Different problems may follow from such a grant of autonomy, such as insufficient involvement of the autonomous entity in the overall state or vice versa, loosely defined competences, competences assigned unrealistically to the autonomous entity, minority in minority constellations, and implementation of human rights. A number of elements that would need to be present in an entity that is designated as a territorial autonomy are identified, such as demographic distinctiveness, devolution as opposed to decentralization, legal entrenchment, legal supremacy, statute-making powers, significant competences, parallel action, limited external relations powers, law-making, executive and judicial institutions, and integrative mechanisms.[80] The point is made that asymmetrical state-building is a feature of the ongoing second wave of post-Cold War settlements to secessionist conflicts,[81] and that a *de jure* approach of the research into such asymmetrical arrangements offers great clarity, because the "existence or extent of asymmetry can be immediately identified through a study of the formal constitutional and legislative instruments establishing the state",[82] although the more political and administrative realities of autonomy arrangements should be taken into account, too.

There exist also a number of examples of international territorial administration, that is, instances where the international community has, in one way or another, separated a certain piece of territory from the original state territory and placed it

---

[75]Kymlicka (2007), pp. 179–180, 234. Kymlicka (2007), p. 237, also makes the point that "it may indeed be correct that granting territorial autonomy to a law-abiding minority increases tensions; while supporting territorial autonomy after it has been seized by a belligerent minority decreases tensions". See also Kymlicka (2007), p. 243.

[76]Kymlicka (2007), p. 241 f.

[77]Kymlicka (2007), p. 263.

[78]See Weller and Nobbs (2010).

[79]Weller (2010a), p. 2.

[80]Weller (2010a), pp. 4–5.

[81]Weller (2010a), p. 7.

[82]Weller (2010a), p. 8.

under international administration as a temporary measure. It could be argued that the Memel Territory was such a territory while it was still administered by France on behalf of the League of Nations and before it was made a territorial autonomy in Lithuania under the Memel Convention. The analysis of Michaela Salamun entitled *Democratic Governance in International Territorial Administration - institutional prerequisites for democratic governance in the constitutional documents of territories administered by international organisations* does not include Memel, but covers instead a number of other international territorial administrations, that is, the Free City of Danzig, the Saar Territory, the Territory of Leticia, the City of Jerusalem, the Free Territory of Trieste, Congo, West Irian, South West Africa/ Namibia, Cambodia, Somalia, Eastern Slavonia, Bosnia and Herzegovina, the City of Mostar, the District of Brcko, East Timor and Kosovo (which is still relevant due to the controlled independence established in the 2008 Constitution of Kosovo). All these international territorial administrations have been created in response to conflict situations. Her approach is legal, with an analysis of the relevant formative or constitutive documents, as concerns the separation of powers, the independence of the judiciary, the principle of popular sovereignty, mechanisms of accountability and judicial review of the executive branch of government, the review of the constitutionality of legislative acts as well as political rights and special participation rights of minorities. Salamun's research comes close to our inquiry by focusing on territories and the specific arrangements for special territories, but it employs a broader scope of elements at the same time as it does not reach very far beyond the "law in books". The issues and concerns raised are, however, similar to the ones dealt with in this inquiry, and the piece may well be understood as a parallel inquiry to ours.

Academic work on territorial autonomy is to a great extent carried out at the national or even at the sub-state level. There is governance related research in virtually all Spanish autonomous communities and also in many of the Italian regions, and the research into the government of Scotland has increased very much during the last few years due to the autonomy created for that part of the United Kingdom (UK). Research with a view to sub-state entities has been carried out by, for instance, Joseph Marko,[83] Yash Ghai,[84] Chris Himsworth,[85] Vernon Bogdanor,[86] and a number of other authors featured in this study. To some extent, this more recent research has adopted a focus which covers governance in a more systematic way than the earlier research.

---

[83]Marko (1995).

[84]Ghai (1999). We will reconnect to the important synthetic analysis presented in Ghai (2000b) in section 9.6 below.

[85]Himsworth and Munro (2000).

[86]Bogdanor (1999).

1.5 Description of the Sub-State Entities Included in the Study as Core Cases

The entities included in our research are, at the outset, predominantly singular entities that can be presumed to be autonomous territories. In principle, sub-state forms of organisation of a federal kind are neutral from the point of view of minorities of all kinds, ethnic, linguistic and religious, although there exist federations where the federal structure is influenced by the wish to cater for the position of minorities. Conversely, there also exist territorial autonomies which are not created for minorities, but where the existence of autonomy is based on other considerations, such as geographical distance. Both approaches are featured in this inquiry: the sub-state entities included here are in many cases premised on the basis of the distinctive features of a population group, but in a few cases, the minority concerns are not predominant in explaining why the autonomy solution was adopted.

Sometimes it is proposed that autonomy (and federalism, for that matter) is a sustainable form of organisation mainly for states which are already developed and which do not suffer from the weaknesses that can be found in many developing states. The autonomous territories included in this study are, nonetheless, found in different continents around the world, that is, in Europe, the Americas, in Asia and in Africa, in a deliberate attempt to make the point that sub-state forms of organisation are not confined to those parts of the world that can "afford" such organisational solutions. Sub-state forms of organisations are not only available in Europe, but also elsewhere in the world.

Sub-state arrangements that take on the form of territorial autonomy or federal solutions are in many ways a Western phenomenon. As pointed out by Kymlicka in a context of territorially concentrated national minorities, "[a]ll groups over 250,000 that have demonstrated a desire for territorial autonomy now have it in the West, as well as many smaller groups (such as the German minority in Belgium)".[87] However, he also points at reasons that decrease the existence of sub-state governance outside Europe. According to Kymlicka, expectations of a certain type of behaviour by the sub-state entities in the West seem to be fulfilled: "For one thing, all of these substate autonomies operate within the constraints of liberal-democratic constitutionalism, which firmly upholds individual rights. They are subject to the same constitutional constraints as the central government, and so have no capacity to restrict individual freedoms in the name of maintaining cultural authenticity or cultural purity. In fact, these substate autonomous governments typically show no wish to adopt such a conservative approach to their culture."[88] At the same time, "no Western democracy that has adopted territorial autonomy for

[87]Kymlicka (2007), p. 69 f.

[88]Kymlicka (2007), p. 144.

its homeland minorities has reversed this decision".[89] In Latin America, indigenous populations have, in fact, been able to secure some autonomy for themselves. In contrast, Africa, Asia and Middle East are identified by Kymlicka as areas that remain interested in the centralisation of states: "Claims for minority autonomy remain off-limits. Any forms of minority autonomy that predated independence have typically been abolished, and any promises to establish autonomies that were made in the process of achieving independence have often been broken. In those few states where some form of territorial autonomy now exists (or is under negotiation), this has typically been the outcome of violent struggle and civil war, and has often been adopted under international pressure (e.g. in Sudan, Indonesia, Sri Lanka, Burma, Philippines, Ethiopia, Iraq, etc.). India is perhaps the only state in Asia, Africa, or the Middle East to have voluntarily and peacefully adopted forms of territorial autonomy for its homeland minorities."[90]

However, the claim of autonomy is not necessarily off-limits in Asia or Africa. The examples of Hong Kong and Macau in China prove that substantial differences, although not of a linguistic or ethnic nature, can be accommodated within an Asian state structure. In fact, mainland China is to a great extent affected by some forms of sub-state governance, although admittedly of a kind which incorporates them in the authoritarian structures of the state, leaving perhaps little or no space for autonomy in the meaning of this piece of research or in the meaning of autonomy as practiced in Hong Kong and Macau. A recent addition to the practice of sub-state governance is Aceh in Indonesia, where a domestic resolution was reached after some private international involvement helped identify common ground.

In a unique resolution of the African Commission on Human and Peoples' Rights, sub-state governance was recommended instead of secession for independence. The pessimistic assessment by Kymlicka can therefore also be qualified as concerns Africa. In the case of *Katangese Peoples' Congress v. Zaire*,[91] such a solution was based in regional international law in Africa, in particular the African Charter on Human and Peoples' Rights. The African Commission held, on the basis of Article 20 of the African Charter on Human and Peoples' Rights, that no such violations of

---

[89]Kymlicka (2007), p. 177 f.

[90]Kymlicka (2007), p. 251. In footnote 7 on p. 251, Kymlicka presents the following examples where promises of autonomy were made but perhaps not fulfilled: Baluchistan in Pakistan, Arakan and Kachinland in Burma, South Moluccas in Indonesia, East Turkestan in China, Bougainville in Papua-New Guinea, Eritrea in Ethiopia, Bioko in Equatorial Guinea, Nkole, Bunyoro and Buganda in Uganda, Ashanti in Ghana, Bamileke in Cameroon, the Druze in Syria and the Berbers in Morocco (Riffians) and Algeria (Kabyles). See also Weller (2010a), who makes the point that while "autonomy has been studied to a considerable extent in relation to Europe, there is a dearth of scholarship addressing cases in Africa".

[91]African Comm. Hum. & Peoples' Rights, Comm. No. 75/92 (not dated). In the communication involving a claim of denial of self-determination, probably in practice to a great extent propelled by the issue of who was to control the natural resources of Katanga, the president of the Katangese Peoples' Congress requested the African Commission on Human and Peoples' Rights to recognise, *inter alia*, the independence of Katanga under Article 20(1) of the African Charter on Human and Peoples' Rights.

human rights had taken place in relation to Katanga that it would be justified, under the right of self-determination, to disturb the territorial integrity and sovereignty of Zaire. Instead, the region of Katanga should look for internal constitutional solutions to satisfy its needs in the political sphere. The African Commission started by concluding that all peoples have a right to self-determination, but that there may be controversy as to the definition of peoples and the content of such a right. It also concluded that the issue in this case is not self-determination for all Zaireoise as a people, but specifically self-determination for the Katangese. The African Commission held that it was not relevant in this context whether the Katangese consist of one or more ethnic groups. It also held that there is no evidence that the people of Katanga would have been denied the right to participate in government as guaranteed by Article 13(1) of the African Charter, nor concrete evidence of violations of human rights to the point that the territorial integrity of Zaire should be called into question. Gross violations of the rights of the Katangese could perhaps have resulted in such doubt, but this was not the claim. Against this background, the African Commission reached the conclusion that Katanga is obliged to exercise a variant of self-determination that is compatible with the sovereignty and territorial integrity of Zaire. Therefore, the wish of Katanga to gain independence had no merit under the African Charter.

What is interesting is that the decision of the African Commission did not only state the existence of the two extremes, the self-determination of Zaire and the possibility of independence. In rejecting the communication, the African Commission held that self-determination can be exercised in any of the following ways: "independence, selfgovernment, local government, federalism, confederalism, unitarism or any other form of relations that accords with the wishes of the people but fully cognisant of other recognised principles such as sovereignty and territorial integrity." Evidently, there are sub-state forms of self-determination which can be created inside an existing state. At least in so far as these forms of self-determination imply law-making powers at a sub-national level, it would be possible to speak about internal self-determination. This would be the case concerning federalism and confederalism as well as for such autonomy arrangements which fall into the category of "any other form of relations" singled out by the African Commission.[92] However, whether or not such institutional structures are created which in one way or another cater for the participatory needs of a people inside a state is a decision which is in the hands of the national legislator. Such decisions have been made, as is shown, for instance, by the examples of Zanzibar in Tanzania and Rodrigues in Mauritius.[93]

The cases studied in our inquiry also represent the main types of legal systems, the civil law system and the common law system. It will be interesting to inquire

---

[92]See the case of *Kevin Mgwanga Gunme et al. v. Cameroon*, African Comm. Hum. & Peoples' Rights, Comm. No. 266/03, May 2009, paras 182–203, confirming the *Katanga* case. See also Suksi (2005b).

[93]The case of Southern Sudan is also important in the context, but it is not dealt with here to any greater extent, because in 2011, it was decided that Southern Sudan will become independent and not continue to exist as a part of Sudan.

into the ways in which the legal orders of the sub-state entities are fitted into the national legal systems.

Often referred to as the oldest existing autonomy in the world, the *Åland Islands* is at least in part a direct result of conflict resolution between two states, Finland and Sweden, by the League of Nations in 1921. Formally speaking, the autonomy arrangement for the Åland Islands was instituted as early as 1920 by the first Self-Government Act,[94] but at this point, the inhabitants of the Åland Islands refused to become involved in the autonomy institutions. Only after the Åland Islands Settlement between Finland and Sweden, approved by the Council of the League of Nations, determined that the Åland Islands would belong to the sovereignty of Finland, and after the Parliament of Finland passed a so-called Guaranty Act in 1922 that complemented the Self-Government Act by the conditions for Finnish sovereignty established by the League of Nations, did the inhabitants start to operate within the autonomy institutions. Today, the 1991 Self-Government Act of the Åland Islands allocates law-making powers to the Legislative Assembly of the Åland Islands, the law-making body for the approximately 28,000 inhabitants (amounting to 0.53% of the total population of Finland of 5.3 million). The aim of the Åland Islands Settlement was to preserve the Swedish character of the Åland Islands and to promote the prosperity and happiness of its inhabitants.[95] It is possible to say that this aim has been realized, because the Åland Islands is still, under section 36(1) of the Self-Government Act, a unilingually Swedish-speaking region, while mainland Finland is organized bilingually with Finnish and Swedish as the national and – as a consequence – official languages. With the entire public sector in the Åland Islands functioning in Swedish, section 37 of the Self-Government Act nonetheless guarantees an individual right for Finnish citizens to use

---

[94]The unofficial translation into English of the current autonomy statute uses the term 'Autonomy Act', but in our inquiry, the literal translation 'Self-Government Act' is used. For the translation into English, see www.finlex.fi/fi/laki/kaannokset/1991/en19911144.pdf. The authoritative versions of the Act have been enacted both in Finnish and in Swedish. In the Self-Government Act, a distinction is made between the legislative powers of the regional entity, for which the Swedish term *landskapet* (Fi: *maakunta*) is used, and the legislative powers of the realm, for which the Swedish term of riket (Fi: *valtakunta*). However, instead of these rather unclear concepts, the distribution of legislative powers is analyzed from the point of view of those of the Legislative Assembly of the Åland Islands, on the one hand, and the Parliament of Finland, on the other.

[95]For a comprehensive treatise of the constitution of the Åland Islands, see Suksi (2005d). Whether the Islanders constitute a minority is debatable. See, e.g., Hannikainen (1993b), p. 20, in which it is concluded that the Swedish-speaking population of the Åland Islands forms a distinct national community which should be considered as qualifying in international law as a national minority or equivalent to national minority, although not all of the most common criteria for minority status are fulfilled by the population of the Åland Islands. Currently the inhabitants of the Åland Islands display a strong "Ålandic" national identity in comparison with the Swedish-speaking population in Finland, which in general strongly identifies itself with Finland. Of a total population of 5.3 million inhabitants in Finland, some 290,000 (5.4%) speak Swedish, which means that the Åland Islanders constitute 10% of the number of Swedish-speakers in Finland. Around 5% of the inhabitants of the Åland Islands are Finnish-speaking, which means that they actually constitute a minority in minority. See also Myntti (1996), p. 1.

Finnish in a matter concerning himself or herself before a court of law and before other state authorities in the Åland Islands. This is important, because around 5% of the inhabitants of the Åland Islands are Finnish-speaking and every year, a large proportion of the tourists visiting the Åland Islands come from mainland Finland. With its Gross Domestic Product (GDP) of 57,700 USD per capita in 2007, the Åland Islands belong to the wealthiest regions in the European Union and exceeds in this respect the general GDP per capita of both Finland (37,700 USD) and Sweden (39,600 USD). An important reason for such a high figure is the position of the shipping sector in the economy of Åland.

Puerto Rico, an island in the Caribbean, has often been referred to as the oldest colony in the world. In 1493, Christopher Columbus arrived on the island during his second voyage to the Americas, and it became a possession of Spain until it was lost to the United States of America in the Spanish-American War of 1898. After the war, the island continued its colonial existence as a possession of the United States.[96] The population of Puerto Rico is currently just below 4 million inhabitants, which represents around 1.2% of the total population of the USA, which is 305.7 million. However, almost as many Puerto Ricans live in mainland United States. The island is heavily dependent on financial transfers from the USA, something that has probably caused its public sector to assume a disproportionately large role in the economy of Puerto Rico, and its GDP per capita, which was under 19,000 USD in 2007, is much lower than that of the US average (45,800 USD in 2007).[97] Ethnically, Puerto Rico is different from mainland USA, with a population which is predominantly Spanish-speaking and culturally relatively distinct. However, by law, Puerto Rico is bi-lingual with Spanish and English as equal official languages in public institutions, in Government and in all its departments, municipalities or other political subdivisions, agencies, public corporations, offices and government dependencies of the executive, legislative and judiciary branches of the Commonwealth of Puerto Rico. The Puerto Ricans have maintained their own characteristics (and seem to wish to continue to do so in the future) despite the fact that there have been several attempts to "Americanize" the population, for

[96]See, e.g., Rivera Ramos (2001), pp. 104–117, Perea (2001), pp. 140–166, Smith (2001), pp. 374–380, Trías Monge (1997), pp. 1–4, 36–44, 160 ff., Carr (1984), pp. 17–104, and Rivera Ramos (2007), pp. 27–54.

[97]The economic dependency of Puerto Rico from the US is very strong, and more than 50% of the population is receiving so-called food stamps, that is, social welfare from the federal government. See Carr (1984), pp. 201–230, in particular p. 215, where Carr explains that in 1980, 60% of the Puerto Ricans were receiving food stamps, that is, were receiving social welfare transfers. See also Rivera Ramos (2007), p. 62 f., 166, who concludes that Puerto Rico is a modern colonial welfare state. See also Rivera Ramos (2007), p. 214 f. For comparisons between Puerto Rico, on the one hand, and other countries and territories, including the US, on the other, see Rosselló (2005), pp. 28–39, 125, 181–195. Currently, the annual tax revenue raised by the Government of Puerto Rico is in the order of 8 billion US dollars, while the transfers from the federal government to the Puerto Rican economy (albeit not via the Puerto Rican budget) approaches 18 billion dollars per year. See also Thornburgh (2007), p. 5 f., who places the federal transfers at a level of 16 billion and who concludes that the figure is growing.

instance, by providing English-only education, during the earlier history of this American possession.[98] Therefore, in reality, the concept of bilingualism is only present as a thin layer in the official context,[99] while the island remains predominantly Spanish-speaking and, in addition, strongly Puerto Rican in terms of national identity.[100]

After a colonial-styled Sultanate during the better part of the nineteenth century and a colonial period under British rule from the 1890s on, *Zanzibar* emerged as an independent State on 10 December 1963.[101] The independent Zanzibar had a Sultan as its head of state and a legislature elected in July 1963 in which the more Arab oriented Zanzibar Nationalist Party/Zanzibar and Pemba People's Party (ZNP/ZPPP) alliance dominated over the African oriented Afro-Shirazi Party (ASP) with 18 to 13 seats elected from single-member constituencies. However, Zanzibar experienced a revolution inspired by the African spirit as early as mid-January 1964 that overturned the Government, abolished the monarchy and revoked the Independence Constitution that had been adopted by a constitutional conference in London in September 1963.[102] After a union treaty entitled the Articles of Union between the Republic of Tanganyika and the Peoples' Republic of Zanzibar was concluded by the President of Tanganyika and the President of Zanzibar on 22 April 1964, Tanganyika and Zanzibar were merged into one State or one sovereign republic, as the new state was characterized in the preamble of the union treaty. The union treaty does not identify the new state as a federation, but as a Union Republic. However, different characterizations of the new structure have often labeled Tanzania as

[98]See, e.g., Álvarez Gonzáles (2001), pp. 289–314, Oquendo (2001), pp. 315–348, and Rivera Ramos (2007), p. 68. The local Puerto Rican reaction to such attempts has been a very unsupportive attitude towards teaching English in schools.

[99]Only approximately 2,000 persons residing in Puerto Rico are English-speaking in the meaning that they do not master Spanish and that they do not belong to the Puerto Rican "nationality", which means that in principle, the bi-lingual arrangement is internally very generous. However, for instance in elections, the ballot papers have not been bi-lingual, that is, in Spanish and English, but only in Spanish, until the elections of 2008, when the unilingual ballot papers were challenged in court. Therefore, the ballot papers in the elections of 2008 were bilingual Spanish and English, in spite of the fact that the parties and candidates are actually identifiable on the basis of symbols or photographs.

[100]In fact, the mentality of the formally bilingual Puerto Rico seems to some extent to be similar to that of the unilingually Swedish-speaking Åland Islands and the French-speaking Quebec: in all of these cases, the main national language, English respectively Finnish and French, is or has been narrated in negative terms. On the issue of national identity, see also Rivera Ramos (2007), pp. 69, 171 f.

[101]Zanzibar was admitted as a member of the United Nations on 16 December 1963. See also Khamis Bakary (2006), p. 1 f. For an account of the historical development of Zanzibar, see Othman (2006), pp. 34–58. For a detailed account of the coming into being of Zanzibar, see Shivji (2008), pp. 1–141. See in particular Shivji (2008), p. 68, who characterizes the Zanzibar revolution as a nationalist one, instead of being a social one. See also Maliyamkono (2000a, b).

[102]After the revolution, a decree under the name the Existing Laws Decree, No. 1 of 1964, was passed, maintaining previously existing legislation in force to a great extent and thus establishing legal continuity. See Shivji (2008), p. 58.

a federation,[103] while others make the point that implicitly, the Constitution of Tanzania expects there to be development in the direction of a unitary state.[104] The reference to federalism is probably at least in part a result of the fact that there existed an overall plan for East-Africa in the beginning of the 1960s to join together the former colonial territories in a federal structure. The population of Zanzibar, encompassing the two larger islands of Unguja (or Zanzibar Island) and Pemba as well as a number of smaller islands, is estimated at 1 million inhabitants, which is around 2.6% of the population of Tanzania.[105] While the two major ethnic identities of the population are the Arab oriented and the African oriented ones, there is also a small Indian minority. The Muslim faith, with a number of internal denominations, is the predominant religion practiced by around 95% of inhabitants. Kiswahili (that is, Swahili) is the language of the population, and all legislation is both passed in Kiswahili and published in the Official Gazette, but the Laws of Zanzibar are also published in English.[106] Both Kiswahili and English are used very much in courts, and a court of law in Zanzibar will hear cases in both languages. The GDP per capita of Tanzania was around 370 US$ in 2007, and it seems as if the figures concerning Zanzibar were more or less at the same level, perhaps some 10% lower.

Since its return to Chinese sovereignty in 1997, *Hong Kong's* 6.93 million inhabitants, representing 0.52% of the total population (1.3 billion) of China, have enjoyed a large measure of autonomy. The Hong Kong autonomy arrangement was created for a special reason: the maintenance of the capitalist system under the principle of "one country, two systems"[107] when China resumed its sovereignty over Hong Kong after British colonial rule. The fact that the arrangement is temporary, formally extending over 50 years until 2047, makes it even more unique. Ethnically, 95% of the inhabitants of Hong Kong are of Chinese descent and speakers of Chinese languages, underlining the non-ethnic nature of the arrangement. However, Chinese in its Cantonese version and English are the official languages of Hong Kong, and from time to time, even the Putonghua language, that

[103] Currently, the Civic United Front (CUF) would like to have a three-government solution which essentially would be organized along federal lines. Dourado (2006), p. 78 ff., makes the point that the then President of Zanzibar, Mr. Karume, had a federation in mind when the Union Republic was created. See also Dourado (2006), pp. 83, 91. On the distinction from a legal point of view, see Khamis Bakary (2006), p. 20 f. Othman (2006), p. 54 f., is of the opinion that the relationship between Tanzania and Zanzibar is not a federal one, nor is it an interim arrangement towards a unitary state: "They intended to create a single state with two authorities, but with one of those authorities having a limited geographical jurisdiction. The idea was to retain the identity of the smaller unit." See also Othman (2006), pp. 67–69.

[104] See also Khamis Bakary (2006), p. 21 f.

[105] The population of the entire Tanzania is estimated to have been 38.7 million in 2008. See Tanzania Human Rights Report (2009), pp. 2, 180.

[106] Locally, the international name of the language is used in the form "Kiswahili". According to art. 87 of the Constitution the official language of the House of Representatives shall be Kiswahili, and all documents of the House shall be written in Kiswahili and, if necessary, in English.

[107] See, e.g., Ghai (1999), pp. 35–64, Xiao Weiyun (2001), pp. 1–47, Horlemann (2003), pp. 1–85.

is, standard Mandarin, is used, although very rarely if ever in the proceedings of the Legislative Council. All legislation is enacted in Chinese and English, and because Hong Kong is entitled to maintain its common law system, the default language in legal proceedings is English, which requires the existence of a legal profession trained in English. The majority of Hong Kong's population is Buddhist or Taoist, and because religious freedoms are circumscribed in Mainland China, Hong Kong serves to some extent as a special area for those Chinese who wish to practice their religion without interference. There is also a concept of indigenous inhabitants in Hong Kong, a term that refers to the descendants of persons who enjoyed certain traditional rights in the New Territories, an area of land which was joined with the British colony of Hong Kong in 1898.[108] In spite of the fact that the ethnicity of the population of Hong Kong is the same as in the adjacent areas of Mainland China, it is clear that the population of Hong Kong has developed its own identity which is distinct from the identity of the population in Mainland China. In 2007, the GDP per capita in Hong Kong was US$ 44,413, which is considerably higher than the national figure of US$ 3,315.

In the United Kingdom, recent constitutional development has resulted in increasing devolution and regionalisation of the country, including *Scotland*.[109] In this context, the devolution of power to Scotland in 1999/2000 could to some

[108]Leung Mei-fun (2006), p. 206 ff. There is a statutory advisory body, the Heung Yee Kuk, established in 1959, that represents the indigenous inhabitants of the New Territories in Hong Kong and that forms one of the functional constituencies for the purposes of elections to the Legislative Council of Hong Kong.

[109]The so-called Channel Islands, that is, Guernsey, Jersey and the Isle of Man have historically speaking a unique relationship to the English Crown. The main interest from an autonomy point of view is currently directed towards the three special areas in the UK, namely, Northern Ireland, Scotland and Wales. Northern Ireland had regional self-government through its own legislative assembly, the Stormont, between 1921 and 1974, but this arrangement was suspended because of the unrest that plagued Northern Ireland. The area was thus placed under direct rule of the central government. A new attempt to establish self-government took place against the background of the so-called Good Friday Agreement between the UK and Ireland in 1998. The Legislative Assembly started its activities in the end of 1999, but the co-operation between the different groupings was difficult and after an infiltration scandal involving terrorist organisations, the basis of co-operation vanished completely. Northern Ireland was again placed under direct rule of London, and the local legislative work and self-government were suspended until further notice. However, after the elections in 2007, the traditional opponents in Northern Ireland have managed to create a joint government for Northern Ireland, which means that this autonomy arrangement is again up and running from May 2007 on. The delegation of power to Wales in 2000 was less comprehensive than that of Scotland and does not involve legislative powers proper, only powers of an administrative nature. The Government of Wales Act of 2006, as amended, increased the law-making powers of the Welsh National Assembly by granting it powers to make Measures. These Measures of the Assembly approach the concept of an act, but they remain at a relatively low norm-hierarchical level, including powers to vary UK legislation subject to the veto of the Secretary of State for Wales, House of Commons or House of Lords, and do not normally contain powers to criminalise actions. At the same time, it seems that the powers granted in 2006 to the Welsh Assembly are clearly of an enumerated nature, leaving the UK level in the possession of residual powers. The National Assembly for Wales is responsible over such areas as education, health care

extent be seen as a partial roll-back of the union that in the case of Scotland was created by means of a treaty signed between two independent States, England and Scotland, in 1706.[110] Autonomy was by no means a new concept that devolution introduced in Scotland, because a certain form of administrative autonomy or functional autonomy existed for Scotland within the UK legal order for the better part of the twentieth century. The population of Scotland was in 2008 approximately 5 million inhabitants, which is around 8% of the total population of the UK, at 62 million. In 2006 its GDP per person was 33,400 US$, which is slightly less than the national figure of 37,400 US$ per person. Linguistically, Scotland is predominantly English-speaking, while Scots, or the Scottish variant of English, may perhaps be considered anything between a dialect and a language and is spoken by 15–30% of the inhabitants of Scotland.[111] The Scottish Government is promoting the use of Scots, although English in practice remains the official language, for instance, for legislation and public administration. Upon ratification of the European Charter for Regional and Minority Languages in 2001, the UK declared Scots as a regional and minority language in the territory of the entire UK for the purposes of chapter II of the Charter and also declared that a number of the provisions in the Charter should also apply to Scottish Gaelic. Hence both languages have gained recognition in the UK. The Scottish jurisdiction recognises to some extent Gaelic as an additional local language.[112] Very few, however, are able to speak Scots Gaelic.[113] Ethnically, close to 90% of the inhabitants identify themselves as being Scottish, while less than 10% identify themselves as English, Irish or Welsh. Sociologically, there seems to exist an identity of being Scottish, potentially cast as a progressive moral value, and a Scottish national identity that may be construed more in communitarian terms than the English national identity, which by contrast seems to be construed in liberal individualist terms. At the same time, recognition at

and culture and is in charge of a budget for these purposes and has a separate executive, the Welsh Assembly Government, which is politically accountable to the Assembly.

[110] In fact, as maintained by Bogdanor (1999), p. 119, devolution to Scotland may be seen as a return to the original ideas, expressed in the treaty of union, of how Scotland should be governed. It is perhaps only now, during modern times, that mechanisms of governance have developed beyond the relatively streamlined and uniform unitary state. For the history of Scottish devolution and the preparation of the Scotland Act, see Bogdanor (1999), pp. 166–202, and Himsworth and Munro (2000), pp. vii–x, 52.

[111] Therefore, it has also be argued that "the Scots language is a Germanic language related to English. It is not Celtic, but has been influenced by Gaelic, as Scottish Gaelic has been influenced by Scots". See Scotland Guide: Scots Language, at http://www.siliconglen.com/Scotland/3_1.html (accessed on 25 March 2009).

[112] See, for instance, section 7.1 of the Rules of Procedure of the Scottish Parliament, according to which the Parliament shall normally conduct its business in English but members may speak in Scots Gaelic or in any other language with the agreement of the Presiding Officer.

[113] In the census of 1991, around 66,000 persons, that is, 1.34% of the population, were Gaelic speakers, and in the census of 2001, the number had fallen to 58,650 persons. See Scotland Guide: Census figures for Gaelic speakers, at http://www.siliconglen.com/Scotland/7_14.html (accessed on 25 March 2009).

the individual level of a Scottish identity does not have to imply that "the Union" is denounced.[114] Evidently, an individual living in Scotland can have layers of identities, some of which are stronger in some situations and others of which, such as the identity of being British or English, are stronger in others.

Aceh is one of the most recent sub-state entities in the world, located in a region of the world which is rich in ethnic, linguistic and religious groups living close to each other and often intermingled with each other. When Dutch colonialism was extended over what is now the Republic of Indonesia, the kingdom of Aceh tried to maintain its independence until it was finally overtaken in 1874 as the last independent territory of colonial times. Since that time, the Acehnese were involved in a lower or a higher level of struggle as well as resistance against the colonial power. When Indonesia became independent in 1945, the Acehnese were perceived as important to the success of decolonization, but at the same time, the former colonial borders were established as the international borders of the new State, and therefore, Aceh remained a part of Indonesia.[115] The independence of Indonesia did not necessarily improve the situation of the Acehnese very much, in particular as Indonesia soon turned into an authoritarian and centrally governed state where a liberalization process was commenced only in 1998. By the time of the authoritarian period under president Suharto, the grievances of the Acehnese, including a multitude of human rights violations, led to an armed struggle against the central government, with the aim of making Aceh an independent state. Although a more serious insurgency commenced as early as in 1976, the armed struggle took place from the late 1980s onwards by the Free Aceh Movement (Gerakan Acheh Merdeka; GAM), which at some point controlled up to 70% of the territory of Aceh. In the aftermath of the tsunami, momentum for a political solution was created that took on the form of a peace agreement between the GAM and the Government of Indonesia and involved an autonomy solution. The population of Aceh is around 4 million, that is, 1.7% of the total population of Indonesia, which was around 237.5 million in 2008. The area has natural resources in the form of, for instance, oil and gas, but the proceeds from these resources have previously tended to go to the central government of Indonesia. While the overall annual GDP per capita of Indonesia is around 2,000 USD, Aceh is clearly less well off, with a GDP per capita of 1,000 USD. Even that figure may be considered high when taking into account the effects of post-tsunami relief and development donations, and if purged of these extraneous funds, the GDP per capita could be as low as 600–700 USD,

---

[114] Condor and Abell (2006), p. 74 f.

[115] On the history of Aceh and Indonesia, see, e.g., Miller (2009), pp. 3–5, and Drexler (2008), *passim*, and pp. 213–236 in particular, who explores the "official" historical narratives of the parties to the conflict, but also the "unofficial" narratives that allege, *inter alia*, that the parties of the conflict in Aceh were, in fact, dependent of each other and that the conflict was, at least to a part, an intentional creation. The conclusion that can be drawn on the basis of Drexler's analysis is that everything in Aceh is not necessarily as it seems to be.

placing Aceh among the five poorest regions of Indonesia.[116] Although almost all of the Acehnese are Muslims, which is something that is reflected in the religious provisions of the autonomy legislation, the population is by no means homogeneous. In fact, there are at least seven linguistically and culturally distinct minority populations in Aceh (the Gayo, Alas, Kluet, Aneuk Jamee, Tamiang, Singkil and Puloe) amounting to more than 20% of Aceh's population,[117] and due to previous settlement, there is also a Javanese population in Aceh of more than 15%.

Without doubt, the six territorial autonomies examined in our research are very different, in particular with respect to their economical situation and their location in the world. A superficial similarity that unites them is their population size in proportion to the population of the state in which they exist, which seems to range from one-half percentage point to a few percentage points, with Scotland having the largest with a population of 8% of the national population. However, the similarities and differences from a legal point of view will reveal themselves after an examination of these cases against the background of the elements derived from the Memel Territory.

[116]According to Miller (2009), p. 180, "[d]espite the massive injection of capital into Aceh since the tsunami, it remains the fourth poorest Indonesian province after Papua, Maluku and Gorontolo, and second only after Papua if the 13 percent of Acehnese who became vulnerable to poverty after the tsunami are included. With 28.5 percent of the local population living below the poverty line (earning Rp. 130,000 or US$14 per month), Aceh's poverty rate is almost the double of the national average of 16.7 percent". According to the introduction to the Explanatory Notes on the Law on the Governance of Aceh, the aim of the law is to accelerate the achievement of prosperity, and several provisions of the law are focused on the development of Aceh.

[117]See Miller (2009), p. 3 f. According to Lindsey and Santosa 2008, p. 4, "[s]ome observers argue that as many as 300 discrete cultures can still be identified, although most scholars agree that they can all be grouped into 19 main categories".

Chapter 2
The Autonomy of Memel

2.1 Link to Minority Rights

There is a clear connection between the autonomy of the Memel Territory and the minority rights of the German population, in particular, a population which lived in a relatively concentrated area in western Lithuania until the Second World War. The minority rights of the population of Memel (or Klaipeda, as the area is called in the Lithuanian language) were guaranteed in the treaty arrangements following the First World War and might therefore be regarded as a part of the League of Nations minority rights arrangement, but with the reservation that there was no formal connection to the League of Nations in the Memel Convention (see below), which was concluded between five different States.[1]

The autonomy of the Memel territory has its roots in section X of the 1919 Treaty of Versailles, whose Art. 99 deals with the transfer of a formerly German piece of territory and the inhabitants thereof to the allied and associated powers:

> Germany renounces in favour of the Principal Allied and Associated Powers all rights and title over the territories included between the Baltic, the north-eastern frontier of East Prussia as defined in Article 28 of Part II (Boundaries of Germany) of the present Treaty and the former frontier between Germany and Russia. Germany undertakes to accept the settlement made by the Principal Allied and Associated Powers in regard to these territories, particularly in so far as concerns the nationality of the inhabitants.

The State of Lithuania had declared independence from Russia in 1918 and was barely in existence at the time of the signing of the Versailles treaty that regulated the former German territories. Therefore, the settlement concerning the area mentioned in Art. 99 was between the principal allied and associated powers. They intended to place Memel under international administration, which in reality was a French administration supported by the presence of French troops in the area.

[1]See also Rogge (1928), p. 176 f., who accounts for a broader role of the League of Nations in the context.

DOI 10.1007/978-3-642-20048-9_2,

Lithuania was in opposition to this plan and occupied the area in 1923,[2] but the State of Lithuania eventually accepted involvement in the settlement referred to in Art. 99 and consequently signed the Convention concerning the Territory of Memel (hereinafter in this chapter: the Convention) and the attached Statute of Memel (hereinafter in this chapter: the Statute) together with the British Empire, France, Italy and Japan.[3] In this way the Statute of Memel became a part of a treaty under international law,[4] a legal document which, according to Art. 8 of the Convention, could be tried in the Permanent Court of International Justice (PCIJ).

The Convention was done approximately 2 years after the Constitution of Lithuania was adopted, which means that the Convention and the appended Statute were ratified by the Lithuanian Parliament, but it seems that no formal amendments were made to the Lithuanian Constitution of 1922. Thus the Memel Statute would have constituted an act of exception in relation to the Lithuanian Constitution, with the effect of setting aside the Constitution in situations of conflict. Robinson commented on the birth of the Memel Territory as an autonomous entity by saying that it was actually dependent on a Lithuanian piece of law, not on an act of international law.[5] The legitimacy of the Statute as an internal domestic act can be grounded in the decision of the constitutional convention of 11 November 1921, which was followed by a declaration of the Lithuanian Government concerning the autonomy of Memel on 7 May 1923. Although the Statute was in many respects modified in comparison with the declaration of 1923, its main objective, that of autonomy, prevailed.[6]

In Art. 1 of the Convention, the principal allied and associated powers transferred the territory to the State of Lithuania, whereas according to Art. 2, "[t]he Memel Territory shall constitute, under the sovereignty of Lithuania, a unit enjoying legislative, judicial, administrative and financial autonomy within the limits prescribed by the Statute set out in Annex I".[7] The formerly German citizens

---

[2]For a detailed account of the events in and the legal status of the Memel area between 1918 and 1924, see Robinson (1934a), pp. 23–37. In principle, Rogge (1928), *passim*, and Robinson argue and interpret the law from two opposing perspectives, Rogge from the point of view of the autonomy arrangement and Robinson from the point of view of the Lithuanian state. For a description of the history of the Memel area before 1919, see Plieg (1962), pp. 1–7, and Kalijarvi (1937), pp. 19–49. For the period between 1920 and 1924, see Plieg (1962), pp. 12–32. See also Lapidoth (1997), pp. 77–85.

[3]For a description of the negotiations around the Versailles peace process and the subsequent measures (the Convention and the Statute) with respect to Memel, see Rogge (1928), pp. 1–20, Robinson (1934a), pp. 37–57, Kalijarvi (1937), pp. 50–196.

[4]Convention concerning the Territory of Memel, signed at Paris, May 8, 1924, 736 *League of Nations Treaty Series* 1924, at p. 87. For the final text of the Convention, see also *Official Journal of the League of Nations*, September 1924, pp. 1201–1223. For an analysis of the political situation concerning Memel, see Kalijarvi (1936), pp. 204–215.

[5]Robinson (1934a), p. 106.

[6]See Robinson (1934a), p. 284 f.

[7]According to the *Memel* case, p. 23, the intention of the autonomy arrangement in Memel was to "ensure to the transferred territory a wide measure of legislative, judicial, administrative and financial *decentralization*, which should not disturb the unity of the Lithuanian State and should

who were resident in the territory became citizens of Lithuania. According to the census of 1910, the last before the war, around 140,000 inhabitants lived in the Memel area, and close to 50% of them were speakers of Lithuanian,[8] thus forming a linguistic minority population in Germany. When the Memel area was then handed over to Lithuania, the Germans in the territory subsequently became a minority in Lithuania, but inside the autonomous Memel Territory, the German population seemed to dominate at least in a political sense, because the German or autonomy-oriented parties enjoyed the support of more than 75% of the vote in the Memel Territory both in the elections to the Assembly of Memel in 1925 and 1927 and also to the Parliament of Lithuania in 1926.[9] This, in turn, provides evidence of the fact that the great majority of the inhabitants of the Memel Territory, even many of those who linguistically were Lithuanian-speakers, nonetheless identified themselves as Germans or as German-minded citizens of the Memel Territory during its existence as an autonomous entity, rather than considering themselves to be citizens of Lithuania in the ethnic sense.[10] It was not easy for Lithuania to accept such

operate within the framework of Lithuanian sovereignty" (italics by author). The use of the term 'decentralization' in the context to describe the transfer of powers is interesting against the background of the more modern term of 'devolution'. For a commentary to the Convention, see Rogge (1928), pp. 173–250.

[8]Rogge (1928), pp. 4–5. However, because of the long separation of the Lithuanian speakers in the German areas from the Lithuanian speakers in the Russian areas, a unified Lithuanian language was only developing as a written language in the beginning of the twentieth century, while a number of different dialects existed. See Rogge (1928), p. 355.

[9]Rogge (1928), p. 4, fn. 6.

[10]See Plieg (1962), p. 34, fn. 122, for population statistics. See also Rogge (1928), pp. 226–229, who does not regard the German speakers in Memel as such a national minority which would come under the declaration relating to protection of minorities that was referred to in Art. 11 of the Convention and which Lithuania had made before the League of Nations. Rogge's point seems to be that both the German and the Lithuanian languages were state languages or official languages in the Memel Territory, as established in Art. 27 of the Statute and that the Germans in Lithuania were a state-forming people together with the Lithuanians. However, according to Art. 26 of the Statute, the authorities of the Memel Territory were supposed to carry out and cause to be carried out in the Territory the provisions contained in the declaration concerning the protection of minorities made by the Lithuanian Government before the Council of the League of Nations in 1922. This indicates that there might have been some concern over the Lithuanian and other minorities in the Territory and that the authorities of the Memel Territory had an obligation *vis-à-vis* such minorities. Hence as concerns the Lithuanian language, although it was an official language in the Memel Territory together with the German language, it could be regarded, from the point of view of international law, a minority language in the Territory. See Rogge (1928), pp. 227, 354 f. However, the position of Rogge was heavily criticized in Robinson (1934a), p. 169, making the point that the national majority, the Lithuanians, cannot really become a minority in the Memel Territory. Instead, Robinson concludes that in the Memel Territory, it is possible to be a member of the majority and the minority at the same time: "So sind katholische Deutsche des Memelgebiets mit Bezug auf die *staatlichen Behörden* konfessionell Mehrheits-, sprachlich Minderheitsangehörige, dagegen sind protestantische Litauer konfessionell Minderheits-, völkisch Mehrheitsangehörige. Mit Bezug auf die *Lokalbehörden* ist es gerade umgekehrt." (italics by MS) There were also Jews in the Memel Territory, according to Plieg (1962), p. 115, some 5,000 in the beginning of the 1930s.

strongly defined linguistic and political characteristics in an area that was merged with the newly independent state. Instead, Lithuania showed a clear interest in asserting its existence as a nation state. The attempts to re-orientate the basically German-speaking Memel Territory towards Lithuania by, for instance, requiring the use of the Lithuanian language in official contexts, preventing German teachers, judges and other professionals from entering Memel, encouraging the migration of Lithuanians from other parts of Lithuania to the Memel Territory and establishing Lithuanian as a compulsory language of instruction became a constant source of contention between the two governments, that of Lithuania and that of the Memel Territory.[11] It is probably fair to conclude that the forcible transfer of the former German territory via the allied and associated powers to Lithuania, in addition to the suspicion within the Government of Lithuania that Germany might wish to re-gain the Memel territory, resulted in a situation in which Lithuania did not spare its efforts to "Lithuanize" the area.

The Preamble of the Statute of Memel underlined the wisdom of granting autonomy to the Memel Territory and of preserving the traditional rights and culture of its inhabitants. It also referred to the grant to the Memel Territory of the status of an autonomous unit and proceeded thereafter to state that "[t]he Republic of Lithuania enacts the [...] Statute". Under Art. 1 of the Statute, "[t]he Memel Territory shall constitute, under the sovereignty of Lithuania, a unit, organised on democratic principles, enjoying legislative, judicial, administrative and financial autonomy within the limits prescribed in the present Statute". Autonomy was thus explicitly mentioned in the Statute and therefore also in the Convention as a concept that was subjected to the higher principle of sovereignty of the state. Interestingly, in addition to the ordinary identification of the three branches of government in existence in the autonomous territory, financial autonomy was also mentioned as a separate category of autonomy.[12] According to Rogge, the autonomy thus defined differed from other arrangements of self-government, particularly illustrated by the fact that the Lithuanian state was not granted any rights of control and influence in the matters of the Memel Territory, save for the right of veto of the Governor as established in Art. 16 of the Statute.[13] This agreement did not, however, resolve the conflicting claims of the state of Lithuania and the inhabitants of Memel. Unrest within the Territory continued, with corresponding measures being

[11]See, e.g., Plieg (1962), pp. 41 f., 44, 175–176, 178, 216 f. Plieg also makes the point that the autonomy arrangement was perhaps seen by Lithuania only as an interim phase in the decentralized fabric of the unitary state, which would evolve in a certain direction and eventually disappear.

[12]Judging from the recurring difficulties of the Memel authorities to adopt a budget in a timely manner in advance of the fiscal year, the financial autonomy was not easy to deal with. See Robinson (1934a), p. 317 ff.

[13]Rogge (1928), p. 269.

implemented by the Lithuanian state in order to curb the German-oriented developments which were taking place in the Memel Territory.

The constitutional life of Lithuania was greatly affected by the authoritarian tendencies of the 1920s and the 1930s, and this domestic authoritarianism was also evident, after the *coup d'état* of 1926,[14] in the Constitutions of 1928 and 1938. Because the Memel Territory became influenced by the Nazi ideology imported from Germany at the beginning of the 1930s, the autonomy arrangement was trying to function under less favorable stars. A central government turning from democracy to authoritarianism is a factor that will negatively affect the "life expectancy" of an autonomous entity,[15] and with the continuously contentious nature of the Memel arrangement as a determining factor, especially after the rise of Germany as a major Central European power in the 1930s, it is no surprise that the Territory was eventually reunited with Germany in May 1939.[16] Actually, the Statute outlived both the first and the second Constitution and stayed in effect, at least normatively, until the spring of 1939. In practice, however, the Statute was often set aside by the Lithuanian authorities.[17] This was the case particularly during 1934–1935, when

[14]For the declaration of the state of emergency (or state of war) by president Antanas Smetonas, see Robinson (1934b), pp. 624 f. See also Plieg (1962), pp. 38, 187 f., about the consequences in the Memel Territory, where the declaration of the state of emergency coincided with a governmental crisis involving the appointment of the President of the Directorate. The state of emergency lasted until 30 July 1938, but when it was lifted, no great changes occurred in the attitudes of the Lithuanian Government toward the Memel Territory.

[15]As stated in Nordquist (1998), p. 71, an "autonomy that is not threatened by outside events and that is implemented with a certain consensus from the area designed as an autonomy, seems to face as its last major threat the central government, which may change its position towards the autonomy". On p. 73, Nordquist makes the point that the "internal conditions for an autonomy seem more important than the external. For instance, autonomies within democratic states are more likely to be durable than other autonomies. Considering the conditions that cause a break-up of autonomies, internal governmental actions take precedence over international factors. Besides the internal dimension, a major threat to autonomies is major structural changes in the state system that affect the central government." On p. 73, he continues to conclude that "[p]olitically weak, or unstable, states may be a greater threat to an autonomy. Having a different political structure within one's borders may provide a tempting excuse for governments that seek explanations for political failures." The conclusion is similar to the point made in Wheare (1964), p. 47: "Dictatorship, with its one-party government and its denial of free election, is incompatible with the working of the federal principle. Federalism demands forms of government which have the characteristics usually associated with democracy or free government. There is a wide variety in the forms which such government may take, but the main essentials are free election and a party system, with its guarantee of a responsible opposition." For a similar argument, see Lapidoth (1997), p. 200.

[16]As a part of Nazi-Germany, the area was evidently not granted any sub-state existence as a "Land", because the sub-state organization of Weimar Germany was abolished and the entire state centralized following the implementation of the Nazi policies in Germany during 1933 and 1934. See Weiss (2004), p. 74. See also Wheare (1964), p. 47.

[17]According to Plieg (1962), p. 217, the autonomy arrangement functioned altogether only 6 years and 6 months in the way intended by the Statute. In practice, as stated by Plieg (1962), p. 219, the Statute was suspended.

many civil servants in the Memel Territory were severed from their posts and the number of mandates in the Chamber of Representatives lowered to 24 on very dubious grounds but with the result that the five Lithuanian-oriented representatives could, by abstaining from participation in the sessions, prohibit the quorum of 20 representatives and thus prevent votes of no confidence towards the Lithuanian-minded President of the Directorate.[18] In the Memel Territory, the authoritarianism and nationalism of Lithuania was clearly evident through the resulting obstruction of the functioning of the autonomous entity, and it seems that such tendency to obstruct did not develop into an implementing practice which was somewhat more faithful to the Statute until the last year of the existence of the autonomy arrangement, in 1938–1939.[19]

Most of the originally German inhabitants probably wanted to remain German or at least to retain close relations with Germany, while Lithuania was determined not to give away any of the territories it had recently acquired. The sense of nationalism that was growing stronger in Germany did not leave Memel unaffected, and over the years, a tide of irredentism developed with requests concerning unification with Germany. This continued until a state of siege was declared for Memel. After the take-over of the German Government by the Nazis in 1933, the Nazi ideology took hold in Memel as well.[20] As a consequence, a number of the Nazi leaders of Memel

[18]Plieg (1962), pp. 138–151. The authorities of the Lithuanian state were really making themselves unpopular in the Memel Territory. According to Plieg (1962), p. 166, when the anti-Memel measures by the Lithuanian authorities reached their peak by 1934–1935, Germany became so agitated by the events that Hitler himself referred, in a speech on 21 May 1935 before the German Parliament, to the restoration by the guarantee powers to the Convention of respect of the most basic *human rights* as a condition for concluding a treaty with Lithuania. Although a relatively early use of the notion of human rights in the context of international politics, it was truly an opportune reference to the concept with a view to the violations of human rights that Hitler's policies caused later on. However, in light of the human rights developed after the Second World War, it seems as if many of the actions of the state authorities in the Memel Territory could have been labeled as violations of human rights. In 1945, the concept of human rights was embedded in the Charter of the United Nations, and the first substantive definition of what human rights are came in 1948 with the Universal Declaration of Human Rights (UDHR). Many of the rights later on recorded in the UDHR were violated in the Memel Territory, such as the independence of the judiciary, the right to fair trial, etc. In December 1935, after an ordinary Directorate reflecting the will of the majority in the Chamber had been instituted, civil servants of German origin were re-instituted in their posts. See Plieg (1962), p. 173.

[19]Plieg (1962), p. 193 f., 214.

[20]According to Plieg (1962), pp. 91, 107–118, two competing political organizations with a national socialistic orientation were constituted. They gained substantial support in the elections to the city council of Memel in 1933, but were not at that point seriously competing with the more established parties at the level of the Memel Territory. Interestingly, the main Nazi party was not negatively disposed towards the Jewish population of the Memel Territory. Members of these organizations were accused of treason before a Lithuanian court martial in 1934, and altogether 83 of them were convicted, while 37 were found not guilty. See Plieg (1962), p. 133 f. See also Plieg (1962), pp. 189, 198, 203–206, 221.

and their supporters were imprisoned.[21] The pressure from Nazi Germany was, however, considerable, and in March 1939, Lithuania finally agreed to cede the Memel territory back to Germany.[22] At that point, it was still not known that Lithuania itself would come to be "re-united" in 1940 with what had become of the Russian Empire after the revolution, that is, with the Soviet Union (starting with the grant of military bases to Soviet troops as early as in the Fall of 1939, only months after the Memel Territory was re-united with Germany). With those measures, however, both the construction of the League of Nations era as well as the small independent republic and the autonomy arrangement had effectively disappeared.[23]

When German armed forces retreated from Lithuania and the Memel area during the final phases of the Second World War, the practical consequence was that all inhabitants of German origin were evacuated from the Memel Territory. It can therefore be said that the end of the Second World War also brought the autonomy of the Memel Territory to an end, because the population for which it had been created did not exist anymore.[24]

Even before the Nazi takeover in Germany, the elected political leadership of Memel looked for ways to interact with Germany directly, or with what was still Weimar Germany at the time, in order to offset the agricultural overproduction occurring in the Memel area and to create income for the region. On 17 December 1931, Mr. Böttcher, the first clearly autonomy or German oriented President of the Directorate of the Memel Territory, that is, the Head of Government of the

[21]Plieg (1962), pp. 91–93.

[22]Plieg (1962), pp. 206–213. In contacts between the Lithuanian and German Governments, the latter obviously gave two options: either to enter into an agreement about the reunion of the Memel Territory with Germany and thus achieve a peaceful solution or to accept the possibility of armed action. The treaty between Lithuania and Germany became effective on 22 March 1939, and 1 day later, Hitler arrived in Memel together with the German fleet and the ground forces. As concluded by Plieg (1962), p. 223, there is no doubt that the reunification was following the will of the great majority of the inhabitants.

[23]The position of the Memel Territory can also be studied from the point of view of the so-called Molotov-Ribbentrop Pact, that is, the non-aggression pact between Nazi Germany and the Soviet Union, concluded on 23 August 1939, that is, after Lithuania ceded the Memel Territory to Germany. According to Art. 1 of the secret additional protocol to the non-aggression pact, "[i]n the event of a territorial and political rearrangement in the areas belonging to the Baltic States (Finland, Estonia, Latvia, Lithuania), the northern boundary of Lithuania shall represent the boundary of the spheres of influence of Germany and U.S.S.R. In this connection the interest of Lithuania in the Vilna area is recognized by each party". This means that according to the original plan, Lithuania would actually remain in the German sphere of influence, although the implementation of the plan resulted in a situation where all of Lithuania except the Memel Territory was transferred to the Soviet sphere of influence.

[24]However, Plieg (1962), p. 225, has argued that of all the areas "taken" by Nazi-Germany, the Memel area was not taken by force in violation of international law and that the Memel area should therefore not have been taken away from Germany after the Second World War.

autonomous territory, appointed by the Governor of the Memel Territory after a series of politically unviable Lithuanian-minded cronies which failed to secure normal political confidence with the Chamber of Representatives,[25] visited the Ministry of Food and the Ministry of Foreign Affairs of the Republic of Germany together with two representatives of the Memel legislature. The aim of the trip was to secure, through direct negotiations with Germany, an agreement on preferential treatment of agricultural produce exported from Memel to Germany. The visit was undertaken without the knowledge of the Lithuanian Government. Mr. Böttcher claimed that the trip was of a private nature, although his travel expenses had been paid out of the public funds of the Memel Territory. In addition, lacking passports, the members of the delegation were given travel documents by the German consulate in the territory with reference to the importance of the trip for Germany. As a consequence of the trip, the Governor of Memel, as a representative of the Republic of Lithuania in the Memel Territory, dismissed the President of the Directorate for violation of the distribution of powers between Memel on the one hand and Lithuania on the other (foreign relations were, under Art. 7 of the Statute of Memel outlining the residual powers of the central government of Lithuania, within the exclusive jurisdiction of the Lithuanian Republic), although the Memel Statute did not contain any provision that would have made such a dismissal possible. In addition, the Governor of Memel appointed a new President of the Directorate, Mr. Simaitis, and dissolved the Chamber of Representatives of Memel, that is, the representative assembly of the autonomous entity. Claims about the violation of the Statute of Memel were raised[26] and the PCIJ was asked to look into the legality of the acts.

The issue was brought before the Permanent Court of International Justice for judicial resolution by the principal allied and associated powers, that is, by the United Kingdom, France, Italy and Japan. Lithuania was the defendant party, and the matter was resolved in the case of *Interpretation of the Statute of the Memel Territory*.[27] It is possible to say that the PCIJ sat in this instance in the capacity of a constitutional court, adjudicating an institutional dispute between state bodies. The core legal question in the case can be summarized as the general issue as to how the

[25]Plieg (1962), pp. 34–49. Böttcher was the first President of the Directorate whose appointment actually reflected the result of the elections to the Chamber of Representatives. The fight over who would be the President of the Directorate, a Lithuanian-minded appointee of the Governor or a regionally established person with support in the Chamber of Representatives was an important political point of contention during the period of the autonomy of the Memel Territory. Several votes of confidence were held in the Chamber of Representatives, indicating a good understanding of the mechanism of parliamentary accountability.

[26]Such claims were raised several times before the League of Nations, *e.g.*, through the German Government. See Plieg (1962), pp. 40, 46, and Kalijarvi (1937), pp. 221–225 concerning international actions and pp. 225–237 for an article-by-article account of the points of contention concerning the implementation of the Statute.

[27]*Interpretation of the Statute of the Memel Territory*, Judgment of 11 August 1932, PCIJ, Series A./B.–Fasc. No. 50, p. 294.

process of government should be carried out when the interests of central government, the government of the autonomous entity and the representative assembly of the latter collide. From the perspective of this case, it can be said that the protection of the external sovereignty of a State was a paramount concern,[28] not easily relinquished to its sub-divisions.[29] However, internal sovereignty, that is, the power to pass laws, is apparently a characteristic that can be divided between the state and its sub-divisions. This divided internal sovereignty translates into the substantive contents of autonomy in the definition of the legislative powers of the autonomous entity over certain subject-matter.

The Court arrived at the more specific conclusion of the case after a vote which was divided (ten against five). The Court departed from the notion that the Governor of the Memel Territory was entitled, in order to protect the interests of the state, to dismiss the President of the Directorate in cases of serious acts which violated the Convention of Paris of 1924, including its annexes, and which were calculated to prejudice the sovereignty of Lithuania, under the premise that no other action could be taken.[30] Against that background, the dismissal of Mr. Böttcher as President of the Directorate had been in order in the circumstances in which it took place, but the dismissal of the President of the Directorate did not in itself involve the simultaneous termination of the appointments of the other members of the Directorate. They could continue in office, awaiting the appointment of a new President, which the Governor of Memel did under somewhat chaotic political circumstances when he appointed Mr. Simaitis to the post.[31] According to the Court, when considering the circumstances, the appointment of the Directorate presided over by Mr. Simaitis was in order. However, the Court also found that the dissolution of the Chamber of

---

[28]See also the case of *Lighthouses of Crete and Samos*, Judgment of 8 October 1937, PCIJ, Series A./B.–Fasc. No. 71., in which the PCIJ developed a political link test to determine on the basis of the constitutive documents whether or not an autonomous territory has seceded from the State, and Kalijarvi (1937), p. 205.

[29]In this context, it should be mentioned that in the *Memel* case, the PCIJ concluded that within the limits fixed by the Statute of Memel, "it certainly was not the intention of the Parties to the Convention that the sovereignty should be divided between the two bodies which were to exist side by side in the same territory". "Their intention was simply to ensure to the transferred territory a wide measure of legislative, judicial, administrative and financial decentralization, which should not disturb the unity of the Lithuanian State and should operate within the framework of Lithuanian sovereignty." The Memel case, p. 23. The point here is that the external sovereignty, or sovereignty of State under public international law, was not divided by the Convention. The Court continued by saying that "[w]hilst Lithuania was to enjoy full sovereignty over the ceded territory, subject to the limitations imposed on its exercise, the autonomy of Memel was only to operate within the limits so fixed and expressly specified". *Ibidem.*

[30]As pointed out in a critical account by Plieg (1962), pp. 68–85, the PCIJ made the decision without knowledge of the fact that earlier Presidents of the Directorate and members of the Memel Government had made similar contacts with the German authorities without any negative reactions by the central government of Lithuania.

[31]It may be inferred from the name of the new President that he was probably not of German origin, but of Lithuanian origin.

Representatives of the Memel Territory by the Governor of the Memel Territory when the Directorate presided over by Mr. Simaitis had not received the confidence of the Chamber was not in order. Hence Lithuania as defendant was vindicated on most of the issues raised before the Court, except on the dissolution of the Chamber of Representatives, but even on the issues that were decided in line with Lithuania's contentions, the interpretation of the PCIJ did not make its full findings in favor of Lithuania, but qualified the issues to a greater or lesser extent.[32]

2.2 The Elements of Autonomy in Memel

2.2.1 *Powers*

The *Memel* case turns to a great extent on the powers granted to the Memel Territory and on the exercise of these powers by the Memel Territory. At the same time, the powers of the Memel Territory are mirrored in the powers of the central government of Lithuania. The PCIJ noted that the Memel Territory had, for the purpose of managing its local affairs as it pleased, been provided under the Statute with a legislature, an executive and a judiciary.[33] The Court concluded, however, that the sovereign powers of the state of Lithuania and the autonomous powers of Memel territory were of quite a different order, and that, as a consequence, the exercise of the powers of the autonomous entity should be based on a legal rule of a positive nature that could not be inferred from the silence of the norm from which the autonomy was derived.[34] This means that the Court was looking in a very positivist manner at the normative interfaces between the state of Lithuania and the Memel Territory, requiring a clear rule for the justification of the powers of the latter. Therefore, according to the Court, the autonomy of Memel existed only within the limits fixed by the Statute, and because there were no provisions to the contrary in the Convention or its annexes, precedence was given to the rights ensuing from the sovereignty of Lithuania. In the case, the PCIJ clearly departed from a distinction between legislative acts on the one hand and executive acts on the other.[35] At the same time, the Court concluded that the "legislature was intended to be completely independent within the prescribed limits of the autonomy, but that it was to have no legislative powers outside those limits".[36]

The legislative powers of Memel were identified in Articles 5 through 7 and 10 of the Statute. In Art. 10, it is established that "[l]egislative power in the Memel

---

[32]The *Memel* case, p. 30.

[33]The *Memel* case, p. 24.

[34]The *Memel* case, p. 23.

[35]The *Memel* case, p. 24.

[36]The *Memel* case, p. 25.

Territory shall, within the limits of this Statute, be exercised by the Chamber of Representatives". A legislative body is thus identified as the holder of the principal normative powers of law-making on subject-matter enumerated in Art. 5 of the Statute.[37] It should be observed that the Statute contains an enumeration of the powers granted to the legislative body of Memel,[38] while the legislature of Lithuania, against the background of the Statute and the *Memel* case, was considered to be the holder of residual powers, that is, lawmaker in the territory of Memel in such substantive areas that were not mentioned in the Statute. This is corroborated by Art. 7, according to which the affairs which, under the Statute, were not within the jurisdiction of the local authorities of the Memel Territory were regarded as being within the exclusive jurisdiction of the competent organizations of the Lithuanian Republic.[39] As mentioned above, the PCIJ regarded this provision important in drawing up the boundaries of the authority of the two jurisdictions, with enumerated powers granted to the Memel Territory and with residual powers remaining with the state of Lithuania.

Although Memel could certainly be characterized as a legal order of its own on the basis of the Statute,[40] the fact of the matter nonetheless seems to be that within the territory of Memel, there existed two legal orders, namely the laws enacted by the Chamber of Representatives of Memel in areas established in the Statute and laws enacted by the Parliament of Lithuania in areas that were not identified in the Statute as subject matter that belonged to the competence of the

[37]According to Art. 12, both the Chamber of Representatives and the Directorate had the right to initiate legislation to be adopted for the Memel Territory by the Chamber of Representatives. For an analysis of the subject-matter belonging to the exclusive legislative competences of Memel, with comparative notes with a view to the division of competence in Germany, see Rogge (1928), pp. 287–297.

[38]For an impression of which kinds of legislative enactments the Chamber of Representatives of the Memel Territory passed between 1926 and 1933, see Robinson (1934b), pp. 556–565.

[39]For an impression of which areas the residual powers of the Lithuanian central government encompassed or in which areas they were found, see Robinson (1934b), pp. 444–481. They contained, *inter alia*, pieces of laws in the following field: constitutional laws, citizenship and passports, security of the state, military service and the army, the Red Cross, the judiciary, criminal law, amnesty and pardon, orders and decorations, state loans, the monetary system, the banking system, the insurance system, the bourses and maritime trade, the monopolies, accises, alcoholic beverages, the customs, foreign trade (imports and exports), import duties, export duties, standards, trade, foreign service, press, assembly and associations, traffic over borders, emigration, aliens, traffic regulations, the educational system, scholarships, lotteries, and the association of agriculture.

[40]Describing the autonomy arrangement in Lithuania as the existence of two legal orders was natural against the background of the fact that the legislation of the Republic of Lithuania that was in effect in the area of the Memel Territory was in effect in its fields of competence at the same time as the legislation of the Memel Territory was in effect in its fields of competence. In fields where the legislation of Lithuania was in force, there was also, if needed, an administrative organization in place to implement the legislation.

Memel Territory.[41] Therefore, while both legislatures possessed exclusive law-making powers, there did not seem to exist many areas of concurring powers, where both legislatures would have been competent to act[42] and where, for instance, a principle of preemption on the part of the Lithuanian lawmaker would have determined how the competences were divided inside the concurring jurisdiction. However, there seemed to exist certain shared powers in areas where the Statute mandated the authorities of Memel to implement general legislation applicable over the entire state of Lithuania (see below, Sect. 2.2.3).[43] Such shared powers were probably mainly of an executive nature in the Memel Territory and placed the executive powers of Memel in the position of an implementing organization in respect of national legislation.

Article 5 of the Statute listed the enumerated powers of Memel which were assigned to the competence of the local authorities of the Memel Territory. It is clear that Art. 5 did not specify that the powers identified were of a legislative nature only. Instead, the general reference to the local authorities of the Memel Territory was of a broader nature, covering also the central executive body of Memel[44] as well as the local government or municipalities of Memel[45] at the

---

[41]This division of the territory in two different legal orders was in principle not reciprocal so that the Lithuanian territory outside Memel would have been affected by the legislation of Memel. However, under Art. 21, the sentences pronounced respectively by the Courts of the Memel Territory and by the other Lithuanian Courts had the force of law in the whole territory of Lithuania, including the Memel Territory, and the same applied to warrants of arrest delivered by the authorities of the Memel Territory and by the authorities of the other parts of Lithuania respectively. The two jurisdictions were thus not exclusive in relation to each other at the level of implementation of law through courts, but instead integrated. This integrated nature of the jurisdictions is apparent also on the basis of Art. 24, according to which the jurisdiction of the Supreme Court of Lithuania extended over the whole territory of the Republic, including the Memel Territory. This Court had a special Section for the affairs of the Memel Territory, mainly composed of judges drawn from the magistrates of the Memel Territory, and it had the possibility hold its sessions in the town of Memel.

[42]See Rogge (1928), p. 302, Robinson (1934a), p. 342.

[43]The notion of shared powers is used in Hannum (1996), p. 383. Such powers were at least in part to be found in the area of public order and police functions. See Robinson (1934a), pp. 602–607.

[44]At the same time, the Court expressed the opinion that "the Lithuanian Government would equally require protection if the act were an executive act and not a legislative act". The *Memel* case, p. 28.

[45]This broad understanding of the concept of authorities of the Memel Territory sparked also a discussion concerning the right to vote and stand for election for municipalities and districts along the lines of whether only those with the regional citizenship of the Memel Territory would have the right or whether the right would belong to all citizens of Lithuania, resident in the Memel Territory. Rogge as well as the administrative court of the Memel Territory seem to have been of the former opinion, while Robinson (1934a), p. 598–601 was of the latter opinion, grounding his inclusive view on Art. 19 of the Statute. Because the Memel Territory had legislative competence over the organization of municipalities and districts and because the right to vote and stand for election was not regarded a civil right of the kind that should be available to all Lithuanians on an equal basis, the former interpretation can probably be regarded as correct.

same time as the broad description would probably have functioned as a definition of the jurisdiction of the courts in Memel. Nonetheless, for a legal order to emerge, legislation has to be passed, and it is safe to assume that the principal aim of Art. 5 was to delineate the legislative competence of the Chamber of Representatives, with secondary effects after legislation had been passed on the executive and the judiciary. However, in Art. 5, some of the powers of Memel were determined so that their exercise presumed the existence of national legislation. This is true in relation to the registration of trading vessels in accordance with the laws of Lithuania and the regulation of the sojourn of foreigners which was also in conformity with the laws of Lithuania, which would seem to result in a situation where legislative action by the legislature of Memel was not required or, if rules are passed, they would have been subordinate to the legislation enacted by the Parliament of Lithuania.[46] This would also have been the effect of the treaty ratification provision in Art. 4 of the Statute, which in the first paragraph of Art. 5 was given precedence over the subject-matter identified in the enumeration: because treaties were to be ratified by the Lithuanian legislature also with a view to the competencies of Memel, it could be said that the powers of Memel were circumscribed by whatever treaties Lithuania chose to ratify (see below, Sect. 2.2.4).

Much of the subject-matter within the competence of the Memel Territory can be placed in the area of public law of a continental European nature, such as the organization and administration of communes (municipalities) and districts, public worship, public education, public relief and health, including veterinary regulations, social welfare, local railways (except those belonging to the Lithuanian state), roads and local public works, police (subject to the provisions of Articles 20 and 21), the acquisition of rights of citizenship (subject to the provisions of Art. 8), the organization of the judicial system (subject to the provisions of Articles 21–24), direct and indirect taxes levied in the Territory (with the exception of customs duties, excise duties, commodity taxes and monopolies on alcohol, tobacco and similar luxury items), and the administration of public property belonging to the Memel Territory.[47]

However, the legislature of Memel also had the possibility to pass norms in areas which normally are regarded as pertaining to so-called private law,

[46]Interestingly, Robinson (1934a), p. 561, makes the point that the legislation adopted by the Chamber of Representatives in the Memel Territory was subordinate to the legislation adopted by the Parliament of Lithuania and that the latter would take precedence in case of conflicting provisions. Such a conclusion is, however, not viable against the background of the Statute, and it would have meant that the autonomy of the Memel Territory was not at all of a legislative nature, but of an administrative nature only, a characterization which is not supported by the documentation. Such an interpretation would defy the entire notion of autonomy in the Statute.

[47]Concerning comments on the substantive powers of the Memel Territory, see Robinson (1934a), pp. 351–468.

such as labor legislation, civil legislation (including proprietary rights) and criminal, agrarian, forestry and commercial legislation (including weights and measures), with the understanding that all operations effected by the credit and the insurance institutions and the exchanges shall be subject to the general law of the Republic, regulations governing organizations officially representing the economic interests of the Territory, and the regulation on Memel Territory of timber-floating and navigation on the rivers (other than the Niémen) and the canals within the Memel Territory, subject to agreement with the Lithuanian authorities in case such watercourses are usable outside the Memel Territory for timber-floating.

It was at least of principal importance that Art. 5 also contained a provision according to which the legislative bodies of the Republic of Lithuania and the Memel Territory could take legal dispositions to effect a unification of laws and regulations. For instance, it would have been possible for the legislature of Memel to incorporate, by way of a reference in a piece of law, an entire act of the Parliament of Lithuania as the law of Memel. It seems, however, as if the main focus of the provision was the material unification of law, for instance, in the field of commercial law, the expected effect of such unification being that norms with the same contents would exist both in the Memel Territory and the rest of Lithuania. It appears that no such unification of law was ever achieved in any area of legislation.[48]

The enumerated sphere of competence of the Memel authorities and, in particular, of the legislative body of Lithuania as the principal organ was hence very broad, and the limitation of Lithuanian sovereignty throughout the Convention and the Statute was therefore very far-reaching. In addition, however, Art. 5 of the Statute made it possible to extend the competence of the authorities of the Memel Territory to other matters through the laws of Lithuania. The reference to the laws of Lithuania does not clearly establish the normative level at which such additional delegation of powers would be possible, but the use of the plural form "laws" indicates that sole use of the Constitution was not the only alternative: the additional delegation of powers to the authorities of Memel could also be effectuated in other norms. In so far as such a delegation would take on the form of ordinary legislation, the possibility would remain that the legislature of Lithuania could revoke the additional delegation by an ordinary legislative decision, because there was no protection under the Statute against such a revocation.[49] Also, such an additional delegation by an ordinary law of Lithuania did perhaps not add to the powers of the legislature of Memel, but instead to the powers of the executive authorities.

[48]Robinson (1934a), p. 469 f.

[49]See also Robinson (1934a), p. 468 f. According to Robinson, an enlargement of competence of this kind occurred only once, within the area of criminal procedure.

The broad law-making powers possessed by Memel did not go unchecked. Under Art. 6 of the Statute, in the absence of provisions to the contrary within the Statute, the local authorities of the Memel Territory, in exercising the powers conferred upon them by the Statute, were under an obligation to conform to the principles of the Lithuanian Constitution.[50] Consequently, it is possible to say that the autonomy arrangement was, at the outset, not placed outside the reach of the Lithuanian Constitution, but that instead the Constitution of Lithuania was also the Constitution of the Memel Territory. However, the provisions of the Statute could certainly in many ways be regarded as exceptions to the Lithuanian Constitution.[51] Therefore, it seems that if a hierarchy of norms were to be constructed, the Constitution of Lithuania came first and, for the Memel Territory, the Statute came second, after which the ordinary legislation adopted by the Memel legislature and the Parliament of Lithuania could be considered as taking third place in the ranking of normative levels.

The more practical implementation of the principles of the Lithuanian Constitution in the area of law-making in Memel was in the last instance the task of the Governor, because he had to promulgate the laws passed by the Chamber of Representatives within 1 month after their submission to him (and laws declared urgent by the Chamber within 2 weeks), unless he decided to exercise his right of veto. According to Art. 16, the Governor had the right to veto laws passed by the Chamber of Representatives of the Memel Territory, if these laws exceeded the competence of the authorities of the Territory as laid down by the present Statute, or if they were incompatible with the provisions of Art. 6 (that is, did not conform with the principles of the Lithuanian Constitution) or with the international obligations of Lithuania. The veto powers of the Governor were of an absolute nature.[52] In addition, the authorities of the Memel Territory, that is, the Chamber of Representatives, the Directorate and the courts of law, were under a duty to give effect to the principles of the Lithuanian Constitution,[53] and this duty was also a guiding principle for the Governor as representative of the Lithuanian Government in a way which would have created a basis for the use of the veto. The veto powers of the Governor were to be used on the basis of legal grounds, not on the basis of practical expediency.[54]

Finally, under Art. 24, the jurisdiction of the Supreme Court of Lithuania extended itself over the entire territory of the Republic, including the Memel

[50]The notion of the Lithuanian Constitution was not limited to the first Lithuanian Constitution of 1922, in force at the time of the conclusion of the Convention, but encompassed also the later constitutions, that is, those of 1928 and 1938. See Robinson (1934a), p. 474 ff.

[51]See, e.g., Kalijarvi (1937), p. 203. But cf. Robinson (1934a), p. 471 f., who vigorously denies the nature of the Statute as containing exception to the Constitution of Lithuania and criticizes Rogge on that point.

[52]For a discussion about the veto powers of the Governor, see Robinson (1934a), pp. 525–528.

[53]Robinson (1934a), p. 471.

[54]Robinson (1934a), p. 560 f.

Territory. This Court included a special Section to deal with the affairs of the Memel Territory, mainly composed of judges drawn from the courts of the Memel Territory, and it was also able to hold its sessions in the town of Memel. Hence complaints that originated on the basis of the legislation of Memel in the courts of Memel were tried at the final instance by the Supreme Court of Lithuania, which was a state court. The highest echelon of the entire legal order of Lithuania was thus united and delivered judgments that at least in principle were designed to harmonize the interpretation of law in the entire territory of the state, while at the same time recognizing the unique source of law of Memel.[55] It seems, however, that the Supreme Court of Lithuania was not the final arbiter of the Statute of Memel but that instead this was the PCIJ. While the Supreme Court remained at the helm of substantive law, constitutional adjudication of at least institutional relationships concerning, e.g., the competencies of the two jurisdictions remained a matter for the PCIJ. This role of the PCIJ was, of course, much limited by the fact that recourse to the PCIJ was through the States signatories to the Convention: for a constitutional case to arise on the basis of the Statute before the PCIJ, a problem of international magnitude was needed. More ordinary constitutional problems would not find their way to the PCIJ, and thus remained outside the realm of judicial review, although the Supreme Court of Lithuania was able to adjudicate on at least some conflicts of competence in concrete cases, while it did not have the power to try the relationship between ordinary legislation and the Constitution of Lithuania.[56] In short, there was no umpire or arbiter designated in the Statute to exercise internal constitutional jurisdiction for Memel.[57] Such a court, empowered to review cases involving the compatibility of the acts of the Memel Government with the Statute, was, however, established by the Parliament of Lithuania in 1935,[58] but due to the complicated

---

[55]See Robinson (1934a), pp. 699–714. This internal judicial separation between Lithuanian and Memel law, reflected in the court organization, is evidently explained by the fact that in the Memel Territory, the German legal system and those German laws that were not specifically revoked or amended after the creation of the autonomy arrangement continued to be applied after the transfer of the territory to Lithuania, whereas the rest of Lithuania had been under the Russian legal system, which did not provide for a solid basis for adjudicating cases arising in the Memel Territory. See Rogge (1928), p. 352 f. and Kalijarvi (1937), pp. 79, 226. See also Plieg (1962), p. 217, who makes the same contrast between the Russian and the German legal systems. On the top of general courts, there were also administrative courts in the Memel Territory, as explained in Robinson (1934a), pp. 588–591.

[56]Robinson (1934a), pp. 704–705.

[57]See Robinson (1934a), pp. 276, 349, and Lapidoth (1997), p. 84 f. See also Robinson (1934a), p. 559, who connects the power of constitutional review to the veto powers of the Governor on the basis of the reference in Art. 16 of the Statute to the requirement of observance of the principles of the Lithuanian Constitution in Art. 6 and who apparently is of the opinion that the exercise of the veto powers is to be understood as constitutional review.

[58]Statutgerichtsgesetz, Amtsblatt des Memelgebietes 20 März1935, pp. 207–210. According to the Act, the statute review court is affiliated with the Supreme Court of Lithuania, and consists of the President of the Supreme Court and four judges, appointed by the Lithuanian president for 7 years, who are knowledgeable in the area of public law. The court would try different cases, such as

political situation in Lithuania at the end of the 1930s, the Statute Court never started to operate. This was probably not entirely negative, because the legislation establishing the Statute Court was very unclear on, for instance, what the consequences of a ruling of the Court would be in a case where an act of the Memel Government, including the Chamber of Representatives, was declared to be in violation of the Statute.[59]

The existence of two different fields of legislative competence in the territory of Memel was the source of some confusion (although the competence of the Parliament of Lithuania was relatively limited) with regard to the material competence of the courts. In principle, only courts of the Memel Territory existed in the area at first instance and at appeal level as well as for administrative matters, so the problem was whether they could also try cases on the basis of legislation adopted by the Parliament of Lithuania. In principle, the issue seems to have followed the principle *cuius legislatio eius iurisdictio*,[60] that is, that the courts of Memel tried cases arising on the basis of the laws of Memel, while the courts of Lithuania tried cases arising on the basis of such laws of Lithuania that were applicable in the Memel Territory. Therefore, in a number of areas, such as the military, the criminal liability of those civil servants of the Lithuanian state who functioned in the Memel Territory and were tried at first instance (for such crimes as treason), parties appeared before the Lithuanian courts, not the courts of the Memel Territory. Ultimately, however, the

conflicts between an act of the Lithuanian Parliament and an act of the Memel Territory, conflicts between a Memel act and the Memel Statute, conflicts of administrative acts of Lithuania and the Memel Statute, conflicts between the acts of the Governor of Memel and the Memel Statute, and conflicts between administrative acts of Memel and the Memel Statute. Because there was no provision that the court could try the relationship between an act of Memel Territory and the Constitution of Lithuania, it seems that constitutional review was not explicitly possible, unless the Constitution was considered an act of the Lithuanian Parliament. Cases could be initiated by the President of the Directorate, the Governor of Memel and the Minister of Justice, and the judgments of the courts were final. It seems clear that the statute review court could not preempt the jurisdiction of the PCIJ under the Memel Statute. See also Hannum (1996), p. 382, and Kalijarvi (1937), p. 243 f., who concludes that there is "serious doubt as to the validity of the decisions of this tribunal, where Lithuania is both judge and party".

[59]For a critical assessment of the Lithuanian Act establishing the Statute Court, see von Freytagh-Loringhoven (1935), pp. 520–525. For instance, it seems that a case could be initiated against a piece of law anytime after its enactment, which made it possible to raise a complaint also for very old legislation, creating a certain measure of legal uncertainty. von Freytagh-Loringhoven (1935), p. 523, draws the conclusion that the Statute Court was created in order to usurp the powers and functions of the League of Nations and the PCIJ.

[60]Robinson (1934a), pp. 633, 636, 638. The judicial autonomy of the Memel Territory was enhanced by the provision in Art. 22 of the Statute, which stipulated that the organization and competence of the tribunals of the Memel Territory shall be determined by a law of the Territory, subject to Art. 24, according to which the Supreme Court of Lithuania was the highest court instance. The judicial autonomy was also sustained by the provision of Art. 23 of the Statute, according to which the judges in the Memel Territory would be appointed by the Directorate. See Robinson (1934a), pp. 694–698.

Supreme Court of Lithuania, with its Memel Section, was in charge of producing the final decisions in the state.[61]

2.2.2 *Participation*

The exercise of public powers, most notably of the legislative powers, is normally legitimized by means of some form of participation. There are two main mechanisms of participation normally associated with the exercise of legislative powers and with national and sub-national decision-making, namely elections and referendums. The Memel Statute does not contain provisions concerning the use of the referendum as a mechanism within the Territory for the purposes of adopting legislation or resolving other issues. Therefore, direct participation by means of a referendum was clearly not the main mode of participation, although the option may have remained whereby the advisory referendum could be used to gauge the opinions of the inhabitants on a certain issue. However, the Statute itself contained in Art. 38 provisions concerning its amendment, and in a case where a proposal to amend the Statute had been approved by the Chamber of Representatives, a minority of one quarter of the Chamber, or 5,000 persons with the right to vote, could require that the amendment was submitted to the people in a referendum before the Parliament of Lithuania had to make the final decision on the amendment issue. An amendment of the Statute required in such cases the approval of two thirds of the citizens of the Memel Territory participating in the referendum.[62]

---

[61] On the competence of the court systems, see Robinson (1934a), pp. 608–677. According to Robinson (1934a), p. 670, there were also some special courts in the Memel Territory, such as "das Kaufmannsgericht, das Gewerbegericht, das Seeamt, das Pachteinigungsamt und die Schlichtungsausschüsse". Evidently, the fact that for most of the time, there was a state of emergency of some sort in force gave space for many encroachments by the authorities of Lithuania into the powers of the courts (and also administrative authorities) of Memel, including the incarceration of inhabitants of Memel during several months in Lithuanian prisons on the basis of Lithuanian norms. See Plieg (1962), pp. 62–67, 182–187.

[62] See Rogge (1928), p. 410–411. In a critical argument against, *inter alia*, Rogge's position, Robinson (1934a), pp. 294–319, 807–812, makes the point that the Memel Territory had no constitutional autonomy of its own, but was entirely dependent on the parliament of Lithuania concerning amendments to the Statute. This being so, the Memel Territory was not a "state" in the meaning of a constituent state of a federation, nor a "Staatsfragment" or an autonomous territorial association or corporation. Robinson seems to come down on regarding the Memel Territory as a protected self-government *sui generis*, designed to function as means of separate implementation such powers in the areas of legislation, administration, judiciary and finances which are grounded in the Lithuanian legal order. Robinson also argued that the referendum legislation would be enacted by the Lithuanian Parliament, that not only those with the regional citizenship would have the right to vote and that the referendum would be of a facultative nature only. Robinson (1934a), p. 537, regarded the provision of the Statute that the Lithuanian Parliament would enact the election law for the Memel Territory as another piece of evidence for the absence of constitutional

Elections to the Chamber of Representatives are only indirectly referred to in the *Memel* case by the Court. In their submissions, the parties to the case make some references to elections,[63] but the contribution of the Court is mainly related to a discussion concerning the dismissal of the Chamber of Representatives, which as a consequence would have necessitated the holding of new elections. This is clear, for instance, on the basis of the reference to Art. 12, para. 5, of the Statute, which deals with the dissolution of the Chamber and the holding of elections to a new Chamber.[64] In commenting on the provision, the Court made the observation that "[d]issensions may well arise between the Chamber and a Directorate duly installed in office, i.e. which had received at the outset of its career the confidence of the Chamber. Such occurrences are common in all countries which are subject to a parliamentary regime. It may well happen in such a case that the Directorate would believe that the policy which it desired to follow was the right policy and the policy which would commend itself to the electorate. The Directorate is in such cases qualified under Article 12 to agree to a dissolution. It would only desire a dissolution because it expected that the electorate would support it."[65] Therefore, elections to the Chamber hover continuously above the actual issues resolved in the case.

After having resolved the case, the Court appended a *dictum* to the judgment concerning the effects of the case. In the Court's opinion, the Governor should not have dissolved the Chamber of Representatives. However, the Court did not intend to say that "the action of the Governor in dissolving the Chamber, even though it was contrary to the treaty, was of no effect in the sphere of municipal law. This is tantamount to saying that the dissolution is not to be regarded as void in the sense that the old Chamber is still in existence, and that the new Chamber since elected has no legal existence."[66] The Court thus gave no *ex tunc* effect to its decision so that the elections held after the dissolution would have been voided: in the judgment, the Court issued the caveat that it only interpreted the Memel Statute in relation to its relationship with the treaty, while it did not want to withdraw the legal effects of the actions of the Governor in the sphere of municipal (that is, domestic) law. The case thus resolved the principal issue and would most likely have affected *ex nunc* similar future situations.

The most common participatory actor in a representative political setting which utilizes elections is the political party. The case recognizes the existence of a party system in the Memel Territory and the importance of the party system in the context of parliamentary accountability, because the appointee of the Governor to fill the

autonomy of the Memel Territory. See also Plieg (1962), p. 215, who is of the opinion that the Memel Territory possessed a statehood of its own which was not dependent on the sovereign will of the Lithuanian state, but on the Convention, that is, on a treaty of international law. For a similar position, see Kalijarvi (1937), pp. 205–218.

[63]See, e.g., the *Memel* case, pp. 16, 17, 20.

[64]The *Memel* case, p. 43.

[65]The *Memel* case, p. 44.

[66]The *Memel* case, p. 46.

post of the President of the Government after the dismissal of Mr. Böttcher was Mr. Simaitis, who was "a person who did not belong to the existing political parties at Memel"[67] and whose appointment further aggravated and complicated the conflict in the Memel Territory. Moreover, it is stated that as the new President of the Directorate, Mr. Simaitis engaged in negotiations with the leaders of the majority parties with a view to forming a Directorate, that is, a government with members acceptable to the majority parties.[68] The Statute, however, does not make reference to political parties, but is entirely silent on the issue. The existence of a multitude of political parties and a multi-party political system in the Memel Territory is thus presumed by the PCIJ.

That presumption can be inferred from the Statute, although the Statute does not mention the political parties in connection with elections. According to Art. 2 of the Statute, the Memel Territory shall constitute, under the sovereignty of Lithuania, a unit, organized on democratic principles. Such principles relate, to a great extent, to the mechanisms of participation and to elections, in particular, and to the exercise of public powers in legislative and executive decision-making. Article 33 of the Statute also provides for the existence of freedom of assembly and association as well as freedom of conscience and of the press, which all are rights essential for a viable party system, this being particularly the case with the freedom of association. However, the main concern seems to have been how these rights could be limited with reference to public order, in particular, from the side of the Lithuanian Government.[69]

As concerns elections to the Chamber, the Statute was, in an interesting way, connecting the Memel Territory to the Republic of Lithuania, by requiring in Art. 11 that elections to the Memel Chamber were carried out in conformity with Lithuanian election law. As a consequence, some of the most salient features of the political system of the autonomous entity were to be directly modeled on that of the so-called mother state. At the outset, there was no need to have any separate election law in place in Memel, because Lithuanian law also applied for the purposes of elections to the Chamber of Representatives. However, in 1925, the Parliament of Lithuania enacted a separate piece of legislation governing elections in Memel, the Act on the Elections to the Chamber of Representatives.[70] The fact

[67]The *Memel* case, p. 41.

[68]The *Memel* case, p. 42.

[69]See Robinson (1934a), pp. 774–784, who even makes the point that the application of the competencies of the Lithuanian state and the Memel Territory could conceivably lead to the imposition of double censorship, one by the state and another by the Memel Territory.

[70]For the election law of Memel, see Robinson (1934b), pp. 503–521. According to Robinson (1934a), p. 530 f., the reason for a separate election law for Memel, adopted by the Lithuanian Parliament, was that the Lithuanian election law was not suitable for the specificities of the Memel Territory. For the text of the Election Act in Lithuanian and German, see Rogge (1928), pp. 114–136. The Election Act was amended several times. See Robinson (1934a), p. 531. The Lithuanian language original of the Act used the term "Seimelis" to denote the Chamber of Representatives, which is a diminutive form of the Lithuanian term "Seim" for Parliament. Ibid., p. 114, fn. 1. See also Rogge (1928), pp. 323–325, for a commentary to Art. 11 of the Memel Statute.

that elections to the Chamber of Representatives in Memel were dependent on Lithuanian election law may have created some measure of uncertainty about the matter, especially after the turn of Lithuania towards authoritarianism.[71]

In principle, however, such a turn towards authoritarianism in Lithuania should not have affected the election rules applicable in the Memel Territory, because under Art. 10 of the Statute, the Chamber of Representatives was to be elected by universal, equal, direct and secret suffrage. The method of election was further specified in Art. 11, according to which the members of the Chamber would be elected for 3 years by the citizens of the Memel Territory in the proportion of one deputy per five thousand inhabitants or for any fraction exceeding two thousand five hundred inhabitants.

The mandate period of 3 years was in no way unusual,[72] but it was quite exceptional that the right to vote (and, presumably, also the right to stand as a candidate) would be restricted to the citizens of the Memel Territory. Eligibility was thus conditioned upon the possession of a special regional citizenship, created actually under Articles 8–10 of the Convention, where the point of departure was that former German citizens, that is, those persons who had been residents of the Memel area from 1918 to 1924, would automatically acquire Lithuanian citizenship and because of their residency in Memel, citizenship of Memel as well. Citizenship of the Memel Territory was also regulated on the basis of Art. 8 of the Statute, which in other articles connected certain specific rights to the possession of the regional citizenship. Early on, the interpretation seems to have existed that the possession of regional citizenship of Memel would have been possible without the simultaneous possession of Lithuanian citizenship and was enough for the right to vote and to stand as candidate.[73] However, this interpretation was convincingly disputed and regional citizenship was made dependent on the possession of Lithuanian citizenship in explicit provisions of the law.[74] For regional citizenship, the

[71]It is, however, worth mentioning in the context that according to Art. 19 of the Statute, elections to the communal and district assemblies were to be held in accordance with the laws of the Memel Territory and electoral laws regulating such elections were to be drawn up following democratic principles. Thus there existed a requirement of election legislation of the Memel territory for the lower echelons of public administration. The fact that the lower echelons (municipalities and districts) were recognized in the Statute signals the fact that the concept of self-government in the context of autonomies is likely to reach far beyond the main decision-making bodies of the autonomous entity.

[72]See also Rogge (1928), p. 326.

[73]Rogge (1928), p. 305 f. As concluded by Rogge (1928), p. 323, Lithuanian citizens who did not possess the regional citizenship of the Memel Territory were not entitled to vote in the elections to the Chamber of Representatives.

[74]Robinson (1934a), pp. 494–510. The construction of the regional citizenship, granted by the authorities of the Memel Territory, so that it would have been independent of the national citizenship was implausible also against the background of Art. 9 of the Statute, according to which persons who were in the possession of the regional citizenship of the Memel Territory were entitled to enjoy the same civil rights as the Lithuanian citizens over the entire territory of Lithuania. See also Robinson (1934a), pp. 514–519 concerning the equal rights of the two groups

conditions were originally the requirement of residency in the Memel Territory and a waiting time of 1 year. The requirement of the waiting time was dropped in 1932.[75]

What was also quite exceptional in Art. 11 was that instead of determining an exact number of mandates or seats in the Chamber of Representatives, the Statute established a ratio of representation, at one member per five thousand inhabitants as a maximum or one member per any number of inhabitants varying between 2,500 and 5,000 inhabitants. This rule led to flexibility in determining the number of seats in the Chamber in a manner that had a bearing on the electoral system, which was described by Robinson as the same *automatische Wahlsystem* (automatic election system) that had been used for the Lithuanian Parliament, that is, a proportional election system using so-called long lists.[76] At the same time, there was a distinction between those who were represented, the inhabitants, which normally was a larger group, and those who were entitled to vote, the citizens of Memel, which was a more restricted group of persons.[77]

The first elections of 19 October 1925 featured candidates from *Memelländische Landwirtschaftspartei*, *Memelländische Volkspartei* and *Sozialdemokratische Partei des Memellandes*, which constituted a union against the opponents to autonomy, in particular against the Lithuanian-minded *Bauernpartei*, *Autonomiebund* and *Arbeiterföderation*. The turnout was as high as 83.52%, and the union of the three Memel-minded parties secured 27 of the 29 seats in the Chamber of Representatives with the 58,756 votes cast for it, while the Lithuanian minded

of citizens in their "non-native" territories. There was an attempt from the side of the election commission to disregard on the basis of the Memel election law the regional citizenship as a qualification for the right to vote, but Art. 37 of the Statute was interpreted by a court of the Memel Territory so that only those in possession of the regional citizenship could vote. See Plieg (1962), p. 35.

[75] Plieg (1962), p. 87.

[76] According to Articles 1 and 72 of the 1935 election law for the Memel Territory, as annotated in 1932 and reproduced in Robinson (1934b), pp. 503–521, Memel was, for the purposes of elections to the Chamber of Representatives, one constituency where the seats were distributed so that the total number of votes cast in the constituency was divided by the number of representatives to be elected from the constituency, after which this remainder was used to divide the number of votes cast for each list, the result being the number of representatives elected from each list. Because the number of inhabitants in the Memel Territory was somewhat over 140000 inhabitants and because under the Statute, there would be 1 representative elected for each 5,000 inhabitants, the number of representatives to be elected was normally 29.

[77] See Robinson (1934a), p. 535. Article 37 of the Statute regulated the first elections in the territory: "The first elections to the Chamber of Representatives shall take place within six weeks from the date of the coming into force of the present Statute. The Chamber will meet 15 days after the elections. Only inhabitants of the Memel Territory over 21 years of age may take part in these elections, provided: i° that, having acquired Lithuanian nationality on the conditions specified in Article 8, paragraph i, of the Convention referred to in the preamble to this Statute, they do not opt for German nationality before the date of the elections ; 2° that at least 15 days before the elections they opt for Lithuanian nationality on the conditions specified in Article 8, (a) and (b), of the said Convention." The age limit was later changed by the Lithuanian Parliament.

parties got only two seats with their 3,761 votes. In addition, there were other parties that participated in the elections, such as *Kommunisten* and *Mieterbund der Stadt Memel*.[78]

The second elections to the Chamber of Representatives were held on 30 August 1927 after the Chamber was dissolved following a persistent conflict between the Governor and the political establishment of the Memel Territory over the appointment of the President of the Directorate.[79] The German-minded *Volkspartei* and the *Landwirtschaftspartei* lost one seat each and the Social Democrats two, while the Lithuanian minded parties gained two seats and the Communists came in with two seats. The division between the two blocs in terms of seats was therefore 25 seats to 4.[80]

The third elections to the Chamber of Representatives were held on 10 October 1930. They were characterized, *inter alia*, by the illegal participation of such Lithuanian voters who did not possess regional citizenship of the Memel Territory. The German or autonomy-oriented *Landwirtscahftspartei*, *Volkspartei*, *Sozialdemokratische Partei* and *Arbeiterpartei des Memelgebiets* secured 24 seats in total, while the Lithuanian minded parties won 5 seats.[81]

The fourth elections to the Chamber of Representatives were held on 4 May 1932. Despite the increase in the number of regional citizens entitled to vote, the German or autonomy oriented bloc of parties once again secured 24 seats in the Chamber of Representatives, while the number of Lithuanian oriented representatives remained at 5.[82]

The fifth elections to the Chamber of Representatives were held on 29 September 1935, and then, the German or Memel-minded political context became even clearer. The 29 seats in the Chamber of Representatives were contested by 187 candidates on the list of the German or autonomy oriented bloc and by candidates on six Lithuanian oriented lists. Each voter received a small binder of slips, and on each slip, alphabetically ordered, the name of one candidate was printed without any reference to which party or list the candidate was representing. The voter had to pick out the preferred 29 names of candidates from this slip, an operation that took approximately 10 minutes per voter and caused the elections to be prolonged by 1 day. In spite of the complicated voting procedure, the turnout rate rose to 91.3%. Out of 1,964,073 votes cast under this method in the election, the great majority, i.e. 1,592,604 votes, that is, more than 81%, were cast for candidates of the *Memelländisch Union*, the main German-minded party. Only 6 of the 29 members of the Chamber were Lithuanians. Many charges were made of election-related

[78]Plieg (1962), p. 35. There was also a party of the civil servants of the Lithuanian state, but it dissolved itself before the elections.

[79]Already at this point, the legal issues underlying the *Memel* case before the PCIJ were becoming visible.

[80]See Plieg (1962), p. 41, and fn. 48 in particular.

[81]See Plieg (1962), p. 46, and fn. 88 in particular.

[82]See Plieg (1962), p. 88, and fn. 23 in particular.

wrongdoing following the elections,[83] such as the inflation by the Lithuanian authorities of the number of persons who were granted regional citizenship,[84] in addition to the fact that the election observers sent by the signatories to the Convention were not satisfied with the complicated voting procedure.[85]

The sixth elections to the Chamber of Representatives were held on 11 December 1938. The turnout on this occasion rose to 96.8%. The *Memeldeutsche Liste*, which replaced the former German or autonomy oriented party lists in the territory and which was led by a national socialistically oriented person who had been imprisoned for treason, won 87% of the votes cast, and most of the candidates elected from that list were standing for Chamber elections for the first time. The large share of votes translated into 25 representatives in the Chamber of Representatives, while the Lithuanian oriented lists secured a total of 4 seats in the Chamber.[86]

As summarized by Plieg (see Table 2.1, below),[87] political sentiments within the Memel Territory were consistently German or autonomy-oriented, while the Lithuanian oriented political forces remained in a minority position:

Table 2.1 Political support of Memel-oriented parties

	1st Chamber, 19 Oct 1925	2nd Chamber, 30 Aug 1927	3rd Chamber, 10 Oct 1930	4th Chamber, 4 May 1932	5th Chamber, 29–30 Sept 1935	6th Chamber, 11 Dec 1938
Total no. of votes cast	62,517	54,756	49,130	65,767	67,657	72,247
For Memel. German parties	58,756	45,968	40,813	53,128	54,917	62,986
In percent	94	84	82.2	80.8	81.2	87.2
Seats of the "Memel people"	27/29	25/29	24/29	24/29	24/29	25/29

Elections were also held at local government level. As concerns the town of Memel, it grew considerably during the era of autonomy, and a good part of the

[83]See Kalijarvi (1936), pp. 210–212.

[84]It seems as if 11,810 voters had cast their votes for the Lithuanian-oriented candidates, and because altogether 10383 persons of Lithuanian origin had been granted regional citizenship by 29 September 1935, Plieg (1962), p. 162, draws the conclusion that the six Lithuanian-oriented representatives in the Chamber of Representatives got elected because of this extraordinary registration of persons who otherwise would have been unqualified as voters. The other conclusion drawn by Plieg is that in practice, the entire resident population of the Memel Territory had supported the candidates of *Memelländisch Union*, that is, the bloc of German or autonomy-oriented parties. According to Plieg (1962), p. 218, altogether 10,000 Lithuanians would have moved to the Memel Territory between 1925 and 1938.

[85]Plieg (1962), p. 162. So also Kalijarvi (1937), p. 241 f.

[86]Plieg (1962), p. 201.

[87]Plieg (1962), p. 218.

explanation for the increase in the number of inhabitants could be attributed to the encouragement by the Lithuanian central government authorities in regard of persons from other parts of Lithuania to move to the Memel Territory. For instance, in the elections to the city council of Memel (see Table 2.2, below),[88] the votes between the German or autonomy oriented candidates and the Lithuanian oriented candidates were distributed as follows:

Table 2.2 Distribution of political support in Memel city council

	German-oriented	Lithuanian-oriented
1924	38	2
1930	34	6
1933	31	9
1936	25	15

For the citizens of Memel who were at the same time citizens of Lithuania, participation through elections was not limited to electing the Chamber of Representatives in Memel or to electing members of the local government. According to Art. 3 of the Statute, the election of deputies representing the Memel Territory to the Lithuanian Parliament would take place in conformity with the Lithuanian electoral legislation.[89] Consequently, all those inhabitants of Memel who had Lithuanian citizenship were involved in the governance of the whole of Lithuania on an equal basis with other Lithuanians.[90] This participation was probably important with regard to those powers that were not granted to Memel, that is, those residual powers that the public authorities of Lithuania in general and the Parliament in particular held on the basis of the Statute. At the same time, it is possible to assume that representation of Memel in the Lithuanian Parliament was important for making sure that the entitlements of Memel on the basis of the Statute were respected by the Lithuanian authorities. However, the main point in this context is that the persons elected from the Memel Territory were not representatives of the special interests of Memel, but members of a legislature acting on the basis of a free mandate in the interests of the entire state.[91]

The 1926 Lithuanian election law identified the Memel Territory as one constituency among the ten constituencies for the purposes of the elections to the Lithuanian Parliament and determined that five representatives out of a total of 85

[88]Plieg (1962), p. 178.

[89]Taking into consideration Articles 1 and 76 of the Lithuanian election law of 1926 the elections to the Lithuanian Parliament were proportional and based on long lists in altogether ten constituencies, where the seats were distributed so that the total number of votes cast in the constituency was divided by the number of representatives to be elected from the constituency, after which this election remainder was used to divide the number of votes cast for each list, the result being the number of representatives elected from each list.

[90]See Rogge (1928), p. 308.

[91]See Rogge (1928), p. 272 f., Robinson (1934a), p. 328.

parliamentary representatives would be elected from the Memel Territory. Hence formally speaking, there were no special seats reserved for the Memel Territory in the Lithuanian Parliament,[92] but parliamentary elections were conducted in the Memel Territory amongst the eligible Lithuanian voters, and the number of representatives to be elected from each constituency was established by the national election commission in proportion to the number of inhabitants. The first general elections in which the Memel Territory participated were held the same year, 1926, and in those elections, the five mandates were divided between various parties connected with autonomy.[93]

Following the election of the representatives of the Memel Territory to the electoral college for the election of the President of Lithuania in 1938, they then declined to participate in the election of the president. This incident showed the extent of the rift that had developed between the Memel Territory, on the one hand, and the state of Lithuania, on the other.[94]

2.2.3 *The Executive*

Although the *Memel* case turns on the powers of an autonomous entity, the core of the case is about the powers enjoyed by the executive branch of government of the autonomous entity. The main thrust of the *Memel* case therefore deals with the actions of the executive, and with whether or not those actions were in keeping with the powers accorded to the Memel Territory in the Statute. In principle, the Statute was limited to the regulation of the position of the authorities of the Memel Territory, in particular the position of the Directorate, but actions by its President made it necessary for the Court to bring into the picture the executive of the central government of Lithuania, as represented by the Governor of the Memel Territory. From that perspective, the case is also about the powers of Lithuania and its executive.

By introducing the central government of Lithuania, as represented by the Governor of Memel,[95] as an actor into the political life of the Memel Territory, the *Memel* case does not only deal with the ordinary horizontal accountability of the government before the parliament, but also with a vertical accountability of a particular kind. This vertical accountability comes into play in the situation in which the central government or the governor perceives that the autonomous entity has overstepped the limits of its competence and acted in a way which contradicts the autonomy statute.

The claim was that the authorities of the Memel Territory, and especially its Directorate, did not have powers to make contacts with foreign countries, because

---

[92]See Robinson (1934a), p. 328.

[93]Rogge (1928), p. 273.

[94]Plieg (1962), p. 198.

[95]For an analysis of the role of the Governor as the representative of the central Government of Lithuania, see Rogge (1928), p. 270 ff.

those powers were reserved to the state of Lithuania. The more specific problem in the context was that the Statute did not outline the specific powers of the Directorate, a legal situation which opened up an opportunity for the Directorate to act under an assumption of the existence of implied powers of some kind. There seems to have been an understanding that the enumeration of competencies in respect of the authorities of the Memel Territory mainly concerned the legislative branch and that the executive branch would have more latitude to act in its own right because of the silence of the Statute. At the same time, the *Memel* case dealt with the powers of the state of Lithuania and of the Governor, its representative in the territory. On the one hand, the powers of the Governor were established in the Statute, but on the other hand, the powers that he could exercise in Memel were relatively few and did not encompass the situation that gave rise to the case. Hence even in the case of the Governor, there could have existed some implied powers. This argument is what the parties appeared to put forward in their submissions.[96]

The Court returned the matter to the spheres of competence of the two entities, those of the state of Lithuania and those of the autonomous entity of Memel, by concluding that on the one hand, under the Statute, Lithuania was to enjoy full sovereignty over the Territory ceded to it under the Peace Treaty, subject to the limitations imposed on its exercise, while on the other the autonomy of Memel was only to operate within the limits so fixed and expressly specified. The Court found that pursuant to Articles 1 and 2 of the Convention and Articles 1 and 7 of the Statute, the powers of the one and the autonomous powers of the other "are of a quite different order in that the exercise of the latter powers necessitates the existence of a legal rule which cannot be inferred from the silence of the instrument from which the autonomy is derived, or from an interpretation designed to extend the autonomy by encroaching upon the operation of the sovereign power".[97]

It seems that Art. 7 is of crucial importance in the context, because it establishes the enumerated powers of Memel and the residual powers of the state of Lithuania (see above, Sect. 2.2.1). The Court denied the general existence of implied powers for the Memel Territory and concluded that the autonomy of Memel "only exists within the limits fixed by the Statute and that, in the absence of provisions to the contrary in the Convention or its annexes, the rights ensuing from the sovereignty of Lithuania must apply".[98] Although the Statute mainly dealt with the powers of the Memel authorities in general, without assigning the powers to the different decision-making bodies of the Memel Territory, such as to the Chamber of Representatives or the Directorate specifically, the Court held that Art. 17 of the Statute, which says that the Directorate shall exercise executive power in the

[96]See the *Memel* case, p. 22.

[97]The *Memel* case, p. 24.

[98]The *Memel* case, p. 24. This message was sustained by the Court on the basis of a consideration of the powers of the Governor, on the basis of which the legislature of the Memel Territory was to be completely independent within the prescribed limits of the autonomy, but that it was to have no legislative power outside those limits". *Ibidem*.

Memel Territory, must be read as restricted to executive power in respect of matters within the competence of the Memel authorities, “otherwise it would be in flagrant contradiction with the provisions in Article 7, which says that affairs which under the Statute are not within the jurisdiction of the local authorities are to be within the *exclusive* jurisdiction of the competent organizations of the Lithuanian Republic”.[99]

Consequently, the executive powers of the Memel Territory were to follow the same delineation of competence in relation to the powers of the state of Lithuania as the legislative powers. Because the President of the Directorate had intruded into a “sphere which was not within the limits of the authority of Memel as defined by the Statute, but fell within the exclusive competence of the Lithuanian Government”,[100] the President could be dismissed. In fact, following Art. 10, delineating the legislative powers of the Chamber, the Court actually formulated a rule that was absent from Art. 17 of the Statute: Executive power in the Memel Territory shall, within the limits of this Statute, be exercised by the Directorate. The same could also be expressed as a (belated) proposal for an amendment to Art. 17: The Directorate shall exercise executive power in the Memel Territory within the limits of this Statute. On the basis of the case, this seems self-evident, but it perhaps lies in the nature of sub-state entities of both the autonomous and federal kind that they from time to time test the boundaries of their powers.

While the applicant States wanted to make the reaction against a Memel executive acting *ultra vires* dependent on a loss of confidence on the part of the Chamber of Representatives, this did not convince the Court, although there were no explicit provisions to deal with a situation in which the Memel executive transgressed the boundaries of competence. The Court could not believe that the respondent State had been left without any protection or remedies in such a situation where the Memel executive went beyond the competences delineated in Art. 7, because that would destroy the general scheme of the Convention. The PCIJ was instead of the opinion that the veto powers of the Governor under Art. 16 regarding legislative acts also entitled the Lithuanian state to protection in relation to executive acts, but instead of a veto on legislation, the mechanism that was approved by the Court was the dismissal of the President of the Directorate. However, such a power of dismissal on the part of the Governor was not without limits. A dismissal could be considered a legitimate and appropriate measure of protection of the interests of the state only in certain specific situations, namely in cases where “the acts complained of were serious acts calculated to prejudice the sovereign rights of Lithuania and violating the provisions of the Memel Statute, and when no other means are available”.[101] Hence the possibility to dismiss the President of the Directorate was very circumscribed and could not be used in every possible situation where discontent with the President existed: the right to dismiss was regarded as an exceptional right

[99]The *Memel* case, p. 26.
[100]The *Memel* case, p. 36.
[101]The *Memel* case, p. 29.

to be exercised only in extreme cases.[102] In addition, the limited right to dismiss the President did not grant the Governor any right to supervise, in a continuous way, the functions and working of the Government of Memel.[103]

The act of dismissal of the President undertaken by the Governor took on the form of revocation of the decree by which the Governor had appointed Mr. Böttcher to be President of the Directorate. There was thus a formal mechanism of appointment which could be reversed: the Governor reversed his earlier decision. When reversing the earlier decision, the reversal only concerned the President, not the other members of the Directorate, who would hold their positions until they were replaced,[104] the assumption being that such replacement would be done by the Chamber of Representatives.

At the same time as the Court established that there may exist a certain vertical accountability of the executive body of the autonomous entity before the national authorities in situations where the executive body at the sub-state level has acted *ultra vires*,[105] the Court outlined the general features of parliamentary accountability in the Memel Territory, that is, the features of horizontal accountability within the autonomous entity. The executive power was defined as the power to carry out all such executive acts as fall within the competence of the Memel authorities, while the right to continue to hold executive office in the Directorate was dependent upon the confidence of the Chamber in the Directorate. It was at this juncture, after the appointment of Mr. Simaitis as President to replace Mr. Böttcher, that the PCIJ started to look into the horizontal mechanism of parliamentary accountability. The Court stated that while the Governor had the power to appoint the President of the Directorate, he would not, in regard to the future functioning of the Memel Government, "forget the provision in Article 17 of the Statute that a Directorate must enjoy the confidence of the Chamber and must resign if the Chamber refuses it its confidence".[106] The Court also asked itself whether the need to take into account the mechanism of confidence "constituted a legal obligation upon the Governor and

[102]The *Memel* case, p. 30.

[103]The *Memel* case, p. 29. It appears that the powers of the Governor were relatively strictly formulated and identified in the Statute and that those powers also were relatively few. See the Memel case, p. 24.

[104]The *Memel* case, pp. 32–33. The other members of the Directorate were appointed by the President without the involvement of the Governor.

[105]According to Wheare (1964), p. 19, such a possibility has apparently also existed in Canada during the time Canada was a Dominion in the British Commonwealth. However, as he explains, "the use of the power of disallowance has not been confined to cases where a provincial act was thought to be *ultra vires*. It had been used also to nullify legislation of which the Dominion executive did not approve." For examples of disallowance both *ultra vires* and *intra vires* in Canada between 1867 and 1939, see Wheare (1964), p. 224 f. While the PCIJ dealt with the disapproval of acts *ultra vires*, it appears that the Governor of Memel, with his direct links to the Government of Lithuania, was also using disapproval of acts *intra vires* in a way which was conditions by perceived national interest.

[106]The *Memel* case, p. 40.

whether, if it can be shown that he has failed to do so, the appointment he has made would not be in order".[107]

The Court was of the opinion that there was no obligation on the part of the Governor to secure in advance the acceptance of the Chamber for the choice of the new President by negotiations with the parties or groups in the Chamber. Instead, the Court found that the confidence of the Chamber is a matter which the Chamber itself will express for itself by its vote at the point when the Directorate starts to function with the Chamber, although a Directorate which has never obtained the confidence of the Chamber may represent no more than the individual will and views of the Governor and of his nominee for the post of President of the Directorate.[108] In addition, the Court pointed out that the Directorate must resign if the Chamber refuses it its confidence. As a practical matter, the PCIJ recognized that the appointee of the Governor, that is, Mr. Simaitis, had engaged in negotiations with the leaders of the majority parties in order to form a Directorate acceptable to them and that if successful, the Chamber would probably have given a vote of confidence to the Directorate at a point when such a vote was required. Had those negotiations been successful, there would have been no dissolution of the Chamber.[109] According to the Statute, so the Court said, the Governor makes the appointment on his own responsibility from amongst the citizens of the Memel Territory and the Chamber gives or refuses its confidence at a later stage.[110] Therefore, the Court arrived at the conclusion that the duty of the Governor to limit his choice of President to persons to whom it may reasonably be expected that the Chamber will accord its confidence is not a legal obligation, although it is a matter of good sense. In the opinion of the Court, any Governor of the Territory would comply with that idea to make the Statute work successfully,[111] but as an issue, the appointment of the President was more a political question than a legal one.

It is fascinating to take note of the argumentation of the PCIJ. As early as 1932 (or, in fact, as early as 1924 when the Statute was annexed to the Convention; see below), the legal formulation of governmental accountability was done in fairly clear terms that expressed the core content of parliamentarism, that is, the requirement of confidence. Within the ambit of the Statute, a horizontal confidence mechanism was apparently in the hands of the Chamber of Representatives, the representative assembly of the Memel Territory, but in situations where the government of the autonomous entity moved outside the legislative powers of the

[107] The *Memel* case, p. 40.

[108] The *Memel* case, p. 43 f. The Court pointed out that there is no guarantee that the views of a Directorate that has not received the confidence of the Chamber represent in any way the views of the local elements in the Memel Territory. *Ibidem*.

[109] The *Memel* case, pp. 39–41.

[110] It is said by the PCIJ that a Directorate comes legally into existence as soon as it is constituted. "From that moment it is entitled to act as the Directorate and to transact business. It need not wait for the Chamber to express its confidence." The *Memel* case, p. 43.

[111] The *Memel* case, p. 40.

autonomous entity as established in the Statute, a vertical confidence mechanism could appear and justify reactions from the national government towards the government of the autonomous entity. It is evident on the basis of the *Memel* case that it deals with the political accountability of government and not with its legal accountability. The latter, excluded in this context, would involve considerations of, e.g., impeachment or criminal and tort procedures in courts of law.

The dissolution of the Chamber of Representatives is a corollary issue in the case. After Mr. Simaitis had formed his Directorate, he presented the Directorate to the Chamber and submitted it to the Chamber for a vote of confidence. "After hearing speeches from the leaders of some of the parties in the Chamber, the vote was taken and the Chamber refused its confidence. Thereupon Mr. Simaitis produced and read to the Chamber the Governor's decree of dissolution."[112] The consent of the Directorate was required under Art. 12 of the Statute for such a dissolution, and the Court was of the opinion that such a requirement had the purpose of ensuring that "the local elements would have some voice in the decision whether or not the Chamber should be dissolved".[113] However, the controversial decision to dissolve the Chamber had received the assent of a Directorate that did not have a proven record of confidence with the Chamber, which as a consequence made the Directorate of Mr. Simaitis devoid of the views of the local elements. In the opinion of the Court, the situation was closely approaching that of according the power of dissolution of the Chamber to the Governor alone, which the Court felt was not the intention of Art. 12 of the Statute.[114] In this context of the dissolution of the Chamber, the Court drew a distinction between the position of a directorate which had previously received the confidence of the Chamber on the one hand, and the position of a directorate that had not received the confidence of the Chamber, on the other.[115] Therefore, and also on the basis of Art. 17 of the Statute, the PCIJ arrived at the conclusion that a Directorate that has never enjoyed the confidence of the Chamber is not entitled to consent to dissolve the Chamber,[116] while the Governor can dissolve the Chamber with the consent of a Directorate which has functioned on the basis of confidence from the Chamber.[117]

In the case, the PCIJ concluded that in the same way as the Governor, a Directorate which has never enjoyed the confidence of the Chamber is not entitled to consent to dissolve the latter. The resolution of the case is interesting because the PCIJ drills right into the heart of parliamentarism, that is, deals with the mechanism of governmental accountability in the context of the confidence mechanism.

[112] The *Memel* case, p. 44.
[113] The *Memel* case, p. 43.
[114] The *Memel* case, p. 44.
[115] The *Memel* case, pp. 44–45.
[116] The *Memel* case, pp. 45–46.
[117] The *Memel* case, p. 46.

The Statute contains a fair amount of provisions that deal with the executive, both at the top of the hierarchy in the Memel Territory and at the level of more practical implementation. The starting point for the executive power in the Territory was Art. 1, according to which the Territory would enjoy administrative autonomy at the top of the legislative, judicial and financial autonomy. According to Art. 10, para. 3, laws enacted by the Chamber of Representatives and promulgated by the Governor would be countersigned by the President of the Directorate. Article 17, paras. 1 and 2, of the Statute stated the following about the Directorate, that is, about the executive body of the autonomous entity:

> The Directorate shall exercise the executive power in the Memel Territory. It shall consist of not more than five members, including the President, and shall be composed of citizens of the Territory.
>
> The President shall be appointed by the Governor and shall hold office so long as he possesses the confidence of the Chamber of Representatives. The President shall appoint the other members of the Directorate. The Directorate must enjoy the confidence of the Chamber of Representatives and shall resign if the Chamber refuses it its confidence. If, for any reason, the Governor appoints a President of the Directorate when the Chamber of Representatives is not in session, it shall be convened so as to meet within four weeks after the appointment to hear a statement from the Directorate and vote on the question of confidence.

It is clear that in its Art. 17, the Memel Statute laid down legal rules concerning governmental accountability.[118] One of the legal questions that the PCIJ was asked to answer was "whether, in the circumstances in which it took place, the appointment of the Directorate presided over by M. Simaitis is in order". The PCIJ explained that "[u]nder Article 17 of the Statute, the Governor appoints the President of the Directorate and the President appoints the other members. Thus there are two stages. The Governor is concerned only with the first. As soon as the appointment of the President is made, the Governor's responsibility with regard to the creation of the Directorate comes to an end. The President alone is responsible for the choice of the other members; he does not have to submit their names to the Governor or obtain the Governor's approval. Their appointment depends on the will and the act of the President alone. If the Governor were to interfere in the appointment of these other members in the sense of endeavoring to dictate to the President whom he should appoint, he would exceed the functions attributed to him by the Statute." Article 17 of the Statute provided that the Directorate shall be composed of citizens of the Territory. This requirement of regional citizenship was, according to the Court, the only qualification for membership of the Directorate which was expressly stated in the Statute.

Although the Directorate had the right under Art. 18 of the Statute to propose legislation to the Chamber and some other functions of the Directorate, and the subordinated administration was mentioned in other provisions of the Statute, the

[118] For a lengthy account of governmental accountability in the Memel Territory, including the formation of the Directorate and its legal liability, see Robinson (1934a), pp. 564–585.

actual tasks of the Directorate were not enumerated anywhere in the document. Interestingly, the Statute does not create any particular powers for the Directorate to issue decrees either for the implementation of the Acts of the Chamber of Representatives or for independent regulation of administrative matters. There was a proposal to grant such a decree power to the Directorate on the basis of an analogous application of former German law and another proposal to follow the old Russian praxis, also implemented within the Government of Lithuania, which presumed such a power for the executive.[119] Because it is not plausible that the reference in Art. 10 of the Statute to legislative powers could mean anything but law in the sense of formal legislation adopted by the legislature, the issuance of law in the material sense could realistically only be grounded on the latter of the two alternatives.[120]

A local police force was created under Art. 20 of the Statute to maintain public order, and in Art. 25 of the Statute, there was a requirement that the educational curricula in the public schools of the Memel Territory would be of the same level as in Lithuania, and the Statute also contained rules concerning the employment of civil servants in general and of teachers in particular. In Art. 27, both the Lithuanian language and the German language were recognized as official languages in the Memel Territory,[121] while Lithuanian of course remained the official language of Lithuania, and in Art. 26, the authorities of the Memel Territory were obligated to carry out and cause to be carried out in the Territory the provisions contained in the Declaration concerning the protection of minorities that was made by the Lithuanian Government before the Council of the League of Nations.[122] This means that there was a clear majority – minority constellation indicated in the Statute, with certain protections also for the minority within the minority, that is, for the Lithuanians in the Memel Territory.[123] However, the main thrust of Art. 27 was that it caused the more or less compulsory use of the Lithuanian language in the Territory, often to the detriment of the German language, something that was a constant source of conflict.[124] It is also evident on the basis of the Statute that the Memel Territory would consist of districts and municipalities, that is, of administrative sub-divisions governed on the basis of principles of self-government. The executive powers and institutions of the Memel Territory were thus relatively well

[119]See Robinson (1934a), pp. 519–525, 567 f.

[120]Perhaps this could be viewed as such a principle of the Lithuanian Constitution referred to in Art. 6 of the Statute.

[121]At least in theory, this should have meant that the officials of the Memel Territory would have been obligated to know not only German but also Lithuanian. See also Robinson (1934a), pp. 721–746.

[122]Meeting of 12 May 1922 of the Council of the League of Nations. However, there was one exception to the obligation: paragraph 4 of Article 4 of the Declaration was not included in the Statute.

[123]However, there may have existed other minorities in the Memel Territory which were not accorded explicit protection under the Statute, although there may have existed other protection mechanisms for them. On the minority issue, see Robinson (1934a), pp. 717–720.

[124]See Plieg (1962), pp. 52–55.

spelled out, but additional individual rights were granted to the inhabitants of the Memel Territory in the Statute concerning the respect of private property,[125] the freedom of meeting, association, conscience and the press as well as the freedom of teaching and right to open schools.

However, the executive power of the Memel Territory was not completely separated from the executive power of the state of Lithuania. Formally speaking, a number of points of contact existed, as spelled out by the Statute, and it can be presumed that the practical operation of autonomy in the Memel Territory also necessitated such contacts and interfaces not regulated by the Statute.[126] The regulation of the sojourn of foreigners in conformity with the laws of Lithuania, mentioned in the enumeration of powers of Art. 5, as well as the registration of trading vessels according to the laws of Lithuania, mentioned in the same provision, were probably areas where contacts between the authorities of Memel and the state of Lithuania were necessary. Under Art. 20 of the Statute, the local police force in Memel could apply for assistance from the Lithuanian Government. At the same time, the necessary police force for the protection of the port was to be detailed by the Memel authorities for service under the Lithuanian authorities, while the frontier and customs police and the railway police were furnished by, and were under the direct authority of, the Lithuanian Republic.[127] Hence in the realm of policing contacts were probably very necessary, as also evidenced by Art. 21, which created an obligation for the courts and police of Memel to execute court judgments and arrest warrants issued in other parts of Lithuania.[128] The curriculum equality in the public schools of Memel in comparison with schools in other parts of Lithuania, as laid down in Art. 25 of the Statute, was also a point of contact,[129] and under Art. 31, school teachers in the Memel Territory who were of foreign nationality could only be engaged with the consent of the Lithuanian Government. Moreover, according to Art. 34, passports were to be delivered to citizens of the Memel Territory by the Directorate of the Territory on behalf of the Lithuanian Republic and in accordance

[125]As indicated by Plieg (1962), p. 181 f., the respect of private property in Art. 32 of the Statute and the possibility to expropriate property for public purposes on the basis of law was seriously violated by the Lithuanian authorities when the Lithuanian expropriation law was applied to expropriate properties, theoretically for the harbor, but in practice for building housing for persons from other parts of Lithuania.

[126]One such forum of contacts was the board of the harbor, which was internationalized under a separate protocol to the Convention and which contained one representative of the Memel Territory, one representative of the Lithuanian state and one neutral person. The harbor matters were a constant source of conflict in the relation between the Memel Territory and the central Government of Lithuania. See Plieg (1962), pp. 50–51.

[127]See Robinson (1934a), pp. 602–607.

[128]See Robinson (1934a), pp. 677–686, who on p. 685 makes the interesting point that in the Lithuanian jurisdiction, issues concerning the names of individuals were an administrative matter, while such issues were a court matter in the jurisdiction of the Memel Territory.

[129]It was pointed out by Robinson (1934a), p. 716, that university education is a matter belonging to the legislative competence of the state of Lithuania, not to the Memel Territory.

with the regulations established by the Lithuanian Government.[130] Also, as provided for in Art. 5, regulation in the Memel Territory of timber-floating and navigation on the rivers, other than the Niémen, and the canals within the Memel Territory, was within the competence of the Memel authorities, but subject to agreement with the Lithuanian authorities in case such watercourses were utilizable outside the Memel Territory for timber-floating. Finally, in the "financial" provision of Art. 35, the Lithuanian Government and the local authorities of the Memel Territory were required, within a period of 1 month from the coming into force of the Statute, to enter into negotiations for the purpose of determining the percentage of the net yield of the customs duties, excise duties and commodity taxes, including revenues from monopolies dealt with in Art. 5, para. 12, which shall be assigned to the Memel Territory.[131] It was also provided that the percentage thus determined could be revised from time to time by the Lithuanian Government in agreement with the local authorities of the Memel Territory.[132]

It is therefore possible to conclude that the autonomy created by the Statute for the Memel Territory did not envision a hermetically insulated and self-contained jurisdiction, but an arrangement of self-government which, at least at some given points, was supposed to interact with the rest of Lithuania in a way that might be denoted with reference to the concept of shared powers.[133] It may well be that the points of interaction were, in practice, more abundant than the ones identified in the Statute. However, it is interesting that neither the Statute nor the Convention contained any provisions concerning control of the powers of the Memel Territory

[130]Interestingly, the passports mentioned both the Lithuanian nationality of the bearer and his status as citizen of the Memel Territory. In practice, the Lithuanian Government prescribed two types of passports, one for domestic purposes and another for international purposes. For the respective norms, see Robinson (1934b), pp. 635–647. Still in 1936, the Lithuanian authorities were creating difficulties for crossing the border to Germany and the Lithuanian passport legislation of the same year abolished the reference to the regional citizenship of the Memel Territory. See Plieg (1962), p. 176 f.

[131]In determining the percentage, the provision stated that account shall be taken: (1) of the average value of imports and exports per head of the population in the Memel Territory and in the other parts of Lithuania respectively during the years 1921 and 1922, special circumstances which may have influenced the returns for those years being allowed for; (2) of the additional revenue and expenditure which the transfer of sovereignty over the Memel Territory to Lithuania involves for the Lithuanian State. See Robinson (1934a), pp. 788–801.

[132]For the agreements of 1926 and 1932 concerning financial equalization between the Lithuanian state and the Memel Territory, see Robinson (1934b), pp. 648–651. According to Plieg (1962), pp. 55, during 1925, 55% of the income to the state budget of Lithuania came from the Memel Territory, but the state of Lithuania was consistently refusing to return but a relatively small fraction of the revenue to the Government of the Memel Territory, placing the Government of Memel in constant economic hardship. At the same time, it should be recognized that the state revenues of Lithuania were not great, either.

[133]Hannum (1996), p. 383. See also Robinson (1934a), p. 786, who makes the point that under Art. 34 of the Statute, both the authorities of the Memel Territory and the authorities of the Lithuanian state had concurring powers to grant passports and that they could do so, which in practice meant that an individual could turn either to the Memel or the state authorities to get a passport.

by the central authorities of the Lithuanian Government,[134] although the position of the Governor certainly could be interpreted as containing not only a negative control (veto powers, dissolution of the Chamber), but also certain positive powers of control.[135] In practice, the Lithuanian authorities were frequently interfering in matters that belonged to the competence of the authorities of the Memel Territory, in particular after the decision of the PCIJ, which was interpreted by the Lithuanian Government as a vindication of its attempts to keep the Memel Territory as part of Lithuania.[136] A significant part of the problems in the Memel Territory during 1934–1935 can, in fact, be attributed to the unwillingness of the Lithuanian authorities to allow the political forces of the Memel Territory, that is, the political majority, to form such a Directorate which would enjoy the confidence of the Chamber of Representatives.[137] In addition, the veto powers of the Governor were obviously frequently used in order to prevent or stall the legislative work of the Chamber of Representatives.[138] According to some pieces of information, of a total of 165 pieces of law enacted by the Chamber of Representatives between 1925 and 1939, as many as 62 laws were vetoed by the Governor, although 19 vetoes were eventually lifted.[139] The 43 pieces of law that were vetoed with final effect meant nonetheless that 26% of the legislative enactments of the Chamber did not enter into force, which seems to be a very high figure, with an even higher share of laws being under the threat of veto.[140]

2.2.4 International Relations

The substantive issue that gave rise to the *Memel* case was the usurpation of the foreign powers of Lithuania by the representatives of the political establishment of Memel. Because Lithuania was to enjoy full sovereignty over the ceded territory,

[134]Robinson (1934a), p. 280 f. Conversely, there was no special ministerial post created in the Government of Lithuania under the heading of Minister for Memel Affairs (or something similar) for tending to such issues arising in Memel that required the attention of the central government. Proposals to that effect were made before 1924, but they were defeated before the final Statute was approved. See Robinson (1934a), p. 320.

[135]Robinson (1934a), pp. 319–327. As pointed out in Plieg (1962), pp. 201, two of the several Lithuanian Governors in the Memel Territory were at the same time ministers in the Lithuanian Government.

[136]See Plieg (1962), pp. 52–67, 90–106.

[137]See Plieg (1962), pp. 152–166, 171 f. Plieg indicates that the situation was normalized in this respect actually only after the elections of 1935.

[138]Plieg (1962), p. 179.

[139]Plieg (1962), p. 180.

[140]Plieg (1962), p. 180, makes, however, the point that the Chamber of Representatives made also a lot of other decisions than pure legislative enactments, and according to him, the share of vetoes is not very great in relation to the entire number of decisions.

subject to the limitations imposed on its exercise by the Statute, and because the Memel Territory had not received any foreign powers through the enumeration of competences in Art. 7, the foreign powers were among those residual competences that belonged to the state of Lithuania. The external sovereignty of Lithuania in all its appearances was to be protected. A visit by the President of the Directorate and two members of the Chamber of Representatives without the knowledge of the Lithuanian Government in the capital of a foreign State for the purpose of negotiations for a preferential treatment of the Memel Territory in trade of agricultural produce together with the Government of the foreign State disregarded the right of the relevant departments of the Lithuanian Government to conduct such negotiations.[141] The Court concluded that "the attempt to secure an arrangement as to the admission of agricultural produce by negotiations with the officials of the competent departments of the German Government falls within the sphere of foreign relations, and consequently M. Böttcher's action exceeded the competence of the Memel authorities and thereby violated the Statute".[142]

The PCIJ placed the direct contacts and negotiations between the Memel authorities and the German authorities in a broader context of foreign relations between Lithuania and Germany and concluded that during the material time, relations were somewhat disturbed between Lithuania and Germany. "The diplomatic correspondence exchanged between the two Governments in January of the same year shows that various causes of friction existed. The sudden grant to Memel of better terms than Lithuania as a whole enjoyed for the admission of agricultural produce into Germany might well embitter the situation at Memel and undermine the feeling of loyalty towards the central authorities."[143] This indicates that the internal coherence of the state of Lithuania was one of the concerns of the Court. Therefore, the dismissal of Mr. Böttcher from the Presidency was in order, not only with a view to the contacts and negotiations that had taken place, but also with a view to possible renewed attempts to engage in direct dealings with Germany. The Court was thus also concerned about the prospect of further disturbances of the same kind and wanted to set a precedent for future presidents and authorities of Memel.[144]

On the basis of the Statute, it appears that the foreign relations and the treaty powers of Lithuania were carefully crafted in a manner which positioned them with the residual competences of Lithuania. No mention of foreign relations is included in Art. 5, and references to the registration of vessels by the Memel authorities under the relevant legislation of Lithuania, to regulation of the sojourn of foreigners in conformity with the laws of Lithuania and to rules governing the waterways other than the river Niémen on the border to Poland to be adopted with the agreement of Lithuanian authorities, consolidate the understanding that the Memel Territory had

---

[141]The *Memel* case, pp. 34–35.

[142]The *Memel* case, p. 35.

[143]The *Memel* case, p. 36.

[144]The *Memel* case, p. 36.

a share only in the internal sovereignty of Lithuania, not in the country's external sovereignty. Therefore, it is no surprise that the PCIJ came down on the side of the defense of the sovereignty of the State of Lithuania in its decision.

This becomes even clearer on the basis of Art. 4 of the Statute, according to which the measures taken by the Lithuanian legislature in the execution of international treaties and conventions shall be applicable to the Memel Territory in so far as the said treaties and conventions are not contrary to the present Statute. This indicates that the central authorities of Lithuania in principle also had full competence to carry out foreign affairs on behalf of the Memel Territory. Article 4 is, nevertheless, making the point that such treaties which Lithuania has entered into may have repercussions for the Memel Territory. Therefore, the provision also stated that in the event that the treaties concluded by Lithuania applied to affairs which, by virtue of Art. 5, came within the competence of the local authorities of the Memel Territory, it was a duty of the authorities of the Memel Territory to take the necessary measures for the application of the said international agreements. The implementation of treaties did not necessarily have to take on the form of an act of the Chamber of Representatives, but could also be accomplished through executive and court decisions.[145] As a consequence, the arrangement appeared to be one in which the Memel Territory had no role in the negotiations and the conclusion of international agreements, that is, in the "upward" flow of the creation of international obligations, but it was given a role in the "downward" flow of the international obligations to the extent that the implementation of a treaty fell within the sphere of competence of the Memel authorities and required domestic measures.[146] Because the implementation in the Memel Territory of treaties concluded by the State of Lithuania was affecting the powers of the Memel Territory, it could be said that the central Government of Lithuania was, at least in theory, able to carve out and perhaps diminish or limit the powers of the Memel Territory through treaties that were concluded.[147]

The relationship of Lithuania to international law was, under the Constitution of Lithuania, apparently of a monist nature. Robinson places Lithuania in the same group of countries as, e.g., the United States, where a ratified treaty is law, because the Lithuanian Constitution of 1922 contained no provisions concerning bringing in the force of the provisions of a treaty in the domestic jurisdiction.[148] Therefore, the domestic jurisdiction was responsible for the implementation of a treaty as agreed.

[145]Robinson (1934a), p. 336, fn. 1.

[146]According to Robinson (1934a) p. 335 f., there is but one instance in which the authorities the Memel Territory were participating in the conclusion of a treaty under international law. That instance dealt with an agreement concerning the evangelic-Lutheran church in the Memel Territory. This participation took place with the knowledge of the State of Lithuania, and the formal conclusion of the treaty was done by the State, not the Memel Territory.

[147]See Robinson (1934a), pp. 332, 356. But see Robinson (1934a), p. 334 f., where he makes the point that Lithuania could not conclude such treaties which are in conflict with the Convention and thus the Statute.

[148]Robinson (1934a), p. 336 f.

For instance, the Convention required in Art. 18 formal ratification by Lithuania and deposition of the instrument of ratification at Paris, which took place on 30 July 1924. In addition, however, the Convention was also promulgated nationally in the Official Gazette of Lithuania on 1 September 1924 and in the Official Gazette of the Memel Territory on 18 September 1924.[149] The pledge on the part of Lithuania to enact the Statute as law was actually already included in the Preamble to the Statute.

2.3 Reflections

The Memel Territory was embedded in the constitutional and legal fabric of Lithuania in a number of ways. The 1922 Constitution of Lithuania as well as the subsequent Lithuanian Constitutions before the Second World War also constituted the supreme law for the Memel Territory, although at the same time, the Statute, established through the Convention in 1924, introduced many exceptions to the Constitution. Many of the political and legal structures of Memel were intermixed with those of the state of Lithuania.

For the purposes of our comparison, what should one expect on the basis of the *Memel* case?

As concerns the element of legislative powers, one could expect that a range of issues would be found in any autonomy statute. Firstly, a natural part of any autonomy statute would be the definition of the competences of the autonomous entity in relation to the central government of the state. Secondly, this enumeration can take on various forms, but in an autonomy context where the point of departure is often the delegation of the constitutional powers of law-making to the sub-state entity, the enumeration would list the law-making powers possessed by the entity, while leaving the legislature of the state in the possession of so-called residual powers.

The element of participation would mainly encompass the mechanism of elections, and it would probably not be very often that one would come across direct popular participation in decision-making by means of the referendum. As a consequence of the mechanism of elections, there would also be in an autonomy statute provisions concerning the organization of the representative body. In addition to the elections, the opposite could be found, that is, the dissolution of the representative body. It would also be possible to find provisions concerning elections from the autonomous territory to the national parliament. Finally, it seems the right to vote in elections to the legislative body of the autonomous entity could be tied to the possession of regional citizenship of some kind.

In respect of the element of executive power, several things could be expected. Firstly, in the vertical dimension, it should be expected that the autonomy act, normally enacted by the national legislature, does not make provisions for

[149] Rogge (1928), p. 249. See also Kalijarvi (1937), p. 203 f.

situations in which the governmental body of the autonomous entity has acted *ultra vires* and threatens the competences and even the sovereignty of the central government. Secondly, it should also be possible to expect that the autonomy act, whatever its official title, creates some norms that deal with the institutional organization of the governmental body in an autonomy. Thirdly, in the horizontal dimension, it should be expected that governmental accountability is based on parliamentarism, that is, one or several mechanisms that align the governmental body of the autonomous entity with the legislative assembly of the same on the basis of confidence between the governmental body and the legislature, expressed by simple majority either when the governmental body is created or dismissed or both. Although the *Memel* case does not dwell on the financial aspects of sub-state organization, issues related to fiscal and budgetary powers would also be interesting in this context, following the reference in Art. 2 of the Convention and Art. 2 of the Statute to the concept of financial autonomy.

Finally, within the context of foreign relations, it would not be warranted to expect too many things, perhaps mainly provisions dealing with the implementation of such international obligations that the central government of the State has entered into.

The judgment in the *Memel* case by the PCIJ was valid at the time of its issuance, but does it have any legal relevance today? The judgment itself was of immediate relevance for the resolution of the legal problems related to the facts in the case, and because the context was that of the Memel Statute, the judgment itself is of limited legal validity at this very moment. It is, however, interesting as a legal opinion concerning the ways in which governmental business should be conducted in an autonomous entity governed by an autonomy statute. In that respect, it could have had relevance in a hypothetical situation where the Åland Islands Government would have used the complaints mechanism available under the League of Nations Settlement and submitted an application via the Government of Finland all the way to the PCIJ. The manner in which the Court reasoned in the *Memel* case would probably have been similar in a hypothetical Åland Islands case. What could perhaps be concluded is that the PCIJ was, in the *Memel* case, protecting the sovereignty of the State from being diluted by actions of a sub-state entity in a situation in which the central government did not agree to granting foreign powers to the sub-state entity. This is probably still a valid point of view today, almost 80 years after the case was resolved by the PCIJ.

From a methodological point of view, the *Memel* judgment is quite interesting. The PCIJ made the observation on the basis of the Lithuanian submissions underlining the importance of the right of supervision of the autonomous entity that the "argument consisted almost entirely of deductions drawn from the contents of constitutions in force in other countries, from the constitutional practice of other countries and from the statements made in the works of authors who have studied these constitutions".[150] However, in the opinion of the Court, it could find sufficient

[150]The *Memel* case, p. 30.

basis in the Convention and the Statute for the conclusion that in certain circumstances the Governor has the right to dismiss the President of the Directorate. Therefore, the Court felt it did not need the comparative information (deductions drawn from the contents of constitutions in force in other countries and from the constitutional practice of other countries) or the *opinio iuris* (statements made in the works of authors who have studied these constitutions). It concluded that it was "unnecessary to consider the extent to which the constitutions of other countries can be used as a guide interpreting the Statute of Memel".[151]

The statement is limited to the case and to the possibility of the Governor to exercise general supervision of the actions of the Government of Memel, something that the Court denied existed, and it should probably not be read as a general repudiation of comparative law: the normative materials that were directly applicable in the matter were sufficient for the interpretation and resolution of the case, and no such uncertainty surfaced that would have made it necessary to search for comparative information or doctrine to support the interpretations that the Court arrived at. However, the statement is at least slightly remarkable against the background of the fact that at least one concept central to the case, that of parliamentary accountability of the government before the parliament and the mechanisms related to the realization of that accountability, had only relatively recently found their way into the written constitutions of various countries. Yet the idea of the parliamentary accountability of government seemed to be a very clear one for the Court, almost as if the contents of the concept were established at the level of customary law. Hence in spite of the methodological rejection of comparative and doctrinary outlooks for the supervision of sub-state entities, the Court had, outside the question of supervision of executive action by the Governor, in fact, taken a look at the functioning of the accountability mechanism or at least at a collateral mechanism, that of the dissolution of the Parliament, in different countries and made the observation that "[d]issensions may well arise between the Chamber and a Directorate duly installed in office, i.e. which had received at the outset of its career the confidence of the Chamber. Such occurrences are common in all countries which are subject to a parliamentary regime."[152] Considering the share of the judgment that is devoted to the exposition and understanding of the parliamentary mechanisms, the Court's denouncement of comparative and doctrinary materials on one of the issues contained in the judgment does not sound completely honest even in the limited context of the supervision by the Governor of the executive actions of the Directorate.

One problem from a comparative point of view would probably have been that the regulation of the concept of parliamentary accountability was very varied, with some unwritten constitutions establishing such accountability in constitutional conventions, with some written constitutions not having explicit provisions on the

---

[151]The *Memel* case, p. 30.

[152]The *Memel* case, p. 44.

matter but allowing nonetheless a practical implementation of the mechanism, and with some written constitutions that explicitly provided for the mechanism in the same way as the Memel Statute.[153] In addition, some of the judges on the bench came from countries where no such accountability mechanism existed. The statement by the Court that a comparative outlook was not necessary was probably also a safe course of action: the complete understanding of the mechanism, so eloquently demonstrated by the Court in the judgment, could have become standard-setting if it had been at least in part premised on the existence of the mechanism elsewhere, which means that the Court probably avoided some political disturbances (even involving Lithuania) by limiting the sources of law in the case to the Statute itself.

For the purposes of our study, there is no need to take into account such national sensitivities. Instead, the comparative method can be utilized throughout the study in order to arrive at deductive conclusions about the structure of territorial autonomy for the purposes of sub-state governance. In the pursuit of conclusions about territorial autonomy, it is, however, necessary to try to formulate a somewhat clearer theoretical understanding of what territorial autonomy is and is not. This is necessary, in particular, in order to separate territorial autonomy from the concept of federalism.

[153]Practical evidence about the functioning of the mechanism of parliamentary accountability in, e.g., the European countries during the 1920s and 1930s was, in fact, pointing in different directions. Especially in the newly independent countries of that era, for instance, those surrounding Lithuania, including Lithuania itself, the mechanism of parliamentary accountability seemed to produce relatively short-lived governments which in a good number of cases were not able to resist the evolution of the political systems in an authoritarian direction. This was true also in the case of Lithuania, which already well before the *Memel* case turned its system of governance into an authoritarian rule. In that perspective, the definition of the PCIJ of parliamentary accountability was clearly pointing in a direction which was opposite to the developments that took place at the state level.

Chapter 3
The Relationship between Federalism and Autonomy

3.1 Terminological Confusion

The terminological clarity in respect of two categories of sub-state existence on a territorial basis, namely federalism and autonomy, is probably less than it should be. Against the background of our analysis of the Memel Territory and on the basis of the *Memel* case, it would seem that territorial autonomy is a relatively straightforward matter, denoting a singular entity in what otherwise would be a unitary state, vested with exclusive law-making powers of an enumerated nature (without preemption possibilities by the national lawmaker) and maintaining governmental institutions of its own. In reality, the concept of autonomy is not quite as clear-cut, but requires specifications in relation to, *inter alia*, adjacent forms of sub-state governance, most notably federalism, which in its classical form denotes a symmetrical extension of constituent states over the entire territory, with institutional representation of sub-state entities at the federal level. Between the "pure" forms of autonomy and federalism, some mixed forms of sub-state governance exist. In addition, there are forms of autonomy of a "lesser" nature, where the powers assigned to the sub-state entity are not of a legislative nature, but perhaps administrative in the main, resulting in regional self-government of a more regular kind.

A number of authors recognize the unclear nature of the concepts of autonomy and federalism. For instance, it has been pointed out by Gamper that "strongly decentralized states, such as Spain and, more recently, Italy and the United Kingdom, nearly approach the – very vague and controversial – standard of what is called a federal system".[1] She feels that it may be difficult to define the key elements of a classic federal system, because legal comparisons show an impressive variety of deviations from any ideal standard. However, her opinion is that there is

[1]Gamper (2004), p. 69, fn. 16.

M. Suksi, *Sub-State Governance through Territorial Autonomy*,
DOI 10.1007/978-3-642-20048-9_3, © Springer-Verlag Berlin Heidelberg 2011

"some common understanding as to the minimum institutional requirements of all federal systems".[2] Henig is of the opinion that federalism "does not stem from a single source and there is no universally accepted definition".[3] Domínguez García refers to a "terminological mess" when discussing sub-state entities and their relationship to concepts such as region, federated community, member state, federal and quasi-federal states, and devolved entities.[4]

In the context of British devolution, Bogdanor concludes that the term 'federalism' is used rather loosely when constitutional change is discussed and that those who discuss federalism actually often mean devolution.[5] Inverting this, Navaratna-Bandara discusses devolution in a conflict-resolution context, but uses the term 'devolution' as a catch-all phrase for solutions that range from federations through territorial autonomy to self-government of a lesser kind.[6] Kymlicka, in turn, uses the terms 'territorial autonomy', 'federal territorial autonomy', 'quasi-federal territorial autonomy' and 'multination federalism' more or less interchangeably, and although he, too, paints with a relatively broad brush, it seems that much of his discussion is focused on asymmetrical autonomy arrangements of the type that our research identifies as territorial autonomies, distinguishable from federations.[7] In a commentary concerning the autonomy of Hong Kong, Ghai discusses the position of the entity in relation to a variation of spatial devolution ranging from confederation via federation to autonomy and administrative decentralization, making the point that these categories are not exclusive and that often, a firm distinction is hard to make.[8]

---

[2]Gamper (2004), p. 57.

[3]Henig (2006), p. 4 f., describes the essence of federalism in the following way: "[T]he vital characteristic of federalism is that governmental institutions at each level 'own' certain powers and competences, and they can act independently in exercising them. If we take a simplified model of a two level structure with 'A' at the highest level and 'B', 'C' and 'D' at the lower level, then the governmental institutions of 'B' have the power to take certain decisions without reference to 'A' and without necessarily acting in the same manner as 'C' or 'D'. Equally, whilst 'B', 'C' and 'D' may be represented at the higher level, 'A' can take decisions within its area of competence without any formal reference to the lower tier." However, it seems that Henig is mainly describing the material dimensions of federalism, without paying sufficient attention to the institutional dimensions. However, it has been pointed out that there may also be a distinction between 'federal' and 'federalism', where 'federal' is a distinct form of institutional organization, whereas 'federalism' denotes a political principle of some kind that advocates the creation of federal governance. See, e.g., Burgess and Gagnon (1993).

[4]Domínguez García (2009), p. 411.

[5]Bogdanor (1999), p. 202, seems to think that the creation of exclusive law-making powers in a sub-state legislature denotes federalism, which also indicates a certain confusion concerning the forms of sub-state governance.

[6]Navaratna-Bandara (1995), p. 21 f.

[7]E.g., Kymlicka (2007), pp. 70–71, 144. However, Kymlicka is also clearly interested in the potential of federations to guarantee minority rights.

[8]Ghai (1999), pp. 182–184.

Lapidoth also makes the point that differences and distinctions between the various concepts of sub-state governance are not always sufficiently clear and that a certain term may have different meanings to different scholars and officials.[9] Benedikter nonetheless makes the point that there is a general consensus in the scholarly world on the essence of the federal principle and of federal systems.[10] Hence although there may not be complete consensus on what constitutes 'federalism', there is probably even less consensus on the notion of (territorial) 'autonomy'.[11] This seems to be supported by Ruiz Vieytez, who states that "[t]he Spanish model should not be confused with a federal system, given the existence of a single Constitutional Law and Sovereignty covering the whole of the country".[12]

In addition, as indicated by Elazar, the emergence of new, asymmetrical forms of governance require new theory-building to give them theoretical expression. The void is also pointed out by Ghai, according to whom "[t]here is no developed or reliable theory of autonomy; modern but contested justifications revolve around the notion of identity. We are, for the most part, hazy about its structures or the mechanisms to capture its potential. We have yet to find a balance between the common and the particular which lies at the heart of autonomy."[13] Ghai uses autonomy as a broad generic term, and includes under it specialized terms such as federalism, regional autonomy, but distinguishes from these constitutionally protected forms of autonomy such notions as regionalism and decentralization.[14] However, he points at a major factor that distinguishes ethnic autonomy from classical federation, namely the asymmetrical features of the arrangement.[15] Therefore, it is of importance in this context to try to create at least some theoretical notions around territorial autonomy, on the one hand, and federalism, on the other, in order to distinguish them from each other and from some other concepts, such as 'devolution', 'regional state' and 'regional self-government'.[16]

However, writing from an Italian regionalist point of view and recognizing the ambiguities connected with the terms 'federation' and 'regional state', Bartole holds the opinion that it will be very difficult and perhaps not even very useful to

---

9 Lapidoth (1997), p. 49.

10 Benedikter (2007), p. 22.

11 For instance, it seems that in Bogdanor (1997), pp. 65–87, Bogdanor is using federations as examples, not territorial autonomies, although much of what he is proposing is relevant also for territorial autonomies.

12 Ruiz Vieytez (2004), p. 135.

13 Ghai (2000b), p. 8.

14 Ghai (2000b), p. 8 f.

15 Ghai (2000b), p. 12. He also concludes that "for many groups, the exact amount of devolved power is less important than that they alone should enjoy some special powers, as a way to mark their status". See Ghai (2000b), p. 14.

16 See Elazar (1987), p. 152.

try to discern clear and evident boundaries between federal and regional states, and that it is neither very easy nor convenient to distinguish federal and regional states from each other.[17] He nonetheless thinks that with a view of constitutional reform in Italy, the direction of which could have been increased federalism,[18] legal scholars have the task of identifying the characteristics of a federal state with regard to a regional state.[19] Because states where a non-federal autonomy regime is extended to the territory of the entire state are very rare (with Italy and Spain as current examples), it remains an important theoretical task to try to identify the characteristics of autonomy arrangements, which are often singular or do not normally extend themselves over the entire state territory, in relation to the characteristics of federal organization.[20] It is possible to say that Olivetti joins in this opinion by making the point that the "modern literature of comparative constitutional law and of general theory of the State has always tried to provide a satisfactory explanation for the various forms of autonomy that cannot be included in the classical phenomenon of the federal state".[21] He also complains that the literature that has studied autonomy arrangements may have started from the assumption that the regional state is a form of constitutional arrangement where the autonomy is somewhat less developed than in the federal state or from the assumption that the regional state is a mix of autonomy and federalism. He attributes such negative assumptions in particular to international lawyers.[22]

---

[17]Bartole (1998), pp. 184, 186.

[18]As explained in Amoretti (2011), pp. 66–69, the constitutional reforms in Italy in 1999 and 2001 reversed the distribution of powers between the central government and the regions so that they now are based on enumeration for the national level and residual powers for the regional level, but the importance of the state-regions conference has remained limited and cannot be regarded a federal chamber proper. The principle of subsidiarity established in the Italian Constitution distributes powers from the centre to the lowest possible level (even to the municipality), while each of the regions has the possibility to request more powers from the national and thus enhance the asymmetrical nature of the Italian state.

[19]Bartole (1998), p. 187. According to Bartole (1998), pp. 183, 187, the Belgian authority, Delpérée, has maintained since 1967 that it is not possible to distinguish the regional state from the federal state and that there is no difference between the two.

[20]This, however, is not quite accepted by Domínquez García, who thinks that identifying particular characteristics of a federal state may cause the category of federations becoming futile, and proposes instead the over-arching concepts of composite or compound states to cover different sub-state existences, dividing the compound states into integral compound states, where the entire territory is divided into politically autonomous sub-states (Germany, Austria, Belgium, Spain, Italy) and into partially compound states (Portugal, Finland, the UK, etc.). See Domínguez García (2009), p. 413 f.

[21]Olivetti (2009), p. 777.

[22]Olivetti (2009), p. 778.

3.2 The Characteristics of Federalism v. Autonomy

3.2.1 Classical Understanding of Federalism

One of the authoritative formulations of the principles of federalism as a distinct principle of organization was proposed by Wheare, who was interested in establishing a definition of federalism which was flexible enough to accommodate a variety of features[23] and stressed the fact that the practice of governance is even more important than the constitutional form recorded in formal constitutions.[24] A starting point of his analysis is that in relation to the individual, there are two different governments, the federal government and the government of each state, which both operate directly upon the people, thus making each individual subject to two governments.[25] The federal principle is based on an association of states where the division of powers is such that the federal and state governments are each, within their own spheres of both exclusive and concurring competence,[26]

---

[23]Wheare (1964), pp. 1, 15, 19 f. One particular method of flexibility accounted for on p. 232 ff. is the "temporary delegation of powers by regional to general government, or vice versa". However, Wheare was criticized by Elazar for regarding federalism as nothing more than a "technique for political integration – occasionally useful, transitory in nature, and ultimately to evolve into a more simple form of decentralization within a strong unitary government". See, e.g., Elazar (1987), p. 149. In the same vein, autonomy is often referred to as a technique of the opposite direction, that of secession. However, both federations (which is the point of Elazar) and autonomy arrangements have proven to be sturdier than the predictions of some observers.

[24]Wheare (1964), p. 20. On p. 223, he considers the importance of practice, conventions and custom as complementary to the formal constitution of the federation. Even more so, Friedrich (1968), pp. 7, 173, is not interested in defining federalism from a legal point of view that illustrates a static design regulated by firm and unalterable rules, but in dynamic terms that illustrate a process. According to Friedrich, "the development (historical) dimension of federal relationships has become a primary focal point, as contrasted with the distribution and fixation of jurisdictions (the legal aspect)," while our inquiry is more focused on the legal aspect, without leaving aside the dynamic side. Instead of what the structure of a federal relationship has Friedrich inquires into what function a federal relationship has, although he does not think that the legal dimension is unimportant.

[25]Wheare (1964), p. 2.

[26]According to Wheare (1964), p. 78, the simplest form of division of powers "is obtained by having one list only and that actually exclusive". In the context, however, it seems clear that when talking about the exclusive list of competencies, he means the powers of the federation, while the powers of the sub-state level would be residual, something that he confirms on p. 80 that the "aim must be to get an exclusive list for the general government which contains as many as possible of the important subjects of general concern", leaving the residual competences to the sub-state level. In the same context, he also considers the possibility that instead, the powers of the sub-state entities are enumerated while the residual powers would be vested in the federal government, but concludes that "objections of a different kind may be imagined". Putting forward the example of Canada, which he has previously qualified as quasi-federal, he writes that the example suggests "that this need not mean that provincial powers will be by any means negligible or progressively whittled down". On p. 96, he gives the powers of customs and excise as examples of exclusive federal competences, while revenue from property, commercial undertakings and monopolies,

co-ordinate and independent.[27] Suitable exclusive powers at the federal level were, *inter alia*, foreign relations and customs and excise.[28] Because of the division of powers, there should exist a designated body of some independence to adjudicate disputes that may arise between the two levels of government[29] as well as a parallel system of courts, one for the federal jurisdiction and another for the jurisdiction of each state, in order to adjudicate in concrete cases arising in the different jurisdictions.[30] He analyzed several federal-like state formations and concluded that, *inter alia*, the formal constitutional determination that a state is federal was greatly mitigated by the fact that the general legislature could amend the federal constitution without the direct participation of the constituent states.[31]

In addition, Wheare thought that federal constitutions and federal government actually were concepts that could be separated from each other for the purposes of analysis so as to bring out those relatively few states that actually were federations and to leave aside nominal federations and states that could not be described as federations at all.[32] To test whether a system of governance can be described as a federal government, Wheare asks the following question: "Does a system of government embody predominantly a division of powers between general and regional authorities, each of which, in its own sphere, is co-ordinate with the others and independent of them?"[33] If so, Wheare thinks the system is federal, provided

grants, loans and taxations could be placed among the concurring competences. However, on p. 126, he resigns before the difficulty of indicating at which level of governance different competences of an economic nature should be placed.

[27]Wheare (1964), pp. 10, 75 f. Wheare concludes that a mere reference to exclusive competences is misleading, because in practice, concurring competences of wider or narrower sort exist between the federal level and the state level. As a consequence, the existence of concurring competences necessitate, according to Wheare, provisions concerning which authority it is that shall prevail in situations of conflict. Normally, the rule should be that when, inside the concurring competences, there is a conflict, the federal norm prevails and the state law gives way.

[28]Wheare (1964), pp. 96, 169 f. Wheare is aware of the problems posed by treaty powers of the federation to the states, because ultimately, they may extend the legislative powers of the federal government "to any subject upon which it can make a treaty". This is particularly so in regard of subject-matter which domestically is placed among the exclusive competences of the constituent states: "[D]oes not this mean that the general government is, through its use of the treaty power, entering the sphere of the regional legislatures? And does not this reduce the regional field considerably? And unexpectedly?"

[29]Wheare (1964), p. 59.

[30]Wheare (1964), p. 68. However, a supreme court of the federation should have the final say.

[31]Wheare (1964), pp. 21, 24. He therefore thought that, e.g., the 1891 Constitution of Brazil and the 1936 Constitution of the Soviet Union were not really federal. Wheare operated with the notion of the quasi-federal constitution, classifying the Weimar Republic, Federal Republic of Germany and the Soviet Union as quasi-federal. See Wheare (1964), p. 25 f.

[32]Wheare (1964), p. 20 f.

[33]Wheare (1964), p. 33. Although the two levels of government are supposed to be independent, they also have to stay in a relationship of co-ordination with each other. That relationship can take on several different forms, such as inter-governmental conferences, meetings of governors, etc., as pointed out in Wheare (1964), pp. 226–232.

that not only the constitutive document but also actual governmental practice supports the conclusion. This, again, seems to require a three-tier test to be united in functions, but not to be unitary: (1) that constituent states desire to be united under a single independent general government for some purposes; (2) that constituent states desire to be organized under independent regional governments for other purposes; and (3) that they are able to operate it.[34] From the point of view of autonomy, it is interesting that Wheare has the additional requirement that the terms of the agreement which distributes powers between the federal level and the state level must be supreme and binding upon them,[35] which means that the federal constitution must be supreme. In autonomies, however, the situation is often such that the autonomy statute, whatever its official name, constitutes an exception to the general constitution of the state and may even place itself in some respects "above" the constitution of the state, at least in cases where the autonomy statute is entrenched in one way or the other in obligations under international law.

In analyzing federal government, Wheare notes that many persons regard it as "essential to a government if it is to be federal that the regions should have equal representation in the upper house of the general legislature".[36] He, however, seems to disagree to some extent and feels that "equal representation is not essential to ensure that the system is federal government", while equal representation "may be essential to ensure that it is effective federal government".[37] The effectiveness of federal government, again, is not clearly spelled out, but it appears that the possibility of an upper federal house to safeguard the interests of the constituent states in matters relating to treaties with foreign countries would be one measure of efficiency of the federal principle.[38] Therefore, an institutional equality mechanism at the federal level, included in the constitution of the country, seems nonetheless to be presumed for the existence of federal government for the sake of guaranteeing co-operation of the constituent states in federal government. The institutional representation of the constituent states at the federal level appears to be a very important characteristic that cannot be left to be developed by practice, but needs to be recorded in the formal constitution. Wheare also underlines the importance of the party system and puts forward the US model with two dominant parties as an explanation for why the government of the United States may be held as being the most successful federal government in the world: "it is the existence of its two-party system which provides a unifying influence through the whole framework of

[34]Wheare (1964), p. 36.

[35]Wheare (1964), p. 53 f.

[36]Wheare (1964), p. 87. See Wheare (1964), p. 88: "States may be reluctant to enter a federal union unless they are guaranteed some safeguard in one house of the legislature against their being swamped by the more populous members of the union."

[37]Wheare (1964), p. 88.

[38]Wheare (1964), p. 180 f.

government (. . .)."[39] Evidently, the existence of the same party system of two dominant parties both at the federal level and in the constituent states is perceived as important, at least in the US context.

On the top of the guaranteed division of power between central and regional governments, Lijphart proposes five additional attributes for federalism[40] that we can put in relation to autonomy arrangements at the sub-state level:

- "A written constitution which specifies the division of power and guarantees to both the central and regional governments that their allotted powers cannot be taken away." The autonomy arrangements are not always detailed in the constitution of the country, but in separate pieces of law that may or may not have constitutional rank, and if they do not, they can, at least in theory, be revoked by the body that enacted the legislation;
- "A bicameral legislature in which one chamber represents the people at large and the other the component units of the federation." In countries where autonomy arrangements exist, the legislatures are normally not bicameral for the purpose of granting representation for the autonomous entities, leaving the one chamber for the representation of the people, either on the basis of ordinary apportionment of seats or on the basis of special mandates created for the autonomous entities;
- "Over-representation of the smaller component units in the federal chamber of the bicameral legislature." Because there is normally no federal chamber in countries with autonomy arrangements, there cannot be any over-representation in a chamber for "institutional" representation of a sub-state entity. However, there might be over-representation in the unicameral legislature for the autonomous entity;
- "The right of the component units to be involved in the process of amending the federal constitution but to change their own constitutions unilaterally." Typically, sub-state entities that take on the form of autonomy arrangements would not have any institutional right to be involved in the amendment of the national constitution, and as concerns their own constitutions, often termed autonomy statutes, they often are enacted and amended by the legislature of the state with the consent of the sub-state entity, although there may exist some space for the autonomous entity to modify its own internal constitutional arrangements;
- "Decentralized government, that is, the regional government's share of power in a federation is relatively large compared to that of regional governments in unitary states." This is also true in respect of autonomy arrangements.

Lijphart also summarizes the opinions of five experts of federalism on the hallmarks of federalism, concluding that a starting point for all is the federal division of powers or decentralization.[41] Elazar is said to emphasize a relatively rigid written constitution, while Finer argues that both a rigid constitution and bicameralism are part of federalism. Riker, in turn, stresses the latter point and thinks that the second chamber is one of the special constitutional features of federalism, sustained by Wheare (see above), who in addition introduces the requirement of a supreme written constitution. Finally, in a listing of ten yardsticks

[39] Wheare (1964), p. 85. On the relationship between federalism and party system, see also Friedrich (1968), pp. 47–51.

[40] Lijphart (1985), pp. 4–5. See also Elazar (1987), p. 22 f.

[41] Lijphart (1985), p. 11. For a comment from the point of view of autonomy concerning the idea of consociationalism proposed by Lijphart, see Lapidoth (1997), p. 173 f.

of federalism, Duchacek includes the rigid constitution and bicameralism and equal representation of unequal states. It thus seems that federalism entails a constitutionally entrenched form of symmetrical governance at the sub-state level with a bicameral mechanism of some sort as an institutional forum for the representation of the sub-state units.

3.2.2 Expanding the Frames of Federalism

Painting with a relatively broad brush, Elazar elaborates his notion of federalism in a manner which not only covers typical federations, but assigns the term 'federation' or 'federacy' to a number of cases that would normally not be understood as federal government. He thinks that federal principles are concerned with the "combination of self-rule and shared rule" in a setting of constitutional distribution of powers between general and constituent governments where "the constituting elements in a federal arrangement share in the processes of common policy making and administration by right, while the activities of the common government are conducted in such a way as to maintain their respective integrities".[42] According to Elazar, a federation is a "polity compounded of strong constituent entities and a strong general government, each possessing powers delegated to it by the people and empowered to deal directly with the citizenry in the exercise of those powers".[43] He also thinks that so-called second federal chambers constitute an important device for maintaining federalism, because they offer the opportunity to protect constituent state interests and also to give the states an effective role in federal government.[44]

What is interesting here from the point of view of autonomy arrangements is that Elazar is referring to the constituent entities in plural form and is assuming a symmetrical organization of federations, implying a more or less voluntary

[42]Elazar (1987), p. 5 f. See also Elazar (1987), p. 12, where he expresses the simplest possible definition of federalism: "self-rule plus shared rule", and thinks that federalism thus defined "involves some kind of contractual linkage of a presumably permanent character that (1) provides for power sharing, (2) cuts around the issue of sovereignty, and (3) supplements but does not seek to replace or diminish prior organic ties where they exist".

[43]Elazar (1987), p. 7. See also Elazar (1987), p. 21: "If a political system is established by compact and has at least two "arenas", "planes", "spheres", "tiers" or "levels" of government, each endowed with independent legitimacy and a constitutionally guaranteed place in the overall system and possessing its own set of institutions, powers and responsibilities, it is deemed to be federal."

[44]See Elazar (1987), p. 184. In this context, Elazar thinks that the German federal chamber is most effective, while the US Senate is one of the least effective federal chambers because its members are elected *ad personum* and are not required to represent their states per se. He also adds that the decorative Canadian Senate does not even pretend to perform a serious federalist function.

association with the constituent units,[45] something which is often not the case with autonomies which often exist as singular units in formally unitary states, thereby introducing a measure of asymmetry in the constitutional fabric of the state which may or may not have a voluntary act behind their emergence. For these latter cases, Elazar develops the notion of federacy as one postmodern application of the federal principle: "In a federacy arrangement, a larger power and a smaller polity are linked asymmetrically in a federal relationship whereby the latter has greater autonomy than other segments of the former and, in return, has a smaller role in the governance of the larger power. The relationship between them is more like that of a federation than a confederation and can be dissolved only by mutual agreement."[46] However, drawing especially from the African experiences with federalism, which have often been negative and not long-lived, he concludes that unbalanced federal arrangements rarely succeed: "Two-unit federations are particularly vulnerable, because they do not offer sufficient opportunities for tension-reduction coalitions. Nor are federal arrangements likely to work where one entity is clearly dominant." The image is created that asymmetrical sub-state arrangements would seem to be at risk, and Elazar thinks that the future of federalism in the Third World may be limited, at least at first glance.[47] However in the particular context of Africa, the authoritarian political environment is probably a greater factor in determining the success and failure of sub-state arrangements than its asymmetrical nature.[48]

In essence, when referring to federacies or to political systems with federal arrangements, Elazar seems to be describing autonomy arrangements. However, he issues a caveat when dealing with technically unitary states that use federal principles (*inter alia*, Portugal with 2 autonomous overseas regions, Spain with 17 autonomous regions,[49] Italy with 15 ordinary and 5 special autonomous regions,[50] Tanzania with 2 constituent units and the United Kingdom with 4 countries and

---

[45]See, e.g., Elazar (1987), pp. 157, 166, 182, 185. See also Elazar (1987), p. 33, where he maintains that federalism has to do "with the need of peoples and polities to unite for common purposes yet remain separate to preserve their respective integrities", that federal principles grow out of the idea that free people can freely enter into lasting yet limited political associations to achieve common ends and protect certain rights while preserving their respective integrities" and that the federal idea itself rests on the principle that political and social institutions and relationships are best established through covenants, compacts, or other contractual arrangements, rather than, or in addition to, simply growing organically". Such voluntary association is often not present in autonomy arrangements.

[46]Elazar (1987), pp. 7, 55, 234–235. He also mentions associated state arrangements and common markets in the context.

[47]Elazar (1987), p. 253.

[48]See Nordquist (1998), pp. 59–77, about the low likelihood of autonomy arrangements to survive in authoritarian countries.

[49]Concerning Spain, Elazar (1987), p. 165, feels that the Spanish system denies the autonomous territories a major role as territories in the national government.

[50]Concerning Italy, Elazar (1987), p. 165, concludes that its constitution "comes closest to that of Spain with its system of regionalization, in which the regions are given certain autonomous powers of home rule without being involved *qua* regions in the general government".

5 self-governing islands). In cases of this kind, the "use of federal principles can have important consequences, but the distinction between them and true federations is made real because such principles do not permeate them".[51] He is of the opinion that "federalism is not omnipresent or coterminous with any exercise of power away from the center, *de facto* as well as *de jure*"[52] and that there indeed exists sub-state governance that is not federal in nature but that introduces asymmetrical features by way of an application of the federal principle (*inter alia*, Åland Islands, Azores and Madeira, Faroe Islands and Greenland, Guernsey, Isle of Man and Jersey, Jammu and Kashmir, Northern Marianas and Puerto Rico).[53] When considering federal solutions in the context of ethnic cleavage, he mentions, *inter alia*, Canada, Italy,[54] Spain[55] and the United Kingdom,[56] thereby indicating that sub-state solutions may be valuable in the context of conflict resolution.

Indeed, Elazar's reference to federacy in the context of autonomy arrangements changed into a distinction between federations, confederations and autonomy arrangements in his later work entitled *Federal Systems of the World*, which according to its specification in the title is *A Handbook of Federal, Confederal and Autonomy Arrangements*.[57] It seems that at least at the level of the title of the handbook, a distinction is made between different arrangements so as to create a separate category of autonomy arrangements. The definitions used in the handbook, however, largely repeat the earlier terminology of federacy without really making conceptual distinctions between federal arrangements, on the one hand, and autonomy arrangements, on the other, although the category of 'autonomy' is now introduced, with Corsica in France as one example.[58] The other two examples mentioned in the category of autonomy are Georgia and Ukraine, but for Georgia, the references intended are probably Abchasia, Adjaria and South Ossetia,[59] and for Ukraine, the reference should be to the autonomous territory of Crimea.[60] If so, it seems that Elazar places sub-state entities other than regular federations in the category of federacy in situations where the entities have law-making powers

[51]Elazar (1987), p. 44. Elazar (1987), pp. 157–168, identifies the following requisites of a federal system: written constitution (with several different constitutional options), non-centralization and areal division of power.

[52]Elazar (1987), p. 46. See also Elazar (1987), pp. 44–46.

[53]Elazar (1987), pp. 54–57, 60. For more contrasting examples in relation to federations, see Elazar (1987), pp. 226–231.

[54]Elazar (1987), p. 237: "regionalism as a protofederal arrangement designed to build publics in a country that has suffered from political alienation on the part of individuals and families."

[55]Elazar (1987), p. 238: "autonomy for national minorities and Spanish unity."

[56]Elazar (1987), p. 238: "devolution of administrative powers and national rights to constituent countries inhabited by separate peoples."

[57]Elazar (1994).

[58]Elazar (1994), p. xix.

[59]Elazar (1994), p. 89.

[60]Elazar (1994), pp. 255–257.

proper, while entities with special administrative powers of self-government, subordinated to the law-making powers of the national legislature, are placed in the category of autonomy.[61] This distinction is probably not helpful in bringing conceptual clarity to the attempts to categorize sub-state entities by way of relating them to federalism. Nonetheless, the handbook is useful for a study of autonomy arrangements, because it contains descriptions of such sub-state entities along with descriptions of federal arrangements.[62]

In comparing different federations, Watts, too, thinks that a "characteristic feature of federations generally is an emphasis upon constitutional supremacy as the ultimate source defining federal and state or provincial jurisdiction".[63] Although he denies the existence of a single pure model of federation that is applicable everywhere, he concludes (following Elazar)[64] that federalism seems to be characterized by a combination of regional self-rule through a common government (collaborative partnership) for some purposes and regional self-rule for the governments of the constituent units (constituent unit autonomy) for other purposes, within a single political system so that neither level of government is subordinate to the other,[65] although the practical application of these features may vary from case to case. Watts uses the term 'federalism' as a normative term which refers to the "advocacy of multi-tiered government combining elements of shared-rule and regional self-rule", based on the "presumed value and validity of combining unity and diversity, i.e., of accommodating, preserving and promoting distinct identities within a larger political union".[66] In its normative understanding, federalism aims at perpetuating both union and non-centralization at the same time. Much in line with Wheare but by adding the participatory element, Watts makes the point that in federations, neither the federal nor the constituent units of government are constitutionally subordinate to the other:[67] "each has sovereign powers derived from the constitution rather than from another level of government, each is empowered to deal directly with its citizens in the exercise of its legislative, executive and taxing powers, and each is directly elected by its citizens." Although

---

[61]This is somewhat surprising against the background that the etymological origins of the term 'autonomy' can be traced back to the Greek terms 'auto', meaning 'self', and 'nomos', meaning 'law' or 'rule'. See Lapidoth (1997), p. 29, and Eide (1998), p. 251. Hence the autonomies in France, Georgia and Ukraine would not necessarily qualify in the core group of autonomies, that is, such entities which have law-making powers proper.

[62]*Inter alia*, Tibet and Xinjiang in China, Faroe Islands and Greenland in Denmark, Åland Islands in Finland, Jammu and Kashmir in India, Azores and Madeira in Portugal, Basque Country, Catalonia and Galicia in Spain, Zanzibar in Tanzania and Puerto Rico in the United States.

[63]Watts (2008), p. xv.

[64]Elazar (1987), pp. 5, 12.

[65]Watts (2008), pp. 1, 8. According to Watts, this definition results in a spectrum of more specific non-unitary forms of government, ranging from "quasi-federations" and "federations" to "confederacies" and beyond.

[66]Watts (2008), p. 8.

[67]Watts (2008), p. 9.

Watts feels that this is more an institutional than a substantive characteristic, he thinks that the constitutional distribution of powers between the federal and regional governments is a fundamental defining characteristic of federations,[68] an observation which is true also with regard to autonomy arrangements.

While not claiming to establish a definition of federalism, Watts nonetheless presents the generally common structural characteristics of federations as a specific form of federal political system,[69] something that we can supplement with contrasting characteristics of autonomy:

- "[at] least two orders of government, one for the whole federation and the other for the regional units, each acting directly on its citizens". This is a dimension of sub-state organization where the regional units of a federation are normally several and spread out over the entire territory of the state, while a state with an autonomy arrangement is normally a territorial entity of a unitary kind;
- "[a] formal constitutional distribution of legislative and executive authority and allocation of revenue sources between the two orders of government ensuring some areas of genuine autonomy for each order".[70] This characteristic is shared by federal and autonomy arrangements, but unlike classical federations, where it seems the federal government generally holds the enumerated powers while the constituent states hold the residual powers, the autonomy arrangements are often designed so that the state holds the residual powers, while the autonomous entity is vested with enumerated powers or that the powers of the territorial autonomy are dependent on a non-entrenched ordinary piece of national law that places the ultimate residual powers with the national lawmaker;
- "[p]rovision for the designated representation of distinct regional views within the federal policy-making institutions, usually provided by the particular form of the federal second chamber".[71] Almost without exception, this is *not* the case with autonomy

[68] Watts (2008), p. 83.

[69] Watts (2008), p. 9. Watts does not, however, claim that all these defining characteristics necessarily have to be present in a case for it to be qualified as a federation, but concludes, e.g., on pp. 18–21, that federations may be differently organized and at times even asymmetrical so as to result in a relatively great variation of forms inside the category of federal organization. As Watts points out on p. 18, there is no single "ideal" or "pure" form of federation.

[70] As concluded by Watts (2008), pp. 84 f. and 92 f., in a manner which is relevant also for autonomy arrangements in their relationship with the national level, it is important to "find a balance between the independence and interdependence of governments within a federation". As concerns the relationship between legislative and executive powers in federations, it seems that often, legislative competence imply executive powers in the area of those competences, but in some federations, the federal level also uses the state level for executive purposes within the sphere of federal legislative competence. See Watts (2008), p. 86 f.

[71] See also Watts (2008), pp. 147, 150, who concludes that the "principle of bicameralism has been incorporated into the federal legislatures of most federations", the only exceptions among 25 federations currently in existence being the United Arab Emirates, Venezuela, Comoros, Micronesia and St. Kitts and Nevis. At least as concerns last of the exceptions, the case could be made that Nevis actually is an autonomous territory in the state (see below, Sect. 3.5.3). As concerns Spain, the chamber of the legislature where there is regional representation is partly elected, partly appointed. The 208 elected representatives are not elected from the autonomous communities, but from provinces, which is an administrative layer below the autonomous territories. However, 51 representatives are appointed by the parliaments of the 17 autonomous communities. The representation of sub-state units in federations is, according to Watts (2008), p. 152, not even in half of the

arrangements, where this institutional link to the governance of the entire state is not present, although there may exist one or more designated seats to the parliament of the state;
- "[a] supreme written constitution not unilaterally amendable and requiring the consent for amendments of a significant proportion of the constituent units".[72] This is not normally the case in constitutional orders that include autonomy arrangements, where the constitution-maker of the state has the right to amend the constitution without the co-operation of the political institutions of the autonomy, at least in so far as the possible autonomy provisions are not affected;
- "[a]n umpire (in the form of courts, provision for referendums, or an upper house with special powers)". Interestingly, an umpire is not always provided for in autonomy arrangements, at least not an independent umpire which would be empowered to strike a balance between the state and the autonomy arrangement; and
- "[p]rocesses and institutions to facilitate intergovernmental collaboration for those areas where governmental responsibilities are shared or inevitably overlap". In autonomies, such processes and institutions are probably less likely to exist than in federations, although in practice, mechanisms of collaboration are needed in relation to autonomy arrangements, as well.

It is clear on the basis of this account of characteristics that autonomies can much more often than not be identified as such a category of constitutional and institutional arrangements which can be distinguished from federations. However, the two forms of governance, federation and autonomy arrangements, often share particular circumstances that lead to their creation,[73] again with comments that contrast autonomies against the background of federations:

- "[t]he degree and distribution of cultural and national diversity that they attempt to reconcile". The reconciliation of diversity is a feature which often is predominant in autonomy contexts, probably more often than in federations;[74]
- "[t]heir creation by aggregation of constituent units, devolution to constituent units, or both processes". For the autonomies, it seems that devolution is mainly relevant, although it is not to be excluded that autonomy arrangements result from the aggregation of units, for instance, as a result of the transfer of territories between two States;
- "[t]he number, relative size and symmetry or asymmetry of the constituent units".[75] An autonomy is normally a singular phenomenon in a state, introducing a profound asymmetry into the fabric of the state (which in most cases identifies itself as a unitary

cases based on an equality of state representation at the federal level, but may instead favor smaller sub-state entities or significant minorities, although sub-state units with larger populations tend to get more seats.

[72]See also Watts (2008), pp. 157–170.

[73]Watts (2008), p. 19.

[74]However, as pointed out in Watts (2008), p. 76, a number of federations contain constituent units marked by different linguistic, ethnic or religious majorities and refers in this respect to, *inter alia*, Belgium, Canada, Ethiopia, India, Nigeria, Russia and Switzerland as evidence for the opening offered by federalism to "accommodate ethnic, linguistic and regional groups by establishing regional units within which they may form a majority with the power to protect and promote their distinctiveness through a measure of self-government".

[75]Although most federations are symmetrical, some asymmetrical federations also exist, such as Canada, the Russian Federation. See Watts (2008), pp. 32 f.

state), while the constituent units of a federation are found over the entire territory of the federal state;[76]
- "[t]he distribution of legislative and administrative responsibility among governments". This distribution is a regular feature of federations and autonomy arrangements alike, but unlike federations, where it seems the federal government generally holds the enumerated powers while the constituent states hold the residual powers,[77] the autonomy arrangements are often designed so that the state holds the residual powers, while the autonomous entity is vested with enumerated powers;[78]
- "[t]he allocation of taxing powers and financial resources". Such allocation takes place both in federations and in respect of autonomy arrangements, but the extent of the allocation may vary greatly;
- "[t]he roles of federal and constituent-unit governments in the conduct of international relations". Foreign powers are in both cases often reserved to the state, but some autonomy arrangements display significant exceptions to the supremacy of the state in the area of foreign powers;
- "[t]he character and composition of their central federative institutions". In autonomies, no such "federative" or national institutions exist or, if they do, they are very weak in relation to similar institutions in federations;
- "[t]he processes and institutions for resolving conflicts and facilitating collaboration between interdependent governments". Such processes, typical for federations, may be absent in autonomy contexts or only weakly developed;
- "[t]he ratification of constitutional amendments by regional legislatures or referendums". It is normally not the case with autonomy arrangements that they would have a say in amending the national constitution, although they normally have the possibility to participate in and ratify the amendments of their own autonomy statutes (which may or may not have some constitutional rank);
- "[t]he degree of political centralization or non-centralization and the degree of economic integration". This is a crucial feature in both federations and in relation to autonomy arrangements and implies the existence of vertical lines of contacts between the state and the sub-state entity.

In federations, the sub-state level may develop different varieties of political systems, depending on the circumstances. As concerns political parties, Watts recognizes that the party systems at the federal and the state levels may be similar

[76]This is supported by the data concerning the constituent units of federations in Watts (2008), pp. 71–76. See also Davis (1978), p. 121 f., who says that in a federation, the business of state is "divided between two popularly elected governments, a national government embracing the whole territory of the nation and a "regional" government for each of the lesser territories", which means that the lesser territories are multiple and cover the entire territory of the country.

[77]For examples, see Watts (2008), pp. 31 (Switzerland), 33 (Australia), 34 (Austria), 38 (Mexico), 39 (Malaysia), 40 (Pakistan), 43 (Brazil), 44 (Belgium), 47 (Argentina), 50 (Nigeria), 59 (Bosnia and Herzegovina), 61 (the Democratic Republic of Congo). Canada, India and Belau are apparently exceptions that confirm the rule, because the major residual powers are vested with the federal government in a division of powers which is based on enumeration both concerning the competences of the federation and the constituent states (or provinces, as the sub-state entities are called in Canada). See Watts (2008), pp. 32, 37. In addition, some federal states (such as the Russian Federation, Comoros, St. Kitts and Nevis, Micronesia, South Africa, Ethiopia and Venezuela) have such distributions of competences which are difficult to place in any of the categories.

[78]According to Watts (2008), p. 43, this distribution of competencies is the case in Spain.

or different, and that there are four different aspects of political organization in federations that may affect the functioning of a federal political system: "(1) the relationship between the party organizations at the federal level and provincial or state party level, (2) the degree of symmetry or asymmetry between federal and provincial or state party alignments, (3) the impact of party discipline upon the representation of interests within each level, and (4) the prevailing pattern of political careers."[79] According to Watts, political systems where parliamentary accountability of the Westminster kind is not practiced, such as in the US and Switzerland, have tended to produce loose confederations of state or cantonal and local party organizations of a decentralized nature. In contrast, the situation could be different in parliamentary federations, where the pressures for effective party discipline within each government in order to sustain the sub-state executive in office have tended to separate federal and provincial or state branches of parties into more autonomous layers of party organization.[80] He makes the observation concerning voting in the second chambers that in "federations where members of the federal second chamber are directly elected, generally they tend to vote along party lines rather than strictly for the regional interests they represent. Where they are indirectly elected by state legislatures they are more likely to regard themselves as representing regional interests, although regional political party interests also can play a significant role".[81]

3.2.3 Institutional and Substantive Dimensions Distinguished

Against the background of the work by Wheare, Lijphart, Elazar and Watts, it is probably possible to distinguish between institutional and substantive dimensions of federalism. For instance, according to Gamper, Austria would seem to meet the demands of the minimum *institutional* requirements of all federal systems: Firstly, both "legislative and administrative competences are distributed between the federation and the Länder". Secondly, the Länder "participate in the legislative process at federal level, as the Länder parliaments elect the members of the Federal Assembly ("Bundesrat"), which is the second legislative chamber at the federal level". Thirdly, under "the Fiscal Constitutional Act and the Fiscal Adjustment Act, the Länder have some budgetary powers". Fourthly, the "State Governors and Independent Administrative Tribunals – instead of federal administrative agencies – are mainly responsible for carrying out federal administration on the federation's behalf ("indirect federal administration")". Fifthly, "there exist a number of formal

[79] Watts (2008), p. 145.

[80] Watts (2008), p. 145. For independent party formations and organizations at sub-state level, Canada and Belgium are presented as examples, while those in Australia, Germany and India show somewhat stronger ties to the party organizations at the federal level.

[81] Watts (2008), p. 151.

and informal instruments of cooperative federalism as well as an umpire (Constitutional Court) that solves conflicts between the federation and the Länder".[82] Although this listing of institutional dimensions of federalism hints at material dimensions in the references made to the distribution of competences, budgetary powers and the conflict-solving mechanism, Gamper makes the point that this is just one side of Austrian federalism, the other one being that "the major part of competences – and the more important – belongs to the federation".[83] There should therefore also be a substantive part to the definition of federalism, not only an institutional one.

The *substantive* dimension of federalism is in Austria described with reference to the competences and responsibilities divided between the federal level and the state level. Firstly, there are exclusive federal competences, where the federation is responsible for both legislation and for the execution of the same matter. Secondly, there are exclusive state competences of a residual nature where the states are responsible for the legislation and execution of the same matter. Thirdly, there are mixed competences. Fourthly, there are areas where the federation is responsible for framework legislation, while the states are responsible for the execution of the matter. Fifthly, there are competences where the federation is responsible for framework legislation, while the states are responsible for implementing legislation and for execution of the matter.[84] As concerns the distribution of the competences, if a competence is not explicitly referred to as a federal competence by way of enumeration, a matter falls into the residual competence of the Länder. Such a residual competence of the constituent states is, according to Gamper, "a common feature to most federal constitutions and is believed to favour the states, but its effect depends on which and how many competences have been enlisted as federal competences".[85] "In the case of Austria, only few and less significant powers are left to the Länder in this way. Neither are the Länder's explicit competences [. . .] of a more fundamental nature."[86]

A related theme is the norm-hierarchical status of the legislative enactment of the sub-state legislative body. According to the description by Gamper relating to Austria, Länder constitutional law must not violate federal constitutional law. In the hierarchy of Austrian law, therefore, "Länder constitutional law is at the top of all kinds of Länder law, it is equal to ordinary federal law, but it is below federal constitutional law."[87] Under the principle of relative constitutional autonomy

[82]Gamper (2004), p. 57.

[83]Gamper (2004), p. 57. Because the Federal Assembly has never vetoed a federal bill because of its centralizing tendency at the expense of the Länder and because of some other characteristics, Gamper feels that the Austrian form of federalism is one of the most centralized of its kind.

[84]Gamper (2004), p. 58.

[85]Gamper (2004), p. 58.

[86]Gamper (2004), p. 58.

[87]Gamper (2004), p. 60.

developed by the Constitutional Court, "Länder constitutions may contain provisions of all kinds as long as they do not violate federal constitutional law".[88]

At the outset, the division of powers between the federal level and the state level in Austria follows the so-called petrification theory, according to which the subject matter is divided according to the division of the pertinent substantive law at the historical moment when the division of competences was determined. This means that new subject-matter, such as certain technological issues, falls within the sphere of competence of the federation.[89] At the level of ordinary legislation, under the principle of different aspects, a matter can, according to the Constitutional Court, fall into several competences and thus be regulated by the federation and the Länder under different aspects.[90] At this juncture, there is also a principle of mutual consideration at play, requiring that the federation and the Länder "must heed each other's interests and not excessively neglect the legislation enacted by the other when enacting their own legislation".[91] However, if there remain doubts about the sphere of competence to which a matter belongs after the application of these interpretation rules, the so-called federalistic interpretation rule will, in the end, be applied, which means that the matter will fall within the competence of the Länder[92] in a manner that indicates the existence of residual powers with the constituent states.

It has been concluded in relation to the federation in Germany that the "Länder are states as the federation is a state. Both have their autonomous, constitutional power. The sovereignty of the Länder does not derive from the federation's sovereignty; the federation has to respect the sovereignty of the Länder. There exist separate constitutional spheres in the federation on the one hand and in the Länder on the other hand. Each Land has the right to adopt its constitution and thereby structure its own political institutions."[93] As concerns the US, the "Constitution confers only limited powers on the federal government, and the Tenth Amendment confirms that all residual powers not prohibited to the states by the Constitution 'are reserved to the States respectively, or to the people'".[94] Thus the powers held in federations at the central government level, on the one hand, and at the level of the constituent states on the other, are important. So much so that some authors maintain that the presence of an explicit division of legislative power in the constitution is the exclusive hallmark of every constitutional system which purports to be federal.[95] However, the representation of the territorial units, the constituent

---

[88]Gamper (2004), p. 60.

[89]See Gamper (2004), p. 58 f.

[90]Gamper (2004), p. 59.

[91]Gamper (2004), p. 62.

[92]Gamper (2004), p. 59.

[93]Weiss (2004), p. 76.

[94]Tarr et al. (2004), p. 90.

[95]See Davis (1978), p. 142. For an exploration of different theories of federalism, see Davis (1978), pp. 121–216.

states, at the federal level is also a defining feature of a federation, because a distinguishing hallmark of a federation is the "accommodation of the constituent units of the union in the decision-making procedure of the central government on some constitutionally entrenched basis".[96]

King is of the opinion that a federation is "most significantly distinguished from other forms of sovereign state by the fact that its structure is grounded in the representation of regional governments within the national or central legislature on an entrenched basis".[97] Obviously, a combination of the material and the institutional dimensions of the federal structure could be used to indicate what is and, more importantly for this piece of research, what is not a federation. From the point of view of (the potential for) federalism in Asia, Galligan makes the point that the "set of essential federal institutions that writers typically identify are the organizational means for putting such a system into political practice. The three key ones are a written constitution that defines the respective powers of the two spheres of government and is hard to amend, a bicameral legislature with a strong federal chamber representing the constituent states or provinces, and a constitutional court to resolve jurisdictional disputes and keep governments within their constitutional limits."[98] He adds a fourth organizational means, a system of intergovernmental institutions to facilitate collaboration between governments in areas of shared or overlapping jurisdiction.

In his elaboration of the phenomenon of federalism, Anderson concludes that if there is an essence of federalism, "it is that there are two constitutionally established orders of government with some genuine autonomy from each other, and the governments at each level are primarily accountable to their respective electorates".[99] Again, this is a very broad statement which may also extend itself to situations the federal nature of which are disputed, such as Spain and Saint Kitts and Nevis. All sub-state forms of organization do not fully meet the criteria for federalism, because some are very centralized and weakly federal, while others have special unitary features that may sometimes permit the central government to override the autonomy of constituent units. He also sees a distinction between federal arrangements, on the one hand, and devolved unitary regimes, on the other.[100] He feels, however, that there is no definitive answer to whether or not the debatable cases are federations. The characteristics of federations nonetheless comprise six different elements:[101]

[96]Burgess (1993), p. 5.

[97]King (1993), p. 94. See also King (1982).

[98]Galligan (2007), p. 293.

[99]Anderson (2008), p. 4.

[100]Anderson (2008), p. 5.

[101]Anderson (2008), p. 3 f.

- "[a]t least two orders of government, one for the whole country and the other for the regions. Each government has a direct electoral relationship with its citizens." This is, by and large, true also for states with autonomies, but the sub-state arrangement often involves only one sub-state entity, not two or more, as in ordinary federal structures. Normally, inhabitants of the sub-state entities in the autonomous territories participate through elections both in the national legislature and the legislative assembly of the sub-state entity, which means that they may develop their own political environments with party structures that differ from that of the federal level;[102]
- "[a] written constitution some parts of which cannot be amended by the federal government alone." Here, the condition is stricter than is the case concerning many autonomous territories, which do not necessarily rely on positive rules of a written constitution, but on other norms, such as ordinary legislation of the national law-making body. Also, territorial autonomies normally do not participate in the amendment of the national constitution;
- "[a] constitution that formally allocates legislative, including fiscal, powers to the two orders of government ensuring some genuine autonomy for each order." As concerns autonomous territories, the allocation of powers often takes place in a special autonomy statute, not in the constitution of the country. That autonomy statute may or may not be of constitutional rank;
- "[u]sually some special arrangements, notably in upper houses, for the representation of the constituent units in key central institutions to provide for regional input in central decision-making, (...)."[103] Typically, autonomous territories do not have institutional representation in key institutions at the national level;
- "[a]n umpire or procedure (usually involving courts, but sometimes referendums or an upper house) to rule on constitutional disputes between governments." Because an autonomous territory is a singular unit in a state which in other respects is unitary, there is often not any constitutional court for such disputes, but instead dispute resolution processes that may be of a more political nature;
- "[a] set of processes and institutions for facilitating or conducting relations between governments." There probably are such processes and institutions for autonomy arrangements in relation to the central government, but because autonomous territories are often singular entities, there would not exist any natural horizontal relationship to similar entities. The relatively typical situation of horizontal discussion between constituent units in federations is therefore lacking in most states with autonomous territories.

As concerns the distribution of powers between the central level and the sub-state level, Anderson distinguishes between two broad approaches, the dualist model and the integrated model: "The dualist model typically assigns different jurisdictions to

[102]Anderson (2008), p. 65: "The party regime is critical. In federations where the political parties are integrated between the two orders of government, the national party leaders may have great influence over candidates and leaders in the constituent units; alternatively, regional barons, with their power bases in the constituent units, may be king makers for the party at the centre."

[103]Anderson (2008), p. 45, makes the point that the "central legislatures of federations usually have some balancing of representation by population with representation by constituent units. This federal dimension of representation is usually embodied in upper houses, but it can be present in lower houses as well". Anderson (2008), p. 46, also puts forward the view that the "prevalence of such upper houses in federations is associated with the idea that both the population and the constituent units are part of what makes a federation, and both dimensions need to be reflected in the central institutions". Hence the institutional dimension of sub-state representation may be understood as central to federations.

each order of government, which then delivers and administers its own programs. The integrated model provides for many shared competences and the constituent-unit governments often administer centrally legislated programs or laws."[104] He goes on to conclude that under the dualist, or classical, model of federalism, constitutional jurisdiction over different subjects is usually assigned exclusively to one order of government,[105] but he also point out that the dualist model does not in practice "achieve a neat separation of powers because so many issues have regional, national, and even international dimensions and many different responsibilities of governments are themselves intertwined".[106] This is probably also due to the fact that in all dualist constitutions, "there are some shared or concurrent powers in which both orders of governments can make laws".[107] Because the distribution of powers is difficult to compartmentalize in a water-tight manner, "residual powers go to the federal government in federations that emerged from previously unitary regimes and to the constituent-unit governments in federations that brought previously separate units together".[108] It seems that territorial autonomies often follow the former model, because they are typically born in situations where there is a previous unitary regime that devolves power to a singular entity.

3.3 The Characteristics of Autonomy v. Federalism

3.3.1 Indications of a Separate Category of Autonomy

In the well-known phrase "autonomy is not a term of art in international or constitutional law",[109] Hannum captures an important characteristic of our study. That is whether or not it is possible to identify elements of autonomy arrangements in a manner which distinguishes such arrangements from federal arrangements. The point of view of Hannum is that of public international law and international human rights law, not primarily the institutional law derived from constitutions, and he does not provide any further definition of autonomy or its relationship to federalism. However, the choice of case studies in his research creates at least an intuitive understanding of the possible differences between the two concepts, perhaps also a more theoretical notion not explicitly developed in his research, but present nonetheless. Hannum is clearly reviewing sub-state entities, in particular of the kind

---

[104]Anderson (2008), p. 21.

[105]According to Anderson (2008), p. 21, in this model, "each order of government normally delivers programs in its area of responsibility, using its civil service and departments; the federal government's departments are thus present throughout the country".

[106]Anderson (2008), p. 21.

[107]Anderson (2008), p. 21.

[108]Anderson (2008), p. 26.

[109]Hannum (1996), p. 4.

which are singular arrangements for the benefit of a minority population or for the resolution of a conflict situation of the kind we would refer to as autonomy arrangements, although he also includes a number of federal arrangements in his inquiry, such as India and Malaysia. It is interesting, however, that in part III of his inquiry on other examples of autonomous arrangements, he includes a chapter on federal and quasi-federal structures (with, *inter alia*, Switzerland and the Soviet Union as examples, while the United States is left out with reference to the good availability of materials),[110] as if such federal arrangements, too, were part of the same concept of autonomy he is fleshing out.

The terminology of enumerated and residual powers, on the one hand, and bicameralism and representation of the constituent states, on the other, is present in Hannum's research, but it is not developed into an institutional theory that would distinguish between autonomy and federalism. This is so probably because his approach is that of international law, not constitutional law, and because the objectives of his research were more functional in the areas of minority protection and conflict resolution. He could therefore arrive at the conclusion that while "each situation is unique, the conflicts in which autonomy is viewed by one party as essential to the guarantee of its survival concern some or all of the following basic issues: language; education; access to governmental civil service, including police and security forces, and social services; land and natural resources; and representative local government".[111] The substantive dimensions of distribution of competences are more important in this context.

The review of the different cases against the background of norms of international law leads Hannum to identify a fully autonomous territory as an entity, mainly within the purview of the Western-oriented democracies based on a separation of powers, which possesses *most* of the following powers:[112]

- There is a locally elected representative body with some independent legislative authority, limited by a constituent document. Unless the exercise of this authority exceeds the local legislature's competence as defined in the constituent document, it should not be subject to veto by the principal/sovereign government. Local competence should generally include control or influence over primary and secondary education, the use of language, the structure of local government, and land use and planning;
- There is a locally selected chief executive, who may be subject to approval by the central government; the executive may have responsibility for the administration and enforcement of state (national) as well as local laws. While the executive may be jointly responsible to the local and central authorities, this structural confusion is probably best avoided in circumstances where strong local identity is asserted;
- There is an independent local judiciary with full responsibility for interpreting local laws. Disputes over the extent of local authority or the relationship between the autonomous and central governments may be within the original jurisdiction of local courts, but final decisions are commonly within the competence of either the state judiciary or a joint dispute-settling body;

---

[110]Hannum (1996), p. 333.

[111]Hannum (1996), p. 458.

[112]Hannum (1996), p. 467 f.

– Areas of joint concern may be the subject of power-sharing arrangements between the autonomous and central governments, in which local flexibility is permitted within the broad policy parameters set by the central government. In addition to local implementation and administration of state norms, joint authority is frequently exercised over such matters as ports and communication facilities, police, and exploitation of natural resources.

Although Hannum refers to powers when proposing this summary of the notion of 'full autonomy', with the qualification that most, but not all, of the dimensions should be present in an arrangement for it to be called an autonomy arrangement, it seems that this account is more institutional than functional. Moreover, he places this account of full autonomy at the end of a progression of rights,[113] as if there existed a range of other alternatives of a "lesser" nature, suited for situations that do not necessarily require the full thrust of delegated powers and sub-state institutions. The fully autonomous sub-state entity seems to be very autonomous and is, indeed, short of independence, while autonomous entities with a less elaborate institutional structure and less powers could exist and could still be called autonomies. From the point of view of the self-determination of peoples, Hannum argues that autonomy arrangements within sovereign States can be viewed as operationalizations of the right to self-determination, for instance, within the framework of the concept of 'any other political status' established in the UN General Assembly Declaration on Friendly Relations.[114]

Lapidoth is more focused on autonomy than on federalism and starts her enquiry by declaring that autonomy is a "means for diffusion of powers in order to preserve the unity of a state while respecting the diversity of its population",[115] that is, the political or cultural aspirations of minorities, indigenous populations and peoples striving for self-determination inside an established State. In defining her object of study, she is comparing territorial autonomy with other arrangements for the diffusion of powers, such as federalism, decentralization, self-government, associate status and self-administration.[116] It therefore seems that Lapidoth regards territorial autonomy as being in a category of its own among the various forms of sub-state governance and also considers that self-determination as a human right can also take on the form of territorial autonomy.[117] She classifies the theoretical discussion concerning autonomy into four categories, which we can combine with indications of the positions of the authorities she is using to create the categories:[118]

---

[113]Hannum (1996), p. 474.

[114]Hannum (1996), p. 41.

[115]Lapidoth (1997), p. 3.

[116]Lapidoth (1997), pp. 5, 10.

[117]Lapidoth (1997), p. 23. She concludes that "[m]ore and more authors seem to consider autonomy as a valid means of self-determination in a world where there is a trend toward federalization and regionalization".

[118]Lapidoth (1997), pp. 29–33. The opinions of the authorities on the matter and the categories are not completely exclusive in relation to each other, and therefore the same person may appear in two categories.

(1) autonomy as a right to act upon one's own discretion in certain matters, either on an individual basis or through an official body (Hauriou, Bernhardt, Oberreuter), (2) autonomy as a synonym of independence (Jellinek), (3) autonomy as synonymous to decentralization (Berthélémy, Steiner) and (4) autonomy as a reference to an entity that has exclusive powers of legislation, administration and adjudication in specific areas (Laband, Carré de Malberg, Duguit, Dörge, Robinson, Sohn, Bernhardt, Crawford, Hannum and Lillich). She calls the fourth category 'political autonomy', seemingly most populated by authorities on the matter, as opposed to 'administrative autonomy', which in her opinion is limited to powers in the sphere of administration. Her own definition of 'political autonomy' is an eclectic description along the following lines: "A territorial political autonomy is an arrangement aimed at granting to a group that differs from the majority of the population of the state, but that constitutes the majority in a specific region, a means by which it can express its distinct identity."[119] However, her definition does not really stop at that, but includes additional elements, such as the division of powers, law-making competence, representation of the population in the autonomous entity and resolution of disputes between the autonomous entity and the central government.[120]

The definition of autonomy serves for Lapidoth as a point of comparison with other arrangements for the diffusion of authority, such as federal systems, decentralization, self-government, associate statehood and self-administration.[121] She characterizes federations as states which base their functioning on a constitutional division of powers between central and regional authorities, which leave the residual powers to the constituent states at least in situations where they have preceded the creation of the federation, which create a mechanism by which the constituent entities participate in the legislative function at the central government level and which set up a special tribunal for dispute resolution for either vertical or horizontal problems between the different entities.[122] This characterization of federations is very much in harmony with the lines of argumentation presented above. Contrasting federations with territorial autonomies by highlighting the significant constitutional differences between the two, she concludes the following:[123]

- Autonomy can be established by a treaty, by a constitution, by a statute, or by a combination of these tools, whereas a federation is usually established by a constitution;
- In most cases, the autonomous entity, as such, does not participate in the activities of the central authorities, whereas the constituent states in federations play an important role in

[119] Lapidoth (1997), p. 33.

[120] Lapidoth (1997), pp. 33–35.

[121] Lapidoth (1997), p. 49. She, however, excludes the term 'devolution' from the analysis, because it denotes the mere act of transferring powers and does not indicate the content or nature of those powers.

[122] Lapidoth (1997), p. 50.

[123] See Lapidoth (1997), pp. 50–51.

the central authorities. The two roles mentioned are membership in the upper house and participation in the process of amending the federal constitution;
- Autonomy is usually established in regions that have a particular ethnic character, whereas the federal structure applies to the entire territory of the country. In addition, even federations can contain autonomous territories which fall outside of the federal structure of the state, and federalism and autonomy have sometimes even been combined;
- For autonomy arrangements, no special tribunals are normally established to resolve disputes between the central government and the autonomous entity, although a system for settling disputes may be set up.

It seems clear for Lapidoth that in spite of the considerable differences between federal and autonomy arrangements, systems of sub-state governance of this sort share some similarities, for instance, in terms of their objectives. Therefore, she feels that it may be useful to draw analogies between them in various areas.[124] In addition, she considers the relationship between autonomy, on the one hand, and concepts such as decentralization, self-government, associate statehood and self-administration, on the other. As concerns decentralization, Lapidoth holds that decentralization involves solely a delegation of powers, while autonomy assumes a transfer of powers and that the former may include limited participation of locally elected persons in the regional authorities, whereas in the case of autonomy, the basic assumption is that all the transferred functions are exercised by the locally elected representatives. An important notion concerning decentralization is that the central government may perhaps revoke the decentralization unilaterally, while the abrogation or amendment of autonomy arrangements are at least in some cases subject to the consent of both the central authorities and the autonomous entity. In the same vein, a regime of decentralization may vest in the central government powers to control, supervise and revise the acts of the decentralized authorities, while it would be only exceptionally possible for the central government to interfere in the actions of the autonomous entity, such as in cases where the autonomous entity has exceeded its powers or endangered the security of the state.[125]

Lapidoth is also of the opinion that the concept of self-government or self-rule is closely related to autonomy, because under self-government, a territorial community manages its own internal affairs by itself, without any external intervention. She feels that the concept of self-government implies a considerable degree of self-rule, whereas autonomy is a flexible concept with material contents that range from limited powers to very broad ones.[126] However, she does not provide any good distinction between self-government and autonomy. Instead, it seems the two concepts are overlapping to a great extent. She also considers the relationship between autonomy and associate statehood and concludes that associated statehood

[124]Lapidoth (1997), p. 51.

[125]Lapidoth (1997), pp. 51–52.

[126]Lapidoth (1997), pp. 52–53.

can be described as autonomy with very broad powers.[127] However, in this case there seems to be a greater difference, because associated statehood may be premised on independence preceding the association or at least a right to independence on the basis of a colonial relationship or trusteeship, which normally is not the case with autonomous entities.

3.3.2 *Autonomy as a Distinct Category*

It seems that Benedikter employs a very clear distinction between federalism on the one hand and autonomy on the other. In his opinion, "[r]egional autonomy is a specific territorial political organization having its own constituent features. It should not be confused with a subcategory of federalism. It is based on a specific formula of the political and legal relationship between a central state and a regional community within its traditional territory. Regional autonomy is a political and constitutional organization *sui generis* that deserves distinct attention and analysis in theory and practice".[128] He points out that autonomy can be established by a mere national act, while a federation can only be created by a state constitution.[129] He therefore thinks that autonomy and federalism are distinguishable and should be distinguished from each other,[130] although there exists some overlap between the two concepts that blurs the boundaries between them.

Benedikter thinks that the basic distinction is as follows: "[I]n a federation, the federated states or regions are generally involved in policymaking, whereas autonomous entities rule themselves, but normally have no special rights regarding the central power. Participating in the national institutions by democratic means, they have no special level of representation at the centre as federations (e.g. with a second chamber composed of representatives of the regions)."[131] On a continuum ranging from an associated state, on the one hand, to territorial autonomy and even administrative decentralization,[132] on the other, he separates between the federation and the autonomous territory by giving a definition of each of them and by giving

---

[127] Lapidoth (1997), pp. 54–55. The concept of self-administration that is considered by Lapidoth (1997), p. 55–57, on the basis of a proposal in 1991 to the UN General Assembly by the Principality of Liechtenstein, seems to be organized in progressive levels from decentralization to territorial autonomy.

[128] Benedikter (2007), p. 2.

[129] Benedikter (2007), p. 23.

[130] Benedikter (2007), pp. 12, 14, 18.

[131] Benedikter (2007), p. 12. See also Benedikter (2007), p. 23.

[132] Benedikter (2007), pp. 14–15. Apparently, the example of Corsica in France slides in this direction: "The mere transfer of administrative powers to regional bodies reduces the 'self-government agencies' to a sort of peripheral branch of the state administration, subordinated to carry out decisions taken at the centre". See Benedikter (2007), p. 27.

examples of each category. A federation is defined as an arrangement in which "[t]wo or more constituent entities enter into a constitutional framework with common institutions. Each member state retains certain delegated powers and the central government also retains powers over the member states".[133] The federal arrangement is exemplified by cases such as Belgium, Germany, Switzerland, the United States, India, Russia, Brazil and Canada. Territorial autonomy (which also may be called "home rule") is defined as arrangements where the sub-state entities are "[i]ntegral parts of a political sovereign state which have legislative and executive powers entrenched by law. Specific solution for one or more units of a state, but not for the whole territorial state structure."[134] The examples mentioned in the context are the Åland Islands, Gagauzia, Aceh, Greenland, and Muslim Mindanao. The basic point of distinction between unitary states with autonomous entities, on the one hand, and federations, on the other, is, according to Benedikter, "that in a federal state, the equality of the constituent units is a predominant feature of the state structure, while in a state with one or more autonomous entities it is not".[135]

Benedikter thinks that a proper use of the term autonomy is motivated whenever only a specific part of the territory of a state acquires a special status with special characteristics.[136] He distinguishes between symmetrical and asymmetrical federalism and makes the point that sometimes the devices of federalism and autonomy are combined. This is the case in, for instance, Canada, India and Russia, which, although federations, also encompass some entities with special powers so as to create these entities as special territorial autonomies in the framework of a federal state.[137] He also holds that the use of the autonomous entities in Spain as an overall feature of state organization makes Spain a disguised federation.[138] He nonetheless sees a distinction between autonomy and asymmetrical federalism, because "federalism is a system in which all regions have equal power, with some exceptions whenever the level of self-governance ensured by the powers of an ordinary federated unit may not be sufficient to accommodate the special needs of a peculiar community which require a major measure of self-government".[139]

Benedikter therefore identifies the following categories as the main features of a modern federal state: "1. A constitutionally entrenched distribution of powers between the central state and the component units; 2. The legal equality of these units: all of them have more or less identical powers and institutional stance in the

[133] Benedikter (2007), p. 15.

[134] Benedikter (2007), p. 15.

[135] Benedikter (2007), p. 25.

[136] Benedikter (2007), p. 13.

[137] See Benedikter (2007), p. 11. Apparently, Quebec and Nunavut in Canada as well as Puerto Rico and Northern Marianas in the United States would be examples of such situations. See Benedikter (2007), p. 13.

[138] Benedikter (2007), p. 24.

[139] Benedikter (2007), p. 24.

federal structure; 3. A governmental structure in all the component units with governments and legislatures of their own (very often also with their own constitutions or statutes); 4. The participation of the component units in the handling of federal affairs in a particular institutional way (second chamber elected in different procedure as the first chamber); 5. The equality of all citizens in federal elections and in other federal affairs."[140]

Benedikter concludes that an autonomy arrangement can be embedded in different ways in the constitutional fabric of a state on a graded scale between a minimum level of power-sharing up to an optimum,[141] which probably is to be understood as a maximal solution short of independence. The proper understanding of territorial autonomy, therefore, "not only encompasses administrative powers of local bodies, but requires the existence of a regional parliament with a minimum power to legislate in some basic domains as well as an independent elected executive which implements this legislation in the given autonomous area".[142] He is of the opinion that an autonomous entity must be endowed with its own parliament or assembly, democratically elected by universal suffrage by the region's population, but in addition, he thinks that the same population must be represented in the national parliament by forming a constituency of its own. The combined effect of these two measures is to ensure political participation on the part of the autonomous region at both levels of governance.[143] As concerns the executive function, he thinks that an autonomous entity must be vested with a government that is independent of the national institutions, elected either by the regional assembly or directly by the regional electorate. He goes on to hold that in a genuine autonomy, the central government cannot have any say in the designation of the head of the autonomous executive, which is not to have any responsibilities of the central government or be member of the offices of the central government, although the central government may delegate the administration of centrally held powers to the regional executive.[144]

The characterizations of territorial autonomy and federalism by Benedikter recognize the existence of legislative powers, but he is mainly focusing on the institutional features and differences of the two forms of organization. He makes reference to institutional representation of sub-state entities in federations and the absence of such representation in cases of territorial autonomy, but he does not develop the idea of the distribution of powers or the substantive dimension into an element of his definition and distinction by making the point that one or the other level of governance should hold the residual powers.

140 Benedikter (2007), p. 27.

141 Benedikter (2007), p. 55.

142 Benedikter (2007), p. 42.

143 Benedikter (2007), p. 55.

144 Benedikter (2007), p. 55.

3.4 The Notions of Regional State, Devolution, and Regional Self-Government

3.4.1 Regionalization and Autonomization

Italy is an interesting example of a state which after the Second World War and in a post-authoritarian context set out to re-create its constitution with a view to maintaining the unitary nature of the state while at the same time creating a level of sub-state governance. One important hurdle that according to Bartole needed to be overcome in the context was the traditional thinking in a unitary state that in the hierarchy of norms, the legislation of the state was supreme to lower norms, for instance, to norms passed by regional assemblies.[145] The establishment of exclusive legislative powers at the sub-state level in a fashion that sets aside the national norms in the sphere of competence of the sub-state entity may, as a consequence, not be a very easy task. In the Italian context, there was, however, a greater problem with the issue of residual powers. The thinking around the federal ideas hovered around the classical opinion that the "federal state had to be based on a compact between the pre-existing states, which were to surrender some of their functions to a new common state organization",[146] while retaining the residual powers for themselves as a reminder of the original sovereign powers they once held. The regions, however, were to have "autonomous powers only, that is to say that they could not purport to hold any state sovereignty", which was convenient and useful to a constituent assembly "which wanted to avoid the difficult task of the creation of a federal state", although the theory itself seemed somewhat ambiguous.[147]

From a modern point of view, this classical point of departure is not necessarily completely representative anymore, because functions of constituent states of federations are also sometimes enumerated.[148] In Italy, the distribution of powers between the national legislature and the regional legislatures was complicated by the concurring powers, created on the basis of relatively ambiguous principles of national interests, compliance with the decisions of the national legislator, and development of social legislation. The residual powers were effectively with the central government, not with the several regions,[149] some of which were special in the meaning that their populations contained minority groups.[150]

---

[145]See Bartole (1998), p. 176. According to Bartole, "the separation of the competences between regional and central authorities does not allow the use of the concept of the hierarchy of the sources of law with regard to the relations between national and regional statutes".

[146]Bartole (1998), p. 173.

[147]Bartole (1998), p. 174. See also Bartole (1998), p. 182 f.

[148]Bartole (1998), p. 174.

[149]Bartole (1998), p. 185 f.

[150]Bartole (1998), pp. 187–193. There is a German-speaking group in the province of Bolzano/Bozen, which is a part of the region of Trentino-Alto Adige, a French-speaking group in Valle

Because the substantive dimension of the distribution of powers presented difficulties for a distinction between a federal state and a regional state, Bartole moves on to consider the institutional dimensions and finds that elements underpinning their possible distinction could be found in the organization of the central bodies of the state. According to Bartole, in federal states, the representatives of the constituent states are present, while in the "regional states the bodies of the central state are usually formed without the presence of the regions".[151] He therefore proposes that against the background of the then Italian constitutional setting, a possible distinction between the notions of federal state and regional state could be based, not on differences in the distribution of powers between the centre and the periphery, but on the idea that "the constitutional subjectivity and the political identity of the member states of a federation are guaranteed in a better way than those of the regions in a regional state. For instance, the representatives of the member state are present in the central bodies of the federal states and take part in the national decision-making process. Not even their borders can be modified without their consent and any revision of the federal constitution very often requires their participation in the necessary process".[152] Evidently, more or less the opposite would be true about a regional state: the representatives of the regions are not present in the central bodies of the state and the regions do not take part in the national decision-making process.

It seems that the regional structure of the Italian state is moving towards a more federal structure. Since 1997, on the basis of ordinary legislation enacted by the Parliament of Italy,[153] the division of competences has been reformed so that national powers are based on enumeration, while regional powers are based on the principle of residual powers, at the same time as the principle of subsidiarity was established in the legislation.[154] These features were confirmed in a particular constitutional law in 2001,[155] which contained some additional features, but which did not transform the Senate into a forum for participation drawn from the regions.

d'Aosta, a Slovenian-speaking group in Friuli-Venezia Giulia and a small Ladinian group in the provinces of Bolzano and Trento in the region of Trentino-Alto Adige. The regional form of organization (and the partition of the region of Trentino-Alto Adige in two autonomous provinces with law-making powers, Trento and Bolzano/Bozen) makes it possible to cater for the needs of the minority groups in the smaller communities, although the regional organization of the Italian state is not primarily motivated by minority concerns.

[151] Bartole (1998), p. 183. However, Bartole returns to the substantive distribution of powers when indicating that in such an institutional setting, the "legal doctrine speaks no more about the sovereignty of the member states and prefers to bestow on them the nature of autonomous constitutional entities, that is, constitutional entities which do not have original powers but are the holders of powers transferred to them by the central state". Hence there seems to exist a connection between the substantive and the institutional dimensions.

[152] Bartole (1998), p. 183.

[153] Palermo (2004), p. 110.

[154] Palermo (2004), p. 110.

[155] See Constitutional law no. 3 of 18 October 2001. Under section 117 of the Constitution of Italy, the state holds enumerated powers, while the regions are vested with residual powers.

Instead, as to its composition, the Senate remained a duplicate of the Chamber of Deputies in the Italian variant of bicameralism. "The new system limits the legislative and administrative powers of the national level, abolishes State control over regional legislation, and establishes a presumption of general regional legislative competence in the constitution. It also establishes a more cooperative regionalism, by creating new bodies for cooperation between Regions and States, although it does not transform the Senate into a Chamber of Regions, as advocated by most scholars. Regions are now also enabled to conclude international agreements (although with the consent of the State) and can freely determine their own form of government. In particular, they can decide how to appoint the President of the Region (in almost all Regions the President is now directly elected by the people and no longer nominated by the assembly) and can approve their own electoral law. As to competencies, the Regions not only received the general legislative competence in all the matters that are not explicitly reserved to the State, but they can also get some additional powers in the fields of culture and security by means of a new negotiation procedure with the State. Last but not least, ordinary Regions are now entitled to approve their own constitutions (while respecting the limits imposed by the national constitution and by EU law), which represents a decisive step, at least from the formal point of view, towards federalism. The new constitutional framework thus makes the Italian regional system so close to a federal system that it is almost impossible to draw a line between the two concepts."[156] However, the institutional dimension still remains incomplete and connects Italy and its regional state at least in part in the category of autonomy arrangements.

Spain is the only country where the constitution identifies a right to autonomy by a recognition and guarantee in Art. 2 of the Constitution of the right to autonomy of the nationalities and regions of which it comprises at the same time as the same provision makes reference to the indissoluble unity of the Spanish nation. Hence there is an ethnic component behind the Spanish model of sub-state governance.[157] However, the framers of the Constitution avoided the difficult task of baptizing the territorial form of the state that was in the process of creation,[158] or at least they did not use the notion of federalism when authoring this supreme norm. Therefore, the indication of the existence of a unitary state in Art. 2 of the Constitution might be the starting point (albeit in a very attenuated form) of a more exact characterization of Spain in relation to the terms 'autonomy' and 'federation'. The doctrinary descriptions of the Spanish state contain notions such as a 'state of autonomies', a 'politically decentralized unitarian state', a 'multi-regional state', a 'decentralized state not far in its structure from federal states', a 'unitarian-federal state' and a

[156]Palermo (2004), p. 110.

[157]As a consequence, the Spanish Constitutional Court held on 28 June 2010 that the interpretative references "Catalonia as a nation" and "Catalonia's national reality" in the Preamble to Organic Law 6/2006 of 19 July 2006 to reform the Statute of Autonomy of Catalonia have no legal effect.

[158]Flores Juberías (1998), p. 196.

'federal-regional state'.[159] The terminological confusion has prompted the conclusion that the structure of the Spanish state "escapes any definition and any precise location in the classification of the forms of the State".[160] However, it is possible to agree with Ruiz Vieyez that the model of sub-state governance opted for in Spain is a widely acknowledged "solution to the territorial diversity of the State"[161] in spite of the fact that the Spanish senate is not a representation of the autonomous communities, but is drawn by means of elections from provinces, which constitute a further territorial sub-division, below the level of the autonomous communities (one autonomous community normally consists of several provinces).

In Spain, "the autonomous parliaments can pass laws, with the same degree of force as State (national) laws, with which they are related by virtue of the principle of competence. Thus, there are areas in which the Autonomous Communities have full executive and legislative powers; areas in which legislative powers are shared between the State and the Communities, which hold executive powers; and finally, areas in which legislation is in the hands of the State and only execution powers are the responsibility of the Autonomous Community."[162] The particularity of the Spanish example is that the state structure is still in the process of change, because the autonomy arrangement is asymmetrical and can – at least in principle – be somewhat different in respect of each of the autonomous communities on the basis of their respective autonomy statutes. However, a division into three main categories of autonomies may still be discerned, namely the historical autonomous communities and the other autonomous communities, which all have law-making powers proper, and the autonomous cities (Ceuta and Melilla on the Northern coast of Africa), which do not have law-making powers proper, but administrative autonomy only.[163] Following Flores Juberías, it can be said that autonomy in Spain is limited in scope, because in addition to the enumeration of competences (that is, functions) which the "autonomous communities may assume, the Constitution also provides a list of those competences reserved for the state".[164] It would therefore seem that the competences of both the state and the autonomous communities are enumerated and that there is actually no area of residual competences. However, Flores Juberías points to the fact that the Spanish system is not one in which "neatly defined matters or areas under state jurisdiction are put under the full control of autonomous communities, while others remain entirely subject to the actions of the central institutions of the state. It is a system in which functions, not matters, are distributed".[165] There exist matters exclusively

[159]See Flores Juberías (1998), p. 196 f., for the sources in the Spanish literature.

[160]See Flores Juberías (1998), p. 197, for the Spanish source.

[161]Ruiz Vieytez (2004), p. 147 f.

[162]Ruiz Vieytez (2004), p. 144.

[163]See Ruiz Vieytez (2004), pp. 139–144 for an overview of the different options of autonomous organization.

[164]Flores Juberías (1998), p. 199.

[165]Flores Juberías (1998), p. 209.

attributed either to the state (such as nationality, defense, justice, etc.) or to the autonomous communities (such as institutions of self-government, forestry, autochthonous language, etc.) over which the relevant authority is entitled to adopt any imaginable kind of measure, but the main bulk of the competences (such as social security, television, environmental protection, etc.) remain in an area where both are competent in one way or another.[166] This, in turn, means that the production of effective governance requires a number of co-ordination measures between the state and the autonomous communities.

Because exclusive state competences are enumerated in Art. 149 of the Spanish Constitution and because the exclusive autonomous competences which the autonomous communities can assume *in toto* outside of the area of exclusive state competences are enumerated in each autonomy statute of every autonomous entity, the scope of which may vary, it would seem that the residual powers reside with the autonomous communities. However, although a particular autonomous community "may enjoy all competences not expressly attributed to the state by the Constitution", "it will only enjoy those expressly contained in its particular Statute". Therefore, the autonomy statute of an autonomous territory, enacted by the Parliament of Spain in the form of an organic law,[167] is "the norm of reference in order to know how far the scope of competence of a community goes",[168] because under Art. 149.3 of the Spanish Constitution, authority over matters not assumed by the autonomy statutes shall belong to the state.[169] Therefore, the residual powers in the Spanish autonomy scheme seem to be vested with the state, although the issue of where the residual powers are ultimately located may lack practical relevance.

Against this background, it seems that in Italy and Spain, the regions and autonomous communities are not institutionally represented at the central level in a bi-cameral legislature through a senate or a corresponding body. As concerns Italy, the reforms during the first decade of the new millennium have not succeeded in developing the Senate into such a Chamber of Regions that would fulfill the criterion of institutional representation of constituent states in a bi-cameral setting, and as concerns Spain, it seems that the senate "does not adequately fulfill its role as a chamber for territorial representation as it does not provide the Autonomous Communities with sufficient channels of participation".[170] In fact, it has been stated

---

[166] Flores Juberías (1998), p. 209. See also Flores Juberías (1998), p. 212, where he outlines the complex distribution of competences in five different categories: integral competences, exclusive but limited competences, shared competences, concurring competences and indistinct competences. See also Ruiz Vieytez (2004), pp. 144–145, for a description of the distribution of powers.

[167] Ruiz Vieytez (2004), p. 138. This is the procedure for the regular autonomous communities, while the historical and more advanced communities participate in the amendment of their respective statutes, *inter alia*, by way of referendum.

[168] Flores Juberías (1998), p. 210.

[169] Flores Juberías (1998), p. 210.

[170] Ruiz Vieytez (2004), p. 149.

that proposals to develop the Spanish system of autonomous communities toward a federal model are met with considerable resistance.[171] The academic and the political discussion in both countries testifies to the fact that the terminological distinction between autonomy arrangements or the regional state, on the one hand, and federalism, on the other, is relevant and that neither of the two countries has yet crossed the line in a definitive manner from the former to the latter, although certain developments in such a direction can be discerned.

3.4.2 *Devolution of Powers*

When speaking about autonomy, references are frequently made to devolution, a notion often used in Britain with respect to creating autonomy arrangements in different parts of the United Kingdom. Devolution can, however, be a problematic term in the context, because it may also be used to describe processes that do not necessarily conform to such federal or autonomy arrangements denoted as sub-state entities in this inquiry. In considering the notion of devolution, Lapidoth, in fact, emerges as somewhat critical of the notion, making the point that it denotes the mere act of transferring powers and does not indicate the content or nature of those powers.[172] As pointed out by Wilson and Stapleton, "[d]evolution is not a cessation of all power from the centre with the establishment of new states; rather it is the redistribution of selected responsibilities, with core state power residing in the national, that is, the British, parliament".[173] With this definition, the residual powers are, in the UK context, left with the national parliament so as to indicate that enumerated powers are granted to regional entities (although this distribution is unclear and will be examined below). They are not specific about the nature of the transferred powers, which means that the powers could be of both legislative and administrative nature. They also conclude that "Bogdanor (1999) sees devolution as comprising three main aspects: 1. The transfer of power to a subordinate elected body; 2. The transfer of power on a geographical basis; 3. The transfer of functions at present exercised by Parliament".[174]

However, this definition is not quite the one used by Bodganor in 1999, at the point when Scotland and Wales were granted their respective sets of powers or, rather, institutions to take care of powers devolved to the two regions. According to Bogdanor, devolution involves at a general level "the transfer of powers from a

[171] Ruiz Vieytez (2004), p. 148. See also Anderson (2008), pp. 4, 10, who claims that Spain is effectively federal and that most experts would classify Spain as federal (such as Máiz and Losada 2011) but that many resist the term because they associate it with undermining national unity. It seems, however, as if most legal commentators would not place Spain amongst the federations.

[172] Lapidoth (1997), p. 49.

[173] Wilson and Stapleton (2006a, b), p. 2.

[174] Wilson and Stapleton (2006a, b), p. 3.

superior to an inferior political authority",[175] and he sustains this by stating that constitutionally, "devolution is a mere delegation of power from a superior political body to an inferior",[176] although "devolution seems to create new independent layers of government", which in reality are not independent but interdependent.[177] This general definition is not limited enough to pinpoint the creation of territorial autonomy, but is instead overbroad for that purpose, also encompassing the regular administrative decentralization of power and functions to administrative entities of regional self-government. The more specific definition of devolution offered by Bogdanor consists of three elements: "the transfer to a subordinate elected body, on a geographical basis, of functions at present exercised by ministers and Parliament",[178] which is slightly different than the one referred to by Wilson and Stapleton, above. The first element of the definition requires that there be a subordinate elected body, which means the creation of an institutional forum based on representation of the inhabitants at the same time as it is implied that such a body is vested with decision-making powers. The reference to subordination is in itself problematic, because it implies a limitation of the decision-making authority of the subordinate body against the background of influence that the superior body wields and because it, as a consequence, does not create real decision-making independence in the subordinate decision-making body. Bogdanor explains that such subordination seeks to preserve intact the central feature of the British Constitution, that is, the supremacy of Parliament.[179] The second element is certainly also one which is present in a definition of territorial autonomy, namely the creation of a jurisdiction which is territorially based. Here, the geographical basis is connected to the functions of an elected body. Therefore as a minimum, the second element requires the definition of an electorate, distinct from the national electorate, from which the members of the elected body are drawn. The third element concerns the material dimensions of devolution and goes on to hold that the functions transferred are those that before devolution takes place are exercised by ministers and Parliament. According to Bogdanor, these functions "may be either legislative, the power to make laws, or executive, the power to make secondary laws – statutory instruments, orders, and the like – within a primary legal framework still determined at Westminster".[180] It therefore seems as if it were possible to devolve only executive functions, thereby creating administrative autonomy of some sort, while

---

175 Bogdanor (1999), pp. 2, 283.

176 Bogdanor (1999), p. 287. He also thinks that constitutionally, the Scottish Parliament will clearly be subordinate, but politically it will be anything but subordinate. See Bogdanor (1999), p. 288.

177 Bogdanor (1999), p. 283.

178 Bogdanor (1999), p. 2.

179 Bogdanor (1999), p. 3.

180 Bogdanor (1999), p. 2 f.

the devolution of law-making powers implies that parallel executive functions are devolved, too.[181]

This definition seems to be a description of a self-governing territorial autonomy with at least some law-making functions placed at the sub-state level, but the reference to a relationship of subordination between the decision-making body of the sub-state entity, on the one hand, and the national decision-making body, on the other, would leave the former in a dependency which does not fit our definition of exclusive law-making powers as a qualification for autonomy proper or the core examples of autonomy arrangements. Instead, such sub-ordination and dependency vests the sub-state entity with powers that perhaps ultimately are of an administrative nature only and that can be revoked by the national decision-making body in the same order that was first used to grant the powers to the sub-state level. At least in respect of Northern Ireland, there actually exist examples of such revocations in situations where the internal political situation in that area has forced the central government of the United Kingdom to suspend the operation of self-government at the regional level,[182] although, by contrast, such revocations would seem to be highly unlikely in the case of Scotland or Wales.[183] Also, according to Bogdanor, the Parliament of England would have only a "more or less theoretical right to legislate on Scotland's domestic affairs against the wishes of the Scottish Parliament, something never done in Northern Ireland".[184] However, if the supremacy of the Parliament of England has turned into a power to "supervise another legislative body which will make laws over a wide area of public policy",[185] the autonomy of the devolved entity is nonetheless relatively attenuated.

Bogdanor expressed his ideas about devolution during a period of time when the devolved institutions had just been instituted, without knowing in which direction such development would lead. Authors who published views on devolution some years later were not quite as sure about the demise of parliamentary supremacy in the UK. Henig, for instance, maintains that the devolved authorities of Scotland, Wales and Northern Ireland do not "own" their powers in the same way as central government: "Competences may be devolved to other tiers of governance, but in all

[181] See also Pilkington (2002), p. 9 f., who distinguishes between executive devolution (power to make decisions; typified by the Welsh Assembly), legislative devolution (power to make laws; typified by the Scottish Parliament) and administrative devolution (power to carry out specific functions; typified by the pre-devolution Scottish, Welsh and Northern Ireland Offices that had a functional autonomy of some kind). Concerning functional autonomy, see Suksi (2008b).

[182] See, e.g., Bogdanor (1999), pp. 97–109, Pilkington (2002), p. 8, and Trench (2007a), p. 58. See also Henig (2006), p. 45, who presents the abolition of the Greater London Council as an example, albeit not as a parallel example directly relevant for the devolved entities.

[183] Bogdanor (1999), p. 292. According to Bogdanor, it would be difficult to abolish the Scottish devolution without organizing a referendum on the matter in Scotland.

[184] Bogdanor (1999), p. 292. It is easy to agree with Bogdanor (1999), p. 294, that a profound constitutional change has taken place in the UK through the enactment of legislation that devolves power to the regions.

[185] Bogdanor (1999), p. 292.

cases the powers and the authorities themselves can be legally removed or altered by decision of the centre. Devolution UK style does not carry with it any constitutional entrenchment."[186] However, the historical roots of devolution in Britain are very interesting, including, *inter alia*, Ireland and Canada as well as a number of former colonies where the de-colonization process was in a number of instances cast in federal terms.[187] It would hence seem to be ignorant to think that the current forms of devolution have sprung from unrelated *ad hoc* responses to different situations in recent times. Instead, there have been relatively many conceptual developments and practical experiences from both federal and autonomy solutions in Britain, including judicial resolution of competence matters, on the basis of which it has been possible to modify current forms of devolution in a manner which conforms with the general features of the UK constitution. Given the fact that the UK constitution is unwritten, the devolution arrangements are not necessarily easy to compare with other forms of sub-state governance, be it in the form of federal solutions or in the form of territorial autonomy.

Bogdanor distinguishes devolution from federalism on the basis of the fact that federalism would "divide, not devolve, supreme power between Westminster and various regional or provincial parliaments. In a federal state, the authority of the central or federal government and the provincial governments is co-ordinate and shared, the respective scope of the federal and provincial governments being defined by an enacted constitution", while by contrast, devolution "does not require the introduction of an enacted constitution".[188] Therefore, he seems to think that federalism is the same as exclusive law-making powers being vested with a sub-state entity, where the "Parliament of the United Kingdom would have power to legislate for Scotland only in certain defined areas, other areas becoming the entire responsibility of the Scottish Parliament".[189] In spite of the distinction, Bogdanor, writing more or less at the time when devolution to Scotland and Wales was being instituted and not knowing of the practical operation of the devolved entities, employs the notion of a quasi-federal relationship to describe the relationship, for instance, between the Scottish Parliament and the Parliament of the United Kingdom.[190] Watts, again, compares the devolved British jurisdictions with other sub-state arrangements, such as federations, regionalized unions and unitary systems. He operates with a graded scale and holds that a "decentralised unitary system may shade into a devolved union, a devolved union into a quasi federation, or a quasi-federation into a federation".[191] Watts feels that in some respects, "the

[186]Henig (2006), p. 23. However, Henig (2006), p. 44, also thinks that a revocation of devolution is more a theoretical alternative than a real one.

[187]For the historical roots of devolution, see, e.g., Mitchell (2007), pp. 24–47, Pilkington (2002), pp. 19–50, Bogdanor (1999), pp. 13–109.

[188]Bogdanor (1999), p. 3.

[189]Bogdanor (1999), p. 202.

[190]Bogdanor (1999), p. 293 f.

[191]Watts (2007).

devolved United Kingdom shares most of the basic institutional features that mark federations",[192] but differs from federations in the lack of a written constitution and a second chamber, that is, in its institutional representation, although he thinks that the position of the Secretaries of State for each of the three devolved entities inside the executive branch of the national government to a certain extent compensates for this. Also, in comparison with federations and devolved unions such as Spain and Italy, the "devolved entities in the UK have a constitutionally subordinate rather than coordinate status".[193]

Following Trench, Watts concludes that the "ultimate maximisation of the UK Parliament's legal authority and the UK Government's dominance of intergovernmental processes mean that the formal authority of the devolved administrations is limited, with legal power remaining firmly in the hands of the UK Government to shape, legislate and implement policy", and because devolution applies only peripherally, to three regions encompassing only around 15% of the UK population, leaving the remainder of the country in a fundamentally unitary system", federalism and even quasi-federalism is out of the question. Watts then proceeds to look for corresponding arrangements in, *inter alia*, so-called federacies and associated states, and makes the observation that in such relationships, there is only a minimal role for the peripheral territories in the government of the larger state, "whereas the devolved territories in the UK have full representation within the House of Commons".[194] In this comparison, Watts is probably wrong, because such peripheral entities as he is referring to normally enjoy ordinary representation or perhaps even over-representation in the national parliament. He is, however, correct in pointing out the remarkable vertical inter-relationships between the national executive, on the one hand, and the executives of the devolved entities in the UK, on the other, including in relation to the funding of the devolved jurisdictions, which generally speaking do not exist to the same extent in federations or territorial autonomies.[195]

His comprehension of the distinct dimensions of the UK devolution does not prevent him from placing the devolved UK within the broad genus of federal political systems which encompasses regionally devolved unions, federations, quasi-federations, confederations, federacies, and some other organizational alternatives. Following Wheare's definition of quasi-federations, Watts thinks that the devolved entities in the UK can not be placed in that category, but after identifying a more limited notion of 'quasi-federation', involving a potential for evolution towards federal forms of organization, he thinks the UK might be placed in that limited category, nonetheless.[196] The best categorization of the UK system

[192]Watts (2007), p. 250.

[193]Watts (2007), p. 250.

[194]Watts (2007), p. 252.

[195]Watts (2007), pp. 252, 257, 260. Horizontal relations between the three devolved entities in the UK are not significant.

[196]Watts (2007), p. 266 f.

Watts finds is among regionalized unions or decentralized unitary systems. He tends to think that Japan, with its symmetrical division of the country into 47 prefectures could come close, at least in terms of powers, while the devolved entities of the UK would seem to have more powers than regional units in decentralized unitary systems like Sweden and certainly France.[197] This means that Watts is actually moving towards considering even clearly administrative forms of regional self-government of a decentralized nature (e.g., Sweden) as a possible categorization for the devolved entities in the UK. This is clearly not satisfactory for him, because he retreats from that position and compares the UK entities with federacies and associated states in unitary systems such as Denmark, Finland, France, New Zealand and Portugal, that is, essentially territorial autonomies (see above), but concludes that the UK entities are "more integrated with the union than those other examples".[198] He therefore arrives at the conclusion that although the United Kingdom has some features resembling those of federations and quasi-federations, it remains predominantly a devolved union. The United Kingdom Government clearly remains dominant in its relations with the devolved territories, while creating in a partial portion of its territory autonomous spheres for devolved institutions within which it has been possible for them to pursue differentiated policies and some territorial diversity.[199] It seems against the background of our study that Watts needs to include yet another category in his graded scale, that of territorial autonomy, in order to better illustrate the position of such singular entities as Scotland, Wales and Northern Ireland in what basically is a unitary state. The language of federalism is clearly not sufficient, but may instead create confusion.[200]

---

197 Watts (2007), p. 267.

198 Watts (2007), p. 267.

199 Watts (2007), p. 268.

200 For the British, it seems clearer that, for instance, Scotland is not a part of a federal structure. While distinguishing the devolved UK entities from federal arrangements, a report in 2009 concerning Scottish devolution points out that "the most obvious similarity is that Scotland enjoys a very substantial degree of autonomy under devolution, and relates to the UK Government in many of the same ways as a state government would to a federal one. In a federal system there are (at least) two constitutionally established levels of government. There is at least one function where each level has exclusive competence, and each level is constitutionally free to exercise its competence without the consent of the other level (and, at the lower level, independently of the other states, regions or provinces). In most federations the same structure applies across the territory of the federation, and the governments at each level are accountable to the relevant electorates (i.e. regional or federal). The constitutional system of the United Kingdom is not federal. Most obviously there is no second level government for its largest sub-national region (England). But also as a matter of constitutional law there are no functions for which the devolved Parliaments or Assemblies have exclusive competence. In most federal systems, not only is state- or provincial-level government operational in all parts of the country, but their powers tend to be broadly uniform, and so the powers of the federal government are uniform throughout its jurisdiction. The UK differs in this respect in that the powers of the Scottish Parliament, Welsh Assembly and Northern Ireland Assembly differ, in some respects substantially, one from another.

In an attempt to distinguish between different models of devolution in the Scottish context, McFadden and Lazarowicz make the point that when sub-state entities are organized, two basic models are available in respect of the powers that are vested in the sub-state entity through a constitution or an act of parliament. The first model is one where the central authority "devolves all of its powers to the local or subordinate body except for certain powers which it specifically reserves to itself".[201] The other one is a model where the "central authority devolves to the local or subordinate body certain specified powers while everything not so specified is, by implication, reserved to the centre". They label the former the retaining model and the latter the transferring model and conclude that "the retaining model spells out what the subordinate or local body *cannot* do and it is implied that it *can* do everything that is not spelled out", while the transferring model "spells out what the local or subordinate body *can* do and it is implied that it *cannot* do anything which is not mentioned".[202] In principle, this characterization corresponds to our distinction between enumerated and residual powers and how they are placed at the national and sub-state levels of governance. According to McFadden and Lazarowicz, the American Constitution is an example of the retaining model, which at least in theory tilts the balance of powers against the centre, as "everything not specified in the Constitution lies within the powers of the individual states".[203] They present the Canadian Constitution as an example of the transferring model, originally designed to produce a strong central government. The first attempt of devolution in relation to Scotland was undertaken in 1978 (see below), at which point the legislation that was adopted could be characterized as an "example of the transferring model, specifying in great detail the legislative and executive powers which were to be devolved from Westminster".[204] However, they maintain that the British Government opted for the retaining model when the Scotland Act 1998 was enacted: "All matters which are not specifically reserved to the UK Parliament are devolved to the Scottish Parliament".[205] For sure, this is the basic structure of the

Most federal systems will have some special arrangement for particular territories with special circumstances, but Spain is an interesting example of more asymmetrical federalism. The system of autonomous communities allows for considerable differences between the powers they all exercise. The autonomous communities do, however, enjoy some exclusive competences and there is now no part of Spain which does not enjoy some decentralised powers. Devolution (in the sense in which we use the term) differs from these sorts of federalism since the devolving authority retains, at least as a matter of law, the power to alter the devolution settlement to impose new or different obligations or constraints on the devolved authorities, even within the scope of their competences." See Serving Scotland Better (2009), p. 60. As pointed out by the report, p. 61, only 15 percent of the population of the United Kingdom live under the devolved governments.

[201]McFadden and Lazarowicz (2002), p. 5.

[202]McFadden and Lazarowicz (2002), p. 5.

[203]McFadden and Lazarowicz (2002), p. 6. Of course, as pointed out above, the different constitutional doctrines in the US and the supremacy clause in particular have resulted in a situation where the sphere of action of the constituent states is, in practice, very limited.

[204]McFadden and Lazarowicz (2002), p. 6.

[205]McFadden and Lazarowicz (2002), p. 7.

arrangement, but as such, it is heavily conditioned by the doctrine of the sovereignty of the UK Parliament, making the Scottish Parliament a sub-ordinate body which is not independent and not co-ordinate with central government as in a federal system. "It may not only be overruled by the UK Parliament, it may even be abolished by it."[206] They issue, of course, the caveat that this is mainly a theoretical possibility and not really a political option, but the outcome of the doctrine of parliamentary sovereignty might nonetheless be that the basic structure of the retention model in the case of Scotland is overshadowed by the ultimate residual power of the UK Parliament to adopt any law it wishes.

Without excluding the possibility that the constitutional structure of the UK could develop into a federal system,[207] Trench says that it is, for the time being, wrong to approach devolution as having established a set of quasi-federal relations in the United Kingdom, because the UK is simply, but in many important respects, fundamentally different from those systems. He also makes the point that politicians and officials involved in territorial matters in the UK are often keen to emphasize that what the UK has is devolution, not federalism: "the UK has established something that is quite different from the sorts of relations that exist between federal governments and constituent units in federal systems".[208] The distinction from federalism can be stated unambiguously by saying that it is "plain in point of form that the scheme of Scotland Act 1998 is devolutionary, not federal. The Scottish Parliament is not a co-ordinate institution, but a subordinate one, restricted to legislating within its conferred powers, and it has no exclusive sphere of competence", at the same time as the concept of parliamentary supremacy, established in a provision of the Scotland Act, should serve "as a symbolic reminder that devolution should not be mistaken for federalism, let alone independence".[209] What the devolved entities of the UK, Scotland, Wales and Northern Ireland, constitute is actually three different territorial

[206]McFadden and Lazarowicz (2002), p. 8.

[207]Such proposals are included, inter alia, in Henig (2006), *passim*, who on p. 15 expresses dissatisfaction with devolution because it does not seem to be derived from belief in any overarching institutional theories or even from a coherent set of ideas. According to Henig, a federalization of the UK would require that England be divided in regions and that they would be given law-making powers and that a regional chamber would replace the House of Lords.

[208]Trench (2007e), p. 284. According to Trench (2007a), p. 70, the clear view among those who designed the institutional framework of devolution is that "what they were devising was not a federal system, by which they understand a clear distinction of functions and governments". Against such a qualification, the distinction between federal and devolved systems would be based on the clarity vs. unclarity of functions and governments, which is probably not a very solid distinction. See also Hazell (2005a), p. 250, who concludes that "Westminster is not the equivalent of a federal legislature".

[209]Himsworth and Munro (2000), p. xviii. However, they move cautiously in the direction of federalism by saying that "[i]n the result, it may not go too far to suggest that the relation between Scotland and the United Kingdom becomes semi-federal. Westminster and Whitehall have legal powers to intervene, but will be loath to impose them on unbiddable Scottish institutions, which may appear (and may claim) to be more representative of the popular will in Scotland". However,

autonomies, to a greater or a lesser extent,[210] although Trench considers the concept of autonomy a related but secondary concept in the UK context.[211] Each of the three devolved entities has its respective relationship of a vertical nature to the central government of the United Kingdom. These vertical relationships are all different as to their content, creating a fundamental asymmetry in the constitutional fabric of the UK as a result of the differences in the nature of the competences devolved to the sub-state entities.[212] This has been described as a "means for the UK to provide varying degrees of regional autonomy to match the differing needs and circumstances of its component parts, without the more fundamental restructuring of the constitution that a move to a fully federal structure would entail".[213] Another way of expressing this is by saying that the "combination of this asymmetry and the particular place of the UK Parliament, in the absence of a written constitutional document allocating some responsibilities exclusively to one level of government or another, is what differentiates the UK from federal countries".[214] At the same time, the horizontal relationships between the three entities seem to be weak.[215]

As pointed out by Trench, autonomy can be formulated in a number of ways, *inter alia*, as something closely related to the concept of power and dependent on that. In such a perspective, "[a] party possesses autonomy if it is able to exercise power in relation to its functions and its own existence without requiring the assent or assistance of the other party in doing so. Thus if a devolved administration can

---

there are few signs of federalism in the arrangement, while the terminology of territorial autonomy seems to illustrate the relationship better.

[210]See Trench (2007a), p. 55, who points out that it is very difficult to generalize about what devolution means because it is different for each of the entities (Scotland, Wales and Northern Ireland): "The devolution arrangements as a whole are profoundly asymmetric."

[211]See Trench (2007c), p. 17.

[212]See Trench (2007a), p. 61, Himsworth and Munro (2000), p. xix f. Trench (2007a), p. 63: "While devolution may have created different governments accountable to different elected bodies, the relations between them would still work much the same way as they had when all were part of a single government accountable to Westminster." See also Hazell (2005a), p. 230, who concludes that "Westminster has one relationship with the Scottish Parliament, and a completely different relationship with the National Assembly for Wales. Westminster continues to a surprising extent to be a three-in-one Parliament; but when legislating for the devolved territories it faces in three very different directions". Of course, the position of Wales has changed with the strengthening the powers of the Welsh Assembly in 2006.

[213]Serving Scotland Better (2009), p. 41.

[214]Serving Scotland Better (2009), p. 51. This report of the so-called Calman Commission makes a comparative point that underlines our difficulty of at all including Scotland in a comparison of constitutional law, e.g., along the dimensions of the chart on different autonomy positions: Internationally the UK's territorial constitution cannot be placed into a pigeon-hole alongside similar arrangements elsewhere. The UK is not a federal state like the US, Canada or Australia. Nor is it particularly like Spain, made up of different autonomous communities with differing levels of responsibility. (...) The UK is, as has been said, not just a Union State, but a State of different unions: different unions which have formed between England and each of its three neighbours". Serving Scotland Better (2009), p. 60.

[215]See also Trench (2007a), p. 61.

introduce and implement its own policies without needing any consent from the UK Government, and without the UK Government being able to hinder it from doing so, it can be said to be autonomous."[216] In this perspective, the autonomy of, for instance, Scotland is complicated at least in part by "the extent to which the structure of the devolution settlements compels the two levels of government to take each other's views into account in a wide range of situations (...)".[217] Therefore, the autonomy of Scotland might not be quite as broad as the autonomy of a number of other sub-state entities in other countries, although it is at the same time evident that the qualification of "absence of the need of assent or assistance of the other party" sets a very high threshold for what is and what is not autonomy. Against the background of that requirement, essentially describing the hallmarks of self-determination, even independent states might fail the test of autonomy, let alone sub-state entities.

3.4.3 *Regional Self-Government in Europe*

The concept of regional self-government, referred to by Watts in his analysis of the UK devolution process, is a very broad term and seems to be in the process of slowly evolving into a legal concept at the European level, provided that the Council of Europe adopts it as a part of a convention. Regional self-government may encompass forms of sub-state governance ranging from constituent entities in federations to administrative decentralization at the regional level. A general point of departure could, in respect of regional self-government, be constituted by the Council of Europe Draft Charter of Regional Government, proposed in 1997 by the Congress of Local and Regional Authorities of the Council of Europe. A 2002 report to the Congress also lists in charts attached to it (Appendices IV and V) constituent units of federations in a manner which would seem to establish 'regional self-government' as the widest and most general normative term concerning governance at the sub-state level.[218] The models that the document uses are as

[216] Trench (2007c), p. 17. Trench (2007c), p. 18 f., identifies the following resources as resources that constitute power: (1) constitutional resources, (2) legal and hierarchical resources, (3) financial resources, (4) organizational resources, (5) lobbying resources, and (6) informational resources.

[217] Trench (2007c), p. 17.

[218] The European Charter of Regional Self-Government - Follow-up given by the Committee of Ministers to Recommendation 34 (1997) on the draft European Charter of Regional Self-Government - CPR (9) 6 Part II, of the report/explanatory memorandum of 3 April 2002 by Peter Rabe, Appendix IV and V. See also Resolution 146 (2002)1 of 6 June 2002 by the Congress of Local and Regional Authorities of the Council of Europe on the draft European charter of regional self-government.

follows[219]: Model 1 (Belgium, Germany, Italy,[220] the Russian Federation and Switzerland) encompasses regions with the power to enact primary legislation, the existence of which is guaranteed by the constitution or by a federal agreement and cannot be questioned against their will, while model 2 (Spain and the United Kingdom[221]) covers regions with the power to enact primary legislation, the existence of which is not guaranteed by the Constitution or by a federal Agreement. Model 3 (the Czech Republic, Hungary and Italy[222])[223] contains regions with the power to enact legislation, according to the framework (principles, general provisions) established by national legislation, the existence of which is guaranteed by the Constitution, whereas model 4 (Poland and the United Kingdom[224]) includes regions with the power to adopt laws or other regional legislative acts, according to the framework (principles, general provisions) established by national legislation, the existence of which is not guaranteed by the Constitution. These four models are clearly ones that could include territorial autonomies. In addition, model 5 (Denmark,[225] France, Sweden, Turkey and the United Kingdom) denotes regions with decision-making power (without legislative power) and councils directly elected by the population, while model 6 (Finland and Latvia) illustrates regions with decision-making power (without legislative power) and councils elected by the component local authorities. In addition, concerning three states (Bulgaria, Estonia and Malta) the point is made that the region is a decentralized part of the state structure or has some other form. The power of the region to enact primary legislation is defined in the report as the power to enact legislation in designated areas of competence, which is to apply to a region, and which for those areas of competence is of the same legal status as legislation enacted by the national parliament for such (other) areas of competence as are the responsibility of that parliament. Here, it is evident that the description points at exclusive law-making powers. The scope of such decision-making power that is not legislative in nature may vary, but according to the report, it consists in general of implementing national legislative measures.

---

[219]The models are explained in Appendix IV: *Models of regional self-government to be prepared* of the above document of the Council of Europe. A good number of European states are missing from the account, such as Greece, the Netherlands, Norway, Portugal, Romania, Slovenia and Slovakia.

[220]Evidently, Italy appears in this context with reference to the special regions.

[221]The United Kingdom appears in this context with reference to Scotland and Northern Ireland.

[222]Evidently, Italy appears in this context with respect to the "ordinary" regions.

[223]It is possible to dispute the conclusion indicated by model 3 that the Czech Republic and Hungary would have regions vested with legislative powers.

[224]The UK appears in this context with respect to Wales.

[225]Interestingly, the autonomous territories of the Faroe Islands and Greenland are not reported at all in relation to Denmark. If they were reported, they would be placed either in model 1 or, more likely, model 2.

Apparently, the Council of Europe may be moving towards adopting a definition of regional self-government which is very broad and can contain very different constitutional arrangements. The creation of such models and perhaps the eventual adoption of a charter of regional self-government spell out what self-government is in both form and substance. This is intrinsically useful for example in different situations of conflict resolution, when examples are sought for possible future arrangements: self-government may thus denote a wide range of organizational options at the sub-state level. At the same time as 'regional self-government' is a very broad term, it seems that each instance of territorial autonomy – and of federation, for that matter – is, at the same time, an instance of self-government. However, the reverse is not true: each instance of self-government can not be labeled as territorial autonomy (or a federation). In fact, only a few of the examples of regional self-government would seem to qualify as constituting territorial autonomy.

3.5 Conclusions

3.5.1 Compiling the Building-Blocks of Autonomy

Our conceptual distinctions indicate that there is a graded scale between classical federalism, on the one hand, and regional self-government of an administrative nature, on the other. While it is relatively easy to distinguish territorial autonomy with exclusive law-making powers from administrative arrangements of regional self-government, the border line between federations and territorial autonomies is more unclear or fluid. It is, however, possible to use the material and institutional features of federalism and try to draw a boundary of some kind between federal forms of organization and territorial autonomies. In doing so, it is necessary to issue the caveat that such a boundary is likely not to be very firm, but instead flexible and subject to interpretations on a case-by-case basis. It is therefore likely that there will be cases of a hybrid nature, which do not conform to the typical categories of federation and territorial autonomy.

Territorial autonomy is a legal construction that appears in a unitary state in a fashion which often is akin to the position of states in federations. While the pure unitary state may still be the regular text-book example of a state, in reality states that display sub-state forms of organization (federal and autonomy arrangements) nowadays constitute a majority of states at least in Europe. Also, even federations may, in addition to their constituent or component states, contain autonomous territories (as is the case with Nunavut in Canada[226] and parts of India[227]) or

[226]See Légaré (2008).

[227]See Hannum (1996), pp. 151–177.

cultural autonomies (as is the case with cultural autonomy in the Russian Federation[228] and to some extent also in India[229]). Therefore, at this juncture, a few reflections on the distinction between federal and autonomy arrangements may be justified.

As pointed out above, although there is no completely coherent theory of federalism, a core definition of a federation might contain two different elements. Firstly, the federal legislative body is organized so as to provide for equal (or sometimes less than equal) representation for the constituent or component states of the federation in one chamber of the federal legislature, elected or appointed, while the other chamber is normally directly elected by the inhabitants of the constituent or component states in a way which guarantees the proportional representation of the population. It is therefore possible to say that the 'Upper House' generally displays symmetry by granting an equal number of seats to all constituent or component states (although in some federations, such as Germany, the size of the constituent unit is taken into account), while seats in the 'Lower House' are distributed according to the number of inhabitants, citizens or voters across the entire territory of the federation.[230]

Secondly, at least in a federation of the classical model, the federal legislature and the central authorities have enumerated powers, which means that they are in the possession of specific jurisdictional competencies or certain specified functions which, at least in theory, have been granted to the federation by the constituent entities. Constituent states, in turn, remain in possession of residual jurisdictional competencies, which allows the characterization of the basis of their powers as a general competence. Hence, the constituent states are empowered to deal with all matters not explicitly reserved to the federal level.

In the context of the American constitution, Wheare is of the opinion that this test of federalism concentrates on a relatively superficial characteristic of the US Constitution, although he at the same time feels that the question of where the residue of power is to rest is an important question in framing a federal government, because it may affect the whole balance of power in a federation:[231] "The essential point is not that the division of powers is made in such a way that the regional governments are the residuary legatees under the Constitution, but the division made in such a way that, whoever has the residue, neither general nor regional government is subordinate to the other." Wheare continues by denying that these points would be essential to the federal principle:[232] "They may be usual characteristics of governments which are federal, but they themselves do not

[228]See Torode (2008).

[229]See Barbora (2008).

[230]There may be some variation to this principle, as for instance in Switzerland, where some small cantons are so-called half cantons, entitled to only one seat in the federal assembly, while the larger cantons have two.

[231]Wheare (1964), p. 11 f.

[232]Wheare (1964), p. 12.

make a government federal." According to Wheare, "the important point is whether the powers of government are divided between co-ordinate, independent authorities or not". Wheare also thinks that a federation can be organized so that the federal level has enumerated powers while the state level has residual powers, or so that both levels of government have enumerated powers. "Both methods can achieve the kind of division of powers which is characteristic (...) of the federal principle. Circumstances will decide which method is to be adopted." [233] It seems, however, as if Wheare did not really consider a situation where residual powers are vested in the federal level and enumerated powers in the state level as constituting federalism.

The idea underpinning the distribution of powers between federal and state levels in a federation like the United States, for example, is that the constituent states have retained at least some traces of their original sovereignty, albeit in a way profoundly circumscribed by the federation.[234] For instance, the amendment of the federal constitution will generally require the participation and consent of the constituent or component states (in a confederation, the constituent states would retain a much more substantial part of their original sovereignty). A consideration of great relevance in the context of residual powers is, of course, the material scope of residual competences, which may be broad or limited, although the notion of residual competences might be of an expansive nature, capable of becoming broader according to the needs that arise, for instance, in the form of new issues that were not at hand when the powers of the central government and the sub-state entities were defined and established.

In the American context, for instance, constitutional development is in this respect a narrative of the expansion of the power of the federal government, although the Tenth Amendment to the US Constitution provides that the states retain those powers not delegated to the federal government. Assisted by the US Supreme Court, the areas of exclusive state control have progressively narrowed, while the federal level has increasingly regulated areas that have traditionally been state matters. The important doctrine in the context is that of federal preemption, found in the so-called supremacy clause in art. VI, clause 2, of the US Constitution, according to which in situations where federal and state laws are in conflict with one another, the federal enactments will prevail and override the state enactments.[235] In the Federal Republic of Germany, the principle of *Bundesrecht bricht Landesrecht*,

---

[233]See Wheare (1964), p. 12 f.

[234]See also Wheare (1964), p. 48.

[235]"This Constitution, and the Laws of the United States which shall be made in pursuance thereof; and all treaties made, or which shall be made, under the authority of the United States, shall be the supreme law of the land; and the judges in every state shall be bound thereby, anything in the constitution or laws of any state to the contrary notwithstanding." See, e.g., Rossum and Tarr (2007), pp. 418–420, and Rotunda and Nowak (1999), pp. 199–231. See also Anderson (2008), p. 26, who makes the point that courts in federal systems "have tended to give broad interpretation to specified powers, whether federal or constituent unit, so the effect of residual power clauses has been less than envisaged by constitutional drafters".

that is, federal law breaks state law, is established in section 31 of the Basic Law of Germany. It means that if there is a conflict between a norm established in state law and a norm established in federal law, the federal norm takes precedence.

Watts also agrees in principle with this above description of the distribution of powers in "classical" federations. "Where the process of establishment has involved the aggregation of previously distinct units giving up some of their sovereignty to establish a new federal government, the emphasis has usually been upon specifying a limited set of exclusive and concurrent federal powers with the residual (usually unspecified) powers remaining with the constituent units. The United States, Switzerland and Australia provide classic examples. Austria and Germany followed this traditional pattern although their reconstruction during the post-war period did involve some devolution by comparison with the preceding autocratic regimes."[236] Watts, however, presents Belgium and Spain as examples of federations where "the creation of a federation has involved a process of devolution from a formerly unitary state".[237] In those instances, he thinks the reverse has been the case: "the powers of regional units have been specified and the residual authority has remained with the federal government".[238] Here we have to disagree, because Belgium has re-defined the powers of its constituent parts in a fashion which more or less behaves as predicted by the theory of classical federalism, placing residual powers with the constituent entities, while Spain actually remains a state which consists of autonomous entities without being a federation, because it seems to leave the residual powers at the central level, albeit in a convoluted way, and refrains from creating an institutional forum for the constituent entities at the central level. The "devolution" alternative probably does not explain the distribution of powers in federations,[239] but more appropriately in autonomy arrangements.

Watts also presents some intermediate cases, such as Canada, India and Malaysia, where there is a combination of the processes of aggregation and devolution. In addition, as concerns the distribution of powers in Canada and India, he concludes that there are specific listings of exclusively federal and exclusively provincial as well as concurring powers with the residual authority assigned to the federal government.[240] On a sliding scale between federations and autonomy arrangements, Canada and India would, therefore, both assume intermediate positions between the two extremes. This is sustained by the conclusion of Watts that in many federations "the exclusive legislative powers of the constituent units are left undefined as residual powers",[241] although in some federations, such as

[236]Watts (2008), p. 84.

[237]Watts (2008), p. 89.

[238]Watts (2008), p. 89.

[239]However, it is not entirely clear in which meaning Watts uses the term 'devolution'. He seems to use it to describe instances of transfer of powers form the central government level to lower levels.

[240]Watts (2008), p. 85.

[241]Watts (2008), p. 87.

Switzerland, Canada, Belgium, India, Malaysia, South Africa and the United Arab Emirates, "fields of exclusive jurisdiction of the constituent units are constitutionally defined". While making some distinctions between concurring and shared authority,[242] Watts concludes that "residual authority represents assignment by the constitution of jurisdiction over those matters not otherwise listed in the constitution. In most federations, especially those created by a process of aggregating previously separate units (although also in some others), the residual power has been retained by the unit governments",[243] that is, by the constituent states of, *inter alia*, the USA, Switzerland, Australia, Germany, Malaysia, Argentina, Brazil, Mexico, Nigeria, Russia, Pakistan and the United Arab Republic.[244] This is, according to Watts, often done in order to "underline their autonomy and the limited nature of powers assigned to the federal government".[245]

Because autonomy arrangements are not normally created by way of (voluntary) aggregation, but by different mechanisms, such as constitutional devolution or treaties between States, the autonomous entities would not normally base their powers on residual powers, although the implied powers of the federal governments have often been interpreted extensively. A point in this direction is made by Watts concerning, *inter alia*, Canada, India and South Africa: "In some federations, however, usually where devolution from a more centralized unitary regime characterized the process of federal formation, the residual powers have been left with the federal government."[246] As concerns Spain, in particular, Watts concludes that "5 of the 17 Autonomous Communities were assigned the residual authority, but for the others it remains with the central government".[247] In respect of the distribution of powers, Spain may therefore be a mixed case in respect of competences, moving into the fringes of autonomy arrangements, displaying stronger features of autonomy for the 17 regular autonomous communities and some features moving towards federalism for the five historical autonomous communities.

No solid theory underpins autonomy or devolution either, perhaps because autonomy arrangements are often very pragmatic *ad hoc* solutions that escape generalizations. However, Rolla approaches the matter by also including other

[242]Concurring powers are competences in the areas of which both the federal level and the state level are competent and where the state level can act until the federal level preempts the competence by its own action, while shared powers are competences occur in areas of "related" powers where both levels of government are competent to act without neither of them being paramount so as to require consent by both levels of governance before actions are taken. See Watts (2008), pp. 87–89, Anderson (2008), p. 26.

[243]Watts (2008), p. 89.

[244]In Europe, the following countries can be described as federations: Germany, Switzerland, and Austria, as well as Russia and Belgium. The latter two, however, display certain features that modify their federalism. Nevertheless, federalism is normally a fairly symmetrical mode of organization.

[245]Watts (2008), p. 89.

[246]Watts (2008), p. 89.

[247]Watts (2008), p. 89.

kinds of sub-state entities, creating three different categories of distribution of powers that constitutions usually follow: "(a) A double list system itemizing the duties that are assigned to the State and to the Regions respectively (Canada), (b) A system based on the inventory of the Central State's competence, which catalogues the matters delegated to the State while implicitly devolving all remaining areas of competence to the decentralized bodies (federal criterion), (c) A system based on the inventory of devolved areas of competence, which entails the constitutional catalogue of the matters specifically delegated to the Regions and thus residually reserving all other areas to the state legislators (regional criterion)."[248] He has carried out a systematic review of the position of Macau in China on the basis of the Basic Law concerning Macau and comes to the conclusion that the criterion used in the context of Macau is the regional criterion, although certain matters have been specifically devolved to the central state. He identifies Art. 18 of the Basic Law concerning Macau as a residual clause that places residual legislative powers with the lawmaker of the central government. This is consistent with our general view of territorial autonomies and would apply to Hong Kong in China, too, although Hong Kong might also be considered for the same category as the Åland Islands in Finland and the provinces in Canada, that is, category (a).

3.5.2 *Constructing a Provisional Definition of Autonomy*

Although no solid theory of autonomy seems to exist, it should be possible to say that if a provisional definition of autonomy were to be developed, compared to federal arrangements the relationships between the central level and the sub-state level would be reversed. Firstly, the state's legislative body would not normally incorporate official representation of the sub-state entity, although the inhabitants of an autonomous region might be granted a certain number of seats filled by means of elections from that particular constituency.[249] Hence, at the same time as the inhabitants of the autonomous territory have the right to elect their own self-governing bodies, they participate in national elections on an equal basis with the other citizens of the state.

Secondly, the legislative powers of the autonomous sub-state entity would be enumerated and specified so that it has special competence in certain fields, while the central government and the state legislature would, at least in principle, retain general legislative competence or residual powers. The idea underpinning this characterization is that the sub-state entities do not possess any original sovereignty: they are constitutionally created and defined entities entrusted with powers transferred to them from the central government. Such autonomies would not

[248] Rolla (2009), p. 476.

[249] See also Olivetti (2009), p. 779.

Material dimensions Institutional dimensions	Enumerated powers at the state level, residual at the sub-state level	Residual powers at the state level, enumerated at the sub-state level
Institutional representation of regional entities at national level + regular representation of voters through elections	1. Classical federation	2. Modified federation
Regular representation of voters through elections	3. Modified territorial autonomy	4. Territorial autonomy

Fig. 3.1 Institutional and material dimensions of sub-state arrangements

1. *Classical federation*, where there is a bi-cameral legislature with a regional chamber and with enumerated powers (coupled with a preemption doctrine) at the state level, leaving the residual powers to the sub-state level.	2. *Modified federation*, where there is a bi-cameral legislature with a regional chamber and with residual powers at the state level, establishing enumerated powers for the sub-state level.	3. *Modified territorial autonomy*, where there is a unicameral legislature with enumerated powers at the state level and residual powers for the sub-state level.	4. *Territorial autonomy*, where there is a unicameral legislature with residual powers (with no preemption doctrine) at the state level and enumerated powers established for the sub-state level.

Fig. 3.2 Four models of sub-state organization

normally have any great influence on such matters as amendments to the national constitution, at least not in cases that do not affect the autonomy arrangement itself.

The institutional and material dimensions of our theory of sub-state governance that encompasses both federations and territorial autonomies can be visualized in the following way (see Fig. 3.1, above).

The figure produces two ideal types of organization, the classical federation (combination no. 1), on the one hand, and the territorial autonomy (combination no. 4), on the other. They can be understood as the extreme positions that mark the two ends of a continuum onto which mixed models or hybrids can be placed. Because it seems as if the existence of joint decision-making organs at the state level would be important for the notion of shared rule in federations, combination no. 2 tips in the direction of federations, while combination no. 3 lacks that defining characteristic and moves its placement on the continuum to a position somewhere between combination 2 and combination 4. As a consequence, the range of organizational options between federation and territorial autonomy could be represented in the following way (see Fig. 3.2, above).

Even these ideal types and hybrids do not represent the entire range of organizational options, because there may exist cases that fall in between the four categories. This would be the case if, for instance, the powers of both the organs of the central state and those of the sub-state entity/entities would be enumerated. Also, the concept of 'regional state' dealt with above would find itself in a hybrid position, perhaps somewhere around model 3, the modified territorial autonomy.

Above, the Memel Territory was explored as a classic example of territorial autonomy. Using the institutional and material criteria expounded above, it seems the Memel Territory did not fulfill any of the criteria for constituting a federation with Lithuania, but instead it fulfilled the criteria developed above for territorial autonomies. This is not, as such, very surprising, because this singular entity, the Memel Territory, can be viewed as an archetype of territorial autonomy. The Memel Territory had no institutional representation in the unicameral Parliament of Lithuania, but instead, Members of Parliament were elected from the Memel Territory pursuant to the same election legislation as from the rest of Lithuania. This means that in principle, the Memel Territory returned representatives to the Parliament of Lithuania in the same proportion as the other parts of Lithuania. As concerns the distribution of powers between the central Government of Lithuania and the Memel Territory, as established in the Statute, the Memel Territory was vested with exclusive legislative powers on the basis of an enumeration, while the powers of the Lithuanian Parliament were of a residual nature. The domestic constitutional or political struggle concerning Memel was very much about the application of national legislation in the jurisdiction of Memel, that is, about whether or not national law was supreme to and preempted the legislative powers of the sub-state entity. Against this background, therefore, at least in the case of the Memel Territory, the test developed above for distinguishing between federations and autonomies seems to work. The test also seems to work with regard to a number of federations, such as the United States of America.

3.5.3 Testing the Autonomy Definition

The test can be applied to other cases, too, perhaps in particular to cases in which federal language has been used to create the impression of a federal relationship between the central government and a singular entity. In such cases, there is reason to suspect that they are of a borderline character and that for this reason there exists interest in determining whether they are federations or states with an autonomous territory. At least two such cases can be pointed to in this context, namely the historical example of Eritrea, which was a "federal unit" in Ethiopia between 1952 and 1962 after being placed under UN trusteeship after the Second World War due to its previous colonial relationship to Italy, and the current example of St. Kitts and Nevis, the constitution of which defines the state as a federation.

Lapidoth has applied several characteristics of federations and autonomy arrangements to the special relationship between Ethiopia and Eritrea that existed between 1952 and 1962, established on the basis of a UN General Assembly resolution.[250] Her conclusion is that Eritrea was a territorial autonomy, not a state in a federation. "Despite the use of the terms 'federation', 'federated', and 'Federal Act', the relationship can hardly be considered as federal in nature. No federal institutions were established, except for the Imperial Federal Council, which had only advisory functions and was to meet 'at least' once a year. Neither a federal legislature nor a federal executive distinct from those of Ethiopia was established. No upper house or federal organ for settling disputes existed. It thus appears that despite the use of the ambiguous 'federal' expressions, Eritrea had the status of an autonomous area, not of a federated district." "Moreover, while there was a limited means of preventing an excess of power by Eritrea, there was no remedy for such an excess by Ethiopia. In addition, the joint organ of consultation was not fit to address all the needs of coordination and cooperation." "[T]he difference of regime in the two partners probably undermined the arrangement: Ethiopia was an absolute monarchy and later a communist dictatorship, while Eritrea strove to be a democratic entity." Lapidoth also refers to other reasons, such as fear of secession, for the ultimate incorporation by Ethiopia of Eritrea. She concludes by saying that "[p]robably, the basic condition for the success of any autonomy was missing: the joint wish for compromise and reconciliation. Because autonomy is, by its very nature, based on cooperation and coordination, it cannot succeed if the parties are unable to overcome their animosity."[251] On the basis of her application of the different principles, in particular the institutional criterion, Lapidoth then argues that Eritrea was not part of a federation between 1952 and 1962, but an autonomous territory of the Ethiopian state[252] until it was merged with Ethiopia as its 14th province without protests from the United Nations after a unanimous vote in the Eritrean Assembly on 15 November 1962 to dissolve the federation and unite Eritrea with the Ethiopian empire.[253]

[250]GA Res. 390 A (V), 2 December 1950. See also Lapidoth (1997), p. 129 f. Eritrea is an independent state since 1993.

[251]Lapidoth (1997), p. 130.

[252]However, see Hannum (1996), pp. 337–341, who follows the federalist terminology of the then Ethiopian legislation concerning Eritrea and does not react to the fact that the singular entity of Eritrea does not seem to be a federation, but instead an autonomy arrangement. For a personal account of how the special relationship between Ethiopia and Eritrea came into being, see Spencer (1984), pp. 223–260, where the use of the federal terminology seems very "intentional". See also Negash (1997), p. 146: "For all intents and purposes, the relationship between Eritrea and Ethiopia was not in the least federal. Even according to the intentions of the UN, Eritrea was not granted a federal status but only a status of autonomy. Yet the UN and its advisors, including the Commissioner for Eritrea, Anze Matienzo, insisted on using the term federation without having to bother about laying down the appropriate infrastructure for its proper functioning." These different interpretations concerning the conceptualization of the Eritrean situation underline the need for theoretical distinctions between autonomy arrangements and federations.

[253]Negash (1997), p. 138. According to Negash (1997), p. 147, the federation was doomed to fail because it did not reflect the conception and exercise of power as understood by the Unionist Party, that is, a party that advocated a complete union between Ethiopia and Eritrea. See also Negash (1997), pp. 184–229, for different documents illustrating the nature of the Eritrean autonomy arrangement, inter alia, the resolution of the General Assembly, the text of the Constitution of Eritrea, reports, election results, economic data, etc.

The conclusion that Eritrea was a territorial autonomy rather than an entity in a federation tends to hold also on the basis of the application of our test based on the institutional and material criteria developed above, but a more precise positioning of Eritrea would probably be that of a hybrid model represented by combination no. 3, that is, a modified territorial autonomy. In fact, on the basis of paragraph 1 of the resolution of the General Assembly of the United Nations, Eritrea shall constitute an autonomous unit federated with Ethiopia under the sovereignty of the Ethiopian Crown.[254] On the basis of paragraphs 2 and 3 of the resolution it seems as if the intention of the UN was to vest Eritrea with exclusive legislative as well as executive and judicial powers in the field of domestic affairs, that is, residual powers, so that the jurisdiction of Eritrea would extend to all matters not vested in the Federal Government, including the power to maintain the internal police, to levy taxes to meet the expenses of domestic functions and services, and to adopt its own budget. In turn, the powers of the Ethiopian state were enumerated, encompassing, for instance, international relations.[255] At the same time, the main mode of representation of Eritrea at the national level was by means of general elections to the legislature of Ethiopia in proportion of the population of Eritrea to the population of the entire state, as established in paragraph 5 of the resolution.[256] The Imperial Federal Council that was mentioned in the resolution

[254]According to Spencer (1984), p. 234, the three-government model of a federation (one overall state government and two sub-state governments) had to be discarded if there were to be any settlement and that the Ethiopian position was soon accepted that "Ethiopia was not to be federated with Eritrea, but the converse, that Eritrea was to be federated with Ethiopia under the sovereignty of the Ethiopian crown". When the autonomy model was designed, the U.S. constitutional model was abandoned in favor of a two-government model of a "federation wherein the Ethiopian government was, at the same time, the federal government". With, e.g., foreign powers vested in the state of Ethiopia, it seems as if Ethiopia was more a unitary state that included a singular autonomous entity. For an account of the diplomatic background to the Eritrean situation, see Okbazghi (1991), pp. 50–176, and Gayim (1993). See also Okbazghi (1991), p. 180, who laments the absence of any neutral arbiter between Eritrea and Ethiopia and concludes that "the imperial government of Ethiopia was designated both as the government of Ethiopia and as the government of Ethiopia and Eritrea, a unity completely alien to the concept of federalism", and Negash (1997), p. 85, who holds that the "federation was not working because there was not distinction between the Ethiopian government and the federal government". In this respect, the problem seems to have been somewhat similar to that of Zanzibar (see below, Chap. 4).

[255]See also Okbazghi (1991), p. 209: "By envisaging autonomy for Eritrea, the federal plan seems to have drawn a distinction between external self-determination, which was denied to Eritrea in view of its association with Ethiopia, and internal self-determination, in which the Eritreans were left to arrange their lives internally in accordance with their wishes." However, the autocratic nature of the Ethiopian Government prevented the proper functioning of the Eritrean autonomy. See Okbazghi (1991), pp. 177, 188, 198 f., 208 f. But see also Negash (1997), p. 144, who maintains that the "federation arrangement had very few committed supporters. The first incursions against the Eritrean constitution were not from Ethiopia or the federal authorities but from the Eritrean Assembly and government."

[256]In the 1956 elections to the Ethiopian parliament, Eritrea was consequently allocated 14 seats in a chamber of 201 members. See Negash (1997), p. 117 f., who also holds that interestingly, the Ethiopian election legislation was more progressive than that of Eritrea, because it introduced direct

was composed of equal numbers of Ethiopian and Eritrean representatives, but it had only advisory functions concerning the common affairs of the Federation, that is, those matters that had been enumerated in paragraph 3 for the entire state. Thus the Council was hardly an effective mechanism of institutional representation of two entities of a federation, and under the Federal Act, the Council would meet relatively seldom, at a minimum rate of once per year, which contributed to the fact that the Council did not emerge as a functioning body.[257]

The contents of the Federal Act were included in the Constitution of Eritrea, which was adopted by the Eritrean Constituent Assembly on 15 July 1952 under at least moderate British and American legal influence and which contained additional provisions concerning the governance of this sub-state entity. It was, however, difficult for the Eritrean autonomy to survive in the context of autocratic and authoritarian rule in Ethiopia, and it seems that the representative of the central Government of Ethiopia in Eritrea, the governor of Eritrea, played a crucial role in undermining the Eritrean autonomy by expanding his own authority far beyond the explicit powers assigned to him.[258] Hence the dispute concerning Eritrea seems to have revolved around preemption under national law. Also, the Eritreans themselves seem to have been, if not ignorant, at least indifferent about the correct functioning of their autonomous system of governance, leaving the scene open for the pro-Ethiopian actors in Eritrea. At the same time, it is also likely that not only the Eritrean Assembly, but also a majority of the population in general was positively predisposed towards full unification with Ethiopia,[259] revealing a rift between the pro-unionist Christians and the "autonomist" Muslims.[260]

---

election with universal suffrage (including women), whereas the Eritrean inhabitants elected their representatives mainly indirectly through electoral colleges and on the basis of male votes only.

[257]See Spencer (1984), p. 235, who concludes that the "Council rapidly became a nonentity". See also Negash (1997), pp. 79 f., 145.

[258]On the role of the Governor of Eritrea, see Okbazghi (1991), pp. 180, 189–194, and Negash (1997), pp. 78, 83 f., 101 f., 106, 118, 128. Apparently, the actual role of the Governor of Eritrea became similar to that of the Governor of the Memel Territory (see above, Chap. 2).

[259]The indifference was perhaps at least in part due to the fact that the autonomy arrangement was externally imposed both on Eritrea and Ethiopia, although such a solution was at the time the most feasible one. See Negash (1997), pp. 71, 144. One persistent problem was, however, the fluid role of the Chief Executive of Eritrea, an office which at times was united de facto if not de jure with the office of the Governor of Eritrea, who was the representative of the Emperor of Ethiopia. On the role of the Chief Executive, see Negash (1997), pp. 86 f., 97–106, 124, 128, 132 f. Remarkably, at a time of conflict between the Chief Executive of the Eritrean Government, that is, the Premier, and the Eritrean Assembly, the autocratic Emperor of Ethiopia himself felt that the Eritrean Assembly should be reminded of the workings of parliamentary assembly and "instructed his representative in Asmara to inform the Eritrean Assembly that the suspension of the regular session was unconstitutional and that the Eritrean assembly had the power to pass a vote of no confidence in those whom it had in the first place elected". Negash (1997), p. 105.

[260]After civil war and the Communist experiment in Ethiopia, Eritrea eventually proclaimed independence in 1993.

The second test case for our constitutional typology concerning sub-state entities, the Federation of St. Kitts and Nevis, still exists as a single state, although there was a failed attempt on the part of Nevis in 1998 to dissolve the relationship and become an independent country.[261] Chapter I of the 1983 Constitution of Saint Christopher and Nevis, issued in a British Constitutional Order in 1983,[262] is entitled "the Federation and the Constitution", indicating that there would exist a federal relationship between the two entities. The same determination is made in section 1(1) of the Constitution on the federation and its territory, according to which the island of Saint Christopher (which is otherwise known as Saint Kitts) and the island of Nevis shall be a sovereign democratic federal state. In spite of the fact that the state consists only of two entities, in this case islands, the constitutional terminology is that of a multi-entity nature. However, the formal relationship between St. Kitts and Nevis seems at least in principle to be similar to that of Ethiopia and Eritrea, although in terms of our typology of sub-state forms, Nevis is a territorial autonomy of a kind which matches model 4 above.

As concerns the institutional dimension, the Constitution of St. Kitts and Nevis establishes a legislature for the entire state, the National Assembly, which is unicameral and draws its elected representatives from both parts of the state, at the same time as there are at least three appointed senators in the Assembly, the number of which can arise up to two-thirds of the elected representatives.[263] With reference to the material dimension, this parliament may, under section 37 of the Constitution, make laws for the peace, order and good government of Saint Christopher and Nevis. However, the power of Parliament to make laws having effect in the island of Nevis shall not extend to any of the specified matters (that is to say, matters with respect to which the Nevis Island Legislature has exclusive power to make laws so having effect). Here, the National Assembly is vested with the residual powers, while the legislature of Nevis has enumerated powers. Under section 103 of the Constitution, the Nevis Island Legislature may make laws, which shall be styled Ordinances, for the peace, order and good government of

[261] On 10 August 1998, 61.83 percent of the voters who participated in a referendum in Nevis voted to secede from the Federation of St. Kitts and Nevis on the basis of section 113 of the Constitution. However, the referendum result was not formally valid due to the failure to reach the two-thirds qualified majority. According to section 113(1), "[t]he Nevis Island Legislature may provide that the island of Nevis shall cease to be federated with the island of Saint Christopher and accordingly that this Constitution shall no longer have effect in the island of Nevis".

[262] Statutory Instruments 1983 No. 881, the Saint Christopher and Nevis Constitution Order 1983, made in the Privy Council at the Court at Buckingham Palace, the 22nd day of June 1983. The Constitution of Saint Christopher and Nevis is found in Schedule 1 of the royal order.

[263] A part of the senators are appointed by the Governor-General upon the recommendation of the Prime Minister and another (greater) part upon the recommendation of the Leader of the Opposition. It seems on the basis of section 41 of the Constitution that the distinction between representatives and senators is only relevant concerning votes of no confidence, whereas the two categories of parliamentarians in other respects, such as voting on legislation, appear to have equal rights.

the island of Nevis with respect to so-called specified matters.[264] Also, the National Assembly can transfer more legislative competences than those enumerated as specified matters to the Nevis Island Legislature by a majority of two-thirds.

In spite of these law-making powers of its own, Nevis can request and consent to the enactment of a national law within the specified matters that normally would belong to the competence of the Nevis Island Legislature.[265] Such enactments or provisions shall accordingly have effect in the island of Nevis as if they had been enacted by the Nevis Island Legislature and may be amended or revoked accordingly. In addition, any time when there is in force a declaration made by the Governor-General by proclamation, upon the advice of the Prime Minister and with the concurrence of the Premier of Nevis, that any provisions of any law enacted by Parliament specified in that declaration (being provisions that relate to a specified matter) are required to have effect in the island of Nevis in the interests of external affairs or in the interests of defense, they shall accordingly have effect in the island of Nevis. If there is any inconsistency between those provisions and the provisions of any law enacted by the Nevis Island Legislature, the provisions of the law enacted by Parliament shall prevail. In addition, a law enacted by Parliament shall not be regarded as extending to a specified matter of Nevis by reason only that it contains incidental or supplementary provisions relating to that matter and having effect in the island of Nevis. Again, if there is any inconsistency between any such provisions and the provisions of any law enacted by the Nevis Island Legislature, the provisions of the law enacted by Parliament shall prevail. A similar provision is contained in section 103(2) of the Constitution in respect of the legislation of Nevis: a law made by the Nevis Island Legislature may contain incidental and supplementary provisions that relate to a matter other than a specified matter but if there is any inconsistency between those provisions and the provisions of any law enacted by

---

[264] Matters with respect to which the Nevis Island Legislature has exclusive power to make laws are listed in part I of schedule 5 to the Constitution as follows: agriculture, amenities for tourists, animals, archaeological or historical sites and monuments, borrowings of money, or obtaining grants of money, for the purposes of the Nevis Island Administration and the making of grants and loans for those purposes, cemeteries, cinemas, conservation and supply of water, dangerous or inflammable substances, economic planning and development other than national planning and development, employment of persons who are not citizens, hotels, restaurants, bars, casinos and other similar establishments, housing, industries, trades and businesses, land and buildings other than land and buildings vested in the Crown and specifically appropriated to the use of the Government, including holding of land by persons who are not citizens, manufacture and supply of electricity, parks and other places for public recreation, prevention and control of fires, roads and highways, sport and cultural activities, the matters with respect to which the Nevis Island Legislature is empowered to make laws by sections 47, 70, 71, 72 and 73, as applied with modifications by section 104, and by sections 102(l) and 113, any matter added by Parliament under section 37(6) and any matter that is incidental or supplementary to any matter referred to in this list.

[265] This is a procedure that resembles very much the Legislative Consent Motion (or the so-called Sewel mechanism) introduced for Scotland almost 20 years later than for Nevis (see Sects. 5.4.1 and 5.4.4, below).

Parliament, the provisions of the law enacted by Parliament shall prevail. Evidently, in situations of unclear competence where there is a so-called positive competence conflict, the national law has precedence. This could indicate the existence of a limited preemption doctrine on the part of national law, but probably mainly in the area of narrowly defined concurring powers. Part 2 of the schedule contains certain interpretations concerning the delimitation of the legislative powers of Nevis.

Against the background of the Constitution of St. Kitts and Nevis, it is possible to say that the state is not really a federation, because it does not fulfill the institutional or the material dimensions of the definition of a federation. It also has a peculiar two-entity construction where the main entity at the same time is in charge of governance for the entire state within the powers reserved to it. A federally organized state would entail the existence of an overall national government and two or more entities at the sub-state level, which is clearly not the case on the basis of the Constitution of St. Kitts and Nevis. What is clear, instead, is that on Nevis, there are two legal orders in existence, that of the entire state created on the basis of the residual powers of the state and that of the sub-state entity created on the basis of the enumerated powers of Nevis, although the legal order of the state seems to have the upper hand in such situations of concurring powers where both have exercised their competence. At the same time, there is no institutional forum for the representation of Nevis in the national parliament, but only representation of the inhabitants of Nevis in the unicameral parliament of the state. On this basis, it is therefore possible to say that Nevis actually is a territorial autonomy within the state of St. Kitts and Nevis.

3.5.4 Formulating a Definition of Territorial Autonomy

It seems that our test of sub-state governance is able to distinguish between different constitutional situations and to specify the constitutional form that a particular sub-state entity has on a continuum between an entity in a classical federation and an entity of territorial autonomy in a unitary state. The combination of the institutional and the material dimension is relevant as a point of departure for a constitutional analysis and also for a comparative analysis, capable of uncovering terminological anomalies created intentionally or unintentionally when the sub-state arrangements have been drafted and adopted. It is probably also possible to indicate a more exact positioning of different sub-state entities on the scale with reference to our typology developed above.

Within the material dimension, the issue of legislative powers is in many ways crucial for the understanding of sub-state entities and their functioning. These powers constitute, at the level of the state, the core of its internal sovereignty. Making laws is equal to the effective exercise of power over the territory of a state. In states where autonomies exist, a share of that internal sovereignty may have been transferred under the constitution of the state in such a way that both the state legislature and the legislature of the autonomous entity have exclusive legislative powers in relation to each other, although they may also have concurring jurisdictions. Therefore, in so far as an autonomy arrangement has been vested with exclusive law-making powers, the powers also constitute a share in the internal self-determination of the entire state.

Within the institutional dimension, it is obvious that the autonomous territories are not participating in decision-making at the central level in the same way as within the federations, but usually depend on regular political representation in the normally uni-cameral national parliament. Because the constituent states of federations implement a principle of shared rule through their institutional representation in a federal chamber, it is also logically possible to justify measures that the federal level takes in relation to the state level by way of joint measures in order to implement uniform national objectives across all the constituent states, often formulated as a preemption doctrine of some sort. When sufficiently justified, the constituent states – or at least a sufficient majority of them – will agree to measures that may make inroads to their powers. In principle, this is precisely what autonomy arrangements are set to avoid: because an autonomous territory does not share decision-making power at the national level, it should also be able to expect that the national government will not attempt to encroach into the sphere of competence of the autonomous entity.

After this theoretical exposé, with terminology drawn from some of the most salient features of federations, we are now in a position to define what the ideal types of a (classical) federation and a territorial autonomy are. A federation is a more or less symmetrical transfer of exclusive law-making powers, on the basis of the constitution, to two or more entities at the sub-state level which vests the federal level with enumerated powers exercised at least in principle in a shared manner with the sub-state entities through institutional representation of the sub-state entities at the federal level. This arrangement leaves the sub-state entities with residual powers at the same time as the powers of the federal level are often enhanced by a preemption doctrine according to which federal law has supremacy over state law.

An arrangement with a territorial autonomy normally involves a singular entity in what otherwise would be a unitary state, introducing thereby an asymmetrical feature in the state through transfer of exclusive law-making powers on the basis of provisions that often are of a special nature. The resulting division of power is one where the national level retains the residual powers, while the sub-state level relies on enumerated powers and there is no institutional representation of the sub-state entity at national level. In addition, there is normally no supremacy clause in operation between the national level and the sub-state level that would, at least as concerns ordinary law and lower enactments, imply that national enactments set aside sub-state enactments. The effect of the absence of a supremacy mechanism would be to underline the exclusive nature of the legislative powers at the sub-state level.

Chapter 4
Conflict Resolution in a Self-Determination Context as a General Frame for Sub-state Arrangements

4.1 Conflict Resolution in Different Contexts of Time and Space

The autonomy solutions reviewed in this inquiry all have very different roots and reasons. As established above, they constitute a species of institutions that differs from federal forms of organization even in cases where the state to which they are attached is a federation. They can also, at least to some extent, be presented in a joint frame of conflict resolution and, within that frame, in a chronological sequence that links in to the concept of self-determination.

The Memel Territory, presented in Chap. 2, is an example of an early instance of conflict resolution in which a formal treaty under international law was concluded in order to regulate the position of Memel in relation to Lithuania. Almost simultaneously, the Åland Islands were on the agenda of the international community for the same reason. Both the Memel Territory and the Åland Islands were instituted and started functioning prior to the Second World War, and Memel even disappeared as an autonomous entity in a prelude to the War. In that historical context, the self-determination and the sovereignty of the State was important and relatively well protected.

Arguably, Puerto Rico developed characteristics of autonomy somewhat later, in 1950, as a result of an evolution that was embedded in a broader self-determination discussion in the aftermath of the creation of the United Nations in 1945. The position of Zanzibar is related to self-determination even more clearly, because the territory emerged as an independent State in 1963 out of a colonial situation and was joined with another State as early as 1964 for the purposes of forming a union. The issue of self-determination is also present in the case of Hong Kong with reference to the colonial past of the territory. At least concerning Puerto Rico and Zanzibar, the self-determination of the people is strongly in the picture, while the Hong Kong issue could be so, too, through the winding up of the colonial relationship.

The granting of law-making powers to Scotland is not as clearly related to conflict resolution as the other cases reviewed here, but it is perhaps possible to entertain the idea that devolution was a preemptive measure designed to defuse an

M. Suksi, *Sub-State Governance through Territorial Autonomy*,
DOI 10.1007/978-3-642-20048-9_4, © Springer-Verlag Berlin Heidelberg 2011

even remotely potential conflict before it started to smolder seriously. In that respect, the resolution of the Aceh conflict came much later, after the point of time when a greater natural calamity had forced the parties to the conflict to reconsider their positions. Hence the two cases can be understood as constituting situations in which a solution to aspirations of self-determination of the inhabitants of an area was sought for through institutional solutions that do not disrupt the territorial integrity of the State.

The chronology of the creation of autonomies is thus illustrative of different conflict scenarios and of different situations of self-determination. Although the main elements of comparison extracted from the *Memel* case are not directly dealt with here, the core issues are, however, embedded in narratives covering the different sub-state entities. After the framework within which the sub-state arrangements exist has been established, an analysis of the various elements related to sub-state governance will be more fruitful.

4.2 The Åland Islands: From Risk of Secession and War to Peaceful Conflict Resolution

4.2.1 Domestic Preliminaries in Anticipation of International Involvement?

The origins or the special position of the Åland Islands in Finland can be found in the events that surround Finland's attainment of independence in 1917. Until 1917, the Åland Islands were administratively an ordinary part of the autonomous Grand Duchy of Finland, while Finland at that time was a special part of the Russian Empire.[1] In 1918, the Åland Islands were made a province of Finland under a Governor appointed by the state. However, there was an international treaty arrangement in place from 1856 onwards that influenced the military position of the Åland Islands, namely the so-called Paris Convention on the Demilitarization of the Åland Islands of 1856. In this treaty the Russian Empire, Great Britain and France agreed, in the aftermath of the Crimean War, that the Åland Islands would not be fortified and that no installation would be created there for the military or the navy. It can be said that this regular part of the Finnish jurisdiction was subject, early on, to international regulation as concerns a narrow field of traditional national competences, namely military policy.[2] Obviously, the Åland Islands are geographically

[1]See Art. 2 of the 1906 Constitution of Russia, according to which "(t)he Grand Duchy of Finland, while it constitutes an indivisible part of the Russian State, is governed in its domestic affairs by special institutions on the basis of a special legislation". Szeftel (1976), p. 84.

[2]During the First World War, Russia deployed troops on the Åland Islands and built military installations. Moreover, the Finnish Civil War at the beginning of 1918 resulted in the presence of military forces of the Whites and Reds, as well as units of the German and Swedish Army. The demilitarization of the Åland Islands was in danger at that point of time.

near Stockholm, the Swedish capital. The Islands' strategic importance for Sweden derived from this close proximity. Moreover, from the Åland Islands, it was possible to control large portions of the Baltic Sea.[3]

By the time of Finnish independence from the Russian Empire at the end of 1917, thoughts were put forward in the Åland Islands concerning a possible reunion with Sweden. Finland became an autonomous part of the Russian Empire in the aftermath of the so-called Great Nordic War of 1808–1809,[4] but before that, Finland, including the Åland Islands as an administrative and court district, had been a regular part of the Kingdom of Sweden from the thirteenth century. Therefore, it is understandable that the Åland Islanders would, in the uncertainties characterizing the world during and after 1917, be interested in finding a safe haven in Sweden, which did not participate in the First World War. In addition, because an independent Finland would, in terms of language, be dominated by a great Finnish-speaking majority, there were uneasy feelings in the Åland Islands about the future. The idea of a transformation from a multi-ethnic and multilinguistic Russian Empire to what at that point could potentially become a unilingual country and a pure nation state of Finland was unsettling. Therefore, seceding from Finland and joining Sweden would have been an attractive option during those turbulent times for the inhabitants of this predominantly Swedish-speaking area.

The attempts to separate the Åland Islands from Finland and to join the area with Sweden manifested themselves, *inter alia*, in two petitions addressed to the state bodies of Sweden, the first one in 1917[5] and the second one in 1919.[6] In these

[3]See also Björkholm and Rosas (1990). With the development of modern weapons systems, the strategic importance of the Åland Islands has diminished.

[4]The Russian occupation of Finland left a Swedish-speaking population in Finland in the coastal areas of Southern, South-Western (including the Åland Islands), and Western Finland that altogether amounted to around 12% of the population of Finland. The inhabitants of the Åland Islands constituted less than 10% of that minority group.

[5]At the end of December 1917, a petition campaign was undertaken on the Åland Islands to establish and support the wishes of the inhabitants to secede from Finland and to join Sweden. Of the approximately 21,000 inhabitants of the Islands, approximately 12,500 persons had the right to vote, and about 8,000 of these were presented with a petition on the issue. 7,135 persons signed the petition addressed to "the king and people of Sweden" asking for measures to be undertaken leading to annexation by Sweden. Already in August 1917, an unofficial assembly of the inhabitants of the Åland Islands had proposed that the area would secede from Finland and join Sweden. See de Geer-Hancock (1986), p. 32 ff.; Modeen (1973), p. 14 ff. The collection of signatures proceeded from house to house and was completed in less than a week's time. See Lindh (1984), p. 38 f. Högman (1981), pp. 41, 43, points out that the petition was formulated as a proxy *in blanco*, which authorized persons to be elected later on to deliver the wishes of the inhabitants of the Åland Islands to the king of Sweden, which happened on 3 February 1918. The final text of the petition was published on 20 March 1918.

[6]The second petition campaign was completed on 29 June 1919. This second petition was signed by 9,735 persons who supported union with Sweden, while 461 persons refused to sign the petition. See Lindh (1984), p. 44 f. Högman (1981), pp. 119, 124 f., points out that every signature was confirmed by two witnesses and that the petition again was a proxy *in blanco* for union with Sweden.

petitions, an overwhelming majority of the inhabitants of the Åland Islands expressed the wish that the Åland Islands should be separated from Finland and rejoined with Sweden.[7] This wish seemed to coincide well with the principle of self-determination that was presented towards the end of the First World War by President Wilson of the United States of America. This principle of self-determination was included among 14 different policy programs presented by President Wilson,[8] and its aim was to function as a guideline for adjudicating the national affiliation of minority groups when national borders were re-drawn. This principle of self-determination was not, however, applied in the case of the Åland Islands, because neither Finland nor Sweden were warring parties in the First World War and for that reason not parties to the peace negotiations at Versailles. In addition, the principle of self-determination was not understood as such a positive rule of public international law that it would recognize, on the basis of a simple declaration of will, the right of a certain part of the population to secede from the State to which the population belonged.

As the relationship between Finland and Sweden continued to develop in a negative direction, with the potential to become a threat to peace, the issue concerning the Åland Islands was taken up in 1920 by the League of Nations upon a British initiative. The League of Nations had after all been created under the Versailles Peace Treaty after the First World War as the international organization that would work for the maintenance of peace in the world.

As early as May 1920, however, the Parliament of Finland adopted the Act on the Self-Government of the Åland Islands (Statutes of Finland, SoF 124/1920), prepared on the basis of Government Bill 73/1919 issued to the Parliament in December 1919.[9] In terms of a timeline, therefore, it is important to note that the

---

[7]These two petitions are sometimes erroneously referred to as referendums or plebiscites. See Hannikainen (2007), p. 54, Austen et al. (1987), p. 145.

[8]In his speech of 8 January 1918 containing fourteen points of American aims for ending the First World War, the exact term 'self-determination' is not used, but many of the formulations are coherent with the principle. It should be noted that the speech also uses the concept of autonomy, but probably in a relatively flexible manner. See Wambaugh (1933), p. 4 f, commenting Wilson's points: "His meaning appears, from the first, to have been that no change of sovereignty must be made by conquest and that such national groups as wished it should be given autonomy within the state to which they belonged." See also Veiter (1984), p. 13, Mattern (1920), p. 176 f. As pointed out in Wambaugh (1933), p. 11, the real endorsement of the principle of self-determination took place in Wilson's speech on 24 January 1918, in which he said, *inter alia*, that national aspirations must be respected, that peoples may be dominated and governed only by their own consent, and that self-determination is not a mere phrase, but an imperative principle of action, which statesmen ignore at their own peril.

[9]See Governmental Committee Report 24/1919, p. 19. In the Report, a review of foreign law was included (e.g., the Isle of Man, Guernsey and Jersey in Britain and those dominions which at that point still were a formal part of Great Britain, such as Canada, Australia, South-Africa and New Zealand, but also Iceland, which was a part of Denmark, Croatia and Herzegovina as parts of the Austro-Hungarian Empire, and Elsass-Lothringen as a part of Germany. The Committee inquired into, *inter alia*, the distribution of legislative powers and their substantive contents as well as into taxation powers of these entities, but found that none of them was suitable, due to differences in circumstances, as a model for the self-government of the Åland Islands. Concerning the historical example of Elsass-Lothringen (Alsace-Lorraine) as a non-federal part of Germany after 1871, see Wolff (2010), p. 18.

work within the governmental structures of Finland towards alleviating the fears of the Åland Islanders began early on, right after the enactment in July 1919 of the Form of Government (Constitution) Act of Finland. A governmental committee was appointed in July 1919 to draft legislation concerning a general scheme of self-government for the provinces of Finland,[10] but due to exceptional reasons, the Government redefined the task of the committee in the Fall of 1919 and directed it to draft special legislation concerning the Åland Islands, dealt with by the Government in its session in October 1919 and handed over to the Parliament in December 1919. This first Act on the Self-Government of the Åland Islands was passed by the Parliament pursuant to the constitutional amendment formula involving a qualified majority in the final adoption without, however, declaring in the Act itself that it would be a constitutional act. Therefore, the Act constituted a so-called act of exception in relation to the Constitution of Finland,[11] but combined with the requirement in section 36(1) that it could only be amended in the order prescribed for constitutional amendments, the Act actually acquired special entrenchment. In addition, section 36(1) of this Act also established a so-called regional entrenchment for the autonomy arrangement by stipulating that any amendment, explanation or revocation of the Act required the consent of the Legislative Assembly of the Åland Islands.[12]

---

[10]When the Form of Government (Constitution) Act was enacted in 1919, provisions providing language rights for the speakers of Finnish and Swedish and provisions making possible general systems of self-government of a higher order were incorporated into the Constitution. The former were realized in the form of linguistic guarantees on an equal footing for both language groups, but the latter never led to anything concrete, probably at least in part for the reason that the Åland Islands were granted autonomy.

[11]The doctrine of acts of exception is based on the understanding that in the legislative life of a nation, there may, for political reasons, exist moments when such a piece of law has to be adopted which is against the formal letter of the constitution. In such situations, the parliament may, by using the same formulas as prescribed for constitutional amendments, adopt an ordinary act of parliament which is, from a material point of view, in breach with the constitution. Such an act of exception introduces limitations or adjusting specifications, embedded in an ordinary act of Parliament, that open up holes in the wall which the formal constitution creates. An act of exception can be defined as an ordinary act of Parliament through which it has been possible to accept a violation of the core meaning of a constitutional provision, provided that this ordinary act is approved by the Parliament in the manner prescribed for constitutional amendments. Hence when a Bill contains an infringement of the formal constitution in a manner that affects the core meaning of the constitutional provision in question, such an enactment can, nevertheless, be approved by the parliament as a so-called act of exception, provided that the decision is made in the manner prescribed for the adoption of constitutional amendments.

[12]In the context of legislating on self-government for the Åland Islands in 1920, the then recent Finnish experience as an entity with (relative) autonomy may be cited as an important factor conducive to the domestic recognition of the autonomy for Åland in 1920 and in 1922. The autonomous Grand Duchy of Finland was created in 1809 and codified in Article 2 of the 1906 Constitution of Russia, which concluded that "(t)he Grand Duchy of Finland, while it constitutes an indivisible part of the Russian State, is governed in its domestic affairs by special institutions on the basis of a special legislation". Szeftel (1976), p. 84.

As early as 1920, the autonomy arrangement was already entrenched in the most unusual way in the constitutional fabric of Finland. According to the Bill, the purpose of the Act was to extinguish all even remotely justifiable reasons for discontent that may have existed on the part of the inhabitants of the Åland Islands and to guarantee to the Åland Islanders the opportunity to arrange their existence as freely as was possible for a region that did not constitute a State. One part of this freedom was evidently the exception in the Act for the inhabitants from the general duty to carry out military service in the Finnish army. Another feature of the 1920 Self-Government Act was that the distribution of legislative powers between the Parliament of Finland and the Legislative Assembly of the Åland Islands was fashioned according to a more "federal" principle that placed enumerated powers with the national parliament, while the residual powers were assigned to the Legislative Assembly of the Åland Islands (see Sect. 5.3.1 below).

4.2.2 Decision by the League of Nations

These background elements indicate that the autonomy arrangement for Åland was, early on, tied to both international and national politics and international and national law. The negotiation process did not actually involve the local population or their representatives to a significant extent, but rather the representatives of Finland and Sweden and also representatives of the Council of the League of Nations. However, the Committee of Rapporteurs visited the Åland Islands, and the Council of the League of Nations heard the representatives of the Åland Islanders.[13]

The option of secession was quickly ruled out by the League, although in its 1920 Report the Commission of Jurists had concluded that the "principle recognising the rights of peoples to determine their political fate may be applied in various ways; the most important of these are, on the one hand the formation of an independent State, and on the other hand the right of choice between two existing States". The principle of self-determination, it said, must "be brought into line with that of the protection of minorities; both have a common object – to assure to some national Group the maintenance and free development of its social, ethnical or religious characteristics". After concluding that the protection of minorities was already provided for in many constitutions and that the body of international law under the League of Nations had resulted in the creation of special legal régimes for certain sections of the population of a state, the Commission suggested that there could be a middle ground between the formation of a new and independent State and choosing between two existing States: "Under such circumstances, a solution in the nature of a compromise, based on an extensive grant of liberty to minorities,

[13]Barros (1968), pp. 276, 310, 324, 328–329.

may appear necessary according to international legal conception and may even be dictated by the interests of peace."[14]

Considering the historical background and Finland's ongoing transformation, the Commission concluded that the "fact that Finland was eventually reconstituted as an independent State is not sufficient to efface the conditions which gave rise to the aspirations of the Aaland Islanders and to cause these conditions to be regarded as if they had never arisen".[15] It was therefore necessary to take into consideration the factual situation on the Islands, such as the fairly homogeneous nature of the inhabitants, the geographical location of the Islands, the racial, linguistic, and traditional links between the Islands and Sweden, and the forcible separation of the Islands from Sweden in 1808–1809. On the basis of these considerations, the Commission concluded that, under public international law, the Åland Islands question should not be left entirely to the domestic jurisdiction of Finland, and that the Council of the League of Nations was competent, on the basis of Art. 15(4) of the Covenant of the League of Nations, to make any recommendations which it deemed just and proper in the case.[16]

The League of Nations then appointed a Commission of Rapporteurs to the Åland Islands question, which concluded that the "right of sovereignty of the Finnish State over the Aaland Islands is (...) incontestable and their present legal status is that they form part of Finland. To detach the Aaland Islands from Finland would therefore be an alteration of its status, in depriving this country of a part of that which belongs to it".[17] Considering the question of whether a minority has the right to separate itself from a State, even when it apparently fulfils the conditions for doing so, the Commission stated: "The answer can only be in the negative. To concede to minorities, either of language or of religion, or to any fractions of a population the right of withdrawing from the community to which they belong, because it is their wish or their good pleasure, would be to destroy order and stability within States and to inaugurate anarchy in international life; it would be to uphold a theory incompatible with the very idea of the State as a territorial and political unity."[18] The Commission formulated what has since become the established position: "separation of a minority from the State of which it forms a part and its incorporation in another State can only be considered as an altogether exceptional solution, a last resort when the State lacks either the will or the power to enact and apply just and effective guarantees".[19]

Because the Commission of Rapporteurs could not find evidence of any gross violations of the rights of the Åland Islanders and because the application of the

---

[14]Official Journal of the League of Nations, Special Supplement No. 3, October 1920, p. 6.

[15]Ibid., p. 12.

[16]Ibid., p. 14.

[17]The Aaland Islands Question (1921), note 26, p. 25.

[18]Ibid., p. 28.

[19]Ibid., p. 28.

Wilsonian principle of self-determination for deciding on the national affiliation of a population group was not a rule of positive public international law, the Commission did not find any immediate reason to recommend either secession or a referendum on the issue in the Åland Islands. The Commission also refrained from recommending a transitional arrangement: "A transitory expedient has also been thought of, which would consist of leaving matters as they are for a number of years, five or less, at the end of which a plebiscite should take place. This arrangement, in the opinion of its sponsors, would have the advantage of ending the state of tension which exists at present and giving time for matters to calm down and for the inhabitants to reflect more dispassionately over the guarantees which union with Finland would offer for the preservation of their Swedish individuality."[20] Instead, the Commission of Rapporteurs, and apparently also the Finnish Government, preferred a comprehensive and immediate solution[21] based on the conditional maintenance of the sovereignty of Finland.

The solution recommended by the Commission of Rapporteurs involved the Self-Government Act of 1920, which the Finnish Parliament had enacted in order to defuse the tension surrounding the Åland Islands question. The Commission was evidently relatively satisfied with the Self-Government Act itself, but recommended certain additions aimed at the preservation of the Swedish language as the language of schools on the Åland Islands. Moreover, the maintenance of real property in the hands of the natives was recommended, and in the area of politics, measures against the premature exercise of the franchise by new inhabitants. The Commission also suggested conditions for the nomination of a Governor of the Åland Islands to ensure the appointee had the confidence of the population.[22] If Finland acted against the expectations of the Commission and refused to grant the guarantees recommended, it proposed an outcome it clearly considered undesirable: "The interest of the Aalanders, the interests of a durable peace in the Baltic, would then force us to advise the separation of the islands from Finland, based on the wishes of the inhabitants which would be freely expressed by means of a plebiscite."[23] This reference to the referendum appears despite the Commission's earlier statement that it would not be an appropriate mechanism of decision-making in this particular context.

[20]Ibid., p. 32.

[21]In the case of Kosovo, a different strategy was adopted. According to UN Security Council Resolution 1244/99, an international administration and substantial autonomy and self-government were instituted, with a view to reaching a final settlement of the issue in the future. The current UNMIK-led administration of Kosovo can therefore be viewed as the kind of transitory arrangement the League of Nations wished to avoid in the Åland Islands case. For a comparison between the international decisions concerning the Åland Islands and Kosovo, see Suksi (2002a). See also Suksi (2005c).

[22]The Aaland Islands Question (1921), note 26, p. 32.

[23]Ibid., p 34.

The Council of the League of Nations took up the matter in 1920 and concluded in its decision of 24 June 1921, against the background of the Report of a Committee of Jurists[24] and the Memorandum of a Commission of Rapporteurs,[25] which both investigated different aspects of the question, that sovereignty over the Åland Islands belonged to Finland, but under certain conditions that related to the interests of the world, future cordial relations between Finland and Sweden and the prosperity and happiness of the Åland Islands themselves. At this point, the Council of the League of Nations established two different strands to achieve these aims: (1) that certain further guarantees should be given for the protection of the Islanders, and (2) that arrangements should be concluded for the non-fortification and neutralization of the Archipelago.[26]

As concerns the second strand, the treaty arrangement concerning the non-fortification and neutralization of the Åland Islands led in October 1921 to the adoption of the Convention on the Non-Fortification and Neutralization of the Åland Islands. In Art. 9 of the Convention, the parties to the convention, including Sweden, recognized that the Åland Islands constituted an integral part of the Republic of Finland. However, it should be noticed that this Convention does not deal with the autonomy arrangement and the internal constitutional structures concerning the Åland Islands, but is limited to international security policy.

[24]The Aaland Islands Question (1920).

[25]The Aaland Islands Question (1921).

[26]The Åland Islands Agreement before the Council of the League of Nations, V. Minutes of the Seventeenth Meeting of the Council, June 27th, 1921. League of Nations Official Journal, September 1921, at 701. In para. 5 of the decision of 24 June 1921, the Council of the League of Nations established the following: "5. An international agreement in respect of the non-fortification and the neutralisation of the Archipelago should guarantee to the Swedish people and to all the countries concerned, that the Aaland Islands will never become a source of danger from the military point of view. With this object, the convention of 1856 should be replaced by a broader agreement, placed under the guarantee of all the Powers concerned, including Sweden. The Council is of the opinion that this agreement should conform, in its main lines, with the Swedish draft Convention for the neutralisation of the Islands. The Council instructs the Secretary-General to ask the governments concerned to appoint duly accredited representatives to discuss and conclude the proposed Treaty." Hence it was the security of the State of Sweden that motivated a specific Convention. Some opinions have been presented that the Åland Islands Settlement and the Åland Islands Convention constituted a package, but at least for the Commission of Rapporteurs, it was clear that issues of autonomy and security should be kept separate, concluding in their report that "[w]e are also of the opinion that the establishment of the political status of Aaland should precede the establishment of its international status. But these are, in our opinion, two different and separate questions. [. . .] The question of sovereignty does not need to be intermingled with that of disarmament and neutralisation. It will be solved immediately if our conclusions are agreed upon, by the maintenance of the existing status quo, in consideration of the addition of special guarantees granted to the population of Aaland. The suggested international Convention should, in our opinion, have as its sole object that of replacing and completing the Convention of Paris." See The Aaland Islands Question (1921), p. 36 f.

As concerns the first strand of the decision of the Council of the League of Nations on 24 June 1921, the Council of the League of Nations established two different guarantee mechanisms:

> 3. The new guarantees to be inserted in the autonomy law should specially aim at the preservation of the Swedish language in the schools, at the maintenance of the landed property in the hands of the Islanders, at the restriction, within reasonable limits, of the exercise of the franchise by new comers, and at ensuring the appointment of a Governor who will possess the confidence of the population.
>
> 4. The Council has requested that the guarantees will be more likely to achieve their purpose, if they are discussed and agreed to by the Representatives of Finland with those of Sweden, if necessary with the assistance of the Council of the League of Nations, and, in accordance with the Council's desire, the two parties have decided to seek out an agreement. Should their efforts fail, the Council would itself fix the guarantees which, in its opinion, should be inserted, by means of an amendment, in the autonomy law of May, 7th, 1920. In any case, the Council of the League of Nations will see to the enforcement of these guarantees.

As is clear on the basis of para. 3 of the Settlement, the Council of the League of Nations was well aware of the existence of an autonomy act, that is, of the 1920 Self-Government Act. Apparently, the arguments of Sweden and of the representatives of the inhabitants of the Åland Islands had made an impression on the Council, because some specific protection mechanisms that Finland would, after more concrete definition of the contents of these protection mechanisms, insert in the Self-Government Act included provisions concerning Swedish as the language of education, the maintenance of real property in the hands of the inhabitants of the Åland Islands, restriction of the right to vote of new inhabitants in the area and the position of the representatives of central government. The discussion concerning these principles between the representatives of Finland and Sweden and the agreement thereupon took place during the days immediately after 24 June 1921 so that the Council of the League of Nations could, on 27 June 1921, register the more concrete guarantees in a separate text which was appended to the decision of 24 June 1921. This Åland Islands Settlement did not become a formal treaty between Finland and Sweden, but the Settlement approved under the auspices of the League of Nations nonetheless resolved the contentious issue. The legal nature of the Settlement under public international law has given rise to a certain discussion about whether the Settlement is a treaty or not, and it seems clear that the latter opinion is now commonly followed, although the Settlement is today understood by Finland as a binding international obligation in the form of customary international law.[27]

In the Åland Islands Settlement, Finland undertook to guarantee, without undue delay, to the population of the Åland Islands the maintenance of its language, culture and local Swedish traditions through incorporation of guarantees for these matters in the Self-Government Act. What is special in this context from the point of view of international politics and public international law is that the Council of the League of Nations referred to autonomy and used the concept of autonomy

[27] See Hannikainen (2004), pp. 19–21, 33–41, 47–52.

when it made reference to the 1920 "Law of Autonomy of the Aaland Islands".[28] Thus there existed a more or less established concept of autonomy under public international law and in connection to the Åland Islands by the time the status of the Memel Territory had to be decided in 1924.[29]

The specific obligations undertaken by Finland were formulated before the Council of the League of Nations as follows:

> 1. Finland, resolved to assure and to guarantee to the population of the Aaland Islands the preservation of their language, of their culture, and of their local Swedish traditions, undertakes to introduce shortly into the Law of Autonomy of the Aaland Islands of May 7th, 1920, the following guarantees:
>
> 2. The Landsting and the Communes of Aaland Islands shall not in any case be obliged to support or to subsidize any other schools than those in which the language of instruction is Swedish. In the scholastic establishments of the State, instruction shall also be given in the Swedish language. The Finnish language may not be taught in the primary schools, supported or subsidized by the State or by the commune, without the consent of the interested commune.
>
> 3. When landed estate situated in the Aaland Islands is sold to a person who is not domiciled in the Islands, any person legally domiciled in the Islands, or the Council of the province, or the commune in which the estate is situated, has the right to buy the estate at a price which, failing agreement, shall be fixed by the court of first instance (Häradsrätt) having regard to current prices.
>
> Detailed regulations will be drawn up in a special law concerning that act of purchase, and the priority to be observed between several offers.
>
> This law may not be modified, interpreted, or repealed except under the same conditions as the Law of Autonomy.
>
> 4. Immigrants into the Aaland archipelago who enjoy rights of citizenship in Finland shall only acquire the communal and provincial franchise in the Islands after five years of legal domicile. Persons who have been five years legally domiciled in the Islands shall not be considered as immigrants.
>
> 5. The Governor of the Aaland Islands shall be nominated by the President of the Finnish Republic in agreement with the president of the Landsting of the Aaland Islands. If an agreement cannot be reached, the President of the Republic shall choose the Governor from a list of five candidates nominated by the Landsting, possessing the qualifications necessary for the good administration of the Islands and the security of the State.
>
> 6. The Aaland Islands shall have the right to use for their needs 50% of the revenue of the land tax, besides the revenues mentioned in Article 21 of the Law of Autonomy.
>
> 7. The Council of the League of Nations shall watch over the application of these guarantees. Finland shall forward to the Council of the League of Nations, with its observations, any petitions or claims of the Landsting of Aaland in connection with the application of the guarantees in question, and the Council shall, in any case where the question is of a juridical character, consult the Permanent Court of International Justice.

---

[28] References to the concept of autonomy had been included already in the 1919 Treaty of Versailles and in a number of other treaties adopted after the First World War. Hence at the level of public international law, there seemed to exist a legal understanding concerning particular jurisdictions created often for the protection of minority populations defined on the basis of ethnic, linguistic or religious characteristics.

[29] See also Suksi (2011).

The Åland Islands Settlement agreed upon by Finland and Sweden before the Council of the League of Nations gave the special rights granted under this autonomy arrangement a collective character, because the focal point of the special rights was the inhabitants of the Åland Islands.

4.2.3 Domestic Implementation by a Special Act

These guarantees and rights for the inhabitants of the Åland Islands were registered in a separate Act containing Special Provisions concerning the Population of the Åland Islands (SoF 189/1922), or the so-called Guaranty Act. The Parliament of Finland did not formally speaking amend the 1920 Self-Government Act, but enacted instead a separate piece of law as a complement to the Act of 1920. The Guaranty Act was enacted in the same order as the Self-Government Act, that is, in the constitutional order with the same special and regional entrenchment stipulations as the Act of 1920. From that perspective, it is possible to say that the Guaranty Act was vested with the same elevated constitutional status as the first Self-Government Act. However, the particular legislation concerning the sale of real property in the Åland Islands, mentioned in sub-section 2 of para. 2 of the Settlement, was enacted by the Parliament of Finland only in 1938 as the Act on the Exercise of the Right of Redemption at Sale of Real Property in the Åland Islands (SoF 140/1938),[30] which means that the particular protection mechanism regarding real property was inoperative during the first 15 years of the autonomy of Åland. It is possible to say against this background that immediately after the entering into force of the 1919 Form of Government (Constitution) Act, the formula of "one state" as well as the newly gained sovereignty of Finland were challenged and that Finland had to agree to and implement special measures in order to protect its territorial integrity.

In terms of the legislative strategy chosen to incorporate the Åland Islands Settlement in the legal order of Finland, it is possible to say that it was not incorporated in the normal way as a treaty under international law. The reason for this is that the Åland Islands Settlement is not a treaty under international law and thus there was no treaty to be incorporated under those constitutional provisions that existed in 1921–1922. Instead, the Settlement was brought into force domestically through another procedure, namely transcription (or, in other words, reception). In this context of the Åland Islands Settlement, this method of incorporation means that the text of the Settlement, which was originally drafted in French and English, was translated in Finland *expressis verbis* into Swedish and Finnish (with the exception that the order of the paragraphs of the Guaranty Act is different from

[30] This Act was replaced in 1951 by an Act with the same title (SoF 671/1951), and the current law is based on the Act on the Limitation of the Right to Acquire and Possess Real Property in the Åland Islands, also entitled the Act on the Acquisition of Real Property on the Åland Islands (SoF 7/1975).

the order of the paragraphs in the Settlement). After the translation was completed, the Government of Finland submitted the text to the Parliament of Finland in the form of a Bill, which was enacted in the Parliament pursuant to the requirements of a qualified majority and in the fast track order of constitutional amendments.[31] The 1951 Self-Government Act incorporated the provisions of the Guaranty Act with some modifications, which means that the method of incorporation actually shifted over from transcription to transformation, and this latter method is also the one that applies to the incorporation of the Settlement in the 1991 Self-Government Act.[32]

On the basis of para. 7 of the Åland Islands Settlement, section 6 of the 1922 Guaranty Act contained provisions for a situation where the Legislative Assembly of the Åland Islands might present complaints or notes about the implementation of the Self-Government Act and Guaranty Act. In such a situation, the Government of Finland would add its own observations to the complaint or note and pass on the issue to the Council of the League of Nations so that the Council could supervise the implementation of the provisions and, in case the matter is of a judicial nature, obtain an opinion from the PCIJ.[33] This procedure became a *desuetudo* when the League of Nations system collapsed as a consequence of the Second World War and the United Nations declared its unwillingness to take over the supervisory function of the League of Nations. The domestic provisions concerning the complaints mechanism were eliminated from Finnish legislation only in 1951, when the second Self-Government Act repealed the Acts of 1920 and 1922.[34] However, despite the disappearance of the mechanism of supervision, the autonomy arrangement itself has been regarded as one of customary law under public international law, still binding on Finland.[35] There has been some discussion

[31]In the third reading on 9 December 1921, the matter was declared urgent by the votes 153 to 23 (meaning that the Bill was not left in abeyance over the next elections for a final consideration by the subsequent Parliament), after which the law was enacted on the same day by the votes 152 to 22.

[32]See Suksi (2008c), pp. 277–279.

[33]The complaint mechanism was never used.

[34]There were plans, recorded in committee proceedings and in a Government Proposal to the Parliament in 1946, to establish a similar procedure under the United Nations. However, under the post-Second World War circumstances, the negative opinions of the Soviet Union concerning such international supervision were also of great relevance. On this, see Modeen (1973), pp. 61–76; Hannikainen (1993a), pp. 41–48.

[35]See Hannikainen (1993a), pp. 79–102. As concerns the unilingually Swedish-speaking school system in the Åland Islands and its relationship to the Finnish-speaking minority there, the *Belgian Linguistics* case of the European Court of Human Rights (Judgment of 23 July 1968, Ser. A, No. 6) seems to indicate that there is no such discrimination against Finnish-speaking pupils in the Åland Islands that would be prohibited under the ECHR: there would seem to exist "legitimate and objective grounds to keep the schools of the Åland Islands monolingually Swedish" at the same time as the present system would not seem to "involve disproportionality between the means employed and the aim sought". The demilitarization and neutralization of the Åland Islands may perhaps be regarded as a so-called objective regime under international law. See also Hannikainen (1993a), pp. 103–130.

concerning the relationship between the arrangement for the Åland Islands and the various human rights conventions binding on Finland. It has been suggested that the 1921 decision by the League of Nations could be considered as a *lex specialis*, but it would seem as if most legal experts gave precedence to Finland's obligations under human rights conventions according to the principle of *lex posterior*.[36]

In 1951, the second Self-Government Act (SoF 670/1951) was enacted by the Parliament of Finland and, in the same form, by the Legislative Assembly of the Åland Islands, following the requirements of a qualified majority. At this juncture, two additions were made to the special rights granted to the Åland Islanders. Firstly, a particular regional citizenship was created as a statutory definition of who was and who was not an inhabitant of the Åland Islands and thereby entitled to a certain legal position which was different from that of other Finnish citizens. Secondly, the general freedom to carry out business operations was made, in the territory of the Åland Islands, dependent on the possession of the regional citizenship. The specific *right of domicile* defined the group of persons who were to be considered beneficiaries of the special features of autonomy, that is, the right to vote and stand as candidate in municipal and provincial elections, acquisition and possession of real estate,[37] the right to carry out so-called regulated branches of trade,[38] and exemption from military service. The definition of the right of domicile created at this point a distinction between the inhabitants of the Åland Islands and those of mainland Finland that was more protective of the former than under the previous legislation, while the definition may have had a discouraging effect on persons from the mainland as concerns their intention to move to the Åland Islands. The special rights connected to the right of domicile do, however, not directly constitute a barrier to the exercise of freedom of movement.

The 1951 autonomy legislation made the contours of autonomy more specific and provided more detailed regulations concerning the powers and functioning of autonomy. At this point, an enumerated list replaced the more general clause in defining the competences of the Legislative Assembly. Within the framework of the legislative powers, the boundaries of the law-making capacity of the Legislative Assembly could be efficiently supervised by the President of the Republic, who could veto an act of Åland upon receiving an opinion from the Supreme Court.[39] However, the authorities of the Åland Islands received no corresponding remedy for situations in which the legislature of the Republic of Finland interfered with the

[36]On the discussion, see Hannikainen (1993b), p. 53 f.

[37]A special Act on the Purchase of Real Estate (SoF 3/1975) was enacted for the first time in 1938 (SoF 140/1938) and amended in 1951 (SoF 671/1951).

[38]However, the right of trade was not exclusively reserved for those who had the right of domicile, but regulated trades could also be carried out by persons who had had uninterrupted legal residence in the Åland Islands for 5 years.

[39]When an act of Åland is presented for the President, it is always accompanied by an opinion of the Åland Delegation.

legislative powers of the Legislative Assembly.[40] This asymmetry is one element that could distinguish the Åland Islands arrangement in Finland from a federal arrangement. As concerns the administrative tasks and possible conflicts between the administrative authorities of the state and the Åland Islands in respect of these, the Supreme Court was given the competence to rule on them upon an opinion of the Åland Delegation (Sect. 5.3.4).

The current Self-Government Act was enacted in 1991. The 1991 Act strengthened the self-government of the Åland Islands and restricted the state's supervision. This was carried out especially by expanding the legislative competences of the Åland Islands (e.g., rules concerning use of the flag of the Åland Islands, leasing, historical sites, social care, sub-soil resources (in respect of which there is "adjacent" competence with the state), the sale of alcoholic beverages, archives, postal affairs, radio and telecommunications) as well as giving the Åland Islands more administrative powers. A more detailed regulation concerning the language of instruction was included in the Act to provide more protection for the cultural identity of the inhabitants of the Åland Islands. Moreover, the acquisition of a certain proficiency in the Swedish language as a condition for the right of domicile was added to the Act. The special rights tied to the possession of the right of domicile were kept more or less in the same form as in the 1951 Self-Government Act, with the exception that the right of a person without the right of domicile to exercise a trade or profession in Åland for personal gain may be limited by an act of Åland.[41]

These substantive developments of the autonomy arrangement were included in 1991 in the current Self-Government Act which was enacted in the same manner as its predecessors.[42] When doing so, Parliament decided explicitly not to qualify the Self-Government Act as a constitutional act, because it contained very detailed provisions of a special kind which were not deemed to be suitable for introduction into a constitutional act.[43] Instead, the Self-Government Act can be viewed as a particular act (somewhat akin to a so-called act of exception) that distributes legislative powers between mainland Finland and the Åland Islands and creates a special and a regional entrenchment of some sort for the arrangement: the Self-Government Act is peculiar in the sense that it can only be repealed or amended by Parliament by use of the procedure prescribed for constitutional amendments, provided that the Legislative Assembly of the Åland Islands makes a similar decision by a qualified

[40]On this, see Jyränki (1995), pp. 13–15. It should be noted that there is only a limited judicial review *post legem* in Finland on the basis of section 106 of the Constitution.

[41]However, under section 11 of the 1991 Self-Government Act, such an act of Åland may not be used to limit the right of trade of a person residing in Åland, if no person other than a spouse and minor children are employed in the trade and if the trade is not practiced in business premises, an office or any other special place of business. Hence a non-Ålander has the right to trade, but limitations to that right may be enacted in an act of Åland.

[42]The preamble to the 1991 Self-Government Act notes that the Act has been enacted in the manner prescribed by section 67 of the Parliament (Constitution) Act and with the consent of the Legislative Assembly of the Åland Islands.

[43]See Palmgren (1997), p. 86.

majority of two thirds. As concerns Ålandic consent to amendments to the Self-Government Act, section 69 of this Act requires materially identical decisions of the Finnish Parliament and the Legislative Assembly, so that the decision is made in Åland by a two-thirds qualified majority. The Property Acquisition Act does not, in the first place, according to section 17, require any super-majority in the Legislative Assembly, but leaves this particular entrenchment and the raising of the decision-making threshold to the two-thirds level to be determined in an act of Åland (which itself must be enacted in that manner). The Act of Åland on the Right to Acquire Real Property and on Permits to Acquire Real Property (Statutes of the Åland Islands, SoÅ 68/2003) was subsequently enacted by a qualified majority of two thirds.

Section 1 of the 1991 Self-Government Act recognizes that the Åland Islands are self-governing, that is, autonomous, in the manner established in the Act. Therefore, the current Self-Government Act is still to be viewed as an implementing act in relation to the 1921 Åland Islands Settlement, which is recognized by Finland as an effective international obligation. Thereby, an international entrenchment of the self-government arrangement of the Åland Islands is created. The Property Acquisition Act (SoF 3/1975) for the Åland Islands, enacted by the Finnish Parliament by a two-thirds qualified majority pursuant to the constitutional amendment formula but without declaring itself a constitutional act, is also a part of the implementation of the Settlement.[44] In respect of property and the right to carry out business operations in the Åland Islands, there is something close to an unamendable core of the Constitution: section 28 of the Self-Government Act lays down that the amendment of the Constitution or another act shall not enter into force in the Åland Islands without the consent of the Legislative Assembly of the Åland Islands insofar as it relates to the principles governing the right of a private person to own real property or business property in the Åland Islands. This means that the Parliament of Finland cannot, by amendments to the Constitution, try to diminish the particular property rights in the Åland Islands if the Legislative Assembly of the Åland Islands is opposed to such a measure. This particular material entrenchment is an extra safeguard, but it has never been needed.

4.2.4 Recognition in the Constitution

Only in 1994 were the Form of Government (Constitution) Act of Finland and the Parliament (Constitution) Act amended so as to make explicit the position of the Åland Islands in the constitutional setting by means of a so-called general entrenchment. Over a period of more than 70 years, it was not possible to discern from the

[44]The important change that took place in 1975 was that under the previous law, anybody could buy real estate on the Åland Islands, but faced, in the absence of the right of domicile, the risk of the property being redeemed. However, under the 1975 Act, an advance permit by the Government of the Åland Islands is required of persons who are not in the possession of the right of domicile before they can purchase the property.

formal constitutional texts that there existed, in Finland, a distribution of legislative powers between the Parliament of Finland and the Legislative Assembly of the Åland Islands. The constitutional definition of the Åland Islands was carried over to sections 75 and 120 of the Constitution of Finland which entered into force in the year 2000. Section 120 of the Constitution recognizes the special status of the Åland Islands by providing that "[t]he Åland Islands have self-government in accordance with what is specifically stipulated in the Act on the Self-Government of the Åland Islands". This creates the general constitutional recognition of the autonomy arrangement and thus also a general entrenchment of that arrangement.

In contrast, section 75(1) of the Constitution on special legislation for the Åland Islands establishes that amendments to the Self-Government Act and the Act on the Right to Acquire Real Estate in the Åland Islands are governed by specific provisions in those acts. This means that the amendment formulas of those acts, establishing the special entrenchment and the regional entrenchment, is returned back to those particular acts from the regular constitutional amendment procedure established in section 73 of the Constitution. Section 75(2) of the Constitution actually contains a recognition of the fact that two legislatures exist in Finland, the Parliament of Finland on the one hand, and the Legislative Assembly of the Åland Islands on the other, because the section lays down that the enactment of acts passed by the Legislative Assembly of the Åland Islands is governed by the provisions of the Self-Government Act. In addition, the provision indicates that the Legislative Assembly of the Åland Islands has a right to submit proposals. It is not clear on the basis of the constitutional provision where such proposals would be placed and what they should concern, but section 22(1) of the Self-Government Act specifies this by saying that the Legislative Assembly may submit initiatives in matters that belong to the legislative competence of the Parliament of Finland and that such initiatives are submitted through the Government of Finland.

In addition, there is a normative level of constitutional law in the internal legal order of the Åland Islands. Originally, the Legislative Assembly itself decided to adopt legislation under the requirement of a qualified majority of two thirds. The Supreme Court of Finland has also, as the oversight body concerning the use of legislative competence in the Åland Islands (but not in mainland Finland), recognized that the Legislative Assembly of the Åland Islands is within its competence if it decides to create acts of Åland under the requirement of a two-thirds qualified majority.[45] Such a recognition was introduced in section 55 of the Act of Åland on the Legislative Assembly (SoÅ 11/1972), according to which it is possible to establish in an act of Åland that a decision about enactment of an act of Åland shall be made by a qualified majority of two thirds of the votes cast in the Legislative Assembly, and an act of Åland containing such a provision shall be enacted in the same order. It is therefore clear that even within the jurisdiction of

[45]See Opinion of the Supreme Court of 20 November 1971, in which the creation of a requirement of a qualified majority for the amendment of acts of Åland was deemed to be in harmony with the legislation concerning self-government. See also Suksi (2005d), pp. 473–479.

Åland, there can be a hierarchy of norms which recognizes a separation between ordinary acts of Åland and acts of Åland of a constitutional nature. The acts of Åland that have been enacted pursuant to this constitutional procedure are the Act of Åland on the Legislative Assembly, the Act of Åland on the Government of the Åland Islands (SoÅ 42/1971), the Act of Åland on the Right to Acquire Real Property and on Permits to Acquire Real Property (SoÅ 68/2003) and the Act of Åland on Certain Fundamentals about the Economy of the Åland Islands (SoÅ 22/1983).

Section 55(1) of the Act of Åland on the Legislative Assembly sets up the general procedure of enactment of constitutional legislation of an internal nature, while section 74(4) of the same Act provides that the Act itself cannot be amended or revoked except by way of the procedure prescribed in section 55 of the Act. Section 67(2) of the Self-Government Act requires separately that the act of Åland that regulates the right to vote of Finnish citizens who lack the right of domicile (regional citizenship) and citizens of Nordic countries and other countries shall be enacted by a qualified majority of two thirds. As a consequence, there is the Act of Åland on the Right to Vote and Eligibility in Municipal Elections for Persons who Lack the Right of Domicile (SoÅ 63/1997). The reason for such a heightened requirement for adoption is probably the fact that the right to participation is a central element of the Åland Islands Settlement. Unlike the ordinary procedure of constitutional amendment in the Parliament of Finland, the procedure in the Åland Islands for creating or amending constitutional legislation of an internal nature does not require an intervening election so that one Legislative Assembly would make the material decision and another one, convening after the next elections, would make the final decision with a qualified majority.

4.2.5 *Involving the Åland Islands in the European Union*

When the accession of Finland to the European Union was prepared and negotiated, Finland recalled that the autonomy of the Åland Islands was constitutionally guaranteed on the basis of the internationally recognized status of the Islands and requested that special measures would be taken so that the autonomy arrangement would not be adversely affected. Consequently, Finland proposed that derogations be inserted into the Treaties on which the European Union is founded by way of special provisions in Articles 227 EC, 79 ECSC, and 198 EAEC through a special Protocol.[46] Without such an arrangement, the assent of the Legislative Assembly of

[46]Firstly, the Åland Islands would, according to the Government proposal to the negotiations, have to be allowed to maintain its legislative powers over the conditions regulating the rights to vote and to stand as a candidate in elections to the Legislative Assembly and to municipal councils, a legislative power that was, under the 1991 Self-Government Act, limited to those enjoying the right of domicile in the islands. According to the Finnish Government, the conditions for obtaining voting rights would not discriminate between Finnish citizens of mainland Finland and citizens of other Member States. Secondly, the right to acquire and hold property, the right of establishment,

the Åland Islands could not be taken for granted, with the risk that the Åland Islands remain outside the European Union altogether.

Of these requests by the Government, Protocol No. 2 on the Åland Islands, attached to the Treaty of Accession of, *inter alia*, Finland to the European Union granted some[47] and denied some others.[48] In granting the exceptions, the European Union took into account the special status that the Åland Islands enjoyed under international law,[49] but only as of 1 January 1994.[50] As a consequence, the final arrangement in respect of the European Union contains an addition to Article 227 EC (and the corresponding Articles 79 ECSC and 198 EAEC) as *littera* d), according to which the Treaty shall not apply to the Åland Islands unless the Government of Finland gives notice by a declaration when ratifying the Treaty that the Treaty shall apply to the Åland Islands in accordance with the provisions set out in Protocol No. 2 to the Treaty concerning the accession of new Member States. This declaration was deposited with the Government of Italy on 9 December 1994, whereupon the Åland Islands' entry into the European Union became effective together with that of Finland on 1 January 1995, albeit with the special conditions referred to above.

---

and the right to provide services would be restricted to natural or legal persons enjoying the right of domicile in the Åland Islands or to those authorized by the competent authorities of the Islands. Thirdly, the Government of Finland requested a permanent exemption from Community tax harmonization legislation for the Islands and the ferry traffic passing through them. Fourthly, a Protocol should include provisions that protect the rights of the inhabitants of the Åland Islands in Finland and that require the authorities of the Åland Islands to treat citizens from all Member States equally. On the accession negotiations, see Fagerlund (1997).

[47]The second and third requests of the Government of Finland were granted (the third request was accepted with a view to maintaining a viable local economy in the Islands) and the latter part of the fourth one, too, thus creating an option for a more or less permanent exception on part of the Åland Islands to the Treaties on which the European Union is founded. In the fields of harmonization of the law of the Member States on turnover taxes and on excise duties and other forms of indirect taxation the exemption may be less permanent, depending on the exemptions not having any negative effects on the interests of the Union nor on its common policies. Protocol No. 2 on the Åland Islands, Art. 2(b). See Fagerlund (1997).

[48]The first request and the first part of the fourth request were not granted. However, in Declaration No. 32 on the Åland Islands of the Final Act on the Accession by the current Member States, the Union recalls in respect of the municipal suffrage and eligibility that Article 8b TEU (since 1 December 2009, Art. 20(2-b) and Art. 22(1) of the Treaty on the Functioning of the European Union (TFEU) and Art. 40 of the Charter of Fundamental Rights of the EU) makes it possible to agree with the requests presented by Finland. According to the Declaration, if Finland declares, according to Article 227(5) ECT (after 1 December 2009, Art. 355(4) of the TFEU), that the Treaty will be applied in the Åland Islands, the Council will, within six months and according to procedures laid down in Article 8b TEU, establish the conditions on which this Article shall be applied to the special circumstances of the Åland Islands. See Fagerlund (1997).

[49]Conference on Accession to the European Union/Finland. Subject: Chapter 29: Other – Union common position on Finland's request concerning the status of the Åland Islands. Agreed by the Council at its meeting on 21 February 1994 (CONF-SF 20/94).

[50]This so-called stand-still clause means that in the area of EU law, no new exceptions may be introduced after 1 April 1994.

The effect of the special arrangement in respect of the Åland Islands is the special tax regime in relation to mainland Finland and the European Union, making the Islands comparable to a third country concerning the indirect taxes included in the arrangement and drawing a certain tax boundary between the Åland Islands and mainland Finland. The exceptions in Protocol 2 in regard of the special rights of the inhabitants of the Åland Islands affect areas which in practice are minor from the perspective of the legislative powers of the Åland Islands. After 1 December 2009, the relationship between the Åland Islands and the European Union is, in addition to the Accession Treaty and Protocol 2, regulated under Art. 355(4) of the Treaty on the Functioning of the European Union (TFEU), which states that "[t]he provisions of the Treaties shall apply to the Åland Islands in accordance with the provisions set out in Protocol 2 to the Act concerning the conditions of accession of the Republic of Austria, the Republic of Finland and the Kingdom of Sweden".

At the end of 1994, the Self-Government Act was amended (SoF 1556/1994) so as to include a new chapter on issues that concern the European Union. According to section 59a, the Government of the Åland Islands shall be informed about issues that belong to the exclusive competence of the Åland Islands that are being prepared within the Union[51] and shall be provided the opportunity to participate in the sessions of the Finnish Council of State when such issues are dealt with. Moreover, according to section 59b, in issues falling under the competence of the Åland Islands, the Government of the Åland Islands shall formulate the Finnish position in respect of the application of the common EU policies on the Åland Islands.[52] Finally, on the basis of section 59c, a candidate selected by the Government of the Åland Islands shall be proposed as one of the Finnish representatives to the Committee of Regions of the EU. Due to the amendments in 2009 to the Treaty on the European Union that created the so-called subsidiarity control according to Art. 6(1) of the Protocol on the Application of the Principles of Subsidiarity and Proportionality,[53] the Rules of Procedure of the Parliament of Finland (SoF 40/1999) were amended so as to require

[51] The Ministry of Foreign Affairs should see to that all proposals by the European Commission concerning new legislative acts are forwarded to the Provincial Government at the same time as the specialized ministries shall, within their field of competence, inform the Provincial Government about matters that they are dealing with. See Government Bill 307/1994 concerning the Position of the Åland Islands in case of a Finnish Membership in the European Union, p. 10.

[52] See Government Bill 307/1994 concerning the Position of the Åland Islands in case of a Finnish Membership in the European Union, p. 11. In such cases, the position of the Åland Islands would be appended to the position of Finland so that the opinion of the Legislative Assembly would become known by the European institutions.

[53] "Any national Parliament or any chamber of a national Parliament may, within eight weeks from the date of transmission of a draft legislative act, in the official languages of the Union, send to the Presidents of the European Parliament, the Council and the Commission a reasoned opinion stating why it considers that the draft in question does not comply with the principle of subsidiarity." From the point of view of sub-state governance, the protocol notes the existence of that level of governance, because the second sentence of the provision continues as follows: "It will be for each national Parliament or each chamber of a national Parliament to consult, where appropriate, regional parliaments with legislative powers."

the Grand Committee of the Parliament, when functioning as the integration committee, to forward information about proposals concerning legal acts of the EU further to the Legislative Assembly of the Åland Islands. The mechanism makes possible for the Legislative Assembly to submit its views on how proposals at EU level relate to the principle of subsidiarity in Art. 5 of the TEU.[54]

4.2.6 *Regional Citizenship and Special Rights*

The 1991 Self-Government Act spells out the details of the autonomy of Åland and creates, in line with its predecessor of 1951, an exclusive characteristic in respect of citizenship: only citizens of Finland may have the right of domicile in Åland.[55] The arrangement amounts to a special regional citizenship, which is possessed, by virtue of section 6 of the Self-Government Act, by a person who at the time of the entry into force of the Act had the right of domicile according to the 1951 Self-Government Act and by a child who is under 18 years of age, is a citizen of Finland and is resident in the Åland Islands, provided that the father or the mother of the child has the right of domicile. The regional citizenship thus follows the principle of *jus sanguinis*. However, according to section 7 of the Self-Government Act, the right of domicile is, in general, granted upon application, to a citizen of Finland who has moved to the Åland Islands, and who has, without interruption, been habitually resident in the Åland Islands for at least five years[56] and who is satisfactorily

[54]See also Government Bill 77/2010 with a proposal to amend section 59a of the Self-Government Act so as to establish a mechanism through which the Legislative Assembly can participate in the so-called subsidiarity control in the EU that the national parliaments are involved in concerning proposals to enact new EU legal acts. The Parliament of Finland has already adopted the amendment proposal once, but as required by the ordinary process of constitutional amendments, the decision was left in abeyance over the next elections, after which the matter will be taken up by the next Parliament.

[55]Based on Rosas and Suksi (1996).

[56]See SAC 1991-II-3, in which the Supreme Administrative Court of Finland (SAC) concluded that the fact that the person applying for the right of domicile had moved from the Åland Islands while his application was pending was not a reason which could be used to deny his application. See also SAC 2002:92, which dealt with a family in which the husband owned a house in Mariehamn in the Åland Islands. Mariehamn was thus their place of domicile. He worked as a medical doctor at the central hospital of the Åland Islands and carried out specialization studies at the University Hospital of Turku in mainland Finland with the aim to function as a specialist at the central hospital of the Åland Islands. His wife was since 1997 employed on a regular basis by the City of Mariehamn as a teacher of Finnish. The specialization studies of the man required that he spent extended periods of time in Turku, and his wife spent longer periods of time in Turku while she was on maternity leave. The apartment in Turku was very small, 30 square meters, intended mainly for overnight stay. The Government of the Åland Islands denied the spouses' application of the right of domicile on the grounds that they had not had their actual place of domicile in the Åland Islands without interruption during five years. The spouses applied the decision at the SAC.

proficient in Swedish.[57] Under EU law, the term *regional citizenship* is, since 1 January 1995, equivalent to the right of domicile (in the Swedish language *hembygdsrätt* and in the Finnish language *kotiseutuoikeus*) on the basis of Art. 1 of Protocol 2 on the Åland Islands of the Act concerning the Conditions of Accession and the Adjustment to the Treaties on which the Union is Founded, attached to the 1994 Treaty of Accession, *inter alia*, of Finland to the European Union.[58] As provided for in section 30 of the Self-Government Act, the word "Åland" shall be incorporated in a passport issued in the Åland Islands, if the holder of the passport has the right of domicile. Therefore, the cover of the passport contains, in addition to the reference to "Suomi – Finland", the word "Åland" as well.

The rules concerning the acquisition of the right of domicile in the Åland Islands may thus be viewed as exclusive in relation to citizens of other countries[59] and

The SAC was of the same opinion that section 7(2) of the Self-Government Act is not clear in how it should be interpreted. The SAC inquired into the *travaux preparatoires* of the 1991 Self-Government Act and found that there is a connection to section 3 of the 1951 Self-Government Act. With reference to the time the spouses lived in Turku and the provisions in section 6(2) about how children acquire the right of domicile and section 8(2) about the loss of the right of domicile on other grounds than temporary relocation from the Åland Islands, the majority opinion of the SAC held that the decision of the Government of the Åland Islands was not against the law and denied the appeal. The SAC was of the opinion that the spouses had not had their actual place of domicile in the Åland Islands at least during five years in the manner to be expected under section 7 (2) of the Self-Government Act. Most applications of the right of domicile are, however, granted by the Government of the Åland Islands, and the applications denied constitute normally between 1 and 10% of all applications. See Suksi (2005d), pp. 39. See also Sjölund (2009), pp. 67, 68–89, who points at unclear practices in the decision-making of the Government of the Åland Islands, indicating that the decision-making concerning the right of domicile may at times be based on arbitrary considerations not established in the law. The analysis of Sjölund also accounts for a number of court cases related to the right of domicile. See also Myntti and Scheinin (1997).

[57]On the situation in respect of the language requirement on the basis of the 1951 Self-Government Act, which did not contain such a requirement, see the so-called *Oinas* case, SAC 1979-I-4. In the case, the Government of the Åland Islands had denied an application of the right of domicile by a Finnish citizen on grounds that his knowledge of the Swedish language was deficient. Because the denial violated the constitutional right of equality and because there was no language proficiency requirement in the 1951 Self-Government Act, the Government of the Åland Islands could not deny the right of domicile on the grounds mentioned in the decision of the Government of the Åland Islands. The SAC therefore revoked the decision of the Government of the Åland Islands and returned the matter for a new decision-making procedure to the Government of the Åland Islands. Section 7(2) of the 1991 Self-Government Act contains the qualification of satisfactory knowledge of Swedish. See also Suksi (2005d), pp. 31–33, Sjölund (2009), pp. 60, 63, 66, 79 f., and Myntti and Scheinin (1997), p. 134 f. According to Myntti and Scheinin (1997), p. 142, "a very strict interpretation of the requirement of proficiency in the Swedish language as a prerequisite for acquiring the Ålandic right of domicile might well amount to a disproportionate limitation and unreasonable restriction of the rights guaranteed in the ECHR as well as the CCPR", at least partly because the 1921 Åland Islands Settlement makes possible restrictions of franchise for newcomers within reasonable limits. No such complaints have been raised so far.

[58]OJ 94/C241/08.

[59]See SAC 2788/1/94 of 2 June 1995 (Docket Nr 2386), in which the SAC declared, upon concluding that the request by the applicant of a preliminary ruling from the EFTA Court was

restrictive as concerns mainland citizens of Finland. However, the right of domicile entitles the possessor of this right under sections 9 through 12 of the Self-Government Act to some material rights that present themselves as exclusive compared with the persons who are not in possession of the right of domicile. These material rights are the right to participation in elections to the Legislative Assembly and municipal boards, including eligibility for office,[60] the right in section 10 of the Self-Government Act to acquire real estate in the manner provided for under the Property Acquisition Act (SoF 3/75),[61] and the right of trade established in section 11 of the

unfounded, that the requirement of equal treatment in Article 126.2.c of the Treaty on the European Economic Area (EEA Treaty) had not been violated by the Government of the Åland Islands when it declined an application for the right of domicile from a German citizen because of the lack of Finnish citizenship. On the part of the Åland Islands, the EEA Treaty contains exceptions with respect to the possession of real estate and trade, concerning which non-domiciled persons may acquire rights on the basis of administrative permits granted by the Provincial Government, which procedure must not be discriminatory, while the Treaty does not affect, *inter alia*, the political rights flowing from the right of domicile. For an illustrative analysis of administrative decision-making concerning the right of domicile, see Sjölund (2009). See also Suksi (2005d), pp. 32–39.

[60]According to section 67 of the Self-Government Act, as amended on 31 December 1994 (SoF 1556/94), an act of Åland enacted by a two-thirds majority in the Provincial Parliament may stipulate that a citizen of Finland without the right of domicile and citizens of Iceland, Norway, Sweden and Denmark shall be granted suffrage and be eligible for office in municipal elections on the prerequisites provided in an act of Åland and that the same rights may be given to *citizens of other states*. The latter part of the section is a reaction to the exception that remained unrealized in the Accession Treaty and to Article 8b of the TEU (now Art. 20(2-b) and Art. 22(1) of the TFEU and Art. 40 of the Charter of Fundamental Rights of the EU), which grants these rights to citizens of Member States in respect of municipal elections in any Member State, albeit on the basis of a Council Directive, which may contain derogations that follow from "problems specific to a Member State". See Council Directive 94/80/EC of 19 December 1994. In an Explanatory Memorandum to a Proposal for a Council Directive (COM(95) 499 Final/11.01.1996) amending the above mentioned Council Directive on municipal elections, the EC Commission points out that "(s)ince a period of residence, irrespective of nationality, is required of all those that do not have the right of domicile it can be concluded that there is no discriminatory treatment incompatible with article 8B (1) of the EC Treaty, between Finnish citizens and other EU nationals as regards to the right to vote and to stand in municipal elections. No specific conditions are therefore necessary to apply article 8B (1) to the Åland islands". According to Ålandic law, citizens of the EU have the right to vote in municipal elections after one year of residence. Please note that the elections to the Legislative Assembly are not covered by the EU law on municipal elections.

[61]See SAC 3941/1/94 of 2 June 1995 (Docket Nr 2385), in which the SAC concluded that a decision by the Government of the Åland Islands, with which it had denied the application of a company resident in Sweden to possess real estate in the Åland Islands, was not discriminatory in respect of companies in other EEA countries. The ruling dealt with the application of Article 126 of the EEA Treaty and section 2 of the Land Acquisition Act. A similar regulation is found in Article 1 of Protocol No 2 on the Åland Islands of the Act concerning the Conditions of Accession and the Adjustments to the Treaties on which the Union is Founded (OJ 94/C241/08), attached to the 1994 Treaty of Accession, *inter alia*, of Finland to the European Union. (Williams) 2009, p. 123, concludes that there is "no inherent conflict between the local restrictions on land acquisition that Finland has obligated itself to upholding in the context of Åland's autonomy, on one hand, and the human rights of individuals interested in selling, purchasing, inheriting or

Act,[62] as well as some exemptions from the general duty to perform military service established in section 12, although there is, for Swedish-speaking conscripts of mainland Finland, a separate Swedish-speaking brigade. Under section 8 of the Self-Government Act, the forfeiture of Finnish citizenship shall also mean the forfeiture of the right of domicile, while the forfeiture of the right of domicile of a person who moves permanently away from the Åland Islands shall be regulated in an act of Åland.[63]

Although the special rights of the Åland Islanders may attract a great deal of interest, their inclusion in the Åland Island Settlement indicates a far more important a position for the special rights in the functioning of the autonomy arrangement than actually is the case at the practical level. In the actual functioning of the self-government and the public authorities of Åland, the management of the special rights is a marginal feature only, the operation of which will be illustrated, for the purposes of our inquiry, in relation to the right to vote in the elections to the Legislative Assembly of the Åland Islands (Sect. 6.2).

As concerns the right of domicile, it is, however, important to underline the fact that this particular right was not a part of the Åland Islands Settlement in 1921, but was introduced in the 1951 Self-Government Act after decades of hard debate between the Åland Islands and mainland Finland, involving politicians, the Åland Delegation and the Supreme Court.[64] The right of domicile has since provided a

---

bequething such land, on the other". Williams also finds that "the existing restrictions on land acquisition are proportional to legitimate government aims and avoid placing an excessive burden on the individuals they negatively impact". For an analysis of praxis concerning administrative decisions by the Government of the Åland Islands on permits to purchase real property, see Suksi (2005d), pp. 326–336. The idea to restrict ownership of real estate in 1921 was probably of a mainland Finland provenance, conceived by Swedish-speaking Finns as one means to protect the traditional Swedish-speaking areas. The idea was, however, not realized in mainland Finland. See von Bonsdorff (1950), pp. 41–46, Suksi (2008c), pp. 73–75.

[62]Under the provision, the right of trade is not exclusively tied to the right of domicile, but dependent on an act of Åland, which, however, shall not limit the right of trade of a person residing in the Åland Islands, if no staff except his spouse and minor children is used in the trade and if the trade is not practiced in business premises, an office or another special place of business. A similar regulation is found in Article 1 of Protocol No 2 on the Åland Islands of the Act concerning the Conditions of Accession and the Adjustments to the Treaties on which the Union is Founded (OJ 94/C241/08), attached to the 1994 Treaty of Accession of, *inter alia*, Finland to the European Union. For an analysis of praxis concerning administrative decisions by the Government of the Åland Islands on permits to purchase real property, see Suksi (2005d), pp. 336–341.

[63]See the Act of Åland on the Right of Domicile (SoÅ 2/1993), according to which a person who during five years has been permanently resident outside of the Åland Islands forfeits his or her right of domicile.

[64]For a legal-historical account of how the right of domicile was introduced into the 1951 Self-Government Act, see Spiliopoulou Åkermark (2009), pp. 19–37, Sjölund (2009), pp. 55–66. As concerns the exceptions granted at the Finnish and Ålandic membership in the EU to the Åland Islanders on the basis of Protocol 2, it is unclear whether the negotiators on the part of the EU (of the Government of Finland, for that matter) understood or were aware of the fact that the right of domicile (that is, the regional citizenship) is actually not based on the 1921 Åland Islands

platform for the management of the other special rights of the Åland Islanders. The right of domicile is therefore a "package" within which the various components of the package exist as separate elements.[65]

4.2.7 *Different Dimensions of the Jurisdiction and Its Funding*

Under section 2 of the Self-Government Act, the territorial jurisdiction of the Åland Islands is established by way of reference to the territory it had at the time of the entry into force of the Self-Government Act and the territorial waters directly adjacent to its land territory according to the enactments in force on the limits of the territorial waters of Finland. This means that the jurisdictional border between the autonomy arrangement and mainland Finland is actually brought back to the jurisdictional definition of the 1951 Act, which in turn refers the jurisdictional issue to the 1920 Act. At the inception of the autonomy arrangement, the jurisdiction was formed on the basis of the jurisdictional border of the Special Province of the Åland Islands, created in 1918 out of the Province of South-Western Finland within the area of those municipalities that constituted the jurisdiction of the court of first instance of the Åland Islands. The concept of 'special province' is unclear, but one interpretation of the concept could be that unlike a regular province, the Special Province of Åland had, for a short period of time, both a civilian and a military governor.[66] The inhabitants of the Åland Islands were uneasy about the construction and therefore the subsequent autonomy arrangement created for the same jurisdictional area in 1920 did probably not feel too convincing until the guarantees of the League of Nations were in place in 1922. Sub-section 2 of the provision contains the possibility that if the jurisdiction and sovereignty of the State are extended beyond the limits of the territorial waters, the jurisdiction and sovereignty of Åland may be likewise extended, as agreed by the state and Åland. Although Finland has extended its jurisdiction through the establishment of an exclusive economic zone (EEZ), the jurisdiction of the Åland Islands has not been extended in the same manner. This means that the norms of mainland Finland apply *in toto* in the EEZ adjacent to the Åland Islands.[67]

Settlement and is thus not directly presupposed by the particular status of the Åland Islands under international law, but has instead been created in domestic law.

[65]Spiliopoulou Åkermark (2009), p. 37, Lindbäck (2009), p. 140. For such an assessment, see Suksi (2008c).

[66]Such a construction with a military governor paired together with a civilian one as the representative of the State was probably necessitated by the military interest showed by, *inter alia*, Germany and Sweden towards the Åland Islands. See also Report of the Commission of Rapporteurs to the Council of the League of Nations 1921, p. 71, where it is pointed out that the special nature of the Province was due to the fact that there was also a military governor in the Special Province. Concerning an analysis of the Province of Åland, see Westerlund (1993), pp. 313–322.

[67]Suksi (2005d), p. 16 f.

According to section 3 of the Self-Government Act, the population[68] of the Åland Islands is represented by the Legislative Assembly of the Åland Islands in matters relating to its self-government. The distinction between matters relating to the self-government of the Åland Islands, on the one hand, and those relating to matters left unmentioned, on the other, is actually a reference to the distribution of legislative competence between the Legislative Assembly of the Åland Islands and the Parliament of Finland. In combination with the territorial application of the Self-Government Act and section 17 of the Act, according to which the Legislative Assembly enacts acts for the Åland Islands, this means that in the area of the Åland Islands, the Legislative Assembly of the Åland Islands exercises legislative powers in relation to the matters identified in section 18 of the Act, while the legislative competence in the territory of the Åland Islands in other matters is vested in the Parliament of Finland. At the same time, the provision lays down that the administration of the Åland Islands is vested in the Government of the Åland Islands and the officials subordinate to it. Because the jurisdiction of Åland is mainly of a public law nature, there is the need for a relatively large implementing organization by way of administrative agencies in the Åland Islands that make, *inter alia*, various allocation decisions concerning public funds in the areas of social affairs, health education and the environment.

Financially, the Åland Islands are very independent as concerns spending decisions,[69] although decisions concerning the funding of the autonomy functions are influenced by the limited taxation powers of the autonomy arrangement. As established in section 44 of the Self-Government Act, the Legislative Assembly confirms a budget for the Åland Islands. On the income side of the budget, the main contribution is the annual equalization amount that the Åland Islands receive under section 45 of the Self-Government Act, but it is also possible for the budget of the Åland Islands to receive extraordinary grants[70] and so-called tax retributions.[71] It is

[68]The Finnish- and Swedish-language original versions of the Self-Government Act use the term 'väestö' and 'befolkning', respectively, to collectively identify the inhabitants of the Åland Islands, while the unofficial translation of the Self-Government Act uses the term 'people', which is not quite correct.

[69]The State Audit Office, which is functioning under the authority of the Parliament of Finland and is empowered generally to oversee any public or private spending that concerns funds paid over the state budget, is not empowered to exercise its control powers to the funds that are paid to the budget of the Åland Islands as the equalization amount. This budgetary independence of the Åland Islands in respect of state funds transferred as a lump sum does not mean that there is no control: there is a separate Audit Office within the Government of the Åland Islands.

[70]Section 48: "An extraordinary grant may be given on the proposition of the Åland Parliament for particularly great non-recurring expenditures that may not justifiably be expected to be incorporated in the budget of Åland. An extraordinary grant may only be given for purposes within the competence of Åland." Such extraordinary grants are rare, and two examples are known, namely the building of a vocational school in hotel and restaurant activities and an electricity project in the Åland Islands.

[71]Section 49: "If the income and property tax levied in Åland during a fiscal year exceeds 0.5 per cent of the corresponding tax in the entire country, the excess shall be retributed to Åland (tax

also possible for the Åland Islands to take up bond loans and other loans in its own name and under its own fiscal responsibility. In addition, under some special circumstances, the Åland Islands may receive so-called special subsidies over the state budget.[72] Finally, the Åland Islands have, under section 18, para. 5, powers of taxation that relate to an additional tax on income and a provisional extra income tax, as well as the trade and amusement taxes, the legal basis of the dues levied for the Åland Islands and the municipal tax. Out of these funding methods, the equalization amount from the state budget to the budget of the Government of the Åland Islands is the most important one (around 54 per cent in 2009), followed by the municipal tax that brings in proceeds to the budgets of the 16 municipalities in the Åland Islands. Bond loans are used to some extent by the Government of the Åland Islands.

The additional tax on income has been used by the Legislative Assembly only a few times, in the 1930s and the 1960s. The Legislative Assembly has enacted an Act of Åland on Åland Islands Tax (SoÅ 58/1993), which establishes a 3.5% tax on income for persons and inheritance, but this Act needs to be activated by a separate annual tax law, and no such activation law has recently been enacted in the Åland Islands. This means that the Legislative Assembly has been wary about imposing such additional taxes on the inhabitants and businesses of the Åland Islands that would increase taxation from the level that the Parliament of Finland has already imposed in the form of general state taxes on income. As a consequence, the provisional extra income tax has never been imposed, while the trade and amusement taxes, when such were imposed, had a marginal role only in the budget of the Åland Islands. Dues levied for public services that the Government of the Åland Islands or the municipalities in Åland provide for inhabitants are normally at a modest level and do not cover the actual cost of the services.

In reality, the main power of taxation under the legislative competence of the Åland Islands is the municipal tax or the local government tax imposed as a flat rate tax on the income of individuals and business enterprises. The Legislative Assembly has the power to establish the law on municipal tax, including the deductions by which the individual tax levels are regulated, but the general rate of municipal tax is established in each municipality on the basis of section 121 of the Constitution of

retribution)." In this way, it is guaranteed that the money raised in the Åland Islands by way of state taxation is not used for funding state activities in mainland Finland. In 2009, the tax retribution paid back over the state budget to the budget of the Government of the Åland Islands was 24 m€, which is around 15 per cent of the equalization amount of 164 m€ and around 8 per cent of the total budget on 305 m€ of the Government of the Åland Islands. See Landskapsregeringens berättelse (2010), pp. 232–233.

[72]Section 51: "Åland shall be subsidised from State funds in order to (1) prevent or remove substantial economic disorders that affect especially Åland and (2) cover the costs of a natural disaster, nuclear accident, oil spill or another comparable incident, unless the costs are justifiably to be borne by Åland." One example of such a special subsidy is known. In 2004, the Åland Delegation decided to give a special subsidy to the Åland Islands for a reserve generator for the production of electricity.

Finland, which establishes this rate as one of the dimensions of constitutionally guaranteed municipal self-government. Against this background, it is possible to conclude that out of the total income tax paid by an average income-earner in the Åland Islands on the basis of his or her salary, slightly over 50 per cent is taken as municipal tax.[73] As a consequence, the legislative powers of the Åland Islands in the area of income tax are considerable, but the political discussion over recent decades has concerned the wish of the Åland Islands to take over such forms of taxation that are now within the legislative competence of the Parliament of Finland, such as indirect taxation (VAT and different duties),[74] taxation related to shipping, property tax, etc. Such an amendment of the fiscal basis of the autonomy arrangement would probably have to be coupled with a transfer of substantive legislative competences from the Parliament of Finland to the Legislative Assembly of the Åland Islands at the same time as the equalization amount would be decreased.

The equalization amount is compensation from the state to the autonomous entity for functions that the Åland Islands takes care of in place of the state. In that sense, the equalization amount corresponds to those taxes mentioned in the 1921 Åland Islands Settlement and that were abolished later on. Therefore, there is a connection between the equalization amount and para. 6 of the Åland Islands Settlement. The final amount of the financial equalization is determined retroactively in a special equalization procedure, but advance payments are made from the state budget. The amount of equalization is established so that the state income for the relevant year, less the new loans that the state has taken,[75] is determined on the basis of the final state accounts and that net sum of state income is multiplied by the factor of 0.45.[76] This factor is the basis for equalization

[73]Because the state income tax is progressive, earners of high income pay a greater proportion in the proportional state income tax and a smaller proportion in the municipal tax, while earners of low income mainly pay municipal tax and only little state income tax.

[74]In this respect, it is should be noted that although Protocol 2 concerning the Åland Islands to the Finnish EU Accession Treaty makes an exception concerning the Åland Islands concerning indirect taxes and thus creates the position for the Åland Islands of a third country in the EU as concerns indirect taxation, the legislation that formulates.

[75]The deduction of the new state loans from the state income has been motivated by the fact that the Government of the Åland Islands can take up loans in its own name under section 50 of the Self-Government Act.

[76]According to section 47, the basis for equalisation shall be altered if the bases for the State final accounts change in a manner that has a considerable effect on the amount of equalization. According to section 47(3), the basis for equalization shall be raised if (1) the expenditures of Åland have increased because administrative duties of the State have been transferred to Åland, or because Åland by agreement with the State pursues in full or for a considerable part an activity that is in the interest of the State, (2) the realization of the purposes of autonomy causes substantial additional expenditures, or (3) other significant expenditures which have not been taken into account when enacting this Act are caused to the Åland administration. Conversely, the basis for equalization shall be lowered if administrative duties of Åland have been transferred to the State and the expenditures of Åland have hence decreased. The alteration of the basis for equalization

pursuant to section 47 of the Self-Government Act and represents an estimate at the end of the 1980s and the beginning of 1990s of how large the transfers from the Åland Islands to the state budget are and how much the Åland Islands should, as a consequence, be compensated in order to reach a balance in the transfers. At that point, it was estimated that the share of the Åland Islands in the net state budget of Finland was 0.45 per cent. The debate between the Åland Islands and mainland Finland has since been about the correctness of this figure, but it seems that the factor of 0.45 is more or less correct, although fluctuations benefitting the Åland Islands and mainland Finland alternate.[77] The equalization amount therefore represents compensation to the Åland Islands for the state functions it takes care of and the funding of which it otherwise would have to cover by raising taxes. The equalization amount introduces a great deal of stability into the budget of the Åland Islands, but at the same time, the Government and the Legislative Assembly of the Åland Islands do not have such financial instruments at their disposal by which they could themselves steer the economy of Åland by means of taxation decisions.

In contrast to the income of the budget of the Government of the Åland Islands, the spending side of the budget is much less affected by rules established in the Self-Government Act. In principle, the Legislative Assembly is, when adopting the budget on the basis of section 44(1), at liberty to make any allocation decisions it sees fit under rules established in an act of Åland.[78] The state authorities of mainland Finland have no competence to interfere in the budgetary processes, and the State Audit Office has no power to audit the accounts of the Government of the Åland Islands. The only statutory limitation that is placed on the budgetary powers of the Åland Islands is established in section 44(2), according to which the Legislative Assembly shall, when confirming a budget, strive to ensure at least the same level of social benefits for the population of Åland as is enjoyed by the population in mainland Finland. This provision was preceded by the Act of Åland on Certain Fundamentals about the Economy of the Åland Islands (SoÅ 22/1983), adopted in the constitutional order by a two-thirds qualified majority by the Legislative Assembly. This Act guarantees the same level of social benefits to the Åland Islanders as for those living in mainland Finland, and also corresponding levels in the areas of special subsidies to business activities in less developed areas and traffic in the archipelago as well as subsidies and loans to municipalities. However, an implicit steering effect on the budget of the Government of the Åland Islands is caused by the fact that the legislative powers allocated to the Legislative Assembly in section 18 of the Self-Government Act are predominantly in the area of public law, as the concept is understood within continental European

shall be provided by an Act of Parliament with the consent of the Legislative Assembly of the Åland Islands. So far, the amount of equalization has not, however, been changed.

[77]See Suksi (2005d), p. 153.

[78]The self-governing entity of the Åland Islands is also a legal person, and as provided in section 66 of the Self-Government Act, this legal entity shall have the same right of exemption from taxes and of comparable benefits as the State.

law. The Åland Islands is competent in such areas as health, social services, education, environment and the police, all of which require explicit administrative implementation through agencies and civil servants. All these functions require relatively significant public funding, and as a consequence, the public sector of the Åland Islands is larger than that of mainland Finland or of Sweden. By implication, those legislative powers that the Parliament of Finland is in charge of in the territory of the Åland Islands are predominantly of a private law nature, requiring less infrastructure in the public administration.

4.2.8 Joint Adjudication of Autonomy Issues

The Self-Government Act creates a number of interfaces between the Åland Islands and the central government of Finland for reaching decisions on, *inter alia*, the equalization amount and the legislative competence of the Åland Islands. The first level of such co-operation is the Åland Delegation, created under section 5 as a joint organ of the Åland Islands and the state, that is, the central government. Section 55 of the Act determines that the Governor of the Åland Islands is the chairperson of the Åland Delegation, and the Council of State and the Legislative Assembly of the Åland Islands shall both elect two persons as members of the Delegation and two deputy members for each Member, which is necessary to fulfill the requirement that the Delegation reaches a quorum only when all the Members are present. Because the Åland Delegation is a joint body, section 57 of the Self-Government Act stipulates that Åland bears those expenses of the Åland Delegation that derive from the delegates elected by the Legislative Assembly, while the other expenses are covered from state funds.

According to section 56 of the Self-Government Act, the Åland Delegation shall, upon request, give opinions to the Council of State, the ministries of the central government, the Government of the Åland Islands and to the courts. One of the main functions of the Åland Delegation relates to the budgetary processes established in the Self-Government Act. The Åland Delegation determines the equalization amount that the Åland Islands is entitled to from the state budget under section 45 as well as the size of the advance payments of the equalization amount. It also determines the tax retribution that the Åland Islands might be entitled to under section 49 of the Act, decides on the extraordinary grant that the Legislative Assembly might have requested under section 48 and, if particular needs arise, awards the special subsidy referred to in section 51 at the same time as it decides upon the possible conditions for the subsidy. In the economic matters listed in section 56(3) (except the advance payments), the President of Finland has, according to section 56(5), to confirm the decision of the Åland Delegation. If such a confirmation decision is not made by the President, the matter is returned to the Åland Delegation for reconsideration. In addition, the Delegation decides upon disputes between the Government of the Åland Islands and the central government about the establishment of new fairways in the sea and about real property that the state might need for its purposes in the Åland Islands. According to section 36(2), the official language of the Åland Delegation is Swedish.

In addition to these functions, the Åland Delegation is involved in the determination of whether the enactments of the Legislative Assembly are within its competence, a task which is performed together with the Supreme Court of Finland (Sect. 5.3.4).

4.2.9 Application of Norms through State Courts

Competence control in relation to Ålandic enactments takes place before the enactment is passed and promulgated (Sect. 5.3.4). The courts in charge of the concrete interpretation of Ålandic and Finnish acts are normally not involved in the competence control, although they may have to make decisions concerning the choice of law, that is, whether they should apply an act of Åland or an act of the Parliament of Finland. Normally, however, it is clear under which of the two bodies of law a case should be resolved. What is particular in this context is that the courts resolving legal issues in the Åland Islands are, under section 35 of the Self-Government Act, part of the court system of Finland, that is, courts of the state, and judges and other employees of the courts are civil servants of the state. Because the courts implement the rule of law under the principle of independence of courts, they do not, of course, favor either of the two legal orders over the other although they deal with cases that originate on the basis of either Ålandic or state norms. As a consequence, each legal order is recognized by the courts as being equally effective within their respective spheres of competence.

However, the court system is divided into general courts and administrative courts, and because of the public law nature of the legislative competence of Åland, a large part of the cases resolved by the administrative court of the Åland Islands originate in the legislative powers of Åland. The Court of First Instance of the Åland Islands and its territorial jurisdiction for the territory of the Åland Islands in civil and criminal cases is established under the court legislation and material law established by the Parliament of Finland.[79] The Court of Appeal of Turku/Åbo is the superior instance for such cases, and in cases where the creation of a precedent is necessary, the Supreme Court of Finland may grant leave for review at the final instance.

As concerns the administrative jurisdiction, decisions of subordinate agencies of the Government of Åland Islands and of municipalities in the Åland Islands are normally appealed at the Administrative Court of the Åland Islands, while the final instance in most administrative cases is the Supreme Administrative Court of Finland (hereinafter: the SAC). Administrative decisions of the Government of the Åland Islands, that is, the cabinet and the departments under its immediate

[79]However, it should be noted that prosecution in criminal matters is a state function, while criminal investigation is mainly a task of the Åland Islands Police.

political control, are appealed directly to the SAC. Appeals over the decisions of the Government of the Åland Islands to the SAC can only be based on grounds of legality, while appeals over decisions of other agencies may also be based on grounds of feasibility. Under section 25(2), a specialized court, the Court of Social Insurance of Finland, deals with complaints over pension decisions made by the Government of the Åland Islands. Under section 25(1), it is, however, possible under an act of Åland to prescribe that decisions made by subordinate agencies to the Government of the Åland Islands are not appealed at the administrative court, but in an "internal" administrative procedure at the Government of the Åland Islands. This is not very frequent, and there is, nonetheless, always the last instance recourse to the SAC over the decisions of the Government of the Åland Islands. The judicial system applicable in the Åland Islands seems more protective of the sub-state jurisdiction than what is the case concerning Puerto Rico, the self-determination of which may be diluted, for instance, by decisions of federal courts.

4.3 Puerto Rico: Conflict Over the Form of Self-Determination

4.3.1 Acquisition of Autonomous Territory by Conquest

While under Spanish rule, the status of Puerto Rico and its inhabitants alternated between different positions, in particular during the nineteenth century. Only five months before the Spanish-American War, in 1897, Spain actually granted Puerto Rico an autonomous position under a charter of autonomy according to which Puerto Rico was vested with self-government and law-making powers.[80] The elections to the bi-cameral Legislative Assembly were held at the start of the war, and the Assembly barely managed to constitute itself before the island was occupied by the US and placed under US military rule. Because the Spanish autonomy charter was not law in the formal sense, but only a royal decree, the norm-hierarchical level of the charter was rather low. In addition, the nature of the law-making powers of the Legislative Assembly, exercised together with the Governor General as the representative of Spain, was not completely clear and was never really tested. However, it might be possible to place this first autonomy experiment in Puerto Rico in section II of the above chart (see table 1, above)[81] and

[80]For an English-language version of the Charter of Autonomy, see http://www.michie.com/puertorico (accessed on 30 January 2009). For an exposé of the autonomy charter, see Trías Monge (1997), pp. 11–15.

[81]It seems as if there was a plan to elevate the entrenchment status of the charter, because the amendment formula of the charter was phrased in a relatively demanding manner: "When the present Constitution shall be once approved by the Cortes of the Kingdom for the islands of Cuba and Puerto Rico, it shall not be amended except by virtue of a special law and upon the petition of the insular parliament." This means that a special statute was envisioned and that the initiative for

to compare it with governance arrangements in the British Dominions, such as Canada, of the same era. The powers of Puerto Rico would have been of a residual nature, while the powers of the Spanish legislature were enumerated in the charter, and Puerto Rico would have had a possibility to participate in the conclusion of such commercial treaties by Spain which were relevant for Puerto Rico.

Under the 1898 Treaty of Paris, that is, the peace treaty between Spain and the United States,[82] Puerto Rico was ceded by Spain to the United States. According to Art. II of the treaty, "Spain cedes to the United States the island of Porto Rico (...)", while Art. IX laid down that "[t]he civil rights and political status of the native inhabitants of the territories hereby ceded to the United States shall be determined by the Congress". Through ratification, the treaty became internally binding in the US, and Art. IX of the treaty actually created a duty on the part of the Congress to pass legislation concerning, *inter alia*, Puerto Rico. Domestically, such a duty was implemented outside of the regular federal structure, probably to a great extent under a wish on the part of the USA to enter the ranks of the other imperial States, because the situation offered a chance to establish the US as a colonial power. At the same time, the idea was to educate the inhabitants of Puerto Rico, *inter alia*, politically so as to reach a suitable level of self-governance, as the term was understood in the American context.

The interpretation soon emerged that Puerto Rico would be governed under the plenary powers of Congress with reference to, in particular, Article IV, section 3(2), of the US Constitution, which constitutes the so-called territorial clause and according to which "the Congress shall have Power to dispose of and make all needful Rules and Regulations respecting the Territory or other Property belonging to the United States". As a possession of the US, Puerto Rico is regarded as a territory that is unincorporated in the federal structure of the State.[83] The political discussion continued between two alternatives, whether or not the US Constitution followed the flag. A third interpretation, a middle ground of some sort, was ultimately the one upon which the legislative approach and later also rulings of the US Supreme Court were based: the concept of the "United States" excludes territories and therefore, the new territories could be governed as colonies if Congress so chose.[84] This interpretation was adopted from the very beginning of the US – Puerto Rico relationship when the Organic Act of Puerto Rico, or the so-called Foraker Act was enacted in 1900.

This interpretation was confirmed in a series of cases collectively known as the so-called *Insular Cases*, decided by the US Supreme Court between 1901 and

---

the enactment would come from the Legislative Assembly of Puerto Rico. For characterizations of the Spanish autonomy charter, see also Trías Monge (2001), pp. 230 f., and Trías Monge (1997), pp. 13–15, 164.

[82]Treaty of Peace, concluded at Paris December 10, 1898 and ratified in 1899. Treaties, Conventions, International Acts, Protocols and Agreements between the United States of America and Other Powers 1776–1909, 1910, pp. 1690–1696.

[83]See Rivera Ramos (2007), p. 129, who accounts for an opinion of the Attorney General of the United States, given as testimony in 1991 before a US Senate committee.

[84]Duffy Burnett and Marshall (2001), pp. 4–6.

1922.[85] The law as outlined in those cases is still in force and makes the point that such possessions of the United States as Puerto Rico and Philippines were, after treaty-based annexation, "foreign to the United States in a domestic sense".[86] In the most important of the Insular cases, *Downes v. Bidwell*,[87] the issue was whether the so-called uniformity clause of the US Constitution applied to goods imported from Puerto Rico to mainland USA so as to prohibit the imposition of a customs duty on such produce. The US Supreme Court found that this would, indeed, not be the case, although the US Constitution in principle applied to Puerto Rico. Under this partial application doctrine, the question is which parts of the US Constitution (and of the US legal order) apply and which do not. Some principles of the US Constitution would apply, such as, *inter alia*, the prohibition of bills of attainder, the prohibition of *ex post facto* laws and the prohibition of titles of nobility, while others, such as the uniformity clause, would not. The basis for the applicability and inapplicability of the rules of the US Constitution was grounded in a distinction between natural and artificial or remedial rights,[88] and the former would be protected everywhere and at all times, including in Puerto Rico,[89] while the latter were regarded peculiar to the American system of jurisprudence and protected only within the United States, that is, in the federal states.[90] However, the distinction is not very clear and it is not always possible to say exactly which rules of the US Constitution apply and which – if any – do not. In fact, it might be safe to assume as a practical matter that all of the constitutional rights of the US Constitution apply also in Puerto Rico. However, there are no special rights, as in the case of some other sub-state entities.

[85]For a complete list of the 23 insular cases, see note 1 in Duffy Burnett (2001), p. 390 f. For a deep analysis and criticism of the cases, see Rivera Ramos (2007), pp. 73–142, Torruella (2007), pp. 283–347, and Duffy Burnett (2005), pp. 797–879. See also Rosselló (2005), pp. 148–180, and Trías Monge (1997), pp. 44–51.

[86]*Downes v. Bidwell*, 182 U.S. 244, at pp. 341–342 (concurring opinion of Justice White). The rationale of "foreign in a domestic sense" is, however, variable and applies differently in respect of different pieces of law. For instance, whether an appellant's conviction in a Puerto Rican court for the possession of marijuana was a "foreign" or "domestic" conviction for the purposes of affecting the provisions concerning the purchase of firearms in mainland USA, the court of appeals considered it not foreign, but domestic. Attempts to buy firearms by claiming that the appellant had never been convicted in a domestic court of law for a crime that carried a jail sentence exceeding one year was therefore deemed as unlawful conduct. See *United States v. Marco Laboy-Torres*, 3rd Circuit, 29 January 2009.

[87]182 U.S. 244, at p. 770.

[88]*Downes v. Bidwell*, p. 282 at 785.

[89]Freedom of religion and conscience, right to personal liberty and individual property, freedom of speech and of the press, access to justice, due process, equal protection, immunities from unreasonable searches and seizures as well as cruel and unusual punishments, and such other immunities as are indispensable to a free government.

[90]Right to citizenship, right to suffrage, right to the particular methods of procedure pointed out in the Constitution, which are peculiar to Anglo-Saxon jurisprudence and some of which have been held by the states to be unnecessary to the proper protection of individuals.

In a series of court cases, the point is made that the American understanding of fairness applies to Puerto Rico,[91] including the free speech clause in the First Amendment, the due process clause of the Fifth or Fourteenth Amendment, the equal protection guarantee of the Fifth or Fourteenth Amendment and the safeguards against unreasonable searches and seizures of the Fourth Amendment as well as the right to travel. Evidently, at least these constitutional rights belong to the fundamental ones.[92] At the same time, there are also cases that conclude that some other constitutional rights are not fundamental and thus not applicable,[93] such as the right to trial by jury.[94] In addition, the right to vote in federal elections is apparently not a fundamental one in an unincorporated territory such as Puerto Rico, because that right is one controlled by the constituent states, which Puerto Rico is not (see below, Sect. 4.3.3). It has also been suggested that the protections afforded to U.S. citizenship (probably those outside of the due process and equal treatment area that do belong to the fundamental constitutional rights), would not be among the fundamental ones because the Puerto Ricans are U.S. citizens on the basis of a statute and not directly on the basis of the U.S. Constitution.[95] As a consequence of the Insular Cases, it can be said that the uniformity clause of the US Constitution does not force the US Government to apply federal law to Puerto Rico in the same manner as to the constituent states.[96]

[91]The "American understanding of fairness", is mentioned in *Small v. United States*, 544 U.S. 385 (2005), at 389, because the fundamental provisions of the US Constitution guarantee fairness apply with equal force in Puerto Rico. The examples mentioned in *United States v. Marco Laboy-Torres* (3rd Circuit, 29 January 2009) are "*Posadas de Puerto Rico Associates v. Tourism Co. of P. R.*, 478 U.S. 328, 331 n.1 (1986) (citing *Balzac v. Porto Rico*, 258 U.S. 298, 314 (1922) (First Amendment Free Speech Clause); *Calero-Toledo v. Pearson Yacht Leasing Co.*, 416 U.S. 663, 668–69, and n.5 (1974) (Due Process Clause of the Fifth or Fourteenth Amendment); *Examining Board of Engineers, Architects and Surveyors v. Flores de Otero*, 426 U.S. 572, 599–601 (1976) (equal protection guarantee of the Fifth or Fourteenth Amendment); *Torres v. Puerto Rico*, 442 U.S. 465, 471 (1979) (Fourth Amendment))".

[92]In *Califano v. Torres*, 435 U. S. 1, 435 U. S. 4 n. 6 (1978), the US Supreme Court assumed, without deciding on the issue, that the constitutional right to travel extends to the Commonwealth. See also Rivera Ramos (2007), p. 212 f., who in addition makes the point that rights which Congress creates by act as federal entitlements apply in Puerto Rico.

[93]*Examining Board of Engineers, Architects and Surveyors v. Flores de Otero*, 426 U.S. at 600 n. 30 (describing the Insular Cases and explaining that "only 'fundamental' constitutional rights were guaranteed to the inhabitants" of Puerto Rico).

[94]*Balzac v. the People of Porto Rico*, 258 U.S. 298, 343 (Sixth Amendment). See Thornburgh (2007), pp. 51–55, for criticism of the *Balzac* case and the unequal situation of Puerto Ricans on the basis of a statutory citizenship. It should be mentioned that Art. II, Sect. 11, of the Constitution of Puerto Rico guarantees the right to trial by jury.

[95]Thornburgh (2001), pp. 357–359, 367. See also Rivera Ramos (2007), p. 177.

[96]However, it seems that federal law is, generally speaking and in practice, uniformly applied to Puerto Rico in the same way as to the constituent states. See below, the section concerning the distribution of powers.

Therefore, as explained in the case of *Murphy v. Ramsey*,[97] the people of the United States have supreme power over the national territories and their inhabitants, because the United States are the sovereign owners of the national territories. Against this background, as laid down in the case of *First National Bank of Brunswick v. County of Yankton*, Congress could, by virtue of its plenary powers, make "a void act of the Territorial legislature valid, and a valid act void".[98] For our inquiry, the latter is particularly relevant; that is, the possibility to make a valid act, enacted by the Legislative Assembly of Puerto Rico, void, because such a conclusion means that a US act supersedes an act of Puerto Rico and thus places the latter in an inferior position in relation to the former.

4.3.2 *Compact of Government?*

Those Puerto Rican inhabitants who chose not to maintain their allegiance to Spain were made citizens of the United States on the basis of the 1917 Act to provide a civil government for Puerto Rico, and for other purposes. In addition to US citizenship, the 1917 Act contained, *inter alia*, a Bill of Rights for the Puerto Ricans. This so-called Jones Act in part superseded the Foraker Act and was in 1950 re-named the Puerto Rican Federal Relations Act through Public Law 600 of the 81st Congress. Public Law 600 was officially entitled an Act to provide for the organization of a constitutional government by the people of Puerto Rico.[99] As concerns citizenship of the Puerto Ricans, it has, however, been maintained that

[97] 114 U.S. 15, at 747.

[98] 101 U.S. 129, at 133. The following was said in the case concerning the plenary powers of Congress: "In the organic Act of Dakota there was no express reservation of power in Congress to amend the Acts of the territorial Legislature, but none was necessary. Such a power is an incident of sovereignty, and continues until granted away. Congress may not only abrogate laws of the territorial Legislatures, but it may itself legislate directly for the local government. It may make a void Act of the territorial Legislature valid, and a valid Act void. In other words, it has full and complete legislative authority over the People of the Territories and all the departments of the territorial governments. It may do to the Territories what the People, under the Constitution of the United States, may do for the States." In a summary of this case concerning the power of Congress to legislate for Territories, that is, concerning the nature of the plenary powers of Congress, it is said that Congress may legislate for Territories as a State does for its municipal organizations.

[99] Act July 3, 1950, c. 446, 64 Stat. 314. The jurisdictional determination of the Federal Relations Act, as included in US Code, Title 48, Chapter 4, Sect. 731. Territory included under name Puerto Rico, lays down that "[t]he provisions of this chapter shall apply to the island of Puerto Rico and to the adjacent islands belonging to the United States and waters of those islands; and the name Puerto Rico, as used in this chapter, shall be held to include not only the island of that name, but all the adjacent islands as aforesaid". It deserves to be emphasized that the Federal Relations Act and Public Law 600 are two different pieces of law. Trías Monge 1997, p. 44, points out that the Foraker Act has actually never been repealed *in toto*: "Although parts have been repealed, some of its sections live to this day as part of the Federal Relations Act."

"[i]nherent in any definition of commonwealth status is the fact that the U.S. citizenship of persons born in Puerto Rico is secured by statute and not by the U.S. Constitution itself".[100] As a statutory category based on the Jones Act, the US citizenship of the Puerto Ricans is a "subcategory of U.S. nationality which can exist side by side with (...) full U.S. citizenship for a person born and residing in the states". Nonetheless, "because of the unincorporated territory status of Puerto Rico", the citizenship of Puerto Ricans is "not fully equal to the citizenship of persons born or naturalized in the states of the Union", who thereby "enjoy citizenship protected by the Fourteenth Amendment".[101] The legal category of "citizen of Puerto Rico", created against the background of the preamble and of Art. I, section 1, and Art. III, section 5, of the Constitution of Puerto Rico, may on this basis be characterized as a "legal residency status with rights and privileges conferred under the local constitution to the extent consistent with federal law".[102] This has not prevented the Government of Puerto Rico from formalizing the status of the inhabitants as citizens of Puerto Rico by way of granting certificates of citizenship of Puerto Rico[103] that, *inter alia*, entitle them to vote in Puerto Rican elections, a claim that was tried in 1997 in the so-called *Mari Bras* case before the Supreme Court of Puerto Rico.[104]

---

[100]Thornburgh (2001), pp. 358, 367.

[101]Thornburgh (2001), p. 367. See also Thornburgh (2007), pp. 51–55 for criticism of the unequal citizenship construction in the *Balzac* case. Rivera Ramos (2007), p. 99, refers to a second-class citizenship when analyzing the U.S. citizenship of the Puerto Ricans. On the citizenship issue, see also Rivera Ramos (2007), pp. 145–189.

[102]Thornburgh (2001), p. 367. See also Thornburgh (2001), pp. 359–371, explaining how the federal government considers invalid such attempts to renounce U.S. citizenship that purport to establish an independent Puerto Rican citizenship for an individual. An attempt to extract recognition for a local citizenship that is independent from U.S. citizenship (and that also could have qualified for eligibility in Puerto Rican elections as "citizen of Puerto Rico") was refused by a federal court. See *Alberto O. Lozada Colon v. U.S. Department of State*, 2 F.Supp.2d 43 (D.D.C., 23 April 1998). Thornburgh (2001), p. 361: "While Puerto Rico has powers of local government which in some respects are like the states to the extent consistent with federal law and the U.S. Constitution, Puerto Rico does not have the sovereignty or constitutional authority to ignore the Supremacy Clause of the federal Constitution by creating a separate nationality." Nonetheless, according to Thornburgh (2001), p. 365, the Supreme Court of Puerto Rico has ruled, evidently without effect, that citizenship of Puerto Rico "constitutes a form of citizenship superior to that of citizenship of a state of the Union". Thornburgh denies that this could be the case and implies actually the opposite instead.

[103]See Decree No. 7347 of 1 May 2007 by the Department of State of Puerto Rico on the evaluation and granting of certificates of citizenship of Puerto Rico (Reglamento del secretario de estado num. 7347 para regir el proceso evaluación y otorgamiento de certificados de ciudania Puertorriquena). The legal basis for the decree is the Law No. 3 of 1 February 1906, the Foraker Act, the Federal Relations Act, and the Constitution of Puerto Rico, all as amended.

[104]*Ramirez de Ferrer v. Mari Brás*, Supreme Court of Puerto Rico, No. CT-96-14 (18 November 1997). See also Rivera Ramos (2007), pp. 174–175. If Puerto Rico were to become independent, there exist different interpretations of whether or not the US Congress could divest the Puerto Rican citizens of their US citizenship.

In section 1 of the current Federal Relations Act, Congress, that is, the legislature of the United States, recognizes the principle of government by consent and establishes that the Act is adopted in the nature of a compact so that the people of Puerto Rico may organize a government pursuant to a constitution of their own adoption. The idea of a compact seems to be present in the manner in which decision-making capacity is in part transferred onto the inhabitants of Puerto Rico in section 2 of the Act, because this Act, which on the basis of the legal situation until 1950 would be directly applicable in Puerto Rico, had to be submitted to the qualified voters of Puerto Rico for acceptance or rejection through an island-wide referendum to be held in accordance with the laws of Puerto Rico. Hence a future contingency involving a referendum on the entering into force of the Act was created, a mechanism that has been disapproved of in other contexts.[105] Nothing was explicitly provided for the possibility that the Act would not be approved by the Puerto Rican voters, but by implication, a rejection would probably have sustained the direct application of national legislation in the same way as until then. In fact, the Act would have been binding on Puerto Rico even without the referendum.

Under section 2, if this Act of the US Congress "is approved by a majority of the voters participating in such referendum, the Legislature of Puerto Rico is authorized to call a constitutional convention to draft a constitution for Puerto Rico, a constitution which shall provide a republican form of government and shall include a bill of rights". In this way, the Federal Relations Act granted a permission for the legislature of Puerto Rico to call a separate constitutional convention to draft and decide upon a constitution that would contain certain set principles. Against the background of section 3 of the Act, such an adoption of the constitution was regarded as an adoption by the people of Puerto Rico. After adoption by a constitutional convention, the President of the United States was authorized by the Act to transmit such a constitution to the Congress of the United States if he found that the constitution conformed with the applicable provisions of the Federal Relations Act and of the Constitution of the United States. As a last stage, therefore, an approval of the Puerto Rican Constitution by the US Congress was required, making the Puerto Rican constitution at least as much an Act of the US Congress as it was a decision of the Puerto Rican people. In addition, the procedure contained the possibility that the constitution would not be approved or be approved only after amendments, because Congress was making its decision on the basis of its plenary powers under the territorial clause. It can be said that in principle, the US Congress could have approved any text as the constitution of Puerto Rico, but chose to involve the people of Puerto Rico in the drafting and adoption of the constitution.

[105] See Suksi (1993), p. 68 (with references included therein) and p. 73 (citing *Santo v. State*, 2 Iowa 164(1855), according to which an Act dependent on a contingent event, such as approval in a referendum, could not, without amendments to the state constitution replace the law-making process prescribed by the constitution).

The actual constitution-making process contained three referendums and two convocations of the constitutional convention in Puerto Rico. In the first referendum on 4 June 1951, the voters of Puerto Rico approved Public Law 600, that is, the procedure that would govern the making of the constitution. Thereafter, on 27 August 1951, the members of the constitutional convention were elected, and they drafted the constitution between September 1951 and February 1952.[106] In principle, under Public Law 600, the convention could have adopted the constitution given the overwhelming majority that existed for it in the convention, but the constitution was nonetheless submitted to a referendum on 3 March 1952, in which 80 per cent of those voting approved it. Because some amendments were made to the text of the constitution when it was being debated in the US Congress and because those amendments were approved by the President of the US when signing the resolution approving the constitution, the previous constitutional convention was convened again to make a decision on the matter. The decision of the constitutional convention to approve the – now amended – constitution on the part of the people of Puerto Rico was made on 25 July 1952, but the two amendments, the one on compulsory education and the other on the amendment of the Constitution, proposed by the US Congress, were submitted to an additional referendum on 4 November 1952, in which they were approved by the people.[107]

In itself, the 1951 referendum (together with the two subsequent referendums on the Constitution of Puerto Rico) could be understood as a first status referendum, followed by three others in 1967, 1991 and 1998. In the first referendum(s), it is clear that the Puerto Ricans chose to be governed within the framework of a status different from that of a state in the federation and that the US Congress agreed to the final product, although questions remained about the legal effect of the measure for the powers of Congress. Congress promised and agreed to a particular status for Puerto Rico, but the conditions and effects of the pledge were not adequately spelled out. Consequently, the status of Puerto Rico remains a problem for the United States today, although attempts to resolve the situation have been made.[108]

---

[106]See Diario de sesiones de la convencion constituyente de Puerto Rico, 1951 y 1952, 2003.

[107]Concerning the constitution-making process, see Trías Monge (1997), pp. 113–118, and Rosselló (2005), pp. 212–213. It may be said that in the *Mari Bras* case, the Supreme Court of Puerto Rico attempted to exercise a *pouvoir constituant* of some kind, that is, a claim of constituent powers of Puerto Rico as a root of its own law-making powers or at least to create a starting point for such an argument, perhaps specified in future rulings. The *Mari Bras* ruling is still good law and constitutes a platform for issuing residence certificates for the citizens of Puerto Rico, although the case did not constitute such a Puerto Rican citizenship which is separate and independent from US citizenship. Interestingly, in Thornburgh (2007), pp. 87–92, it is indicated that the federal courts could, if Congressional action is not forthcoming, correct the (by modern standards) erratic *Balzac* case and recognize voting rights in federal elections to Puerto Ricans. However, the right to vote in federal elections is actually a right controlled by the constituent states.

[108]See Report by the President's Task Force on Puerto Rico's Status, December 2007, at http://www.usdoj.gov/opa/documents/2007-report-by-the-president-task-force-on-puerto-rico-status.pdf (accessed on 26 March 2009), which reiterates the position of a similar report from 2005 in which

The English language translation of the name of the document is the Constitution of the Commonwealth of Puerto Rico,[109] but the drafting in Spanish produced an entirely different title for the document that links the entity to the concept of self-determination: Estado Libre Asociado de Puerto Rico, that is, the Free Associated State of Puerto Rico.[110] The Spanish language name of the entity can be understood as emphasizing the idea of a compact between the US and Puerto Rico as two entities, while the English language version might have a slightly different connotation, understood as emphasizing more the idea of a compact between the inhabitants of Puerto Rico.[111]

Article 1 of the Constitution of Puerto Rico clarifies that the compact is represented in the terms agreed upon between the people of Puerto Rico and the United States of America, but the compact was actually already made through the joint adoption of Public Law 600 in 1950,[112] not through the joint adoption of the Constitution of Puerto Rico. Anyway, it is possible to argue that at least a practice, if not law, of regional entrenchment of the sub-state constitutional space available to Puerto Rico was created.[113] Within that space assigned in the Federal Relations Act and in the approval by Congress of the first constitution, the legislature and people of Puerto Rico could amend and vary its constitution without engaging the US Congress in amendment processes. For amendments which reach further than the so-called compact between Puerto Rico and the United States,

---

the US executive branch concluded that Puerto Rico is a territorial possession (in fact, property) of the United States and could be disposed of without further consultation.

[109]The use of the term "Commonwealth" is not without historical precedence, because the constitutions of Massachusetts, Pennsylvania, Virginia and Kentucky identify these constituent states of the US as commonwealths. They are, however, regular states in the federation since 1789, whereas Puerto Rico is not a state. The eighteenth century use of the term may be explained by the wish of the two entities to distance themselves from the State, that is, the British Empire, when drawing up their constitutions and to indicate a political existence on a new footing, perhaps in the form of a compact, recorded in the constitutions, between their respective inhabitants.

[110]The terminological choices in the Spanish and the English versions were those of the constitutional convention. See Resolution No. 22 of Constitutional Convention: To determine in Spanish and in English the name of the body politic created by the Constitution of the people of Puerto Rico, of 4 February 1952, in which the specific point was made that "Estado Libre Asociado" is equivalent to and an appropriate translation of the English word "commonwealth". The Spanish-language terminology is therefore not necessarily an equivalent of the term "free association" in the decolonization context of the international politics and international law in the 1960s.

[111]A compact or covenant was used as a background assumption on several occasions when state constitutions were enacted during the latter part of the eighteenth century. See Suksi (1993), pp. 56–58, 69–74, and Elazar (1998), pp. 7 f.,19, 24, 26, 75–98, 108–112, 179, 194, 248, 259, 263, 265, 266–270.

[112]See Public Law 447, 82d Congress: Joint Resolution approving the Constitution of the Commonwealth of Puerto Rico which was adopted by the people of Puerto Rico on March 3, 1952.

[113]See also Smith (2001), p. 382, who makes a similar point with reference to the compact. However, the notion of a genuine compact is very problematic and very much disputed. See, e.g., Rosselló (2005), pp. 214–217.

Congress should presumably be engaged.[114] However, the compact construction has drawn sobering criticism: "The 'compact' referred to in Article 1, Section 1, of the constitution of Puerto Rico is subject to and exists only as permissively allowed at the discretion of Congress. Under the Supremacy Clause (Article VI) of the U.S. Constitution and Section 734 of Title 48 of the U.S. Code, federal law nullifies incompatible local law, not *vice versa*. Thus, the constitution of Puerto Rico does not accord to the residents of Puerto Rico any meaningful form of consent to the promulgation and application in Puerto Rico of federal law, which remains the supreme law of Puerto Rico. Furthermore, by adopting amendments to Puerto Rico's constitution to require that future changes in the local constitution conform to federal law, Congress rejected any suggestion that, as a 'commonwealth', Puerto Rico had achieved nonterritorial association with the United States that was not subject to principles of federal supremacy."[115]

4.3.3 The Ambiguous Position in Relation to the Federation

It should be noted that the Federal Relations Act, adopted in 1917 and as amended, remained in force after the adoption of the Constitution of Puerto Rico, with the exception of some provisions, identified in section 5 of the Act as provisions that were repealed by the time the Constitution of Puerto Rico entered into force. Consequently, in an order of legal norms, the Constitution of Puerto Rico is based on the Federal Relations Act which in turn is based on the territorial clause of the US Constitution. This seems to leave the Constitution of Puerto Rico in an inferior position in relation to the Federal Relations Act and to place the statutory enactments of the legislature of Puerto Rico at an even lower level in a hierarchy of norms. In comparison with the beginning of the twentieth century, it nonetheless was not out of line by the US Congress to state in the preamble of the Act in 1950 that it had, by a series of enactments, progressively recognized the right of self-government of the people of Puerto Rico and caused an increasingly large measure of self-government to be achieved. However, although the idea of a compact is there, the compact is not entrenched in the Constitution of the USA, which means that at least in theory, Congress could, with reference to its plenary powers under the territorial clause, repeal the Federal Relations Act and erase the basis for the

[114]See also Smith (2001), p. 382, who argues that the compact requiring that changes occur only with the agreement of both U.S. and Puerto Rican authorities actually "perpetuates a U.S. veto power over Puerto Rican decisions to alter their internal governing arrangements".

[115]Thornburgh (2007), p. 16 f. The supremacy clause contains three different standards for federal preemption of the legislative powers of states, namely express preemption, field preemption and conflict preemption. See The Constitution of the United States of America – Analysis of Cases Decided by the Supreme Court of the United States to June 28, 2002 (2004), pp. 261–271. See also Rotunda and Nowak (1999), pp. 199–231.

Constitution of Puerto Rico. This is particularly so given that any subsequent Congress after the one that adopted the Act is not bound by the previous one, but is sovereign in relation to a territory such as Puerto Rico. Thus the powers devolved or delegated to Puerto Rico by the US Congress could at least in theory be repealed with reference to the plenary powers of Congress.[116]

In the case of *United States v. Sanchez*,[117] the federal court of appeals found it had to decide "whether the creation of the Commonwealth of Puerto Rico pursuant to the Federal Relations Act so changed the status of Puerto Rico that it must now be considered a separate sovereign for the limited purpose of the dual sovereignty exception to the Double Jeopardy Clause". The court found that this was not the case: Congress' decision to permit self-governance in Puerto Rico does not make Puerto Rico a separate sovereign for double jeopardy purposes in the way the states in the federation are. Puerto Rico is, after the enactment of a constitution for itself, still constitutionally a territory, and not a separate sovereign, and as a territory, "Puerto Rico remains outside an exception to the Double Jeopardy Clause which is based upon dual sovereignty" of the federation and the constituent states. "The authority with which Puerto Rico brings charges as a prosecuting entity derives from the United States as sovereign." "The development of the Commonwealth of Puerto Rico has not given its judicial tribunals a source of punitive authority which is independent of the United States Congress and derived from an 'inherent sovereignty' of the sort supporting the Supreme Court's decisions involving the states (...) and Native American tribes (...). Congress may unilaterally repeal the Puerto Rican Constitution or the Puerto Rican Federal Relations Act and replace them with any rules or regulations of its choice. Despite passage of the Federal

---

[116]See Thornburgh (2001), p. 361: "Puerto Rico's local sovereignty is a statutory delegation of the authority of Congress to govern territories, and is not a vested, guaranteed, or permanent form of sovereignty like the states have under the Tenth Amendment." Also Trías Monge (1997), pp. 112–113, 115 f, makes the point that when the US Congress chose the compact construction, its intention was never to alter the basis of the relationship of Puerto Rico to the United States under the US Constitution. See also Thornburgh (2007), p. 17, Neuman (2001), pp. 194–196, Alvarez-Gonzales (1991), pp. 21–42 (giving some judicial evidence on the existence of an autonomy arrangement based on a mutual compact), and Trías Monge (2001), p. 238, who, however, refers to the case of *Figueroa v. People*, 232 F.2d 615 (1956) that rejects the complete sovereignty of Congress and agrees to the compact construction by saying that the Constitution of Puerto Rico is not just another Organic Act of the Congress (and makes the point that to argue otherwise would be to accuse the US Congress of fraud; the court found that"[w]e find no reason to impute to the Congress the perpetration of such a monumental hoax".). A similar Puerto Rican point, raising ultimately the question of the *pouvoir constituant* or the independent constitution-making powers of Puerto Rico, was inherent in the case of *Ramirez de Ferrer v. Mari Brás*, Supreme Court of Puerto Rico, No. CT-96-14 (18 November 1997), in which the local supreme court detached the local citizenship of Puerto Rico from the U.S. citizenship. See Smith (2001), p. 381, who makes the point that the case was not correctly argued.

[117]*United States v. Rafael Sanchez and Luis Sanchez*, 992 F.2d 1143 (1993). The case was decided by the 11th Circuit, which is not the federal appeals court to which Puerto Rico belongs. Instead, Puerto Rico is under the 1st Circuit, which has viewed the matter differently (see *infra*, notes 118–120 in this Chap.).

Relations Act and the Puerto Rican Constitution, Puerto Rican courts continue to derive their authority to punish from the United States Congress and prosecutions in Puerto Rican courts do not fall within the dual sovereignty exception to the Double Jeopardy Clause." This, however, can be challenged by making the point that actual practice does not operate in this way in Puerto Rico. Also, in the early case of *Puerto Rico v. Shell Co.*,[118] a lower court had concluded that an act of Congress preempted the ground occupied by a local act and superseded it and that the local district court, as a consequence, was without jurisdiction as concerns the offense. The Supreme Court disagreed with this and rejected the assumption that a congressional statute penalizing specific local behavior and a statute of Puerto Rico to the same effect cannot coexist. Consequently, an alleged crime could be tried either on the basis of the US Act or the very similar Puerto Rican Act without risk of double jeopardy. This means that Congress and the Legislative Assembly of Puerto Rico actually could have concurring or virtually overlapping legislative competences within which enactments by both can be valid at the same time. This position appears to have been followed in the case of *United States v. López Andino*,[119] which confirmed the validity of the concept of dual sovereignty for the purposes of separate prosecutions and trials for offenses similarly identified in the two jurisdictions.[120]

The (at least theoretical) issue of the weak position of constitutional rights of the US Constitution in Puerto Rico is paralleled by the relationship between federal legislation and Puerto Rican legislation, where the former supersedes the latter in cases of conflict. According to section 9 of the Organic Act of Puerto Rico *alias* the Jones Act, that is, the subsequent Puerto Rican Federal Relations Act,[121] "the statutory laws of the United States not locally inapplicable (...) shall have the same force and effect in Puerto Rico as in the United States", except if otherwise provided and with the exception of some tax legislation (where the phrase "not locally inapplicable" is the same as in temporally limited incorporation legislation enacted by Congress with a view to admitting particular territories to the federation as states).[122] Hence it is possible for the US Congress to make explicit exceptions

[118]302 U.S. 253, at p. 260, 261.

[119]831 F.2d 1164 (1st Circuit, 1987).

[120]However, the dual sovereignty construction was criticized by Judge Torruella in his concurring opinion (later followed in the case of *United States v. Rafael Sanchez and Luis Sanchez*, 992 F.2d 1143 (1993), *supra* note 117 in this Chap., because Puerto Rico is not sovereign in the same way as a state is, but instead dependent in the exercise of its legislative powers on the sovereignty of Congress. From that perspective, the plenary powers of Congress could also be interpreted so as to make the federal and Puerto Rican norms one legal order, with the sovereign Congress at the top, in which an aborted prosecution by Puerto Rican authorities preclude a new prosecution by federal authorities. This is, however, not the actual situation.

[121]See also US Code, Title 48, Sect. 734.

[122]Apparently, the concept of "not locally inapplicable" has historical roots in incorporation legislation that Congress enacted for new territories, such as Utah and Hawaii. The phrase was used *expressis verbis* in section 5 of Organic Act to Provide for a Government for the Territory of Hawaii of 30 April 1900 (C 339, 31 Stat 141), that is, the same year as the Foraker Act was

for the application of US federal legislation in Puerto Rico, and such exceptions have been made, *inter alia*, in the Internal Revenue Code.[123] However, if there is no such explicit exception in a piece of federal legislation, it in principle applies in the same way as in any state of the US, provided that it is not locally inapplicable. The scope of what is not locally inapplicable, in turn, is determined by courts, in the last instance by federal courts, which means that the defense of local inapplicability becomes a matter of legal interpretation (Chap. 5).

4.3.4 Through Self-Determination to International Politics

Because of its colonial background, Puerto Rico has remained on the agenda of the United Nations.[124] After the Second World War, Puerto Rico was placed on a list of territories over which States should, according to Art. 73(e) of the UN Charter, submit information to the United Nations. However, on 27 November 1953, the UN General Assembly decided that the United States could cease sending information on Puerto Rico after the attainment of self-government in the form of an autonomous political entity.[125] Somewhat later, the decolonization issue gained

enacted: "[. . .] the Constitution, and, except as otherwise provided, all the laws of the United States, including laws carrying general appropriations, which are not locally inapplicable, shall have the same force and effect within the said Territory as elsewhere in the United States [. . .]." The phrase was also used for, e.g., Oklahoma and Wisconsin. Hence the doctrine of distribution of powers between the federation and different territories, incorporated or unincorporated, was muddled from the very beginning, but acceptable probably because it was anticipated that it would not remain in force very long. The phrase was also used in section 1891 of the Revised Statutes of 1878. See Rivera Ramos (2007), p. 89 f., as well as Duffy Burnett (2005), pp. 825–827 (and footnote 129 on p. 826), who thinks that Puerto Rico was, in 1898, implicitly exempted from the application of the US Constitution and Sect. 1891 of the US Revised Statutes, not explicitly, as the Philippines. See also *Cordova & Simonpietri Insurance Agency Inc. v. Chase Manhattan Bank N.A.*, 649 F.2d 36, footnote 34 (1981), for a historical exposé of the phrase, where a link to the so-called "compromise of the thirteen" in 1950 is made.

[123]It seems, however, that some of the exceptions have been revoked later, in particular, in the area of corporate taxation.

[124]See Trías Monge (2001), p. 233. The point is made by Rivera Ramos (2007), p. 223, in the following way: "Thus, a regime of internal democracy coexists with a system of undemocratic colonial subordination."

[125]See UN GA Res. 748 (VIII) of 27 November 1953. In the decision, the UN General Assembly concludes that the people of Puerto Rico has achieved a new constitutional status. The General Assembly also recognized that, "in the framework of their Constitution and the compact agreed upon with the United States of America, the people of the Commonwealth of Puerto Rico have been invested with attributes of political sovereignty which clearly identify the status of self-government attained by the Puerto Rican people as that of an autonomous political entity". This was decided in spite of the fact, reported in Thornburgh (2007), p. 17, that "[i]n advance of the vote in the United Nations adopting Resolution 748, the United States circulated to the General Assembly a legal memorandum stating that the precise legal and political nature of Puerto Rico's 'commonwealth' was subject to the supremacy of federal law as 'interpreted by judicial

new momentum in the UN through two resolutions of the General Assembly, Resolution 1514 (XV) and Resolution 1541 (XV) in 1960, through common Article 1 in the CCPR and the CESR and through the so-called Friendly Relations Declaration of 1970. In this context, the General Assembly and the Decolonisation Committee of the United Nations adopted several resolutions which affirmed the inalienable right of the people of Puerto Rico to self-determination and independence. In this way, the issue of the self-determination of Puerto Rico was actually re-initiated. It is noteworthy that the UN processes were limited in scope in their focus on independence as the outcome of decolonization, without leaving much space for sub-state solutions as possible operationalizations of self-determination.[126] However, just as independence is desired in the context of decolonization in order to secure law-making powers for a new state, sub-state expressions of self-determination should probably result in the creation of exclusive legislative powers in the sub-state entity in a manner which is freely accepted by the population of the colonial area. Therefore, the "present arrangement seems to be acceptable until a formula is found to gain greater political power (through greater autonomy or full incorporation into the United States) without losing the connection to the United States".[127]

The concrete solution to the problem of colonialism has been sought by way of three different alternatives, independence, statehood and improved commonwealth status. The option of independence falls outside of the scope of our inquiry,[128] but

decision' of U.S. courts." See also Thornburgh (2007), p. 62 f., as well as Trías Monge (1997), p. 124 f., according to whom the US opposed the paragraph in the resolution in which the General Assembly affirmed its competence to decide whether a Non-Self-Governing Territory has or has not attained a full measure of self-government, but lost in the vote.

[126]For an account of the issue of Puerto Rico before the United Nations, see Trías Monge (1997), pp. 136–140, Carr (1984), pp. 339–365, Rosselló (2005), pp. 85–98, and Thornburgh (2007), pp. 17, 61–69. For relevant UN committee resolutions, see also Blaustein (1991), pp. 203–234. For an interesting discussion in the United Nations in 2008, bringing the internal differences on status to the UN bodies and problematizing the predominant focus of the UN on independence, see Statement by Hon. Kenneth D. McClintock, President of the Senate of Puerto Rico, before the UN Special Committee on the Situation with Regard of the Declaration on the Granting Independence to Colonial Countries and Peoples, 9 June 2008 at the United Nations Headquarters in New York.

[127]Rivera Ramos (2007), p. 221 f. As pointed out by Rivera Ramos (2007), p. 225, "Congressional refusal to increase Puerto Rican participation in federal legislation or to grant a greater degree of autonomy than is now vested in the Puerto Rican government, absent a substantial change in the political status of the island, is grounded in the view that Congress may not relinquish its plenary powers over Puerto Rico as long as the latter remains unincorporated territory of the United States". This means that avenues indicated by the US Constitution must be used to move Puerto Rico from the ambit of the territorial clause to some other existence in conjunction with the United States.

[128]However, as pointed out by Thornburgh (2001), p. 365, citizenship independent of that of the United States is "an essential characteristic of the status option of independence; it does not exist under the other two options that may be presented to the voters of Puerto Rico". If independence really was an option in the context, it could be effectuated by means of the *pouvoir constituant*, that is, by means of exercising the constituent powers through adopting an independent constitution for an independent country, on the basis of which the sovereignty of the new state and its legislative powers are based. After the establishment of sovereignty, the new sovereign state would, of course, be at liberty to, for instance, conclude a treaty of association with the United States. As maintained

the two other options can be dealt with under the sub-state terminology of this study. The statehood option means that Puerto Rico would be re-constituted as a state in the federation of the United States of America, thus becoming a regular constituent state not subject to the plenary powers of Congress under the territorial clause.[129] In such a situation of integration into the US federal structure, Puerto Rico would perhaps be placed in section I of Fig. 1.1 (Sect. 1.3) or perhaps between sections I and III, with law-making powers of a certain kind entrenched in the US Constitution. Constitutionally, such a solution would be relatively clear-cut, with many historical precedents to fall back on. The improved commonwealth status is much more difficult to envision within the US constitutional structure, but is seems as if such a remodeling of the arrangement would have to involve the creation of exclusive law-making powers for Puerto Rico in a normative framework that is entrenched in one way or the other in the constitutional fabric of the United States. Such measures would move Puerto Rico from section IV in the above table to section I (or perhaps II) of the same, but they would most likely have to be effectuated through amendments to the federal constitution, which is a very difficult way to go,[130] in particular because of the fact that if exclusive legislative powers would be vested in the Legislative Assembly of Puerto Rico by way of enumeration, Puerto Rico would probably have to be exempted from the application of at least the supremacy clause in Art. VI of the US Constitution.[131] Therefore, an enhanced commonwealth may not be at all realistic as a solution.

Because the options of statehood and improved commonwealth status both require decision-making action on the part of the constitutional institutions of the US, the political discussion is constantly focused on the organization of a binding self-determination referendum in Puerto Rico, the alternatives of which would be defined in an act adopted by the US Congress. In the case of independence, the people of Puerto Rico have the right to exercise their self-determination, and at least in principle, no "permission" by the United States is needed. However, only a small minority of Puerto Ricans are in favor of independence, while the large majority of

in Rosselló (2005), p. 272, by way of analogy, the issues in Quebec is whether to get out of Canada, while in Puerto Rico, the issue is whether to team up totally with the United States.

[129]Several proposals from Puerto Rico or the Resident Commissioner of Puerto Rico to adopt Puerto Rico as a state in the federation have been placed with the US Congress during the period of US rule over Puerto Rico, and the matter has been supported also by, *inter alia*, several US Presidents and congressional bills, but to no avail. See Rosselló (2005), pp. 218–228, 242.

[130]As explained in Thornburgh (2001), p. 365, the Puerto Rican judiciary has probably attempted such maneuvers without constitutional basis when ruling that the citizenship of Puerto Rico constitutes a form of citizenship superior to that of citizenship of a state of the Union. However, he also is of the opinion that a "territory with a local commonwealth constitution authorized by an act of Congress (P.L. 81–600) does not have greater sovereignty than a state of the Union".

[131]A provision similar to that in Art. 120 of the Finnish Constitution could be possible: "Puerto Rico will be governed under a special statute, specifying the legislative powers which the Legislative Assembly of Puerto Rico is exercising independently according to the Constitution of Puerto Rico" (Sect. 4.2.4).

Puerto Ricans seems to be in favor of either the statehood option or the developed commonwealth option. In case one of the two internal options for self-determination would gain a clear majority in the future, it would probably not be impossible for the United States and its Congress to work out a normative framework for its realization,[132] although the developed commonwealth option may be unrealistically difficult to fit into the constitutional fabric of the United States.[133] In this respect, the association of Zanzibar with Tanganyika may provide some food for thought.

---

[132]That the federal government remains seized by the matter is obvious on the basis of Executive Order No. 13183 of 23 December 2000 (65 F.R. 82889, as amended by Ex. Ord. No. 13209, Apr. 30, 2001, 66 F.R. 22105; Ex. Ord. No. 13319, Dec. 3, 2003, 68 F.R. 68233) on the Establishment of the President's Task Force on Puerto Rico's Status: "Section 1. Policy. It is the policy of the executive branch of the Government of the United States of America to help answer the questions that the people of Puerto Rico have asked for years regarding the options for the islands' future status and the process for realizing an option. Further, it is our policy to consider and develop positions on proposals, without preference among the options, for the Commonwealth's future status; to discuss such proposals with representatives of the people of Puerto Rico and the Congress; to work with leaders of the Commonwealth and the Congress to clarify the options to enable Puerto Ricans to determine their preference among options for the islands' future status that are not incompatible with the Constitution and basic laws and policies of the United States; and to implement such an option if chosen by a majority, including helping Puerto Ricans obtain a governing arrangement under which they would vote for national government officials, if they choose such a status." For those ends, the President's Task Force on Puerto Rico's Status was established, with the task to "seek to implement the policy set forth in section 1 of the order. It shall ensure official attention to and facilitate action on matters related to proposals for Puerto Rico's status and the process by which an option can be realized. It shall provide advice and recommendations on such matters to the President and the Congress. It shall also provide advice and recommendations to assist the Executive Office of the President in fulfilling its responsibilities under Public Law 106–346 to transfer funding to the Elections Commission of the Commonwealth of Puerto Rico for public education on and a public choice among options for Puerto Rico's future status that are not incompatible with the Constitution and the basic laws and policies of the United States." The Task Force shall report on its actions to the President as needed, but no less frequently than once every 2 years, on progress made in the determination of Puerto Rico's ultimate status. The US Government is hence at least in principle involved in a dynamic process with Puerto Rico concerning Puerto Rico's future status, something which is also referred to by the U.S. Supreme Court in the case of *Reid v. Covert*, 354 U.S. 1, at 15 (1957), where the status as unincorporated territory is viewed through the *Insular Cases* and described as a temporary form of territorial government and which is also expounded in Trías Monge (1997), pp. 125–135. See Thornburgh (2001), p. 368, who adds that this temporary nature continues "until full integration or independence is achieved through the constitutional process of self-determination", and Thornburgh (2007), p. 18, who requires action by Congress for a political resolution of the matter. However, Trías Monge (1997), p. 51, is of the opinion that under the territorial clause, Puerto Rico could be held and governed indefinitely. Concerning the dynamic nature of the issue, see also Duffy Burnett and Marshall (2001), pp. 18–23, Jiménez Polanco (1998), pp. 106–115.

[133]See Thornburgh (2001), pp. 351–359, and Rosselló (2005), pp. 248–261. See also Trías Monge (1997), p. 170, who says that "[s]overeignty, like the atom, can be split", thereby confirming the point of departure in our study.

4.4 Zanzibar: Appeasing Internal Conflict by Uniting for Sub-state Status

4.4.1 A Treaty as the Fundament

By the time Zanzibar gained independence in 1963, there was a plan to create an East-African federation which never materialized (see below), but which may nevertheless have influenced the leaders of Tanganyika and Zanzibar, whose agreement in 1964 produced a new State which was unitary in form for the mainland part of the country, while creating a particular jurisdiction for those islands in the Indian Ocean that are commonly referred to as Zanzibar. The creation of the agreement was very swift and consensus was reached during a secluded meeting of the then leaders of the two countries, President Julius Nyerere of Tanganyika and Sheikh Abeid Karume of Zanzibar.[134] Evidently, the matter of concluding such an agreement was not prepared in advance, but came as a surprise,[135] and the exact provisions were drafted within a matter of days after the principal decision concerning the union had been reached.[136]

The Articles of Union may be defined as a treaty under public international law,[137] because Art. viii foresees ratification of the Articles of Union and domestic implementation of the Articles through legislation in both Tanganyika and Zanzibar.[138] The treaty was thus concluded between two sovereign States.[139] It is

[134]President Karume was then leader of the Afro-Shirazi Party, which was the driving force behind the revolution on 12 January 1964 and which was made into the only party in Zanzibar through the Afro-Shirazi Party Decree, Decree No. 11 of 1965. The revolution of Zanzibar took place at the height of the cold war, and therefore, as explained in Shivji (2008), p. 55 ff., 101–107, 243 f., the Union issue also has connections to the world politics of that time. The suspicion in the West was that the East was in the process of making Zanzibar into the Cuba of Africa and therefore, the West was in support of Tanganyika and the Union.

[135]See, e.g., Dourado (2006), p. 73 f. It is maintained by Shivji (2008), p. 98, that a majority of the members of the Revolutionary Council of Zanzibar would have been opposed to the union with Tanganyika, hence president Karume was hard pressed to act in disregard of the requirement of the law.

[136]See, e.g., Othman (2006), pp. 51–54. For a detailed analysis, see also Shivji (2008), pp. 76–82.

[137]See, e.g., Khamis Bakary (2006), p. 4 f. It seems that the Articles of Union have not been deposited with the United Nations Treaty Series.

[138]In Tanganyika, the Act to ratify the Articles of Union was enacted on 25 April 1964, number 22 of 1964.

[139]Khamis Bakary (2006), p. 24: "Hence the Revolutionary Government of Zanzibar is subordinate to no other power, body or organ of state. Thus Zanzibar is and shall remain a sovereign state, and shall exist as an integral part of the United Republic of Tanzania, in accordance with the terms and conditions stipulated in the Articles of Union between the State of Zanzibar i.e Peoples Republic of Zanzibar and the Republic of Tanganyika."

debatable whether proper ratification has been carried out in Zanzibar,[140] but the passage of time could at least be referred to as a qualification for the current validity of the arrangement on the part of Zanzibar.[141] The treaty background positions Zanzibar in the state of Tanzania in a manner reminiscent of the position of Scotland in the United Kingdom. However, the integration of Zanzibar into the Union Republic was less complete than in the case of Scotland and left Zanzibar with its own law-making body in charge of matters not transferred to the Union when the Articles of Union were concluded.

The birth of the new state was also meant to entail the enactment of a constitution for the united republic by a constituent assembly, as provided for in Art. ii.[142] However, it is debatable as to whether such a constituent assembly has ever been called together.[143] On the one hand, the country could, with reference to the

[140] See Cole and Denison (1964), p. 1512, who state that "a Law to ratify the Articles of Union between the two countries, entitled the Union of Zanzibar and Tanganyika Laws, 1964, was passed in Zanzibar and published as Government Notice No. 243 in the Gazette of the United Republic of Tanganyika and Zanzibar on May 1, 1964". However, according to Khamis Bakary (2006), p. 7 f., no Act to ratify the Union is to be found in the statute book or the official gazette of Zanzibar, that no such legislative decision has been taken, and that there hence has been no ratification on the part of the People's Republic of Zanzibar. Because the basic requirement of ratification of Art. viii of the Articles of Union was not adhered to, the Union is said to have no legal basis. Dourado (2006), p. 76, explains that he was Attorney General of Zanzibar at the material time and that the normal procedure of requesting the legal advice of the AG was not followed when the law to ratify the Articles of Union, 1964 was enacted. However, Othman (2006), p. 51 f., advances the opinion that the Articles of Union was ratified by both the Tanganyika National Assembly and the Revolutionary Council of Zanzibar, because two persons who were in the Revolutionary Council at the time have confirmed that the matter was discussed in the council, during which discussion opinions against the Union were quashed. According to Othman, the union agreement is valid in law. Shivji (2008), p. 92, is of another opinion: "The inescapable conclusion, therefore, is that the Union of Tanganyika and Zanzibar Law, 1964, which *purports* to be the law ratifying the Articles, was never made by the body invested with legislative capacity in and for Zanzibar, and that the body, the so-called Supreme Authority, which purported to make the Law did not have the legislative capacity to make it since the Supreme Authority was superseded once it made the Legislative Powers Law. (...) [T]he law thus made should have been signed by all the members of the Revolutionary Council as was done in the case of the Legislative Powers Law, 1964. It was not." In spite of the legal problems, Shivji (2008), p. 93, arrives at a similar conclusion as Othman: "The notification that such a law had been made by the 'Revolutionary Council of Zanzibar in conjunction with the Cabinet of Ministers thereof' was simply untrue. Thus, the relevant Zanzibari authorities did not ratify, in law and in fact, the Articles of Union. Whether the non-ratification affects the legal validity and political legitimacy of the Union some forty years later is a different matter (...)." See also Shivji (2008), p. 248.

[141] For an argument from the point of view of quiet passive assent, see Khamis Bakary (2006), p. 8 f.

[142] Article vii created a procedure for constitution-making for the entire state according to which a commission would be adopted to make proposals for a constitution for the United Republic, after which a constituent assembly would be summoned within 1 year from the commencement of the union so that the assembly would contain representatives of both Tanganyika and Zanzibar. No such constituent assembly has ever been called together. See Shivji (2008), pp. 108 f., 163–170.

[143] For instance, the constituent assembly that adopted the 1977 Constitution of Tanzania was the regular Parliament that turned itself into a constituent assembly. For a detailed account of this issue,

Articles of Union, still be regarded as being in the interim period specified in the Articles of Union. The constitutional amendments that have taken place have been enacted pursuant to constitutional provisions that could be traced back to the Constitution of Tanganyika, as modified by the Articles of Union.[144] On the other hand, the 1977 Constitution of the United Republic of Tanzania was passed by a Constituent Assembly on 25 April 1977. However, that Constituent Assembly seems not to have been instituted in the manner contemplated by the Articles of Union: the Parliament of the Union declared itself a Constituent Assembly and adopted the 1977 Constitution.[145] Again, the passage of time may have regularized the situation, and several constitutional amendments have occurred in the mean time, indicating at least some level of acceptance and legitimacy of the *de facto* situation also as a *de jure* situation. After the adoption of the 1984 Constitution of Zanzibar,[146] the 1977 Constitution of Tanzania incorporated the position of

see Shivji (2008), pp. 163–170, which concludes that the establishment of one party was the single most significant and decisive moment in the loss of Zanzibar's autonomy at the same time as the 1977 Constitution of Tanzania was enacted in utter breach of the Articles of Union. See also Shivji (2008), p. 172, who makes the point that the single authority of the party made nonsense of the principle of distribution of power between two legislatures and two executives, which he understands to be the core of the federal principle underlying the Articles of Union and the basis of Zanzibar's autonomy. "Zanzibar was left with a shell of autonomy while the substance was drained away."

[144]See, e.g., Dourado (2006), p. 82, who characterizes this instance of constitution-making on 11 July 1965 that led to the enactment of the, actually second, Interim Constitution of Tanzania as a breach of the treaty obligations contained in the Articles of Union. According to Dourado 2006, p. 82 f., the Interim Constitution of 1965 "was passed in order to implement the recommendations of the Presidential Commission on the One-Party State". See also Shivji (2008), p. 125, who points out that "[t]he Act was passed by a special majority under Section 35 of the then existing 'interim constitution'; thus it was treated as a constituent act". Shivji continues by saying that "[i]mplicitly the effect of the Act was to amend the provisions of the Articles of Union and the Acts of Union. The question that arises in law is whether the Union parliament had the authority to amend the Articles and the Acts of Union. As for the Articles, clearly it was an international treaty and therefore could only be amended by the original signatories none of which existed after the Union. (...) At the same time, an Act of the Union parliament could not amend the Acts of Union because the Acts of Union were actually two pieces of law, one passed (purportedly) by the Revolutionary Council and the other by the then Parliament of Tanganyika." Ironically, Karume, who as the President of Zanzibar was, at the same time, the vice-president of Tanzania was the one to assent to the Act by which the Interim Constitution was approved, as explained in Shivji (2008), p. 134: "The Interim Constitution (Amendment) Act (No. 21 of 1965) making currency, foreign exchange and exchange control a Union matter was passed by the National Assembly on 10 June 1965, was assented to by Karume, in absence of Nyerere, on the same date and came into force on that very day. Clearly, Karume did not know what he was signing; Zanzibaris in the parliament hardly appreciated the implication of what they were passing. (...) As usual, Karume did not care about legalities and went ahead to appoint a Bank Commission to look into the modalities of setting up a state bank for Zanzibar." As argued by Shivji (2008), p. 140, the addition of item 12 on the list of Union matters was in breach of the Articles of Union and Acts of Union and therefore invalid.

[145]According to Art. 151(1) of the Constitution of Tanzania, "Parliament" means the Parliament of the United Republic referred to in Art. 62 of the Constitution.

[146]The version used for the purposes of this study is the Constitution of Zanzibar 1984, the Revised Edition of 2006, published by the Revolutionary Government of Zanzibar on the basis of a grant

Zanzibar into the common constitutional fabric. The 1977 Constitution of Tanzania is the national constitution currently in force.[147] It identifies socialism as one of the founding principles of the Government in the preamble and states in Art. 3(1) that the United Republic is a socialist state, which, however, adheres to multi-party democracy.

Article iii of the Articles of Union created a governance solution for the interim period that established the Constitution of Tanganyika as the Constitution of the Union Republic, but in a modified form.[148] The modifications introduced a separate legislature and executive in and for Zanzibar, constituted in accordance with the existing law of Zanzibar. This structure was to have exclusive authority within Zanzibar for matters other than those reserved to the Parliament and Executive of the Union Republic.[149] The indication is therefore that the Union Republic would have enumerated powers, while Zanzibar would possess the residual powers.[150] As concerns the enumerated powers of the Union Republic, Art. iv of the Articles of Union contains a list of eleven matters which shall be reserved to the Parliament and Executive of the United Republic and where they shall have exclusive authority, namely (a) the Constitution and government of the United Republic, (b) external affairs, (c) defense, (d) police, (e) emergency powers, (f) citizenship, (g) immigration, (h) external trade and borrowing, (i) the public service of the United Republic, (j) income tax, corporation tax, customs and excise, and (k) harbors, civil aviation, posts and telegraphs. As a consequence, the distribution of powers

from the UNDP. This version is current as of February 2010. In addition, the constitutional amendments of July 2010 are incorporated in the text on the basis of the Act to Amend the Constitution of Zanzibar of 1984 (the Tenth Zanzibar Constitutional Amendments Act of 2010).

[147]The version used for the purposes of this study is the 1977 Constitution of Tanzania as amended until 30 June 1995. This version is the current one as of February 2010.

[148]On the Interim Constitution, see Shivji (2008), pp. 94–97.

[149]See also Dourado (2006), p. 81 f., who is of the opinion that residual powers were vested not only in Zanzibar, but also in Tanganyika, with the consequence that the Articles of Union created three jurisdictions, and that the temporary fusion of two jurisdictions, the United Republic and Tanganyika) "in one Government has been the cause of confusion and its continuance has resulted in the erroneous thinking that Tanganyika is the United Republic and the United Republic is Tanganyika". "Persons including Government and Party leaders were unable to appreciate that the Government of the United Republic exercising powers over "union matters" in respect of the whole territory of the United Republic was a separate Government from that of the United Republic exercising powers over non-union matters in respect of Tanganyika. In essence therefore there were three governments." See also Dourado (2006), pp. 83 f., 86 ff. In addition to Dourado's wish to promote a federal interpretation of the Articles of Union, his criticism also seems to be based on ignorance of some sort about the existence and function of territorial autonomy, where one of the salient features is that the national parliament is charged with a full competence outside of the territorial autonomy, while the national parliament has a limited competence only inside the autonomy jurisdiction.

[150]See Dourado (2006), pp. 80–81, who also points out that "the Parliament and Executive of the United Republic were given exclusive authority in respect of all other matters in and for Tanganyika". This quality, of course, speaks in favour of a non-federal organisation of the state, although Dourado advocates a federal arrangement.

between Zanzibar and the Union Republic seems federal in nature from the very beginning, although federalism is not referred to in the context. In addition, with a view to the exclusive nature of the powers at the national level, it seems that no concurring powers were envisioned.[151] The two areas of competence would be mutually exclusive, and the national level would also be competent to act within its powers in the territory of Zanzibar.

There have been several attempts in the East African space to coordinate the policies of the various states. At the beginning of the 1960s, there was a plan to create a federation within the area, and there was an East African Common Services Organization between 1961 and 1967 which evolved into the East African Community,[152] but it was dissolved in 1977. Cooperation in the area did not diminish, and in 1999, the Treaty for the Establishment of the East African Community was signed. In 2000, the Treaty was ratified by the three original members, Kenya, Uganda and Tanzania, and it entered into force.[153] The headquarters of the Community are in Arusha, Tanzania. Tanzania joined the Community as a State and brought with it Zanzibar into the Community. Unlike the Åland Islands in the EU context, the Treaty does not mention Zanzibar and does not seem to contain any accommodation for the specific characteristics of Zanzibar. In fact, the functions of the Legislative Assembly of the East African Community as well as the commitments of the States parties, such as Tanzania, are materially speaking overlapping with much of the legislative powers of Zanzibar, while they also cover parts of the Union Matters.

4.4.2 Disputed Amendments to the Union Constitution

Later in the history of Tanzania and Zanzibar, the list of matters attributed to state level has been increased through amendments to the Interim Constitution, but without formal changes to the Articles of Union.[154] The addition of new matters to the list of Union matters without formal amendment of the treaty has continued to function as a source of contentious discussion. It has also reduced the legitimacy of

[151]See *S.M.Z. v. Machano Khamis Ali & 17 Others*, Court of Appeal of Tanzania at Zanzibar, Criminal Application No. 8 of 2000 on 3 April 2000, in which the Court denies that there is a list of concurrent jurisdiction.

[152]See, e.g., Othman (2006), p. 46.

[153]Treaty for the Establishment of the East African Community (as amended on 14th December, 2006 and 20th August, 2007).

[154]As pointed out by Khamis Bakary (2006), p. 3, this is formally speaking not in order, because the Articles of Union "may be amended only through a consensus of the two contracting sovereign parties, and no other body may do so, not even the Parliament of the United Republic". He also makes a reference to the Treaty of Union between England and Scotland. See also Khamis Bakary (2006), p. 9 f.

the Union in the minds of the inhabitants of Zanzibar.[155] The original eleven Union matters became 22 Union matters through these amendments. The additional ones were: 12) all matters concerning coinage, currency for the purposes of legal tender (including notes), banks (including savings banks) and all banking business; foreign exchange and exchange control, 13) industrial licensing and statistics, 14) higher education, 15) mineral oil resources, including crude oil and natural gas, 16) the National Examinations Council of Tanzania and all matters connected with the functions of that Council, 17) civil aviation, 18) research, 19) meteorology, 20) statistics, 21) the Court of Appeal of the United Republic, and 22) registration of political parties and other matters related to political parties.[156] If taken separately, the various Union Matters might add up to more than 30 matters, although the list itself numbers 22. By the end of the 1970s, the residual powers of Zanzibar consisted substantively, *inter alia*, of the following matters: information, agriculture, natural resources, environment and cooperatives, trade, industry, marketing, tourism, education, culture and sports, health and social welfare, water construction, energy and land, communication and transport, as well as youth, employment and women and children's development.[157]

The federal-like distribution of powers, with enumerated powers established for the Union and residual powers for Zanzibar, continues under Art. 4(3) of the 1977 Constitution of Tanzania. The distinction in the Constitution of Tanzania between Union matters and non-Union matters is in principle leading to the creation of legislative jurisdictions that are exclusive in relation to each other,[158] but the growth of the list of union matters has been perceived as a problem, because such a growth erodes the legislative authority of Zanzibar.[159] This is a legitimacy issue arising from the divergent definition of Union Matters as established in the Articles of Union, on the one hand, and the Constitution of Tanzania, on the other, affecting

---

[155]See Shivji (2008), p. 128 f., according to whom the technique of amending the list in the definition section was used to increase the list of Union matters. "By the death of Karume in 1972, the list of union matters had expanded from the original 11 to 16, including significantly the sixteenth item which was 'mineral oil resources including petroleum, its relative hydrocarbons and natural gas."

[156]'Zanzibar: Key Historical and Constitutional Developments' by Eastern Africa Centre for Constitutional Development, at www.kituochakatiba.co.ug/zanz%20const.htm (accessed on 5 February 2010).

[157]For the list, see 'Zanzibar: Key Historical and Constitutional Developments' by Eastern Africa Centre for Constitutional Development, at www.kituochakatiba.co.ug/zanz%20const.htm (accessed on 5 February 2010).

[158]According to Art. 151(1) of the Constitution of Tanzania, "Union Matters" means all public affairs specified in Article 4 of this Constitution as being Union Matters. Hence it seems that the term "matter" is not limited to the identification of legislative powers, but encompasses also executive powers and other public affairs. The consequence is that the division of powers between Mainland Tanzania and Tanzania Zanzibar is of a general nature and not limited to the legislative powers.

[159]Dourado (2006), p. 91: "Every increase in Union matters involves an erosion of Zanzibar's sovereignty over matters reserved to its exclusive jurisdiction."

the relationship between Mainland Tanzania and Zanzibar: "Since appending the list of Union matters to the Interim Constitution of 1965 as a schedule, the practice developed that the Union parliament increased the list by amending the schedule without reference to the Articles of Union. The distribution of power (. . .) between the Union and Zanzibar could be unilaterally changed by the union parliament."[160]

In sub-section 2 of Article iv of the Articles of Union, there is a very particular feature that counters the federal characteristics of the distribution of powers: the legislature and the executive of the Union Republic, that is, the national level, was at the same time the legislature and executive of Tanganyika or mainland Tanzania in respect of all other matters. Hence there would be, under the Articles of Union, only two legislatures and executives in Tanzania, one for mainland Tanzania in respect of the union matters and all other matters and another for Zanzibar in respect of all other matters than union matters.[161] Evidently, mainland Tanzania or former Tanganyika remained a unitary state, while Zanzibar introduced a sub-state feature to the entire state. The sub-state features were visible also through the institutional arrangements. According to Art. iii(b), the principal vice-president of the Union Republic would be the head of the executive of Zanzibar, and under Art. iii(c), there should be representation of Zanzibar in the Parliament of the Union Republic, although the exact form of such representation was unspecified.

This institutional set-up was also commented on by the Court of Appeal of Tanzania in the case of *Seif Sharif Hamad v. S.M.Z.*,[162] which dealt with, *inter alia,* the issue of whether the prosecuting authorities of Mainland Tanzania have the authority to appear before the High Court of Zanzibar for the enforcement of such material legislation that has been enacted within the framework of Union Matters. The Court stated that the "President of the Union has, under Art. 34(3) of the Union Constitution, two hats; that of the United Republic for Union Matters and that of Mainland Tanzania for non-Union matters. Under both hats there are public officers with delegated authority. The crux of the matter is to determine under [which –MS] hat is any public officer operating. The D.P.P. in this case was operating under the hat of Mainland Tanzania on procedural matters which are non-Union matters and so should not have authority to represent the President of the United Republic before the High Court of Zanzibar."

[160]Shivji (2008), p. 173 f.

[161]As pointed out by Khamis Bakary (2006), p. 19, "we have two Constitutions but three jurisdictions, in other words, three governments". In the same vein, see Khamis Bakary (2006), p. 30 f. For features that speak for a federal nature of the arrangement, see Khamis Bakary (2006), pp. 22–27. Those would be the name of the state (Tanzania as a United Sovereign Republic), the existence of three different entities (Tanganyika, Zanzibar and the United Republic), the restriction of the executive authority of the United Republic to the Union Matters only, division of powers between the federal level and the sub-state level, and the (amended) system of picking the vice-President of the Union from one part of the Union if the President comes from the other part. According to Khamis Bakary (2006), p. 31, the Articles of Union are a written, federal, rigid and supreme Constitution.

[162]Court of Appeal of Tanzania, [1998] T.L.R. of 24 February 1993.

4.4.3 Zanzibar's Own Constitution within the Union

Although there were constitutional developments at the national level, it lasted until 5 October 1979 before the first Constitution of Zanzibar was enacted by the Revolutionary Council of Zanzibar,[163] then controlled by the successor of the ASP, the CCM (Chama Cha Mapinduzi). In principle, the 1979 Constitution of Zanzibar followed those provisions in the Union Constitution that relate to Zanzibar, and only minor modifications were made at that point.[164] Essentially, the Zanzibari Constitution was a replica of the national constitution. At this point, a House of Representatives was introduced as the legislative body of the territory, but it had only 10 directly elected members out of a total membership of 109 persons.[165] The House of Representatives started to operate in January 1980. The current rule on the basis of which the House of Representatives exists is Art. 63(1) of the 1984 Constitution of Zanzibar. The provision actually creates a Legislative Council that consists of two parts, the President of Zanzibar, on the one hand, and the House of Representatives on the other.

After some political difficulties, the current Constitution of Zanzibar was enacted in 1984 in the then one-party setting, and it went into operation in 1985.[166] It has been stated that the "1984 Zanzibar Constitution differed very much from the 1979 one, for it had a bill of Rights, defined a Zanzibari, stipulated state directives and made a House of Representatives that consists mostly of elected members",[167] but on the same grounds, it also differed very much from the Constitution of Tanzania,

---

[163]The revolutionary spirit started to fade in 1970, when the first president of Zanzibar was assassinated. The new president started to normalize things by reinstating the common law and the courts instead of the people's courts and by reintroducing a constitution, although not the independence constitution as such, but at least the idea of one. Originally, as pointed out by Othman (2006), p. 44, the idea was to call a constituent assembly within one year after the revolution, but no such body was ever brought into existence. On this, see also Shivji (2008), p. 61 f. For a detailed account of the enactment of the 1979 Constitution of Zanzibar, see Shivji (2008), pp. 186–201.

[164]See 'Zanzibar: Key Historical and Constitutional Developments' by Eastern Africa Centre for Constitutional Development, at www.kituochakatiba.co.ug/zanz%20const.htm (accessed on 5 February 2010).

[165]'Zanzibar: Key Historical and Constitutional Developments' by Eastern Africa Centre for Constitutional Development, at www.kituochakatiba.co.ug/zanz%20const.htm (accessed on 5 February 2010).

[166]In Shivji (2006), pp. 170, 184, the following intriguing question is posed in the context of a treason trial: "What is it that the Constitution of Zanzibar constitutes?".

[167]'Zanzibar: Key Historical and Constitutional Developments' by Eastern Africa Centre for Constitutional Development, at www.kituochakatiba.co.ug/zanz%20const.htm (accessed on 5 February 2010). The liberal tone of the 1984 Constitution of Zanzibar seems, according to Shivji (2008), p. 228, to a great extent be based on the draftsman, then Attorney General Abubakar Khamis Bakary.

to which the Bill of Rights was added only later on.[168] Following the adoption of the Constitution in 1984, the first elections after the 1964 revolution were held in Zanzibar on 13 October 1985.[169] Those elections concerned both the president of Zanzibar and the House of Representatives[170] and were conducted in the one-party setting. As with the Constitution of Tanzania, the Constitution of Zanzibar 1984 also contains a reference to socialism. However, there is little left of that principle in the society of Zanzibar.

In 1992, amendments were made both to the Constitution of Tanzania and the Constitution of Zanzibar towards transforming Tanzania into a multi-party state,[171] and the first multi-party elections in 30 years were held on 29 October 1995.[172] In the elections in Zanzibar, the CCM prevailed with 26 seats, while the CUF (Civic

---

[168] Shivji (2008), p. 227, indicates that the bill of rights was added to the Constitution of Tanzania because "it would have been too embarrassing to have a bill of rights in the Zanzibar constitution and not have one in the Union constitution".

[169] 'Zanzibar: Key Historical and Constitutional Developments' by Eastern Africa Centre for Constitutional Development, at www.kituochakatiba.co.ug/zanz%20const.htm (accessed on 5 February 2010).

[170] According to Art. 151(1) of the Constitution of Tanzania, "the House of Representatives" means the House of Representatives of Zanzibar referred to in Article 106 of this Constitution and which performs its functions in accordance with this Constitution and the Constitution of Zanzibar, 1984. As pointed out in Othman (2006), p. 61, the constitutional discussions of 1983/1984 resulted in major amendments to the 1977 Union Constitution and the formulation of a new Zanzibar Constitution. "But they also resulted in the resignation of Aboud Jumbe from all his state and party positions, the sacking of a Zanzibari Chief Minister and the serious warning given by the ruling party to a number of prominent Zanzibar figures." For a detailed account of the downfall of Jumbe, see Shivji (2008), pp. 201–225.

[171] The transition was made pursuant to recommendations of the so-called Nyalali Commission, or the Presidential Commission on Single Party or Multiparty System in Tanzania. According to Othman (2006), p. 65, one of "the major recommendations of the Nyalali Commission was for the replacement of the present Union set-up with a federal one". Amongst the 11 Zanzibari members of the Commission, "7 wanted the present Union set-up, with some major changes, to remain, 3 wanted a federal and 1 was undecided", but what was important in the context was that both sides agreed that there were problems within the Union. In the work of the Commission, some cases from the Nordic space were presented, namely Denmark (with Faroe Islands and Greenland) and Finland (with Åland Islands) as examples of entities that have "full autonomy in a number of areas which they exercise within a non-federal state". See Othman (2006), p. 65 f. Shivji (2008), p. xviii, makes reference to a colonial-type relationship between Britain and Northern Ireland as a model for the Articles of Federation. Also Dourado (2006), p. 83, accounts for some comparisons with Northern Ireland as a part of the United Kingdom, but denies the validity of the comparison on the basis that Northern Ireland would have been conquered by an imperial power, while Zanzibar was never conquered. Also, Dourado (2006), p. 89, says that in order to "accord with the Articles of Union, 1964 the Constitution should clearly reflect a federal status and not a devolved status (as in the case of Northern Ireland) as desired by NEC" (the NEC is the National Executive Committee of the CCM). See also Dourado (2006), p. 98, who concludes that the "Articles of Union, 1964 did not adopt an intermediate method of setting up two governments or a devolved status as in Northern Ireland".

[172] According to Art. 151(1) of the Constitution of Tanzania, "Political Party" means a political party which has been granted full registration in accordance with the Political Parties Act, 1992.

United Front) secured 21, and the candidate of the CCM won the presidential election by a margin of 1%. The final result was that the CCM gained 26 out of the 50 seats, while the CUF gained 24. The general understanding was that the elections were marred by various irregularities, and as a consequence, violence broke out and the CUF declined to participate in the House of Representatives.[173]

The political opposition was subjected to repressive measures by the public authorities. Some changes were made to the Constitution of Zanzibar in 1998 following recommendations by a Committee appointed by the President of Tanzania, but the political situation did not improve much. After the Commonwealth had involved itself as a mediator between the two parties,[174] the CCM and the CUF, a first agreement (the Muafaka I) was signed, involving pledges to reform, *inter alia*, the election law and the Zanzibar Election Committee. The CUF ended its boycott, but the independence of the Zanzibar Election Committee was not achieved, so the elections of the year 2000 also resulted in violence, deaths and large-scale repression.[175] An internal peace deal (the Muafaka II) was signed between the two parties in 2001 and was implemented, *inter alia*, through amendments no. 8 and 9 to the Constitution of Zanzibar. Since the implementation of the Muafaka II, the Zanzibar Election Committee now includes two members of the official opposition, an office of Director of Public Prosecutions was established,[176] and the leaders of the two parties pledged to develop cordial relationships.[177]

According to the distribution of powers between the Union Republic and Zanzibar, the party legislation is a Union matter.

[173]'Zanzibar: Key Historical and Constitutional Developments' by Eastern Africa Centre for Constitutional Development, at www.kituochakatiba.co.ug/zanz%20const.htm (accessed on 5 February 2010).

[174]According to Art. 151(1) of the Constitution of Tanzania, "Commonwealth" means the organization whose members include the United Republic and every country to which the provisions of section 7 of the Citizenship Act, 1961, apply.

[175]'Zanzibar: Key Historical and Constitutional Developments' by Eastern Africa Centre for Constitutional Development, at www.kituochakatiba.co.ug/zanz%20const.htm (accessed on 5 February 2010).

[176]The idea concerning an independent, impartial and politically neutral Director of Public Prosecutions did actually not come originally from the Muafaka II, but from a study of the legal systems of Tanzania and Zanzibar, carried out in 1994. The so-called Bomani report made such a proposal, but it was not implemented at the time. The Attorney General at the time was actually a politician and a member of Government, and went forward with charging 18 senior political figures of the opposition with treason in a manner which set a negative example of prosecutorial discretion. No-one was convicted on the basis of the charges.

[177]'Zanzibar: Key Historical and Constitutional Developments' by Eastern Africa Centre for Constitutional Development, at www.kituochakatiba.co.ug/zanz%20const.htm (accessed on 5 February 2010).

4.4.4 *Zanzibar in the Union Constitution*

Article 1 of the Constitution of Tanzania identifies Tanzania as one state and as a sovereign United Republic, and continues in Art. 2 to define the territory of Tanzania so that it consists of the whole of the area of Mainland Tanzania[178] and the whole of the area of Tanzania Zanzibar,[179] including the territorial waters. As concerns the latter part of the Union, a similar identification of territory is included in Art. 1 of the Constitution of Zanzibar 1984 (as amended on 9 August 2010), according to which the area of Zanzibar consists of the whole area of the Islands of Unguja and Pemba and all small islands surrounding them and includes the territorial waters that before the Union during a few months formed the People's Republic of Zanzibar.

The state authority is divided between Mainland Tanzania and Tanzania Zanzibar so that there are two organs vested with executive powers, two organs vested with judicial powers and two organs vested with legislative and supervisory powers over the conduct of public affairs.[180] This results in one set of organs for Mainland Tanzania and in another set of organs for Tanzania Zanzibar. The United Republic has its Government, judiciary and legislature, while in Tanzania Zanzibar, the executive powers lie with the Revolutionary Government of Tanzania Zanzibar (RGZ), the judicial powers with the judiciary of Tanzania Zanzibar, and the legislative and supervisory powers with the House of Representatives of Zanzibar.[181] All this is placed in Art. 152(3) under the Constitution of Tanzania, which shall apply to Mainland Tanzania as well as Tanzania Zanzibar. What is notable in this context is that the Constitution of Tanzania recognizes the Constitution of Zanzibar.

A number of provisions of the 1977 Constitution of Tanzania create a focus on the United Republic as the possessor of the sovereignty of the state. According to Art. 28(1), every citizen has the duty to protect, preserve and maintain the independence, sovereignty, territory and unity of the nation, while Art. 28(4) identifies treason, as defined by law, as the most grave offence against the United

[178] According to Art. 151(1) of the Constitution of Tanzania, "Mainland Tanzania" means the whole of the territory of the United Republic which formerly was the territory of the Republic of Tanganyika. Dourado (2006), p. 91 f., criticizes this and is of the opinion that "the Constitution is muddled by using interchangeably Tanzania and the United Republic and the muddle is further compounded by substituting Mainland Tanzania for Tanganyika".

[179] According to Art. 151(1) of the Constitution of Tanzania, "Tanzania Zanzibar" means the whole of the territory of the United Republic which formerly was the territory of the People's Republic of Zanzibar and which was previously referred to as "Tanzania Visiwani".

[180] According to Art. 151(1) of the Constitution of Zanzibar, "state authority" includes the Executive and the Legislature of the United Republic, as well as the Executive and the House of Representatives of Zanzibar.

[181] According to Art. 151(1) of the Constitution of Zanzibar, the term "the Government" is a general term and includes the Government of the United Republic, the RGZ or a District Council or Urban Authority, and also any person exercising any power or authority on behalf of the Government or local government authority.

Republic.[182] In addition, under Art. 32, the state of emergency can be declared by the President, that is, the leader of the United Republic, in relation to Zanzibar also.[183] Finally, it is stated in Art. 46B(1), that the principal executive leaders of the organs vested with executive powers in the United Republic mentioned in Art. 4 of the 1977 Constitution Act shall be duty bound, each of them in the exercise of the powers conferred on him by the 1977 Constitution or the Constitution of Zanzibar 1984, to ensure that he protects, strengthens and preserves the integrity of the United Republic. Because sub-section (3) of the provision identifies not only the President, Vice-President and Prime Minister of the United Republic but also the President of Zanzibar as the principal leaders to whom the duty applies, the latter is supposed to promote the good of the United Republic rather than such particular interests of Zanzibar that could potentially lead to a violation of the integrity of the United Republic. It thus seems as if the protection of Tanzanian sovereignty was established as a principle at the level of the Tanzanian Constitution.

Opinions in Zanzibar may differ from this, but it seems as if it had been, earlier on, impermissible to even discuss different organizational options, including secession, for the position of Zanzibar.[184] This was sustained until 2010 by Art. 1 of the Constitution of Zanzibar 1984, which provided that Zanzibar was an integral part of the United Republic of Tanzania. However, after the constitutional amendment on 9 August 2010 of Art. 1, the special characteristics of the entity are now underlined by the statement that "Zanzibar is a state". Also, Art. 8 of the Constitution of Zanzibar formulates the observance of the principle of independence (ostensibly the independence of Tanzania, at least until 2010) as a fundamental objective of the Government, whatever organizational form that government might assume, and Art. 9(3) continues by requiring such a structure of government of the RGZ which takes into account the need to promote national unity. Therefore, at least normatively, the sovereignty of the state is protected, actually by both constitutions. However, in Art. 23(4) and (5), a constitutional duty is established for every Zanzibari to protect, preserve and maintain the independence, sovereignty, territory

[182]This provision was used by the Court of Appeal of Tanzania in the case of *S.M.Z. v. Machano Khamis Ali & 17 Others* to declare treason a Union Matter.

[183]According to Art. 151(1) of the Constitution of Tanzania, "Zanzibar" has the same meaning as Tanzania Zanzibar.

[184]However, for a published opinion on the matter, see Khamis Bakary (2006), p. 32. For a legal evaluation of the matter, see also Maalim (2006). See, in particular, Maalim (2006), p. 142, and also p. 148, where he advocates the position that the massive election irregularities in the elections of the year 2000 did not reach the threshold of triggering the exercise of the right of secession. Although arguing from the point of view of international law but referring to the Quebec case of the Supreme Court of Canada, Maalim (2006), pp. 149–156, 160, holds it possible that a secession of Zanzibar would be possible only through agreement of the two component parts and advocates that the right and possibility of secession should be recognized in the Constitution of Tanzania. See also Maalim (2006), p. 159: "Zanzibar was once a sovereign state which was brought into the union by its executives and if it seeks to re-establish itself as a sovereign state it will be seeking 'dissolution' and not secession."

and unity of Zanzibar, as if it were Zanzibar that is the independent entity and as if Zanzibar were not a sub-state entity of Tanzania. The Constitution of Zanzibar is therefore not internally entirely consistent, and the relationship between the Union Republic and Zanzibar remains muddled.

The 1977 Constitution of Tanzania contains a two-tiered amendment procedure. Firstly, under Art. 98(1), sub-section a, Parliament may enact legislation to alter any provision of the Constitution, except those relating to paragraph (b) of Art. 98(1), or any provisions of any law specified in List One of the Second Schedule to this Constitution by the support of no less than two-thirds of all the Members of Parliament.[185] The qualified majority required is thus drawn not just from among the MPs present and voting, but from all 323 MPs, which results in the relatively high requirement of 216 MPs. A particular procedure of amendment relates to alteration of any provision of the Constitution or any provisions of any other law that relate to any of the matters specified in List Two of the Second Schedule to the Constitution. Such an amendment shall be passed only if it is supported by the votes of not less than two thirds of all Members of Parliament from Mainland Tanzania and not less than two thirds of all Members of Parliament from Tanzania Zanzibar. This amendment procedure, involving separate majorities of different segments of the membership of Parliament, requires that it is divided into two categories, those drawn from Mainland Tanzania and those drawn from Tanzania Zanzibar. In the former case, the number of MPs is 248,[186] while in the latter case, the number of MPs is 75.[187] Consequently, in order to amend formally or materially List Two of the Second Schedule,[188] 166 mainland MPs and 50 MPs from Zanzibar need to

[185] See also Khamis Bakary (2006), p. 17, who is of the opinion that these Union matters should require the support of two thirds of MPs from Mainland Tanzania and Zanzibar, each, because it would otherwise be easy for the MPs from Mainland Tanzania to alter those Acts.

[186] 182 + 55 (30% of women) + 10 appointees of the President + Attorney General = 248. It is, of course, fully possible that there will be persons from Zanzibar among the 10 appointees of the President. There is no requirement that they have to be recruited from Mainland Tanzania, and in practice, there are Zanzibaris among the appointees of the President.

[187] 50 + 15 (30% of women) + 5 members appointed by the House of Representatives of Zanzibar = 75. Khamis Bakary (2006), p. 16, makes the point in a critical vein that the House of Representatives of Zanzibar does not have the power to introduce legislation on Union matters, but this is probably not quite justified as a point of criticism with a view to the fact that the House of representatives appoints 5 MPs on the top of the overrepresentation of Zanzibar in Parliament.

[188] The list contains the following items that can be characterized as protected or entrenched constitutional matters: the existence of the United Republic, the existence of the Office of President of the United Republic, the authority of the Government of the United Republic, the existence of the Parliament of the United Republic, the authority of the Government of Zanzibar, the High Court of Zanzibar, the list of Union Matters, and the number of Members of Parliament from Zanzibar. It is notable that different dimensions of Zanzibar are strongly featured in this list. Khamis Bakary (2006), p. 16 f., makes the observation that while the number of MPs from Zanzibar is entrenched, the number of MPs from Mainland Tanzania is not so and that Parliament formally speaking could, by simple majority, increase the number of MPs from Mainland Tanzania, thereby rendering the representation of Zanzibar marginal.

support the measure. This procedural requirement amounts to a very peculiar entrenchment clause which is of a general nature, but with a regional dimension. However, it seems that this separate majority procedure has not been used even once in the Union Parliament to pass a law after 1977. This could perhaps be interpreted as evidence for the protective nature of the amendment clause with its heavy weighting in favor of Zanzibar.[189]

The two-tiered amendment procedure with qualified majorities of different kinds in respect of the matters that may concern Zanzibar seems relatively straightforward. However, confusion is created by Art. 64(4) of the Constitution of Tanzania. The provision commences with a disclaimer: any law enacted by Parliament concerning any matter shall not apply to Tanzania Zanzibar. However, there are three exceptions to this listed in the provision, the first of which may amount to substantive changes in the relationship between Mainland Tanzania and Zanzibar and that at least in theory could amount to a certain preemption mechanism. Firstly, if a law explicitly states that it shall apply to Mainland Tanzania as well as to Tanzania Zanzibar or it replaces, amends or repeals a law which is in operation in Tanzania Zanzibar, then the law adopted by Parliament applies to Zanzibar. Secondly, if a law replaces, amends or repeals a law which was previously in operation in Mainland Tanzania and also in operation in Tanzania Zanzibar pursuant to the Articles of the Union of Tanganyika and Zanzibar, or pursuant to any law which explicitly stated that it shall apply to Mainland Tanzania as well as Tanzania Zanzibar, then the law adopted by Parliament applies to Zanzibar. Thirdly, if a law relates to Union Matters, then the law adopted by Parliament applies to Zanzibar. If reference is made to the term "Tanzania" in any law, such a law shall apply in the United Republic in accordance with the three points of departure.

The third category is uncomplicated from the point of view of amendment, because it establishes the reach of the Union legislation within the framework of the Union matters according to the First Schedule of the Constitution of Tanzania, as referred to in Art. 4. Such laws can be enacted pursuant to the ordinary enactment procedure without a qualified majority. However, the first category is problematic from the point of view of the distribution of powers (Sect. 5.5). The second category is uncomplicated at least to the extent that it concerns the reference to the Articles of the Union, while the latter part of the category is unclearly expressed, because there cannot exist very many pieces of law except the Constitution of Tanzania pursuant to which legislation could be passed. In that case, qualified majorities apply. The first category is thus the most problematic one, because Parliament cannot simply enact a law which falls outside the sphere of Union matters and declare it applicable in Zanzibar. On the contrary, such a law is null and void under Art. 64(3) of the Constitution of Tanzania because of encroachment into the sphere of competence of the House of Representatives of Zanzibar. In effect, this latter provision amounts to a denial of supremacy and preemption.

---

[189]See Othman (2006), p. 59.

At the same time, the constitutional situation of Zanzibar is autonomous in its own right. After the revolution in 1964, there was no constitutional document for Zanzibar until 1979. The first sub-state constitution of Zanzibar was enacted in 1979 and replaced in 1984 by the current Constitution of Zanzibar. It can be asked whether it emanates from the Union constitution or whether it exists on the basis of the Articles of the Union. The Articles of Union in a way presuppose the existence of a constitutional structure of Zanzibar as one part of the Union Republic, so at least from the point of view of Zanzibar, the Constitution of Zanzibar emanates in its own right from the Articles of Union.[190] In addition, the Constitution of Zanzibar of 1984 was enacted independently of the Union constitution, because the Union constitution did not, at that point, require a Constitution of Zanzibar or make any reference to it. In fact, the Constitution of Zanzibar can be amended and repealed by the House of Representatives of Zanzibar without the confirmation of Parliament, although it has to conform to the Union Constitution. This, therefore, is one important dimension of autonomy.

Later amendments to the Constitution of Tanzania specifically recognize the 1984 Constitution of Zanzibar. With reference to the conformity of the Constitution of Zanzibar with the Constitution of Tanzania, Art. 64(5) of the latter contains a provision of a *Grundnorm* nature which states that without prejudice to the application of the Constitution of Zanzibar in accordance with the Constitution of Tanzania concerning all matters pertaining to Tanzania Zanzibar which are not Union Matters, the Constitution of Tanzania shall have the force of law in the whole of the United Republic. If in that set up any other law conflicts with the provisions contained in the Constitution of Tanzania, the Constitution of Tanzania shall prevail and the other law shall be void to the extent of the inconsistency with the Constitution. Of course, the Articles of Union may be regarded as such a *Grundnorm*, too, because the Articles of Union constitute a "parent Act from which all other legislative Acts (including the two Constitutions [. . .]) have derived their authority".[191] In this light, the amendments in August 2010 to Art. 1 of the Constitution of

[190]As pointed out by Shivji (2006), p. 184, "[t]he Constitution of Zanzibar is made by the people of Zanzibar through the Revolutionary Council. It does not derive its legal authority or political legitimacy from the Union Constitution nor it is subordinate to the Union Constitution. This is stated very explicitly in the Preamble of the Zanzibar Constitution." Shivji (2006), p. 186, draws the conclusion that "the Constitution of Zanzibar constitutes State Power which is the sum of executive, legislative and judicial power".

[191]Khamis Bakary (2006), pp. 2, 28–29, where he also laments the fact that the Articles of Union, in their capacity as the *grundnorm*, were not taken into consideration when the cases of *Seif Sharif Hamad* and *Machano and 17 others* were decided. See also Khamis Bakary (2006), pp. 30 ff., where he argues that the Articles of Union are a supreme law of the land and form a written Constitution of the Union. Shivji (2006), p. 184, draws the following conclusion: "The Articles of the Union, through the Acts of Union, are part of the Constitution of the Union and that of Zanzibar. Both the Constitution of Zanzibar and the Union Constitution are subordinate to the Acts of Union and in case of conflict the Acts of Union prevail." However, according to Shivji (2008), p. 178, the 1977 Constitution of Tanzania has been understood as departing from the idea that the Government of Zanzibar derives its authority from the 1977 Constitution, but he considers this

Zanzibar that identify Zanzibar as a state cannot purport to amend the relationship between Zanzibar and the Union as the relationship is defined in the Articles of Union or in the Constitution of Tanzania. Therefore, the amendment is confined to Zanzibar alone.

4.4.5 *The Distinctiveness of the Zanzibari Jurisdiction*

There is also a superiority clause in Art. 4 of the Constitution of Zanzibar of 1984, and it is similar to the superiority clause in the Union Constitution. According to the provision, the Constitution has the force of the law throughout the country, which at face value seems to imply direct legal effect within the territory of Zanzibar. In that respect, the Constitution forms a higher norm in relation to any other norm passed within the jurisdiction of Zanzibar, and if any legislation is found to be in conflict with the Constitution, it shall prevail and the lower norm shall be null and void to the extent that it conflicts with the constitution. However, there is one part of the Constitution which contains only fundamental principles and directive principles and policies of the RGZ, namely chapter 2 of the Constitution, that is, Articles 8-10A. According to Art. 10A, the provisions of this general chapter shall not be enforced by any court. The provision goes on to hold that no court in the country shall have the power to decide any matter either to be done or not to be done by any person or authority or law or any judgment which is in accordance with the provisions in Articles 8–10. Therefore, the objectives, while they probably should be perceived as binding on the RGZ, are declared unjusticiable by an explicit provision of the Constitution.

This is not the case as concerns the Bill of Rights of the Constitution of Zanzibar, that is, Articles 11-25A.[192] On the contrary, and with effect beyond the Bill of Rights, Art. 25A creates an individual right for any person to institute a suit in the High Court if he sees that the Constitution has been violated or is being violated or is likely to be violated.[193] In such a situation, the High Court is empowered to

understanding as erroneous, because the Government of Zanzibar derived its authority from the revolution and the subsequent laws passed by the Revolutionary Council.

[192] See also Tanzania Human Rights Report (2009), p. 202, where the distinction between justiciable and unjusticiable rights is confirmed.

[193] This is sustained by Art. 23(1), according to which every person has the duty to observe and abide by the Constitution of Zanzibar and the laws of Zanzibar, and to take legal action to ensure the protection of the Constitution and the laws of the land. The violent reaction against demonstration by the opposition party CUF on 27 January 2001, reported in Maalim (2006), p. 146, seems to have been carried out in spite of the right of free and peaceful assembly in Art. 20(1) of the Constitution of Zanzibar. Also in conjunction to the elections of the year 2000, limitations of human rights were put in place without a declaration of any state of emergency.

declare and order that the Constitution has been violated, is being violated or is likely to be violated, and as a consequence, the High Court may give an order to the officer or government organ concerned. There is a more specific redress mechanism of the same kind attached to the Bill of Rights in Art. 24(2), on the basis of which the High Court has the power to declare and order compensation to any person whose rights have been violated. It seems, however, as if these constitutional remedies, of potentially monumental importance, have not been used very much, if at all. One reason for this could be the limitation clauses in Art. 24(1) and Art. 24 (4), according to which the guarantees and remedies may be varied through legislation enacted by the House of Representatives.

As provided for in the Articles of Union, Zanzibar has its own judiciary which is independent from the judiciary of Mainland Tanzania.[194] This is facilitated under the 1977 Constitution of Tanzania under Art. 114, according to which provisions that create the judiciary of the Union Republic do not prevent the continuance or establishment, in accordance with the law applicable in Zanzibar, of the High Court of Zanzibar or courts subordinate to it.[195] The High Court is based on Art. 93(1) of the Constitution of Zanzibar. It is identified as a superior court of record with unlimited jurisdiction on criminal and civil cases and other powers as may be conferred.[196] According to Art. 100 of the Constitution of Zanzibar and on the basis of the High Court Act 1985, there shall, in addition to the High Court itself, be Regional Magistrate's Courts,[197] District Magistrate's Courts, and Juvenile Courts. In addition to the regular courts, there is, according to the High Court Act, also a separate court organization in Zanzibar based on Islamic conceptions.

[194]According to Art. 151(1) of the Constitution of Tanzania, "Judiciary of Zanzibar" means the Zanzibar Judiciary which includes all the courts within the RGZ. For a detailed account, see Peter and Sikand (2006).

[195]According to Art. 151(1) of the Constitution of Tanzania, "High Court" means the High Court of the United Republic or the High Court of Zanzibar, while the "Chief Justice of Zanzibar" means the Chief Justice of the High Court of Zanzibar who, pursuant to the Constitution of Zanzibar, 1984, is the head of the Zanzibar Judiciary. It should be noted that the Chief Justice of Zanzibar and the members of the Zanzibar High Court are appointed by the President on the recommendation of the Judicial Service Commission.

[196]For instance, under Art. 72(1) of the Constitution of Zanzibar, the High Court of Zanzibar has exclusive jurisdiction and authority to hear and determine all cases concerning the elections in Zanzibar, except elections of the President of Zanzibar. Hence election complaints are tried by the High Court, and the reliefs that can be claimed are a declaration that the election is void a declaration that the nomination of the person elected was invalid a declaration that any candidate was duly elected where the seat is claimed for an unsuccessful candidate on the ground that he had a majority of lawful votes, a scrutiny. Election petitions shall be presented within fourteen days from the date of the declaration of the results of the election by the Returning Officer, and the High Court shall hear and determine each election petition within two years from the date of presentation of the election petition before it.

[197]The Magistrates' Court Act 1985, Act No. 6 of 1985.

These so-called Kadhis' courts, introduced already during the British colonial era, deal with legal problems of Islamic personal status, marriage, divorce and inheritance, provided that both parties are Muslims.[198] The law of evidence and also procedure to some extent is that applicable under Muslim law (generally, however, the common law provides for the procedure), and the jurisdiction of Kadhis' Courts is connected to the High Court of Zanzibar through the possibility of appeals.[199] However, cases originating in Kadhis' Courts cannot be brought to the Court of Appeal of Tanzania, so the High Court of Zanzibar is the final instance in those matters.

The jurisdictional relationship between the court systems of Mainland Tanzania and Zanzibar is established in Art. 115(1) of the Constitution of Tanzania. According to the provision and subject to Articles 83 and 116 of this Constitution, the jurisdiction of the High Court of Zanzibar shall be as specified in the laws applicable in Zanzibar. In addition, sub-section (2) of the provision stipulates that, subject to the provisions of the Constitution of Tanzania or of any other law enacted by Parliament, where any law enacted by Parliament which is applicable in Mainland Tanzania and also in Tanzania Zanzibar vests any power in the High Court, then the High Court of Zanzibar may exercise that power concurrently with the High Court of the United Republic.[200] This means that the judiciary of Zanzibar implements both the laws of Zanzibar and those laws of the Union that are applicable in Zanzibar,[201] with some

[198] The Kadhis' Courts Act, 1985, Act No. 3 of 1985.

[199] As pointed out in Tanzania Human Rights Report (2009), p. 187 f., there is an unclear situation as concerns law of procedure in Kadhi's courts that results in restrictions of access to justice.

[200] As stated by the Court of Appeal of Tanzania in the case of *Seif Sharif Hamad v. S.M.Z.*, [1998] T. L.R., the High Court of Zanzibar has concurrent jurisdiction with the High Court of Tanzania over legislation which applies to both parts of the United Republic, as provided by Art. 115(2) of the Constitution of Tanzania. Therefore, the trial of an applicant on the basis of the National Security Act 1970 was conducted in the High Court of Zanzibar. Also, the Court established that because the High Court and the courts subordinate thereto are not Union Matters, the procedure and processes in those courts are not Union Matters. On this basis, the prosecution in Zanzibar of a crime that is based on the National Security Act 1970 is not the responsibility of the Director of Public Prosecutions of Mainland Tanzania, but of the prosecutorial officer of Zanzibar. Hence the point of the provision is that the administration of justice is not a union matter. When an act is committed in Zanzibar in violation of Union laws, the matter has to be brought for trial in a Zanzibar court.

[201] This is also supported by Art. 101 of the Constitution of Zanzibar, according to which documents containing court orders issued by courts in Mainland Tanzania and courts in Zanzibar in cases of whatever civil nature and criminal matters of all kinds (including warrants of arrest) may be served and may be executed in any place in Tanzania, subject to certain conditions established in the provision. In practice this means that criminal law on such areas which is within Union matters, e.g., armament control and firearms, is prosecuted under the authority of the Director of Public Prosecutions of Zanzibar, and the situation is similar as concerns immigration law. If the criminal or illegal act has taken place in Zanzibar, then also the enforcement of the applicable law takes place there. Shivji (2008), p. 116 f., accounts for the control that Zanzibar exercised over immigration during the first three decades of its Union time and makes the point that the fully integrated Union law on immigration was passed only in 1995.

exceptions.[202] However, the laws of the Union applied by the courts of Zanzibar constitute a clear minority amongst the norms applied, perhaps less than 5%. Most of the normative materials applied by the courts of Zanzibar therefore originate in the legal order of Zanzibar. Although the two judiciaries are separate, the apex of the two court systems is united, because the Court of Appeal of Tanzania is the appeals court also for the purposes of cases that arise on the basis of norms in the legal order of Zanzibar, except those of a Muslim origin[203] and those relating to the interpretation of the Constitution of Zanzibar, as stated in Art. 99 of the Constitution of Zanzibar. In the instances where the legal problem arises on the basis of norms within the legal order of Zanzibar, the Court of Appeal applies the laws of Zanzibar, not those of the Union.[204] In fact, the Court of Appeal sits in Zanzibar once a year to hear cases originating in Zanzibar, normally around five cases per year. The President of Tanzania appoints the Justices of Appeal from among persons who qualify to be appointed Judges of the High Court of the United Republic or from among persons who qualify to be appointed Judges of the High Court of Zanzibar in accordance with the laws applicable in Zanzibar.[205] In this context, Zanzibar thus has the possibility to set its own qualification requirements for the judges of its own courts.

[202]As stated in the case of *Haji v Nungu and Another*, Court of Appeal of Tanzania, [1987] LRC (Const) of 27 September 1986, "the Election Act 1985 has to be read together with article 83 of the Constitution and that fact precludes the High Court of Zanzibar from acquiring jurisdiction concurrently with the High Court of the United Republic", because the Court of Appeal was specifically vested with the jurisdiction to hear appeals from the High Court of the United Republic in matters including election petitions. The High Court of the United Republic has no territorial jurisdiction over Zanzibar and cannot sit in Zanzibar to hear election petitions, but has to do so in the mainland, although its material jurisdiction in election matters also covers Zanzibar.

[203]Even so, under Art. 116(2) and (3), the Chief Justice of the Court of Appeal shall have no power over any matter concerning the structure and administration of the day-to-day business of the courts established in accordance with the Constitution of Zanzibar, 1984, or any law of Tanzania Zanzibar. The Chief Justice shall from time to time consult with the Chief Justice of Zanzibar concerning the administration of the business of the Court of Appeal in general, and also concerning the appointment of Justices of Appeal.

[204]This unification of the legal order at its apex is also reflected in Art. 45(1) of the Constitution of Tanzania, according to which it is the Union President who has the grant pardons, less severe punishment, etc., also in respect of persons convicted and punished in Tanzania Zanzibar and in respect of punishments imposed in Tanzania Zanzibar under legislation enacted by Parliament which applies to Tanzania Zanzibar, in the same manner he is authorized to exercise those powers in Mainland Tanzania.

[205]See, however, Khamis Bakary (2006), pp. 14–15, who presents critical remarks concerning the composition and functioning of the Court of Appeal of Tanzania.

4.4.6 *The Unimplemented Constitutional Jurisdiction and Other Joint Bodies*

Although the Court of Appeal of Tanzania is the highest court instance of the state, it has been excluded in Art. 117(2) from adjudication of competence issues that might arise between the Government of the Union Republic and the RGZ. Instead, the 1977 Constitution of Tanzania creates a particular court instance for that purpose, the Special Constitutional Court referred to in Art. 125 through 128 of the Constitution of Tanzania. Its sole function is to hear and give a conciliatory decision over matters referred to it concerning the interpretation of the Constitution of Tanzania where such interpretation or its application is in dispute between the Government of the United Republic and the RGZ, which means that its mandate is relatively limited and excludes, for instance, claims of unconstitutionality that arise amongst private individuals.[206] However, so far, the court has not been constituted.[207] The decisions of the Court are final.

The Special Constitutional Court does not have the power to inquire into or to alter the decision of the High Court or the decision of the Court of Appeal which has been given in accordance with the provisions of Art. 83 of the Constitution or the decision of the Court of Appeal which has been given in accordance with Art. 117 of the Constitution.

Half of the members shall be appointed by the Government of the United Republic and the other half shall be appointed by the RGZ from among judges of the two High Courts or Justices of Appeal. In principle, the Special Constitutional Court is composed of equal numbers of persons from the two parts of Tanzania, the Union Republic and Zanzibar, which gives a strong position to Zanzibar. A person may be appointed to be a member of the Special Constitutional Court for the purposes of hearing one dispute only or for hearing two or more disputes should they arise, but the Court shall hold sittings only when there is a dispute to be heard.

However, so far, not one single case has been dealt with by the Special Constitutional Court.[208] Therefore, it is not possible to know how the complicated decision-making procedure of the Court would operate in practice: a decision shall be determined on the basis of the opinion of two thirds of the members appointed from Mainland Tanzania and two thirds of the members appointed from Tanzania Zanzibar, that is, by separate qualified majorities, as if the resolution of the dispute amounted to a constitutional amendment affecting Zanzibar.[209]

---

[206]See, e.g., Khamis Bakary (2006), p. 13.

[207]Shivji (2008), p. 180.

[208]Khamis Bakary (2006), p. 18. He reports a case in 1984, when the then President of Zanzibar was determined to call for the Special Constitutional Court, but the one Party "frustrated his efforts and he was forced to resign from the CCM Party and the Government".

[209]See Khamis Bakary (2006), p. 13 f., and Shivji (2008), p. 180, who think that the Special Constitutional Court would not be capable of operating under such requirements of super-majorities.

In addition to the redundancy of the Special Constitutional Court, Art. 99(1)(a) of the Constitution of Zanzibar declares that the Court of Appeal shall not have the power to hear cases relating to the interpretation of the Constitution of Zanzibar.[210] No Union institutions thus seem to have the competence to make determinations concerning the internal constitutional issues of Zanzibar.[211] The Constitution of Zanzibar, however, identifies in Art. 99A the High Court of Zanzibar as the instance at which constitutional interpretation of the Constitution of Zanzibar takes place. If a lower court deals with a suit in which the interpretation of the Constitution of Zanzibar arises, the case shall be immediately referred to the High Court of Zanzibar. In case there is an appeal against the decision of the High Court in such a constitutional case, the case shall be heard by three judges of the High Court, as appointed by the Chief Justice and excluding the judge who heard the case on the first occasion. There have, however, been very few cases of a constitutional nature that the High Court of Zanzibar has dealt with, and they seem to have ended up in the Court of Appeal of Tanzania because they have involved individual parties who have been able to bring their cases all the way to the Court of Appeal as the problematic issues have been based on material law in ordinary acts below the level of constitutional law.

For the determination of the level of ethical conduct within the two governments, Art. 129 of the Constitution of Tanzania creates the Permanent Commission of Enquiry, which shall, upon the conclusion of an enquiry and pursuant to the procedure prescribed by a law enacted by Parliament in that regard, submit to the President or to the Head of the RGZ, as the case may be, a report on the proceedings of the enquiry, the views of the Commission on the whole matter, and its recommendations. Such enquiry may in principle be instituted in relation to persons employed in the service of the Government of the United Republic and those in the RGZ, employees and leaders of political parties who deal with public affairs, members and employees of all Commissions in the Government of the United Republic and the RGZ, persons holding office in the departments of those governments, public corporations, and such other public authorities as may be specified in a law enacted by Parliament. However, two persons are excluded from the range of such enquiry, the President of Tanzania and the Head of the RGZ.

The Special Constitutional Court of the United Republic and the Joint Financial Committee of the United Republic as well as the National Electoral Commission of

[210] In addition, it is excluded from hearing matters of Islamic law which have arisen at a Kadhis' court and such matters which the Constitution of Zanzibar or a law enacted by the House of Representatives identifies.

[211] In the case *Seif Sharif Hamad v. S.M.Z.*, dealing with the application of material criminal law of the Union by the courts of Zanzibar, the Court of Appeal also touched upon constitutional issues, and raised a specific constitutional point on the basis of the then Art. 98(2) of the Constitution of Zanzibar, repealed in 2002. The Court wondered, in case of any inconsistency between the two Constitutions, "which body would have the authority to reconcile the two provisions or declare one inappropriate"? With a view to Art. 99 of the Constitution of Zanzibar, the question is still relevant.

the United Republic are, under Art. 124 of the Constitution of Zanzibar, identified as such institutions which, in accordance with their establishment pursuant to provisions in the Union Constitution, are authorized to perform their functions in Zanzibar in terms of the procedure stipulated in the Union Constitution and any other law enacted by either Parliament or the House of Representatives. For those functions, as performed in Zanzibar, the three institutions shall, under the Constitution of Zanzibar, be construed as institutions of the RGZ. This results in that the national elections carried out in Zanzibar are actually carried out under the authority of the National Election Commission.

4.4.7 Unclear Funding Arrangements

The budget of the Union Republic is in principle a matter of the Union Republic, and according to Art. 133 of the Constitution of Tanzania, the Government of the United Republic shall maintain a special account to be known as "the Joint Finance Account". It forms a part of the Consolidated Fund of the United Republic,[212] and to that Joint Finance Account, all the moneys contributed by the two Governments shall be paid in such proportions as shall be determined by the Joint Finance Commission in accordance with legislation enacted by Parliament for the purposes of the business of the United Republic in relation to Union Matters.[213] The seven member Joint Finance Commission, appointed by the President, shall analyze the revenue and expenditure arising from, or relating to the management of affairs concerning Union Matters, and make recommendations to the two Governments concerning the contribution by, and the allocation to, each of the Governments.

The Commission has, however, not functioned consistently, and it has therefore not fulfilled its task to keep under constant scrutiny the fiscal system of the United Republic and also relations between the two Governments concerning financial matters. The consequence of this has been that the RGZ has not contributed any funds to the management of Union matters, while the Government of Tanzania has made transfers to the RGZ that amount to 4.5% of the Consolidated Fund per year, including the same share of development funds from donor countries to Tanzania. The RGZ has its own Consolidated Fund under Art. 104 of the Constitution of

[212]According to Khamis Bakary (2006), p. 12, Mainland Tanzania does not have its own Consolidated Fund for matters other than Union Matters which relate to Mainland Tanzania only, which underlines the asymmetrical nature of the Tanzanian arrangement. From the perspective of Zanzibar, this is a problem, because according to Khamis Bakary (2006), p. 12, "all expenditure in respect of non-Union matters in Mainland Tanzania should not be met by the Consolidated Fund of the United Republic".

[213]According to Khamis Bakary (2006), p. 12, this contains a further asymmetrical problem, because "it is only the governments of the United republic and that of Zanzibar, which are bound to contribute for the servicing and maintenance of the Union. Mainland Tanzania does not contribute anything and in fact is not bound under the Constitution to do so".

Zanzibar to which all revenue derived from various sources shall be paid. It is, under Art. 114 of the Constitution of Zanzibar, from the Consolidated Fund of Zanzibar that the contribution of the RGZ to the Union should be paid.[214]

The economic advantages of the Union for Zanzibar become even more apparent when the tax powers are taken into consideration. According to Art. 138 of the Tanzanian Constitution, the Union Parliament enacts tax legislation, but the House of Representatives of Zanzibar is, at the same time, not precluded from exercising its power to impose tax of any kind. This means in practice that Parliament enacts tax legislation for Mainland Tanzania, while the House of Representatives enacts particular forms of tax legislation for Zanzibar. While it can be said that the Union is, in many ways, irrelevant in Zanzibar because most of the matters leading to legislation are the responsibility of Zanzibar, the Union brings in a clear economic benefit for Zanzibar that might not be there if, for instance, Zanzibar became independent.

4.4.8 *The Category of Zanzibari and the Special Rights*

The Constitution of Tanzania departs from the fact that there are citizens of Tanzania. However, the Constitution of Zanzibar distinguishes between three categories of persons, namely everyone for the purposes of most of the constitutional rights established in the Constitution of Zanzibar,[215] as well as citizens, and Zanzibari. The category of everyone has the broadest coverage. The category of citizens, apparently in the meaning of citizens of Tanzania, seems to be relevant

[214]According to Art. 115 of the Constitution of Zanzibar, the contribution from the RGZ to the Union shall not be expended until the Joint Finance Commission has analysed the revenue and expenditure and made its recommendations to relevant institutions on the allocation of the expenditure and the RGZ agrees with the said recommendations and allocation. This provision of the Zanzibar Constitution functions thus as a restriction on the part of the RGZ in relation to the Union as concerns the funding of the Union, leaving the Union budget in principle dependent on Mainland Tanzania. The finances of Zanzibar are managed by the Zanzibar Revenue Board. The revenue is partly originating in the tax powers of Zanzibar, and although the income taxation is a Union Matter, there is an understanding that whatever is collected in Zanzibar by the Tanzania Revenue Authority, the tax remains in Zanzibar and is transferred to the Government of Zanzibar. Development aid is by default going to Mainland Tanzania, as is pointed out by Dourado (2006), p. 101, but a solution has been worked out that gives a share of 4.5% of whatever is received to Zanzibar, more or less on the same basis as transfers are made to a regular region of Tanzania. Zanzibar would, however, like to have 11.5%, because that was the share of Zanzibar towards the creation of the Central Bank of Tanzania and also to the currency board of the East African Community in the 1960s. On the dissolution of the currency board and the assets that should have returned to Zanzibar up to 11.05%, see Shivji (2008), p. 132.

[215]The great majority of the Zanzibari are Muslim, but the Constitution of Zanzibar tries to establish a relatively secular state. In Art. 19(1) of the Constitution, every person is accorded the right to freedom of thought or conscience, belief or faith and choice in matters of religion. It is remarkable that the provision also guarantees the freedom to change religion or faith.

only in respect to one constitutional right in the bill of rights, that is the right to be informed about events both within the country and in the world at large in Art. 18 (2), but most of the fundamental objectives and directive principles and policies are also intended to cover all citizens. However, as concerns the category of Zanzibari, there are clear connections in the Constitution of Zanzibar to the mechanisms of participation in Zanzibar. This is the case, for instance, in respect of Art. 7(1), according to which any Zanzibari who has attained the age of eighteen years shall have the right to vote in the elections taking place in Zanzibar, as specified in ordinary law. Article 21(1) and (2) contain further references to the right of a Zanzibari to participation. At the same time, the Constitution presupposes in its Art. 6 that a specific legislative definition of the category of Zanzibari is established by the House of Representatives.[216] This is done in the Zanzibari Act, 1985.[217]

According to the Zanzibari Act, the term 'citizen' means a citizen of the United Republic of Tanzania as defined in the Citizenship Act of the United Republic, while a 'Zanzibari' means a Zanzibari person as defined in the Constitution of Zanzibar. The dates of independence and conclusion of the Articles of Union are cutting points for defining the status of a Zanzibari as a regional citizenship of some sort. In principle, the starting point is citizenship of Tanzania, in accordance with both *jus soli* and *jus sanguinis* at the inception of the current Zanzibar. According to Art. 3 of the Act, any person who is a citizen of Tanzania in accordance with the Tanzanian citizenship law and who has been residing in Zanzibar before and up to 12 January 1964 shall be a Zanzibari, which means that by the time of independence, the citizenship of the new state was created as a summary measure for everyone within the jurisdiction. This is continued by providing that any person who, as from 26 April 1964, is a citizen of Tanzania and who was born in Zanzibar shall be a Zanzibari if both of his parents or his father or his mother is a Zanzibari in accordance with the Zanzibari Act. In addition, it is declared that any person who is a citizen and who, before 26 April 1964, was a Zanzibari shall be a Zanzibari if he has not lost his Tanzanian citizenship.

The starting point for determining who has regional citizenship of Zanzibar is thus relatively generous, although after this point in time, the status of Zanzibari will be based on *jus sanguinis*. The picture, however, changes when considering persons who might want to become Zanzibari without qualifying for the above-mentioned fundamental conditions. Some of the requirements for becoming a Zanzibari by naturalization, that is, through a separate decision by the Government of Zanzibar (or a Minister, as the case may be) on the basis of an application by the prospective person, are quite stringent. Such a person must have resided in Zanzibar for a consecutive period of fifteen (15) years, he or she must have sufficient

[216]Article 6(1) of the Constitution of Zanzibar creates the category of the Zanzibari person as a distinctive status definition who, under sub-section 2 of the provision, shall enjoy rights and privileges befitting a Zanzibari and shall also be obliged to perform duties, functions and responsibilities as provided in the Constitution or in ordinary legislation.

[217]Act No. 5 of 1985.

knowledge to write and read Kiswahili, he or she must be of good character, he or she must have entered Zanzibar lawfully and obeyed all prevailing laws and regulations of Zanzibar, he or she must be of full age, and he or she shall have the intention to continue residing in Zanzibar. Such a naturalized person may also lose his or her Zanzibari status, if he or she is deprived of Tanzanian citizenship or if a Minister deprives him or her of Zanzibari status. The Government issues identity cards to persons who qualify as Zanzibari that function as identity cards for various purposes in the private sphere, but the card is also evidence of the person's right to vote.

There are some rights outside the scope of participation, understood in the broad sense of the concept so that it also encompasses appointments to at least the most important public offices, that seem to depend on the status of being a Zanzibari. These are the right to work,[218] equal opportunity and the right to hold on equal terms any office or discharge any function under the state authority of Zanzibar, established in Art. 21(3) of the Constitution of Zanzibar.[219] However, the Constitution of Zanzibar creates in Art. 23(4) the duty of every Zanzibari to protect, preserve and maintain the independence, sovereignty, territory and unity of Zanzibar. Such a constitutional duty is not completely unusual in constitutions of independent states, but to establish a constitutional duty of regional citizens to uphold a number of characteristics of sovereignty for a sub-state entity may be regarded as a provision that may run counter to the interests of the State to maintain its sovereignty and integrity.[220] As a consequence, the legislator of Zanzibar may, under Art. 23(5), enact appropriate laws to enable the people to serve in the forces and in the defense of the nation. Again, the language used is such that would normally be found in the constitution of a state, but not in the constitution of a sub-state entity. Furthermore, the implementation through legislation of the duty has resulted in the creation of so-called special departments of the RGZ, namely a Zanzibar militia called the special force, the coast guard unit and the youth service (Sect. 7.4.3).

There is one important area where Zanzibari status is a legal requirement for achieving a "benefit". In principle, Art. 3(1) of the Land Tenure Act of 1992 declares as public land all natural land within the islands of Zanzibar, whether occupied or unoccupied. Real property is thus mainly public. According to Art. 7 of the Land Tenure Act, a Zanzibari may, however, achieve a right of occupancy, but on certain conditions outlined in Art. 8 of the Act. One of the preconditions is that the holder of the interest in the land is a Zanzibari over the age of eighteen. If this is not the case, the tenant risks forfeiture, that is, that the occupancy is terminated

[218]It is noteworthy that in Art. 22(1), there is a work-related provision that is phrased both in the terms of a duty and a freedom, according to which every person has a duty to participate voluntarily and honestly in lawful and productive work.

[219]In addition, it is mentioned in Tanzania Human Rights Report (2009), p. 197, that according to Education Act, 1982, every Zanzibari has the right to education up to basic education.

[220]For a discussion of allegiance, see also the case of *S.M.Z. v. Machano Khamis Ali & 17 Others*, *supra*, note 151 in this Chap.

according to provisions in Art. 57 of the Act. In such a situation, the Minister shall issue an order of termination, after which the land shall be vacated. Nevertheless, there is a procedure for compensating the tenant for different aspects of the property included in Art. 64. The purpose of the requirement of the status of Zanzibari seems to be to keep land in the hands of the original Zanzibaris so that it will not be transferred into the hands of persons who might move in from the more populated Mainland Tanzania and settle in Zanzibar. Historically, there has been migration from the mainland to Zanzibar, and such a provision concerning real property is probably to be understood as an attempt to discourage migration, in particular because of the scarcity of land.[221]

Apart from the three categories of individuals (persons, citizens and Zanzibari), the Constitution of Zanzibar contains references to the term "people". The term is found in Art. 9 among the fundamental objectives as well as in Articles 11(1), 11(5), 22(1), 23(2–3), 23(5) of the Bill of Rights. While in some contexts, such as Art. 11 (1) concerning the declaration that all people are born free and equal, the reference to people is not made in the collective sense, but in the meaning of a group of persons or individuals, it is evident that some of the references are intended as a legal description of the people of Zanzibar as a collective term. It is not surprising that "the people of Zanzibar" would appear as a collective term in the Constitution of Zanzibar. After all, Zanzibar emerged as an independent State in January 1964, and it could be argued, by using the terminology of the 1970 UN Friendly Relations Declaration, that the people of Zanzibar traded in their independence as one form of self-determination for another form, that of "any other political status", while choosing not to become completely integrated into the new State of Tanzania.[222] There is even a reference to the sovereignty of the people in Art. 9(2)(a), that is, in the non-justiciable part of the Constitution, at the same time as other sub-sections of the provision deal with the security and welfare of the people and with participation of the people in governmental affairs. There is also a reference to the well-being of the people in Art. 22(1), to property that is collectively owned by the people in Art. 23(2), and to the attitude of people who are masters of the destiny of their nation in Art. 23(3). Therefore, it is possible to maintain that the Constitution of Zanzibar departs from the understanding that there exists a separate people of Zanzibar that forms the basis for the existence of this sub-state entity.[223] This is by no means the case with all sub-state entities, such as Hong Kong, the Åland Islands, or Scotland.

---

[221] See also Shivji (2008), p. 16 f., who accounts for the migration from mainland to Zanzibar, and Shivji (2008), p. 71 f., on the fears in Zanzibar concerning an unrestricted freedom of movement from mainland Tanzania.

[222] Under the terminology of Resolution 1514(XV) of the United Nations General Assembly with the Declaration on the Granting of Independence to Colonial Countries and Peoples, Zanzibar emerged in 1964 as a sovereign independent State out of a colonial situation with Great Britain as the former colonial power.

[223] See also Maalim (2006), p. 140 f., who argues that the population of Zanzibar constitutes a people.

4.5 Hong Kong: Resolving a Colonial Conflict through Autonomy

4.5.1 Treaty-Based Decolonization

China attracted great interest amongst the colonial powers during the eighteenth and nineteenth centuries, and the Empire was forced to open up for trade and other contacts with the outside world. This led to armed confrontations between China and the United Kingdom. After being part of the Chinese Empire, the island of Hong Kong on the south-eastern coast of China was transferred to the United Kingdom under Art. III of the 1842 Treaty of Nanking,[224] ending the so-called Opium War of 1840. Due to further disturbances between the two empires, British possessions were enlarged on the basis of Art. VI of the 1860 Convention of Peking to the township of Kowloon,[225] which is actually a peninsula of the Chinese mainland. Finally, British possessions on the mainland were extended to the so-called New Territories through a 99-year lease on the basis of the 1898 Convention of Peking,[226] a period of time that would elapse in 1997.

Throughout the twentieth century, the Chinese governments irrespective of political orientation held these treaties to be unequal and argued for a return of the Chinese territories of Hong Kong.[227] The aggravation of the Chinese was increased by the fact that Hong Kong was a colony of the United Kingdom, ruled by a Governor appointed by the UK Government. The colonial government of Hong Kong was created under the Hong Kong Letters Patent 1917–1995[228] and the Hong Kong Royal Instructions 1917 To 1993 (Nos. 1 and 2).[229] The system did not leave

---

[224]Treaty Between China and Great Britain, Signed at Nanking, 29 August 1842, Art. III: It being obviously necessary and desirable that British subjects should have some port whereat they may careen and refit their ships when required, and keep stores for that purpose, [China] cedes to [Great Britain] the Island of Hong Kong, to be possessed in perpetuity by Her Britannic Majesty, her heirs and successors, and to be governed by such laws and regulations as Her Majesty [. . .] shall see fit to direct."

[225]Convention of Friendship between Great Britain and China Signed in Peking, 24 October 1860, Art. VI: "With a view to the maintenance of law and order in and about the harbour of Hong Kong, [China] agrees to cede to [Great Britain] to have and to hold as dependency of Her Britannic Majesty's Colony of Hong Kong, that portion of the township of Cow loon, in the Province of Kwang-tung, of which a lease was granted in perpetuity to Harry Smith Parkes, Esquire, Companion of the Bath, a member of the Allied Commission at Canton, on behalf of her Britannic Majesty's Government, by Lan Tsung Kwang, Governor-General of the Two Kwang. It is further declared that the lease in question is hereby cancelled; [. . .]."

[226]Convention between Great Britain and China Respecting an Extension of Hong Kong Territory, Signed at Peking, 9 June 1898.

[227]See also Leung (2006), pp. 4 f., 16 f. The colonial problem existed, of course, also in relation to Portugal, which had established itself as a colonial power over Macau.

[228]For the Letters Patent, see Leung (2006), pp. 371–380.

[229]For the Royal Instructions, see Leung (2006), pp. 381–390.

much space for the participation of the Chinese population of Hong Kong in the public affairs of the colony. The Legislative Council was appointed by the Governor from three different "constituencies" and had mainly advisory powers, while the Executive Council, established as the highest policy-making body, had even less connection to the population. Towards the end of the colonial period there were attempts to develop mechanisms to enhance political participation (*inter alia*, in 1991, the first direct elections of a portion of the Legislative Council were held).[230] These reforms were, in part, a response to criticism from the UN Human Rights Committee of Hong Kong's lack of democratic institutions.[231] In principle, however, the issue of political reform was deferred to the period following the return of sovereignty over Hong Kong to China. Of course, colonialism constitutes a denial of self-determination,[232] that is, a denial of the meta-norm of participation, so whatever would have been done by the UK within the colonial structure short of ending colonialism would not have been a sufficient remedy.

In the 1980s, as the UK's 99-year lease of the New Territories came closer to its end, the Chinese and the UK Governments began discussions about the future of Hong Kong. On 19 December 1984, China and the UK Government concluded the Joint Declaration on the Question of Hong Kong in which the UK Government agreed to return the entirety of Hong Kong to China on 1 July 1997 and thus end the colonial period with respect to that area. Although the agreement between China and the UK is entitled the "Joint Declaration", the document is formally to be understood as a bilateral treaty under international law,[233] creating legal obligations

---

[230]See Leung (2006), pp. 60–70, 257 f.

[231]See UN Human Rights Committee, Concluding Comments in 1995, CCPR/C/79/Add.57, para. 19: "The Committee is aware of the reservation made by the United Kingdom that Article 25 does not require establishment of an elected Executive or Legislative Council. It however takes the view that once an elected Legislative Council is established, its election must conform to Article 25 of the Covenant. The Committee considers that the electoral system in Hong Kong does not meet the requirements of Article 25, as well as Articles 2, 3 and 26 of the Covenant. It underscores in particular that only 20 of 60 seats in the Legislative Council are subject to direct popular election and that the concept of functional constituencies, which gives undue weight to the views of the business community, discriminates among voters on the basis of property and functions. This clearly constitutes a violation of Articles 2, paragraph 1, 25 (b) and 26. It is also concerned that laws depriving convicted persons of their voting rights for periods of up to 10 years may be a disproportionate restriction of the rights protected by article 25." See also the Human Rights Committee's report to the General Assembly, A/44/40 (44th session, 1989), paras 140–189.

[232]In the context of decolonization and self-determination of colonial territories, the General Assembly of the United Nations removed on 8 November 1972 Hong Kong from of the list colonial territories on the proposal of China. See Weiyun (2001), p. 67. According to China, Hong Kong was a Chinese territory occupied by Britain.

[233]Joint Declaration of the Government of the United Kingdom of Great Britain and Northern Ireland and the Government of the People's Republic of China on the Question of Hong Kong, 19 December 1984, 1399 UNTS 33. See also Ghai (1999), pp. 53–56.

on both of the parties after ratification.[234] In the Joint Declaration, the UK and China also agreed to implement the separate annexes to the Joint Declaration.[235]

The Joint Declaration is a unique treaty about an internal governance structure because of the temporal nature of its commitments. According to Art. 3(12) of the Joint Declaration, the autonomy arrangement concerning Hong Kong is limited in time, lasting 50 years from the Chinese resumption of sovereignty over Hong Kong on 1 July 1997. A similar Joint Declaration from 1987 exists between China and Portugal concerning Macau.[236] The temporal nature of the autonomy arrangements distinguishes Hong Kong and Macau from the other autonomy arrangements dealt with in our study, but it is difficult to predict how the temporal nature of the arrangement affects its contents. Although the treaty contains many obligations for China, it is debatable whether the UK will feel compelled to monitor the observance of the treaty now that the British part of its implementation is complete.[237] The question of what will happen after the fifty year period is, of course, already very topical now, in 2011, but there have been signs that the autonomy arrangement may continue to exist after the period that guarantees autonomy for Hong Kong.[238] Autonomy could continue, in one form or another, but in such a case, the arrangement would be purely internal and solely based on the Constitution of China, without any international guarantee for its continued existence.

It is possible to argue that Hong Kong's return by the United Kingdom was an exercise of China's right to self-determination. However, the population of Hong

[234] According to Art. 8, the Joint Declaration is subject to ratification and shall enter into force on the date of the exchange of instruments of ratification, which shall take place in Beijing before 30 June 1985. The same provision says that the Joint Declaration and its Annexes shall be equally binding, which seems to imply that the entire document was intended to have normative effects between the parties. See also Weiyun (2001), p. 70. See also Mushkat (1997), p. 172, according to whom the Joint Declaration and its Annexes were not incorporated into the local law of Hong Kong: "As pronounced by the High Court, neither the Hong Kong Act 1985 nor the Application of English Law Ordinance bestowed upon the Joint Declaration the force of law in Hong Kong." Therefore, the Joint Declaration could not, as such, give rise to justiciable claims in Hong Kong. On the treaty nature of the Joint Declaration, see also Mushkat (1997), p. 140 ff.

[235] Annex I: Elaboration by the Government of the People's Republic of China of its basic policies regarding Hong Kong; Annex II: Sino-British Joint Liaison Group; Annex III: Land Leases. The English and the Chinese versions of the Joint Declaration are equally authentic.

[236] Joint Declaration of the Government of the Portuguese Republic and the Government of the People's Republic of China on the Question of Macao, 13 April 1987, 1498 UNTS 195.

[237] As pointed out by Chan (2010), p. 129, there is "no enforcement mechanism under the Joint Declaration or at the international level" for conflict resolution by an external mechanism.

[238] See Huang (2009). See also Weiyun (2001), p. 112, quoting Deng Xiaoping for saying the following: "This law shall be effective for at least 50 years. I would like to add here, after 50 years, there would be less need for Hong Kong to change. Our policies regarding Hong Kong shall not change." However, as pointed out by Ghai (1999), p. 143, the amendment restriction included in Art. 159(3) of the Basic Law prohibiting amendments that contravene the basic principles would presumably disappear after the 50 year period. See also Chan (2010), p. 129, who concludes that it is not clear "whether the model will ultimately (or within 50 years) lead to the merger or the retention of 'two systems'".

Kong did not participate in decisions about the transfer of sovereignty from the UK to China or in the ending of the colonial period by extending Chinese self-determination over Hong Kong. No referendum was held on the transfer of Hong Kong to China and the option of granting independence to Hong Kong was never on the agenda.[239] However, it can be argued that the high degree of autonomy granted to Hong Kong under Art. 3(3) of the Joint Declaration as a special administrative region constitutes a grant of internal self-determination to Hong Kong and, in fact, to the population of Hong Kong, or at least a grant of a share in the internal self-determination of China. According to the provision, foreign affairs and defense are the responsibility of the Central People's Government, while Hong Kong takes care of the rest and enjoy executive, legislative and independent judicial powers. In addition, Hong Kong can also be said to possess some features of external self-determination, because under Art. 3(10) of the Joint Declaration, the Hong Kong Special Administrative Region (HKSAR) may, on its own, maintain and develop economic and cultural relations and conclude relevant agreements with states, regions and some international organizations by using the name "Hong Kong, China" and may, also on its own, issue travel documents for entry into and exit from Hong Kong.

4.5.2 *The Broad Constitutional Frames for Autonomy*

Constitutionally, it might have been possible to try to fit Hong Kong into the scheme of self-governing autonomous areas provided for in Articles 112–122 of China's Constitution. In national autonomous areas, people's congresses and people's governments of autonomous regions, autonomous prefectures and autonomous counties may be created, but the basis for these institutional structures is nationality (that is, ethnicity or language), while the main characteristics that separate Hong Kong from the rest of China are not ethnic or linguistic, but economic and legal. Although the autonomous institutions are expected to implement the laws and policies of the state, people's congresses of national autonomous areas have the power to enact autonomy regulations and specific regulations in light of the political, economic and cultural characteristics of the nationality or nationalities in the areas concerned. Such autonomy regulations and specific regulations of autonomous regions shall be submitted to the Standing Committee of the National People's Congress (NPCSC) for approval before they enter into force. The regulations of autonomous prefectures and counties shall be submitted to the next higher level, the standing committees of the people's congresses of provinces or autonomous regions for approval before they enter into force, and they shall be reported to the Standing Committee of the National People's Congress for the record.

---

[239] On the issue, see Ghai (1999), pp. 41–45, and Ghai (2004), p. 444.

The autonomous institutions thus have regulatory powers, but not genuinely exclusive legislative powers when they independently administer educational, scientific, cultural, public health and physical culture matters in their respective areas, protect the cultural legacy of the nationalities and work for the development and prosperity of their cultures. In addition, the organs of self-government of the national autonomous areas may, in accordance with the military system of the state and concrete local needs and with the approval of the State Council, organize local public security forces for the maintenance of public order. According to Art. 121 of the Constitution, the organs of self-government of the national autonomous areas, in accordance with the autonomy regulations of the respective areas, employ the spoken and written language or languages in common use in the locality. The Chinese Constitution is therefore very open to ethnic variants of sub-state governance by means of regional autonomy, although the Chinese concept of autonomy can mainly be placed in section III of our chart concerning various autonomy positions (see Fig. 1.1 above in Sect. 1.3).[240] It should be noted that the issue in respect of Hong Kong did not involve nationality, in the sense of differing ethnicity or language, but instead, the issue was the differing economic and legal systems. However, Annex I to the Joint Declaration includes a pledge from the Chinese Government that in addition to Chinese, English may also be used in organs of government and in the courts in the HKSAR.

While regional autonomy and other forms of minority protection are regular features of the Chinese Constitution in relation to the 55 recognized minority ethnic groups of China, the situation with respect to Taiwan may have been the main reason for amending the Constitution in 1984 so as to allow the creation of special administrative regions. It is likely that Hong Kong and Macau were also in the picture early on.[241] The existence of a constitutional provision concerning special administrative regions was a suitable normative framework for the re-incorporation of Hong Kong and for assigning the autonomy arrangement a legal basis in the constitutional fabric of the country. Article 31 of the Constitution of the People's Republic of China (PRC) grants the state the power to establish special administrative regions when necessary. In addition, the social, economic and legal systems to

[240]For the 55 recognised ethnic minorities in China, different structures of regional autonomy are used in many instances. See Ghai (1999), pp. 113–125, and Ghai (2000a), pp. 77–98. According to Ghai (2000a), p. 78 f., minorities in China constitute only 8% of the population, but in absolute numbers, they amount to as many as 60 million persons. Their size varies from the mere 5,000 Tartars to the nearly nine million Hui, but on the top of ethnic minorities, the 55 national minorities also comprise religious minorities, such as Muslims and Buddhists. On the functioning of regional ethnic autonomy in China, see Chunli (2009).

[241]See Ghai (1999), p. 56 f., Weiyun (2001), pp. 9–11, and Leung (2006), p. 19 as well as Chen (2009), p. 755 ff. and Chan (2010), p. 126. As pointed out by Hualing et al. (2007), p. 2 f., the concept of "one country, two systems" was by no means new in the Chinese political thinking in the beginning of the 1980s, but it has its root in the 1930s and the 1940s, first in the distinction between areas controlled by the Communists in relation to areas controlled by the Nationalist Party and later on in the relationship between China and Tibet during a short time after 1949.

be instituted in special administrative regions shall be prescribed by law enacted by the National People's Congress in light of the specific conditions.[242] The constitutional provision is open and does not say much about the powers granted to a special administrative region (hereinafter: SAR), but the reference to "administrative" indicates that the powers to be exercised could be at least regulatory in nature.

It was evidently deemed necessary to establish such SARs as a means to facilitate the transfer of sovereignty over Hong Kong and Macau from the UK and Portugal to China, as recorded in the Joint Declarations between the Governments of the three countries. The requirement of regulation through law was fulfilled by the National People's Congress on 4 April 1990, when it adopted the Basic Law of the Hong Kong Special Administrative Region of the People's Republic of China.[243] The specific condition that was taken into account was the need to return Hong Kong to China, a place with a different economic and legal system. Through the Basic Law, the capitalist system of Hong Kong with the British styled common law tradition was fitted into the overall socialist system of China both in the area of economics and law by creating an exception to what the Chinese Constitution required.

An explicit reference to Art. 31 of the Constitution of China was included in section 3(1) of the Joint Declaration concerning Hong Kong, which creates an international commitment for the internal solution. The legal basis for the domestic solution is established in the Basic Law which spells out in detail the contents of the arrangement under Art. 31 of the Constitution and creates, *inter alia*, exclusive

[242]"The state may establish special administrative regions when necessary. The systems to be instituted in special administrative regions shall be prescribed by law enacted by the National People's Congress in the light of the specific conditions." A special administrative region is apparently to be distinguished from such autonomy arrangements which are created on the basis of Art. 4 on minority rights: "Regional autonomy is practiced in areas where people of minority nationalities live in concentrated communities; in these areas organs of self- government are established to exercise the power of autonomy. All national autonomous areas are integral parts of the People's Republic of China."

[243]Adopted on 4 April 1990 by the Seventh National People's Congress of the People's Republic of China at its Third Session. The Basic Law was promulgated on the same day by Decree No. 26 of the President of the PRC. On the same day, perhaps to dispel any doubts about the constitutionality of the Basic Law, the NPC made the "Decision of the National People's Congress on the Basic Law of the Hong Kong Special Administrative Region of the People's Republic of China, according to which the Basic Law "is constitutional as it is enacted in accordance with the Constitution of the People's Republic of China and in the Light of the Specific Conditions of Hong Kong". See Weiyun (2001), pp. 75, 81. See also Decision of the Standing Committee of the National People's Congress on the English Text of the Basic Law of the Hong Kong Special Administrative Region of the People's Republic of China, according to which the 14th Meeting of the 7th NPCSC decided the following: "the English translation of the Basic Law of the Hong Kong Special Administrative Region of the People's Republic of China, examined and approved under the aegis of the Law Committee of the National People's Congress, shall be the official English text and shall be equally authentic as the Chinese text. In case of any discrepancy in the meaning of wording between the English text and the Chinese text, the Chinese text shall prevail." For the decision, see Leung (2006), p. 464.

law-making powers for the legislature of Hong Kong (and Macau, too).[244] In comparison, other autonomous areas created in Mainland China, such as Tibet, based on Articles 4 and 116 of the PRC Constitution, seem to enjoy a form of autonomy which is mainly of a regulatory nature, although the autonomous entity also has the power to modify national legislation, a power which appears to be, in practice, seldom exercised. In cases where an autonomous area in Mainland China wishes to modify national law, the modification can be approved by the authorities of the autonomous area, but there is the additional requirement that such modifications must be approved by the central government in order to take effect. Hence the effect of Art. 31 of the Constitution is to place the system of special administrative regions outside of the framework of the regular regional autonomies and to distinguish the SARs from the regular regional autonomies.

The Joint Declaration mentions Art. 31 of the Constitution in Art. 3(1) of the Joint Declaration when elaborating the basic policies applicable to Hong Kong in connection with its transfer to Chinese sovereignty. Article 3(1) of the treaty provides that the PRC, while upholding national unity and territorial integrity and taking account of the history of Hong Kong and its realities, has decided to establish, in accordance with the provisions of Article 31 of the PRC Constitution, a Hong Kong Special Administrative Region upon resuming the exercise of sovereignty over Hong Kong. Somewhat differently from regional autonomies in Mainland China, Art. 3(2) states that the Hong Kong Special Administrative Region will be directly under the authority of the Central People's Government of the People's Republic of China, but at the same time, the HKSAR will enjoy a high degree of autonomy, except in foreign affairs and defense which are the responsibilities of the Central People's Government. This creates the impression that the HKSAR may exercise the residual powers, while the national government holds a minimum of enumerated powers, those central to preserving national unity and territorial integrity. In addition, the reference in the Joint Declaration to a high degree of autonomy may be contrasted with the concept of autonomy in Articles 112–122 of the PRC Constitution. *Prima facie*, it seems that the high degree of autonomy granted to Hong Kong amounts to more autonomy than that which has been granted to the autonomous regions elsewhere in China because the HKSAR is vested with executive, legislative and independent judicial power,[245] including that

[244]The term "Basic Law" is in this context not a reference to a special enactment and amendment formula (although the initiation of amendments from Hong Kong is a more difficult procedure), because the Basic Law does not appear to have been adopted by the National People's Congress of China by any qualified majority or special procedure. Moreover, section 159 of the Basic Law does not prescribe any more complicated amendment formula for the Basic Law than for any other act, but it does prevent such amendments to the Basic Law that are in contravention with the basic principles, found in the Joint Declaration. Therefore, the references in the Basic Law to the Joint Declaration could be interpreted as an elevation of the normative status of the Basic Law to a level above that of ordinary acts of China.

[245]On issues of separation of powers in the HKSAR, see Wesley-Smith (2004), pp. 83–107, and Hsu (2004), pp. 279–302, which both raise critical points about the relationship between the

of final adjudication, and because the laws in force in Hong Kong remained basically unchanged by the transition, as provided by Articles 8 and 18 of the Basic Law. Similarly to the regional autonomies, Art. 3(4) of the Joint Declaration establishes that the Government of the HKSAR will be composed of local inhabitants. Finally, Art. 3(12) of the Joint Declaration provides that the basic policies established in Art. 3(1–12) of the Joint Declaration – and elaborated in Annex I to the treaty, a declaration made by China – are to be stipulated in a Basic Law of the Hong Kong Special Administrative Region by the National People's Congress and will remain unchanged for 50 years from 1 July 1997.

Pursuant to the Joint Declaration, reinforced by Annex I, the National People's Congress of China was obligated, after ratification, to enact and promulgate a Basic Law of the Hong Kong Special Administrative Region of the People's Republic of China (hereinafter: the Basic Law) in accordance with the Constitution of the People's Republic of China. The obligation stipulates that after the establishment of the HKSAR, the socialist system and socialist policies shall not be practiced in the HKSAR and that Hong Kong's previous capitalist system and life-style shall remain unchanged for 50 years. Because the two social orders would normally be understood as antagonistic, the "NPC adopted a formal decision on the same day it passed the Basic Law, declaring that the Basic Law is consistent with the PRC Constitution".[246] Also, Annex I declared that apart from displaying the national flag and national emblem of the PRC, the HKSAR may use a regional flag and emblem of its own and is in charge of the maintenance of public order in the HKSAR. Although military forces may sent by the Central People's Government to be stationed in the HKSAR for the purpose of defense, they shall not interfere in the internal affairs of the HKSAR.[247]

Annex I also contains a section on basic rights and freedoms according to which the Government of the HKSAR shall protect the rights and freedoms of its inhabitants and other persons according to law and maintain the rights and freedoms as provided for by the laws previously in force in Hong Kong. These basic rights include, according to section XIII of Annex I, freedom of the person, of speech, of the press, of assembly, of association, to form and join trade unions, of correspondence, of travel, of movement, of strike, of demonstration, of choice of occupation, of academic research, of belief (that is, of religion, which is of importance in this context), inviolability of the home, the freedom to marry and the right to raise a family freely. Many of these basic rights are such that have been and in many cases still are denied in Mainland China. Every person shall also have the right to confidential legal advice, access to the courts, representation in the courts by a

executive and the judiciary, the first one because of appointment of judges to tribunal-like and administrative positions, the latter one because of the strong position of the executive in the appointment of judges to the bench.

[246]See Hualing et al. (2007), p. 3.

[247]Expenditure for these military forces shall be borne by the Central People's Government.

lawyer of his choice, and to obtain judicial remedies, and every person shall have the right to challenge the actions of the executive in the courts.

These basic rights are reinforced by the pledge that the provisions of the International Covenant on Civil and Political Rights and the International Covenant on Economic, Social and Cultural Rights as applied to Hong Kong shall remain in force.[248] These basic rights are also reinforced by section II of Annex I which promises that the laws previously in force in Hong Kong shall be maintained, except for any that contravene the Basic Law[249] or is amended by the HKSAR legislature. The 'laws previously in force in Hong Kong' include the common law, rules of equity, ordinances, subordinate legislation and customary law, which means that the common law system is granted protection under both national constitutional law (e.g., Art. 31 of the Constitution) and international law. This is important with a view to the fact that China maintains a socialist legal system with a legal order evolving toward a civil law system. Finally, Annex I contains provisions concerning the right of abode, travel and immigration.

The Joint Declaration (including its Annexes), as a formal treaty under international law which has been ratified by China, entrenches the autonomy arrangement in international law and provides an international guarantee for upholding the obligation. The guarantee is, formally speaking, bilateral and not multilateral, since the UK is the only other party to the international commitment. The Joint Declaration does not stipulate a supervisory mechanism, which means that China is expected to implement its obligations in good faith on the basis of the treaty[250]

[248]The CCPR was incorporated into Hong Kong's domestic law already in 1991 through the Bill of Rights Ordinance. On the CCPR as well as the UN Convention Against Torture, the Convention on the Elimination of All Forms of Discrimination Against Women and the International Covenant on Economic, Social and Cultural Rights, see Petersen (2007), pp. 33–53, who makes the point that in contrast to the other human rights treaties, the CCPR enjoys an elevated status in Hong Kong's judicial discourse. Noting the link between the CCPR and the Bill of Rights Ordinance, Weiyun (2001), p. 228, denies the possibility that the Bill of Rights Ordinance would be higher than all other laws. See also Leung (2006), pp. 185–205.

[249]See Decision of the Standing Committee of the National People's Congress on Treatment of the Laws Previously in Force in Hong Kong in Accordance with Article 160 of the Basic Law of the Hong Kong Special Administrative Region of the People's Republic of China. Adopted by the Standing Committee of the Eighth National People's Congress at its 24th Sitting on 23 February 1997 (as reproduced in Ghai (1999), pp. 571–576). The previous legislation that was not allowed to remain in force comprised of surprisingly few enactments, only 14 ordinances, and only a handful of provisions in ten other ordinances. However, many of the ordinances and provisions were of a "liberal" nature that the Chinese Government apparently disliked.

[250]In case a dispute arose between China and the UK about the implementation of the Joint Declaration, Ghai (1999), p. 72, is of the opinion that there seems to exist no basis for effective action in case of its breach. Because China has not recognized the compulsory jurisdiction of the International Court of Justice, such a dispute could be litigated before the Court only if China agrees to such litigation on a case-by-case basis. Interestingly in the context, the Sino-British Joint Liaison Group agreed, in advance of the transfer of sovereignty, that a number of international treaties, among them the Statute of the International Court of Justice, would continue to apply to the HKSAR after 1 July 1977. See Leung (2006), p. 417.

by means of national law explicitly mentioned in the treaty itself: Art. 3(12) of the Joint Declaration stipulates that implementation will take place by means of a Basic Law of the HKSAR enacted by the National People's Congress. In this way, China committed itself in the Joint Declaration to implementing an unusually detailed set of treaty provisions in its domestic legislation by means of a legislative decision of the highest law-making body in a piece of law which is specifically named in the treaty.[251]

However, the Joint Declaration provided nothing specific about the normative level at which the Basic Law should be enacted, nor was it understood by the Chinese Government so that it should be turned into national law *expressis verbis*: although the main bulk of the Basic Law, including its name, comes from the Joint Declaration, it contains provisions which are not prescribed by the Joint Declaration[252] at the same time as some provisions of the Joint Declaration are not explicitly featured in the Basic Law, although one can always find an implicit connection. While the title of the law, the Basic Law, could imply that it has an elevated normative status which falls between the Constitution and ordinary legislation or as an organic law of some sort, it seems that the Basic Law was enacted under the Constitution of China as an ordinary piece of legislation.[253] From that perspective, the Basic Law is, in the Chinese legal order, a piece of ordinary legislation, sometimes attributed with the characteristics of a "special law" in the hierarchy of norms because the general legal principles of China imply that special laws prevail over ordinary laws: "At the national law level, laws which have the status of a special law prevail over ordinary pieces of law", and the Basic Law is considered to be such a law.[254] Hence the Basic Law seems to have some sort of elevated status.[255]

---

[251]See also Weiyun (2001), p. 13, who concludes that the Joint Declaration is not domestic law, but that China would, after signature and ratification, start implementing it. "Naturally, it has legal status and effect." See Weiyun (2001), pp. 76, 200 f, 213.

[252]See Weiyun (2001), p. 289, Ghai (1999), pp. 67–70.

[253]See Leung (2006), pp. 40–42, according to whom the norm hierarchy in China is as follows: the Constitution, the national legislation, administrative regulations and local regulations. The Basic Law is placed on the second level, among the national legislation. See also Morris (2007), p. 105, who points out that the "Basic Law is not, as many common-law commentators have declared, a constitution or "mini-constitution" for Hong Kong. It is merely another law – a statute – enacted by the NPC. It is subordinate to the PRC Constitution and does not occupy the entire field, as much of the PRC Constitution applies in Hong Kong as well."

[254]Leung (2006), p. 42. See also Leung (2006), pp. 45–47, 244 f.

[255]On the concept of basic law in China, see Ghai (1999), p. 101, making the point that it can be understood as referring to statutes, that is, ordinary national laws enacted by the NPC. As pointed out by Dowdle (2007), p. 71, "China has more than sixty 'basic laws' in force at present, of which the Basic Law of the Hong Kong SAR is simply one. Contrary to what many in Hong Kong's interpretative community presumed, at least in the 1990s, simply calling the Hong Kong Basic Law a 'Basic Law' did not endow it with some uniquely 'constitutional' essence per se." Nonetheless, according to Weiyun (2001), p. 177, "the HKSAR Basic Law is regarded as a

4.5.3 The Basic Law as an Autonomy Statute

In spite of perhaps not having solid constitutional status in the Chinese legal order on the highest level of the Chinese hierarchy of norms, the Basic Law functions, in the jurisdiction of Hong Kong, as a constitution from which the powers and competences of the organs of authority of Hong Kong are derived, such as the powers to legislate, execute legislation and adjudicate disputes.[256] This is established in Art. 11 of the Basic Law, which stipulates that, in accordance with Art. 31 of the Chinese Constitution, the systems and policies practiced in the HKSAR, including the social and economic systems, the system for safeguarding the fundamental rights and freedoms of its residents, the executive, legislative and judicial systems, and the relevant policies, shall be based on the provisions of the Basic Law and that no law enacted by the legislature of the HKSAR shall contravene the Basic Law. Article 11 of the Basic Law thus "settles the difficult problem of specifying what articles of the Constitution shall not be applied to the HKSAR".[257]

As a consequence, in the Hong Kong legal order, the Basic Law is the supreme norm from which the competences of the organs of the SAR are derived. Nonetheless, at the same time, together with the Joint Declaration, the Constitution of China constitutes the national normative basis for the Basic Law[258] and it can also find application within the jurisdiction of the HKSAR, at least to the extent that the generally comprehensive Basic

fundamental law established by NPC; any amendment should be made by NPC", which statement of course may be limited to the amendment procedures of the Basic Law.

[256] Leung (2006), p. 33, is of the opinion that from a legal point of view, "the Basic Law should not be considered as the Constitution of Hong Kong, although it may have certain functions of a Constitution for the territory", but see Leung (2006), p. 55 f., where she writes that "[n]evertheless, from the broad delegation of powers by the Constitution and the comprehensive legal system it prescribes, as far as Hong Kong is concerned, the Basic Law is the supreme law of the territory in addition to the Constitution, no matter what name it may be given". However, although the Basic Law is a piece of national law in China, according to Leung (2006), p. 10, it is nonetheless at the same time a special law, apparently because it has been enacted within the framework of Art. 31 of the Chinese Constitution. See also Weiyun (2001), p. 54, who seems to feel that the Basic Law assumes an intermediate position, with much of its contents of a non-constitutional nature but also with some similarities in form to constitutional law: "It could refer to the framework of constitutional law where it is proper to do so." However, he adds on p. 129 that "the Constitution is indispensable to the Basic Law in respect of its birth and existence", and on p. 131 that the Basic Law is not the supreme law of the HKSAR or that it would have the supreme legal effect, because the Chinese Constitution has that position in China, including the HKSAR.

[257] Weiyun (2001), p. 130 f.

[258] See also Ghai (1999), p. 71, who concludes that the Joint Declaration is effective in Chinese laws, and probably also that it is superior to the Basic Law when their provisions conflict. But see Weiyun (2001), p. 85 f., who denies that the Joint Declaration would at all constitute the legal basis for enacting the Basic Law. Instead, the legal basis comes via Art. 31 from the Constitution of China, and therefore, it is according to him incorrect to say that the Joint Declaration is the legal basis for enacting the Basic Law. He continues by saying that the Joint Declaration is only written in an international instrument, not a domestic law, and it seems he says so because the Constitution of China lacks a provision regulating the relationship, although there exists ordinary legislation in the area of civil law that grants precedence to international treaties concluded by China.

Law might leave something unregulated.[259] However, it should be noted that Art. 159 (4) of the Basic Law contains a limitation clause concerning amendments which stipulates that no amendment to the Basic Law shall contravene the established basic policies of the People's Republic of China regarding Hong Kong.[260] This limitation clause seems to be a reference to Art. 3 of the Joint Declaration, where the basic policies are laid down in a comprehensive and relatively detailed manner in twelve points, and to Annex I of the Declaration, which according to its preamble is a further elaboration of Art. 3 of the Joint Declaration. The limitation clause concerning amendments seems, therefore, to rely on strong international entrenchment of the autonomy arrangement and therefore elevates the Basic Law to above the level of ordinary law – at least for the purposes for our scheme concerning different autonomy positions (see Fig. 1.1 in Sect. 1.3) – if not in a strict norm-hierarchical sense within the Chinese legal order. Because China has chosen to resume sovereignty over Hong Kong by means of an international treaty that foresees the implementation of a set of principles in domestic legislation and because the subsequent domestic legislation contains a prohibition of amendments that contravene the basic principles in the treaty, it can be argued that the self-limitation should be considered constitutionally relevant as long as the self-limitation is not formally abolished.[261]

Undoubtedly, the Chinese Constitution, including its law-making provisions, provided the basis for enacting the Basic Law, but when it was enacted, the contents of the international obligation in the Joint Declaration were channeled through the broad language of Art. 31 of the Constitution into the Basic Law, which defines, in a non-exclusive list in Art. 11, the exceptions to the Chinese Constitution. These exceptions, like the basic principles of the Joint Declaration, are broad and leave large "areas" of the Chinese Constitution empty, only to be filled for the purposes of the territory of Hong Kong by the provisions of the Basic Law, which is protected by way of a re-connection in Art. 159(4) to the international obligation in the Joint Declaration. This means that almost none of the provisions of the Basic Law could be amended if the proposed amendment contravened the basic principles.

---

[259]See Weiyun (2001), p. 84, who concludes that when it is said that the Constitution should apply to HKSAR, it "does not mean that every part, every article of the Constitution can apply to the HKSAR, but its entirety and many of its articles must apply to HKSAR". But see Weiyun (2001), p. 163, where he states the contrary by saying that "[o]f course, the Constitution as the highest among all National Laws shall be applicable as a whole to the HKSAR". See also Leung (2006), p. 13, who seems to advocate a limited application of the Chinese Constitution in the HKSAR. She says that those provisions of the Chinese Constitution that contradict the principle of "one country, two systems" shall not be directly applicable to Hong Kong and recommends that "one should not adopt a totality approach to the issue of whether other provisions of the Chinese Constitution apply to Hong Kong. Decisions must be based on the principle of 'one country, two systems' and be made after detailed classification of the nature of the provision."

[260]On the substantive restraints on the NPC concerning amendments to the Basic Law, see Leung (2006), p. 90 f. See also Weiyun (2001), p. 179 f.

[261]On the existence of such a notion of self-limitation at the top of the CPG, see Chang (2007), pp. 351–362.

Because the Basic Law is regarded as a piece of ordinary legislation in the Chinese legal order, the provision in Art. 159 stipulating that the power of amendment of the Basic Law shall be vested in the National People's Congress may seem somewhat unnecessary. However, the provision is significant since it indicates that the NPCSC cannot and should not be able to amend the Basic Law,[262] not even through its interpretations. Instead, the provision allocates an initiative-making function to the NPCSC, granting the NPCSC along with the Chinese State Council and the HKSAR the power to propose amendments to the Basic Law. Because the potential initiators of amendments to other Chinese legislation include a broader range of actors, the Basic Law, in fact, employs a special amendment formula.[263]

Should the need to amend the Basic Law arise in Hong Kong, there is a complicated procedure for bringing the bill before the National People's Congress. According to an interpretation by the NPCSC,[264] such an amendment has to be initiated by the Government of Hong Kong, not by the Legislative Council, which means that the Chief Executive of Hong Kong must also support it because he or she has to defend a proposed amendment before the central authorities. If and when initiated, an amendment must receive the support of two thirds of all the members of Hong Kong's Legislative Council. At the central level, the HKSAR delegation to the National People's Congress is responsible for submitting an amendment bill to the NPC after obtaining the consent of two thirds of the deputies in the delegation to the NPC. However, before a bill to amend the Basic Law is put on the agenda of the NPC, the Basic Law Committee shall study it and submit its views. It is therefore difficult to bring amendment proposals arising in Hong Kong to the attention of the NPC, and there seems to be a fundamental imbalance in relation to the NPCSC and the State Council in that respect, since those two bodies have easier access to the NPC for the purposes of amending the Basic Law. The procedures also contain an internal "contradiction" because the Basic Law Committee, which plays a role when Hong Kong initiates the procedure, is a subcommittee of the NPCSC, which has a separate, independent avenue for proposing amendments. The NPCSC therefore may affect the amendment procedures initiated by the Hong Kong side when an amendment bill is dealt with by the Basic Law Committee.

---

[262]See also Weiyun (2001), p. 177, who thinks that the "HKSAR Basic Law is regarded as a fundamental law established by NPC; any amendment should be made by NPC".

[263]See Leung (2006), pp. 82–84.

[264]In the *Interpretation of 6 April 2004* of the NPCSC of Art. 7 of Annex I and Art. III of Annex II to the Basic Law, the NPCSC determined that the Chief Executive shall, according to the Interpretation, make a report to the NPCSC as regards whether there is a need to make an amendment. Thereafter, the NPCSC makes a determination on the need on the basis of Articles 45 and 68 of the Basic Law, in the light of the actual situation in the HKSAR and in accordance with the principle of gradual and orderly process. If there is such a need, the NPCSC will authorize the Government of Hong Kong to file an amendment bill with the Legislative Council. This procedural determination by the NPCSC may, in fact, amount to an amendment of the Basic Law, as pointed out in Ghai (2007b), p. 398.

Of course, it can be argued that the Hong Kong initiated procedure should be complicated because amendments to the constitutional arrangement should not be made lightly. Nevertheless, it seems that any amendment bill originating in Hong Kong would require massive consensus before being placed on the agenda of the NPC, almost to the extent of excluding any reasonable chance of ever reaching the national legislative body.[265] However, once the amendment proposal has reached the NPC, the amendment requires only a simple majority.[266] Hong Kong has no veto over unwanted amendments passed by the NPC, and the only protection lies in the international obligation established by the Joint Declaration and specified in Art. 159(4) of the Basic Law that those basic policies reflected in the Basic Law cannot be amended even by the NPC. Arguably, Annex I to the Joint Declaration does not express a minimalist understanding of those basic policies, but instead provides a broad and detailed expression of the basic policies. As a result, most of the substance of the Basic Law is shielded from amendments which might attempt to vary the basic policies during the 50 year period: much of the Basic Law reflects such basic policies and can therefore not be amended in a negative direction.

The three Annexes appended to the Basic Law specify their own amendment formulas.[267] They are all less stringent than the general amendment formula that requires a legislative decision by the NPC, and they also place varying degrees of decision-making power in the hands of the HKSAR. Annex I deals with the selection of the Chief Executive. According to section 7 of Annex I, if there is a need to amend the method for selecting the Chief Executive for the terms subsequent to the year 2007, such amendments must be endorsed by a two-thirds majority of all of the members of the Legislative Council, receive the consent of the Chief Executive, and be reported to the NPCSC for approval.[268] Here, an explicit approval decision by the NPCSC is required, not by the NPC. Amendments to Annex II concerning the election of the Legislative Council follow a similar procedure but without the need for approval by the NPCSC. Instead, under section III of Annex II, amendments have to be reported to the NPCSC for the record, much in the same way as is the case for regular legislative decisions in the HKSAR.[269] Finally, a potentially important amendment procedure is prescribed by Art. 18(3) of

[265]See also Leung (2006), p. 88, who argues in a similar vein.

[266]See also Leung (2006), p. 89.

[267]See Leung (2006), p. 241.

[268]However, according to the decision of the NPCSC of 26 April 2004, amendments to Annex I cannot be initiated in the Legislative Council, but are to be submitted by the Government of Hong Kong after the need for a reform has been determined by the NPCSC. This interpretation may amount to a *de facto* amendment of the Basic Law or at least of its Annex I and has been criticised in that vein in Ghai (2007a), pp. 134–137. See also Leung (2006), p. 240 f. On 28 August 2010, the NPCSC approved an amendment to Annex I concerning the election of the CE from 2012 so that he is elected by an Election Committee with 1200 members divided into four different sections of equal size.

[269]See Weiyun (2001), p. 325, Leung (2006), p. 239 f. Apparently, against the background of that comparison, a decision made in the HKSAR to amend Annex II of the Basic Law could be returned by the NPCSC to the HKSAR. On 28 August 2010, the NPCSC recorded the amendment that in

the Basic Law which empowers the NPCSC to add to or delete from the list of Mainland Chinese laws to be applied in the HKSAR enumerated in Annex III within the areas of defense, foreign affairs, and other matters outside the limits of Hong Kong's autonomy. The NPCSC must first consult the Basic Law Committee and the Government of the HKSAR on such matters.[270] Therefore, in theory, the Basic Law includes a measure of flexibility within its overall scheme by opening up three particular amendment formulas within certain areas which do not require a legislative decision of the NPC.

Above, the obligation to implement the Joint Declaration was discussed. A reference to the implementation obligation in respect of the Joint Declaration is included in the preamble of the Basic Law. After recounting the historical events leading up to the resumption of Chinese sovereignty over Hong Kong and referring to upholding national unity and territorial integrity, the maintenance of the prosperity and stability of Hong Kong, and taking account of its history and realities, the preamble mentions the decision to establish a Hong Kong Special Administrative Region in accordance with the provisions of Art. 31 of the Constitution of China and, under the principle of "one country, two systems",[271] not to apply the socialist system and policies in Hong Kong. It then recognizes that the basic policies of the People's Republic of China regarding Hong Kong were elaborated by the Chinese Government in the Sino-British Joint Declaration. Thus a direct link is established between the Basic Law and the Joint Declaration, and the legislative decision to enact the Basic Law was made in order to ensure the implementation of the basic policies of the People's Republic of China regarding Hong Kong. Finally, the preamble makes the point that the National People's Congress enacted the Basic Law of the HKSAR in accordance with the Constitution of the People's Republic of China.[272]

2012, the LegCo shall have 70 members, of which 35 are returned by functional constituencies and 35 by geographical constituencies.

[270]See also Leung (2006), p. 89 ff. See also Chan (2010), p. 129, who gives a critical assessment of the Basic Law Committee and concludes that a decade after the establishment of the HKSAR, "the Basic Law Committee is still generally perceived as nothing more than a rubber stamp".

[271]Concerning the political notion of the concept, see Xiaoping (2004). See also Ghai (1999), pp. 140–142.

[272]For instance, Weiyun (2001), p. 64, concludes that it is "necessary to trace the background to such an unprecedented law, to define its relations with the JD, and to set down all the reasons for enacting such a law". The special status for Hong Kong is a clear deviation from the four fundamental principles of the Chinese Constitution, as established in the preamble of the Constitution, namely the socialist road, the rule of the proletariat, the leadership of the Communist Party and the guidance of Marxism-Leninism and Mao Zedong thought. See also Leung (2006), p. 3, making the point that Deng Xiaoping's thoughts were added to the preamble in 1999 and Ziang Jeming's three basic thoughts in 2004. Evidently, they may used to justify the particular system granted to the HKSAR through the Joint Declaration and the Basic Law. As explained by Morris (2007), pp. 98–106, the "one country, two systems" concept, including the two separate legal orders and the common law system practiced in Hong Kong, is an expression of the Marxist dialectics that is expected at the end to produce a merger between the two in a synthesis the contents of which are not known at this point of time. In this light, the autonomy of Hong Kong

4.5.4 Guarantee of Capitalist Economy and Common Law to Residents

A number of provisions among the general principles enumerated in the Basic Law establish the normative understanding of the position of the HKSAR within the Chinese state system and under Chinese sovereignty. According to Art. 1, the HKSAR is an inalienable part of the People's Republic of China, but under Art. 2, the National People's Congress authorizes the HKSAR to exercise a high degree of autonomy and to enjoy executive, legislative and independent judicial power, including that of final adjudication, in accordance with the provisions of the Basic Law. The insignia of sovereignty to be used by the SAR is the national flag and the national emblem of the People's Republic of China, but the HKSAR may also use a regional flag and a regional emblem, the descriptions of which are determined in Art. 10. Significantly, when regulating the relationship between the central authorities of China and the HKSAR, the Basic Law provides in Art. 12 that the HKSAR shall be a local administrative region of the People's Republic of China, which shall enjoy a high degree of autonomy and come directly under the Central People's Government. While the autonomy granted to Hong Kong is greater than that which is accorded to a local administrative region, the latter part of the provision means that, unlike Chinese provinces, there is no intermediate layer of government and Hong Kong reports directly to the central government.[273]

According to Art. 24 of the Basic Law, residents of the HKSAR ("Hong Kong residents") shall include permanent residents and non-permanent residents. The Basic Law thus creates an exclusive category of permanent residents of the HKSAR who are entitled to some rights that other Chinese citizens – and others – who are non-permanent residents are not entitled to. For instance, Article 3 of the Basic Law stipulates that the executive authorities and legislature of the HKSAR shall be composed of permanent residents of Hong Kong in accordance with the relevant provisions of the Basic Law. However, as stated in Art. 25 of the Basic Law, all Hong Kong residents – including non-permanent residents – shall be equal before the law, and they shall enjoy other fundamental rights enumerated in Articles 27–40. In addition, Art. 41 stipulates that persons in the HKSAR other than Hong Kong residents shall, in accordance with law, enjoy the rights and freedoms of Hong Kong residents.[274] As a consequence, it seems that although fundamental

could be extinguished, first in an incremental manner through the interpretations of the NPCSC and later, supposedly after 2047, by legislative decision of the NPC.

[273]See Weiyun (2001), p. 137. See also Weiyun (2001), p. 262, according to whom although "the HKSAR will enjoy a high degree of autonomy, it will still be a local administrative region and it cannot be taken as an exception at all".

[274]The freedoms of the residents of the Hong Kong Special Administrative Region (and also of other persons in the region) shall be safeguarded by the HKSAR in accordance with law, which is a general reference in Art. 4 of the Basic Law covering not only the rights established in the Basic Law, but also in the common law applicable in the HKSAR.

rights and freedoms are seldom absolute, the rights of those persons who are non-residents could, by legislative decision, be made less absolute than those of residents.

Articles 27 – 40 contain further fundamental rights of residents, that is, of both permanent and non-permanent residents, as originally established in Annex I to the Joint Declaration. Hong Kong residents have the freedom of speech, of the press and of publication, of association, of assembly,[275] of procession and of demonstration, of marriage and family life, of conscience, of religious belief and practice (including freedom to preach) and of occupation and of academic research, literary and artistic creation and other cultural activities, of confidential legal advice and access to courts as well as the right to institute legal proceedings against the acts of the executive authorities and their personnel, and the right and freedom to form and join trade unions, and to strike. They have the freedom of the person and of movement and travel,[276] and no Hong Kong resident shall be subjected to arbitrary or unlawful arrest, detention or imprisonment or to arbitrary or unlawful search of the body or home or other premises or deprivation or restriction of the freedom of the person or to torture, arbitrary or unlawful deprivation of the life. The freedom and privacy of communication of Hong Kong residents shall be protected by law. Hong Kong residents also have the right to social welfare in accordance with the law. The welfare benefits and retirement security of the labor force shall be protected by law. Hong Kong residents also enjoy other rights and freedoms safeguarded by the laws of the HKSAR. Finally, the lawful traditional rights and interests of the indigenous inhabitants of the "New Territories" shall be protected by the HKSAR. The Basic Law also stipulates that the provisions of the International Covenant on Civil and Political Rights, the International Covenant on Economic, Social and Cultural Rights, and international labor conventions as applied to Hong Kong remain in force and shall be implemented through the laws of the HKSAR.[277] The rights and freedoms enjoyed by Hong Kong residents can be

[275]See *Leung Kwok Hung & Others v HKSAR* [2005] 3 HKLRD 164, at 199, in which a peaceful procession not notified in advance as required by the law was aborted by the police and the persons in charge tried in court. The case deals with the way in which the requirements of the ICCPR (prescribed by law, necessary in a democratic society and proportionality) are brought into the ambit of the fundamental rights of the Basic Law. The convictions of the defendants were upheld, but the concept of public order was limited so as to confine the discretion of the Police Commissioner to regular public order under a proportionality consideration, excluding thereby the broader implications of "*ordre public*".

[276]See the case of *Gurung Kesh Bahadur v Director of Immigration* [2002] 2 HKLRD 775, in which the freedom to travel was interpreted directly on the basis of Art. 31 of the Basic Law and in which restrictions of the freedom were not found permissible. See also Young (2004), pp. 109–132.

[277]See also the case of *Hong Kong Special Administrative Region v Ng Kung Siu* (1999) 2 HKCFAR 442, the so-called national flag desecration case, in which, according to Petersen (2007), p. 35, "the government accepted in court that Article 19 is incorporated into the Basic Law by its Article 39". On p. 36, Petersen concludes that it is noteworthy that the government was so ready to concede that even legislation implementing Art. 23 of the Basic Law (see below)

restricted only as prescribed by law, that is, by a legislative enactment of the Legislative Council. Such restrictions shall not contravene the provisions of the international obligations applicable in HKSAR.[278]

According to Art. 24, the permanent residents of the HKSAR shall include Chinese citizens who are born in Hong Kong or who have ordinarily resided in Hong Kong for a continuous period of not less than seven years or their descendants. Nationals of other countries may also become permanent residents after ordinarily residing in Hong Kong for a continuous period of not less than seven years. At the same time, Art. 22 prescribes that for entry into the HKSAR, people from other parts of China must apply for approval.[279] Thus the Basic Law differentiates between Chinese citizens in Mainland China and Chinese citizens who are permanent residents of the HKSAR. These permanent residents shall have the right of abode in the HKSAR and shall be qualified to obtain, in accordance with the laws of the region, permanent identity cards which state their right of abode. The non-permanent residents of the HKSAR shall be persons who are qualified to obtain Hong Kong identity cards in accordance with the laws of the HKSAR but who have no right of abode. Understandably, the right of abode in Hong Kong is attractive as a status definition for an individual, and related administrative decisions made by the Hong Kong Government have been challenged several times before the courts of Hong Kong. These cases have led to a number of constitutionally relevant decisions concerning the interpretation of the Basic Law.[280]

One of the most significant controversies concerning the right of abode did not concern an operative part of a judgment of the Court of Final Appeal (CFA),[281] but

---

concerning national security legislation must be struck down if it cannot be interpreted so as to comply with the ICCPR. In the case, the CFA upheld the restrictions that the national flag legislation, as implemented in Hong Kong, imposed.

[278] As pointed out in *Gurung Kesh Bahadur*, *supra* note 276 in this Chap., at 783, when interpreting the fundamental rights in chapter III of the Basic Law, "[a] generous approach should be adopted to the interpretation of the rights and freedoms whilst restrictions to them should be narrowly interpreted". The CFA based itself on similar interpretation statements made earlier in *Ng Ka Ling*, *infra* note 281 in this Chap., and *Ng Kung Siu*, *supra* note 277 in this Chap. as well as in *Leung Kwok Hung*, *supra* note 275 in this Chap.

[279] As laid down in Art. 22 of the Basic Law, the number of persons who may enter the HKSAR from Mainland China for the purpose of settlement shall be determined by the competent authorities of the Central People's Government after consulting the Government of the HKSAR.

[280] See, e.g., Leung (2006), pp. 92–174. See also the case of *Kong Yunming v The Director of Social Welfare* [2009] 4 HKLRD 382, challenging social welfare policies which require 7 years of residency before receiving benefits.

[281] *Ng Ka Ling and Others v Director of Immigration* (1999) 2 HKCFAR 4, at pp. 26–28. See also the case of *A Solicitor v Law Society of Hong Kong (SJ, intervening)* [2004] 1 HKLRD 214, in which the Court of Final Appeal again asserted its constitutional jurisdiction, but apparently without ramifications in relation to the NPCSC or the Central Government. For a comment, see P.Y. Lo, 'Master's of One's Own Court', in Hong Kong Law Journal, vol. 34, part 1 of 2004, pp. 47–65.

occurred in response to *obiter dicta*, in which the CFA presented its opinion that it could also examine acts of the NPC and NPCSC to determine their conformity with the Basic Law. The CFA essentially corrected this opinion in a subsequent "clarification" which had been requested by the Hong Kong Government. The CFA established that it does not hold itself above the NPC or the NPCSC.[282] However, the substantive issue resolved by the CFA's judgment – which concerned the right of abode of the children of Hong Kong permanent residents born on the mainland – caused the Government of the HKSAR to request an interpretation from the NPCSC. The Hong Kong Government feared that more than 1.6 million persons could seek residence in Hong Kong as a consequence of the court's decision. The NPCSC's interpretation overturned a portion of the CFA's judgment and applies to future cases of a similar nature, although the individuals who were party to the original case were not affected.[283] The interpretation raised doubts about the finality of the CFA's decisions and the independence of the judiciary, in particular because the court had previously declared that it is not above the NPCSC and would, consequently, find the interpretations of NPCSC binding on itself.

According to its preamble, the Basic Law prescribes the systems to be practiced in the HKSAR, that is, the capitalist economic system and the common law legal system. The former is preserved by way of negation since Art. 5 provides that the socialist system and policies shall not be practiced in the HKSAR, but this provision also states the same in positive terms: the previous capitalist system and way of life shall remain unchanged for 50 years.[284] In addition, under Art. 6 the HKSAR shall protect the right of private ownership of property in accordance with the law.

In 1984 and even when the Basic Law was enacted in 1990, the ideological belief that the socialist economic system is a viable alternative to the capitalist system and that it might even prevail still existed. At the end of the first decade of the twenty-first century, however, it seems obvious that it is not the capitalist system of Hong Kong that has experienced any considerable change. Instead, the socialist system of Mainland China is rapidly moving towards a capitalist system. There is, however, a "collective" basis in the area of real property, because according to Art. 7 of the Basic Law, the land and natural resources within the HKSAR are state property.

---

[282] *Ng Ka Ling & Others v Director of Immigration (No 2)* [1999] 1 HKLRD 577, at 578. The clarification judgment is very short, altogether two pages.

[283] The *Interpretation of 26 June 1999* by the Standing Committee of the National People's Congress of Articles 22(4) and 24(2)(3) of the Basic Law of the Hong Kong Special Administrative Region of the People's Republic of China. See Davis (2007), pp. 88–90, Ghai (2007a), pp. 132–134, and Chan et al. (2000), pp. ix–215 for academic analysis and pp. 219–532 for documents that materialised in the public debate after the Interpretation was issued. See also Chan (2010), p. 130 ff. with other case examples.

[284] Leung (2006), p. 32, makes the point that "[s]cholars of Chinese constitutional law appear to agree that Article 5 of the Constitution is a general provision and Article 31 is a special provision, and that according to rules of interpretation, special provisions should prevail over general provisions".

The Government of the HKSAR is responsible for their management, use and development and for their lease or grant to individuals, legal persons or organizations for use or development. The revenue derived from the use of this public property shall, according to the provision, be exclusively at the disposal of the government of the region.[285]

Article 8 of the Basic Law preserves the common law system as a defining characteristic of the HKSAR together with a number of other dimensions of the legal order.[286] At the outset, Art. 8 provides that the laws previously in force in Hong Kong shall be maintained, although the NPCSC was empowered to determine which of Hong Kong's laws would not apply after the transfer of sovereignty. The term "laws previously in force in Hong Kong" includes the common law, rules of equity, ordinances, subordinate legislation and customary law.[287] The common law is important in this context because it determines the way in which the other dimensions of law are interpreted.[288] However, the provision contains an exception for such laws, provisions or dimensions of the Hong Kong legal order that contravene the Basic Law and that are subject to any amendment by the legislature of the HKSAR. The ultimate source of norms is therefore the Basic Law.

The common law nature of the legal order of the HKSAR also has a linguistic component, because under Art. 9, the English language may, in addition to the Chinese language, be used as an official language by the executive authorities, legislature and judiciary of the HKSAR. As a consequence, legislative enactments in Hong Kong are carried out and published in the two official languages, that is, in both Chinese and English. Because the common law roots of the Hong Kong legal order are British, court proceedings are conducted in English, although increasingly, proceedings in the lower courts are conducted in Chinese. This, in turn, makes it necessary to provide English-medium legal training. Since the overwhelming majority of the residents of Hong Kong are not English speakers, they are

---

[285] See also Weiyun (2001), p. 121 f.

[286] See Leung (2006), p. 7: "Hong Kong practices the common law tradition and follows the doctrine of binding precedents." Concerning the continuity of legislation previously in force, see Leung (2006), pp. 70–74. As pointed out by Dowdle (2007), p. 56, "Hong Kong may be the only jurisdiction in the modern world to elevate a particular legal system to the status of a constitutional right". See also Ghai (2009).

[287] The Sino-British Joint Liaison Group agreed in advance of the transfer of sovereignty on 28 matters previously regulated by UK law that would continue to be regulated by way of local legislation after 30 June 1997, on a large number of bilateral treaties between Hong Kong and various countries which would continue to be in force after 30 June 1997, and on 211 international conventions that would continue to be applied to the HKSAR after 30 June 1997. For the lists of the documents, see Leung (2006), pp. 413–416, 417–430.

[288] As pointed out by Leung (2006), p. 301, "[o]ne of the major differences between the common law system and the Chinese legal system is that the former places greater emphasis on 'due process' while the latter concentrates on 'substantial justice'. Procedural justice is always more time-consuming and expensive, but its end result is usually nearer justice and farther away from injustice. That is the great value of a common law system."

linguistically prevented from participating, in particular, in court proceedings, leaving litigation in the hands of a very exclusive group of persons who on the basis of their training master both the English language and the law.[289] While in Hong Kong, the common law jurisdiction functions in two languages, English and Chinese, the Scottish jurisdiction functions in one language, but in a manner that combines common law and civil law (see also section 5.8.2 below).

4.6 Scotland: Avoiding Even a Remote Possibility of Conflict by Granting Autonomy

4.6.1 Deepening the Pre-existing Treaty-Based Autonomy

After ratification of the Treaty of Union by the English and Scottish parliaments in 1706, the new kingdom of Great Britain emerged in 1707.[290] It is significant in the context that Scotland was never conquered by England, but instead, the independence of the Kingdom of Scotland was recognized by England as early as 1328. During medieval times, the population of Scotland consisted of Celtic and non-Celtic populations, forming together the Scottish nation.[291] By personal union in 1603, Scotland and England became constitutionally linked with each other under the same king, and after the restoration of constitutional government in England in 1689, a more complete union between Scotland and England started to appear relatively natural and realistic (although some forceful persuasion was exercised by the English).[292] However, the UK did not come into existence through the "growth of a single national or linguistic consciousness, but as the outcome of a series of historical contingencies".[293]

The fact that in 1707, the union abolished the Scottish parliament was not in itself a very dramatic measure, because the increase in the power of the old Scottish parliament was a relatively recent phenomenon, only less than two decades old.[294] At the same time, however, the Scots were granted certain special status definitions, such as the preservation of a church of their own[295] as well as their own legal

---

[289] See Dowdle (2007), pp. 56, 62 ff.

[290] Bogdanor (1999), p. 4.

[291] Bogdanor (1999), p. 8.

[292] Bogdanor (1999), p. 9 f. For a detailed description of the Scottish history from the Roman times until the Act of Union, see Pilkington (2002), pp. 25–29.

[293] Bogdanor (1999), p. 4. For a description of the historical background, see Bogdanor (1999), pp. 3–18.

[294] Bogdanor (1999), pp. 8–9, Himsworth and Munro (2000), p. viii.

[295] The Church of Scotland Act 1921 recognises the denomination as the national church of Scotland, but it is not an established church and it is independent of state control in matters spiritual.

order[296] and court system[297] in exchange for joining the union. The result of the union was therefore a unitary country with some functional autonomy accorded to the Scots in certain material fields of law.[298] "Thus the Treaty created a new state with one parliament, but two systems of law and two established churches."[299] It has, against this background, also been suggested that the state was actually not a unitary state in which all parts were treated in the same way, but instead a union state that made it possible to have different rules for different parts of the country (although the union agreement was amended several times).[300]

Functional autonomy (or autonomies) denotes in this context that both the executive power and the legislative power in the UK developed special structures and procedures for dealing with the Scottish affairs.[301] In the executive, the Scottish Office was created in the 1880s, and by the 1990s, its position had evolved so as to involve membership of the Scottish Secretary of State in the UK Cabinet with overall responsibility over Scottish matters, in particular with a view to the five main departments of the Scottish Office (with a main seat in Scotland and a branch office in London). Those departments were agriculture, environment and fisheries, development, education and industry, health, and home affairs.[302] "The Scottish Office thus became the department of government administering Scotland's domestic affairs and the real heart of executive government in Scotland. Moreover, the Secretary of State became the focus of Scotland's political identity. He came to be seen in a wider sense as 'Scotland's minister' and thus held accountable for all government decisions affecting Scotland, whether or not they lay within his area of statutory responsibility."[303]

In the UK Parliament, bills relating exclusively to Scotland were dealt with by one of the two Scottish standing committees, each comprising between 16 and 50 MPs, of which at least 16 were Scottish MPs, and reflecting the party balance of the House of

---

[296] The treaty of union distinguished between "public right", i.e., public law that would be regulated by the parliament of Great Britain, on the one hand, and "private right", which would remain unaltered except if it became necessary, from the point of view of Scotland, to alter it. See Bogdanor (1999), p. 10.

[297] The Scottish Court of Session and other Scottish courts were guaranteed with the pledge that no Scottish lawsuit would be tried before an English judge. See Bogdanor (1999), p. 10.

[298] As reported by Bogdanor (1999), p. 11 f., and Himsworth and Munro (2000), p. viii, there were also some proposals to create a confederation with two parliaments.

[299] Bogdanor (1999), p. 11.

[300] Bogdanor (1999), pp. 14–15.

[301] Himsworth and Munro (2000), p. x, use the term administrative devolution and conclude that aspects of central government would be "conducted by a department which is defined territorially rather than functionally". See also Pilkington (2002), p. 57 f. Also the separate Scottish court system could be understood to constitute a functional autonomy. Concerning administrative devolution allowing for a degree of administrative autonomy with functional responsibilities, see Mitchell (2007), pp. 35–40. On the forms of autonomy in Britain before the Good Friday Agreement concerning Northern Ireland and the devolution to Scotland and Wales, see also Leopold (1998), pp. 223–250.

[302] Bogdanor (1999), p. 111.

[303] Bogdanor (1999), p. 111 f.

Commons. In addition to the two regular Scottish committees, there was a Scottish Grand Committee comprising of all of Scotland's then 72 MPs that could take charge of certain parts of the second and third readings of non-controversial Scottish bills, receive reports and question Scottish ministers during question time. Finally, there was a Select Committee on Scottish Affairs to scrutinize government departments.[304] Hence there was already a Scottish sub-system in the House of Commons. Devolution transferred that sub-system to Edinburgh and placed it under direct electoral control.[305] The matters and functions transferred by devolution to Scotland were generally such that had already been exercised by the Scottish Office.[306]

4.6.2 Devolution by Referendum

A first attempt to institute devolution in Scotland was undertaken after the elections to the UK Parliament in February and October of 1974, but in February 1977, the bill failed in Parliament.[307] The second attempt in the UK Parliament was successful in January 1978, at which point the Act contained a combined referendum and repeal clause that amounted to a support threshold of some kind:[308] "If it appears to the Secretary of State that less than 40 per cent of the persons entitled to vote in the referendum have voted 'yes' . . . he shall lay before Parliament the draft of an Order in Council for the repeal of this Act."[309] In the referendum on 1 March 1979, 51.6 per cent of those voting (that is, 32.85 per cent of the electorate) supported the

[304] Bogdanor (1999), p. 115 f. As concluded by Hazell (2005a), pp. 226, 239 f., although these procedures still exist, they are, after devolution, disused in the case of Scotland.

[305] Bogdanor (1999), p. 116. As concluded in Bogdanor (1999), p. 117, before devolution "Scotland was in the anomalous if not unique position of having a separate legal system, together with separate arrangements for the handling of executive business, but no separate legislature to which the Scottish executive could be held responsible". In addition, there was a separate court system for Scotland.

[306] Trench (2007a), p. 55. This is probably also the reason why Trench (2007d), p. 173 f., is able to indicate that the UK Government's internal administrative arrangements have been largely a continuation of those from before the devolution and lacks in overall co-ordination between the different UK departments.

[307] Bogdanor (1999), pp. 177–183. At the same time, a parallel administrative devolution to Wales was planned and carried out. Devolution has, however, a long history in Britain, starting from a short-lived devolution scheme for Ireland between 1782 and 1801 and continuing in the end of the nineteenth century in the devolution or home rule plans of Gladstone. See Trench (2007c), p. 3 f., and Pilkington (2002), pp. 41–44, who in fact makes the point that Gladstone developed a distinction between powers devolved to different territories and powers reserved to Parliament and did so to a large extent against the background of the British experience with dominions such as Canada. See also Pilkington (2002), p. 9, according to whom the original concept of devolution "was put forward by Edmund Burke at the end of the eighteenth century and formed part of his solution to the problems of the British government in dealing with the revolutionary American colonists and the Irish Catholics who were disenfranchised by the 1801 Act of Union".

[308] Bogdanor (1999), pp. 183–188.

[309] As quoted in Bogdanor (1999), p. 188.

Scotland Act, while it was opposed by 48.5 per cent of those voting (that is, 30.78% of the electorate).[310] Thus the 'yes' vote fell clearly below the requirement of 40 per cent, and as a consequence, the Labour-led UK Government collapsed. The new Conservative Government and Parliament, elected in May 1979, thereafter repealed the Scotland Act.[311] Therefore, it appears that the provision with the support threshold actually managed to make the referendum a politically binding advisory referendum that ultimately led to the repeal of an existing Act, which, in addition to the demise of the Government, is quite extraordinary.

The devolution idea was resurrected through the work of the non-elected and thus informal Scottish Constitutional Convention (not to be confused by the constitutional term 'constitutional convention'), a body which was comprised of Scottish representatives of Labour, the Liberal Democrats, labour unions, churches, and local government as well as of other bodies.[312] Before the general election of May 1997, Labour made devolution and a devolution referendum an election issue. After winning the elections, Labour saw to it that the Referendum (Scotland and Wales) Act was passed and the referendums held. The Scottish referendums were held on 11 September 1997, and on the first question, whether the voter agreed that there should be a Scottish Parliament, 74.3 per cent of the voters gave an affirmative answer, which means that the measure would have been carried even in the event that the 40 per cent support threshold from 1979 had been in effect. The second referendum on the issue of whether or not the voter agreed that a Scottish Parliament should have tax-varying powers resulted in 63.5 per cent in support of the tax varying powers. Consequently, the Government prepared the Bill for the UK Parliament, where it was adopted without any problems.[313]

Devolution to Scotland was brought about by the Scotland Act 1998 of 19 November 1998.[314] The Scotland Act, initially prepared by the informal body

---

[310]Bogdanor (1999), p. 190, and Himsworth and Munro (2000), p. xi, who make the point that the referendum results led indirectly to a change of government, after defeat on a vote of confidence. For a break-down of the results, see also Pilkington (2002), p. 187.

[311]Bogdanor (1990), pp. 190–191. See also Pilkington (2002), pp. 58–64.

[312]Bogdanor (1999), pp. 196–198, and Himsworth and O'Neill (2003), p. 84 f. As pointed out by Bogdanor (1999), p. 196, the Conservatives and the Scottish National Party refused to participate in the Convention. The latter "declared that it could support only a directly elected convention prepared to draw up a constitution for an independent Scotland". See also Pilkington (2002), pp. 68–71.

[313]See Pilkington (2002), p. 95 f. It is possible to say that due to the electoral victory of Labour in 1997 and its promises and pledges concerning devolution during the election campaign, it was relatively speaking easy to pass the Scotland Act in 1998 with less scrutiny in the UK Parliament than would have been the case later into the governmental period of Labour or if the Conservative Party had been in power, in which case the Scotland Act would not have been enacted at all.

[314]Its descriptive title is "an Act to provide for the establishment of a Scottish Parliament and Administration and other changes in the government of Scotland; to provide for changes in the constitution and functions of certain public authorities; to provide for the variation of the basic rate of income tax in relation to income of Scottish taxpayers in accordance with a resolution of the Scottish Parliament; to amend the law about parliamentary constituencies in Scotland; and for connected purposes".

Scottish Constitutional Convention on the basis of negotiations between Labour and the Liberal Democrats[315] and enacted by the legislature of the United Kingdom, is a very detailed set of norms that specifies, *inter alia*, the distribution of powers between the parliament of the United Kingdom and the parliament of Scotland, the method of election, the legislative procedure, and the implementation of Scottish legislation by the administrative infrastructure. It has been stated that devolution is the most radical constitutional change seen in the United Kingdom since the Great Reform Act of 1832.[316] The reason for such radicalism is that devolution "seeks to reconcile two seemingly conflicting principles, the sovereignty or supremacy of Parliament and the grant of self-government in domestic affairs" to, *inter alia*, Scotland.[317] However, devolution to Scotland does not imply a revocation of the treaty of union, but it instead "provides for a parliament which is constitutionally subordinate to Westminster",[318] as created by section 1 (1) of the Scotland Act, according to which "[t]here shall be a Scottish Parliament". From 1999 on, the Scottish Parliament has had legislative powers within internal matters such as education, health care, housing, transportation and criminal law, and a Scottish budget is administered by the Government of Scotland. The British central government has responsibility over the national economy, the currency, defence and foreign policy, and there continues to be a Scotland Office in the UK Government, but since 2003 as a part of the Department for Constitutional Affairs. The position of the Secretary of State for Scotland with a seat in the UK Cabinet is preserved but merged with another ministerial post.[319] The main branch of the Scotland Office is in Scotland and there is a branch office in London.

---

[315]Bogdanor (1999), p. 219, and Himsworth and Munro (2000), p. xii. The Scottish Constitutional Convention was not an elected body, but instead a collection of interested parties and persons, including members of the UK Parliament and the European Parliament, which produced a blueprint of Scottish devolution, completed by civil servants, and it also functioned as an effective pressure group for the plan.

[316]Bogdanor (1999), p. 1. For the passing of the Scotland Act 1998 in the UK Parliament, see also Himsworth and Munro (2000), pp. xiii–xvii, 5–6.

[317]Bogdanor (1999), p. 1.

[318]Bogdanor (1999), p. 15. For the political debates leading up to devolution, see Bogdanor (1999), pp. 166–202.

[319]See McFadden and Lazarowicz (2002), p. 92 f. The Scotland Office is now a part of the UK Ministry of Justice, and the Secretary of State is a full-time position, not anymore combined with another ministerial post, a development that reflects the new political situation that emerged when the SNP came to power after the Scottish parliamentary elections in 2007. According to Bogdanor (1999), p. 205, the Secretary of State for Scotland has no governor-general functions in the jurisdiction of Scotland and will not act as an intermediary between the Scottish Parliament and the Queen. In fact, according to Pilkington (2002), p. 119, the tasks of the Scottish Secretary have diminished so much that the post is not needed anymore in the form it has existed until recently. It is also possible to say that the Scottish Office patrols the border line between the two competences. See also Serving Scotland Better (2009), p. 125. However, it seems that formerly, the Scotland Office had more functions as a channel of communication, but they have been increasingly replaced by direct contacts between substance officials in Scotland and the UK.

The tax varying powers of Scotland imply that an additional tax of up to 3% can be imposed on top of regular income taxation, but generally speaking the government of Scotland is almost entirely dependent on budgetary transfers from the UK Government in the form of a block grant.[320] However, the power to fix a basic rate for Scottish taxpayers also makes it possible to decrease the income tax by the same amount.[321] So far, however, the tax varying powers have never been used. Instead, the funding of the Scottish budget is dependent on the block-grant over the UK budget, calculated on the basis of a so-called Barnett formula.[322] As a consequence, the Scottish Parliament controls 60% of identifiable public spending in Scotland and is able to do so without interference from central government, but Scotland is in

[320]See also Himsworth (2006), p. 213 f., Himsworth and Munro (2000), pp. 80–91, and Pilkington (2002), pp. 112–114, as well as Bogdanor (1999), pp. 235–254, making the point on p. 239 that the tax-varying power of Scotland is minimal. See also Bell and Christie (2007), p. 77, according to which the block grant, determined on the basis of the so-called Barnett formula, "is part of a political process that allows the centre to retain tight control over the resources available to the devolved administrations and thus the extent to which they can differentiate their policies". For a similar argument, see also Trench (2007b), p. 92, and Himsworth and O'Neill (2003), p. 395. Bell and Christie (2007), p. 77, also make the point that the Barnett formula is unique in the developed world, because there is no country other than the UK that allocates resources at a subnational level using a formula based on changes in spending elsewhere, rather than allocating levels of spending in relation to assessed need". However, at least in the case of the Åland Islands, the block grant to the Åland Islands from the Finnish budget is determined on the basis of a percentage counted on the basis of the expenditures of the State, less the loans that the State has borrowed. While recognising that the block grant offers real autonomy in spending, Trench (2007b), p. 94 f., concludes that the block grant and the Barnett formula "makes the devolved administrations purely spending agencies, not fully functioning governments", which the marginal tax-varying powers could not really save, placing the financial integration of Scotland in marked contrast to the generous legal and administrative powers devolved to Scotland. The consequence of the funding system can, along the lines indicated by Trench (2007b), pp. 96–112, be summarized by saying that the UK Treasury retains a high degree of power, on both the high constitutional level (for instance, organisational resources in comparison to the devolved administrations, control over the Barnett formula and economic and spending information) and the day-to-day operational one (for instance, lobbying, concrete spending decisions). See also Greer (2007), p. 153 f., according to whom the Barnett formula "distributes changes in spending on a strict per capita basis and thereby drives the whole UK towards equal per capita expenditure over time". He also makes the point on p. 155 that the "vast bulk of devolved funding simply does not depend on agreeing with Whitehall on policy issues, as Scotland has shown by spending its Barnett funds on policies London rejected". After all, there seems to exist a measure of independence in the spending decisions.

[321]See Himsworth and Munro (2000), pp. 91–101. The tax varying power could amount to up to 1 billion pounds in 2009, out of a total budget of the Scottish Parliament 27.4 billion pounds. See Serving Scotland Better (2009), pp. 71, 73.

[322]What is particularly problematic concerning the Barnett formula is that it is not very solidly established in the Scotland Act, because Art. 64(2) only says that the "Secretary of State shall from time to time make payments into the [Scottish Consolidated –MS] Fund out of money provided by Parliament of such amounts as he may determine". This is in stark contrast to, e.g., the Åland Islands, where the lump sum is determined according to a formula established in the Self-Government Act. For an example of how the Barnett formula works, see Serving Scotland Better (2009), p. 265.

practice responsible for deciding only 10% of the taxation levied in Scotland.[323] In addition, the powers of Scottish Ministers to borrow money are very limited.[324]

4.6.3 A Constitutional Convention as the Safeguard

A constitutional characterisation of the British areas where devolution has been practiced is not very simple because the country does not have any written constitution, but departs from, *inter alia*, constitutional conventions for the structure of the government. The point of departure seems to be that the legislation that emerges is understood as delegated or devolved legislation and that the legislation of the Parliament of the United Kingdom takes precedence in cases where the regional autonomy legislation stands in conflict with an act enacted by the UK Parliament.[325] In the extreme, the UK Parliament could abolish the entire basis of the legislative competence of the Scottish Parliament, the Scotland Act 1998, pursuant to its supreme powers: "Legally, therefore, there is no reason why the Scottish Parliament could not be abolished by a later act of the United Kingdom Parliament."[326] The reason for this is the fact that the UK Parliament "has voluntarily transferred a number of its law-making powers to the Scottish Parliament without relinquishing its own supreme authority or sovereignty".[327] Therefore, at least in principle, the sovereignty of the UK Parliament is preserved.[328] However, the relevant constitutional convention regulating the matter, the so-called Sewel Convention, holds that the UK Parliament will not normally legislate with regard to

[323] Serving Scotland Better (2009), p. 66. See also Serving Scotland Better (2009), pp. 70–106.

[324] Serving Scotland Better (2009), p. 112.

[325] See, in particular, point 13 in *Devolution. Memorandum of Understanding and Supplementary Agreements between the United Kingdom Government Scottish Ministers, the Cabinet of the National Assembly for Wales and the Northern Ireland Executive Committee*. Presented to Parliament by the Deputy Prime Minister by Command of Her Majesty, December 2001/CM 5240. See also Leopold (1998), pp. 223–250; Himsworth (2006), p. 213; Himsworth (2007), *passim*.

[326] Himsworth and Munro (2000), p. xviii, and Himsworth and O'Neill (2003), pp. 93 f., 149, 164 f. See also Himsworth and Munro (2000), p. 49, making the point that this could theoretically take place in the last resort.

[327] McFadden and Lazarovicz (2003), p. 5. According to them, this means at the same time that the Scottish Parliament is not independent and not free to make laws in any area which it chooses.

[328] See Bogdanor (1999), p. 202, who makes the point that devolution rejects "both separatism, under which the Parliament of the United Kingdom would no longer have power to legislate for Scotland at all; and federalism under which the Parliament of the United Kingdom would have power to legislate for Scotland only in certain defined areas, other areas becoming the entire responsibility of the Scottish Parliament". It thus seems that the Scottish Parliament would not have genuinely exclusive law-making powers, a point which is indirectly made in Trench (2007a), p. 54: "[e]xecutive devolution – unlike legislative devolution – is exclusive".

devolved matters in Scotland without the consent of the Scottish Parliament.[329] The scope of the Sewel Convention may even have been widened during the first decade of Scottish autonomy, because it can be said that the Convention now covers any UK provision in a UK Parliament Bill that 1) falls within the devolved legislative competence of the Scottish Parliament; 2) alters the executive competence of Scottish Ministers; or 3) alters the legislative competence of the Scottish Parliament.[330] The political (if not legal) implication of the Convention is that the UK Parliament will not unilaterally and intentionally intrude into the area of the Scottish legislative competence. The more practical effect of the Sewel Convention is to create a mechanism of discussion between the UK Parliament and the Scottish Parliament, in practice managed through contacts between the UK Government and the Scottish Government, in which the Scottish Parliament can either give or withhold its consent to such legislation being prepared in the UK Parliament that actually belongs to the Scottish legislative competence. If the consent is withheld, the expectation is that the UK Parliament will not extend the law to the jurisdiction of Scotland.[331]

With reference to our two-dimensional scheme concerning different autonomy positions (see above, Fig. 1.1 of Sect. 1.3), it is clear that in the absence of a written constitution as a basis for the Scottish devolution arrangement, Scotland is positioned in the lower part of the chart. However, the Sewel Convention, albeit only

[329]"We [the Government] envisage that there could be instances where it would be more convenient for legislation on devolved matters to be passed by the United Kingdom Parliament. However, ... we would expect a convention to be established that Westminster would not normally legislate with regard to devolved matters in Scotland without the consent of the Scottish Parliament." As quoted in The Sewel Convention, volume 1: Report. Procedures Committee Report, 7th Report, 2005 (Session 2), SP Paper 428, PR/S2/05/R7, at http://www.scottish.parliament.uk/business/committees/procedures/reports-05/prr05-07-vol01.htm (accessed on 13 March 2009). See also Lords Hansard text for 21 July 1998, column 791, at http://www.publications.parliament.uk/pa/ld199798/ldhansrd/vo980721/text/80721-20.htm#80721-20_spnew2 (accessed on 12 March 2009). See also para. 13 of the Memorandum of Understanding, in which the contents of the Sewel convention are reiterated, and Hazell and Rawlings (2005), p. 6, and Winetrobe (2005), pp. 43–44.

[330]Serving Scotland Better (2009), p. 48.

[331]Therefore, as pointed out by Bogdanor (1999), p. 291, it is perhaps "in constitutional theory alone that full legislative power remains with Westminster. It is in constitutional theory alone that the supremacy of Parliament is preserved. For power devolved, far from being power retained, will be power transferred; and it will not be possible to recover that power except under pathological circumstances, such as those of Northern Ireland after 1968. Thus the relationship between Westminster and Edinburgh will be quasi-federal in normal times and unitary only in crisis times. For the formal assertion of parliamentary supremacy will become empty when it is no longer accompanied by a real political supremacy. (...) In Scotland then, the supremacy of Parliament will bear a very different and attenuated meaning after the setting-up of her parliament. It will certainly not mean the supremacy over 'all persons, matters and things' of the 1920 Government of Ireland Act". However, it seems that the mechanism of legislative consent from the Scottish Parliament to the UK Parliament to legislate on devolved matters cuts at least materially if not formally into the position of the Scottish Parliament (see below).

political, should be weighed in the context so as to elevate the position of Scotland somewhat in the lower part of the chart. Because at least in theory, if not in practice, there is the possibility that the UK parliament could override a Scottish act within the legislative competence of Scotland and because the UK Parliament may, in the Scotland Act, thus have reserved to itself the ultimate residual power, it seems that the legislative powers of Scotland are not completely exclusive in nature.[332] At the same time, the law-making powers of Scotland are strong in the meaning that individual rules established in Scottish Acts can constitute the sole basis for an administrative decision or a court sentence. Therefore, the Scottish powers are not merely of an administrative nature, subordinated to the national legislature, but real and enforceable in their compelling effect on, for instance, individuals and business corporations.[333] Against this background, it is possible to say that Scotland is best placed around the border-line area that divides sections II and IV of the chart. Taking into consideration the so-called Sewel convention, Scotland could perhaps be placed in the upper part of section II of the chart.

4.6.4 Parliamentary Sovereignty and Constitutional Review

Because of the concept of the sovereignty of Parliament, the courts have not undertaken any judicial review, for instance, concerning compliance of acts of Parliament with the treaty of union, in spite of the fact that the treaty can be regarded as one of the documents forming the constitution of the United Kingdom.[334] In this respect, the position of Scotland in the United Kingdom is currently determined in ways which are fundamentally different from the traditional approach and, for instance, from the predominantly judicial determination of the position of Puerto Rico in the United States, although the plenary powers of the US

[332] See also Himsworth and Munro (2000), p. xviii, according to whom the Scottish Parliament is "restricted to legislating within its conferred powers, and it has no exclusive sphere of competence. The continuing competence of the United Kingdom Parliament to legislate for Scotland, not merely on reserved matters but on any matter, is explicitly restated in section 28(7) of the Act". However, it remains unclear what happens if the Scottish Parliament chooses not to legislate in a sphere where the UK Parliament has created legislation. If such a "white spot" emerges and the UK Parliament can not fill it with legislation, then the Scottish powers would be exclusive, but that is probably not the case at least in situations where the UK Parliament would feel that there is a national interest to make sure that even the Scottish jurisdiction has a rule for such a matter and decides to extend the application of UK law to Scotland, thereby filling the "white spot".

[333] See, e.g., Page (2005), p. 7, who concludes that the Scottish Parliament does not have any claim of unlimited legislative competence, but "its law making powers are extremely broad, so broad in fact that there are few aspects of Scottish life that do not fall within its competence. Acts of the Scottish Parliament also have exactly the same force of law as Acts of the Westminster Parliament".

[334] See Bogdanor (1999), p. 14, Himsworth and Munro (2000), p. ix, and Himsworth and O'Neill (2003), pp. 152–156.

Congress in relation to territorial possessions are in many ways couched in terms similar to the concept of the supremacy of Parliament in the UK. While the Scottish Parliament is constitutionally subordinate, it seems that it has the political capacity of being anything but subordinate.[335]

It has been pointed out that the position of the UK Parliament, which was based on supremacy and a real power to make laws affecting Scotland's domestic affairs, is the power to supervise another legislative body which will make laws over a wide area of public policy. In such a context, the supremacy of the UK Parliament would be highly attenuated and include the following: (1) the more or less theoretical right to legislate on Scotland's domestic affairs against the wishes of the Scottish Parliament, and (2) the right to abolish the Scottish Parliament, which would be very difficult against the wishes of the Scottish Parliament and the people and without another referendum in Scotland.[336] For that reason, it can be said that the grant of legislative competences to the Scottish Parliament is perhaps not entirely a unilateral measure on the part of the UK Parliament.[337] It might instead be viewed as a devolution scheme with two parties in which one of the parties is weaker.

The Scotland Act also affects the underlying assumptions of the sovereignty of Parliament in other ways. The Scotland Act not only distributes powers but also introduces a judicial element into the determination of that distribution which makes the Scotland Act, in effect, an enacted constitution and provides for a constitutional court instance, the UK Supreme Court (until October 2009 the Judicial Committee of the Privy Council),[338] to interpret the distribution of

---

[335]Bogdanor (1999), p. 288. As stated by Bogdanor (1999), p. 288, the most important power of the Scottish Parliament will be one not mentioned in the Act at all (or at least not among the devolved powers), "that of representing the people of Scotland. The basic premiss of devolution, after all, is that there is a separate political will in Scotland".

[336]Bogdanor (1999), p. 292. As pointed out by Bogdanor (1999), p. 292: "It will not even be easy for Westminster unilaterally to alter the devolution settlement to Scotland's disadvantage. (...) For, although the provisions of the Scotland Act can in theory be altered by a simple Act of Parliament at Westminster, it would in practice be very difficult to do so on a matter which the Scots regard as affecting their interests without the consent of the Scottish Parliament. Thus, in practice, the supreme body with the power to alter the provisions of the Scotland Act will be not Westminster alone, but Westminster together with the Scottish Parliament. In so far as any major amendment of the Scotland Act is concerned, Westminster will have lost its supremacy." See also Henig (2006), p. 45, who makes the point that "in the absence of a written or codified constitution, the sole legal basis for the devolved institutions is Westminster statute which can be repealed or amended". However, he admits that the probability is that "political factors would almost certainly inhibit any unilateral action", although he at the same time refers to the abolition of the Greater London Council by the Conservative Government as an example of an instance where a lower tier has been abolished. The same political conclusion is drawn by Himsworth and Munro (2000), p. xviii.

[337]See also Himsworth and Munro (2000), p. xix.

[338]The Judicial Committee's jurisdiction was transferred to the UK Supreme Court under section 40(4) and Part 2 of Schedule 9 to the Constitutional Reform Act 2005. As concluded in Bogdanor (1999), pp. 206, 293, the Judicial Committee of the Privy Council actually assumed functions of a constitutional court for devolution issues, both in the pre-assent and the post-assent stage. See also Bogdanor (1999), p. 293, making the point that the Judicial Committee is able to

powers.[339] Both are arranged in the form of abstract advance review before the bill passed by the Scottish Parliament is promulgated and in the form of concrete review of implementation. From the point of view of the hierarchy of norms, this could be expressed so that under the legislative authority of the UK Parliament, the Scotland Act functions as a constitutional document for the Scottish jurisdiction,[340] and the Scottish legislative enactments and subsequent secondary legislation are based on the Scotland Act in such a way that judicial review of a constitutional kind in concrete cases becomes possible with the Scotland Act as the yardstick. This is underlined by the fact that under section 103 of the Scotland Act, any decision of the Supreme Court in proceedings under the Scotland Act are binding in all legal proceedings (other than proceedings before the Supreme Court itself). The UK Supreme Court thus has the position of a constitutional court in devolution matters.[341] The constitutional jurisdiction is organized in much more unclear or fluid ways in, for instance, Aceh, the Åland Islands and Hong Kong.

4.7 Aceh: Resolution of Internal Conflict by Internal Agreement

4.7.1 Particular Form of Decentralisation

The Constitution of the Republic of Indonesia was enacted in 1945 as a constitution for a unitary state.[342] The ideology of "unitarism", which may be understood as a reaction

---

pronounce only on Scottish and not on Westminster legislation. It is able to "declare that a Scottish statute is repugnant to the constitution, i.e. that it contravenes the Scotland Act, but not that an Act of the Westminster Parliament is repugnant to it, since the supremacy of the Parliament is in theory preserved. Nevertheless, if the Judicial Committee decides a dispute in Scotland's favour, it would be difficult for Westminster to legislate for Scotland on that matter when the Judicial Committee had ruled that it lay within the scope of Scotland's transferred powers. The decisions of the Judicial Committee, therefore, may well have the consequence that the prerogatives of Westminster are diminished. If that happens, Westminster will lose yet another of the characteristics of a supreme parliament, the right to make any laws it wishes."

[339] Bogdanor (1999), p. 294. Some interlocutors have pointed out hat at least so far, devolution has not reshaped the way in which the UK is governed in such a fundamental manner as predicted by Bogdanor in 1999.

[340] See Himsworth and O'Neill (2003), p. 145.

[341] See Himsworth and Munro (2000), p. 128, and Himsworth and O'Neill (2003), pp. 465, 507.

[342] One reason for the clear choice of the unitary state was the fact that "[o]nly Java-based delegates attended the principal opportunity to debate the shape of the future independent Indonesia, the Body for the Investigation of Indonesian Independence (Badan Penjelidik Kemerdekaan Indonesia, or BPKI) at the end of May 1945. Although a tenth of its 62 members had been born outside Java, there was no voice at that meeting for the concerns of the ethnic minorities. Not surprisingly, the body voted for a unitary republic." "After independence was hastily proclaimed in a manner the Japanese could accept on 17 August, the Japanese-sponsored Committee for the Preparation of Indonesian Independence (PPKI) was called upon to authorize the constitution prepared earlier in Java, and lay

against the proto-federal models of governance under Dutch colonialism and which was strengthened by the attempts of the Dutch to create, after the mid-1940s, a counter-revolution of a federal kind in the newly independent country,[343] has been invoked against later arguments for federalism in Indonesia. Therefore, the decentralization that was first commenced in 1945[344] was deepened and framed in 1999–2000 as a delegation of power to the provinces and further sub-divisions from the central government[345] within the framework of the unitary state. In its amended form, the Constitution of the Unitary State of the Republic of Indonesia establishes a division of the state into provinces and their sub-divisions[346] as regulated by law. These provinces, regencies and municipalities shall, according to Art. 18(2) of the Constitution, administer and manage their own affairs according to, *inter alia*, the principle of regional autonomy which involves self-government at all levels through elected representatives. The concept of regional autonomy is central to the constitutional provision, but it is not clear on the basis of the Constitution what the concept means.

---

the basis for the new state in a hurried three-day meeting." See Anthony Reid, 'Indonesia's post-revolutionary aversion to federalism', in Baogang 2007, p. 149.

[343]See also Lindsey and Santosa (2008), p. 8, and Reid (2007), p. 150 ff. In fact, the Netherlands transferred sovereignty unconditionally on 27 December 1949 to a federal republic, the Republic Indonesia Serikat (RIS), known in English as the Republic of the United States of Indonesia (RUSI), which had emerged as a negotiated compromise and lasted only eight months, before the Republicans won over the Federalists. As explained by Reid (2007), p. 152: "Unitarism became a part of the victorious nationalist package, and hence something that was not negotiable."

[344]See law No. 1 of 1945 concerning local autonomy/decentralization.

[345]According Art. 1, para. 1, of the LoGA, the central government is identified as the President of the Republic of Indonesia empowered with the power of governance over the Republic of Indonesia as referred to under the 1945 Constitution of the Republic of Indonesia.

[346]According to Art. 1, para. 3, of the LoGA, a district/municipality is a part of a province constituting a legal social unit granted with special authority to manage and administer its local governance and social interests in accordance with the laws of and within the system and principles of the Unitary State of the Republic of Indonesia pursuant to the 1945 Constitution of the Republic of Indonesia, headed by a regent/mayor. Interestingly, decentralization in Indonesia goes actually from the national level directly to the district/municipality level, that is, to the sub-provincial level. Aceh is an exception in this respect, because there, devolution goes to the provincial level. However, funds of the central government are in many cases allocate directly to the district/municipality level, and the province of Aceh is not really satisfied with it. District/municipality governance is the administration of government-related affairs exercised by the district/municipality government and the district/municipality House of Representatives in accordance with their respective functions and authorities. Districts and municipalities are according to Art. 1, paras. 18–20, and Arts. 112–114 divided into several sub-divisions: *Kecamatan* (subdistrict) is the operational jurisdiction of the *camat* as a district/municipality apparatus for administrating governance of the *kecamatan*. *Mukim* is a legal social unit under the *kecamatan* consisting of a group of *gampong* with a set geographical boundary, led by an *imeum mukim*, or any other name such person may be called, who is positioned directly under the *camat*. *Gampong*, or any other term it may be called, is a legal social unit under a *mukim* and led by a *keuchik* or any other name such person may be called, having the authority to manage its own affairs. The self-government of Aceh hence consists of several layers and is, in principle, not only focused on the regional level. For the development of the Indonesian constitutional order from 1945, see Lindsey and Santosa (2008), pp. 8–22, and Lindsey (2008), pp. 23–45.

Under Art. 18(5) of the Constitution, the regional authorities shall exercise wide-ranging autonomy, except in matters specified by law to be the affairs of the central government, and in exercising their autonomy, the regional authorities have, under Art. 18(6), the authority to adopt regional regulations, that is, bylaws. Therefore, within the unitary state, there is a constitutional basis for a far-reaching decentralization. Although the central level retains the law-making authority in the House of Representatives, the implementation of national law takes mainly place at lower levels of administration through self-government, that is, through self-governing entities which are not formally part of the state administration. The great ethnic, linguistic and religious variety of the population of Indonesia can be taken into account on the basis of Art. 18A, according to which the power relations between the central government and the regional authorities of the provinces, regencies and municipalities shall be further regulated by law having regard to the particularities and diversity of each region.

The regional nature of the unitary state is also reflected in the Regional Representative Council (DPD), to which each province sends an equal number of members which shall not exceed one third of the number of members of the House of Representatives (DPR) and which are directly elected. Although the construction is somewhat reminiscent of a senate in a federation, its powers are mainly related to the issues relevant for regional autonomy and decentralization, with the possibility to propose bills to the House of Representatives concerning, *inter alia*, regional autonomy, the relationship of central and local governments, the formation, expansion and merger of regions, and financial issues with relevance to the regions.[347] The Regional Representative Council is thus not a senate, as would be the case in a federal structure, but perhaps more correctly understood as a consultative body with respect to legislation which is of direct relevance from a decentralization perspective.[348] In addition, the Council has a role in amending the Constitution, because its members are joined together with the members of the

[347] See Lindsey (2008), p. 35 f., 39, who denotes the organ with the name 'senate', with quotation marks.

[348] As concluded by Lindsey (2008) p. 39, only one of the two houses, the House of Representatives of Indonesia (the Indonesian parliament) has legislative powers, while the Regional Representative Council can only refer laws to the former. It is, according to Lindsey, therefore not clear where the Regional Representative Council stands in the hierarchy in relation to the parliament and other constitutional bodies. "Like senates in, for example Australia and the United States, it could claim a special status as the legitimate voice of regional communities, rather than just political parties. This has the potential to create political difficulties later. The fact that the DPD members are elected as individuals while the DPR members are nominated by parties after the election, means that DPD members might reasonably claim that they are more legitimate representatives of the people than are the members of the DPR. This could become critical in any MPR debate over decentralisation and regional autonomy, where the DPD could be expected to align with the regions, while DPR party control means its members are likely to be more centralist. To date, however, the DPD has been largely a passive institution and has struggled to assert political influence." See also Schmit (2008), p. 167, concerning the structure of the DPD. Each province elects four members to the DPD.

House of Representatives in the People's Consultative Assembly (MPR), which is the body vested with the functions of, *inter alia*, amending the Constitution.

More specifically, under Art. 18B, the state shall recognize and respect units of regional authorities that are special and distinct, and such units shall be further regulated by law.[349] Arguably, Aceh and Papua are such units, and they have each been granted special status by law.[350] Thus the general scheme of decentralization recognizes the special and distinct nature of some regional units and creates a platform for a particular body of legislation for such units. When legislation to that effect is passed, the state is under the obligation to recognize and respect the traditional communities in these units along with their traditional customary rights. However, the Constitution makes this possible under the condition that the communities and the rights that exist remain in accordance with the societal development and the principles of the Unitary State of the Republic of Indonesia.[351] The reference to principles of the unitary state is actually a reference to the *Pancasila*, that is, to the five constitutional principles that constitute the official philosophical foundation of the Indonesian state and that are recorded in para. 4 of the preamble of the Constitution of Indonesia. The five principles are viewed as inseparable and interrelated and they are placed at the helm of the normative order: 1) belief in the one and only God,[352] 2) just and civilized humanity, 3) the unity of

---

[349]Hence in principle, the state respects the local traditional society with its rights as long as such rights exist and they do not conflict with the national law. Historically, all regions had local law which was respected, but after 1960s, national law became more prominent and pushed aside local law. With the constitutional amendments 1999–2003, more variety in the legal order is accepted. What this could mean in concrete terms is that where the national law is already established, such as in much of the area of so-called public law, Aceh would probably not be able to establish deviating rules (such as driving on the right hand side), but in the area of so-called private law, deviations would be possible and they would also be most likely in the area private law, because the *adat* (i.e., customary law) exists mainly in the area of private law.

[350]See Schmit (2008), p. 148, who refers to the Special Autonomy Law for the Province of Papua (Law No. 21/2001).

[351]The five principles of the *Pancasila*, created by Professor Raden Supomo and launched by President Sukarno in 1945, at the time when Indonesia became independent. From the point of view of legal theory, the positioning of *Pancasila* is linked to the normative constructions of Hans Nawiasky, and the effect of the *Pancasila* is that the legal order and the hierarchy of norms does not become too positivistic, but retains features of more substantive justice. See Gueci (1999), and Bourchier (2008), p. 101 f. See also Fitzpatrick (2008), p. 510: "Although the precise boundaries of the *Pancasila* are unclear, in its core conception it encompasses the primacy of national unity, social, stability and a patrimonial state. All social organisations, including religious and legal entities, were obliged – in theory – to adopt *Pancasila* as their governing ideology (Law No. 8 of 1985). It has been, until recently, a compulsory subject in schools and universities. Indeed, in all fields of activity in contemporary Indonesia, notions such as *Pancasila* state, *Pancasila* democracy and *Pancasila* law are still the malleable metanorms by which law, civil activities and people-state relations are judged."

[352]Having the largest Islamic population of all states in the world, there has been a discussion in Indonesia since the independence of Indonesia in 1945. The discussion has continued even past the decision by the MPR in 2002 not to amend the Constitution so as to give *shari'a* constitutional status. See Salim (2008), p. 1–2.

Indonesia, 4) democracy guided by the inner wisdom in the unanimity arising out of deliberations amongst representatives, and 5) social justice for the whole of the people of Indonesia.

Such special and distinct status that is contemplated in Art. 18B is not self-executing, but shall be further regulated by law, which means that particular legislation needs to be enacted by the House of Representatives of Indonesia to give effect to a particular status of self-government. Essentially, the particular status is, nonetheless, a part of the larger decentralization scheme of the Indonesian Constitution. Because Articles 18, 18A and 18B of the Constitution were enacted by way of the second amendment to the Constitution in 2000, the constitutional platform, with the language of (regional) autonomy was available when the political will of the insurgents in Aceh and the Government of Indonesia converged in 2005 in the aftermath of the tsunami. It is also important to consider the fact that a Constitutional Court was created on the basis of the third amendment to the Constitution in 2001. The Constitutional Court was established in 2003 through the Act on the Constitutional Court to try, *inter alia*, the relationship between acts of the House of Representatives and the Constitution (that is, constitutional review of legislation), conflicts of interest among state institutions relating to constitutional powers, actions for the dissolution of political parties, actions with respect to election results, and motions of impeachment.[353]

The development of the constitutional framework coincided with the general decentralization in Indonesia and with consideration of the particular position of Aceh from 1999 on.[354] Limited political, economic and administrative authority was devolved to the sub-provincial administrations, that is, to the districts, already in 1999,[355] by means of legislation on regional government[356] and on fiscal balance

---

[353]Lindsey (2008), p. 34.

[354]For an analysis of the decentralization legislation in Indonesia, see Schmit (2008), pp. 146–187. The legislation on regional administration passed in 1974 during the authoritarian period effectively ended regional autonomy and contributed to creating a negative image for the concept of regional autonomy. See also Miller (2009), p. 44. As concluded in Schmit (2008), p. 150, decentralization was severely criticized because it was "linked to break-away tendencies of entire provinces, like Aceh, former Irian Jaya (now Papua) and Maluku".

[355]Miller (2009), p. 41. In Schmit (2008), p. 147, the point is made that the form of the reform was coincidentally similar than the decentralization in the beginning of the twentieth century by the Dutch colonial power.

[356]Law Number 22 of 1999 on Regional Government. Decentralization was demanded by the reform movement after the end of the authoritarian reign of Suharto, and the first president after Suharto, President Habibie, who had little legitimacy after serving as vice-president of Suharto, responded with a policy of wide-ranging regional autonomy. See Lindsey (2008), p. 30 f. The regionalization legislation of 1999 was, however, criticized by the regions on the grounds of insecurity, because the laws were seen as "gifts from the centre that could be revoked at any time", and the criticism led subsequently to the enactment of Articles 18, 18A and 18B of the Constitution. However, Schmit (2008), p. 147, makes the point that in the reform, the hierarchical position of the provinces above the regencies and cities was abolished, leaving provinces in an ambiguous dual position as autonomous regions and as extended administrative units of the central

between the central government and the regions[357] that entered into force in 2001. Thereafter, a more general decentralization of Indonesia commenced and the legislation concerning the regional governance of Indonesia from 2004 resulted in the creation of altogether 33 regions called provinces, with several layers of subdivisions.[358] The regionalization was supported by other pieces of law on, for instance, general elections at the national level and in the decentralized entities,[359] political parties[360] and financial contributions from the Government of Indonesia.[361]

Although the first special piece of legislation devoted to the issue of Aceh was already passed in 1956 in a way that recognized Aceh as an autonomous region and re-established the border towards other provinces in Sumatra,[362] the modern recognition of the special characteristics of the governance of Aceh was established in 1999,[363] that is, one year before the above-mentioned constitutional rules were in place[364] and before the other regions of Indonesia could start to implement the

government. As is evident on the basis of our inquiry, this dual position is present also in the case of Aceh. For an analysis of the role of *adat* customs in regionalization of Indonesia during the reformation era after 1998, see Avonius (2004).

[357]Law Number 25 of 1999 on Fiscal Balance between the Central Government and the Regions.

[358]Law Number 32 of 2004 on Regional Governance (State Gazette of the Republic of Indonesia Year 2004 Number 125, Supplemental State Gazette Number 4437) as amended by Law No. 8 of 2005 on Enactment of Government Regulation in Lieu of Law Number 3 of 2005 on Amendment to Law Number 32 of 2004 on Regional Governance (State Gazette of the Republic of Indonesia Year 2005 Number 108, Supplemental State Gazette Number 4548).

[359]Law No. 12 of 2003 on the General Election of Members of the House of Representatives (DPR), Regional Representative Council (DPD), Provincial House of Representatives (DPRD Propinsi) and District/Municipality House of Representatives (DPRD Kabupaten/Kota) (State Gazette of the Republic of Indonesia Year 2003 Number 37, Supplemental State Gazette Number 4277).

[360]Law Number 31 of 2002 on Political Parties (State Gazette of the Republic of Indonesia Year 2002 Number 138, Supplemental State Gazette Number 4251).

[361]Law Number 33 of 2004 on Financial Balance between the Central Government and Regional Governments (State Gazette of the Republic of Indonesia Year 2004 Number 126, Supplemental State Gazette Number 4438).

[362]Law Number 24 of 1956 on the Formation of the Autonomous Region of Atjeh and Amendment to the Regulation of the North Sumatera Province (State Gazette of the Republic of Indonesia Year 1956 Number 64, Supplemental State Gazette Number 1103). See also Miller (2009), who points out that the central government failed to honor the terms of the Darul Islam settlement of the 1950s, in particular those related to religion. According to Reid (2007), p. 153, the practical grievances that led to strife in Aceh in the beginning of the 1950s "were all about the loss of the total autonomy and control of local resources which they had enjoyed in the period 1946-50", with demands of a federal state. At that point, the central government also realized that it had been a mistake to try to amalgamate Aceh into a North Sumatra Province.

[363]Law Number 44 of 1999 on the Exercise of Special Authority of the Special Province of Aceh (State Gazette of the Republic of Indonesia Year 1999 Number 172, Supplemental State Gazette Number 3893).

[364]In addition, the Indonesian legislature created in the year 2000 the free port of Sabang on an island in the immediate vicinity to the north of Banda Aceh, the capital of Aceh, under Law

general regionalization legislation.[365] Although the 1999 legislation concerning Aceh in principle dealt with autonomy and introduced such features in the jurisdiction of Aceh which were not present in any other province at that time, including such areas as religion, education and customary law,[366] the arrangement did not function to the satisfaction of the inhabitants of Aceh, many of whom continued to require independence for Aceh.[367] The situation did not improve with the 2001 special autonomy law concerning Aceh, the so-called NAD law (see below).[368] By this time, the term 'autonomy' was already well established in the context of Aceh as a part of its legal language.

4.7.2 A Special Solution for a Special Place

Negotiations towards ending the armed conflict in Aceh had been carried out in Geneva since the year 2000, but the process was difficult and stalled sometime in 2003. In February 2004, contacts were made from Indonesia to the Crisis Management Initiative (CMI), a Finnish NGO functioning under the leadership of Mr. Martti Ahtisaari, former President of Finland, and only days before the tsunami that struck Aceh on 24 December 2004, a new negotiation process was initiated by the CMI.[369] The parties to the negotiations, the GAM and the Government of Indonesia, were both confronted with a humanitarian catastrophe in the form of the tsunami, an incident which brought the parties to the realization that the concrete situation demanded political reconciliation.[370] In a series of meetings during a relatively short period of time, the parties were able to come to an agreement involving self-government for Aceh, established in a Memorandum of Understanding (MoU) signed in Helsinki on 15 August 2005.

Number 37 of 2000 on the Enactment of Government Regulation in Lieu of Law Number 2 of 2000 on Free Trade Area and Free Seaport of Sabang to become a Law (State Gazette of the Republic of Indonesia Year 2000 Number 525, Supplemental State Gazette Number 4054).

[365] Miller (2009), p. 50.

[366] Miller (2009), p. 42.

[367] See Miller (2009), p. 47.

[368] Law No. 18/2001. See also Schmit (2008), p. 148, and Reid (2007), p. 154 f.

[369] Miller (2009), p. 155 f., Drexler (2008), p. 41. For the initial contacts before the Tsunami, see also Husain et al. (2007), pp. 1–74.

[370] The sense of urgency created in the aftermath of the Tsunami is also recorded in the preamble of the Memorandum of Understanding, according to which the parties are "deeply convinced that only the peaceful settlement of the conflict will enable the rebuilding of Aceh after the tsunami disaster on 26 December 2004 to progress and succeed". As pointed out by Miller (2009), p. 183, the resolution of the conflict through self-government "stemmed from the recognition by both parties that they could not militarily defeat each other, as well as their genuine desire to reach a negotiated settlement". For a personal account of the negotiations, see Husain et al. (2007), pp. 77–133.

It should be noted that the term "autonomy" is not featured in the MoU. One reason for the omission of the term may be the fact that the term autonomy had, after the negative experiences from different governance schemes that were labeled autonomies, a bad reputation.[371] The GAM was probably not keen to connect the model of governance it was negotiating to the description of the general decentralization scheme of Indonesia by placing Aceh in the constitutional concept of regional autonomy. There is also no reference in the text of the MoU to the term "self-government"[372] or to the concept of "self-determination".[373] It appears that the parties avoided terms over which a variety of different interpretations exist (even between the parties) and preferred to define the contents of those terms without using the terms.[374] However, the MoU does refer to the term "people" in five different instances. In the preamble to the MoU, there is a reference to the "government of the Acehnese people", in para. 1.1.6 to the "historical traditions and customs of the people of Aceh", in para. 1.2.1 to the "aspirations of Acehnese people for local political parties", in para. 1.2.2 to the right of "the people of Aceh" to nominate candidates for the positions of all elected officials, and in para. 1.2.6 to the guarantee of "[f]ull participation of all Acehnese people in local and national elections". Without doubt, these references create the impression that a distinct people of Aceh exists within Indonesia, and this impression is particularly strong in

[371] See Miller (2009), p. 158, who points out that the "first round of talks were almost derailed by GAM's refusal to accept the Indonesian government delegation's demand that the rebels accept 'special autonomy' as a final solution to the conflict" and that during the second round of negotiations, the Indonesian delegation agreed to replace 'special autonomy' with the less politicized term of 'self-government'". As pointed out by Reid (2007), p. 155, "[i]n relation to the unitary bias of Indonesian state nationalism since 1945, the peace agreement was a remarkable reversal".

[372] The omission of the term "self-government" is certainly interested against the background of the fact that the negotiations actually focused on the form of self-government in Aceh. See, e.g., Miller (2009), p. 158, who makes the point that after the break-through, the talks were devoted to "focusing on what self-government would mean in an Acehnese context and how it could be achieved without compromising Indonesia's territorial sovereignty".

[373] The exclusion of the term self-determination from the MoU was understandable against the background that the GAM dropped its demand of independence for Aceh when the Helsinki process progressed past the Tsunami.

[374] The exclusion of the term autonomy from the MoU did not prevent the inclusion of that term in the LoGA in several provisions, in particular concerning the Special Autonomy Fund, but also as a reference to the special autonomy of Aceh. See below. The term autonomy is also used in the Explanatory Note to the LoGA, for instance, in its introduction: "This situation has motivated the creation of a Law on the Governing of Aceh based on the principle of broad autonomy. The granting of broad autonomy in the political sector to the Aceh people and the administration of regional governance according to the principles of good governance – that is, transparent, accountable, professional, efficient and effective – is aimed at achieving the maximum prosperity for the people of Aceh. In the implementation of this broad autonomy, the people of Aceh shall play an active role in formulating, deciding, implementing and evaluating regional governance policies." It deserves to be mentioned already in this context, that the LoGA does not utilize the terms "self-government" or "self-determination".

the area of participation: the concept of the people of Aceh is here used in a collective sense, with more than allusions in the direction of the existence of an entity of self-determination. It therefore seems that the peace agreement is focused on the internal self-determination of the people of Aceh without using the institutional terminology of autonomy, self-government and self-determination to characterize the arrangement.

The agreement is particular amongst similar peace deals for several reasons, *inter alia*, because it was facilitated by a private conflict resolution institution, because an Aceh Monitoring Mission (AMM) was established by the European Union and ASEAN contributing countries with the mandate to monitor the implementation of the commitments taken by the parties and to resolve disputes between the parties[375] (although the AMM remained in Aceh for a limited period of time only) and because the ultimate arbiter of disputes between the parties was the Chairman of the Board of Directors of the Crisis Management Initiative (in effect Mr. Ahtisaari), who was granted the function to make a ruling which would be binding on the parties. However, the agreement is not a treaty under public international law, which meant that Indonesia was not under any obligation to incorporate the agreement through ratification and to implement the text of the treaty as an international legal obligation. In addition, the agreement was not guaranteed by any third parties (States or inter-governmental organizations), although the EU and the ASEAN were involved in the monitoring of the agreement.[376] The fact that the peace agreement was a "domestic" agreement that became internationalized only to some extent but not fully, probably gave the government and the House of Representatives of Indonesia some degree of freedom to argue for certain constitutional constraints when the implementing legislation was enacted in 2006. In fact, in the preamble to the agreement, the parties committed themselves to creating conditions within which the government of the Acehnese people can be manifested through a fair and democratic process within the unitary state and constitution of the Republic of Indonesia. In this way, the doctrine of the unitary state and the constitutional framework, completed just before the peace negotiations with the regionalization provisions, were brought in to constitute the guiding values of the implementation of the peace agreement. In addition, it should also be remembered in the context that any legislative processes in the House of Representatives of Indonesia would be affected by the fact that the recently created Constitutional Court could receive before it legislation for constitutional review.

In para. 1.1.1 of the MoU, the parties agreed that a new Law on the Governing of Aceh would be promulgated and would enter into force as soon as possible and not later than 31 March 2006. The agreement thus contained a pledge of a legislative process which, according to para. 1.1.2 would be based on four principles that can

[375] See Miller (2009), p. 159.

[376] The Aceh Monitoring Mission, a joint operation by the European Union and the ASEAN, was finished on 15 December 2006. For the final report, see http://www.aceh-mm.org (accessed on 14 June 2009). After that point of time, the international involvement in the matter has been less formal.

be viewed as touching upon the distribution of powers, the foreign affairs and the relationship between the executive branches of Aceh and the central government. In addition, the Law on the Governing of Aceh would implement a large number of substantive provisions in the Memorandum of Understanding.

The Law of the Republic of Indonesia No. 11 of 2006 on the Governing of Aceh (LoGA) was enacted several months beyond the deadline established in the agreement, due to the delays experienced in the legislative process in the House of Representatives. The LoGA was ratified by the President of Indonesia on 1 August 2006,[377] three months after the deadline, 31 March 2006, established in the Memorandum of Understanding.[378] However, no serious claims were raised that the delay would cause the agreement to become ineffective, because progress in the legislative implementation of the agreement could be demonstrated. As provided in Art. 272 of LoGA, the previous autonomy act, Law No. 18 of 2001 on Special Autonomy for the Special Territory of Aceh as the Province of Nanggroe Aceh Darussalam (the so-called NAD law) was revoked at that point in time and declared as no longer being in force. It is also possible to say that the LoGA can, in the domestic Indonesian context, be seen as a further elaboration of the governance legislation both of the national order and concerning Aceh in particular that had been created since the end of the 1990s,[379] and some features of the LoGA, such as the position of Islamic law in Aceh and its governance and the financial provision with the rules concerning revenue allocation between the central government and Aceh are to a large extent carry-overs from the NAD law to the LoGA,[380] although the latter feature was also an element of the MoU.

Upon the passing of the LoGA in the Indonesian parliament, the GAM and other organizations in Aceh protested against the discrepancies between the MoU and the LoGA, while some elements of the Indonesian political establishment and the military were of the opinion that too many concessions were granted to Aceh. The point has been made that the special autonomy legislation concerning Aceh (and also Papua) has been (and probably still is) incompatible with the decentralization

---

[377]In researching and writing on the autonomy of Aceh, an unofficial translation of the Law on the Governing of Aceh and the corresponding Explanatory Notes, as enacted by the Government of Indonesia on 1 August 2006, were used. The final English version was compiled by USAID by using, *inter alia*, documentation and preliminary translations of the LoGA provided by Aceh Monitoring Mission (AMM) and International Organization for Migration (IOM).

[378]See Miller (2009), p. 159. It should be noted that the LoGA was prepared in a participatory manner. For instance, at the provincial level, three local universities, the Syiah Kuala University, Malikusaleh University and the Ar-Raniry State Islamic Institute, were asked to make contributions to the LoGA (which actually led to a number of inconsistencies in the law and in unnecessary repetitions of such substantive law that would anyway be in force elsewhere in national law). In the Indonesian parliament, different NGOs could contribute to the legislative process with their comments.

[379]See also Miller (2009), p. 186.

[380]See Miller (2009), pp. 171 f., 177 ff.

legislation.[381] In a more positive vein it has been stated that the LoGA "granted Aceh far more autonomy than Indonesia's other provinces and redressed some of the key weaknesses in the NAD law before it".[382] The self-governing powers of Aceh are greater than they were in the NAD law, "especially in relation to political rights and representation", and with the introduction of the LoGA, "Aceh became Indonesia's most autonomous province and the first to enjoy broad self-governance".[383] However, it seems clear that there remain discrepancies between the MoU, on the one hand, and the LoGA, on the other. The Indonesian Government is of the opinion that there are, in fact, several elements of the MoU (perhaps up to twelve) that have not yet been properly implemented, while the GAM, on the other hand, is of the opinion that up to 17 provisions of the MoU are still awaiting proper implementation. Both parties to the MoU identify several issues that are relevant for this study and which create pressures for amending the LoGA.[384] As a consequence, the political environment surrounding the LoGA is not quite stable yet.

It should be noted that Art. 269(3) of the LoGA contains an amendment formula for the LoGA that purports to create a regional entrenchment of some sort by requiring that any planned amendment of the LoGA must first undergo consultation by and receive considerations from the DPRA, that is, from the House of Representatives of Aceh. Hence although the LoGA is an ordinary act of the Indonesian parliament and although the LoGA could, in that perspective, be amended by the Indonesian House of Representatives at any time pursuant to the legislative process of the Indonesian parliament, the LoGA introduces a procedural requirement that adds an external element of consultation and consideration by involving the DPRA in the process. Supposing that the amendments sought by the GAM are carried out, they would be protected at least to some extent under the requirement of

[381]See Schmit (2008), p. 152.

[382]Miller (2009), p. 165.

[383]Miller (2009), p. 167. See also Miller (2009), p. 186: "The omission from the LoGA of key provisions in the Helsinki MoU is an ongoing source of dispute between Aceh and Jakarta and a potential basis for future conflict."

[384]*Inter alia*, that there should be a reference to the MoU in the preamble of the LoGA, that the reference in Art. 11(1) to norms, standard and procedure of national supervision should be omitted, that the term "consideration" in Art. 8 should be changed to "consent", that the role of the Indonesian military should be only external defense and that it should be prevented from internal activities in Aceh, that Aceh should be allowed to commit to external loans directly and not only via the central government, and that the direct international access of Aceh should be guaranteed. See the matrix entitled 'Implementation of the Helsinki MoU – GoI and GAM version', at http://www.bra-aceh.org/mi_matrix.php (accessed on 14 June 2009). While many of the provisions of the MoU have been implemented, the lack of implementation or erroneous implementation of several provisions has been identified by the Helsinki MoU Watch as critical, important or requiring clarification. See 'Compilation of Most Serious Concerns Regarding The Implementation of the Helsinki MoU, at http://www.braaceh.org/download/archive/helsinki_mou/Compilation_of_Most_Serious_Concerns_Regarding_The_Implementation_Of_The_Helsinki_MoU.pdf (accessed on 14 June 2009). See also Miller (2009), p. 167.

consultation and consideration in a manner that amounts to a weak regional entrenchment of the LoGA.

The requirement of consultation and consideration is not very strong, and it certainly does not imply that a consent of the Acehnese legislative assembly should be acquired before any amendment can be validly passed. The requirement of consultation and consideration is, however, a compulsory moment in passing an amendment to the LoGA, intended to supply information to the Indonesian parliament on the opinion of the legislative assembly of Aceh. The reference to consultation does not mean that the opinion is legally binding, although it might be politically decisive by activating the role of Aceh as an interested beneficiary and guardian of the terms of the Memorandum of Understanding and the existing LoGA. However, the reference to consultation should mean that information on the planned amendment and its reasons are passed over to the DPRA. The reference to consideration should, for its part, be interpreted as a requirement of a deliberative process in the DPRA, the outcome of which is received by the House of Representatives of Indonesia for the record and treated with appropriate respect. In relation to other instances when the House of Representatives of Indonesia might consult when a piece of law is being enacted, the requirement of consultation and consideration in the LoGA is more formal and may amount to an act of self-constraint by the House of Representatives of Indonesia. Whether this leads to a higher norm-hierarchical status for the LoGA in relation to ordinary legislation is an open question, but it means at least that amendments to the LoGA cannot be made without due notice to the Acehnese and, consequently, to the so-called international community.

If the amendment formula of the LoGA is read together with Art. 18B(1) of the Constitution, a case could perhaps be made for an elevated norm-hierarchical position for the LoGA,[385] but it is doubtful whether the Indonesian legal order

[385] Lindsey (2008), p. 31, approaches the issue from a somewhat different point of view after noting the regionalization laws were criticized by the regions for the reason that they could be revoked at any time. "Constitutional form was therefore demanded to provide a hedge against policy reversal by a future government", something which was granted in Articles 18, 18A and 18B in a manner which mirrors the spirit of the regionalization laws. This interpretation would indicate that the regionalization legislation, including the LoGA, could not be easily revoked by a future parliament, that is, that in the case of Aceh, Art. 18B, in particular, would protect the LoGA against attempts to amend it in the Indonesian parliament. This, in turn, could give reason to conclude that the LoGA is not an ordinary piece of law enacted by the Indonesian parliament that could be revoked at any time by the parliament. From that perspective, the effect of Art. 18B of the Constitution on the LoGA could well be that the position of the LoGA is elevated in our chart describing different autonomy positions, more specifically on the continuum between ordinary law and constitution. The introduction to the Explanatory Notes on the LoGA sustain his by saying that the "broad autonomy is fundamentally not merely a right, but more than that; it is a *constitutional obligation* to be used to the maximum extent for the welfare of Aceh" (italics by MS). It might be possible to think that the LoGA is an organic law of some sort, implementing the constitutional provision, in particular because the LoGA introduces a weak regional entrenchment in respect of its own amendment which requires the "consultation and consideration" by the DPRA in Aceh.

recognizes such an intermediate normative level between the Constitution and the ordinary acts of parliament. However, in spite of the consultation and consideration process, the Indonesian House of Representatives could make a decision which is in contradiction with the opinion of Aceh. If such a decision is in breach of the provisions of the Memorandum of Understanding, the consultation and consideration process will work towards making such discrepancies public and known to the international community.

When the LoGA was enacted, references to Art. 1(1), Art. 5(1), Art. 18, Art. 18A, Art. 18B, and Art. 20 of the Constitution of Indonesia were made in the preamble to the LoGA. In essence, the references underline the importance of the unitary nature of the state, the power of the president of Indonesia to issue regulations and the position of the various regional authorities in the state structure of Indonesia. In addition, the references made to the previous autonomy and regionalization legislation creates the impression that the position of Aceh is evolving against the background of the historical examples of the (often failed) special autonomy arrangements. There is, however, no explicit reference in the preamble or the provisions of the LoGA to the Memorandum of Understanding, but only an implicit one, according to which "the earthquake and tsunami disasters that struck Aceh generated solidarity among all potential components of Indonesian society to rebuild Acehnese communities and the Aceh region and to resolve the conflict in a peaceful, holistic, sustainable, and dignified manner within the framework of the Unitary State of the Republic of Indonesia".[386] There is thus recognition of the fact that a violent conflict existed and that it had to be resolved, but the Indonesian legislature did not record the peace process and the peace agreement as such in the LoGA. The preamble summarizes the historical, political, administrative and religious dimensions concerning Aceh by saying that "it is deemed necessary to establish a Law on the Governing of Aceh", as if the necessity was a purely internal matter, perhaps even something that the Indonesian parliament acknowledged without external interests and impulses.

4.7.3 A Multi-layered Jurisdiction

When the LoGA was enacted, it did not disrupt the continuity of the previously applicable legal norms, because according to Art. 269 (1) of the LoGA, laws and regulations that were in place at the time of the enactment of the LoGA would

[386] However, in the introduction to the Explanatory Notes to the LoGA, an explicit mention of the MoU is included: "The Memorandum of Understanding between the Government and the Free Aceh Movement, which was signed on August 15, 2005, signified a new step in the history of Aceh Province and in the life of its people, towards a peaceful, just, thriving, prosperous, and dignified condition. What should properly be understood is that the Memorandum of Understanding is a form of honorable reconciliation with the objective of sustainable social, economic, and political development in Aceh."

continue to be in force provided they did not contravene the provisions of the LoGA. The situation was somewhat different concerning regulations under laws that related directly to the special autonomy of Aceh and its districts and municipalities, because Art. 269(2) required that they be adapted to conform with the LoGA.

In many respects, the Indonesian Government remains in charge of matters that fall within the sphere of the LoGA, and it is therefore essential to notice that under Art. 270(1), the Government's national authority and the implementation of the LoGA relating to the Government's authority shall be governed by prevailing laws and regulations.[387] There is therefore an expectation that the central government will be called upon to act in different respects in relation to Aceh. In particular, this is true concerning the implementing provisions of the LoGA that are the responsibility of the Indonesian Government. As provided in Art. 270, such implementing provisions shall be formulated no later than two years following the enactment of the LoGA. In principle, the implementing provisions should have been ready by August 2008, but most of the altogether eleven presidential and governmental regulations that the LoGA presupposes were still awaiting the making of final decisions in June 2011. Hence the autonomy of Aceh is so recent that its full operation is not yet known.[388] In addition, the Government of Aceh and also the district and municipal governments are expected to enact their own *qanuns*, that is, bylaws which specify the way in which these entities operate in the implementation of the LoGA.[389]

---

[387] In fact, the introduction to the Explanatory Notes to the LoGA places the governance of Aceh in the larger context of Indonesian governance: "This Law expressly regulates that the Aceh Government is an inseparable part of the Unitary State of the Republic of Indonesia, and that the broad autonomy applied in Aceh based on this Law constitutes a subsystem within the national system of governance."

[388] Some caveats are necessary in relation to our research concerning Aceh. The analysis of the autonomy of Aceh is carried out in a somewhat uncertain normative environment. So far, there are only two norms that have been issued, namely the Government Regulation No. 20/2007 on Local Political Parties and the Presidential Decree No. 75 of 2009 concerning the Consultation Procedure and the Recommendation made by the DPRA and Aceh Government. The lack of secondary legislation about the details of the autonomy arrangement should nonetheless not produce any such result in this inquiry that would be completely overturned after the secondary legislation is in place and is being implemented. Because the autonomy of Aceh is so recent, there is also a lack of doctrinary writings and court judgments that would specify the position of Aceh in the Indonesian state system. Therefore, interviews with a number of experts on the Acehnese autonomy were carried out in May 2009 both in Aceh and in Jakarta to acquire information about the contents of the autonomy arrangement and the different interpretations that exist at the moment. See also an assessment by May 2006, which touches on many of the issues included in our study.

[389] According to Art. 1, para. 21, of the LoGA, an Aceh *qanun* is defined as a "legal regulation equivalent to a provincial regulation governing the conduct of governance and social life in Aceh". The term *qanun* is hence not a reference to anything very unique, but only a denomination from a local perspective of what is enacted as regulations at the provincial level elsewhere in Indonesia. A *qanun* and a provincial regulation are thus norms of a generally applicable nature within the provincial jurisdiction the enactment of which should have a legal basis in national law. Under Art. 1, para 22, similar bylaws under the name *qanun* can be enacted at the district/municipal level in Aceh: "District/municipality *qanun* is a legal regulation equivalent to a district/municipality

A definition of Aceh is given in Art. 1, para. 2, of the LoGA: "Aceh is a province constituting a legal social unit having unique characteristics and granted with a special authority to manage and administer its local governance and social interests in accordance with the laws of and within the system and principles of the Unitary State of the Republic of Indonesia pursuant to the 1945 Constitution of the Republic of Indonesia, headed by a Governor." Para. 4 of the same provision summarizes the notion of governance in Aceh: "Aceh governance is the administration of government-related affairs of a provincial region within the system of the Unitary State of the Republic of Indonesia pursuant to the 1945 Constitution of the Republic of Indonesia, exercised by the Aceh Regional Government and the Aceh Regional House of Representatives in accordance with their respective functions and authorities." These definitions (and the corresponding definitions of the districts/municipalities in Aceh) seem to imply a far-reaching integration of Aceh in the state structure of Indonesia. The authority of Aceh consists of certain powers to be exercised in accordance with the laws of and within the system and principles of the unitary state, and the powers of the organs of Aceh shall be exercised in accordance with their respective functions and authorities.

Article 3 of the LoGA defines the territorial jurisdiction of Aceh by establishing its borders.[390] To the north, the border is adjacent to the Straits of Malacca, to the south, the border is adjacent to the Province of North Sumatra, to the east, the border is adjacent to the Straits of Malacca, and to the west, adjacent to the Indian Ocean.[391] The international borders relevant for Aceh are, however, those of Indonesia.

Internally, the jurisdiction of Aceh is under Art. 2 divided into several subdivisions. Firstly, there is a division of the region of Aceh into 18 districts/municipalities (*kabupaten*), which are divided into sub-districts (*kecamatan*). *Kecamatan* are further divided into *mukim*, which consist of *kelurahan* and *gampong*.[392] Of these levels of government, the provincial or regional level is

regulation governing the conduct of district/municipality governance and social life in Aceh." According to Art. 21(3), the organizational structures and procedures for the governance of Aceh and its districts/municipalities shall be governed by *qanun*, which means that each of the two levels of governance seem to have some authority over its own organization, because it is empowered to pass a *qanun* of its own dealing with organizational matters.

[390] There is an issue about the possible secession of two provinces from Aceh, which is partly an ethnic issue involving the Gayo people (the central government plays in part politically on this), partly a development issue.

[391] According to para. 1.1.4 of the Memorandum of Understanding, the borders of Aceh correspond to the borders as of 1 July 1956. The territorial jurisdiction of Aceh as determined in the LoGA is not entirely in keeping with this pledge, and the GAM has expressed dissatisfaction about the situation, but has chosen to go forward with the implementation of the LoGA. See Miller (2009), p. 164.

[392] Concerning the national organization of the lower levels of local government, see Schmit (2008), p. 168 f., who concludes that through Government Regulation No. 8/2003, *kecamatan* and *kelurahan* were effectively placed under central government control, leaving regencies and cities with less power. Finally, it seems that *mukim* will merely consist of *gampong*, because under Art. 267 of the LoGA, *kelurahan* will be gradually replaced with *gampong*. The possibility to eliminate *gampong* is a decision made by means of a *qanun* of a district/city.

probably the most important for Aceh. According to Art. 21 of the LoGA, the implementing bodies for the governance of Aceh comprise the Aceh Government and the DPRA, that is, the executive branch and the part of the autonomy arrangement which has the power to pass the regional bylaws or *qanuns*. The LoGA establishes a similar denomination for the districts/municipalities, where the implementing bodies for their governance comprise the district/municipality governments and the district level representative assembly (the DPRK).

The organization of governance in Aceh is thus relatively hierarchical, but there is also an enumeration of general principles of governance that must, according to Art. 20, be followed at the provincial and district/municipal level. These principles contain the following: the principle of Islam, the principle of legal certainty, the principle of public interest, the principle of orderly government administration, the principle of openness, the principle of proportionality, the principle of professionalism, the principle of accountability, the principle of efficiency, the principle of efficacy and the principle of equality.

Although the principle of Islam is mentioned among the general principles of governance in Aceh and although the overwhelming majority of the inhabitants of Aceh are Muslims, the LoGA may be making the religious component in Aceh more important in law than it in reality would have to be by including a multitude of provisions of a religious nature that make Aceh relatively unique amongst sub-state entities. It should be noted that it was the Indonesian parliament that created the religious provisions in the LoGA and established the denominational character of Aceh and that religious matters were not strongly on the agenda of the GAM during the peace negotiations. In fact, it seems as if the GAM were less interested in denominational matters, such as the *Syari'yah*, and more in substantive issues that can be promoted by means of self-government.[393]

The LoGA also contains a number of provisions that aim at allocating the symbols of sovereignty and distinctiveness between the state of Indonesia and the Government of Aceh.[394] As provided in Art. 246, there shall be a national flag of Indonesia, but in addition, the Aceh Government may also determine and affirm on the basis of a *qanun* a regional flag of Aceh as a symbol of its special and unique characteristics. However, the regional flag of Aceh as a symbol shall not constitute

[393] As pointed out by Miller (2009), p. 171 ff., the GAM, when it participated in the political process during the implementation of the LoGA, "remained fundamentally opposed to what it saw as Jakarta's imposition of *Syari'ah* on the Acehnese people", and it seems that the Partai Aceh, the political formation of the previous GAM, has continued to remain opposed to the Islamic law. The Syari'ah provisions in the LoGA are in principle a carry-over from the previous NAD law, and a basic Islamic law framework had already been established in accordance with the NAD law and on the basis of some Islamic *qanun* of Aceh. The Islamic law was therefore implemented already from 2003 on, although the implementation was limited in the beginning. A broader implementation of Islamic law started only after the Tsunami of 2004, which many Acehnese interpreted as a divine punishment for failure to abide by Islamic law. See also Salim (2008), p. 163 f.

[394] As established in para. 1.1.5 of the MoU, Aceh has the right to use regional symbols including a flag, a crest and a hymn.

a symbol of sovereignty and shall not be treated as flag of sovereignty in Aceh. A similar right to distinct symbols is established in Art. 247 concerning a coat of arms and in Art. 248 concerning a regional hymn. Finally, in Art. 251, Aceh is granted the right to establish its own name as a province within the system of the unitary state of Indonesia, as based on the Constitution of Indonesia, and the titles of elected government officials, but only after the general elections to the DPRA in 2009,[395] until which the name of the province was Nanggroe Aceh Darussalam. In advance of the decision concerning the name of the province of Aceh, the Governor of Aceh enacted an Aceh Government regulation on 7 April 2009 according to which the province of Aceh should be known by reference to the name 'Aceh'.[396]

The LoGA charges the Government of Aceh and the districts/municipalities with a multitude of tasks and services that they should provide. As concerns the provincial level, Art. 178 prescribes that the execution of governmental affairs that fall under the jurisdiction of the Government of Aceh shall be funded from the Aceh Income and Expenditure Budget (APBA) (the districts/municipalities have their own budgets). Remarkably, Art. 193(1) prescribes that the budget for the provision of education shall total at least 20% of the APBA and shall be allocated for school-level education.[397] In addition, the execution of such governmental affairs that are delegated to the Governor of Aceh as a representative of the Indonesian Government shall be accompanied by funding from the national budget for the implementation of deconcentration[398] and also for the implementation of

[395] This is based on para. 1.1.3 of the MoU, according to which the name of Aceh and the titles of senior elected officials will be determined by the legislature of Aceh after the next elections.

[396] The decision of the Governor is likely in contravention with national norms and decisions, because according to the Indonesian legal system, the decision made by a lower authority (in this case Governor's regulation) should not contradict a decision made by a higher authority (in this case Art. 251 of the LoGA).

[397] This mechanism is also a carry-over from the previous NAD law and is, in fact, also featured in Art. 31(4) of the Constitution of Indonesia as a rule for the state budget, which indicates that Indonesia is involved in a serious investment in education. As concerns Aceh, the mechanism is according to Miller (2009), p. 179, expected to result during the financial year of 2008–2009 alone to amount "to a staggering US$360 million". "Since the introduction of the NAD law, however, Aceh's education system has seen few improvements. School attendance rates in Aceh have remained well below the national average, in part because of corruption and financial mismanagement at all levels of the state bureaucracy, and in part because of the conflict, when hundreds of schools were burnt down and tens of thousands of Acehnese families were displaced by the violence. The biggest blow to Aceh's education system, however, was delivered by the tsunami, which killed some 2,000 school teachers and more than 200 university lecturers, and disrupted the education of about 140,000 elementary school students and 20,000 high school students."

[398] As established in Art. 198, every delegation of authority by the Indonesian Government to the Governor of Aceh as a representative of the Indonesian Government in Aceh shall be accompanied by relevant funds. Article 199 expresses the principal point that all goods procured using deconcentration funds shall become state property. However, state property referred to in paragraph (1) may be granted to the Government of Aceh. The same is true under Art. 201 concerning goods procured using assistance task funds.

assistance tasks.[399] The tasks that are transferred from the Indonesian Government to the Government of Aceh, delegated to the Governor of Aceh or assigned to the Government of Aceh shall, according to Article 15, be complemented by funding from the budget of the central government in accordance with the appropriate principle, that is, in accordance with decentralized management, deconcentrated management or assistance tasks.

Revenue to the budget of Aceh can, according to Art. 179, be derived from different sources, such as regional taxes, regional charges, proceeds from the management of regional assets,[400] *zakat* (that is, mandatory charity) and other legal real income of Aceh and its districts/municipalities as well as equalization funds,[401]

---

[399] According to Art. 200, every support task given by the Indonesian Government to the Government of Aceh (and to the governments of districts/municipalities and *mukim/gampong*) shall be accompanied by funds.

[400] Funds from shared earnings derived from hydrocarbon and other natural resources, namely share of earnings from forestry, in the amount of 80%, share of earnings from fisheries, in the amount of 80%, share of earnings from general mining, in the amount of 80%, share of earnings from geothermal energy, in the amount of 80%, share of earnings from oil mining, in the amount of 15% and share of earnings from natural gas mining, in the amount of 30%. In addition to the Shared Earnings Funds, the Government of Aceh shall receive additional Shared Earnings Funds from oil and natural gas that shall constitute a portion of the revenues of the Government of Aceh, namely share of earnings from oil mining, in the amount of 55% and share of earnings from natural gas mining, in the amount of 40%. See also Miller (2009), p. 166, according to whom the natural resource revenue (and the right to implement Islamic law) was essentially a reconstituted version of the previous law on special autonomy. As pointed out by Miller (2009), p. 167, under the LoGA, "Aceh's natural resources continued to be collected by the Finance Ministry in Jakarta and redistributed back to Aceh". In addition, Miller (2009), p. 177, points out that Aceh's revenue-sharing arrangements with Jakarta from the fiscal year of 2008–2009 on "are slightly more generous than those outlined in the NAD law". Hence it seem that most of the financial arrangement in the LoGA is a carry-over from the former NAD law. The problem in the context is the transparency in determining the total earnings collected in Jakarta. For transparency and efficiency, gas and oil extracting in Aceh shall be managed jointly by the central government and the Government of Aceh according to a procedure that is regulated through a government regulation. This condition is different in comparison with other provinces in which gas and oil extraction is fully under central government authority. Hence in relation to other parts of Indonesia, the revenue sharing in Aceh seems generous and they certainly should have the effect of placing Aceh in a different economic league altogether. As pointed out in Schmit (2008), p. 175, allocations between the centre, province and local government vary between different categories: "In the oil and gas sectors the state shares are high at 85 and 70 per cent and provincial shares relatively low at 3 to 6 per cent, leaving 6 to 12 per cent to local governments and another 6 per cent to other local governments in the same province. In the mining, forestry and fishery sectors, local host government shares can run as high as 32 per cent to 64 per cent, with the remaining 16 per cent and 20 per cent for the provinces and the centre and nothing for fellow local governments within the province."

[401] Equalization funds consist of funds from shared tax proceeds, namely share of revenues from the Land and Building tax, in the amount of 90%, share of revenues from Land and Building Right Purchase Duty, in the amount of 80% and share of revenues from Income Tax (Income Tax from Articles 25 and 29 for domestic personal tax subjects, and Income Tax from Article 21), in the amount of 20%.

special autonomy funds[402] and other legal revenues. It is also possible for the Government of Aceh to obtain loans, but from foreign sources only via the Indonesian Government (although para. 1.3.1 of the MoU might indicate otherwise) and from domestic sources only upon consideration of the Minister of Home Affairs. According to Art. 187 the Government of Aceh (and the district/municipality governments, too) may issue regional government bonds in accordance with prevailing laws and regulations. The Government of Aceh may also receive grants from foreign sources, provided that the Government of Indonesia is informed about such grants. It seems that the first years of the new autonomy arrangement in Aceh have been very well funded with generous budgetary allocations from the Indonesian state budget, first collected in the territory of Aceh and later on allocated as prescribed by the LoGA to the Government of Aceh. The provisions concerning the budget and the revenue of Aceh indicate that Aceh is an entity with juridical personality that makes it capable of owning property and entering into agreements and other legal relationships, which of course is important for the economic independence of the entity.

4.7.4 Islamic Characteristics of the Jurisdiction

There is no direct reference to Islamic law in the Memorandum of Understanding, but a reference in the agreement to *qanun* in Aceh and historical traditions and customs can be understood as an implied dimension of a religious nature.[403] Most of the provisions of Islamic law were, however, part of the rules already applicable in Aceh on the basis of legislation enacted prior to the LoGA, although the international interest towards the matter arose only in the wake of the attention that Aceh received after the tsunami catastrophe. According to Art. 125 of the LoGA, the *Syari'at* Islam (which could be translated by reference to Islamic *shari'a*) implemented in Aceh shall consist of a broad range of religious principles, the *aqidah* (faith), *syariah* (law) and *akhklak* (morals), and the law includes the substantive areas of *ibadah* (devotion), *ahwal alsyakhshiyah* (family law),

[402] According to Art. 183, the Special Autonomy Fund referred to in Article 179 paragraph (2) point c shall constitute revenue of the Aceh Government to be used to pay for development, especially construction and maintenance of infrastructure, community economic empowerment, poverty eradication, and funding for education, social programs, and health. The Special Autonomy Fund is, however, of a temporary nature and shall be available for a period of 20 years, the amount of which from the first to the fifteenth years shall be equal to 2 percent of the National General Allocation Fund ceiling, and from the sixteenth through the twentieth years shall be equal to 1 percent of the National General Allocation Fund ceiling. See also Miller (2009), p. 177.

[403] In para. 1.1.6 of the MoU, it is said that "Kanun Aceh will be re-established for Aceh respecting the historical traditions and customs of the people of Aceh and reflecting contemporary legal requirements of Aceh".

muamalah (civil law), *jinayah* (criminal law),[404] *qadha'* (courts), *tarbiyah* (education), *dakwah* (lecture), *syiar* (religious teachings), and the defense of Islam. Further provisions related to the implementation of Islamic Law shall be governed by Aceh *qanuns*, but in principle and under Art. 126, every person of the Islamic faith in Aceh must adhere to and practice Islamic law, while every person residing or located in Aceh must respect the implementation of Islamic law.

The governments of Aceh and its districts/municipalities are given in Art. 127 the responsibility for the implementation of Islamic law, and the Indonesian Government, the Aceh Government and district/municipality governments shall allocate funds and other resources for the implementation of Islamic law. At the same time, however, the governments of Aceh and of its districts/municipalities shall guarantee freedom, foster harmony, respect the religious values practiced by the various religious faiths, and protect the followers of various religious faiths so as to allow them to practice their faiths according to their religions. The LoGA, however, contains some particular substantive guarantees for Islam as the dominant faith in Aceh. For instance, according to Art. 153, the Aceh Government shall have the authority to set provisions based on Islamic values for the press and broadcasting,[405] which means that the Government of Aceh can, if it so wishes, control the contents of expression, potentially through prior censorship. Under Art. 227, every resident shall have the freedom to, *inter alia*, engage in academic research, creative arts, literature, and other cultural activities that do not contravene Islamic law, a provision which seems to lead to a restriction of the freedom rather than to a guarantee of it.

For the implementation of Islamic law, there is an Aceh *Syari'yah* Court as the court of appeals and District/Municipality *Syari'yah* Courts as courts of first instance exercising judicial powers within the jurisdiction of the religious court

[404] As provided in the rules concerning criminal jurisdiction in Art. 129, in the event of a criminal act (*jinayah*) committed jointly by two or more persons, among whom are one or more non-Muslims, the alleged non-Muslim perpetrator(s) may choose to submit themselves to *jinayah* law instead of the National Criminal Code. However, any non-Muslim person committing a criminal act (*jinayah*) that is not governed by the National Criminal Code or by criminal provisions outside the National Criminal Code shall have *jinayah* law applied to his/her case. Acehnese residents committing a *jinayah* criminal act outside Aceh shall be subject to the provisions of the National Criminal Code. In September 2009, the outgoing DPRA adopted a *Jinayat Qanun*, that is, an Islamic criminal code, which introduced such punishments as stoning. The Governor of Aceh refused his assent to the *qanun*, and returned the enactment to the DPRA, which in effect means that the new DPRA, in office since October 2009, will reconsider the draft.

[405] For the purpose of implementing the provision, the Aceh Government shall coordinate with the Indonesia Broadcasting Commission for the Aceh Region to set guidelines for broadcasting ethics and broadcast program standards. According to the Explanatory Note to the LoGA, what is meant by the authority to set provisions related to the press and broadcasting is the "oversight of the content or circulation of press and broadcast products to ensure they do not contravene Islamic values". The Aceh Government is thus empowered to control the contents of the freedom of expression.

constituting a part of the national judicial system,[406] with the Supreme Court of Indonesia as the court of final instance.

There is also a Cleric Consultative Assembly (the MPU), whose membership consists of Muslim clerics and scholars who are working partners of the Aceh Government and the DPRA. In addition, the institution of *Wali Nanggroe*, which is the office of one designated individual, is an institution of cultural authority as the unifier of the people and preserver of traditional and cultural life,[407] perhaps best

[406]For instance, the judges of the *Syari'yah* courts are appointed by the President of Indonesia. As stated in Art. 128, the administration of Islamic Law in Aceh shall be a part of the national judicial system under the jurisdiction of the religious judiciary that is executed by the *Syari'yah* Court, which is free from any external influence. The *Syari'yah* Court is a court of law for all persons of the Islamic faith located in Aceh and it has the authority to examine, try, rule upon, and resolve cases that fall into the areas of *ahwal al-syakhshiyah* (family law), *muamalah* (civil law), and *jinayah* (criminal law), based on Islamic Law, the further provisions of which are governed by Aceh *qanun*. A *qanun* shall, under Art. 132, also govern the procedural law in *syari'yah* courts. However, implementation of other aspects of *syari'at* Islam, such as *ibadah* (worship), *akhlak* (conduct) and *dakwah* (Islamic summons) is not the authority of the *Syari'yah* courts, but the authority of the Government of Aceh and of the government of district/city, as mentioned in Art. 128(3) of the LoGA. It should be noted that, according to Art. 133, the tasks of conducting inquiries and investigations for the enforcement of Islamic Law with respect to *jinayah* falling under the jurisdiction of the *Syari'yah* Court shall be performed by the Indonesian National Police and Civil Service Investigators, whose functions and recruitment shall be governed by an Aceh *qanun*. On the *Syari'yah* Court, see Salim (2008), p. 164 f. Miller (2009), p. 176, points out that the implementation of Islamic law in Aceh is not of the most rigorous kind, but employs practices that are leaner than, for instance, those practiced in the Malaysian provinces of Kelantan, Negeri Sembilan and Kedah. However, several *qanun* prescribe caning as punishment for crimes. See, e.g., the report by the International Development Law Organization entitled 'Review on the Revisions being made to the Three Qanuns on Jinayah' of 1 November 2008, at http://www.aceheye.org/data_files/english_format/issues/issues_women/women_2008_11_01.pdf (accessed on 11 June 2008), in which the Government proposed amendments to existing *qanuns* in order to specify the implementation. According to Salim (2008), pp. 159, 166, before the Tsunami in 2004, not a single person had been caned. However, after the Tsunami, even public canings have taken place, but probably not without the authorization of the national Government. See also Salim (2008), p. 167, who concludes that "as both the police and the public prosecution are not decentralized but remain Jakarta-based, nationwide institutions, the actual implementation of *shari'a* in Aceh remains more or less entirely under the control of the nation-state of the Republic of Indonesia".

[407]The *Wali Nanggroe* is based on para. 1.1.7 of the MoU, according to which the institution of *Wali Nanggroe* with all its ceremonial attributes and entitlements will be established, but the institution is actually a carry-over from the NAD law. Under Art. 96, the *Wali Nanggroe* institution constitutes a traditional customary (*adat*) leadership as a unifier of the people that is independent, has authority, and has the jurisdiction to develop and oversee the implementation of *adat* institutions and *adat* affairs, the awarding of titles and honors, and the exercising of other *adat* rites. The *Wali Nanggroe* institution shall be neither a political nor a government institution in Aceh. The *Wali Nanggroe* institution shall be led by a person, the *Wali Nanggroe*, who acts on an individual and independent basis. Further provisions regarding candidacy requirements, election procedures, electorates, terms of office, position protocols, finances, and other matters concerning the *Wali Nanggroe* shall be governed by Aceh *qanun*. According to Art. 97, the *Wali Nanggroe* shall be entitled to award honorary titles or *adat* designations to individuals or organizations, whether domestic or overseas, pursuant to criteria and procedures governed by Aceh *qanun*.

understood as an honorary president of Aceh within the area of customary law and practices. However, in principle, the *Wali Nanggroe* is extraneous to the governmental structures of Aceh. Connected to the institution of *Wali Nanggroe*, the different *adat* or customary institutions shall,[408] according to Art. 98, function and serve as a means for public participation in the governing of Aceh and the governing of districts/municipalities in the areas of security, peace, harmony, and public order. Resolution of community social problems through traditional means shall be carried out by *adat* institutions, such as the Aceh *Adat* Council, the *imeum mukim* or by any other name it is referred to, the *imeum chik* or by any other name it is referred to and another ten traditional institutions. Hence in principle, the *adat* and its institutions may occupy an important position in Acehnese society, including as a means of participation. Further provisions regarding the duties, authority, rights and obligations of *adat* institutions, empowerment of *adat*, and *adat*-related affairs shall according to the LoGA be governed by Aceh *qanun*, which at the same time may mean that the customary practices and law of the *adat* become positivized.

4.7.5 Rights of Persons, Residents and Citizens

Article 211 of the LoGA creates a generic category of Acehnese persons by prescribing that an individual who is born in Aceh or of Acehnese descent, whether located within or outside Aceh, and who acknowledges himself/herself as an Acehnese person shall be an Acehnese person. Presumably, this category of Acehnese persons covers Muslims and non-Muslims as well as the different ethnic groups that are represented in Aceh, in particular because the Indonesian Government, the Aceh Government, and district/municipality governments shall recognize, respect, and protect the ethnic diversity of Aceh. In addition, the Aceh Government and district/municipality governments shall, according to the provision, recognize and protect the right of all ethnic groups in Aceh to be treated equally in political, economic, social and cultural affairs. In so far as minorities in Aceh are concerned, on the basis of Art. 221(4), regional languages shall be taught as local content in school education.

There is, according to Art. 212 of the LoGA, also a distinct legal category of the Aceh resident, who shall be any person permanently domiciled in Aceh regardless of ethnicity, race, religion and descent.[409] This status does not seem to amount to a regional citizenship of an exclusive kind, because any person who moves to Aceh to live there becomes an Aceh resident, but it can function as a basis for the exercise of certain rights, such as the right to vote. An Aceh resident would thus have a legal

---

[408] Concerning *adat* law, see, e.g., Holleman and Sonius (1981), Avonius (2004), p. 6.

[409] As agreed in para. 1.2.5 of the MoU, all Acehnese residents will be issued new conventional identity cards prior to the elections of April 2006.

position to which it is possible to combine certain legal rights, while the collective determination of who is an Acehnese person would not constitute a basis for legal rights and obligations, except in the area of equality (and presumably also non-discrimination).

It is difficult to say what the distinction between Acehnese persons and Aceh residents implies in terms of law. It may be that the former are incorporated into the concept of the protection and promotion of Acehnese culture that the Government of Aceh is in charge of on the basis of Art. 221 of the LoGA so that even Acehnese persons who are not residents of Aceh may be approached by the Government of Aceh in matters cultural. However, residents of Aceh are, under Art. 227 of the LoGA, entitled to certain rights on the basis of LoGA.

In comparison with many other autonomy statutes, the LoGA is particular in this respect because it contains a list of human rights in spite of the fact that Articles 26–32 of the Constitution of Indonesia, which include the bill of rights established through the second amendment, provides for a number of constitutional rights for the citizen and for everyone residing in the territory of Indonesia. Against this background, the separate human rights provisions in the LoGA and the obligation to create a human rights court would seem unnecessary, because it should be possible to raise similar rights issues before the Indonesian courts. Therefore, the human rights issues meant in this context should probably be something different.[410] Under Art. 227, in the chapter on human rights, every resident shall have the right to equal standing before the law, freedom of speech, freedom of the press and publication,[411] freedom of association, freedom of assembly, freedom of movement, to conduct peaceful demonstrations, and the right to create and join labor unions and to conduct labor actions, freedom to engage in academic research, creative arts, literature, and other cultural activities that do not contravene Islamic law,[412] elect and be elected pursuant to requirements set out in prevailing laws and regulations, and receive legal services and assistance, facilitation through the judiciary, and choice of legal attorney/legal counsel for the defense of his/her legal rights and

[410]Human rights violations that could be tried as violations by such a human rights courts could be, *inter alia*, mass killings, displacement of civilians, etc., that have occurred after the signing of the LoGA.

[411]There is a potentially serious claw-back clause regarding freedom of expression in Art. 153, according to which the Government of Aceh shall have the authority to set provisions related to the press and broadcasting, based on Islamic values (the national free speech legislation seems to have a somewhat similar provision). Further provisions related to the control of content of speech shall be governed by Aceh *qanun*, which makes it possible at least in theory to implement the wish of the Acehnese to maintain a certain life-style. For the purpose of implementing the control the content of speech, the Government of Aceh shall coordinate with the Indonesia Broadcasting Commission, Aceh Region, to set guidelines for broadcasting ethics and broadcast program standards. However, attempts to impose such control may be impracticable, because the relatively secular Jakarta TV is seen in Aceh, too.

[412]In Aceh, the freedom of religion seems to translate, on the basis of the LoGA, into a freedom to be Muslim.

interests before a court of law. These are matters that can be tried by the human rights court to be established under Art. 228.[413] The separate human rights provisions and the human rights court to be created seem to indicate that claims of violation of human rights can be raised directly on the basis of the LoGA without there being any need to connect the claims to other Indonesian legislation. It remains unclear, however, from where the substantive contents of the different human rights are brought,[414] but one alternative could be that the interpretation of the substantive contents of the human rights is derived from the UN Covenants on civil and political and on economic, social and cultural rights, which Indonesia has ratified.[415] Such an extraneous source of law would, however, seem to contradict the wish of Indonesia to maintain its sovereign integrity.

Under Art. 216, every resident has the right to quality and Islamic education in line with developments in pedagogy and technology, a provision which is sustained by the duty of Aceh residents between 7 and 15 years of age to undergo primary education.[416] Every Aceh resident shall also have an equal right to receive health

[413]However, the human rights court has not been established as of May 2009. One piece of criticism in the context is that the human rights court would evidently not be empowered to try past violations of human rights. See Miller (2009), p. 167. In addition, the establishment of the national Truth and Reconciliation Commission was halted by the decision of the Constitutional Court of Indonesia No. 006/PUU 4/2006, which revoked the Law No. 27 of 2004, which has to some extent affected the work of the sub-national branch of the same in Aceh, although there is a legal basis for the latter in Art. 229 of the LoGA.

[414]The Explanatory Notes attached to the LoGA indicate that the provision creating the human rights in the LoGA is sufficiently clear.

[415]Indonesia ratified both the International Covenant on Civil and Political Rights and the International Covenant on Economic, Social and Cultural Rights on 23 February 2006. In a Declaration worded similarly for both covenants, filed with ratification, Indonesia made an explanation that is of relevance for Aceh: "With reference to Article 1 of the International Covenant on Civil and Political Rights [and of the International Covenant on Economic, Social and Cultural Rights – MS], the Government of the Republic of Indonesia declares that, consistent with the Declaration on the Granting of Independence to Colonial Countries and Peoples, and the Declaration on Principles of International Law concerning Friendly Relations and Cooperation Among States, and the relevant paragraph of the Vienna Declaration and Program of Action of 1993, the words 'the right of self-determination' appearing in this article do not apply to a section of people within a sovereign independent state and can not be construed as authorizing or encouraging any action which would dismember or impair, totally or in part, the territorial integrity or political unity of sovereign and independent states." The explanation does not concern the other substantive rights of the two covenants, so at least in principle, these covenantal rights could be available as a source for the human rights court.

[416]The primary (and apparently also secondary) education is free of charge and shall be provided based on the principles of democracy and justice, with full respect for upholding human rights, Islamic values, local culture, and societal pluralism. As explained by the International Development Law Organization in its report 'A Brief Account on the Qanun on Education in Aceh' from November 2008, at http://www.aceh-eye.org/data_files/english_format/ngo/ngo_idlo/ngo_idlo_2008_11_00.pdf (accessed on 11 June 2009): "The Aceh government's promise of providing free education to children from 7–18 years of age has been fulfilled by means of Qanun No. 5 year 2008 on Education, which has recently been passed by the Aceh parliament

services. Every worker shall, under Art. 175, have an equal right to obtain reasonable employment in Aceh, and according to Art. 180, every worker shall have the right to form and become a member of a workers'/labor union in accordance with prevailing laws and regulations. Coupled with such economic and social rights, the public sector, that is, the Indonesian Government, the Government of Aceh and the districts/municipalities have the duty to provide, *inter alia*, social services, health services and educational services, all formulated in a manner which indicates the existence of a relatively large public sector in Aceh that is supported by economical and financial provisions concerning, *inter alia*, the budget and revenue of Aceh (see below). On the basis of Art. 231, the Indonesian Government, the Government of Aceh and district/municipality governments as well as Aceh residents must promote and protect the rights of women and children and carry out empowerment efforts based on values. At the same time as the economic, social and cultural rights receive attention in the LoGA, Articles 163 and 165 also establish the freedoms of trade and investment as well as commercial activity, albeit in a number of instances on the basis of licenses granted by the Government of Aceh.

It should be noted that the LoGA creates at least one distinction between residents and citizens of Indonesia: Art. 213 recognizes the right of every Indonesian citizen in Aceh to land in accordance with prevailing laws and regulations. This seems to put foreign nationals at a disadvantage concerning land ownership. At the same time, the provision recognizes the existence of certain faith-based community lands, presumably by way of collective ownership. In spite of the fact that the right to self-determination may be a sensitive issue in the context against the background of the claim of self-determination by way of independence that was presented in the first phase of the negotiations between the GAM and the Indonesian Government, there are references in Art. 143 to the people, most likely in their collective capacity. Sub-section 2 of Art. 143 creates the duty for the Indonesian Government, the Government of Aceh and district/municipality governments, in formulating and implementing sustainable development, to take into account, respect, protect, fulfill, and uphold the rights of the Acehnese people.

Most of the rights for residents are such that are contained among the Indonesian constitutional rights and which, with reference to Articles 26(3) and 28 of the Constitution, should be regulated by law. Consequently, the constitutional provisions containing individual rights are not self-executing or justiciable as such, but seem to require implementing legislation enacted by the House of Representatives of Indonesia. Because the LoGA is an ordinary act of parliament, it may be understood as such to be a piece of legislation that implements the

(DPRA). The *Qanun* provides the guarantee for Acehnese children to have access to education, at least until secondary school level. Free education is also provided for children with mental disabilities and the government has provided special schools for this purpose. The *Qanun* on Education becomes even more interesting not only because it aspires to provide education of a national character but also because it regulates on the need for a special Acehnese local content to be taught as a school subject as well for example the unique status of Aceh and its enforcement of Syar'iah." The *Qanun* was proposed by the Aceh Government.

constitutional rights in the territory of Aceh and brings the constitutional rights into force either with or without reference to human rights. Moreover, because Art. 26 (2) of the Constitution concludes that residents shall consist of Indonesian citizens and foreign nationals living in Indonesia, the reference to residents in the LoGA is actually a reference to every individual within the jurisdiction of Aceh. In addition, a number of statutory injunctions prohibit certain actions against residents of Aceh. Residents must not be subjected to any form of arbitrary or unlawful search of their persons, residences, or clothes, or to the revocation or elimination of their rights, or the restriction of their individual freedoms, and they must not be subjected to arbitrary torture or the unlawful removal of their right to life, and be unlawfully arrested, detained, prosecuted and imprisoned.

4.8 Reflections

It is evident on the basis of the different cases above that autonomy is an unusual and often also a problematic solution to various organizational needs in a state. The asymmetry introduced by territorial autonomy may be confusing and defy the logic of what may be perceived as the rational (and thus symmetrically hierarchical) organization of a state.

An initial issue is a terminological one. Although the international documentation related to the two cases of autonomy that preceded the Second World War, the Åland Islands and the Memel Territory, makes reference to autonomy, it seems that the autonomy statutes of various kinds do not employ the term autonomy. Instead, reference is made to such concepts as self-government (even in the constitutional norms relating to the Åland Islands) or special administrative region, and it is also possible to omit a descriptive reference to the entity and denote the entity by its geographical name only, as is the case with Zanzibar, Scotland and Aceh. Although it may be maintained that autonomy is an established legal term at the level of international law, it appears that autonomy is not necessarily a term of art at the level of national constitutional law.[417] In fact, this particular term is perhaps even avoided, sometimes because it may be confused by aims to organize the state in a federal way, and sometimes perhaps because the term may be too strong an implication of independence for the territory. Instead, other strategies of description are used for these entities that often break out from the ordinary pattern of state organization, *ad hoc* terminology being the main option. There is also variation amongst the states involved in this study in recognizing the existence of an autonomous territory within the framework of its sovereignty, perhaps for reasons that imply a challenge to the sovereignty of the State.

[417] Autonomy is a legal term in some domestic jurisdictions, such as Spain, where a right to autonomy is formulated in Art. 2 of the Constitution.

Another feature that is apparent on the basis of the study is that the constitutional imagination of the national lawmaker seems to be very broad and amounts to surprising institutional flexibility concerning the organization of the state. It is not only terminology that is *ad hoc*, but often also the sub-state institution itself. There may exist certain national structures against the background of which an autonomy arrangement is modeled, such as the regional organization in Indonesia, the broad understanding of devolution in the United Kingdom and the non-federal entities in the United States, but in most cases (and even in the examples mentioned) it seems that each autonomy arrangement is unique in terms of organization. The reason for this is probably the fact that each autonomy arrangement is an answer to specific regulatory needs in the context in which it emerged.

There is an evident need to regulate the position of these asymmetrical institutions in autonomy statutes and in constitutions of the states in which they exist. Here, strategies vary to a great extent. Separate autonomy statutes adopted by the national legislature for the regulation of the position of the autonomous territories exist in all cases but Zanzibar, where the national constitution contains quite detailed norms about the position of Zanzibar in the Constitution of the Union Republic and leaves the rest to be regulated in a constitutional document adopted by the legislature of Zanzibar. The reason for this can be found in the coming into being of Tanzania: two independent States decided to form a union, and the constitution of the Union Republic is therefore the natural normative platform for common rules. Even in a case where the autonomous territory is mentioned in the constitution of the state, as is the situation in the Åland Islands, there is a separate autonomy statute (which in this case preceded the formal constitutional mention by 75 years). Most written constitutions do not, however, mention the autonomy arrangement, but leave the matter entirely to be determined in the separate autonomy statute. Internally, the terminology of a constitution is used in Zanzibar and Puerto Rico, while the internal basic documents of the other autonomous territories use varying terminology when identifying the most important normative enactments.

The connection to international law and international politics is characteristic of most of the autonomy arrangements studied here. Starting from Puerto Rico and the Åland Islands (and the Memel Territory, of course) and continued by Hong Kong and Zanzibar, decisions made at the international level either through formal treaties or other agreements signal the creation of international obligations for individual States to set up autonomy arrangements in their internal legal orders. However, all autonomy arrangements, such as Scotland, do not have any immediate international or treaty background, but are domestic or domestic with a relatively weak international dimension, such as Aceh. The extent of international involvement can thus vary from formal supervisory functions by international bodies (the Åland Islands and the Memel Territory before the Second World War and Puerto Rico from the 1950s on) through potential (but not necessarily practiced) bilateral oversight over treaty implementation (Puerto Rico, Hong Kong) to domestic pledges before a more informal international audience (Aceh). The level of efficiency of these commitments of various kinds can be debated: *de jure*, formal commitments in, for instance, treaties may be presumed to be strong, but *de facto*, there is nothing that prevents a purely domestic pledge from being effective. It seems, however, as if domestic pledges could leave more latitude to the national lawmaker and the national government in choosing the course of action when setting up an autonomy arrangement. The consequence of this is that it depends completely on the good faith of the state in question to implement the autonomy arrangement as intended.

Entrenchment of an autonomy arrangement in the entirety of the legal order is a consequence of the combined operation of the domestic and international dimensions. In some cases, namely Scotland and Aceh, the autonomy arrangement relies solely on domestic law, while in respect of the other areas, international law is involved, too. Therefore, the entrenchment is, at the outset, often two-layered and is based upon the assumption that the State implements its commitment under international law to institute an autonomy arrangement in the domestic jurisdiction in good faith and, if a margin of appreciation on behalf of the State exists, in suitable ways that do not thwart the purpose of the autonomy arrangement. The domestic jurisdiction comes normally with a distinction between norms at the constitutional level, on the one hand, and norms at the level of ordinary legislation, on the other. Therefore, the actual entrenchment of territorial autonomy would often be multi-layered. Autonomy is constitutionally entrenched in a very detailed manner as concerns Zanzibar, while the formal constitutional norms concerning the Åland Islands are more general in nature. There is no particular reference to Hong Kong (or Macau) at the constitutional level, but a general norm concerning special administrative regions that creates the framework for the autonomy statute. Puerto Rico and Aceh do not feature at all in the constitutional norms of their home states, but rely on autonomy statutes passed as ordinary legislation. This would also seem to be the situation for Scotland, where no written constitutional framework exists, while a certain entrenchment effect could be recognized to the mechanism of constitutional convention, in this case the Sewel convention.

The normative space that is left to the autonomy arrangement for the purposes of enacting institutional legislation by means of its own legislative decisions varies quite considerably and is to some extent a function of the distribution of powers (see Chaps. 5, 6 and 7). However, already at this stage, it is possible to conclude that the normative space is relatively broad in respect of the Åland Islands, Zanzibar and Puerto Rico, which seem to have wide frames for passing legislation of their own concerning the internal organization of the autonomous entity. In all these cases, the wide frames have also been filled by institutional legislation, so the autonomous entities have utilized the opportunity to set up their own structures of government. There is less space in this respect for Hong Kong, Aceh and Scotland, where the autonomy statutes establish relatively detailed rules on the institutional structure of autonomy and leave less normative space to the autonomous entity itself to organize its activities as it sees fit. As a consequence, the autonomy of the latter group could be somewhat more constrained than that of the former group. However, as a consequence of the strong federal supremacy and the plenary powers of the national lawmaker, it seems that the Puerto Rican arrangement is subordinated to national norms also in this respect.

The normative space to organize the institutional structure of autonomous entities does not necessarily seem to be tied to the power of taxation as the method of producing the revenue of the autonomous entity. Aceh and Scotland do not have significant tax powers of their own and would thus not have much leeway to, for instance, vary their governmental bodies according to their own economic strength (or weakness, as it could be), and therefore, it would seem to be only natural that much of the government is regulated in the autonomy statute. However, the Åland Islands also has somewhat limited taxation powers, and still the revenue for the governmental entities (with the exception of the municipalities) is not directly produced on the basis of taxation of the inhabitants of the autonomous territory. Even in the case of broader tax powers, it seems that the autonomies are, at least to some extent, dependent on transfers from the central government of the state, except in Hong Kong. Therefore, complete fiscal autonomy seems difficult to achieve, but the budgetary transfers from the state to the autonomous entity may be organized in different ways, for instance, without any controls, as is the case with the Åland Islands, or with control, which would seem to be the case in most other cases where transfers take place. Hong Kong, again, brings in evidence of the opposite to the Åland Islands: although there is fiscal capacity on the basis of tax powers, the institutions are established to a considerable extent in the autonomy statute, not in internal legislation of the sub-state entity. When considering the GDP/capita figures, it seems that the Åland Islands and Hong Kong, followed closely by Scotland, fare best amongst the six entities, while Puerto Rico, Aceh and Zanzibar have been less successful, at least so far, in making use of their position to their own benefit. The economic success of a sub-state entity, however, would not seem to depend very much on whether the entity has its own law-making powers or not in the area of taxation (although the caveat needs to be issued that this research is not designed to answer questions concerning economic performance).

Territorial autonomies may often have courts of law of their own that are separate from the court organization of the state. This is so concerning Zanzibar, Puerto Rico, Hong Kong, and Scotland (although the Scottish judiciary is to some extent also a UK competence), while the Åland Islands and also Aceh do not have courts of their own (although the religious courts in Aceh may perhaps be perceived as such). However, the existence of an independent court organization in the autonomies does not seem to be altogether complete, because in all cases but Hong Kong, the highest appellate court instance is actually a state court, normally a Supreme Court or a Supreme Administrative Court. Hence the apex of a dual court system nonetheless features a national court as the final interpreter of disputes and appeals (the issue of constitutional jurisdiction will be discussed separately, because it presents an entirely different scenario). As was pointed out in Chap. 3, a separate court system for the autonomous entity has sometimes been regarded as a defining feature of autonomy. However, assuming that the courts operate under the principle of the independence of the judiciary, it should not matter much that the courts are state courts, although at least in Puerto Rico, some issues have been decided differently depending on whether the court is a court of Puerto Rico or a federal court. In cases where the state courts are in charge of interpreting the legislation produced by the legislature of the autonomous entity, it is, of course, important that the state court recognizes the legislation of the sub-state entity as relevant law and implements it in the case at hand.

On the basis of the examples studied here, territorial autonomies emerge as a result of two different mechanisms, through fragmentation and through integration, as a response to different needs that are often embedded in an environment of conflict resolution and even self-determination. An autonomous entity emerges through fragmentation where the state delegates normative powers of a particular kind to the regional level so as to create a unique sub-state entity. As pointed out above, the delegation of powers may be done on the basis of the constitution or on the basis of ordinary legislation, and situations of this kind can often be denoted by the term devolution. Examples of fragmentation as a reason for the emergence of autonomous entities are the Åland Islands, Scotland, and Aceh. An autonomous entity emerges through integration where the State incorporates a territory which it has not previously governed and which is vested with law-making powers on the basis of an autonomy statute of some sort. As examples of emergence through integration it is possible to point to Hong Kong, Zanzibar and Puerto Rico, and the Memel Territory would also belong to this category. The mode of emergence links at least to some extent to the terminological complications presented above: where the autonomous entity is created through fragmentation within the state, it is more plausible than in cases of integration that there is a conceptual framework, for instance, in the constitutional doctrine that facilitates the creation of the autonomous entity, such as self-government, devolution or regional self-government of a special kind. Such conceptual preparedness is probably lacking in cases where the autonomous entity is integrated from an exogenous position into the structures of the state, something which is apparent on the basis of our review of those autonomies that have emerged due to integration. In the cases of Hong Kong, Zanzibar and Puerto Rico, it is relatively clear that the constitutional framework of the state lacks a conceptualization of both territorial autonomy and the implications of the term, so, too, in the case of the Memel Territory. This is not to say that fragmentation is an uncomplicated way to produce autonomous entities, but because the methods of setting up autonomous entities in situations of fragmentation are more clearly in the hands of national interests relying on pre-existing conceptual tools, there may exist at least some understanding of territorial autonomy prior to the legislative drafting work.

The emergence of a territory as an autonomous entity may have a stronger or a weaker connection to the issue of self-determination. In the case of Zanzibar, the integration is clearly connected with the concept of self-determination because two independent States, Zanzibar and Tanganyika, decided to join together in the Union Republic of Tanzania. It seems as if Zanzibar is the only case where it would be possible to make the point that an entity is more or less genuinely federated with another entity, although the end result was an autonomy arrangement rather than a federal arrangement. Hong Kong is illustrative of the self-determination issue from another perspective, where the full territorial self-determination of China demanded the unwinding of the colonial relationship between the United Kingdom and Hong Kong. Finally, Puerto Rico has been discussed among such colonial territories where the range of institutional choices goes from full integration in the state through an enhanced autonomy status to independence. In contrast, there is probably a weaker connection to self-determination in the other cases, all of which came into being through fragmentation. As concerns the Åland Islands, the argument of self-determination, with implications for a referendum and an ultimate secession, was not recognized in the post-First World War setting, and in Scotland and Aceh, there is a limited connection only to the issue of self-determination. Yet at the same time, the normative powers, which in most of these cases amount to significant law-making powers (see Chap. 5), can be understood as a grant of a share of the entirety of self-determination of the State to the autonomous territory.

As is already evident on the basis of the above discussion of self-determination, the chronology in which the autonomous territories were presented is actually of some importance. After the First World War, the starting point was established that a minority population inhabiting a particular territory cannot freely secede from an existing State by reference to their wish to exercise self-determination (the Åland Islands). After the Second World War, non-self-governing territories were dealt with in the United Nations system (Puerto Rico), and the right of former colonies to become independent or to assume some other political status was specified in the 1960s (Zanzibar). The injustice of colonial relationships was still relevant in the 1980s (Hong Kong), while in the 1990s and thereafter, the application of the principle of self-determination emphasized that the solution to possible problems of governance should be sought for in internal arrangements that do not disrupt the territorial integrity and sovereignty of the State (Aceh, and possibly also Scotland).

The self-determination issues are relevant in relation to many of these autonomous territories from the perspective of the inhabitants of those territories. In so far as the terminology of "the people" is utilized in the context, such a reference may imply a direct connection to the right of peoples to self-determination. Evidently, the notion of the people is used in the collective sense at least in connection to Zanzibar, Puerto Rico and Aceh, although in the case of Aceh, the concept of the people might exist for domestic purposes only. For the other two, there probably exists a link to the concept of the people in international law. A collective circumscription of the population is also produced by such regional citizenship as is established for Zanzibar, Hong Kong and the Åland Islands (and also to some extent in Aceh) and which manifests itself in certain exclusive or special rights in the territory, such as the right to vote in the elections to the legislative organ and the right to possess property in the territory. At the same time, the residency requirements for the achievement of the status of regional citizenship may be very lengthy (ranging from 5 through 7 to 15 years). As concerns Hong Kong and the Åland Islands, neither the status of permanent residency nor that of right of domicile amount to a recognition of the inhabitants as a 'people' under international law. This is almost reversed in relation to Puerto Rico: the unequal position of Puerto Rico as an entity outside the US federation actually results in special non-rights because of the territorial dimension, although the population can be qualified as a people. However, federal law grants citizenship of Puerto Rico to such US citizens who reside at least one year in the jurisdiction, so a concept of a separate regional citizenship also exists in this context.

Self-determination can, in its current form, assume different forms. In the 1970 UN Friendly Relations Declaration,[418] three institutional categories for implementing the right of self-determination by a people are identified, namely the establishment of a sovereign and independent State, the free association or integration with an independent State, or the emergence into any other political status. The first category, independence, can be excluded from the scope of this study, while all of the entities involved can be placed in the third category, emergence into any other political status. In addition, Zanzibar might also qualify for the category of free association or integration with an independent State. These institutional modes of self-determination should be freely determined by a people through a suitable procedure. To the extent a people is the beneficiary of self-determination towards the creation of a sub-state entity, it can be asked how and under which forms the exercise of such self-determination has taken place. It is evident on the basis of the 1975 *Western Sahara* case[419] of the International Court of Justice (ICJ) that, in addition to referendums or elections, also other forms of the exercise of self-determination can be possible. The ICJ refers in this context to decisions of the United Nations, more specifically to decisions of the General Assembly.

As concerns referendums as a procedural device for self-determination, such have been organized in Puerto Rico and Scotland, but under terms set by the national legislative bodies. Also, it can be argued that in Puerto Rico, the process of self-determination is still incomplete in spite of the three status referendums (see section 6.5 below). Surprisingly, it seems as if elections had not been used for the initial exercise of self-determination, although all entities involved have elected assemblies, of which at least the one in the Åland Islands has been granted a decisive role in decision-making concerning the autonomy statute and international treaties applicable in the jurisdiction in a manner potentially relevant in a self-determination context. In relation to other forms of self-determination decisions than by referendum or elections, it seems that only the 1921 decision about the Åland Islands Settlement by the Council of the League of Nations could qualify in this category, pending another UN decision about Puerto Rico. The creation of Zanzibar, Hong Kong and Aceh as sub-state entities would seem to fall outside of the procedural frames established by the ICJ. The President of Zanzibar cut a quick deal with the President of Tanganyika without wider consultations (and perhaps without even ratifying the Articles of Union), while

---

[418]Declaration on Principles of International Law concerning Friendly Relations and Co-operation among States in accordance with the Charter of the United Nations, adopted by the U.N. General Assembly on 24 October 1970 (G.A. Res. 2625/XXV).

[419]*Western Sahara*, Advisory Opinion, I.C.J. Reports 1975, at 59.

the People's Republic of China and the United Kingdom concluded a treaty about the transfer of sovereignty over Hong Kong, albeit clearly in the traditional self-determination context of decolonization. Finally, the internal peace deal between the Indonesian Government and the GAM was implemented in national law by the Parliament of Indonesia without the direct involvement of the Acehnese. Overall, it seems that the procedural guarantees for the exercise of self-determination have not been too well catered for even in relation to those sub-state entities the inhabitants of which are designated as peoples. Thus in practice, there is no clear connection between sub-state entities in the category of "any other political status" and the procedures by which self-determination should be exercised.

Against this background, the exercise of self-determination in one institutional form or another actually becomes the core content of conflict resolution. The broad and – admittedly – relatively permissive concept of self-determination has catered for different kinds of needs but produced, in the cases studied, relatively clear-cut expressions of territorial autonomy, that is, singular entities with at least some measure of law-making powers without disrupting the unitary nature of the states within which they exist. The material contents and the material extent of the intern al self-determination accorded to these entities may, however, vary greatly.

Chapter 5
The Distribution of Powers

5.1 From Enumeration through Residual Powers to Open Arrangements

The various constitutions and autonomy statutes included in this study employ different mechanisms for the distribution of powers between the national legislature, on the one hand, and the sub-state legislature, on the other. Against the background of the example of the Memel Territory and the *Memel* case before the PCIJ, and also with a view to our more theoretical distinction between federations and autonomies developed above, it could be expected that the powers of the sub-state entities would, in most cases, be attributed on the basis of enumeration, leaving residual powers to the national level. However, the entities studied in our inquiry are only more or less in harmony with this starting point; in fact, most entities are less so. The entities may actually be viewed as forming groups of two entities so that the first group contains Hong Kong and the Åland Islands, the second group Scotland and Zanzibar, and the third group Aceh and Puerto Rico. In addition, this ordering of the entities would also seem to illustrate the proximity to or the distance from the Memel example in the area of the distribution of powers.

Arguably, Hong Kong comes closest to the "original" autonomy arrangement of Memel, because its powers seem to be based on enumeration. It is possible to hold the view that the national lawmaking powers with respect to Hong Kong are enumerated, too, but the mainland Chinese position seems to be that the powers of the national legislature are, under the Constitution of China, of a residual nature. If this were the case, the arrangement in Hong Kong would be very close to Memel, but this is, at least to some extent, debatable. In the light of the documentation studied for the purposes of this inquiry, no indications seem to exist that the drafters of the Joint Declaration would have had the Statute of Memel in mind, although this cannot be altogether excluded either, given that Great Britain was one of the parties to the Memel Convention and the Memel Statute.

The Åland Islands display a model of the distribution of powers in which the competences of both the sub-state legislature and the national legislature are

M. Suksi, *Sub-State Governance through Territorial Autonomy*,
DOI 10.1007/978-3-642-20048-9_5,

enumerated in the autonomy statute. This is taking the Åland Islands one step away from the original Memel arrangement and organizes the distribution of powers in a manner similar to that which exists between the Canadian federation and its provinces. As such, the use of two lists of powers is not federal by origin, but in fact to some extent natural from the point of view of the theory of autonomy, at least in so far as the intention is to create lawmaking competences that are mutually exclusive in relation to each other.

As regards Scotland, the exercise of the devolved powers is organized from a different point of view in comparison with Hong Kong and the Åland Islands so that Scotland is vested with residual powers and the UK Parliament with enumerated powers. This is at least how the arrangement tends to look, although at the same time, the UK Parliament is still in possession of the ultimate residual powers on the basis of the concept of parliamentary sovereignty. In order to "regulate" this characteristic, the unwritten British constitution has developed mechanisms of advance conflict resolution that are uniquely British.

The most federal-like determination of lawmaking powers amongst all the examples reviewed here is displayed by Zanzibar, which holds residual powers, while the Parliament of the Union Republic holds enumerated powers in respect of Zanzibar. No doubt, Zanzibar is a sub-state entity, but whether it is a federal entity or an autonomous entity has been a contentious issue over recent decades. A point frequently made by the Zanzibari side is that the partnership has turned out to be very unequal because of the additions by the Union Republic to the enumerated matters of the national parliament.

In spite of the intention to organize the governance of Aceh from the point of view of residual powers so that the national level would be left with some enumerated powers, the actual outcome of the implementation of the peace agreement seems to be a very muddled definition of powers: the norms issued in Aceh exist at a normative level below the enactments of the national parliament, and the powers of Aceh and the powers of the national level seem overlapping to such a great extent as to create a huge area of concurring powers. In order to know who does what, an additional agreement has to be negotiated, the result of which is recorded in a decree of the national government. The arrangement is thus very open-ended.

As concerns Puerto Rico, it seems that there are different definitions of powers. Depending on the point of view, they may be enumerated for Puerto Rico and residual for the national level or enumerated for both levels of governance. It seems, however, that the Puerto Rican arrangement is the most open-ended one, because it exists under the plenary powers of the national lawmaker, vesting the national level with the ultimate residual powers under all circumstances. As a consequence, it is possible to hold that the entire area of Puerto Rican legislative competence, at least in theory, concurs completely with national lawmaking powers and that the national powers always have precedence whenever they are exercised.

It seems on the basis of our study that the core function of sub-state governance, the exercise of powers, is very differently organized in different entities. At the outset, it appears that not all instances of sub-state governance can qualify as having a high degree of autonomy.

5.2 Hong Kong: Enumeration (or Delegation under the Plenary Powers of the National Legislature?)

5.2.1 *High Degree of Autonomy*

As pointed out above, the high degree of autonomy accorded to the HKSAR is not comparable to other entities of local administration in China (except Macau, which is another SAR). Annex I of the Joint Declaration established the HKSAR's legislative powers which would be vested in the legislature of the HKSAR. According to the Annex, the legislature may on its own authority enact laws in accordance with the provisions of the Basic Law and legal procedures, and report them to the NPCSC for the record. Annex I also includes language to the effect that laws enacted by the legislature which are in accordance with the Basic Law and legal procedures shall be regarded as valid. Against this background, Annex I defines Hong Kong's legal order and specifies that the laws of the HKSAR consist of the Basic Law, the laws previously in force in Hong Kong and laws enacted by the HKSAR legislature.

Article 3(2) of the Joint Declaration states that the HKSAR will enjoy a high degree of autonomy, except in foreign affairs and defense which are the responsibility of the Central People's Government,[1] while Art. 3(3) frames the general characteristics of autonomy by vesting the HKSAR with executive, legislative and independent judicial powers. This is re-stated in Annex I to the Joint Declaration which provides that except for foreign affairs and defense which are the responsibilities of the Central People's Government, the HKSAR shall be vested with executive, legislative and independent judicial power, including that of final adjudication. In addition, Art. 3(3) of the Joint Declaration states that the laws in force in Hong Kong at the time of the signing of the Declaration will remain basically unchanged. The continuity of the legal order of Hong Kong is specified in Annex I since after the establishment of the HKSAR, the laws previously in force in Hong Kong (i.e. the common law, rules of equity, ordinances, subordinate legislation and customary law) shall be maintained, save for any that contravene the Basic Law and subject to any amendment by the HKSAR legislature, which, according to Art. 66

[1] The allocation of these powers to the CPR is sustained by the fact that according to Art. 19(3), the courts of the HKSAR shall have no jurisdiction over acts of state such as defence and foreign affairs. The wording of the provision is not making an exclusive list of acts of state, but also some other acts of state may be included than those relative to defence and foreign affairs. The Chief Executive has a central position in the context of defining what is and what is not an act of state, because the courts of the Region shall, according to the provision, obtain a certificate from the Chief Executive on questions of fact concerning acts of state such as defence and foreign affairs whenever such questions arise in the adjudication of cases. Such a certificate is binding on the courts. Before issuing such a certificate, the Chief Executive shall obtain a certifying document from the Central People's Government. The act of state could potentially constitute a way to limit the autonomy of the HKSAR. On the issue, see Leung Mei-fun (2006), pp. 279–300.

of the Basic Law, holds legislative powers. This position is articulated in greater detail in Art. 160 of the Basic Law, which provides that upon the establishment of the HKSAR, the laws previously in force in Hong Kong shall be adopted as laws of the Region except for those which the NPCSC declares to be in contravention of the Basic Law.[2] If any laws are later discovered to be in contravention of the Basic Law, they are expected to be amended or cease to have force in accordance with the procedure as prescribed in the Basic Law (see below, Sect. 5.2.3).

Documents, certificates, contracts, and rights and obligations valid under the laws previously in force in Hong Kong shall continue to be valid and be recognized and protected by the HKSAR, provided that they do not contravene the Basic Law. In practice, this meant that an almost complete legal order was transferred from the sovereignty of the UK to the sovereignty of China and maintained in force even in its details. Its norms range from criminal law to social legislation, from property law to health care legislation, and from financial regulations to tax legislation.[3]

This created an understanding that the central government retains certain enumerated powers to itself, namely authority over foreign affairs and defense matters as well as the power to enact and amend of the Basic Law itself. In contrast, residual powers would be assigned to the HKSAR to be exercised by its organs, by the executive power and by the legislature of the HKSAR.[4] Even the Basic Law supports such an understanding by assigning foreign affairs and defense to the central government in articles 13 and 14, respectively, while identifying several substantive areas in which legislative competences of the HKSAR are confirmed. In fact, the confirmation of the different substantive areas as powers of Hong Kong could also be interpreted as enumerations, although their function seems to be to dispel any doubts about where the competence is vested.

However, the central government of China as well as Chinese doctrine seem to be strongly opposed to the characterization of the distribution of powers by reference to the fact that the central government would hold a few enumerated powers, while the residual powers, that is, the vast bulk of the legislative powers, would be vested in the HKSAR. The argument put forward by the Mainland Chinese authorities and academics is that China is not a federal state in which the federation would hold enumerated powers and the states the residual powers on the

---

[2]See Ghai (1997), p. 355: "The initial review of the compatibility of laws was undertaken by the Preliminary Working Committee in 1994 and 1995 which took a much broader view of 'compatibility' than mere legal validity. It recommended that 26 ordinances should be repealed in their entirety and 12 partially. These included 6 amendment ordinances that had been passed to bring the primary ordinances into conformity with the Bill of Rights Ordinance, although the Bill of Rights Ordinance was to be kept except for provisions dealing with its effect on other legislation." See also the NPCSC decision of 23 February 1997, and Leung (1999).

[3]As pointed out by Leung Mei-fun (2006), p. 14, because the Basic Law is a piece of written law, it changes the unwritten constitutional culture to a "written" one in Hong Kong.

[4]However, see Ghai (1997), p. 149 f., who expresses doubts about the concept of residual powers in the context and feels that the Basic Law may have diluted the guarantees of the Joint Declaration.

basis of a distribution of powers. Instead, so the argument goes, China is a unitary state, and because the Basic Law is a piece of ordinary legislation in the legal order of China, the residual powers are actually held by the central government, not by the HKSAR. Because the NPC has the plenary powers of the sovereign lawmaker, the NPC could revoke the Basic Law. Consequently, so the argument continues, there is no distribution of powers as in a federal system, but a delegation of powers on the basis of the Basic Law from the central government to the HKSAR. Instead, the ultimate residual powers are held by the NPC.[5] In this respect, the position of the Mainland Chinese doctrine concerning the congressional sovereignty of the NPC is akin to the concept parliamentary sovereignty in, e.g., the United Kingdom or the concept of plenary powers of the US Congress.

From the point of view of the HKSAR, things can be understood differently, supported by the stipulations in the Joint Declaration and its Annex I: the international commitment signals an intention on the part of China to distribute powers between the central government and the HKSAR, not only to devolve powers in a manner which allows a withdrawal of those powers at the will of the central government.

---

[5]See Leung Mei-fun (2006), pp. 34–36, Ghai (1999), pp. 148–153, and Weiyun (2001), pp. 60, 92–95, 98–101, 134 f., where the claim is repeatedly made that the HKSAR uniquely enjoys a higher degree of autonomy in many respects than a member state of a federal country. Apparently, the variant of sub-state organisation looked into in this inquiry, that of territorial autonomy, was not considered when the Joint Declaration and the Basic Law were adopted. See also Leung Mei-fun (2006), p. 20 f. On p. 21 f., Leung concludes against the background of a statement by Deng Xiaoping about the "one country, two systems" principle that "the special administrative regions may have a high degree of autonomy only to the extent authorized by the central government. Matters which are not within the authority of special administrative regions will be dealt with by the central government." Also Weiyun (2001), p. 134 f., concludes that because China is a unitary state, each administrative region, including the HKSAR, is only a local administrative region. However, against the background of the Joint Declaration and the granting of legislative powers to Hong Kong in the Basic Law, a reference to authorisation by the central government sounds like an understatement. See also Ghai (1999), pp. 62, 68. The aversion towards any opening towards a federal-like state organisation is generally explained by Galligan (2007), p. 304 f., by saying that "[f]ederalism requires limited government, so if the country requires strong government, either because of its poverty or fragmentation, or because the ruling party is committed to imposing a new social order, federalism is an unsuitable instrument". See also Baogang (2007), p. 9, where the point is made that "Hong Kong's special status has weakened the traditional unitary model of China", and pp. 13 and 15, where, *inter alia*, China is characterised as a state that has built up hybrid federalism with the key characteristics of regional autonomy, defined as an institutional configuration that combines a unitary system with federal elements which has the capability of achieving stability and peace at the cost of inter-group equality and even democracy. See also Yongnian (2007), p. 217, in which the definition of the Chinese unitary state is brought beyond its formal boundaries and, following the behavioural tradition, the central-local relations are characterised as de facto or behavioural federalism. See also Cheung (2007), p. 249, where it is stated that "[t]he OCTS model has not made the PRC a federal state, because it is after all a constitutionally unitary state", although the arrangement "exhibits certain federalist characteristics". See also Chan (2010), p. 129, according to which the high degree of autonomy conferred on the HKSAR is to be exercised only in the framework of a unified country, and the central government retains all essential powers over the operation of the HKSAR".

Therefore, while the theory of the devolution of power of the Chinese Government seems entirely plausible after the 50 year period has lapsed, at which point the legislature of China is free to amend the autonomy arrangement as it pleases or to continue or discontinue the arrangement, China's international obligation based on the Joint Declaration to uphold the high degree of autonomy of the HKSAR with the distribution of powers established in the Joint Declaration and its Annex I points in the other direction.[6] It seems, namely, that the autonomy arrangement of Hong Kong has been created in a manner that is by and large in line with our theoretical models that juxtapose autonomy with federalism: China is not a federal state, and while some of the competences of the central government are enumerated (with ultimate residual powers kept by the central government), so are many, perhaps all of the competences of the HKSAR.

When considering the issue from the level of the Chinese constitution, the picture may change because Art. 31 of the Constitution of China does not offer any substantive protection for any arrangement created on that basis and does not even mention the concept of autonomy. The fact that Art. 31 excludes a special administrative region from the regular structures of regional autonomy, which certainly do not have any residual powers independent of the powers of the central government, sustains the argument that the special arrangements created under Art. 31 could also be different with respect to the allocation of powers. On its face, Art. 31 could be so broad as to contain not only administrative devolution of the sort regulated in articles 112-122 of the Constitution but also a number of other possible arrangements. In fact, the reference to "special" in Art. 31 should probably mean something besides administrative devolution, which as a maximum contains law-varying powers subject to approval by the central government.

5.2.2 *Complete Legal Powers by Enumeration in Almost All Areas*

The competences of the central government in the area of foreign affairs will be dealt with separately below, but suffice to say in this context that the HKSAR has also been granted powers in that area, according to both the Joint Declaration, its Annex I and in the Basic Law. In the area of defense, however, the central government holds the entire measure of powers as laid down in Art. 14 of the Basic Law. The provision stipulates that the Central People's Government shall be responsible for the defense of the HKSAR. This is evidently a responsibility only in relation to defense against external aggression, because sub-section 2 of the provision stipulates that the HKSAR is responsible for the internal dimension, the maintenance of public order. According to Art. 14(3) of the Basic Law, military

[6] Interestingly, the legal effect of the reference in the Basic Law to the Joint Declaration is denied by Leung Mei-fun (2006), p. 31. She also states that the Joint Declaration "does not add anything to (or perhaps the correct formulation would be that it does not detract anything from -MS) the legislative power of China and, therefore, has little to do with the validity of the Basic Law".

forces that are stationed by the Central People's Government in the HKSAR for defense purposes shall not interfere in the local affairs of the Region. However, the Government of the HKSAR may, when necessary, ask the Central People's Government for assistance from the garrison for the maintenance of public order and disaster relief. The provision also contains some other rules that pertain to the Chinese defense forces in the HKSAR. In addition to abiding by national laws, members of the garrison shall abide by the laws of the HKSAR, which means that they are not granted immunity. Also, expenditure for the garrison shall be borne by the Central People's Government, which means that the Chinese defense forces do not burden the budget of the HKSAR.

As indicated above, the Joint Declaration and its Annex I as well as the Basic Law contain several confirmations or enumerations of the powers of the HKSAR.

The Joint Declaration can be understood as making reference to, *inter alia*, the following areas of competences: social and economic systems, fundamental rights and freedoms, private property, ownership of enterprises, inheritance, foreign investment, free port, customs, financial services, currency, taxation, budget, immigration and maintenance of public order as well as foreign powers in the area of economic and cultural relations. Similar areas of competence, allocated to the HKSAR, are found in Annex I, *inter alia*: the judicial system, prosecutions, legal practitioners, reciprocal juridical assistance with foreign states (this is probably to be envisioned as a shared competence, because the central government shall assist or authorize the HKSAR in the area), financial matters, taxation and public expenditure, economic and trade system, ownership of property, the monetary system, shipping (some shared powers), civil aviation (shared by way of authorization from central government), culture, education, science and technology, including policies regarding the educational system and its administration, the language of instruction, the allocation of funds, the examination system, the system of academic awards and the recognition of educational and technological qualifications, institutions of all kinds, including those run by religious and community organizations.

Much of the same substance appears in the enumeration of the Basic Law,[7] as faithfully established by the Chinese lawmaker against the background of the Joint Declaration and its Annex I, but there are also a number of specifications of competences in the Basic Law.[8]

The competences include the following: safeguarding of the rights and freedoms of residents, private ownership of property, amendments to the areas of law that shall be maintained (the common law, rules of equity, ordinances, subordinate legislation and customary law), laws prohibiting any act of treason, secession, sedition, subversion against the Central People's Government, or theft of state secrets, laws prohibiting foreign political organizations or bodies from conducting political activities in the HKSAR, and laws prohibiting political organizations or bodies of the HKSAR from establishing ties with foreign political organizations or bodies, adopting legislation to implement some of the

[7]See Ghai (1997), p. 147, who finds information supporting the conclusion that "residual powers are indeed not with the HKSAR". This could, in turn, be supporting the conclusion that the powers of the HKSAR are of an enumerated nature, although the definition of the enumerated powers of the HKSAR is not very clear in all instances. See Ghai (1997), pp. 148–151.

[8]Ghai (1997), p. 68, is of the opinion that there are formulations in the Basic Law which suggest a smaller area for autonomy than in the Joint Declaration. See also Ghai (1997), pp. 144–147.

rights and freedom guaranteed to the residents, adopting the structure, powers and functions of the courts, prescribing the powers and functions of the district organizations and the method for their formation, protection of the right of individuals and legal persons to the acquisition, use, disposal and inheritance of property and their right to compensation for lawful deprivation of their property, protection of ownership of enterprises and the investments from outside the HKSAR, adopting tax legislation, prescribing the monetary and financial systems of the HKSAR, formulating monetary and financial policies, safeguarding the free operation of financial business and financial markets, and regulating and supervising them, providing rules for the issue of Hong Kong currency and the reserve fund system, safeguarding the free flow of capital within, into and out of the HKSAR, maintaining the status of a free port and imposition of tariffs, pursuing the policy of free trade and safeguarding the free movement of goods, intangible assets and capital, recognition and protection of land leases extending beyond 30 June 1997, expiration of leases of land without a right of renewal, taking care of matters of routine business and technical management of civil aviation, including the management of airports, the provision of air traffic services within the flight information region of the Hong Kong Special Administrative Region, and the discharge of other responsibilities allocated to it under the regional air navigation procedures of the International Civil Aviation Organization, formulating policies on the development and improvement of education, including policies regarding the educational system and its administration, the language of instruction, the allocation of funds, the examination system, the system of academic awards and the recognition of educational qualifications, providing rules under which community organizations and individuals may run educational undertakings of various kinds in the HKSAR, developing Western and traditional Chinese medicine and improving medical and health services, providing various medical and health services through community organizations and individuals, formulating policies on science and technology and protecting achievements in scientific and technological research, patents, discoveries and inventions, deciding on the scientific and technological standards and specifications applicable in Hong Kong, formulating policies on culture and protecting the achievements and the lawful rights and interests of authors in their literary and artistic creation, providing for religious organizations the rights to acquire, use, dispose of and inherit property and the right to receive financial assistance, assessing the qualifications for practice in the various professions, formulating policies on sports and for non-governmental sports organizations, formulating policies on the development and improvement of the social welfare system in the light of the economic conditions and social needs, adopting labor legislation, enacting an electoral law, and adopting rules and procedures for the Legislative Council.

These legislative powers cover a wide range of areas and encompass most of the legal order. They are supported by appropriate criminal provisions in Hong Kong law. The Basic Law is generally silent on criminal provisions passed within the legislative powers of the HKSAR (except in Art. 23 of the Basic Law), which may be interpreted as evidence of the inapplicability even in the most serious cases of Mainland Chinese criminal law in the HKSAR. According to Art. 23 of the Basic Law, the HKSAR shall enact laws on its own to prohibit any act of treason, secession, sedition, subversion against the Central People's Government, or theft of state secrets, to prohibit foreign political organizations or bodies from conducting political activities in the Region, and to prohibit political organizations or bodies of the Region from establishing ties with foreign political organizations or bodies (see below). This demonstrates that the Mainland Chinese lawmakers do not have lawmaking powers with regard to the jurisdiction of the HKSAR even in this core area of provisions connected to the sovereignty of the State.

Clearly, these enumerated powers cannot be withdrawn or repealed by the Chinese Central Government before 2047 without breaching its international obligations, in particular when considering the direct link established in the preamble of the Basic Law to the Joint Declaration.[9] It is difficult to understand how the enumerated competences of the central government, on the one hand, and the competences of the HKSAR, on the other, would not constitute a distribution of powers on a more permanent basis than is the case with a mere administrative devolution. Certainly some of the competences mentioned in the Basic Law are of a devolved nature. Provisions which grant powers to the HKSAR as authorized by the central government indicate the existence of an administrative devolution, perhaps also of a shared competence. However, for the most part, it would seem that exclusive legislative powers are established for the HKSAR by way of enumeration on the basis of Annex I of the Joint Declaration.

This conclusion is supported by Art. 18, according to which national laws shall not be applied in the HKSAR except for those listed in Annex III to the Basic Law, which shall be applied locally by way of promulgation or legislation by the HKSAR.[10] Hence the Basic Law prohibits the application of national legislation in the HKSAR in all areas of law but a few which are explicitly mentioned. Even in the case of the national legislation listed as applicable in the HKSAR, the authorities of the HKSAR may choose whether to promulgate the national law in question *expressis verbis* in the jurisdiction of the HKSAR or adopt the content of the national law in the laws of the HKSAR. Until May 2009, incorporation of national law has mainly been achieved by Hong Kong legislation in order not to stir up uncertainty and emotions amongst the residents of the HKSAR. The method of adapting provisions of national law by passing legislation in the HKSAR is probably preferable because it ensures that the material contents of the Mainland Chinese legislation appear in the legislation of the HKSAR in a coherent and logical

[9]The situation becomes different if a state of war or a state of emergency has to be declared under Art. 18 of the Basic Law for reasons of turmoil. In such a context, the application of national legislation could be extended to the jurisdiction of the HKSAR. See Weiyun (2001), pp. 148, 165 f.

[10]Annex III of the Basic Law mentions the following national laws: (1) Resolution on the Capital, Calendar, National Anthem and National Flag of the People' Republic of China, (2) Resolution on the National Day of the People's Republic of China, (3) Declaration of the Government of the People's Republic of China on the Territorial Sea, (4) Nationality Law of the People's Republic of China, (5) Regulations of the People's Republic of China Concerning Diplomatic Privileges and Immunities, (6) Law of the People's Republic of China on the National Flag, (7) Regulations of the People's Republic of China concerning Consular Privileges and Immunities, (8) Law of the People's Republic of China on the National Emblem, (9) Law of the People's Republic of China on the Territorial Sea and the Contiguous Zone, (10) Law of the People's Republic of China on the Garrisoning of the Hong Kong Special Administrative Region, (11) Law of the People's Republic of China on the Exclusive Economic Zone and the Continental Shelf and (12) Law of the People's Republic of China on Judicial Immunity from Compulsory Measures concerning the Assets of Foreign Central Banks.

manner.[11] Mainland Chinese legislation has been directly promulgated only in a few cases. Such promulgation introduces national law into the HKSAR legal order without adaptation, which means that the national law is not embedded in the systematic and material environment in which it is supposed to be functioning in the HKSAR. The Basic Law therefore departs from the principle that relevant national laws must be implemented in the legal order of Hong Kong in a manner similar to various implementation methods of international law in domestic legal orders. In the former case, promulgation, the implementation method used is that of incorporation, while in the latter case, legislation, the implementation method is that of transformation. In this respect, there is a certain similarity with the Åland Islands, although there, it is the Legislative Assembly that decides whether or not it will use national law (see below, Sect. 5.3.3). Such a requirement of implementation is premised on the understanding that the two legal orders are separate from each other and that the legislative powers exercised in them are mutually exclusive. Therefore, if the legal order of the HKSAR does not regulate a certain matter and leaves a legal vacuum, national law cannot be used to fill the vacuum, unless the national law is added to Annex III under the special conditions of Art. 18(3) and is confined to matters relating to defense and foreign affairs as well as other matters outside the limits of the autonomy of the region as specified by the Basic Law. The avenue provided by Art. 18 and Annex III is thus of an exceptional nature and has relatively narrow and clear limits.

5.2.3 Possibility to Expand National Powers and to Return Hong Kong Legislation

It is important to acknowledge that on the basis of Art. 18(3) of the Basic Law, Annex III constitutes, at least in theory, potentially problematic flexibility for the legislative competence of the HKSAR. The provision holds that the NPCSC may add to or delete from the list of laws in Annex III after consulting its Basic Law Committee and the Government of the HKSAR. Deleting laws from Annex III could conceivably increase the legislative competence of the HKSAR to some extent, while adding laws to the list could in principle diminish its legislative competence.

[11] For example, according to some interlocutors, a treaty between China and Russia concerning the estates of Russian nationals has been incorporated by means of an Ordinance of the HKSAR, and on the basis of the Ordinance, a regulation of the Chief Executive has been issued with more detailed implementation provisions. Also, when the United Nations Security Council decided on sanctions against terrorism in the aftermath of 11 September 2001, new national legislation was adopted in China because of terrorism concerns, whereupon an Ordinance was enacted in the HKSAR, and subsequently a regulation by the Chief Executive was issued. The particular Ordinance was criticised because it gives the Chief Executive the power to agree with the Central People's Government on implementation measures in the HKSAR so as to create a wholesale opening for executive action by the central government in the area of criminal law and leaves the Legislative Council sidelined.

However, the provision contains a material limitation clause according to which laws listed in Annex III shall be confined to those relating to defense and foreign affairs as well as other matters outside the limits of the autonomy of the HKSAR as specified by the Basic Law. Even the material content of Annex III is therefore constrained by the general distribution of powers between the central government of China and the HKSAR, and Annex III cannot actually be used to encroach on the competences of the HKSAR.[12] By May 2009, a total of six Mainland Chinese laws had been added to the list in Annex III. Since some of the laws originally mentioned were taken off the list and modified by new legislation, the substantive or material effect of the alterations is not very great,[13] except in the cases of the Nationality Law and the Flag Law. The former applies to the HKSAR by way of promulgation, which means that it is applied to the HKSAR in the same way as to the rest of China.[14] The National Flag Law, by contrast, was incorporated into the legal order of the HKSAR by way of the National Flag Ordinance in a manner that adapted the contents of the national law to the circumstances of the HKSAR.[15]

The above conclusion is also supported by Art. 17, which requires that laws enacted by the legislature of the HKSAR must be reported to the NPCSC for the record. The reporting for the record does not affect the entry into force of such laws, but the reporting procedure opens up a possibility for the NPCSC to consider the conformity of the enactment of the Legislative Council with the Basic Law in two

[12]However, according to Leung Mei-fun (2006), p. 48, the provision is important, because it "determines the ultimate power of the central government to add certain PRC laws into the Hong Kong SAR, even in peaceful times". There is a provision in Art. 18(4) of the Basic Law for state of war or states of emergency, at which times the central government could extend the application of national law to the HKSAR: "In the event that the Standing Committee of the National People's Congress decides to declare a state of war or, by reason of turmoil within the Hong Kong Special Administrative Region which endangers national unity or security and is beyond the control of the government of the Region, decides that the Region is in a state of emergency, the Central People's Government may issue an order applying the relevant national laws in the Region."

[13](1) Resolution on the Capital, Calendar, National Anthem and National Flag of the People' Republic of China, (2) Resolution on the National Day of the People's Republic of China, (3) Declaration of the Government of the People's Republic of China on the Territorial Sea, (4) Nationality Law of the People's Republic of China, (5) Regulations of the People's Republic of China Concerning Diplomatic Privileges and Immunities, (6) Law of the People's Republic of China on the National Flag, (7) Regulations of the People's Republic of China concerning Consular Privileges and Immunities, (8) Law of the People's Republic of China on the National Emblem, (9) Law of the People's Republic of China on the Territorial Sea and the Contiguous Zone, (10) Law of the People's Republic of China on the Garrisoning of the Hong Kong Special Administrative Region, (11) Law of the People's Republic of China on the Exclusive Economic Zone and the Continental Shelf, and (12) Law of the People's Republic of China on Judicial Immunity from Compulsory Measures concerning the Assets of Foreign Central Banks. See also Leung Mei-fun (2006), pp. 48, 92 f.

[14]Leung Mei-fun (2006), p. 93. For the text of the Nationality Law, see Leung Mei-fun (2006), pp. 442–444.

[15]Leung Mei-fun (2006), p. 175. See also the case of *Hong Kong Special Administrative Region v Ng Kung Siu, supra* note 277 in Chap. 4, before the CFA in a case dealing with the criminalization of flag desecration.

respects. Firstly, the NPCSC can consider whether the enactment falls under the affairs within the responsibility of the Central Authorities, that is, national defense and foreign affairs. This is a relatively straightforward indication that the legal order of Mainland China is separate from the legal order of the HKSAR. Secondly, the NPCSC can consider whether the enactment is in conformity with the relationship between the central authorities and the HKSAR. This dimension seems to be a reference to possible attempts on the part of the HKSAR to change procedures established in the Basic Law by means of its own legislative decisions. If the NPCSC, after consulting the Basic Law Committee under it, considers that any law enacted by the legislature of the HKSAR is not in conformity with the provisions of the Basic Law, the NPCSC may return the law in question to the HKSAR but shall not amend it.[16] Any law returned by the NPCSC shall immediately be invalidated, that is, invalidation is a legal consequence of the decision to return the law to the HKSAR. In effect, the law of the HKSAR loses its validity as a result of a decision by the NPCSC to return a law. Therefore, it is possible to say that a decision by the NPCSC to return a law to the HKSAR is actually a veto decision. After a decision by the NPCSC to return a law to the HKSAR, it would, in the first place, be the task of the Legislative Council to resume its decision-making in the matter and to produce a new law that would enter into force subject to approval by the Chief Executive.[17]

Between July 1997 and May 2009, no piece of legislation has been returned to the HKSAR by the NPCSC,[18] but were such a decision to return to be made, it would not have retroactive effect *ex tunc*, unless otherwise provided for in the laws of the HKSAR. Consequently, none of the laws of the HKSAR have so far been invalidated as a result of the return policy. The provision concerning the possible return of laws of the HKSAR is formulated in a very open manner, because it does not establish any deadline for the decision of the NPCSC by which a law of the HKSAR should be returned. It would probably be unreasonable to assume that the NPCSC could return very old laws of the HKSAR or that the NPCSC could return, for instance, all laws enacted during a certain year or a term of office of the Legislative Council, because the return of such laws could upset in fundamental ways the functioning of the legal order of the HKSAR. Therefore, a more reasonable understanding of the possibility to return laws to Hong Kong could be that only in some individual cases could such return take place, and only within a reasonable time, such as within 3 months after the law was passed. Such an understanding of a dead-line would enhance legal certainty.

[16] See also Weiyun (2001), p. 160 f.

[17] However, according to Leung Mei-fun (2006), p. 248, if a law is returned, it becomes void immediately, which would mean that the NPCSC has a veto power over all legislation of Hong Kong which is of an absolute nature and which, in the absence of an explicit time-limit, does not promote legal certainty. However, the NPCSC does not have the power to amend the piece of law that is returned. See also Leung Mei-fun (2006), p. 247, who reports, against the background of Art. 90 of the Law on Legislation of Mainland China, the authority that has enacted a regulation has a two-month time-limit to decide on whether or not to make any amendments.

[18] As concluded by Chen (2009), p. 762, "the central government has not established any machinery for the systematic scrutiny of each SAR law when it is passed, and has never queried any SAR law".

The possibility to return laws to the HKSAR by the NPCSC could actually be understood as a veto power on the part of the central government for situations in which the legislative powers of Hong Kong have been exercised in a manner that constitutes a transgression into the competences of the lawmaker of Mainland China. Because the lawmaking powers of Hong Kong are very broad, the material scope of the veto power would thus seem to be very limited. Because none of the laws enacted by Hong Kong have been returned so far, it should be possible to conclude that the legislative activities of HKSAR have succeeded well in remaining within the legislative powers of Hong Kong.

In addition, the above conclusion is supported by Art. 20 of the Basic Law, according to which the HKSAR may enjoy other powers granted to it by the National People's Congress, the NPCSC or the Central People's Government. This provision means that powers other than those included in the Basic Law may be devolved to the HKSAR, and because the central government authorities may choose to do so, they may also choose to withdraw such powers without any limitations imposed by the Basic Law.[19] The Basic Law itself thus contains a

[19]It seems that the NPCSC gave its blessing under Art. 20 of the Basic Law to the enactment in the HKSAR of the Co-location bill introduced to advance the creation of joint entry points for immigration and import purposes where the administrative procedures of Mainland China and the HKSAR in respect of immigration and import can be carried out at the same time. Legislative Council, Official Record of Proceedings, statement by Ms. Miriam Lau, 7 May 2008, p. 7153: "The implementation of the co-location arrangement at SBP [Shenzen Bay Port–MS] is made possible after the Standing Committee of the National People's Congress conferred powers on the SAR under Article 20 of the Basic Law for enforcement and jurisdiction under Hong Kong law in the Hong Kong port area situated at the SBP." See Decision of the Standing Committee of the National People's Congress on Authorizing the Hong Kong Special Administrative Region to Exercise Jurisdiction over the Hong Kong Port Area at the Shenzhen Bay Port of 30 October 2006. See also the Official Reply of the State Council concerning the Area of the "Hong Kong Port Area at the Shenzhen Bay Port" over which the Hong Kong Special Administrative Region is Authorized to Exercise Jurisdiction and the Land use Period, Letter No. 132 [2006] of the State Council on 30 December 2006. Hence art. 20 has been used to grant extraterritorial application of public authority of the HKSAR in the area of Mainland China. The measure was effectuated by means of the Shenzhen Bay Port Hong Kong Port Area Ordinance, Ord. No. 4 of 2007. However, there is no reciprocity here, granting Mainland Chinese authorities the right to apply national law in the jurisdiction of the HKSAR. If co-location would be Hong Kong-based (which is not the case in 2009; a Bill to that effect was not approved by the Legislative Council on 7 May 2008 after voting in which the functional constituency representatives secured a majority for the Bill, but the representatives of the geographical constituencies did not, which meant that the prescribed joint majority in the Council was not achieved), a joint inspection building would be located in Hong Kong and would involve the exercise of Mainland statutes and powers pertaining to border and customs clearances within the territory of Hong Kong. Such an arrangement would, however, mean that the co-location arrangement is implemented within the boundary of Hong Kong, and therefore, fundamental constitutional difficulties would arise because Mainland law enforcement officers responsible for boundary control would enforce Mainland law within the boundary of the HKSAR. Under the principle of "one country, two systems", Mainland Chinese law cannot be implemented in the HKSAR, and the Basic Law does not contain any good answer to the question of how a reciprocal co-location arrangement could be achieved. A law of the HKSAR granting such powers to Mainland Chinese authorities would probably face legal challenges in the HKSAR.

provision which makes administrative devolution possible, leaving the central government organs in the possession of the original powers in respect of the devolved functions. Therefore, *e contrario*, the powers granted in the Basic Law should be understood as competences based on a distribution of powers between the central government and the HKSAR in an arrangement that satisfies that part of our definition of an autonomous territory which deals with the competences. Because the scope of the legislative competences of the HKSAR is so broad that according to one estimate, more than 99% of the laws enacted by the central legislature are not applicable to the HKSAR,[20] it is not easy to indicate what other powers could be granted by the central government authorities. It seems that such other powers would have to be within the two areas of national powers, defense and foreign affairs, and of the two, the latter is more likely to contain functions that could be transferred to the HKSAR under Art. 20 of the Basic Law.

In terms of our scheme concerning different autonomy positions (see Fig. 1.1 in Sect. 1.3, above), a holistic assessment that takes into consideration not only the domestic legislation concerning Hong Kong (the Constitution of China and the Basic Law, including the constitutional self-limitation in Art. 159(4) barring any amendment to the Basic Law which contravenes the established basic policies of the People's Republic of China regarding Hong Kong) but also the international obligation through the Joint Declaration and its Annex I would therefore place the HKSAR in section I of the figure. The competences vested in the HKSAR are exclusive lawmaking powers, but on the vertical dimension of the figure, it seems that the international nature and background of the arrangement places Hong Kong somewhere in the lower part of section I.[21]

This should be the case until the end of the 50-year period in 2047. After that period, supposing that the legislature of China does not amend the Basic Law, the HKSAR would probably be featured in section II of the scheme. Currently, only a smaller part of the competences relating to the HKSAR seem to be of a concurrent or shared nature, leaving at the outset the major part of the competences in the ambit of exclusive lawmaking powers. However, as indicated above, there exist areas of law where both the central government and the HKSAR are expected to act. Such "adjacent" areas include, for instance, the maintenance of a shipping register of the HKSAR (Art. 125), civil aviation (Arts. 128–135) and the incorporation of the national laws mentioned in Annex III of the Basic Law (Art. 18).

---

[20]Chen (2009), p. 759.

[21]By contrast, the general scheme of ethnic regional autonomy in the Chinese Constitution would seem to fit section III of our chart concerning different autonomy positions, because the powers of those entities are mainly regulatory. See Leung Mei-fun (2006), p. 41.

5.2.4 *Interpreting the Basic Law: 1 + 1 = 1?*

There is a certain contradiction between the common law system practiced in Hong Kong and the Chinese legal system, which could be characterized as a civil law system. Article 158 charges both the NPCSC and the courts of the HKSAR with the task of interpreting the Basic Law. On the one hand, the power of interpretation of the Basic Law is vested in the NPCSC, which holds the plenary power of interpretation under Art. 158(1).[22] On the other hand, the courts of the HKSAR are authorized to interpret on their own, in adjudicating cases, the provisions of the Basic Law which are within the limits of the autonomy of the SAR.[23] In this context, the distribution of powers between the national government and the HKSAR is obviously highly relevant.[24] The provision raises several issues. Firstly, it seems as if the power of interpretation between the NPCSC, on the one hand, and the courts of Hong Kong, on the other, overlap, which creates a need for coherence within the system.[25] Secondly, these potentially overlapping powers of interpretation create a risk of conflict between different interpretations rendered by each body. Thirdly, when interpreting the Basic Law, the NPCSC is operating in its own normative environment, which is of a civil law nature, although the body itself is political and not bound by principles of legal interpretation. The Hong Kong courts, however, approach the interpretations from the point of view of the common law,

[22]The position of the NPCSC could therefore, with reference to the constitutional position of the NPC, be recognized with reference to the concept of parliamentary sovereignty, which a common law court is not authorized to question. The CFA clarification decision *Ng Ka Ling & Others v Director of Immigration (No 2), supra* note 282 in Chap. 4, at p. 576, could well be understood in such a manner. See also Ghai (2007a), pp. 374 ff. See also Chan (2010), p. 130.

[23]For the different interpretation situations in which the NPCSC may be called to issue an interpretation, see Ghai (1999), p. 193 f. See Leung Mei-fun (2006), p. 38, who makes the point that Mainland China and the HKSAR have their own court systems which are not subordinate to each other: "The only common channel happens to be, in the eyes of common law experts, the controversial exercise of legislative interpretation power by the NPCSC. In other countries having a single sovereign system and several jurisdictions, it is common to have only one court of final appeal."

[24]As stated by Leung Mei-fun (2006), p. 52, the interpretation system under Art. 158 means that the power of interpretation is divided between the NPCSC and the court system of Hong Kong: "The former is in charge of interpreting those provisions relating to matters that are the responsibility of the central government and the issues concerning the relationship between the central government and the SAR government, while the latter is authorised to interpret the rest of the provisions." See also Ling Bing (2007), pp. 624, 645 f., making the point that the NPCSC does not really have any general overall power of interpretation, but one which is limited to the excluded matters, while the CFA is authorised to interpret independently all other matters arising under the Basic Law.

[25]As pointed out in the CFA decision *Director of Immigration v Chong Fung Yuen* [2001] 2 HKLRD 533, at p. 544, the "power of the Standing Committee extends to every provision in the Basic Law and is not limited to the excluded provisions referred to in art. 158(3)". See Hualing et al. (2007), p. 1.

because they are common law courts.[26] In that capacity, the Court of Final Appeal seems to adopt an interpretive approach to the Basic Law which gives primary attention to the text of the Basic Law when read in the light of its context and purpose,[27] while the NPCSC's approach to interpretation is less clear. Fourthly, sub-section 2 of Art. 158 states in its English language version that the NPCSC shall authorize the courts of Hong Kong to interpret the Basic Law. However, when the provision was drafted in the 1980s, constitutional review was not anticipated by the central government of China, and the understanding of constitutional review was not well developed. This may have resulted in the relatively ambiguous formulation that seems to presuppose a particular authorization decision by the NPCSC before the courts of Hong Kong are entitled to review the constitutionality of the legislation enacted by the Legislative Council of Hong Kong. However, the correct translation of the phrase seems to be that the NPCSC hereby authorizes the courts of the HKSAR to interpret provisions of the Basic Law.[28] Any further authorization

[26]The common law approach for the interpretation of the Basic Law was established through the case of *Director of Immigration v Chong Fung Yuen* [2001] 2 HKLRD 533. See also Leung Mei-fun (2006), p. 30: "Since members of the Basic Law Drafting Committee were from China, a civil law jurisdiction, and Hong Kong, a common law jurisdiction, the final version of the Basic Law does represent compromise and co-operation of both legal systems." Furthermore, according to Leung Mei-fun (2006), p. 43, the Basic Law was mainly drafted following three principles, the principle of sovereignty, the principle of autonomy and the principle of stability and maintenance of the existing system. See also Chan (2010), pp. 130, 132, who underlines the political nature of the NPCSC and that it is not, in its interpretation function, an organ of an independent judiciary. Therefore, the interpretation of the NPCSC should be treated as a legislative act, not as a judicial decision.

[27]*Director of Immigration v Chong Fung Yuen*, *supra* note 26 in this Chap., at pp. 545–547, referring to extrinsic materials, including the Joint Declaration and the Explanations on the Basic Law (draft) given at the NPC on 28 March 1990 shortly before the adoption of the Basic Law, that is pre-enactment materials. See also Young (2007), p. 17. However, as pointed out by Ghai (2007a), p. 387, the use of a purposive approach is difficult, because "the *travaux preparatoires* of the Joint Declaration or the Basic Law are not publicly available, and protected under secrecy laws of China", at least not all of them. How much such statutory interpretation in a common law system differs from statutory interpretation by courts in a civil law system is an open question, but the difference does not have to be very great, because the Basic Law with its relatively detailed rules does not seem to open up very many common law dimensions in the area of the "constitutional law of Hong Kong". Granted that the Basic Law contains some typically common law concepts, such as the right to abode, most of the provisions in this piece of law do not display any great relationship to common law. However, there may be a quantitative difference between Hong Kong and Mainland China, as observed by Ghai (2007a), p. 401: "There are relatively few rules of interpretation in China (so far as one can tell) while the common law prides itself on a highly developed science of interpretation." See also Ghai (2009), pp. 21–49.

[28]According to Leung Mei-fun (2006), p. 54, the provision observes, on the one hand, "the constitutional requirement that only the NPCSC has the power to interpret the laws of China. On the other hand, it requires the NPCSC to delegate, so far as the Basic Law is concerned, the interpretation powers to courts of Hong Kong in adjudicating cases. Thus, the existing powers of the courts in Hong Kong in relation to the interpretation of law will be observed." See also Leung Mei-fun (2006), p. 246. According to Davis (2007), p. 88, both "the Joint Declaration and the Basic Law implicitly require the exercise of constitutional judicial review by the Hong Kong courts".

by the NPCSC is therefore not needed for the courts to interpret legal issues that pertain to the competences of Hong Kong.[29]

This is confirmed in Art. 158(3), according to which the courts of the HKSAR may also interpret other provisions of the Basic Law in adjudicating cases. Obviously, the other provisions are mainly such provisions of the Basic Law which are outside the limits of the SAR's autonomy, but within the powers of the central government.[30] However, if the courts of Hong Kong, in adjudicating cases, need to interpret the provisions of the Basic Law concerning affairs which are the responsibility of the Central People's Government, or concerning the relationship between the Central Authorities and the HKSAR, and if such interpretation will affect the judgments on the cases, the courts of Hong Kong shall, before making their final judgments which are not appealable, seek an interpretation of the relevant provisions from the NPCSC through the Court of Final Appeal of Hong Kong.[31] This means that the Basic Law singles out two excluded categories (CPG matters and matters involving the relationship between the CPG and the HKSAR), and if a need to interpret them arises in litigation, the Court of Final Appeal (CFA) has an obligation to request an interpretation from the NPCSC. When the NPCSC interprets the provisions concerned, the courts of Hong Kong, in applying those provisions, shall follow the interpretation of the NPCSC. However, judgments previously rendered shall not be affected.[32] In this respect, the normative position of an interpretation by the NPCSC seems to be close to that of a legislative act of the NPC, that is, the same lawmaker that enacted the Basic Law.[33] From that point of

[29]However, as pointed out by Po Jen (2007), p. 453, this may have repercussions on the status of the Hong Kong courts in relation to the NPCSC: "Therefore, since pursuant to Article 158(2), the power of Interpretation granted to the Hong Kong courts is a delegated power from the NPC, it is legally untenable for the grantee to possess the powers to override the Acts of the grantor." He also says on p. 453 that "the judiciary is therefore deprived of the power to invalidate NPC decisions for being inconsistent with the Basic Law". As pointed out by Ling Bing (2007), p. 633, under Art. 158(2), "the relationship between the NPCSC and the Hong Kong courts in regard to the power of interpretation is that of *shouquan*, which may be translated either as 'authorisation' (as in the official English text) or "delegation of powers".

[30]See Chan (2010), p. 131: "Yet the ambit of what is outside that autonomy is only vaguely defined."

[31]As pointed out by Leung Mei-fun (2006), p. 49 f., only the Court of Final Appeal is under a clear obligation to seek an interpretation from the NPCSC under certain circumstances, but the lower courts do not have a clear obligation in this respect, which could in practice result in a situation where "the power of interpretation by the courts in Hong Kong may go beyond what is stipulated by the Basic Law". See also Young (2007), p. 18. The obligation to seek interpretation is akin to the mechanism of preliminary rulings in the European Community, which system may have served as a prototype for the drafters of the Basic Law. See Hualing et al. (2007), p. 7, and Lo (2007), p. 164 ff. However, Ghai (2007b), p. 128, regards this analogy inappropriate, because the NPCSC is part of a power-structure of a Socialist state governed under the principle of democratic centralism.

[32]See also Leung Mei-fun (2006), p. 46.

[33]See Chan (2010), p. 132.

view, the presence of a supremacy doctrine might be indicated, something that in a common law system of British provenance would place the courts under the sovereignty of the lawmaker.

The NPCSC has, between 1 July 1997 and 2010, issued only three interpretations concerning the Basic Law, and the Court of Final Appeal has not yet asked the NPCSC for any interpretations: "One was in response to a CFA ruling, on the request of the Government of the HKSAR; the second was issued without any court proceedings having been instituted but in the midst of a public debate about the pace of democratization in the region; and the third was made in anticipation of the commencement of legal proceedings on the issue of the term of office of a new chief executive."[34] Although requests of interpretation have not been presented by the CFA, the interpretations have touched upon the independence and jurisdiction of the courts in the HKSAR and upon the true extent of the region's autonomy.[35] This is, naturally, a source of concern, because the requests for interpretations within the general powers of the NPCSC may come from executive or non-judicial organs, including the State Council, the Central Military Committee, the Supreme People's Procuratorate and all special committees of the NPCSC (such as the Legislative Affairs Commission). The Supreme People's Court is also entitled to request an interpretation.[36]

The Basic Law creates a particular body, the Basic Law Committee, to assist the NPCSC in the interpretation of the Basic Law as a permanent committee. When instances of interpretation arise, the NPCSC shall consult its Committee for the Basic Law of the Hong Kong Special Administrative Region before rendering an interpretation of the Basic Law. The Basic Law thus contains an obligation to consult the Basic Law Committee, and because half the membership of the Basic Law Committee is from Hong Kong, it should be possible for the viewpoints of Hong Kong to be taken into account when decisions about the interpretation of the Basic Law are made. It seems, however, that the NPCSC (and, consequently, the Basic Law Committee) has not been requested to exercise its power of interpretation frequently, and so far, only three interpretations concerning the HKSAR have

[34] Hualing et al. (2007), p. 4. For the texts of the Interpretations, see http://www.basiclaw.gov.hk/en/materials/index.html (accessed 22 August 2009). See also Lo (2007), pp. 157–164. For an analysis of the three interpretations, see also Cheung (2007), pp. 252–258.

[35] Hualing et al. (2007), p. 4. In addition, the NPCSC has issued two decisions on the time-table for broadening of the electoral rights in relation to the elections of the Chief Executive and the Legislative Council, confined to Annexes I and II of the Basic Law, where the NPCSC is given an express role in the procedure of amending the electoral systems (see below, Sect. 6.7.1). However, these decisions, although they are authoritative, should be distinguished from the interpretations, because the decisions are confined to specific areas, whereas the interpretations may touch upon a multitude of matters in the relationship between Mainland China and the HKSAR.

[36] See Yang (2008), pp. 265, 279. This means that it should not be too difficult to persuade one of the organs of public power to approach the NPCSC with a request is a controversy about the application of the Basic Law emerges.

been issued.[37] The Basic Law Committee also has a role in the Basic Law's amendment procedures. Consequently, the Basic Law Committee might be viewed as a guardian of the Basic Law and of the status of the HKSAR, albeit within its institutional limits as a committee of the NPCSC.[38] Hong Kong is not the only sub-state entity where the interpretation of the relevant legislative instruments is placed in the hands of both a political and a judicial body. The Åland Islands and also Scotland display such mechanisms.

5.3 The Åland Islands: Two Enumerations

5.3.1 From Residual to Enumerated Powers

Section 75(2) of the Constitution of Finland contains a recognition of the fact that two legislatures exist in Finland, the Parliament of Finland, on the one hand, and the Legislative Assembly of the Åland Islands, on the other, because the section lays down that the enactment of acts passed by the Legislative Assembly of the Åland Islands is governed by the provisions of the Self-Government Act. Under the 1991 Self-Government Act, this distribution of legislative competence is established by means of an enumeration of two spheres of legislative competence, one for the Legislative Assembly of the Åland Islands and another for the Parliament of Finland. Neither the constitutional recognition nor the double enumeration formed a part of the original arrangement in 1920–1922.

Originally, the distribution of powers was fashioned in a more "federal" manner in the 1920 Self-Government Act so that the legislative powers of the Parliament of Finland for the purposes of producing legal norms for the jurisdiction of Åland were enumerated, while the legislative powers of the Legislative Assembly of the Åland Islands were of a residual nature.[39] This attribution changed in the 1951 Self-Government Act so that the lawmaking powers of both legislatures were

[37]The interpretation power of the NPCSC is in principle a regular feature of the Chinese legal order, extending itself to any legislation in effect in Mainland China, but the power has, since 1949, not been used very much. See Leung Mei-fun (2006), p. 39. See also Yang (2008), pp. 255–285, who makes the point that there is an emerging trend of the NPCSC wishing to blur the distinction between legislative amendment and legislative interpretation so as to make the concept of legal interpretation more powerful, while the interpretative techniques and motivations of the interpretations remain still quite undeveloped. On the Basic Law Committee, see Leung Mei-fun (2006), pp. 85–88.

[38]See also Ghai (1999), p. 180 f. As pointed out by Ghai (2009), p. 21, the Basic Law Committee might be regarded as a quasi-judicial body when it is consulted for the purposes of implementing Art. 17 (return of an Ordinance by the NPCSC to Hong Kong), Art. 18 (adding or deleting a national law in the list of Annex III), Art. 158 (interpreting the Basic Law) and Art. 159 (amending the Basic Law).

[39]Suksi (2005d), p. 172.

enumerated, and this is also the point of departure in the 1991 Self-Government Act. From a practical point of view, the shift in the strategy concerning the distribution of legislative powers was probably not very dramatic, but from the point of view of principle, the issue is of some importance, because the arrangement indicates that a preemption of some sort was built into the 1920 Self-Government Act. Generally speaking, therefore, it is not always beneficial to operate under the assumption that a residual competence for the sub-state entity is a better option, because such a "residual" point of departure may open up the need to recognize or accept a smaller or a greater window for national preemption.

The main problem with the original determination of the legislative competences was that the practical operation of paras. 12 and 13 in section 9(2) of the 1920 Self-Government Act introduced unforeseen limitations to the competence of the Åland Islands. According to para. 12, the competence of the Parliament of Finland included such issues that were regulated through international treaties. Today, such a provision would, in the highly internationalized normative environment, have seriously threatened the legislative competence of Åland and transferred competence to the Parliament of Finland. In para. 13, the Parliament of Finland was given legislative competence in such areas which had not been normatively regulated in an ordinary act by the time of the enactment of the 1920 Self-Government Act. This would have affected great parts of such modern activities and issues that have been invented or surfaced later on, and as a consequence, the regulation of new activities and issues would automatically have been placed within the legislative competence of the Parliament of Finland. In retrospect, it is possible to conclude that the legislative competence of the Åland Islands would have been severely circumscribed and exposed to a continuous leakage of competence in the direction of the Parliament of Finland.

With such a definition of the competence of Åland that existed between 1920 and 1951, the legislative competence of the Åland Islands would today have been much more limited, while the legislative competence of the Parliament of Finland in the territorial jurisdiction of the Åland Islands would have been much broader. It was therefore in the interests of the Åland Islands to develop another system of distribution of legislative powers, and proposals in that direction were made as early as 1946. The technique of enumeration of the legislative powers of both legislatures resolved the problematic issues, but when the 1951 Self-Government Act was being drafted, it was also recognized that the transition to a new system involving an enumeration of the competences of both legislatures could lead to new disputes concerning the interpretation of the competence line. Eventually, section 11 of the 1951 Self-Government Act listed the substantive areas in which the legislative power in regard of the jurisdiction of Åland would rest with the Parliament of Finland, while section 13 listed those substantive areas where the legislative power could be exercised by the Legislative Assembly of the Åland Islands.[40] This enumeration of the two spheres of competence is actually a method for the

[40]Suksi (2005d), p. 173 f.

division of powers followed in the Canadian federation, where both the powers of the federation and those of the provinces are based on enumeration.[41]

The 1991 Self-Government Act followed the principle of enumeration of both spheres of competence. According to section 17, the Legislative Assembly of the Åland Islands shall enact legislation for Åland, and the actual legislative powers of the Legislative Assembly are listed in section 18 of the Self-Government Act. The conclusion that the legislative powers of the Åland Islands are exclusive in relation to the powers of the Parliament of Finland means that the Parliament of Finland cannot, by its own enactments, fill a normative void within the competence sphere of the Legislative Assembly. Conversely, authorities of the Åland Islands cannot use legislation from the competence sphere of the Parliament of Finland to fill a void in the competence of the Åland Islands.[42]

This is also established in a number of cases by the Supreme Administrative Court. For instance, in SAC 2003:1, the Court concluded that in the absence of a provision concerning the self-rectification of an administrative decision in legislation of the Åland Islands, the Government of the Åland Islands could not, by means of a decision of its own, carry out such a self-rectification, and the provision in the Administration Act applicable in mainland Finland could not be applied. In SAC 1982-A-II-1, the Court stated that provisions which in mainland Finland were included in an Act concerning the steering of agricultural production had not been enacted in the Åland Islands within the legislative competence of the Legislative Assembly. Therefore, corresponding steering measures could not be undertaken in the Åland Islands. Hence, in concrete instances, the parallel existence of the two legal orders is based on mutual exclusivity, which does not permit the use in one jurisdiction of such norms that belong to the other jurisdiction.

The incapacity of the Parliament of Finland to enact legislation for the Åland Islands within the legislative competences of the Legislative Assembly means in effect that the national parliament cannot act on the basis of any principle of preemption in relation to the Åland Islands when enacting ordinary legislation.

Although the Legislative Assembly may exercise its legislative powers within the enumerated area designated for the Åland Islands, it does not have a general obligation to do so in relation to each matter established in the list.[43] Insofar as the Legislative Assembly has chosen not to adopt a norm that regulates a specific issue, it cannot be expected or compelled to do so, except in three situations. An expectation of enactment of legislation follows from the regulatory tasks that the Constitution of Finland places upon the lawmaker, in particular, in the constitutional

---

[41]There is, however, no evidence in the *travaux preparatoires* concerning the 1951 Self-Government Act that the Canadian model would have been considered in the context of the Åland Islands.

[42]See also Palmgren (1997), p. 88.

[43]However, see Jääskinen (2003), p. 16, who is of the opinion that the Åland Islands has, on the basis of the general foundational solutions in the Self-Government Act, a duty to legislate within areas that belong to the legislative competence of the Åland Islands if a non-regulated situation is considered unacceptable.

rights established in chapter 2 of the Constitution. Most of the several constitutional rights in the Constitution require the lawmaker to act in the area of a constitutional right either under a qualified legislative reservation[44] or a regulation reservation[45] or that it be under a duty to secure and promote a constitutional right, which amounts to a duty to undertake positive action. Each constitutional right is not of such a nature that it would touch upon the legislative competence of Åland and thus create an expectation of enactment of legislation, but the economic, social and cultural rights as well as the environmental issues are such that affect the legislative competence of the Åland Islands. Therefore, it could be argued that there are constitutional rights that require legislative action by the Legislative Assembly. In fact, at the level of constitutional provisions of this kind, the Parliament of Finland could, at least in theory, affect the jurisdiction of Åland by enacting very detailed constitutional provisions in those sections of the Constitution that apply in the Åland Islands.

Secondly, the Self-Government Act contains provisions that require the Legislative Assembly to enact acts of Åland, such as section 7(3) concerning particular grounds for granting regional citizenship, section 8(2) on the loss of regional citizenship in some cases, section 15 on the right of the Legislative Assembly to dissolve itself and call new elections, section 16 on the procedure for appointing the Government of the Åland Islands, and section 24(1) on the possibility to appoint individuals other than Nordic citizens to public office.

A third category of obligation to legislate in the Ålandic sphere of legislative competence follows from such EU law that takes on the form of a directive and that does not find any other normative channel of implementation than an act of Åland. If the EU norm that requires national implementation is not implemented in the Åland Islands within the time-frame specified in the relevant directive or if the implementation in the Åland Islands is materially incorrect, the non-implementation is, under EU law, interpreted as a breach of the EU treaties. Such a breach would result in a legal process in the EU Court where the European Commission would bring charges against Finland as a Member State of the EU (see below, Sect. 8.6.3).

5.3.2 *Competence of Åland Mainly in Public Law*

The Self-Government Act, apart from mentioning the governmental institutions at the autonomous level, leaves these institutions and organs to be regulated by enactments of the Legislative Assembly. It specifies in section 3(2) that the administration of Åland is vested in the Government of Åland and the officials

[44] A qualified legislative reservation limits the discretion of the lawmaker to the area which is mentioned in the relevant constitutional right.

[45] A regulation reservation imposes a duty on the lawmaker to create by means of legislation an environment in which the relevant constitutional right can be fulfilled.

subordinate to it. It further stipulates in section 3(1) that the population of the Åland Islands is, in matters relating to autonomy, represented by the Legislative Assembly. The members of this Legislative Assembly shall, according to section 13, be elected by direct and secret ballot, through universal and equal suffrage. Because only persons with the right of domicile shall be entitled under section 9 to participate in these elections, universal suffrage is implemented within that group of persons. In addition, section 17 of the Self-Government Act provides that the Legislative Assembly shall enact legislation for Åland. Thus the internal structures of government are determined by Ålandic legislation. However, the scope of the internal authority of the Legislative Assembly to pass legislation on these issues is laid out in section 18, according to which Åland shall have legislative powers in respect of the following issues:

> 1) the organization and duties of the Åland Parliament and the election of its members, the Government of Åland and the officials and services subordinate to it; 2) the officials of Åland, the collective agreements on the salaries of the employees of Åland and the sentencing of the officials of Åland to disciplinary punishment; 2 a) the employment pensions of the employees of Åland and the elected representatives in the administration of Åland, as well as of the head teachers, teachers and temporary teachers in the primary and lower secondary schools in Åland; 3) the flag and coat of arms of Åland and the use thereof in Åland, the use of the Åland flag on vessels of Åland and on merchant vessels, fishing-vessels, pleasure boats and other comparable vessels whose home port is in Åland, without limiting the right of state offices and services or of private persons to use the flag of the state; 4) the municipal boundaries, municipal elections, municipal administration and the officials of the municipalities, the collective agreements on the salaries of the officials of the municipalities and the sentencing of the officials of the municipalities to disciplinary punishment; 5) the additional tax on income for Åland and the provisional extra income tax, as well as the trade and amusement taxes, the bases of the dues levied for Åland and the municipal tax; 6) public order and security, with the exceptions as provided by section 27, paras. 27, 34 and 35; the firefighting and rescue service; 7) building and planning, adjoining properties, housing; 8) the appropriation of real property and of special rights required for public use in exchange for full compensation, with the exceptions as provided by section 61; 9) tenancy and rent regulation, lease of land; 10) the protection of nature and the environment, the recreational use of nature, water law; 11) prehistoric relics and the protection of buildings and artifacts with cultural and historical value; 12) health care and medical treatment, with the exceptions as provided by section 27, paras. 24, 29 and 30; burial by cremation; 13) social welfare; licenses to serve alcoholic beverages; 14) education, apprenticeship, culture, sport and youth work; the archive, library and museum service, with the exceptions as provided by section 27, para. 39; 15) farming and forestry, the regulation of agricultural production; provided that the state officials concerned are consulted prior to the enactment of legislation on the regulation of agricultural production; 16) hunting and fishing, the registration of fishing vessels and the regulation of the fishing industry; 17) the prevention of cruelty to animals and veterinary care, with the exceptions as provided by section 27, paras. 31, 33; 18) the maintenance of the productive capacity of the farmlands, forests and fishing waters; the duty to transfer, in exchange for full compensation, unutilized or partially utilized farmland or fishing water into the possession of another person to be used for these purposes, for a fixed period; 19) the right to prospect for, lay claim to and utilize mineral finds; 20) the postal service and the right to broadcast by radio or cable in Åland, with the limitations consequential on section 27, para. 4; 21) roads and canals, road traffic, railway traffic, boat traffic, the local shipping lanes; 22) trade, subject to the provisions of section 11, section 27, paras. 2, 4, 9, 12–15, 17–19, 26, 27, 29–34, 37 and 40, and section 29, paragraph 1, paras. 3–5, with the exception that also the

Åland Parliament has the power to impose measures to foster the trade referred to in the said paragraphs; 23) promotion of employment; 24) statistics on conditions in Åland; 25) the creation of an offence and the extent of the penalty for such an offence in respect of a matter falling within the legislative competence of Åland; 26) the imposition of a threat of a fine and the implementation thereof, as well as the use of other means of coercion in respect of a matter falling within the legislative competence of Åland; 27) other matters deemed to be within the legislative power of Åland in accordance with the principles underlying this Act.

The list of legislative powers of the Åland Islands comprises a total of 27 paragraphs. Because most of these powers are in the sphere of so-called 'public law', they clearly imply the need and the existence of a relatively broad administrative decision-making machinery in individual cases of implementation of the acts of Åland. In fact, the public sector of the Åland Islands appears, proportionally speaking, to be greater than that of the mainland, partly because of this 'public law' orientation and partly because of the independent Ålandic control over state grants to the Åland Islands. These grants saw a steady increase during the 1990s, resulting in a corresponding enlargement of the public administration of the Åland Islands.

Because the number of opinions by the Supreme Court in matters related to the competence control on the basis of the Self-Government Act is very high, it is not possible to undertake any extensive analysis of each paragraph in section 18 of the Act.[46] Therefore, the presentation here is limited to the Opinion of the Supreme Court nr 1339 of 22 June 2000 concerning the Act of Åland on the Police (SoÅ 49/2000).[47]

On 15 October 1999, the Government of the Åland Islands issued proposal no. 1/1999-2000 concerning police legislation for the Åland Islands to the Legislative Assembly which the Legislative Assembly adopted without very many substantive changes. The proposal was to a great extent based on the Police Act of mainland Finland, and probably for that reason, almost no explanatory text was attached to the various sections included in the proposal. The report of the Legislative Committee was presented to the plenary in the third reading on 20 March 2000 and adopted without a vote. The legislative decision was sent to the Ministry of Justice and to the Åland Delegation on 21 March 2000. The Åland Delegation issued an opinion on the Police Act of Åland on 11 May 2000 in which it found that the law was within the competence of Åland, with the exception of some provisions. As concerns the provisions which it found would fall outside of the competences of Åland, the Åland Delegation held that they should be ordered to lapse. As a consequence, the Ministry of Justice requested on 25 May 2000 an Opinion from the Supreme Court, which the Court gave on 22 June 2000. The Supreme Court stated that the substantive area to which police legislation belongs is actually divided, because the Åland Islands has competence on the basis of section 18, para. 6, concerning public order and security with those exceptions that are mentioned in section 27, paras. 27, 34 and 35. The Court concluded that some of the provisions that the Åland Delegation had found to be outside of competence were actually within competence, but found that eight provisions were outside competence, one of which was not identified by the Åland Delegation, but only by the Supreme Court. As concerns section 8(2) in the police legislation, the Court noticed that the Government of the Åland Islands could give, on the basis of the Consent Decree about Police Administration in the Åland Islands (SoF 828/1998), a civil servant the authority to carry out criminal investigation

[46]For a deeper analysis, see Suksi (2005d), pp. 167–247.

[47]For the entire decision-making chain in relation to the Police Act of the Åland Islands, see Suksi (2005d), pp. 121–148.

in relation to crimes that have a connection with the administrative branch within which the civil servant is functioning. The Court referred to the Police Act of mainland Finland, according to which only the Ministry of Interior can give a civil servant the authority to carry out a criminal investigation that has a connection with the administrative branch within which the civil servant is functioning. Against this background, the Supreme Court opined that the Government of the Åland Islands cannot be given the right included in the provision because it belongs to the legislative competence of the Parliament of Finland. The Court held that to this extent, there was an excess of competence in the legislative decision, but held also that a provision about criminal investigation in such cases could probably be included in a consent decree. Because the Legislative Assembly had been, as concerns the eight particular provisions, outside of its competence, the Supreme Court recommended to the President of Finland that the provisions would be ordered to lapse. In the decision of the President of 30 June 2000, the President used the partial veto to order the eight provisions to lapse, whilst also concluding that no other obstacle exists for the entering into force of the Police Act of Åland. The Government of the Åland Islands decided on 10 August 2000 on the basis of a letter from the President that the Police Act of the Åland Islands should enter into force on 1 September 2000, but without those provisions that were outside of the competence.

As mentioned above, the spheres of legislative competence of the Åland Islands on the one hand and the state (or the mainland) on the other are exclusive in relation to each other and based on the enumeration of powers. The lists of legislative competence are perceived as a more or less complete demarcation of the two legislative competencies, but reference is made to 'other matters' that are deemed to be within the legislative power of the Legislative Assembly or of the Parliament of Finland according to the principles underlying the Self-Government Act, indicating that for matters which are difficult to allocate through the listing of express competences, the question of competence may be resolved on the basis of a principle of affinity.[48] According to section 18, para. 27, the legislative competence of the Legislative Assembly comprises other matters than those listed in section 18 deemed to be within the legislative power of Åland in accordance with the principles underlying the Self-Government Act, while section 27, para. 42, makes reference to other matters that are deemed to be within the legislative power of the Parliament of Finland according to the principles underlying this Act. The provisions can be said to constitute implied powers of some sort for both the Legislative Assembly and the Parliament of Finland, but they have not been invoked to any great extent.[49]

---

[48]For an example, see the Opinion of the Supreme Court No. 3169 of 9 October 1994 concerning the holding of an advisory EU referendum, below.

[49]See Suksi (2005d), p. 242 ff., mentioning Opinion of 19 October 1996 on Ålandic legislation concerning forestry associations, which was considered to be within the legislative powers of the Åland Islands under section 18, para. 27. However, in Opinion of 21 March 1996 concerning Ålandic legislation on genetically modified organisms, the Supreme Court held that some provision in the legislative decision of Åland was outside of competence because on the basis of section 27, para. 42, the matter belonged to the legislative competence of the Parliament of Finland (although the Court admitted that some parts of the matter touched upon Ålandic competences). From the beginning of the 1970s, some seven enactments of Åland have been regarded to belong to the legislative competence of Åland on the basis of the affinity principle, while three enactments of Åland were outside competence because of affinity to the legislative competence of the Parliament of Finland.

What is particular in the case of the Åland Islands in relation to the ideal type of autonomy as exemplified by the Memel Territory, in addition to the enumerated powers of the autonomy, is that the powers of the state are also enumerated. Therefore, under section 27 of the Self-Government Act, the following issues are under the legislative competence of the Parliament of Finland:

> 1) the enactment, amendment or repeal of the Constitution and an exception to the Constitution; 2) the right to reside in the country, to choose a place of residence and to move from one place to another, the use of freedom of speech, freedom of association and freedom of assembly, the confidentiality of post and telecommunications; 3) the organization and activities of state officials; 4) foreign relations, subject to the provisions of chapters 9 and 9 a; 5) the flag and coat of arms of the state and the use thereof, with the exceptions provided by section 18, para. 3; 6) surname and forename, guardianship, the declaration of the legal death of a person; 7) marriage and family relations, the juridical status of children, adoption and inheritance, with the exceptions provided by section 10; 8) associations and foundations, companies and other private corporations, the keeping of accounts; 9) the nationwide general preconditions on the right of foreigners and foreign corporations to own and possess real property and shares of stock and to practice a trade; 10) copyright, patent, copyright of design and trademark, unfair business practices, promotion of competition, consumer protection; 11) insurance contracts; 12) foreign trade; 13) merchant shipping and shipping lanes; 14) aviation; 15) the prices of agricultural and fishing industry products and the promotion of the export of agricultural products; 16) the formation and registration of pieces of real property and connected duties; 17) mineral finds and mining, with the exceptions as provided by section 18, para. 19; 18) nuclear energy; however, the consent of the Government of Åland is required for the construction, possession and operation of a nuclear power plant and the handling and stockpiling of materials therefore in Åland; 19) units, gauges and methods of measurement, standardization; 20) the production and stamping of precious metals and trade in items containing precious metals; 21) labor law, with the exception of the collective agreements on the salaries of the Åland and municipal officials, and subject to the provisions of section 29, paragraph 1, para. 6, and section 29, para. 2; 22) criminal law, with the exceptions provided by section 18, para. 25; 23) judicial proceedings, subject to the provisions of sections 25 and 26; preliminary investigations, the enforcement of convictions and sentences and the extradition of offenders; 24) the administrative deprivation of personal liberty; 25) the Church Code and other legislation relating to religious communities, the right to hold a public office regardless of creed; 26) citizenship, legislation on aliens, passports; 27) firearms and ammunition; 28) civil defense; however, the decision to evacuate residents of Åland to a place outside Åland may only be made with the consent of the Government of Åland; 29) human contagious diseases, castration and sterilization, abortion, artificial insemination, forensic medical investigations; 30) the qualifications of persons involved in health care and nursing, the pharmacy service, medicines and pharmaceutical products, drugs and the production of poisons and the determination of the uses thereof; 31) contagious diseases in pets and livestock; 32) the prohibition of the import of animals and animal products; 33) the prevention of substances destructive to plants from entering the country; 34) the armed forces and the border guards, subject to the provisions of section 12, the actions of the authorities to ensure the security of the state, state of defense, readiness for a state of emergency; 35) explosive substances, as to the part relating to state security; 36) taxes and dues, with the exceptions provided by section 18, para. 5; 37) the issuance of paper money, foreign currencies; 38) statistics necessary for the state; 39) archive material derived from state officials, subject to the provisions of section 30, para. 17; 40) telecommunications; however, a state official may only grant permission to engage in general telecommunications in Åland with the consent of the Government of Åland; 41) the other matters under private law not specifically mentioned in this section, unless the matters relate directly to an area of legislation within

the competence of Åland according to this Act; 42) other matters that are deemed to be within the legislative power of the Parliament of Finland according to the principles underlying this Act.

The legislative powers of the Finnish Parliament are numerous, and in addition to mainland Finland, the acts enacted by the Parliament of Finland within these matters apply also to the Åland Islands. As can be seen from the enumeration of the powers of the Parliament of Finland for the purposes of the jurisdiction of Åland, they are to a greater extent focused on rules that in the continental European doctrine are placed in the area of so-called private law. This is also sustained under para. 41, according to which other matters under private law not mentioned in section 27 belong to the legislative competence of the Parliament of Finland, unless the matter relates directly to an area of legislation within which the competence is on the Legislative Assembly. The presumption therefore in the jurisdiction of Åland is that private law is mainly for the Parliament of Finland, while public law remains mainly a responsibility of the Legislative Assembly of the Åland Islands. In addition, the presumption of competence for the Parliament of Finland is sustained in the area of criminal law and the deprivation of individual liberty by the fact that the general power of criminalization in respect of the criminal code is allocated under section 27, para. 22, to the Parliament of Finland, while the Legislative Assembly is empowered under section 18, para. 25, to criminalize conduct which falls within the legislative competence of the Åland Islands. As is evident on the basis of section 27, para. 23, the competence to regulate courts and the administration of justice is vested in the state, and therefore state courts exercise jurisdiction on the Åland Islands. Hence the administration of justice is provided for under legislation enacted by the Parliament of Finland. However, the state courts try cases not only on the basis of acts of the Parliament of Finland, but also on the basis of acts of the Legislative Assembly. This has functioned well, because the courts are, naturally, independent in relation to both the Åland Islands and the state of Finland.

The Parliament of Finland also holds the legislative powers in respect of the Åland Islands in matters that are listed in section 29(1) of the Self-Government Act, but contrary to the matters listed in section 27, the matters listed in section 29 can be transferred from the Parliament of Finland to the Legislative Assembly of the Åland Islands by means of ordinary legislation. These matters are as follows: (1) the population registers; (2) the trade register, the association register and the shipping register; (3) the employment pensions of the employees of the municipalities and the elected officials of the municipalities, and the employment pensions of other persons, with the exceptions as provided by section 18, subparagraph 2 a, as well as other social insurance; (4) other alcohol legislation than that referred to in section 18, subparagraph 13; (5) the banking and credit services; (6) employment contracts, with the exception provided for apprenticeship by section 18, subparagraph 14, and co-operation in enterprises. The idea with the list is that with the consent of the Legislative Assembly, the Parliament of Finland may enact an ordinary act (requiring a simple majority) by which the legislative authority in these matters is transferred to the Åland Islands in full or in part. In spite of this more flexible manner of transfer of legislative powers, the section has not been used a single time. Instead, the limited adjustment of competences that took place in 1996 was completed through a formal amendment to the Self-Government Act. There is no corresponding mechanism of a transfer of legislative powers from the Legislative Assembly of the Åland Islands to the Parliament of Finland. In case such a transfer should need to be carried out, it would only be possible by way of a formal amendment to the Self-Government Act.

5.3.3 *Acts of Mixed Nature and Acts of Reference*

Although the Ålandic and the mainland Finnish legislative competences are exclusive in relation to each other, it is not prohibited for the Legislative Assembly to take in provisions from Finnish law. Under section 19(3) of the Self-Government Act, it is possible, for the purposes of achieving uniformity and clarity of an act of Åland, to include provisions in acts of Åland on matters relating to the legislative powers of the Parliament, provided that in their substance, they coincide with the corresponding provisions of an act of Parliament. The inclusion of such provisions in an act of Åland shall not alter the separation of the legislative powers of the Legislative Assembly and the Parliament of Finland.

Such inclusion of provisions from laws enacted by the Parliament of Finland in the acts of Åland results in the enactment of acts of a mixed nature in the Åland Islands. This "mixity" is a result of the fact that the exercise of legislative powers in the Åland Islands does not always produce clear-cut regulation of legal relationships within the Ålandic sphere of competence only, but spills over to the other side of the competence line. The consequence is that a part of the provisions that should be included in the act of Åland with a view to the regulatory logic of the enactment might not belong to the legislative competence of the Legislative Assembly. Therefore, section 19(3) makes it possible to enact coherent and systematically structured acts of Åland by using in the act of Åland such norms that belong to the legislative competence of the Parliament of Finland and that materially coincide with the corresponding norms in an act enacted by the Parliament of Finland.[50] The possibility to enact mixed legislation tries to ensure that an act of Åland is informative in relation to all those individuals and business operations to whom the act is applied. The incorporation of provisions from acts enacted by the Parliament of Finland into acts of Åland does not, however, change the legislative competence between the two lawmakers in any way. If a deviation from the competence has taken place, then the Legislative Assembly has made an incursion into the legislative competence of the Parliament of Finland. A deviation in the

[50] In Scotland, a similar result may be produced through adjudication of the competence line by courts. In Scotland and the UK, courts of law may interpret the purpose of a Scottish act through the "pith and substance" test so that a Scottish act is considered to be within competence even when containing a provision that belongs to UK competence.

choice of words only does not constitute a breach of competence unless it at the same time involves a material deviation from competence.

The consequence of section 19(3) of the Self-Government Act is that an act of Åland can contain provisions that originally have been enacted within the competence of the Parliament of Finland. In such a situation, the provision originally enacted by the Parliament of Finland continues to be applicable in the Åland Islands on the basis of the legislative competence of the Parliament of Finland. The further consequences of this become apparent if the Parliament of Finland amends the original provision, because then the provision amended by the Parliament of Finland applies in the Åland Islands as amended. At such a point, the good aim of producing an informative act of Åland is, of course, countered. In order to satisfy the need of an individual or a business enterprise to always receive correct information about the contents of legal provisions, acts of Åland of a mixed nature should be automatically amended if the Parliament of Finland amends provisions that have been incorporated into acts of Åland

As concerns the quantity of "mixity" in an act of Åland, it has sometimes been suggested that the proportion of provisions stemming from an act enacted by the Parliament of Finland should not exceed 50%. There is no such rule in the Self-Government Act, and the interpretations of the Supreme Court do not indicate that such a rule of proportion would be imposed in practice. However, there exist some opinions of the Supreme Court that indicate that Ålandic enactments that consist entirely or mainly of provisions that belong to the legislative competence of the Parliament of Finland cannot be passed by the Legislative Assembly.[51]

It is also important to take note of the fact that the Legislative Assembly may, within its legislative competence, enact so-called acts of reference (Swedish: *blankettlag*), which means that an act enacted by the Parliament of Finland is made applicable in the Åland Islands within the legislative competence of Åland by means of an act of Åland. The situation is in this respect different from the acts of a mixed nature, because the acts of reference are enacted within the competence of Åland. This method of enactment is often used to legislate on technical standards, such as foodstuffs, product safety, chemicals and motor vehicles.[52] By choosing to enact an act of reference, the Legislative Assembly has decided to apply the same provisions as in mainland Finland, and in such a situation, it is beneficial if the normative situation in the Åland Islands can follow the development of the provisions in mainland Finland. Typically, an act of Åland of this sort makes reference to the act or acts enacted by the Parliament of Finland by mentioning the name and number of the act or acts and declares that future

[51] See, e.g., the following Opinions of the Supreme Court: HDu 5.4.1963, HDu 19.6.1979.

[52] See also Silverström (2008b), p. 45, who makes the point that the implementation of technical EU directives may cause the Legislative Assembly to choose such a legislative strategy that directives are implemented by way of referring to the relevant state implementing legislation. "However, there are also many directives requiring Ålandic legislation which are not simple copies of State legislation".

amendments made by the Parliament of Finland to the act or acts will also apply in the Åland Islands.

The method of act of reference has also often been used in the implementation of EU law, because the short implementation period prescribed by an EU directive may leave such a narrow time-frame that the law-drafting mechanism of the Åland Islands does not have the time to react. In such situations, the Government and the Legislative Assembly of the Åland Islands may choose to enact the act of Åland according to the wording it received in the Parliament of Finland, which leads to certain savings in time and resources. The capacity to draft laws in such quantities as required by changes in the formal legal environment (the EU, international treaties) and by changes in society is, after all, limited in the Åland Islands.[53] Therefore, from time to time, acts of reference are used in a manner which incorporates by Ålandic legislative decision the contents of an act passed by the Parliament of Finland.

Sometimes, acts of reference are enacted by the Legislative Assembly so that they not only make reference to an act passed by the Parliament of Finland, but also contain one or a couple of material provisions, such as an exception of some sort to the act of the Parliament of Finland. In such cases, the act of reference actually becomes of a mixed nature, too, albeit of a different kind than the above-mentioned acts of a mixed nature. One example of such a legislative technique could be the Act of Åland on the Application on the Åland Islands of some Acts on Re-Districting of Municipalities (SoÅ 76/1997). According to this Act of Åland, the Act on Re-Districting of Municipalities (SoF 1196/1997) of mainland Finland shall be applied in the Åland Islands, but with exceptions specified in the Act of Åland. The exceptions mentioned in the particular Act of Åland transfer those functions that in mainland Finland were held by the Ministry of the Interior, the provincial government and the Council of State to the Government of the Åland Islands. In addition, this Act of Åland prescribes that costs that are caused by the implementation of the legislation on the re-districting of municipalities in the Åland Islands are payable out of the means of the budget of the Åland Islands instead of being paid from the state budget. The use of acts of reference may thus from time to time lead to normative situations which are not easy to understand for the individual or even the public authorities and courts that implement such acts of reference.

5.3.4 Bipolar Competence Control

Under section 19 of the Self-Government Act, the Åland Delegation, which is a joint body for different administrative and economic matters (see above,

[53]As pointed out in Silverström (2008b), p. 45, only eight civil servants are responsible for the drafting of legislation in the Government of the Åland Islands, which is very little in comparison with any Member State, although the volume of EU norms relevant for the Åland Islands is almost at the same level as the volume of EU norms relevant for a Member State.

Sect. 4.2.8), also has a role in the determination of whether or not an act of Åland is within the competence of the Legislative Assembly as stipulated by section 18 of the Act. After the Legislative Assembly has made the decision on the adoption of an act of Åland, that decision is delivered both to the Ministry of Justice in the central government and to the Åland Delegation. The latter shall, according to section 19, give its opinion to the former before the decision is presented to the President of the Republic by the Ministry of Justice. This opinion of the Åland Delegation is actually the first instance at which an external body exercises competence control, actually in two different ways, both in respect of excess of powers and in respect of problems caused for the internal or external security of the state. If the Åland Delegation does not find any problems with the competence or security issues, the Ministry of Justice does not normally refer the matter to the Supreme Court for an opinion, but presents the act of Åland to the President.[54] From the point of time when the Ålandic piece of law arrives at the Ministry of Justice, the President has a period of four months at her disposal to react to a competence problem in the enactment and inform the Government of the Åland Islands of her decision that there exist obstacles for the entering into force of the act of Åland in full or in part. If the President does not react within four months,[55] the enactment is published by the Government of the Åland Islands in the Statutes of Åland, after which it enters into force on a day specified by the Government of the Åland Islands.

However, if the Åland Delegation finds a competence problem or if a vote in the Delegation indicates that there might be one, or if the matter decided by the Legislative Assembly is new or if the issue is otherwise unclear on the basis of the Self-Government Act, the Ministry of Justice requests an opinion from the Supreme Court.[56] Such an opinion of the Supreme Court is not a decision in an individual case concerning a real dispute between individuals or legal persons, but instead an abstract opinion *ante legem* about the application of section 18 of the Self-Government Act,[57] perhaps in some ways comparable to the constitutional review performed in France by the *Conseil Constitutionnel*. According to section 36 (2) of the Self-Government Act, opinions and also other decisions that the Supreme

[54]See also Palmgren (1997), p. 89 f.

[55]As pointed out in Silverström (2008b), p. 45, the waiting time due to the competence control may result in breaches of EU law because of incomplete implementation within the prescribed time, which may be shorter than the time reserved for competence control.

[56]See also Koskelo (2009), p. 11. However, Palmgren (1997), p. 91, remarks that in practice, "problems concerning the division of powers are usually solved by more or less informal consultations between the authorities". Such consultations probably takes place when prospective the enactment is still being formulated into a Bill of the Government of the Åland Islands or, at the latest, while the Bill is being dealt with by the Legislative Assembly.

[57]See Koskelo (2009), p. 13, who makes the personal reflection as the President of the Supreme Court that in this review, "it is not always easy to understand how the new law is intended to operate in practice".

Court makes concerning the Self-Government Act are to be made in Swedish.[58] Opinions of the Supreme Court in matters of competence control in relation to the Åland Islands can be said to have binding status under customary law, because the President always follows these opinions,[59] although it has also been pointed out in authoritative sources that the opinions of the Supreme Court do not bind the President.[60] However, there is no administrative or political discretion in the decision-making (except perhaps to the extent the matter might deal with the internal or external security of the state, which is very rare). Instead, the President makes her decisions on legal grounds.[61] The President would not veto an Ålandic enactment, or parts of it, on the grounds that she felt the enactment was not in the interests of the Åland Islands or that the enactment was poorly drafted.

It is therefore possible to conclude it is the review by the Supreme Court that makes the legal determination concerning particular enactments where there is an excess of competence on the part of the Legislative Assembly of the Åland Islands. In such situations, the Court identifies those provisions in the act that it finds fall outside the competence of the lawmaker of the Åland Islands. Three main categories of cases appear in which the Supreme Court has had reason to propose that the President should exercise her veto: 1) the enactment of the Legislative Assembly is in breach of the Constitution of Finland;[62] 2) a provision in an

---

[58]For the procedure of drafting of the opinions of the Supreme Court and making decisions on them in the Court, see Koskelo (2009), p. 12: "The matters are referred from the plenary meeting to a three-member committee and are then presented in a department consisting of five justices of the supreme court. The person presenting the matter assists in drafting the opinion at the committee and department stages. The committee's task is thus to do preparatory work and produce a draft opinion pending its final adoption at the department. The differences of opinion that sometimes arise generally become apparent already at the committee stage. If necessary, the opinion is put to a vote."

[59]Suksi (2005d), p. 142. See also Koskelo (2009), p. 12, who concludes that to date, the president has followed the proposals of the Supeme Court and has generally also adopted the Court's reasoning.

[60]Koskelo (2009), p. 10. Koskelo is the President of the Supreme Court. According to her, the opinions of the Supreme Court serve as guidance, and although they are a prerequisite for a decision to exercise the veto, her opinion is that they are not binding. For such opinions, see also Suksi (2005d), p. 141, fn. 52, where reference is made to the *travaux preparatoires* to the 1991 Self-Government Act. Therefore, in the face of continuous practice that normally would amount to a norm of a customary law nature, there are significant denials of the normative effect of such practice. See also Koskelo (2009), p. 12, for the comment that at least in one case dealing with an enactment of the Legislative Assembly that limited the right of certain officials to perform public duties in the Åland Islands, the President of Finland has not uncritically accepted the position of the Supreme Court. Instead, while not vetoing the enactment, she expressed her view on how the law should be applied so that it is in harmony with the Constitution.

[61]As pointed out by Koskelo (2009), p. 10, "the supreme court thus does not express an opinion on whether the legislation is appropriate or comment on the quality of the legislative product".

[62]According to Koskelo (2009), p. 11, these are generally minor, inadvertent infringements and deal, for instance, with the lack of constitutional authorization in the enactment to pass subsidiary norms through decrees. See also Suksi (2005d), p. 246, where, in addition to this delegation issue, the issue of Ålandic regulation in the area of constitutional rights is pointed out as an area that relatively frequently creates problems in competence control.

enactment by the Legislative Assembly falls outside of the competence of the Åland Islands and thus remains within such a legislative matter that is within the competence of the Parliament of Finland;[63] and 3) the enactment of the Legislative Assembly is not in compliance with the legal norms of the European Union.[64] After having obtained an opinion from the Supreme Court the President of the Republic may, under section 19(2), order the Ålandic enactment to be annulled in full or in part, if she considers that the Legislative Assembly has exceeded its legislative powers or that the enactment relates to the internal or external security of the state. The veto powers of the President in relation to the Ålandic enactment are therefore of an absolute nature, while the powers of the President in relation to the enactments of the Parliament of Finland are, at best, of a suspensive nature.

After the entering into force of the current Self-Government Act in 1993, it became possible for the President to use a partial veto, which means that it is not necessary to veto the entire Ålandic enactment. As a consequence of the reform, in almost all instances where the President has used the veto, the veto has been partial and dealt with only those provisions in the enactment that fell beyond the legislative competence of the Legislative Assembly.[65] Combined with the empirical fact that

---

[63] According to Koskelo (2009), p. 11 f., these infringements are very rare, but because such new legal institutions are continuously created that were not foreseen during the drafting of the 1991 Self-Government Act, the Supreme Court has the task to determine whether the new area is comparable in nature to the competencies of either the Legislative Assembly or the Parliament of Finland. See also Suksi (2005d), p. 242 f., where reference is made to the issues of the Ålandic EU referendum and gene technology.

[64] According to Koskelo (2009), p. 12, Finland as a Member State is in breach of its international obligations if an Ålandic law conflicts with mandatory EU legislation. Because legislative power on issues relating to Finland's relations with foreign powers belongs to the Parliament of Finland, the Supreme Court has argued that the Legislative Assembly does not have the authority to pass laws that would place Finland in breach of a treaty, that is, in breach of its obligations as a Member State of the EU. For interpretations of the Supreme Court in this regard, see also Suksi (2005d), pp. 264–271.

[65] Since 2004, it is possible under section 20(3) of the Self-Government Act to pass into law and to promulgate such acts of Åland without submitting them to the competence control of the President that are related to the budget of the Åland Islands and that cannot be left pending during the four month period of presidential competence control. In such cases where there are particular reasons for the introduction of an act of Åland, the Government of the Åland Islands may decide that the act of Åland shall enter into force already before the President has had an opportunity to use her veto powers. If the President decides to use either the total or partial veto in relation to such an act that has been brought into force, the Government of the Åland Islands, the Government of the Åland Islands is under the duty to publish a declaration that the act or a part thereof ceases to apply from the day the declaration is published in the Statutes of Åland. This amendment to the Self-Government Act provoked serious criticism, because it could lead to legal uncertainty if a budget law were later repealed by the President. However, this possibility relating to budget laws has so far been used very sparingly and in a limited manner, mainly as a technical tool for adjusting levels of social allowances from the beginning of the budget year. The mechanism means that the Government of the Åland Islands declares, under an authorization of the Legislative Assembly based on particular reasons, that the act of Åland enacted by the Legislative Assembly is such that it shall enter into force before the regular competence control has been undertaken.

the President has exercised the veto powers in relation to 1–3% of the Ålandic enactments per year, the limitation of the competences of Åland is at a modest level. At the same time, the Legislative Assembly is politically active and interested in pushing the boundaries of its own competences. Therefore, at least some of the instances in which the veto has been used are likely to have been test cases designed more or less intentionally by the Legislative Assembly with the purpose of claiming new legislative "territory". When the veto has been recommended, the Supreme Court also formulates an opinion on whether the provisions that remain in the Ålandic enactment, that is, those which have not been found to be beyond competence, can enter into force.[66]

While the Supreme Court is in the driver's seat concerning competence control under section 18 of the Self-Government Act over Ålandic enactments before they are promulgated as acts of Åland, the situation is very different – and at the same time normatively confusing – concerning enactments of the Parliament of Finland. According to section 74 of the Constitution of Finland, the Constitutional Committee of the Parliament is the authoritative organ for abstract constitutional review *ante legem* of draft laws. While this normally functions surprisingly well, in spite of the fact that the Constitutional Committee is composed of regular MPs, including the one representing voters in the Åland Islands, the constitutional review may also touch upon the issue of whether the Parliament is within its competence as concerns the jurisdiction of Åland on the basis of section 27 of the Self-Government Act. This competence control is mainly done in respect of international treaties that Finland has entered into and that may or may not have to be consented to by the Legislative Assembly of the Åland Islands. However, from time to time, ordinary enactments are also dealt with by Parliament that may produce questions about their constitutionality in relation to the Self-Government Act. A case in point was the enactment of the Lotteries Act in 2001, where the Constitutional Committee formulated an amendment to the draft that it considered could be passed by the Parliament as an ordinary law. After being passed, the enactment was submitted to the President of Finland, who used her powers to seek an opinion from the Supreme Court on the matter. After the Supreme Court had established that the enactment encroached onto the legislative competence of the Åland Islands,[67] the President returned the enactment to the Parliament for reconsideration. The Parliament re-enacted the Lotteries Act with the same contents as before, thereby overriding the position of the President, but enacted at the same time an amendment to the Lotteries Act that entered into force at the same time as the Act itself and that erased the competence problem.

The constitutional convulsions revealed the bipolarity of the constitutional review as concerns the competence line between the Legislative Assembly and the Parliament and juxtaposed the Supreme Court and the Constitutional

---

[66] Koskelo (2009), p. 12.

[67] See Koskelo (2009), p. 16, for a cautious comment on the case 2001:79 of the Supreme Court.

Committee as the supervisors of the two enumerations. It is highly unusual from the normative point of view that different provisions of one act have different interpreters and that situations may arise where the two interpreters express positions that are contrary to each other. The inherent asymmetry of any autonomy arrangement is elevated to an entirely new level in Finland through the asymmetry related to the interpretation of the two enumerations of legislative powers where neither of the main actors is identified as the stronger one. The general principle of coherence in the legal order would, however, seem to require that one of the interpreters would be recognized as the one having the upper hand, and in that respect, it would probably have to be the Supreme Court in relation to both enumerations of legislative powers, not the Constitutional Committee, because the Parliament of Finland as a political body should not be recognized as having a superior position in relation to its counterpart in the Åland Islands, the Legislative Assembly. In spite of the confusing arrangement in terms of the control of the two legislative competencies, the system has functioned surprisingly well,[68] and it is unusual for the Parliament of Finland to try and interpret its powers in the territory of the Åland Islands in a manner that encroaches onto the legislative powers of the Legislative Assembly.

Although the legislative competences of both the Legislative Assembly and the Parliament of Finland are based on enumeration, in practice, however, only one of the enumerations is systematically checked for possible transgressions, namely that of the Legislative Assembly of the Åland Islands. Each of the enactments of the Legislative Assembly is first scrutinized by the Åland Delegation, and if problematic issues are detected, the Supreme Court is asked to deliver an opinion before the enactment is scrutinized by the President. This means that the competence control is, in practice, performed in a one-dimensional manner, as if the Åland Islands actually were following the ideal type of autonomy as a form of organization, with residual powers at the national level, because each enactment of the Parliament of Finland does not undergo the same scrutiny in a systematic manner for transgressions into the legislative competence of the Åland Islands.

5.3.5 *Making Ålandic Norms and Consent Decrees: Some Peculiarities of Norm Hierarchy*

Two acts of Åland of an internal constitutional nature are essential for the creation of the structures of government, namely that on the Organisation of the Legislative

[68] See also Jääskinen (2006), whose report arrives at the conclusion that it is not necessary to create any separate court instance of an independent nature to deal with the competence conflicts. See also Koskelo (2009), p. 17, for a comment on the questioning of the position of the Supreme Court after 80 successful years, concluding that there does not appear to exist any strong support for a modification of the system.

Assembly of the Åland Islands (SoÅ 11/1972) and that on the Government of the Åland Islands (SoÅ 42/1971). The Act of Åland on the Organisation of the Legislative Assembly of the Åland Islands determines that the Legislative Assembly is composed of 30 representatives and that they are elected by means of proportional representation from the single constituency of the Åland Islands. This Act also determines which standing committees the Assembly has and the procedures for lawmaking. As concerns the legislative initiatives, either the Government of the Åland Islands or a member of the Legislative Assembly may propose legislation. After review by one of the standing committees of the Legislative Assembly, the proposal is subjected to three readings in the Legislative Assembly. At the third reading, the proposal is either approved or rejected by a simple majority of those voting, except when the act is of an internal constitutional nature and requires a qualified majority. After the completion of the legislative procedure in the Legislative Assembly, the decision of the Assembly is sent to the Government of the Åland Islands for publication in the collection of the Statutes of Åland, and to the national Ministry of Justice and the Åland Delegation, as provided for in sections 19 and 20 of the Self-Government Act (see above, Sect. 5.3.4). The Self-Government Act has very few provisions concerning the lawmaking institutions and processes except that it prescribes that there shall be a Legislative Assembly and a Government in the Åland Islands. This shows that the Legislative Assembly is independently in charge of enacting the organisational legislation that regulates the position of not only its own functions, but also the functions of the Government of the Åland Islands.

Under section 106 of the Finnish Constitution, courts of law can, in individual cases before them, conclude that the application of an act in the case is in apparent conflict with the Constitution. If so, the court can, in concrete judicial review *post legem*, set aside the act and apply the constitutional provision directly, but the court cannot declare the act itself unconstitutional. In principle, the provision underlines the norm-hierarchical difference between the Constitution, on the one hand, and the ordinary legislation, on the other. So far, section 106 has only been used in a handful of cases, all of them in relation to acts of the Parliament of Finland, but it has been argued that this section could also apply to acts of Åland. Undoubtedly, from the perspective of an individual, such a position is completely justifiable. However, the different control mechanisms created in the Self-Government Act, which itself is of an exceptional nature, mean that it is not totally clear that section 106 is among the constitutional provisions applicable to the Åland Islands.[69] An amendment to the Self-Government Act clarifying this matter would be advisable, not only from a general point of view, but also from the point of view of the hierarchy of norms.

Under section 21(1) of the Self-Government Act, it is possible for the Government of the Åland Islands to issue decrees in matters that belong to the competence of the Åland Islands, provided that the relevant act of Åland has authorized the

[69] See Suksi (2005d), pp. 502–508 and sources mentioned therein.

Government to do so. However, the decree powers cannot be exercised in respect of the basic provisions concerning the rights and obligations of individuals and in respect of such matters that otherwise are of a legislative nature under the Constitution or the Self-Government Act. This means that the decree powers of the Government of the Åland Islands are relatively circumscribed and that they do not contain any executive prerogative to pass rules on different matters. The subordinate position of the decrees is emphasized in section 60 of the Self-Government Act, according to which such a provision of a decree of Åland shall not be applied which is in conflict with an act of Åland or with such an act enacted by the Parliament of Finland that is in force in the Åland Islands. This is a particular Ålandic provision that parallels a provision in section 107 of the Constitution of Finland for the purposes of application of decrees in mainland Finland. In this respect, section 60(1) constitutes an exception to section 107 of the Constitution of Finland.

In section 32, a particular normative procedure is established that normally should not affect the formal distribution of powers but that distributes administrative tasks between the Åland Islands and state authorities. The procedure uses so-called consent decrees, issued by the President of Finland after the Åland Delegation has given an opinion on the draft. The purpose of consent decrees is to make possible transfers of duties belonging to the state administration to administrative agencies of the Åland Islands or duties of an agency of Åland to the state administration. Such transfer may be agreed upon by the Government of the Åland Islands and the transfer may be arranged for a certain period of time or until further notice. If notice is given on an existing agreement by either of the two parties, the relevant consent decree shall be amended or repealed as soon as possible and in any case within one year from the date of the notice. Unless the decree is amended or repealed within the said time, the agreement shall be deemed to have been terminated one year after the notice. This means that it is the agreement between the parties that controls the validity of the decree. The mechanism of consent decrees has, however, some normative implications for the legislative powers of the Legislative Assembly, because under sub-section 2 of the provision, an act of Åland which is contrary to a consent decree shall not apply to the extent the act of Åland is contrary to the consent decree while the decree is in force. Here the principles of the hierarchy of norms are, at least to some extent, turned upside down, but in practice, the Åland Islands can always terminate an agreement which has resulted in such an application of a consent decree that raises competence problems.

Consent decrees are prepared jointly by the executive organs of the Åland Islands and mainland Finland, and they deal typically with such public functions that in one way or another leave the inhabitants of the Åland Islands without public services in certain matters that belong either to the legislative competence of the Legislative Assembly or the Parliament of Finland. Examples of matters where consent decrees exist are tasks related to the production of the list of voters for elections of the Legislative Assembly and municipal boards in the Åland Islands by the population registry authorities of the state of Finland and the emergency transportation of persons for medical reasons on vessels belonging to the Coast Guard. In these cases, organs of the Finnish state administration have agreed to take care of functions which otherwise are the responsibility of the Åland Islands.[70] The example of Åland already shows that the executive agencies of autonomies and the state may need to cooperate to achieve an expedient management of certain issues, but the relationship between the Scottish Government and the UK Government takes such contacts to an entirely different level.

5.4 Scotland: Lawmaking Against the Background of Parliamentary Sovereignty

5.4.1 The Pledge of the Sewel Convention

The Scottish Parliament is established on the basis of section 1 of the Scotland Act, while section 28 provides that the Parliament of Scotland may make laws within its area of competence known as acts of the Scottish Parliament, provided that Bills of the Scottish Parliament receive Royal Assent.[71] The Scotland Act also provides that every act of the Scottish Parliament shall be judicially noticed. However, an act of the Scottish Parliament is not law insofar as any provision of the act is outside the legislative competence of the Scottish Parliament, which means that courts of law may find themselves in a position of ruling on issues of *ultra vires*, and if a Scottish act is found to be *ultra vires*, it seems to imply that such an act has entered into the area of the legislative competence of the Parliament of the United Kingdom.[72]

---

[70] Decree on the Taking Care of some Tasks that Relate to Elections to the Legislative Assembly and to Municipal Elections as well as to Advisory Municipal Referendums in the Åland Islands (SoF 375/1999) and Decree of the President of the Republic concerning the Tasks of the Border Guards in the Åland Islands (SoF 420/2004).

[71] According to the section, a Bill receives Royal Assent at the beginning of the day on which Letters Patent under the Scottish Seal signed with Her Majesty's own hand signifying Her Assent are recorded in the Register of the Great Seal. The date of Royal Assent shall be written on the act of the Scottish Parliament by the Clerk, and shall form part of the act. The Scottish acts and other normative enactments by the Scottish authorities are published through Queen's Printer for Scotland, as established in section 29 of the Scotland Act.

[72] According to section 29, a provision is outside that competence so far as any of the following applies: it would form part of the law of a country or territory other than Scotland, or confer or remove functions exercisable otherwise than in or as regards Scotland; it relates to reserved matters; it is in breach of the restrictions in Schedule 4; it is incompatible with any of the Convention rights or with Community law; or it would remove the Lord Advocate from his position as head of the systems of criminal prosecution and investigation of deaths in Scotland. The question whether a provision of an act of the Scottish Parliament relates to a reserved matter is to be determined by reference to the purpose of the provision, having regard (among other things) to its effect in all the circumstances. In addition, a provision which would otherwise not relate to reserved matters, but makes modifications of Scots private law, or Scots criminal law, as it applies to reserved matters, is to be treated as relating to reserved matters unless the purpose of the provision is to make the law in question apply consistently to reserved matters and otherwise.

However, according to section 28(7) of the Scotland Act, the legislative powers of the Scottish Parliament do not affect the power of the Parliament of the United Kingdom to make laws for Scotland. Therefore, although the legislative matters reserved to the UK Parliament as defined in Schedule 5 of the Scotland Act are based on an enumeration, leaving the residual competences to the Scottish Parliament, it nonetheless seems as if the UK Parliament has kept to itself the ultimate residual powers even to overrule a piece of Scottish legislation, if need be.[73] In such situations, parliamentary sovereignty would prevail: the Scottish Parliament cannot prevent the UK Parliament from enacting a UK law. This means that ultimately and under the concept of the legislative supremacy of the UK Parliament, the legislative competences of the Scottish Parliament are not exclusive.[74] Under the Sewel Convention, which is a pledge of constitutional order in the UK system of governance, it is, however, established that "Westminster would not normally legislate with regard to devolved matters in Scotland without the consent of the Scottish parliament" (see below).[75]

The idea that the UK Parliament is supreme, albeit with the Sewel Convention exception for normalcy, is confirmed by a Memorandum of Understanding between the UK Government and the devolved administrations from 1999. According to the MoU, the UK Parliament "retains authority to legislate on any issue, whether devolved or not. It is ultimately for Parliament to decide what use to make of that power. However, the UK Government will proceed in accordance with the convention that the UK Parliament would not normally legislate with regard to devolved matters except with the agreement of the devolved legislature. (...)".[76] At its most extreme, the supremacy of the UK Parliament can be expressed by saying that by passing an act, the UK Parliament can "override or nullify any act of the Scottish Parliament and if the Scottish Parliament refuses to pass an act which the

[73]As pointed out by Bogdanor (1999), p. 202, "[t]he Act thus, in theory at least, preserves parliamentary supremacy, and Westminster can, if it wishes, continue to legislate on matters devolved to Scotland". However, Bogdanor (1999), pp. 287–294, expresses strong reservations about the political and even constitutional capability of the UK Parliament to do so, leading the reader to the conclusion that the UK Parliament is not anymore sovereign. "This is because it does more than devolve powers. It divides the power to legislate for Scotland between Westminster and Edinburgh (...)." See also Pilkington (2002), p. 98, and Hazell (2005a), p. 299, who makes the point that "Westminster's sovereignty remains intact, expressly preserved by the devolution statutes. The only respect in which it is fettered is by the Sewel convention, a self-denying ordinance which constitutionally Westminster could abrogate at any time". See also McFadden and Lazarowicz (2002), p. 5, according to which the UK Parliament has voluntarily transferred law-making powers to the Scottish Parliament without relinquishing its own sovereignty and without making the Scottish Parliament independent so that it would be free to make laws in any area which it chooses.

[74]Himsworth and Munro (2000), pp. xviii, 36 f.

[75]Lords Hansard text for 21 July 1998, column 791, at http://www.publications.parliament.uk/pa/ld199798/ldhansrd/vo980721/text/80721-20.htm#80721-20_spnew2 (accessed 12 March 2009).

[76]As laid before the Scottish Parliament by the Scottish Ministers, January 2002, SE/2002/54. See http://cci.scot.nhs.uk/Publications/1999/10/MofU (accessed 16 March 2009).

government at Westminster wishes it to pass, the UK Parliament will simply pass one for it"[77] or amend the Scotland Act itself.[78] Provided that a good working relationship and goodwill exists on the part of the central government and Scotland, "it is unlikely that the UK Parliament would wish to assert its sovereignty in this way".[79]

However, there is a possibility under section 30 for the Queen to make modifications to schedules 4 or 5 outlining the competences of the UK Parliament. For instance, she can, by an Order in Council, determine functions which are to be treated, for such purposes of the Scotland Act as may be specified, as being, or as not being, functions which are exercisable in or as regards Scotland. This seems to mean that matters reserved to the UK Parliament could be devolved by executive decision to Scotland, if need be, without modifying the Scotland Act. This procedure, which has been used quite a lot (perhaps mainly areas of competence where the two spheres meet), is intended to allow some adjustment of the distribution of powers between the UK Parliament and the Scottish Parliament in both directions, that is, from Scotland to the UK or from the UK to Scotland. The use of this mechanism requires affirmative decisions by both houses of the UK Parliament and by the Scottish Parliament.[80] By 2009, a total of nine orders had been made under section 30, with none of the orders transferring competence from Scotland to the UK,[81] which means that the section 30 orders were used exclusively to increase the competence of Scotland.

5.4.2 *The Area of Residual Powers Dotted with UK Competence*

The determination of the powers of the UK Parliament is done on the basis of two different regulatory strategies. Schedule 5 of the Scotland Act, on the one hand, enumerates the areas of law where the UK Parliament is competent to enact legislation applicable also in the Scottish jurisdiction, while Schedule 4, on the other hand, determines the provisions enacted by the UK Parliament that cannot be modified by an act of the Scottish Parliament, although such provisions might, in principle, exist in areas of law where the Scottish Parliament is empowered to act on

[77] McFadden and Lazarowicz (2002), p. 8.

[78] McFadden and Lazarowicz (2002), p. 85.

[79] McFadden and Lazarowicz (2002), p. 8. See also McFadden and Lazarowicz (2002), p. 84.

[80] See Gee (2005), p. 297, according to whom the mechanism has been used five times between 1999 and 2002. See also Himsworth and Munro (2000), p. 43 f. Himsworth and O'Neill (2003), p. 180, conclude that the mechanism has been used for minor technical amendments, but that it could also be used as a vehicle to make more substantial amendments to the devolution settlement as a whole.

[81] Serving Scotland Better (2009), pp. 45–46.

the basis of its legislative powers.[82] Therefore, in the territory of Scotland, two domestic legal orders co-exist, one determined under UK law and another determined under Scottish law.

As concerns the enumerated powers of the UK Parliament in Schedule 5 of the Scotland Act, they contain both general reservations and specific reservations. The general reservations are enumerations of subject matter, while the specific reservations consist of enumerations of legislation.

The general reservations contain, *inter alia*, the following: the constitution (the Crown, including succession to the Crown and a regency,[83] the Union of the Kingdoms of Scotland and England, the Parliament of the United Kingdom, the continued existence of the High Court of Justiciary as a criminal court of first instance and of appeal and the continued existence of the Court of Session as a civil court of first instance and of appeal), the registration and funding of political parties, foreign affairs (international relations, including relations with territories outside the United Kingdom, the European Communities and their institutions and other international organisations, regulation of international trade, and international development assistance and co-operation),[84] the civil service of the state, defense (the defense of the realm, the naval, military or air forces of the Crown, including reserve forces, visiting forces, international headquarters and defense organizations, trading with the enemy and enemy property),[85] and treason (including constructive treason), treason felony and misprision of treason.

Hence the areas reserved to the UK Parliament include the devolution legislation and the constitution of the Scottish Parliament, which cannot really alter the terms of devolution even for internal matters by its own enactments, with the exception of relatively minor matters, such as the enactment of standing orders.[86]

The specific reservations to the UK Parliament encompass a broad range of particular legislation and policy.

The specific reservations include fiscal, economic and monetary policy (including the issue and circulation of money, taxes and excise duties, government borrowing and lending, control over United Kingdom public expenditure and the exchange rate and the Bank of

[82]See also Himsworth and Munro (2000), pp. 38–42.

[83]However, the provision does not reserve, *inter alia*, Her Majesty's prerogative and other executive functions, functions exercisable by any person acting on behalf of the Crown, or any office in the Scottish Administration as well as property of the Queen and the Crown in Scotland and certain other entitlements.

[84]However, observing and implementing international obligations, obligations under the Human Rights Convention and obligations under Community law is not reserved, nor is assisting Ministers of the Crown in relation to any matter to which the reservation concerning foreign affairs applies.

[85]Except, *inter alia*, the exercise of civil defence functions by any person otherwise than as a member of any force or organisation listed in the reserved issues.

[86]Trench (2007b), p. 57. As pointed out by Trench, issues such as the number of members of the legislatures, the electoral system used, the nature of executive power and its relation to the legislature are outside devolved competence. Any change in them would require action by the UK Parliament. On the general reservations, see also Himsworth and O'Neill (2003), pp. 172–176.

England),[87] the currency (coinage, legal tender and bank notes), financial services (including investment business, banking and deposit-taking, collective investment schemes and insurance),[88] financial markets (including listing and public offers of securities and investments, transfer of securities and insider dealing), money laundering, misuse of drugs, data protection, elections (elections for membership of the House of Commons, the European Parliament and the [Scottish -MS] Parliament, including the subject-matter of the European Parliamentary Elections Act 2002 the Representation of the People Act 1983 and the Representation of the People Act 1985, and the Parliamentary Constituencies Act 1986, so far as those enactments apply, or may be applied, in respect of such membership, the franchise at local government elections), firearms, entertainment (the subject-matter of the Video Recordings Act 1984, and sections 1 to 3 and 5 to 16 of the Cinemas Act 1985 (control of exhibitions), that is, the classification of films for public exhibition by reference to their suitability for viewing by persons generally or above a particular age, with or without any advice as to the desirability of parental guidance), immigration and nationality (including asylum and the status and capacity of persons in the United Kingdom who are not British citizens; free movement of persons within the European Economic Area; issue of travel documents), scientific procedures on live animals, national security, interception of communications, official secrets and terrorism, betting, gaming and lotteries, emergency powers, extradition, lieutenancies, public access to information held by public bodies or holders of public offices (including government departments and persons acting on behalf of the Crown), business associations (the creation, operation, regulation and dissolution of types of business association (except the creation, operation, regulation and dissolution of particular public bodies, or public bodies of a particular type, established by or under any enactment, and charities), insolvency, competition, intellectual property, import and export control, sea fishing outside the Scottish zone (except in relation to Scottish fishing boats), consumer protection, product standards, safety and liability, units and standards of weight and measurement, telecommunications and wireless telegraphy, postal service, research councils,[89] designation of assisted areas, protection of trading and economic interests, electricity, oil and gas, coal, nuclear energy and energy conservation as well as road transport, rail transport, marine transport, and air transport.

In addition, there is an enumeration of "other matters" in the area of specific reservations, including subject-matter in the sphere of, *inter alia*, transport of radioactive material, social security schemes, child support, occupational and personal pensions, war pensions, regulation of the professions (such as architects, health professions, auditors), employment, job search and support, abortion, xeno-transplantation, embryology, surrogacy and genetics, surrogacy arrangements, human genetics, medicines, medical supplies and poisons, media and culture (including broadcasting), public lending rights, government indemnity scheme,

[87]Except local taxes to fund local authority expenditure (for example, council tax and non-domestic rates).

[88]Except bank holidays.

[89]As pointed out by Trench (2007b), p. 56, "[w]hile higher education is devolved, the Research Councils are reserved matters and subject to direction from the UK Government. This means that universities in the devolved territories receive a substantial amount of their funding from a UK source and not the devolved funding councils, are assessed for their research (but not for their teaching) by a UK body, and consequently may find it hard to respond to devolved priorities or policies". Although there in principle is a separation between the competences, some areas nonetheless appear to be characterised as concurring competences.

judicial remuneration, equal opportunities, control of weapons (nuclear, biological and chemical weapons and other weapons of mass destruction), time, and outer space.[90]

Evidently, based on the above enumerations, the powers of the UK Parliament are quite considerable in spite of the fact that Scotland at least in principle has been granted the residual powers.[91] Notably, social security is a matter which is kept with the UK and not devolved to Scotland.[92] It should be considered, of course, that the passage of time may introduce new issues that have not been considered amongst the issues involved in the devolution scheme, and it is possible that such new issues would, by default, be added to the devolved issues because they are not mentioned among the reserved issues. In addition, there are certain general reservations and identifications of shared powers (for instance, in cross-border contexts)[93] as well as "negative reservations", which make the point that although a certain subject matter has been identified as being reserved to the UK Parliament, some exceptions exist (for instance, financial assistance to industry) which may establish competence for the Scottish Parliament. It seems as if such areas could be described as shared competence. In fact, from the point of view of the supremacy of the UK Parliament, a case could be made for regarding the devolved area in its entirety as an area of shared competence.[94] In addition, it is also possible to argue that the supremacy and sovereignty of the UK Parliament constitutes a preemption power with regard to the powers of the Scottish Parliament.

At the same time, the issue of legislative competences is also approached from the point of view of the Scottish Parliament by way of negative enumeration by listing enactments and measures that are protected from modification by the Scottish Parliament or by executive decisions. Under schedule 4, related to sections 29 and 53(4) of the Scotland Act, a number of such enactments are mentioned. For instance, an act of the Scottish Parliament cannot modify, or confer power by subordinate

[90]On the specific reservations, see also Himsworth and O'Neill (2003), pp. 177–179. The specific reservations are arranged in part II of schedule 5 under a series of "heads" as follows: (a) Financial and Economic Matters, (b) Home Affairs, (c) Trade and Industry, (d) Energy, (e) Transport, (f) Social Security, (g) Regulation of the Professions, (h) Employment, (i) Health and Medicines, (j) Media and Culture, and (k) Miscellaneous.

[91]See also Trench (2007b), p. 64, who makes the point that the competence of the Scottish Parliament is general, and McFadden and Lazarowicz (2002), p. 7 f. See also Serving Scotland Better (2009), pp. 15–17, 158–214, for a detailed account of legislative competence of the UK Parliament with a view to what could be transferred to Scotland. The report identified some areas as suitable, such as some forms of taxation, administration of elections to the Scottish Parliament and rules concerning air guns.

[92]Serving Scotland Better (2009), p. 52. In the report, several references are made to the UK as a Social Union, the implication being that the social transferences from the central government to individuals living in different parts of the UK form one part of the glue that keeps the UK together. See, e.g., Serving Scotland Better (2009), pp. 63–65.

[93]On the cross-border public authorities, see Himsworth and Munro (2000), pp. 107–114.

[94]However, the report Serving Scotland Better (2009), p. 126, makes the point that there are only very limited areas of shared or concurrent competence.

legislation to modify articles 4 and 6 of the Union with Scotland Act 1706[95] and of the Union with England Act 1707 insofar as they relate to freedom of trade and to the Private Legislation Procedure (Scotland) Act 1936. The same prohibition exists in relation to a number of provisions of the European Communities Act 1972, provisions concerning the designation of enterprise zones in the Local Government, the Planning and Land Act 1980, provisions on rent rebate and rent allowance subsidies and council tax benefits in the Social Security Administration Act 1992, and the Human Rights Act 1998. The prohibition is also extended to judicial salaries, powers exercisable by a Minister of the Crown in certain situations, and the law on reserved matters (except when modifications are incidental to, or consequential on, provisions made which do not relate to reserved matters, and do not have a greater effect on reserved matters than is necessary to give effect to the purpose of the provision). In addition, an act of the Scottish Parliament cannot modify, or confer power by subordinate legislation to modify, the Scotland Act itself, except that it is possible to modify certain sections explicitly identified.[96] It is also important to recognize that within the area of Scottish legislative powers, the Scottish Parliament has the "power to amend or repeal existing Acts of the UK Parliament which relate to devolved matters".[97] A need to undertake such measures arises, for instance, in relation to such UK legislation which was in force within the Scottish jurisdiction at the time when the devolution arrangement entered into force on 1 July 1999. For reasons of continuity of the legal order, the point of departure was that such "old" UK legislation would remain in force until amended by the Scottish Parliament on the basis of its legislative competence.

After such a determination in the Scotland Act of a relatively detailed nature of the legislative competences of the UK Parliament, supplemented by the negative enumeration of matters that the Scottish Parliament cannot modify, it can generally be said that the Scottish Parliament is vested with the remainder of legislative powers, that is, the residual powers.[98] The material areas in which they exist are,

[95] As pointed out by McFadden and Lazarowicz (2002), p. 84, a "Scottish Executive dominated by parties in favour of independence, therefore, would not be able to pass a valid Act of the Scottish Parliament declaring Scottish independence".

[96] Sections 1(4), 17(5), 19(7), 21(5), 24(2), 28(5), 39(7), 40 to 43, 50, 69(3), 85 and paragraphs 4(1) to (3) and 6(1) of Schedule 2 as well as some other sections specifically mentioned in the Act. As concluded by Page (2005), p. 8, the Scottish Parliament has no power to legislate other than for or in relation to Scotland, in relation to the reserved matters set out in Schedule 5, in breach of restrictions in Schedule 4, contrary to the Convention rights or Community law and to remove the Lord Advocate as head of the system of criminal prosecution and investigation of deaths. See also McFadden and Lazarowicz (2002), p. 18.

[97] McFadden and Lazarowicz (2002), pp. 15, 17.

[98] According to Bogdanor (1999), p. 204, the abortive Scotland Act of 1978, attempted to create enumerated powers for Scotland. While the plan in 1978 was closer to the ideal type of autonomy in terms of distribution of powers, the current Scotland Act is different and moves somewhat toward federalism. See also McGarry (2010), p. 153 f., who thinks that the powers of Scotland may be defined in a residual way, although he seems to be in some doubt because of the reason that Westminster retains the ultimate authority to legislate for Scotland in all matters.

inter alia, education (both in schools and colleges or universities), the health service and public health, local government (including holding of local government elections, although franchise is a competence of the UK Parliament), housing and planning, personal social services, the environment, agriculture and fisheries, public transportation and roads, cultural matters, the courts and the legal system generally, and criminal law,[99] prosecutions and policing, all sustained by a Scottish budget competence.[100] Within these areas, the Scottish Parliament can in principle do anything that has not been explicitly forbidden in the lists of reserved matters and of matters the modification of which has been blocked,[101] except when the matters are also a part of the competences of the EU, as in the case of the environment as well as agriculture and fisheries. In fact, there have been policy choices in Scotland that at the level of legislation concerning, for instance, social policy, policing and criminal justice, local government, and education have led to some arrangements that are different from the corresponding arrangements in England.[102]

However, with the patchy delineation of the competence of the UK Parliament, creating "islands" of UK competence in areas which otherwise would seem to fall within the sphere of competence of Scotland,[103] there is a constant risk that the Scottish Parliament is *ultra vires* when legislating on various matters. Therefore, the Scotland Act contains a number of mechanisms for resolving competence conflicts, some of which are embedded in the legislative procedure and some of which are of a more judicial nature.[104] From a more empirical point of view, it

[99]According to Hazell (2005b), p. 230, criminal law has been an important area of Scottish law-making after devolution.

[100]Trench (2007b), p. 54. See also McFadden and Lazarowicz (2002), pp. 15–17.

[101]Trench (2007b), p. 51.

[102]Trench and Jarman (2007), pp. 114–116, who mention university tuition fees, abolitions of a criminalization of promotion of homosexuality, health care for the elderly and salary increases for teachers. See also Pilkington (2002), pp.115–129, 132–135.

[103]According to Trench (2007b), p. 70, "there remains a close relationship between devolved and reserved or non-devolved functions", and that "devolved governments can do little without affecting non-devolved functions", while "non-devolved matters have a huge impact on devolved territories in general and devolved matters in particular. He also concludes that within devolved matters, "what the UK Government does in or for England will have a major impact on the devolved administrations". Pilkington (2002), p. 119, concludes that certain anomalies stand out, for instance, that all health issues are devolved to Scotland except for abortion and that all matters related to culture and the arts are devolved except for broadcasting. He therefore recommends a reconsideration of the division between reserved and devolved powers. An effect of such reconsideration would be that the islands of UK competence inside the overall Scottish competence would diminish and the impression of a patchy distribution of competence would be mitigated.

[104]In the case of *Martin v. Her Majesty's Advocate*, [2010] UKSC 10, para. 2, five different mechanisms are identified: "section 31 (scrutiny of Bills before introduction), section 32 (the responsibility of the Presiding Officer), section 33 (reference of Bills to the Judicial Committee – now the UK Supreme Court – for scrutiny) and sections 98–103 and Schedule 6 (post-enactment adjudication of issues about legislative competence by the courts). A As pointed out by Bogdanor (1999), "the operation of the Scotland Act will continually raise questions about the limits of authority of both Edinburgh and Westminster. A constitution which divides powers requires

seems that the pre-assent abstract review of competence is not used very much (or at all between 1999 and 2005),[105] and the review on the basis of court cases relatively little, placing the burden of competence control on the pre-legislative stage that takes place in contacts between the UK Government and the Scottish Government (see below).

5.4.3 *Multiple Competence Control of the Scottish Powers*

5.4.3.1 Administrative Mechanisms

As concerns mechanisms of competence control embedded in the legislative procedure, there shall be, under section 31 of the Scotland Act, a scrutiny of Bills before their introduction by the member of the Scottish Executive in charge of the Bill. He or she shall, on or before introduction of the Bill to Parliament, state that in his or her view the provisions of the Bill would be within the legislative competence of the Parliament.[106] What happens if a Scottish Minister states that the Bill is within competence without it being so has not been tested and has perhaps no legal answer. In addition, the Presiding Officer of the Scottish Parliament shall, on or before the introduction of a Bill to Parliament, decide whether or not in his view the provisions of the Bill would be within the legislative competence of the Parliament and state the reasons for his decision.[107] This has happened on two occasions, but not in relation to Bills submitted by the Scottish Government, rather in relation to Members' Bills.[108] An additional pre-introduction competence screening by the Scotland Office has been put in place, too, which means that the UK Government

therefore a court to police the division". Devolution cases before the Judicial Committee of the Privy Council have, however, been relatively few, and the pre-assent procedure has not been used at all. See Hazell and Rawlings (2005), p. 6.

[105] Trench (2007b), p. 68, Gee (2005), pp. 260–265, who compares the pre-assent procedure with judicial review before the French *Conseil Constitutionnel*.

[106] See Page (2005), p. 25, according to which it actually is the Lord Advocate who clears executive bills for introduction. A minister cannot make a statement on legislative competence without such clearance, but the statement of the minister to the Parliament is normally very short and uninformative. For the process, see, e.g., Scottish Ministerial Code (2008), para. 3.3.

[107] According to Bogdanor (1999), p. 205, this mechanism is not without potential for complications: "It would be perfectly possible for the Presiding Officer to take the view that a proposed bill is *ultra vires*, while the majority in the Parliament takes a different view. It is not clear what would happen in the case of such a disagreement." Such problems have not been reported by Page (2005), p. 26, but if the Presiding Officer detects a competence problem, there may arise a need to rotate the bill back to the Scottish Government for amendments. See also Himsworth and O'Neill (2003), p. 316, and McFadden and Lazarowicz (2002), p. 55.

[108] Himsworth (2007), pp. 398 ff.

may actually get actively involved in the determination of whether or not a bill of the Scottish Government is within the powers of the Scottish Parliament.[109]

It is the Presiding Officer of the Scottish Parliament who submits bills for Royal Assent under the assumption that the Bill approved by the Scottish Parliament is within the competence of the Scottish Parliament. However, according to section 32 of the Scotland Act, he or she shall not submit the Bill for Royal Assent if the Advocate General, the Lord Advocate or the Attorney General could make or has made a reference in relation to the Bill under section 33 to the UK Supreme Court,[110] if the Secretary of State makes an order in relation to the Bill under section 35 of the Scotland Act, or if the Supreme Court has determined that the Bill or any provision of it is not within the legislative competence of the Scottish Parliament. At this stage, in practice, "[t]o ensure that no bill exceeds that competence, the UK Government's Scottish lawyers (in the Office of the Solicitor to the Advocate-General) examine each bill in detail, and check across Whitehall by what is known as a 'section 33 trawl' to ensure that the UK Government is satisfied that the [Scottish –MS] Parliament has not exceeded its competence (. . .)".[111]

[109]Page (2005), p. 27. According to Page, the "Office of the Solicitor General to the Advocate General ('OSAG') within the Scotland Office examines bills before they are first introduced, as well as formally when they have completed their parliamentary stages, with a view that the UK government has 'early warning of issues of competence of bills of the Scottish Parliament or actings of the Scottish Executive, and can engage in constructive dialogue with the Scottish Executive to address them'".

[110]Until October 2009, the referral was made to the Judicial Committee of the Privy Council. As stated in Serving Scotland Better (2009), p. 45, by 2009, this referral procedure has not been used at all. The Advocate General, the Lord Advocate or the Attorney General may refer the question of whether a Bill or any provision of a Bill would be within the legislative competence of the Parliament to the Judicial Committee for decision. The referring official may make a reference in relation to a Bill at any time during the period of 4 weeks beginning with the passing of the Bill, and any period of four weeks beginning with any subsequent approval of the Bill in accordance with standing orders made by virtue of section 36(5). He shall not make a reference in relation to a Bill if he has notified the Presiding Officer that he does not intend to make a reference in relation to the Bill, unless the Bill has been approved as mentioned in sub-section (2)(b) since the notification. Section 34 of the Scotland Act also provides for the possibility that the Judicial Committee has sought a preliminary ruling from the European Court of Justice in a related matter that has a connection to a reference of a Scottish Bill the Judicial Committee should deal with. In such a situation, the Presiding Officer of the Scottish Parliament may state that the Parliament wishes to reconsider the Bill and request the referring officer to withdraw the Bill from the Judicial Committee. According to Bogdanor (1999), p. 206, the mechanism puts the "courts and the Judicial Committee of the Privy Council in the position of deciding a question of *vires* in the abstract rather than in the context of a concrete case, without which there may be an incomplete understanding of the facts". According to Trench (2007e), p. 194, the devolution issues schedules to the Scotland Act "give the courts the jurisdiction (unusually) to consider the lawfulness of legislation between completing its Parliamentary passage and enactment, before it has had any actual effect". See also Himsworth and Munro (2000), pp. 45–47, Himsworth and O'Neill (2003), pp. 320–323, and McFadden and Lazarowicz (2002), p. 55.

[111]Trench (2007e), p. 185. According to Trench, so far "no bill has been challenged by any of these procedures (. . .), but this close scrutiny of legislation by another government indicates a

There are also openings for reaction at the central government level under section 35 of the Scotland Act, if a Bill contains provisions which a UK Secretary of State has reasonable grounds to believe would be incompatible with any international obligations or the interests of defense or national security or which make modifications of the law as it applies to reserved matters and which a UK Secretary of State has reasonable grounds to believe would have an adverse effect on the operation of the law as it applies to reserved matters. In such situations, the Secretary of State may make an order prohibiting the Presiding Officer from submitting the Bill for Royal Assent within four weeks from the passing of the Bill. Such an order must identify the Bill and the provisions in question and state the reasons for making the order. Section 35 of the Scotland Act is therefore central to limiting the legislative powers of the Scottish Parliament and preventing it from legislating on certain domestic matters so as to "influence the administration of matters reserved to Westminster in a manner harmful to the public interest".[112] As a consequence, the UK Government can, in certain circumstances, prevent the enactment of legislation by the Scottish Parliament. The Secretary of State for Scotland would presumably in practice have the leading role in this, and he could even be characterized as the "guardian of devolution",[113] although a good number of other organs of the public administration are involved in issues that arise on the basis of devolution. However, this mechanism has not been used even once during the first decade of devolution to Scotland.[114]

5.4.3.2 Judicial Mechanisms

As concerns mechanisms for competence control of a more judicial kind, section 101 of the Scotland Act could provide the starting point for an analysis. It gives a rule of interpretation to a court of law faced with a situation where a provision in a Scottish Act or a provision created by the Scottish Executive could be *ultra vires* (and thereby void according to section 29(1) of the Scotland Act): a provision is to be read as narrowly as is required for it to be within competence, if

surveillance of autonomy that is not to be found in many other areas of devolved government". See Page (2005), p. 31, who makes the point that no pre-assent references have been made. See also Page (2005), p. 27, who makes the point that "[f]aced with the threat of a six month delay to a bill and the consequent disruption to its legislative programme that a referral to the Judicial Committee would entail, it would seem that the Scottish Executive has preferred to move offending sections or redraft the legislation rather than invite the UK government to test its arguments in court".

[112] Bogdanor (1999), p. 203. According to Page (2005), p. 31, no such ministerial interventions have taken place during the first five years of Scottish devolution. See also Himsworth and Munro (2000), pp. 323–324, and McFadden and Lazarowicz (2002), p. 84.

[113] See also Himsworth and Munro (2000), p. 49 f., and McFadden and Lazarowicz (2002), p. 55 f., according to whom it is, in practice, the Secretary of State for Scotland who is informed about the enactment of each Bill by the Scottish Parliament.

[114] Serving Scotland Better (2009), p. 45.

such a reading is possible, and is to have effect accordingly. The point has been made that the main purpose of the provision "must be to urge a court to tend towards a construction of the Scotland Act which places a particular matter outside the scope of the reserved matters in Sched. 5 and, therefore, within the competence of the Parliament".[115] The interpretation rule asks thus a generous view to be taken concerning the extent of the devolved matters, which are of a general nature, as opposed to those reserved, which may be viewed as being of a special nature.[116] As stated in section 29(3) of the Scotland Act, a question whether a provision of an act of the Scottish Parliament relates to a reserved matter is primarily to be determined, subject to sub-section (4), by reference to the purpose of the provision, having regard (amongst other things) to its effect in all the circumstances.

If the interpretation of the Scottish provision does not have an effect within the reserved UK competences, it should thus be within Scottish competences and valid even in cases where a *prima facie* reading might bring it over to the UK competences.[117] Here, a so-called "pith and substance test" is elaborated: "[A]ny question whether a provision 'relates to' a reserved matter should be determined by reference to its 'pith and substance' or its purpose and if its purpose was a devolved one then it would not be outside legislative competence merely because it incidentally affected a reserved matter. A degree of trespass into reserved areas was inevitable because reserved and other areas were not divided into neat watertight compartments."[118]

In addition, there may at least in theory exist a situation where there is a valid Scottish rule, enacted within Scottish competence, and a rule in a UK law, applicable on the same factual circumstances, enacted intentionally by the UK Parliament but without consent from the Scottish Parliament. In such a situation, the UK Parliament would have enacted the Act with, for instance, the territorial description that "this Act extends to England, Wales and Scotland",[119] and a clear conflict would exist between the two norms. When the UK provision is intentionally extended to the Scottish jurisdiction, it can be argued that parliamentary supremacy

[115]Himsworth and Munro (2000), p. 125.

[116]See Himsworth and Munro (2000), p. 125.

[117]According to Trench (2007b), p. 65, "this is a form of a blue-pencil rule to preserve legislation which might otherwise be beyond the Parliament's competence".

[118]Himsworth and Munro (2000), p. 40, where a reference is made to a case concerning Northern Ireland from 1937 in which the pith and substance test was used. A similar pith and substance test is used in Canada. Examples provided by Himsworth and O'Neill (2003), p. 191, contain the following: "[A]n Act of the Scottish Parliament could legitimately affect coal mining, provided that its purpose is to prevent pollution. That Act could not, however, modify UK legislation whose subject matter is the coal industry." "[A]n Act of the Scottish Parliament cannot in principle amend the Coal Industry Act 1994, even if the general purpose of the legislation is to prevent pollution. If, however, the amendment can be treated as merely 'incidental', and 'necessary' to achieve the pollution prevention purpose, such an amendment *is* permitted."

[119]See Hazell (2005b), pp. 228–230, for a general explanation for the territorial extension of UK legislation.

should apply. However, the situation would probably be different if the UK law was unintentionally, that is, by mistake made effective in the Scottish jurisdiction. A situation that could produce such an outcome would be for UK legislation in the "islands of UK competence" within the general Scottish competence to be amended so as to become broader than the law currently is which would mean that UK law would transgress into Scottish competence. A court would thus be faced with a situation of the choice of law. While the Scottish Parliament is not sovereign, the prevailing doctrine holds that the UK Parliament is, and judges may "find themselves in the unfamiliar territory of reviewing *primary* legislation passed by a democratic but not sovereign legislature. That is, primary legislative outputs will be subject to judicial control".[120]

It has been pointed out that there is no rule on how to make the choice of law in the United Kingdom in such a hard case: "while there may be a belief that Westminster could oust devolved legislation on the ground that it is a species of secondary legislation, that has little legal basis."[121] From that perspective, the *lex superior* principle would not suffice, although the Scotland Act, enacted by the UK Parliament constitutes the legal norm from which the authority of the Scottish rule is derived. A proposal that has been made is to use instead the *lex posterior* principle, that is, that the later law supersedes the earlier.[122] *Lex posterior* is possible as a construction against the background of the fact that the Scottish Parliament has the power to amend such UK legislation which has been enacted prior to devolution but which is within the powers of the Scottish Parliament.[123] Therefore, if the Scottish Parliament has the power to influence the contents of an act of the UK Parliament, the Scottish Parliament should be in a position to enact rules in its own sphere of competence that set aside previous rules in UK legislation. A third proposal to resolve the norm conflict could be the *lex specialis* principle.

The *lex posterior* and *lex specialis* principles for resolving the norm conflicts are perhaps not suitable, because the source of law for application in the same legal situation is not the same lawmaker, whereby the question is returned back to the distribution of powers between the two lawmakers. Therefore, the *lex superior*

---

[120] Gee (2005), p. 279.

[121] Trench (2007b), p. 66. For instance, in the case of *Axa General Insurance Limited and Others v. Scottish Government*, [2010] CSOH 2, of 8 January 2010, paras. 88–145 (appeal pending), the Outer House of the Court of Session was of the opinion that an act of the Scottish Parliament is primary legislation in a way similar to an act of the UK Parliament and that it is not secondary legislation subject to judicial review on common law grounds except under very narrowly drawn circumstances. As a consequence, the common law argument of irrationality could not be used against an act of the Scottish Parliament but in the extreme situations of bad faith, improper motive or manifest absurdity (para. 142). However, the court pointed out that "if, hypothetically, a Scottish Parliament were ever to legislate in a manner which could be described as flagrant and unconstitutional abuse of power, it is to my mind unthinkable that the court should have no option but to hold themselves powerless to intervene".

[122] Trench (2007b), p. 66.

[123] See McFadden and Lazarowicz (2002), pp. 15, 17.

principle would nonetheless seem to be the most suitable of the three: because the Scottish rule that conflicts with a UK rule is found in an act of the Scottish Parliament which has been enacted on the basis of the Scotland Act, which in turn is an enactment of the UK Parliament under the principle of parliamentary supremacy, norm hierarchy will therefore dictate the resolution of hard cases that escape the narrow interpretation of section 29(3) of the Scotland Act by reference to *lex superior*.[124] Such an interpretation would give the existing UK law an upper hand in the hard cases[125] and would preserve the power recognized to the UK Parliament in section 28(7) of the Scotland Act to make laws for Scotland, something that has been suggested in some court proceedings.[126] What would save the Scottish jurisdiction is the declared intent on the part of the UK Government not to normally legislate within the framework of the Scottish competence.

The application of the *lex superior* principle in such a situation can be criticized, because it invokes, in the fashion presented above, the ultimate power of the UK Parliament to make a subsequent constitutional decision, although a court of law is trying to make a decision in a hard case that involves two rules of equal substantive validity: in principle, the UK Parliament can regulate the competence of the Scottish Parliament and remove it, but that particular consideration is not intended to take place at a point where a court tries to determine which one of the two valid substantive rules it should use to resolve a case. In such a situation, the *lex posterior* rule could, nonetheless, be the better one, because a court should perhaps not use the constitutional argument of *lex superior*, but instead leave that determination to the UK Parliament. A *lex posterior* position at an instance where a court resolves a hard case would not detract from the sovereign power of the UK Parliament to change, if need be, the constitutional parameters of the devolution arrangement.[127] This question is, however, difficult to answer in the absence of a written constitution.

The mechanisms of a judicial kind to try claims concerning competence turn on the identification of so-called devolution issues in court proceedings, that is, the identification of problems or conflicts between UK law and Scottish law that are of

[124]This interpretation actually finds support in section 28(7) of the Scotland Act, according to which the legislative powers of the Scottish Parliament do not affect the power of the Parliament of the United Kingdom to make laws for Scotland. Perhaps there could also be constructions along the lines of implied powers in the context.

[125]The praxis of the Judicial Committee of the Privy Council between 1999 and February 2009 does not lend itself to broad characterisations concerning the strategies of the choice of law (see below), because the Judicial Committee treated the issues as distribution of competence between Scotland and the UK rather than as conflicts of law. It seems, however, as if the Scottish provisions could, in many instances, be saved because their effects were not repugnant to Art. 6(1) of the European Convention on Human Rights.

[126]See Gee (2005), p. 279 f.

[127]Some support for the *lex posterior* principle could perhaps be found in the reasoning of the Outer House of the Court of Session in the case of *Axa General Insurance Limited and Others v. Scottish Government*, [2010] CSOH 2, of 8 January 2010, paras. 88–145, now in the process of being appealed.

a real, not abstract, nature. In addition, a devolution issue also arises if Scottish law fails to conform with rights guaranteed by the ECHR, or with EU law. The above-mentioned choice of law situations could produce devolution issues when the court chooses to apply Scottish law, while the disadvantaged party might prefer UK law. According to section 98 of schedule 6 to the Scotland Act, a "devolution issue" may mean six different things, the first one being the question whether an act of the Scottish Parliament or any provision of an act of the Scottish Parliament is within the legislative competence of the Parliament, while the remaining five pertain mainly to officials and functions of the Scottish executive.[128] As a consequence, a devolution issue deals with the material contents of action taken by a Scottish institution, making the range of possible legal challenges very wide.[129] Such devolution issues may arise before courts in Scotland or before courts in England and Wales, and in both cases, the rules differ from each other at least as concerns the names of the courts, although the general characteristics seem to be similar.

The UK Supreme Court can receive devolution issues before it on the basis of three different mechanisms. Firstly, under section 4 of schedule 6, proceedings for the determination of a devolution issue in Scottish courts may be instituted by the Advocate General or the Lord Advocate,[130] and the Lord Advocate may defend any such proceedings instituted by the Advocate General. Therefore, devolution issues may also arise in proceedings in which an individual is involved (in which case the Advocate General and the Lord Advocate shall be notified of the proceedings before a court or tribunal, whereupon they may decide to take part in the case). Secondly, according to section 7 of schedule 6, a court, other than the House of Lords or any court consisting of three or more judges of the Court of Session, may refer any devolution issue which arises in proceedings (other than criminal proceedings) before it to the Inner House of the Court of Session, while a tribunal from which there is no appeal shall refer any devolution issue which arises in

[128]"b) a question whether any function (being a function which any person has purported, or is proposing, to exercise) is a function of the Scottish Ministers, the First Minister or the Lord Advocate, c) a question whether the purported or proposed exercise of a function by a member of the Scottish Executive is, or would be, within devolved competence, d) a question whether a purported or proposed exercise of a function by a member of the Scottish Executive is, or would be, incompatible with any of the Convention rights or with Community law, e) a question whether a failure to act by a member of the Scottish Executive is incompatible with any of the Convention rights or with Community law, f) any other question about whether a function is exercisable within devolved competence or in or as regards Scotland and any other question arising by virtue of this Act about reserved matters." For a visual comparison of this set of issues concerning Scotland with Northern Ireland and Wales, see Gee (2005), p. 291.

[129]Gee (2005), p. 258, and Himsworth and O'Neill (2003), pp. 510–507.

[130]For a case that has been initiated through referral by the Lord Advocate, see *David Spiers, Procurator Fiscal v. Kevin Gerald Ruddy (Scotland) and Her Majesty's Advocate General for Scotland* Judicial Committee of the Privy Council, 12 December 2007, at http://www.privy-council.org.uk/output/Page535.asp (accessed 18 March 2009).

proceedings before it to the Inner House of the Court of Session.[131] Any other tribunal may, too, make such a reference. In addition, a court, other than any court consisting of two or more judges of the High Court of Justiciary, may refer any devolution issue which arises in criminal proceedings before it to the High Court of Justiciary.[132]

In addition to this possibility of the lower courts to refer devolution issues to higher courts, sections 10 and 11 contain the possibility that higher courts can refer devolution issues to the Supreme Court. Any court consisting of three or more judges of the Court of Session or of two or more judges of the High Court of Justiciary may refer any devolution issue which arises in proceedings before it to the UK Supreme Court (otherwise than on a reference under paragraphs 7,8 or 9). Thirdly, there is a right to appeal the decisions of superior courts dealing with the determination of a devolution issue to the Supreme Court. According to section 12 of schedule 6, an appeal against a determination of a devolution issue by the Inner House of the Court of Session or the High Court of Justiciary on a reference shall, under certain conditions, go to the Supreme Court. Most of the cases before the Supreme Court (formerly the Judicial Committee of the Privy Council) have arisen on the basis of appeals in Scottish criminal cases.[133] Apparently, there is also a possibility that proceedings involving a devolution issue could arise before courts in England or Wales, too, that is, outside of the jurisdiction of Scotland.[134] In such situations, similar referral and complaint mechanisms apply.

Finally, there is the possibility that proceedings in the Supreme Court of the United Kingdom, created by the Constitutional Reform Act of 2005, can deal with

---

[131] This reference mechanism is similar to the one that exists on the basis of Art. 234 of the EC Treaty concerning preliminary rulings of the European Court of Justice. See also Gee (2005), p. 266.

[132] The High Court of Justiciary is the highest Scottish court instance in the area of criminal law.

[133] See also Gee (2005), p. 267.

[134] According to section 15 of schedule 6, proceedings for the determination of a devolution issue may be instituted by the Attorney General., and the Lord Advocate may defend any such proceedings, and the existence of devolution issues shall be brought to the attention of the two officials. Under section 18, a magistrates' court may refer any devolution issue which arises in proceedings (other than criminal proceedings) before it to the High Court, and under section 19, a court may under certain conditions refer any devolution issue which arises in proceedings (other than criminal proceedings) before it to the Court of Appeal. A tribunal from which there is no appeal shall refer any devolution issue which arises in proceedings before it to the Court of Appeal, and any other tribunal may make such a reference. In addition, according to section 21, a court, other than the House of Lords or the Court of Appeal, may refer any devolution issue which arises in criminal proceedings before it to the High Court (if the proceedings are summary proceedings), or the Court of Appeal (if the proceedings are proceedings on indictment). The Court of Appeal may, under section 22, refer any devolution issue which arises in proceedings before it (otherwise than on a reference under paragraph 19, 20 or 21) to the Judicial Committee (from the end of 2009 the UK Supreme Court), and an appeal against a determination of a devolution issue by the High Court or the Court of Appeal on a reference under paragraph 18, 19, 20 or 21 shall lie to the Judicial Committee, but only with leave of the High Court or (as the case may be) the Court of Appeal or, failing such leave, with special leave of the Judicial Committee.

devolution issues.[135] Most devolution cases before the UK Supreme Court, which before 2009 dealt with them in institutional form of the Judicial Committee of the Privy Council, have originated by way of appeal from the High Court of Justiciary[136] and have dealt with the issue of whether or not acts of Scottish authorities and especially of the prosecutorial authorities of the Scottish Government have been in conformity with the rights guaranteed in the European Convention on Human Rights, in particular in relation to Art. 6 on the right to fair trial, with the length of proceedings as the most frequently occurring area of dissatisfaction. When deciding an appeal, the Judicial Committee has actually answered two questions, whether the matter is a devolution issue (that is, whether the Judicial Committee has jurisdiction to try the matter) and whether there is a breach of law. A majority of the appeals have been dismissed, which means that the claims of the applicants that either a provision in a Scottish act or actions of the Lord Advocate were in breach of the European Convention and thus in breach of the Scotland Act and, as a consequence, null and void, were not granted.[137] The mechanism thus also

[135]See Gee (2005), pp. 252 f., 255, for a description of appeals in Scottish cases to the Appellate Committee of the House of Lords. However, Gee (2005), pp. 260, 266, says that there was no obligation on the part of the Law Lords to refer a devolution issue to the Judicial Committee, because the Appellate Committee of the House of Lords could determine under the law that it is more appropriate that it should determine the issue. Bogdanor (1999), p. 207, has expressed doubts about whether the House of Lords, as a part of the UK Parliament, is a proper body to deal with devolution issues.

[136]By February 2009, out of 20 cases, only one has originated in the Inner House of the Court of Session, that of *Karl Anderson, Alexander Reid and Brian Doherty v. The Scottish Ministers and Advocate General for Scotland* (DRA Nos. 9, 10 and 11 of 2000, decided by the Judicial Committee on 15 October 2001) concerning administrative detention, raising issues under Art. 5 of the European Convention on Human Rights. The Judicial Committee dismissed the appeal, which was the first to ask that a provision enacted by the Scottish Parliament would be stricken down. See Gee (2005), p. 293, Himsworth and Munro (2000), p. xxii, and Himsworth and O'Neill (2003), p. 512 f. From 2003 on, the number of appeals to the Judicial Committee seems to have stabilised itself at a level of 2 appeals per year, although in 2008, there were no appeals at all. See http://www.privy-council.org.uk/output/Page31.asp (accessed 17 March 2009). As pointed out by Trench (2007e), p. 171, "[t]his is not because the parties to litigation consider that devolution issues are rare – between 600 and 1000 a year are notified to the UK Government, mostly from Scotland – but the law officers involved seldom decide to intervene (and those cases are seldom appealed to the higher courts)". See also Gee (2005), pp. 267–274, for analysis of the cases, making the point that the praxis during the first 5 years of devolution issues is looking for its direction and that focus on the Judicial Committee only is not sufficient in the context, because devolution issues arise in ordinary proceedings and can apparently also be resolved in such proceedings without reference to the Judicial Committee. According to Hazell (2005a), p. 299, the hundreds of devolution issues have "forced a more rapid harmonisation of Scots criminal law and procedure with human rights norms than has been the case in England".

[137]See, e.g., *Patrick Anthony Flynn, Peter Mitchell Meek, John Gary Nicol and Peter McMurray v. Her Majesty's Advocate*, Judicial Committee of the Privy Council, 18 March 2004, at http://www.privy-council.org.uk/output/Page472.asp (accessed 19 March 2009). See also Himsworth and O'Neill (2003), p. 518 f., and McFadden and Lazarowicz (2002), pp. 95 f, 98.

makes it possible to place a direct complaint concerning an act of the Scottish Parliament so as to create judicial review of Scottish legislation.[138]

The Scottish authorities have in most cases been found to be within their powers as determined by the Scotland Act, while a smaller number of cases were remanded back to the appropriate courts with the necessary instructions concerning the interpretation arrived at by the Judicial Committee.[139] It needs to be underlined that during the first decade of devolution to Scotland, no act of the Scottish Parliament was struck down on the basis of being *ultra vires* and no claims were presented in legal actions before courts claiming that the Scottish Parliament had acted unreasonably. This may well be interpreted as meaning that the Scottish Parliament respects the devolution arrangement and does not intentionally try to push issues that are on the other side of the competence line.

A first purely constitutional trial without connection to the ECHR arose in the case of *Logan and Other v. Procurator Fiscal*,[140] resolved by the High Court of Justiciary. The case dealt with the increase through a Scottish Act of the sentencing powers of the sheriff court in summary judgment from six to twelve months. The devolution issue was whether those powers were part of the reserved powers or the devolved powers, and the Scottish court concluded that the purpose of the Scottish provision was to make Scots criminal law with regard to penalties, procedure and jurisdiction in the sheriff court apply consistently to both common law offences and statutory offences. The modifications made by the Scottish Act to the UK Act on Road Traffic Offences "were merely incidental to, and consequential on, the more general aspect of the provision, which relates generally to the powers of the sheriff in relation to statutory offences, whatever their origin; and the modifications do not have a greater effect upon reserved matters than is necessary to give effect to that purpose of the provision"[141] in the Scottish Act. In another case, *Martin v. Her Majesty's Advocate*,[142] the situation was almost exactly the same and dealt with the same Acts and issues, but the case was resolved by the Supreme Court of the United Kingdom upon appeal against a judgment of the High Court of Justiciary in Scotland. It has, in fact, been pointed out that the *Martin* case is essentially an appeal against the *Logan* case, perhaps for the purposes of allowing an overturn of *Logan*. This did not take place. Instead, the Supreme Court decided its first

---

[138]See, e.g., *DS v. Her Majesty's Advocate* (Appeal No. 12 of 2006), Judicial Committee of the Privy Council, 22 May 2007, at http://www.privy-council.org.uk/output/Page535.asp (accessed 19 March 2009).

[139]See, e.g., *David Spiers, Procurator Fiscal v. Kevin Gerald Ruddy (Scotland) and Her Majesty's Advocate General for Scotland* Judicial Committee of the Privy Council, 12 December 2007, at http://www.privy-council.org.uk/output/Page535.asp (accessed 18 March 2009). See also Gee (2005), pp. 292–294, for a list of cases before the Judicial Committee between October 2000 and December 2004.

[140][2008] HCJAC 61.

[141]*Logan v. Procurator Fiscal*, para. 24.

[142][2010] UKSC 10.

devolution case soon after starting to operate in October 2009. In the *Martin* case, the Supreme Court materially speaking confirmed the result of *Logan*, although by means of a more elaborate reasoning and by a slim majority of three justices against two, which in itself indicates that the *Martin* case might not be a very clear leading case but that there might exist such uncertainty about the borderline between the two legislative competences that the result could be different in a future case.

In the *Martin* case, the Supreme Court concludes that it is for the courts to decide whether an act which is challenged is within or outside competence.[143] The attribution of legislative powers to two lawmaking bodies is, however, not possible so that the reserved and devolved areas would be divided into precisely defined, watertight compartments. Instead, some degree of overlap is inevitable, as is the case, for instance, in federal systems. Such situations would be resolved by using the so-called "pith and substance" test,[144] that is, a test that is designed to find out the "true nature and character" of the provision that was being suspected of breach of competence in order to "determine whether it was legislation 'with respect to' matters that were in the prohibited or permitted sphere".[145] At the outset, it was clear that the Scottish provision came into the area of reserved matters, as established in Schedule 5, Head E – Transport, section E1 on Road Transport, which contains, in letter d, the Road Traffic Act 1988 and the Road Traffic Offenders Act 1988. The Supreme Court, however, considered that section 29(4) of the Scotland Act "deals with a special category of overlap between reserved matters and matters which are not reserved that is in point in this case",[146] and made reference to section 126(5) of the Scotland Act about Scots criminal law that includes criminal offences, jurisdiction, evidence, procedure and penalties and the treatment of offenders.

The Supreme Court concluded that the Scottish provision under review dealt with penalties. In spite of this, it was possible that the Scottish provision would pass the boundary of reserved matters, and therefore, the "purpose" test had to be applied: "The key word here is 'consistently'. If the purpose is to make the relevant rule of Scots criminal law apply consistently to reserved matters and otherwise, it will pass the test."[147] The Supreme Court reached the decision that this was the case, and in doing so, it inquired into the purpose of the problematic provision in the Scottish act by studying the relevant *travaux preparatoires*.[148] According to the Court, the purpose of the Scottish provision was to contribute to the reform of the

---

[143] Para. 5.

[144] As pointed out in para. 15, the phrase "pith and substance" does not appear in any provision of the Scotland Act, although the phrase was used while the Act was being debated.

[145] Para. 11.

[146] Para. 18.

[147] Para. 19. Here, it is possible to discern a similarity with the acts of Åland of a mixed nature. See above, Sect. 5.3.3.

[148] Paras. 25–30.

summary justice system by reducing pressure on the higher courts by means of provisions that belong to the area of Scots criminal law. Thereafter, the majority opinion asked whether the Scottish provision had the consequence to make the law apply consistently, which it did both as concerns common law and statutory offences.[149]

Finally, the majority opinion asked whether the Scottish rule was special to a reserved matter. The rule that the overall maximum sentence for the offence is twelve months is special to the Road Traffic Act and thus a reserved matter of the UK Parliament, while the rule which determines the procedure under which the maximum sentence can be imposed is a rule about Scots criminal jurisdiction and procedure, which is not reserved. The rule that was modified was therefore a rule of procedure within Scottish competence, not the maximum sentence for the offence, which would be within the competence of the UK Parliament.[150] To alleviate any doubt, the opinion also invoked the principle of a generous application of para. 2(3) of Schedule 4 which favours competence, as opposed to an interpretation which applies competence narrowly, in particular as the purpose of the provision under scrutiny supported a conclusion that the Scottish Parliament had the competence to pass the provision.[151] In addition, the material rules that had been enacted by the UK Parliament were left untouched[152] and when passing the Act, the Scottish Parliament only intended to regulate the Scottish legal system,[153] not the UK legal system. Therefore, the appeal was dismissed and the legislative provisions enacted by the Scottish Parliament found to be within Scottish competence.

5.4.4 *Consenting to Lawmaking by the UK Parliament within Scottish Powers*

While the Scotland Act creates several procedures, both political and legal, for making sure that the Scottish Parliament stays within its sphere of competence,[154] it is striking that the Act does not address the issue from the point of view of the UK Parliament,[155] but leaves instead a very asymmetrical impression concerning the legislative powers of the two legislatures. Because the UK Parliament is sovereign

---

[149] Paras. 32–33.

[150] Paras. 34–37.

[151] Para. 38.

[152] Para. 59.

[153] Para. 66.

[154] See also Trench (2007b), p. 67, and Gee (2005), p. 257 for a graphic illustration of mechanisms for checking legislative competence.

[155] See also Trench (2007b), p. 71, who makes the point that the UK control of Scottish legislation is reinforced by the fact that there are no parallel mechanisms for UK legislation, and Trench (2007e), p. 180.

and does not limit its successors by way of positive domestic law, such as a written constitution, the ordinary British response to an issue of constitutional order is the creation of a so-called convention. Hence to remedy the asymmetry in the determination of legislative competences, the Sewel Convention provides a platform for establishing a consent procedure by which the Scottish Parliament makes a formal decision concerning legislative consent to a Bill under consideration in the UK Parliament that makes provision applying to Scotland for any purpose within the legislative competence of the Parliament, or which alters that legislative competence or the executive competence of the Scottish Ministers.[156] However, the process of legislative consent motions (LCM) by the Scottish Parliament is not a legislative process, but an agreement proposed by the Scottish Government that certain matters within the legislative competence of the Scottish Parliament instead be dealt with by the UK Parliament.[157]

The Sewel Convention establishes a mechanism that at least to some extent corrects the asymmetry created in the Scotland Act and thus respects the position of the Scottish Parliament, but it seems that situations where consent is necessary arise relatively often.[158] Therefore, those instances are relatively frequent where the UK Parliament may feel a need to have to act outside of the Sewel concept of "normally" and pass legislation which is within the legislative competences of

[156] Rule 9B.1. of the Standing Orders of the Scottish Parliament. For the entire procedure of legislative consent, see also rules 9B.2. and 9B.3.

[157] Winetrobe (2005), p. 49. For summarizing criticism, see Winetrobe (2005), p. 50, Himsworth and O'Neill (2003), pp. 195–199. According to Winetrobe, there is an assurance on the part of the UK Government after the grant of consent by the Scottish Parliament "that (a) any subsequent legislation will be properly scrutinised at Westminster, and (b), in this task, Scotland's MPs will play a central role, just as they would when participating in scrutiny of legislation covering non-devolved matters, or as they did with legislation affecting Scotland prior to devolution". This assurance has not, however, materialized in full. For critical points of view, see Winetrobe (2005), pp. 50–58. A mechanism similar to the Sewel Convention exists for Nevis in St. Kitts and Nevis (see Sect. 3.5.3 above).

[158] During the 2008–2009 Session of the Scottish Parliament, legislative consent was decided, *inter alia*, in relation to the following bills in the UK Parliament: Apprenticeships, Skills, Children and Learning Bill, Borders, Citizenship and Immigration [HL] Bill, Coroners and Justice Bill, Local Democracy, Economic Development and Construction [HL] Bill, Marine and Coastal Access [HL] Bill, Policing and Crime Bill, and Welfare Reform Bill, while during the 2007–2008 session, legislative consent was decided in relation to the following Bills: Climate Change Bill, Criminal Justice and Immigration Bill, Dormant Bank and Building Society Accounts Bill, Education and Skills Bill, Energy Bill, Football Spectators and Sports Grounds Bill, Health and Social Care Bill, Housing and Regeneration Bill, Pensions Bill, and Statute Law (Repeals) Bill [HL]. See http://www.scottish.parliament.uk/business/legConMem/index.htm (accessed 13 March 2009). According to Serving Scotland Better (2009), p. 49, "[s]ince 1999, 101 Sewel Motions or LCMs have been moved in the Scottish Parliament on a wide range of policy areas. For example, legislation which has been subject to a LCM has included the Proceeds of Crime Act 2002, the Health Act 2006 and the Dormant Bank and Building Societies Accounts Act 2008. All have been passed, although in some cases after amendment.

Scotland.[159] In cases where the legislative consent is decided upon and given, the Scottish Parliament agrees that the relevant provisions in the UK Bill, insofar as the matters fall within the legislative competence of the Scottish Parliament, should be considered by the UK Parliament. However, the Scottish Parliament could probably also not agree that the provisions should be considered by the UK Parliament, and in such cases, following the Sewel Convention, the UK Parliament should normally not include such provisions in UK legislation that purport to apply in the Scottish jurisdiction. In theory, the legislative consent motions may deal with competence issues both in the general area of devolved competence and in relation to the determination of negative competence in schedule 4. However, because schedule 4 identifies certain UK Acts in a relatively clear manner, the legislative consent motions have only dealt with issues within the general area of devolution, not with the negative list of UK Acts and the possible enlargement of their scope.

Although the option of the withholding of consent exists, statistics from 12 May 1999 until the beginning of March 2009 show that all legislative consent motions (formerly called Sewel motions) have actually been passed by the Scottish Parliament.[160] It can therefore be said that the consent mechanism has started to appear as the default position and has not really produced any such material protective function for the Scottish legislative competence that tests whether the pledge in the Sewel Convention that the UK Parliament will not normally legislate on matters within the Scottish legislative competence is effective.[161] Instead, the mechanism appears to have made it possible to open up inroads for the UK legislative competence into the Scottish legislative competence,[162] as if there existed concurrent

[159]Some interlocutors have also made the point that the LCMs are sometimes used in situations where the Scottish Parliament feels that the issue is controversial in Scotland. This means that the reason for the use of an LCM is not always to be found at the UK level. As pointed out in the BBC News of Friday, 17 December, 2004, entitled ‘Apology after Westminster blunder’ (accessed 1 April 2010), “Scotland Act mastermind Murray Elder claimed in October that measures on topics such as the rights of gay couples are being sent to Westminster in a way never intended. He said the Scottish Executive may be using a legal loophole to avoid debates on controversial issues. Under the arrangement, MSPs can avoid debating non-controversial issues”.

[160]Session 1 (1999–2003): 39 motions; Session 2 (2003–2007): 38 motions; Session 3 (2007–>): 11 motions so far. See Legislative Consent Memorandums and Motions. Statistics by Session, at http://www.scottish.parliament.uk/business/legConMem/LCM-Stats.htm (accessed 13 March 2009). See also Trench (2007e), pp. 185–187, who at least at the time of writing (2005) does not seem to discern any clear patterns in how different issues are ending up in the Sewel process.

[161]As put in The Sewel Convention, volume 1: Report 2005, para. 128, “[b]y deciding to establish a new Parliament specifically to handle legislation on devolved matters, the UK Parliament implicitly recognized the need for its own law-making powers in Scotland to be subject to a self-denying ordinance, notwithstanding its continuing formal sovereignty in all parts of the UK. Put simply, it would be pointless, and destructive of the spirit of devolution, to create a new law-making institution and then routinely to step on its toes.” See also Winetrobe (2005), p. 41 f., and McFadden and Lazarowicz (2002), p. 88.

[162]See The Sewel Convention, volume 1: Report 2005, para. 2: “A principal criticism has been that the convention has been over-used, with nearly as many Sewel motions passed as there have been Acts of the Scottish Parliament (ASPs). A related perception is that powers are being “handed

legislative powers, even if the material competences are separate.[163] However, at the same time, the material issues where the UK Parliament has legislated on Scottish matters are supposedly of a minor or even marginal nature, without important implications for the core competences of the Scottish Parliament or Executive.[164]

The use of the consent mechanism is also a sign of the fact that the UK Government[165] and the UK Parliament know where the boundaries of the UK legislative competences run in relation to the Scottish competences.[166] Finally, it is not clear on the basis of the Sewel Convention what will happen if the UK Parliament either by mistake or intentionally enacts a piece of UK law which extends itself to the legislative competence of the Scottish Parliament.[167] The presumption arising on the basis of the notion of parliamentary sovereignty is that in such a situation, the UK Act will prevail, because in the Scottish jurisdiction, no procedure exists to override a UK Act, except perhaps for the enactment of a corresponding "corrective" act for the jurisdiction of Scotland. The consequence of a potential norm collision could thereafter ultimately be tried in courts, where the matter would be adjudicated on the basis of the provisions of the Scotland Act. However, in actual practice, there was one occasion in which the UK Parliament

back" to Westminster, and that use of the Sewel process is a kind of "counter-devolution". In some instances, the criticism has been that the convention has been used inappropriately, to impose a general UK solution on a subject where a distinctively Scottish approach would be preferable. More recently, Lord Sewel himself (among others) has suggested that what was originally meant to be an inter-Parliamentary convention has instead been "hijacked" by government, and used for purposes for which it was never intended."

[163] Trench (2007b), p. 54.

[164] See The Sewel Convention, volume 1: Report 2005, para. 45.

[165] One of the points of criticism against the Sewel Convention has been that it has created an executive-driven procedure between the UK Government and the Scottish Executive which has relegated the UK Parliament and the Scottish Parliament to a secondary position, although it is exactly the two parliaments which should be the central actors in matters of legislation. See, *inter alia*, The Sewel Convention, volume 1: Report 2005, paras. 54–59, Winetrobe (2005), p. 66, Hazell (2005a), p. 304.

[166] See The Sewel Convention, volume 1: Report 2005, para. 134: "Close liaison between the [Scottish – MS] Executive and [the UK – MS] Government, mediated through the Scotland Office and operating at official and Ministerial level, has very largely succeeded in preventing Government legislation straying inadvertently into devolved areas, and has also ensured that where there is a case for crossing the line deliberately, this is discussed and agreed between the administrations from an early stage."

[167] See The Sewel Convention, volume 1: Report 2005, para. 145, which reports one situation of inadvertent UK legislation within Scottish competences: "The possibility exists, therefore, that Westminster will legislate without the Parliament's consent, or even against a deliberate refusal of consent. On the one occasion we are aware of where this has so far happened – a minor and entirely inadvertent breach of the Convention – the Executive rightly provided a prompt explanation. It is clearly important that this should happen, so that the Parliament can consider the implications of what has happened (including, where appropriate, the case for passing corrective legislation of its own)."

enacted a piece of law within Scottish competence without the LCM procedure. In this case, the UK Parliament was very apologetic, and later on repealed the UK position.[168]

5.4.5 *Joint Discussions as a Mechanism for Resolving Competence Issues in Advance*

In the scheme of UK intergovernmental relations, the mechanisms established in the Scotland Act are not the only ones available to manage the "islands of UK competence" and their relationship to the (in principle) residual competence of the Scottish Parliament and Government. There actually exists a more informal and preparatory platform for dealing with devolution issues which is activated on the basis of "early warning" in relations between the appropriate branches of the UK Government and the Scottish Government. In fact, the stated policy of the UK Government is to primarily rely on these informal advance mechanisms and to utilize the formal actions of the Secretary of State and the referrals of the Law Officers only a last resort.[169] The point of departure for such preparatory discussions is a Memorandum of Understanding and Supplementary Agreements on devolution, concluded between the United Kingdom Government, Scottish Ministers, the Cabinet of the National Assembly for Wales and the Northern Ireland Executive Committee. The first Memorandum of Understanding was concluded on

[168]See BBC News of Friday, 17 December, 2004, entitled 'Apology after Westminster blunder' (accessed 1 April 2010). The UK legislation consisted of sections 209–211 of the Housing Act 2004 which only extended to England and Wales, because housing belongs to the competence of Scotland, except that any amendments made by the Act have the same extent as the Act being amended. Sections 209–211 amended the Caravan Sites Act 1968, Part 1 of which extends to Scotland. Therefore, amendments made to part 1 of that Act by the 2004 Act extend to Scotland as well – by accident. One consequence of the amendment was that section 209 introduced a new exemption from requirement for a caravan site licence by reference to paragraph 11A of the Caravan and Control of Development Act 1960 which effectively removes requirement for licence for local authority land providing accommodation as a camp site for Roma. Subsequently, the Scottish Parliament reversed this arrangement in section 171 of the Housing (Scotland) Act 2006.

[169]Memorandum of Understanding and Supplementary Agreements on devolution, concluded between the United Kingdom Government, Scottish Ministers, the Cabinet of the National Assembly for Wales and the Northern Ireland Executive Committee, para. 26, as laid before the Scottish Parliament by the Scottish Ministers, January 2002, SE/2002/54. See http://cci.scot.nhs.uk/Publications/1999/10/MofU (accessed 16 March 2009). For a referral of the Lord Advocate, see *David Spiers, Procurator Fiscal v. Kevin Gerald Ruddy (Scotland) and Her Majesty's Advocate General for Scotland* Judicial Committee of the Privy Council, 12 December 2007, at http://www.privy-council.org.uk/output/Page535.asp (accessed 18 March 2009). Trench (2007e), p. 197, concludes that "intergovernmental relations are not merely informal, but also take place almost entirely in the private".

1 October 1999, with some subsequent amendments.[170] The Memorandum and the subsequent agreements entitled Concordats are not intended to be legally binding, but may have the status of soft law.[171]

The purpose of the Memorandum and the Concordats is to ensure smooth management of the interfaces between the different jurisdictions so that conflicts and problems could be avoided before lawmaking in the UK or in Scotland enters the formal stages or the implementation phase.[172] The procedures established under the Memorandum are based on the principles of communication, consultation, co-operation, exchange of information, statistics and research, and confidentiality (albeit with due regard to access to information as provided by different regimes of publicity). In practice, this means that the Scottish Executive stays continuously in close contact with the UK Government in most of its areas of competence. The political consensus between the governments involved and the dominance of the UK Government in the equation have, as a consequence, ensured that few disagreements between the two layers of government have entered the public domain.[173]

The Memorandum of Understanding provides for the establishment of a Joint Ministerial Committee (JMC), which is a discussion forum and ultimately also a dispute resolution mechanism between the UK Government and the devolved administrations[174] if their bilateral discussions do not lead to a satisfactory result.

[170] As laid before the Scottish Parliament by the Scottish Ministers, January 2002, SE/2002/54. See http://cci.scot.nhs.uk/Publications/1999/10/MofU (accessed 16 March 2009). On the Memorandum and the Concordats, see Trench (2007b), pp. 61–64.

[171] Trench (2007b), p. 62, who also makes the point that the Memorandum and the Concordats lack any sort of enforcement mechanism. As stated in para. 2 of the general part of the MoU, it "is a statement of political intent, and should not be interpreted as a binding agreement. It does not create legal obligations between the parties. It is intended to be binding in honour only. (. . .)." The same is true for the Concordats: they are, according to the Memorandum, intended to serve as working documents. See para. 3 of the MoU. See also Serving Scotland Better (2009), p. 121 f.

[172] According to Trench (2007b), p. 63, the Memorandum "appears to impose largely equal obligations on all the parties to it, the UK Government as much as the devolved administrations", and on p. 64, he concludes that many of the so-called soft-law provisions of the Memorandum and the Concordats "work to the benefit of the UK Government far more than they do to that of the devolved administrations", mentioning the principle of confidentiality as one example, because for the UK government, a breach of confidentiality might only be embarrassing, while for a devolved administration it might result in a critical loss of information. See also Trench (2007e), p. 196, according to whom disagreements or differences are defused by officials or by ministers before they might reach the formal framework of dispute resolution.

[173] See Trench (2007e), However, some interlocutors have indicated that the Memorandum of Understanding and the bilateral concordats are not quite as important in practice as they might seem.

[174] The JMC consists of the UK Government as well as Ministers from Scotland, Wales and Northern Ireland to "provide some central co-ordination of the overall relationship". Serving Scotland Better (2009), p. 122. Hence there is also a certain measure of horizontal contacts between the devolved areas. In addition, there is a British-Irish Council that brings together the three sub-state entities of Britain, the Channel Islands and the Isle of Man and the two sovereign States, the UK and Ireland.

Unlike the competence allocation mechanisms of the Scotland Act, which display an asymmetry by not focusing on the competences of the UK Parliament, the Joint Ministerial Committee is based on reciprocity and can also consider the competences of the UK, thus establishing in principle a symmetrical approach to the competence issues.[175] Because the JMC was not convened during the five first years of its existence to resolve policy disputes, it seems that the JMC would be engaged only as a last resort, if normal administrative channels and the good offices of the relevant Secretary of State do not suffice.[176] The JMC seems, however, influenced by the political background of the UK Government and the Scottish Executive. When Labour was the dominant party in both jurisdictions, it was normally possible to deal with competence issues at the level of officials of the two governments.[177] After the electoral gains of the SNP in 2007 and the creation of the minority Government in Scotland, political views concerning competence issues may have changed,[178] and as a consequence, the JMC has actually been used as a forum for discussion, but probably still less frequently than originally envisaged.[179] The JMC has a number of sub-committees that have worked more actively than the JMC plenary. It seems that the JMC mechanism is there primarily for advance discussion

[175]Trench (2007a), p. 276.

[176]See Trench (2007b), p. 61, Hazell and Rawlings (2005), p. 6. See Trench (2007e), pp. 162–168, on the functioning of the JMC and its sub-committees, that is, JMC Plenary and the different JMCs established for health, knowledge economy, poverty, and Europe, some of which have met more frequently and some not at all. The sub-committee JMC(Domestic) was established as late as in 2008. See also Serving Scotland Better (2009), p. 123, and McFadden and Lazarowicz (2002), p. 90.

[177]According to some interlocutors, there was a surprising amount of conflict during the time when Labour was in Government both at the UK level and in Scotland, but the conflicts and – to some extent – personal animosities could be and were managed behind the scenes because those involved belonged to the same party. With the change of Government in Scotland in 2007, there is more Government-to-Government dialogue.

[178]The SNP-led Government is perhaps less willing to share draft laws than the previous Governments, a feature that probably also is present on the UK side and which shows itself so that everybody waits until there is a set ministerial decision on one side before it is communicated to the other side. However, the SNP Government has led to less conflict than could be expected. According to some interlocutors, while some political tensions exist, some may be deliberately engineered. What might be a greater problem is a lack of understanding amongst officials on both sides concerning how the system is intended to work. However, such misunderstandings existed already before 1998, so they are not necessarily a creation of devolution. In practice, there is a lot of constructive discussions between the two administrations, constant exchange of letters between UK ministers and Scottish ministers, and relatively few areas of serious dispute, although the media depicts the relationship as one of constant conflict.

[179]See Serving Scotland Better (2009), pp. 122–124. It is probably possible to say that the SNP is partly playing by the rules, partly trying to push the boundaries, but the SNP is not necessarily a source of conflict. What may be more important is the fact that the economic situation was benign during the first decade of Scottish devolution, with rising prosperity and without serious challenges concerning money between the UK and Scotland. In 2010, the situation became different, and the test of devolution might be in the reduction of public expenditure and the political choices that need to be made.

so that legal disputes, resolved by the Supreme Court *ex post facto*, could be avoided.

Five separate overarching Concordats apply broadly uniform arrangements across the UK Government with respect to all devolved areas, namely (1) the Joint Ministerial Committee,[180] (2) the handling of matters with an EU dimension,[181] (3) financial assistance to industry,[182] (4) international relations touching on the responsibilities of the devolved administrations,[183] and (5) statistical work across the UK.[184] In addition, individual UK Government Departments and their counterparts in the devolved administrations have agreed and published bilateral Concordats, and for Scotland, a large number of different bilateral Concordats with the central government exist, some more general and some fairly specific as concerns the subject-matter.[185] The Secretary of State for Scotland also has

[180]Ministerial responsibility within the UK Government for the MoU and JMC agreements lies with the Deputy Prime Minister in his capacity as Chairman of the Cabinet's Committee on the Nations and Regions.

[181]See chapter B1 of the Memorandum of Understanding: Concordat on Co-ordination of European Union Policy Issues – Scotland. The UK Foreign and Commonwealth Secretary is responsible for the Concordat on the Co-ordination of European Union Policy Issues.

[182]See chapter C of the Memorandum of Understanding: Concordat on Financial Assistance to Industry, with a section on the implications of EU law. The UK Chief Secretary to the Treasury is responsible for the Concordat on Financial Assistance to Industry.

[183]See chapter D1 of the Memorandum of Understanding: Concordat on International Relations – Scotland. The UK Foreign and Commonwealth Secretary is responsible for the Concordat on International Relations.

[184]See chapter E of the Memorandum of Understanding: Concordat on Statistics. The UK Economic Secretary is responsible for the Concordat on Statistics.

[185]For instance, Concordat on the Implementation of Directive 2001/18/EC and Regulation 1946/2003/EC (An agreement between the Department of the Environment in Northern Ireland, the National Assembly for Wales, the Scottish Executive and the UK Government), Concordat between the Department for Transport and the Scottish Executive, Concordat: Sharing Information About Sex Offenders, Concordat Between the Scottish Executive And the Department For Constitutional Affairs, Concordat between HM Treasury and the Scottish Executive, Concordat Between the Department for Transport and the Scottish Executive, Concordat Between the Office of the Deputy Prime Minister and the Scottish Executive, Specific Concordat Between the British Cattle Movement Service and the Scottish Executive Rural Affairs Department, Concordat between the Ministry of Agriculture, Fisheries and Food (MAFF) and the Scottish Executive (SE) in respect of the State Veterinary Service (SVS) and Animal Disease Compensation, Concordat between the Scottish Ministers and the Secretary of State for Defence, Concordat between Department of Social Security and the Scottish Executive, Concordat between the Department of Social Security and the Scottish Executive, Concordat between HM Treasury and the Scottish Executive, Concordat between the Home Office and the Scottish Executive, Concordat between the Scottish Executive and the Lord Chancellor's Department, Concordat between the Scottish Ministers and the Secretary of State for Defence, Concordat on Health and Social Care, Concordat between Department for Culture, Media and Sport and the Scottish Executive, Concordat between the Health and Safety Executive (HSE) and the Scottish Executive (SE), Concordat between the Scottish Executive (SE) and the Department of Trade and Industry, Concordat on Co-ordination of EU, International and Policy Issues on Public Procurement, Concordat between the

responsibilities within the UK Government for promoting the devolution settlement, for ensuring effective working relations between the UK Government and the devolved administrations, and for helping to resolve any disputes which may arise.[186] At the level of higher officials, "the Cabinet Secretary and Head of the Home Civil Service chairs a weekly meeting to which the Permanent Secretaries of the devolved administrations are invited",[187] and there are also contacts on a personal level between officials in Scotland and London. In fact, if there are discussions between Scotland and the UK about competence, for instance, in such a situation where Scotland feels that it has competence while the UK Government is of the opinion that Scotland does not, the emphasis is on the level of officials rather than on the political level.[188] Finally, another mechanism for competence control has started to emerge within the House of Lords on the basis of legislative practice. The House of Lords has developed particular committees for the purpose of scrutinizing the compatibility of European law with Scottish law. This mechanism is not foreseen in the Scotland Act, but falls outside of the established procedures and is in the formative stage.[189]

On the basis of the multifarious control of legislative competence, the picture emerges that the Scotland Act caters for a variety of situations in which devolution issues, that is, competence problems may arise. The Scotland Act creates an extraordinary number of safeguards, political as well as judicial, to make sure

Cabinet Office and the Scottish Administration, Concordat between the Scottish Ministers and the Secretary of State for Education and Employment, Main Concordat between the Ministry of Agriculture, Fisheries and Food and the Scottish Executive, and Subject Specific Concordat between MAFF and the Scottish Executive on Fisheries.

[186]See the Memorandum of Understanding and Supplementary Agreements on devolution, paras. 24–26. Trench (2007e), p. 168, points out that "[f]inancial disputes are to be dealt with in the first instance bilaterally between the UK Treasury and the devolved administration. A first 'appeal' lies to Treasury ministers, and if the devolved administration remains dissatisfied, the matter may be referred to the UK Cabinet. While the devolved administration can raise the matter at the JMC as well, it is for the UK Cabinet to make a 'final decision', so raising it at the JMC would simply be a way of indicating concern or annoyance and not a direct means to a resolution." According to some interlocutors, a taxation matter involving the UK Treasury emerged into a discussion between the UK taxation perspective and the Scottish perspective, which was of an environmental nature. Ultimately, in the discussion at the level of the officials, the Scottish officials gave in, but if the discussion would have progressed to the ministerial level, it is possible that the Scottish minister would have had a harder line.

[187]Serving Scotland Better (2009), p. 124.

[188]It is possible to say, on the basis of discussions with interlocutors, that in practice, competence decisions between the UK Government and the Scottish Government are muddled through. As a consequence, there are no records of where the dividing line is drawn in individual situations (and the legal consideration of the competence line seems to prefer to deduce the decision of where the line should be drawn from statutory evidence). This means that individual officials could have a considerable impact on the matters and that there is no institutional memory when staff is changing. In addition, even the LCMs are not recorded very precisely as concerns their content.

[189]See also Serving Scotland Better (2009), p. 128 f.

that the Scottish lawmaker stays within its own sphere of competence and that it does not threaten the competence of the UK Parliament. At the same time, the Sewel Convention approaches the matter from the point of view of the UK Parliament and creates a mechanism for securing that the UK Parliament, when entering the legislative competence of the Scottish Parliament, does so only with the consent of the Scottish Parliament. Primarily, the line of demarcation between the two jurisdictions is, however, adjusted in a manner not determined by the Scotland Act or the Sewel Convention, but by mutual contacts between the relevant executive agencies in a manner that takes on the form of advance notification and consideration of potentially problematic proposals.[190]

A judicialization of the competence problems has thus not taken place, but the difficult issues have been dealt with through inter-governmental procedures in a less "hostile" or adversarial way.[191] It may be speculated as to why there has not been more litigation in the constitutional area, but one reason could be the absence of a written constitution and, as a consequence, there is a need to focus more on the political process through the advance review mechanisms. Another reason could be the fact that Labour was in control of both the UK Government and the Scottish Government until 2007, thereby diminishing the likelihood of conflicts over legislative policy.[192] There exists in Scotland a political constitution rather than a

[190]The issues escalate as necessary from the level of officials to the sub-committees of the JMC and even to the JMC plenary, and according to some interlocutors, the Marine Environment Bill could be a good example of how the inter-governmental discussion progresses on both sides. However, one general problem that seems to exist is that there are a lot of officials in the UK Government who do not understand that there is devolution and who, as a consequence, do not recognize the need of the contact with the devolved administration. The multifarious arrangement is commented in a critical vein by Trench (2007e), p. 191: "The outcome has avoided both conflict and internal chaos, but at the price of huge amounts of work by those directly involved, and an increasingly convoluted, even unwieldy, set of legislation which requires specialist skills to comprehend or even find." See also Trench (2007a), p. 287, making the point that policing of the activities of the devolved administrations is time-consuming, demands vast resources of highly skilled civil servants in the UK central government and duplicates the work already done by the lawyers of the Scottish Parliament and the Scottish Government. In addition, some interlocutors makes the point that intergovernmental relations between the UK Government and a single devolved administration are sometimes of an ad hoc, bilateral and informal nature.

[191]Hazell (2005a), p. 300. The "instinct" dictates a non-litigation and advance negotiation approach.

[192]However, according to evidence given by interlocutors, at least one example of executive interaction between a UK Minister and a Scottish Minister, both Labour, exists where the Scottish party wanted to make a point that was squarely in conflict with the position of the UK Minister. In the situation, the Scottish Minister expressed his policy point, but was compelled to back down, and the UK position prevailed. This indicates that it is possible for the inter-governmental process to tip in favour of the UK Government even with Labour in power on both sides. Such political conflicts behind the scenes might be more common with the SNP on the Scottish side making its own policy points. However, it also seems that before 2007, there was more contacts between the UK Government and the Scottish Government, while after 2007, there is less contact and not so close co-operation as before.

judicial one, which means that there is no instant legal response to difficult issues, but instead a result from negotiations between the two governments. It seems, however, as though the number of transgressions of competence have been very few in number. A problem that such a multifarious control of legislative competence creates is that different parts of the control framework may arrive at different conclusions concerning the interpretation of where the borderline between the competences runs. For sure, the UK Supreme Court (until October 2009 the Judicial Committee of the Privy Council) is the ultimate judicial referee of the devolution settlement, but there is nonetheless the risk that the political and the judicial channels of conflict resolution produce different end results.[193] The wealth of arrangements for competence control in Scotland can be contrasted with the dearth in Zanzibar.

5.5 Zanzibar: Clear Residuality but Unclear Implementation

5.5.1 *Federal-Type Residual Competences*

There is a federal-type distribution of powers established in the Constitution of Tanzania for matters that belong to the Union Republic, on the one hand, and Zanzibar, on the other. The point of departure is Art. 4(3) of the Constitution of Tanzania: "For the purposes of the efficient conduct of public affairs in the United Republic and for the allocation of powers among the organs specified in this Article, there shall be union matters as listed in the First Schedule and there shall also be non-union matters which are all other matters not so listed." The enumeration of Union Matters in the First Schedule is thus complemented by an attribution of residual matters for Zanzibar.

The first schedule of the Constitution of Tanzania, referred to in Article 4 of the Constitution, enumerates the Union Matters as follows:

> The Constitution of Tanzania and the Government of the United Republic.
> Foreign Affairs.
> Defence and Security.
> Police.
> Emergency Powers.
> Citizenship.
> Immigration.
> External borrowing and trade and borrowing.

[193] One instance which could be problematic is at hand after the Presiding Officer of the Scottish Parliament has certified that the bill proposed by the Scottish Government is within competence and the bill advances to the different legislative stages where amendments could be introduced and agreed upon that are outside of competence. In such a situation, it is at least in theory possible that there would be court action against the act that would put the competence certification to a test. Because the Scottish Parliament in itself is not a legal person, the legal action would have to be brought against the Scottish Parliament Corporate Body, which would, though its organs, be in a position to formulate the opinion of the Scottish Parliament on a legislative issue.

Service in the Government of the United Republic.

Income tax payable by individuals and by corporations, customs duty and excise duty on goods manufactured in Tanzania collected by the Customs Department.

Harbours, matters related to air transport, posts and telecommunications.

All matters concerning coinage, currency for the purposes of legal tender (including notes), banks (including savings banks) and all banking business; foreign exchange and exchange control.

Industrial licensing and statistics.

Higher education.

Mineral oil resources, including crude oil and natural gas.

The National Examinations Council of Tanzania and all matters connected with the functions of that Council.

Civil aviation.

Research.

Meteorology

Statistics

The Court of Appeal of the United Republic.

Registration of political parties and other matters related to political parties.

Point 3 of the list of Union matters is further underlined in Art. 147, according to which it is prohibited for any person or any organization or any group of persons except the Government to raise forces or maintain in Tanzania an armed force of any kind, at the same time as the Government of the United Republic has the recognized right, in accordance with the law, to raise and maintain in Tanzania armed forces of various types for the purposes of the defense and security of the territory and the people of Tanzania. This, however, has not prevented Zanzibar from establishing, on the basis of the Constitution of Zanzibar, security forces and border guards that are militarily organized and that have even been accorded the right to carry arms (see below, Sect. 7.4.3).[194]

In addition, there are acts of the Parliament of Tanzania that require for their amendment a qualified amendment procedure in Parliament. By implication, therefore, these acts also belong to the legislative competence of Parliament and could be said to constitute Union matters. Article 98(1)(a) makes reference to the Second Schedule of the Constitution of Tanzania, in which such laws or particular provisions are enumerated and the amendment of which requires the support of at least two thirds of all Members of Parliament. These acts and provisions are the Republic of Tanganyika (Consequential, Transitional and Temporary Provisions)

[194]See Maalim (2006), p. 145, who is of the opinion that the competence of the Union in the area of defence and security creates an overall liability and responsibility of the Union Government over, e.g., human rights violations, even when they are acting on the instruction of the Zanzibar Government officials. This is, of course, true as concerns the application of international law in the area of human rights: the State of Tanzania is responsible before international treaty bodies for violations of human rights that might take place through acts or omissions of the authorities of Zanzibar. Constitutionally, the matter could be different. Because defence and security is a Union Matter, the legality of the security organisations of Zanzibar could be doubted, and as a consequence, there could exist an enhanced liability and responsibility on the part of the Government of Zanzibar for the actions of such forces.

Act, 1962, sections 3, 17, 18, 23 and 26 (Cap.500), the Civil Service Act 1962, sections 22, 23 and 24 (Cap.509), the Judicial Service Act, 1962, sections 22, 23 and 24 (Cap.508), and the whole Act of Union between Tanganyika and Zanzibar (Cap.557). These Acts and provisions obviously contain a considerable overlap with the Union Matters as defined in the First Schedule.[195]

This overlap is even clearer in List Two of the Second Schedule, which contains an enumeration of matters that constitute the definitional core of the entire Union Republic. Article 98(1)(b) lists matters the amendment of which requires to be supported by two thirds of all Members of Parliament from Mainland Tanzania and two thirds of all Members of Parliament from Tanzania Zanzibar, that is, a double qualified majority. This extraordinarily strict requirement that has never been applied in practice concerns the existence of the United Republic, the existence of the Office of the President of the United Republic, the authority of the Government of the United Republic, the existence of the Parliament of the United Republic, the authority of the Government of Zanzibar, the High Court of Zanzibar, the list of Union Matters, and the number of Members of Parliament from Zanzibar. Evidently, the aim of this constitutional protection is to ensure for the Zanzibaris the continuance of the Union according to the terms of the agreement so that Mainland Tanzania cannot unilaterally change the arrangement, for instance, to the detriment of Zanzibar. However, the requirement also cuts in the other direction and would prevent unilateral action on the part of Zanzibar towards breaking the Union Republic and re-emerging as an independent State. Therefore, the amendments in 2010 to the Constitution of Zanzibar should have no effect in this greater scheme of things and remain internal to Zanzibar.

5.5.2 *The Principle of Duality*

The Parliament, that is, the Parliament of Tanzania, is designated in Art. 64(1) of the Constitution of Tanzania as the holder of legislative powers in relation to all Union Matters and also in relation to all other matters concerning Mainland Tanzania. Sub-section 2 of the same provision vests the legislative powers in Tanzania Zanzibar over all matters which are not Union Matters in the House of Representatives. A restatement of this is established in Art. 106(3) of the Constitution of Tanzania, according to which "[a]ll legislative authority in Zanzibar over all matters which are not Union Matters is hereby vested in the House of

[195] According to Shivji (2008), p. 175 f., laws that require a two-thirds majority for amendment include the Acts of Union (Cap. 557 of the Revised Laws 1965) which ratified the Articles of Union. "This means that the union parliament could amend the Acts of Union, and therefore indirectly the Articles of Union, thereby changing the structure of the union including the distribution of power. This is exactly what it has been doing by adding to the list of Union matters."

Representatives of Zanzibar".[196] There is hence a distribution of legislative powers between two legislatures, apparently in an exclusive manner, because according to sub-section 3, any law enacted by the House of Representatives concerning any matter in Tanzania Zanzibar which is within the legislative jurisdiction of Parliament shall be null and void. The same is true concerning any law enacted by Parliament concerning any matter which is within the legislative jurisdiction of the House of Representatives: such a law shall be null and void.[197] This guarantees the autonomy of the jurisdiction of Zanzibar in the different areas of residual matters, such as the administration of criminal justice, the judiciary, etc.

The distribution of legislative powers has been identified as a principle of duality in the case of *Haji v Nungu and Another*, decided by the Court of Appeal of Tanzania in 1986.[198] According to the case, there are three dimensions or characteristics of that duality: (1) matters which concern exclusively that area which before the Union constituted what was then known as Tanganyika, and is presently referred to under the Constitution of Tanzania as Tanzania Mainland, that is, matters which fall under the exclusive domain of the Government of the United Republic and over which the RGZ has no jurisdiction; (2) matters which concern exclusively Zanzibar and which fall within the exclusive domain of the RGZ and which are matters over which the Government of the United Republic has no jurisdiction whatsoever; (3) matters which concern both sides of the Union, that is, both Tanzania Mainland as well as Zanzibar. According to the *Haji* case, the third dimension of duality is dealt with in three different ways in the Constitution of the United Republic: (a) some matters of common concern are listed in the First Schedule to the Constitution, as provided under articles 4 and 64 of the Constitution;[199] (b) other matters of concern both to Zanzibar and Tanzania Mainland and which are not listed in the First Schedule, but which are specifically provided for under the Constitution of the United Republic;[200] (c) non-union matters which

[196] Although the official language of Zanzibar is Swahili, the bills are actually drafted in English by the Government, after which the bill is translated into Swahili. The representatives are given the draft in Swahili, and the bill is passed in Swahili, while the assent of the President is actually given on the English version. The act is published in the Official Gazette in Swahili, but they are also published in English in the Laws of Zanzibar. When the law is applied by the courts, judges will hear cases both in English and in Kiswahili. The version of the Laws of Zanzibar used in preparation of this text is the Revised Edition of 2006, if not otherwise indicated.

[197] See Othman (2006), p. 59.

[198] Court of Appeal of Tanzania, [1987] LRC (Const) of 27 September 1986 (Nyalali, C.J.; the concurring opinions of the two other judges contain specifications to the main opinion).

[199] The Court of Appeal makes the point that historically, this list has not stood still but has gradually increased. The Court opined that such an increasing trend may be an indication of a healthy growing confidence and trust between the people and leadership on both sides of the Union.

[200] The Court of Appeal mentions the right of audience of the Attorney General of the United Republic in any court in Tanzania, even the court of Zanzibar, the jurisdiction of the High Court of the United Republic to hear and determine election petition cases, which was the root of the *Haji* case, the jurisdiction of the Permanent Commission of Enquiry, which extends itself over the entire territory of Tanzania, including Zanzibar, and certain legislation of the Parliament of the United

concern both sides of the Union but which the Constitution of the United Republic does not contain provisions for dealing with.[201]

As a consequence, the legislative powers of Zanzibar and Mainland Tanzania are in principle mutually exclusive. This conclusion was reached by the Court of Appeal of Tanzania in the case of *S.M.Z. v. Machano Khamis Ali & 17 Others*[202] by the words that "a matter is either exclusively for Zanzibar or it is for the Union", at the same time as the Court denies the existence of a list of concurrent jurisdiction. In addition, sub-section 4 concludes that any law enacted by Parliament concerning any matter shall not apply to Tanzania Zanzibar except in three situations.[203] Firstly, such a law shall have expressly stated that it shall apply to Mainland Tanzania as well as to Tanzania Zanzibar or it replaces, amends or repeals a law which is in operation in Tanzania Zanzibar. Secondly, such a law replaces, or amends or repeals a law which was previously in operation in Mainland Tanzania and also in operation in Tanzania Zanzibar pursuant to the Articles of the Union of Tanganyika and Zanzibar, or pursuant to any law which expressly stated that it shall apply to Mainland Tanzania as well as Tanzania Zanzibar. Thirdly, such a law relates to Union Matters, and whenever reference is made to the term "Tanzania" in any law, such law shall apply in the United Republic in accordance with the interpretation contained in the provisions of Art. 64. The Union parliament has increasingly enacted legislation that should apply to Zanzibar, too. For instance, an act of the Union Parliament was enacted in 1995 as a Union matter that stated that the vice-president of Tanzania does not have to be a person from Zanzibar.[204] The Act was, however, not passed by the double qualified majority established for matters in List Two of the Second Schedule, and therefore, the Members of Parliament from Zanzibar were not accorded the importance that the special amendment procedure actually implied.[205]

Republic which is enacted in accordance with the provisions of Art. 64(4) of the Constitution of Tanzania, such as the Election Act 1985.

[201]The Court of Appeal mentions as an example of such matters the fishing activities in the territorial waters of Tanzania in the Indian Ocean, but is of the opinion that there may exist other matters, too, some of which might, in the course of time, "as the people of Tanzania continue to mature in their nationhood, will find their place either as union matters listed in the First Schedule to the Constitution or as matters specifically provided elsewhere under the Constitution of the United Republic and that of Zanzibar". Such an increase of the Union Matters either through additions to the First Schedule or through constitutional amendments would seem to drain the legislative competence of Zanzibar and to potentially constitute incremental moves towards a unitary state.

[202]Court of Appeal of Tanzania at Zanzibar, Criminal Application No. 8 of 2000 on 3 April 2000.

[203]See Othman (2006), p. 59.

[204]See Shivji (2008), p. 176.

[205]Shivji (2008), p. 177, also makes the point that the Zanzibari MPs have themselves failed in protecting the constitutional autonomy of Zanzibar in the Parliament in situations where a two-thirds majority was required, because they "hardly ever took a robust stand in the Union parliament in any case", probably mainly because "the relationship between the two parts of the Union was determined in the close chambers of the Party not by public deliberations in the National Assembly".

As stated in 1999 by the High Court of Zanzibar in the case of *S.M.Z. v. Machano Khamis Ali & 17 Others,*[206] sovereignty is divisible. Therefore, the determination of which of the two Governments exercises sovereignty over any given matter requires the determination of whether the matter is a Union matter or a non-Union matter. The question in the case is whether treason can be committed in Zanzibar or perhaps only in Tanzania as a state. This issue was originally the focal point in the case that was before the High Court of Zanzibar,[207] but it was withdrawn, only to be dealt with by the Court of Appeals of Tanzania.

The Court of Appeal of Tanzania reviewed, in the case of *S.M.Z. v. Machano Khamis Ali & 17 Others,*[208] the constitutional issue of whether or not treason can be committed against the RGZ. The Court of Appeal was of the opinion that four matters have to be proved in an indictment for treason: that an act has been committed, that the act is treasonable, that the act is against a sovereign or a state, and that the act was done by a person who owes allegiance to the sovereign or the state. Against this background, the Court asked itself two questions: is Zanzibar a state and is the RGZ sovereign? The answer was no. According to the Court of Appeal, the United Republic of Tanzania is a state: "The two parts forming the United Republic of Tanzania can neither separately go to war against a foreign power nor can war be made against one of them separately (...). The United Republic of Tanzania is the treaty-making power." Because security is a Union Matter according to para. 3 of the First Schedule of the Constitution, overthrow of the Head of the Revolutionary Government of Zanzibar or, as he is also called, the President of Zanzibar, is a Union Matter and not a matter of exclusive jurisdiction of the RGZ. Treason is a matter for the Union and not a matter for the exclusive jurisdiction of Zanzibar because there is a matter, security, which is specifically provided for under the Union Constitution and which concerns both sides of the Union. Treason is a breach of security, which is a Union Matter, and "treason can only be committed against a sovereign".

However, it could be argued, and has indeed been argued from the Zanzibar side in the case of *S.M.Z. v. Machano Khamis Ali & 17 Others*, that treason is a normal crime that can be defined by the criminal legislation of both Tanzania and Zanzibar. The applicability of the provisions of treason would then depend on whether the legislation has defined that particular crime. Against this background, it could be argued that treason can be committed both against the Tanzanian Government and

---

[206] *S.M.Z. v. Machano Khamis Ali & 17 Others* (High Court of Zanzibar, Session Case No. 17 of 1999).

[207] See *S.M.Z. v. Machano Khamis Ali & 17 Others*, in which the RGZ charged the defendants with treason. The High Court of Zanzibar ruled "that the commission of treason is very possible in Zanzibar". This was determined in a preliminary ruling, pending the final verdict. However, before the High Court of Zanzibar gave its judgment in the matter, the prosecution withdrew the charges. Therefore, because the matter was constitutionally important, the Court of Appeal of Tanzania decided to review the case.

[208] Court of Appeal of Tanzania at Zanzibar, Criminal Application No. 8 of 2000 on 3 April 2000. The decision of the High Court of Zanzibar was overturned.

the Government of Zanzibar.[209] The decision of the Court of Appeal of Tanzania has, however, determined the matter so that treason is a Union matter. In fact, because treason is, by reference to security, a Union matter, it has been asked whether or not the National Security Act 1970, after security had become a Union matter in 1984, extends to Zanzibar. In the case of *Seif Sharif Hamad v. S.M.Z.*,[210] the Court of Appeal of Tanzania decided that the substantive security legislation of 1970, originally adopted for Mainland Tanzania, has to be construed with such adaptations that bring it into conformity with the constitutional amendment of 1984 that made security a Union matter. Therefore, the National Security Act 1970 was deemed to extend to Zanzibar by virtue of the constitutional amendment.

5.5.3 Problems in Implementing Competences

Evidently, the distribution of powers between the Parliament of Mainland Tanzania (the Union Parliament) and the House of Representatives is not completely without problems. Some points of contention and clashes exist, because in line with the above-mentioned court cases, it may be asked whether the list of Union matters in the First Schedule is exhaustive. The Court of Appeal of Tanzania distinguishes between three different categories: (1) matters classified in the First Schedule as a Union Matter, (2) matters specifically provided for under the Union Constitution to concern both sides of the Union, and (3) matters regulated by a legislation enacted under Art. 64(4) extending to the entire Union.[211] One example in point is the Elections Act 1985, supposedly enacted under Art. 64(4)(a) of the Constitution of Tanzania. The Court of Appeal opined that "[u]ndoubtedly, this legislation does not concern a union matter listed under the First Schedule to the Union Constitution and would appear to infringe the provisions of Article 78(1) of the Constitution of Zanzibar, which provides, in effect that: 'All legislative power in Zanzibar over all non-union matters is vested in the House of Representatives'". It is not far-fetched to suggest that the third category, in particular, could function in a way reminiscent of a preemption clause in federal settings. This, in itself, would be a characteristic that is capable of moving Zanzibar some steps towards federal arrangements on the scale between federations and autonomies.

The distribution of powers is problematic in particular concerning the implementation of international treaties that Tanzania concludes, because in most cases, such treaties would affect the legislative powers of Zanzibar and require

---

[209] Shivji (2006), p. 186, points out that "[a] *Mzanzibari* owes allegiance to the state of Zanzibar and therefore an offence of treason can be committed against the state of Zanzibar".

[210] Court of Appeal of Tanzania at Zanzibar, [1998] T.L.R., of 24 February 1993 (criminal appeal No. 171 of 1992, from the ruling of the high court of Zanzibar, at Zanzibar, of 28 August 1992, criminal sessions case No. 1 of 1991).

[211] *Haji v Nungu and Another*, [1987] LRC (Const) of 27 September 1986.

that at least some measures of domestic implementation take place by way of legislative decision-making in Zanzibar. For instance, in the area of the international law of shipping, such as the Law of the Sea Convention, Marine Pollution Convention and the Convention concerning Safety of Life at Sea, Zanzibar has its own legislative competence relative to merchant shipping. As a consequence, Zanzibar has its own Merchant Shipping Act and the Union its own, and for the domestic administration of, for instance, registration of vessels and inspection of vessels, Zanzibar has its own administrative authorities and the Union its own. The situation is the same concerning intellectual property, where Zanzibar has had its own intellectual property legislation since 2007. Evidently, the domestic implementation of international treaties in Zanzibar is an area where the constitutional law governing the Union does not establish any clear position.

The ratification of international treaties is a Union matter taken care of by the Union Parliament, but because domestic implementation is in most cases a responsibility of both the Union for Mainland Tanzania and of Zanzibar, the end result concerning the position of the State could vary. There is sometimes divergent legislation in the two entities, but most matters have been dealt with under party discipline, in particular, during the one-party system. Therefore, no great differences have emerged, at least not of such magnitude that the State of Tanzania would have been considered to be in breach of its international obligations because of Zanzibar. Should a case arise in which there was a difference between the political parties in charge of the two governments, in Mainland Tanzania and Zanzibar, there would be no guarantee that the persons in charge could talk to each other, and the outcome of domestic implementation could be different.

Today, the greater part of legislation emanates from consultancies offered by inter-governmental organizations, regional organizations, non-governmental organizations, etc., for instance, concerning the environment, drug trafficking and other global themes where the interests are universal. Therefore, most of the legislation passed in Zanzibar is similar to the legislation of Mainland Tanzania: the material similarities are striking, and, for instance, the penal provisions in Zanzibar and Mainland Tanzania are mostly similar. The legislation where there are differences deals with governance and the administrative framework, that is, governmental structures.

In certain areas, there are greater differences, in particular in areas which are influenced by religious beliefs and cultural considerations that are related to the identity of Zanzibar. Zanzibar is under the influence of Islamic religion and culture, but the Islamic culture is not brought to an extreme version. Therefore, there is, for instance, a particular court system, the Kadhis' courts, in place in Zanzibar for the adjudication of issues related to Islamic personal law (marriage, gifts, inheritance). Although Zanzibar is in principle, under Art. 19(2), secular as concerns the government, the Zanzibar mufti is based on Zanzibari legislation, the Establishment of the Office of Mufti Act, 2001, which makes the Mufti a department of the Government and the officeholder an appointee of the President of Zanzibar. The functions of the Mufti relate to the administration of Islamic matters in Zanzibar, including the issuing of *fat-wa* on any matter raised with him relating to any Islamic question which needs to be decided and to keep record of all *fat-wa* issued by the office of the Mufti. The Mufti also has the function of settling any religious dispute arising among Muslims, to settle any religious dispute arising between Muslims and other religions in consultation with other leaders of that other religion and to organize research and education in the area of religious matters of Muslims. In Zanzibar, there is also the *Wakf* Commission, that is, an Islamic charity (originally established by the British in 1907), for supervising the estates of deceased Muslim persons.

5.5.4 Weak Forms of Consultation and Consent

Article 64(5) of the Constitution of Tanzania establishes a *Grundnorm* of some kind by providing that without prejudice to the application of the Constitution of Zanzibar in accordance with the Constitution concerning all matters pertaining to Tanzania Zanzibar which are not Union Matters, the Constitution shall have the force of law in the whole of the United Republic, and in the event that any other law conflicts with the provisions contained in the Constitution, the Constitution shall prevail and that other law, to the extent of the inconsistency with the Constitution, shall be void.[212] This is echoed and sustained by Art. 132 of the Constitution of Zanzibar, according to which no law enacted by the Union Parliament shall apply to Zanzibar unless that law relates to Union affairs only and having complied with the provisions of the Union Constitution. The provision underlines further the legitimacy issues that seem to burden the relationship between Mainland Tanzania and Zanzibar.[213]

However, sub-section (2) of the provision appears to establish a consent mechanism of some sort by providing that the enactment of the Union Parliament shall be submitted to the House of Representatives by the responsible Minister of the RGZ.[214] On one single instance, there has been a reaction on the part of the House of Representatives, and after information submitted by the House of Representatives to the Union Parliament concerning encroachment through an act of the

[212] This mechanism of invalidation was referred to in the case of *S.M.Z. v. Machano Khamis Ali & 17 Others*, where the Court of Appeal of Tanzania concluded that the combined effect of Art. 28(4) of the Constitution of Tanzania and Art. 64(5) "is to repeal section 26 of the Penal Decree" of Zanzibar. "Indeed, the moment security was added to the list of Union Matters, then, first, security should have been defined and two, treason should have been provided for and defined in a law applicable to both parts of the Union as stated in Article 28(4)".

[213] As Shivji (2008), p. 230, states, "[o]n the face of it, the Union parliament can pass a law on a non-Union matter and extend its application to Zanzibar".

[214] The Court of Appeal of Tanzania seems to be addressing this issue in the case of *Seif Sharif Hamad v. S.M.Z.*, [1998] T.L.R., when asking what the import of Art. 131(2) [should probably be Art. 132(2) –MS] of the Zanzibar Constitution is and how it corresponds with Art. 64(4) of the Union Constitution. See also Shivji (2008), p. 230, who refers to the requirement to table such enactment by the Parliament of Tanzania in the House of Representatives.

Union onto the legislative powers of Zanzibar, it seems that the Union Parliament amended the Act which caused the problem. It could therefore be said that there is almost no relationship between the two legislatures, the Parliament and the House of Representatives. The Union Parliament deals with Union Matters and such non-union matters which apply in Mainland Tanzania, while the House of Representatives deals with non-union matters relating to Zanzibar. Sometimes, there are consultations between the House of Representatives and Parliament, but very infrequently.[215] When such consultation takes place, the procedure is in principle such that Parliament starts the enactment procedure concerning a Bill and holds the first reading. If the Bill concerns Zanzibar, it can be sent to the House of Representatives for debate, at which point it is introduced by the relevant minister (which probably would be the Second Vice-President) and debated. After the debate (which is not a legislative procedure), the Bill is sent back with comments and proposed amendments to Parliament, at which point Parliament continues with the second reading and makes the necessary modifications. Finally, in the third reading, the Bill is adopted.

It is also possible to indicate what might happen if consultations are not undertaken. The Union Parliament had already passed a human rights commission bill, providing that it would be applicable in Zanzibar, when the authorities of Zanzibar discovered that no consent had been requested by Parliament from the House of Representatives of Zanzibar. When the human rights commission started to work, the authorities of Zanzibar prevented the activities of the commission in the territory of Zanzibar, partly because of the encroachment into the legislative competence of Zanzibar, but perhaps to a greater extent for a politically sensitive reason, that is, because of the human rights violations that have taken place in Zanzibar. Article 132 also controls the passing of subsidiary legislation within the respective legislative competences. In this respect, it seems that the subsidiary legislation passed on the basis of the original act has to conform to the same delimitation of the legislative competences as the regular acts. At the same time, it also seems that a legal basis in an act is required for the passing of subsidiary legislation.

5.5.5 *Two Lawmakers with a Joint Pool of Sovereignty*

On the top of the distribution of legislative competences by way of enumeration for Parliament and by way of residual implication to the House of Representatives, the Constitution of Tanzania contains some particular specifications of legislative competence that actually amount to enumerations of legislative competence of Zanzibar. In Art. 114, it is recognized that the Constitution of Tanzania does not prevent, in accordance with the law applicable in Zanzibar, the continuance or

[215] According to some interlocutors, such consultations took place when the Maritime Code of Tanzania was enacted.

establishment of the High Court of Zanzibar or courts subordinate to it, and Art. 115 states that the jurisdiction of the High Court of Zanzibar shall be as specified in the laws applicable in Zanzibar.[216] The legislative competence of Zanzibar to create its own court system is thus recognized.

There is also a recognition of the taxation powers of both the Parliament and the House of Representatives in Art. 138. According to sub-section 1, Parliament has the right to enact tax legislation, but under sub-section 2, these powers shall not preclude the House of Representatives of Zanzibar from exercising its power to impose taxes of any kind in accordance with the authority of that House. This means that Zanzibar has its own taxation powers in areas that remain outside the sphere of income tax, customs duty and excise duty designated for the Union in point 10 of the First Schedule.[217] The taxation powers of Zanzibar are exercised on the basis of Art. 133 of the Constitution of Zanzibar, according to which no tax of any kind shall be imposed except in accordance with a law enacted by the House of Representatives or according to a lower norm enacted on the basis of a law. However, the provision at the same time sustains the taxation powers of the Union by concluding that the taxation powers of Zanzibar shall not preclude the Union Parliament from exercising its power to impose tax of any kind in respect of Union matters in accordance with the powers of the Union Parliament. There is nonetheless the condition imposed by the Constitution of Zanzibar that consultations between the RGZ and the Government of the United Republic have been made and agreed to before the Union Parliament enacts the relevant tax law. In addition, although income tax powers are a union issue, there is an understanding that whatever is collected in Zanzibar from individuals and business corporations, the tax collected in Zanzibar remains in Zanzibar and is used for the purposes of the government of Zanzibar. As a practical matter, the income tax is collected by the Tanzania revenue authority, but the funds are transferred to the Ministry of Finance of Zanzibar.

Finally, according to Art. 145(1) of the Constitution of Tanzania, either Parliament or the House of Representatives shall establish local government authorities in each region, district, urban area and village in the United Republic. This is sustained in sub-section (2) of the same provision, according to which Parliament or the House of Representatives, as the case may be, shall enact a law providing for the

[216]Article 115(2) of the Constitution of Tanzania creates a concurrent jurisdiction for the High Court of Zanzibar and the High Court of the United Republic for situations where any law enacted by Parliament and which is applicable in Mainland Tanzania and also in Tanzania Zanzibar vests any power in the High Court. Hence the relevant High Court is the one within whose jurisdiction the law is applied, either Mainland or Zanzibar.

[217]The tax legislation of Zanzibar includes the Value Added Tax Act, 1998, Act No. 4 of 1998 (which avoids double taxation with Mainland by prescribing that if the VAT is already paid in the Mainland, the goods or services are not anymore taxable in Zanzibar, except to the extent the VAT is lower in the Mainland), the Port Service Charges Act, 1999, Act No. 2 of 1999, the Hotel Levy Act, 1995, Act No. 1 of 1995, the Stamp Duty Act, 1996, Act No. 6 of 1996, the Petroleum Levy Act, 2001, Act No. 7 of 2001, and the Zanzibar Social Security Fund Act, 2005, Act No. 2 of 2005.

establishment of local government authorities, their structure and composition, sources of revenue and procedure for the conduct of their business. The provision seems to place an exclusive lawmaking competence with the House of Representatives of Zanzibar as regards local government in Zanzibar.

Under Art. 63(1) of the Constitution of Zanzibar, the legislative powers are actually exercised by a Legislative Council which consists of two parts, the President of Zanzibar, on the one hand, and the House of Representatives, on the other. Article 78 of the Constitution of Zanzibar departs from the existence of a set of Union Matters when stating that legislative power in relation to all matters that are not Union Matters in Zanzibar is vested in the House of Representatives, exercised in principle by means of passing Bills. After a bill is passed by the House of Representatives it is presented to the President of Zanzibar for his assent, after which it becomes law and is printed in the Official Gazette. The bill is, at the outset, drafted in English, after which it is translated into Kiswahili for the purposes of scrutiny in the House of Representatives. It seems that the President records his assent onto the English-language version, but the act is published in its Kiswahili-language version in the Official Gazette. It is possible for the President to deny assent to a bill, but when returned to the House of Representatives, the House may try to override the veto of the President by a two thirds qualified vote of the Members of the House. The position of the President is, however, very strong in this context, because he may, instead of accepting the overriding of his veto, dissolve the House of Representatives.

The decision-making formula in the House of Representatives is, according to Art. 83(1) of the Constitution of Zanzibar, in principle a simple majority amongst those present and voting. There are, however, decisions that have to be taken by other majorities. Under Art. 80(1), amendments to the Constitution of Zanzibar are passed by the House with support both at the first and the second reading by votes equaling not less than two thirds of all votes of Members of the House of Representatives. Consequently, a constitutional amendment has to secure a qualified majority twice, something which is made even more difficult by the fact that the majority seems to be counted from all Members, not of those present and voting. However, there is a reservation for a constitutional referendum of a decisive nature as an amendment method in Art. 80A concerning certain parts and sections of the Constitution as defined in sub-section 2 of the provision, including section 80A itself.[218]

It is also possible to analyze the position of Zanzibar against the background of the principle of self-determination and to characterize the Union arrangement, its constitutional evolution and the position of Zanzibar from that perspective. Under the 1960 UN General Assembly Resolution 1514 on the Granting of Independence to Colonial Countries and Peoples, Zanzibar exercised its right to self-determination in 1963 by becoming independent from a colonial situation under British rule. The decision to form the union with Tanganyika in 1964 was another application of

[218] However, Art. 80A(3) allows for certain technical amendments of the particular provisions without a referendum, pursuant to a qualified majority of two-thirds. Article 80A(4) lays down the expectation of the enactment of a referendum act for the purposes of constitutional amendments.

the right to self-determination, that of free association or integration with another independent State. If self-determination is understood as the competence to exercise lawmaking powers, independence in 1963 signified the establishment of complete lawmaking powers for Zanzibar, while the Union in 1964 implied that some of the original lawmaking powers of Zanzibar were transferred to the Union. However, Zanzibar did not hand over all of its lawmaking powers in 1964 and did not agree to a complete integration of itself into Tanzania. Instead, Zanzibar transferred a relatively small portion of lawmaking powers to the Union, while keeping for itself most of the lawmaking powers. For instance, in the area of criminal law, the Penal Decree Act specifies the extent of the legislative competence of Zanzibar by way of a complete definition of offences and penalties. From that perspective, the additions to the Union matters after the conclusion of the Articles of Union actually diminish the internal self-determination that was left to Zanzibar in the Articles of Union.

Although the range of legislative powers of Zanzibar is vast, with matters of the Union mainly in the areas of foreign affairs, defense and financial issues, and Zanzibar matters in such areas as health, agriculture, construction, etc., it nevertheless seems as though the legislative activities of the House of Representatives did not result in very many pieces of law on an annual level. During the period of 1984 to 2006, the House of Representatives passed around ten (10) acts per year, some of which were acts amending existing laws. The lowest number of acts passed was in 1987 and 2000, when three acts were enacted each year, while the highest number of acts passed has been 17, which took place in 1986 and 1992. One reason for this may be the fact that the statutory law or positive law norms count only for a smaller part of the overall norms of the legal order, while the common law is probably the source of the main part of the norms. The Muslim law applied by the Kadhis' Courts is also relatively limited in scope, and its scope is further limited by the fact that the law of procedure applied in those courts is that of common law. In comparison with Zanzibar, the arrangement in Aceh stands in many respects on weaker ground.

5.6 Aceh: Unclear Implementation of the Settlement

5.6.1 Residual Powers as the Starting Point?

When considering the starting point for the distribution of powers between the central government of Indonesia and Aceh, one is easily led to believe that the central government has kept for itself six substantive areas, while the residual powers are vested in the organs of Aceh. According to para. 1.1.2 (a) of the MoU, "Aceh will exercise authority within all sectors of public affairs, which will be administered in conjunction with its civil and judicial administration, except in the fields of foreign affairs, external defense, national security, monetary and fiscal matters, justice and freedom of religion, the policies of which belong to the Government of the Republic of Indonesia in conformity with the Constitution". This is certainly to a large extent the way in which the GAM understood the distribution of powers when the peace agreement was concluded and on the basis of which the heirs of the GAM still today argues for the improvement of the position of Aceh.

The reality in respect of the distribution of powers is, however, much more confusing, in particular when studying the provisions of the LoGA, most of which actually deal with public powers. It appears that Aceh is not vested with all authority within all sectors of public affairs, but rather that Aceh exercises some authority in all sectors of public affairs that are identified as the residual portion of authority outside of the enumerated powers of the central government. The reality is even more confusing, because according to the LoGA, Aceh exercises some authority even in such areas of public affairs that are designated as areas of the central government, with religion, justice and fiscal matters being such examples.[219]

Article 7(1) of the LoGA grants Aceh and district/municipality governments the power to govern and administer governmental affairs in all public sectors except for governmental affairs falling under the jurisdiction of the Indonesian Government. Hence in principle, the LoGA is allocating a residual sphere of authority to Aceh, while operating on the basis of enumeration when concluding in sub-section 2 that the Government's authority as referred to in sub-section 1 shall include governmental affairs at the national level, overseas politics, defense, security, judicial matters, monetary matters, national revenues, and certain aspects of religious affairs.[220] The

[219]Although police is a national function, the Governor of Aceh (and regent/mayor at the local level) is nonetheless granted the power, under Art. 244, to form a civilian police unit for enforcing a *qanun* related to public order and community tranquillity. In addition, the Governor (and the regent/mayor at the local level), may form a *Wilayatul Hisbah* police unit as a part of the civilian police unit for enforcing *syari'yah qanuns* passed for the implementation of Islamic law. Hence, on the top of state police, there is also provincial and local police forces in Aceh. As concerns courts, there exist in Aceh both general courts of the Republic of Indonesia and shari'a courts, and the case has been made that after the Tsunami, in particular, the shari'a courts have gained more competence, while the general court's competence has diminished. In the area of, e.g., criminal law, petty crimes (jinayah) is governed by Aceh *qanun* and tried by the *shari'a* court, while "the status of other criminal matters, such as theft, murder, and rape, which are currently not yet dealt with a *qanun*, remain unclear, and so, at present, they remain under the jurisdiction of the civil court". If the competences of Aceh to enact *qanun* (bylaws) is extended further, one future prospect is that the material jurisdiction of the civil court is reduced to labour law and land disputes without connection to inheritance matters, making it a special court for these purposes and for persons who are not Muslims. See Salim (2009), p. 11.

[220]According to the Explanatory Notes on the LoGA, the meaning of "governmental affairs at the national level" in the provision "includes policies in the sector of national planning, policies in the sector of national development control, balance of finances, state administration, national economic institutions, establishment and development of human resources, strategic high technology, and national conservation and standardization. What is meant by policies is the Government's authority to carry out the establishment, facilitation, determination, and implementation of national governmental affairs. The authority of the central government as concerns national issues will be determined by a government regulation, the draft of which is undergoing, during the summer of 2009, a review process involving the central government and the Governor of Aceh. The draft covers the authority of the central government in Aceh in all the relevant government

powers that the provision deals with seem, however, to be of a regulatory nature, at least insofar as the powers of Aceh and district/municipality governments are concerned. Article 12 of the LoGA enhances at least in principle the distribution of powers by providing that the Aceh Government and district/municipality governments shall administer governmental affairs under their authority except those constituting the authority of the Indonesian Government as referred to in article 7(2), thereby excluding the enumerated national powers from the ambit of provincial or local government. The administration of the "provincial" affairs shall be governed and managed by the Aceh Government and the district/municipality governments themselves, which seems to mean that the functions of the provincial level cannot be transferred to the Indonesian Government to be taken care of by its administration.

According to Art. 23 of the LoGA, the Aceh Regional House of Representatives, that is, the DPRA, shall have a large number of duties and powers. The DPRA shall, *inter alia*, formulate *qanuns* of Aceh in consultation with the Governor so that joint approval is achieved, supervise the implementation of *qanuns* of Aceh and other legal regulations, supervise the policies of the Government of Aceh for implementing development programs in Aceh, and manage natural and other economic resources, as well as capital investment and international cooperation. The DPRA shall also make recommendations for the appointment and dismissal of the Governor/Vice Governor of Aceh to the President of Indonesia through the Minister of Home Affairs, inform the Governor and the Aceh Election Committee (KIP) regarding the upcoming expiration of the term of office of the Governor/Vice Governor, and select a Vice Governor in the event that the Vice Governor position becomes vacant. In addition, the DPRA shall grant approval for planned international cooperation to be entered into by the Government of Aceh, provide consideration on planned international cooperation to be entered into by the Indonesian Government that directly involves Aceh, provide consideration on planned legislative actions of the Indonesian House of Representatives that directly involve the governance of Aceh, grant approval on planned inter-provincial cooperation and/or cooperation with third parties that pose a burden on the people and region, and request an accountability report from the Governor with respect to the execution of government administration,[221] to evaluate government performance. Finally, the DPRA shall provide recommendations for the establishment of the Aceh KIP and the Elections Supervisory Committee, and supervise and request an accountability report on the implementation of activities and use of budget by the Aceh KIP with respect to the general election of Governor/Vice Governor. The DPRA shall also

sectors, while the rest of the matters are supposed to fall under the authority of the Government of Aceh and the government of district/city.

[221] It should be noted that the Explanatory Notes to the LoGA interpret the function of the accountability report as follows: "The accountability report constitutes a progress report on the implementation of governance and is not intended to bring down the governor." This is yet another indication of the fact that there is no mechanism of parliamentary accountability between the Governor and the DPRA.

exercise other authorities as governed by prevailing laws and regulations. The DPRA has, under Art. 23(2), the powers to adopt bylaws, with guidance from prevailing laws and regulations, for the implementation of the duties and powers that the DPRA has. There is thus a presumption that the DPRA may adopt its own rules of procedure.

As concluded in Art. 22 of the LoGA, the DPRA has legislative, budgetary and supervisory functions and is entitled to form its own organizational structure in accordance with the special characteristics of Aceh.[222] It seems, however, as if the DPRA did not have very much leeway in formulating its own internal rules and procedures.[223] Instead, the LoGA also appears to be relatively specific concerning the internal operation of the DPRA. The main functions of the DPRA are to discuss and approve draft *qanuns* regarding Aceh and income and expenditure budgets, together with the Governor.[224] The DPRA has the function of utilizing the budget as determined in the APBA/APBK and administered by the council secretary in accordance with prevailing laws and regulations.

[222]The same provisions apply to the DPRK at the local government level.

[223]However, articles 30–35 of the LoGA nevertheless prescribe a number of internal dimensions of the DPRA, leaving relatively little to the rules and procedures adopted by the DPRA itself in the form of a *qanun*. According to the LoGA, the DPRA shall consist of a chairperson, commission, deliberating committee, budget committee, honor council, legislative committee, and other organs as required. The DPRA may form at least 5 (five) but no more than 8 (eight) commissions. The Legislative Committee is apparently a mandatory permanent committee that shall exist, and it shall serve as the center for drafting *qanuns*. The Legislative Committee of the DPRA shall formulate regional legislative programs containing a list of draft *qanuns* for 1 (one) membership session and priorities for each budget year, to be subsequently reported in a Plenary Session for affirmation through DPRA decrees, prepare draft *qanuns* submitted through the initiative of the DPRA based on established priority programs, harmonize, integrate, and finalize draft *qanun* concepts submitted by the members, commissions, and joint commissions prior to such drafts being submitted to the DPRA leadership, provide advice with respect to submission of draft *qanuns* by members, commissions, and joint commissions, other than draft *qanuns* listed in the regional legislative program or priority draft *qanuns* for the ongoing year, carry out deliberations and revisions/improvements to draft *qanuns* as specifically instructed by the Deliberation Committee, disseminate and gather inputs on draft *qanuns* currently being and/or to be deliberated, and socialize draft *qanuns* that have been approved, keep up with developments and conduct evaluations regarding the subject matter of *qanuns* by way of coordination with the commissions, receive inputs from the community, both written and verbal, regarding draft *qanuns*, provide advice on draft *qanuns* under deliberation by the Governor and the DPRA, and make an inventory of legal issues and regulations at the end of the DPRA membership sessions to be used as materials by the succeeding Legislative Committee. Hence it appears that the Legislative Committee of the DPRA is the engine of the normative activities of the DPRA.

[224]The DPRA has the function to draft budgets in accordance with the function, duties, and authorities of the DPRA as a part of the Aceh income and expenditure budget using standard price benchmarks agreed between the Governor and DPRA, as affirmed by Gubernatorial Regulation.

5.6.2 *Large Amount of Overlap to Be Negotiated*

In spite of the boundaries thus created between the Indonesian Government and Aceh, the Indonesian Government may, when executing the governmental authorities within its power as referred to in sub-section 2 of Art. 7, choose between different options. According to Art. 7(3) the Indonesian Government may exercise its enumerated powers and authorities by itself, transfer a portion of its authority to the Aceh Government and district/municipality governments, delegate a portion of its authority to the Governor as a representative of the Government and/or governmental agencies, or assign a portion of its authority to the Aceh Government and the district/municipality and *gampong* governments based on the principle of assistance tasks. As a consequence, although there exist national powers that are enumerated, it does not mean that they are necessarily exercised solely at the national level, but they may also be taken care of at the level of Aceh or its districts/municipalities. The attitude towards the enumerated national powers is, therefore, in principle very flexible and dependent upon consultation and consideration by the Acehnese, that is, those powers would appear at the provincial level on the basis of negotiations.

The LoGA identifies for Aceh a number of mandatory matters and also creates a sphere of discretionary matters. Article 16 enumerates the mandatory matters that fall under the authority of the Aceh Government as matters on an Aceh-wide scale.

> These matters include planning, utilization, and supervision of zoning, planning and control of development/construction, maintenance of public order and community tranquillity, provision of public facilities and infrastructure, health sector management, administration of education and allocation of potential human resources, handling of inter-district/municipality social problems, inter-district/municipality services for the employment and labor sectors, facilitation of the development of cooperatives and small and medium enterprises, including inter-district/municipality aspects, environmental management, land services including inter-district/municipality aspects, population and civil registry services, general government administration services, administration services related to investments including interdistrict/municipality aspects, and provision of other basic services that are not provided by the district/municipality governments.

There is a list of other mandatory affairs falling under the authority of the Aceh Government that constitute the implementation of the special authorities of Aceh, including administration of religious affairs in the form of implementing Islamic law for Muslims in Aceh while continuing to maintain interfaith harmony, administration of customary (*adat*) affairs that hinge on Islam,[225] administration of quality education and the incorporation of local content in educational materials in accordance with Islamic law, role of clerics in the determination of policies in Aceh, and administration and management of the *Hajj* pilgrimage in accordance with prevailing laws and regulations.

---

[225] As pointed out by Salim (2009), pp. 3 f., 14 f., the customary adat law and shari'a law contain similar norms which make the Acehnese version of the two sets of norms overlapping and intertwined in many areas. Together with the positivised Indonesian and Acehnese norms, adat law and shari'a law create an interesting setting of legal pluralism in Aceh.

In addition, the LoGA contains a large number of specific provisions which outline the substantive areas within which Aceh (and also its districts/municipalities) may exercise authority. These substantive areas are labor (e.g., granting of licenses for foreign workers, protection of workers, etc.), finance (management of different funds, imposition of regional taxes and charges, issuance of regional government bonds), education (which, however, shall be an integral part of the national educational system as locally adapted and with Islamic education), culture, social affairs, health, telecommunications, management of natural resources and normative powers (*qanun*, gubernatorial regulations and regent/mayor regulations). Although education is a substantive area that would seem to be within the powers of Aceh, it appears that the definition of education covers education from the primary level to the high school level, leaving university education to the state. The appointment and functioning of the Truth and Reconciliation Committee in Aceh, created under articles 229 and 230 of the LoGA, is largely the responsibility of the Aceh Government, although a national Truth and Reconciliation Committee also exists.[226]

Article 16(3) of the LoGA recognizes matters of the Aceh Government that are discretionary in nature. They include such governmental affairs that have the clear potential to enhance community welfare in line with the conditions, uniqueness, and superior potential of Aceh. This means that the Government of Aceh has general competence within its jurisdiction and that it may perform functions which are additional to the ones listed in sub-sections 1 and 2 of Art. 16. In principle, the Aceh Government could do this by identifying an area where its actions are needed and decide to act within such an area. It is hence possible to say that the Aceh Government has both a special and a general competence.

There is an interesting implementation provision in Art. 16(4) concerning the matters referred to in paragraphs (1), (2), and (3), that is, concerning matters that are either mandatory for the Government of Aceh or discretionary. They shall be governed further by Aceh *qanun*, with guidance from prevailing laws and regulations. All of these matters that the Government of Aceh shall or may deal with have to be specified by bylaws enacted by the DPRA, but the bylaws are not independent or decided upon on the basis of some prerogative of the Aceh Government. Instead, they have to be adopted with guidance from prevailing laws and regulations. This, again, seems to mean that the bylaws of Aceh that implement the mandatory and discretionary powers of Aceh cannot deviate too much from the national norms. This is underlined in respect of the mandatory matters in Art. 14(3), according to which the implementation of mandatory governmental affairs shall be conducted with reference to the minimum standards of service, carried out in phases, and stipulated by the Indonesian Government.

[226] The reference to prevailing laws and regulations in the context of the Truth and Reconciliation Committee are, according to the Explanatory Notes to the LoGA, the provisions of Law Number 27 of 2004 concerning the Truth and Reconciliation Commission. It appears, however, that the Constitutional Court has ruled it unconstitutional.

In addition, the role of the national norms is underlined in a great number of provisions of the LoGA that deal with the substantive matters, such as social affairs, health and education. In most of these fields, the powers of Aceh must be exercised in accordance with the prevailing laws and regulations, that is, in accordance with the legislation enacted by the Indonesian parliament and presidential and governmental regulations adopted by the central government authorities. For instance, Art. 141(1) prescribes that comprehensive development planning for Aceh and its districts/municipalities shall be prepared as a component of the national development planning system within the framework of the Unitary State of the Republic of Indonesia, with attention given to Islamic values, socio-cultural issues, sustainability and environmental concepts, justice and equality and necessity. Conformity with national norms is thus expected, and it is difficult to estimate at this point in time how wide the sphere of autonomy might be. It appears, however, that there is not very much room for decisions that deviate from the rules at the national level. This impression is strengthened by the requirement in many substantive fields that the decisions of Aceh are made according to or guided by norms, standards, and procedures, that is, by so-called national standards.[227] In some provisions of the LoGA, there are also explicit requirements that the action at the level of Aceh be based on a regulation by the central government (in five instances) or by the president (in at least three instances).

However, the LoGA also contains a number of provisions that outline substantive areas in which the Indonesian Government exercises authority without much involvement by the Aceh Government. These are the Indonesian armed forces, the police (although the approval of the Governor of Aceh shall be sought when the chief of police in Aceh is appointed), and public prosecution (although the approval of the Governor of Aceh shall be sought when the head of Aceh's prosecution office is appointed). Because the judiciary is a function of the central government, the establishment of the human rights court referred to in Art. 228 of the LoGA is a task of the central government authorities. So are the Sabang Free Trade Area and Free Port that are separated from the customs and excise jurisdictions, as provided for in Art. 167 of the LoGA.[228] Under Art. 172, safety in shipping and air traffic for public

[227]According to the introduction to the Explanatory Notes on the LoGA, the "existence of provisions in this Law concerning the need for norms, standards, procedures, and matters that are strategic and national in nature and are the authority of the Government, is not intended to diminish the authority held by the Aceh Government and its district/municipality governments, but rather it constitutes a form of establishment, facilitation, enactment, and implementation of national governmental affairs". In spite of this intention, there may be pressures from the direction of the unitary state to apply same national standards in Aceh as in all other regions, and because Aceh is a relatively small part of Indonesia, it may also be easily forgotten about when national standards are applied. National standards may thus, in the context of Aceh, amount to claw-back clauses that retain the power with the national government.

[228]However, under Art. 169, the Indonesian Government and Aceh Government shall jointly develop the Sabang Free Trade Area as a centre for regional economic growth. At the same time, the Governor of Aceh is designated as the representative of the Indonesian Government in the area and is empowered in Art. 168 to prohibit certain goods from entering or exiting the Sabang area.

seaports and airports falls under the responsibility of the Indonesian Government in accordance with prevailing laws and regulations. In addition, under Art. 4(1), the central government or its agencies may exercise authority in the establishment of special zones in Aceh and/or in districts/municipalities to carry out certain government functions of a special nature.[229] According to Art. 142(1), the Indonesian Government shall have the authority to determine norms, standards, and procedures for zoning (spatial or physical planning) in the formulation of the zoning plan for Aceh and its districts/municipalities, while taking into account issues of sustainable development and preservation of environmental functions. The reliance on national standards is not only limited to zoning, but as indicated above, it is a feature of a number of other substantive areas as well.

What the LoGA in effect creates is a large area of overlapping or shared powers, where the central government of Indonesia and the Government of Aceh have to agree on how material powers are distributed. The agreement about the distribution of powers is evidently a matter which falls under the consultation and consideration procedure between the central government and Aceh, and the result of the agreement is recorded in a regulation of the central government in a very detailed manner. The Indonesian central government regards the distribution of powers as a particular devolution of powers from the centre to the province rather than as a separation of powers of a "federal" nature. The shared nature of the powers is indicated at least in the 15 or so provisions of the LoGA through reference to the role of the Indonesian Government, Aceh Government and district/municipal governments in taking care of a matter, but it seems that the shared nature of most of the powers recognized in the LoGA is simply presumed. In some instances, like the management of oil and gas resources, joint management is explicitly prescribed by the LoGA. According to Art. 160, the Indonesian Government and Aceh Government shall jointly manage the oil and gas resources located on land and in the sea within Aceh territory, and as concerns the Sabang free trade area, Art. 169 provides that the Indonesian Government and Aceh Government shall jointly develop it as a centre for regional economic growth. At the same time, the Governor of Aceh is designated as the representative of the Indonesian Government in the area. To implement the joint management, the Indonesian Government and Aceh Government may appoint or form an implementing agency to be jointly affirmed. The shared nature of the powers and the different mechanisms of interaction that the LoGA prescribes create the impression that the Government of Aceh

[229] According to para. 4 of Art. 4 of the LoGA, special zones established for trade purposes and/or to serve as free ports shall be governed by prevailing laws (undang-undang), that is, legislation enacted by the House of Representatives. Special zones other than those referred to in para. 4 and the division of authority among the Indonesian Government, Aceh Government and/or district/municipality governments, and the special zone authorities shall be governed by Government Regulation (Peraturan Pemerintah).

and the Government of Indonesia are to a great extent intertwined, not only in theory but also in practice.[230]

5.6.3 *'Consultation and Consent' or 'Consultation and Consideration'?*

A key provision of the LoGA with a view to the distribution of powers is Art. 8, which deals with three categories of decisions at the national level with direct relevance for Aceh, namely (1) drafts of international treaties that directly involve the governance of Aceh and that the central government is planning to conclude, (2) drafts of laws prepared by the DPR, that is, the Indonesian parliament, that directly involve the governance of Aceh, and (3) administrative policies that directly involve the governance of Aceh and which the central government is planning to adopt.[231] In case of all these three categories, decisions at state level shall be developed with the consultation and consideration of Acehnese institutions. As concerns draft treaties and draft laws, the consultation and consideration is sought from the DPRA, while in the case of the administrative policies prepared by the central government, the consultation and consideration is sought from the Governor of Aceh.[232]

The contents of Art. 8 of LoGA are contentious against the background of the MoU, which in para. 1.1.2 refers to the concepts of consultation and consent of the appropriate Acehnese bodies within the three areas. While the concept of consultation may be understood as a fair opportunity to be heard, the concept of consent in the MoU should, in its ordinary meaning, be understood as constituting formal permission to go forward with a decision-making process. If the consent is not

[230]This impression is strengthened by the statement in the Explanatory Notes to the LoGA, according to which "[m]atters to be included in Government Regulations as referred to in this provision are matters that have been jointly agreed by the Government and Aceh Government, including among others the appointment or formation of implementing agencies, procedures for negotiation, drafting of cooperation agreements, setting of target amounts for oil and natural gas production and for production that is sold (lifting), production cost recovery, profit sharing, supervision, community development, reclamation obligations, and appointment of independent auditors".

[231]As stipulated in Art. 42(2), the Governor shall consult and provide consideration on administrative policies established by the Indonesian Government that directly involve Aceh, in accordance with the provisions of the LoGA. The Explanatory Notes to the LoGA state that "[w]hat is meant by administrative policies in this provision are policies directly related to Aceh governance, for example, matters provided for in this Law such as the expansion of territory, formation of special zones, and planning for the formulation and amendment of laws and regulations directly related to the Aceh region".

[232]However, there does not seem to exist yet any working relationship between the national parliament and the DPRA, while there seems to be one between the Government of Aceh and the central government.

granted, the planned measure should not be realized, at least not in the exact form it was first proposed.

Effectively, the concept of consent in the MoU would have created a regional entrenchment for the benefit of Aceh as concerns treaties, national legislation and administrative policies that are decided at the level of the central government. During the preparation of the LoGA, the concept of consent was, however, changed to the concept of consideration (sometimes even to be understood as advice). Although the MoU established principles for domestic implementation, consideration would seem to be fundamentally different from consent. The reason for such an amendment was ostensibly the fact that a requirement of consent from Acehnese institutions would have impaired the sovereignty of the legislature of Indonesia and the position of the central government. This seems to be correct, but at the same time, the shift from consent to consideration can be understood as a breach of the MoU,[233] because "although the Aceh parliament may not agree to certain policies, the national government still has the final say with regard to policies on Aceh, including administrative policies, and international relations and legal policies".[234] In addition, under Art. 8(4), further provisions concerning procedures for consultation and consideration shall be stipulated in a Presidential Regulation.[235] Hence ultimately, the contentious procedure is outlined in a regulation enacted at the level of central government, a regulation which in itself is part of the requirement of consultation and consideration in Art. 8(3).

As concerns the negotiations about the actual scope of the authority to be exercised by Aceh, the bottom line is probably the authority allocated to the 32 other provinces of Indonesia under the general regionalization legislation and the substantive law of Indonesia.[236] Because Aceh is a special entity in that context and

[233]The explanation for the discrepancy between the MoU and the LoGA seems to be that the MoU was negotiated by the Government of Indonesia, at which stage the concept of consent was used, but the LoGA would not have been enacted by the Indonesian parliament if the draft of the LoGA had not used the concept of advise (or consideration, as the term actually seems to translate) instead. See, e.g., Miller (2009), p. 161. This seems plausible against the background of the fact that normally, the Indonesian parliament strives to make its decision by unanimity, as actually expected under the fourth principle of the *Pancasila*. On the issue of unanimity and the consensus-seeking decision-making praxis in the context of constitutional amendment, see Lindsey (2008), p. 23.

[234]International Development Law Organisation, Judicial Assessment of Political Parties' Programs in Aceh towards the 2009 General Election, Report, 22 September 2008, p. 2 f.

[235]See Presidential Regulation No. 75/2009 on the Procedure of Consultation Concerning Legislation, Regulations and International Agreements that Concern Aceh.

[236]For other provinces, there is the Governmental Regulation No. 38/2008, which determines the sphere of authority of the central government, the authority of the provincial government and the authority of the district/city government. The draft Government Regulation on the authority of the central government in Aceh, undergoing preparation during the summer of 2009, merely attempts to stipulate the authority of the central government of Indonesia, while the rest seems to become the authority of the Government of Aceh and the district/city government as determined in a separate *qanun* of Aceh.

has its own special law, that is, the LoGA, as the basis for its governance, the powers accorded to Aceh should be greater than the powers granted to the regular provinces. However, the powers of Aceh can probably not be so great that they could completely preempt the powers of the central government in any of the substantive areas that are relevant for Aceh. Therefore, the solution for each substantive area is probably to be sought somewhere in the middle ground between the powers of the regular provinces and the central government. As laid down in the LoGA, the distribution of powers between the central government and Aceh is therefore very fluid. To establish a clearer distribution of powers, a government regulation was being drawn up in May 2009, with some 100 pages of provisions, but as of June 2011, the negotiations about the distribution of powers were still going on. In comparison to other sub-state entities, the situation is thus unusual: a more exact borderline between the central government and Aceh is determined in separate negotiations, not in the autonomy statute, under the format of consultation and consideration. The negotiations should result in an additional agreement between the central government and Aceh which is formalized in a government regulation. Because the procedure of consultation and consideration is applied,[237] the government regulation may become somewhat more permanent than would be the case if the regulation was just an ordinary government regulation operating in the ordinary regions of Indonesia.

Formally speaking, the authority that para. 1.1.2 (a) of the MoU refers to is a very open concept, ranging from legislative powers to the authority to make an administrative decision in individual cases. In addition, para. 1.4.1 of the MoU prescribes the separation of powers between the legislature, the executive and the judiciary as if the Acehnese legislature referred to was actually a lawmaking body exercising exclusive legislative powers in Aceh. The same impression is created by para. 1.4.2, according to which the legislature of Aceh will redraft the legal code for Aceh on the basis of the universal principles of human rights as provided for in the United Nations International Covenants on Civil and Political Rights and on Economic, Social and Cultural Rights. Also, under para. 1.2.4, the legislature of Aceh will not be entitled to enact any laws until 2009 without the consent of the head of the Aceh administration, a provision which creates the impression of legislative powers proper. Because the sole legislative body in Indonesia is, according to the Constitution, the House of Representatives of Indonesia, the authority Aceh is exercising is, however, not legislative power proper, but the possibility to pass bylaws called *qanun* that in part are based on and required by the LoGA, in part on substantive national legislation. The bylaws are therefore to be characterized as secondary legislation based on a delegation of powers from the central government to Aceh. This nature of secondary legislation of the *qanun* has not prevented the Indonesian lawmaker from using language in the LoGA which

[237] As stated in para. 1.1.2 (d) of the MoU, administrative measures undertaken by the Government of Indonesia with regard to Aceh will be implemented in consultation with and with the consent of the head of the Aceh administration. The consultation and consideration procedure of government regulations with direct effect for Aceh is thus ultimately grounded in the MoU.

refers to legislative powers vested in the DPRA. For instance, Art. 22 of the LoGA lays down that the DPRA has legislative, budgetary and supervisory functions, while Art. 30 establishes the legislative committee of the DPRA.

5.6.4 Bylaws Issued under National Law and National Standards as the Normative Tool

The nature of the autonomy arrangement in Aceh is, of course, greatly affected by the distinction between exclusive legislative powers or legislative powers proper, on the one hand, and powers to make bylaws on the basis of national legislation, on the other. While the MoU may create the impression that Aceh actually has legislative powers proper, the LoGA in reality implements the MoU by granting Aceh the power to pass province-wide bylaws and by granting the district/municipal level the power to pass local bylaws. The powers that are distributed are not legislative powers, because the legislative powers proper belong to the House of Representatives of Indonesia and cannot be divided under the prevailing national doctrine, but instead powers at the level of secondary legislation. As a consequence, the normative powers that may be exercised in Aceh are of a regulatory nature only, subject to the requirements of conformity with national legislation.

At the same time as the normative powers of Aceh are of a secondary nature, the LoGA grants the DPRA the competence to enact bylaws which carry criminal sanctions, mainly for petty crimes. As laid down in Art. 241(2) a *qanun* may contain the potential punishment of imprisonment for up to 6 (six) months and/or a fine up to Rs. 50,000,000.00 (fifty million rupees, that is, 5,000 US$). Under sub-section 3 of the provision, a *qanun* may contain a potential punishment or fine other than that referred to in sub-section 2 in accordance with punishments that are governed by other laws and regulations, that is, in national law. However, sub-section 4 prescribes that a *qanun* concerning *jinayah* violations, that is, violations of Islamic criminal law, shall be exempted from the provisions of sub-sections 1, 2 and 3, which may mean that criminal sanctions under Islamic criminal law are determined with reference to religious concepts of the levels of punishment that may be different and perhaps in excess of the limits mentioned in Art. 241(2). At the same time, however, the national penal code is applicable to a wide range of crimes, although in the future, the competences of Aceh may become wider in the area of criminal law.

The LoGA creates different supervision mechanisms that give the central government a superior role in relation to the Government of Aceh. A general supervision power is established in Art. 11 of the LoGA. According to the provision the Indonesian Government shall establish norms, standards, and procedures and conduct supervision of the administration of affairs carried out by the Government of

Aceh and its districts/municipalities.[238] However, these norms, standards and procedures shall not diminish the authority of the Government of Aceh and the district/municipality governments as referred to in article 7(1), that is, the "residual" sphere of competence of Aceh. In the execution of such supervision the Indonesian Government may implement the function by itself and/or delegate the function to the Governor as a representative of the Indonesian Government to supervise the districts/municipalities.

The general supervisory power that the Indonesian Government holds is supplemented by a power under Art. 235 to supervise bylaws (*qanuns*), which supervision shall be conducted in accordance with prevailing laws and regulations.[239] Within that particular supervision framework, the Indonesian Government may invalidate a *qanun* that contravenes public interests, another *qanun* or superseding laws and regulations, unless otherwise provided for in the LoGA.[240] The reference to invalidation of a bylaw because of contravention of public interest is probably mainly intended to safeguard the territorial integrity of Indonesia in such a situation where Aceh would try to press a separatist agenda ultimately aimed at a declaration of independence. Interestingly, the power to harmonize the norms of the provincial legal order by means of invalidating bylaws at the same hierarchical level that are in contravention with each other is, in the case of Aceh, primarily held by the Indonesian Government, although the expected mechanism would, in this respect, be the courts of law when trying concrete cases.

However, even the Supreme Court is charged with the control of bylaws, because it can review a *qanun* in accordance with prevailing laws and regulations. Because a bylaw that governs the implementation of Islamic law may only be

---

[238] As stated in the Explanatory Notes to the LoGA, norms are rules or stipulations that are used as a system for the implementation of regional governance. While standards are references that are used as guideposts in the implementation of regional governance. Procedures are methods or approaches for the implementation of regional governance. On the basis of LoGA, the Indonesian Government watches over Aceh and it is under tangible supervision. The impression is that Aceh is kept on a relatively short leash without much room for own maneuvers.

[239] An act of principal importance is Law No. 10/2004 on the Making of Legislation. If Aceh drafts a bylaw according to the guidance in Law No. 10/2004, the local law is valid. Hence Law No. 10/2004 is a general piece of law that directs all drafting of legislation at national, provincial and local level. The supervision of the drafting of a *qanun* is, with reference to Art. 235(1) of the LoGA, regulated by the Law No. 32/2004 as long as the LoGA does not introduce deviating provisions concerning supervision.

[240] By May 2009, one *Qanun* of Aceh, No. 7/2006, has been invalidated by the Government of Aceh. Arguably, it is not in line with the MoU to have such an invalidation provision. In addition, if the separation of the legislative and the executive powers were taken seriously and it could be said that the DPRA holds legislative powers proper, it would be intolerable that the executive (GoI) could overrule *qanun* of the legislative power. However, because the *qanun* are bylaws, the problem does not present it from that perspective. Instead, the power of the Indonesian government to overrule *qanun* sustains our impression that Aceh is not really in possession of legislative powers proper, but of regulatory powers that may, in many instances, amount to powers to adopt material rules of law.

invalidated through a material review by the Supreme Court, that is, in the process of trying concrete cases, it would seem by implication that the Supreme Court has a broader function of judicial or constitutional review concerning bylaws that do not deal with the implementation of Islamic law.[241] Such a general judicial review could therefore also cover procedural aspects and claims that are not part of the concrete implementation of a bylaw. The Constitutional Court has no role to play directly in relation to the *qanun,* but if the situation presents itself, it would be possible for the Constitutional Court to exercise constitutional review in relation to the LoGA. Finally, there is, in Art. 235(5), a special prior review by the Indonesian Government of such drafts of bylaws that deal with the regional budget of Aceh (APBA) and that the DPRA is about to adopt.[242] The results that the Indonesian Government arrives at in its review of the draft *qanun* concerning the budget are binding for the Governor of Aceh.[243] When it comes to identifying which organ it is that has the final word about a bylaw, it therefore seems as if the Indonesian Government with the president would hold that power in most cases. In practice, however, it may be the Minister of Home Affairs.

The LoGA contains relatively comprehensive provisions concerning the enactment of the bylaws. As stated in Art. 233, *qanuns* shall be formulated within the framework of executing the governance of Aceh and of its districts/municipalities and in the performance of assistance tasks, that is, within the framework of the

[241]Excluding the Indonesian Government from reviewing *qanuns* with Islamic content can probably be described as one dimension of the respect of traditional ways in Art. 18B of the Constitution.

[242]Practice concerning review of *qanun* as opposed to draft *qanun* that deal with the budget seems at least in one case to be going in different directions. As stated in the Report by the International Development Law Organization entitled 'Judicial Review of *Al-Qur'an* Reading Test for Candidates for Members of the Parliament' of 6 September 2008: "In compliance with the prevailing procedure, the draft qanun was sent to Jakarta for approval by the Department of Home Affairs. It is a standard legislation procedure that every qanun or local regulation (Peraturan Daerah/Perda) produced by local legislatures should be approved by the Department of Home Affairs before its enactment and enforced in the community. This is stipulated in the National Law No. 32 year 2004 on Local Government. Article 145 paragraph (2) and (3) of the Law state that the Central Government, in this case the Department of Home Affairs, reserves the rights to annul a local regulation: first, if it is in opposition to the interests of the general public and/or the higher legislation, and second, the decision of the annulment should be legalised through a presidential regulation (Peraturan Presiden/Perpres) at the latest 60 days from the acceptance of the aforementioned Local Regulation." It seems, therefore, that the legal basis for sending the draft *Qanun* was found in Law No. 32/2004 on Local Government and not in Art. 235 of the LoGA. Based on the 2004 legislation, the Department of Home Affairs conducted a review of the draft *Qanun,* The Central Government saw a controversy in Article 36 of the draft *Qanun* and was of the view that *Qanun* No. 3 year 2008 should not regulate legislative candidates nominated by national parties, although they were nominated for the DPRA and DPRK. The Government of Aceh and the Governor himself were opposed to the provision in the draft *Qanun,* but the DPRA refused to remove it. Although the Government of Indonesia, too, was opposed to it, the President of Indonesia did not exercise his right to disapprove the actual draft *Qanun* during the established period of 60 days, so the provision entered into force and was applied in conjunction with the DPRA elections of 2009.

[243]A similar review of the budget *qanun* of district/municipality by the Governor of Aceh is prescribed, too.

powers granted by LoGA to Aceh and its districts/municipalities. The different provisions of the LoGA require that the DPRA enacts around 60 *qanuns* only for the implementation of the LoGA. Other pieces of national law may contain additional requirements for regulation through *qanuns*.

Article 236 ties the preparation of bylaws to the drafting of national norms by saying that *qanuns* shall be formulated so that they are based on the principles of formulating laws and regulations, including the clarity of purpose, an appropriate drafting institution or apparatus, parity between form and content matter, feasibility, benefits and results, clarity of text and openness. In addition, article 237(1) prescribes that the material content of *qanuns* shall incorporate the principles of protection, humanity, nationality, solidarity, diversity, justice, non-discrimination, equality before the law and government, legal order and certainty and/or balance, harmony, equality and conformity. The national legislator has hence determined a general approach to any matter that is to be regulated by means of a *qanun*.[244] In addition to the principles mentioned, a *qanun* may incorporate other principles in accordance with the content of the relevant *qanun*. A draft of a bylaw may, according to Art. 239, be initiated in the DPRA either by the DPRA itself or by the Governor of Aceh.[245] In cases where the DPRA initiates a bylaw, it shall form the basis of the discussion, while the draft of the Governor shall be used as an accompaniment. Because further provisions related to the procedures of the preparation of draft *qanuns* initiated by the Governor shall be governed by *qanun*, there should exist a bylaw for rules and procedures for parliamentary work in Aceh and in the DPRA.[246] When a bylaw has been initiated by the DPRA, the dissemination of the draft for the purposes of public consultation is the responsibility of the secretariat of the DPRA, while drafts initiated by the Governor are disseminated by the Aceh regional secretariat.

The enactment of a bylaw requires the joint agreement of the Governor and the DPRA, and after such an agreement has been reached, the Governor shall ratify the bylaw[247] and publish it in the Aceh Regional Gazette, whereupon it enters into force. It may be necessary to implement a bylaw with a regulation or decree of the Governor, published in the Aceh Regional Proceedings by the Aceh Regional Secretary. According to Art. 243(5), the Government of Aceh must disseminate Aceh *qanuns* and gubernatorial regulations that have been promulgated in the Aceh Regional Gazette or the Aceh Regional Proceedings. The relatively open definition of the powers of Aceh is not unique, but may exist also in other sub-state entities, such as Puerto Rico.

---

[244] When passing a *qanun* on, e.g., education, Aceh looks at the national standard and then adapts it to the needs in Aceh. If there is a blank spot or a normative vacuum, it can probably be filled by a national standard, if that contains a solution to the problem.

[245] The same provisions apply for *qanun* decided at the level of districts/municipalities.

[246] Such a manual for drafting of *qanun* is established in *Qanun* No. 3/2007.

[247] If the ratification by the Governor is not forthcoming within 30 days from the joint agreement concerning a bylaw, it shall enter into force nonetheless upon publication in the Aceh Regional Gazette in accordance with provisions in Art. 234 of the LoGA.

5.7 Puerto Rico: Residual Powers under Pressure of the Plenary Powers of Congress

5.7.1 *Matters Not Locally Inapplicable: Vast Area of Concurring Powers*

It seems as if both the Federal Relations Act and the Constitution of Puerto Rico tried to establish both a general competence and a special competence in Puerto Rico. As concerns the general competence, the Federal Relations Act departs from the point that the legislative authority of Puerto Rico "shall extend to all matters of a legislative character not locally inapplicable, including power to create, consolidate, and reorganize the municipalities so far as may be necessary, and to provide and repeal laws and ordinances therefore; also the power to alter, amend, modify, or repeal any or all laws and ordinances of every character in force in Puerto Rico or municipality or district thereof on March 2, 1917, insofar as such alteration, amendment, modification, or repeal may be consistent with the provisions of this chapter".[248] Because there is no particular provision in the Puerto Rican Constitution that would formulate the lawmaking powers of the Legislative Assembly at a more general level, it should be possible to conclude that the legislative competence of Puerto Rico is primarily determined in the Federal Relations Act.

In comparison with the formulation of the legislative powers of Congress, the same formulation of "not locally inapplicable" is used for the legislative powers of Puerto Rico. Having said that, it should, however, be mentioned that according to Art. II Sect. 19 of the Constitution, entitled "liberal construction of rights of people and powers of legislative assembly", that is, in a provision that puts the human rights provisions in relation to the powers of the Legislative Assembly, "the power of the Legislative Assembly to enact laws for the protection of the life, health and general welfare of the people shall likewise not be construed restrictively."[249] Thus

[248]US Code, Title 48, Sect. 821. Interestingly, the terminology, "not locally inapplicable", is the same for describing the sub-state competence in Sect. 821 as the state competence in Sect. 734. Logically, the legislative competence of Puerto Rico thus extends to all matters locally applicable, that is, to all matters that necessarily need to be regulated by means of legislation at the sub-state level. The same may be true for the federal law-making powers: they extend themselves as far as Congress feels is necessary.

[249]The Constitution of Puerto Rico contains a relatively comprehensive, albeit non-exhaustive, Bill of Rights, including some economic and social rights, and, in addition, a more programmatic commitment to a number of human rights of an economic and social rights nature in Art. II Sect. 20. As stated by Rivera Ramos (2007), p. 213, this bill of rights "replaced the statutory scheme of basic civil rights adopted in the Jones Act". The constitutional rights were to a great extent modeled against the background of the Universal Declaration of Human Rights, adopted only a few years before the Constitution of Puerto Rico. See Trías Monge (1997), p. 116 f. Hence the impression prevails that the jurisdiction of Puerto Rico attempted to present itself more as a so-called social state than a liberal state by way of characterisation of constitutional strategies. Some of the characteristics of the social state were amended by the US Congress in 1952 when the Constitution was being ratified by it.

at least in the area of constitutional rights, the internal normative point of departure is an extensive interpretation of the lawmaking competences of Puerto Rico. However, the scope of "all matters of a legislative character not locally inapplicable" is fluid and places the point of departure in situations of interpretation within the Federal Relations Act.

At the same time as there seems to be a wish to identify a general lawmaking competence for Puerto Rico, the federal lawmaker, as joined by the constitution-making population of Puerto Rico, seems to be interested in pointing out that the Puerto Rican lawmaker shall have lawmaking competences in some special fields. The above provision in the Federal Relations Act mentions the power to create, consolidate, and reorganize the municipalities so far as may be necessary, and to provide and repeal laws and ordinances in that context as well as the power to alter, amend, modify, or repeal any or all laws and ordinances of every character in force in Puerto Rico or municipality or district thereof on 2 March 1917, provided that such alteration, amendment, modification, or repeal is consistent with the provisions of the relevant chapter. In addition, the Act lays down that the people of Puerto Rico may organize a government pursuant to a constitution of their own adoption,[250] which means that the enactment of the local constitution, too, is within the purview of the powers. In fact, the Federal Relations Act has numerous special provisions of the same nature, empowering specifically the Puerto Rican Legislative Assembly to pass norms on different matters. Such special competences include income tax law and other taxes and duties,[251] the power to create, for the purposes of slum clearance and urban redevelopment, public corporate authorities and vest them with certain powers,[252] to create public commissioners for such tasks,[253] to authorize public loans and spending for such projects[254] and to provide for the use by or disposal to such authorities of any public lands or other property held or controlled by the people of Puerto Rico, its municipalities, or other subdivisions without regard to any federal acts restricting the disposition of public property or lands in Puerto Rico.[255] Apparently, the potential need to undertake measures in relation to slum clearance and urban redevelopment went further than provided for by the federal legislation of that time, so a specific mandate had to be formulated in the Federal Relations Act. In addition, according to the Federal Relations Act, all legislation that had been enacted before the entering into force of the Federal Relations Act by the Legislature of Puerto Rico dealing with slum

---

[250] US Code, Title 48, Sect. 731b: "Fully recognizing the principle of government by consent, sections 731b to 731e of this title are now adopted in the nature of a compact so that the people of Puerto Rico may organize a government pursuant to a constitution of their own adoption."

[251] US Code, Title 48, Sect. 845.

[252] US Code, Title 48, Sects. 910, 911.

[253] US Code, Title 48, Sect. 912.

[254] US Code, Title 48, Sects. 913, 914.

[255] US Code, Title 48, Sect. 913.

clearance and urban re-development and not inconsistent with the Act was specifically ratified and confirmed under the Act.[256]

Parallel to this, the Federal Relations Act also indicates a few fields where, apparently, the federal lawmaker is competent to act. The law of procedure in the federal courts dealing with such federal matters that arise in Puerto Rico is obviously a federal competence, as is the power to legislate on the language of procedure in federal courts, which is English.[257] By implication, the organization of the federal courts is, of course, a federal matter, too, while the organization of the Puerto Rican courts is a sub-state matter.

As a consequence, on the basis of the Federal Relations Act, there seems to be a general competence of the federal lawmaker in respect of matters of a legislative character that are not locally inapplicable and a special competence of the federal lawmaker in respect of the organization of and procedure within federal courts dealing with Puerto Rican matters of a federal nature. At the same time as there seems to be a general competence of the lawmaker of Puerto Rico in respect of matters of a legislative character that are locally applicable, a number of special competences are identified, in particular, in the field of slum clearance and urban redevelopment.

With reference to our terminology of residual and enumerated powers, it appears that the Federal Relations Act is trying to create both types of powers at both the federal level and the sub-state level: the US Congress holds both residual and enumerated[258] powers in respect of Puerto Rico at the same time as Puerto Rico holds both residual and enumerated powers in respect of the legislation it can enact for its jurisdiction. The consequence of this is that in the area where both lawmakers have residual powers, the legislative powers are at least in principle of a concurring nature, which seems to mean that *most* legislative powers are of a concurring nature. The potential area of concurring powers is thus very large and means that the two legal orders overlap on most issues. Furthermore, where the federal lawmaker has exercised its powers, the Legislative Assembly of Puerto Rico cannot successfully entertain its own lawmaking powers. Instead, Puerto Rican law will yield to federal law. If there is a conflict of laws that is tried in court, the federal courts, which are the arbiters of the relationship between the two sets of norms, will depart from federal law when determining whether or not the Puerto Rican legislation is within its established realm. If not, then federal law will be applied.

---

[256]US Code, Title 48, Sect. 916.

[257]US Code, Title 48, Sect. 864: "The laws of the United States relating to appeals, certiorari, removal of causes, and other matters or proceedings as between the courts of the United States and the courts of the several States shall govern in such matters and proceedings as between the United States District Court for the District of Puerto Rico and the courts of Puerto Rico. All pleadings and proceedings in the United States District Court for the District of Puerto Rico shall be conducted in the English language." See also Sect. 874 on the judicial process, the citizenship requirement of officers of courts and the oath of office.

[258]On the basis of the US Constitution, the exclusively federal areas of law are, for instance, admiralty, bankruptcy, immigration, money, naturalisation, post office and foreign relations as well as war powers.

In the case of *Moreno Rios v. United States*,[259] the federal appeals court concluded in as early as 1958 that since "since the terms of the Narcotic Drug Import and Export Act would affect Puerto Rico in the same manner as they do the States of the Union, and since the problem dealt with is a general one, certainly not 'locally inapplicable' to Puerto Rico, it is clear that Congress has the power to apply the Act to Puerto Rico". Here the question is what the goal of the national legislation is and whether that goal is relevant to Puerto Rico, that is, is the crime rate so much lower in Puerto Rico that the Act cannot be assumed to be applicable to Puerto Rico? This test has been applied several times since and turns on the issue of whether or not Congress intended to include Puerto Rico among those jurisdictions to which the federal act in question would be applicable.[260] Hence, when Congress fails explicitly to refer to Puerto Rico, courts must nonetheless inquire as to whether it intended to do so.[261] In conducting such an inquiry, courts have routinely concluded that Congress intended to include Puerto Rico even when a statute is silent on that issue.[262] The application of federal law in Puerto Rico is

---

[259] 256 F.2d 68, 71 (1st Cir. 1958). The case also deals with the continuity of federal legislation after the enactment of the Constitution of Puerto Rico in 1952.

[260] For a recent determination of "intention of Congress", see *United States v. Marco Laboy-Torres*, 3rd Circuit, 29 January 2009.

[261] *United States v. Marco Laboy-Torres*, 3rd Circuit, 29 January 2009 with the following examples: *Puerto Rico v. Shell Co. (P. R.), Ltd.*, 302 U.S. 253 (1937) (determining a statute's applicability to Puerto Rico is a question of congressional intent); *Acosta-Martinez*, 252 F. 3d *infra* notes 265, 293 at 11 (when determining the applicability of a federal statute to Puerto Rico, courts must construe the language [. . .] to effectuate the intent of the lawmakers. "If Congress has made clear its intent that a federal statute apply to Puerto Rico, then the issue of whether a law is otherwise 'locally inapplicable' does not, by definition, arise."). On the issue of whether or not Congress intended to grant federal jurisdiction in civil rights cases (in the case concerning the position of alien civil engineers) arising in Puerto Rico and how the Supreme Court determined the intent of Congress to do so, see *Examining Board of Engineers, Architects and Surveyors v. Flores de Otero*, 426 U.S. at 580. In doing so, the Court said it would examine the language of the jurisdictional provision, the purposes of Congress in enacting it and the circumstances under which the words were employed. At the same time, it conceded that these methods of statutory interpretation may be inconclusive, and it indeed appears that the Court used to a great extent a comparative argument (internal to the USA with respect to territories and states) and a historical argument when arriving to the conclusion that civil rights cases arise in Puerto Rico belong to the federal jurisdiction despite the classification of Puerto Rico as a territory or a state. Therefore, subjected to strict scrutiny, the three justifications for legislation in Puerto Rico for an almost total ban on aliens to engage in civil engineering were not effective.

[262] *United States v. Marco Laboy-Torres*, 3rd Circuit, 29 January 2009, with the following examples: *Examining Board of Engineers, Architects and Surveyors v. Flores de Otero*, 426 U.S. at 597 (defining 'state' to include Puerto Rico for purposes of 42 U. S. C. Sect. 1983 and 28 U. S. C. Sect. 1343(3)); *Americana of Puerto Rico, Inc.*, 368 F. 2d, at 437 (federal statute that referred to the proceedings of any "State, Territory, or Possession," applied to Puerto Rico even though Puerto Rico was not a State, Territory, or Possession); *U.S.I. Properties Corp. v. M.D. Constr. Co.*, 230 F. 3d 489, 499–500 (1st Cir. 2000) (defining 'state' to include Puerto Rico for purposes of diversity jurisdiction under 28 U. S. C. Sect. 1332); *Cordova & Simonpietri Insurance Agency Inc.v. Chase Manhattan Bank N. A.*, 649 F. 2d 36, 38 (1st Cir. 1981) (treating Puerto Rico as a 'state' under the Sherman Antitrust Act).

thus assumed.[263] However, during the past 10–15 years, most acts of Congress mention Puerto Rico explicitly as a Commonwealth to which the act shall apply. Consequently, by way of positive law, the application of federal law is normally also extended to Puerto Rico, because today, there exist only few federal acts that do not explicitly mention the Commonwealth. Local inapplicability of federal law could exist in some special areas, for instance, in relation to federal highway legislation containing provisions requiring the construction of highways to take into consideration space for snow by the roadside, which obviously would not arise in the tropical conditions of Puerto Rico.

5.7.2 Treated as a State in the Federation

It seems that the case-law makes an argument *mutatis mutandis* or by way of analogy, comparing Puerto Rico with the constituent states of the US. Puerto Rico is said to possess "a measure of autonomy comparable to that possessed by the States",[264] while Congress is said to maintain similar powers over Puerto Rico as it possesses over the federal states.[265] The Government of Puerto Rico enjoys the same immunity from suit as the states,[266] but like the states in the federation, Puerto Rico lacks "the full sovereignty of an independent nation", for example, the power to manage its "external relations with other nations", a power which was retained by the Federal Government.[267] As concluded in the *United States v. Marco Laboy-Torres* case, "[i]t is thus not surprising that although Puerto Rico is not a state in the federal Union, 'it ... seem[s] to have become a State within a common and accepted meaning of the word'" and that "consistent with this common and accepted understanding, Congress frequently uses the term 'State' to refer also to Puerto Rico".[268] Therefore, when an issue is general enough to warrant federal

[263] In commenting the Puerto Rican case of *Ramirez de Ferrer v. Mari Brás*, Supreme Court of Puerto Rico, No. CT-96-14 (18 November 1998), Smith (2001), p. 382, makes the point on the basis of the citations of the court opinion that the courts and Congress of the United States decide what matters are "internal" enough to be free of congressional regulation.

[264] See *United States v. Marco Laboy-Torres*, 3rd Circuit, 29 January 2009, and *Examining Board of Engineers, Architects and Surveyors v. Flores de Otero* 426 U.S. 572 at 597.

[265] *United States v. Acosta-Martinez*, 252 F.3d 13, 18 (1st Cir. 2001).

[266] *Ramirez v. Puerto Rico Fire Service*, 715 F.2d 694, 697 (1st Cir. 1983).

[267] *Americana of Puerto Rico, Inc. v. Kaplus*, 368 F.2d 431, 435 (3rd Cir. 1966).

[268] *United States v. Marco Laboy-Torres*, 3rd Circuit, 29 January 2009, with the following examples from federal law: 15 U. S. C. Sect. 1171(b) (transportation of gambling devices); 16 U. S. C. Sect. 3371(h) (transportation of illegally taken wildlife); 18 U. S. C. Sect. 891(8) (extortionate credit transactions); 18 U. S. C. Sect. 1953(d)(1) (interstate transportation of wagering paraphernalia); 18 U. S. C. Sect. 1955(b)(3) (illegal gambling); 18 U. S. C. Sect. 1961(2) (racketeering influenced and corrupt organizations); 28 U. S. C. Sect. 1332(d) (defining 'state' for purposes of diversity jurisdiction). See also *United States v. Steele*, 685 F. 2d 793, 805 n. 7 (3d Cir.

legislation by Congress, such legislation is also normally applicable in Puerto Rico.[269] An "additional persuasive reason" for finding a federal act applicable in Puerto Rico is its possible relation to international treaty obligations that the US has entered into: if a federal act can be connected to the implementation of a treaty, it should not be possible to find that the act is not applicable in Puerto Rico.[270]

More or less in the same manner as citizens of the different states, Puerto Rican citizens are accorded United States citizenship and the fundamental protections of the United States Constitution,[271] and the rights, privileges and immunities that follow from United States citizenship are "respected in Puerto Rico to the same extent as though Puerto Rico were a State of the Union",[272] although some modifications seem to apply. Judgments by Puerto Rican courts of law are guaranteed the same full faith and credit as are those of the states.[273] As pointed out above, like the states in the federation, Puerto Rico, too, has a republican form of government, organized pursuant to a constitution adopted by its people, and a bill of rights. Consequently, the federal courts seem to proceed from the notion that when adopting legislation that is applicable in the states of the federation, Congress also intends such federal acts to be applicable in Puerto Rico. This is also the position of the Federal Government according to 1992 guidance by the US President on the Administrative Treatment of Puerto Rico as a State: "Because Puerto Rico's degree of constitutional self-government, population, and size set it apart from other areas also subject to Federal jurisdiction under Article IV, section 3, clause 2 of the Constitution, I hereby direct all Federal departments, agencies, and officials, to the extent consistent with the Constitution and the laws of the United States, henceforward to treat Puerto Rico administratively as if it were a State, except insofar as doing so with respect to an existing Federal program or activity would increase or decrease Federal receipts or expenditures, or would seriously disrupt the operation of such program or activity. With respect to a Federal program or activity for which no fiscal baseline has been established, this memorandum shall not be construed to require that such program or activity be conducted in a way that increases or decreases Federal receipts or expenditures relative to the level that would obtain if Puerto Rico were treated other than as a State."[274]

1982) (quoting *Mora v. Mejias*, 206 F. 2d 377, 387 (1st Cir. 1953)) and *Calero-Toledo*, 416 U.S. at 672). In *Calero*, at 671, the Supreme Court said that the purpose of Congress in the 1950 and 1952 legislation was to accord to Puerto Rico the degree of autonomy and independence normally associated with states of the union.

[269]See also *U.S. v. Acosta-Martinez*, 252 F.3d 13 (1st Cir. 2001).

[270]*Moreno Rios, supra*, note 259 in this Chap. at 73.

[271]*Americana of Puerto Rico, Inc. v. Kaplus, supra,* note 267 in this Chap. at 11, 434.

[272]US Code, Title 48, Sect. 737.

[273]28 U. S. C. Sect. 1738; *Americana of Puerto Rico, Inc. v. Kaplus*, 368 F.2d at 437.

[274]Memorandum of President of the United States (George H.W. Bush) of 30 November 1992 (57 F.R. 57093).

In some instances, however, Congress has made an explicit provision about the applicability of a federal act in the jurisdiction of Puerto Rico.[275] The intention in those instances is apparently not to indicate that such federal acts that do not have a provision of applicability in Puerto Rico would lack legal force in Puerto Rico. In *Caribtow Corporation v. Occupational Safety and Health Review Commission*,[276] the court of appeal noted that the Federal Occupational Safety and Health Act was one of those pieces of legislation which the Congress could make and had made applicable to the Commonwealth explicitly, and it could also do so in the future with some other pieces of law, as in a number of provisions in the Federal Death Penalty Act, accounted for in the case of *U.S. v. Acosta-Martinez*.[277]

As established in the above cases based on comparisons between Puerto Rico and the states in the federation, Congress is also at liberty to leave out any reference to Puerto Rico, and the federal act should apply nonetheless. In addition, generally applicable federal legislation can, according to the *Caribtow* case, be adopted with no provision for prior local consent, although in some pieces of law, such a consent provision has been used.[278] By the same token, "the fact that certain laws exclude Puerto Rico from the scope of their operation indicates no more than that Congress thought them 'locally inapplicable' or otherwise inappropriate for the Commonwealth",[279] which seems to underline the fact that where Congress has not explicitly excluded Puerto Rico from the application of federal acts, the presumption is that Congress intended such acts to be applied in Puerto Rico.

As indicated above, federal legislation exists that explicitly excludes Puerto Rico from its application. Such is the case, for instance, in respect of the Internal Revenue Code, where individuals who have been residents of Puerto Rico for the entire tax year are exempt from federal income tax for income that originates

[275]Such is the case, for instance, in respect of the block grant paid out of the federal budget to Puerto Rico on the basis of US Code Title 7, Sect. 2028. See also section 205 of the Federal-State Extended Unemployment Compensation Act of 1970, at US Code Title 26, Sect. 3304: "(8) The term 'State' includes the District of Columbia, the Commonwealth of Puerto Rico, and the Virgin Islands."

[276]493 F.2d 1064 (1st Cir. 1974).

[277]252 F.3d 13 (1st Cir. 2001).

[278]For the use of a consent procedure, see section 1503 of Public Law 106–398, Appendix, 114 STAT. 1654A–353 (Floyd D. Spence National Defense Authorization Act for Fiscal Year 2001) and Sect. 5.7.3 below. See also *Moreno Rios*, *supra*, note 258 in this Chap., at 72, concerning an addition of provisions to the Internal Revenue Code of 1954, which made the point that the provisions "shall not apply to the Commonwealth of Puerto Rico unless the Legislative Assembly of the Commonwealth of Puerto Rico expressly consents thereto in the manner prescribed in the constitution of the Commonwealth of Puerto Rico for the enactment of a law". The Puerto Rican legislature gave such a consent in Joint Resolution No. 1 of 25 July 1956, 1 L.P.R.A. preceding Title 1. "However, this amendment had no reference to the provisions of the Narcotic Drugs Import and Export Act, which remains applicable to Puerto Rico without the necessity of the legislature of Puerto Rico manifesting its consent thereto."

[279]*Caribtow Corporation v. Occupational Safety and Health Review Commission*, 493 F.2d 1064 (1st Cir. 1974).

in Puerto Rico[280] and where the Commonwealth of Puerto Rico is, because of its position as a possession of the United States, exempted from tax credit concerning domestic corporations under certain circumstances.[281] Another example is the so-called Medicare Act, where payments to Puerto Rican hospitals for inpatient hospital services are calculated at a lower rate than for other parts of the United States.[282] In the case of *Harris v. Rosario*,[283] which concerned supplementary social benefits, the US Supreme Court was of the opinion that the lower level of reimbursement provided to Puerto Rico under the Aid to Families with Dependent Children program did not violate the Fifth Amendment's equal protection guarantee. "Congress, pursuant to its authority under the Territory Clause of the Constitution to make all needful rules and regulations respecting Territories, may treat Puerto Rico differently from States so long as there is a rational basis for its actions. Such a rational basis was evidently found against the background of three circumstances: Puerto Rican residents do not contribute to the federal treasury; the cost of treating Puerto Rico as a state under the statute would be high; and greater benefits could disrupt the Puerto Rican economy."[284] Because Puerto Rico is not part of the federal territory of the United States but continues to exist as an unincorporated territory, there appears to exist some legal basis for maintaining that no discrimination exists in relation to Puerto Rico and its inhabitants.

The determination of the various dimensions of the legislative competence of Puerto Rico is thus quite confusing. Starting from the legislative powers of the Puerto Rican Legislative Assembly, the reasoning concerning the legislative competences could thus have the following logical progression. The Legislative Assembly is empowered to adopt legislation that is locally applicable. Territorially, this means that the legislation is intended to be in force within the jurisdiction identified in section 1 of the Federal Relations Act and Art. I, section 3, of the Constitution of Puerto Rico. The Legislative Assembly cannot enact legislation which has extra-territorial effect either in relation to other jurisdictions of the United States, federal or state, or in relation to foreign jurisdictions. Materially, this means that the Legislative Assembly can adopt laws within the area that is left unregulated by the federal lawmaker.[285] The federal lawmaker, as a general rule,

---

[280]US Code, Title 26, Sect. 933. However, although the Puerto Ricans do not pay federal income tax, they are paying some other federal taxes, which means that they are not completely exempt from the fiscal authority of the federation.

[281]US Code, Title 26, Sect. 936.

[282]US Code, Title 42, Sect. 1395ww.

[283]446 US 651 (1980) (per curiam).

[284]The reasoning was found in *Califano v. Torres*, 435 U. S. 1 (1978) (per curiam), in which the US Supreme Court concluded that a similar statutory classification was rationally grounded in such circumstances. See also Baralt (2004), p. 555, and Rivera Ramos (2007), p. 128.

[285]In principle, as concluded in *Puerto Rico Department of Consumer Affairs v. Isla Petroleum*, 485 U.S. 495 (1988), the same preemption doctrine of the supremacy clause applies to the constituent states and Puerto Rico. However, in *Puerto Rico v. Shell Co.*, 302 U.S. 253, at 260, 261, a lower court had concluded that an act of Congress pre-empts the ground occupied by a local

only adopts legislation which is applicable throughout the United States and should in principle not enter the lawmaking competences of the constituent states.

Therefore, Puerto Rico can be relatively sure that it has lawmaking powers to the same extent as the constituent states, although there is the (not merely theoretical) possibility that Congress would enact legislation that does not apply to the constituent states, but only to Puerto Rico.[286] In the area of, for instance, tax provisions affecting American companies conducting business in Puerto Rico, the federal lawmaker has unilaterally determined that such funds, when transferred to the US, are not tax exempt under federal tax law, although the income may have been so under Puerto Rican law and the effect of the previous federal tax break was beneficial to Puerto Rico.[287] There are also other instances in which Congress has unilaterally and without consulting Puerto Rico amended federal legislation that has been applicable in Puerto Rico and where the amendment has discontinued the beneficial position of Puerto Rico.[288] At the same time, some federal legislation may exempt Puerto Rico from its application, leaving Puerto Rico in a worse

act and supersedes it and that the local district court, as a consequence, was without jurisdiction as concerns the offense. The Supreme Court disagreed with this and rejected the assumption that a congressional statute penalizing specific local behaviour and a statute of Puerto Rico to the same effect cannot coexist. Hence an alleged crime could be tried either on the basis of the US act or the very similar Puerto Rican act without risk of double jeopardy. This means that Congress and the Legislative Assembly of Puerto Rico actually could have concurring or virtually overlapping legislative competences within which enactments by both can be valid at the same time. This appears to be followed in the case of *United States v. López Andino*, 831 F.2d 1164 (1st Circuit, 1987), which confirmed the validity of the concept of dual sovereignty for the purposes of separate prosecutions and trials for offenses similarly identified in the two jurisdictions. However, the dual sovereignty construction was criticized by Judge Torruella in his concurring opinion (later followed in the case of *United States v. Rafael Sanchez and Luis Sanchez*, 992 F.2d 1143 (1993), because Puerto Rico is not sovereign in the same way as a state is, but instead dependent in the exercise of its legislative powers on the sovereignty of Congress. From that perspective, the plenary powers of Congress could also be interpreted so as to make the federal and Puerto Rican norms one legal order, with the sovereign Congress at the top, in which an aborted prosecution by Puerto Rican authorities preclude a new prosecution by federal authorities. This is, however, not the actual situation.

[286]For such a federal act, see section 1503 of Public Law 106–398, Appendix, 114 STAT. 1654A–353 (Floyd D. Spence National Defense Authorization Act for Fiscal Year 2001) and Sect. 6.5.4 below.

[287]For reasons for the elimination of the tax break, see *Puerto Rico and the Section 936 Tax Credit*. Report to the Chairman, Committee on Finance, U.S. Senate. United State General Accounting Office GAO/GGD-93-109. Washington, D.C.: General Accounting Office, 1993. See also Rivera Ramos (2007), p. 64, on eliminating in 1996 section 936 of the Internal Revenue Code.

[288]Such federal legislation has been enacted unilaterally, that is, without consultation of the Puerto Rican Government. The consent construction in relation to the Constitution of Puerto Rico can thus not be regarded a contract that would be binding within the area of the law-making powers of Puerto Rico and that would set aside the supremacy clause of the US Constitution. In fewer instances, the Congress has actually consulted the Puerto Rican authorities before taking measures.

position in comparison with the regular states.[289] While this unequal treatment is disturbing, it is evidently something that the US Supreme Court tolerates with reference to the plenary powers of Congress.

The area of the legislative powers of the states in the federation can thus be regarded as generic for the indication of the lawmaking powers of Puerto Rico, but not legally conclusive. Puerto Rico is not a constituent state of the US for the purposes of the Tenth Amendment, according to which the powers not delegated to the United States by the Constitution, nor prohibited by it to the states, are reserved to the states respectively, or to the people. Therefore, although the sphere of competence the states still may have within their residual powers has been shrinking, Puerto Rico would not have such a constitutional guarantee or recognition of its powers. The Tenth Amendment therefore constitutes another formal distinction between Puerto Rico, on one hand, and the constituent states, on the other. In addition, the constituent states of the federation cannot be "commandeered" by the Federal Government to implement federal policies or to enforce federal regulations,[290] and at least after the enactment of the Constitution of Puerto Rico in 1952, the situation should be similar concerning Puerto Rico, were it not for the territorial clause that actually makes it possible for Congress to carry out measures in respect of Puerto Rico that would not be possible in respect of the states in the federation. Hence the plenary powers of Congress in respect of Puerto Rico seem to make it possible to govern Puerto Rico in ways which are not symmetrical with governance in relation to states and which in fact amount to "commandeering" (although general practice gives evidence of symmetry and non-commandeering). The plenary powers of Congress may even make it possible, at least legally if not politically, to unilaterally repeal the Constitution of Puerto Rico or the Puerto Rican Federal Relations Act, that is, the foundation of the internal legal order of Puerto Rico with all of its material legislation.

What the material contents of the residual powers of constituent states are, is, however, not very easy to establish. On the basis of Art. I, section 10, of the US Constitution, states are prohibited from carrying out certain measures, namely entering into treaties, alliances or confederations, issuing money and similar instruments, passing bills of attainder (creating a negative obligation for a person who is more or less explicitly implicated in the legislation) and *ex post facto* laws,

[289]As a Congressional report described the situation: "Like other territories, Puerto Rico exercises authority over local government matters that is similar to the authority that states possess, but unlike states, territories do not have a zone of reserved sovereignty that is beyond the reach of Congress in the latter's exercise of its territorial powers. Thus, the Constitution's Territorial Clause continues to apply with respect to Puerto Rico, as has been determined by the Supreme Court", e.g., in *Harris v. Rosario*, 446 U.S. 651 (1980). See Puerto Rico Democracy Act of 2007, Report together with Additional Views [To accompany H.R. 900] of 22 April 2008 by Mr. Rahall, from the Committee on Natural Resources, committed to the Committee of the Whole House on the State of the Union, p. 6, at http://frwebgate.access.gpo.gov/cgi-bin/getdoc.cgi?dbname=110%5Fcong%5Freports&docid=f:hr597.pdf (accessed 13 February 2009), p. 5.

[290]*New York v. United States*, 505 U.S. 144 (1992).

affecting the regular basis of contracts, duties on exports or imports, privilege taxes, inspection laws, tonnage duties and keeping troops as well as interstate compacts without the consent of Congress.[291] In contrast, however, the material contents of the legislation of a constituent state, such as Massachusetts, is very broad (as is that of Puerto Rico), ranging from the administration of the government through real and personal property and domestic relations, courts, judicial officers and proceedings in civil cases to crimes, punishments and proceedings in criminal cases and further on to general laws and express repeal of certain acts and resolves.[292]

5.7.3 Attenuated Power to Make Constitution and Laws

Because the power to enact a constitution for Puerto Rico is a part of the lawmaking powers of Puerto Rico (although those powers are not assigned to the Legislative Assembly, but to the people or to a constitutional convention) and because the material substance of the Constitution extends itself to such areas where the federal legislator may be competent, the problem of concurring powers and the subsequent possibility of precedence for federal norms of a statutory kind is relevant even in relation to the Puerto Rican Constitution: individual provisions in the Constitution of Puerto Rico may be set aside with reference to federal supremacy, although there in principle is a guarantee of local constitution-making power through the compact construction.

This has happened in relation to two provisions of the Puerto Rican Constitution, namely the prohibition of the death penalty in Art. II, section 7, and the prohibition of wiretapping in Art. II, section 10. The appeals court concluded that "the Constitution of Puerto Rico governs proceedings in the Commonwealth courts; this is true of state constitutions and proceedings in state courts. (...) Those constitutions do not govern the definitions or the penalties Congress intends for federal crimes. Indeed, Puerto Rico is not alone in its abhorrence of the death penalty. Some twelve states join it in its views. But those state constitutions do not trump federal criminal law when Congress intends otherwise".[293] The non-exclusivity of Puerto Rican legislative powers thus also applies to its Constitution. This is interesting against the background of the fact that Congress approved the Constitution of Puerto Rico in 1952, including the provisions on the prohibition of death penalty and wiretapping.[294] Therefore, it has been concluded that the bill of

[291] See The Constitution of the United States of America – Analysis of Cases Decided by the Supreme Court of the United States to June 28, 2002 (2004), pp. 379–427.

[292] See *The General Laws of Massachusetts*, at http://www.mass.gov/legis/laws/mgl/ (accessed 5 March 2009).

[293] *United States v. Acosta-Martinez*, 252 F.3d 13 (1st Cir. 2001).

[294] On the death penalty issue, see Baralt (2004), pp. 584–589.

rights of the Puerto Rican Constitution is generally understood "to limit only the actions of the Puerto Rican government and not those of the government of the United States".[295]

The creation of both general and special competences for Puerto Rico is also clear on the basis of the Constitution of Puerto Rico, although, as was pointed above, there are no explicit provisions concerning the general lawmaking competence of the Legislative Assembly of Puerto Rico. Puerto Rico can apparently make laws for the protection of the life, health and general welfare of the people,[296] but also create, consolidate or reorganize executive departments and to define their functions,[297] create and abolish courts, except for the Supreme Court, in a manner not inconsistent with the Constitution, and determine the venue and organization of the courts,[298] create, abolish, consolidate and reorganize municipalities and change their territorial limits subject to referendum, determine their organization and functions and authorize them to develop programs for the general welfare and to create any agencies necessary for that purpose,[299] impose taxes and authorize bonds,[300] and pass provisions concerning the flag, the seal and the anthem of the Commonwealth.[301]

The Constitution of Puerto Rico establishes the lawmaking procedure for a bicameral legislature. At a general level, every bill shall be approved by a majority of the total number of members of which each house is composed. After approval by both houses, a bill shall be submitted to the Governor, and it becomes law if he signs it or if he does not return it, with his objections, to the house in which it originated within ten days of receiving it.[302] The Legislative Assembly can break the veto of the Governor by a two-thirds majority for the bill in each house.

An inductive account of the legislative powers of Puerto Rico could be made on the basis of the Puerto Rican code of laws. A rough idea of which areas of law the

---

[295] Rivera Ramos (2007), p. 57.

[296] Const. Art. II Sect. 19.

[297] Const. Art. III Sect. 16.

[298] Const. Art. V Sect. 2. According to the provision, the courts of Puerto Rico shall constitute a unified judicial system for purposes of jurisdiction, operation and administration. As pointed out by Oquendo (2001), p. 323, the original civil law system of law has "adopted U.S. common law methods, precedents, and doctrines. The result (...) was an amorphous and incoherent legal amalgam", although attempts have been made during the latter part of the twentieth century to return to the civil law style of law in courts. While private law is more clearly rooted in the original civil law tradition of the Puerto Rican legal order, constitutional and administrative law, while codified, have been more influenced by common law. For instance, according to Rivera Ramos (2007), p. 70, "the Penal Code, the Political Code, and the Codes of Civil and Criminal procedure were replaced with analogous bodies of legislation taken from the states of Montana, California, and Idaho".

[299] Const. Art. VI Sect. 1.

[300] Const. Art. VI Sect. 2.

[301] Const. Art. VI Sect. 15.

[302] Const. Art. III Sect. 19. See also Art. III Sect. 17.

legislative competence of Puerto Rico covers could be obtained by listing the different headings of the code:[303]

> Agriculture, non-profit associations, banking, public welfare and charitable institutions, highways and traffic, commerce, workmen's compensation, conservation, taxation and finance, private corporations, sports and parks, election and registration, housing, education, negotiable instruments, examining boards and professional colleges, municipalities, public works, public planning and development, health and sanitation, internal security, insurance, public service, public lands, labor, mortgage law and regulations, civil code, civil procedure, criminal code, criminal procedure, and rules of court as well as the legislature, the executive and the judiciary.

From a European point of view and against the background of a distinction between public law and private law, it seems that the legislative authority of Puerto Rico extends itself to both areas of law. Only the exclusively federal areas of law, that is, admiralty, bankruptcy and immigration, are clearly excluded from the range of lawmaking powers of Puerto Rico. In addition, it seems on the basis of legislation adopted in Puerto Rico that the lawmaking powers of Puerto Rico are very wide, and they are perhaps used in a fashion that in practice make them even broader than the lawmaking powers of a constituent state of the United States.

The constitution-making powers of Puerto Rico are not vested in the Legislative Assembly alone, but also in two other organs, the people and a constitutional convention. A limited number of amendments, a maximum of three at a time, can be dealt with upon the initiative of the Legislative Assembly, which submits the proposals to a referendum, where approval is dependent on a simple majority of those voting.[304] A more comprehensive revision of the Constitution may be undertaken by a constitutional convention, if both houses of the Legislative Assembly so decide by a two-thirds vote. The constitutional convention then drafts the revisions, which are submitted to a referendum for ratification or rejection by a majority of the votes cast.[305] There is a limitation of the material scope of possible amendments that prohibits the alteration of the republican form of government established by the Constitution itself or the revocation of the Bill of Rights.[306] The provision looks like a relatively ordinary self-limitation of the amending powers often found in national constitutions, but it is actually a restatement of the constitutional requirements of the Federal Relations Act and would apply even without being included in the Constitution.[307]

[303]Based on the Internet site Michie's Legal Resources, Titles of the Laws of Puerto Rico, at http://www.michie.com/puertorico/lpext.dll?f=templates&fn=main-h.htm&cp= (accessed 4 February 2009).

[304]Const. Art. VII Sect. 1.

[305]Const. Art. VII Sect. 2.

[306]Const. Art. VII Sect. 3.

[307]The Federal Relations Act lays down that the constitution "shall provide a republican form of government and shall include a bill of rights". See US Code, Title 48, Sect. 731c.

A more fundamental requirement, inserted by the US Congress in the process of approval of the Constitution back in 1952, is that "any amendment or revision of this Constitution shall be consistent with the resolution enacted by the Congress of the United States approving this Constitution, with the applicable provisions of the Constitution of the United States, with the Puerto Rican Federal Relations Act, and with Public Law 600, of the Eighty-first Congress, adopted in the nature of a compact".[308] In effect, this requirement, together with the requirement of a republican form of government and of a bill of rights, amounts to a stand-still clause which effectively prevents Puerto Rico from expanding its internal constitutional space without amendments to the Federal Relations Act. While constitutional amendments are possible, they are only possible within the boundaries of the Federal Relations Act. Any enlargements of the constitutional space of Puerto Rico or changes implying the creation of exclusive lawmaking powers for the Legislative Assembly would therefore have to be made with the consent of Congress and after amendments to the Federal Relations Act.

Against this background, it can be said that the Puerto Rican jurisdiction has few possibilities to assert itself if federal legislation exists in the same area as Puerto Rican legislation. Hence in principle the extent of the lawmaking competences of Puerto Rico is comparable to the lawmaking competences of any state in the federation, and federal statutory law also supersedes the Constitution of Puerto Rico in situations where its provisions are in conflict with federal legislation. Puerto Rican legislation therefore assumes in its entirety a secondary nature in relation to federal law,[309] except in situations where the federal lawmaker has chosen to insert a territorial limitation clause to a piece of federal law, thereby excepting Puerto Rico. In addition, according to the US Judiciary Act, "[f]inal judgments or decrees rendered by the Supreme Court of the Commonwealth of Puerto Rico may be reviewed by the Supreme Court by writ of certiorari where the validity of a treaty or statute of the United States is drawn in question or where the validity of a statute of the Commonwealth of Puerto Rico is drawn in question".[310] Consequently, it seems altogether impossible in a situation in which there is a conflict between a Puerto Rican act and a federal act, that the Puerto Rican act would prevail. Instead, it is the federal act that will prevail.

Combining the normative level at which Puerto Rico is created as a sub-state entity with the relationship between Puerto Rican and federal law, it seems that

[308] Const. Art. VII Sect. 3. Concerning the discussion in Congress on the amendment clause, see also Trías Monge (1997), p. 117 f.

[309] See Oquendo (2001), p. 323.

[310] 28 U.S.C. 1258. According to the provision, this can be done if a final judgment or decree of the Puerto Rican Supreme Court or a statute of the Commonwealth of Puerto Rico is repugnant to the Constitution, treaties, or laws of the United States, or where any title, right, privilege, or immunity is specially set up or claimed under the Constitution or the treaties or statutes of, or any commission held or authority exercised under, the United States. Review and reversal by U.S. Supreme Court has taken place, for instance, in the such decisions of the Puerto Rico Supreme Court as *El Vocero de Puerto Rico v. Puerto Rico*, 508 U.S. 147 (1993) and *Torres v. Puerto Rico*, 442 U.S. 465 (1979).

Puerto Rico has relatively weak status in comparison with a number of other sub-state entities. Evidently, a positioning of Puerto Rico in section IV of the chart for the comparison of different autonomy positions (see Fig. 1.1, above) may be an appropriate illustration of the current situation. Puerto Rico is a sub-state entity with self-government, but in comparison, for instance, with states in the US Federation or with the Åland Islands in Finland, it does not display the features of exclusive lawmaking powers established at the level of the national constitution. Nonetheless, it could be said that in the area where the constituent states are competent to exercise lawmaking powers, Puerto Rico has the same possibility, which means that the positioning of Puerto Rico could move towards section II of the chart.[311] However, Puerto Rico does not have the protection of the Tenth Amendment to the US Constitution, which recognizes a certain residual competence to the constituent states, although that competence has diminished considerably in a way that brings the constituent states closer to Puerto Rico in terms of what the federal level may do in respect of the states. It seems also incorrect to indicate that the normative powers of the Legislative Assembly are of an administrative nature only, because the Legislative Assembly is empowered to enact norms which can be used in courts as a basis for a judgment concerning an individual. This is the case, for instance, with respect to the criminal code and also other norms in the jurisdiction of Puerto Rico. This should not be possible if the powers were of an administrative nature only, as is the case in, for instance, Corsica. Therefore, because individuals can, for instance, be sentenced to jail on the basis of the norms enacted by the Legislative Assembly, the positioning of Puerto Rico should probably be moved from the middle of section IV towards section II, although its position should not reach as far as the far left hand side of the chart.[312]

In terms of constitutional entrenchment, the situation of Puerto Rico is at least to some extent comparable to the two Danish autonomies, the Faroe Islands and Greenland, in which cases the autonomy statutes adopted by the Danish Parliament without any explicit entrenchment in the Constitution of Denmark make in their respective preambles reference to an agreement of some sort between each of the autonomous entities on the one hand and Denmark on the other. However, the grant of lawmaking competence to the Faroe Islands and Greenland involves exclusive lawmaking powers that render national legislation inapplicable, which is not the

[311] For a comparison of Puerto Rico with former colonies in the Caribbean area and with other national territories (French, Dutch) in the Caribbean, see Trías Monge (1997), p. 3, who argues that the other areas have achieved improvements, either independence or some other reasonable status, while Puerto Rico is still "far from the status of an American state". For a comparison of decolonisation in the Caribbean space, see Trías Monge (1997), pp. 141–159.

[312] Interestingly, federal courts refer relatively often to Puerto Rico by using the term 'autonomous'. See, e.g., cases mentioned in Alvarez-Gonzalez (1991), pp. 21–42. Hence the terminology of autonomy in connection to territory has been viewed as relevant in connection to Puerto Rico and the federal courts have often described the legal order of Puerto Rico as something that could be denoted an autonomy arrangement, probably because of the fact that Puerto Rico is not a state in the federation.

case with Puerto Rico. In addition, in the Faroe Islands, new national legislation enacted by the Parliament of Denmark which in principle should be applicable in the Faroe Islands needs to be approved by the Faroese institutions, something that they have often refused to do. This local veto over national legislation is (or was at least until the grant of broader lawmaking powers in 2005) particular from the point of view that as new national legislation is prevented from entering into force in the Faroe Islands, the old pieces of law remain in force, rendering at least part of the Faroese legal order to be old in relative terms.

5.8 Reflections

5.8.1 Construction of Separate Legal Orders

As may be evident on the basis of our inquiry concerning the distribution of powers, certain patterns emerge on the basis of the different sub-state entities. Obviously, at this level of detail, each example studied here is different, yet at the same time instructive as to the general characteristics of how the distribution of powers is dealt with in relation to different sub-state entities.

A juxtaposition that seems unavoidable is between legislative powers proper and administrative powers. In that respect, it is possible to say that all entities reviewed here except Aceh have lawmaking powers in the meaning of law in the formal sense. Acts are passed in Hong Kong, the Åland Islands, Scotland, Zanzibar and Puerto Rico, while the normative level available to Aceh is that of a decree or bylaw. In that capacity, the *qanuns* of Aceh are expected to conform to national law and also, in many instances, to national standards. Therefore, at the outset, it is possible to express doubts about the position of Aceh among the territorial autonomies. This qualification may change somewhat if the powers within the area of criminal law are taken into account, because the Indonesian legal order clearly recognizes a competence to Aceh as concerns criminalization, in particular in matters related to the implementation of Islamic law. The definition of crimes in the law of the autonomous entities is thus present in all of them, although in Aceh at a low normative level that is not satisfactory from a human rights perspective. However, it seems that the Puerto Rican legal order is open to action from the national level, too, in a manner that casts doubt on the autonomous position of Puerto Rico. The federal legislature can pass any act that sets aside Puerto Rican legislation, and the federal courts implement federal law so that in situations of conflict, Puerto Rican law is set aside.

Against this background, it would seem that neither Aceh nor Puerto Rico have lawmaking powers proper and that for this reason, it has not been necessary to create any particular forms of competence control comparable to the mechanisms present in the other sub-state entities. Despite the fact that the Special Constitutional Court established by the Constitution of Tanzania for constitutional review is not functioning, the mechanism nevertheless exists. In relation to Hong Kong and the Åland Islands, there is a very asymmetrical competence control, in the former by means of interpretations of the NPCSC and in the latter by means of opinions of the Supreme Court that are observed in the decision making by the President of Finland concerning Ålandic enactments and by means of opinions of the constitutional committee of the Parliament. Finally, as concerns Scotland, competence control is multifarious and contains political, administrative and judicial aspects. As concerns the role of the Supreme Court of Finland in relation to the legislative enactments of the Legislative Assembly of the Åland Islands, on the one hand, and the role of the UK Supreme Court in the pre-assent reference procedure, on the other, these procedures are reminiscent of the French constitutional review that can take place by the *Conseil Constitutionnel* before the enactment is promulgated as an act. In both cases, the *ante legem* competence review can be distinguished from other judicial functions of the supreme court instance. Competence control with regard to such sub-state entities that have legislative powers proper seems thus to be organized in particular ways. At the same time, it should not be forgotten that in spite of a formal mechanism of competence control, ordinary courts of law might have to perform different operations in the area of choice of law when resolving concrete cases. In such instances, the choice between the national legal order and the legal order of the sub-state entity may sometimes amount to something akin to a determination of competence. Against the background of the defunct Special Constitutional Court of Zanzibar, the Court of Appeal of Tanzania, from time to time, adjudicates cases in this light, and Finnish courts may also have to make choices between laws in concrete cases, although the competence line is established in such a manner that normally there should be no need to do so.

As concerns the issue of whether a sub-state entity is vested with lawmaking powers proper or only with powers of an administrative or regulatory nature, one important consideration is the possibility of the sub-state entity to criminalize the conduct of individuals. If such a power exists, the entity can probably be distinguished from ordinary administrative jurisdictions of, for instance, a decentralized kind. The power to criminalize conduct seems to be of a general nature at least in Hong Kong, Zanzibar, Scotland and Puerto Rico, while the competence is more specific in Aceh and in the Åland Islands. In the latter, the national parliament is empowered to define general crimes, while the Legislative Assembly may criminalize such conduct which violates enactments within the legislative competence of Åland. As concerns Aceh, the powers within the area of criminal law are to a greater extent tied to the implementation of the Islamic faith. Obviously, Puerto Rico is in a particular position here, because the national legislature could always, in light of its plenary powers, enact definitions of crimes that set aside the Puerto Rican definitions (and which has taken place in relation to the prohibition of the death penalty in the Puerto Rican Constitution). Therefore, the autonomous nature of Puerto Rico can be qualified even from the point of view of the power to define crimes.

An important consideration in this context is also whether the legislative powers of the sub-state entity are exclusive in relation to the national legislation or not. A case in point is the Åland Islands, where the legislative powers are exclusive so as to completely rule out the possibility of the Parliament of Finland enacting legislation with the purpose of filling normative voids within the Ålandic competence and also to completely rule out the possibility of administrative agencies of the Åland Islands or courts implementing law in concrete cases which would by means of interpretation fill gaps in the legal order of Åland by incorporating norms, for instance, from the legal order established by the Parliament of Finland. The two legal orders are thus mutually exclusive in the areas in which they exist. This is clearly also the case in relation to Hong Kong and Zanzibar. It would seem that Scotland fits this category, too, but with the point of departure being parliamentary sovereignty, the legislative powers are probably best characterized by reference to their non-exclusive nature. As concerns Aceh and Puerto Rico, the situation is even clearer: the national legislature is in the position to override enactments of the sub-state entity in a manner that indicates a non-exclusive role of the norms of those jurisdictions. In these two cases, the powers held by the sub-state entity are based on delegation in a clearer manner than in the other cases, which instead depart from the distribution of powers between two legislatures. Distribution of powers is also the case in Hong Kong, although there are mainland Chinese opinions emphasizing delegation instead of distribution of powers. In fact, the distinction between exclusive and non-exclusive powers may stem from the fact that the powers of the two sub-state entities are to a great extent overlapping or concurring with the national powers and, whenever there is a conflict between the national powers and the sub-state powers, the national powers take precedence. The exclusivity or non-exclusivity of the lawmaking powers may also be related to the normative level at which the distribution of powers is established. If the distribution of powers is done at the level of the constitution of the state or in an autonomy statute that has a quality of that kind (as in the case of the Åland Islands), the likelihood is greater that the legislative powers will assume an exclusive nature in relation to the legislative powers of the national parliament. In contrast, the establishment of the distribution of powers at a normative level below the level of constitutional law or even in governmental regulations (as in the case of Aceh) might tend to lead to a situation of non-exclusive normative powers.

Here the discussion may be taken towards the issue of supremacy or preemption. This discussion is originally a theme of federal forms of organization, but as pointed out in Chap. 3, the absence of preemption or supremacy may be understood as a corner-stone of territorial autonomy. This can be contrasted with federal forms of organization, which normally include a concept of preemption or supremacy. Absence of preemption as concerns so-called ordinary legislation is clear in the cases of the Åland Islands and Zanzibar and also Hong Kong. In respect of these sub-state entities, the national legislature is not in a position to encroach into the legislative competence of the autonomy arrangement and to set aside legislation established by the lawmaker of the sub-state entity. There is also a spirit of non-preemption concerning Scotland, but legally, the issue is open due to the principle of parliamentary sovereignty, within which the Scottish autonomy arrangement functions. National preemption or supremacy is present in the cases of Puerto Rico and Aceh, leaving their legal orders more or less open for action at the national level. There should normally not exist any need to take active measures at the national level that would result in preemption of the normative space that the sub-state entity has on the basis of the distribution of powers, but the risk that this could take place is ever present and will influence the relationship between the sub-state entity and the national government.

The preemption issue may change somewhat if the normative level at which preemption could take place is raised from the level of ordinary law to the level of constitutional law. For instance, concerning the Åland Islands, the situation is such that the 1991 Self-Government Act makes exceptions to the Constitution of Finland in many areas, but in those areas the Self-Government Act does not introduce exceptions, the Constitution applies to the Åland Islands in the same manner as it applies to the rest of Finland. Theoretically speaking, if the Parliament of Finland wanted to enforce its view upon the Åland Islands in, for instance, social rights or the environment, which are areas that belong to the legislative competence of the Åland Islands but which are not a part of the Åland Islands Settlement and thus not specifically protected in the Self-Government Act, the Parliament of Finland could amend the Constitution so as to make very detailed provisions about these matters in the Constitution. As a consequence, the Legislative Assembly would be under a duty to legislate accordingly. This has never happened in relation to the Åland Islands, and there is even a particular protection in the Self-Government Act against this kind of *mala fides* amendment for a certain property-related area. However, Zanzibar has been affected by amendments to the Union Constitution in a manner that could be termed preemption through constitutional amendments. A constant source of irritation in the relationship between the Union Republic of Tanzania and Zanzibar is the additions to the list of matters that are Union matters, because those additions have retracted from the competence of Zanzibar as defined in the Union Treaty. The additions to the list of Union matters were done under the one-party rule, so consideration of these matters was not taking place in an environment of freedom, and the over-representation of Zanzibar amongst the representatives in the Parliament of Zanzibar was, for that reason, of no avail. Anyway, the use of preemption at the level of the constitution is nonetheless a reality in this particular context. As concerns Hong Kong, there may be a possibility opened up for such a construction, too, if the mechanism of expanding the applicability of national legislation was used by means of an addition of matters to Annex III of the Basic Law, but here, the mechanism is materially circumscribed in such a manner that the sphere of competence of Hong Kong should be reasonably well secured at least during the 50 years duration of the autonomy arrangement. Also, the mechanism of interpretation has so far been used sparingly, and it does not seem that it could result in constitutional preemption. For Scotland, constitutional preemption is clearly a possibility, should the UK Parliament choose to enact legislation that extends itself to Scotland: in the absence of a written constitution, the autonomy arrangement hinges on parliamentary sovereignty on the basis of which the UK Legislature might even disregard the political convention that protects the legislative competence of Scotland. In the cases of Aceh and Puerto Rico, in particular, it is actually unnecessary to even discuss constitutional preemption, because their legislative competences are already wide open to preemption at the level of ordinary national legislation.

It is another matter that institutions or representatives at the national level may have a veto power in relation to such enactments that have been produced in the autonomous territory. The veto power is an ordinary part of competence control in respect of the enactments by the Legislative Assembly of the Åland Islands, but as a practical matter, excess of competence is relatively infrequent and results only a few times per year in the use of the so-called partial veto. In the case of Hong Kong, legislation enacted by the Legislative Assembly has, until now, never been returned from the national level to Hong Kong, which means that the veto power has not been used. As concerns Scotland, it seems that the advance contacts between the Scottish administration and the UK administration and the pre-assent competence control has managed to sift potentially problematic issues so that there has been no need to deny assent. The Indonesian Government plays a general supervisory role in relation to Aceh, but is also specifically empowered to invalidate *qanuns* of Aceh on certain grounds, which means that there is a particular veto power in operation at the national level. The Åland Islands, Hong Kong and Scotland as well as Aceh thus form a group of four sub-state entities operating under the influence of at least some national-level veto powers. In addition, there is a group of entities without any formal veto mechanisms. In this group, Zanzibar is an oddity, because it has a strong lawmaking autonomy, but is completely independent in its exercise of its legislative powers not only in the area of ordinary law, but also in the area of internal constitutional law. The national government is not at all involved in competence control in the Zanzibari jurisdiction through a veto mechanism, and for this reason, the Constitution of Zanzibar could be amended independently so that many of its provisions are now in conflict with the Union Constitution. In addition, the governmental structures of Zanzibar contain militarily organized institutions that should not be possible under the Union Constitution. It is not only the absence of a national competence control with veto powers that results in this situation, but also the non-operational provisions in the Union Constitution concerning the Special Constitutional Court. Finally, the enactments of Puerto Rico are not checked by federal authorities from the point of view of making a veto possible. Legislation of Puerto Rico is simply void if it is found to be in violation of federal law. Therefore, two of the entities, Zanzibar and Puerto Rico, are not under any national veto arrangements, but for different reasons and with different consequences. Perhaps this is a characteristic that moves the two in a more "federal" direction.

The existence of veto powers of some sort is also indicative of at least some contacts between the national level and the sub-state level. Contacts in advance of legislative enactments are potentially very broad and multifarious in Scotland, and also in the case of Aceh, there may exist a need to discuss issues with the national level before normative enactments are issued. It seems that lawmaking takes place more independently in the case of the Åland Islands and that the enactment is processed in a joint bi-partisan body only after the actual lawmaking in the Legislative

Assembly. In Hong Kong, the legislative process seems very independent, save for contacts by the executive power to the national level (see Chap. 7 below), while contacts with the national level with respect to legislation to be adopted at the sub-state level is almost non-existent in the cases of Zanzibar and Puerto Rico.

As asymmetrical governance arrangements with lawmaking powers, territorial autonomies pose a challenge not only to the conceptualizations of how a state should be constructed in the most rational way, but also to the mechanisms of constitutional review. This, in particular, expresses itself in many of the entities reviewed as an additional asymmetry. Autonomy implies in itself a high degree of asymmetry, but the constitutional review may also be constructed in an asymmetrical manner. Such asymmetrical structures of constitutional review exist in the context of the Åland Islands and Hong Kong, and also in the context of Scotland. In these cases, competence control regarding the legislative enactments of the sub-state entities is organized in manners that are completely different from the control of competence of the national lawmaker. In fact, it may be said that in Finland, China and the UK, only attenuated forms of competence control, if any, exist with respect to the powers of the national lawmaker in relation to the sub-state lawmaker. In Zanzibar, constitutional review is altogether defunct to the extent that the Court of Appeal of Tanzania has felt itself compelled to present ideas of how problematic issues of a constitutional nature should be resolved while adjudicating concrete cases on the basis of ordinary legislation.

From a material point of view, it is natural to assume that the use of powers at the sub-state level expresses the needs and wishes of the inhabitants who live within the territory. In Hong Kong, the contents of legislation are not given any political content, except by implying the point that in that territory, socialism and the socialist legal order of mainland China shall not be practiced. The law of Hong Kong is thus not enacted with any particular political content, but is the outcome of seemingly neutral political processes of participation (see below, Chap. 6). The same is true concerning the Åland Islands, but the peculiarity of that area is that the Legislative Assembly does not always enact "original" Ålandic legislation, but may, by means of its own legislative decision, incorporate provisions and even entire acts from the ambit of the Parliament of Finland. This method of legislation is also sometimes used in Hong Kong in respect of such national legislation that has to be brought into effect within the narrow sphere of Annex III of the Basic Law. The point of departure for legislative work is neutral also for Scotland and Puerto Rico and for Zanzibar as well, although one could expect the religious component to have a stronger role because of the Muslim orientation of the population of Zanzibar. In this respect, Aceh stands out as the only sub-state entity where the contents of normative enactments is supposed to be of a confessional nature, namely that of the Islamic *Shari'yat*. At least in the cases of the Åland Islands and Zanzibar, it seems that the sphere of legislative competence of the sub-state entity is being constantly grinded against the legislative competence of the national lawmaker so as to assume a confrontational potential, less so in the Åland Islands, more so in Zanzibar.

The material extent of the legislative or normative powers of the different sub-state entities is difficult to measure, but some general reflections may be allowed in this context along a descending line ranging from Hong Kong to Aceh. On the basis of our study, it seems that the most extensive legislative powers are held by Hong Kong, which at the same time means that the powers of the national lawmaker are the most limited in relation to Hong Kong. Zanzibar is not very far behind Hong Kong in this respect, but has nonetheless a somewhat more limited scope for lawmaking, while the Union Parliament has slightly more powers than the national legislator in China. It is another matter that Zanzibar has *de facto* expanded its powers by enacting legislation which is not fully in compliance with the current listing of Union matters. It is probably a matter of taste as to whether the Åland Islands or Scotland should be characterized as a territory having more powers than the other, but the main point is that both have significant lawmaking powers over a multitude of legal disciplines. The powers vested in Puerto Rico are important and similar in terms of material extent to those of a state in the US federation, but more limited than the powers of the entities previously mentioned in this context. Also, the material scope of the powers of Puerto Rico are not fixed in any autonomy statute in the same way as for the other entities just mentioned, which means that the federal lawmaker can, as a practical matter, modify the material scope of the lawmaking powers of Puerto Rico simply by enacting federal legislation. Finally, it seems that the powers of Aceh are more subordinated to those of the national lawmaker and government than one might think when discussing the position of Aceh in the context of territorial autonomy. Compliance with national law and standards leaves less material scope for the decision makers in Aceh than in any of the other entities.

What the actual powers of the sub-state entities are will vary between the different entities, but generally speaking, it seems that social affairs, as well as health and education are such that autonomy statutes identify them as matters where sub-state decision-makers at least are competent to act. Foreign affairs and defense seem to be matters that as a minimum are kept at the national level. However, for all these matters, important exceptions prevail, so it is probably not possible to establish any firm rule on where each type of matter should be placed, at the sub-state level or at the national level. The distribution of powers would normally depend on the unique features of the situation.

Looking at this progression from the vantage point of the Memel Territory, it seems that this descending line of distribution of powers is also relevant for an ordering of the sub-state entities on a continuum between autonomies and other entities. Hong Kong comes closest to the Memel Territory, followed by the Åland Islands, Scotland and Zanzibar (which at least to some extent appears to be approaching a federal form of organization). Our inquiry also indicates the existence of at least a few sub-state entities that perhaps should not be regarded as autonomies proper, namely Puerto Rico and Aceh, mainly because of the very open nature of these arrangements, leaving the legal orders in a clearly non-exclusive position in relation to the national lawmaker and the national government. For the individual living in a sub-state entity, a diversified organization of the state by means of a distribution of powers in an exclusive and even a non-exclusive manner means normally that he or she will have to abide by the norms of two different lawmakers, that of the sub-state entity and that of the national level (as concerns the Åland Islands and Scotland, there is a third lawmaker at the level of the European Union, which adds a further degree of complexity to the equation). From the point of view of a unitary state, this is unusual and may, when a new sub-state arrangement is created, require some adaptation. However, a situation with two lawmakers in unitary states with a sub-state arrangement is similar to a federal arrangement and in that respect not unusual, except when a federal structure is complemented with a sub-state entity outside of the federal structure. From the point of view of the individual (or a business enterprise, for that matter), it is of course important that the legislative powers of a sub-state entity are exercised in a manner that is legally correct so as to maintain a good level of legal certainty.

5.8.2 *Accommodation of Different Legal Systems through Sub-state Jurisdictions*

While in principle it is possible to say that Memel was and the Åland Islands, Aceh and Hong Kong are sub-state entities in civil law countries and that Scotland, Zanzibar and Puerto Rico are sub-state entities in common law countries, the legal orders of the sub-state entities themselves may be at a greater or lesser variance with the national legal order (see Table 5.1 below).

As the table indicates, the cases dealt with in our inquiry cover a variety of different legal systems and their combinations. Puerto Rico is a special case in this respect, because its internal legal order, originally rooted in the Spanish civil law system, has grown more common law oriented, in particular under the influence of the application of federal legislation, which takes place through federal courts. At times, the local courts of Puerto Rico, in applying Puerto Rican legislation, have tried to strengthen the civil law orientation, but it is nonetheless somewhat uncertain in which category Puerto Rico should be placed. This uncertainty is also present in relation to Scotland, the legal order of which is often described as a hybrid system

Table 5.1 The principal conceptual relationship between the national legal order and the legal order of the sub-state entity

	National legal order	
Sub-state legal order	Civil law	Common law
Civil law	1. Åland Islands Memel Territory Aceh	2. Scotland (Puerto Rico) (Quebec, Louisiana)
Common law	3. Hong Kong (Aceh)	4. Puerto Rico (?) Zanzibar

that displays characteristics of both civil law and common law.[313] Scotland has had its own civil law influenced legal order since the union with the common law oriented England in 1707, and it has been held that "much of Scots public law is modeled on the common law, insofar as it is not regulated by statute" and that judicial review of administrative action, and criminal law and criminal procedure would not be "recognizably civilian in character".[314] Hence the sub-state legal order also recognizes common law. As concerns Hong Kong, article 8 of the Basic Law of the Hong Kong Special Administrative Region of the People's Republic of China actually explicitly declares that the common law shall remain in force when sovereignty over Hong Kong is passed over from the United Kingdom to China.[315]

In fact, one indirect, if not direct, reason for the creation of sub-state arrangements may be that it is possible to preserve such legal characteristics of the sub-state entity which may be more or less alien to the national legal system. While the direct reason for creating an autonomy arrangement may be the minority issue (which it is not in the case of Hong Kong), an underlying consequence of the minority issue may be differences in the understanding of the way in which the legal order should be constructed. Therefore, such variance should actually not be surprising, but almost expected. As concerns Aceh as a part of Indonesia, the Indonesian law is "often described as a member of the 'civil law' or 'Continental' group of legal systems found in European countries such as France and Holland, as opposed to 'common law' or 'Anglo-Saxon' legal systems, such as those in the United Kingdom and its former colonies. This description is true to the extent that much of Indonesia's legal system is derived from Dutch models and continues to rely on many surviving Dutch colonial statutes. It would be wrong, however, to assume that Indonesia simply adopted the Dutch system. As in many other former colonial countries, the Indonesian legal system is, in fact, a complex amalgam of

---

[313]Gloag et al. (2001), p. 2.

[314]Gloag et al. (2001), p. 3. Quebec, a province in the Canadian federation, was guaranteed the right to maintain its own civil law system of French origin within the area of private law in the Canadian federation in which all other provinces and the federation itself are of a common law orientation and where constitutional law is normally referred to the area of common law. A similar set-up applies in the relationship of Louisiana and the rest of the USA. See Himsworth (2009), pp. 119 f., 122–127. On p. 122 f., he points out that "the Scottish system is inadequately described simply as a mix of common law and civil law. Instead we are talking about a system which, like so many, is mixed in other ways as well. The Scottish system retains signs of the historical period which predated the arrival of the civilian influence. More recently, there has been added the systemic influence of the twentieth-century creations of European Community and Human Rights laws, as well as the more sporadic influence of other countries including those in other parts of the Commonwealth."

[315]It should, of course, be remembered that the legal system of mainland China is not really a civil law system in the so-called continental tradition, but still a system of law which tries to expound the socialist ideals and principles, a system of socialist law. For a criticism of the equation of civil law and socialist law, see Ghai (2007b), pp. 125, 127 and in particular p. 138, where he concludes that China's political system is not governed by civil law.

several legal systems, mainly because the Dutch colonial legal model inherited in 1945 was, in fact, a complex combination of *adat* (traditional customary law), *syariah* (Islamic law) and an incomplete local permutation of the legal system of the Netherlands."[316] "In fact, Indonesian law is made up of several legal systems interwoven with each other and operating simultaneously."[317] Evidently, despite the civil law nature of the Indonesian legal order, it is at least to some extent of a hybrid nature, and the prominent position that is given in Aceh to Islamic law underlines this feature at least for Aceh.

The value of the distinction between common law and civil law may not be very great, because today, "it is legislation, not historical judge-made doctrine, that is the principal foundation of legal order throughout the common-law world".[318] In fact, in all the cases reviewed here, the sub-state legal orders are statute-based, delegating lawmaking powers to the sub-state entities in certain areas in a manner that makes adjudication of the autonomy statute itself statutory interpretation. Statute-based legal orders of sub-state entities normally also tend to drive adjudication of the legislation of the sub-state entity itself in the direction of statutory interpretation in a manner that imposes limits to what the area of common law and relevance of common law concepts could be in the context. The positive law established by the legislator in a written provision is the predominant source of statutory interpretation in such cases, not any common law principle found by the court outside of the realm of positive law. Nonetheless, the variance between the national legal order and the sub-state legal order at this fundamental level may increase the potential for tension between the two orders of the legal systems.

As is often the case in the area of public law, the relevance of so-called legal families as an explanatory factor is relatively low, because the legal families are mainly constructed along the lines of the legal "style" or way of doing things in the area of private law. Therefore, the focus of this inquiry on a number of constitutional elements does not seem to bring out much explanatory value along the lines of legal families or legal systems.

[316] Lindsey and Achmad Santosa (2008), p. 2 f. It is perhaps possible to say that Indonesia is predominantly a civil law country, but increasingly, some common law influences are felt in contract law and in criminal tort. Before colonial times, Indonesia was common law oriented, but today, it is perhaps best described as a hybrid system of some sort, mainly because of the colonial background, but also because of influences from common law neighbours. From *adat* law, the common law influences grow stronger, and legal pluralism growing. From "new order" of the 1960s, more norms have been given from the top in the form of positive law.

[317] Lindsey and Achmad Santosa (2008), p. 3.

[318] Dowdle (2007), p. 61.

Chapter 6
Participation in Decision-Making

6.1 Elections, and Some Referendums

One of the main elements of autonomy is participation, in particular, participation in the decision-making concerning the exercise of those competencies with which the sub-state entity has been vested. Without exception, all entities included in our inquiry have an elected body which is in charge of using the powers assigned in the autonomy statute. This is certainly something that can be expected on the basis of the example of the Memel Territory.

The electoral systems used in determining the composition of the highest decision-making body in a sub-state entity vary quite considerably. Against the background of the ordinary variation of the electoral systems at the national level, the variation at the sub-state level is similar, except in the case of Hong Kong, where the use of the so-called functional constituencies for the selection of half of the Legislative Council is a distinctive feature. Otherwise, the sub-state entities rely on proportional elections, first-past-the-post elections and electoral systems that mix features of the two. Departing from the proportional election system in the Memel Territory, the Åland Islands and Aceh place themselves closest to this position, followed by Scotland and Puerto Rico with mixed systems. Zanzibar has a traditional majoritarian system, while in Hong Kong, the majoritarian system is combined with functional constituencies in a manner that places Hong Kong far away from the original position of direct proportionality. This order of the sub-state entities will also constitute the structure of this chapter.

In addition to election of the main decision-making body in a sub-state entity, direct elections may also be carried out in respect of the head of the executive power in the sub-state entity, such as a governor or a president. This is the case in Aceh, Puerto Rico and Zanzibar, while in the Åland Islands and Scotland, the head of the executive power is determined in the parliamentary process by the popularly elected body (although the national heads of state have formal functions in relation to both entities). Finally, in Hong Kong, the chief executive is selected indirectly.

M. Suksi, *Sub-State Governance through Territorial Autonomy*,
DOI 10.1007/978-3-642-20048-9_6, © Springer-Verlag Berlin Heidelberg 2011

In all the cases reviewed here, most of the populations of the sub-state entities are also represented at the national level in the national law-making body through elections. There are two exceptions to this pattern, namely Puerto Rico and Hong Kong, where particular forms and procedures apply for representation at the national level. Obviously, there is no institutional representation in an upper chamber or a federal chamber for the sub-state entities. One exception might be Aceh in relation to Indonesia, where the Regional Representative Council at the national level could be a step in a federal direction, were it not for the explicit aim of incorporating regions of Indonesia in a consultative process limited to matters of direct interest for the regions. Election of the president of the state is a relevant platform of participation, too, for individuals resident in sub-state entities, except again in the cases of Puerto Rico and Hong Kong. Local government within the sub-state entity is also an important forum for participation, and elected organs of local government or municipalities exist in all sub-state entities.

The expectation of a low level of referendums is, by and large, correct, but direct participation by the population of the sub-state entity through popular votes is not quite as rare as one would expect. Referendums have been used, for instance, in the creation of the sub-state jurisdiction, to determine the position of the autonomous territory in relation to European integration, for the purposes of inquiring into the opinions of the population concerning constitutional amendments, and to gauge sentiments concerning different alternative forms of self-determination. It seems, however, as if the so-called ordinary laws enacted in the autonomous territories were an area which is not dealt with by means of referendums. Finally, it is also possible to point out some other mechanisms of public participation, such as consultations, as means to ascertain the opinions of the people.

6.2 The Åland Islands: Legitimacy from Regional Citizenship

6.2.1 Two Levels of Participation and Different Constituencies

The issue of participation constitutes a core provision in the 1921 Åland Islands Settlement. According to para. 4, "[i]mmigrants into the Aaland archipelago who enjoy rights of citizenship in Finland shall only acquire the communal and provincial franchise in the Islands after 5 years of legal domicile. Persons who have been 5 years legally domiciled in the Islands shall not be considered as immigrants". Hence the right to vote and to stand as a candidate was internationally guaranteed as a special right for those inhabitants of the Åland Islands who had continuous residence in the Åland Islands for 5 years. In addition, that guarantee indicated two levels of participation, namely the Legislative Assembly of the Åland Islands and the municipal boards in the 16 municipalities of the Åland Islands. What the Åland Islands Settlement did not cover explicitly were the parliamentary elections to the Parliament of Finland. In that respect, section 37 of the 1920 Self-

Government Act provided that the Act did not affect the right of the inhabitants of the Åland Islands to participate in the elections of the President of Finland and the Parliament of Finland. In addition, as concerns the national affiliation of the Åland Islands, there seems to have been no intention by the League of Nations to organize a referendum on the issue. In its report on the Åland Islands, the Commission of Rapporteurs was clearly of the opinion that the dispute should not be submitted to a referendum, concluding in their report that "we have rejected from our conclusions the idea of recourse to a plebiscite".[1]

According to section 13 of the 1991 Self-Government Act, the members of the Legislative Assembly are elected by direct and secret ballot, and the suffrage is universal and equal amongst those who have the right of domicile. Section 3(1) of the Act establishes that the Legislative Assembly represents the population of the Åland Islands in matters that relate to its self-government. The population of the Åland Islands is, however, not a general reference to everybody who lives in the area of the Åland Islands. Instead, under section 9 of the Act, only a person with the right of domicile may participate in the elections of the Legislative Assembly.[2] Because the possession of the right of domicile is either by birth or after 5 years of residence, there is a substantial number of persons living on the Åland Islands, *inter alia*, citizens of Finland, without the right to vote and to stand for election in the Åland Islands, who thus cannot participate in the exercise of the legislative powers of the Åland Islands. The number of persons with the right to vote in elections to the Legislative Assembly was 19,418 in 2007,[3] while the total number of persons with the right to vote in the 2007 elections in the Åland Islands of the Parliament of Finland was 25,111.[4] However, in practice, the discrepancy is

---

[1]The Aaland Islands Question (1921), p. 36 f.

[2]See also *Gillot v. France*, UN Human Rights Committee, Comm. 932/2000, UN Doc. CCPR/C/75/D/932/2000 and *Py v. France*, ECtHR, Judgment of 11 January 2005. Both cases deal with the situation in New Caledonia and the delimitation of the group of persons with the right to vote in a referendum and in elections with reference to a residence requirement, but in the case of New Caledonia, the delimitation was accepted with reference to the fact that the inhabitants are a particular population, probably an indigenous people, which the inhabitants of the Åland Islands are not.

[3]Of those, 18,343 lived in the Åland Islands and 1,075 outside of the Åland Islands. The reason for a lower number of persons outside of the Åland Islands in the possession of the right to vote in the elections to the Legislative Assembly than to the Parliament of Finland is explained by the fact that the right of domicile (regional citizenship) expires after 5 years of residence elsewhere than in the Åland Islands. In the municipal elections organized at the same time, the number of eligible persons was 21,058, which is a significant difference explained by the fact that the right to vote is open to other citizens of Finland, of the Nordic countries and of the EU resident in the Åland Islands during at least 1 year before the elections.

[4]Of the total number of 25,111 persons with the right to vote, 5,371 Finnish citizens with a municipality in the Åland Islands as their home municipality were living outside the Åland Islands during the elections. Therefore, in the elections of 2007, there were 19,740 Finnish citizens living in the Åland Islands who had the right to vote. This would indicate that the group of Finnish citizens resident in the Åland Islands that does not have the right to vote in the elections to the Legislative Assembly is 1,397 persons, both Finnish and Swedish speakers.

not quite of this magnitude, because the number of persons who at the moment of the elections were resident in the Åland Islands and who thus were most likely to vote was 18,343 for the Legislative Assembly elections and 19,740 for the Parliamentary elections.

It is significant for the autonomy of the Åland Islands that most institutional rules, such as the choice of the electoral system, are issued under the authority of the Åland Islands in legislation of Åland, not in the Self-Government Act or through legislation of the Parliament of Finland. Some formal links to the state and to the Self-Government Act remain, however, such as the provision in section 14 of the Self-Government Act, according to which the sessions of the Legislative Assembly are opened and closed by the President of the Republic or, on his or her behalf, by the Governor. In most cases, it is, in fact, the Governor who does this. Under the same section, it is the task of the Governor to present the proposals and statements of the President to the Legislative Assembly, while most of the draft laws are submitted to the Legislative Assembly by the Government of the Åland Islands. The proposals referred to in section 14 consist mainly of treaties that Finland is about to ratify and that require, under section 59 of the Self-Government Act, the consent of the Åland Islands for their entering into force in the jurisdiction of Åland.[5] Because the President is in charge of the treaty competence of Finland in relation to third States, proposals seeking Åland's consent to treaties are submitted by the President through the Governor. There is a further possibility, formulated in section 15 of the Self-Government Act, for the President to become involved in the operation of the Legislative Assembly. If there were a parliamentary crisis in the Åland Islands, it is possible that the President, after consultation with the Speaker of the Legislative Assembly, would dissolve the Legislative Assembly and order a new election. So far, this has never taken place. There are further provisions in the Act of Åland on the Legislative Assembly on the procedures surrounding a dissolution of the Assembly.

6.2.2 *Proportional Elections with Political Groupings*

According to the Act of Åland on the Legislative Assembly, the elections to the Legislative Assembly, organized every 4 years, are proportional. For the distribution of mandates, the formula used is that of d'Hondt, which is the same as for the

[5] In a similar manner, there is a particular protection, perhaps related to some dimension of para. 3 of the 1921 Åland Islands Settlement, in section 28 of the Self-Government Act. According to the provision, an amendment of the Constitution or another act passed by the Parliament of Finland shall not enter into force in Åland without the consent of the Åland Parliament, insofar as it relates to the principles governing the right of a private person to own real property or business property in Åland. In addition, an opinion shall be obtained from the Legislative Assembly before the enactment of an act of special importance to Åland. In this way, one could say, the Legislative Assembly can, nonetheless, influence law-making in the area of property law, which otherwise is a competence of the Parliament of Finland.

Table 6.1 Elections to the Legislative Assembly of the Åland Islands between 1983 and 2007[6]

Political grouping/ year and turnout	1983 64.4%	1987 64.3%	1991 62.4%	1995 62.5%	1999 65.9%	2003 67.6%	2007 67.8%
Centre	11	9	10	9	9	7	8 (+1)
Liberals	9	8	7	8	9	7	10
Social democrats	5	4	4	4	3	6	3
Liberal co-operation	5	5	6	6	4	4	3
Independent cooperation		2	3	3	4	3	4
Green		2					
Progress of Åland					1	1	
Future of Åland						2	2 (−1)
	30	30	30	30	30	30	30

Parliament of Finland. So, too, is the system with open lists of candidates, which means that on a list of candidates of a political grouping, voters determine the order of the candidates in proportion to the votes cast for each candidate.[7] On a practical level, a voting system with open lists also allows for the impact of a geographical component in the elections, because it would be a consideration of some relevance whether the candidate comes from the main island of the Åland Islands or from the other, sometimes remote, parts of the archipelago. The open list system makes it possible for the voters to also take this into account when making their political choices concerning who is their preferred candidate in the Legislative Assembly. Naturally, their choices are limited by the decisions of the political groupings to select certain candidates for their lists, but within the various lists, the voters actually determine who is elected and who is not by affecting the order of the candidates on the list. Because the entire territory of the Åland Islands is one constituency for the purposes of electing the 30 members of the Legislative Assembly, the distribution of seats between mainland Åland and the archipelago parts of the Åland Islands is therefore of some importance in the context (see Table 6.1 above).

The turnout figures show a declining trend at the end of 1980s and the beginning of the 1990s, but that negative trend was broken sometime in the early 1990s, at

[6]The information is collected from the home-page of Ålands statistik- och utredningsbyrå at www.asub.ax (accessed 28 September 2010) and – as concerns 2007 – also from the home page of the Legislative Assembly at www.lagtinget.ax (accessed 28 September 2010).

[7]The proportional election is established in concrete terms through sections 62 through 64 of the Act of Åland on Elections to the Legislative Assembly and on Municipal Elections (SoÅ 39/1970). According to the provisions, the internal order of candidates on a list of candidates who do not belong to an electoral association and candidates on a list from an electoral association is determined on the basis of their individual number of votes. The different candidates are accorded comparison quotas so that the first candidates receives the total number of votes cast for the list of candidates, the second candidate half of the votes of the list, the third candidate one third of the votes, the fourth candidate one fourth of the votes, etc. If the number of votes or the quotas are equally large, the order of such candidates is determined by lot. In the final phase, the names of all candidates are listed in the order of descending quotas, and out of the candidates thus listed, such a number of candidates is selected from the top as should be elected as members of the Legislative Assembly (which is 30 members).

which point political participation measured by turnout started to increase somewhat. The reason for that may be the discussion about the impact of EU membership and the subsequent emergence of a debate on whether the Åland Islands should break away from Finland and constitute itself as an independent country with some special arrangement with the EU (a debate which manifested itself in the emergence of a political grouping that advocates independence) or whether the autonomy of the Åland Islands should be deepened. The interest in politics that the turnout figures might reflect could also be a consequence of political division in the Åland Islands that can be seen in the entry of new political groupings into the Legislative Assembly over the years. Also, after the introduction of parliamentary accountability in government in 1988, the elections probably matter more for the practical operation of Åland's autonomy, because the Government actually changes as a consequence of elections. Because the proportional system of election results in a distribution of seats among several parties, none of which can normally gain the absolute majority in the Legislative Assembly, the Government which is formed after the elections is bound to be a coalition government of several political groupings. An ordinary legislative environment is ensured, *inter alia*, by section 9 of the Act of Åland on the Legislative Assembly, which prohibits the imperative mandate and thus protects the independence of the members in their legislative work.

Legislation concerning political parties is considered to belong to the legislative competence of the Parliament of Finland, and therefore, there is no act of Åland on the political parties featured in the Legislative Assembly. Because the conditions laid down by the Political Parties Act (SoF 10/1969) require such a high number of supporters for registering a political party (5,000 voters with the right to vote) that it would not be realistic to use that legal avenue, the political formations competing over political power in the Åland Islands are not parties proper, but rather political groupings that function under the regular Associations Act (SoF 503/1989). In practice, they nonetheless function as political parties, particularly when campaigning for elections to the Legislative Assembly. The Government of the Åland Islands also provides some subsidies for their political activities, part of which comes from a grant via the state budget intended for support of political parties and their activities. However, the political system of the Åland Islands has almost no connection to the parties on the mainland; only the Åland Social Democrats have some contacts with the mainland Social Democratic Party. Consequently, the political system of the Åland Islands is very home-grown and is in no way under any influence from the mainland.

The political coloring of the Åland Islands is original in comparison with mainland Finland and also with Sweden: in the Åland Islands, the role of the political organizations on the left side of the political spectrum is limited, represented only by the Social Democrats, while in Finland and in particular in Sweden, there is more support for parties on the left. As a consequence, the political system of the Åland Islands mainly consists of parties occupying the center-right spectrum of politics, and it is symptomatic that the Social Democrats have only recently been in Government for the first time. Although the issue of secession was dealt with in a conclusive manner by the League of Nations in 1921, disillusionment with the slow development of a deeper autonomy and with the negative consequences of the EU accession to the Åland Islands prompted the creation of a new political grouping towards the end of the 1990s, the Future of Åland, that has demanded independence for the Åland Islands. In the elections of 2003, this new group gained two seats in the Legislative Assembly, and it was able to renew these two seats in the elections of 2007 (but after the elections in 2007, one member of this group left to join the Center).

6.2.3 The Use of the Referendum in the EU Context

While elections are the main mechanism of participation in the governance of the Åland Islands, referendums have clearly been an exception. In 1917–1921, the direct participation of the population of the Åland Islands was very much on the agenda, but only the accession of Finland to the EU in the mid-1990s prompted issues of such magnitude that a popular consultation was actualized. With the accession of Finland to the European Union and with the emerging principle of integration by referendum, it was asked whether the Åland Islands should hold an advisory referendum on the EU issue before the Legislative Assembly of the Åland Islands gives its formal consent to the Islands' membership of the EU, which actually involves a special EU status on the basis of the separate protocol on the Åland Islands.[8] The reason for the concerns were that EU law sets aside Ålandic norms and interferes with the jurisdiction of Åland especially within the areas of trade, agriculture and fisheries, and therefore, it could be argued that EU membership would have the effect of diminishing the autonomy of the Åland Islands. Lacking specific referendum provisions, one issue that arose on the basis of the Self-Government Act in this respect was whether the Åland Islands are at all permitted to organize popular votes of any kind. The Government of the Åland Islands submitted a legislative proposal containing a draft for an act of Åland on an advisory referendum about the EU accession, and the Legislative Assembly passed it. However, during the competence control, doubts were expressed about the power of the Legislative Assembly to enact such a piece of law.

In an Opinion to the President of the Republic, the Supreme Court of Finland emphasized the fact that the referendum is only advisory, and that it does not constitute any infringement of the decision-making procedures. Therefore, the advisory referendum does not deprive the Legislative Assembly of its right to represent the Åland Islands. On that basis, the Court found that regulations concerning an advisory referendum do not violate the Self-Government Act. The Court concluded that provisions concerning advisory referendums are not of a constitutional character in the sense that they would, under section 27, para. 1,

---

[8]The Act concerning the Conditions of Accession and the Adjustments to the Treaties on which the Union is Founded, Protocol No 2 on the Åland Islands, OJ 94/C 241/08.

deviate from the competence of the Republic to enact laws at the constitutional level. On the contrary, the Supreme Court ruled that in this case, Ålandic legislation concerning an advisory referendum could be enacted under section 18, para. 27, because the matter fell under the competence of the Åland Islands.[9] In this rare reference to the "implied powers" of the Legislative Assembly to enact an act of Åland which is within the legislative profile of the Åland Islands although not materially enumerated amongst the legislative powers, the advisory referendum was found to be within its competence. As a consequence, the President of Finland did not veto the Act of Åland on the advisory EU referendum and therefore, an advisory referendum could be held.[10] Another reason that could be put forward in support of a referendum on the EU membership issue is that the conditions of accession were not a theme during the 1991 elections to the Legislative Assembly.

The Ålandic advisory referendum on membership of the EU was organized on 20 November 1994. Only those with the right of domicile had the right to vote in this regional referendum. The EU referendum, the first referendum ever on the Åland Islands and the only one so far, produced a low turnout of only 49.1%. Of those voting, 73.6% voted for the EU, while 26.4% opposed joining the Union together with Finland.[11] The Legislative Assembly of the Åland Islands accordingly made its final decision on 2 December 1994, applying the required two-thirds qualified majority, because Finland's accession to the European Union was made according to the procedure of limited constitutional exceptions, requiring the same qualified majority in the Parliament of Finland for the final decision.[12] Had EU membership been rejected, the Åland Government would probably have needed to

[9]Opinion of the Supreme Court, 9 September 1994, Nr 3169 (Dnr OH 94/104).

[10]A decisive referendum would clearly require an amendment of the Self-Government Act. However, the Opinion of the Supreme Court can be criticized for placing too much emphasis on the title of the Act of Åland on the Advisory Referendum concerning the Accession to the European Union, because the question formulated in the Act that would be submitted to the people indicated that the Legislative Assembly would have to vote according to the opinion of the people. Hence the question in the referendum, as established in the Act, gave the impression that the result is binding on the Legislative Assembly, and as a consequence, it could be argued, the law-making powers of the Legislative Assembly would be disturbed in a manner which would require a formal amendment to the Self-Government Act permitting referendums. In the same vein, but in another situation, if the Åland Islanders would like to carry out a referendum on the independence of the Åland Islands by means of a referendum created under an act of Åland, the result would be similar: an act of Åland with norms about an independence referendum would clearly be contrary to section 27, para. 1, of the Self-Government Act and therefore, such a law would be reviewed negatively by the Supreme Court and, as a consequence, be vetoed by the President under section 19(2) of the Self-Government Act on that ground and also because the said act would deal with the external or internal security of the state.

[11]Folkomröstningarna om anslutning till Europeiska Unionen (1994), p. 12.

[12]According to section 58 of the Self-Government Act, the Government of the Åland Islands has the possibility to participate in negotiations concerning international treaties. However, the Åland Islands are not a subject of public international law but have a very limited international legal capacity. See Hannikainen (1993a), p. 172. See also Bring (2007).

resign and the Islands would not have become a part of the European Union by 1 January 1995, but assumed a status comparable to that of the Faeroe Islands. The Åland Islanders, including those citizens of Finland who did not have the right of domicile, of course also participated in the nation-wide advisory EU referendum, which was arranged before the Ålandic referendum. The turnout on the Åland Islands in this national referendum was 61.2%, and of those voting, 51.9% supported EU membership. The reason for the greater support for EU membership in the later Åland referendum was probably that by the time of the regional referendum, it was known that both Finland and Sweden would become members of the Union.

6.2.4 Presidential and Parliamentary Elections

At the national level, the President of Finland exercises the most significant powers in relation to the Åland Islands through the possibility of legislative veto, while in mainland Finland, the office of the President has been divested of many of the powers that were originally attached to it, including the absolute veto. Therefore, it should be of great interest for the Åland Islanders to participate in the presidential elections. In realistic terms, however, the inhabitants of the Åland Islands are so few that a candidate from Åland would be unlikely to win the presidential elections, and therefore, the election of the President is about voting for a national candidate, of whom at least some visit the Åland Islands during the election campaign. The turnout in presidential elections is generally speaking lower in the Åland Islands than in the elections to the Legislative Assembly, and also lower than in presidential elections in mainland Finland. However, the turnout in the second round between the two final candidates seems to be higher than in the first round,[13] probably because of the greater focus in the second round on the two candidates that are available, one of whom will be elected.

Under section 25(2) of the Constitution of Finland, for the parliamentary elections, the country is divided, on the basis of the number of Finnish citizens, into at least 12 and at most 18 constituencies. In addition, the Åland Islands form a constituency of their own for the election of one representative. Article 68 in the Self-Government Act contains a similar provision, according to which in parliamentary and also in presidential elections, Åland constitutes an electoral district. In the Election Act (SoF 714/1998), section 6(1) creates the Åland Islands as one constituency from which one MP shall be elected to the Finnish Parliament.[14]

[13]The turnout in presidential elections since 1994 is as follows: 1994/I: 70.3% and 1994/II: 74.3%; 2000/1: 59.1% and 2000/II: 61.6%; 2006/I: 57.5% and 2006/II: 61.9%. See www.lagtinget.ax (accessed 28 September 2010).

[14]In addition, section 36(2) in the Rules of Procedure of the Parliament (SoF 40/1999) states that the MP from Åland shall always have the right to be present in the meetings of the Grand Committee of Parliament, which is the central body in Parliament dealing with EU integration matters.

The one Åland representative in the Finnish Parliament can thus be viewed as an example of so-called special representation. This arrangement was not a part of the Settlement before the League of Nations, but was incorporated into domestic legislation in 1947 without external pressure and put into effect in the elections of 1948. A mandate in the Finnish Parliament represents in mathematical terms approximately 25,600 citizens. As a consequence, because the MP elected from the Åland Islands would represent approximately 26,000 citizens, the special representation does not result in any significant disproportionality.

However, since the electoral system in Finland is based on the principle of proportional representation in multi-member constituencies,[15] the one MP elected from the Åland Islands is an anomaly. Instead of the regular first-past-the-post election in a single member constituency, the Åland representative to the Finnish parliament is actually returned by means of a modified proportional election which could be called a first-*list*-past-the-post system, provided that lists are used in a particular election.[16] Thus the election of the Åland representative to the Finnish parliament can be described as partially proportional. Although it is in no way insignificant who the MP for Åland is in the Parliament of Finland, the turnout figures in parliamentary elections are lower than in the elections to the Legislative Assembly and also lower than generally in mainland Finland. After the beginning of the 1990s, the turnout has, however, experienced an increase.[17]

The MP for Åland represents all citizens in the area, not only persons who are in the possession of the regional citizenship of the Åland Islands. For this reason, it is natural that the one Åland MP is not prevented from participating in deliberations concerning such national legislation which, according to the Self-Government Act, belongs to the legislative competence of the Åland Islands.[18] From this point of view, the special mandate in the Parliament to represent Finnish citizens resident on

[15]Under the Election Act, section 110, sub-section 1, 30 persons with a right to vote in parliamentary elections may found an electoral association for the purpose of nominating a candidate in the parliamentary elections and two or more electoral associations may present a joint list, which may include a maximum of four candidates.

[16]Under the Election Act, the election of the one MP takes place under a very peculiar electoral system which in principle replicates the system of proportional elections with open lists in multi-member constituencies distributed according to the d'Hondt method used in mainland Finland. In the Åland Islands, under the expectation that lists of maximum four persons are submitted, persons with the right to vote, that is, persons who fulfill the qualification of being citizens of Finland of at least 18 years of age (and who thus do not have to be in the possession of the regional citizenship), vote for one person on the list. The person on the list who gets the most votes in the election will, for the purposes of establishing the relative numbers of votes, receive all votes of the list, the second one half of the votes, the third one one-third of the votes and the fourth one one-fourth of the votes. The person ranked first on the list which receives most votes will receive the mandate as MP, while the rest are considered as substitutes in case the ordinary member would for some reason resign his or her seat.

[17]The turnout in parliamentary elections in the Åland Islands since 1983 is as follows: 1983: 56.0%; 1987: 52.8%; 1991: 50.8%; 1995: 52.1%; 1999: 54.8%; 2003: 60.3%; 2007: 57.1%. See www.lagtinget.ax (accessed 28 September 2010).

[18]On the 'West-Lothian Question' in the United Kingdom, see Leopold (1998), p. 227.

the Åland Islands is one part of a regular representation scheme in law-making at the national level, not an avenue for the autonomy arrangement. In his or her task as a representative, the Åland parliamentarian should observe the prohibition of the imperative mandate in section 29 of the Finnish Constitution and avoid becoming an arm of the governmental institutions of the Åland Islands in the Finnish Parliament. The MP for Åland is a representative of citizens in the Parliament of Finland, not of the Government of the Åland Islands or of the Legislative Assembly.

6.2.5 Initiatives to the National Parliament

Because the MP for Åland in the Parliament of Finland should not be seen as the prolonged arm of the governmental structures of Åland and their special interests, it is important to notice that an institutional channel of participation, additional to the formal requirements of consent by Åland concerning treaties and legislation that affect Åland's interests, is placed in section 22 of the Self-Government Act. According to the provision, the Legislative Assembly may submit initiatives in matters that belong to the legislative competence of the Parliament of Finland and which are of particular relevance for Åland as a territorial jurisdiction. In other words, if the Legislative Assembly of the Åland Islands feels that it should take action within those enumerated matters that are established under sections 27 and 29 of the Self-Government Act, it could do so by presenting an initiative to that effect to the Government of Finland. The Government of Finland acts in this context as a mere intermediary, having the task to present the initiative for the consideration of the Parliament of Finland.[19] Similarly, the Government of the Åland Islands may submit initiatives on matters within the legislative powers of the Parliament of Finland when there is a need to issue a decree or perhaps some other regulation for the Åland Islands.

The mechanism of initiatives from the Legislative Assembly of the Åland Islands to the Parliament of Finland is not used very often, and when it is used, it is historically a vehicle for proposing amendments to the Self-Government Act or to the legislation concerning limitations to the right to own real estate. However, in 2006, there was an initiative to amend the Election Act with the proposal to reserve one of the Finnish seats in the European Parliament for an MEP from the Åland Islands. The cases before the ECJ implicating the Åland Islands in the actions against Finland had confirmed the belief of the authorities of the Åland Islands that the European Union only talks to the Member States and does not pay much attention to the specific situations and special legal orders at a sub-state level. Against the background of this understanding, the Legislative Assembly of the Åland Islands decided to use its right under section 22(1) of the Self-Government Act to present a Bill to the Parliament of Finland on issues that belong to the legislative autonomy of

[19]As explained by Palmgren (1997), p. 90, the Åland Islands has the possibility to bring a matter to the Parliament of Finland even if the Government of Finland does not agree.

the Finnish Parliament,[20] requesting that the Election Act (SoF 714/1998) be amended so as to reserve one seat of the 14 MEPs to be elected from Finland for a particular constituency of the Åland Islands.[21] Under the rule that existed at the material time, Finland was one constituency for the purposes of electing the 14 MEPs, but the Ålandic proposal made the case for electing 13 MEPs from mainland Finland and one from the Åland Islands.[22] In this way, it was perceived that the Åland Islands would gain compensation for its loss of legislative competence and a political voice in the European Union. The disillusionment with the EU is perhaps also visible in the turnout figures concerning elections to the European Parliament, which remain at a very low level in the Åland Islands,[23] even lower than in mainland Finland.

The system proposed by the Legislative Assembly as concerns the elections to the European Parliament is essentially the same as the one which has been in place since 1947 at the national level for elections to the Parliament of Finland. The question is whether this same system would work in the elections to the European Parliament. The Bill initiated by the Legislative Assembly did not involve a proposal to amend either the Self-Government Act or the Constitution of Finland so as to create the Åland Islands as a single-member constituency for the purposes of the European Parliament elections. Thus the Bill contained no proposal to create a constitutional basis for the guaranteed seat in the European Parliament. This can be viewed as a problem under the current Constitution, although that was not the case in 1946. From the point of view of EU law relevant for the matter, reference can be made to Council Decision of 25 June and 23 September 2002 amending the Act concerning the election of the representatives of the European Parliament by direct universal suffrage, annexed to Decision 76/787/ECSC, EEC, Euratom, which in Art. 1 establishes that the elections to the European Parliament shall be carried out by way of proportional representation, using the list system or the single transferable vote, and which in Art. 7(1) stipulates that the electoral procedure shall be governed by the national provisions of each Member State subject to the provisions of the Council Decision.

[20] Övrigt ärende 3/2006, Regeringens skrivelse till Riksdagen med anledning av Ålands lagtings initiativ som innehåller förslag till lag om ändring av vallagen. In another legislative area, the Legislative Assembly submitted, on 8 March 2011, to the Parliament of Finland a proposal deals with the amendment of the sex crimes of the Criminal Code that is of a general nature and not linked to the particular needs of Åland or to the autonomy of Åland.

[21] The initiative also raised two other issues, namely the participation of the Government of the Åland Islands in the control of the implementation of the principle of subsidiarity and the standing of the Åland Islands before the ECJ. However, these additional issues were not framed in the form of legislative proposals. See Suksi (2007), pp. 398–400.

[22] There is one similar arrangement in place, namely concerning the German-speaking population of Belgium, which has one reserved seat in the European Parliament. See Loi du 23 mars 1989 relative a l'election du parlement europeen (coordination officieuse jusqu'au 1 mars 2004)/Wet van 23 maart 1989 betreffende de verkiezing van het europese parlement (officieuze coördinatie tot 1 maart 2004), articles 9 and 10.

[23] The turnout in elections to the European Parliament in the Åland Islands since 1996 is as follows: 1996: 44.4%; 1999: 21.8%; 35.6%. See www.lagtinget.ax (accessed 28 September 2010).

On the one hand, Art. 2 of the Council Decision allows that a Member State establishes constituencies for elections or subdivides its electoral area in a different manner, however, without generally affecting the proportional nature of the system. This is sustained by Art. 7(2), which underlines that the national provisions may, if appropriate, take account of the specific situation in the Member State. However, such a specific situation shall not affect the essentially proportional nature of the voting system. Against this background, it is possible to raise doubts about the conformity of the proposed Ålandic election system with EU law, because it would have created a massive imbalance in the proportion of representation per mandate in the European Parliament between the one mandate designated for the Åland Islands with around 28,000 inhabitants, on the one hand, and the thirteen mandates designated for mainland Finland with around 5.3 million inhabitants, on the other.[24] It can be concluded that there existed serious legal complications in relation to the Bill proposed by the Legislative Assembly of the Åland Islands.

In its Report to the plenary of the Parliament,[25] the Constitutional Committee concluded that the Finnish Government represents the Åland Islands in the Council of Ministers at the EU level when the Council deals with matters which also belong to the competence of the Åland Islands. The Committee found that the initiative of the Åland Islands is understandable and that the legal order of the Åland Islands should be taken into account in the context. However, the Constitutional Committee was of the opinion that the initiative does not fit well the requirement of proportional elections and the principle of equal suffrage. At the same time, the Constitutional Committee nonetheless established that the issue of Åland's representation in the European Parliament cannot be decided on the basis of principles of international law or rules of the Constitution but that the issue is ultimately dependent on a political solution. This may perhaps be interpreted as a life-line that the Parliament is throwing in the direction of the Åland Islands. However, on the basis of the legal grounds and because the number of Finnish MEPs would, due to amendments to the EU Treaty, be diminished from 14 to 13, the Constitutional Committee proposed that the initiative be rejected. The Committee, nonetheless, appended an additional statement according to which it would be important to continue the discussions about the mechanisms of influence for the Åland Islands in the European Parliament at a European level, *inter alia*, because the position of the Åland Islands in Europe is special and unique. On 13 February 2007, the initiative was defeated in the Parliament without a vote.

[24]It is also possible to refer to a potential source of complication in Article 25 of the U.N. Covenant on Civil and Political Rights, which in letter b) establishes a human right to participate in elections and in c) a right to have access, on general terms of equality, to public service in his country. In the matter of *Istvan Mátyus v. Slovakia* (U.N. Human Rights Committee, Comm. 923/2000, U.N. Doc. CCPR/C/75/D/923/2000). The U.N. Human Rights Committee concluded that Slovakia had violated Article 25 of the Convention when allowing a town to be divided for the purposes of local elections into a number of constituencies of very different sizes, some of which sent one representative for more than one thousand inhabitants to the local council, while others sent one representative for as few as two hundred inhabitants to the local council.

[25]Grundlagsutskottets betänkande 13/2006.

6.2.6 Expanding Participation in Local Government

While the voting rights and eligibility in relation to the Legislative Assembly have remained limited in the manner established in the 1921 Åland Islands Settlement, the voting rights and eligibility at the municipal level have undergone an evolution that has lowered the thresholds of participation for those persons who are not in the possession of the right of domicile (the right of regional citizenship). In principle, the point of departure in section 9 of the 1991 Self-Government Act is still a restrictive one concerning the elections to municipal councils and appointments to other positions of trust in the municipal administration. However, as indicated by section 9, municipal suffrage, as established in section 67 of the Act, can be implemented in relation to citizens of Finland without the right of domicile in the Åland Islands and also in relation to citizens of Iceland, Norway, Sweden and Denmark and to citizens of other States in a manner that deviates from the requirement of the right of domicile. In addition, the EU accession had an impact in this area by opening up suffrage within local government (but not concerning the Legislative Assembly) also for those persons resident in the territory of the Åland Islands who are EU citizens. Although the Parliament of Finland enacted the provision in the Self-Government Act, the final decision on the matter is actually left to the Legislative Assembly, which is under the requirement to enact an act of Åland that provides for a deviation from the main rule by a majority of two-thirds of the votes cast in the Legislative Assembly. As a consequence, the Act of Åland on the Right to Vote and Eligibility in Municipal Elections for Persons who Lack the Right of Domicile (SoÅ 63/1997) has been enacted by the Legislative Assembly. The decision to open up the eligibility requirements at the local government level is therefore at least in principle in the hands of the Åland Islanders themselves, although the EU law would, if the Ålandic provisions are not in harmony with EU law, set aside the Ålandic norm. On the basis of this particular Act, section 30 (2) of the Local Government Act of Åland (SoÅ 73/1997) was amended so that the residency requirement for eligibility in municipalities is now 1 year before the day of municipal elections.

While elections to the Legislative Assembly are held on the basis of political platforms offered by the political groupings, the same groupings do not have much activity at all at the local government level. This may, in part, be a consequence of the fact that the municipalities of Åland have somewhat fewer functions than, e.g., municipalities in mainland Finland, but also of the fact that the municipalities in Åland are, in most cases, very small. Therefore, politics in the municipalities are more person-oriented than party-oriented, and in the elections, party groupings are not really needed as intermediaries, although the candidates in municipal elections make clear their affiliation to the political groupings when nominated by groups of individual voters. This may, however, change in the future, if the Legislative Assembly adopts a proposal submitted by the Government of the Åland Islands in 2010 according to which the political groupings shall also have a right to nominate candidates in municipal elections, provided that this is done under the auspices of a local association of an Åland-wide political grouping. Because the municipal elections are organized at the same time as elections to the Legislative Assembly, the turnout figures presented for the Legislative Assembly are indicative also for participation in the municipal elections, but because the number of persons with the right to vote is larger than in the Legislative Assembly elections, the actual turnout is normally somewhat lower in most of the municipalities. In the municipal elections of 2007, the number of persons with the right to vote was 21,058 and the turnout was 66.4%, with a variation of between 62.3% for Mariehamn and 85.9% in the smallest municipality, Sottunga, with only 99 persons with the right to vote.

At the local government level, elections to the municipal board is the main method of participation available to the inhabitants of each municipality, because it seems that no referendums have ever been organized in any of the municipalities. If referendums were organized, they would, under section 34 of the Local Government Act of Åland, be advisory, not decisive. However, the initiation of an advisory referendum could be undertaken not only by the municipal council, but also through a popular referendum initiative undersigned by 5% of the voters, as established in section 35 of the Act. In the case of a referendum initiative, the municipal council would nonetheless have the power to decide whether a municipal advisory referendum shall be held. There is another important dimension to participation at the local level, which is the appointment of persons to positions of trust. After the municipal elections, the municipal council constitutes the municipality for the next 4 years by electing the decision-makers of the lower organs of municipal administration, such as the municipal board and the various committees. The eligibility requirements are by and large the same as for the elections to the municipal council.

Taken together, the elections to the municipal council and the appointments to the other municipal organs constitute a core dimension of the right of municipalities to self-government, guaranteed under section 121 of the Constitution of Finland. Although the Åland Islands Settlement originally limited eligibility to those with the right of domicile, the constitutional right of self-government of municipalities was actually not affected very much. However, the enlargement of eligibility at the municipal level has widened the base of those persons in the Åland Islands who can participate in the exercise of the constitutional right of municipal self-government.

Although the autonomy of the Åland Islands is essentially a participatory frame, guaranteed to the inhabitants of the Åland Islands in several ways, the turnout in the various elections in the Åland Islands at elections to the Legislative Assembly, the Parliament of Finland, the European Parliament and the municipal councils as well as in elections of the President of Finland shows a relatively low level of activity. It is apparent on the basis of the turnout figures that the inhabitants of the Åland Islands perceive the Legislative Assembly as their main political forum (including probably also the municipal councils), followed by their interest in the office of the President. The Parliament of Finland is not understood as quite as significant, perhaps in particular because the main decisions concerning public services and allocation of public funds are made in the Åland Islands by the Legislative Assembly. Finally, the low turnout in elections to the European Parliament sends a clear message about the perceived importance of that organ (but as of 1 December

2009, the European Parliament has a share in the law-making powers of the EU more or less on a par with the Council of Ministers). The thinking seems to be that the most important decisions for the Åland Islanders are made in the Åland Islands by the Legislative Assembly and the municipal councils. These patterns of participation that have evolved during decades of autonomy are so far less established in most other sub-state entities, such as in Aceh.

6.3 Aceh: Creating a Regional Polity

6.3.1 Participation at the Core of the Peace Agreement

It is not very surprising that the LoGA contains a large number of provisions concerning participation. After all, Aceh experienced a separatist insurgency that claimed independence, that is, both external and internal self-determination, which, if realized, could have maximized the participation of the Acehnese in all areas of legislative powers. The peace agreement was premised upon the dropping of the claim of external self-determination by the GAM,[26] but the questions to be resolved were how the internal dimension of self-determination would be incorporated within the framework of the Indonesian state structure and how the members of the GAM would be incorporated in the political structures of Aceh (and, ultimately, of Indonesia). Therefore, there are provisions in the LoGA concerning elections of the Governor of Aceh, the DPRA, and the Indonesian parliament.

However, it deserves to be repeated that the term self-determination is not referred to in the MoU. The main reason may be that the Acehnese, including the GAM, had demanded that an independence referendum be held in Aceh in a manner comparable to that of East Timor. The President of Indonesia, Abdurrahman Wahid, went so far as to suggest that it would be unfair to only allow the East Timorese to decide their political status,[27] in effect promising that a referendum could be held in Aceh, too. Subsequent presidents have retracted that pledge, but reference to the term 'referendum' is still colored by that promise: a referendum is understood as a mechanism to decide about independence. That is probably the reason why the LoGA creates an entirely representative structure of decision-making for Aceh, without any provisions on participation through referendum at any governmental level.

[26]See Miller (2009), p. 158.

[27]Miller (2009), p. 67. See also Drexler (2008), pp. 50 f., 65, 77, 130, 133 f., 150–155, 180–186, 211, reporting, *inter alia*, on the peaceful mass rally on 8 November 1999 in Banda Aceh, when one million persons gathered in Banda Aceh to demand a referendum. The event made the SIRA, that is, the Central Committee for Referendum Aceh, a strong political force in Aceh that ultimately converged with the GAM in the gubernatorial elections, where Mr. Nazar, the leader of the SIRA, was featured as the candidate for the post of the Vice-Governor.

The MoU contains an entire chapter of provisions concerning political participation of the people of Aceh. In para. 1.2.1, the Government of Indonesia agreed to and promised to facilitate the establishment of Aceh-based political parties that meet national criteria. The possibility to create local political parties as opposed to the national ones, which are the only ones that can nominate candidates in any election elsewhere in Indonesia, was one of the main aspirations of the Acehnese in the peace negotiations but also one of the main objections of the Indonesian Government.[28] The Indonesian Government nonetheless agreed to create the political and legal conditions for the establishment of local political parties in Aceh in consultation with the Indonesian parliament. This includes the right to nominate candidates for the positions of all elected officials in the elections of April 2006 and thereafter, the organization of free and fair local elections in 2006 for the head of the Aceh administration and in 2009 for the legislature of Aceh, and the guarantee of the full participation of all Acehnese people in local and national elections according to the Constitution of Indonesia.

6.3.2 Local Political Parties

The constitutional and political order of Indonesia channels the opinions of the population to the decision-making fora of the state of Indonesia through political parties, mentioned in Art. 22E(3) of the Indonesian Constitution, according to which the participants in the general election for the election of the members of the House of Representatives and of the Regional House of Representatives are political parties. The focus on political parties is strengthened in the party legislation, which establishes the requirements of national political parties and by default prevents regional political parties, because of the risk of secessionist tendencies if regional or local political parties were allowed. However, in the case of Aceh, the Indonesian legislation specifically allows for local political parties, although they are not allowed anywhere else in Indonesia.

According to Art. 75 of the LoGA, residents of Aceh may establish local political parties.[29] This is important, because the requirements for establishing a national party are such that a group interested in promoting specific Acehnese interests would never be able to form a national party because of the small size of

[28]Miller (2009), p. 158: "The most divisive issue throughout the talks, however, concerned the formation of Aceh-based political parties. GAM's demand to establish local political parties had been highly contentious during the peace talks in 2001 and 2002, and had ultimately been rejected by Jakarta on the grounds that local political parties contravened Indonesia's Law No. 31/2002 on political parties, which required parties to have regional boards in at least 50% of Indonesia's provinces."

[29]According to Miller (2009), p. 168, this provision went well beyond the previous NAD law, which had only allowed the election of candidates who were members of parties with a national presence.

Aceh in comparison with the rest of the country.[30] In the definitions of Art. 1, paras 13 and 14, of the LoGA, a distinction is made between political parties (evidently in the meaning of national political parties), on the one hand, and local political parties on the other. While a political party is defined as a "political organization voluntarily formed by a group of Indonesian citizens based on a common goal and aspiration to fight for the interest of the members, society, nation and country through the general elections", a local political party is defined as a "political organization voluntarily formed by a group of Indonesian citizens domiciled in Aceh based on a common goal and aspiration to fight for the interest of the members, society, nation and country through the elections of DPRA/DPRK, Governor/Vice Governor, regent/deputy regent, and mayor/deputy mayor". This distinction would seem to indicate that the local political parties are not expected to be able to promote candidates at the national level and to send members to the national political organs. However, the opposite is not true concerning politics at the provincial level: the national political parties may participate in the political life of Aceh on the same terms as the local political parties. In addition to the LoGA, Art. 312 of the national election law[31] mentions the local political parties in Aceh for the purposes of electing the members of the DPRA and the DPRKs and makes the point that as long as they are not specifically regulated in the LoGA, the provisions of the national election law shall be applied. There is hence a special recognition of the Acehnese local political parties in the national election law. Interestingly, on top of the fairly detailed rules in the LoGA concerning local political parties, Art. 95 stipulates in addition that further provisions related to local political parties shall be governed by government regulations,[32] making it possible for the executive power of Indonesia to have a say in the right to participation through political parties.

Local political parties may be formed and established by at least 50 Indonesian citizens who are at least 21 years of age and are permanently domiciled in Aceh. In addition, a local political party must consist of at least 30% women. The LoGA also prescribes that the leadership of local political parties shall be located in the capital city of Aceh and that of the leadership of local political parties, at least 30% shall be women. Local political parties shall have clearly distinguishable names, symbols and logos and they shall have permanent offices, which indicates that they are established as juridical persons, a quality brought about through registration and validation as legal entities provided that they have chapters in at least 50% of the districts/municipalities and 25% of *kecamatans* in each district/municipality. The membership of a local political party shall, according to Art. 83 of the LoGA,

---

[30]Concerning local political affairs elsewhere in Indonesia, see Schmit (2008), p. 172. The case could be made the Indonesian nationalists were fearing that demands for a regional party structure could spread from Aceh to the rest of the country.

[31]Law of the Republic of Indonesia No. 10/2008 concerning General Election for Members of People's Representative Council, Regional Representatives' Council, and Regional People's Representative Council.

[32]See Government Regulation No. 20/2007 concerning Local Political Parties.

consist of Indonesian citizens permanently domiciled in Aceh who have reached the age of 17 years or are/have been married. Membership of a local party shall be voluntary, open and non-discriminatory for all Indonesian citizens permanently domiciled in Aceh who agree to the articles of association and bylaws of a given local political party. The finances of a local political party shall, according to Art. 84, be derived from members' dues, lawful contributions and assistance from the APBA and APBK. As concerns the subsidies from APBA and APBK, they shall be granted proportionally to political parties that gain seats in the DPRA and the DPRK, as provided by an implementing *qanun*. As concerns contributions from members and non-members as well as from business enterprises and other corporate entities, Art. 85 of the LoGA sets an annual ceiling for such contributions.

Although local political parties are allowed in Aceh, they are under Art. 77 of the LoGA nevertheless tied to the national principles by the requirement that the underlying principles of a local political party must not violate the *Pancasila* or the 1945 Constitution of the Republic of Indonesia, although such a party may incorporate certain characteristics that reflect the aspirations, religion, local customs, and philosophy of the Acehnese people. The alignment of local parties with the national principles is underlined by Art. 78, according to which the general objectives of a local political party shall be to achieve the national ideals of the Indonesian people as described in the preamble of the 1945 Constitution of the Republic of Indonesia, to promote a democratic society based on the *Pancasila* and uphold the people's sovereignty within the Unitary State of the Republic of Indonesia and to achieve prosperity for all Acehnese people. In addition, the LoGA prescribes that the specific objectives of a local political party shall be to increase the political participation of the Acehnese people in the implementation of regional governance and to advance the ideals of the local political party as part of society, the people, and the state, in accordance with the uniqueness and special nature of Aceh. Finally, the objectives of local political parties must, according to the provision, be pursued in a constitutional manner.

Although a local political party has, after its registration, the right to carry out ordinary political activities, in part listed in Art. 80 of the LoGA,[33] such a party is also under particular obligations that on their part underline the alignment of political work with the national principles. As stated in Art. 81, a local political

[33] According to Art. 80 of the LoGA, a local political party shall have the right to receive equal and fair treatment from the Aceh Government and district/municipality governments, manage and administer its internal organizational affairs independently, retain copyright title over its party name, symbol, and logo from the department in charge of legal and human rights affairs, participate in the general elections of DPRA and DPRK members, nominate candidates to fill seats in the DPRA and DPRK, recommend the dismissal of its members from the DPRA and DPRK, recommend the replacement of its members in the DPRA and DPRK, nominate candidates to be elected as Governor and Vice Governor, regent and deputy regent, and mayor and deputy mayor in Aceh; and enter into affiliations or other forms of cooperation with another local political party or national political party. The nominations and cooperation with other parties shall be specified by a *qanun*.

party shall have the obligation to adhere to the *Pancasila* and implement the 1945 Constitution of the Republic of Indonesia and other laws and regulations, maintain the integrity of the Unitary State of the Republic of Indonesia, participate in the development of Aceh and national development, uphold the supremacy of the law, democracy, and human rights, provide political education and channel the political aspirations of its members and ensure the successful conduct of general elections at regional and national levels.[34]

The provisions concerning local political parties are complemented by a number of prohibitions and sanctions. According to Art. 82, a local political party shall be prohibited from using a name, symbol, or logo that resembles the flag or coat of arms of the Republic of Indonesia, the symbol of a state institution or the Government, the regional symbol of Aceh, the name, flag, or symbol of other nations or of an international institution/agency, or the name or picture of a person, the name, symbol, or logo of another political party or local political party, whether in principal or in their entirety. In addition, a local political party shall be prohibited from undertaking activities that contravene the *Pancasila*, the 1945 Constitution of the Republic of Indonesia, or other laws and regulations, undertaking activities that endanger the integrity of the Republic of Indonesia, accepting contributions from or giving contributions to foreign entities in any form whatsoever that contravene prevailing laws and regulations, accepting contributions, whether cash or in kind, from any person without clearly stating such a person's identity, receiving contributions from individuals and/or corporate entities exceeding the limit set by prevailing laws and regulations, soliciting or accepting funding from state-owned enterprises, region-owned enterprises, village-owned enterprises, or by any other name they may be referred to, or from cooperatives, foundations, nongovernmental organizations, community organizations or humanitarian organizations. A local political party is also prohibited from establishing a business enterprise and/or holding shares in a business enterprise and from adopting, developing, or disseminating the teachings of communism or Marxism-Leninism. Thus there is an additional prohibition connected to the *Pancasila* and to the Constitution and laws of Indonesia and also a prohibition concerning the ideological content of the political work that a local political party may undertake.

In conjunction with the prescriptions concerning the activities of the parties and the prohibitions that limit their activities, there are provisions in the LoGA concerning the supervision of local political parties. According to Art. 93, the regional departmental office in charge of legal and human rights affairs, that is, an agency of the central government, shall exercise supervision with respect to the following duties specified in Art. 92: implementation of both administrative and substantive examination of the

[34] In addition, a local political party shall compile and maintain its membership data, maintain bookkeeping, lists of contributors, and records of amounts of contributions received, and be open to providing this information to the public and the government, prepare periodic financial reports and maintain a special bank account for party funds. These obligations are apparently in keeping with para. 1.2.8 of the MoU that says that there will be full transparency in campaign funds.

articles of establishment and the requirements for establishing local political parties as referred to in Articles 75 and 77, examination of local political party chapters as presented in the articles of establishment of the political parties and their chapters, and checks of the names, symbols, and logos of political parties. The Independent Elections Commission (KIP Aceh) is charged with the supervision of respect for requests for results of annual financial audits of local political parties and audit reports concerning general election campaign funds, and the Governor as the representative of the Indonesian Government is responsible for the examination of the possibility of violations of prohibitions for local political parties as concerns, *inter alia*, activities that contravene the *Pancasila*, the 1945 Constitution of the Republic of Indonesia, or other laws and regulations, activities that endanger the integrity of the Republic of Indonesia, accepting, receiving or soliciting funds in violation of the LoGA, establishing a business enterprise and holding shares in one, and adopting, developing, or disseminating the teachings of communism or Marxism-Leninism.[35]

Articles 86–88 of the LoGA contain an elaborate sanctions regime for situations where the provisions concerning local political parties have been violated. Persons who violate the contribution ceilings by giving excess funds may be sentenced to a prison term of up to 6 months and/or fined up to a significant amount of money, and so, too, may directors of the local political parties who accept such excessive contributions (and the excess of such a contribution shall be deemed confiscated to the state). If the directors of a local political party use their party to engage in adopting, developing, or disseminating the teachings of communism or Marxism-Leninism, they shall, under Art. 86 be charged with a crime against state security pursuant to Article 107, points c, d, and e of the Indonesian Criminal Code, and may have their party dissolved on the basis of a ruling by the Constitutional Court. A local political party may also be temporarily suspended on the basis of a decision by the Constitutional Court as provided in Art. 88 of the LoGA for undertaking activities that contravene the *Pancasila*, the 1945 Constitution of the Republic of Indonesia, or other laws and regulations and for undertaking activities that endanger the integrity of the Republic of Indonesia. The LoGA also prescribes a number of administrative punishments that deal with the substantive requirements placed on local political parties by the LoGA. It is therefore possible to say that local political parties are subject to a strict legal regime that is aimed at aligning them with the national constitutional and political order and at preventing them from pursuing subversive activities under the guise of a legitimate political formation. This regime concerning local political parties seems problematic against the background of the freedom of association in, for instance, the CCPR.

---

[35]There is a restriction of the supervision activities in Art. 94 concerning the Indonesian Government, the Government of Aceh and the district/municipality governments. They shall not carry out supervision of the implementation of functions and rights of local political parties specified in articles 79 and 80 of the LoGA, that is, as concerns the general political activities of the local political parties, such as the general political work, nomination of candidates, and the internal affairs of the parties.

6.3.3 *Elections Administered within the National Frame*

The organization of elections is charged to the Independent Election Commission (the Aceh KIP), which according to Art. 56 of the LoGA is a body responsible not only for the elections of the DPRA and Governor and vice-Governor in Aceh, but also for the national elections, that is, elections of the president and vice-president of Indonesia, members of the Indonesian House of Representatives and members of the Indonesian Representative Council of Regions.[36] The district/municipality has its own election commission which for its part participates in the organization of the national and Aceh-wide elections and organizes the elections at the local government level. The Aceh KIP and the local KIPs are not organs of the Government of Aceh, but constitute instead an integral part of the National Elections Commission (KPU).[37] There is a separate Elections Supervisory Committee at the Aceh level and also at the local government level, formed by the national Elections Supervisory Committee. Such a Committee supervises the execution of the election of Governor/Vice Governor, regent/deputy regent, and mayor/deputy mayor and carries out other duties and authorities as set out in prevailing laws and regulations.[38] In addition, according to Art. 64 of the LoGA, election observation at elections of

[36]Article 58 lists the duties and authorities of KIP: (a) plan and carry out the election of Governor/Vice Governor, regent/deputy regent, and mayor/deputy mayor, (b) determine procedures for the election of Governor/Vice Governor, regent/deputy regent, and mayor/deputy mayor, (c) coordinate, implement, and control all stages in the election of Governor/Vice Governor, regent/deputy regent, and mayor/deputy mayor, (d) determine dates and implementation procedures with respect to campaigns and voting for the elections of Governor/Vice Governor, regent/deputy regent, and mayor/deputy mayor, (e) accept the registration of candidate tickets as participants in the election, (f) examine the requirements of nominated candidates for Governor/Vice Governor, regent/deputy regent, and mayor/deputy mayor, (g) determine candidate tickets that have met the established requirements, (h) accept the registration of and announce the campaign teams, (i) conduct audits of and publicize the reports on campaign fund contributions, (j) affirm the result of vote recapitulations and announce the results of the election of Governor/Vice Governor, regent/deputy regent, and mayor/deputy mayor through a plenary meeting, (k) conduct an evaluation and submit a report to the DPRA/DPRK on the election of Governor/Vice Governor, regent/deputy regent, and mayor/deputy mayor, and (l) carry out other duties and authorities as set out in relevant laws and regulations. Miller (2009), p. 168, points out that the KIP Aceh and the Aceh Election Supervisory Body were already included in the NAD Law, but the elections component of the special autonomy legislation was never implemented.

[37]Although both the KIP of Aceh and the KIPs of district/city are all part of the national KPU, they are different from the KPUD, established for the purposes of the national elections, in certain respects. Firstly, the members of a KIP are decided by the KPU on the basis of recommendation from the DPRA/DPRK, while the members of a KPUD are decided by the KPU on the basis of recommendation from the government of the provincial/district/city levels. Secondly, the KIP of Aceh consists of seven members, while the KPUD consists of five members.

[38]The supervision of the elections to the multi-member representative bodies is in principle similar, as set out in articles 103–128 in the national election law.

Governor/Vice Governor, regent/deputy regent, and mayor/deputy mayor may be carried out by local, national and international monitors.[39]

After an election, the KIP of Aceh submits the election results to the DPRA, which in its turn forwards the results to the President of Indonesia, who, on the basis of Art. 69 of the LoGA, affirms the election of the Governor and Vice-Governor. The inauguration and swearing-in of the Governor and Vice-Governor is carried out in a DPRA plenary session in the presence of the Chairperson of the *Syari'yah* Court by the Indonesian Minister of Home Affairs on behalf of the President of Indonesia. The procedure of confirming the election result by the representatives of the Indonesian state is a further indication of the fact that at the same time as the Governor of Aceh is a representative of the population of Aceh, he or she is also a representative of the Indonesian state in the province, charged at the same time with tasks which actually are functions of the Indonesian Government.

Under Art. 72 of the LoGA, voters in Aceh are granted a wide spectrum of participatory rights, namely the right to elect their Governor/Vice-Governor, to monitor the process of such an election, to propose policies with respect to the governing of Aceh and the governing of the districts/municipalities, to propose improvements and amendments to *qanuns*, and to supervise the use of the budget. A problematic dimension concerning the implementation of the gubernatorial election is that such elections shall, according to Art. 73 of the LoGA, be further governed by *qanun* with guidance from prevailing laws and regulations. The provision thereby delegates the specification of a constitutional right to the level of bylaws, beyond reach of, for instance, the constitutional review performed by the Constitutional Court of Indonesia. As concerns the election results as such, complaints in concrete cases may be filed directly at the Supreme Court of Indonesia, which issues final decisions in such matters as specified in Art. 74.

6.3.4 Post-conflict Elections of the Governor

The first elections after the peace agreement and the tsunami were the elections of the Governor in 2006. According to Art. 65 of the LoGA, the Governor/Vice Governor, regent/deputy regent, and mayor/deputy mayor are elected in a direct election by way of single tickets once every 5 years. The incumbent may be re-elected only once to the

[39]Monitors of elections of Governor/Vice Governor, regent/deputy regent, and mayor/deputy mayor must adopt an independent approach and possess a clear source of funding. International monitors must follow the procedures set out in prevailing laws and regulations. Monitors of elections of Governor/Vice Governor, regent/deputy regent, and mayor/deputy mayor must be registered with the KIP in accordance with prevailing laws and regulations. The prevailing law in the area in election observation, including the position of international election observers, is found in articles 231–243 in the national election law. For the organization of the KIP Aceh during the elections of 2006 and the activities of the Election Supervisory Body (the so-called PANWASHLIH), see Miller (2009), p. 168 f.

same position. The LoGA contains provisions concerning the different stages of elections from nomination to vote counting and declaration of results. Candidate tickets for the election of the above-mentioned executive positions can be nominated by national political parties or coalitions of political parties, local political parties or coalitions of local political parties, coalitions consisting of national political parties and local political parties, and/or by individual persons.[40] The eligibility requirements for candidates for the executive positions are very elaborate and contain, *inter alia*, both a constitutional and a religious component.[41] In addition to the eligibility requirements referred to in Art. 67(2) of the LoGA, individual candidates must, according to Art. 68, obtain support from at least 3% of the population located over at least 50% of the number of districts/municipalities in the case of the election of Governor/Vice Governor, and 50% of the number of sub-districts in the case of the elections of regent/deputy regent, and mayor/deputy mayor.[42] This means that already the candidates in executive elections have to command a substantive overall support in much of Aceh. As concerns the Governor and Vice Governor, the popular election is not, however, the final verdict on the matter, because the election has to be affirmed under Art. 69 of the LoGA by the President of Indonesia.[43]

The first election held in Aceh after the peace agreement and the tsunami was the election of the Governor and Vice Governor on 11 December 2006. The election was organized on the basis of articles 66–72 of the LoGA,[44] which detail the

[40]As pointed out by Miller (2009), p. 168, the possibility to nominate independent candidates went well beyond the NAD law, which had only allowed the election candidates who were members of parties with a national presence, and it was also more than was mandated by the MoU. The provisions in the LoGA concerning local political parties and the possibility to nominate independent candidates "made Aceh's new electoral system more participatory and inclusive than Indonesia's other provinces, although in July 2007 the Constitutional Court amended Law No. 32/2004 on Regional Government (which amended Law No. 22/1999) to allow independent candidates to contest direct local elections nationwide".

[41]Candidates must be Indonesian citizens, carry out the values and practices (*syari'at*) of their religions, adhere to the 1945 Constitution of the Republic of Indonesia, have a minimum high school education or its equivalent, be at least 30 years of age, be in good physical and mental condition and free from any illicit drugs, based on a comprehensive physical screening by the medical team, have never been convicted of a crime punishable by a prison term of at least 5 years based on a court ruling having permanent legal force, except in cases of the crime of treason or a political crime for which an amnesty/rehabilitation has been granted, not currently have voting rights revoked by a court ruling having permanent legal force, have never committed an indecent act, have knowledge of their regions and be known by the communities in that region, present a list of personal assets and consent to the list being publicized, not be currently serving as acting Governor/regent/mayor, and not be liable for a financial debts personally, or on behalf of a legal entity under his/her charge, which cause losses to the state.

[42]The support for nomination shall be evidenced through proof of identity and written statements from the supporting persons.

[43]After affirmation by the Minister of Home Affairs, the Governor inaugurates and swears in the local executive leaders in Aceh.

[44]According to the definitions of Art. 1, para. 7, of the LoGA, the election of the Governor is based on the principles of directness, openness, freedom, confidentiality, honesty and fairness. Such

different stages of the election and indicate that further provisions concerning the elections are provided in bylaws. Tickets consisting of two candidates, one for the post of Governor and another for the post of Vice-Governor,[45] were presented. The requirements placed on candidates in Art. 67 of the LoGA are very high,[46] and some requirements, in particular the requirement of a minimum level of education and the test of religion, which in the predominantly Muslim region translated into a reading test of the Koran, drew criticism. The reading test was problematic for the potential female candidates, who failed on it and caused the gubernatorial election to be contested by male tickets only.[47]

---

prevailing laws and regulations that were in effect during the gubernatorial elections were, according to the Explanatory Notes to the LoGA, the Nanggroe Aceh Darussalam Provincial *Qanun* Number 2 of 2004 concerning the election of Governor/Vice Governor, regent/deputy regent, and mayor/deputy mayor in Nanggroe Aceh Darussalam Province, as amended by Nanggroe Aceh Darussalam Provincial *Qanun* Number 3 of 2005 concerning the Amendment to Nanggroe Aceh Darussalam Provincial *Qanun* Number 2 of 2004. The latest amendment to the elections *Qanun* was done by means of *Qanun* No. 7/2006.

[45]Similar provisions concerning nomination of candidates are included in the LoGA concerning regents and deputy regents in districts and concerning mayors and deputy mayors in municipalities.

[46]Candidates must be Indonesian citizens, carry out the values and practices (*syari'at*) of their religions, adhere to the 1945 Constitution of the Republic of Indonesia, have a minimum high school education or its equivalent, be at least 30 years of age, be in good physical and mental condition and free from any illicit drugs, based on a comprehensive physical screening by the medical team, have never been convicted of a crime punishable by a prison term of at least 5 years based on a court ruling having permanent legal force, except in cases of the crime of treason or a political crime for which an amnesty/rehabilitation has been granted, not currently have voting rights revoked by a court ruling having permanent legal force, have never committed an indecent act, have knowledge of their regions and be known by the communities in that region, present a list of personal assets and consent to the list being publicized, not be currently serving as acting Governor/regent/mayor, and not be liable for a financial debts personally, or on behalf of a legal entity under his/her charge, which cause losses to the state.

[47]European Union Election Observation Mission (2007), pp. 6, 13. The reading test requirement surfaced again in relation to the DPRA elections. The requirement was included in *Qanun* No. 3/2008 on Local Political Parties, which made the reading test only be applicable to DPRA candidates from local political parties, creating the question of whether the test will be applicable also to candidates from national parties. As stated in the Report by the International Development Law Organization entitled 'Judicial Review of *Al-Qur'an* Reading Test for Candidates for Members of the Parliament': "In compliance with the prevailing procedure, the draft qanun was sent to Jakarta for approval by the Department of Home Affairs. It is a standard legislation procedure that every qanun or local regulation (Peraturan Daerah/Perda) produced by local legislatures should be approved by the Department of Home Affairs before its enactment and enforced in the community. This is stipulated in the National Law No. 32 year 2004 on Local Government. Article 145 paragraph (2) and (3) of the Law state that the Central Government, in this case the Department of Home Affairs, reserves the rights to annul a local regulation: first, if it is in opposition to the interests of the general public and/or the higher legislation, and second, the decision of the annulment should be legalized through a presidential regulation (Peraturan Presiden/Perpres) at the latest 60 days from the acceptance of the aforementioned Local Regulation. Based on this legislation, the Department of Home Affairs conducted a review of Qanun No. 3 year 2008. The Central Government saw a controversy in Article 36 of the draft qanun. The

The role of local political parties in the nomination process is further specified in Art. 91 of the LoGA. Such a party, a coalition of local political parties, or a coalition consisting of national political parties and local political parties may register their candidate tickets upon having obtained the required 15% of the seats in the DPRA or 15% of the total valid votes in the general election of the DPRA in the given region. The provision contains the requirement that there should be written vision, mission, and program statements for the candidate ticket. A local political party, coalition of local political parties, or coalition consisting of political parties and local political parties may only nominate one candidate ticket, and this pair of candidates may not be nominated again by another local political party or coalition of local political parties. In practice, this means that persons who are not satisfied with the candidate ticket of a party or a coalition are advised to nominate candidates on an independent ticket. As concerns independent candidates, they are, according to Art. 68 of the LoGA, under the additional requirement that they must obtain support from at least 3% of the population located over at least 50% of the number of districts/municipalities.[48]

According to Art. 71, the right to vote in gubernatorial elections is held by Indonesian citizens domiciled in Aceh or its districts/municipalities, who as of the date of the voting are at least 17 years of age or are/have been married, do not suffer any mental debilitation, do not have voting rights revoked by a court ruling with permanent legal force, and are registered as voters. In connection with the elections of 2006, there was criticism of the fact that members of the Indonesian armed forces and the Indonesian police force were excluded from suffrage on the basis of Art. 230 of Law No. 32/2004 regarding Regional Governance.[49]

In the gubernatorial election of 2006, the GAM was divided between the leadership based outside Aceh that sought to broaden its appeal by endorsing one set of candidates with other party affiliations, on the one hand, and the Aceh-based younger leaders and members, who backed two GAM members standing as independent candidates, on the other. The former were supporting the ticket of Mr. Humam Hamid, who was not a GAM member, and who was also the candidate of the United Development Party (PPP), a national party with an Islamic orientation that served as the loyal opposition during the dictatorship of President Suharto. The latter supported Irwandi Yusuf, a US-educated former insurgent and prisoner. The

National Government was of the view that Qanun No. 3 year 2008 should not regulate legislative candidates nominated by national parties, although they were nominated for the DPRA and DPRK." The Government of Aceh and the Governor himself were opposed to the provision in the *Qanun*, but the DPRA refused to remove it. Although the Government of Indonesia, too, was opposed to it, the President of Indonesia did not exercise his right to disapprove the *Qanun* during the established period of 60 days, so the provision remained in force and was applied in conjunction with the DPRA/DPRK elections of 2009.

[48] In the regent/mayor elections at the local government level, the support level is 50% of the number of sub-districts.

[49] European Union Election Observation Mission (2007), p. 12.

Table 6.2 Election results for elections of Governor of 2006 in Aceh[50]

No.	Name of governor/vice governor candidate	Total of valid ballots	Percentage of valid ballots
1	Ir. H. Iskandar Hoesin, MH; Drs. H.M. Saleh Manaf	111,553	5.54
2	H. Tamlicha Ali; Drs. Tgk. Harmen Nuriqmar	80,327	3.99
3	Drs. H. A. Malik Raden, MM; H. Sayed Fuad Zakaria, SE	281,174	13.97
4	Dr. Ir. H. Ahmad Humam Hamid, MA; Drs. H. Hasbi Abdullah, M. Si	334,484	16.62
5	H. Muhammad Djali Yusuf; Drs. H. R. A. Syauqas Rahmatillah, MA	65,543	3.26
6	Drh. Irwandi Yusuf, M. Sc; Muhammad Nazar, S. Ag	768,745	38.20
7	Ir. H. Azwar Abubakar, MM; M. Nasir Djamil, S. Ag	213,566	10.61
8	Drs. H. Ghazali Abbas Adan; H. Shalahuddin Alfata	156,978	7.80
	Total of valid ballots cast	2,012,370	
	Total of invalid ballots cast	92,369	4.39
	Total on final voters' list (FVL)	2,632,935	
	Turnout in percent (based on FVL)		79.94

other party tickets were the *Partai Amanat Nasional*'s candidate Azwar Abubakar, and Malik Raden of *Golkar*, the ruling party under Suharto. The candidates for Vice-Governor on the various tickets were often from other parties than the main candidate, confirming that alliances between parties are a real phenomenon in Aceh.[51]

In the elections of 11 December 2006, the Acehnese elected Mr. Irwandi Yusuf to be Governor of Aceh and Mr. Muhammad Nazar to be Vice-Governor.[52] It seems on the basis of the result that the independent candidates were carried by the electorate, while the party-affiliated ones were unsuccessful. At a turnout of almost 80%, the winning ticket of candidates received 38.2% of the votes cast. Because the winning ticket exceeded the support threshold of 25%, the candidates were elected directly without any second round. Therefore, the election can be characterized as a first-past-the-post election, but with the potential for a run-off election (see Table 6.2 above).[53]

[50]As officially announced by KIP Aceh on 29 December 2006. See European Union Election Observation Mission (2007), p. 31.

[51]See BBC News at http://news.bbc.co.uk/go/pr/fr/-/2/hi/asia-pacific/6217318.stm, published on 11 December 2006 (accessed 3 June 2009). For the split within the GAM, see also Miller (2009), p. 171, Drexler (2008), p. 211.

[52]As pointed out by Miller (2009), p. 168, the primary legal instruments for Aceh's first direct elections of the Governor after the tsunami were the LoGA and the 1945 Constitution, supported by a central government regulation on Aceh-based parties (No. 20/2006; Miller gives the year 2007 for the regulation) and a *Qanun* on local elections and political parties (originally No. 2/2004, as amended by No. 3/2005 and 7/2006).

[53]At the local government level, three districts/municipalities in Aceh ended up organizing run-off elections between the two front-running tickets for regents/mayors because in the first round, none of the candidate tickets received more than 25% of the votes. See European Union Election Observation Mission (2007), p. 33 f.

Mr. Irwandi Yusuf campaigned with a "mission and vision" based on peace and progress and won the majority of votes in 16 of the 21 districts. Interestingly, only a few of the districts were previously known as strongholds of the GAM. In three districts (Pidie, Aceh Tamiang and Bener Meriah) Irwandi and Nazar came in second, in Aceh Tengah third, and in Aceh Singkil fourth. In the provincial capital, Banda Aceh, where the turnout was the lowest (59.5%), Irwandi and Nazar received only 15.5% of the votes.[54] If the support for GAM in the broad sense is gauged by combining the results of Mr. Irwandi and Mr. Hamid, it could be said that the GAM succeeded in gaining the support of around 55% of those voting.

6.3.5 *Post-conflict Representation through an Elected Body*

The second election in Aceh was that of the DPRA, that is, the House of Representatives of Aceh, on 9 April 2009 (and also of the members of the DPRK, DPRRI, and DPDRI, that is, lower levels of representation). In Art. 1(10) of the LoGA, the Aceh House of Representatives (DPRA) is defined as an element of the Aceh regional government whose members are elected through general elections.[55] However, the LoGA does not contain provisions, *inter alia*, concerning the term of office of the DPRA or the method of election. Therefore, according to Art. 4 of the national election law, the election shall be held once every 5 years. In addition, under Art. 5(1) of the national election law, election of members of the DPRA, as well as election to the Indonesian parliament and to the regency/municipality DPRDs shall be conducted through an open proportional system.[56] The same proportional electoral system is thus applied both in Aceh and in the parliamentary elections. In Art. 19 of the national election law, the right to vote is granted to any Indonesian citizen who has reached the age of 17 years or more on the polling day or who has been married, which is the same as in the LoGA for the gubernatorial election. The candidates are required, under Art. 50 of the national election law, to fulfill conditions similar to the candidates in the gubernatorial elections, with the exception of the nomination by a number of voters, because the parties nominate the candidates. The parties nominate the candidates through procedures outlined in articles 50 and 51 of the national election law, arranging the nominees in a list of

[54]European Union Election Observation Mission (2007), p. 31. On the election result, see also Miller (2009), p. 169 f.

[55]Provisions similar to those concerning the DPRA are included in the LoGA for district/municipality House of Representatives (DPRK), which is defined as an element exercising district/municipality governance whose members are elected through general elections.

[56]As will be explained below, the electoral system is partly open, because candidates who do not succeed in exceeding a certain threshold attributed to the party list but where the votes cast for the party nonetheless allocates more seats to the party than have been assigned to the candidates who exceeded the threshold, the candidates will be allocated seats according to the numerical order on the list of candidates, as originally determined by the party.

nominees for each party, observing the requirement that according to Art. 52 of the national election law, at least 30% of the nominees on each list have to be women. In addition, the nominees are listed in numerical order and at least every third nominee must be a woman.

According to Art. 89(1) of the LoGA, a local political party must meet a number of requirements, enforced by Aceh KIP, in order to run in the general election of the DPRA/DPRK. It has to have been validated as a legal entity, it has to have chapters in at least two-thirds of the districts/municipalities in Aceh and in at least two-thirds of the *kecamatans* in those districts/municipalities, it has to have a membership of at least 1/1,000 of the total population in each of its chapter locations, as evidenced by local political party membership cards, and it has to have permanent offices for its chapters. In addition, it has to register its name and symbol with the KIP. Evidently, the stringent conditions apply only as entry requirements, because under Art. 90, the requirements for participating with candidates in subsequent elections are different: if a local political party has obtained at least 5% of the seats in the DPRA or obtained at least 5% of the seats in the DPRK throughout at least one-half of the districts/municipalities in Aceh, the local political party may continue to participate in the subsequent elections at the respective level of governance.

The local political parties of Aceh which qualified for participating in the elections to the DPRA were the Prosperous and Safe Aceh Party (*Partai Aceh Aman Sejahtera*, PAAS), the Aceh Sovereignty Party (*Partai Daulat Atjeh*, PDA), the Independent Voice of the Acehnese Party (*Partai Suara Independen Rakyat Aceh*, SIRA), the Aceh People's Party (*Partai Rakyat Aceh*, PRA), the Aceh Party (*Partai Aceh*) and the Aceh Unity Party (*Partai Bersatu Aceh*, PBA). At the same time, however, also national parties, such as *Partai Demokrat*, *Partai Golongan Karya* (*Golkar*), *Partai Amanat Nasional* (PAN) and *Partai Keadilan Sejahtera* (PKS) contested the provincial elections in Aceh,[57] collecting votes among the Acehnese voters. The campaigning in elections is relatively rigorously regulated. For instance, as stipulated in Art. 84, the campaign operator, participants, and party officers shall be prohibited to dispute, *inter alia*, the state ideology, that is, the *Pancasila*, and the Preamble of the 1945 Constitution, conduct activities that endanger the integrity of the Unitary State of the Republic of Indonesia and defame an individual, religion, ethnic group, society, other group as well as other parties.[58]

---

[57] Originally, altogether 38 national political parties were set to participate in the elections in Aceh. See International Development Law Organisation on 'Judicial Assessment of Political Parties' Programs in Aceh towards the 2009 General Election' (2009), p. 1.

[58] Other actions prohibited are provoke and instigate conflicts among individuals or groups in the society, violate public orders, threaten to use violence or incite people to use violence against an individual or a group of people and/or in other contesting political parties, destroy and/or remove visual displays of other contestants, use state facilities, places for worship, educational facilities, bring or use picture logo and/or in other attributive materials other than the logo and/or in other attributive materials belonging to their own contesting party and promise or give money or in other materials to the campaign participants.

In the 2009 DPRA elections, the number of persons with the right to vote was 3,009,965, and altogether 2,266,713 voters exercised their right to vote, which means that the turnout was 75%. The number of valid votes was 2,146,845, which means that there were as many as 119,868 invalid votes. That is more than the support of some smaller parties that got seats in the DPRA and thus not a healthy sign of the state of the electoral system.

The DPRA consists of 69 seats, which is more than the 55 seats the DPRA should have in Aceh on the basis of Art. 23 of Law No. 10/2008 of the Republic of Indonesia concerning General Election for Members of People's Representative Council, Regional Representatives Council, and Regional People's Representative Council.[59] However, the LoGA grants in Art. 22(3) an exception to Aceh concerning this national rule by providing that the number of DPRA members must not exceed 125% of the number stipulated by law. Aceh has adopted the absolute maximum number of seats for its own House of Representatives. With a proportional election system, a higher number of seats to be contested in the election makes it easier for smaller parties to gain seats in the assembly, but a possibility to vary the number of seats in this way is quite unique. At the same time, the exception for Aceh from the national scheme underlines two features, firstly, the fact that in principle, the governmental institutions of Aceh are constituted in much the same way as elsewhere in the regions of Indonesia, and secondly, that the LoGA is a *lex specialis* in relation to the *lex generalis* found in such Indonesian legislation of a national character that applies to regions elsewhere in Indonesia. If a matter related to the governance of Aceh is not regulated in the LoGA, an applicable legal rule to fill a vacuum would in most cases be found in the national regionalization legislation, that is, in Law 32/2004 on Regional Government. Also in other areas, such as the electoral system including the distribution of mandates in the DPRA, the situation is similar: the LoGA does not regulate the matter, and therefore, the rule for the distribution of the mandates is the same as for the national parliament, as established in the national election law.

The mandates in the 2009 election were distributed as follows:

1. Partai Aceh (PA), 1,007,173 (46.91%), 33 mandates
2. Partai Demokrat, 232,728 (10.84%), 10 mandates
3. Partai Golongan Karya (Golkar), 142,411 (6.63%), 8 mandates
4. Partai Amanat Nasional (PAN), 83,060 (3.87%), 5 mandates
5. Partai Keadilan Sejahtera (PKS), 81,529 (3.80%), 4 mandates
6. Partai Persatuan Pembangunan (PPP), 74,429 (3.47%), 4 mandates
7. Partai Keadilan dan Persatuan Indonesia, 41,278 (1.92%), 1 mandate
8. Partai Daulat Atjeh (PDA), 39,706 (1.85%), 1 mandate
9. Partai Bulan Bintang (PBB), 37,336 (1.74%), 1 mandate
10. Partai Kebangkitan Bangsa (PKB), 30,257 (1.41%), 1 mandate
11. Partai Patriot, 15,054 (0.70%), 1 mandate

[59] In a province with the population of more than 3,000,000 to 5,000,000 people, 55 seats shall be allocated.

Of the local political parties, only two could secure seats in the DPRA, while the rest of the parties represented in the DPRA are constituted as national political parties, although their representatives in the DPRA are, naturally, Acehnese. This means that the national political establishment has a significant number of followers in Aceh.[60] At the same time, however, it is clear that close to 50% of the Acehnese support the *Partai Aceh*, that is, the party that has largely been created by transforming the former GAM into a political organization. The combined support for the two Acehnese parties did not, however, lead to a majority of the seats. The representatives in the DPRA feature very few women, which is curious with a view to the requirement of at least 30% of female candidates. Apparently, in the (partly) open list-proportional election, the male candidates attracted sufficient numbers of votes for the female candidates to be sidelined.[61] The low number of female members of the DPRA is a challenge for the future, given the fact that the LoGA deals in several provisions with the empowerment and participation of women.

Of the local political parties that participated in the elections, only PA qualified for automatic participation in the subsequent DPRA elections, while the other parties will have to go through the relatively rigorous qualification procedure prescribed in Art. 89(1) of the LoGA. How effectively the thresholds established in the provision will discourage local political parties from contesting the next elections is difficult to estimate at this point of time, but such an entry threshold may be very effective in limiting the number of parties in the political system, and the expectation of the national legislator may have been that such limitations work to the benefit of the national party system and for the coherence of the political system in Aceh. At the same time, such stringent entry requirements may, however, amount to an unreasonable restriction of political rights.

Once elected to be a member of the DPRA, each member must, according to Art. 36 of the LoGA, associate himself or herself with a fraction, which is yet another requirement that the LoGA places on the internal structures of the DPRA. The total number of members in each fraction must be at least equal to the minimum number of commissions in the DPRA, which means that the minimum size of a fraction is five members. Such DPRA/DPRK members who come from either national political parties or local political parties that do not fulfill the requirements to form one fraction must join with an existing fraction or form a joint fraction. Correspondingly, existing fractions must accept DPRA/DPRK members from other political parties/local political parties that do not fulfill the requirements to form one

---

[60]Originally, the PA estimated it could win up to 59 seats in the DPRA. According to the spokesperson of the PA, "[t]he seat allocation method caused my party to lose many seats. Many of our candidates who gained 10,000 votes failed to secure a seat, while candidates from other parties who gained only 7,000 votes secured one seat each". As reported in 'Aceh Party wins election, without celebration', in The Jakarta Post, Tuesday, May 19, 2009, p. 2. Apparently, in the (partly) open list system, the divisors used to allocate seats produced a smaller quota to the candidate of the PA than to the candidates of the rival parties in spite of the fact that the PA candidate received more individual votes.

[61]See Art. 214 of the national election law.

fraction, and in the event a joint fraction, after being formed, no longer meets the requirements of a joint fraction, all of the members of the joint fraction must join other fractions that fulfill the requirements. National political parties or local political parties that meet the requirements to form a fraction may only form one fraction, which means that a qualifying fraction cannot be split into two, and a joint fraction may be formed by national political parties and local political parties. This forced alignment of members of the DPRA with internal fractions of the DPRA is probably intended to work against the fragmentation of the political scene in the same way as the requirements on parties for submitting candidates in elections. However, the rules seem to be such that they may, in effect, also force such parties to work together in a fraction which do not have much in common in terms of the political platform or supporters, thereby potentially distorting the will of the electors.

Persons elected to be members of the DPRA have, under Art. 26, the right to submit draft *qanuns*, to submit questions, to issue recommendations and opinions, to protocol, financial and administrative rights, to elect and be elected, to defend themselves, and to immunity. The right to submit draft *qanuns* is very important from a principal point of view as a counterweight to the Government's right to submit drafts, while the other rights are either self-explanatory or somewhat unclear. What the extent of immunity of a member of the DPRA is has not been spelled out in the LoGA, but it seems that the DPRA can itself, by means of a *qanun*, regulate the matter within the framework of the existing laws and regulations. In contrast to the rights, members of the DPRA also have a number of responsibilities. Importantly, the members have to abide by the *Pancasila* (the five values) that constitutes the formative principles of the Indonesian state. In addition, the members of the DPRA have to implement the Indonesian Constitution of 1945 and to comply with all laws and regulations, which are requirements that align the decision-making in the DPRA with the national legal order. The members are also required to promote democracy in the execution of Aceh governance and to fight for the enhancement of the people's welfare and prosperity and to take into consideration and channel people's aspirations, receive people's complaints and grievances, and facilitate follow-up actions to bring about their resolution. Finally, the members are required to comply with the bylaws, codes of ethics, and oaths of office for DPRA members, place the interests of the country above personal, group and class interests, submit an accountability report regarding their duties and performance as members of the DPRA as a manifestation of their moral and political obligations towards their constituents, and to uphold norms and ethics in work relationships with relevant institutions.

The exercise of the rights and responsibilities of the DPRA members shall be governed by the bylaws of the DPRA with guidance from prevailing laws and regulations, which means that the DPRA may itself adopt rules of procedure and conduct for its activities. There is, however, a great emphasis on the ethical conduct of the duties of the member of the DPRA in the LoGA, because its provisions require the adoption of a Code of Ethics for the DPRA members and the creation of an Honor Council with, *inter alia*, powers of investigation.

There is a set of *de facto* legal requirements in Art. 37 for candidates when they are elected to be members of the DPRA (or, alternatively, prohibitions for inaugurated DPRA members to serve in a certain capacity).[62] DPRA members who do not fulfill these obligations shall be recommended for dismissal based on the results of an examination by the DPRA Honor Council, and the implementation of these restrictions shall be governed by the DPRA bylaws with guidance from prevailing laws and regulations.

Apart from death and stepping down on the basis of a written resignation as ways of terminating the office of a member of the DPRA, a member may also be dismissed from office under Art. 38 during his or her term in office upon recommendation from the nominating national political party or local political party.[63] Any dismissal of DPRA members shall be submitted for official validation by the DPRA leadership to the Minister of Home Affairs through the Governor. Dismissal of DPRA members in cases other than those related to the will of the political parties shall be executed following a DPRA decree based on a recommendation by the DPRA Honor Council, and the implementation of the provisions concerning termination of office and dismissal shall be governed by DPRA bylaws with guidance from prevailing laws and regulations.

6.3.6 Local Government and National Elections

In the simultaneous local government elections to the DPRK in 2009, there was somewhat more variation in the election results, but the list of parties did not change much, although the local political parties SIRA, PRA, PAAS and PBA got some

---

[62]They are prohibited from concurrently serving in certain positions, to the effect that they probably would have to resign from their other posts if elected or, alternatively, refrain from running as candidate. Such situations encompass state officials, judges with a judicial institution, civil servants, members of the National Armed Forces and National Police and employees of state-owned enterprises and province-owned enterprises, and/or other entities whose budgets come from the public funds managed by different layers of government. There is another set of professions which according to the provision must be relinquished by DPRA members during their membership terms in the DPRA. Such occupations that members of the DPRA are also prohibited from performing are duties as structural employees at state or private educational institutions, public accountants, consultants, advocates/lawyers, notaries, practicing physicians, journalists, and managers of mass media as well as other occupations that have any connection to their duties, authorities, and rights as DPRA members. These prohibitions are very wide and far-reaching and may be problematic. At the same time, they are understandable against the background of the prohibition of corruption, collusion and nepotism included in the same provision.

[63]This can be done for continuously failing to perform his/her duties or being hindered for a consecutive period of 6 months, for no longer meeting the requirements of a DPRA member, after being declared as having violated his/her oath of office and/or the DPRA code of ethics, after failing to fulfill the obligations of a DPRA member, after violating prohibitions applicable to a DPRA member, or after being convicted by a court ruling having permanent legal force of committing a crime punishable by imprisonment of 5 years or more.

seats in the DPRKs. Consequently, it seems as if the old party-political alignments with roots at the national level were surprisingly strong and could only be broken by the more active supporters of the former GAM, while new political forces on the political arena of Aceh may find it difficult to establish themselves.

The elections in Aceh were held at the same time as the national elections to the two elected bodies at the central government level of Indonesia, namely to the 132-seat Regional Representative Council (DPD) and 560-seat House of Representatives (DPR). In both elections, the province forms the constituency. At the same time, elections to the regional houses of representatives were held in other provinces of Indonesia. The Aceh-based parties were not participating in the national elections to the Indonesian House of Representatives, because only national political parties can participate in those elections due to the rigorous requirements in Art. 7 and 8 of the national election law (in addition, there is a support threshold of 2.5% in Art. 208 of the national election law which would effectively prevent any Aceh-based local political party from ever getting a seat in the national parliament). As demonstrated above, at the same time, however, national parties were able to contest the DPRA elections in Aceh, collecting votes from among the Acehnese voters. Many Acehnese declined to vote in the national elections, thereby reducing their electoral participation to the DPRA and the DPRKs of Aceh only. Nonetheless, the 13 seats of the constituency of Aceh in the Indonesian House of Representatives were divided between the national political parties as follows, with 1,838,915 valid votes and 427,798 invalid votes[64] cast in the partly open party-list proportional voting system:[65]

1. Partai Demokrat 751,475 (40.87%)
2. Partai Golongan Karya (Golkar) 193,631 (10.53%)
3. Partai Keadilan Sejahtera (PKS) 130,278 (7.08%)
4. Partai Persatuan Pembangunan (PPP) 113,580 (6.17%)
5. Partai Amanat Nasional (PAN) 107,953 (5.87%)

Candidates for the Regional Representative Council have to run as independents without party platforms, elected on the basis of Art. 5(2) of the national election law through a district system with multiple representatives.[66] The four independent

[64]The number of invalid votes cast is surprisingly high and should be a source of concern, although there is the possibility that at least some of the invalid votes may have been cast in protest against the central government. The Aceh KIP has resolved the disputes and seems to have concluded that everything was in accordance with the rules.

[65]According to Art. 214 of the national election law, candidates who acquire votes that correspond to at least 30% of a quota determined in the basis of the votes cast in relation to the seats available are first allocated the seats, and if no candidates achieve the quota of 30%, the seats are allocated in the order of the list of candidates, as originally determined by the party. The provision was later modified by the Constitutional Court so that the winning candidate is the one who gains more votes.

[66]The requirements placed by Art. 12 upon a candidate for the DPD are as follows: citizen of the Republic of Indonesia who is 21 years of age or more, believing in the Almighty God, having domicile in the territory of the Unitary State of the Republic of Indonesia, able to talk, read, and

candidates who were elected to the Regional Representative Council were supported as follows, with 1,763,811 valid votes cast and 502,902 invalid votes cast:

1. Abdurrahman BTM 234,118 (13.27%)
2. Bachrum Manyak 172,417 (9.78%)
3. Ahmad Farhan Hamid 121,747 (6.90%)
4. A Khalid 101,808 (5.77%)[67]

As Indonesian citizens and on the basis of Law No. 42/2008 concerning Presidential Election, the Acehnese also participate in the elections of the president and vice-president of Indonesia. The presidential election is a direct election, potentially in two rounds, if no ticket of candidates receives more than 50% of the votes over least 20% of the vote in more than half of the provinces of Indonesia. If a second, run-off round is needed, the ticket that receives more than half of the valid votes cast returns the president and vice-president. In the presidential elections of 8 July 2009 in Aceh, the results were divided as follows between the different tickets with candidates for president and vice-president:

Megawati Soekarnoputri; Prabowo Subianto: 53,835 (2.40%)
Soesilo Bambang Yudhoyono; Boediono: 2,093,567 (93.25%)
Jusuf Kalla; Wiranto: 97,717 (4.35%)

The result in Aceh was overwhelmingly in favor of the incumbent president of Indonesia, with a support level far exceeding his support at the national level, although he was elected in the first round after receiving 60.80% of the vote nationwide. The support for Yudhoyono probably reflected the role he played

write in the Bahasa Indonesia, at least graduate from Senior High School (SMA), Religious High School (*Madrasyah Aliyah*/MA), Vocational High School (SMK), Religious Vocational High School (*Madrasyah Aliyah Kejuruan*/MAK), other schools of the same level, loyal to Pancasila as the state foundation and the Constitution of 1945 and the goals of the Proclamation of August 17, 1945, never been sentenced or imprisoned based on a legitimate and legally binding verdict for a criminal act threatened by an imprisonment sanction of 5 years or more, physically and mentally healthy, having been registered as a voter, willing to work full time, resigning from the positions of civil servant, member of Indonesian National Army, or member of the State Police of the Republic of Indonesia, board of administrators in a state owned company and/or region owned company or any entity of which the budget expense is financed by APBN and/or APBD which is proven by a letter of withdrawal that cannot be revoked, willing not to practice as a public accountant, lawyer, notary, land certificate issuing authority (PPAT), and not to become a supplier of goods and services related to the state finance and other occupations that may cause conflict of interests with the duties, authority and rights as a member of DPD in line with the regulations of laws, willing not to couple position as other state authorities, or as board of administrator at a state owned corporation (BUMN)/Region owned corporation (BUMD), or in other entities financed by APBN and /or APBD, nominated only in one representative institution, nominated in one electoral district; and acquiring minimal support from voters in the electoral district. According to Art. 13, such minimal support referred to in Art. 12 is, for a province like Aceh with the population between one million and five million inhabitants, is at least 2,000 voters;

[67]This result was revoked by the Constitutional Court of Indonesia and the fourth candidate to be elected was Mr. Mursyid.

during his first period as president of Indonesia in securing special status for Aceh and in promoting the LoGA when it was being enacted. Conversely, the low support in Aceh for Megawati Soekarnoputri in comparison with her 26.79% vote at the national level is probably explained by the fact that under her period as president, the military campaign against the GAM reached a high point.

6.3.7 Other Forms of Public Bodies

The denominational character of Aceh includes the recognition of the position and powers of the Clerics' Deliberation Council (MPU) in Art. 138 of the LoGA at the Aceh provincial level and at the local government level. The membership of MPUs consists of clerics and Muslim intellectuals who have a deep understanding of the Islamic religion, and the provision requires that attention is given to the representation of women in the MPUs. The MPUs are supposed to be independent and their leadership is selected through a deliberation session among *ulamas*, that is, traditional religious leaders.[68] Hence membership in such councils is by appointment, not by election. One of the tasks of the MPUs is to be partners to the Government of Aceh and the DPRA as well as to the local government institutions,[69] and this task includes the affirmation of *fatwas* (religious decrees).[70] The *fatwas* may serve as one of the points of departure in considerations concerning the formulation of policies by regional governments in the areas of governance, development, community development, and economy, as provided by *qanun*. The MPUs may thus have a role as initiators and inspirers of governmental activities. In that capacity, the MPUs may be understood as vehicles of participation, although the MPUs also have

[68] On the political role of the Acehnese *ulamas* since 1945, see Salim (2008), pp. 143–156, 165–167.

[69] Potentially, the partnership between the MPUs and the governmental institutions of Aceh may be very far-reaching, because according to the Explanatory Notes to the LoGA, "[w]hat is meant by partner in this provision is a position of equality and parallelism in providing considerations on policies for the implementation of governance in Aceh". In fact, the MPU may, from this perspective, become an effective counterweight to the Government of Aceh. In addition, according to the Explanatory Notes, "[i]n carrying out its duties and functions the MPU shall receive financial support from the APBA/APBK and other legitimate sources, pursuant to the law". According to Salim (2008), p. 155, the "legal drafting process in Aceh has been dominated by the *shari'a* jurists while the involvement of non-Islamic law experts with experience in legal drafting was very small", but this conclusion may be disputed, because in reality and in comparison with other legal experts, there seem to be fewer *shari'a* jurists involved in decision-making.

[70] According to Art. 140, the MPUs have the function to issue *fatwas*, either solicited or unsolicited, regarding issues of governance, development, community development, and the economy. The fatwa can be understood as an opinion issues for the consideration of a governmental entity. Interestingly, the political establishment in power in Aceh is the GAM reconstituted in the form of a local political party, the PA, and as such, the party which controls the DPRA and is the party of the current Governor, is opposed to what it understands as Jakarta's imposition of the *Syari'ah* on the Acehnese people. See Miller (2009), p. 171.

spiritual functions.[71] In addition to the MPUs, the above-mentioned institutions of *adat* or customary practices and law, including the *Wali Nanggroe*, may serve as mechanisms of participation.

The mechanisms of participation included in the LoGA contain several other non-electoral forms of participation. According to Art. 238, the community shall have the right to submit verbal and written inputs to the preparation and discussion of draft *qanuns*, which seems to mean that the DPRA, and the DPRK at the local government level, have a duty to receive such communications for the record and even to demonstrate at least some action on the issues submitted. In fact, the provision opens up the preparation of normative decisions by stipulating that every stage in the preparation and discussion of a *qanun* must have guaranteed opportunities for public participation. What this could mean in concrete terms is hinted at in the LoGA in the provisions that require the dissemination of draft *qanuns* for public information, but public hearings could also be a method of guaranteeing public participation.

According to Art. 143, the community shall have the right to participate actively in the implementation of sustainable development and the right to obtain information on zoning that has been determined by the Government of Aceh and district/municipality governments. Planning and implementation of programs that relate to rehabilitation, psycho-social recovery and mental health programs in response to conflicts and natural disasters shall, according to Art. 226, be carried out with attention given to Acehnese culture and to maximizing local community participation, as further provided by *qanun*. In the area of education, there shall, according to Art. 220, be a Regional Education Council, which constitutes one of the vehicles for community participation in the field of education in a manner provided by a *qanun*. Non-electoral modes of participation are also found in Scotland, where the rules for adopting legislation by the Parliament contain explicit provisions on, for instance, the publication of drafts for public consideration.

6.4 Scotland: The British Electoral Tradition Modernized

6.4.1 Elections, Referendums and Consultations

The main mode of political participation in Scotland is through elections, both to the Scottish Parliament and to the UK Parliament as well as to the EU Parliament and local governments, while referendums are not explicitly recognized in any of

[71] According to Art. 140, the MPUs have the function to provide guidance for resolving differences of opinion on religious matters among community members. According to Salim (2008), p. 156, "there are two ways the MPU engages in the regional legislation. First, the MPU prepares a draft of qanun at the preparation stage. Second, the MPU takes part at the formal meetings conducted at the legislative chamber. In these meetings, along with the provincial legislature, the MPU discusses the draft qanun as proposed by the provincial government". Between 2000 and 2006, at least 17 *qanun* were enacted for the implementation of *shari'a* in Aceh.

their forms in the Scotland Act.[72] The predominance of participation through elections does perhaps not, however, entirely rule out the possibility that the Scottish Parliament would decide to organize an advisory referendum on a matter that belongs to its legislative competence,[73] while the absence of positive rules on decisive referendums should be interpreted as an exclusion of binding popular votes. With a view to the fact that the right to vote in elections in Scotland is a legislative matter reserved to the UK Parliament, the presumption would, however, seem to be that even advisory referendums could perhaps be made impossible in Scotland by measures of the UK Parliament. Decisive referendums that resolve a legislative matter belonging to Scottish competence with normatively binding force could only be held after proper amendments to the Scotland Act.

On top of ordinary general elections to the Scottish Parliament held at least every 4 years, extraordinary elections may be held under certain circumstances of political crisis or dead-lock, such as if two-thirds of the membership of the Scottish Parliament vote for dissolution of the Parliament or if the nomination procedure for the First Minister has not been successful within the time-frame provided.[74] In principle, such extraordinary elections do not postpone the next ordinary elections, unless the extraordinary elections are held within 6 months before the next scheduled ordinary elections. The 4-year electoral cycle is also translated into a 4-year session of the Scottish Parliament, with no annual cut-off as is the case with the UK Parliament. The consequence is that important legislative projects are prevented from being aborted before their consideration has been finished, but the practice of the legislative proceedings has not entirely given up the thinking around the 1-year session, because the Scottish Government nonetheless presents legislative

---

[72]The election legislation and the electoral systems are, however, so indistinctively allocated as competence areas between the UK level and Scotland that functionally, the area of elections almost appears as a shared competence where different facets of competence are intertwined with each other.

[73]See Himsworth and Munro (2000), p. 124 f., who explain a discussion concerning the possibility enacting a Scottish act that enables the Scottish Ministers to hold a referendum on any matters. "Such an Act could be read as permitting a referendum on reserved matters such as independence (for Scotland) or the monarchy. The Act would (. . .) be in danger of being held *ultra vires* to that extent but, to preserve its validity, [section 101 of the Scotland Act -MS] requires the courts to read it as narrowly as is required for it to be *intra vires*, so far as that is possible. In this case they could read the Act as enabling only the holding of referendums on matters within the Parliament's competence and the Act would, therefore, not be rendered *ultra vires* to any extent." See also Himsworth and O'Neill (2003), pp. 186, 510, where it is stated that because the purpose of such a bill could be interpreted as testing of opinion rather than the amendment of the constitution, such a bill would almost certainly be within the powers of the Scottish Parliament. A draft bill on an advisory referendum for gauging several options of developing Scottish self-government, including independence, was submitted for public discussion in March 2010, but it is uncertain whether the Scottish Government will submit any bill proposing such a referendum to the Scottish Parliament. See Scotland's Future: Draft Referendum (Scotland) Bill Consultation Paper, 2010. It seems that around 1/3 of the Scottish would be in favour of independence.

[74]See also Bogdanor (1999), p. 216 f., Himsworth and O'Neill (2003), p. 97, and McFadden and Lazarowicz (2002), p. 24.

programs on an annual basis, that is, altogether four during the 4-year session.[75] The intention has also been to publish bills for consultation before they are presented for the Scottish Parliament, thereby facilitating a broader participation in the preparation of legislation by the wider society, but not all bills have been submitted for consultation.[76] In addition, the Scottish Parliament receives public petitions brought by individuals or other legal formations to the Public Petitions Committee,[77] and the committee meetings of the Scottish Parliament are open to the public. It is thus possible to say that the founding principles of the Scottish Parliament – power-sharing, accountability, accessibility and equal opportunities – are being implemented.[78]

6.4.2 *Combining Majoritarian and Proportional Elections under UK Law*

The 129 members[79] of the unicameral parliament are elected by way of a mixed majority-proportional election,[80] that is, both from 73 single-member constituencies and from eight multi-member regional constituencies returning 56 members to the Scottish Parliament.[81] The territories of the two different sets of

[75] See Page (2005), pp. 17–20.

[76] See Page (2005), pp. 21–23, and McFadden and Lazarowicz (2002), p. 50 f.

[77] Himsworth and O'Neill (2003), pp. 381–384.

[78] See, e.g., Para. 3.1. of Scottish Ministerial Code (2008).

[79] Under section 27 of the Scotland Act, the two Scottish law officers, the Lord Advocate and the Solicitor General for Scotland may, if they are not members of the Parliament, participate in the proceedings of the Parliament and treat them also otherwise as members of the Parliament to the extent permitted by standing orders with the exception that they may not vote.

[80] The MMP system is also referred to as the mixed member proportional system. The system is in Scotland termed the Additional Member System (AMS), probably because it contains a corrective mechanism that grants fewer mandates from regional lists to those parties that are strong in constituencies and more mandates from regional lists to parties that are weak in constituencies. See Herbert et al. (2007), p. 4. See also Himsworth (2006), p. 204, and Himsworth and Munro (2000), p. 14 f., 16, and McFadden and Lazarowicz (2002), p. 23, as well as Bogdanor (1999), p. 203, who makes the point that the system is similar to the one used in Germany. For an explanation of the reasons for choosing a mixed majority proportional system instead of a pure first-past-the post system or an STV system, see Pilkington (2002), p. 101 ff.

[81] According to section 1 of the Scotland Act, one member of the Parliament shall be returned for each constituency (under the first-past-the-post system) at an election held in the constituency, while Members of the Parliament for each region shall be returned at a general election under the additional member system of proportional representation. See Bogdanor (1999), p. 221. The parties with representation in the Scottish Parliament are, on the basis of the elections in May 2007, the Scottish National Party (47 mandates), the Scottish Labour Party (46 mandates), the Scottish Conservatives (17 mandates), the Scottish Liberal Democrats (16 mandates), the Scottish Green Party (2 mandates), and one independent.

constituencies are determined by a Boundary Committee for Scotland constituted under UK legislation in a manner provided for by schedule 1 to the Scotland Act.[82] The constituencies should be of more or less the same size with regard to population. According to section 2 of schedule 1 to the Scotland Act, there shall be eight regions for the purposes of elections to the Scottish Parliament (two of which shall be the Orkney Islands and the Shetland Islands), namely the eight European Parliamentary constituencies which were provided for by the European Parliamentary Constituencies (Scotland) Order 1996 and the Parliamentary Constituencies Act 1986. The section also provides that seven regional members shall be returned for each region, and this part of the election is managed by means of a closed list system, in which the parties place the candidates in the order from which they will be elected to the Scottish Parliament. There is no legal disqualification for persons that might wish to sit as members of both the Scottish Parliament and the UK Parliament at the same time, and this has also taken place in practice, but a political understanding has developed that dual mandates should be avoided.[83] Once elected, a Member of the Scottish Parliament is required to take an oath of allegiance to the Crown before he or she can participate in the proceedings of the Parliament, something that has caused some protest but has not caused individual MSPs to leave the Scottish Parliament.[84]

Under section 5 of the Scotland Act, the candidates may stand for return as constituency members or regional members or both, but may be returned to the Scottish Parliament from only one of the two circumscriptions, with preference

[82]Under section 7 of schedule 1 to the Scotland Act, the following rules apply: 1. A constituency shall fall wholly within a region; 2. The regional electorate of any region shall be as near the regional electorate of each of the other regions as is reasonably practicable having regard, where appropriate, to special geographical considerations; 3. So far as reasonably practicable, the ratio which the number of regional member seats bears to the number of constituency member seats shall be 56 to 73; 4. The number of regional member seats for a region shall be (a) one eighth of the total number of regional member seats, or (b)(if that total number is not exactly divisible by eight) either one eighth of the highest number which is less than that total number and exactly divisible by eight or the number produced by adding one to one eighth of that highest number. If the total number of regional member seats is not exactly divisible by eight, the Commission shall calculate the difference between (a) the total number of regional member seats, and the highest number which is less than that total number and exactly divisible by eight, and that is the number of residual seats to be allocated by the Commission. The Commission shall not allocate more than one residual seat for a region. The Commission shall divide the regional electorate for each region by the aggregate of (a) the number of constituencies in the region, and (b) one eighth of the highest number which is less than the total number of regional member seats and exactly divisible by eight, and, in allocating the residual seat or seats for a region or regions, shall have regard to the desirability of allocating the residual seat or seats to the region or regions for which that calculation produces the highest number or numbers. Under section 8 of the schedule, the regional electorate is the number of persons (a) whose names appear on the enumeration date on the registers of local government electors, and (b) who are registered at addresses within a constituency included in the region.

[83]See Himsworth and O'Neill (2003), p. 104, and McFadden and Lazarowicz (2002), pp. 23 f., 28.

[84]McFadden and Lazarowicz (2002), p. 31.

given to the constituency member. As concerns the constituency candidates, a person may not be a candidate to be a constituency member of the Scottish Parliament for more than one constituency and a candidate for a regional list for more than one region. The candidates to be regional members shall either be persons included in a list determined and submitted by political parties in so-called closed lists where the voters can not influence the order of candidates[85] or persons who are running as individual candidates. The Members of the Scottish Parliament to be returned from the regional lists are determined on the basis of the d'Hondt method,[86] and thus the proportionality is actually created at the regional level in Scotland, not at the level of the entire Scottish jurisdiction,[87] although the proportionality created in regions is probably relatively close to the overall proportionality. In comparison with the UK Parliament, it is noteworthy that the Scottish Parliament is not organizationally a copy of its "parent" parliament, but instead modeled against the background of legislative assemblies in contemporary unitary states or, perhaps even more appropriately, in most European sub-state entities. At the same time, the electoral system is not the same as for the UK Parliament, but modified by an addition of a proportional dimension to it.

The right to vote in the Scottish elections is regulated in the Scotland Act so that the right is linked to the possession of the right to vote in local government elections. Under section 11 of the Scotland Act, the persons entitled to vote as electors at an election for membership of the Scottish Parliament held in any constituency are those who on the day of the poll would be entitled to vote as electors at a local government election in an electoral area falling wholly or partly within the constituency, and are registered in the register of local government electors at an address within the constituency. The practical consequence of connecting the right to vote to local government elections is that the electorate is broadened beyond UK citizens to those of the Member States of the European Union who are resident in Scotland.[88] This is quite special, because participation in the exercise of law-making powers is normally restricted to the citizens of the country in question. However, the broader approach in the case of Scotland may be a consequence of the fact that the Scottish Parliament is, after all, legally understood as a subordinate legislative assembly in relation to the UK Parliament.

As a consequence of the fact that the legislative competence in the electoral area is to a great extent vested in the UK Parliament (with the exception of the holding of

[85]See Bogdanor (1999), p. 226, Himsworth and Munro (2000), p. 12 f., 14, McFadden and Lazarowicz (2002), pp. 21–23.

[86]Bogdanor (1999), p. 221 f. On p. 223, Bogdanor makes the point that while there is no explicit threshold in the proportional election at the regional level, there is an implicit threshold: "Any party of candidate failing to win 5.7% of the vote will not win a seat."

[87]Bogdanor (1999), p. 223. In this respect, the proportional electoral system of Scotland is similar to that of Finland, where the proportionality is produced in the regions, while in Germany and New Zealand, proportionality is produced at the national level.

[88]McFadden and Lazarowicz (2002), p. 26.

local government elections, although franchise in those elections is a UK matter), the administration of elections in the territory of Scotland to the Scottish Parliament, to the UK Parliament and to the European Parliament is taken care of by the Election Commission, which is a UK-wide public body. It seems, however, as if the Scottish Parliament wanted the Scottish Parliament elections to be held on the basis of a Scottish norm. Local government elections do not have any election commission, and therefore, there is, in principle, no guidance and no election reports for those elections, but the Election Commission is in effect administering the elections on the basis of an agency agreement with the Scottish Government, because the legislative competence concerning local government elections in Scotland belongs to Scotland (for agreements about exercise of competence in Åland, see section 5.3.5 above). The Election Commission is an independent body, the employees of which are not civil servants, but public servants. It has a UK-wide presence with an office in Scotland, but it reports directly to the Speaker's Committee in the UK Parliament and it is funded by the UK Parliament under the Fees and Charges Order, not on the basis of the regular UK budget allocated by the UK Government.

Because franchise in local government elections is a matter specifically reserved to the UK Parliament (although the holding of local government elections are within Scottish competence), it is possible to say that the Scottish political system cannot create any electorate of its own definition for the purposes of the elections to the Scottish Parliament.[89] However, the distribution of competences and the legislation concerning different elections is quite confusing.[90] There are ties to the general UK rules in the electoral sphere also as concerns the disqualification from membership of the Scottish Parliament. Under section 15 of the Scotland Act, a person is disqualified from being a member of the Parliament (subject to exceptions in section 16[91]) if he is

[89] In addition, the UK Secretary of State for Scotland has explicit and at the same time relatively broad powers under section 12 of the Scotland Act to make provision about elections as to the conduct of elections for membership of the Parliament, the questioning of such an election and the consequences of irregularities, and the return of members of the Parliament otherwise than at an election. Such provisions may be, *inter alia*, about the registration of electors, for disregarding alterations in a register of electors, about the limitation of the election expenses of candidates, for the combination of polls at elections for membership of the Parliament with polls at other elections, etc. In addition, for the purposes of the Scotland Act, the regional returning officer for any region is the person designated as such in accordance with an order made by the Secretary of State for Scotland as determined in section 12. Finally, the return of a member of the Parliament at an election may be questioned only under Part III of the Representation of the People Act 1983 as applied by an order issued by the Secretary of State under section 12. Hence it can be said that the Secretary of State for Scotland and the UK central government level have an important formal role to play in elections to the Scottish Parliament.

[90] See Scottish Elections 2007 (2007), pp. 10–19.

[91] Under section16, a person is not disqualified from being a member of the Parliament merely because he is a peer (whether of the United Kingdom, Great Britain, England or Scotland). A citizen of the European Union who is resident in the United Kingdom is not disqualified from being a member of the Parliament merely because of section 3 of the Act of Settlement (disqualification of persons born outside the United Kingdom other than Commonwealth citizens and

disqualified from being a member of the House of Commons under paragraphs (a) to (e) of section 1(1) of the House of Commons Disqualification Act 1975 (judges, civil servants, members of the armed forces, members of police forces and members of foreign legislatures), if he is disqualified otherwise than under that Act (either generally or in relation to a particular parliamentary constituency) from being a member of the House of Commons or from sitting and voting in it, if he is a Lord of Appeal in Ordinary, or if he is an office-holder of a description specified in an Order in Council made by Her Majesty under this sub-section.[92]

6.4.3 National Parties

The Scotland Act recognizes political parties in section 5, in which the concept of "registered political party" is connected to a party registered under Part II of the Political Parties, Elections and Referendums Act 2000.[93] Because this Act belongs to the legislative competence of the UK Parliament, it is again possible to say that elections in Scotland are conditioned by the definitions and norms of the UK, without allowing the emergence of a normatively independent party structure in Scotland. The tie to the UK party legislation becomes relevant because of the requirement that only registered political parties may submit to the regional returning officer a list of candidates to be regional members for a particular region, that is, a so-called regional list.[94] Although so-called independent candidates are

citizens of the Republic of Ireland). In addition, the Scottish Parliament may resolve to disregard any disqualification incurred by that person on the ground in question if it considers that the ground has been removed, and it is proper to disregard any disqualification so incurred.

[92]An office-holder of a description specified in an Order in Council made by Her Majesty under this sub-section is disqualified from being a member of the Parliament for any constituency or region of a description specified in the Order in relation to the office-holder (a term that includes employee or other post-holder).

[93]In fact, the Scotland Act even recognises opposition parties, in particular, in keeping with the British parliamentary tradition by providing in section 97 rules for financial assistance for opposition parties. Her Majesty may by Order in Council provide for the Parliamentary corporation (that is, the legal subject that represents the Scottish Parliament, which in itself is regarded an unincorporated association) to make payments to registered political parties for the purpose of assisting members of the Parliament who are connected with such parties to perform their Parliamentary duties. However, such payments shall in principle not be made to a party in pursuance of such an Order if any of the members of the Parliament who are connected with the party are also members of the Scottish Executive or junior Scottish Ministers, unless the Order specifies otherwise. See Himsworth and Munro (2000), pp. 9, 121 f., and McFadden and Lazarowicz (2002), p. 31.

[94]A regional list of a party can contain between one and twelve candidates, and if vacancies occur among the candidates elected from the regional lists, the position is filled from the list where the vacancy occurred in the order determined by the elections. A person can be featured as a candidate only on one regional list or in one single-member constituency. As concerns vacancies among constituency members, such seats are filled by means of by-elections as situations arise. For two examples of such situations, see Pilkington (2002), p. 117 f.

possible, a political grouping which is seriously competing for political power in the Scottish Parliament is normatively compelled to constitute itself as a political party under UK legislation.

Apparently, the rules that tie the Scottish parties to the UK party legislation are effective: judging on the basis of the names of parties in the Scottish Parliament, the party structure of Scotland displays a considerable affinity with the party structure of England, evidently as a carry-over from the times before devolution,[95] although the Scottish National Party (SNP), of course, is an exception to the regular pattern. The real reason for the affinity is historical. Because of the political integration of Scotland into parliamentary decision-making since 1707 through the Parliament of the United Kingdom, the British party system with two main parties, Labour and the Conservatives, alternating in power and with a third party, the Liberal Democrats, trying to challenge the two main parties, has been relevant in Scotland, too. Politically speaking, it seems that Scotland was, most of the time, solidly Labour in terms of political affiliation.[96] The challenge to this traditional party structure with direct links with the national parties came since the 1970s onward from the SNP, which gained the largest share of the votes in the elections of 2007 and 2011 to the Scottish Parliament, and there is also a small Scottish Green Party. The resemblance of the Scottish Parliament to the Parliament in London and the existence of a party structure prior to devolution that could be carried over to the new political arena seem to have perpetuated the national party structure in Scotland,[97] but with the obvious exception of the SNP. However, although the same parties are present in both Scotland and at the UK level, the political platforms could differ quite considerably from each other within the same party.

It has, however, been stated that in policy terms, the Scottish parties "enjoy significant freedom against a background of little pressure from the party centrally

[95]The Political Parties, Elections, and Referendums Act requires that a party has a constitution, pays a registration fee, and maintains a party office. Some of the Scottish parties, such as the Scottish Green Party, are regional ones, while a number of the parties are national level parties, such as the Conservatives and the Labour, operating in Scotland through branches that under the Act can have up to 12 brand names (such as the Scottish Labour). The Scottish Liberal Democrats is a Scottish entity of its own and is federated at the UK level with the Liberal Democrats.

[96]See Bogdanor (1999), pp. 119–143, 194. As pointed out by Greer (2007), p. 140, different governments face different problems and opportunities, fighting on one flank in England and different ones in Scotland and Wales: "The Conservatives, Labour and the third-place Liberal Democrats vie for power in England. Scotland and Wales have marginal Conservative parties and strong nationalist parties to the left of Labour committed to loosening or eliminating the bond with the UK. Scotland also has left and libertarian parties that challenge both the nationalist SNP and Labour from their left flank. More proportional electoral systems in Scotland and Wales strengthen all the small parties, greatly strengthening Plaid Cymru and the SNP and making possible the rise of the Scottish Greens and the Scottish Socialist Party while keeping the unpopular Conservatives alive. The result is that Labour and the Liberal Democrats face very different strategic challenges in the three different parts of Great Britain."

[97]However, it is likely that in the UK Parliament elections of 2010, the Scottish Labour will run on a policy platform that differs from the one of the national Labour, e.g., in the area of education.

over devolved matters".[98] For instance, Labour has changed considerably in Scotland and become re-invigorated, while it has, at the UK level, moved in a centralized direction over the last 20 years, although it was, originally, the party of devolution.[99] For the Liberal Democrats, devolution has provided a platform where it can be more visible than in national politics.[100] It is therefore possible to say that devolution has "had mixed impact on the political parties but has generally started to produce cross-border national parties whose Scottish incarnations are very different from those adopted in London".[101] In the new party political landscape, it seems that devolved government has become more consensual (partly as a consequence of the electoral system), the devolved assemblies are more concerned with regional matters than with UK policy issues, parties in the devolved regions resent the centralizing control of Westminster, and party allegiances are different at the devolved level and give rise to anomalous voting patterns.[102] In so far as the political power in Scotland is controlled by a different party than the one in power in the UK Government, there is obviously also a certain risk of such conflict that may lead to disruptions in the working relationship between the Scottish Government and the UK Government.[103] So far, however, no such conflict has emerged, although it seems as if there had been more contact between the UK Government and its Scottish counterpart before the change of Scottish Government in 2007 than there is after the change.

6.4.4 Counting Votes in the Additional Member System

Each person with the right to vote has the opportunity of casting two votes in the elections to the Scottish Parliament, a constituency vote and a regional vote, as determined by section 6 of the Scotland Act.[104] The result of the elections departs

[98]Laffin et al. (2007), p. 201 f.

[99]Laffin et al. (2007), p. 206.

[100]Laffin et al. (2007), p. 211 ff.

[101]Pilkington (2002), p. 120. One of the ironies is that while the proportional representation in the Scottish Parliament has saved the political existence of the Conservatives in Scotland, the party remains opposed to proportional representation at the UK level.

[102]Pilkington (2002), p. 182 f. See also Henig (2006), p. 33, who makes the point that partly for reasons of distance, "Scottish and English political structures have always been less integrated than Welsh and English".

[103]See Trench (2007e), p. 180. See also Trench (2007a), p. 287: "Particularly if parties come to office which do not have a strong interest in making devolution work (and be seen to work), this system is highly vulnerable". This is true both for the UK level and for Scotland. In fact, due to the difference in the electoral system, with FPTP to the UK Parliament and MMP to the Scottish Parliament, the two parliaments are based on different political legitimacies.

[104]See also section 11(2) of the Scotland Act, according to which a person is not entitled to vote as elector in any constituency more than once at a poll for the return of a constituency member, or more than once at a poll for the return of regional members, or to vote as elector in more than one constituency at a general election.

from the counting of the constituency votes, because the calculation of the so-called regional figures, that is, the divisors for the proportional elections among the regional lists under section 7 of the Scotland Act, is determined by the constituency votes cast for the political parties that have regional lists. For each registered political party which has submitted a regional list, the regional figure or divisor for the purposes of determining the regional result is the total number of regional votes given for the party in all the constituencies included in the region divided by the aggregate of one plus the number of candidates of the party returned as constituency members for any of those constituencies. Each time a seat is allocated to the party under section 8, that figure is recalculated by increasing (or further increasing) the aggregate by one. For each individual candidate to be a regional member for the region, the regional figure for the purposes of section 8 is the total number of regional votes given for him in all the constituencies included in the region. The actual allocation of seats to regional members is determined under section 8 of the Scotland Act.

The first regional member seat shall be allocated to the registered political party or individual candidate with the highest regional figure, while the second and the subsequent regional member seats shall be allocated to the registered political party or individual candidate with the highest regional figure, after any recalculation required by section 7 has been carried out. Seats for the region which are allocated to a registered political party are then filled by the persons in the party's regional list in the order in which they appear in the list (see Table 6.3 below).[105]

This method of seat allocation, also called the Additional Member System, seems to result in a significant correction of the "bias" of the FPTP election at the constituency level and produce a relatively neat overall proportionality (see Table 6.4 below).

It appears on the basis of the information in the two tables and the elections of May 2011 that the support for Labour has steadily decreased in the Scottish parliamentary elections, while the support of SNP has fluctuated (possibly as a consequence of fluctuations in voter turnout) and spiked in 2011 with an overall support of 44.7%, resulting in absolute majority with 69 seats in the Scottish Parliament. The support of Conservatives seems relatively stable. It also appears as if the Scottish electoral system at least in 2007 would have favored the larger parties and disadvantaged the mid-sized and smaller parties, a tendency which in 2011 favored the SNP. It is not, however, clear to which dimension of the electoral system that effect could be attributed, but what can be said is that the proportional dimension of the electoral system is not strong enough to fully compensate the inequalities of the FPTP system in the single member constituencies. In spite of the

[105] The d'Hondt method employs the following divisors for determining the ranking within a list: the top candidate receives all of the votes cast for the list, the second one 1/2 of the votes, the third one 1/3, the fourth one 1/4, and the other divisors are 1/5, etc., of the votes cast for the list. For a constructed illustration of the allocation of seats, see *Appendix*. For illustrations of how the proportional election system works in the Scottish elections to the European Parliament, see Bogdanor (1999), p. 222, and Pilkington (2002), p. 188 f. as well as McFadden and Lazarowicz (2002), pp. 23 f., 32–37.

Table 6.3 Seats in the Scottish Parliament and electoral support in 2007 of Scottish parties by constituency and list seats[106]

	Constituency MSPs			Regional List MSPs		
	1999	2003	2007	1999	2003	2007
Labour	53	46	37 32.1%	3	4	9 29.1%
SNP	7	9	21 32.9%	28	18	26 31.0%
Liberal Democrats	12	13	11 16.2%	5	4	5 11.3%
Conservatives and Unionist Party	0	3	4 16.6%	18	15	13 13.9%
Green Party	0	0	0 0.1%	1	7	2 4.0%
Socialist Party	0	0	0 0%	1	6	0 0.6%
Others	1	2	0%	0	2	1 4.3%
Total	73	73	73	56	56	56

Table 6.4 Total seats in the Scottish Parliament and electoral support in 2007 of Scottish parties[107]

	Total MSPs elected			Share of seats (%)	Overall support (%)
Party	1999	2003	2007	2007	2007
Labour	56	50	46	35.7	31.83
SNP	35	27	47	36.4	33.21
Liberal Democrats	17	17	16	12.4	14.25
Conservat. and Unionist Party	18	18	17	13.2	15.83
Green Party	1	7	2	1.6	2.18
Socialist Party	1	6	0	0.0	0.34
Others	1	4	1	0.8	2.33
Total	129	129	129		
Turnout	58.16%	49.42%	51.72%		

focus on parties, also independent candidates were elected to the Scottish Parliament over the years. The Scottish political system has grown more varied and fragmented than the UK one, with several small parties in addition to the four main parties, creating a situation where there is a greater potential that challengers to the traditional parties emerge.

[106] In 2003, seven elected Labour MSPs were Labour Co-operative members. Source: 2007 Elections. Results Analysis, at http://www.scottish.parliament.uk/MSP/elections/2007/analysis.htm (accessed 25 March 2009).

[107] In 2003, seven elected Labour MSPs were Labour Co-operative members. Source: 2007 Elections. Results Analysis, at http://www.scottish.parliament.uk/MSP/elections/2007/analysis.htm (accessed 25 March 2009).

6.4.5 The Scottish Parliament in Relation to the UK Parliament: The West Lothian Question

While the Scotland Act presupposes that the Scottish Parliament adopts standing orders to regulate its internal procedures, it seems that the Scotland Act already in itself contains a relatively detailed description of the internal structure of the Parliament.[108] There are provisions concerning the Presiding Officer and the Clerk, and also provisions concerning the creation of a corporate body inside the Parliament with the powers of contract and determination of liabilities. There are also provisions in the Scotland Act on how to call for witnesses and documents to the Parliament for making investigations into different matters. However, it seems that the concept of the free mandate, that is, the prohibition of the imperative mandate is not established at the level of positive law, but is presumed and taken as a self-evident feature of the political system.[109]

The creation of a Scottish parliament implied at the same time that the number of the Scottish MPs in the House of Commons of the Parliament of England was diminished. In fact, from 1922 until devolution, there was a Scottish over-representation in the UK Parliament with 72 MPs returned from Scotland to the UK Parliament, while devolution brought about a representation that is in the same proportion as in England, returning around 59 MPs from Scotland to the UK Parliament.[110] Hence although the Scottish voters continue to vote in the elections to the UK Parliament and to send MPs from Scottish constituencies, their numbers are now adjusted from what used to be an over-representation of Scotland in the UK Parliament to what can be considered an equitable representation with a view to the legislative powers reserved to the UK Parliament and exercised also over the jurisdiction of Scotland. The reduction in the number of Scottish MPs has a background in the so-called West Lothian question, which has been a part of the British devolution discussion for quite some time and which asks "whether it is justifiable for Scottish MPs, after devolution, to continue to be able to vote for English domestic affairs when non-Scottish MPs will no longer be able to vote on Scottish domestic affairs".[111] As a consequence, it has

[108]According to McFadden and Lazarowicz (2002), p. 38, the Scottish Parliament is given a relatively free hand by the Scotland Act in deciding how it should work, because the Act does not set out detailed requirements for the Parliament's method of operation. In comparison with, for instance, the Åland Islands, Puerto Rico and Quebec, it nonetheless seems that the Scottish Parliament is somewhat more constrained as concerns its internal structure and function than the other legislative assemblies of sub-state entities.

[109]As based on the speech of Edmund Burke to the electors in Bristol in 1774. See Kurland and Lerner (2000), ch. 13, doc. 7.

[110]Bogdanor (1999), pp. 211, 232.

[111]Bogdanor (1999), p. 227. Bogdanor (1999), p. 234, makes the point that the West Lothian question may be falsely posed, because "English MPs have little interest in Scottish domestic affairs, while England's dominant position in the United Kingdom means that there are hardly any wholly 'English' domestic issues of no concern to MPs from Scotland and Wales". See also Pilkington (2002), pp. 165–167.

also been asked whether it is appropriate, after devolution, "for a Scottish MP to become a minister in a British government exercising functions, which, in Scotland, were the responsibility of the Scottish Parliament". Apparently, the answer to the latter question is not negative.[112]

One response to the problem posed by the West Lothian question could be to make the entire UK a federal state by providing for a UK Parliament (perhaps with a bicameral structure) and devolving legislative powers to a Parliament of England, in charge of a jurisdiction of England and making sure that the devolved powers of the other parts of the UK are more or less symmetrical within the common structure. Because of the size of England in relation to the other parts of the UK, such a solution may be unrealistic.[113] Another response to the problem is that a special legislative procedure for "English" legislation is created within the current UK Parliament, but such procedures seem impracticable because of the fact that the entire House of Commons would anyway be the ultimate legislative body.[114] While it is not possible to think that Scottish MPs would be excluded from the House of Commons, some thinking has revolved around the idea that the Scottish MPs would not participate in the legislative matters that concern England. Constitutionally, such an "in and out" solution would be unworkable because the Government would have different majorities depending on whether the Scottish MPs are in or out, which would contain the potential that the Government would lack the political majority in the House of Commons on English issues, leaving the constitutional system in an impossible situation.[115] In addition to these thoughts, a response to the question could perhaps be at least in part looked for in the concept of the free mandate (that is, the prohibition of the imperative mandate), which actually prohibits the influence of special interests in the exercise of the parliamentary mandate but which also as a consequence underlines the importance of the national interest in the legislative work. With reference to such national interest, the MPs from devolved jurisdictions would be expected to take interest in the overall common good also when participating in decisions at the UK level that belong to the area of devolved competences.[116]

---

[112]Bogdanor (1999), p. 227, who reports that Mr. Robin Cook actually resigned from the post of Minister of Health in the UK Government (health being a devolved matter; however, he has consequently not found it problematic to function as the Minister of Foreign Affairs, which is a matter reserved to the UK Government). However, former Prime Minister and former Chancellor of the Exchequer, Mr Gordon Brown was elected to the UK Parliament from Scottish constituencies.

[113]Bogdanor (1999), p. 228. See also Bogdanor (1999), pp. 235, 276, presenting ideas of a quasi-federal state.

[114]Bogdanor (1999), p. 228 f.

[115]Bogdanor (1999), p. 229 ff.

[116]In fact, as pointed out by Trench (2007a), p. 273, the Scottish MPs in the UK Parliament have not become advocates for the devolved institutions, which seems to indicate that they do not feel obliged to take into consideration the special interest of the devolved jurisdiction.

6.4.6 *Elections at Other Levels: UK, Europe, and Local Government*

Elections to the UK Parliament are held at a different pace than the Scottish Parliament. Where the term of mandate of the Scottish Parliament is 4 years, the UK Parliament has a maximum term of 5 years, which means that general elections can be held (and are often held) before the term of mandate has lapsed. In Scotland, after the correction of the over-representation of Scotland, there are, since the 2005 elections, 59 constituencies for the purposes of general elections to the UK Parliament, while the method of election continues to be that of first-past-the-the-post. The Scottish constituencies in the UK elections are thus not the same as in the elections to the Scottish Parliament.

Table 6.5 Seats and support in general elections to UK Parliament in Scotland 1992–2010[117]

Party	1992	1997 – Total votes: 2,812,439 – Turnout: 71.3%	2001 – Total votes: 2,315,703 – Turnout: 58.2%	2005 – Total votes: 2,333,882 – Turnout: 60.6%	2010 – Total votes: 2,465,722 – Turnout: 63.8%
Labour	49 seats 39%	56 45.65%	56 43.9%	41 39.5%	41 42.0%
Lib. Democrats	9 seats 13.1%	10 13%	10 16.4%	11 22.6%	11 18.9%
SNP	3 seats 21.5%	6 21.96%	5 20.1%	6 17.7%	6 19.9%
Conservative	11 seats 25.6%	0 17.54%	1 15.6%	1 15.8%	1 16.7%
Green	0	0 0.06%	0	0 <2%	0 0.7%
Others	0 0.8%	0 0.80%	0	0 <2%	0 1.7%

It seems that the position of Labour is relatively solidly around 40% in the UK Parliament elections and so, too, is the support for the Liberal Democrats and the SNP, while the Conservatives fare less well in Scotland (see Table 6.5 above). It is also evident that voter turnout is generally somewhat higher in elections to the UK Parliament than in Scottish elections, although it could be expected that turnout in Scottish elections, which focus more on the immediate Scottish issues, would be higher. Perhaps the Scottish voters nonetheless consider the UK Parliament as the primary one.[118]

[117]Source: Scotland Guide: Government and Politics – General Elections, at http://www.siliconglen.com/Scotland/19_10.html (accessed 26 March 2009), BBC: UK Election 2010, Scotland Results. http://news.bbc.co.uk/2/shared/election2010/results/region/7.stm. Accessed 18 November 2010.

[118]This may be a consequence of the more national focus of, in particular, the television.

Table 6.6 Elections to the European Parliament in Scotland

	1999 – Turnout: 24.8%	2004 – Turnout: 24.7%	2009 – Turnout 28.8%
Labour	29.6%, 3 MEPs	26.4%, 2 MEPs	20.8%, 2 MEPs
SNP	27.1%, 2 MEPs	19.7%, 2 MEPs	29.1%, 2 MEPs
Lib. Democrats	9.8%, 1 MEP	13.1%, 1 MEP	11.5%, 1 MEP
Conservatives and Unionist Party	19.7%, 2 MEPs	17.8%, 2 MEPs	16.8%, 1 MEP
Green Party	5.8%, –	6.8%, –	7.3%, –
Socialist Party	4.0%, –	5.2%, –	–
Others	5.8%, –	11.1%, –	14.5%, –

As concerns elections to the European Parliament, the method of election is, due to the EU rules, to be proportional or based on the STV, which means that the FPTP system in single member constituencies is not possible. In the UK, the 78 members of the European Parliament are elected on a regional basis, with the entire Scottish jurisdiction as one constituency for the purpose of electing 6 members to the EU parliament by way of proportional election on the basis of closed lists (Table 6.6).[119]

As in most countries, participation in the European Parliament elections is a problem also in Scotland, although the EU has law-making powers which reach to the legislative competence of not only the UK Parliament but also the Scottish Parliament and override them. Again, the main Scottish parties seem to prevail in the European Parliament elections, but the Conservatives come out stronger than in other elections. Also, the fragmentation of the party map among the smaller parties is more apparent.

In addition, there are 32 council areas in Scotland in which local government elections are held,[120] for the first time in 2007 following the STV system.[121] However, while franchise in local government elections (as in any UK elections) is a competence of the UK Parliament, the holding of the local government elections is a Scottish competence, although election to the Scottish Parliament is a UK competence. The multitude of participatory forums available to the inhabitants of Scotland stands in stark contrast to Puerto Rico, where participation is confined to the sub-state entity.

---

[119]See The 2004 European Parliament Elections in the United Kingdom (2004) , p. 14. Prior to the EP elections of 2009, the number of MEPs elected from Scotland was reduced from 7 to 6 due to the revision of the fundamental treaties of the EU, which meant that the lower national quota of UK resulted in the loss of one Scottish MEP.

[120]See Local Government Boundary Commission for Scotland (1995).

[121]See Scottish Elections 2007 (2007), p. 6.

6.5 Puerto Rico: Participation Confined to the Territory

6.5.1 No Representation at the Federal Level

There are few areas in the world where participation in political matters through elections and referendums exceeds the levels of Puerto Rico. This is so mainly in terms of the internal system of participation in Puerto Rico, because the island does not have any voting members in the Senate or the House of Representatives of the US Congress, only a Resident Commissioner in the House of Representatives. In addition, the US presidential elections are not held in Puerto Rico.

Starting with the representation of Puerto Rico at the federal or national level, the Federal Relations Act stipulates that "the qualified electors of Puerto Rico shall choose a Resident Commissioner to the United States at each general election",[122] that is, every 4 years of the federal electoral cycle. This means that the citizens of Puerto Rico, although at the same time citizens of the United States, do not have the right to vote in the ordinary elections to the federal Senate and Chamber of Representatives, because Puerto Rico, not being a state in the federation, does not have any seats allocated to itself in those bodies, where the representation of the population is based on an allocation of seats to states, two for each in the Senate and a varying number for each in the House based on the number of inhabitants of the state.[123] Although the Puerto Ricans do not participate in the election of senators and representatives, the election of the Resident Commissioner is nonetheless a federal election. However, the unequal status of the Puerto Ricans in respect of federal elections in relation to the states in the federation may be regarded from the American point of view as a statement of the fact that the right to vote is a constitutional right that does not apply to Puerto Rico under the US Constitution and is therefore not one of those fundamental rights guaranteed by the US Constitution that apply to Puerto Rico,[124] although a case can be made for considering the

[122]US Code, Title 48, Sect. 891. Under Sect. 892, the eligibility requirements of the Resident Commissioner are that the person is a bona fide citizen of the United States, more than 25 years of age, and is able to read and write the English language.

[123]If Puerto Rico were a state, it would be entitled to two senators and six representatives and it would participate fully in the election of the President and Vice President with an eight-member Electoral College delegation. See Puerto Rico Democracy Act (2007), p. 6. The possible grant of these mandates to Puerto Rico would at least to some extent influence the relative position of the current states, which may or may not affect their attitude towards the statehood of Puerto Rico. See Rosselló (2005), pp. 266, 298–303.

[124]In this respect, the situation is indeed strange: a mainland USA resident who moves to Puerto Rico loses his or her right to vote upon taking up residency in Puerto Rico and cannot vote even by mail from Puerto Rico, although the same person could cast a vote by mail from anywhere in the world. At the same time, a Puerto Rican inhabitant who takes up residence in the US is entitled to vote in, *inter alia*, federal elections. In terms of participation in federal elections, Puerto Rico is thus territorially speaking an excluded zone. See, e.g., Rosselló (2005), pp. 67 f., 318. See also Rosselló (2005), pp. 72–74, 304–305, 308, in which he analyses the (already third similar) case of

right to vote as one of the fundamental rights under the US Constitution that should apply in Puerto Rico.[125] Without doubt, a situation of this sort in which a group of individuals is barred from participating in elections to the representative institutions that possess the national law-making powers is contrary to both Art. 1 and Art. 25 of the CCPR.[126] However, before federal courts, a demand in the case of *Igartúa de la Rosa v. United States* that Puerto Ricans be granted the right to vote in presidential elections was, in 2005, deemed to be a political question that could not be tried by the courts, while the CCPR was not regarded a treaty which is self-executing in a manner that could be used to resolve the legal issues before courts.[127]

The only link to the legislative power at the federal level is therefore the Resident Commissioner, who may become a member of House committees, but does not have the formal right to vote on bills on the House floor.[128] In addition, the Puerto Ricans do not have the right to participate in the US presidential elections, because the membership of the Electoral College is allocated on the basis of the states in the federation. In spite of this fact, the presidential primary elections of the two main US parties, the Republicans and the Democrats, are arranged in Puerto Rico. This means that the Puerto Ricans are not entitled to anything except "advisory" contributions to the process of federal law-making and the exercise of federal executive powers, although the federal legislation and federal government may affect Puerto Rico in a profound way. However, as concerns taxation, it should be emphasized that because the powers of taxation are on Puerto Rico under an enumerated competence and because the Internal Revenue Code explicitly exempts Puerto Rico from the application of federal income tax, there is no grave situation of "taxation without representation" at the federal level, although Puerto Ricans are subject to federal payroll taxes (which include federal unemployment tax and

---

Gregorio Igartúa de la Rosa, et al. v. United States, *infra* note 127 in this Chap. in which the federal district court of Puerto Rico concluded that it was unconstitutional to deny voting rights to US citizens in presidential elections (however, the Court of Appeals reversed the decision on the basis that the case concerned a political issue) and indicates that change in the constitutional status of Puerto Rico could also be effectuated through court action and that such action could involve the reversal of the discriminatory contents of the *Insular Cases*, *supra* notes 85 and 87 in Chap. 4. Mr. Igartúa has filed his case with the Inter-American Commission for Human Rights, which means that there may, in the future, be a case that examines the relationship between the Inter-American human rights system and the US law.

125 See also Rosselló (2005), p. 97.

126 See also Rosselló (2005), p. 97.

127 417 F.3d 145 (1st Circuit, 3 August 2005). The case was the third *Igartúa* case with the same result, although the 2005 case produced a divided court of 5–2. See also Thornburgh (2007), pp. 3, 63–67. The Court of Appeals was of the opinion that the right to vote in presidential elections was not turning on the possession of US citizenship, but rather on the fact that such elections are organized by the states in the federation (which Puerto Rico is not).

128 However, in practice and without support in any norm, the House of Representatives allows the Resident Commissioner to sit in the House and vote on Bills, except in situations where the vote of the Resident Commissioner could affect the result of the vote. Hence he or she has an advisory presence on the House floor.

employer's share of social security and Medicare) and income taxes on United States and foreign-source income.

It is also important to underline that the Resident Commissioner is entirely created under the Federal Relations Act and is not at all mentioned in the Constitution of Puerto Rico.[129] At least to some extent, the Resident Commissioner has served as a vehicle of protest from Puerto Rico towards the existing relationship between Puerto Rico and the U.S. and as a symbol of the people of Puerto Rico for the limits on the governance of Puerto Rico, but perhaps even more as an "ambassador" of Puerto Rico in Congress, although his/her salary and expenses are paid from the federal budget.[130]

6.5.2 Bicameral Representation through Voting in a Mixed System

Under the Puerto Rican Constitution, the laws of Puerto Rico shall "guarantee the expression of the will of the people by means of equal, direct and secret universal suffrage and shall protect the citizen against any coercion in the exercise of the electoral franchise".[131] That right to vote is exercised at the level of the sub-state entity in elections to the two houses of the Legislative Assembly, in elections of the Governor of Puerto Rico and in referendums concerning different matters.[132] In

[129]See Anderson (1998b), p. 51.

[130]Anderson (1998b), p. 51. For testimonies of Resident Commissioners on the status issue before the bodies of Congress, see, *inter alia*, the statements of Carlos Romero Barceló (Joint Hearing on examination of the political preferences of the U.S. citizens of Puerto Rico before the Subcommittee on Native American & Insular Affairs of the Committee on Resources and the Subcommittee on the Western Hemisphere of the Committee on International Relations, House of Representatives, 17 October 1995, Serial No. 104–56 (Committee on Resources)), Jaime B. Fuster (Hearing on S. 712 to provide for a referendum on the political status of Puerto Rico before the Committee on Agriculture, Nutrition, and Forestry, United States Senate, 9 November 1989; Hearings on S. 712 before the Committee on Finance, United States Senate, 14–15 November 1989; Hearing on H.R. 4765 Puerto Rico self-determination act before the Subcommittee on Insular and International Affairs of the Committee on Interior and Insular Affairs, House of Representatives, 28 June 1990, Serial No. 101–83, part II), and Jaime Benitez (Hearing on S. 2998 a bill to amend the Puerto Rico Federal Relations Act before the Committee on Interior and Insular Affairs, United States Senate, 12 April 1976; Hearings on H.R. 11200 and H.R. 11201 to approve the compact of permanent union between Puerto Rico and the United States before the Subcommittee on Territorial and Insular Affairs of the Committee on Interior and Insular Affairs, House of Representatives, 20 January 1976 and 9 February 1976, Serial No. 94–44, part I).

[131]Const., Art. II Sect. 2.

[132]In November 2008, there were six different elections organized at the same time: the Resident Commissioner, the Governor of Puerto Rico, the Senators, the Representatives, the mayors and the councilmen in local government. For the voters, this meant that they were requested to fill in three ballot papers of different colors with two elections on each ballot paper.

addition, that right to vote is relevant at the level of local government. The people in its political composition consists of citizens, which is normally not difficult to determine with regard to the native population of the island. However, as concerns persons who have moved to Puerto Rico from other parts of the United States and taken up residence there, the Federal Relations Act makes the determination that US citizens who reside in Puerto Rico for 1 year shall be citizens of Puerto Rico.[133]

As concerns the so-called general elections, that is, elections of the Governor, the members of the Legislative Assembly and other officials whose election on that date is provided for by law, every person over 18 years of age has the right to vote provided that he fulfills the other conditions determined by law.[134] However, no person shall be deprived of the right to vote because he does not know how to read or write or does not own property. The electoral process and the registration of voters, political parties and candidates are matters to be determined by Puerto Rican law.[135]

According to Art. III, section 1, of the Puerto Rican Constitution, "the legislative power shall be vested in a Legislative Assembly, which shall consist of two houses, the Senate and the House of Representatives whose members shall be elected by

---

[133]US Code, Title 48, Sect. 733a. See also Thornburgh (2001), pp. 359–371, who relates an attempt to recognize a citizenship of Puerto Rico by the Puerto Rican judiciary and, in the last instance, by the Supreme Court of Puerto Rico, which would be independent from U.S. citizenship and which would qualify the holder of the local citizenship to vote in Puerto Rican elections without having U.S. citizenship. The case of *Ramirez de Ferrer v. Juan Mari Brás*, Supreme Court of Puerto Rico, No. CT-96-14 (18 November 1997), which Thornburgh regards an example of judicial separatism in Puerto Rico, became actually partly obsolete already shortly before the Supreme Court of Puerto Rico made its decision, because the Legislative Assembly of Puerto Rico amended the law so as to make clear that a citizen of Puerto Rico is a person with United States nationality and citizenship who is a lawful resident of Puerto Rico. The "people of Puerto Rico" are not, according to Thornburgh (2001), p. 366, a separate nationality, but a body politic consisting of persons with U.S. nationality and citizenship who reside in Puerto Rico. This includes those born there and those who were born or naturalized in a state of the Union and reside there". The renunciation of U.S. citizenship therefore also affects the right to vote in Puerto Rican elections. See also Smith (2001), pp. 373 f., 380–386.

[134]On the basis of the *Mari Brás* case of the Puerto Rican Supreme Court, it can be said that a citizen of Puerto Rico who is not, at the same time, a citizen of the United States, is entitled to vote in Puerto Rican elections. See *supra*, note 104 in Chap. 4. On the other hand, there should actually not exist any such separate citizens of Puerto Rico who are not, at the same time, US citizens.

[135]In contrast with elections in the United States, the Puerto Rican elections are carried out by using paper ballots instead of voting machines of all kinds, and after the initial count, there is a systematic island-wide recount of all ballots by the Commonwealth Election Commission that determines the final result. In every municipality, there is an office of the election committee with three employees, one for each main party, and there is a computerized system for a continuous registration of voters so that the list of voters is checked against the population register. Hence there is no procedure of registration for voting for every election, as in mainland US. The Commonwealth Election Commission handles the nomination of the candidates, which procedure is a source of legal complaints because candidates not satisfying the nomination requirements (10,000 signatures, documents over income tax, property, debts, criminal record, etc.) are regularly appealing the negative decisions of the Election Commission.

direct vote at each general election".[136] No free mandate or prohibition of the imperative mandate is established, and the plurality voting system practiced in Puerto Rico has actually led to a strong clientelism in which the elected politicians are perceived as persons who are expected to cater for the needs of their voters in the constituencies.[137] At the same time, a relatively strong party discipline is imposed in the two houses of the Legislative Assembly.

The senate has 27 members and the house of representatives 51 members,[138] but in case one party or list of candidates receives more than two-thirds of the seats in each house, the number of members of the opposition may be increased under certain circumstances from among those opposition candidates in the elections that did not receive enough votes to be seated in the Legislative Assembly.[139] Thus there is a peculiar balancing mechanism in place in the Constitution that prevents the Legislative Assembly from being turned into a one-party organ that could at any time be able to, for instance, meet the requirements of qualified majorities established for constitutional amendments. The balancing mechanism guarantees that there should, at all times, be an opposition to the dominant party in the Legislative Assembly and an avenue of participation also for the opposition or political minorities.[140] Without doubt, the artificial enhancement of the seats of the political minority in the legislature without the support of the actual votes cast is not in compliance with the rules concerning participation of, e.g. Art. 25 of the CCPR, and if there were a wish to remedy the situation by amending the electoral rules, a change to a more proportional electoral system would probably be the way to go.

The minority protection mechanism was activated in the elections of 2008 when the NPP won a landslide victory in both houses of the Legislative Assembly, with an aggregated support of approximately 988,000 votes against the 780,000 votes of the PDP. For instance, for the senate, the first 16 seats were filled with the winning candidates from the districts, none of which came from the PDP. Thereafter the six senators-at-large were seated after the elections, five of which came from the PDP. After the activation of the minority enhancement mechanism, the PDP was granted four more mandates. With the activation of the minority enhancement mechanism, the PDP got altogether nine seats in the senate. A similar enhancement procedure was undertaken concerning the House of Representatives. Because of the plurality

[136] As concerns eligibility to the Legislative Assembly, it is required under Const., Art. III, section 5, that the person is able to read and write the Spanish or English language, is a citizen of the United States and of Puerto Rico, has resided in Puerto Rico at least 2 years immediately prior to the date of his election or appointment and has resided in his or her constituency at least 1 year before elections. For Senate membership there is a requirement of over 30 years of age, and for the House of Representatives over 25 years of age.

[137] See also Rivera Ramos (2007), p. 227 f.

[138] Const. Art. III, section 2.

[139] For the mechanism, see Const. Art. III, section 7.

[140] The legislative history of this mechanism has its root in the dominance of the then Popular Party, which had swept the local elections with a 100% victory.

election, the NPP had swept both houses of the Legislative Assembly in spite of the fact that the PDP has substantial support in Puerto Rico, which proves that the risk of complete one-party dominance is real.

Such a balancing mechanism designed to maintain proportionality may be important with a view to the fact that under Art. III, section 3, the elections to the House of Representatives proceed from single-member constituencies, and even the senatorial elections, where two members are elected from one constituency, could return a significant number of candidates of the dominant party. That risk is, however, at least to some extent mitigated by the fact that each house of the Legislative Assembly is not only elected on the basis of constituencies into which Puerto Rico is divided, but also on the basis of one Puerto Rico-wide general constituency, from which 11 senators-at-large and 11 representatives-at-large are elected.[141] The effect of the members-at-large is to allow a certain proportionality in the two chambers, which may be heavily influenced by the first-past-the-post or plurality method of election. In effect, the electoral system could be described as a mixed-member proportionality system. Because of this combination of majority vote and proportional vote, the electoral system of Puerto Rico differs from the electoral systems that are in use for elections to the US Congress or to the legislatures of the constituent states. More concretely, the method of distribution of the seats of the members-at-large is the Single-Non-Transferable-Vote (SNTV).[142]

[141]Const., Art. III, section 3. A voter may only vote for one candidate on the list of senators-at-large and for one candidate on the list of representatives-at-large.

[142]For an exposé of the election law of Puerto Rico, see Anderson (1998a), pp. 59–82. As explained by the Internet source Elections in Puerto Rico, the "[a]t-large voting as implemented in Puerto Rico is known internationally as the Single Non-Transferable Vote (SNTV) system". "Incidentally, the non-transferability of the vote refers to the fact that voters in Puerto Rico do not indicate transferable second, third, fourth and successive preferences, as they would do under the Single Transferable Vote (STV) system used in parliamentary elections in Ireland and Malta, as well as the Australian Senate." "Under this procedure, parties may nominate up to eleven candidates in each house, but voters may choose only one at-large Senate candidate, and one at-large House candidate. At-large candidates run as individuals rather than as a list, but parties determine the ballot order of their at-large candidates, which varies across Puerto Rico's election precincts in order to insure each candidate has an approximately equal chance of being elected. A voter casting a straight-ticket ballot automatically chooses the at-large candidates placed at the top of his or her party's Senate and House lists; nonetheless, voters may choose any single at-large candidate from any party or independent ticket (or even vote for a write-in candidate) for each legislative body. It should be noted that the distribution of at-large seats is determined to a degree by the number of candidates nominated by each party: there have been instances in which minor parties have failed to win a single at-large seat in either house because their vote was divided among too many candidates, as well as cases in which parties have lost the opportunity to secure additional at-large seats because they nominated too few candidates. In practice, Puerto Rico's two major parties – the Popular Democratic Party (PPD) and the New Progressive Party (PNP) – nominate six candidates for each house, while the Puerto Rican Independence Party (PIP), which has a much smaller following, fields single candidates for both the Senate and the House." See http://eleccionespuertorico.org/referencia/system.html (accessed 5 February 2009).

Since the methods of electing the senate and the house of representatives are the same, because the representatives are drawn from constituencies that are subdivisions of the constituencies of the senate and because elections to both houses are held at the same time for the same mandate period, it is possible to say that the composition of both houses coincides, by and large. Doubts can be expressed about the need to duplicate the political profile of the people in two houses. As a matter of fact, in an advisory referendum held in 2005, a clear majority of the voters preferred to have a unicameral legislature (see below), but the low turnout in the referendum withheld legitimacy from the vote. In addition, the vote was brought about by the more leftist oriented political majority, but the proposal submitted to the vote failed to define the meaning of unicameralism. For these reasons, and because of changes in government, the advice of the people has not yet resulted in any legislative activity on the matter that would lead to a constitutional amendment establishing unicameralism, and by 2009, the issue seemed to be dead.

A first-past-the-post method of election is mandated for the officials that are elected in general elections by reference in Art. VI, section 4, of the Constitution. According to the provision, every popularly elected official shall be elected by direct vote and any candidate who receives more votes than any other candidate for the same office shall be declared elected. This is certainly so for the Resident Commissioner (see above), but also, for instance, for the Governor of Puerto Rico, who has been an elected official since 1948, before which time the Governors were appointed by the federal government, that is, by the US President.[143] The Governor is central to the constitutional fabric of Puerto Rico, because under Art. IV, section 1, of the Constitution, the executive power shall be vested in a Governor, who shall be elected by direct vote in each general election.

6.5.3 Party Constellations According to the Status Issue

It is notable that the concept of a political party is explicitly mentioned in the Constitution of Puerto Rico. A party structure developed early on in Puerto Rico, and it was carried over from the "old" system to the new one in the beginning of the 1950s, partly supported by Art. IX, section 6, of the Constitution, which guaranteed for the political parties continuity in all rights recognized by the election law, provided that on the effective date of the Constitution they fulfilled the minimum requirements for the registration of new parties contained in the election law. The political parties are also recognized as a basis for the nomination system of candidates because of their role in the possible enhancement of the opposition in the Legislative Assembly in situations where one of the parties gains more than two-thirds of the seats in the Legislative Assembly.

[143]See Trías Monge (1997), pp. 101–106.

The party system of Puerto Rico has been relatively stable in terms of which parties are involved in the political system of Puerto Rico, and they are also more active in between the elections than the two main parties in the mainland USA, which in comparison are more campaign organizations revived every 4 years on the occasion of the elections.[144] However, their size and importance in relation to each other and also their platforms have changed somewhat over time. Four parties exist at the moment, the Popular Democratic Party (PDP), the New Progressive Party (NPP), the Puerto Rican Independence Party (PIP)[145] and the Party of Puerto Ricans for Puerto Rico. The main issue that distinguishes the different parties from each other is their attitude towards the so-called status issue,[146] that is, towards the three options for the permanent status of Puerto Rico. The PDP supports (enhanced) commonwealth status, while the NPP supports full statehood,[147] and the PIP is for the independence of Puerto Rico. Finally, the most recent addition to the political environment, the Party of Puerto Ricans for Puerto Rico, wants to side-track the status issue until other, more practical and pressing issues have been resolved.

However, it also seems that behind that basic issue, the two national parties are at least to some extent reflected in the two main parties of Puerto Rico so that the PDP is mainly to be regarded as a Puerto Rican equivalent of the Democratic party, while the NPP is not as clearly to be regarded as the Republican party of the island, because also Democrats are members of the NPP. Therefore, it is also possible to say that the Republican – Democrat dichotomy cuts across the Puerto Rican party system in a way which does not facilitate a clear comparison between the two party systems. Perhaps for that reason, it appears as if none of the parties were directly connected to any of the two mainland parties. A certain social stratification of the Puerto Rican parties is to some extent recognizable. The "middle class", if it exists in Puerto Rico, could vote for both the PDP and the NPP, while the NPP has a

---

[144]See Anderson (1998b), p. 50.

[145]The position of the PIP has been negatively affected by the at least partial criminalization and repression of independence activists that took place from the first decades of the 20th century until at least the end of the same century. See Rivera Ramos (2007), pp. 199–204.

[146]For an elaborate study of the relationship of the political parties to the status issue, see Carr (1984), pp. 107–198. However, as maintained by Anderson (1998b), pp. 43, 54, the status issue is not particularly central in explaining electoral behavior, while concerns related to, *inter alia*, criminality, drug addiction, corruption, the personalities of the candidates and the certainty about federal transfers are issues that influence the preferences of the voters, although the dilemma concerning the status issue regularly reminds of itself. For a nuanced consideration of the status issue in relation to the political parties, see also Meléndez (1998), pp. 119–143.

[147]In terms of strategy, the NPP is viewing the status issue as a civil rights issue because of the inequalities embedded in the present colonial arrangement. Therefore, the primary aim is to persuade Congress to organize a binding referendum with the different status options, hoping that the statehood option will prevail. Secondarily, the representative institutions of Puerto Rico could submit a membership application with Congress. Finally, there is also the remote possibility that Puerto Rico would follow the so-called Tennessee example by sending the two senator candidates and six representative candidates to Congress, asking for recognition of their membership in the two houses.

Table 6.7 Support differences between the PDP and the NPP between 1968 and 2008[148]

Year	PDP	NPP	Difference (%)
1968	40.0	42.7	2.7
1972	48.7	41.1	6.6
1976	43.4	46.6	3.2
1980	47.0	47.2	0.2
1984	47.8	44.6	3.2
1988	48.7	45.8	2.9
1992	45.3	49.3	4.0
1996	44.5	51.1	6.6
2000	46.7	47.7	1.0
2004	43.6	52.1	8.5
2008	42.3	53.6	11.3

proportionally higher number of supporters from the lower social classes, such as the poor from the slums and from the poorer parts of the inside of the island, leaving the PDP somewhat more as a party of those who are, proportionally speaking, better off. In this context, the PIP is different as it is mainly composed of intellectuals and academics who perhaps are not connected with the people quite in the same way as the other two parties.

The first elections after American occupation were held in Puerto Rico already in the year 1900 with elections to the House of Representatives, while the senate remained appointed until 1917. Since that time, elections have been held regularly for both chambers. After a re-shuffling of the party structure in the aftermath of the 1967 status referendum, the political system of Puerto Rico has evolved towards a virtual two-party system consisting of PDP and NPP as the main parties (see Table 6.7 above), alternating in power in an almost predictable manner, except during the more recent elections during the last two decades, in which the NPP has managed to strengthen its relative position. In fact, the difference in the popular support between the two parties is so small that even slight movements in the electorate affect the outcome of the elections.

In the elections of 2008, the two smaller parties got less than 3% of the vote each,[149] which means that they lost their status as parties until possible re-registration of the parties is approved by the Commonwealth Election Commission.[150] It is

[148]For the period 1968–1996, see Anderson (1998b), p. 26. For the period of 2000–2008, see Cómision Estatal de Elecciones (2008).

[149]The support threshold of 3% is counted on the basis of votes cast in the election of Governor, held simultaneously.

[150]A formation that wishes to register itself as a political party has to collect signatures of supporters up to at least 5% of the total vote cast for the Governor, which is around 100,000 signatures after the 2008 elections. Registration as a party entitles the party to public funds given as an annual contribution of around 300,000 dollars per year (in election years 600,000 dollars) and specifically for campaigning (each party gets 3 million dollars, but even more if the party collects more by itself, so that there might be around 9 million altogether). In addition, status as a party entitles the party to be represented in the election bodies at the central and the local level. The

Table 6.8 Elections of Governor in Puerto Rico between 1968 and 2008[152]

Year	Party	Support (%)
1968	NPP	43.6
1972	PDP	50.7
1976	NPP	48.3
1980	NPP	47.2
1984	PDP	47.8
1988	PDP	48.7
1992	NPP	49.9
1996	NPP	51.1
2000	PDP	48.6
2004	PDP	48.4
2008	NPP	52.8

notable that the pro-independence PIP attracted only 30,000 votes in the 2008 elections.

The first elected Governor of Puerto Rico was elected in 1948. Also in the office of the Governor, the representatives of the main parties have alternated, and with them, the position on the status issue.[151] In much the same manner as in the Legislative Assembly, the representatives of the two main parties have alternated in the post of the Governor of Puerto Rico (see Table 6.8 above).

The elections of 2004 are of particular interest in this context because the margin by which the PDP candidate won them was only slightly more than 3,000 votes. As a consequence, the counting was challenged in both Puerto Rican courts and in federal courts. For the latter, the matter was ultimately decided by the Court of Appeals in the case of *Rosselló-Gonzáles v. The Puerto Rico Electoral*

defeat of PIP in the elections of 2008 meant that the party in principle lost the public funding and that its 475 staff members in the election commissions were fired.

[151] See also the testimonies on the status issue of various Governors before the appropriate organs of Congress, *inter alia*, Mr. Pedro Rosselló (Joint hearing on the Puerto Rico status plebiscite before the Subcommittee on Native American & Insular Affairs of the Committee on Resources and the Subcommittee on the Western Hemisphere of the Committee on International Relations, House of Representatives, 17 October 1995, Serial No. 104–56 (Committee on Resources); Hearing on H.R. 3024 to provide a process leading to full self-government for Puerto Rico before the Subcommittee on Native American & Insular Affairs of the Committee on Resources, House of Representatives, 23 March 1996, Serial No. 104–87), and Rafael Hernandez Colon (Hearings on S. 710, S. 711, and S.712 to provide for a referendum on the political status of Puerto Rico before the Committee on Energy and Natural Resources, United States Senate, 1–2 June 1989, and Hearing on S. 712 to provide for a referendum on the political status of Puerto Rico before the Committee on Agriculture, Nutrition, and Forestry, United States Senate, 9 November 1989; Hearings on S. 244 to provide for a referendum on the political status of Puerto Rico before the Committee on Energy and Natural Resources, United States Senate, 7 February 1991; Hearing on H.R. 4765 Puerto Rico self-determination act before the Subcommittee on Insular and International Affairs of the Committee on Interior and Insular Affairs, House of Representatives, 28 June 1990; Hearings on S.712 before the Committee on Finance, United States Senate, 14–15 November 1989; Hearing on the compact of permanent union between Puerto Rico and the United States before the Committee on Interior and Insular Affairs, United States Senate, 3 December 1975).

[152] Source: www.eleccionespuertorico.org (accessed 20 February 2009).

Table 6.9 Elections of Resident Commissioner in Puerto Rico between 1980 and 2008[153]

Year	Party	Support (%)
1980	NPP	47.7
1984	PDP	48.7
1988	PDP	49.0
1992	NPP	48.6
1996	NPP	49.8
2000	PDP	49.3
2004	NPP	48.6
2008	NPP	52.7

Commission,[154] which concluded that federal subject matter jurisdiction did not really exist over a local electoral dispute although district courts shall have original jurisdiction of any civil action that tries to redress the deprivation, under, *inter alia*, state law of any right, privilege or immunity secured by the Constitution of the United States or by any act of Congress providing for equal rights of citizens. It is therefore possible that federal courts have jurisdiction over claims arising out of a state or local electoral dispute if, and to the extent that, the complaint contains a set of facts that indicates the violation of a constitutionally guaranteed right. The court concluded that the case alleged the violation of a constitutionally guaranteed right, because the federal constitution protects the right of all qualified citizens to vote in local elections. However, election law, as it pertains to state and local elections, is for the most part a preserve that lies within the exclusive competence of the courts of the constituent states and the federal courts should not intervene in that competence. Because the method of counting of the votes that allowed so-called split votes on the ballot papers had been established before the elections and because the method did not disenfranchise a distinguishable group of voters, the federal court concluded that no federal case arose on the basis of the facts. The controversy was therefore subsequently decided by the Supreme Court of Puerto Rico within the Puerto Rican jurisdiction, in which case the Puerto Rican court did not grant any change of the counting method, and hence the election result first determined by the election commission of Puerto Rico remained in effect.

A similar profile as for the governorship can be observed with regard to the elections of the Resident Commissioner, elected at the same time as the Governor and the two chambers of the Legislative Assembly. The position of the Resident Commissioner has also alternated between the two main parties (see Table 6.9 above).

The period of the Commonwealth of Puerto Rico was preceded by substantial experience in participation through elections, a practice that was enhanced and deepened by the time of the introduction of the Commonwealth by the election of the Governor. It seems on the basis of the election statistics that the one of the two

[153] Source: www.eleccionespuertorico.org (accessed 20 February 2009).

[154] United States Court of Appeals for the 1st Circuit, 04–2611, 28 January 2005 (joined cases). See also Rosselló (2005), p. 323.

main parties that wins the elections normally wins them with regard to all of the posts, that is, the Legislative Assembly, the Governor and the Resident Commissioner.[155]

6.5.4 Referendums on the Status Issue, Constitutional Amendments and Other Matters

However, the people of Puerto Rico do not only participate through elections, but also directly in the resolution of political and constitutional issues. According to the Constitution of Puerto Rico, the people have a role in adopting or rejecting constitutional amendments which is decisive in nature, that is, normatively binding. In fact, the Constitution has been amended several times through the referendum in the more limited process of constitutional change. The number of referendums concerning individual amendments to the Constitution has been limited to three at a time. As concerns the complete revision involving a constitutional convention, also subject to approval in a decisive referendum, the Constitution has not undergone any such processes. Several referendums have been held in Puerto Rico after the two referendums in conjunction with the constitution-making process in 1951 (Public Law 600) and 1952 (the Constitution), three of which have dealt directly with the issue of the status of Puerto Rico (see Table 6.10 below).

The three so-called status referendums (1967, 1993 and 1998) form an interesting pattern with regard to this prevalent and dominant issue in the political and constitutional life of Puerto Rico. The two earlier status referendums indicated only a marginal support for the independence alternative,[156] while the status referendum in 1998 resulted in an interesting and unusual limbo: all three alternatives were rejected by 50.3% of the voters.[157] Hence at the same time as the status referendums

[155]It seems that only in 2004, the elections for the Governor and the Resident Commissioner were won by different parties.

[156]The status referendum of 1967 was boycotted by the supporters of independence, and therefore the figures were even lower than the actual support. See Trías Monge (1997), p. 130, and Jiménez Polanco (1998), p. 104.

[157]The ballot paper included four different substantive options and a fifth option "none of the foregoing", and it was this last alternative that was supported by most voters. The reason for submitting five alternatives in one referendum was the fact that the then Governor, supportive of statehood, caused the referendum to be held on the basis of three alternatives that he defined in a manner that the supporters of the commonwealth felt were misleading. A law-suit was brought against the referendum, demanding that the three alternatives would be re-defined, but the court did not re-define the alternatives. Instead the court added two new options, "associated status" and "none of the other alternatives" (the latter seems to have been a part of the original bill in the House of Representatives). The supporters of the commonwealth status thereafter decided to campaign for the last option. The statehood alternative received 46.5% of the votes, which share demonstrated a steady support over time for this alternative. However, the statehood option, which implies that Puerto Rico is in all respects aligned with the regular state organization in the US, may pose great risks for the linguistic and cultural characteristics of Puerto Rico because of the dominant role of the English language. See also Baralt (2004), pp. 539–542, Rivera Ramos (2007), p. 58 f., and Rosselló (2005), p. 227.

Table 6.10 Referendums in Puerto Rico since 1951[158]

Year	Nature	Issue	Result	Support (%)	Turnout (%)
1951	Advisory	Public Law 600	Approved	76.5	65
1952 3 March	Advisory	Constitution	Approved	82	58
1952 4 Nov.	Advisory	Constitution (amendm. after US Congress decision)	Approved	88	54
1960	Binding	Constitutional amendment	Approved	78	52
1961	Binding	Constitutional amendment	Approved	83	58
1964	Binding	Constitutional amendment	Approved	78	40
1967	Advisory	Status of Puerto Rico	– Statehood	39.0	
			– Commonw.	60.4	
			– Indep.	0.6	66
1970	Binding	Voting at 18	Approved	59	35
1991	Binding (?)	Claim of democratic rights	Rejected	53.0	61
1993	Advisory	Status of Puerto Rico	– Statehood	46.3	
			– Commonw.	48.6	
			– Indep.	0.6	73.6
1994	Binding	Two constit. amendm.	Both rej.		
			– La Fianza	53.6	
			– Aum. de Jueces	54	63
1998	Advisory	Status of Puerto Rico	Rejected, none of the three alt.	50.3	71.3
2005	Advisory	Unicam. or bicam.?	Unicameralism	83.4	22.3

can be seen as an indication of the level of support for the three traditional parties in Puerto Rico because their main platforms were represented as alternatives in the status referendum,[159] the result from the referendum of 1998 is probably an indication by the population of Puerto Rico of the fact that it is of no use to continue organizing advisory status referendums as long as the US Congress has not enacted legislation that creates a binding referendum for submitting all or at least one of the

[158] See Jiménez Polanco (1998), pp. 87–88. The information has been complemented through statistics from the Commonwealth Election Commission. The first referendum ever held in Puerto Rico was organized in 1917 concerning the so-called Seca Law on the prohibition of alcoholic beverages, approved by 61% of those voting with a turnout of 68%. There have been several proposals to hold referendums on the top of the ones actually held. See Jiménez Polanco (1998), pp. 91–95, 106–115. However, as concluded by Jiménez Polanco (1998), p. 98 f., the turnout rate in the referendums has generally been lower than in general elections of the same era. For the 1991 referendum, see Baralt (2004), pp. 535–539, and Rivera Ramos (2007), pp. 185–187.

[159] See also Anderson (1998b), p. 55.

alternatives to the people.[160] After all, there are implications of a change of status for the internal constitutional order of the United States, except in the case of independence, which is least favored at the moment. A favorable situation for a status referendum is politically speaking not at hand before a sufficiently large portion of the population, perhaps in clear excess of 60%, has coalesced behind one of the "internal" alternatives, that is, either statehood or enhanced commonwealth status.[161]

The 1991 referendum on the claim of democratic rights could perhaps also be added to the status referendums, but because the aim was to achieve an internal platform by way of amendments to the Puerto Rican Constitution for petitioning the US Congress for a status decision, this particular referendum is not normally presented as one of the status referendums. Although the 1991 proposal to amend the Constitution was rejected by the people, it is worth mentioning that the amendment dealt with the inalienable right to freely and democratically determine Puerto Rico's political status, the right to choose a dignified, non-colonial, non-territorial status not subordinate to plenary powers of Congress, the right to vote for three alternatives, the right that only results with a majority will be considered triumphant in a plebiscite, the right that any status would protect Puerto Rico's culture, language and identity, and continued independent participation in international sports events, and the right that any status guarantees the individual's right to

---

[160]The 1998 referendum had also undertones unrelated to the issue, and it has been held that the 1993 referendum may be the best gauge so far concerning the opinions of the people. The federal organs have expressed a continued interest in the matter. As indicated by a Memorandum of President of the United States (George H.W. Bush) of 30 November 1992 (57 F.R. 57093) entitled 'Administrative Treatment of Puerto Rico as a State', the US Government will remain seized by the status issue and will continue to be open for status referendums: "As long as Puerto Rico is a territory, however, the will of its people regarding their political status should be ascertained periodically by means of a general right of referendum or specific referenda sponsored either by the United States Government or the Legislature of Puerto Rico." "This guidance shall remain in effect until Federal legislation is enacted altering the current status of Puerto Rico in accordance with the freely expressed wishes of the people of Puerto Rico." Hence the US Government is not opposed to changing the status of Puerto Rico, and periodic status referendums could therefore be expected until the status question is resolved by a final vote. See also Duffy Burnett and Marshall (2001), pp. 20–23, outlining the Congressional attempts to introduce legislation concerning a binding referendum, Thornburgh (2007), pp. 73–75, on the efforts of the US executive branch to resolve the political status of Puerto Rico, Thornburgh (2001), pp. 352–359, illustrating the constitutional difficulties related to the determination of the final status, in particular, inside the constitutional fabric of the United States, Thornburgh (2007), pp. 18–21 on the results of the three referendums, and Puerto Rico Democracy Act (2007), p. 6, for a recent attempt to regularize the situation. Definite Congressional action is, however, lacking.

[161]However, the value of the "internal" options, at least of the statehood option, might be greatly lessened if the issue was presented in the way of a choice between becoming Americans or remaining Puerto Ricans. In such a set-up, the alternative of becoming independent and entering thereafter into a relationship of associated statehood with the US could attract more support than has been the case. This is said to be due to the fact that if the "surface" of a Puerto Rican is scratched a little bit, an *independista* will be discovered under the skin in spite of the fact that the declared position is that of statehood or developed commonwealth status. See Carr (1984), p. 13.

American citizenship.[162] If the proposal had been passed in the referendum as an amendment to the Constitution, it is difficult to say what effect, if any, such a provision would have had on the US Congress.[163]

As concerns independence, the default alternative on the basis of the right to self-determination of colonized peoples under international law, it is possible to interpret the results from the three referendums so that the people of Puerto Rico have, in free expressions of their will three times over, decided not to opt for independence. It should be observed, however, that none of the status referendums have been binding, which implies that the independence option has yet to be submitted to the people in a binding referendum. The above interpretation on the basis of the advisory referendums also indicates that the solution to the status issue has to be looked for among the other options for the exercise of self-determination, such as free association or any other political status, as outlined in the UN Friendly Relations Declaration. In so far as free association may imply that a territory associates itself with an existing independent State by giving up its independence in exchange for a position as a constituent state in a confederation or a federation, that would not seem to be the case for Puerto Rico. Instead, the solution would have to be looked for in the category of 'any other political status freely decided by the people', that is, integration through statehood (in which case the people of Puerto Rico give up their right to self-determination in the meaning of exclusive legislative powers of their own in exchange for shared sovereignty and self-determination in the federation) or any other political status through enhanced commonwealth status (which would grant a sufficient amount of exclusive law-making powers to Puerto Rico so that they can be exercised independently of the legislative powers of Congress, but under the constitutional rights of the US Constitution).[164]

How would such a binding status referendum, which at the same time can be understood as a free choice by the people within the right to self-determination, come about? Probably on the basis of an act of Congress,[165] which in the case of

---

[162] Translations of the amending sentences from http://en.wikipedia.org/wiki/Puerto_Rican_status_referendums#1991_Constitutional_Amendment_Referendum (accessed 27 March 2009).

[163] The point can be made that the referendum actually violated the restriction concerning constitutional amendments by the referendum, according to which only three amendments are permissible by the referendum at the same time. A greater number of amendments should be made by using the method of constitutional convention. The same argument could have been true also for the 2005 unicameralism referendum in the case it had been passed.

[164] As pointed out by Carr (1984), pp. 104 f., 406–409, the matter can also be viewed differently, because the existing commonwealth position is untenable. According to Carr, the real options are "statehood or independence". This is also the position expressed in Rosselló (2005), p. 269 f., 320, and Thornburgh (2007), pp. 4, 77–81, 86 f., who makes the remark on p. 62 that the 1998 referendum indicates that the "residents of Puerto Rico have withdrawn their consent to be governed under the current 'commonwealth' status", which, however, could indicate support for some sort of enhanced commonwealth status, not favored by Thornburgh.

[165] For a recent move in that direction with an account of the legislative history, see Puerto Rico Democracy Act (2007), p. 6. See also Rosselló (2005), p. 319: "The federal government must offer a U.S. statehood enabling act, along with a blueprint for future U.S. relations with a separately

enhanced commonwealth status should take on the form of an amendment to the US Constitution, drafted in cooperation with the Government of Puerto Rico. The normal way to submit such an issue to the referendum would be to formulate one substantive alternative and one zero alternative, that is, a "Yes" or "No" constellation. Because two relatively clear internal alternatives have taken shape at a general level, it would also be possible to submit the two status positions as the sole alternatives to the referendum, with the natural consequence that one of the alternatives will muster the majority of votes cast. However, for leaving the ambit of the territorial clause of the US Constitution, the material contents of both alternatives must be ready from the federal level, that is, that there must exist a decision to admit Puerto Rico as a state in the federation and that there exists a constitutional amendment concerning the special status of Puerto Rico that will enter into force after the amendment has been approved in the status referendum.[166] This is so because only with such clear alternatives, offered by the United States in a binding manner, can there be an informed choice by the people of Puerto Rico within their right to self-determination. This is so also because the statehood alternative already exists as a procedure outlined in the US Constitution and has been tested several times over when states have been admitted to the federation: equality between the internal alternatives requires that the enhanced commonwealth option is specified in the US Constitution in a manner similar to the

sovereign Puerto Rico. The implications of each options must be communicated effectively to the people of Puerto Rico. The voters of Puerto Rico must then assume the duty of making an informed, binding choice."

[166]An amendment to the US Constitution on the special status of Puerto Rico could be phrased, e.g., in the following way: "Puerto Rico will have its own exclusive legislative powers exercised under its own Constitution on the basis of an Act of Congress that can only be amended if both Congress and the people of Puerto Rico make corresponding decisions to that effect." Obviously, the contents of such an act of Congress would have to agreed upon, too, before the status issue is resolved so that the voters know what the alternatives are. A legislative package of this kind would remove Puerto Rico from the territorial clause of the US Constitution, revoke the Federal Relations Act and establish an enumerated list of legislative powers to be exercised by Puerto Rico (that is, replace the general formula of "not locally inapplicable", leaving residual powers to the US, for instance, in the area of defense, monetary issues, and at least greater parts of foreign relations). It would address, *inter alia*, the problematic issues of representation in the U.S. Senate and House of Representatives and the electoral college on the basis of US citizenship and identification of the final arbiter for competence conflicts between the federal government and Puerto Rico, and it would seem that the US citizens of Puerto Rico should have a final recourse to the US Supreme Court on the basis of the constitutional rights guaranteed in the US Constitution (although Puerto Rico could continue to have its own internal constitutional rights with a broader material scope). However, the value of the enhanced commonwealth option in a set-up of this kind is greatly diminished by the difficulty of effectuating such an amendment to the US Constitution, partly because of procedural reasons, partly because the constituent states could be reluctant to grant exclusive law-making powers to an entity that would, thereafter, be in a better position than the states, for instance, because the supremacy clause would not anymore extend itself to Puerto Rico in the manner it extends itself to the states. On the difficulties that can be regarded as almost insurmountable, see Rosselló (2005), pp. 248–261, and pp. 264–266 (concerning the statehood option) as well as Thornburgh (2007), pp. 77, 80 f.

statehood option.[167] In addition, this conclusion can be grounded in the right to self-determination in a colonial situation, on the basis of which it can be argued that the United States owes to Puerto Rico the creation of a fair framework for the making of an informed decision in the matter.[168] Thus the onus is on the US Congress.

There is actually one interesting example of an attempt to organize a binding referendum in a part of Puerto Rico, but the plan was ultimately aborted. A local referendum with links to the federal level was planned to be held in November 2001 amongst the registered electors of the municipality of Vieques concerning the existence of a live-fire shooting and training range of the US Navy on the island of Vieques east of the main island of Puerto Rico. The area was a source of conflict between Puerto Rico and the United States, and an agreement about the procedure to deal with the area was reached between the Governor of Puerto Rico and the US President. The voters were to be given the possibility to choose between the two options provided in section 1503 of Public Law 106–398, that is, the National Defense Act for Fiscal Year 2001,[169] namely 1) the ceasing of the Navy training not later than 1 May 2003, with conveyance of the federal property to the Puerto Ricans, and 2) the continuation of the training, including training using live ammunition, under the terms proposed by the Navy that included pecuniary compensation to the Puerto Ricans. In the provision of the Act, the US president was charged with the duty to provide for a referendum on the island of Vieques in Puerto Rico to determine by a majority of the votes cast by the Vieques electorate whether the people of Vieques approve or disapprove of the continuation of the conduct of

[167]However, this is not the position taken in the Report by the President's Task Force on Puerto Rico's Status, December 2007, at http://www.usdoj.gov/opa/documents/2007-report-by-the-president-task-force-on-puerto-rico-status.pdf (accessed 26 March 2009), p. 10 f., which proposes two plebiscites. The first one would be on the issue of whether to retain the current status as a territory (i.e., commonwealth) or to emerge into a non-territorial status (i.e., statehood or independence). If the latter wins, then a second plebiscite would be held to choose between these alternatives which the US Constitution recognizes and Puerto Rico would emerge either as the 51st state in the federation or as an independent country. However, if the former alternative, continued territorial status as a commonwealth would win, the report proposes that the praxis of plebiscites is repeated in the future "periodically as long as that status continues, to keep congress informed of the people's wishes".

[168]See Rivera Ramos (2007), pp. 225, 244, which can be interpreted as support for a constitutional amendment for an enhanced commonwealth status, because such an amendment, together with the procedure for admission as a state would hold the potential to remove Puerto Rico from the territorial clause and thus from the colonial relationship. See also Rosselló (2005), p. 269: "Whether deliberately or unintentionally, Uncle Sam has been perpetrating cruel hoaxes upon the hopeful peoples of its non-traditional territories ever since 1898. If a meaningful procedural methodology is at last to be applied to them, it must begin with explicit Congressional definitions of the available colonial exit strategies. Given that there is nothing 'manifest' about the destinies of these territories, Congress must overtly articulate destiny alternatives that it deems to be acceptable."

[169]Public Law 106–398, Appendix, 114 STAT. 1654A–353 (Floyd D. Spence National Defense Authorization Act for Fiscal Year 2001). On the Vieques issue, see also Baralt (2004), pp. 617–639, Rivera Ramos (2007), pp. 67, 248a, 248b.

live-fire training, and any other types of training, by the Armed Forces at the Navy's training sites on the island under certain conditions laid down in the Act. According to section 1503, the term "Vieques electorate" meant in the context of the referendum the residents of the island of Vieques, Puerto Rico, who, on the dates specified in the sub-section, were registered to vote in a general election held for casting ballots for the election of the Resident Commissioner of the Commonwealth of Puerto Rico. The proclamation of the results was the task of the president, and according to sub-section e, the outcome of the referendum, as proclaimed by the president on the basis of the results returned from the island of Vieques, was binding. What is important here from the point of view of principle is that the US Congress created a binding referendum for the determination at the local level of a matter which admittedly was of a federal nature. The Act was executed through a Presidential Directive,[170] which in para. 1 made the point that it is "understood that the full implementation of this directive is contingent upon the Government of Puerto Rico authorizing and supporting this referendum, and the cooperation of the Government of Puerto Rico as specified in paragraph 5(a)", which presupposed co-operation between the Puerto Rican and federal authorities. The plan was to hold the referendum on 6 November 2001.

From the point of view of division of powers, this piece of federal law may be regarded as one example of how Congress can legislate for Puerto Rico with effects within the legislative competence of Puerto Rico concerning its legislation concerning participation. Following the ordinary distribution of powers, the organization of a local government referendum in a municipality of Puerto Rico, which implied the activation of the Puerto Rican election administration, would normally have been a matter attributed to the legislative competence of Puerto Rico.[171] From the point of view of the federal distribution of powers, such a measure would probably not be possible in an ordinary constituent state, because such a state is vested with the legislative powers concerning elections and referendums and with control of its own election administration.[172] The federal lawmaker would not have the authority to activate the election administration of a state in the same way as it

[170]Directive to the Secretary of Defense by the President of the United States on 31 January 2000: Resolution Regarding Use of Range Facilities on Vieques, Puerto Rico (Referendum).

[171]In Puerto Rico, the federal action necessitated, *inter alia*, the approval on 28 December 28, 2000 the Act (No. 457) to amend Sections 1, 2, 3, 4, 8, 12, 20 and 22 of Act No. 423 or October 27, 2000, in order to clarify several of its provisions and harmonize these with the Directive of President William Jefferson Clinton of January 31, 2000 and Public Law 106–398 of October 30, 2000, known as the "Floyd D. Spence National Defense Authorization Act for Fiscal Year 2001".

[172]See Suksi (1993), p. 68. However, the retrocession of the county of Alexandria from Washington, D.C. in 1846 was effectuated by means of a referendum in which the inhabitants of the area to be ceded from the federal district to Virginia would approve the measure. See Suksi (1993), p. 63. Hence there exist at least one example of a federal referendum, but that dealt with inhabitants under direct federal authority.

arguably could do in Puerto Rico.[173] Of course, a consideration that affects the situation is that Puerto Rico did not oppose the organization of such a referendum.

However, due to the conflict concerning the issue between Puerto Rico and the federal government (the Navy, in particular), and after the election of a new Governor who was negatively disposed towards the agreement on procedure, the Legislative Assembly eventually adopted legislation for an advisory referendum in Vieques on the basis of its own legislative competences. The legislation identified three different alternatives that were submitted to the voters of Vieques, the second one of which was not at all included in the federal Act:[174] 1) continuation of the military exercises and bombings by the Navy on Vieques, using inert ordnance, until their conclusion, no later than 1 May 2003. The ouster of the Navy from Vieques and the transfer of the land of the eastern part of Vieques to the Department of the Interior of the United States of America; 2) immediate and permanent ceasing of the military exercises and bombings by the Navy on Vieques. The ouster of the Navy from Vieques, the cleaning and return of the land of Vieques to its people; and 3) permanently continue the military exercises and bombings of the Navy and the Armed Forces on Vieques with the option of using live ordnance. In the "indigenous" advisory referendum held on 29 July 2001 in the municipality of Vieques, alternative no. 1 received 1.7% of the votes, alternative no. 2 altogether 68.2% and alternative no. 3 altogether 29.9% at a turnout of 80.9% out of 5893 persons with the right to vote.[175]

After the advisory referendum, the binding referendum was postponed until 25 January 2002. Even that date was not met, but the Navy instead proposed that its activities on the island would cease, which eventually happened in 2003, and made also the point that the referendum provisions in the Act be repealed.[176] Congress passed and President Bush signed on 12 December 2001 the 2002 Defense Appropriations bill,[177] which canceled the referendum and required the Navy to

---

[173] As a practical matter and in reality, there was an agreement between the Governor of Puerto Rico and the President of the United States on how the resolution of the matter would progress.

[174] On 13 June 2001, the Legislative Assembly adopted the Act (No. 34, the enabling act of the referendum) to direct and regulate an electoral referendum process in the Municipality of Vieques under the provisions of the Puerto Rico Electoral Act, Act No. 4 of December 20, 1977, as amended, in order to ascertain the sense of the residents of Vieques regarding the military exercises and bombings of the Navy of the United States of America on said island municipality; to enable the vote of the duly registered and active electors of the Municipality of Vieques so that they may state in a free and democratic manner, and free from coercion, in the exercise of their electoral prerogative, on the options provided in this Act; authorize the Commonwealth Elections Commission of Puerto Rico to carry out said referendum pursuant to the terms provided in this Act; to appropriate the needed funds; and for other purposes.

[175] See http://www.ceepur.org/consulta2001/escrutinio/summary.html (accessed 4 February 2009).

[176] United Press International, 15 July 2001: Navy wants to avoid Vieques referendum, at http://www.highbeam.com/doc/1P1-45237522.html (accessed 4 February 2009).

[177] See the Defense Authorization Act for 2002 (Public Law 107–107; S. 1438), which contains in Section 1049 provision that cancels the requirement for holding the January 2002 referendum. See CRS Report for Congress (Order Code RS20458, Updated on 20 August 2003): Vieques,

find a suitable replacement for Vieques before abandoning it in May 2003. As a consequence, the federal referendum was never held. However, the plan to organize a binding referendum in a part of the territory of Puerto Rico on the basis of federal legislation that had been drafted in cooperation between the Puerto Rican Government and the US Government may provide a model for such a possible status referendum that is organized on the basis of federal law and that is binding. This is so because Congress apparently considers itself empowered to enact such legislation, probably on the basis of its plenary powers under the territorial clause. Together with the strong tradition of elections, the different status referendums, which link into the political organization of Puerto Rico, the Vieques referendum and the constitutional referendums indicate that participation is a central feature of the constitutional system of Puerto Rico. This is the case in Zanzibar, too, but mainly through the mechanism of elections.

6.6 Zanzibar: Troubled Forms and Practices of Participation

6.6.1 From One Party to Two Parties and Beyond (or Back?)

Historically, Zanzibar was, since colonial times, divided between two main parties, the ZNP of more Arab provenance and the ASP of more African provenance.[178] The ZNP/ZPPP Government was overthrown by the ASP in the revolution of 1964,[179] and as a consequence, the ASP became the only party in Zanzibar, controlling the Revolutionary Council.[180] In 1977, in conjunction with the adoption of the Constitution of Tanzania, the ASP merged with the TANU, the ruling party of the mainland, and formed the CCM.[181] Hence there was a profound political

Puerto Rico Naval Training Range: Background and Issues for Congress by Ronald O'Rourke, at https://www.policyarchive.org/bitstream/handle/10207/3340/RS20458_20030820.pdf?sequence=7 (accessed 4 February 2009).

[178]Othman (2006), pp. 41, 42, 44.

[179]As pointed out by Othman (2006), p. 42 f., the supporters of the ASP felt that their role as the leading party had been stolen by the British when they granted the independence of Zanzibar with a ZNP/ZPPP led Government under the monarchical form of government with the Sultan at the top. The same point is made by Shivji (2008), p. 35 f., indicating that the British handed over power to a political minority rather than to a political majority.

[180]As a consequence of the revolution, the ZNP/ZPPP Government was overthrown, the monarchy was abolished and the independence constitution of 1963 was abrogated. See Othman (2006), p. 43. According to Othman (2006), p. 56, during the period between 1964 and 1977, Zanzibar and Tanganyika were ruled by different political parties, ASP and TANU respectively, with each political party operating in its own geographical areas as the single party. However, "at the approach of every general election, the two parties held a joint congress where they nominated a joint presidential candidate for the elections".

[181]See Othman (2006), p. 56 f., Shivji (2008), pp. xix,152–163, and 'Zanzibar: Key Historical and Constitutional Developments' by Eastern Africa Centre for Constitutional Development, at www.kituochakatiba.co.ug/zanz%20const.htm (accessed 5 February 2010).

integration of the party structures of the two parts of the union. The integration of the two parties into one also affected the manner in which politics were done in the two parts of Tanzania, leading to an alignment of Zanzibar as a part of the greater Tanzanian polity ruled by the one party.[182] Although both Mainland Tanzania and Zanzibar have since given up the one-party system and introduced a multi-party system with a number of parties competing for political power, the CCM still has a strong position both in Mainland Tanzania and in Zanzibar and it continues to be a party with a leftist orientation. There is another major party in Zanzibar, the Civic United Front (CUF), which is a liberal party and has been close to gaining a majority position but has not managed quite yet, although its support is almost equal to that of the CCM.[183] If the current constellation changes so that Zanzibar is ruled by a different party than Mainland Tanzania, the political dynamics could change drastically. Things have gone "smoothly" with one party running both governments, but the day there are different parties in power in the two parts of the country, there might be problems. At such a point, it will be very interesting to follow the reaction of Mainland Tanzania, the hope being that it will be peaceful and reasonable.

The political life of Zanzibar has traditionally been very divisive, and it is possible to make a case for a continuation of the division between the ASP and the ZNP/ZPPP in the beginning of the 1960s in a similar fashion and on the basis of some (imagined) racial markers between the CCM and the CUF after the re-introduction of the multiparty system.[184] As a society, Zanzibar is probably over-politicized, to the extent that practically speaking every Zanzibari is a member of one of the two political parties or at least an active supporter of one of them. Other parties have had difficulties in even entering the political scene of Zanzibar. It is obvious that the CCM has the advantage of being the old party with established

[182]In fact, according to Dourado (2006), p. 89, already the 1965 Interim Constitution of Tanzania was enacted as a consequence to create a one-party state, but the one party was the TANU in Mainland Tanzania and the ASP in Zanzibar until the merger of the two into the CCM in 1977. Dourado (2006), p. 95, is critical of this and maintains that by "granting party supremacy over the organs of Government we have breached one of the fundamental provisions of the Articles of Union, 1964". On the one-party state and its limitation of the actual autonomy of Zanzibar, see also Shivji (2008), pp. 107–110, 211–212. On the creation of the one-party state of Tanzania in 1965 through the second Interim Constitution, see Shivji (2008), pp. 124–129, 145–149.

[183]See Shivji (2008), p. 232. There are also other parties in Zanzibar, although the CCM and the CUF are the only ones in the House. The smaller parties are present in Zanzibar probably because of the requirement of the Political Parties Act, 1992, that a party be present in all parts of the country.

[184]Shivji (2008), pp. 3, 5–40, 246. However, Shivji regards such an explanation too simplistic, and introduces also other dividing lines, which, however, seem to coalesce to some extent. See also Shivji (2008), p. 25 f.: "Although dominated by mainlanders, ASP was not a mainland African party just as ZNP, with a significant Arab component, was not an Arab party. It was the ZPPP which came close to an ethnic party in that it derived its overwhelming support from the Shirazis." The Shirazis are a group of Zanzibaris who are believed to be, in part, descendants of Persian immigrants. See also Maliyamkono (2000a, b), p. 246 f.

organizational structures for political mobilization. For the same reason however, it probably also has difficulties to relinquish the powers it has amassed and to turn over them to the opposition, in this case the CUF.[185] What was suddenly proposed in the Spring of 2010 by the leaders of the two parties was to create a government of national unity,[186] a measure that would make it necessary to amend the Constitution. The proposal included a plan to organize a referendum on the issue of "Do you want to have a government of national unity?"[187] However, no referendum had ever been organized in Zanzibar before 2010,[188] and the Constitution did not make any reference to a referendum before the amendments of 2010. Therefore, the plan to organize a referendum on the issue of a government of national unity had to be effectuated through the enactment of a separate referendum act, enacted on 30 March 2010.[189] Even so, it would seem that the referendum would have to be qualified as an advisory one, because the Constitution of Zanzibar placed the decision-making powers concerning constitutional amendments in the hands of the House of Representatives.

The referendum on the government of national unity was held on 31 July 2010. With a turnout of 71.9%, altogether 66.4% of the voters supported the formation of a government of national unity, while 33.6% opposed the measure.[190] After the referendum, the House of Representatives was called into an extraordinary session

---

[185]As pointed out in Tanzania Human Rights Report (2009), p. 193, "[t]he right to participate in governance is very controversial in Zanzibar. It is commonly known in the whole world that Pemba is a stronghold of the opposition party Civic United Front (CUF) but under the system of 'a winner takes all', the ruling party monopolises power on its own. The opposition parties and their followers are sidelined when it comes to governance."

[186]The government of national unity would seem to follow principles of power-sharing similar to those in Northern Ireland. The winning party would get the office of the President, while the second party would nominate the Vice-President, after which the winning party would get the second Vice-President, who would sit in the House of Representatives. The President and the Vice-President would together appoint the ministers, while junior ministers would be drawn from the two parties in proportion to their seats in the House. For earlier plans for such a government of national unity, see Othman (2006), p. 49, Shivji (2008), p. 33.

[187]On the web-site of the Zanzibar Election Commission, the question is worded in the following way: "Do you accept the new Government structure after the General Election 2010?" See http://referendum.zec.go.tz/ (accessed 19 October 2010).

[188]See, e.g., the comments in Othman (2006), p. 52, and Dourado (2006), p. 75 f., on the issue of and concerning reasons for why there was no referendum on the Articles of Union in 1964. Nonetheless, reference is sometimes made to the inquiries of the Nyalali Commission as an unofficial referendum, because the commission had the mandate to solicit consultations, e.g., through questionnaires and meetings in villages. By an estimated ratio of 8:2, the population did not support the introduction of a multi-party system. See also Maalim (2006), p. 144, who advances the speculative opinion that if a fair and open referendum were organized on the exercise of the right of secession, "the chances for the majority opting for secession are high". See also Shivji (2008), p. 249 on the absence of ideas to consult the people on the constitution.

[189]Amendments to the Elections Act would be necessary also with a view to the fact that the Election Commission would not, at the moment, have any mandate to organize a referendum.

[190]See Zanzibar Referendum (2010).

for the adoption of the constitutional amendments, which took place on 9 August 2010. The norms concerning the government of national unity became operative after the elections on 31 October 2010. The constitutional amendment introduced a new mechanism of participation, the constitutional referendum, in Art. 80A of the Constitution of Zanzibar. According to the provision, it is not enough that the House of Representatives decides on amending certain provisions of the Constitution, but in addition, a referendum is required to effectuate the amendment.[191] This entrenchment of, in particular, the fundamental rights and individual freedoms as well as the presidential system of government, covers also the constitutional amendment procedure. According to the provision, a separate referendum act is to be enacted by the House of Representatives for the purposes of carrying out constitutional referendums.

6.6.2 *The Right to Vote in Divisive Elections*

The starting point for political participation is Art. 5(1) of the Constitution of Tanzania, according to which every citizen of the United Republic who has attained the age of 18 years is entitled to vote in any public election held in Tanzania as provided by law. Parliament may enact a law that, for instance, imposes conditions restricting a citizen from exercising the right to vote on grounds specified in Art. 5(2).[192] In addition, there is a general participation clause in Art. 21 of the Constitution of Tanzania. Although the Constitution of Tanzania did not originally contain references to the Constitution of Zanzibar, the amendments to the Tanzanian Constitution made after the enactment of the 1984 Constitution of Zanzibar recognize the existence of Zanzibar and its governmental structures. As provided in Art. 106 of the Constitution of Tanzania, there shall be a House of Representatives of Zanzibar. However, deviating terminologically from the description of the Legislative Council of Zanzibar in Art. 63(1) of the Constitution of Zanzibar, the Tanzanian Constitution makes the point that the House of Representatives shall comprise two parts, namely the elected or appointed Members

[191] The requirement of a referendum is established in Art. 80A for the amendment of articles 1 through 5A concerning the general characteristics of Zanzibar, Art. 9 concerning the government and the people, articles 11 through 25A concerning the fundamental rights and individual freedoms, Art. 26 concerning the office of the president and the qualifications for election of President, Art. 28 concerning the term of office of President, all articles in part II of the Constitution concerning the First and the Second Vice-President, all articles in part III of the Constitution on the ministers, deputy ministers and the revolutionary council, except articles 49 and 50, and Art. 80A on constitutional amendments through the referendum.

[192] There is an explicit prohibition in Art. 113A of the Constitution of Tanzania concerning a Justice of the Court of Appeal, a Judge of the High Court or a magistrate of any grade to join an political party. The same rule is recorded in Art. 97 of the Constitution of Zanzibar. Because party membership is a precondition for candidacy in elections, the rule prohibiting party membership effectively bars members of the judiciary from political office. They do, however, have the right to vote in elections.

of the House, on the one hand, and the Head of the RGZ, on the other. The contribution of both parts is required for a valid decision.[193]

Matching these national provisions at the sub-state level, Art. 9(2)(a) of the Constitution of Zanzibar declares that "sovereignty resides in the people and it is from the people that the Government through this Constitution shall derive all its power and authority". The provision elevates the security of the people and their welfare to be the primary objective of the government, and therefore, it is provided that "the people shall participate in the affairs of their Government in accordance with the provisions of this Constitution".[194]

The right to vote in Zanzibar is regulated in Art. 7 of the Constitution of Zanzibar. The right to vote is in principle general, but the House of Representatives may enact a law and make provisions which may bar a Zanzibari from exercising a right to vote for such reasons as having the citizenship of another country, having a mental disease certified by the High Court, having been convicted of a criminal offense and serving his sentence in the Education Center, that is, in the prison in Zanzibar (however, a person in custody could vote). There is an exclusion clause in Art. 121(4) of the Constitution of Zanzibar that refers to persons in service with the so-called Special Departments of the Revolutionary Government of Zanzibar. Such persons are prohibited from taking part in political activities except voting in any election in accordance with the provisions of Art. 7 of the Constitution. The House of Representatives is also given the task of enacting election legislation that relates to the elections and eligibility of the President, Members of the House of Representatives and Councilors for Local Government. The Election Law is required under Art. 7(3) to regulate the establishment of a permanent register of voters and the procedure of correcting the content of that register.

It is clear that the one-party elections in Zanzibar did not fulfill the requirements of international election norms, but the multi-party elections seem to have been marred with problems, too. For instance, the elections of the year 2000 were characterized by massive irregularities and were disapproved of by international election observation missions.[195] In this respect, the elections of 2010 for the

[193]The general functions of the House of Representatives are outlined in Art. 88 of the Constitution of Zanzibar and they comprise, inter alia, the following: to enact legislation where implementation of that matter requires legislation, to debate the performance of each Ministry during the annual budget session in the House of Representatives to put different questions to the Revolutionary Government of Zanzibar in the House of Representatives and to approve and oversee development plans of the Government in similar manner that Government budget is approved. Article 107 of the Constitution of Tanzania reproduces these tasks of the House of Representatives and mentions also the basic function of the President of Zanzibar as the second part of the legislature of Zanzibar.

[194]The elections in Zanzibar are governed by the Elections Act, 1984, Act No. 11 of 1984, enacted by the House of Representatives of Zanzibar (as amended in 1990 by Act No. 4, in 1992 by Act No. 8, in 1992 by Act No. 14, in 2000 by Act No. 3, in 2001 by Act No. 3, in 2002 by Act No. 12, in 2004 by Act No. 3).

[195]See, e.g., Maalim (2006), p. 147. See also Hamad (2007), pp. 40–49, 51, who notes that there is a big gap between the electoral laws, on the one hand, and the implementation of the laws, on the

Table 6.11 Elections to the House of Representatives between 1995 and 2010 by seats allocated to the two parties in the elections[196]

Party	1995	2000	2005	2010
CCM	26	34	30 (31)	28
CUF	24	16	19 (17)	22

purposes of constituting the government of national unity seem to be a great improvement.

As concerns the House of Representatives of Zanzibar, that is, the primary law-making body for the approval of Bills, Zanzibar is, under Art. 65(1) of the Constitution of Zanzibar, divided for the purposes of the election of 50 Representatives into 50 constituencies,[197] all of which elect one person to be member of the House of Representatives for a 5-year mandate period in a manner laid down by the Constitution and the Elections Act, 1984. The determination of the result of the election follows the method of first-past-the-post, because under Art. 88 of the Elections Act, the returning officer shall declare after the counting of the votes that candidate to be elected for whom the majority of the votes has been cast (see Table 6.11 above).[198]

As the results of the various elections show, the two-party system produces a result which is relatively even, and it is possible that the CUF could have come out

---

other. In particular, it is problematic that as a rule, the aftermath of the elections seem to revert to violent action, arrests and detentions, fabricated charges against political opponents of the main party.

[196]Source: African Elections Database, at http://africanelections.tripod.com/zanzibar.html (accessed 8 July 2010) and Zanzibar Electoral Commission: Results for House of Representative Candidates – 2010 Zanzibar General Election, at http://www.zec.go.tz/docs/results_representatives2010.pdf (accessed 8 December 2010). Turnout figures are not available. In the referendum on the government of national unity on 31 July 2010, the turnout was reported to have been 71.9%, representing 293,039 voters. This figure is based on the number of persons with the right to vote registered in the general register of voters, which is 407,669. This is a relatively low figure with respect to the total population of Zanzibar of around one million inhabitants. Allowing for a large portion of young persons in the population, the total number of 400,000 would nonetheless seem to indicate that there is a good number of non-Zanzibaris living in Zanzibar. That group is excluded from voting in Zanzibar elections, but would have the right to vote in national elections. For the turnout figure, see Zanzibar Referendum (2010), p. 18503.

[197]Under Art. 120 of the Constitution of Zanzibar, the Zanzibar Electoral Commission divides Zanzibar into election constituencies, the number of which may vary between 40 and 55, as determined by an act. All constituencies shall as far as possible have an equal number of residents as the Commission may determine. However, the Commission does not have to follow this condition to the extent deemed appropriate, taking into consideration the size of the population particularly ensuring appropriate representation in urban areas and towns in rural areas thinly populated, population growth, the means of communication and administrative demarcations. As provided for in the Elections Act, the residence requirement for ordinary residency in a constituency is 36 months. The legislation thus expects a relatively great measure of immobility of the electorate, which may be criticized. See Hamad (2007), p. 53.

[198]Because the two main parties of Zanzibar, the CCM and the CUF, are almost equally strong and at the same time entrenched in an almost perpetual position in relation to each other, it has not been possible to agree on changing the FPTP system into a system of proportional election.

as the winner in at least some of the elections, if only the elections had been truly free and fair.[199]

In addition to the elected representatives, there shall, according to Art. 66(1), be ten nominated members of the House of Representatives. They are appointed by the President from amongst persons who upon nomination shall be qualified to be member of the House of Representatives. The provision contains the limitation of the powers of the President of Zanzibar that not less than two persons shall be appointed in consultation with the opposition leader in the House of Representatives or in consultation with the political parties if there is no opposition leader. This means that in appointing the additional members, the President is tied to that political balance of the House of Representatives which was produced through the elections. Finally, as laid down in Art. 67, 40% of the number of elected members in the House of Representatives shall be female. Such female members are supposed to be Zanzibaris and they are to be proposed by political parties in the House that have won at least 10% of the constituency seats in the elections to the House. The female members are appointed by the Zanzibar Election Committee in proportion to the parliamentary strength of the political party proposing the female members. In this way, the proportions between the main parties represented in the House are not disrupted, but it seems that the rule works to the detriment of the smaller parties.

In addition to the more regular requirements concerning the right to stand for election and to become a member of the House of Representatives, such as the requirement of being at least 20 years of age, the right to vote, nominations,[200] and the status of being a Zanzibari,[201] Art. 68 of the Constitution of Zanzibar expects

[199]For a summary of problems related to the elections of 1995, 2000 and 2005, see Hamad (2007), pp. 40–49.

[200]For elections to the House of Representatives, a person must be nominated as a candidate in writing by not less than twenty-five voters registered in the polling districts within the constituency for which he is a candidate, and a candidate must deposit a sum of money with the Returning Officer. The deposit is forfeited to the Government if the candidate withdraws his candidature after nomination day or if the number of votes counted in his favor at the election is less than one tenth of the total number of votes counted for the seat which he was a candidate, save that such deposit shall not be forfeited if the candidate dies. In other cases, the deposit shall be returned to the candidate even if he is not elected. However, no person shall be nominated as candidate in more than one constituency, but any party may, notwithstanding any provision or requirement in the Elections Act, field any person to be a candidate in any constituency and such candidate may register and vote at such constituency. Hence the political parties are very clearly favored in the nomination of candidates.

[201]In addition, it is evidently so that the lawmaker can, under Art. 68(e) create additional exclusions. Some limitations of political activities apply to civil servants. While civil servants may be members of any political party under the Civil Servants (Participation in Politics) Act, 1992 (Act No. 15 of 1992), they shall not be politically active during office hours. However, they may participate in demonstrations organized by the Government. There is also the particular restriction of political activities in Art. 121(4) of the Constitution of Zanzibar, pertaining to any person in service with the Special Departments of the Revolutionary Government of Zanzibar. This special category of personnel belonging to the Marine Militia and to the para-military forces (see below) are prohibited from taking part in political activities except voting in any election in accordance with the provisions of Art. 7 of the Constitution.

that a candidate is literate[202] and that he or she is a member and candidate proposed by a political party that has permanent registration in accordance with the Political Parties Registration Act, 1992, which is a piece of national law. Compulsory membership of a political party is underlined by Art. 71 (1), according to which a representative shall cease to be a member of the House if he or she ceases to be a member of the party that proposed him to stand for elections. The central role of the political party is apparent on the basis of Art. 134(1) of the Constitution of Zanzibar, according to which the term 'party' means a political party officially registered in accordance with the Political Party Act 1992.[203] This means that the party as a political organization is tied to the Union legislation by the Constitution of Zanzibar as intended by point 22 of the first schedule to the Constitution of Tanzania and that, as a consequence, a political party has, on the basis of the Political Party Act, to establish itself in the whole of Tanzania. The eligibility grounds are further sustained in Art. 69 by some grounds of exclusion from candidacy, such as the possession of the citizenship of any other country, a High Court decision attesting a mental disease, not being a member and candidate nominated by a party, and conviction of criminal offense and imprisonment in the Educational Center or prison in the Mainland for the period of 6 months or more or for election offenses regarding honesty during a period of 5 years before election.[204]

In addition to the above-mentioned categories of non-eligible persons, the Chairman of the Revolutionary Council, that is, the President of Zanzibar, is not eligible for the House of Representatives. This is a natural consequence of the fact that the constitutional and political system of Zanzibar is very presidential, identifying the President as the Head of State of Zanzibar, the Chairman of the Revolutionary Council and the Head of the Revolutionary Government in Art. 26 (1) of the Constitution of Zanzibar. For instance, the President may summon the House of Representatives at any time to continue its functions and also dissolve the House under certain relatively generous conditions.[205]

---

[202] For persons with impaired vision or other physical infirmity, the requirement is ability to speak Kiswahili.

[203] While the political parties is a Union Matter, association legislation remains within the legislative powers of Zanzibar. Reportedly, there have been difficulties created for parties and associations, and as concerns associations, it should be possible to resolve the problems by means of such legislative amendments that the House of Representatives has at its disposal. See also Tanzania Human Rights Report (2009), p. 192.

[204] Once elected, a Representative enjoys relatively broad immunities under Art. 86(3) of the Constitution of Zanzibar.

[205] According to Art. 91(2), the conditions are as follows: "(a) if the life of the House of Representatives has expired in terms of Article 92 of the Constitution; or (b) at any time within the last 12 months of the life of the House of Representatives for the purposes of calling an earlier general election; (c) if the House of Representatives has refused to approve Government Budget; or (d) if the House of Representatives refuses to approve a Bill in terms of Article 79 of the Constitution; or (e) if the House of Representatives declines to pass a motion which is of fundamental importance of Government policies and the President considers the way out in the National interest is not to dissolve the cabinet or appoint a new Chief Minister but to call for a

Article 20(2) of the Constitution of Tanzania contains explicit restrictions on the operation of political parties, because it shall not be lawful for any political entity to be registered which according to its constitution or policy aims at promoting or furthering the interests of any religious faith or group, of any tribal group, place of origin, race or gender, or of only a particular area within any part of the United Republic. This is already and in itself relevant from the perspective of Zanzibar, but the provision also goes on to prohibit the registration of a party that advocates the break-up of the United Republic, accepts or advocates the use of force or violent confrontation as means of attaining its political goals, advocates or intends to carry on its political activities in only one part of the United Republic, or does not permit periodic and democratic election of its leaders. Parties organized in a military fashion or under totalitarian rule are thus forbidden, which is understandable, but from the point of view of Zanzibar and a (theoretical) break-up of the Union, the Constitution of Tanzania is very limiting. In addition, the provision requires any party to carry out its activities in several parts of Tanzania, which means that locally confined parties are not possible.

6.6.3 Electing the Powerful Executive

The system of government of Zanzibar is very presidential, combining in the person of the President also the offices of Head of Government and the Chairman of the Revolutionary Council, that is, the main executive organ. Particular qualifications therefore exist for the election of the President of Zanzibar each 5 years.[206] The elections of the President and of the House of Representatives do not, however, coincide. For candidacy, it is required under Art. 26(2) of the Constitution of Zanzibar that the person is a Zanzibari by birth, has attained the age of 40 years, has qualifications that enable him to be elected as member of the House of Representatives, and is a member of and a candidate nominated by a political party duly registered in accordance with the Political Parties Act, 1992. In addition to the nomination of a party, it is required by Art. 34(2) that the candidacy for president is, in addition, supported by a certain number of voters, determined in the Election Act to be not less than two hundred nominators who are registered voters for the purposes of elections under the Election Act from each of the five regions of

general election; or (f) if having regard to the proportional representation of political parties in the House of Representatives, the President considers that it is no longer legitimate for the Government in power to continue in office, and it is not feasible to form a new Government."

[206]The provisions concerning the election of the President of Zanzibar are largely reproduced in Art. 104 of the Constitution of Tanzania, which provides that the Head of the RGZ shall be elected by the people in Tanzania Zanzibar in accordance with the provisions of the Constitution of Zanzibar, 1984, and in accordance with the procedure prescribed by legislation enacted by the House of Representatives of Zanzibar which relates to the election in general or to the election of the Head of the RGZ. The provision also regulates the situations where the presidency has become vacant.

Table 6.12 Presidential elections in Zanzibar between 1995 and 2010 by party of the contestant in per cent[207]

Party	1995 – Turnout: 95.7%	2000 – Turnout: N/A	2005 – Turnout: 90.8%	2010 – Turnout: 89.5%
CCM	50.24	67.04	53.18	50.1
CUF	49.76	32.96	46.07	49.1
Other parties	–	–	0.75	0.6

Zanzibar. During the one-party rule, the eligibility requirements were in practice controlled by the one party, placing the selection of the candidate effectively in the hands of or at least under the strong influence of Mainland Tanzanian interests in a way that might not always have promoted such candidates that the Zanzibaris themselves thought would be best for them.[208]

For elections of the President, Zanzibar forms one constituency, and according to Art. 27(4), the right to vote in presidential elections is accorded to the same group of persons that has the vote in the elections to the House of Representatives. The presidential election of Zanzibar is a two-round election: if in the first round nobody receives more than 50% of the total valid votes cast, the Zanzibar Election Committee shall appoint a day for the second ballot of the presidential election, which is a run-off election between the two best candidates of the first round. The one who receives more than 50% of the total valid votes cast shall be declared to have been elected. The presidential elections are placed under a particular exclusionary clause concerning legal challenges, because Art. 34(7) of the Constitution of Zanzibar stipulates that when a candidate has been declared by the Zanzibar Election Commission to have been elected President, no court whatsoever shall be empowered to inquire into that candidate's election. Hence although the High Court of Zanzibar is empowered to try election complaints, the presidential elections are not within its jurisdiction (see Table 6.12 above).

As shown by the results of the presidential elections in Zanzibar, the political divide between the supporters of the CCM and the CUF is relatively even, at least in

[207] Source: African Elections Database, http://africanelections.tripod.com/zanzibar.html (accessed 8 July 2010) and Zanzibar Electoral Commission, 2010 General Election – Presidential Results, http://http://www.zec.go.tz/docs/Election%20Results%202010.pdf (accessed 18 November 2010). Other parties are such as Jahazi Asilia, DP, NRA, SAU, AFP, NCCR, TADEA.

[208] See, e.g., Othman (2006), p. 57, explaining the consequences of the forced resignation of President Jumbe of Zanzibar: "it was the party's NEC [National Executive Committee –MS] which appointed Ali Hassan Mwinyi as an Interim President and later nominated him for election as the President of Zanzibar. (. . .) Since NEC's Zanzibari membership is no more than a third of the total, this meant therefore that a Zanzibar President could be chosen by a forum which is predominantly non-Zanzibari." See Shivji (2008), p. 226 f. See also Othman (2006), p. 58, according to which the CCM has amended its constitution to allow the re-introduction of the special committee on Zanzibar that is under the party's Central Committee. The dominant position of the one party indicates that instead of the Special Constitutional Court, the NEC was the final arbiter of problematic issues between Mainland Tanzania and Zanzibar, something also indicated by Dourado (2006), p. 84.

the elections of 1995, 2005 and 2010, and candidates of other parties have been completely marginalized under the overwhelming weight of the two main parties. What is striking is the turnout in the presidential elections, which hovers around or above 90%. Such a level of participation is very high and testifies to the extremely politicized nature of Zanzibari society. Also, the presidential elections of 1995, 2005 and 2010 testify to the fact that the two main contestants, the CCM and the CUF, are very close to each other. The candidate of the CCM has, however, been able to secure more than 50% of the votes, which means that a second round of voting has not been necessary. This may change if the other parties become more active and create more substantial support in the future.

6.6.4 Over-Representation at the National Level

As concerns the election of the President of Tanzania, Art. 47(2) of the Constitution of Tanzania provides for a system of election in which both the President and the Vice-President appear on the same ticket. The nomination of the Vice-President is, however, arranged on a territorial basis: if the President of the United Republic comes from one part of the United Republic, then the Vice-President shall be a person who comes from the other part of the Union. The provision tries to maintain a balance between the two parts of the Union Republic, or at least a situation in which the other part is not forgotten about. Most of the time, this has meant that the President has been from Mainland Tanzania and the Vice-President from Zanzibar, but the territorial origin of the two office holders was reversed once, with the President of the United Republic, Mr. Ali Hassan Mwinyi coming from Zanzibar and the Vice-President from Mainland Tanzania. The system is, however, such that the candidate elected as President of Tanzania would not necessarily have to receive one single vote from Zanzibar in order to be elected. Moreover, it would not be too far-fetched to suggest that the vice-president of the Union is normally not politically attached to Zanzibar, and is not a part of the Government of Zanzibar, which makes him more or less irrelevant in Zanzibar. Although Art. 47 explicitly makes it possible to nominate the President of Zanzibar for the election of Vice-President, there are some incompatibilities under the provision (that is, being the President of Zanzibar or the Prime Minister of the United Republic, Member of Parliament), and if the holders of the office of the Prime Minister of Tanzania or of the President of Zanzibar are appointed or elected to be Vice-President of the United Republic he or she shall cease to hold these offices.

The Parliament of the Union Republic consists according to Art. 66(1) of the Constitution of Tanzania of different categories of MPs, namely members elected to represent constituencies (including the 50 constituencies in Zanzibar, the same constituencies that are used as the basis for the elections to the House of Representatives of Zanzibar), five additional members from Zanzibar elected by the House of Representatives from among its members, the attorney general, and at least 15% female members of the total number of the three previous categories.[209] The female members are nominated by the political parties represented in the Parliament as provided for in Art. 78 of the Constitution and on the basis of proportional representation amongst those parties. The President and the Vice-President shall not be MPs. Because the election in the constituencies is, according to Art. 77 of the Constitution of Tanzania, a first-past-the-post election, the proportional representation of women in Parliament could perhaps be thought as implying an MMP system of elections. This is not, however, the case, because the appointment of female MPs does not influence the political strength of the parties in Parliament, created through the FPTP method in the constituency elections. Instead, the function of the appointment of female MPs seems to be to balance up the expected male dominance in the constituency elections and introduce a system of guaranteed seats for women. The fact that there are 50 constituencies in Zanzibar for the purposes of the election of the MPs is explained by the creation of the Union Republic:[210] both parts of the Union were joined together in a situation where both had been sovereign States, and the Union respected that form of association by not changing the internal structure of the two entities, such as the division of Zanzibar into 50 constituencies.[211] The dramatic over-representation of Zanzibar can be well illustrated by reference to the constituency size, which ranges between 10,000 and 15,000 voters in Zanzibar, while in Mainland Tanzania, it could be as high as 200,000 voters. This is clearly a problem from the point of view of the equality of vote, as established in Art. 25(b) of the CCPR.[212]

There is a quorum requirement in Art. 94(1) of the Constitution of Tanzania as concerns the organization of a valid meeting of Parliament, which is half of all the Members of Parliament. If that is fulfilled, legislative decisions and other decisions can, in the great bulk of cases, be made on the basis of simple majority. However, there are special qualified majorities required in some provisions

[209] According to Shivji (2008), p. 172 f., out of a total of 239 members of the Parliament under the 1977 Constitution of Tanzania, around 55 could come from Zanzibar, leading to a considerable over-representation. "In reality, though, the overwhelming presence of Zanzibaris in the National Assembly meant for little because the powers of the National Assembly had been grossly eroded and shifted to the party."

[210] The women appointed to Parliament in proportion to the strength of the political parties should also include women from Zanzibar.

[211] As reported in Dourado (2006), p. 78, the then President of Zanzibar, Mr. Karume said to Mr. Dourado at the moment when the Union Republic was created more or less the following in Kiswahili: "Don't worry, we have the right to be represented on their National Assembly, but they don't have the right to be on our Revolutionary Council." From this, Dourado draws the conclusion that the President of Zanzibar had a federation in mind. See also Shivji (2008), p. 128.

[212] For a comment concerning the over-representation under the 1965 Interim Constitution, see Shivji (2008), p. 128: "Of the total 204 members, some 55, or over one-fourth were to be from Zanzibar. Mainlanders quietly resented this over-representation of Zanzibaris although in practice it mattered little since Zanzibaris hardly participated in the deliberations of the National Assembly nor, during Karume's time, did they care as to what happened in the National Assembly. For Karume and his colleagues, what mattered was 'their' Revolutionary Council (...)."

of the Constitution, such as for constitutional amendment and for the amendment of issues mentioned in the two schedules to the Constitution. In addition, there is a special decision-making requirement concerning votes of no confidence, where the requirement is an absolute majority. That requirement may make the mechanism of parliamentary accountability quite attenuated. The large number of MPs from Zanzibar gives, at least in theory, a relatively great leverage to them by way of affecting the quorum of Parliament and the qualified majorities. At least in these respects, the current multi-party political system of Tanzania would have to take into account the position of the Zanzibar politicians on different matters to a greater extent than perhaps was the case during the one-party system. In fact, the strong Zanzibari representation in Parliament is unprecedented, and it could even be argued that the five Members of Parliament appointed to Parliament by the House of Representatives introduces a federal dimension in the relationship between Mainland Tanzania and Zanzibar. However, it is still a singular entity holding exclusive legislative powers that at least in principle are not affected by any doctrine of preemption, although the complaint on the part of Zanzibar is that Parliament has adopted legislation which breaks into the legislative competence of Zanzibar. Also, it seems that no West Lothian issue has been raised in Parliament, but the MPs from Zanzibar vote on all legislation adopted by Parliament, even legislation which only applies in Mainland Tanzania (which is most of the legislation enacted by the national parliament), although they might not have any political interest in influencing Mainland issues.

6.6.5 Two Different Election Commissions

For the purposes of organizing the elections in Zanzibar, a Zanzibar Electoral Commission (ZEC) is created under Art. 119 of the Constitution of Zanzibar. The Electoral Commission is established as an autonomous department and it is headed by the Director of Elections, who is the secretary to the Commission and who is appointed by the President.[213] The Electoral Commission of Zanzibar is an independent authority, not obliged to follow any orders or directions from any person or any department of the Government or the opinion of a political party. However, it is expected, from time to time, to consult with the National Electoral Commission of the United Republic. The reason for this is the fact that the Zanzibar Election Committee implements, within the jurisdiction of Zanzibar, the election law and party legislation enacted by the Union Parliament. As a

[213]Zanzibar Electoral Commission Act, 1992, Act No. 9 of 1992. Under the Act, the Electoral Commission is charged with the over-all supervision of the general conduct of all Presidential, Member of the House of Representatives and Local Authorities elections in Zanzibar. It has been recommended by Hamad (2007), p. 52, that the power of the President to appoint the chairperson and other members of the ZEC be reduced in order to preserve the independence of the ZEC and to build confidence among the inhabitants of Zanzibar towards the electoral process.

consequence, the national elections of the President of Tanzania and of the Parliament are carried out by the ZEC.

The ZEC is granted immunity from court action, because no court has jurisdiction to inquire into anything done by the ZEC in the performance of its functions in accordance with the provisions of the Constitution. This is a significant provision, because elections in Zanzibar have traditionally been controversial. For instance, the elections carried out in the 1990s were widely deemed to have not been fair nor free.[214] As concerns the elections of 2010, media discussion has pointed at certain problems with the identity cards that voters should possess as a concrete proof of the identity of the voter and his/her right to vote. Early on, prospective voters had applied for cards, but their applications had not been processed or perhaps misplaced or lost, as was been claimed by higher authorities. Hundreds of persons, in particular in Pemba, faced disenfranchisement, because in the absence of identity cards, they could not be registered to vote in their *Shehia* in the register of voters, the creation and maintenance of which is the task of the Electoral Commission.[215] At the end of February 2010, the delay had, in some cases, been as long as 3 months. In Zanzibar, there is also local government organized on the basis of elected municipal councils.

For the purposes of the elections at the national level, there shall, according to Art. 74 of the Constitution of Tanzania, be an Electoral Commission of the United Republic which shall consist of members to be appointed by the President. Here, the same principle applies as with the formation of the tickets to the election of the President and Vice-President: The President shall appoint the Vice-Chairman of the Electoral Commission so that if the Chairman of the Commission comes from one part of the Union, the Vice-Chairman shall be a person who comes from the other part of the Union. The Electoral Commission of the Union is in charge of organizing the Union elections, but under Art. 74(13) of the Constitution of Tanzania, the Electoral Commission of the United Republic shall, from time to time, consult with the Electoral Commission of Tanzania Zanzibar. The constituencies in Zanzibar for the purposes of both national elections and Zanzibar elections are divided according to Zanzibar electoral laws by the ZEC, which acts as an agent of the national electoral commission.

Incredible as it sounds, every state in the world does not have a national election administration. This is the situation in China. For Hong Kong, the absence of a national election administration means that the organization of elections in Hong Kong is entirely the responsibility of Hong Kong, but the national government is nonetheless in a position to influence issues related to the right to vote in Hong Kong.

---

[214] For an at least partly critical analysis of the Zanzibar Election Committee, see Rugalabamu (2000), pp. 105–132. As pointed out in Rugalabamu (2000), p. 108, the ZEC has not made an impression on anybody for its independence, and this seems to be the conclusion also in Hamad (2007), pp. 42, 46.

[215] As reported in Rugalabamu (2000), p. 110, there were difficulties with registration also during the preparations for earlier elections. This was confirmed by Hamad (2007), pp. 40–42, concerning the elections of 1995, 2000 and 2005.

6.7 Hong Kong: Participation Contained

6.7.1 Towards Universal Suffrage

The participatory mechanisms of Hong Kong revolve around the requirement in Art. 68 of the Basic Law that the legislature of the HKSAR shall be constituted by elections for a 4 year term of office. Under Art. 26 of the Basic Law, permanent residents of the HKSAR have the right to vote and the right to stand for election with the specification that these rights must be exercised in accordance with law. In this context, it is evident that the reference to law means Hong Kong legislation, not Mainland Chinese legislation, except in the case where the Basic Law, which is a Chinese law, contains provisions concerning elections. This is the case, for instance, in Art. 68 of the Basic Law and in Annex II of the Basic Law, entitled "Method for the Formation of the Legislative Council of the Hong Kong Special Administrative Region and Its Voting Procedures". The local piece of legislation which specifies the participatory rights and mechanisms concerning the legislature of Hong Kong is the Legislative Council Ordinance of 1997.[216] However, the Bill of Rights Ordinance contains language, *inter alia*, within the area of political rights that replicates the provisions of the International Covenant on Civil and Political Rights within the legal order of the HKSAR, such as the right and the opportunity to vote and to be elected at genuine periodic elections which shall be by universal and equal suffrage and shall be held by secret ballot, guaranteeing the free expression of the will of the electors.[217]

When Hong Kong was re-united with China, it could be expected against the background of the limited right to participation during colonial times that the target concerning elections would be the full realization of the right to participation through popular vote. Although the initial system of election to the legislative council was not in conformity with this target, Art. 68(2) of the Basic Law is

[216]Chapter 542 of the Laws of Hong Kong, Gazette Nr 134 of 1997, 3 October 1997, with the long title To provide for the constitution, convening and dissolution of the Legislative Council of the Hong Kong Special Administrative Region; to provide for the election of Members of that Council; and to provide for related matters (as amended).

[217]As stated by Weiyun (2001), p. 225, "the UK did not inform China beforehand of the enactment of the Hong Kong Bill of Rights Ordinance 1991, neither did the two sides reach a consensus afterwards. The UK's unilateral action was inconsistent with the spirit of the JD. As this was a major legal change made unilaterally after May 1985, China decided it could not undertake the obligation of keeping everything fundamentally unchanged after 1997." On p. 227, he identifies provisions of the Ordinance on national defence, military and foreign affairs which could be deemed to be in contravention with the Basic Law. However, the enactment of the Bill of Rights Ordinance in 1991 was understandable against the background of the Tiananmen Square massacre in June 1989, when it already was clear that China would re-gain its sovereignty over Hong Kong. Of course, the references in the Basic Law of 1990 to the CCPR may be seen as an additional platform for specifying the human rights of the population of Hong Kong. See Leung Mei-fun (2006), p. 185 f.

formulated in a forward-looking manner, making it possible to modify the electoral system in the light of the actual situation in the HKSAR. The "dynamic" nature of the electoral system is clear from the principle of gradual and orderly progress, and the ultimate aim is the election, at some point of time during the 50 years period, of all of the members of the Legislative Council by universal suffrage.[218]

Therefore, the main efforts concerning future constitutional development in the HKSAR will be in the area of universal suffrage, for both the legislative council and the chief executive elections (see below). The aim is to broaden the electorate, although the Chinese Government may still be of the opinion that the UK reservation to the CCPR will continue.[219] The timetable for such constitutional development was set by the NPCSC, which issued on 29 December 2007 a decision on issues relating to the methods for selecting the Chief Executive and for forming the Legislative Council in the year 2012 and on issues relating to universal suffrage.[220] Although some measures in the direction of universal suffrage will most likely be taken in 2012, they will be preparatory to the direct election in 2017 of the Chief Executive under Art. 45 and of the Legislative Council in 2020 under Art. 68. Amendments to Annexes I and II of the Basic Law concerning elections of the two organs (see above) as well as amendments to the relevant election ordinances in the HKSAR would be needed.[221]

---

[218]In section 4 of the *Interpretation of 6 April 2004* of the NPCSC of Art. 7 of Annex I and Art. III of Annex II to the Basic Law concerning amendments to the method of selection of the Chief Executive (see below), it seems as if the amendments to the voting procedures of the Legislative Council were conditional to first amending the selection procedure of the Chief Executive. For the text of the *Interpretation of 6 April 2004*, see Leung Mei-fun (2006), pp. 459–461. See also Davis (2007), p. 79 ff., and Leung Mei-fun (2006), p. 238 f. After the *Interpretation of 6 April 2004* was issued, the NPCSC made an additional decision on 26 April 2004, in which it stated that in the 2007 election of the Chief Executive and the 2008 election to the Legislative Council, the method of universal suffrage shall not be applied, but that the method of election could be modified thereafter. For a comment, see Chen (2004), pp. 215–225.

[219]Upon ratification of the CCPR, the Government of the UK declared that it reserves "the right not to apply sub-paragraph (b) of article 25 in so far as it may require the establishment of an elected Executive or Legislative Council in Hong Kong". See http://sim.law.uu.nl/SIM/Library/RATIF.nsf/ (accessed 13 January 2010).

[220]See Decision of the Standing Committee of the National People's Congress on Issues Relating to the Methods for Selecting the Chief Executive of the Hong Kong Special Administrative Region and for Forming the Legislative Council of the Hong Kong Special Administrative Region in the Year 2012 and on Issues Relating to Universal Suffrage Adopted by the Standing Committee of the Tenth National People's Congress at its Thirty-first Session on 29 December 2007, at http://www.basiclaw.gov.hk/en/materials/doc/2007_12_29_e.pdf (accessed 14 January 2010). The background to the Decision can be found in the 2007 Green Paper on Constitutional Development, at http://www.cmab.gov.hk/en/issues/electoral4.htm (accessed 14 January 2010), and subsequent developments. The issue of democratic reform has been dealt with further in Hong Kong, see http://www.cmab.gov.hk/en/press/press_2201.htm (accessed 14 January 2010), and it has stirred the emotions of the population of Hong Kong, which would seem to wish a more rapid progress towards direct elections of the Legislative Council.

[221]For a comment concerning the decision of the NPCSC, see Chen (2008a), pp. 1–13.

6.7.2 *Elections through Geographical and Functional Constituencies*

6.7.2.1 Different Franchise Requirements

Article 67 of the Basic Law contains certain eligibility requirements for members of the Legislative Council. The Council must be composed of Chinese citizens who are permanent residents of the SAR with no right of abode in any foreign country.[222] Permanent residents of the SAR who are not of Chinese nationality or who have the right of abode in foreign countries, however, may also be elected members of the Legislative Council of the Region, provided that the proportion of such members does not exceed 20% of the total membership of the Council.[223] This provision is relatively generous towards persons of foreign origin, which is rare in contexts where formal legislative decisions are made. Although the Basic Law opens up such a possibility, sections 27–28 of the Legislative Council Ordinance limit the right to vote of natural persons to those who have permanent residency in Hong Kong.[224] The rights directly related to elections are supplemented under Art. 27 by other political rights, guaranteed for the residents of Hong Kong, namely the freedom of speech, of the press and of publication and the freedom of association, of assembly, of procession and of demonstration. A horizontal connection to the local executive is provided under articles 50 and 70 of the Basic Law, according to which it is possible for the Chief Executive to dissolve the Legislative Council once during his or her term of office, followed by new elections of members of the Legislative Council within 3 months. No such dissolution has taken place during the first decade of the existence of the HKSAR.

Two different types of constituencies elect members of the Legislative Council. The electorate in the geographical constituencies is broad and inclusive, encompassing 3.372 million persons with the right to vote in the elections of 2008, while the electorate in the functional constituencies is limited and contained only a total of 229,861 natural persons or corporate bodies with the right to vote in their

[222] According to Leung Mei-fun (2006), p. 28, it is not in the eyes of the Chinese authority an empty slogan to state that only patriotic people may govern the HKSAR: "It is one of the criteria for the selection of the leaders of the special administrative region."

[223] For the right to vote in elections, see also sections 24–25 and 27–30 of the Legislative Council Ordinance.

[224] In addition, section 31 of the Legislative Council Ordinance explicitly disqualifies the following natural persons from exercising the right to vote: those found under the Mental Health Ordinance (Cap 136) to be incapable, by reason of mental incapacity, of managing and administering his or her property and affairs, those who are members of the armed forces of the Central People's Government or any other country or territory. It should also be mentioned that according to Art. 24 (2), sub-section 4, permanent residents may include foreign nationals who have continuously resided in Hong Kong for 7 years. Hence it is not necessary to be a Chinese citizen to vote.

respective functional constituencies in the same elections.[225] Therefore, there is a fundamental imbalance between the two electorates in relation to the number of members in the Legislative Council they return.[226] There is also a stark imbalance between the functional constituencies. Because each functional constituency returns one member to the Legislative Council – and the membership of such constituencies ranges from hundreds of persons to tens of thousands – the voting power of a voter in, for instance, the Insurance functional constituency is several times higher than that of a voter in the Education functional constituency. In addition, as determined in section 21 of the Legislative Council Ordinance, the Labour functional constituency has three seats in the Legislative Council (see Table 6.13 below).[227]

---

[225]According to section 20 of the Legislative Council Ordinance, the functional constituencies are as follows: (1) Heung Yee Kuk (which is a statutory advisory body representing the indigenous inhabitants of the New Territories); (2) agriculture and fisheries; (3) insurance; (4) transport; (5) education; (6) legal; (7) accountancy; (8) medical; (9) health services; (10) engineering; (11) architectural, surveying and planning; (12) labour; (13) social welfare; (14) real estate and construction; (15) tourism; (16) commercial (first); (17) commercial (second); (18) industrial (first); (19) industrial (second); (20) finance; (21) financial services; (22) sports, performing arts, culture and publication; (23) import and export; (24) textiles and garment; (25) wholesale and retail; (26) information technology; (27) catering; (28) District Council. The corporations included in each functional constituency are established in sections 20A – 20ZB of the Legislative Council Ordinance. See also Hong Kong 2007 (2008), p. 9 f. Evidently, the functional constituencies can change over time after amendments of the law. As explained in the Report on the 2008 Legislative Council Election, p. 12, at http://www.eac.gov.hk/pdf/legco/2008/en/report/2008lce_full_lc_report_e.pdf (visited on 7 August 2009), the functional constituency electorate consists of both natural persons and corporate bodies. A requirement for a natural person to be a functional constituency (FC) elector is that the person must be a geographical constituency (GC) elector. "Among the 28 FCs, 18 of them consist of corporate electors. A corporate elector is required to cast its vote through an authorised representative ("AR") who is a natural person and a GC elector appointed by the corporate elector to vote on its behalf." "The appointment or replacement of the AR must be registered with the Electoral Registration Officer ("ERO"). An FC elector cannot be an AR for the same FC, but can be an AR for another FC. An AR of a corporate elector cannot be appointed as the AR of another corporate elector at the same time. A person who is qualified to be an elector of more than one FC can only become an elector of one of the FCs of the person's choice. If a person is eligible to register as an elector in one of the four special FCs, namely, Heung Yee Kuk, Insurance, Transport and Agriculture and Fisheries, the person can only be registered as an elector of that special FC." For the problems attached to the functional constituencies, see Ghai (1999), p. 251 ff.

[226]In the 1999 Concluding Comments of the CEDAW Committee concerning Hong Kong's initial report under the UN Convention on the Elimination of Discrimination against Women, para. 319, the point is made that the electoral system of Hong Kong "contains structural obstacles to the equal political participation of women, which is indirect discrimination against women, especially with respect to the functional constituencies". Consequently, the CEDAW Committee urged the Government "to take all measures necessary to ensure the equal representation of women in all constituencies, including rural committees, on the basis of the principle universal and equal suffrage, [...]". See Report of the Committee on the Elimination of Discrimination against Women, 20th and 21st session, 1999, G.A.O.R., 54th session, suppl. No. 38 (A/54/38/Rev.1).

[227]According to section 36 of the Legislative Council Ordinance, by-elections shall be held to fill vacancies in the Legislative Council. Three by-elections have so far been held, in 2000 (Hong Kong Islands geographical constituency), 2001 (election committee) and 2007 (Hong Kong Island geographical constituency). See http://www.eac.gov.hk/en/about/chairman.htm, accessed 9 August 2009. In a geographical constituency, a single-member by-election essentially becomes a first past the post election although it would be carried out by way of lists normally used in a proportional election.

Table 6.13 Elections to the Legislative Council of Hong Kong 1997–2009[228]

Membership	1st term (1998–2000)	2nd term (2000–2004)	3rd term (2004–2008)	4th term (2008–2012)
Elected by geographical constituencies through direct elections	20 – Turnout: 53.29%	24 – Turnout: 43.57%	30 – Turnout: 55.64%	30 – Turnout: 45.20%
Elected by functional constituencies	30 – Turnout: 63.50%	30 – Turnout: 56.50%	30 – Turnout: 70.10%	30 – Turnout: 59.76%
Elected by an election committee	10 – Turnout: 98.75%	6 – Turnout: 95.53%	– N/A	– N/A
Total	60	60	60	60

The expansion of the numbers of Legislative Council members returned by geographical constituency elections, organized for the first time in 1991 under British rule, represents minor progress towards universal suffrage. For the first and second Legislative Council terms, some members were selected by an 800-member election committee,[229] but this system was phased out by the third term elections and members who had been elected by the election committee were replaced by directly elected members. By 2007, there were around 3.3 million registered voters in Hong Kong for the purposes of electing half of the members of the Legislative Council from five geographical constituencies. Each constituency returns between four and eight members of the Legislative Council, selected on the basis of a closed list voting system which operates on the basis of the Hare quota[230] and, if seats are left unfilled, is complemented by the largest remainder formula, as specified in section 49 of the Legislative Council Ordinance. Each list submitted for election may consist of candidates up to the number of seats allocated to the constituency in which the list is registered, and a voter casts his or her vote for a list in his or her constituency. The seats for the constituency are distributed among

[228]Hong Kong 2007 (2008), p. 9. See also 2008 Legislative Council Election, at http://www.elections.gov.hk/legco2008/eng/facts.html (visited on 7 August 2009), and Turnout Rate, at http://www.elections.gov.hk/legco2008/eng/turnout/tt_gc_GC.html (visited on 7 August 2009). For a final report concerning the 1998 elections, see http://www.info.gov.hk/info/98eac-e.htm (visited on 7 August 2009).

[229]The election committee consisted of 600 representatives of the functional constituencies, 36 Hong Kong deputies to the NPC, 60 members of the Legislative Council, 41 Hong Kong members of the National Committee of the Chinese People's Political Consultative Conference, 21 representatives of the corporate body Heung Yee Kuk, 21 members of the Hong Kong and Kowloon District Councils, and 21 members of the New Territories District Councils.

[230]The quota is determined by dividing the total votes cast in a constituency for all lists by the specified number of seats for the constituency concerned, and the candidate(s) whose votes exceed the quota are elected. For the elections of 2012, the LegCo amended Annex II to the Basic Law, and the NPCSC recorded it on 28 August 2010, so as to increase the number of members of the LegCo from 60 to 70, 35 of whom are elected directly from geographical constituencies and 35 indirectly from functional constituencies.

the lists according to the number of votes they receive, which produces a proportional result at the level of the constituencies which is conducive to a multi-party outcome for the composition of the Legislative Council.[231] This means that the vote is a closed-list proportional election.

6.7.2.2 Corporatism through Functional Constituencies

While the elections from the geographical constituencies are, from the point of view of the right to participation, performed in a regular manner, the election of the other half of the Legislative Council from functional constituencies challenges the ordinary understanding of participation by introducing a corporatist element in the system of decision making in Hong Kong. The system has attracted the criticism that it violates, *inter alia*, Art. 25 of the CCPR. According to the interpretation of the NPCSC, this functional constituency-based form of elections will be discontinued by 2020, as indicated by the Decision of the NPCSC of 29 December 2007 (see Sect. 6.7.1 above). The functional constituencies are constructed so that each of them represents an economic, social or professional group important to the HKSAR. This part of the Legislative Council election is essentially corporatist, representing special interest groups in society. "The electorate of functional constituencies representing economic or social groups is generally made up of corporate members of major organizations representative of the relevant sectors. Each corporate member appoints an authorized representative to cast the vote on its behalf in an election."[232]

According to section 51, in almost all functional constituencies, the first past the post system is used to elect the one member of the functional group to the Legislative Council, but there is a striking variance in the voting methods that adds up to altogether four different voting systems that are used in the election of the Legislative Council.[233] The electoral system(s) used for the functional constituencies seems to be open to at least some measure of control by the central government and to special interests not normally found in elections to legislative bodies. Because each (corporatively organized) functional constituency has its own membership of varying size, it may be problematic to list the overall turnout rates for the functional constituencies, but it is noteworthy that the turnout rate in the functional constituency elections has been higher than in the geographical constituency elections. One possible explanation could be that because one vote of an eligible voter in any functional constituency weighs more and has more effect on the election of one member of the Legislative Council than in a geographical

---

[231] Hong Kong 2007 (2008), p. 9.

[232] Hong Kong 2007 (2008), p. 10. See also sections 25–26 of the Legislative Council Ordinance.

[233] In four small special functional constituencies, a preferential elimination system of voting is used as specified in section 50 of the Legislative Council Ordinance, while the Labour functional constituency actually uses the block vote method, because it elects three members to the Legislative Council by following in principle the first past the post method.

constituency, the functional constituency election may be perceived as more meaningful and attractive for those who are eligible to vote in the functional constituencies. Voters (natural persons) of functional constituencies also have the right to vote in the geographical constituencies. This means that such persons actually cast two votes in the election of the same body, the Legislative Council, in violation of the principle of one person, one vote.[234]

6.7.2.3 The Political Environment in the Legislative Council

The principle expressed in the Joint Declaration that "the Socialist system and Socialist policies shall not be practiced in the HKSAR and that Hong Kong's previous capitalist system and life-style shall remain unchanged for 50 years" has a bearing on the political structures of Hong Kong. While China is a one-party state which does not allow any competing political parties aside from the Communist Party, Hong Kong, even with the current limitations on participation, has a multi-party system where different parties compete for seats in the Legislative Council. The political competition in elections is not only limited to the portion of the Legislative Council elected by geographical constituencies, but it also exists in functional constituency elections since candidates in the functional constituencies are in most cases affiliated with political parties or groupings. Therefore, the party structure of Hong Kong crosses, at least to some extent, over the two constituencies, making it somewhat complicated to visualize the development of the support of the various parties in the Legislative Council over time. In the elections of 2008, around 14 different parties and political groupings could be identified, while three candidates were elected as independents, that is, without a formal affiliation to a political party.[235]

A main division between the parties is actually not based on the distinction between geographical and functional constituencies, but on the attitude towards the central government in Beijing. The result of this divide is two groups of parties, the pan-democrats, who emphasize the broad autonomy of Hong Kong, and the

[234] According to Young and Law (2006), p. 103, in 2004, "only 5.76% of all registered GC electors had an additional right to vote in the FC election. There were over 3 million GC registered electors who were not entitled to vote as an FC elector". In addition, the "system of FCs breaches the 'one person, one vote' principle since individual FC electors are entitled to vote twice in the LegCo election, while GC electors ineligible to vote in an FC are entitled to vote only once".

[235] In the elections of 2004 to the Legislative Council, out of the 30 mandates contested in the direct election in geographical constituencies, *inter alia*, the Democratic Party got 7 mandates, the Democratic Alliance for Betterment of Hong Kong 8 mandates, the Liberal Party 2 mandates, the Article 45 Concern Group 3 mandates, and pro-Government individuals and others 1 mandate, while the total number of mandates controlled by these in the Legislative Council is 9 for the Democratic Party, 12 for the Democratic Alliance for Betterment of Hong Kong, 10 for the Liberal Party, 4 for the Article 45 Concern Group and 12 for the pro-Government individuals. This means that the functional constituencies have a significant impact on the political landscape of the Legislative Council of Hong Kong.

pro-China camp, who wish to maintain good relations with the central government. The pan-democrats won 19 of their 23 seats in the Legislative Council from the geographical constituencies and only 4 from the functional constituencies, and are represented by such parties as the Democratic Party (7 from geographical constituencies + 1 functional constituency = 8 seats), the Civic Party (4 + 1 = 5), the League of Social Democrats (3 + 0 = 3), Neighbourhood and Workers Service Centre of Senators (1 + 0 = 1), Hong Kong Federation of Trade Unions (1 + 0 = 1), Hong Kong Association for Democracy and People's Livelihood (1 + 1 = 2), the Frontier (1 + 0 = 1), and Civic Act-up (1 + 0 = 1), and then there is also a grouping of Pro-democracy individuals and others (0 + 1 = 1). The pro-China camp has stronger support in the Legislative Council on the basis of its significant support in the functional constituencies, where it received 24 out of its 34 seats. The pro-China camp consists of the Democratic Alliance for the Betterment and Progress of Hong Kong (9 geographical constituency + 4 functional constituency = 13 seats), the Liberal Party (0 + 7 = 7), the Hong Kong Federation of Trade Unions (0 + 1 = 1), the Alliance (Hong Kong) (0 + 3 = 3), and a grouping of Pro-China individuals and others (1 + 9 = 10). As a result, the pro-China camp is currently the stronger of the two groups of parties. The independent members have made an inroad into the Legislative Council by taking two seats from the pan-democrats and one seat from the pro-China camp (2 + 1 = 3).[236] It seems that none of the parties of Hong Kong has any organic relationship to the one party in Mainland China, the Communist Party.

The Basic Law contains several provisions dealing with the internal organization of the Legislative Council, although the Legislative Council may, under Art. 75(2) of the Basic Law, make rules of procedure for itself, provided that they do not contravene the Basic Law. Under Art. 71, the president of the Legislative Council shall be elected by and from among the members of the Legislative Council,[237] and he or she shall be a Chinese citizen of not less than 40 years of age, who is a permanent resident of the Region with no right of abode in any foreign country and has ordinarily resided in Hong Kong for a continuous period of not less than 20 years. This specification concerning the qualifications of the president of the Legislative Council excludes any such member of the Legislative Council from the presidency who might have been elected from among the above-mentioned group of persons that lacks Chinese nationality and has right of abode in a foreign country. The presidency is hence strongly tied to local Hong Kong circumstances.

[236] It has not been possible to obtain similar breakdowns of the election results from earlier elections.

[237] According to Art. 72, the President of the Legislative Council has the following powers and functions: to preside over meetings, to decide on the agenda, giving priority to government bills for inclusion in the agenda, to decide on the time of meetings, to call special sessions during the recess, to call emergency sessions on the request of the Chief Executive, and to exercise other powers and functions as prescribed in the rules of procedure of the Legislative Council.

Article 75 of the Basic Law specifies that a quorum for a meeting of the Legislative Council must not be less than one half of all of its members, which is a relatively high requirement. The voting patterns in the Legislative Council have been influenced by the division of the constituencies into geographical and functional ones. While decisions concerning bills submitted by the Government of Hong Kong are normally made by a simple majority (meaning, in effect, that the pro-Beijing and presumably also pro-Chief Executive members of the current Legislative Council have the ability to determine the outcome of any decision), proposals to amend the Basic Law as well as its Annexes I and II require a two-thirds majority in the Legislative Council. Decisions of the latter kind therefore would need the co-operation of the minority bloc in the Legislative Council.[238] The same co-operation need is true in respect of so-called private members' bills introduced in the Legislative Council, which need to be adopted by a majority of members within both parts of the Legislative Council, that is, by more than half of the members elected from the geographical constituencies and by more than half of the members elected from the functional constituencies. It can therefore be said that in some respects, the division in geographical and functional constituencies introduces features of bicameralism in the Legislative Council.[239]

Article 73 of the Basic Law lists the powers and functions of the Legislative Council, the most important of which is to enact, amend or repeal laws in accordance with the provisions of the Basic Law and legal procedures. Members of the Legislative Council of the Hong Kong Special Administrative Region may, according to Art. 74 of the Basic Law, introduce bills in accordance with the provisions of the Basic Law and legal procedures. Bills which do not relate to public expenditure or political structure or the operation of the Government may be introduced individually or jointly by members of the Council. In case motions, bills or amendments to government bills are introduced by individual members of the Legislative Council, their passage shall, according to section II of Annex II, require a simple majority vote by each of the two groups of members present: members returned by functional constituencies and those returned by geographical constituencies through direct elections.[240] Hence the distinction between the geographical and functional constituencies has relevance also after the elections, inside the Legislative Council, making it potentially more difficult to undertake certain

---

[238]As stated by Leung Mei-fun (2006), p. 261, "[u]nder normal circumstances, it is nearly impossible to get a two-thirds majority in the LegCo. This is believed to be the rationale of this voting system".

[239]Attempts from the Government of Hong Kong in 2005 to bring about incremental changes to improve the participatory situation were deemed insufficient by the pro-Hong Kong parties, which led to the result that the vote on the political reforms in the Legislative Council did not obtain the prescribed qualified majority because the more "democratically" minded part of the Legislative Council did not vote for the bill. See Chen (2005), p. 537.

[240]See Weiyun (2001), p. 323 f., and Leung Mei-fun (2006), p. 261.

measures.[241] In addition, the written consent of the Chief Executive shall be required before bills relating to government policies are introduced.[242]

Taken together, this means that the independent powers of the Legislative Council and its members are to a great extent circumscribed in a manner which does not correspond to the regular position of members of legislative bodies. The power to define the direction of the policies of Hong Kong is, as a consequence, seriously tipped in favor of the Chief Executive (CE), who is not only an official of the HKSAR but also a representative of the central government in Hong Kong. Because a bill passed by the Legislative Council may, according to Art. 76, take effect only after it has been signed and promulgated by the CE, it is possible to say that the CE is certainly in a very strong position in relation to the Legislative Council.

If the Chief Executive of the HKSAR considers that a bill passed by the Legislative Council is not compatible with the overall interests of the Region, he or she may, according to Art. 49, return it to the Legislative Council within 3 months for reconsideration. If the Legislative Council passes the original bill again by not less than a two-thirds majority of all the members, the CE must sign and promulgate it within 1 month. Alternatively, he or she may, after consultations, dissolve the Legislative Council. Dissolution also may occur, according to Art. 50, if the Legislative Council refuses to pass a budget or any other important bill introduced by the Government, and if consensus still cannot be reached after consultations. The CE must consult the Executive Council before dissolving the Legislative Council, but the use of the power of dissolution is circumscribed by the provision that the CE may dissolve the Legislative Council only once in each term of his or her office.[243] However, such a dissolution has not taken place at least up until 2010.

Other powers and functions of the Legislative Council are, *inter alia*, to examine and approve budgets introduced by the Government, to approve taxation and public expenditure, to debate any issue concerning the public interest, and to endorse the appointment and removal of the judges of the CFA and the Chief Judge of the High Court. The Legislative Council also receives and handles complaints from Hong

[241]As pointed out by Leung Mei-fun (2006), p. 261, "[t]his separate voting system has been severely criticised ever since it was designed. It is quite obvious that the system was designed to safeguard the passage of government bills. With such restrictions, after the handover, a very limited number of private bills would be able to win enough support in the LegCo. One can see that if a private bill can win over the LegCo under such a system, the bill must be a very popular bill with very few members objecting to it. Based on that design, it would be very difficult for a government bill, such as the budget or other important bills, to fail in the LegCo; at the same time, it would be very easy to block the passage of an anti-government bill." See also Chan (2010), p. 134.

[242]See Davis (2007), p. 85, who also points out that amendments to government bills and motions or bills introduced by individual members of the Legislative Council require majority approval by each of the two different groups of legislators, that is the thirty members from functional constituencies and the thirty members from the geographical constituencies. This makes the law-making process even more difficult and moves the Legislative Council even further away from regular law-making bodies.

[243]See Leung Mei-fun (2006), p. 258 f., who discusses this from the point of view of checks and balances.

Kong residents. In addition, the Legislative Council has powers and functions in relation to the executive power of Hong Kong, that is, in the horizontal dimension, instituting a certain measure of checks and balances (see below, Chap. 7).

The functions of the Legislative Council are supported by the possibility to summon, as required when exercising the above-mentioned powers and functions, persons concerned to testify or give evidence. Such testimonies would be important especially in the context of trying to resolve complaints from residents and examining the actions of the CE and other representatives of the executive power. Its functions are also supported by the fact that under Art. 77, the members of the Legislative Council shall be immune from legal action in respect of their statements at meetings of the Council, and according to Art. 78, they shall not be subjected to arrest when attending or on their way to a meeting of the Council. In some situations specified in Art. 79, it is, however, possible for the President of the Legislative Council to declare that a member of the Council is no longer qualified for the office.[244]

6.7.3 *Indirect Election of the Chief Executive*

As explained above, half of the Legislative Council is not elected on the basis of universal suffrage. Against that background, it is not surprising that the election of the Chief Executive (CE) is indirect at the moment, and might remain so in view of the interests of the central government to control the actions of the very powerful institution in the governmental structure of Hong Kong, although the ultimate aim is direct election. As provided for in Art. 45 of the Basic Law and its Annex I on the selection of the Chief Executive, the person is currently selected by an election committee, which is composed of 800 members drawn from four sectors[245] (which are in turn composed

[244]These circumstances are the loss of the ability to discharge his or her duties as a result of serious illness or other reasons, absence with no valid reason from meetings for three consecutive months without the consent of the President of the Legislative Council, loss or renouncement of his or her status as a permanent resident of the Region, accepting a government appointment and becoming a public servant, becoming bankrupt or failing to comply with a court order to repay debts, conviction and sentencing to imprisonment for 1 month or more for a criminal offence committed within or outside the Region and being relieved of his or her duties by a motion passed by two-thirds of the members of the Legislative Council present, and being censured for misbehaviour or breach of oath by a vote of two-thirds of the members of the Legislative Council present.

[245]The four different sectors have each 200 members in the election committee, the sectors begin as follows: industrial, commercial and financial sectors, the professions, labour, social services, religious and other sectors, and members of the Legislative Council, representatives of district-based organizations, Hong Kong deputies to the National People's Congress, and representatives of Hong Kong members of the National Committee of the Chinese People's Political Consultative Conference. See section 8 of the Chief Executive Election Ordinance, L.N. 187 of 2001 of 21 September 2001, which prescribes the specific election method of the CE. See Hong Kong 2007 (2008), p. 10, which describes the election in the following way: Altogether 664 members of 35 subsectors are returned through elections in the subsectors, while 96 members in the election committee are *ex officio* members who are Hong Kong deputies to the National People's Congress (NPC) and members of the Legislative Council under the NPC subsector and the Legislative

of altogether 38 subsectors, as provided for by law). Article 45(1) actually refers to consultations as an alternative to election. As long as the CE is not directly elected by the population of Hong Kong, the method of selection of the CE is probably closer to a consultation than a proper election, although the Election Committee does perform an election amongst its members. The term of office of the Election Committee is 5 years, which means that it is a permanent body that may be called to perform its selective function even before the 5-year term of office of the CE has ended. Candidates for the office of CE may be nominated jointly by not less than 100 members of the Election Committee (from 2012, 150 members), and each member may participate in the nomination of only one candidate. On the basis of the list of nominees, the Election Committee elects the CE designate by secret ballot on a one-person-one-vote basis. A candidate must, according to section 27 of the Chief Executive Election Ordinance, secure a majority of those voting in order to be elected. Although members of the Election Committee represent different sectors, they vote in their individual capacities.

According to Art. 44 of the Basic Law and section 13 of the Chief Executive Election Ordinance, the CE must be a permanent resident of the HKSAR, a Chinese citizen, have no right of abode in any foreign country, be at least 40 years of age and have ordinarily resided in Hong Kong for a continuous period of not less than 20 years. He or she shall also be a person of integrity, dedicated to his or her duties. After the election, the person designated as the next CE shall declare that he or she is not and will not become member of any political party, and upon assuming office, he or she shall declare his or her assets to the Chief Justice of the CFA of the Hong Kong Special Administrative Region. According to Art. 46 of the Basic Law, he or she can be re-elected only once for a consecutive period. The mid-term resignation of one CE prompted a consideration of whether the new office holder should be selected for the remainder of the original period, which in the actual case was 2 years, or if the new office holder should have a full 5-year term of office. The matter was pursued in court in Hong Kong, but the Hong Kong Government seems to have wanted to expedite the decision, so it asked the Central People's Government to request an interpretation from the NPCSC. In its third interpretation, issued on 27 April 2005, the NPCSC came to the conclusion that the vacancy would be filled for the remainder of the original period.[246]

Council subsector. Finally, 40 members of the election committee are nominated within the religious subsector by six designated bodies. For the elections of 2012, the NPCSC amended Annex I to the Basic Law on 28 August 2010 so as to increase the number of members of the election committee from 800 to 1200, divided into four sectors, each with 300 members. At the same time, the nominations requirement was raised to 150 members.

[246]See *Interpretation of 27 April 2005* of the NPCSC of Paragraph 2, Article 53 of the Basic Law of the Hong Kong Special Administrative Region of the People's Republic of China by the Standing Committee of the National People's Congress. For a comment, see Feng and Lo (2007), pp. 143–153. The method of bringing about this Interpretation is calling into question the exercise of independent judicial powers within the area of constitutional review in the HKSAR, as was the *Interpretation of 26 June 1999*. See Marsden (2006), pp. 117–141. The vacancy in the office of the CE resulted apparently from the fact that the first CE, Mr. Tung Chee Hwa, turned into a political liability for Beijing and was – most likely – induced to file for a voluntary resignation in

The method for selecting the CE is framed in a similarly "dynamic" way to the election of the Legislative Council. The method shall, under Art. 45 of the Basic Law, be specified in the light of the actual situation in the HKSAR and in accordance with the principle of gradual and orderly progress.[247] The ultimate aim is the selection of the CE by universal suffrage upon nomination by a broadly representative nominating committee in accordance with democratic procedures. Thus although the election of the CE is to be transferred to a popular vote, the nomination procedure will not be open but in the hands of a nominating committee, which makes the composition of the committee a major issue. This is problematic given the strong position of the CE: Beijing probably needs to ensure that the CE elected in Hong Kong is acceptable in Beijing, too, and not only amongst the voters of Hong Kong. Therefore, a nomination committee may have the effect of restricting the candidates to those which are to the liking of the central government of China. Article 25(b) of the CCPR, however, could provide the basis for opening up a general nomination procedure.

However, the election currently carried out by the 800-member election committee (from 2012, 1200 members) is not final, but according to the Basic Law, the nominee elected in this manner by the election committee must be appointed to the position by the central government of China, that is, the State Council of the PRC. This appointment makes the election of the Chief Executive even more problematic in comparison with a direct election and furnishes the CE with a "gubernatorial" image that links him or her closely to the central government of China. However, the election of the Chief Executive is scheduled to become direct on the basis of universal suffrage by 2017. At least for the time being, it cannot be said that there exists any constitutional convention indicating that the State Council should always follow the election result of the election committee.[248] Therefore, a more direct

the beginning of 2005. He was replaced on the post by Mr. Donald Tsang, Former Chief Secretary for Administration, first as the Acting CE and subsequently as the one with 2-year tenure. In 2008, he was selected and appointed for his second term for a full 5-year period.

[247]In the *Interpretation of 6 April 2004* of the NPCSC of Art. 7 of Annex I and Art. III of Annex II to the Basic Law, the NPCSC concluded that motions to the effect of amending the method of selection of the CE may be made from the year 2007 on, provided that there is a need to amend the selection, which means that the method may be amended or remain un-amended. The CE shall, according to the Interpretation, make a report to the NPCSC as regards whether there is a need to make an amendment. Thereafter, the NPCSC makes a determination on the need on the basis of articles 45 and 68 of the Basic Law, in the light of the actual situation in the HKSAR and in accordance with the principle of gradual and orderly process. An amendment bill is introduced by the Government of HKSAR into the Legislative Council, in which the matter requires the supports of two-thirds of all the members of the Legislative Council, after which the decision is submitted to the NPCSC for approval or recording. On the basis of section 4 of the *Interpretation of 6 April 2004*, it seems as if the amendments to the voting procedures of the Legislative Council were conditional to first amending the selection procedure of the CE. For the text of the *Interpretation of 6 April 2006*, see Leung Mei-fun (2006), pp. 459–461, and for an analysis, see Leung Mei-fun (2006), pp. 250 ff., and Davis (2007), pp. 78–84. For the subsequent developments, see Chen (2008a), *passim*.

[248]See Weiyun (2001), pp. 145, 275 f., who holds that the appointment decision concerning the Chief Executive and the principal officials by the central authorities is not a mere formality without

election of the CE in Hong Kong from 2017 onward will not completely remedy the situation with respect to the realization of the right to participation: the CE is still, formally speaking, appointed by a state organ, the legitimacy of which is highly questionable, and in making the appointment decision, it is fully possible that the State Council could refuse to appoint a Chief Executive that the voters of Hong Kong have elected, creating a problem in the face of Art. 25 of the CCPR.[249]

The Basic Law or its Annex I do not make any provision for the removal of the Chief Executive, except that in the case of impeachment decided by the Legislative Council, the final decision shall be made by the Central People's Government in Beijing. Article 4 of the Chief Executive Ordinance specifies that one way in which a vacancy in the high office can be created is by removal of the office holder by the Central People's Government. If the office of the Chief Executive becomes vacant for any reason, the election committee shall elect a new office-holder for the remainder of the period, and that remainder counts as one term of office towards the limit of two terms of office for any person holding the office of the Chief Executive, as provided in section 3 of the Chief Executive Election Ordinance.

6.7.4 Elections in Local Government and within the Indigenous Community

The 18 district councils, that is, advisory local government units, are organized under the District Councils Ordinance[250] and composed of elected members and members appointed by the Chief Executive as well as some *ex officio* members. In the 18 district councils, there are currently altogether 405 elected members and 102 appointed members as well as 27 *ex officio* members (chairmen of rural committees in the New Territories). As prescribed by section 41 of the District Councils Ordinance, the elected members are elected by way of a simple majority vote for a 4 year period, which means that the territory of the HKSAR was divided into 405 constituencies.[251] The function of the appointed members, such as lawyers, is to ensure certain expertise within the district councils. In the third district council election (for the term 2008–2012), the turnout was 38.83%.[252] The fact that one-fifth of the district council members are not directly elected can be said to constitute a deviation from general patterns of participation at the level of local government.

---

practical significance. Instead, the power of appointment has practical significance, because they are acts of state and legally binding. Hence the selection of the Chief Executive by the Election Committee (or, in the future, election by the voters of Hong Kong) does not have to lead to an appointment decision by the Central People's Government. Concerning the possibility of existence of constitutional conventions of British provenance in the HKSAR, see Leung Mei-fun (2006), p. 9.

[249] According to Weiyun (2001), p. 275, the appointment decision is an expression of national sovereignty.

[250] Gazette Nr L.N. 77 of 1999, 19 March 1999.

[251] See Hong Kong 2008 (2009), p. 12.

[252] Hong Kong 2007 (2008), p. 11 f.

While the main function of the district councils has been to advise the Government on matters affecting the well-being of the people living and working in the districts as well as on the provision and use of public facilities and services within the districts and to serve as organs of consultation when the Government wishes to discuss an issue, the functions of the district councils have recently been enhanced somewhat. They have been charged with minor environmental improvement and community involvement projects and funds for these activities have been made available.[253]

There is a third layer of elected persons at the village level, where a Village Representative and, if the village is an indigenous village, an Indigenous Inhabitant Representative are elected for 4 years under the Village Representative Election Ordinance,[254] following the first past the post system of election. Such representatives are, under the ordinance, also members of Rural Committees.

In addition, there is the special formation of the Heung Yee Kuk, a statutory advisory body, which may be understood as a platform for the participation of the indigenous population of the New Territories. According to section 9 of the Heung Yee Kuk Ordinance,[255] it has the function to promote and develop mutual co-operation and understanding among the people of the New Territories, to promote and develop co-operation and understanding between the Government of Hong Kong and the people of the New Territories, to advise the Government of Hong Kong on social and economic developments in the interests of the welfare and prosperity of the people of the New Territories, to encourage the observance of all such customs and traditional usages of the people of the New Territories as are conducive to their welfare and to the preservation of public morality, and to exercise such functions as they may be invited to from time to time by the Chief Executive. The Councilors of the indigenous organization often run in uncontested elections and are even co-opted in situations provided by law. As explained above, the Heung Yee Kuk is itself one of the functional constituencies which elects a member to the Legislative Council. In that respect, the one functional constituency seat could be regarded a special mandate or reserved seat for the indigenous population.

In Hong Kong, no referendums have ever been organized, but proposals in that direction have been made by some political groups, although the legal order does not contain provisions concerning referendums of any kind.[256] However, there are many

---

[253]See Hong Kong 2008 (2009), p. 8 f., at http://www.yearbook.gov.hk/2008/en/pdf/E01.pdf (accessed 18 August 2009).

[254]Gazette Nr 2 of 2003, 14 February 2003.

[255]Gazette version date 30 June 1997.

[256]A proposal to organise a consultative referendum on the political reforms, that is, on the issue of the universal suffrage was presented in the Legislative Council in October 2004, when it had become clear on the basis of the Interpretation of 6 April and the subsequent Decision by the NPCSC that the Government of the HKSAR had probably misrepresented the wish of the population of Hong Kong to change the electoral system in its communications to the NPCSC. The proposal was effectively killed, not only in the Legislative Council, but also by the Chief Executive and through the surprisingly strong involvement of the central government in Beijing. For an analysis of the events, see Ghai (2004), pp. 433–449.

forms of public consultation used in Hong Kong, such as public hearings and publication of draft legislation and, in particular, consultation papers for general discussion.

6.7.5 Selection of Delegates to the NPC and to the NPCSC

Under the Basic Law, the HKSAR is also entitled to send delegates to the National People's Congress. The point of departure for participation of the population of Hong Kong in the decision-making of the entire country is article 21(1) of the Basic Law, according to which Chinese citizens who are residents of the HKSAR shall be entitled to participate in the management of state affairs according to law. Evidently, the law referred to here is the national law, not legislation passed by the HKSAR. The method of participation is, however, not by direct election, but by selection, as indicated by Art. 21(2) of the Basic Law: In accordance with the assigned number of seats and the selection method specified by the National People's Congress,[257] the Chinese citizens among the residents of the Hong Kong Special Administrative Region shall locally elect deputies of the Region to the National People's Congress to participate in the work of the highest organ of state power. However, it has been pointed out that the "people's congress system does not form part of the political system of Hong Kong, since the 'one country, two systems' doctrine is based on the isolation of the Hong Kong system from the socialist system practiced in the Mainland. Furthermore, Hong Kong deputies are a special political group created and imposed by the NPC on Hong Kong without substantive linkage to Hong Kong's political structure and community at large".[258]

While the elections of the Legislative Council and the CE are scheduled to become direct at some future point, there is no such plan for national elections or specifically for the deputies that Hong Kong sends to the NPC.[259] Instead, the election is performed by an Election Council with a relatively limited membership,[260] which

[257]For the specification, see Measures for Election of Deputies of the Hong Kong Special Administrative Region of the People's Republic of China to the Ninth National People's Congress, which, according to Art. 1 of the Measures, was enacted in accordance with the Chinese Constitution, the Basic Law, the provisions of the third paragraph of Art. 15 of the Electoral Law of the National People's Congress and Local People's Congresses of the People's Republic of China and in view of the actual conditions of the HKSAR. For the text, see Leung Mei-fun (2006), pp. 465–467. According to Art. 2 of the Measures for Election of Deputies, the election shall be carried out under the direction of the NPCSC.

[258]Hualing and Choy (2007), p. 202.

[259]But see Leung Mei-fun (2006), p. 85, who thinks that such election is foreseeable in the near future.

[260]According to Art. 5 of the Measures for Election of Deputies, the "Election Council shall be composed of Chinese citizens from among the members of the Selection Committee for the First Government of the Hong Kong Special Administrative Region, as prescribed by the Decision of the National People's Congress on the Method for the Formation of the First Government and the

does not genuinely represent the electorate of Hong Kong and which gives the upper hand in the election of NPC delegates to the electors of the CE and through them, to the pro-Beijing faction in Hong Kong.[261] Groups of ten or more members of the Election Council may jointly nominate members, which means that nominations are not open amongst the Chinese residents of Hong Kong, but confined to a particular category of persons,[262] although there is no requirement that the members be members of the Communist Party. Because the membership of the Election Council also contains members of the Legislative Council of the HKSAR, therefore even members of Hong Kong political parties are nominated and consequently selected, albeit only persons who are pro-Beijing. The competitive nature of the elections is ensured by the provision in Art. 8 of the Measures for Election of Deputies according to which the number of candidates shall be 20% more than the number to be elected. The method of election seems, on the basis of articles 8 and 10, to be based on the plurality of the vote if the nominees exceed the number to be elected by 20–50%, and it seems that a run-off voting system requiring a simple majority was used in the case of a greater number of nominees.[263] At any rate, the voting in the Election Council is secret, and after the results of the election have been announced by the presidium of the Election Council

First Legislative Council of the Hong Kong Special Administrative Region, the members of the Eighth National Committee of the Chinese People's Political Consultative Conference from among residents of the Hong Kong Special Administrative Region who are not members of the Selection Committee and the members of the Provisional Legislative Council of the Hong Kong Special Administrative Region who are Chinese citizens. However, those who have expressed their unwillingness to become members of the Election Council shall be excepted." In spite of the existence of the Election Council, Leung Mei-fun (2006), p. 85, concludes that the deputies of the NPC from the HKSAR are appointed by the central government.

[261]See Hualing et al. (2007), p. 9. According to Hualing and Choy (2007), p. 204, only 435 and 1,029 persons were eligible to vote in the Ninth (1998–2003) and Tenth Hong Kong NCP elections.

[262]For the procedure, see Choy and Hualing (2007), p. 584 ff.

[263]According to Choy and Hualing (2007), p. 585 f., "[e]ach voter may vote for any number of deputies from one to 36 in the preliminary vote. Ranking the candidates according to the number of votes received in the preliminary vote, the candidates with the greatest number of votes will fill the quota of formal candidates until the maximum number of candidates allowed is met." Thereafter, "unlike in the preliminary vote, each voter is required to vote for all the 36 seats available in the final vote", and "[a]ny ballot in which the number of candidates selected is more than or less than the number of seats available will be invalid". The seat is allocated to a candidate "only if he or she got the highest number of votes *and* at the same time obtained a simple majority vote", but if the "number of candidates receiving simple majority votes is greater than the number of seats available, seats would be filled in order of the candidates' vote totals. If there is more than one candidate fulfilling the requirements to fill the last seat (...), another vote will be held for those candidates and the candidate that receives the greatest number of votes will fill the last seat". "[I]f the number of candidates receiving simple majority votes is less than the number of seats available, another vote will be conducted to select candidates to fill the remaining seats." However, although internal campaigning may be fierce, public campaigning in the society is not possible, and vote trading seems to be rampant. See Choy and Hualing (2007), pp. 594–597, and p. 600, where they conclude that the "result of an election is therefore pre-determined not by Beijing manipulating the electoral process, but by the packing of the Electoral Conference with Beijing's supporters".

and transmitted to the Credentials Committee of the NPCSC, the NPCSC shall affirm the qualification of the deputies and publish the name list of the deputies.

The number of deputies from Hong Kong in the NPC is 36,[264] which is more than Hong Kong's population – as a percentage of the Chinese population – would warrant (29), and thus there is an over-representation of Hong Kong in the NPC by seven deputies. It is legally possible for a person to be simultaneously a member of the Legislative Council of Hong Kong and the NPC, and in fact a number of Hong Kong delegates of the NPC have been members of the Legislative Council at the same time.[265] In their capacity as delegates of the NPC, the Hong Kong delegates participate in the functions of the NPC at the national level in the same way as other delegates. They also have a particular function since they help residents of Hong Kong who may have experienced problems on the mainland. Under the instructions they have received from the NPC, they are, in fact, specifically forbidden to carry out inspections and inquiries into local matters in their area, that is, in Hong Kong, in the same manner as the Mainland Chinese delegates are empowered to do in their respective areas. Instead, the delegates from Hong Kong are from time to time invited to participate in inspections and inquiries in Mainland China, that is, outside their own area.[266]

It is also important to recognize that Hong Kong has one member in the NPCSC,[267] which is a powerful body in the constitutional structure of Hong Kong and even more so in the state structure of China. Hong Kong is therefore formally taken well into account in the context of Chinese governance. At the same time, however, China remains a one-party state in which the policies of the Communist party are implemented by the legislative bodies at the central level. Previously, criticism was rare in the NPC, but the delegates have become more vocal, and it seems that the delegates from Hong Kong are, generally speaking, relatively active in discussing policy issues in the NPC.[268]

---

[264]Article 3 of the Measures for Election of Deputies. See Leung Mei-fun (2006), p. 465.

[265]As pointed out in Hualing and Choy (2007), p. 221, "many of the deputies have been members of both the NPC and Legislative Council, which has acted assertively to ensure the accountability of the Hong Kong government. The two positions may be difficult to distinguish, as some have predicted, and the role a deputy has in Hong Kong will affect his or her behaviour in the NPC activities. One cannot quarantine one's pattern of political behaviour".

[266]See Hualing and Choy (2007), p. 207 ff.

[267]The NPCSC Member from Hong Kong is Mrs. Fan. The other special autonomous region, Macau, also has a member in the NPCSC.

[268]However, as pointed out by Hualing and Choy (2007), p. 205, the Hong Kong delegation to the NPC is led by officials of the Liaison Office of the CPG in the HKSAR and the delegation contains no representatives of democrats or even moderate professionals, although there is no explicit exclusion of them. See also Choy and Hualing (2007), p. 586 f., who make the point that the Liaison Office controls the Hong Kong delegation to the NPC. Representatives of the Liaison Office are permitted to participate in the elections of the delegation to the NPC and they have been very successful, but they are of course not part of the actual inhabitants of Hong Kong and therefore lack the genuine capacity to represent Hong Kong. Also, in such cases, there may exist conflict of interest issues.

The focus on the autonomy of the HKSAR as a part of Mainland China may hide the fact that there are different layers of participatory structures in Hong Kong. Apart from a proportionately strong participation in national affairs, the limited nature of Legislative Council elections and participation within the Legislative Council is supplemented by the participatory structures at the district and village level. As our review has shown, these different dimensions of participation are often formally or informally interconnected, which may be a problem in itself. Members of the Legislative Council may at the same time be delegates to the NPC, and the existence of functional constituencies and appointed memberships in various bodies of public authority, including the appointment of the Chief Executive by the Central People's Government, present problems from the point of view of participation, because they limit the scope of such participation which should take place through elections by universal vote.

6.8 Reflections

It seems very clear on the basis of our study that participation is a core issue in relation to any sub-state entity. Participation is often a central point in agreements or other settlements that deal with the position of a sub-state entity, such as in relation to the Åland Islands, Aceh and Zanzibar, but participation is in no way absent from any of the other sub-state arrangements. The participatory frame of a sub-state arrangement is important in particular in relation to the exercise of those law-making powers that have been accorded to the sub-state entity: the same requirements concerning participation apply at the sub-state level as at the national level when law-making powers are exercised. In institutional terms, unicameralism seems to be the main form of organizing the sub-state legislature, with only Puerto Rico following the principle of bicameralism, which, however, in practice may move towards unicameralism because the same method of election is applied for both chambers. A hint of bicameralism is produced in Hong Kong by the electoral system that divides the legislature into two equally large parts on the basis of the constituencies from which the members have been elected.

As can be expected, election is the main form of participation, but it is from time to time complemented by referendums or by other forms of participation, such as consultations. All sub-state entities except Hong Kong create participatory mechanisms that are in compliance with international norms concerning the right to participation. However, many characteristic differences prevail, and it is not an exaggeration to say that although the different forms of participation at the national level may be relatively varied, the sub-state entities can still add to this variation. In particular, the introduction of sub-state entities to a state structure often means that a special layer of government and public affairs is created where the needs of participation have to be met, often perhaps in ways that differ from the ordinary. For the individual living in a sub-state entity, this normally means that there may be additional elections and other forms of participation that are added on to the ordinary forms of participation.

The right to vote is a natural starting point for the right to participation, and at the outset, it does not seem as if there would be significant differences between the right to vote and the right to stand as a candidate that would create these two election elements in very different ways. The right to stand for election seems normally to follow from the right to vote, although some additional qualifications, such as a higher age requirement, may be imposed. Therefore, the right to vote and the determination of the constituency or the various constituencies on the basis of the right to vote is a major issue in the delineation of the right to participation in the sub-state entities. Citizenship is normally one of the requirements, but as concerns elections in Scotland, citizenship is actually not required, and under the Basic Law, non-Chinese residents could be elected in Hong Kong, but the local law does not allow for such an enlargement of the electorate.

The creation of a sub-state entity may be combined with a wish to guarantee to the original population of the jurisdiction a protected position in the exercise of the law-making powers accorded to the entity by way of establishing a particular constituency consisting of the "original" inhabitants of the area. This was the case with the Åland Islands already back in 1921, and this is also the situation some 70 years later with Hong Kong. Also in Zanzibar, the right to vote in Zanzibari elections is restricted to a particular group. In all these cases, the right to vote is connected to the possession of a particular residency or citizenship of the area. At least in the case of the Åland Islands, it is possible to refer to justifiable reasons to do so, and in the other cases, it seems understandable that a particular circumscription of the electorate has been established. Whether all these cases would stand a critical examination can be doubted, although there exists some praxis from human rights treaty bodies that indicates a certain margin of appreciation for the protection of populations that are regarded as indigenous and that are in the process of exercising the right to self-determination. Therefore, a less protective course of action, as in Scotland and Aceh and also Puerto Rico, is probably to be recommended (although in Puerto Rico, there have been attempts to connect the right to vote as an exclusive right to the possession of a separate citizenship of Puerto Rico). In Puerto Rico, however, the electorate could be defined in a more limited way for the specific purpose of exercising the self-determination that Puerto Rico has. It may be mentioned as a special feature in this context that the indigenous population in Hong Kong has one guaranteed seat in the Legislative Council through one of the functional constituencies.

As concerns the dissolution of the representative organ at the sub-state level, it seems that the national government, that is, the national executive, has less of a role in the context than one perhaps could expect. In Zanzibar, Hong Kong, Puerto Rico, Scotland and Aceh, it seems clear on the basis of the norms that it is not possible for the national government to cause the dissolution of the sub-state parliament or legislative assembly. Such a possibility is included in the case of the Åland Islands, but it has never been used and the power of the President of Finland in that respect is delineated so that it is dependent on action by the Speaker of the Legislative

Assembly and should only be exercised when there is an internal parliamentary reason in the Åland Islands for a dissolution in the form of a political crisis. This means that the national governments cannot effectuate a dissolution of the sub-state assembly for reasons that are extraneous to the sub-state entity. This means also that the sub-state autonomies reviewed here seem to be organized in harmony with the *Memel* case, where it was not correct by the national government to dismiss the representative assembly of the Memel Territory. Our findings thus support the conclusion that the national executive cannot meddle with the representative organ elected by the voters of the sub-state entity. Instead, the dissolution of the highest decision-making body in a sub-state entity is an internal matter for these entities.

While the main focus of the right to participation is on the election of the main decision-making body in the sub-state entity, such as a Legislative Assembly, Legislative Council or Parliament, sub-state entities normally also contain other layers of government that operate on the basis of participation. In relation to the Åland Islands, municipalities of the Åland Islands were even one part of the 1921 Åland Islands Settlement in terms of the restriction of the right to vote to the local inhabitants. The position of local government under the sub-state level is not as prominent in any of the other cases, but it is nonetheless possible to say that to a greater or a lesser extent, local government is a sub-state issue, too. However, in respect of Scotland, franchise at the local government level is a specific national competence (in fact, with respect to EU citizens, the right to vote in the local and the European Parliament elections is an EU competence), although the actual holding of local government elections is a Scottish competence. In Aceh, the sub-state jurisdiction is internally multi-layered and presupposes elected decision-making bodies at different levels, while in Hong Kong and perhaps Zanzibar, local government seems least developed of all the entities reviewed here. However, generally speaking, it seems that the sub-state entity itself is the focal point of political participation, perhaps because of the fact that it is the highest decision-making body for a relatively small jurisdiction, while the importance of local government may become proportionally speaking smaller than in other parts of the state, which perhaps do not have the sub-state level established in the same manner. Nordic co-operation and, later on, membership in the European Union has compelled the Åland Islands to open up its right to vote in municipal elections from the regional citizens to Nordic citizens resident in a municipality of the Åland Islands and further on to citizens of the European Union and to citizens of other countries. The example of the Åland Islands shows that the fundamental elements of the autonomy arrangement, first established in a fundamental document of particular solemnity, may actually undergo changes due to developments in the political and legal environment surrounding the autonomy arrangement.

In addition to elections in the sub-state entity itself, the inhabitants normally also have the right to participate in elections at the national level. However, there are two exceptions, namely Hong Kong and Puerto Rico. Because in China, no elections are held at the national level, the representatives of Hong Kong to the NPC are selected in an indirect manner. Because Puerto Rico is not a part of the federation, the Resident Commissioner elected to the House of Representatives of the US Congress does not fulfill the normal purpose of participation in law-making, but appears only in an "advisory" capacity. In the case of Aceh and Scotland, the constituency is the same as in elections to the representative body of the sub-state entity. However, due to the franchise requirements in the Åland Islands and Zanzibar, the constituencies for national elections are larger than for sub-state elections. The discrepancy, which is around 5.5% in the Åland Islands and much higher in Zanzibar, potentially somewhere around 25–50%, is a source of concern, obviously mainly in relation to Zanzibar.

The political organization in sub-state entities through parties displays greater variation than one would expect. In some sub-state entities, the political formations are national, in some they are both national and home-grown, and in others entirely home-grown in a manner that does not display much affinity to the national party-systems. As concerns legislative competence within the area of political parties, the national parliaments seem to have that competence in the cases of the Åland Islands, Scotland, Zanzibar, and Aceh, while in Hong Kong and Puerto Rico, the party legislation has emerged at the sub-state level. The importance of the issue is underlined by the Aceh peace process, where the possibility to create regional political parties was one of the core issues. The matter was dealt with so that national law established a rule according to which regional parties are possible in Aceh, although elsewhere in Indonesia, only national parties are allowed. Although the Åland Islands cannot legislate on political parties in the jurisdiction, the political system there is operated on the basis of political organizations constituted as regular associations and given under Ålandic law the right to submit lists of candidates. Therefore, a political infrastructure of *de facto* political parties has emerged. Of course, it has also to be recognized that due to demographics, the numbers of potential supporters of parties in autonomous territories are often so small that they would not be able to meet national criteria, for instance, concerning the number of supporters.

Generally speaking, the political parties or organizations in the sub-state entities show a greater or a smaller affinity to the national party structures. For obvious reasons, the smallest affinity exists in Hong Kong, where the multi-party setting is not in any way related to the one-party structure of the national government. The organizational structure of the Åland Islands in terms of party politics is also surprisingly remote from the national level and certainly very indigenous, which is the situation in Puerto Rico, too. The political parties active in Scotland, Zanzibar and Aceh are closer to the national political arena, but probably for different reasons. In Scotland, the pre-devolution political landscape of the UK level was transferred to the new political setting created around the Scottish Parliament, while in Zanzibar, the past era of one-party rule, the incorporation of both of the main parties in Zanzibar in the national parliament, and the requirement that political parties are established throughout the national territory have resulted in a situation where the two parties are involved in both national and sub-state politics. In Aceh, only two regional political parties have so far been able to break the dominance of the national parties, one of which can be regarded as the heir of the former rebel movement. Hence although it could be expected that the party structures and – as a consequence – the political systems of the sub-state entities are home-grown, the reality may be quite different: many of the sub-state entities are relatively integrated with politics at the national level, and this may even be the aim of politics at the national level. In spite of the fact of how much or little the politics of the sub-state entities are connected with the national level, each of the entities reviewed here appear as "microcosms" of political participation and political life with their own particular dynamics. The powers exercised by the decision-making bodies at the sub-state level are significant for the populations of those entities and therefore, the political focus created by the arrangement at the sub-state level means that this level competes with the national level for the population's political attention.

The electoral systems used in the autonomies vary from proportional election to the first-past-the-post method of election and from there further on to the use of functional constituencies in Hong Kong for the purposes of electing half of the Legislative Council. Proportional election, also followed in our historical starting point, the Memel Territory, is used in the Åland Islands and Aceh, while a system mixing proportional and first-post-the-past election is used in Scotland and Puerto Rico. Zanzibar is the only sub-state entity that uses the first-past-the-post election in its pure form. Together with Puerto Rico, Zanzibar also seems to be the only entity to have a portion of members appointed, which is a doubtful arrangement from the point of view of participation in decision-making. In Puerto Rico, the potentially justifiable aim of the appointment of members to the law-making body is to maintain at least some opposition in situations where the winning party has swept almost all places in the FPTP election, while in Zanzibar, both the majority and the minority is enhanced by appointment of non-elected persons. Hong Kong is a particular entity because of its combination of constituencies of direct election and functional constituencies, and within these constituencies, different electoral systems are practiced. In the constituencies of direct election, the Hare quota is used as the method of allocating seats in the Legislative Council, while the functional constituencies use four different methods. The d'Hondt method is used in the Åland Islands, while the mixed systems of Scotland and Puerto Rico use the Additional Member System in combination with the d'Hondt divisor and the single non-transferable vote, respectively, for the production of the proportional effect in elections.

The choice of the electoral system in the various sub-state entities is dependent on where the legislative competence is placed as concerns election law. It seems clear that in the Åland Islands, Zanzibar and Puerto Rico, the competence in enacting electoral legislation for the sub-state entity and thus also the choice concerning the electoral system is in the hands of the respective law-making bodies of the sub-state entities, while in Aceh, Scotland and Hong Kong, the choices are made at the national level, either through provisions in the autonomy statute or, as in the case of Hong Kong, through political choices at the national level that enables the Legislative Council to carry out amendments in local legislation through an Annex to the Basic Law. In this respect, the first group of sub-state entities, the Åland Islands, Zanzibar and Puerto Rico, are found outside of the frames of the historical starting point of the Memel Territory, whereas the other three are within the frames of this starting point. Obviously, it should be of great importance for sub-state entities to be in possession of the entire electoral system relating to the sub-state entity itself, but this does not always seem to be the case. Where the election administration in charge of the sub-state elections belongs is a corollary issue and the division of the entities is almost the same as in respect of the general competence concerning election law, except that Hong Kong has an election administration of its own, probably for the reason that no national elections are organized in China. Therefore, the independence and impartiality of the election administrations in charge of elections in Scotland and Aceh are of great importance for the two sub-state entities and for the legitimacy of their highest decision-making bodies. There is, however, one particularity in the context of the electoral systems: although the Åland Islands and Zanzibar are in their full freedom to select any electoral system, they have chosen the same system as is in place at the national level. The fact that Zanzibar has not moved away from the FPTP system may be a factor that contributed to the unusual attempt to counter political division between the two parties by means of a government of national unity. On the other hand, in Scotland, another electoral system is practiced for the Scottish Parliament than nationally for the UK Parliament, although it is the latter that has enacted the contents of the autonomy statute. This indicates that the national lawmaker is not in all situations interested in establishing exactly similar institutions at the sub-state level even if the national lawmaker is in control of the contents of the autonomy statute. Puerto Rico is the only entity that has used its competence in the area of election law to deviate at least to some extent from the national electoral system.

In sub-state entities, there may, on top of the election of the highest decision-making body, be elections also to the highest executive office. In the Åland Islands and Scotland, no election of governor or local president takes place because there is no such office. Instead, it is the head of the national executive that assumes a role, albeit only a very formal one, in the legislative and also some political processes within those entities. Elections of Governor or President of the sub-state entity are organized in Aceh, Puerto Rico and Zanzibar. In the context of Aceh, such elections are particular in that the Governor of Aceh is not only an executive representative of Aceh, but also of the national government. The indirect elections of the Chief Executive of Hong Kong is an exception in the context, but as is the case with the elections to the Legislative Council of Hong Kong, the selection of the Chief Executive is also due to develop in the direction of a direct election, probably within the next 10 years. The feature uniting Aceh and Hong Kong is that the national government is vested with the power of final endorsement of the chief executive after the popular election. This is obviously very problematic from the point of view of participation because of the risk the mechanism creates that the will of the people is set aside by means of executive decisions at the national level.

All sub-state entities involved in our inquiry are also represented at the national level in one way or the other, except obviously not institutionally in the manner that constituent states in federations are represented through seats in a federal chamber or a similar structure at the level of the federal government. The normal method of involvement is election by voters in national elections, but the ways in which these elections are organized may differ very much, and in the case of Hong Kong, the mechanism crosses over to the area of selection, perhaps even appointment. Voters in Puerto Rico are not allowed to participate in the regular elections at the national level, but instead, they elect a Resident Commissioner to the House of Representatives of the US Congress. Hence the voters of Puerto Rico can be said to have no real powers of participation in national government. In the other four entities, the populations participate in elections at the national level, sometimes even at a supra-state level, as is the case with the European autonomies. In such situations, the participatory scheme made available to the voters is multi-layered, encompassing local government, the sub-state level, the state level and the supra-state level. The relevance of each layer of decision-maker is perhaps indicated by the turnout in the various elections, and generally speaking, it seems to be so that elections at the sub-state level are the most interesting ones for the voters in the sub-state entities. Elections at this level seem to matter most for the inhabitants of the sub-state entities, although the Scottish voters still seem to view the UK Parliament as the more important political forum for themselves than the Scottish Parliament.

In terms of sub-state representation in the national parliament, sub-state entities are often in a somewhat preferential position. The Finnish citizens resident in the Åland Islands are guaranteed one seat in the Finnish Parliament, although in a manner that does not create any discriminatory treatment of the voters in mainland Finland, while the residents of Hong Kong have an over-representation in the NPC of China. Of all sub-state entities reviewed here, Zanzibar has the strongest position at the national level with its massive over-representation in the Union Parliament. It seems, however, as if that over-representation has not helped much to improve the position of Zanzibar, at least not during the one-party regime, when the interest represented in the parliament was not so much that of Zanzibar, but that of the one party, as defined by the central policy-making body of that party. At the same time, the arrangement is open to criticism from the point of view of equality. The over-representation of Scotland in the UK Parliament was corrected at the point when the Scottish Parliament started to function, and it seems that Scotland and also Aceh are represented in their respective national parliaments in proportion to their population. The Puerto Rican situation falls completely outside of this frame of representation at the national level because the voters in Puerto Rico are not voters in federal elections in the USA. Instead, they elect a Resident Commissioner to act in an advisory capacity in relation to the federal structures in a manner that cannot even be regarded as a guaranteed seat. In fact, if the Puerto Rican voters were able to participate in federal elections, they would be entitled to vote in six members to the US House of Representatives and two to the Senate as well as eight members to the US Electoral College for the purposes of the presidential elections. Here, the inequality is negative in comparison with the positive inequality in Hong Kong and Zanzibar. It also seems that there may exist a tendency to separate terminologically the lawmaker at the sub-state level from the lawmaker at the national level by avoiding a similar description of the two law-making bodies. This is so at least in Zanzibar, the Åland Islands, Puerto Rico and Hong Kong, where the terms 'House of Representatives', 'Legislative Assembly' (In Åland the *Lagting*, in Puerto Rico the *Asamblea Legislativa*), and 'Legislative Council' are used instead of Parliament, *Riksdag*, Congress or National People's Congress. In Aceh and Scotland, the description of the highest decision-making body of the sub-state entity follows the terminology of the national lawmaker.

As concerns the actual participation in legislative work at the national level, the so-called West-Lothian question, a discussion that emerged in a Scottish context, has not caused any disqualifications in any of the five legislatures where representatives from sub-state entities participate. Representatives from the sub-state entities are not limited in their parliamentary mandates to partake in decision-making at the national level only as concerns such matters that belong to the legislative competence of the national lawmaker. Instead, the members of parliaments elected from the sub-state entities are involved in all matters dealt with by the national parliaments, and it seems that such participation is also possible in the national executive, at least in the case of British MPs elected from Scottish constituencies.

The position of women in political participation is relevant also at the sub-state level. In spite of a quota of female candidates to be nominated, it seems that the elections in Aceh brought in only a few women into the Acehnese assembly. This was the first time the elections were carried out to the assembly after the entry into force of the piece of law that created the assembly, so there may have been some hesitance on the part of women to vote for female candidates. However, in subsequent elections, only one development should be expected, that is, an increase in the number of female representatives in the Acehnese assembly. Women are also accorded special treatment in Zanzibar, where the elected membership of the House of Representatives is always to be complemented by a component of 40% female representatives, appointed in proportion to the political strength of those parties that secured a minimum of 10% of the constituency seats (this appointment of women is additional to the appointment in Zanzibar of persons to the President's liking). Apparently, the rule works under the assumption that women will never or almost never win in a constituency and that they therefore are in need of preferential treatment. If this preferential treatment at the same time means that women always abstain from running in a constituency, the mechanism is probably not a healthy sign of the political environment in which elections take place. In the other sub-state entities reviewed here, women compete for political positions on an equal basis with men and are also elected into the legislative organ. It seems, however, as if the female component amongst the political decision-makers in sub-state entities is still at a lower level than the proportion of women in the population in the sub-state entities, a problem which is known also from national parliaments.

Because the right of self-determination may be regarded as a meta-right of participation, underlining the position of the people in determining its political status and in pursuing its economic, social and cultural development, the concrete forms of participation outlined here are operationalizations of how these matters are to be dealt with. The sub-state entities reviewed here are all exercising their self-determination, in so far as the populations can be attached to the concept of a people, in the form of internal self-determination. Because internal self-determination takes on the form of legislation when it is exercised, the matters which the sub-state entities are vested with should be turned into legislation at the sub-state level in a manner that is in harmony with the human rights provisions to which the State in question has acceded. Participation at sub-state level should therefore not be allowed to revert to fiefdoms where the individuals' right to participation is set aside.

At the same time as each of the sub-state entities has a highest decision-making body that determines, in the political process, how the competences concerning different matters granted to the entity should be exercised, almost every one of the sub-state entities reviewed here also displays a particular divisive issue. That particular divisive issue marks much of the political debate in the entity and determines, at least to some extent, how the political process exercises its decision-making powers concerning the competences with which the sub-state entity is vested. In Zanzibar, the deep rift has traditionally been between the CCM and the CUF, and at least in part, the discord has been over the issue of the status of Zanzibar in the Union Republic. It remains to be seen how the government of national unity will succeed in bridging the differences. More recently, the issue of independence has been discussed more openly than during the era of the one-party state. In Puerto Rico, the independence of the island under the principle of self-determination was, for a long time, a major issue, but that has, more recently, turned into a discussion about the form under which the internal self-determination of the entity could be secured, as a state in the federation supported by the PNP or as an autonomous territory outside of the federal structure supported by the PDP. This division is the turning point of most political debate in Puerto Rico. In Scotland, too, there is a discussion concerning independence in a way that draws a dividing line between those who advocate more or less full sovereignty, in particular the SNP, and those who favor an improvement of the devolution arrangement, which would be the other political parties. Although the question of independence has been raised in the Åland Islands, it appears as if it were not anywhere near the levels of support the idea finds in, for instance, Scotland, but is overtaken by the wish of nearly all political groupings to develop the concept of self-government further and to diminish the legislative powers of the national parliament in the area of the Åland Islands. In Hong Kong, the dividing line is constituted by the attitudes of the political parties toward Beijing, parting the political scene between a pro-Beijing camp and the so-called pan-democrats, while independence is not at all on the agenda. Also in Aceh, independence seems to be off the agenda due to the (at least partially) successful implementation of the peace agreement. In Aceh, some of the differences between the PA, on the one hand, and some other parties, on the other, seem to revolve around the issue of how important a role religion should play at the expense of the more material or real needs of the population.

As is evident on the basis of this account of the divisive issues the sub-state entities need to deal with, sub-state existence involves a constant grinding against the counterpart, the national level. While it may be human to wish for a calm political environment, sub-state entities are, in this respect, no different from constituent states in federations. Conflict with the national level is a regular part of the daily life of a sub-state entity, perhaps even more so outside of the regularized federal frame, in jurisdictions that might exist as territorial autonomies. The fact that the conflict over some of the main political issues is constant does not have to mean that the level of conflict has to be high. In fact, in most cases, perhaps in all of the cases reviewed here, the conflict is at a relatively low level and certainly tolerable, and normally, the issues could be dealt with through the political process and discussion. While at least some of that discussion takes place, for instance, through the representatives elected from the sub-state entity to the national parliament, the day-to-day contacts are normally between the executive bodies of the sub-state entities, on the one hand, and the national executive bodies, on the other.

Chapter 7
The Executive Power

7.1 Both Parliamentary and Presidential Governance

Against the background of the situation in the Memel Territory, it would be natural to expect that a system of government with parliamentary accountability between the legislature and the executive body is used as a connecting mechanism between the two. This may very often be so in a European setting, but the sub-state entities reviewed in this study display strong presidential features. In fact, it seems as if the governmental system at the central level of the state in question would serve as a model of how the governmental system at the sub-state level is constructed. In most of the sub-state entities reviewed here, the central government relies on a strong executive, and it is this philosophy that is reflected also at the sub-state level. In fact, the difficulties that the Memel Territory experienced might in part be related to the president-led authoritarianism of the Lithuanian central government: it must have been incomprehensible for the central government under those circumstances that a sub-state entity is not organized under a one-man principle, and as a consequence, the mechanism of parliamentary accountability made the decision-making of the sub-state entity dependent on the Chamber of Representatives in a manner that was difficult to control and anticipate by the central government.

As regards the executive, the Åland Islands and Scotland are hence in line with the starting point formed by the Memel Territory. It may be a matter of taste which one of them is presented "closer" to the point of departure, but the Scottish Government is, through inter-governmental mechanisms, more aligned with the UK Government than is the case between the Government of the Åland Islands and the Finnish Government. The ordering could therefore start with the Åland Islands and continue with Scotland. The switch from the systems of parliamentary accountability to presidential forms of organization is almost dramatic in nature, because there are actually no intermediary forms that would even try to combine the two, although Zanzibar has an explicit provision on accountability. Instead, presidentialism in its pure form exists in Zanzibar and Puerto Rico. Presidentialism is

M. Suksi, *Sub-State Governance through Territorial Autonomy*,
DOI 10.1007/978-3-642-20048-9_7, © Springer-Verlag Berlin Heidelberg 2011

brought to even higher levels in the cases of Aceh and Hong Kong through connections of the chief executive officer to the national government.

Against the background of the Memel example, it could be expected that the autonomy statute would not make provision for national intervention situations where the governmental body of the autonomous entity has acted *ultra vires* so as to threaten the competences and sovereignty of the national government. Also, it could be expected that the autonomy statute would contain some norms that deal with the institutional organization of the executive at the sub-state level and that the horizontal dimension accountability within the sub-state entity would prevail within that context. Therefore, no vertical dimensions of accountability would be expected.

In reality, however, our study reveals differently organized executive powers that range from classical parliamentary accountability to extreme presidentialism and executive-led governments, and some of the executive branches are integrated in the national governmental structures in manners that might not be in harmony with the notion of autonomy.

7.2 The Åland Islands: Normal Parliamentarism with a Slight Modification

7.2.1 Implementing Three Legal Orders

In the Åland Islands, three different legal orders are applied: that of the Åland Islands, that of the state of Finland and that of the European Union. The European Union does not have any administration of its own at the level of Member States, but expects the Member States to take care of the implementation of its legal order through, *inter alia*, the administrative authorities of the Member States. The state administration of Finland implements the legislation that originates in the Parliament of Finland on the basis of section 27 and section 29 of the Self-Government Act and that requires administrative action. Section 3(2) of the Self-Government Act determines, for the purposes of the legal order of Åland, that the administration of the Åland Islands is vested in the Government of the Åland Islands and the officials subordinate to it. The specific principle that administrative competence follows from legislative competence is established in section 23, according to which officials of the Åland Islands shall conduct the administration of matters within the legislative powers of the Åland Islands, subject to some limited exceptions[1] and to the possibility that the administrative competence distribution

[1]The exceptions are (1) statistical information that is necessary for the state and in the possession of officials of the Åland Islands shall on request be made available for state officials; (2) statistical information for the use of the Åland Islands shall be collected in co-operation with the state officials concerned; (3) the Government of the Åland Islands shall obtain opinions from the state officials concerned before undertaking measures regarding a non-movable prehistoric relic; (4) the

is re-arranged by means of so-called consent decrees. Occasionally, however, the European Commission, too, is involved in the concrete application of EU norms in the territory of the Åland Islands.

The existence of three legal orders, that of the Åland Islands, mainland Finland, and the EU, is clarified in a judgment by the Supreme Court of Finland in a case involving liability of public bodies under chapter 3, section 2, of the Damages Act (SoF 412/1974).[2] The Government of the Åland Islands had issued quotas of salmon to fishing boats in the Åland Islands on the basis of Council Regulation 2847/93 EEC about the introduction of a control system for the common fisheries policy. The regulation was binding and directly applicable. The Finnish Ministry of Agriculture issued a decision on 18 October 1997, forbidding all Finnish vessels to fish for salmon, because the national quota was full. On 22 October 1997, the European Commission issued Regulation 2231/97/EEC about the discontinuance of salmon fishing from Finnish boats. The Government of the Åland Islands decided on the basis of the Act of Åland concerning the implementation of the common fisheries policy in the European Community (SoÅ 40/1995) that it would be prohibited to fish for salmon in the waters of the Åland Islands between 30 October and 31 December 1997. After the decision of the Government of the Åland Islands, the fisherman who owned a fishing boat discontinued the salmon fishing. Out of his total quota of 5281 salmon, 2604 salmon remained uncaught. The Government of the Åland Islands agreed to compensate a greater part of the uncaught salmon, but the fisherman claimed damages also for the rest, referring to losses due to failures in the exercise of public powers. The lower courts granted some damages, but the Supreme Court reversed the judgments of the lower courts in its judgment 2004:65, which confirmed the existence of three different legal orders in the territory of Finland and, consequently, also the existence of three different administrative jurisdictions.

The Supreme Court concluded that the fisherman was under an obligation to discontinue fishing at the latest on the basis of the binding regulation of the European Commission, but actually already on the basis of the decision of the Ministry of Agriculture of Finland. Therefore, the decision of the Government of the Åland Island could actually not have caused any harm to the fisherman. The Court nonetheless opined that the Government of the Åland Islands had had insufficient information about the system with quotas for salmon fishing and the national character of the quota. Therefore, the Government of the Åland Islands had, on false premises, issued fishing quotas of an individual nature. Because the relevant Council Regulation is binding and directly applicable, the Government of the Åland Islands should have been aware of the provisions in the Council Regulation and understand their clear contents. Actually, the Government of the Åland Islands was acting *ultra vires* when granting the salmon-fishing quota to the fishermen. In addition, although the fisherman also should have known the content of the law in this case, it could not be expected that he would have known the contents of the Council Regulation better than the Government of the Åland Islands. Therefore, the fisherman had good reason to trust the quota decision that the Government of the Åland Islands had issued to him.

The Supreme Court concluded that the Government of the Åland Islands had acted in a manner, which created a liability for the Government in relation to the fisherman. In addition, the Court concluded that the fisherman had a personal share in the emergence of the economic loss because of his ignorance about applicable legal rules and because the fisherman had taken upon himself a business risk with regard to making sure that he catches

---

Government of the Åland Islands shall obtain an opinion from the National Archives before the officials of the Åland Islands or the municipal or ecclesiastical officials render a decision on the destruction of documents in an archive located in the Åland Islands.

[2]SC 2004:65.

salmon up to the full limit of his quota before the national quota is fulfilled. Therefore, the Court did not grant the fisherman the additional damages he had sought.

The case is informative to a person in the jurisdiction of Åland about the fact that, depending on legislative competence, the administration of a matter may be the responsibility of two other jurisdictions other than the Government of the Åland Islands. An Ålandic individual has good reason to assume that the primary source of administrative decisions concerning their concrete situation is the Government of the Åland Islands or a municipality of Åland, but he or she cannot exclude the possibility that the administration of a matter is, in some cases, the responsibility of a state authority, in most cases situated in the Åland Islands and only sometimes in mainland Finland. In addition, there is the relatively rare possibility that executive decisions are made by the European Commission, which is the implementing organ of the European Union (although the EU does not have much of an executive function in relation to individuals and businesses in the Member States). Instead, the EU uses the administrative authorities and also courts of the Member States to implement its norms in individual cases. In spite of the complications for an individual person residing within the jurisdiction of the Åland Islands in separating between the three legal orders, the fact remains that the population has the duty to know the law produced by these three different sources and to understand the competence relationships between the various executive powers.

For the purposes of implementing the "public law" that emerges from the legislative decisions of the Legislative Assembly, there is therefore an executive power in the Åland Islands organized on the basis of acts of Åland.[3]

7.2.2 Political Accountability

The Act of Åland on the Organisation of the Legislative Assembly of the Åland Islands (SoÅ 11/1972) contains provisions concerning the relationship between the Legislative Assembly and the Government of the Åland Islands. The starting point of that relationship is the principle of parliamentarism, in other words, the government must be accountable to and enjoy the confidence of the Legislative Assembly.[4] The confidence is both collective and individual in respect to the five to seven

[3]This is established in section 16 of the Self-Government Act, according to which the Government of Åland shall be appointed as provided by an act of Åland.

[4]Historically speaking, however, governmental accountability has not always been organized in this manner in the Åland Islands. From the 1920s until 1988, the Government of the Åland Islands was appointed by means of proportional election, which means that the Government always was an all-inclusive coalition government in which more or less all political groupings participated, with the consequence that there was no clear distinction between the political majority carrying the political responsibility and the political opposition criticizing the policies of the majority. In addition, during this early period of the Government of the Åland Islands, the members of the government were perhaps regarded more as civil servants than politically answerable ministers

members of the Government. The important matter from the point of view of governmental accountability is that under the above-mentioned general provisions of the Self-Government Act, the lawmaker of the Åland Islands is itself in the position of formulating the different mechanisms of governmental accountability without the interference of the central government.[5]

In its internal construction of governmental accountability, the Legislative Assembly of the Åland Islands has, naturally, only created mechanisms of accountability between the bodies of the autonomy arrangement, not between autonomy bodies on the one hand and bodies of the central government on the other. Hence, only the horizontal accountability is of relevance, not the vertical.[6] The Organisation of the Legislative Assembly Act of Åland contains provisions concerning the relationship between the Legislative Assembly and the Åland Government. The starting point of that relationship is the principle of parliamentarism, in other words, the Government must be accountable to and enjoy the confidence of the Legislative Assembly.

The First Minister, who heads the Government of the Åland Islands, is in many ways the most visible political figure on the islands. After elections, the Legislative Assembly elects the First Minister, who then proposes the composition of the government, and this proposal is submitted to a vote in the Assembly. Due to proportional election resulting in a multi-party composition of the Legislative Assembly, the Government of the Åland Islands is normally a coalition government.[7] If the proposal is supported by a simple majority of the members, the Government is approved and can start to function. While the Government is in office, a motion of no confidence can be filed by individual Legislative Assembly members, and if an absolute majority of the members approve it, the Government (or a member thereof, if the motion is directed towards an individual member of the government) shall resign. The Government of the Åland Islands Act (SoÅ 42/1971) contains

---

proper. It is only during the last two decades that such a governmental accountability has developed which was the topic of the *Memel* case.

[5]The legal accountability of the members of the Government of the Åland Islands must be distinguished from their political accountability. As provided for in section 60 b of the Self-Government Act, charges against the First Minister of the Government of Åland or one of its members for an offence in office shall be brought in the Court of Appeal of Turku/Åbo.

[6]The President of Finland has, under section 19 of the Self-Government Act, an absolute power to veto legislative decisions of the Legislative Assembly in *toto* or in part when the decision violates the law-making competence of the Parliament of Finland as defined in section 27 of the Act. This takes place in relation to 2–4% of the legislative decisions of the Legislative Assembly *per annum*, in most cases by way of partial veto, thus leaving major parts of the legislative decision to be promulgated by the Åland Islands Government. However, apart from that control of legislative competence (in which the Åland Delegation and the Supreme Court of Finland also play a role), the President of Finland cannot influence the exercise of the law-making powers of the Åland Islands.

[7]The current (November 2010) composition of the Åland Islands Government is the Liberals with four ministers and the Centre with three ministers. The Government is a majority government, controlling 19 seats in the Legislative Assembly.

corresponding provisions on accountability to the parliament, but these are supplemented by a provision allowing the Government itself to declare that it will consider a defeat in a vote on a legislative proposal a motion of no confidence and resign. It is a somewhat unusual feature of parliamentarism in Åland that the members of the government do not, after their election to ministers, hold seats in the Legislative Assembly, but instead, substitutes are called in to the Legislative Assembly.

While the Åland Government is in office, a motion of no confidence can be filed by a group of five Legislative Assembly members, and if 16 members (absolute majority) approve it, the Government (or a member thereof, if the motion is directed towards an individual member of the Government) shall resign. Therefore, there is an asymmetry in the mechanism of parliamentary accountability that functions in the horizontal dimension. The requirement of absolute majority for an expression of no confidence in the Åland Islands can be compared with the national Government of Finland, which for the purposes of governmental accountability is based on a simple majority both at the formation of the government and at the dissolution of the government. The requirement of a simple majority for the appointment of the government and an absolute majority for the expression of no confidence, as established in section 60(3) of the Act on the Legislative Assembly, would also make it possible to run a minority government as long as the required absolute majority is not found for a clear opposition.

7.2.3 The Implementing Organs of the Government

As concerns the Åland Islands, the Self-Government Act, apart from mentioning the governmental institutions at the autonomous level, leaves these institutions and organs to be regulated through enactments of the Legislative Assembly. Thus, the internal structures of government are determined by Ålandic legislation.[8] The scope of the authority of Legislative Assembly to pass legislation on these issues is laid out in section 18, according to which Åland shall have legislative powers in respect to, *inter alia*:

(1) The organisation and duties of the Legislative Assembly of the Åland Islands and the election of its members, the Government of the Åland Islands and the officials and services subordinate to it.
(2) The officials of the Åland Islands, the collective agreements on the salaries of the employees of the Åland Islands and the sentencing of the officials of the Åland Islands to disciplinary punishment.

As a consequence, the Legislative Assembly has the full range of powers to organize not only itself, but also the executive bodies and offices of the Åland Islands. However, section 121 of the Constitution of Finland creates the

[8] See Suksi (2005d), pp. 198–210.

requirement that municipalities shall exist, and because section 18 of the Self-Government Act vests legislative authority over municipalities in the Åland Islands in the Legislative Assembly, the lawmaker of Åland cannot choose to abolish the municipalities, in case such an idea was presented.

The list of legislative powers of the Åland Islands places the main bulk of Ålandic norms within the sphere of so-called 'public law', which as a consequence implies the existence of a relatively broad administrative machinery for decision-making in individual cases of the implementation of acts of Åland. In fact, proportionally speaking, the public sector of the Åland Islands appears greater than that of the mainland, partly because of this 'public law' orientation, partly because of the independent Ålandic powers to decide on the allocation of the block grant from the state budget to the Åland Islands.

Various offices and administrative bodies operate under the Åland Government. While the Government as a collective body is in charge of more political decision-making, individual members as heads of different departments—including those belonging to the offices of the Åland Government—participate in making administrative decisions on the basis of acts of Åland. The political accountability of the Government before the Legislative Assembly extends itself at least to the actions of the Departments of the Åland Islands Government, that is, Finance, Administrative Affairs, Law Drafting, Commerce, Social Affairs and the Environment, Traffic, Education and Culture. However, the political answerability of the Government of the Åland Islands is weaker in respect to the independent agencies of the Åland Islands, such as the Police of Åland, the Health Care of Åland, the Board of Environment, and the schools of Åland, and it becomes very thin and attenuated when moving towards local government and into the area of so-called indirect public administration. The civil service of the Åland Islands is, on the basis of section 24 of the Self-Government Act, open also to other individuals than those residents of the Åland Islands who have the right of domicile, as provided by an act of Åland. However, only a citizen of Finland may be employed in the police force. As is indicated by the listing of the departments of the Government of the Åland Islands, the competence of the Government is of a general nature, akin to that of an independent State. The independent agencies of Åland operating under the various departments reinforce this view.

Although the special rights of those who have the right of domicile constitute an important dimension of the autonomy arrangement, the decision-making related to the management of the special rights, including the granting of the right of domicile, is of a minor nature in the greater bulk of governmental affairs and decisions made by the governmental structures of the Åland Islands. The granting of the right of domicile, which is a platform for the free enjoyment of the special rights of, *inter alia*, purchase of real estate, carrying out a business operation, and the right to vote and to stand as a candidate in the Åland Islands, are handled by the general office of the Department of Administrative Affairs. The clear and more technical decisions concerning the grant of the right of domicile are made by the civil servants of the Åland Islands, while more complicated matters and matters involving issues of principle are dealt with by the First Minister, and sometimes even by the plenary meeting of the Government of the Åland Islands.[9]

Those who are not in the possession of the right of domicile may apply for exceptions to the restrictions on grounds established in acts of Åland. Therefore, the same general office also decides on permits to those not in the possession of the right of domicile to purchase real estate and to carry out business operations in the jurisdiction of the Åland Islands. The more complicated issues, however, are dealt with by an individual minister of the Government or sometimes even by the entire Government. The central point in the context is that matters involving the special rights of the Åland Islanders are dealt with by the governmental structures that ultimately base their legitimacy on the political will of those who possess the right of domicile. The individual administrative decisions concerning the management of these special rights are thus in the hands of the Åland Islanders themselves.[10]

One of the salient features of the 1921 Åland Islands Settlement was the municipalities, which constitute an essential part of the autonomy scheme, because they are based on the principle of the self-government of their inhabitants. At the moment, there are 16 municipalities, many of them very small, counting their population in the hundreds. The town of Mariehamn, the capital of the Åland Islands, is the biggest with more than 10,000 inhabitants. The municipalities also have their own constitutionally guaranteed power of taxation (although the competence to regulate municipal taxation in the Åland Islands rests with the Legislative Assembly). Compared with the municipalities on the mainland, the municipalities in Åland have fewer functions, because the Åland Government takes charge of such important functions as health care and education above the primary level. Most of the public functions performed by the municipalities have their legal basis in Ålandic legislation, but in some respects, the municipalities of Åland also implement national legislation enacted by the Parliament of Finland. This is so, for instance, with respect to the protection of children, which may imply decisions that limit the freedom of the individual, and the provision of services to persons with some disabilities.

7.2.4 Contacts with the National Government

The governmental functions in the Åland Islands are, however, not exclusively in the hands of the institutions of the autonomous entity. Because administrative competence follows from legislative competence, the general principle is therefore that the Government of the Åland Islands is responsible for implementing Ålandic legislation, while the administrative structures of the state are responsible for implementing legislation enacted by the Parliament of Finland. Although there

[9]See Suksi (2005d), p. 35 f.

[10]However, the decisions may be appealed on legal grounds at the SAC, but not on the basis of feasibility or practicability. See Suksi (2005d), pp. 423–425.

are some exceptions to this general rule, there exists two different administrative structures in the Åland Islands, those of the Åland Islands and those of the state. However, because the legislative powers of Åland are mainly of a public law nature (education, health, social affairs, environment, local government), the presence of the state in the Åland Islands is relatively weak.

Nonetheless, there is, according to section 4 of the Self-Government Act, a Governor in the Åland Islands who represents the Government of Finland and who at the same time is, according to section 16 of the Act on Regional Administrative Agencies (SoF 896/2009), the head of the State Agency in the Åland Islands. The State Agency in the Åland Islands is in charge of such administrative matters that under this Act and the Self-Government Act belong to the competence of the state.[11] This means, at the same time, that the Governor is not a part of the Government of the Åland Islands, but assumes instead, the role of a civil servant of the state, which is an external role in relation to the Government and the Legislative Assembly of the Åland Islands.[12]

The appointment of the Governor for the Åland Islands was framed in a particular manner already in para. 5 of the Åland Islands Settlement, and therefore, section 52 of the Self-Government Act stipulates that the President of the Republic appoints the Governor after having agreed on the matter with the Speaker of the Legislative Assembly.[13] If a consensus is not reached, the President shall appoint the Governor from among five candidates nominated by the Legislative Assembly of the Åland Islands. A person is suitable for the post if he or she has the necessary qualifications for conducting the administration of Åland well and for attending to state security. In the event that the President would have to dismiss the Governor of the Åland Islands from the office, the Speaker of the Legislative Assembly shall be heard before a decision is made.

A number of governmental functions in the Åland Islands are taken care of by the state administration. Such functions are, *inter alia*, the population registry, tax collection, the coast guard, labor protection, investigation of the most serious

[11] *Inter alia*, civil defense, population registry, ship register, motor vehicle tax, change of name, registration of foreigners, voting register, marriages and registered partnerships between persons of same sex, licenses of different sorts.

[12] However, for formal occasions of opening and closing the session periods of the Legislative Assembly, the Governor is seated in the meeting hall of the Legislative Assembly.

[13] See Decision of the Chancellor of Justice in his Report of 1999, p. 43, concerning the appointment of the Governor from the point of view of conflict of interest. In the media, there had been speculations about the possibility that the then Speaker of the Legislative Assembly might declare his candidacy for the post of Governor. According to section 52(2) of the Self-Government Act, the Governor is appointed by the President on the basis of an agreement with the Speaker of the Legislative Assembly. If consensus is not reached, the President shall appoint the Governor from among five persons proposed by the Legislative Assembly. The Chancellor of Justice held it clear that the Speaker cannot participate in an agreement that he would himself be appointed as Governor. The Chancellor took into account, *inter alia*, such principles of conflict of interest that are based in the European Convention on Human Rights.

crimes, the land registry, the Social Insurance Institution, the prosecutor's office, the bailiff's office, customs, and the legal aid office. If the state would need real estate for such functions, the Government of the Åland Islands is, according to section 61, under duty to allocate suitable lots for the purpose, and the provision also creates a procedure to that end.

There is a host of different co-operation procedures for resolving practical and day-to-day issues, relevant especially to the administrative competencies of the state authorities, as outlined in the Self-Government Act.[14] This requires that state

[14]According to section 30 concerning administrative authority and procedure, state officials shall conduct the administration of matters within the legislative power of the state, with regard to the following: (1) when making an appointment to a state office in Åland, special weight shall be given to the fact that the appointee has knowledge of the local conditions in Åland or resides in Åland; (2) the word "Åland" shall be incorporated in a passport issued in Åland, if the holder of the passport has the right of domicile; (3) the Åland officials shall partake in civil defence, as provided by a Consent Decree; (4) a person with the right of domicile may be assigned only to civilian duties within Åland by virtue of the general obligation of the citizenry to work; (5) statistics relating to the local conditions in Åland that are in the possession of state officials shall on request be handed over to the appropriate Åland officials; (6) state officials shall ensure that Åland gain access to the necessary frequencies for radio and television broadcasts; (7) the Government of Åland shall decide on granting foreigners or foreign corporations permission to acquire ownership or possession of real property in Åland or to practice a trade in Åland; before making a decision it shall request an opinion from the state official concerned; (8) the duties that according to legislation on contagious diseases in humans or pets and livestock, legislation on the prevention of substances destructive to plants from entering the country and legislation on the production and use of poisons belong to state officials, shall in Åland be performed by the Government of Åland or by another official as provided by an act of Åland; (9) (repealed); (10) the duties that in the state belong to the Consumer Complaint Board shall in Åland be performed by a special board appointed by the Government of Åland; (11) the duties that according to legislation on consumer counseling belong to local administration of the state shall in Åland be performed by authorities of the Åland Islands, as agreed between Åland and the state; (12) a new merchant shipping lane may only be opened in Åland with the consent of the Government of Åland, subject to the provisions of section 62; (13) a matter relating to the permission to conduct merchant shipping in Åland or between Åland and the rest of Finland in a foreign vessel shall be negotiated on with the Government of Åland; (14) the speed limits for merchant vessels on the lanes in Åland and the other matters relating to shipping that are of special importance to Åland shall be negotiated on with the Government of Åland; (15) matters relating to the right to practice air traffic in Åland shall belong to the Government of Åland; however, an opinion on such matters shall be obtained from a state official; (16) when considering matters relating to air traffic that are of special importance to Åland, state authorities shall consult the Government of Åland; (17) archive material deriving from state authorities in Åland may be removed from Åland only after negotiations with the Government of Åland; (18) a decision of the Bank of Finland that may be presumed to be especially important for the economic life or for employment in Åland shall, if possible, only be made after negotiations with the Government of Åland; (19) the Government of Åland shall have the right to be represented together with the Council of state in the negotiations with the central organisations of the producers on income from agriculture and the fishing industry and on the regulation of agricultural production and the fishing industry; (20) the Government of Åland shall be heard before a decision is reached on changes in import regulations that may be especially important to the agricultural production or fishing industry in Åland; (21) an opinion shall be obtained from the Government of Åland before granting a licence to practice a licenced trade, if a state official has the competence to

authorities, in conducting the administration of matters within the legislative power of the state, should undertake different forms of co-ordination, consultation, and contacts with authorities of the Åland Islands. Depending on the matter, this could imply anything from a phone call between the relevant civil servant of the Åland Islands Government and his or her counterpart in the governmental structures of mainland Finland, to the appointment of a joint committee of civil servants to draw up principles for dealing with a matter. Such mechanisms can be understood as methods for resolving the tensions that are a natural consequence of the aspirations of two different governmental systems and of the application of law in two separate (although similar) legal orders.[15] There is a liaison agency of the Åland Islands in Helsinki, the capital of Finland, through which the Government of the Åland Islands manages at least a part of its contacts with the Government of Finland.

There is also a general obligation for the state authorities, established in section 31 of the Self-Government Act, to assist, within their general competence, the authorities of the Åland Islands in the performance of duties related to autonomy. Also, in section 33, a duty is placed on the President of the Republic, the Council of State, a Ministry or some other authority to obtain an opinion from the Government of the Åland Islands if any of these mainland organs issues provisions that only concern the Åland Islands or that otherwise are especially significant to the Åland Islands.

The exercise of executive powers by the Åland Islands Government is tied under section 23 of the Self-Government Act to the legislative powers of the Åland Islands so that the executive powers flow from and originate in the legislative powers of the Åland Islands. This means that the Government of the Åland Islands does not have any executive prerogative, but is instead circumscribed by the legislative powers. This is sustained by section 21 of the Self-Government Act, which ties the exercise of the decree powers of the Government of the Åland Islands to an authorization in an act of Åland, and which means that the Åland Islands Government does not have any independent normative powers outside the area specified by Ålandic legislation.

---

grant the licence; (22) the Government of Åland shall be heard before a decision is reached on closing down an institution or permanent post of local administration of the state in Åland; (23) statistics on Åland that are necessary for the state shall be collected in co-operation with the appropriate Åland officials.

[15]There has also existed an important informal mechanism, although the practice has been discontinued during the last few years. Between the end of the 1930s and 2010, it was customary for the government of Finland, that is, the Council of State, to meet for an 'evening school' each Wednesday, to engage in informal discussions on issues on the political agenda. During the past decade, the Åland Islands has twice been the topic of the evening school, with the First Minister of the Åland Islands, other politicians, and staff from the Åland Islands participating in the discussions. In this way, the highest political bodies of the two jurisdictions can meet to discuss joint issues. For the most part, it seems that these contacts have dealt with reforms to the Self-Government Act and EU issues. From time to time, the President of Finland, Finnish ministers or Government representatives visit the Åland Islands.

Where the exact competence line goes in each situation that the administration of either the Åland Islands or the state tries to deal with may be difficult to know. In unclear situations, the Supreme Court can issue an opinion concerning conflicts of competence in the application of legislation, and the Åland Delegation also has responsibilities within this area. According to section 60(2) of the Self-Government Act, if a conflict of authority arises between Åland officials and state officials on a given administrative function, a decision on the matter shall be rendered by the Supreme Court on the proposal of the Government of Åland or the state official.[16] Before rendering the decision, the Supreme Court shall obtain opinions from the appropriate official and the Åland Delegation.[17] In addition, in section 62 of the Self-Government Act, the Åland Delegation is charged with the duty to resolve certain administrative competence issues.

7.2.5 *The Role of the Language*

According to section 36 of the Self-Government Act, the official language of the Åland Islands is Swedish and the administration is unilingually Swedish-speaking. However, skills among central government officials in the Swedish language are in

[16] On this form of administrative competence control, see Koskelo (2009), pp. 14–15. Section 60(2) has been applied on two occasions only during the last decade, in cases 1998:8 and 2001:38 of the Supreme Court, which fact caused her to wonder whether this means that the distribution of powers on the basis of the Self-Government Act works well. Although the cases deal with the distribution of administrative competence, Koskelo makes the point that in the two cases, principles of general civil procedure have been applied. She also makes the point that in reality, the process in this first and at the same time last instance in the Supreme Court "has many similarities to an arbitration process". In the case 1998:8, dealt with upon the request by the Ministry of Agriculture and Forestry in the Government of Finland, the Supreme Court came to the conclusion that the Ministry of the Finnish Government "does not have the authority, without the consent of Åland, to implement a time-based or regional breakdown of Finland's *salmon quota*", but the Ministry does have the authority to impose a fishing ban under EU law that also applies in the Åland Islands. In the case 2001:38, the Ministry of the Interior in the Government of Finland requested an opinion on whether the decision of the Government of the Åland Islands to grant the slot-machine company of Åland a permit to sell gambling services over the Internet to consumers throughout the territory of Finland was within the authority of the Åland Islands. The Supreme Court found that the decision of the Government of the Åland Islands was delineated so that it did not violate the rules applicable in mainland Finland and thus the Government of the Åland Islands had not exceeded its authority.

[17] A basis for distribution of competence in the area of public enterprises is established in section 65 of the Self-Government Act. If the right to practice a trade, regulated in legislation enacted by the Parliament of Finland according to section 27 or section 29, is reserved to the state, an independent state institution or a corporation where the state holds the power of decision, a decree may be issued to the effect that the Government of the Åland Islands or a corporation where Åland holds the power of decision be entitled to practice the same trade in the Åland Islands, unless there are substantial reasons for the contrary.

decline and increasingly government documents, especially related to the EU, are solely provided in Finnish. This has become a source of irritation in the relationship between the Åland Islands and mainland Finland. Although the Self-Government Act contains a number of provisions on the use of the Swedish language (sections 36 through 42), they are clearly not being properly implemented. This criticism is valid at a general level, but as concerns the competence control at the Ministry of Justice as well as the Ålandic financial matters dealt with at the Ministry of Finance, there are specific provisions in section 34 of the Self-Government Act that guarantee materially and, as a consequence, also linguistically, a good level of knowledge of the Swedish language within the central government of Finland, because for the presentation of decision-proposals within those functions for the President, the Council of State shall appoint civil servants with a good knowledge of the autonomy of the Åland Islands.

The aim of the Åland Islands Settlement in 1921 was, according to the Council of the League of Nations, to maintain the Swedish character of the Åland Islands. There are several mechanisms to that effect in the Settlement, but only one, the language of instruction in para. 2, is specifically focused on the maintenance of the Swedish language. Although the provision in section 40 of the Self-Government Act is worded in a manner different from the original text of the Settlement, the material content is more or less the same: the language of education in schools maintained by public funds or subsidized from such funds shall be Swedish, unless otherwise provided by an act of Åland. If need be, it should therefore be possible to establish a school operating in Finnish, provided that it is entirely funded from private sources. Although the Act of Åland on the Comprehensive School allows for also other than public schools, the provisions of the Act are written in a way that they actually would not apply if, for instance, an association of parents filed an application for a license to establish a private school that follows the Ålandic curriculum, but that operates in the Finnish language.

The monopoly of the Swedish language on the Åland Islands may, however, create a so-called 'minority in a minority' problem in respect to Finnish-speaking persons (about 1,100 or 4.5% of the population) residing there.[18] The population of Finnish-speakers in the Åland Islands appears to be relatively stable, as the ratio of Finnish-speakers today is more or less at the same level as in 1920. The Ålandic language provisions would appear to be in conflict with the provisions of the 1960 UNESCO Convention Against Discrimination in Education.[19] However, following the logic of the European Court of Human Rights *Belgian Linguistics Case*,[20] there

[18]The relationship between the Ålandic arrangements and the various human rights conventions binding on Finland has been the subject of some debate. It has been suggested that the 1921 Åland Islands Settlement, decided by the League of Nations, should be considered a *lex specialis*, but most legal experts give precedence to Finland's obligations under human rights conventions according to the principle of *lex posterior*. Hannikainen (1993b), see note 35, p. 53 f.

[19]Hannikainen (1993b), note 35, pp. 22 f., 41–49.

[20]ECtHR, judgment of 9 February 1967, Ser. A, No. 6.

is no such discrimination against Finnish-speaking pupils in the Åland Islands that would be prohibited under the European Convention on Human Rights; there would seem to exist "legitimate and objective grounds to keep the schools of the Åland Islands monolingually Swedish" at the same time as the present system would not seem to "involve disproportionality between the means employed and the aim sought".[21]

After the completion of school in the Åland Islands, the person's proficiency in Finnish would normally not be at a very high level. Yet at the same time, young persons from the Åland Islands might want to continue their studies in mainland Finland,[22] where some measure of Finnish is required by the educational institutions at admission and also as a practical matter during their studies. Therefore, section 41 of the Self-Government Act prescribes that a graduate of an educational institution in the Åland Islands may, as further provided by a decree, be admitted to a state-maintained or state-subsidized Swedish-language or bilingual educational institution and be graduated from there, even if he or she does not have the proficiency in Finnish required for admittance and graduation.

The Self-Government Act, however, contains additional provisions concerning the Swedish language and also concerning the use of the Finnish language in the Åland Islands and in relation to the authorities of the Åland Islands. It is clear under section 36(1) of the Self-Government Act as a point of departure that the language used in the state administration, within the administrative structures of the Government of the Åland Islands and within local government in municipalities is Swedish.[23] In addition, a private party in Åland has the right under section 39(3) to receive an enclosed Swedish translation with his copy of the document in matters that are considered by a state authority in mainland Finland, such as the Council of State, the central state agencies and such superior courts and other state authorities whose jurisdictions include the Åland Islands or a part thereof, and within which the document shall, according to general language legislation, be written in Finnish.

However, there is an exception to this main rule in section 37 of the Self-Government Act: a Finnish citizen has the right to use the Finnish language in his

[21] Hannikainen (1993b), note 35, p 38 f.

[22] However, a clear majority of the Ålandic students continue their studies in Sweden (for an analysis of special treatment in this respect, see below, Sect. 8.6.5). This is facilitated under section 64, according to which a decree may be issued to the effect that a degree required for a state office in Åland may be substituted with a comparable degree earned in Iceland, Norway, Sweden or Denmark. For positions in the Government of the Åland Islands and the municipalities of Åland, this applies on the basis of Ålandic legislation.

[23] Actually, this was the point of departure already in sections 29–31 of the 1920 Self-Government Act, and as a consequence of para. 1 of the 1921 Åland Islands Settlement, it can be argued that this was confirmed as one part of the autonomy of the Åland Islands. In addition, section 36(3) of the current Self-Government Act provides that he provisions of the Act on the language used in state administration shall also apply, where appropriate, to the officials of the Evangelical Lutheran Church, unless otherwise provided by the Church Code.

or her own case before courts of law and before other state authorities in the Åland Islands. This grant to use Finnish in the unilingually Swedish jurisdiction in contacts with state authorities is not as particular as it may seem, because the same would apply in mainland Finland under the Language Act (SoF 423/2003),[24] if there existed unilingually Swedish-speaking administrative districts of state authorities. Also, under section 39, the courts and the State Agency in the Åland Islands shall, on the request of a party, enclose a translation into Finnish in their documents. Further, if a document submitted to a court or another state official is written in Finnish, the official shall see to its translation into Swedish, if necessary.

The language in the institutional relations is dealt with in section 38 of the Self-Government Act. Letters and other documents between authorities of the Åland Islands and the state authorities in the Åland Islands shall be written in Swedish. The same applies also to the correspondence between the authorities of the Åland Islands and the Åland Delegation, and between the authorities of the Åland Islands and the Council of State, the authorities in the central government of Finland and the superior courts and other state authorities to whose jurisdiction Åland or a part thereof belongs. The same rules concerning correspondence between the different authorities also apply to municipal authorities in the Åland Islands.[25] The main principle is thus that the institutional contacts between the governmental entities of the Åland Islands, on the one hand, and the various state authorities and courts, on the other, take place in the Swedish language. For that reason, section 42 stipulates that provisions on the linguistic proficiency of a state official in the Åland Islands shall be issued by decree with the consent of the Government of the Åland Islands. The point of departure is that any person employed in the service of the state in the Åland Islands has to be proficient in the Swedish language. For that reason, the Self-Government Act also lays down that the state shall organize training in Swedish for the persons in its service in the Åland Islands.

Normally, the linguistic rules apply in the vertical dimension between the public authorities of all sorts and an individual. However, section 43 of the Self-Government Act contains a platform also for horizontal rules, but in a particular context. The provision requires the Council of State to take suitable measures to have the necessary product and service information distributed to the consumers in the Åland Islands in Swedish. The Council of State shall also see to that the rules and instructions to be followed in the Åland Islands are available in the Swedish language.

The focus on language that can be discerned in the Åland Islands is not an important concern in Scotland.

---

[24]The Language Act applies only in mainland Finland, not in the Åland Islands.

[25]However, in some situations, treaties that are to be submitted for approval by the Legislative Assembly under section 59 of the Self-Government Act may be sent to Åland in the original language, if the treaty by law is not to be published in Swedish. Also, a position document relating to EU matters that is notified to Åland on the basis of section 59a may be sent to the Government of the Åland Islands in the original language, if it has not yet been translated into Swedish.

7.3 Scotland: Traditional Parliamentary Environment

7.3.1 Horizontal Political Accountability

A separate Scottish administration is created under Part II of the Scotland Act of 1998. According to section 44 of the Scotland Act, the Scottish Executive[26] shall consist of a First Minister,[27] such Ministers as the First Minister appoints as well as the Lord Advocate and the Solicitor General for Scotland. In addition, there may be Junior Ministers in the Scottish executive, that is, in the Government of Scotland. The members of the Scottish Executive, that is, the Scottish Government as it also is called since 2007, are referred to collectively as the Scottish Ministers,[28] and they shall be members of the Scottish Parliament. The First Minister is, under section 45 of the Act, appointed by the head of the executive of the United Kingdom, that is, Her Majesty, and the other ministers are appointed by the First Minister with the approval of Her Majesty, which introduces a formal (although practically non functional) vertical dimension between the devolved executive and the national executive. The First Minister is nominated on the basis of section 46 of the Act by the Scottish Parliament, apparently by simple majority,[29] within 28 days from elections or the resignation of the previous First Minister. It should be noted that the Scotland Act does not create a Scottish Cabinet as a specific organ of the executive power.

Within the framework of this horizontal dimension, the members of the Scottish executive are normally selected from the party or parties that control the majority of the seats in the Scottish Parliament, although a minority government is possible, too. Because the Scottish Parliament is elected by way of a mixed majority-proportional election,[30] there is a possibility of fragmentation of the support for the different

[26]Although the Scotland Act and the UK Government continues to refer to the concept of the "Scottish Executive", the name was re-branded in 2007 by the SNP-led Government to read the "Scottish Government".

[27]Under section 95 of the Scotland Act, the First Minister has important functions, *inter alia*, in recommending the appointment and removal of judges, although such decisions are formally done by Her Majesty. As concluded by Bogdanor (1999), p. 288, the First Minister is likely to be seen as the real leader of political opinion in Scotland and as the Prime Minister of Scotland.

[28]A person who holds a Ministerial office may not be appointed a member of the Scottish Executive; and if a member of the Scottish Executive is appointed to a Ministerial office he shall cease to hold office as a member of the Scottish Executive. In this context, the notion of "Ministerial office" has the same meaning as is established in section 2 of the House of Commons Disqualification Act. Hence here, too, there is a connection to UK legislation. It seems on the basis of section 59 that the collective of Scottish Ministers, that is, the Government of Scotland, is a legal person of its own, because it can hold property and liabilities in its own name.

[29]See also rules 4.1. through 4.8. of the Standing Orders of the Scottish Parliament.

[30]The MMP system is also referred to as the mixed member proportional system. The system is in Scotland termed the Additional Member System (AMS). See Herbert et al. (2007), p. 4. See also Himsworth (2006), p. 204.

parties in a way that may lead to a coalition government between several parties.[31] The practical operation of the devolution in Scotland started, in fact, with a coalition government between Labour and Liberal Democrats.[32] On 16 May 2007, the Scottish Parliament selected the leader of the Scottish National Party as the nominee for First Minister for recommendation to Her Majesty in a process, which under rule 11.10 of the Standing Orders of the Scottish Parliament follows the principle of simple majority.[33] Because his nomination received in the final round only 49 votes against the 46 votes of his opponents with 33 abstentions,[34] the Government thus created was a minority government that could have suffered a vote of no-confidence at any time in the Scottish Parliament, leading potentially to new elections at any major disagreement about the policies of the government. With elections held in principle every 4 years, with some limitations on when intervening elections could occur, the majority in opposition should, in such a case, probably have an action plan at hand with a view to forming a new government to replace an ousted minority government. Perhaps for the reason that no alternative plan existed, the minority government of the SNP did not suffer any motion of no confidence between 2007 and 2011. In the elections of 2011, the SNP secured a majority in the Scottish Parliament and formed a majority government alone without any coalition partners.

In comparison with Northern Ireland, governmental accountability in Scotland displays a clear affinity to governmental accountability of the central government.[35] However, unlike the formation of the UK Government, the formation of the

---

[31] See also Bogdanor (1999), p. 215, and McFadden and Lazarowicz (2002), p. 74 f, who also point out that there is one crucial difference between the UK Government and the Scottish Government in that the former will almost always have a one-party majority to rely on in the UK Parliament, while the latter will almost always be a coalition government. Even minority governments are possible, as is the case in the third parliamentary period of Scotland.

[32] Pilkington (2002), pp. 104–107, Himsworth and O'Neill (2003), pp. 232–244. For the composition of the cabinets appointed in 1999 and 2000, see Pilkington (2002), p. 190.

[33] See McFadden and Lazarowicz (2002), p. 78. See also Rule 11.11. on simple and absolute majority, which states that any decision of the Parliament shall, if taken by division, require a simple majority unless otherwise expressly states in any enactment or in these rules. The rule also specifies the exact meaning of simple and absolute majority. Himsworth (2006), p. 203, points out that the Scottish Cabinet as a collective term denoting the members of the executive with the exception of the law officers is a non-statutory body.

[34] The parties with representation in the Scottish Parliament are, on the basis of the elections in May 2007, the Scottish National Party (47 mandates), the Scottish Labour Party (46 mandates), the Scottish Conservatives (17 mandates), the Scottish Liberal Democrats (16 mandates), the Scottish Green Party (2 mandates), and one independent.

[35] See also Himsworth (2006), p. 195, who concludes that in principle, "the aim has been to produce by statute a modified form of government of the 'Westminster model'". As pointed out by Himsworth (2006), p. 205, at least two features cater for this, namely that the Scottish Parliament is given an express role in government formation by nominating the First Minister and approving the nomination of the other ministers and that the resignation of ministers is required if the Parliament resolves that they no longer enjoy the confidence of the Parliament. Unlike the relationship between the UK Government and the UK Parliament, the First Minister of Scotland cannot dissolve the Scottish Parliament. See Himsworth and Munro (2000), pp. 59, 209.

Scottish Government, that is, the appointment of ministers, is statutorily established through provisions in the Scotland Act.[36] The important position of the Government of Scotland is illustrated by the fact that the great majority of legislation passed by the Scottish Parliament is based on executive bills submitted to the Parliament,[37] often on the basis of the legislative program of the Scottish Government.[38] However, with the minority government in power after 2007, the bills submitted have often been heavily amended by the Scottish Parliament, where the SNP had a politically weaker position. After the elections of 2011, the situation is quite different and favorable to the SNP.

In addition, the First Minister shall hold office at Her Majesty's pleasure and shall according to section 45 tender his resignation to Her Majesty if the Scottish Parliament resolves that the Scottish Executive no longer enjoys the confidence of the Parliament.[39] Here, too, the principle of simple majority should be the decision-making rule. Again, the solution brought about by devolution for the Scottish jurisdiction is not a complete copy of the UK model, but instead a variation of it.[40] More or less the same procedure concerning no confidence applies on the basis of section 47 to the other members of the Scottish Government, including the Junior Ministers, although it is the First Minister who is the appointing instance. Under section 47, the First Minister may, with the approval of Her Majesty, appoint Ministers from among the members of the Parliament, provided that the Parliament has agreed to the appointments.[41] Such a minister holds office at Her Majesty's pleasure, and may be removed from office by the First Minister. He or she may also at any time resign and shall do so if the Parliament resolves that the Scottish Executive no longer enjoys the confidence of the Parliament.

The confidence in the Scottish Executive denotes a collective responsibility that causes the resignation of all ministers if the Scottish Parliament votes for no confidence that would focus on the First Minister. However, an individual minister may also be implicated by means of an advisory vote, which does not carry with it any legal obligation to resign, but which in practice should lead to the resignation of such a minister.[42] The singular form used when describing the minister who is to resign after a decision of no confidence suggests the latter, that is, that it is only the implicated minister (or ministers) who has to resign, unless the decision focuses on

---

[36]Himsworth and Munro (2000), pp. 59–62, raising also the question whether the statutory basis might make formation of government in Scotland justiciable.

[37]Page (2005), p. 14.

[38]See Page (2005), pp. 17 f.

[39]If the First Minister loses a vote of no confidence, he or she must tender his or her resignation to the Queen and, in such an event, all ministers in the Scottish Executive must also resign. See Himsworth and O'Neill (2003), p. 233, and McFadden and Lazarowicz (2002), p. 80.

[40]Bogdanor (1999), p. 213.

[41]According to Himsworth and O'Neill (2003), p. 236, the requirement of parliamentary involvement is a feature which distinguishes Scotland from the formation of the UK Government.

[42]McFadden and Lazarowicz (2002), pp. 46, 80 f. See also Himsworth and Munro (2000), p. 68.

the entire Government. However, the interpretation seems to be that in principle, the other ministers resign *en bloc* in a situation of loss of parliamentary confidence because they are originally appointed *en bloc*.[43] The political (and perhaps also legal) responsibility of Scottish ministers reaches to the actions of all branches of the Scottish executive, because according to section 59(4), a document shall be validly executed by the Scottish Ministers if it is executed by any member of the Scottish Executive.

The Scottish Government also contains two law officers, the Lord Advocate and the Solicitor General, which at the same time have a prominent position in the Scottish Parliament and may even be members of the Scottish Parliament. The two law officers are recommended by the First Minister for appointment or removal to Her Majesty, and the First Minister needs the agreement of the Parliament also for these two offices. They, too, must resign if the Parliament resolves that the Scottish Executive no longer enjoys the confidence of the Parliament. The law officers can therefore have a double or even a triple role in the Scottish structures of public authority as persons who participate in making rules and implement them.[44] Because of criticism towards this role, the Lord Advocate has given up his right to vote in the Scottish Executive, but remains a member of the Scottish Executive.[45]

Hence, there is a horizontal dimension of governmental accountability, which is clearly codified in the Scotland Act,[46] and which seems to be a primary one. In addition to political accountability through the mechanism of confidence, there are other procedures devoted to executive scrutiny in Scotland, namely parliamentary

---

[43]See McFadden and Lazarowicz (2002), p. 78. See also Scottish Ministerial Code (2008), paras. 1.1., 2.1., 2.2. and 2.7., which all emphasize collective responsibility of the Scottish Government even in the situation that a decision has been taken by an individual minister. See also Guide to Collective Decision-Making (2008).

[44]See also Himsworth and Munro (2000), pp. 34 f., 59, 74. Although under section 57(2) of the Scotland Act a member of the Scottish Executive has no power to do certain acts so far as the act is incompatible with any of the rights guaranteed by the European Convention of Human Rights, a decision to prosecute by or under the authority of the Lord Advocate after a long delay, allegedly violating the right to a reasonable length of proceedings under the Convention, is not prevented under the Scotland Act. *David Spiers, Procurator Fiscal v. Kevin Gerald Ruddy (Scotland) and Her Majesty's Advocate General for Scotland*, Judicial Committee of the Privy Council, 12 December 2007, and *David Shields Montgomery and Andrew Alexander Marshall Coulter v. Her Majesty's Advocate and The Advocate General for Scotland*, Judicial Committee of the Privy Council, 19 October 2000, at http://www.privy-council.org.uk/output/Page535.asp (accessed 18 March 2009). This would seem clear also under section 57(3), which says that sub-section (2) does not apply to an act of the Lord Advocate in prosecuting any offence, or in his capacity as head of the systems of criminal prosecution and investigation of deaths in Scotland, which, because of sub-section (2) of section 6 of the Human Rights Act 1998 is not unlawful under sub-section (1) of that section. It is for the courts to determine whether or not a prosecution shall proceed to trial, although there may exist no primary legislation that compels a representative of the Scottish Executive to proceed to prosecution.

[45]McFadden and Lazarowicz (2002), p. 79.

[46]According to Himsworth (2006), p. 205, "[t]he Parliament is given an express role in government formation which the Westminster Parliament does not enjoy".

questions by the MSPs for either an oral or a written answer by a member of the Scottish Executive, debates on the initiative of opposition parties or of individual members, the work of select or subject committees (with the possibility that a minister of the Scottish Executive participates in it), and the possibility for the First Minister to make a statement to the Parliament outlining a policy or legislative issue.[47]

7.3.2 *Integration with the National Government*

Formally speaking, the governmental structures of Scotland are, in addition, vertically aligned to the national executive by the appointment and release of the ministers of Scotland by Her Majesty. The vertical line of accountability is therefore, at least formally, fairly strong in the case of Scotland and its autonomy, although in actual practice, the vertical dimension should not weigh much in comparison with the horizontal accountability, because the role of the Sovereign is that of a figurehead controlled by the political forces. The formal vertical alignment does not, however, mean that the Scottish ministers become ministers of the Crown.[48]

It is also to be taken into account in the vertical dimension that the members of the staff of the Scottish Administration, that is, the civil servants of the autonomous entity, are members of the Home Civil Service, that is, Her Majesty's Home Civil Service or the national civil service.[49] This is so in spite of the fact that it is the Scottish Ministers who may, under section 51 of the Scotland Act, appoint persons to be members of the staff of the Scottish Administration. The highest echelon of Scottish officials, however, is appointed or approved by the UK Prime Minister after consultation with the First Minister of Scotland, because the UK Prime Minister is also the Minister for the Civil Service.[50] The norms applied on the administrative staff are those of the Home Civil Service by or under any Order in

[47]Himsworth and O'Neill (2003), p. 358 f., 361–366, 370–374, and McFadden and Lazarowicz (2002), p. 46. See also Scottish Ministerial Code (2008) and Guide to Collective Decision-Making (2008).

[48]Himsworth (2006), p. 197, Himsworth and O'Neill (2003), p. 230.

[49]See also Himsworth (2006), pp. 203, 214, Himsworth and Munro (2000), p. 66, Himsworth and O'Neill (2003), p. 261, and McFadden and Lazarowicz (2002), p. 81. As pointed out by Trench (2007b), p. 68 f., staff of the Scottish Government "are part of the Home Civil Service in the same way as staff of any Whitehall department, even though they serve quite different political masters", although their position is tempered by the fact that the devolved administrations have considerable autonomy for matters including grading structures, staffing and pay levels and by the fact that the "Civil Service Code was amended in 1999 to provide that officials owe their loyalty to the administration in which they serve, not a single UK Government, though what that means has never been put to the test publicly".

[50]Serving Scotland Better (2009), p. 125.

Council, and there is a connection to the UK Civil Service (Management Functions) Act of 1992 (delegation of functions by Ministers), according to which salaries or allowances payable to or in respect of such staff of the Scottish administration (including contributions to any pension scheme) shall be payable out of the Scottish Consolidated Fund. The Scottish Ministers also make payments to the UK Minister for the Civil Service of such amounts as he may determine in respect of the provision of certain pensions, allowances or gratuities by virtue of section 1 of the Superannuation Act of 1972, to or in respect of persons who are or have been in particular administrative service.

The integration of the Scottish administration in the national civil service is not only an organizational matter, but also a functional one, because under section 52 of the Scotland Act, the statutory functions[51] conferred on the Scottish Ministers, the First Minister or the Lord Advocate are exercised on behalf of Her Majesty. In addition, statutory functions of the Scottish Ministers shall be exercisable by any member of the Scottish Executive, which functions are consequently also exercised on behalf of Her Majesty. Such a functional connection to the UK central government is, of course, rational, because section 53 of the Scotland Act makes possible a general transfer of functions to the Scottish Ministers from a Minister of the Crown, provided that the functions are exercisable within the devolved competence. Such functions are those of Her Majesty's prerogative and other executive functions which are exercisable on behalf of Her Majesty by a Minister of the Crown, other functions conferred on a Minister of the Crown by a prerogative instrument, and functions conferred on a Minister of the Crown by any pre-commencement enactment,[52] but do not include any retained functions of the Lord Advocate. In addition, Her Majesty may, by Order in Council, pursuant to section 63 of the Scotland Act, transfer functions and modify functions of the central government in Scotland: any functions, so far as they are exercisable by a Minister of the Crown in or as regards Scotland can be transferred to be exercisable by the Scottish Ministers instead of by the Minister of the Crown, by the Scottish Ministers concurrently with the Minister of the Crown, or by the Minister of the Crown only with the agreement of, or after consultation with, the Scottish Ministers.[53]

[51]According to section 52 of the Scotland Act, the concept of statutory functions mean functions conferred by virtue of any enactment. However, there is no direct alignment between the distribution of functions of ministers of the Scottish Government and the departments of the Scottish Administration, and Himsworth and O'Neill (2003), p. 357, feel that this may dilute the idea of responsibility of one for the other.

[52]The concept of "pre-commencement enactment" means in the Scotland Act (a) an act passed before or in the same session as this act and any other enactment made before the passing of this act, (b) an enactment made, before the commencement of this section, under such an act or such other enactment, (c) subordinate legislation under section 106 of the Scotland Act, to the extent that the legislation states that it is to be treated as a pre-commencement enactment.

[53]See also Himsworth and Munro (2000), p. 79, who make the point that it was always clear that the central government would transfer some of its executive functions to the Scottish Executive

Thus beyond the legislative devolution, there also exist broad possibilities of so-called executive devolution, and this mechanism has been used more often than the procedure established in section 30 (see Sect. 5.4.1 above).[54] This means that the Scottish executive is the implementing agency not only of Scottish legislation, but also of UK legislation, and that the scope of the executive powers in Scotland stretches beyond the legislative competences of Scotland. In principle, executive functions that have been devolved from the UK Government to the Scottish Government are not matters that would be discussed in the Scottish Parliament, but it has been held that the mechanism of parliamentary accountability in Scotland also covers functions and issues that the Scottish Government is carrying out in Scotland on behalf of the UK Government and that such matters, too, could be raised by the Scottish Parliament.[55]

However, a number of safeguards involving consent from the central government may be added to such transfers to the Scottish Ministers. In addition, under section 108 on the agreed redistribution of functions exercisable by the Scottish Ministers and others, Her Majesty may, by Order in Council, provide for any functions exercisable by a member of the Scottish Executive to be exercisable by a Minister of the Crown instead of by the member of the Scottish Executive, by a Minister of the Crown concurrently with the member of the Scottish Executive, or by the member of the Scottish Executive only with the agreement of, or after consultation with, a Minister of the Crown.[56]

The flexibility in the integration of the two administrations, where transfer of functions can go in both directions, reaches even further through the mutual agency arrangements provided for in section 93 of the Scotland Act. A Minister of the Crown, including a department of the UK Government, may make arrangements for any of his specified functions to be exercised on his behalf by the Scottish Ministers, and the Scottish Ministers may make arrangements for any of their specified functions to be exercised on their behalf by a Minister of the Crown.[57] However, making, confirming or approving subordinate legislation is not included in the mutually transferable functions, and UK ministers are not authorized to discharge the functions of the Scottish Ministers.[58]

---

and that this possibility is an important feature of the devolution scheme. See also Himsworth and O'Neill (2003), p. 248.

[54]Serving Scotland Better (2009), p. 46.

[55]McFadden and Lazarowicz (2002), p. 15.

[56]See also Himsworth and Munro (2000), p. 133, and Serving Scotland Better (2009), p. 46.

[57]The functional integration is also present in section 106 concerning the power to adapt functions, in particular as concerns the implementation of international obligations. See also Himsworth and Munro (2000), p. 130 f.

[58]Himsworth and O'Neill (2003), p. 248.

7.3.3 Implementation of Devolved Competence

Despite the functional integration through executive devolution from the UK government to the Scottish government, the functions exercised by the Scottish executive, that is, decisions of both a normative and individual kind, are in principle limited in section 54 of the Scotland Act to the sphere of legislative competence of the Scottish Parliament.[59] According to the provision, it is outside devolved competence to make any provision by subordinate legislation, which would be outside the legislative competence of the Parliament if it were included in an act of the Scottish Parliament, or to confirm or approve any subordinate legislation containing such a provision. There is also a limitation of Scottish executive powers in section 57: despite the transfer to the Scottish Ministers by virtue of section 53 of functions in relation to observing and implementing obligations under EU law, any function of a Minister of the Crown in relation to any matter shall continue to be exercisable by him as regards Scotland for the purposes specified in section 2(2) of the European Communities Act of 1972. In addition, under section 118 on subordinate instruments, it may be necessary in certain cases for the Scottish Executive to present subordinate legislation for the UK Parliament for confirmation.[60]

In the case of any function other than a function of making, confirming or approving subordinate legislation, it is outside devolved competence to exercise the function (or exercise it in any way) in so far as a provision of an act of the Scottish Parliament conferring the function (or, as the case may be, conferring it so as to be exercisable in that way) would be outside the legislative competence of the Scottish Parliament. As a consequence, both the normative powers and the powers to pass individual decisions of the Scottish Executive are tied to the sphere of the legislative competence of the Scottish Parliament (while the central government seems to retain a general power to make subordinate legislation as specified in the Scotland Act).[61] In addition, it should be possible to expect, against the background

[59]See also Trench (2007b), p. 53, Himsworth and Munro (2000), p. 70, Himsworth and O'Neill (2003), p. 247.

[60]For detailed specifications, see schedule 7 to the Scotland Act.

[61]See sections 112–116 of the Scotland Act on the powers, functions and procedures relating to subordinate legislation by Her Majesty and other agencies of the central government. Actually, because executive functions are transferred under the Scotland Act, the UK Government cannot use any "preemption" powers by intruding into the competence of the Scottish Ministers. It seems that there is no overlap between the two spheres of competences and thus no need of a Sewel-Convention-like arrangement in the area of executive powers.

of sections 104[62] and 107,[63] that such powers of the executive are exercised only with appropriate legal basis, and with the observance of section 57 of the Scotland Act, according to which a member of the Scottish Executive has no power to make any subordinate legislation, or to do any other act, so far as the legislation or act is incompatible with any of the rights guaranteed on the basis of the European Convention of Human Rights or with European Community law.

In practice, the making of subordinate legislation is a very important function of the Scottish Executive, at least quantitatively, because in its first term between 1999 and 2003, the Scottish Executive issued nearly two thousand Scottish Statutory Instruments, while the Scottish Parliament passed 62 Scottish acts.[64] Finally, section 56 of the Scotland Act identifies a range of shared powers of the executive, where both Scottish Ministers and Ministers of the Crown can take action in spite of the fact that the functions may have been transferred to the Scottish executive.[65]

The Scotland Act vests a broad control competence in the Secretary of State, that is, any Secretary of State of the UK Government, who according to section 58 has both the power to prevent action or to require action of the Scottish Executive under certain circumstances (although the power has not been exercised between 1998

[62]According to the section, the legislation is subordinate legislation under an act of Parliament made by (a) a member of the Scottish Executive, (b) a Scottish public authority with mixed functions or no reserved functions, or (c) any other person (not being a Minister of the Crown) if the function of making the legislation is exercisable within devolved competence. Subordinate legislation may make such provision as the person making the legislation considers necessary or expedient in consequence of any provision made by or under any act of the Scottish Parliament or made by subordinate legislation.

[63]The section holds that subordinate legislation may make such provision as the person making the legislation considers necessary or expedient in consequence of an act of the Scottish Parliament or any provision of an act of the Scottish Parliament which is not, or may not be, within the legislative competence of the Parliament, or any purported exercise by a member of the Scottish Executive of his functions which is not, or may not be, an exercise or a proper exercise of those functions. See also Himsworth and Munro (2000), p. 132.

[64]McFadden and Lazarowicz (2002), p. 70. For the different categories of making subordinate legislation, see McFadden and Lazarowicz (2002), p. 70 f.

[65]For example, any Order in Council under section 1 of the United Nations Act 1946 (measures to give effect to Security Council decisions), section 9 of the Industrial Organisation and Development Act 1947 (levies for scientific research, promotion of exports, etc.), section 5 of the Science and Technology Act 1965 (funding of scientific research), section 1 of the Mineral Exploration and Investment Grants Act 1972 (contributions in respect of mineral exploration), sections 10 to 12 of the Industry Act 1972 (credits and grants for construction of ships and offshore installations), sections 2, 11(3) and 12(4) of the Employment and Training Act 1973 (power to make arrangements for employment and training etc. and to make certain payments), sections 7 to 9 and 11 to 13 of the Industrial Development Act 1982 (financial and other assistance for industry), and sections 39 and 40 of the Road Traffic Act 1988 (road safety information and training). These functions shall be exercisable by a Minister of the Crown as well as by the Scottish Ministers in the Scottish jurisdiction. See also Himsworth and Munro (2000), p. 72.

and 2009).[66] If the Secretary of State has reasonable grounds to believe that any action proposed to be taken by a member of the Scottish Executive would be incompatible with any international obligations, he may by order direct that the proposed action shall not be taken, and if the Secretary of State has reasonable grounds to believe that any action capable of being taken by a member of the Scottish Executive is required for the purpose of giving effect to any such obligations, he may by order direct that the action shall be taken. In this context, "action" may include making, confirming or approving subordinate legislation and even introducing a Bill in the Scottish Parliament.[67] In addition, if any subordinate legislation made, or which could be revoked by a member of the Scottish Executive contains provisions, which the Secretary of State has reasonable grounds to believe to be incompatible with any international obligations or the interests of defence or national security, or which make modifications of the law as it applies to reserved matters and which the Secretary of State has reasonable grounds to believe to have an adverse effect on the operation of the law as it applies to reserved matters, the Secretary of State may by order stating the reasons for it revoke the subordinate legislation.

It is therefore possible to say that the executive branch of the national government has broad powers to control the performance of the Scottish Executive concerning the compliance with international obligations. Knowing that, for instance, issues relevant under EU law may emerge within virtually any area of legislative competence, these control powers are substantial. Adding to that, under section 96 of the Scotland Act, the UK Treasury may require the Scottish Ministers to provide such information, in such a form and prepared in such a manner, as the Treasury may reasonably specify, which means that, in particular, the revenue and spending information of the Scottish autonomy is not a matter that even in its details could be kept within the Scottish autonomous entity.

Against this background, it is possible to conclude that the governmental structures and functions of Scotland are determined in national legislation to a greater extent than is the case with, for instance, the Åland Islands and the Faroe Islands. In spite of this clear link to the national executive, it appears that the Government of Scotland mainly exercises its executive powers in relation to those legislative powers that have been devolved, but not very much in relation to national legislation.[68] However, as explained above, some executive powers

---

[66]See Himsworth and Munro (2000), p. 75, Himsworth and O'Neill (2003), p. 258 f., Serving Scotland Better (2009), p. 47 f.

[67]See also McFadden and Lazarowicz (2002), p. 85.

[68]See Himsworth (2006), p. 194. In addition, as concluded in Himsworth (2006), p. 199, "[t]here is no sense in which a residual power to exercise the functions is left also in the hands of the UK ministers. In the case of devolved functions, it would be unlawful for the Secretary of State to purport to exercise them". However, Himsworth (2006), p. 213, points out that "[t]he Secretary of State has available powers under the Scotland Act to intervene, on specified grounds, to prevent the passing of laws by the Parliament or to prevent the exercise of executive powers by the Scottish

outside the devolved powers have been transferred from ministers of the central government to the Scottish executive. In this context, it has been stated that "[i]t might be that these extensions of executive power beyond the scope of the Parliament's own competence could be viewed as converting the Executive into a mere agent of the UK Government, but there is no sign that the Executive's accountability to the Parliament is affected".[69] In addition, a certain executive prerogative is likely to exist also in the Government of Scotland.[70]

It also seems that the vertical relationship between the government of Scotland and the UK Government is designed in a somewhat different fashion than in Northern Ireland or other constitutional settings where the monarch of Britain is designated as the head of the executive.[71] It is therefore possible to conclude that the Scottish administration is integrated with the UK civil service in a manner which is unusual in comparison with other sub-state entities, and it is not immediately clear on the basis of the Scotland Act to whom the allegiance of the civil servants of the Scottish administration is directed. Presumably, that would be the person or body that exercised the appointment powers and that also could, if need be, exercise the powers of dismissal, which would place Scottish ministers in the front position.[72] However, the integration with the home civil service may also create (or maintain) other allegiances, loyalties and ties. No such vertical alignment exists in Zanzibar, although the system of government there is of British provenance.

Ministers. Neither of these powers has so far been invoked". The vertical dimension is thus quite important, at least in theory.

[69] Himsworth (2006), p. 199.

[70] Himsworth (2006), pp. 200–202. The scope of executive prerogative with the Scottish Government is difficult to identify, because it is minimal in comparison with statutory functions, but it would encompass, e.g., the power to enter into contracts. The civil service is managed on the basis of prerogative in the UK, and there could exist a similar prerogative in the Scottish Government.

[71] Himsworth (2006), p. 196 f.: "It may or may not have any practical consequences but it is clear that Scotland has gone down a different track from that adopted in Northern Ireland and the Commonwealth independence constitutions. Whilst powers exercisable on behalf of the Queen are transferred to the Scottish Executive, there is no overarching concept of the Queen's being the ultimate repository of executive authority in Scotland."

[72] In this respect, it should be noted that para. 6.1. of the Scottish Ministerial Code concludes that Scottish ministers have a "duty to give fair consideration and due weight to informed and impartial advice from civil servants, as well as to other considerations and advice, in reaching decisions; a duty to uphold the political impartiality of the Civil Service, and not to ask civil servants to act in any way which would conflict with the Civil Service Code; (. . .)".

7.4 Zanzibar: Presidential Governance in a Power-Sharing Context

7.4.1 *Presidentialism with the Opposition Involved or Revolutionary One-Man Government?*

As established in Art. 34(1) of the Constitution of Tanzania, the two governments that exist in Tanzania implement the legislation that has originated within their respective sphere of legislative matters. The Government of the United Republic has authority over all Union Matters in the United Republic, and over all other matters concerning Mainland Tanzania. In addition, the Government of the United Republic is in charge of the application and upholding of the Constitution of Tanzania and is also in charge of all other matters over which the Parliament has the power to legislate. There also seems to exist a certain executive prerogative for the President of the United Republic in Art. 34(3), in that all other authority of the Government of the United Republic over all Union Matters in the United Republic and also over all other matters concerning Mainland Tanzania, is vested in the President of the United Republic. It is also established in Art. 105(2) of the Constitution of Tanzania that the executive powers follow the distribution of legislative competence.[73]

The system of government of Zanzibar is very presidential, and it is according to Art. 5A of the Constitution of Zanzibar based on the separation of powers.[74] A particular feature concerning the executive power of Zanzibar is, however, that it is regulated extensively not only in the Constitution of Zanzibar, but also in the Constitution of Tanzania. The latter incorporated rules about the Government of Zanzibar after the Constitution of Zanzibar had been enacted. In fact, the references to government in Art. 6 of the Constitution of Tanzania may, interchangeably and depending on the context, mean the Government of the United Republic, the RGZ, local governmental authorities and any person who exercises power or authority on behalf of either Government. This indicates that there is, at least on the part of Mainland Tanzania, a wish to apply a holistic view to government and to the exercise of the executive power. *Inter alia*, Art. 8(1) of the Constitution provides that the government shall be accountable to the people and that the people shall

[73]"Without prejudice to the powers of the Chairman of the Revolutionary Council as Head of the Revolutionary Government of Zanzibar, the Revolutionary Council shall be the principal organ for advising the Head of the Revolutionary Government of Zanzibar regarding all matters concerning the exercise of his functions of leadership and supervision over the affairs of the Executive for Zanzibar and also in the discharge of his functions over all affairs of Government concerning all matters which are not Union Matters in accordance with the provisions of this Constitution and those of the Constitution of Zanzibar, 1984."

[74]Article 5A(2) allocates the executive authority to the Revolutionary Government of Zanzibar, the legislative authority to the House of Representatives and the judicial authority to the Court.

participate in the affairs of their government in accordance with the provisions of the Constitution. In addition, under Art. 8(2) of the Constitution of Tanzania, the structure of the Government of the United Republic and the RGZ, or any of their organs, and the discharge of their functions shall be so effected as to take into account the unity of the United Republic and the need to promote national unity and preserve national dignity. Therefore, also the executive of Zanzibar is expected to work towards national unity.[75]

As provided in Art. 102 of the Constitution of Tanzania, there is, in addition to the Government of Tanzania, an Executive Government also for Zanzibar which is known as "the Revolutionary Government of Zanzibar". The RGZ has authority in Zanzibar over all matters which are not Union Matters in accordance with the provisions of the Constitution of Tanzania, exercised as provided for in the Constitution of Tanzania and the Constitution of Zanzibar of 1984. Through the amendments in August 2010 to the Constitution of Zanzibar, a legal basis was created for a government of national unity, apparently as an attempt to counter the division that the political and constitutional system of Zanzibar has experienced. Under Art. 39, the President of Zanzibar appoints the First Vice-President and the Second Vice-President. This is essentially a power-sharing arrangement, the effects of which are unknown, but it could be compared with the method of composition of the Government of Northern Ireland, where the parties of the elected assembly are represented in proportion to their political strength in the government.

As concerns the First Vice-President, there is a dimension of power-sharing in the appointment, because he or she shall be appointed after consultation with the party that gets the second position in the results of the election of the President. It is not necessarily so that the presidential candidate of the "opposition" is always headed towards the position of the First Vice-President, but this seems to be the consequence of the mechanism. In practice, under the political constellation that has prevailed until 2010, this would seem to mean that the CUF would be the party that could count on receiving at least the position of the First Vice-President. However, the First Vice-President shall not be a member of the House of Representatives, but he shall be an adviser to the President in the execution of the presidential functions. The First Vice-President shall also perform all other functions that will be assigned to him or her by the President.

In contrast to the First Vice-President, the Second Vice-President shall be appointed by the President from among such members of the House of Representatives who belong to the same party as the President. Also in contrast to the First Vice-President, who shall be an adviser to the President, the Second Vice-President shall be the principal adviser to the President, which is only natural because of the position of the Second Vice-President as the leader of the Ministers. At the same time, however, there is a certain ranking of the Vice-Presidents

[75]According to Tanzania Human Rights Report (2009), pp. 186 f., 222, one of the most pressing human rights issues in Zanzibar is that of corruption, which is seems to be serious within public administration, but exists also in courts of law.

expressed in section 39 of the Constitution of Zanzibar, as amended in 2010. The Second Vice-President is also the leader of Government business in the House of Representatives, and under section 41, possible expressions of no confidence are directed at him or her by the House of Representatives.

Under Art. 51 of the Constitution of Zanzibar, the authority of the Government of Zanzibar is vested in the President of Zanzibar.[76] He may exercise those powers directly or by delegating that authority to subordinate leaders,[77] but he is not obliged to take the advice given to him by any person in the performance of his functions. Under Art. 53, the president has the power to establish and abolish offices in Zanzibar and appoint, promote and dismiss officers.[78] For instance, the President of Zanzibar appoints, under Art. 50, the Principal Secretaries that are heads of office of the President, of the two Vice-Presidents and, if need be, also of the Ministries.

7.4.2 *Impeachment and Accountability*

The presidential system established in Zanzibar is coupled with the powers of the House of Representatives to impeach the President according to provisions in Art. 37 of the Constitution of Zanzibar. For a motion of impeachment, it is required that the President has committed acts which generally violate the Constitution or that he has conducted himself in a manner that lowers the esteem of the Union between Tanganyika and Zanzibar. If a Special Committee of Inquiry reports to the House of Representatives that the charges preferred against the President have a basis, the issue of impeachment of the President shall be brought to the full house of the House of Representatives and, after debate, the House of Representatives may, by a vote of no less than two thirds majority of all the members of the House of Representatives, pass a resolution that the impeachment charges have been proven and that he is unworthy of continuing to hold the office of the President. In such a case, the President is obliged to resign.

[76]As pointed out in Art. 134(1) of the Constitution of Zanzibar, 'President' means the President of Zanzibar and Chairman of the Revolutionary Council.

[77]It is also possible under the Constitution of Zanzibar to delegate powers to any other public authority or entity or person than the President.

[78]The provisions concerning the office of the President of Zanzibar are largely replicated in Art. 103 of the Constitution of Tanzania: "(1) There shall be a Head of the Executive for Zanzibar who shall be the President of Zanzibar and Head of the RGZ and also the Chairman of the Zanzibar Revolutionary Council. (2) The head of the RGZ shall, before assuming office, subscribe the oath before the Chief Justice of Zanzibar to protect and defend the Constitution of the United Republic and any other oath in accordance with the Constitution of Zanzibar in connection with the execution of his duties, and then shall assume office and discharge those functions in accordance with the provisions of this Constitution and the Constitution of Zanzibar, 1984. (3) In addition to his other powers, the Head of the RGZ shall have the power to appoint and assign responsibilities to Ministers and Deputy Ministers of the RGZ.

The larger governmental body in Zanzibar is the Revolutionary Council, which is a collective cabinet[79] organ that under Art. 43(1) of the Constitution of Zanzibar consists of the President and the Second Vice-President (who until 2010 was termed Chief Minister) and Ministers together with other members as the President determines. The Second Vice-President is appointed by the President to be the principal adviser to the President, and he is drawn from amongst the members of the House of Representatives. Specifically, the Second Vice-President shall be drawn from the party to which the President belongs. The other Ministers of the RGZ are appointed by the President under Art. 41(2), upon consultation with the two vice-presidents from amongst the members of the House of Representatives according to the proportion of seats of political parties in the House of Representatives. This should mean that the RGZ would consist not only of ministers of the CCM, but also of those of the CUF, and the ministers from the two parties would control various ministries. As pointed out above, this system is similar to that of Northern Ireland. It is also possible to appoint Deputy Ministers from the membership of the House.[80] The Second Vice-President has the authority over the control, supervision and execution of the day-to-day function of RGZ, and he is also the Leader of the Government business of the RGZ in the House of Representatives.

In spite of the fact that the Constitution of Zanzibar is very presidential and operates at least in principle under the doctrine of the separation of powers, some measure of parliamentary accountability is built into the constitutional fabric of the entity. Already the Preamble to the Constitution of Zanzibar contains a reference to principles that can "only be realised in a democratic society in which the Executive is accountable to a House of Representatives". This is specified in Art. 43(5), according to which the Ministers under the leadership of the Second Vice-President are collectively responsible to the House of Representatives in the execution of the business of the RGZ, which competence is of a general nature. Although Art. 48 may create the impression that a lack of confidence established by the House of Representatives would not be a reason to vacate a ministerial seat in the Revolutionary Council,[81] Art. 41(1) nonetheless makes clear that the House of Representatives may pass a resolution of no confidence in the Second Vice-President.

[79] According to the definition in Art. 134(1) of the Constitution of Zanzibar, the term 'Revolutionary Council' includes the Cabinet. See also Shivji (2008), p. 229 f., according to whom the composition of the Revolutionary Council shows that it is virtually a cabinet, but under another name.

[80] These provisions concerning the Revolutionary Council are largely reproduced in Art. 105 of the Constitution of Tanzania.

[81] "The Office of a Minister, Member of the Revolutionary Council and Deputy Minister shall be vacant: (a) where the President shall remove him from office in writing and signified by Government Seal; (b) if a member ceases to be member of the House of Representatives for any reason other than dissolution of the House of Representatives; (c) if the President accepts the resignation of the person concerned; (d) immediately before the President assumes office." A vote of no confidence is not mentioned as a reason to leave the government in this context, but the reason may be that the grounds in Art. 48 are individual rather than collective.

The vote of no confidence is, however, quite an attenuated phenomenon, because a written notice to that effect must first be supported by no less than one half of all members of the House of Representatives, that is, by absolute majority, and the resolution for a vote of no confidence in the Second Vice-President is passed only if it is supported by a two thirds majority of all the members of House of Representatives, which places the mechanism behind almost as high thresholds as the impeachment of the President. Even the Government of Tanzania is easier to bring down through a vote of no confidence, because according to Art. 53A of the Constitution of Tanzania, the Tanzanian Government can be voted out of office by an absolute majority. It can thus be concluded that the possibility of no confidence is a very remote one, and the mechanism, as established in Zanzibar, has little in common with the mechanism of no confidence in other autonomies, such as Scotland or the Åland Islands. There may even be the possibility to conclude that the accountability referred to in the Preamble of the Constitution cannot be effectively realized, at least through the mechanism of no confidence. The horizontal accountability is thus not present in a realistic way in the constitutional fabric of Zanzibar, at least not after the amendments of August 2010, which introduced a government of national unity appointed from the parties represented in the House of Representatives in proportion to their seats in the House. It is another matter that the accountability of the ministers of the government may be realized by the President, because under Art. 48, the ministers are actually accountable to him.

Although the horizontal accountability within the constitutional structures of Zanzibar seems to be absent, there potentially exists a vertical channel of accountability on the basis of Art. 54(1) of the Constitution of Tanzania. The provision creates the cabinet of Tanzania and mentions as members of it the Vice-President of Tanzania, the Prime Minister, the President of Zanzibar, and all the Ministers.[82] The position of the President of Zanzibar in the cabinet may amount to a vertical mechanism of accountability, but the cabinet of Tanzania is normally not a very relevant forum for policy making for the President of Zanzibar, although in formal terms, the recognition of a representative from Zanzibar in that context is important. In fact, the incorporation of the two territorial entities of Tanzania in the cabinet of Tanzania may be regarded as a wish to underline national unity between the two parts of the Union in a manner that goes in a federal direction. The role of Zanzibar in the cabinet of Tanzania is enhanced by the fact that the Vice-President of Tanzania, who in most cases would come from Zanzibar, is also a member of the Tanzanian cabinet.

[82]According to Khamis Bakary (2006), p. 10, Art. 54(1) and Art. 47(b) of the Constitution of Tanzania, as amended by the 11th amendment, abolished the special status of the President of Zanzibar, and therefore, "the Zanzibar President is treated just like a Cabinet Minister". A similar mechanism exists for the Gagauzian autonomy in Moldova: the Governor, who is the highest executive figure of Gagauzia, elected by the population of Gagauzia, is also a member of the Moldovan government. See Suksi (2009), p. 124.

7.4.3 Particular Governmental Structures

For the purposes of the administration of Zanzibar, the Constitution of Zanzibar creates different administrative structures. Firstly, under Art. 42(1) the President may establish ministries of the RGZ. According to Art. 55(1) there shall also be an Attorney General for Zanzibar who in addition shall be an *ex officio* member of the House of Representatives, a function also found in Scotland. According to Art. 56A (1)(a), there is a Director of Public Prosecutions (DPP; see above, Sect. 4.4.2) appointed by the President. This office was established on the basis of the negotiations leading up to the Muafaka II political agreement and is intended to guarantee an independent prosecutorial function in Zanzibar for the enforcement of legislation. There is also a provision concerning civil servants and public officers in Art. 54 according to which a person holding office in the Government of Zanzibar occupies that position at the pleasure of the President. An office-holder is evidently understood in the broad sense of the term "office", so that also so-called para-statals are included.

A particular feature of the governmental structures of Zanzibar is the existence of so-called special departments. Such organs can be created under Art. 23(5) of the Constitution of Zanzibar by enacting appropriate laws to enable the people to serve in the forces and in the defense of the nation. Most of the special departments, in fact, have a direct legal basis in the Constitution of Zanzibar. According to Art. 121, there shall be three special departments, the Economic Development Force (the JKU), the Special Force for Prevention of Smuggling (the KMKM), and the Educational Centre for Offenders (the Chuo cha Mafunzo), that is, the prison. Under the provision, the President of Zanzibar may, when he deems it fit, establish any other department and designate it a special department.[83] This legal basis was used when the *Kikosi cha Valantia* was created. The President is, under Art. 123(1), the Commander-in-chief of the Special Departments and has the power to do anything he sees fit to do in the interest of the Nation. These powers of the President include the power to order anything to be done by a Special Department in the interest of the nation. This means that the President of Zanzibar has powerful tools in his hands, and the special departments are perceived by the population to be anything but politically neutral[84] at the same time as they are allegedly in some respects functioning outside the law.[85]

---

[83]Tanzania Human Rights Report (2009), p. 213, mentions also the Zima Moto, that is, the fire department, amongst the special departments, created under Act No. 7 of 1999. In addition, the report mentions a general act produced to ensure better working conditions in the special departments, the Special Department Service Commission Act, 2007 (Act No. 6 of 2007).

[84]See, e.g., Tanzania Human Rights Report (2009), p. 214.

[85]According to Tanzania Human Rights Report (2009), p. 217, the special departments are "number one perpetrators of deforestation and no action is taken against them", although they carry out logging without permission.

While it might not be necessary to touch upon the special department of the prison, that is, the Educational Centre for Offenders,[86] the other ones are relevant from the point of view of the fact that Art. 147 of the Constitution of Tanzania forbids the raising of forces, a prohibition which might be interpreted as preventing the creation of a formal army or other forces which have the right to use force or which are organized according to a military hierarchy. In addition, point 4 of the first schedule to the Constitution of Tanzania establishes the police as a Union Matter. The interpretation in Zanzibar seems to be that the prohibition against raising forces should be understood in a limited sense, because three of the special departments are militarily organized and have the right to possess small arms. At the same time, at least some of the special departments created would seem to perform an assisting function in relation to the national police.

The Zanzibar Youth Service or the Economic Development Force (*Jeshi la Kujenga Uchumi* or JKU)[87] is one of the constitutionally mandated special departments of the Government of Zanzibar. The functions of the JKU are to train the young Zanzibaris to serve the nation and, in particular, to employ them in instructions in the basic principles of economy and their application in agriculture, small-scale industries, fisheries and other vocational training, civic education, social and cultural activities including social development, defense of the nation, to join forces with the Tanzanian Police Force where necessary in maintaining security and order, to join force with the Tanzania People's Defense Forces when mobilized in the defense of the United Republic, to provide security guard services to public institutions (such as the vital security installations, public enterprises of the Government, public corporations of the United Republic, and private areas of vital economic importance), to join hands with other security and defense forces in fulfilling their national duties, which in one way or another the JKU is required to fulfill by any law in existence, and to do any other thing which may be given or ordered by the President. The JKU consists of professionals and voluntary servicemen and has the power and right to possess and use arms or ammunitions in the performance of its functions as shall be provided in the JKU Act and regulations made under the Act. The President is the Commander-in-Chief of the JKU and has the powers and the authority as stipulated in the Constitution and the JKU Act. Persons who have served on the JKU constitute a reserve that may be called on in emergency situations.

The *Kikosi Maalum cha Kuzuia Magendo* (the KMKM)[88] is a coast guard unit (or perhaps a maritime militia) of the Government of Zanzibar and, as such, a special force. The KMKM has the legal right to own and use various weapons and armament required to carry out its functions. The tasks of the KMKM are to ensure

[86] On problems in relation to prisons in Zanzibar, see Tanzania Human Rights Report (2009), p. 183.

[87] Jeshi la Kujenga Uchumi Act, 2003.

[88] Kikosi Maalum cha Kuzuia Magendo Act, 2003. According to Shivji (2008), p. 186, the KMKM "continues to be a paramilitary force contrary to the provisions of the Union constitution".

the security of the territorial waters of Zanzibar, to protect and defend marine natural resources, to protect and defend the security of the country from spies and saboteurs coming from the sea, to prevent smuggling activities in the country by all means to protect convoys of Government vessels transporting members of the public, national leaders or valuable goods in the event of a war or public emergency, to transport troops when called upon to do so, to cooperate with the Tanzanian People's Defense Forces, when mobilized in the defense of the United Republic of Tanzania, to counter crimes committed at sea, including illicit drugs trafficking and pirates, to undertake search and rescue operations at sea and the protection of the marine environment, to come to the aid of the Government during public emergencies, and to undertake any assignment given by the President, taking into consideration the duties, expertise and resources of KMKM. The KMKM has the power to search, impound, and apprehend a vessel, vehicle or premises in the vessel, vehicle or premises in the vicinity of landing places involved in or suspected of engaging in the smuggling of goods and other exported cash crops.[89] The KMKM functions under the authority of the President and a Minister of the Government.

The most controversial of the special departments might be the *Kikosi cha Valantia* (the Valantia).[90] The Valantia is a Zanzibar militia or special force, established as a special department of the Government. The duties of the Valantia are to cooperate with the defense and security forces or any other institution in the defense of the United Republic of Tanzania, or the security of citizens and their properties, or to undertake other duties which the Valantia is responsible for under any existing law, to counter any disaster which may arise and affect society, to protect the property of the Government, to maintain peace and security in the country, to discharge all military functions for the purposes of controlling emergency situations in defense and security, and to undertake any assignment given or directed by the President or Minister or any appointed authority. Under the Act, a servant of the Valantia has legal immunity from prosecution of criminal offences while exercising his duties. The servants of the Valantia may carry small weapons and they have also the right of arrest and search. The President is the Commander-in-Chief of the Valantia and he has those powers as prescribed in the Constitution of Zanzibar, 1984. Allegedly, during elections, members of the Valantia are bussed around to polling stations around Zanzibar to vote in the elections, under instructions that the Valantia members should vote multiple times in different

[89]According to Tanzania Human Rights Report (2009), p. 216, in 2008, "more than five hundred bags of cloves which are estimated to fetch Millions of shillings were intercepted by members of Anti-Smuggling Unit (KMKM) who confiscated the proceeds and the vessels". In addition, as pointed out in Tanzania Human Rights Report (2009), p. 223, fn. 1133, although the KMKM Act of 2003 "requires that after KMKM has arrested any smuggled goods they have to surrender the same to police for investigation. That is not done; instead Regional Commissioners, particularly those from Pemga, order the goods to be sold."

[90]Kikosi cha Valantia Act, 2004, Act No. 4 of 2004.

locations, evidently in favor of the incumbent. The activity appears to have been carried out completely openly, and everybody seems to know about it.[91]

7.4.4 Regional and Local Government

In addition to the administrative bodies at the "autonomy level", Art.145 of the Constitution of Tanzania prescribes the establishment of local government authorities in each region, district, urban area and village in the United Republic. Such administrative entities shall be of the type and designation prescribed by law, enacted either by Parliament or by the House of Representatives. It seems that the legislative competence is, in this area, shared, the consequence being that Zanzibar has its own legislation concerning lower levels of administration, while Mainland Tanzania has its own legislation. Article 2A of the Constitution of Zanzibar stipulates that for the purposes of the efficient discharge of the functions of Government, the President, may divide Zanzibar into Regions, Districts and any other areas in accordance with an act enacted by the House of Representatives.[92] At the same time, article 61(1) of the Constitution of Zanzibar requires that there is a Regional Commissioner for every region of Zanzibar who shall be appointed by the President,[93] and that there also is a District Commissioner for every district in Zanzibar who shall be appointed by the President of Zanzibar.[94] Both civil servants are the chief executives of their respective jurisdictions. In theory at least, the Regional Commissioner may, under Art. 61(5), be an implementing organ of both Union law and of the law of Zanzibar, although the latter is more relevant for regional administration, while the presence of the Union is not felt very much at all.

---

[91]This is also reported in Hamad (2007), pp. 45, 53. The special departments should not be used by a political party to perpetrate human rights violations to the political opponents in order to maintain the political status of that party.

[92]The power to introduce administrative sub-divisions is concentrated on the President of Zanzibar on the basis of the constitutional amendment of 2010. Before the amendment, the President of the Union had this power, albeit in consultation with the President of Zanzibar.

[93]A similar provision is included in Art. 61 of the Constitution of Tanzania, creating the office of the Regional Commissioner for all regions of Mainland Tanzania, appointed by the President of Tanzania. The provision, however, also makes the point that the Regional Commissioners in Tanzania Zanzibar are to be appointed by the President of Zanzibar, after consultation with the Union President. Here the constitutional amendments in Zanzibar in 2010 have emphasized the role of the President of Zanzibar as the sole decision-making authority.

[94]The position of the District Commissioner is apparently central in the dominance of the ruling party of the structures of government, as is pointed out in Tanzania Human Rights Report (2009), p. 193: "Currently issues of employment in government departments are under the control of District Commissioner's office. For one to be employed he/she must have a strong recommendation from his/her Sheha. The Shehas are known for their strong support to the ruling party." It should be mentioned that the public sector is the most important source of income in Zanzibar.

In practice, the regional authorities in Zanzibar are controlled by the President of Zanzibar, not by the Union President.

The Regional Administration Authority Act of 1998, creates the offices of the Regional Commissioner, District Commissioner and *Sheha* as representatives of the Government and as the executive arms of the Government. As provided in Art. 3(1) of the Act, the President of Zanzibar in consultation with the President of the United Republic may provide for the administrative division of Zanzibar into regions, districts and other administrative areas as he may deem necessary. Currently, there are five regions in Zanzibar, each headed by a Regional Commissioner, and each of them divided into districts. Every district is further subdivided into *shehias* as determined by administrative convenience, population distribution, management and delivery of services, existence of common facilities, and historical ties. In this context, the regional commissioner has the tasks of monitoring, supervising and assisting in the execution of the functions of the Government in his region assuring that the policies, plans and directives of the Government are observed, maintaining of law and order in the region in collaboration with law enforcement agencies, and assuring that resources, both material and manpower, are used for development in the economy and welfare. Both regional commissioners and district commissioners have the power to arrest a person.

Local government is regulated in both constitutions. Under Art. 128 of the Constitution of Zanzibar, there shall be local governments with elections of their leaders, their powers and functions prescribed by an act enacted by the House of Representatives. According to Art. 146 of the Constitution of Tanzania, the purpose of having local government authorities is to transfer authority to the people, and they are tasked with, for instance, the planning and implementation of development programs within their respective areas. Generally speaking, most administrative matters are not on the local government, but instead on the Government of Zanzibar. This is the case with such areas as schools, health, etc.[95] Municipal government in Zanzibar is organized on the basis of the Zanzibar Municipal Council Act, 1995,[96] and the District and Town Councils Act, 1995. According to the Acts, local government takes place in municipalities and districts and towns, where the inhabitants of a constituency elect the councilors who form the council of a municipality, a district or a town. However, a Minister of the RGZ is in addition charged with appointing no more than three persons amongst lawyers, economists and persons with adequate knowledge and experience in the management of government or public affairs. The term of mandate of a municipal council is 5 years after being elected under the Elections Act, 1984. The mayor is elected

[95] Local government has the following tasks in Zanzibar: maintenance and building of offices, etc., control streets and public roads, lighting of roads and places, maintenance of environment, control of public space, creation and maintenance of recreation grounds, refreshment rooms, cafés and restaurants in recreation grounds, as well as sewage and drainage and public markets. In principle, the organization of a town is similar, but the powers and functions of a town are broader.

[96] Act No. 3 of 1995 and Act No. 4 of 1995.

from amongst the councilors of the municipality, but he is not the chief executive of the council. Instead, the President of RGZ appoints a director who is the chief executive officer in a municipality, while the mayor is, instead, the chief advisor to the council.

A municipality is a corporate body and can enter into contracts,[97] but it can also make bylaws in matters that belong to its sphere of competence. A municipality has some taxation power, such as the property tax and the motor vehicle tax, and the municipality can also collect fees for licenses granted under different acts, but the RGZ also gives subsidies to the municipalities of Zanzibar. The degree of self-government that the municipalities of Zanzibar have is probably relatively limited, because it is the duty of the council to take such action as the minister may from time to time require to safeguard and promote public health. For this purpose, the council shall be responsible for the administration within the municipality of such parts of the Public Health Decree and any other act as the minister may from time to time determine.

In addition to municipal government at the local level, also the Government of Zanzibar is active there through administrative areas called *Shehia*, led by a *Sheha*. These are created under the Local Government Act, 1984, and are representatives of the Regional and District Commissioners (and ultimately the Government of Zanzibar) at the local level, which makes them state agents. According to Art. 64 of the Elections Act, 1984, every *Sheha* shall be an *ex officio* polling agent of the Zanzibar Election Commission, which is problematic against the background of the fact that the "Shehas are known for their strong support to the ruling party".[98]

The multifarious regional and local administrative structures of Zanzibar are only paralleled, amongst the sub-state entities studied here, by the administrative structures of Aceh.

7.5 Aceh: Regional Authority and National Presence through the Governor

7.5.1 Broad Powers of the Governor

As defined in Art. 1, paras. 6–7, of the LoGA, the Aceh Government is an element that exercises the governance of Aceh and that consists of the Governor and

[97]In addition to the power to enter into contracts, a municipality can purchase, lease, gift or exchange land within the municipality,

[98]Tanzania Human Rights Report (2009), p. 193. As recommended in Hamad (2007), p. 52, Sheha should be totally excluded from the process of registration of voters, because they have caused many problems in all elections, although in the elections of 2005, they were already formally excluded from the registration of voters.

Acehnese regional apparatus. The Governor is, according to Art. 39(1), the head of the Aceh Government,[99] elected pursuant to Art. 65 for a period of 5 years, and in leading the Acehnese Government, he or she shall be assisted by a Vice-Governor. The Governor has an overall role and is responsible for establishing the policies of the Government of Aceh in all sectors of governance including public services and community order and tranquility as determined in *qanuns*.

Article 42 of the LoGA identifies a number of duties and powers for the Governor. He is to lead the execution of governance based on policies established jointly by the Governor and the DPRA, to propose draft *qanuns*, to enact *qanuns* that have obtained joint approval from the Governor and DPRA, to prepare and propose draft *qanuns* regarding the APBA to the DPRA for deliberation, approval, and joint enactment, and to implement and coordinate the full implementation of Islamic law. In addition, the Governor is tasked to submit an accountability report on the execution of governance to the DPRA, submit a report on the execution of Aceh governance to the Indonesian Government,[100] provide information on the execution of governance in Aceh and its districts/municipalities to the people, strive toward the full execution of government authorities, represent the region inside and outside and in a court of law, which functions may be delegated to a third party as a legal representative in accordance with prevailing laws and regulations, and execute other duties and authorities in accordance with prevailing laws and regulations.

The Vice-Governor, elected on the same ticket as the Governor, assists the Governor in a number of specific ways, which give the Vice-Governor a somewhat independent role in the governance of Aceh.[101] The Vice-Governor is accountable to the Governor for the performance of his or her duties. If the Governor dies, resigns, is dismissed or is unable to fulfill his or her duties for a consecutive period of 6 months during the period of tenure, the Vice Governor shall replace the Governor until the end of the Governor's term of office.

In carrying out their duties, the Governor and also the Vice-Governor have certain obligations listed in Art. 46 of the LoGA. They must strictly adhere to and implement the *Pancasila*, abide by the 1945 Constitution of the Republic of Indonesia and maintain the sovereignty and protect the integrity of the Unitary

---

[99]Similar provisions are included in Art. 1, paras. 8–9, of the LoGA concerning the district/municipal government and the regent/mayor as the leader of district/municipal government.

[100]In a corresponding manner, the regent/mayor shall submit a report on the execution of district/municipality governance to the Governor as the representative of the Indonesian Government.

[101]According to Art. 44(1), the Vice-Governor shall have the duty of assisting the Governor in the execution of governance, the coordination of the activities of government apparatus in the implementation of Islamic law, the following up reports and/or findings from supervision conducted by supervisory apparatus, the empowerment of women and youth, the local custom (adat) empowerment, cultural development, environmental conservation, monitoring and evaluation of the execution of district/municipality governance, the execution of the duties and authorities of the Governor in the event the Governor becomes unavailable, and the execution of other governmental duties and authorities conferred by the Governor.

State of the Republic of Indonesia. In addition, they have the duty to implement the *syari'yat* of his/her religion (which seems to indicate that there may exist several forms of the *syari'yat*, potentially in different religions or at least different denominations of Islam), enhance the welfare of the people, maintain community tranquility and public order, promote democracy, follow the principles and procedures of clean and good governance free from corruption, collusion and nepotism, carry out and be accountable for the financial management of Aceh and its districts/municipalities in a transparent manner, submit plans for the governance of Aceh and the governance of its districts/municipalities to plenary sessions of the DPRA, and maintain close working relationships with government agencies (evidently in the meaning of the agencies of the Indonesian Government). They shall also submit a report on the governing of Aceh and its districts/municipalities to the Indonesian Government, to provide an accountability report to the DPRA, and to disseminate the reports on the governing of Aceh and its districts/municipalities to the public. In addition, Art. 47 lists a number of prohibitions, including corruption, discrimination, engaging in business activities of a public or private kind, abuse of power and serving in other public capacities, such as a member of the Indonesian parliament, the Regional Representative Council or the DPRA.

7.5.2 *Link to National Government*

However, the Governor of Aceh has a double role, because he or she is not only an elected representative of the people of Aceh, but at the same time, according to Art. 40, a representative of the Indonesian Government in Aceh. In this latter capacity, the Governor is accountable to the President of Indonesia. As stated in Art. 43 concerning the Governor's role as a representative of the Indonesian Government, he or she has the duty and authority to coordinate the development and supervision of district/municipality governance, the execution of governmental affairs in Aceh and its districts/municipalities, the development and supervision of the execution of assistance tasks in Aceh and its districts/municipalities, the development in the execution of activities related to the special and unique characteristics of Aceh, and the efforts toward and maintenance of inter-district and inter-municipality equity in development activities in Aceh.[102]

In carrying out these duties and authorities, the Governor shall be entitled to bestow commendations to and/or administrative sanctions on regents/mayors in

[102]Further provisions related to the mechanisms for executing these duties and authorities of the Governor shall be governed by Government Regulations, supplemented by Aceh qanun. In fact, the Governor of Aceh has seven tasks that the other 32 governors do not have, such as to give opinion on the appointment of the head of police and the prosecutor and to handle the recruitment of police officers.

accordance with prevailing laws and regulations, and as provided in Art. 43(2), the Governor, as the representative of the Indonesian Government, may assign duties to the Aceh regional apparatus. Therefore, both the Aceh Government and also the district/municipality government may be understood as implementing organs for policies of the central government. Funding for the implementation of the Governor's national duties and authorities shall be covered from national funds as established in regulations of the Indonesian Government.[103]

The double role of the Governor of Aceh, created by the LoGA, connects the Government of Aceh to the Indonesian Government both substantively (that is, in the areas mentioned above) and also procedurally. For instance, as established in Art. 249, the establishment and supervision of the implementation of governance of Aceh and its districts/municipalities shall be carried out by the Indonesian Government in accordance with prevailing laws and regulations, as if Aceh was, in terms of its governance and the state supervision of it, just an ordinary region of Indonesia. Although Art. 7 and Art. 12 make reference to a sphere of competence within which Aceh shall take care of its own affairs, Art. 11 of the LoGA nonetheless grants the Indonesian Government a seemingly general authority to establish norms, standards, and procedures and conduct the supervision of the administration of affairs carried out by the Aceh Government and its districts/municipalities. It seems therefore as if the Indonesian Government was able to establish so-called national standards in all spheres of competence, also those which in principle could be considered as being assigned to Aceh under the "residual" notion of competences, and to supervise their implementation. At the same time, however, such norms, standards and procedures that the Indonesian Government establishes shall not diminish the authority of the Government of Aceh and the district/municipality governments as referred to in Art. 7(1). This latter provision seems to indicate that the establishment of norms, standards and procedures as well as the supervision by

[103] As established in articles 198 and 200, every delegation of authority and every support task given by the Indonesian Government to the Governor as a representative of the Indonesian Government in Aceh or to the Government of Aceh, respectively, shall be accompanied by relevant funds, and deconcentration and assistance task activities in Aceh shall be implemented by a regional apparatus working unit established by the Governor, a unit which apparently is working separately from the Government of Aceh in implementing the competencies of the central government. The Governor shall keep the DPRA informed regarding the delegated matters and assistance task administered on behalf of the Indonesian Government and their respective budgets. Article 15 of the LoGA makes a similar point by providing that Indonesian governmental affairs transferred to the authority of the Government of Aceh and the district/municipality governments shall be complemented by funding and the assignment of facilities, infrastructure and staff, in accordance with decentralized management, while governmental affairs delegated to the Governor shall be complemented by funding in accordance with deconcentrated management and governmental affairs assigned to the Aceh Government, district/municipality governments, and *gampongs* shall be complemented by funding in accordance with the principle of assistance tasks. Hence the principle seems to be that transfer, delegation and assignment of matters and tasks from the Indonesian Government is always matched by resources from the Indonesian budget.

the Indonesian Government should be directed towards the national functions potentially delegated or transferred to Aceh or its sub-divisions. The powers held by Aceh on the basis of the LoGA and the governmental decree detailing these powers should probably not be affected by these national standards, unless the agreement on the distribution of powers includes such a dimension.

7.5.3 *Complicated Impeachment and Weak Forms of Accountability*

Breach of the duties and prohibitions that are placed upon the Governor and the Vice-Governor may, under Art. 48, lead to dismissal from office. The reasons for dismissal contain the continued inability to carry out the duties or sustained unavailability for a consecutive period of 6 months, that the requirements placed on the office holder are no longer fulfilled, that he or she is declared as having violated the oaths of office, the failure to perform their obligations and the violation of the prohibitions, as well as a court decision sentencing him to at least 5 years of imprisonment for committing a crime. The motion of dismissal shall be submitted by the DPRA leadership to be resolved in a plenary session[104] and formally recommended by the DPRA leadership to the President of Indonesia based on a ruling by the Supreme Court on the basis of the opinion of the DPRA that the Governor or Vice-Governor (or the heads of the local government[105]) have violated their professional oaths and/or failed to perform their respective obligations.

The process is quite long and arduous, because the Supreme Court must first examine, judge, and rule with a final and binding effect on the DPRA opinion no later than 30 days after the request filed by the DPRA is received by the Supreme Court. If the Supreme Court rules that the Governor or Vice-Governor have violated their oaths of office and/or failed to perform their obligations, the DPRA must hold a plenary session attended by at least three-fourths of the DPRA members and pass a resolution approved by at least two-thirds of the DPRA members present in order to propose formally to the President that the Governor or Vice-Governor be dismissed. After receiving the formal proposal to dismiss the relevant official, the President of Indonesia must process the motion to dismiss within 30 days. The final decision concerning the dismissal of the popularly elected Governor of Aceh and the Vice-Governor is therefore in the hands of the President of Indonesia as a result of an impeachment process of some sort. Although the motion to dismiss the Governor has its roots in Aceh, the actual decision is not made in Aceh. In fact,

[104]The opinion of the DPRA shall be issued through a resolution of a DPRA plenary session attended by at least three-fourths of the total members of the DPRA, and the resolution shall be adopted by at least two-thirds of the DPRA members present.

[105]Heads of districts are not really responsible to the Governor, but to the president of Indonesia, who can dismiss them (actually, it is the minister of home affairs who holds that power).

there is an explicit reference in the LoGA to impeachment in Art. 51(6) on grounds of criminal conviction against the Governor or Vice-Governor for a crime that carries a minimum sentence of 5 years.

Temporary removal from office is also possible, but such a decision can be made by the President of Indonesia without prior motion form the DPRA under articles 49 and 50, if the Governor or Vice-Governor have been convicted of a crime with a minimum sentence of at least 5 years in prison, if they have been indicted for a crime of corruption, terrorism, treason, and/or a crime against state security, or if they have been convicted by a court ruling with permanent legal force of the crimes of corruption, terrorism, treason, and/or crimes against state security, and/or other crimes. However, under Art. 51(4), the DPRA may also motion for temporary removal if the Governor or Vice-Governor have been found guilty of a crime that carries the minimum sentence of 5 years.

In the implementation of its functions, the DPRA is entitled under Art. 24 to, *inter alia*, conduct an interpellation. The interpellation is in this context not to be understood as a reference to parliamentary accountability, effectuated by way of a vote of confidence through which it would be possible to dismiss the Governor or the secretaries of the department. The interpellation mechanism can be used to compel the Government of Aceh to explain its position on different matters before the DPRA, but unlike the ordinary mechanism of parliamentary accountability initiated through interpellation, the interpellation cannot in this situation lead to the resignation of the Government. In addition, the DPRA is entitled to conduct an inquiry,[106] to issue statements of opinion, as well as to submit draft *qanuns*. This means that the DPRA has independent powers to submit proposals and to make amendments to draft *qanun*. Hence the DPRA can change the contents of draft *qanuns* from what, for instance, the Government of Aceh has proposed in a manner that would give the DPRA some clout in relation to the Government of Aceh. At the end, however, a draft becomes a *qanun* only if the Governor of Aceh agrees to it, so it is not possible to say that the DPRA would be in a particularly strong position in relation to the executive structures of Aceh.

There is a slight allusion in the direction of parliamentary accountability in Art. 51, according to which the DPRA shall exercise its right to inquiry if the Governor or Vice-Governor have faced a widespread public crisis of confidence due to an allegation of a crime involving their professional obligations. However, this accountability mechanism is not connected to the regular parliamentary notion of interpellation, but instead to the right to inquiry, exercised upon approval by a DPRA plenary session attended by at least three-fourths of the number of DPRA members and based upon a resolution passed by at least two-thirds of the DPRA members present in that session. The decision thus made is to conduct an investigation of the Governor and/or

[106] As detailed in Art. 25, sub-sections 2–9, the powers to conduct inquiry are broad, including a possibility to call witnesses to be heard. The decision to launch an inquiry requires the approval of a DPRA plenary session attended by at least three-fourths of the total DPRA membership and approved by at least two-thirds of the number of DPRA/DPRK members present.

Vice-Governor. If evidence is found that the crimes have been committed, the DPRA shall hand over the case for resolution to the proper law enforcement authorities in accordance with prevailing laws and regulations.

7.5.4 The Upward Connection of Governmental Departments

While the Governor and the Vice-Governor constitute the highest executive offices, the LoGA provides also for an administrative sub-structure, as provided more in detail by *qanun*.[107] According to Art. 100, there is the Aceh Provincial Secretariat, Aceh *Dinas* offices, that is departments, and Aceh technical agencies.[108] On the basis of Art. 101, the Aceh Provincial Secretariat is chaired by the Aceh Provincial Secretary, that is, a non-elected civil servant, appointed from among civil service employees, who assists the Governor in formulating policies and is accountable to him, coordinates the *Dinas* offices (that is, the departments), institutions and agencies of Aceh Province, and develops the civil service employees in Aceh. Under Art. 102(2)-(4), the Governor shall present his appointee as the Aceh Provincial Secretary to the President of Indonesia, who affirms the candidate through a Presidential Decree. More or less the same procedure applies to the dismissal of the Provincial Secretary. Further provisions related to the requirements and procedures for the appointment and dismissal of the Aceh Provincial Secretary are provided by Government Regulations.

The departments of the Government of Aceh, that is, the *Dinas*, are identified in Art. 110, as the implementing organs of the Government of Aceh. As laid down in Art. 10, the Government of Aceh may establish institutions, agencies, and/or commissions pursuant to the LoGA with the approval of the DPRA and as provided in *qanun*, except on matters that belong to the authority of the Indonesian Government. The *Dinas* are headed by department heads appointed from among civil

[107] More or less the same structure is used for districts/municipalities.

[108] Under the DPRA, there is a separate secretariat. According to Art. 108 of the LoGA, the DPRA Secretariat shall be chaired by the DPRA Secretary who is appointed and dismissed by the Governor upon consultation with the DPRA leadership. Although serving operationally under the DPRA leadership and being accountable to it, the DPRA Secretary shall administratively serve under the coordination of the Aceh Provincial Secretary. Hence the DPRA as a body exercising the normative powers in Aceh is not independent from the executive power. The DPRA Secretary has the duty to execute the secretariat administration of the DPRA, formulate the DPRA Secretariat budget plan and carry out financial administration, manage and administer the DPRA expenditure budget, support the implementation of DPRA duties and functions and provide and coordinate expert staff required by the DPRA in carrying out its functions, taking into account the region's financial resources.

service employees who meet the requirements set out in relevant laws and regulations, that is, in Indonesian norms concerning civil servants.[109] They are appointed and dismissed by the Governor upon the recommendation of the Aceh Provincial Secretary.[110] In performing his/her duties, the Aceh department head shall be accountable to the Governor through the Aceh Provincial Secretary. In addition to departments (*Dinas*), there are the technical institutions of Aceh, which are bodies supporting the Governor's duties to formulate and implement specific Aceh policies. They may exist in the form of an agency or office, and they are headed by directors or heads of office appointed from among civil service employees. Such directors or heads are appointed and dismissed by the Governor upon the recommendation of the Aceh Provincial Secretary, and they are accountable to the Governor through the Aceh Provincial Secretary.

The civil servants in Aceh all are part of the national civil service, although they form one managerial unit. Appointment, transfer, and dismissal from and within Echelon II positions in the Aceh Government shall be determined by the Governor, and the transfer of Civil Service Employees between districts/municipalities within Aceh shall be determined by the Governor, while the transfer of Civil Service Employees between districts/municipalities of different provinces, or between provinces, shall be determined by the Minister of Home Affairs. The same is true concerning transfers of civil servants from Aceh/districts/municipalities to Ministries/Non-departmental State Institutions and vice versa. Transfers of Civil Service Employees are carried out on the basis of the norms, standards, and procedures established by the Head of the State Civil Service Agency. Career development for Civil Service Employees in Aceh/districts/municipalities is carried out through the consideration of issues of integrity and morality, education and training, rank, transfer of position, inter-provincial transfer, and competence. The salaries and benefits of Civil Service Employees in the region are paid out of the APBA and derived from the basic allocation within the general allocation funds.[111] The development and supervision of Civil Service Employees in Aceh/districts/municipalities is coordinated at the national level by the Minister of Home Affairs, and at the Aceh/district/municipality level by the Governor as determined by Government Regulations.

The LoGA contains few provisions concerning individual matters to be decided upon by the Government of Aceh. As concerns disputes that arise in relation to the

---

[109]At a practical level, the close relationship between the Government of Aceh, on the one hand, and the central government agencies, in particular the military, is evidenced by the fact the military has a representative in departmental meetings: when a call for a meeting is issued under the heading "directors +", it means directors and a representative of the military. In Aceh, there is also very much intelligence officials from the military.

[110]The word "cabinet" is not known in the context of the Government of Aceh, but there are high-ranking civil servants (Echelon IIa) and the secretary of the province (Echelon Ib) who may be regarded as a "cabinet". However, there is no collective responsibility; the Governor bears the responsibility for the governance of Aceh.

[111]Calculation of the basic allocation referred to in paragraphs (1) and (2) is based on the Law on Financial Balance between the Central and Regional Governments.

execution of government functions among districts/municipalities in the province of Aceh, such as issues of territorial jurisdiction, they are, according to Art. 127, to be resolved by the Governor, while the Indonesian Minister of Home Affairs is charged with resolving disputes between the province and a district/municipality in Aceh, as well as between the province of Aceh, on the one hand, and a province or a district/municipality outside of its territory. In addition, as laid down in Art. 127, the construction of a house of worship requires a license either from the Government of Aceh and/or from the respective district/municipality government, but the choice of where the decision is made can be included in a *qanun*, which means that the decision to grant a building permit for a house of worship is not necessarily made on the basis of the LoGA.

As in Aceh, also in Puerto Rico, the elected Governor is central to the administration of the sub-state entity, although the office is not connected to the federal government.

7.6 Puerto Rico: The Model of the National Executive Duplicated

7.6.1 Executive Powers Detailed in the Constitution

The Puerto Rican executive is in many respects modeled after its continental counterparts, the US federal government and the governments of the constituent states. The Governor of Puerto Rico is, according to Art. IV, sections 1 and 2, of the Constitution, elected by the voters of Puerto Rico for a period of 4 years.[112] The Office of the Governor is the highest executive office, and the Governor is, under Art. IV, section 4, of the Constitution charged with the task of, *inter alia*, executing the laws and causing them to be executed. In principle, this task of execution of laws is only effective in relation to the laws of Puerto Rico, while federal laws are executed by the federal government through federal agencies. However, there may exist some executive matters of a federal nature, which require the involvement of the Governor of Puerto Rico, such as extradition to other states in the US on the basis of the extradition clause of Art. IV, section 2, of the US Constitution.[113]

The Governor also has other powers and tasks, such as calling the Legislative Assembly or the Senate into special session when the public interest so requires, appointing those officers whose appointment he is authorized to make, being the

[112]According to Art. IV, section 3, of the Constitution, the eligibility requirements for the Governor are that he or she is at least 35 years of age and is and has been during the preceding 5 years a citizen of the United States and a citizen and bona fide resident of Puerto Rico.

[113]As specified in18 U.S.C. 3182, that is, the extradition act.

commander-in-chief of the militia,[114] proclaiming martial law when the public safety requires it in the case of rebellion or invasion or imminent danger of such calamities, suspending the execution of sentences in criminal cases and granting pardons, commutations of punishment, and total or partial remissions of fines and forfeitures for crimes committed in violation of the laws of Puerto Rico, approving or disapproving in accordance with this Constitution the joint resolutions and bills passed by the Legislative Assembly, presenting to the Legislative Assembly, at the beginning of each regular session, a message concerning the affairs of the Commonwealth and a report concerning the state of the Treasury of Puerto Rico,[115] and the proposed expenditures for the ensuing fiscal year and exercising the other powers and functions and discharging the other duties assigned to the Governor by the Constitution or by law. This means that the popularly elected Governor has a wide array of powers vested in him or her.

In the American tradition, the Governor is assisted in his or her role as a head of the executive by secretaries, that is, heads of administrative sectors whom the Governor appoints after the elections.[116] The so-called spoils system practiced in the American-styled government means that the highest echelon of executive officers are political appointees that will be changed with the change of government. However, the Governor is not free to appoint the secretaries at his or her own will, but Art. IV, sections 4 and 5, of the Constitution makes their appointment subject to the advice and consent of the Senate. The appointment of the Secretary of State shall in addition require the advice and consent of the House of Representatives.[117] This means that there is at least a minimum of horizontal link between the Government and the two houses of the Puerto Rican Congress.

7.6.2 Impeachment in Its Original Form

Under Art. IV, section 5, the various secretaries collectively constitute the Governor's advisory council, officially designated as the Council of Secretaries. However, despite the fact that the senate is involved in the confirmation of the secretaries, the council so formed is not politically accountable to the senate, but

[114]The Governor has the power to call out the militia and summon the *posse comitatus* in order to prevent or suppress rebellion, invasion or any serious disturbance of the public peace.

[115]According to Art. IV, section 4, the report shall contain the information necessary for the formulation of a program of legislation.

[116]According to Art. IV, section 6, of the Constitution, at least the following executive departments shall exist: State, Justice, Education, Health, Treasury, Labor, Agriculture and Commerce, and Public Works. In addition, the Legislative Assembly can create other executive bodies.

[117]According to Art. IV, section 5, of the Constitution, the Secretary of State shall fulfill the same eligibility criteria as the Governor. That qualification is important in light of Art. IV, section 7, according to which the Secretary of State of Puerto Rico is the temporary governor until the end of the term of office if the office of the Governor of Puerto Rico becomes vacant.

only legally accountable to both the Senate and the House of Representatives by way of impeachment (see below). Therefore, in spite of the fact that the council of secretaries is a collective body, there exists no collective or individual accountability of a political nature of the collective or of the individual secretaries before the Legislative Assembly.

Instead, the general impeachment powers of the legislature may be used in situations where there is a more serious violation of conduct to remove the implicated person from office. Impeachment proceedings on the basis of Art. III, section 21, of the Constitution can be initiated by the House of Representatives against the Governor, and against each of the secretaries individually or any other civil servant of the government. An impeachment may be caused by treason, bribery, other felonies, and misdemeanors involving moral turpitude, that is, on the basis of legal grounds, not because of loss of political confidence. The indictment is brought by the House of Representatives with the support of two-thirds of the total number of members, which is a very high threshold. The indictment is brought before the senate, which has the power to try and to decide impeachment cases.[118] An impeachment decision requires the majority of three-fourths of the total number of members of the senate. Because impeachment is limited to removal from office, the person who is impeached may be separately liable and subject to indictment, trial, judgment and punishment before a court of law.

7.6.3 General and Special Inter-governmental Contacts

The Government of Puerto Rico maintains an office of its own in Washington, D.C., which is not integrated in the office of the Resident Commissioner, but is officially connected to the office of the Governor of Puerto Rico. The task of the office in Washington and the other liaisons with the federal government is to keep and to intensify the interest of the federation towards Puerto Rico, but this inter-governmental activity has little bearing on the internal politics of Puerto Rico. Generally speaking, it can be said that Puerto Rico conducts its relations to the federal government in the same manner as the states.[119] In addition, the Governor of Puerto Rico participates in the national meetings of governors in the same way as the governors of the states. Hence, the inter-governmental relations of a vertical and

---

[118]However, if the Governor is being impeached, the Chief Justice of the Supreme Court shall preside in the senate at the impeachment trial of the Governor.

[119]See Rosselló (2005), p. 143, who also makes the point that the Office of Insular Affairs at the U.S. Department of the Interior is not the avenue for Puerto Rico's federal relations, while the Office is such an avenue for the other territories (e.g., Guam, US Virgin Islands, Commonwealth of the Northern Mariana Islands, and American Samoa). Also for other reasons than this, "Puerto Rico cannot be fairly lumped together with its sister territories".

horizontal kind of Puerto Rico and the constituent states in the US federation are similar.

There is no federal office in Washington D.C. which would be permanently and exclusively devoted to Puerto Rico. Instead, with different presidents in office, the variation in federal administration results in different strategies with respect to Puerto Rico. The range of options is from no attention at all through task forces appointed by the President to more high profile presidential advisors charged with matters that relate to Puerto Rico. At the same time, the federal government is present in Puerto Rico through the same federal agencies as in any state of the federation.

While the Resident Commissioner is mainly active in the US House of Representatives, he or she in principle has a broader mandate to represent Puerto Rico at the federal level, because he shall be entitled to receive official recognition as the Resident Commissioner by all of the departments of the federal government.[120] In fact, the functions of the office of the Resident Commissioner might warrant the characterization that he or she has a double role, one of which is the participatory role of an advisory nature in the US House of Representatives, and the other of which is that of a federal representative of Puerto Rico to the federal government.[121] However, in practice, the Resident Commissioner is only active in the US House of Representatives, where the principal task is to ensure that the federal legislation[122] and the federal funding decisions also apply to Puerto Rico. Because the Resident Commissioner is not a regular Representative in the House of Representatives, his or her influence is severely circumscribed.

In comparison with both Puerto Rico and Aceh, the executive power of Hong Kong may display the most particular relationship with the national government.

7.7 Hong Kong: National Interest in the Executive

7.7.1 Little Horizontal Accountability

The executive power of Hong Kong is greatly focused on the Chief Executive, an institution which makes the governmental system of Hong Kong very presidential

[120]US Code, Title 48, Sect. 891.

[121]This double role is to some extent sustained by the fact that the salary of the Resident Commissioner is paid out of the federal budget by the House of Representatives in the same way and to the same amount as the salary of a regular member of the House of Representatives in the US Congress. See US Code, Title 48, Sects. 893 and 894.

[122]As a constructed example of the opposite, the Resident Commissioner might, if federal legislation concerning the protection of animals were to be enacted, want to make sure that a possible federal provision prohibiting cockfighting, which is a national sport in Puerto Rico, would not be applied to Puerto Rico.

or, to distinguish it from the national governmental system, an executive-led system under the Central People's Government.[123] Such a characterization follows from the peculiarities of the model conditioned by the weak horizontal lines of accountability and by the interest of the central government of China to establish a vertical line of accountability. Therefore, the governmental structures of Hong Kong may be interpreted as a highly gubernatorial system of governance, paralleled elsewhere by presidential systems of government[124] with various mechanisms of checks and balances.[125] This is sustained by the fact that the Chief Executive is, under section 31 of the Chief Executive Election Ordinance, expected not to be affiliated to any political party. However, as laid down in Art. 64 of the Basic Law, the Government of the HKSAR must abide by the law and be accountable to the Legislative Council of the Region: it shall implement laws passed by the Council and those already in force, but more importantly from an accountability point of view, it shall present regular policy addresses to the Council, it shall answer questions raised by members of the Council, and it shall obtain approval from the Council for taxation and public expenditure. Thus there are indications of

[123]Leung Mei-fun (2006), p. 29, an "executive-led" government has been incorporated in the various provisions of the Basic Law. The system of governance of Macau is probably even more executive-led than that of Hong Kong.

[124]According to Ghai (1999), p. 291, the relationship between the Chief Executive and the Legislative Council "follows no recognizable form of government, being neither parliamentary nor presidential", and p. 177, where he notes that "the region has no power to alter the formal relationship between the executive and the legislature". See also Ghai (1997), pp. 264, 265. According to Weiyun (2001), p. 253, the relationship between the executive and legislative authorities in Hong Kong is that of checks and balances in accordance with realities in Hong Kong. When the Basic Law was drafted, the drafters looked into the issue of parliamentary accountability, but it seems that such a relationship between the executive power and the legislature was rejected because it could potentially, in a multi-party setting with no party holding the majority of seats in the legislature, lead to frequent changes of cabinet and, subsequently, to instability of the system. The HKSAR, "covering a very small land area, a local administrative region of the PRC, enjoying a high degree of autonomy, is not a sovereign state", and therefore," it is not suitable for it to adopt the system of Cabinet accountability as if it were a sovereign state, nor is it suitable for it to adopt the method of casting votes of no-confidence; nor should Legco be easily dissolved". At the same time, on p. 257, he denies that the office of the Chief Executive is gubernatorial, because he will not have legislative and military powers and because he will not be a representative of the Central People's Government. It seems, however, that the Chief Executive has an unusually large share in the legislative powers of the HKSAR and that he also is, after appointment by the State Council, a representative of the central government. On the basis of p. 258 f., the conclusion may be drawn that the office of the Chief Executive was mainly modelled against the background of heads of states and presidents of presidential systems. However, there was no requirement of affiliation to a political party which is unusual.

[125]Ghai (1999), p. 263 f.: "[W]hile a key function of the legislature is to supervise the executive, the Chief Executive has power to dissolve the legislature, and, in the legislative area, the basic responsibility for the initiation of legislation lies with the executive although its enactment requires the consent of the Legislative Council with a veto in the Chief Executive. Checks and balances are also built into the relationships between Hong Kong and the Central Authorities."

horizontal accountability mechanisms, too, in the Basic Law, although they seem to be quite weak.

While the legislative powers of the Legislative Council of Hong Kong (and also those of the legislature in Macau) are very broad, in fact, among the broadest of all of the autonomies considered in this study, subject only to the signature and promulgation of the act by the Chief Executive under Art. 76 of the Basic Law, the constitutional system of Hong Kong is designed in a way which creates minimal horizontal mechanisms of accountability,[126] emphasizing instead the vertical line of accountability.

On the top of such powers as the enactment of laws and approval of budgets, taxation and public expenditure,[127] the Legislative Council is entitled, under Art. 73 of the Basic Law, to receive and debate the policy addresses of the Chief Executive, to raise questions on the work of the Government and to debate any issue concerning the public interest. These forms of contact between the legislature and the executive are repeated in Art. 64 of the Basic Law, according to which the Government of Hong Kong, the head of which is the Chief Executive, must be accountable to the Legislative Council.[128] The performance of the executive can therefore become the object of parliamentary scrutiny through the initial stages of the impeachment procedure, questions (oral questions) and inquiries by committees of the Legislative Council. Although the accountability of the Chief Executive and the subordinate governmental functions is promoted through the free media and public discussion in Hong Kong, the formal line of accountability goes actually from the Chief Executive to the Central People's Government in Beijing.

The Legislative Assembly may receive and debate the policy addresses of the Chief Executive and raise questions on the work of the Government. The work of the executive branch, in particular, that of the Chief Executive, may create dissatisfaction of different magnitudes. A high level of dissatisfaction may lead to an investigation into the actions of the Chief Executive if a motion is initiated jointly by one-fourth of all of the members of the Legislative Council. As will be pointed out below, such a process towards impeachment is only a preparatory decision, because the final decision in such a matter is made by the Central People's Government. This impeachment structure can thus also be interpreted as support for the Chief Executive at the expense of the Legislative Council. Generally, it

[126]Ghai (1999), p. 285: "The council has no power to pass a vote of confidence which would lead to the dismissal of the Chief Executive. According to a Mainland drafter, the provision for a vote of no confidence (which is the principal device for a legislature's control over the executive) was ruled out on the grounds that it would produce frequent changes of government, and would be bad for economic prosperity and social stability. Presumably the continuity of the executive was rated more highly than the continuity of the legislature since the Chief Executive has been given limited powers to dissolve the Legislative Council."

[127]In so far as the bill has been submitted by the Chief Executive, the Legislative Council votes together as a collective body and makes the decisions following the principle of simple majority. See Ghai (1999), p. 279.

[128]See also Ghai (1999), p. 283 ff.

seems that "[t]he office of the Chief Executive is intended to be very powerful, dominating over the legislature".[129]

7.7.2 *Impeachment in the Hands of the National Government*

The only formal way to react against the Chief Executive is by way of an impeachment procedure prescribed in Art. 73(9) of the Basic Law. According to the provision, if a motion initiated jointly by one-fourth of all the members of the Legislative Council charges the Chief Executive with a serious breach of law or dereliction of duty and if he or she refuses to resign, the Council may, after passing a motion for investigation, give a mandate to the Chief Justice of the Court of Final Appeal to form and chair an independent investigation committee. The committee shall be responsible for carrying out the investigation and reporting its findings to the Council. If the committee considers the evidence sufficient to substantiate such charges, the Council may pass a motion of impeachment by a two-thirds majority of all its members and report it to the Central People's Government for a decision. This means that the Legislative Council is not in possession of the final decision-making power regarding impeachment, but instead the central governmental body of China has the authority to make the final decision.[130] In any case, it is unlikely that the Legislative Council in its current form, rooted in a corporatist system of election and not entirely directly elected by the population of Hong Kong, would arrive at an impeachment decision. The Legislative Council has the function to set the impeachment process in motion before the final decision is considered by the central government.[131]

The power of the central government to make the final impeachment decision is, however, not surprising, since, according to Art. 45 and Annex I on the method for the selection of the Chief Executive, the Central People's Government appoints the Chief Executive, subject to local selection by a corporately composed election committee of 800 members.[132] This means that there is no direct election of the

[129]Ghai (1999), p. 291.

[130]Ghai (1999), p. 289: "Particularly striking is the veto that has been reserved to the CPG over the impeachment of the Chief Executive. It highlights the high degree of dependence of the Chief Executive on the CPG (. . .)."

[131]Ghai (1999), p. 285: "However, the adoption of the motion does not necessarily lead to the removal of the Chief Executive, since it has to be reported to the CPG 'for decision'. This form of wording indicates that the final decision is made with the CPG, which might wish to shield the Chief Executive, although it is hard to see how the CPG could disregard the overwhelming majority of the legislature (and the procedure preceding its vote) without causing a major crisis in Hong Kong and in the relationship of the Central Authorities with its residents."

[132]From 2012, the election committee will comprise 1200 members (see Sect. 4.5.3 above). In the 2007 Chief Executive election, the incumbent received more than 81% of the votes in the electoral college of 800 persons. According to Ghai (1999), p. 258, the Basic Law does not specify if the

Chief Executive, although the explicitly stated aim is to develop the selection procedures in that direction sometime after 2007. Such a development would change the set-up concerning governmental accountability and make it more traditionally presidential in nature.

According to Art. 43 of the Basic Law, the Chief Executive is the head of the SAR and he or she also represents the SAR, and under Art. 60 of the Basic Law, the Chief Executive is the head of the Government of Hong Kong. In this capacity and when exercising the powers of the Chief Executive, he or she is, under Art. 43(2), accountable to the Central People's Government and to the HKSAR in accordance with the Basic Law. The CE's accountability to the HKSAR was already discussed above, but the Basic Law does not clarify how the accountability of the Chief Executive in relation to the central government should function.[133]

The central government appoints the Chief Executive under Art. 15 of the Basic Law, but the Basic Law does not contain any provision on the dismissal of the Chief Executive by the central government, although section 4 of the Chief Executive Election Ordinance mentions that the CPG's removal of the Chief Executive may be one reason for vacancy in the office. Instead, according to Art. 52 of the Basic Law, a dispute between the Chief Executive and the Legislative Council may, if the former has refused twice to promulgate a bill enacted by the latter and the Legislative after dissolution and new elections still chooses to enact the legislation, the Chief Executive must resign.[134] Therefore, there exists an attenuated form of governmental accountability in the horizontal dimension, but because it involves a very complicated procedure and also a requirement of a qualified majority of two-thirds, it has little to do with the principle of parliamentarianism.[135]

Central People's Government has a veto; "the language of art. 45 would suggest that it does not, and no procedure is provided for in case a veto is exercised". Ghai supports an interpretation according to which the role of the central government is purely formal, which evidently means that the central government would not have any veto power, but would have to appoint the person selected in Hong Kong.

[133]According to Ghai (1997), p. 224, the "relationship between the executive and the legislature would depend significantly on the meaning and scope of 'accountability', of which the Chinese had a more restricted understanding than the British". See also Ghai (1999), p. 67. As pointed out by Leung Mei-fun (2006), p. 255, "from the angle of the nation, the Chief Executive is an official of the state; and from the angle of Hong Kong, he is the head of the region".

[134]As stated by Leung Mei-fun (2006), p. 262, "even with Articles 50 and 52, it is hardly feasible to force the Chief Executive to resign through the political pressure of the LegCo". However, the National Security (Legislative Provisions) Bill on crimes against the Central People's Government on the basis of Art. 23 of the Basic Law (see below, Sect. 8.7.3) resulted in massive demonstrations on 1 July 2003 and the Government of Hong Kong faced a real risk of not having its bill approved in the Legislative Council. "No Chief Executive can afford such a risk subject to the existence of Articles 50 and 52. Not having a choice, the government had to announce the postponement of the bill indefinitely."

[135]As reported by Leung Mei-fun (2006), 263, there has been a discussion in that vein: a "[f]ormer Basic Law drafter insisted that LegCo has no power to discuss a motion on a non-confidence vote upon any government official subject to Article 64 of the Basic Law while some others argued that it is still debatable". In fact, against advice to the contrary, the Legislative Council has allowed at

In addition, taking into account the corporatist manner of selection of the Legislative Council, the resignation of the Chief Executive because of problems in the horizontal dimension of accountability is only a remote possibility.[136]

7.7.3 The Chief Executive as the Focal Point in the Executive Council

The Chief Executive presides over the Executive Council (ExCo) and appoints and removes its members, which currently amount to 29. According to Art. 55(1) of the Basic Law, its members are drawn from among the principal officials of the executive authorities, members of the Legislative Council and public figures. The mandate of the members of the Executive Council is tied to the mandate of the Chief Executive, not to the mandate of the Legislative Council.[137] In addition, Art. 60(2) requires that there be departments of administration, finance, and justice and that various bureaus, divisions and commissions shall be established in the Government of the HKSAR.[138] The principal officials are nominated by the Chief

least one vote of no confidence against a Secretary of Justice. In addition, below the cabinet level, the release of findings of hearings may cause the implicated official to draw conclusions of his or her conduct and resign voluntarily, which seems to be relatively common. See Leung Mei-fun (2006), p. 266. Yet another example of accountability where the consequences are taken at a personal level may be the resignation of the Secretary of Security Mrs. Regina Ip on 25 July 2003, in the wake of the failed attempt by the Government of Hong Kong to have the National Security (Legislative Provisions) Bill passed in the Legislative Council. See Hualing et al. (2005a, b), pp. xv-xvi. All this may perhaps be interpreted as indicating that a horizontal accountability culture is emerging, although the Basic Law itself does not really support it.

[136] As concluded by Ghai (1997), p. 244, “the process is weighted in favour of the Chief Executive and the final decision lies with the CPG”, and by Ghai (1999), p. 292 that “[t]he extent of accountability of the executive to the legislature is severely limited”. However, in Art. 52, there are three absolute grounds of resignation of the Chief Executive, the second and the third ones that may be realised in the horizontal sphere of accountability: (1) When he or she loses the ability to discharge his or her duties as a result of serious illness or other reasons, (2) when, after the Legislative Council is dissolved because he or she twice refuses to sign a bill passed by it, the new Legislative Council again passes by a two-thirds majority of all the members the original bill in dispute, but he or she still refuses to sign it, and (3) when, after the Legislative Council is dissolved because it refuses to pass a budget or any other important bill, the new Legislative Council still refuses to pass the original bill in dispute. See Leung Mei-fun (2006), p. 259 f.

[137] Ghai (1999), p. 274: "However, none of these provisions suggest that the Chief Executive is bound to take the advice of officials or Executive Councillors or that the Basic Law provides for collective decision making, as in a parliamentary system. The executive therefore is more akin to a presidential system, with the ultimate responsibility for policies and implementation in the Chief Executive. The government falls with the impeachment of the Chief Executive.”

[138] For an organisational chart of the Government of the HKSAR, see http://www.gov.hk/en/about/govdirectory/govchart/index.htm (accessed on 19 August 2009).

Executive, and he or she also has the power to dismiss them from office.[139] As indicated in Art. 55(1) of the Basic Law, the membership of the Executive Council is at least to some extent drawn from the Legislative Council, but this feature probably does not have very much influence on governmental accountability, except that it may keep the Legislative Council, at least to some extent, informed of how the Executive Council works internally. Hence, although some members of the Legislative Council are members of the Executive Council, they are members in their personal capacity, that is, they are persons who are friendly with the Government, but they are not primarily members of the ExCo because of their political party affiliation.[140]

As explained above, the Chief Executive will be appointed by the Central People's Government on the basis of the results of elections or consultations to be held locally, while principal officials or secretaries will,[141] under Art. 15 of the Basic Law, be nominated by the Chief Executive for appointment by the Central People's Government. This means that the central government plays a key role in the construction of the Government of Hong Kong. Chinese and foreign nationals previously working in the public and police services in the government departments of Hong Kong could remain in employment after the transfer of sovereignty from the UK to China. Even after that point of time, British and other foreign nationals may be employed to serve as advisers or hold certain public posts in governmental departments of the HKSAR.

The Chief Executive is the head of the HKSAR and represents the HKSAR in relation to the central government and also in other respects. His or her more specific functions are laid down in Art. 48 of the Basic Law. He or she leads the Government of the HKSAR, decides on government policies, is responsible for the implementation of the Basic Law and other laws which, in accordance with the Basic Law, apply in the HKSAR, signs bills passed by the Legislative Council to promulgate laws, signs budgets passed by the Legislative Council and reports the budgets and final accounts to the Central People's Government for the record, and

---

[139] See also Ghai (1999), p. 275.

[140] However, there exist examples which speak for an emerging political connection between the Executive Council and the Legislative Council along the lines of accountability. The Government of Hong Kong introduced the National Security (Legislative Provisions) Bill to the Legislative Council on 26 February 2003. During the months between March and June, there are massive protests in Hong Kong against the Bill, and on 7 July 2003, James Tien, chairman of the Liberal Party, which at that time dominated eight functional constituencies, resigned from the Executive Council and announced that the Liberal Party will not support the Bill. "Without the votes of the eight functional constituencies controlled by the Liberal Party, the government did not have enough support in LegCo to pass the Bill," as noted in 'Chronology and Abbreviations' in Hualing et al. (2005a, b), p. xv. The Government deferred the resumption of the Second Reading of the Bill and then also the Secretary for Security resigned from her post. The National Security Bill was withdrawn from the Legislative Council on 5 September 2003.

[141] Secretaries and Deputy Secretaries of Departments, Directors of Bureaux, Commissioner Against Corruption, Director of Audit, Commissioner of Police, Director of Immigration and Commissioner of Customs and Excise.

issues executive orders.[142] The Chief Executive also has the task of implementing the directives issued by the Central People's Government with respect to the relevant matters provided for in the Basic Law. This probably covers at least foreign affairs and national security.[143]

Outside of this "normative" sphere, the Chief Executive nominates and reports to the Central People's Government the appointment of the principal officials, that is, the various secretaries and, if need be, recommends to the Central People's Government the removal of these high officials of the HKSAR. He or she also has the function to appoint or remove judges of the courts at all levels in accordance with legal procedures and to appoint or remove holders of public office in accordance with legal procedures. He or she has the task of approving the introduction of motions regarding revenues or expenditure to the Legislative Council, to decide, in the light of security and vital public interests, whether government officials or other personnel in charge of government affairs should testify or give evidence before the Legislative Council or its committees,[144] to pardon persons convicted of criminal offences or commute their penalties, and to handle petitions and complaints. Finally, the Chief Executive has the function to conduct, on behalf of the Government of the HKSAR, external affairs and other affairs as authorized by the Central Authorities (see below).

7.7.4 *Hierarchically Led Administrative Structures*

Although the focus of the Basic Law is very much on the Chief Executive, it also contains provisions concerning other executive bodies. As explained above, directly in relation to the Chief Executive, there is an Executive Council under his or her chairmanship, which according to Art. 54 is an organ for assisting the Chief Executive in policy-making. Members of the Executive Council of the

[142]Executive orders are a kind of prerogative and evidently, such orders are used very restrictively. As a rare example of its use, it could be said that when a law on eavesdropping had been struck down in court, the Chief Executive used the executive prerogative to decree a temporary rule on the use of such devices by the police, which means that the effect of the executive order was mainly within the executive branch. The executive order was revoked by the Chief Executive once a new ordinance was in place. See the Law Enforcement (Covert Surveillance Procedures) Order of August 2005).

[143]See Ghai (1997), pp. 267, 365. However, as pointed out by Ghai, there may also be other areas of directives, such as issues related to the dissolution of the Legislative Assembly.

[144]It is hence possible for the Chief Executive to prevent a public servant from appearing before the Legislative Council or its committees, and there has even been some discussion on whether the Chief Executive himself could do so. However, Art. 73(10) of the Basic Law is unclear about the power of the Legislative Council to summon the Chief Executive, too. See Leung Mei-fun (2006), pp. 263, 266 f. Because the basic assumption is that the Chief Executive is accountable before the Legislative Council, the Chief Executive should not be able to excuse himself.

HKSAR shall according to Art. 55 be appointed by the Chief Executive from among the principal officials of the executive authorities, members of the Legislative Council and public figures, and their removal shall also be decided by the Chief Executive. The term of office of members of the Executive Council is tied to the term of office of the Chief Executive who appoints them. According to Art. 56(2), the Chief Executive is under an obligation to consult the Executive Council before making important policy decisions, introducing bills to the Legislative Council, making subordinate legislation, or dissolving the Legislative Council. The obligation is only to consult, not to decide in accordance with the advice possibly received, and the obligation does not extend itself to the appointment, removal and disciplining of officials and the adoption of measures in emergencies. However, if the Chief Executive does not accept a majority opinion of the Executive Council, he or she shall put the specific reasons on record. This means that there should exist evidence concerning discrepancies on major policy issues, which may be important for the control functions of the executive power by the Legislative Council.

As laid down in Art. 62, the Government of the HKSAR formulates and implements policies, conducts administrative affairs, conducts external affairs as authorized by the Central People's Government under the Basic Law (see below), draws up and introduces budgets and final accounts, drafts and introduces bills, motions and subordinate legislation, and designates officials to sit in on the meetings of the Legislative Council and to speak on behalf of the Government. As stated in Art. 64, the Government shall implement the laws passed by the Legislative Council and the laws already in force. The Department of Justice of the HKSAR has, according to Art. 63, the special task to control criminal prosecutions, free from any interference. The Government may also establish advisory bodies. However, the executive power of the HKSAR and its different departments do not implement Mainland law, although there are certain partnership agreements between HK and Beijing in the areas of tourism (one border point is jointly managed) and taxation (HK goods exported to the mainland receive beneficial tax treatment in relation to foreign imports), which create interfaces between the authorities of the HKSAR and Mainland China.

According to the Basic Law, it is possible to create a second layer of administration, namely so-called district organizations, which, under Art. 97, are not organs of political power. Such district organizations may be established in the HKSAR to be consulted by the Government of Hong Kong on district administration and other affairs, or to be responsible for providing services in such fields as culture, recreation and environmental sanitation. Their powers and functions and the method of their formation shall be prescribed by law.[145] In Hong Kong, more than 4,000 members of the public, including representatives of the relevant professions or the community, are also serving on about 400 advisory bodies.[146]

[145] According to Weiyun (2001), pp. 370–376, there exists a multitude of district organisations.

[146] As reported in the yearbook Hong Kong 2008 (2009), p. 16.

The executive authorities of the Government of the HKSAR function under the direction of the Chief Executive, as assisted by the Executive Council. Under the Chief Executive, a Department of Administration, a Department of Finance, a Department of Justice, and various bureaus, divisions and commissions are established within the governmental framework.[147] The principal officials of the HKSAR shall, according to Art. 61 of the Basic Law, be Chinese citizens who are permanent residents of the Region with no right of abode in any foreign country and have ordinarily resided in Hong Kong for a continuous period of not less than 15 years.

Public servants[148] serve in all governmental departments of the HKSAR and they must, according to Art. 99 of the Basic Law, be permanent residents of the Region, except in cases where British and other foreign nationals are specifically allowed under Art. 101, including those below a certain rank as prescribed by law.[149] Foreigners cannot serve among the highest echelon of public servants, that is, as principal officials. According to the Basic Law, public servants are expected to be dedicated to their duties and responsible to the Government of the HKSAR. When assuming office, the Chief Executive, principal officials, members of the Executive Council and of the Legislative Council, judges of the courts at all levels and other members of the judiciary in the HKSAR must, in accordance with law,

[147] According to the yearbook Hong Kong 2008 (2009), p. 16, "[t]here are currently 12 bureaux, each headed by a Director of Bureau. Together, they form the Government Secretariat. There are 58 departments whose heads are responsible to the Directors of Bureaux for the direction of their departments and the efficient implementation of approved policies. The Audit Commission, the Independent Commission Against Corruption (ICAC) and the Office of The Ombudsman report directly to the Chief Executive. The Chief Secretary for Administration, the Financial Secretary, the Secretary for Justice and the 12 Directors of Bureaux (also known as Secretaries of Bureaux) are politically appointed Principal Officials. They are held accountable for matters falling within their respective portfolios."

[148] As reported in the yearbook Hong Kong 2008 (2009), p. 18, on 31 December 2008, "the total strength of the civil service was 154 300 (excluding about 1 500 judges and judicial officers and ICAC officers)", which was around 4% of the labour force of Hong Kong. This would seem to suggest that the public sector is relatively small in the HKSAR.

[149] According to Art. 101, the Government of the HKSAR may employ British and other foreign nationals previously serving in the public service in Hong Kong, or those holding permanent identity cards of the Region, to serve as public servants in government departments at all levels, but only Chinese citizens among permanent residents of the Region with no right of abode in any foreign country may fill the following posts: the Secretaries and Deputy Secretaries of Departments, Directors of Bureaux, Commissioner Against Corruption, Director of Audit, Commissioner of Police, Director of Immigration and Commissioner of Customs and Excise. The Government of the HKSAR may also employ British and other foreign nationals as advisers to government departments and, when required, may recruit qualified candidates from outside the Region to fill professional and technical posts in government departments. These foreign nationals shall be employed only in their individual capacities and shall be responsible to the government of the Region. According to Art. 92, judges and other members of the judiciary of the Hong Kong Special Administrative Region shall be chosen on the basis of their judicial and professional qualities and may be recruited from other common law jurisdictions, which opens up the courts of the HKSAR for foreign nationals, except, as provided in Art. 90, in the cases of the Chief Justice of the Court of Final Appeals and the Chief Judge of the High Court, where the requirement is Chinese citizenship.

swear to uphold the Basic Law of the HKSAR and swear allegiance to the HKSAR of the People's Republic of China.[150]

The structure of the executive power of Hong Kong has been influenced by the political appointment system introduced in 2002. Under that system, twelve senior secretaries were politically appointed for 5 years, that is, for the term of the Chief Executive. The system was extended in 2008 to two more tiers and now encompasses the secretaries as well as under secretaries and political assistants. Currently, there are altogether around 40 persons who are political appointees in a manner which is reminiscent of a "spoils" system. They can be subjected to political pressure and can resign or be dismissed, something which was not really possible in the previous system with regular civil servants. The creation of such new executive offices, including accountable positions, is subject to a decision by the Legislative Council, which means that the new system increases the political clout of the Legislative Council.[151]

Under articles 57 and 58, the Basic Law creates the legal basis for two independent commissions, namely a Commission Against Corruption and a Commission of Audit. They are expected to function independently, but at the same time, they are accountable to the Chief Executive. In addition, there is an independent Electoral Affairs Commission for overseeing the elections of Hong Kong as well as an office of the Ombudsman, established in 1989, as an independent statutory authority under the Ombudsman Ordinance,[152] to redress grievances arising from maladministration in the public sector.

7.7.5 Reciprocal Administrative Presence of the Central Government and the HKSAR

Within the executive power, the administrative affairs of the HKSAR shall, according to Art. 16 of the Basic Law, be conducted in accordance with the relevant

[150] As one example of the operation of common law in Hong Kong, the crime of misconduct in public office could be mentioned in relation to a Senior Government Officer. In the case of *Shum Kwok Sher v HKSAR* [2002] 2 HKLRD 793, at pp. 798, 817–818, the person was convicted for the crime, but alleged in his complaints that the crime was not prescribed by law, that the law was not accessible and that the law was not foreseeable and that there was no legal certainty. The CFA recognized the existence of a common law crime of misconduct in public office, consisting of four elements [(1) A public official; (2) who in the course of or in relation to his public office; (3) wilfully and intentionally; (4) culpably misconducts himself and the misconduct is serious] and dismissed the appeal.

[151] When the system was extended in 2008, it was discovered that many of the under secretaries and some of the political assistants were also holders of foreign passports and citizenships. Although technically under the Basic Law there was no absolute requirement that the person only is a Chinese citizen, the matter led to a political controversy where, following demands from the general public, the under secretaries terminated their foreign citizenships, while the political assistants known to be foreign citizens did not. See Chen (2008b), pp. 325–331.

[152] See the Ombudsman Ordinance, see Cap. 397 at http://www.legislation.gov.hk/blis_pdf.nsf/4F0DB701C6C25D4A4825755C00352E35/323E49E4C8D2EF6C482575EF0002885C/$FILE/CAP_397_e_b5.pdf (accessed 14 January 2010).

provisions of the Basic Law. Such provisions have, in part, an extraneous nature since they direct themselves towards the executive authorities of Mainland China. In Art. 22 of the Basic Law, there is a prohibition forbidding any department of the Central People's Government or province, autonomous region, or municipality directly under the Central Government from interfering in the affairs, which the HKSAR administers on its own in accordance with the Basic Law. The prohibition aims at insulating the executive power of the HKSAR from the influence of the different structures of the Mainland Chinese executive power,[153] perhaps in particular those geographically adjacent to Hong Kong. However, the provision takes into consideration that there may arise a need for departments of the central government, or for provinces, autonomous regions, or municipalities directly under the central government to set up offices in the HKSAR. In such an event, they must obtain the consent of the Government of the HKSAR and also the approval of the Central People's Government. Consequently, the HKSAR has control over the creation of Mainland Chinese executive offices in Hong Kong and over potential attempts to enlarge the jurisdiction of Mainland China to Hong Kong. In the case that such offices are set up in the HKSAR, they and their personnel shall abide by the laws of the HKSAR, not by Mainland Chinese legislation.

Whereas Mainland Chinese executive offices cannot be established in Hong Kong without permission, the Basic Law contains in itself the basis for establishing some central government functions in the HKSAR. Currently, there exist three offices of the CPG in the HKSAR, namely the defense office (People's Liberation Army and its garrison on the basis of Art. 14 of the Basic Law), which evidently has very limited contacts with any counterparts in the HKSAR, the Foreign Affairs Office, established on the basis of Art. 13(2) of the Basic Law, which probably is mainly collaborating with those branches of the Government of Hong Kong that have international relations, but which otherwise seems to have very limited contacts in Hong Kong,[154] and the Liaison Office of the CPG, which is more visible in the HKSAR than the other bodies.[155]

---

[153]As concluded by Leung Mei-fun (2006), p. 13, Art. 22 of the Basic Law "also binds the Chinese government and the Chinese leaders; otherwise it is very difficult to maintain Hong Kong as a special administrative region".

[154]According to the yearbook Hong Kong 2008 (2009), p. 13, the contacts included "(a) participation in international organisations and conferences, such as obtaining the CPG's approval for HKSAR Government officials to participate as members of the PRC delegation in international conferences limited to states; (b) negotiation and conclusion of international agreements, such as obtaining the CPG's specific authorisation for the negotiation and conclusion of agreements with foreign states in accordance with the relevant provisions of the Basic Law; (c) consular protection for Hong Kong people in distress overseas; and (d) matters relating to consular missions in the HKSAR. The establishment of foreign consular and other official or semi-official missions is a matter for the MFA Office. The HKSAR Government is responsible for the day-to-day management of the consular corps."

[155]It has happened that the representative of Mainland China in the HKSAR has tried to meddle in the politics of Hong Kong by concluding, *inter alia*, on the issue of the holding of a consultative referendum in Hong Kong that it would be in breach of the Basic Law. See Ghai (2004), p. 441 f.

Article 22 allows the HKSAR permission to establish an office in Beijing, thus providing representation for Hong Kong before the Mainland authorities. The Beijing Office of the HKSAR plays a two-way role in linking Hong Kong and Beijing. Its functions include providing information about the HKSAR to the CPG, other Mainland authorities and non-governmental bodies, taking necessary action with the Mainland authorities on specific issues on the basis of the instructions of the relevant bureaus and departments of the Government of the HKSAR and liaising with the CPG and other Mainland authorities, such as counterparts in relevant CPG departments on immigration and nationality matters. The Beijing Office also connects back to Hong Kong by keeping the relevant bureaus and departments of the Government of the HKSAR informed about the latest developments in the Mainland and by providing logistical support to visiting delegations of the Government of the HKSAR. In addition, it liaises with non-governmental bodies from Hong Kong (e.g. Mainland officers of the Hong Kong Trade Development Council and Hong Kong Tourism Board) in the Mainland.

The Beijing Office has a PR function in the Mainland with a view to enhancing the Mainland authorities' and general public's understanding of Hong Kong's systems and latest developments, strengthening trade and economic links, and facilitating exchanges between Hong Kong and the Mainland (including information on immigration-related matters). This is important since the Office also processes applications for entry to Hong Kong for visit, employment, investment, training, residence and education in accordance with the prevailing immigration policies and procedures. Because there would, at any given time, be numerous Hong Kong residents in the jurisdiction of Mainland China, the Beijing Office also handles requests for assistance from them and provides practical assistance to such Hong Kong residents who are in distress in the Mainland. In the area of foreign relations (see Sect. 8.7 below), the Office conducts negotiations on visa-free access with foreign diplomatic missions, which have embassies only in Beijing but do not have representatives in the HKSAR and liaises with diplomatic corps in Beijing on immigration matters relating to the HKSAR.[156] In addition to the Beijing Office, Hong Kong has three economic and trade offices in Mainland China, namely in adjacent Guangdong as well as in Shanghai and Chengdu.

As a part of the Central People's Government in Beijing, the State Council of China has established the Hong Kong and Macao Affairs Office, which deals with matters related to Hong Kong (and Macao, too). The formal contacts between the Government of the HKSAR and its Chief Executive, on the one hand, and the CPG, on the other, are in principle directed via that office, including the issuance of reports by the Chief Executive twice per year to the CPG.[157] Also, proposals concerning Annexes I and II to the Basic Law, and probably other similar proposals,

---

Representatives of the Liaison Office have also frequently featured among the deputies that are selected from Hong Kong to the NPC. See Choy and Hualing (2007), pp. 586–589.

[156]See http://www.bjo.gov.hk/eng/pgm_zhineng_e.htm (accessed 18 August 2009).

[157]See Leung Mei-fun (2006), p. 256.

are dealt with by this office.[158] In terms of schedule, one of the above-mentioned reports of the Chief Executive to the CPG is delivered while the NPC is in session. In addition to formal contacts, there are also informal contacts. However, the problem with the contacts in general and with the informal contacts, in particular, is that they lack transparency.

7.8 Reflections

As was concluded in the introductory part to this chapter, the sub-state entities reviewed here are surprisingly presidential in their organization in comparison with the starting point, the Memel Territory. The main mode of organization seems to be one which emphasizes the strong position of the executive of the sub-state entity. Because presidentialism, or the strong and independent executive power, denotes a particular organizational point of departure with its own internal logic, the mechanisms normally embedded in the other main option, parliamentary accountability, are not present in the presidentially organized sub-state entities. In Zanzibar, Aceh, Puerto Rico and Hong Kong, simple majorities in the sub-state legislatures could not be used for the purpose of realizing the political accountability of the executive bodies. Instead, such political accountability is normally established through different forms of impeachment, perhaps also for the reason that the executive head is popularly elected in Zanzibar, Aceh and Puerto Rico, while that development is pending in Hong Kong. It remains to be seen how the recent introduction of the government of national unity will start to function in Zanzibar, but a first impression is that it could further strengthen the presidential nature of the Government of Zanzibar, in spite of the fact that it is created as a power-sharing arrangement between the two political power-houses in Zanzibar. In the Åland Islands and Scotland, political accountability is created on the basis of support in the parliamentary body of the sub-state entity in a manner similar to the operation of horizontal accountability in the Memel Territory. In the two entities, there is no such executive officer that would be elected in an election separately from the elections to the legislative assembly. Instead, the party commanding most support on the basis of the legislative elections is thought to be entitled to the position as the first minister.

In spite of the concepts of parliamentary accountability and presidentialism, the terminology used to describe the holders of the various executive offices may use the notion of governor or other designation to identify a central office-holder. As was the case in the Memel Territory, and also in the case of the Åland Islands, the representative of the central government in the sub-state entity is called governor and is a civil servant of the state. A similar position, although not terminologically coinciding, is held by the Secretary of State for Scotland, who is institutionally

[158] See Leung Mei-fun (2006), p. 256.

present in Scotland through the Scotland Office. In their functions, they are not directly involved with the government of the sub-state entity, except in relatively few particular situations as determined in the autonomy statutes. An opposite position is present in the cases of Puerto Rico and Zanzibar, where the highest executive office, the Governor of Puerto Rico and the President of Zanzibar, is held by a person elected by the population of the autonomous territory to be a representative of that population without any link with the national government. In this form of internal organization of the sub-state entity, the gubernatorial form of organization is premised on the strong involvement of the office-holder in the administration of the autonomous territory. Between these pure positions, typical of their respective organizational points of departure, there exists an anomalous position where the governor-like office is at the same time both a representative of the territory and a representative of the national government. This dualistic executive exists in Aceh and Hong Kong. While the national level may, for reasons of control, justify such an integration of the sub-state entity in the national structures of governance, this model may prove to be problematic from the point of view of the interests of the sub-state entity, because the population electing the main executive officer is not necessarily of the same opinion as the national government about the person of the office-holder. The model chosen for Aceh and Hong Kong may therefore be a source of conflict between the sub-state entity and the central government.

It appears that the executive of the sub-state entity is often created against the background of the model within the central government of the state, potentially because of the intuitive feeling that this is the manner in which the executive should be organized. In Zanzibar, the starting-point was different, because the independent State of Zanzibar, already presidentially organized because of the internal revolution soon after independence, was joined as such in the greater context of Tanzania. Also in Hong Kong, the pre-autonomy format of the executive, with a colonial governor under the direct control of the UK Government, suited the organizational needs of the central government of China. The model effect of the central government is clearest in the case of Puerto Rico, but somewhat less so in Aceh, because the gubernatorial solution there is also in harmony with the general regional administration of the state. As concerns Scotland, the model effect of the central government is probably strong, but this was initially not the case with the Åland Islands, where the introduction of parliamentary accountability of the kind practiced at the level of the central government took place only at the end of the 1980s. Hence the evolution of the current Ålandic model of parliamentary accountability took a long time. It remains to be seen how the introduction in Hong Kong of a spoils system of some kind concerning the secretaries and the under-secretaries will unfold in respect to political accountability, but the first signs indicate that these secretaries are sensitive to a lack of confidence in the horizontal dimension.

Because of the dominance of the presidential executive in our review, the horizontal mechanisms of accountability thus emphasize impeachment or similar mechanisms as the main form of reaction towards the executive head of government, while decisions by the legislative assembly of no confidence in the government of the sub-state entity are used less. Impeachment is normally a dramatic decision because it overrides the will of the people when the popularly elected head of the executive is voted out of office. Certain grounds of impeachment, established in the autonomy statute, normally apply at a level of precision that borders to requirements for criminalization, and the impeachment decision has to be made by a qualified majority, most often of two-thirds of the membership of the legislature. Impeachment is therefore exceptional and not used very much. In fact, it seems that impeachment has not been used even once in any of the sub-state entities reviewed here.

With regard to the problems in Hong Kong concerning how the terms of office of the Chief Executive are counted, the situation that emerged underscores, in comparison with Aceh and Puerto Rico, that it is important to provide a statutory back-up for the governor in case he or she is no longer taking care of the duties of the highest level of the executive power. In Aceh, the candidate ticket for the election of the Governor contains, at the same time, a candidate for the Vice-Governor, which means that the position is in principle filled for the entire term of office even in the case that the Governor is not taking care of his or her duties. In Puerto Rico, no vice-governor is elected in the gubernatorial elections, but the constitutional provisions of Puerto Rico contain a rule that the secretary of state shall take care of the position until end of the term of office if the Governor for some reason would be unable to do it. In Zanzibar, the second vice-president will fill the position during vacancy.

The use of the mechanism of no confidence is not more frequent in the two cases reviewed here than the use of impeachment in the other entities, although the formation of the government after elections is certainly influenced by the principle of parliamentary accountability. At the stage of forming the government, the principle of parliamentary accountability is at work, and motions of no confidence have been presented in both the Åland Islands and Scotland, although the decisions in the legislatures have not resulted in declarations of no confidence and in dismissals of government. In particular, as concerns the previous minority government in Scotland, such a decision would have been possible in case the other parties had managed to agree on how to replace the minority government. In the Åland Islands, parliamentary accountability is created in an asymmetrical way. It requires a simple majority for the formation of the government after elections, but absolute majority for a decision of no confidence. This is special and such a requirement is not found, for instance, at the level of central government in Finland. This asymmetry would make it, relatively speaking, easier to run a minority government than in a regular parliamentary context, if such a government would be formed.

In addition to the horizontal mechanisms of accountability, the sub-state entities studied here also reveal some vertical mechanisms of accountability. The clearest cases in this respect are Hong Kong and Aceh, where the heads of the executive have to be confirmed in their offices by the national government and where the possible impeachment or dismissal decisions, too, have to be made by the national government. In these two cases, the accountability of the holder of the highest executive office display clear vertical dimensions in a manner that connects the executive head to the national government. This is a feature that aligns the sub-state executive and government with the national government and may greatly influence policy-making at the sub-state level. A presidential government is not, as such, the reason for this, because Zanzibar and Puerto Rico do not display this vertical bond, although at least in theory, Zanzibar is also linked to the national government through the position of its president. Instead, the reason for the vertical accountability structures may be looked for in the national constitutional structures, which in the case of both China and Indonesia emphasize the unitary nature of the state and the central control of regions and other sub-divisions of the state. In China, this is probably mandated by the idea of democratic centralism, and in Indonesia by the ideological foundation of the state, the *Pancasila*.

Governmental accountability in the vertical dimension is relevant amongst the autonomy solutions reviewed here regarding the relationship to the central government. The *Memel* case indicated that a vertical dimension may exist, but in that specific context only with a view to actions *ultra vires* of the governmental body in an autonomous entity. The vertical dimension exists in the cases included in our study, but in the form of *intra vires* mechanisms by way of statutory rules concerning the relationship of the governmental body to the central government (notably Aceh and Hong Kong). It is clear that a relationship between the governmental body of the sub-state entity and the central government can condition the extent of the autonomy very much, in fact so much as to potentially threaten the existence of the autonomy. For the concept of autonomy, it is reassuring that there also exist autonomy arrangements where the autonomy acts create no vertical mechanisms of governmental accountability on a statutory basis. This means that the central government can not threaten the existence of the autonomy by means of executive interference, at least not as long as the autonomous entity and its government is acting *intra vires*.

It is evident on the basis of our study that legislative competence gives administrative competence. This principle, known already from the Memel context, is established in the autonomy statutes of, for instance, the Åland Islands, Scotland and Zanzibar, as well as in Hong Kong, where this principle seems to be very strict. Of course, in Zanzibar, political and constitutional reasons have led to a situation where the independent space of Zanzibar is demonstrated through the creation of special executive departments that probably contravene the reservation of the creation of armed and security forces to the Union, but in principle, also in Zanzibar, legislative competence gives rise to administrative competence. In addition, there may exist separate mechanisms of transferring administrative competence from the government of the state to the sub-state entity, as in the cases of the Åland Islands, Scotland, Hong Kong and Aceh, while the opposite direction would seem to be possible with regard to the Åland Islands (although it has not really been used) and, by default, in the case of Aceh, where sub-state competence is actually a matter that is negotiable between Aceh and the central government. In this respect, it is possible to establish that in some cases, the governments of sub-state entities may also act as executive agencies of the national government for the purposes of implementing national norms. This is the case at least in Aceh and also in Scotland, while in Zanzibar, the various regions and local government can be in such a position. In the Åland Islands, the Government can agree to take upon itself such implementing functions on the basis of particular consent decrees (see above, Chap. 5), while the municipalities of Åland implement national law in a few situations.

The provisions that regulate the executive power at the sub-state level are mainly found in two different sources: in the autonomy statute or in sub-state law. However, as concerns Zanzibar, the level of regulation is relatively high, with provisions concerning the Zanzibar Government in the Constitution of the Union Republic. This is probably quite unusual amongst all sub-state entities in the world. As concerns provisions in the autonomy statute, rules about the executive power are found in the Basic Law concerning Hong Kong and in the LoGA concerning Aceh, as well as in the Scotland Act. In Puerto Rico, the matter is regulated under the Constitution of Puerto Rico which, of course, could be understood as an autonomy statute because it has been enacted jointly by Puerto Rico and the US Congress. However, there is virtually nothing about the executive power in the Self-Government Act concerning the Åland Islands, except a short reference to the fact that there shall be a Government of the Åland Islands, while the actual norms relating to the operation of this Government are to be given in acts of Åland. In this respect and in comparison with the three other entities mentioned above, the legislature of the Åland Islands is at great liberty in passing the institutional and material norms concerning the sub-state executive of the Åland Islands. This liberty is at its largest with respect to Zanzibar, where no particular autonomy statute exists at all. The constitutional space available to the sub-state entities for the purposes of determining through their own decisions how the executive is organized and run, varies from narrow in Aceh, Scotland and Hong Kong to wide in the Åland Islands and Zanzibar (and probably also Puerto Rico).

The sub-state entities are, to a greater or a lesser extent, incorporated in the functioning of the central government so as to produce, depending on the case, a certain alignment of the sub-state entity with the national government. This alignment seems to be greatest with respect to Aceh, and it is perhaps followed by Hong Kong because of the position of the Chief Executive, although the alignment is not quite as apparent as one might expect. Surprisingly, the inter-governmental contacts between the Scottish Government and the UK Government are so multifarious that at least some measure of integration is produced, not only from the point of view of Scotland, but also from the point of view of the UK Government, with a ministerial post reserved for the Scotland Office in the UK Government.[159] Aceh and Scotland are exceptional in their integration with the national government also because the

[159]The integration of the executive branches of Hong Kong, Aceh and Scotland into the national executives by means of different mechanisms might at least in principle open up possibilities for so-called executive preemption by which the national government, either the lawmaker or the national executive, could "commandeer" the executive organs of the sub-state entity to undertake or refrain from undertaking measures of an administrative nature. In Hong Kong, the national government would mainly have a more veiled and political channel for influence of that sort, while in the cases of Aceh and Scotland, the system itself contains mechanisms or structures that provide that possibility. In the relationship between the constituent states and the federation in the United States, such commandeering has negatively perceived of in the constitutional jurisdiction in such cases as *New York v. the United States*, 505 U.S. 144 (1992), and *Prinz v. United States*, 521 U.S. 898 (1997).

civil service of those autonomous entities is part of the national civil service, in Aceh to a greater extent than in Scotland, because not only the Governor of Aceh but also the principal secretary of Aceh has to be confirmed by a decision of the central government. The contact between the executive agencies of sub-state entities of, for instance, Hong Kong and Scotland, and probably also Aceh, can be divided into formal and informal contacts. With respect to the formal contacts established on the basis of the autonomy statutes, the three entities can be said to be relatively well incorporated in the decision-making structures of the national government. However, on top of the formal contacts, there is probably also a layer of informal contacts, the extent of which is difficult to estimate. The level of transparency with respect to the formal contacts appears to be relatively low, but there is probably a substantial lack of transparency concerning the more informal contacts.

As concerns Zanzibar, the Åland Islands and Puerto Rico, the situation is probably very different. From the point of view of the Constitution of Tanzania, Zanzibar would seem to be integrated in different ways into the national government, but in reality, the mechanisms designed in the Union Constitution are not functioning in the manner they may have been intended to, and therefore, in practice, Zanzibar seems to be the sub-state entity that is the least aligned with the national government. There is a low level of alignment also concerning the Åland Islands (although there might exist a wish to maintain better contacts with the governmental authorities of Finland in the Swedish language), while the alignment of Puerto Rico is actually approached from the federal level by means of pledges to treat Puerto Rico administratively in the same way as a state in the federation is treated.

Of the entities studied in this context, only Zanzibar and Aceh are expected to be institutionally involved in certain parts of the national government, while the other entities are not. The institutional involvement of the two entities is not, however, of a federal nature, but is instead organized in a particular manner.

If the focus is shifted from the executive power at the level of the sub-state entity to administrative sub-divisions in those entities, local governments of various kinds can be found in all sub-state entities. In the Åland Islands, local government and the right to vote at that level of governance was an important component of the international guarantee, and under the Finnish Constitution, the municipalities of the Åland Islands have the same right to self-government as the municipalities in mainland Finland, making them relatively autonomous in themselves in relation to the state, or to the sub-state level of the Åland Islands, for that matter. The importance of municipalities or other units of local government may vary between the different sub-state entities, and it seems as if they were the least developed in Hong Kong, which is sufficiently small and homogeneous for more centralized governance through the autonomy arrangement itself, and they seem to have a lesser role in Zanzibar, too. In the other sub-state entities, local government may be relatively important for the provision of public services. However, in the Åland Islands, for instance, the sub-state entity is taking care of some of those public functions at the "regional" level that in mainland Finland are managed by the municipalities. Therefore, it may be so that in territorial autonomies generally, local government through municipalities or similar units is less prominent than outside of the territorial autonomies. The reason for this would be that the territorial autonomy itself stands out as the main provider of public service and does not leave quite the same space for the functions of its local government in comparison to local government in other parts of the state.

As pointed out in the introduction, territorial autonomy is not necessarily a minority protection mechanism, but may be created also for other reasons. In the case of Aceh, the minority protection dimension is perhaps of most relevance, because the entire arrangement is created for the self-government of the Acehnese, who have traditionally emphasized their distinctiveness not only as a minority, but also as a people. Although religion is an important characteristic of Aceh and is also implemented through the governmental structures of the arrangement, it does not make Aceh a particular mechanism of a religious minority, because Islam is a major religion in the entirety of Indonesia. A minority dimension can perhaps be detected in the case of the Åland Islands, because the entire arrangement is premised on the maintenance of the Swedish character of the territory (however, it is another matter if the Swedish-speaking inhabitants of the Åland Islands are a minority of their own or a part of the Swedish speaking population of Finland). This becomes very concrete through the provisions on the use of the Swedish language, not only in relations between the individual on the Åland Islands and the governmental structures of the Åland Islands, but also in relations between the institutions of the Åland Islands and the institutions of the state, which operate with Finnish as the majority language, but with the requirement of a good level of Swedish. To some extent, a similar position is relevant internally in the case of Puerto Rico, which is predominantly Spanish-speaking, although the contacts with the federal structures take place in English. The Scottish autonomy is also premised on the distinctiveness of the Scots, but that distinctiveness does not express itself in a linguistic manner in the administration. The position of the population of Zanzibar as a people is natural against the background of the creation of Tanzania as a Union, but minority protection does not seem to be a consideration except from a religious perspective, resulting in some public bodies and court instances that are of a religious nature. In Hong Kong, the presence of the minority dimension is almost non-existent in the autonomy arrangement (with the exception of the internal recognition of an indigenous group), because the inhabitants of Hong Kong are predominantly Chinese and do not differ from the population of mainland China in any particular manner.

If the narrow minority rights perspective is broadened into a general human rights discussion concerning sub-state entities, then an entirely new scenario emerges: the executive power in the sub-state entities is implementing norms established by the legislative assembly of the autonomous territory has passed. Those norms are implemented by the executive power in concrete cases, involving concrete individuals and business enterprises and other subjects of law. Through these decisions, public powers are exercised to determine the rights, benefits and duties of the private parties. The norms enacted by the law-making authorities of the sub-state entities should, of course, be in compliance with those human rights commitments that the State and perhaps also the sub-state entity itself have agreed to. By the same token, the implementation of law through executive decisions should comply with the human rights, too. However, it is at this level of concrete implementation of law that the risk of violations of human rights is actualized. Therefore, from the point of human rights, the sub-state entities actually assume the role of the State in relation to the individuals that the implementation decisions concern. This is not always uncomplicated. Although sub-state governance through territorial autonomy is in itself a positive opportunity, *inter alia*, from the perspective of the right to self-determination and the right to participation, violations of human rights of individuals is by no means a possibility that should be excluded in a sub-state context.

Chapter 8
International Relations

8.1 From Exclusion to Inclusion

The main issue in the *Memel* case dealt with the direct contacts made by the Directorate of the Memel Territory with a third State, and the PCIJ found that such contacts were not in compliance with the autonomy statute. With this denial of the possibility of international relations in the background, it is evident that this issue is still a source of major concern for States in which autonomous territories exist.

The *Memel* situation is well-established in relation to Puerto Rico and Zanzibar. In the case of Puerto Rico, the incapacity of Puerto Rico to have international relations follows from the operation of federal law, while in Zanzibar, international relations are defined as an exclusive union matter in the Articles of Union and the Constitution of Tanzania. As a consequence and in line with the *Memel* case, Zanzibar has been prevented from participation in an international organization. Although in the case of Aceh, sovereign sensitivities were demonstrated by Indonesia, the sub-state level is nonetheless furnished with a very limited scope of action in the international arena. Scotland is already in a different position, in particular as regards EU matters, while the broadest inclusion of sub-state entities in the international relations of States has taken place in the Åland Islands and, in particular, Hong Kong. While in the case of Hong Kong, the international competence is carefully delineated in the Basic Law, the Åland Islands has engaged in direct contacts with governmental representatives of foreign powers that in principle fall outside of the framework of the Self-Government Act. However, no such commitments have, at least so far, resulted from those contacts in the Nordic space that would be relevant under public international law and that would have created a complication. Therefore, the *Memel* facts have not been tested.

In all of these cases, be they excluded or included in the exercise of the State's international relations, it remains clear that the State is responsible for the international commitments in which the sub-state entities are involved. This is also the position of Denmark in relation to the Faroe Islands on the basis of the

M. Suksi, *Sub-State Governance through Territorial Autonomy*,
DOI 10.1007/978-3-642-20048-9_8,

self-governance legislation of 2005. A state with sub-state entities is likely to be unwilling to give away its international competence entirely, because that would imply the emergence of the autonomous territory as an independent State.[1] However, also the international community is likely to be interested in knowing who, in the final instance, is responsible for international commitments, and here, the starting point is that it is the State within which the sub-state entity exists, which is responsible as an international legal person.[2] This main rule has not prevented Denmark from adopting in 2009 such an autonomy statute for Greenland, in which it is left to the discretion of Greenland to decide, on the basis of the right to self-determination, whether the entity is willing to opt for independence and thus assume the position of an independent State.[3]

Hence if the state is willing to make possible the emergence of a sub-state entity as an independent State, this is possible, but in most cases, it is probably safe to assume that the state is not interested in diminishing its sovereignty and territorial

[1]In two separate Danish acts enacted in 2005, the Act concerning the entering into agreements under international law by the Government of the Faroe Islands, on the one hand, and a similar Act for Greenland, on the other, exceptions are made to the treaty-making power of the State of Denmark and a certain capacity is granted to the two autonomous territories to conclude treaties or treaty-like relationships with third States. In such situations, the State of Denmark is, according to the Acts, ultimately responsible for the international obligation. As concluded in Silverström (2008a), p. 260, "[t]he ability of autonomous entities to participate in international affairs depends primarily on whether the entity has been authorized by the state to do so. It is not surprising if demands for domestic authorizations will increase due to the greater impact and effect of international affairs on autonomies."

[2]The State responsibility is sometimes regulated through so-called federal clauses, as in Art. 28 of the 1969 American Convention on Human Rights, which places a general implementation obligation on the national government and imposes a duty on the national government to take suitable measures for the implementation of the Convention in constituent states in situations where the provisions of the Convention belong to the competence of the constituent states. Apparently, the provision is constructed against the background of the idea that federal supremacy or preemption applies. Sub-section 3 of Art. 28 contains a provision that may, in some situations, become relevant for the creation of autonomous territories: "Whenever two or more States Parties agree to form a federation or other type of association, they shall take care that the resulting federal or other compact contains the provisions necessary for continuing and rendering effective the standards of this Convention in the new state that is organized."

[3]See the Danish Act on the Self-Government of Greenland of 12 June 2009. A similar provision, albeit in a federal setting, was included in Art. 60 of the Constitutional Charter of the State Union of Serbia and Montenegro of 2002, for the purpose of formulating procedures for the withdrawal of one member state from the State Union of Serbia and Montenegro. On the basis of the provision, the three units of the federation, the Federal Republic of Yugoslavia, Serbia and Montenegro, agreed on 14 March 2002 on the Proceeding Points for the Restructuring of Relations between Serbia and Montenegro. The starting point was that in the event of a disintegration of the union, Serbia would be considered the successor State of the international commitments of the Federal Republic of Yugoslavia and that the sub-state entity that is exercising its right to leave the union would not inherit the international legal personality of the Federal Republic of Yugoslavia. As a consequence, Montenegro was able to adopt a declaration of independence through a referendum organized on 21 May 2006 and emerge as an independent State by way of voluntary secession from the Federal Republic of Yugoslavia. See Suksi (2004), p. 47 f.

extension. In situations where the sub-state entity continues to be a part of the state, international law departs from the point of view that the State is internationally responsible for everything taking place under its auspices that have a bearing on commitments at the level of public international law.[4] For the management of the international dimension of sub-state entities that continue to exist within a state, the various states have, however, opted for different solutions.[5]

8.2 Puerto Rico: No Involvement in Foreign Powers

Puerto Rico is not involved in the exercise of the foreign powers of the United States and it is fair to say that the Federal Relations Act does not seem to leave space for Puerto Rico in this respect. The Legislative Assembly has the competence to enact norms that are not locally inapplicable, that is, which are locally applicable. Therefore, decisions of a normative kind within the field of foreign powers are probably not within the competence of the Legislative Assembly or, for that matter, of the Government of Puerto Rico.

The case of *Americana of Puerto Rico, Inc. v. Kaplus*[6] makes it clear that like the states in the federation, Puerto Rico lacks "the full sovereignty of an independent nation", for example, the power to manage its "external relations with other nations", which was retained by the federal government. On the basis of the case, it seems that concerning Puerto Rico, foreign relations are a competence of a

[4]In Bring (2007), p. 40, comments concerning the Faroe Islands and Greenland are made, according to which the international treaties they have concluded bind legally the entire State and the responsibility under international law for possible breaches of the treaties is therefore attributed to Denmark. As pointed out by the author, the Faroe Islands and Greenland have some international rights but lack corresponding duties. As a consequence, they are not subjects of international law in the ordinary meaning of the word. According to Bring, this is would not prevent them and the Åland Islands from being international subjects of a lower dignity than subjects of international law. According to Silverström (2008a), p. 270, the Åland Islands, however, belong to the group of autonomous entities that has no separate legal personality in international law.

[5]Silverström (2008a), p. 271, makes the point that the participation of sub-state entities in international relations makes the conduct of international affairs more fragmented. "The active participation of autonomous entities on the international level certainly makes the international community more complex and cumbersome. However, greater complexity should not be an excuse for a gradual erosion of the competences of autonomous entities." The point here is that the sub-state entity should, at the same time as it might be given the authority to act at the international level, also be entitled to manage the full space of its domestic powers. The grant of powers in the area international relations should not mean that the State at the same time gets a position which allows it to meddle with the powers of the sub-state entity. See also Spiliopoulou Åkermark (1998), pp. 139–150, on the ability of autonomous entities to participate in judicial or quasi-judicial proceedings at the international level.

[6]368 F.2d 431, 435 (3d Cir. 1966).

residual nature held by the federation, not an enumerated one as in the case of the constituent states.

This means that Puerto Rico is not entitled to participate in two core activities of foreign relations, namely the process that leads to the conclusion of international obligations that the United States is party to (for instance, through formal or informal procedures of consultation in advance of the conclusion of treaties by the federal government), on the one hand, and the incorporation of such international obligations that the United States has agreed to, on the other.[7] As concerns the first area, the normative framework contains no explicit provisions on the basis of which Puerto Rico could make an input when the US executive engages in negotiations with third States. It is, however, conceivable that the Resident Commissioner could, on the basis of his or her entitlement to receive official recognition for the office by all of the departments of the federal government,[8] liaise with the State Department on such foreign relations matters that have a bearing on Puerto Rico. Even so, it appears that the role of the Resident Commissioner would be only advisory, not formal.

As concerns the second area, it is clear on the basis of the US Constitution that the US Senate recommends the ratification of treaties, and if ratified by the President, they become domestically binding in a manner that affects the law-making powers of Puerto Rico. In *Moreno Rios*, it was concluded that the US Congress has the undisputed power to apply the Narcotic Drugs Import and Export Act to Puerto Rico, but the court added that "an additional persuasive reason for not imputing to the Congress an intention to render the Act inapplicable to Puerto Rico is the fact that provisions of the Act, for instance, 21 U.S.C.A. § 182(a), were enacted in pursuance of international treaty obligations assumed by the United States".[9] An international treaty duly ratified thus applies to Puerto Rico in the same way as to the constituent states of the federation. The fact that Puerto Rico does not have any representation in the US Senate underlines the inequalities of the present system of governance.

In addition, the lack of full sovereignty evidently also means that Puerto Rico has no competences in the area of foreign relations, not even partial competences. When Puerto Rico tried to create so-called "intermediate boundaries" to counter the influx of weapons and narcotics, the measure was supported by an analogy to the freedom of the federal authorities to search incoming international travelers. In *Torres v. Puerto Rico*,[10] the permissibility of such an "intermediate border" between the Commonwealth and the rest of the United States was examined by the

[7]Trías Monge (1997), pp. 161–163. This does not exclude the possibility that Puerto Rico would be specifically empowered by the federal government to conclude, in individual cases, a treaty on such matters that are relevant to Puerto Rico. However, it is not known that such situations would have existed.

[8]US Code, Title 48, Sect. 891.

[9]*Moreno Rios supra* note 259 in Chap. 5, at 73.

[10]442 U. S. 465 (1979).

US Supreme Court. In support of this proposal, Puerto Rico pointed to its unique political status and to the fact that its borders as an island are, in fact, international borders with respect to all countries except the United States. However, the Supreme Court held that the Puerto Rican law could not be justified by any analogy to customs searches at a functional equivalent of the international border of the United States, because "the authority of the United States to search the baggage of arriving international travelers is based on its inherent sovereign authority to protect its territorial integrity. By reason of that authority, it is entitled to require that whoever seeks entry must establish the right to enter and to bring into the country whatever he may carry. (...) Puerto Rico has no sovereign authority to prohibit entry into its territory; as with all international ports of entry, border and customs control for Puerto Rico is conducted by federal officers. Congress has provided by statute that Puerto Rico must accord to all citizens of the United States the privileges and immunities of its own residents." The territory of Puerto Rico is US territory and the constitutional status of the Commonwealth has no bearing on the power of the federal authorities to enforce the federal legislation relevant to international borders. Any attempt by Puerto Rico to act differently was therefore pre-empted by the federal powers.

Puerto Rico is not a member of any inter-governmental organization, because such membership would entail the exercise of the federal treaty powers and also the possibility that a membership might be interpreted as the creation of a separate sovereignty contrary to the US sovereignty, recognized in the Treaty of Paris and the territorial clause.[11]

There is an exogenous link between Puerto Rico, on the one hand, and international law and international relations, on the other, through the concept of self-determination, which is still relevant at the level of the United Nations (see above, Sect. 4.3.4).

8.3 Zanzibar: Clearly a Union Matter

As stated in the case of *S.M.Z. v. Machano Khamis Ali & 17 Others*,[12] in 1964 two independent States, Tanganyika and Zanzibar, "merged to form a new international person called the United Republic of Tanzania", at which point "both Tanganyika and Zanzibar, and not Zanzibar alone, surrendered their treaty-making powers to the United Republic of Tanzania". According to point 2 of the first schedule to the Constitution of Tanzania, foreign affairs is a Union Matter. It is therefore relatively easy to conclude that Zanzibar has no powers in that area and cannot, for instance,

[11] Puerto Rico can, however, be a member of non-governmental international organizations, such as the Olympic movement.

[12] Court of Appeal of Tanzania at Zanzibar, Criminal Application No. 8 of 2000 on 3 April 2000. In the same decision, the Court stated that "in modern times, sovereignty is divisible".

establish direct diplomatic contacts with third States or become member of international organizations.[13] For instance, in 1992, Zanzibar applied for membership in and was actually admitted to the Organisation of Islamic Conference (OIC), but because of the opposition on the part of Tanzania to the measure, Zanzibar had to withdraw from the organization.[14] The traditional field of foreign relations is thus excluded for Zanzibar. For instance, a minister of the Government of Zanzibar cannot legally approach a foreign State, but has to do so as a part of a delegation of the Government of Tanzania to the third State. This is sometimes the case when the President of Tanzania travels abroad to meet heads of foreign States. At such occasions, ministers from the Government of Zanzibar have sometimes been invited to the delegation.

This does not mean that Zanzibar is entirely without any role in the totality of foreign affairs. When Tanzania concludes an international treaty, such a commitment normally also entails domestic implementation measures. The ratification of treaties is a union matter, done by Parliament against the background of the principle of dualism. The domestic enforcement of the international commitment is, however, another matter, and on the basis of the dualistic principle, the treaty does not become part of the law of the land upon ratification, but a separate implementation act is required for the treaty to have effect in the domestic legal order. Because the legislative competences are divided between the Union Parliament and the House of Representatives of Zanzibar, it is not immediately clear what the course of action should be as concerns the domestic implementation. The question is, what happens if the parliament ratifies an international treaty within a non-union matter (such as drug trafficking, corruption)? Does the union legislation enforcing the treaty in Mainland Tanzania extend its applicability to Zanzibar?

The answer on the part of Zanzibar to the latter question is negative, both from the point of view of law and practice. The consequence is that Zanzibar regards itself under an obligation to enact its own law for the implementation of the international treaty. This may create difficulties,[15] in particular if no advance consultations have taken place between the Governments of Zanzibar and Tanzania. The situation is not made easier by the fact that no mechanism of consultation has been institutionalized, but takes instead place on an *ad hoc* basis only. For

[13]However, Khamis Bakary (2006), p. 12, fn. 26, makes the point that out of approximately 20 Ambassadors of Tanzania to foreign States, three (3) are Zanzibaris, which he seems to feel is a low figure.

[14]Shivji (2006), p. 176, asks questions about the nature of the measure: "Was the attempt aborted legally or politically? After all, we know that Zanzibar was accepted in the OIC; it attended a couple of meetings, and, we do not know if it ever withdrew, or, if it did withdraw, whether it withdrew for political or legal reasons. More research could well show that Zanzibar withdrew, if at all, because of political pressure rather than because it was legally incompetent to make a treaty." See also Shivji (2008), p. 232.

[15]Problematic issues that have arisen have dealt with, e.g., the CEDAW Convention and the Convention on the Rights of the Child, in which cases Zanzibar feels that consultations should have taken place. Enforcement is still problematic within the material scope of these treaties.

instance, there often is no relationship between a minister of the Government of Mainland Tanzania and a minister of the Government of Zanzibar. Therefore, taking the area of agriculture as an example, development aid is by default going to the Mainland Tanzanian Government, although a solution has finally been reached: whatever is received by Tanzania, 4.5 % of the aid is given to Zanzibar. This is not entirely satisfactory for Zanzibar, because this share indicates that Zanzibar is treated as any other region of Tanzania.

Evidently, a consultation procedure should be created. If problematic areas can be identified before the treaty is signed and ratified, it might be possible for Tanzania to avoid problems before international law by means of, for instance, territorial reservations to the treaty concerning Zanzibar, by which Zanzibar would be exempted from the application of some particular provisions in the treaty.[16] It is another matter that such exemptions should perhaps not be favored, for instance, within the area of human rights.

The distribution of powers between the Union Republic, on the one hand, and Zanzibar, on the other, mentions foreign affairs as a matter which is the responsibility of the Union, and at the same time, the Union is charged, for instance, with civil aviation, which typically is a field where international treaty arrangements are prevalent. Merchant shipping is another area, which is subject to vast international regulation through conventions and through the International Maritime Organisation (IMO). However, as a matter subject to the distribution of powers, maritime traffic is not amongst the Union powers, although the treaty arrangements concerning merchant shipping and maritime traffic are dealt with by the Union. As a consequence, the powers within the maritime area are divided between the Union and Zanzibar so that both have their exclusive authorities in this area. In Mainland Tanzania, Parliament has adopted the Merchant Shipping Act of 2003, and on the basis of this Act, a Maritime Safety Administration has been instituted for Mainland Tanzania. Conversely, in Zanzibar, the legislature has enacted the Marine Transport Act of 2006,[17] the administration, implementation and enforcement of which is entrusted to the Zanzibar Maritime Safety Administration. The Act implements in the jurisdiction of Zanzibar, *inter alia*, the Convention on the Safety of Life at Sea, the International Convention for the Prevention of Pollution From Ships and the Load Line Convention.

[16]According to Shivji (2006), p. 177, the position of Zanzibar in the Tanzanian union is a Real Union and that "therefore, in international law the United Republic is not a state but a composite International Person and that Zanzibar is a State and although it cannot conclude treaties it can enter into treaties". This is a novel idea in the context, not supported by existing practice. The idea works towards limiting the international competence of the Union to what is absolutely necessary in terms of representation of the Union at the international level and recognizing an original sovereignty in the two parts of the Union. Shivji (2006), p. 186, draws the conclusion "that Zanzibar is a sovereign and a state, albeit its sovereignty is limited and the jurisdiction of the Executive and the Legislature is limited to non-union matters in Zanzibar, while its Judiciary, as epitomized by the High Court, has unlimited jurisdiction".

[17]Act No. 5 of 2006.

In addition, the Marine Transport Act establishes the Tanzania Zanzibar International Register of Shipping for ocean-going ships and the Tanzania Zanzibar Register of Shipping for coastal ships, including the function of ship surveying. Through registration, a ship is identified as a Tanzania Zanzibar ship. On the basis of the Marine Transport Act, Zanzibar is also exercising such port state control over foreign vessels that enter the ports of Zanzibar as the international conventions require. The complication in this context is, of course, that Tanzania as a State is the party, which is internationally bound by the treaty arrangements and is also the party that participates in the IMO, while Zanzibar lacks established legal possibilities to participate in the activities at the international level.[18]

The current plans to create an East-African Federation as a follow up to the East-African Community that existed in the 1960s are relevant from this point of view. In 2008, a national consultative process was organized in five countries, the populations of which were consulted on whether they want a federation or not and on which conditions.[19] The question from the side of Zanzibar is whether Zanzibar could participate in the Federation independently with equal status in comparison with other parties to the federal structure or whether Zanzibar would participate in the Federation as a part of Tanzania. The reply in 2010 in Zanzibar seems to be that it should be able to participate directly in the Federation and its decision-making in matters that do not belong to the Union, but to Zanzibar. The situation would be different in Union Matters, where Zanzibar could participate through the State of Tanzania, where Tanzania can represent the entire Union with respect to the Union Matters. In principle, Zanzibar may have some political leverage here, because it might be able to prevent Tanzania from participation in case membership in the Federation requires any of the constitutional processes of decision-making and thus qualified majorities in Parliament.

As the cases of Puerto Rico and Zanzibar show, sub-state entities may be precluded from any participation in the area of international relations, although their actions may imply at least a certain role. Other sub-state entities, such as Aceh and Scotland, may have at least some avenues for participating in international relations.

[18]Zanzibar is not even an associate member of IMO, although such membership has been created for Hong Kong, Macao, both Chinese special autonomies, and the Faroe Islands in Denmark.

[19]It appears that Tanzania has entered into the East African Community without consulting Zanzibar. Zanzibar is contemplating filing a case with the East African Court of Justice, claiming that Tanzania alone has no power to conclude and implement the treaty, in particular, because most of the domestic implementation of the treaty would take place within the competence of Zanzibar.

8.4 Aceh: Low-Level Activity Permitted

In para. 1.1.2 of the MoU, it was agreed as one of the fundamental principles of the peace agreement that international agreements entered into by the Indonesian Government which relate to matters of special interest to Aceh will be entered into in consultation with, and with the consent of the legislature of Aceh. This provision is implemented through Art. 8(1) of the LoGA, according to which draft international treaties that directly involve the governance of Aceh to be entered into by the Government shall be developed with the consultation and consideration from the DPRA, as specified in a presidential regulation.[20]

However, as pointed out above (see Sect. 5.6.3), the concept of consent included in the MoU was dropped during the drafting of the LoGA and changed into a weaker notion of consideration. Although the current formulation of the LoGA may be interpreted as giving a firm role to Aceh in terms of procedure and sincere consideration of the position of Aceh in relation to an international treaty that is being drafted or entered into by Indonesia, the provision does not grant Aceh any strong position to press for, for instance, a territorial exception in a treaty by way of requiring a reservation by Indonesia. Also, the provision does not amount to any regional entrenchment of treaties that Aceh might want to maintain. It is also unclear what the phrase "directly involve the governance of Aceh" could mean in the context of concluding treaties. It might imply that the consultation and consideration has to be sought only in cases where Aceh is explicitly implicated, which is a very narrow interpretation, or that consultation and consideration has to be sought in cases where the domestic implementation of the treaty requires action on the part of the institutions of Aceh, perhaps specifically by the DPRA in its capacity of norm-maker that can enact *qanuns*.

Although the LoGA has reduced consent to consideration in the context of treaty-making, the LoGA goes further than the MoU in certain other respects established in Art. 9, as specified by a Presidential Regulation. According to the provision, the Government of Aceh may enter into cooperation with foreign organizations or agencies except cooperation falling under the authority of the Indonesian Government. Here, again, there seems to be a reference to the enumerated competences allocated in Art. 7(2) of the LoGA to the Indonesian Government. The areas excluded from international cooperation would thus be at least governmental affairs at the national level, overseas politics, defense, security, judicial matters, monetary matters, national revenues, and certain aspects of religious affairs. However, because of the blurred division of competence between the central government and Aceh, the areas in which it might engage in international cooperation could, in fact, be more limited. The provision is limiting the cooperation to foreign

[20]According to Presidential Regulation No. 75/2009, the procedure for consultation and recommendation by DPRA in drafting the law regarding the issue about Aceh is regulated by the DPRRI guideline.

organizations or agencies, which seems to imply that cooperation with foreign States, that is, sovereign entities outside of Indonesia, is excluded and that Aceh cannot conclude treaties or agreements with third States. Aceh cannot commit the sovereignty of Indonesia in dealings with foreign organizations and agencies. Nevertheless, it might be able to enter into *other* forms of cooperation with agencies of third States, and certainly with inter-governmental and non-governmental organizations. In the event of entry into cooperation arrangements of this kind, the document governing such cooperation shall include a stipulation stating that the Government of Aceh is a part of the Unitary State of the Republic of Indonesia. Ultimately, the sovereignty of Indonesia should thus be recognized and protected even in the case of a lesser level of international engagement that Aceh may develop.

There is an interesting example of such cooperation in the Memorandum of Understanding on Environmental Cooperation between the Province of Aceh of the Republic of Indonesia, and the States of California, Illinois and Wisconsin of the United States of America, signed on 18 November 2008 by the Governors of the four sub-state entities.[21] In this document, not designated as a treaty or an agreement, but as a Memorandum of Understanding, the four sub-state parties express their interest in cooperation by recognizing that they are parts of two sovereign States, Indonesia and the United States. The four sub-state parties also deal with a matter in the Memorandum which appears to be within their jurisdiction, namely the environment in general and climate change in particular, with the focus on the reduction of greenhouse gas emission from deforestation and land degradation, and the sequestration of additional carbon through the restoration and reforestation of degraded lands and forests and on development of rules within this area. The parties express their willingness to cooperate in the search of joint actions that improve the environmental quality and optimize the quality of life in the relevant sub-state entities. The concrete actions contemplated in Art. 3 of the document include exchange of information, design, implementation and joint financing of studies and projects, development and dissemination of publications, technology transfer, exchange of scholars and experts, development of capacity building programs, joint development of seminars, workshops, conferences, courses, technical visits and certificate courses. The intention is to develop a joint action plan to promote these actions. In Art. 12 of the Memorandum of Understanding, the parties acknowledge that it does not create any legally binding rights and obligations.

In the LoGA, there is an additional grant of a "non-essential" governmental sphere of international activity for Aceh in Art. 9(2), according to which the Government of Aceh may participate directly in international arts, cultural, and sporting events. This sphere of international activity is not specified as one where presidential regulations would be required for the specific forms of the international

[21]The signatories are Governor Yusuf Irwandi for the Province of Aceh of the Republic of Indonesia, Governor Arnold Schwarzenegger for the State of California of the United States of America, Governor Rod Blagojevich for the State of Illinois of the United States of America, and Governor Jim Doyle for the State of Wisconsin of the United States of America.

activity, which means that the Government of Aceh can operate directly on the basis of the provision in the LoGA. Apparently, international arts, and cultural and sporting events are in many cases events in which individuals or teams of individuals participate, but they could do so as representatives of Aceh, perhaps on the basis of funding from the Government of Aceh. As concerns arts and culture, the provision could facilitate, for instance, the opening of a pavilion of Aceh at the Venice biennale, while the reference to sporting events may be interpreted as an option for the Government of Aceh to support a team of its own, for instance, in the international Olympic movement or in football championships.

8.5 Scotland: Some Involvement

It is clear, on the basis of schedule 5 of the Scotland Act, that foreign relations and foreign powers are a matter reserved for the UK competence, and that the Scottish jurisdiction has no competence in that area. Nonetheless, the Scottish jurisdiction comes into contact with issues within that area, for instance, with respect to EU law,[22] as concerns rights that are guaranteed under the European Convention of Human Rights, and in relation to other international obligations, in particular in situations where the implementation of these international or supra-national legal commitments are at issue. Because the implementation of international commitments may have to be done within the Scottish jurisdiction, there is, understandably, a corresponding Scottish interest to participate in the conclusion of those obligations. This interest and the role that, for instance, Scotland plays in the implementation of such obligations is recognized by the Memorandum of Understanding in its section on international and EU relations. In para.18 of the Memorandum of Understanding, it is stated that arrangements for the handling of devolved administrations' interests outside the United Kingdom are set out in the international relations and EU concordats. Therefore, while binding law is silent on the matter of Scottish participation in the exercise of foreign powers, the commitments that the UK and Scottish executive branches have entered into create a legally non-binding framework for such activities at a practical level.

As concerns the creation of obligations, in para. 19 of the Memorandum, the UK Government pledges to involve the devolved administrations as fully as possible in discussions about the formulation of the UK's policy position on all EU and international issues which touch on devolved matters. The involvement of the devolved administrations is subject to mutual respect for the confidentiality of those discussions and adherence to the UK line that has emerged during the process. One part of this pledge is the possibility for Scotland to nominate its share of UK

[22]EC law is in schedule 5 to the Scotland Act regarded as a part of foreign powers, although the practical nature of the commitment lies more within the area of domestic public law. See also McFadden and Lazarowicz (2002), p. 130.

representatives to the Committee of the Regions and the Economic and Social Committee of the European Union.[23] A similar recognition applies to the creation of international obligations outside of the EU framework.

As concerns implementation of obligations, para. 20 of the Memorandum makes the point that the devolved administrations are responsible for implementing international, ECHR and EU obligations which concern devolved matters. As a reminder of section 29, sub-section 2(d), according to which Community law must prevail, it is stated that UK ministers have powers to intervene in order to ensure the implementation of EU obligations, and the wider provisions for resolution of competence disputes through reference to the UK Supreme Court applies, with the UK parliament and UK ministers retaining the power, as provided under the devolution legislation, to legislate in order to implement EU obligations throughout the UK.[24] However, there is also a softer approach to this dimension for cases where the devolved administrations may feel that they do not want to act: if they wish, it is open to them to ask the UK Government to extend UK legislation to cover their EU obligations, something that has taken place in practice. Such a request activates the legislative consent mechanism at the Scottish Parliament at such a stage when the UK Parliament is dealing with the matter. As a practical matter, a fair amount of "behind-the-scenes" discussion would be required.

According to the Concordat with Scotland on co-ordination of European Union policy issues, the interfaces between the UK Government and the Scottish Government contain at least the following dimensions: provision of information, formulation of UK policy, attendance at Council of Ministers and related meetings,[25]

---

[23]Para. B4.29 of the Common Annex to the Concordat on Co-ordination of European Policy Issues, in Memorandum of Understanding and Supplementary Agreements between the United Kingdom Government Scottish Ministers, the Cabinet of the National Assembly for Wales and the Northern Ireland Executive Committee. Presented to Parliament by the Deputy Prime Minister by Command of Her Majesty, December 2001/CM 5240. See also Pilkington (2002), p. 108, and McFadden and Lazarowicz (2002), p. 131 ff.

[24]See Memorandum of Understanding, Concordat on Co-ordination of European Union Policy Issues - Scotland, Common Annex, para. B4.8.

[25]See Memorandum of Understanding, sections B4.12 to B4.15 of the Common Annex to the Concordat on Co-ordination of European policy issues: "Ministers and officials of the devolved administrations should have a role to play in relevant Council meetings, and other negotiations with EU partners. Decisions on Ministerial attendance at Council meetings will be taken on a case-by-case basis by the lead UK Minister. In reaching decisions on the composition of the UK team, the lead Minister will take into account that the devolved administrations should have a role to play in meetings of the Council of Ministers at which substantive discussion is expected of matters likely to have a significant impact on their devolved responsibilities. Policy does not remain static in negotiations and continuing involvement is a necessary extension of involvement in formulating the UK's initial policy position. The role of Ministers and officials from the devolved administrations will be to support and advance the single UK negotiating line which they will have played a part in developing. The emphasis in negotiations has to be on working as a UK team; and the UK lead Minister will retain overall responsibility for the negotiations and determine how each member of the team can best contribute to securing the agreed policy position. In appropriate cases, the leader of the delegation could agree to Ministers from the devolved administrations

implementation of EU obligations, and infraction proceedings. Although the co-ordination of the EU issues takes place in a similar way to the co-ordination of the domestic issues, it seems that Scotland is highly integrated in the management of EU issues in the UK, including participation in the meetings of the Council of Ministers, and in the proceedings before the European Court of Justice on such legal issues where Scotland is either partly or fully implicated for a breach of EU law. A Scottish minister can be designated as the one of the UK team participating in the Council meetings who presents the position of the UK to the Council. However, it is the UK minister, who in case of disagreement has the ultimate responsibility of formulating the UK position.[26] Hence, although Scotland does not have the competence under the Scotland Act to involve itself in EU matters, the Memorandum of Understanding and the Concordat establish a very strong profile for Scotland in this area,[27] with the understanding of a corresponding liability.

Because a breach of EU law may carry with it pecuniary consequences for the Member State, that is, for the United Kingdom, the Memorandum reminds the devolved administrations that they are directly accountable through the domestic courts, in the same way as the UK Government is, for shortcomings in their implementation or application of EU law. For such situations, and evidently also for situations where the ECJ holds the UK liable for an infraction of EU law,[28] all

speaking for the UK in Council, and that they would do so with the full weight of the UK behind them, because the policy positions advanced will have been agreed among the UK interests. Attendance by officials of the devolved administrations at EU meetings will continue, as at present, to be agreed bilaterally with the lead Whitehall Department. Such agreement would also cover attendance at Presidency and Commission chaired meetings, including those discussing implementation matters. The role of officials from the devolved administrations will be to support and advance the single UK negotiating line which they will have played a part in developing." For an analysis of the collaboration between the UK level and Scotland level on EU matters, see also Hazell (2005b), p. 237 f.

[26] For instance, the submission of the United Kingdom to the Convention charged with drawing up the constitutional structures of the European Union was submitted to the European Convention on behalf of the UK Government and the Devolved Administrations in Scotland and Wales. See Jeffery and Palmer (2007), p. 235 f.

[27] In fact, Scotland has carried out direct negotiations with the European Commission in the area of agriculture.

[28] See Memorandum of Understanding, sections B4.22 – B.24 of the Common Annex to the Concordat on Co-ordination of European policy issues: "Where the European Commission instigates informal or formal proceedings against the UK for alleged breaches of EC law, the Cabinet Office will commission and co-ordinate the UK response, which will be sent by UKRep on behalf of the UK Government. Where a case relates solely to implementation in Scotland, Wales, or Northern Ireland in relation to a matter falling within the responsibility of a devolved administration, the draft reply will be prepared by the appropriate devolved administration and agreed at official, and where necessary Ministerial, level with interested Whitehall departments. It will be submitted through UKRep in the normal way as outlined in Paragraph B4.19. Where a case partly concerns implementation of a devolved matter in England and one or more of the devolved regions, the lead Whitehall department will prepare the draft reply in bilateral consultation, at official or Ministerial level as appropriate, with the relevant devolved administrations. Such a procedure will also be followed where a case concerns implementation in Scotland, Wales or

four administrations, including Scotland, have agreed that, to the extent that financial penalties are imposed on the UK as a result of any failure of implementation or enforcement, or any damages or costs arise as a result, responsibility for meeting them will be borne by the administration(s) responsible for the failure. Therefore, a breach of EU law that can be attributed entirely to the Scottish jurisdiction might result in heavy damages for Scotland to the UK, which is the primary payee of the damages.[29] Impliedly, the fine could probably be shared between Scotland and the UK if the breach of EU law can be attributed to both, in particular because ministers of the UK Government have the power to intervene in Scottish decision-making in this area on the basis of section 57 of the Scotland Act.[30] In practice, the distribution of the damages would probably not arise before any court of law because the Memorandum of Understanding is not enforceable in judicial proceedings. Instead, the compensation would be determined by way of political negotiation.

In contrast to EU matters, traditional international relations and exercise of foreign powers display a different profile of involvement, although the UK Government recognizes the legitimate interests of Scotland even in this field.[31] According to the Concordat with Scotland on international relations, the interfaces between the UK Government and the Scottish Government contain at least the following dimensions: exchange of information, formulation of United Kingdom policy and conduct of international negotiations, implementation of international obligations, co-operation over legal proceedings, representation overseas,[32] secondments and training co-operation, visits, public diplomacy, the British Council and BBC World Service, trade and investment promotion, and diplomatic and

Northern Ireland in relation to a non-devolved matter. Where a case partly or wholly involving implementation by a devolved administration is referred to the European Court of Justice, the devolved administration will contribute to the preparation of the UK's submissions to the Court. The devolved administration would take the lead in doing so for cases wholly concerned with implementation in relation to a matter falling within its responsibility, agreed as appropriate with the relevant Whitehall departments. The Cabinet Office and the Treasury Solicitors Department will co-ordinate the UK's submissions to the Court."

[29]See also Trench (2007b), p. 63, who considers this a remarkable provision to impose on the devolved administrations as a price for their autonomy.

[30]See Himsworth and Munro (2000), p. 74.

[31]Unlike the EU matters, in which the Scottish views have to be sought by the relevant UK departments, the traditional foreign affairs such as conclusion of treaties, declaration of war, etc., would be an area where advance contacts with Scotland would be less likely. It is possible that the requirement of efficiency (in the broad sense of the term) in the area of foreign affairs is not easy to combine with accountability. Within foreign relations, Scotland has, however, moved cautiously into the area of development co-operation (e.g., Malawi, Changdung area in China), which indicates that a sub-state entity can undertake some activities and sharing of state power without challenging the state. The expectation is, however, that Scotland does not undertake anything in the realm of foreign relations completely independently, but links such actions to the UK structures. This is reflected, inter alia, in Scottish Ministerial Code (2008), paras. 9.11–9.13.

[32]At the UK Embassy in Washington, D.C., there is a Scottish person seconded by the Scottish Government, and there is a Scottish Representation also in Brussels.

consular relations. In addition, the UK Government and Scottish ministers will maintain full and detailed working-level contacts in regard to international relations. The Secretary of State for Foreign and Commonwealth Affairs and the First Minister or their nominees are expected to meet annually, or at the request of either party to review co-operation in regard to international relations (which is a mechanism that at least partly may overlap with the regular mechanism of the Joint Ministerial Committee and its dispute resolution function, although that mechanism is available too). However, the foreign relations of the UK are exercised through the appropriate agencies of the UK Government also in situations where the interests might be predominantly Scottish,[33] except the relations to the EU institutions and to regional governments in other EU countries, for which Scotland may maintain a representation in Brussels.[34]

It is thus possible to say that the Scottish authorities can utilize a broad framework of consultation for participation in foreign affairs, which in the case of EU matters is more far reaching than in the case of regular international relations. The framework does not contain the possibility of preventing the UK from supporting a measure at the EU level or concluding an international treaty, nor does it contain the possibility of opting out from the implementation of an EU obligation or an obligation that is based in international law. Even so, the incorporation of Scotland into the UK foreign relations, including EU relations in particular, is substantial, if not always very visible.[35]

The relevance and visibility of international relations of sub-state entities is brought to an entirely other level in the cases of the Åland Islands and Hong Kong.

---

[33]According to some interlocutors, the Scottish Government has not received guests at the ministerial level of government from other states.

[34]Under Memorandum of Understanding, para. B4.27 of the Common Annex to the Concordat on Co-ordination of European policy issues, this is possible so far as it serves the "exercise of their powers and the performance of their functions as laid down in the devolution legislation and so far as it is consistent with the responsibility of the UK Government for relations with the EU. If such an office is established, it will work closely with, and in a manner complementary to, UKRep which remains responsible for representing the view of the United Kingdom to the European Institutions, and will respect the responsibility of the UK Government for non-devolved areas, including overall responsibility for relations with the EU. Both UKRep and any office of the devolved administrations will develop working procedures which reflect the need to balance the interests of all parts of the UK."

[35]See also Jeffery and Palmer (2007), pp. 236–238.

8.6 The Åland Islands: Involvement with Some Problems

8.6.1 Conclusion and Implementation of Treaties

The origins of the autonomy of the Åland Islands can be found in a wish of the inhabitants of the islands to secede from Finland and to join with Sweden, and in the conflict between Finland and Sweden about the islands. In para. 7 of the 1921 Åland Islands Settlement, a collective complaints procedure was established for the Åland Islands in case Finland would not live up to its obligations under the Settlement. The 1920 Self-Government Act placed international relations amongst the legislative powers of the Parliament of Finland in a way that affected the legislative powers of the Åland Islands in a negative way (see above, Sect. 5.3.1). Against this background and the sensitivities of sovereignty, it could be expected that the islands would have no share at all, or only a very limited share in the exercise of the external dimensions of sovereignty and self-determination of Finland. However, the situation has evolved differently, and the normative development of the various Self-Government Acts and other legislation within the area of international relations has provided the Åland Islands with a relatively wide measure of functions and safeguards within this area.

While the Self-Government Acts of 1920 and 1951 did not contain any special provisions concerning the participation of the Åland Islands in international matters, the 1991 Self-Government Act adopted a different point of departure and gave a certain position to the Åland Islands in relation to treaty matters. At the time of Finnish EU membership, the standing of the Åland Islands in relation to the preparation of the Finnish position and the implementation of EU law was specified through amendments to the Self-Government Act. The Self-Government Act provides for a complex web of participation for the Åland Islands in decision-making concerning EU matters. There is a somewhat similar mechanism in the Self-Government Act with respect to treaties, which provides that the Government of Åland may propose negotiations on a treaty or other international obligation to the appropriate state officials. The Government of Åland should be informed about negotiations on a treaty or another international obligation if the matter is subject to the competence of Åland, or otherwise relates to matters of special importance to it. The Government of Åland shall have the opportunity to participate in the negotiations, if there is a special reason for this. It is noteworthy in this context that under section 59b(4), the Government of Åland is allowed to make direct contact with the European Commission regarding matters falling within its powers and concerning the implementation of EU decisions there, but it shall notify the Council of State of such contacts. In addition, the Helsinki Agreement between the five Nordic countries constitutes an important development through which the Åland Islands, together with the Faroe Islands and Greenland as the other two Nordic self-governing territories, gained a formal position in Nordic co-operation as early as 1984.

Sometimes, the issue of the demilitarization and neutralization of the Åland Islands is confused with the issue of autonomy. The two issues were, however, handled separately, the former by the states that concluded the 1921 Åland Convention and the latter by the Council of the League of Nations, by deciding on the Settlement after Finland and Sweden had agreed to the contents of it. Therefore, the autonomy of the islands is actually not attached to demilitarization and neutralization.[36] Nonetheless, some have argued that the two different regimes for the Åland Islands form one package.[37] In fact, the behavior of the population and the Government of the islands points in that direction: they pay great attention to monitoring the demilitarization and neutralization, despite the fact that the connection between the autonomy and security issues is very thin and that activities relating to foreign relations are a competence of the state.[38] Although the Government of the Åland Islands does not have any formal supervisory role in relation to the demilitarization and neutralization issue, the Finnish ministries of foreign affairs and defense have remained sympathetic and responsive to its interest in this matter and to the interest of the population of the islands.[39]

As concerns international treaties, the Self-Government Act applies a dual approach involving provisions concerning negotiations, on the one hand, and provisions concerning the implementation of international agreements, on the other. As concerns negotiations, the Government of the Åland Islands may, according to section 58 propose negotiations on a treaty or another international obligation to the appropriate state officials. This would seem to mean that the Ministry of Foreign Affairs is contacted, but because the President is, under the Constitution, in charge of the international relations of Finland, the initiative could also be passed directly to the President. The more likely situation to occur within the sphere of international treaties is, however, that the Finnish Government becomes involved in such treaty negotiations with third States where the subject matter touches upon the legislative competences of the Åland Islands. In such situations, the Government of the Åland Islands shall be informed of negotiations on the treaty or another international obligation. If the negotiations otherwise relate to matters of special importance to the islands, the Government of the Åland Islands shall be informed of the negotiations, if this can be done in a feasible way. If there

---

36 On the demilitarization and neutralization of the Åland Islands, see Björkholm and Rosas (1990), Rosas (1997), Ahlström (1997).

37 Fagerlund (1993), pp. 112–119. See also Spiliopoulou Åkermark (2007), p. 80.

38 See Spiliopoulou Åkermark (2007), p. 91, who gives a vivid account of this attitude.

39 For the ratification of the Open Skies agreement, see Rotkirch (2003), p. 88. For an account, see also Bring (2007), pp. 34–36, where the author accounts of different contacts between the Government of the Åland Islands and the governmental bodies of Finland from a more politological perspective. One of the communications accounted for relates to the so-called Open Skies agreement, which was ultimately not found to be in breach of the demilitarized status. See also Spiliopoulou Åkermark (2007), pp. 80–90, for an account of contacts between authorities of the Åland Islands and Finland concerning the implementation of the demilitarization and neutralization of the Åland Islands, including the Open Skies agreement.

are special reasons that justify the participation of the Government of the Åland Islands in the negotiations, it shall be given the opportunity to do so.[40]

Through the participation of the Åland Islands already at the stage of the negotiations, it could be possible to avoid legal problems at the point when the treaty, if concluded, is implemented in the domestic legal order, which in the Finnish case would often mean bringing into force a treaty within two jurisdictions, that of mainland Finland and that of the Åland Islands. In case there are weighty objections presented from the Åland Islands, the treaty with a third State could even be concluded so that there is a territorial exception for the Åland Islands.[41] An example of this is Protocol No. 2 to the Accession Treaty of Finland in the European Union, prepared with the involvement of the Government of the Åland Islands already during negotiations.

When a treaty has been concluded between Finland and a third State, the dualistic point of departure causes the treaty to be handled in two separate processes that in practice coincide to a large extent. The ratification procedure may involve an acceptance decision by the Parliament of Finland, but in any case, the decision to ratify a treaty is made by the President of Finland, after which Finland becomes bound to the treaty at the level of international law. The Åland Islands are not involved in the actual ratification process. However, ratification of a treaty does not mean that the treaty enters into force within the Finnish jurisdiction. For the legal consequences to occur in the domestic jurisdiction, the treaty has be to brought into force by a separate decision, which is often of a legislative nature. If a treaty or another international obligation binding on Finland contains a provision which under the Self-Government Act concerns a matter within the competence of the Åland Islands, the Legislative Assembly of the Åland Islands must, according to section 59(1), consent to the statute implementing that provision so that it will enter into force in the jurisdiction of Åland.[42] In practice, most of the treaties dealt with in this order, averaging around ten per year, are treaties about the prevention of double taxation or about social benefits. If the Ålandic consent is not given, the treaty does not enter into force within the jurisdiction, only in mainland Finland.[43]

---

[40] As pointed out by Silverström (2008a), p. 262, the "competences of Åland related to the negotiating of treaties or international obligations are not extensive and in practice usually limited to consultation only".

[41] The legislative competence of the Åland Islands is often taken into account in treaty negotiations so that a reference is made in the text of the treaty to the fact that the treaty is not applied to the Åland Islands but that the Government of Finland can file a declaration to the treaty stating that the treaty shall also be applied to the Åland Islands. By using this method, Finland can sign the treaty and wait with filing the declaration until the matter has been dealt with in the Åland Islands. See Palmgren (1995), pp. 22–32.

[42] According to section 59(3), the Legislative Assembly may authorize the Government of the Åland Islands to issue such a consent, but this possibility of delegation is actually not used.

[43] Silverström (2008a), p. 264, makes the point that in practice, the consent mechanism could work as a veto, although it is defined in legal terms only as a treaty-implementing power. The Legislative Assembly has refused its consent only a few times, but such refusals of risk thereof could

A similar procedure applies to treaties or treaty provisions that contain a conflict with the Self-Government Act and that are brought into force by an Act of the Parliament of Finland, which is passed by a majority of two-thirds in the so-called limited constitutional order. In principle, such a conflict of a constitutional nature in relation to the Self-Government Act would primarily be identified by the Constitutional Committee of the Finnish Parliament. In such situations, if a provision of the treaty is contrary to the Self-Government Act, the treaty will, according to section 59(2), enter into force in the jurisdiction of Åland only if the Legislative Assembly gives its consent by a qualified majority of two-thirds of those voting. For this reason, the Finnish Accession Treaty to the European Union had to be passed in the Legislative Assembly in this order. In addition, because of this decision-making hurdle, the Legislative Assembly could also have prevented the so-called Lisbon Treaty from entering into force in the entire territory of Finland on 1 December 2009, thereby placing Finland in a very complicated and legally conflicting situation with respect to the implementation of the Treaty on the European Union and the Treaty on the Functioning of the European Union. In fact, the Legislative Assembly of the Åland Islands was the last law-making body in Europe to give its consent, by 24 votes for and 6 votes against, to the Lisbon Treaty on 25 November 2009, or actually, its consent to the entering into force of the provisions in the Åland Islands to the extent the treaty falls within the competence of Åland.

8.6.2 The Åland Islands in the European Union

During the preparations for Finland's accession to the European Union, Finland recalled that the autonomy of the Åland Islands is constitutionally guaranteed on the basis of the internationally-recognized status of the Islands and requested that special measures be taken so that the autonomy arrangement would not be adversely affected. Consequently, Finland proposed (and the EU agreed) that derogations be incorporated into the relevant EU treaties.[44] Without such an arrangement, the assent of the Åland Legislative Assembly could not have been taken for granted, and thus there was a risk that Åland might remain outside the European Union altogether. The Åland Islands joined the European Union as a part of Finland on 1 January 1995, but with some exceptions formulated in Protocol 2 to the Accession Treaty.[45] It is a

---

affect the Government of Finland when commencing negotiations about other treaties or obligations.

[44]These were to be in Art. 227 of the Treaty on European Communities, Art. 79 of the Treaty on the European Coal and Steel Community, and Art. 198 of the Treaty on the European Atomic Energy Community and a Special Protocol. On the accession negotiations of Finland and the special provisions concerning the Åland Islands in the context of EU law, see Fagerlund (1997), pp. 189–256.

[45]On 1 December 2009, the Treaty on the Functioning of the European Union entered into force, and in that Treaty, Art. 355(4) makes reference to the Accession Treaty and Protocol 2 as follows: "The provisions of the Treaties shall apply to the Åland Islands in accordance with the provisions

matter of taste whether legal matters after accession to the EU are understood as international issues or semi-domestic issues of some sort, but for the purposes of sub-state governance, they often seem more international than semi-domestic. In any case, the constitutional order of Finland recognizes that the Åland Islands have a particular position both in the preparation of national positions in relation to the EU and in the national implementation of EU obligations. In this respect, the mechanism is somewhat similar to the treaty negotiations and implementation of treaty obligations, but due to the specificities of EU law, the rules are more detailed.

It is important to recognize that due to Finnish (and Ålandic) membership in the European Union, since 1 January 1995, a third separate legal order applies to the Åland Islands, that of the European Union. While EU membership does not formally alter the allocation of legislative competence between Åland and the Parliament of Finland according to the Self-Government Act, legislative competence from both legal orders has been transferred to the EU to be exercised by the EU bodies.[46] As a consequence, an individual (or a business enterprise) on the Åland Islands is potentially subject to the norms of three different lawmakers. Because the structures of the EU address themselves to the Member States, sub-state entities like the Åland Islands have also experienced a *de facto* loss of competence, in this case to Finland. Nonetheless, the three legal orders can be understood as separate and exclusive in relation to each other and, as a consequence, as parallel legal orders based on a separation of competencies without any hierarchical ordering between them (although the EU legal order presents itself as a supra-national legal order, at least when looking at it from an EU law point of view). The parallel existence of three legal orders may be confusing: for the individual residing on the Åland Islands, it may be difficult to know exactly which law to obey.[47] At the same time, it underlines the need for Åland both to influence the EU rules when they are being drafted, and the importance of the correct implementation of those EU rules that have been adopted by the lawmaker of the EU. This is important, in particular, when the legislative tool of the directive is used by the EU, because the Legislative Assembly or the Government of the Åland Islands are expected to issue norms on the basis of the directive, in so far as the directive deals with subject matter which falls within the competences enumerated in section 18 of the Self-Government Act among matters that the

set out in Protocol 2 to the Act concerning the conditions of accession of the Republic of Austria, the Republic of Finland and the Kingdom of Sweden." On the position of the Åland Islands and other autonomous territories in the EU, see Silverström (2008a), pp. 265–267, 268.

[46]On the EU issue, see Jääskinen (2003) and Nauclér (2005), pp. 108–109. For the Åland Islands, the transfer of law-making powers to the EU is particularly important in the fields of agriculture and fisheries, transport policy and subsidies to business enterprises and industries.

[47]See, e.g., case number 2004:65 of the Supreme Court of Finland (see section 7.2.1 above), which deals with the implementation of the salmon fishing quotas and makes the point that the individual fisherman and the Åland Government should have followed EC law, rather than decisions of the Åland Islands Government or the Finnish Government, because the EC had the competence to regulate the matter.

Legislative Assembly is in charge of. Only a minority of the directives enacted by the EU fall completely outside of the legislative competence of the Legislative Assembly, because the EU competences, as they are exercised, are mainly in the area of public law. The Ålandic matters affected are agriculture and the environment in general, as well as technical issues such as chemicals and foodstuffs.[48]

However, after accession to the EU, it has become completely clear to the Åland Islanders that membership in the Union affects the legislative powers of the Legislative Assembly in a most profound way. Although the Government of the Åland Islands has the right to participate in many ways in the preparation of Finnish positions concerning decisions of the EU and the European Court of Justice,[49] although the Government of the Åland Islands appoints one of the Finnish representatives in the Committee of Regions,[50] and although one civil servant of the Åland Islands is included among the staff of the Permanent Representation of Finland to the EU, the conviction has grown in the islands that the legislative competences that belong to Åland under the Self-Government Act have been drained and transferred, not only to the EU, but also in practice to the Government of Finland. The main reason for this perception is the fact that the EU is mainly engaging in a dialogue with the Governments of the Member States, leaving the sub-national actors aside, although section 59b(4) of the Self-Government Act specifically allows the Government of the Åland Islands to make direct contact with the European Commission regarding matters falling within the powers of Åland and concerning the implementation of EU decisions there.[51]

The negative perception about the EU is also supported by Commission statistics concerning the implementation of EU law in Member States, which normally faults Finland as the Member State for insufficient implementation in its territory of a number of directives because of the failure of the Åland Islands authorities,

---

[48]Silverström (2008b), p. 45.

[49]The Government of the Åland Islands has the right under section 59a(1) to participate in the national preparation in the Council of State of the Finnish position concerning decisions to be made in the European Union, formulates under section 59a(2) the Finnish position in respect of a decision of the EU on the implementation of the common EC policy concerning the Åland Islands to the extent it would belong to the competence of the Legislative Assembly, shall under section 59a(3) be informed by preparation of matters within the EU that affect the competence of the Legislative Assembly and given the possibility to participate in the work of the Finnish delegation to the EU on such matters.

[50]According to Silverström (2008a), p. 267, the Committee of Regions has been a disappointment for the autonomous territories because of its limited advisory role and its very diverse membership.

[51]A symbolic recognition of the position of the Åland Islands in the EU context is the decision by the Minister of Foreign Affairs of Finland in December 2010 to fly the flag of Åland alongside the flag of Finland outside the Finnish EU representation in Brussels. The initiative stems from the Åland Islands, but the example to do so comes, in particular, from Denmark, which flies the flags of the Faroe Islands and Greenland alongside the national flag outside the Danish EU representation.

including the Legislative Assembly, to enact implementing legislation within the time-frame established in a directive, or up to the established minimum contents of a directive.[52] In a number of cases regarding the implementation of EU law, the responsibility of Finland in respect to issues that are under the control of the Legislative Assembly and the Government of the Åland Islands has been established through judgments of the European Court of Justice. These cases have reinforced the opinion among a good portion of the islanders that membership in the EU is not beneficial for them.

The Government of the Åland Islands has, according to section 59a(1) of the Self-Government Act, the right to participate in the preparation of the national positions of Finland within the Council of State preceding decision-making in the European Union, if the matter would fall within the powers of Åland or otherwise have special significance for it, and to be notified if such issues are pending.[53] If a decision to be made in the European Union pertains in full or in part to the application of a common EU policy in the islands, the Government of the Åland Islands shall formulate the position of Finland, in so far as the matter would in other respects fall within the legislative powers of Åland. If the positions of Åland and the state cannot be harmonized or reconciled regarding a matter falling within the powers of Åland, the Government of the Åland Islands can request that its view be declared when the Finnish position is being presented to EU institutions.[54]

Upon request, the Government of Åland shall also be reserved an opportunity to participate in the work of the Finnish delegation when matters falling within the powers of Åland under the Self-Government Act are being prepared in the

[52]As pointed out in Silverström (2008b), p. 45, the implementation problems are mainly due to the small number of staff working with law-drafting in the bodies of the Åland Islands. The issues arising on the basis of directives are complex and require a high input of personal resources for a materially and timely implementation, but if this cannot be done, one feasible solution that has been used is to bring into force the text of the directive, for instance, by a reference to the directive itself or by enacting an act of Åland which brings into force in the Åland Islands the provisions of an act enacted by the Parliament of Finland for mainland Finland. See also Ålands landskaps-regerings meddelande till lagtinget nr 1/2006-2007, Sect. 4.2.2. EU membership thus affects very much the status of Åland. Åland is a territorial autonomy in relation to the state of Finland, but not in relation to the EU, except in the limited areas where exceptions exist on the basis of Protocol No. 2 to the Finnish Accession Treaty. Within that exception, the Åland Islands could live out some of its pre-membership autonomy, but in the vast area of law-making powers of Åland, the supremacy of EU law actually preempts legislative competence or constitutes a constant potential for preemption.

[53]The Ministry of Foreign Affairs should ensure that all EU proposals for new legislative acts in the EU are forwarded to the Government of the Åland Islands, while specialized ministries should inform the Åland Government about matters that they are dealing with. See Government Bill 307/1994 to the Parliament of Finland concerning the Position of the Åland Islands in case of a Finnish Membership in the European Union, p. 10. The preparatory bodies in the different ministries are also expected to allow representatives of the Åland Islands to participate in the proceedings.

[54]See Nauclér (2005), p. 110.

European Union. As a consequence, one post as a special adviser or councilor at the Finnish representation to the European Union in Brussels is reserved to an Åland Islander. In practice, it has happened at least once that a Minister of the Government of the Åland Islands has represented Finland in the Council of Ministers of the EU, although that would normally be a forum reserved for ministers of the national government. Such an authorization to participate in, for instance, the so-called Agricultural Council, as was the case in one instance, demonstrates a pragmatic stance on the part of the Finnish Government towards the problem of representation. In addition, under section 59e of the Self-Government Act, a candidate selected by the Government of the Åland Islands is to be among the Finnish representatives to the Committee of Regions, the powers of which have increased somewhat in the institutional structure of the EU as a consequence of the Lisbon Treaty, which was concluded in 2009.

The European Union uses two types of legislative acts to achieve its regulatory purposes, namely the regulation and the directive. While the EU regulation is generally binding and directly applicable in the same manner as national or sub-state legislation, the directive requires normally some particular implementation measures by the national lawmakers. In the implementation of directives at the national level, the distribution of legislative powers follows, according to section 59b(1) of the Self-Government Act, the distribution of legislative competences established in sections 18 and 29 of the Act. Hence, in the area of "public law" in broad terms, there are two implementing agencies of EU directives, the authorities of the Åland Islands, on the one hand, and of the state, on the other. The distribution of the administrative powers follows the same distinction. Sometimes, however, the measures of the two implementing agencies may be interdependent, and in such situations, section 59b lays down the expectation that they have to consult each other.

In the event that only one measure can be taken in a Member State in an administrative matter on the basis of EU law, which under the Self-Government Act would fall within the powers of both the Åland Islands and of the state, the decision in the matter shall be made by the state authority. Before such decision-making, as established in section 59b(2), the Ålandic authority shall be consulted in good faith and the positions put forward by it shall be taken into account as far as possible. If the authorities of the Åland Islands and the state do not agree on the measures necessary in situations of this sort, a recommendation for the resolution of the disagreement may be requested from the Åland Delegation. If, under EU law, a Member State may designate only one administrative authority in a situation where both the Åland Islands and the state have powers, the authority shall under section 59b(3) be designated by the state. This does not leave the Åland Islands at the mercy of the state authorities, because a decision by such an authority in a matter that would in other respects fall within the powers of the Legislative Assembly shall be consistent with the position put forward by the Government of the Åland Islands.

The position of the Åland Islands has, however, the potential of becoming more prominent, as is shown by a 2004 memorandum of understanding between Finland, Sweden and the Åland Islands concerning the implementation of the Interreg III A

Archipelago Programme under the auspices of the EU.[55] In the MoU, the Government of the Åland Islands appears as a party alongside with the Governments of Finland and Sweden, the signatures of which appear at the bottom of the MoU. The Government of the Åland Islands is designated in the document as both the managing authority and the paying authority for the purposes of the project, which extends itself across the border between Finland and Sweden and encompasses the archipelagic areas on the western coast of mainland Finland, on the eastern coast of Sweden and the Åland Islands. The secretariat of the program was placed in Mariehamn, the capital of the Åland Islands, and as the managing authority, the Government of the Åland Islands was tasked to exercise powers of control within the program both in mainland Finland and in Sweden, in collaboration with Finnish and Swedish authorities, and to also exercise other public powers, such as to repay, on behalf of both Member States, such subsidies that the Member States may be obliged to return to the EU and to recover subsidies paid to a recipient of EU funds within the program. Here, cross-border cooperation within the EU frame has actually promoted the position of a territorial autonomy geographically positioned on the border of two Member States. The problems that can be identified in the context are of a constitutional nature and relate to the exercise of public powers in the territory of another sovereign, in this case Sweden,[56] while the exercise of control powers in mainland Finland should probably have been regulated through a consent decree (see above, Sect. 5.3.5; section 59b(3) of the Self-Government Act, which regulates the distribution of administrative responsibilities under EU law and places the main responsibility on the state administration, was enacted only after the agreement with the Åland Islands and Sweden). Arguably, the public powers exercised in the management of an Interreg program stem from regulations of the EU, which are directly applicable without national implementation through norms, but the fact remains that in this case, one administrative institution was entitled to cross over to other jurisdictions for the purposes of exercising public powers. The MoU also made possible specific agreements between the Government of the Åland Islands, on the one hand, and the Provincial Government of Stockholm and the appropriate authorities in mainland Finland, on the other.

[55]See Sveriges internationella överenskommelser SÖ 2004:4 (Avtal i form av Memorandum of Understanding med Finland för genomförande av Interreg III A Skärgården-programmet. Stockholm den 17 februari 2004). The MoU is not published in the treaty series of Finland. The program period of the EU was between 2000 and 2006, but it appears that the program extended itself to 2007–2008.

[56]See Persson (2005), pp. 128–130, 323–335, for an analysis of the Swedish law concerning international contractual relations of public authorities. In light of the analysis, the competence of the Swedish public authority to conclude the MoU can be doubted.

8.6.3 *Breaches of EU Law*

In spite of the various consultation mechanisms between the Åland Islands and the state, the normative action or inaction in the islands may result in infringements of EU treaties. A normal consequence of such infringements is that the European Commission initiates legal proceedings in the European Court of Justice against the Member State that is alleged of a violation. In so far as the obligation to fulfill an EU rule alleged to be in breach of EU treaties falls within the powers of the Åland Islands, the state authorities shall, according to section 59c of the Self-Government Act, prepare the response of Finland in co-operation with the Government of the Åland Islands for submission to the ECJ. In case the positions of the Åland Islands and the state cannot be coordinated, the reply from Finland and the position concerning the request of the Government of the Åland Islands shall be prepared so that the position of the Åland Islands can be assessed from the documentation. If the proceedings originated on the basis of action or inaction on the part of the Åland Islands, a representative of the Åland Islands shall be given the right to take part in the oral proceedings before the ECJ.

A number of actions for failure to fulfill obligations have actually been brought by the European Commission against the Republic of Finland before the ECJ because of implementation problems in the Åland Islands.[57] In these cases, the Republic of Finland was found to be in violation of EC law because of lack of

[57]Case C-344/03 on failure to fulfill the condition laid down in Article 9(1)(c) of Council Directive 79/409/EEC on the conservation of wild birds, as amended by the accession treaty (the so-called *Spring hunting* decision; this case also dealt with spring hunting in mainland Finland); C-327/04 on failure to implement Council Directive 2000/43/EC implementing the principle of equal treatment between persons irrespective of racial or ethnic origin (*Equal treatment*); C-107/05 on failure to Implement Directive 2003/87/EEC establishing a scheme for greenhouse gas emission allowance trading within the Community and amending Council Directive 96/61/EC (*Greenhouse gases*); C-343/05 on failure to ensure transposition by Åland of Article 8a of Directive 89/622/EEC on the approximation of the laws, regulations and administrative provisions of the Members States concerning the labelling of tobacco products, as amended by Council Directive 92/41/EEC, amended by Article 8 of Directive 2001/37/EC on the approximation of laws, regulations and administrative provisions of the Member States concerning the manufacture, presentation and sale of tobacco products, and observance on vessels registered in Finland of the prohibition on placing on the market of snuff laid down by that provision (*Oral tobacco*); C-152/06 on failure to implement Directive 2002/95/EC on the restriction of the use of certain hazardous substances in electrical and electronic equipment (*Hazardous electrical equipment*); C-154/06 on failure to implement Directive 2003/108/EC amending Directive 2002/96/EC on waste electrical and electronic equipment (WEEE) (*Waste electrical equipment*); C-159/06 on failure to implement Directive 2001/42/EC on the assessment of the effects of certain plans and programmes on the environment (*Assessment of environmental effects*). The case C-99/05 was stricken out of the list of cases after the Åland Islands had implemented the directive while the case against Finland was pending at the Court. See also Silverström (2008b), p. 46, who points out that while the main part of the pre-litigation proceedings concern the mainland only, "Åland's proportional share of Finnish infringement proceedings is significantly higher when the proceedings reach the ECJ".

implementation or faulty implementation in the Åland Islands.[58] Two of these judgments of the ECJ, the *Spring hunting* case and the *Oral tobacco* case have caused animated reactions on the Åland Islands, because they touch upon Ålandic traditions or deep-rooted habits.

In the *Spring hunting* case, the problem dealt with the traditional hunting of seven species of migratory sea-birds during their return to the rearing grounds and during their period of reproduction. The local population in the Åland Islands (and also in the South-Western parts of mainland Finland) have traditionally hunted these species in the spring, but the directive only allows this if there is no other satisfactory solution other than spring hunting and if the birds are taken in small numbers, defined by a committee (the ORNIS Committee created under the directive) to mean around 1 percent of the average annual mortality rate of the species in question. The Government of the Åland Islands and the Government of Finland run separate régimes of hunting licenses on the basis of their respective legislative competences under sections 18 and 27 of the Self-Government Act, and the hunting authorities of both jurisdictions have granted proper permits for shooting of the birds. However, the Commission received complaints concerning the spring hunting and therefore, action was brought before the ECJ. Already during the first stages of the process involving the formal notice and the reasoned opinions from the Commission to the Government of Finland, those affected in the Åland Islands, that is, mainly men who in modern society have hunting as a hobby, made the point that this is an intolerable intrusion into their right to hunt and into the historical tradition of spring hunting in the archipelago, something that had always existed and that had an importance for subsistence (the issue of spring hunting was always less important in mainland Finland and never reached the same intensity of political discussion). The point was also made that the hunters contribute to the preservation of the species by decimating such small predators, which threaten especially the nesting and by assisting in the creation of nesting places. The ECJ, however, found that only one species of the seven fulfilled the condition that there was no other satisfactory solution, but that species was not among those for which the condition of taking of birds in small numbers was fulfilled. It thus seems that spring hunting is allowed under EC law in relation to one species, but in much smaller numbers than previously and, as also required by art. 9(1)(c) of the Directive, under strictly supervised conditions and on a selective basis. As concerns the other species and hunting of them in the spring, the court ruled that Finland had failed to fulfill its obligations under the relevant directive. As a consequence, the tradition of spring hunting has decreased drastically.[59]

[58] In addition, case number C-292/03 on failure implement Directive 2000/53/EC on end-of-life vehicles concerns both mainland Finland and the Åland Islands and mentions the late implementation on the Åland Islands, which eventually took place, but later than in mainland Finland. On the top of these cases on failure to implement, it should be mentioned that the Administrative Court of the Åland Islands, which is a state court and as such a part of the ordinary court system of Finland, has requested on preliminary ruling from the ECJ. The case C-42/02 dealt with the question of whether Article 49 EC prohibits such legislation in a Member State under which winnings from games of chance organized in other Member States (in this case Sweden) are treated as income of the winner chargeable to income tax, whereas winnings from games of chance conducted in the Member State in question are not taxable. The ECJ found that this indeed was the case.

[59] Suksi (2007), pp. 394–395.

The *Oral tobacco* issue deals to some extent with the relationship between the Åland Islands and Sweden, and it also involves Finland as the State party responsible for the implementation of EU rules in the entire territory.[60]

The case deals with the fairly widespread habit in Sweden and amongst the Swedish-speaking population in Finland to use oral tobacco instead of or parallel to smoking cigarettes. The habit of using oral tobacco is evidently so important that it caused an exception to be inserted for Sweden on the basis of art. 151 of the Accession Treaty.[61] In effect, this means that whereas oral tobacco is a legal product in the Swedish market, oral tobacco is forbidden elsewhere in the EU, including the Åland Islands and the Swedish-speaking parts of Finland. Oral tobacco is, however, a product that is and has been for sale on the ferry-boats operating between Sweden and Finland. The ferry-boats that have been offering oral tobacco for sale have been registered both in Sweden and in Finland.[62] After a formal notice and a reasoned opinion by the Commission, the Government of Finland replied that the prohibition of marketing of oral tobacco had been implemented and observed in mainland Finland. However, the Government concluded that under the Self-Government Act, the matter belongs to the legislative competence of the Åland Islands. The Government of Finland thus agreed with the findings of the Commission that the prohibition of marketing of oral tobacco is not implemented in the Åland Islands and that the prohibition is not observed on vessels registered in the Åland Islands. The ECJ found in its judgment that Finland had failed in its obligation to comply with its obligation under the Treaty and the directive, because Finland, as a Member State 1) has not ensured that the Åland Islands has made the contents of article 8a of the directive a part of its legislation and, 2) has not ensured that the prohibition of the marketing of oral tobacco is complied with on vessels registered in the Åland Islands. It is interesting in the context that it seems to be completely clear for the ECJ that the registration of vessels in the separate ship register of the Åland Islands, a register which is not maintained by the authorities of the self-government or autonomy, but by the state of Finland on the Åland Islands, has the legal consequence that the legal order of Åland follows on board of the vessels registered in the islands, even when the vessel is outside the territorial waters of Finland and the Åland Islands.

The case in principle means that while ferryboats registered in Sweden and trafficking on the Åland Islands can continue to sell oral tobacco on the basis of the exception established for Sweden in the Accession Treaty, the Ålandic vessels operating on the same routes are prohibited from selling the oral tobacco. The economic interest of the sale of oral tobacco on the Ålandic vessels has been estimated to be around 6 million euros, which is in danger of being lost, while the Swedish competitors can develop the sale of oral

---

[60] Suksi (2007), pp. 395–398.

[61] OJ C 241, vol. 37, 29 August 1994. The provision is specified in Annex XV, letter X (Miscellaneous), to the Accession Treaty, concerning Council Directive 89/622/EEC on the labelling of tobacco products and the prohibition of the marketing of certain types of tobacco for oral use, as amended by Article 8 of Directive 2001/37/EC on the approximation of the laws, regulations and administrative provisions of the Member States concerning the manufacture, presentation and sale of tobacco products.

[62] In so far the vessel is registered in Sweden, it can be asked whether or not Sweden is complying with one of the conditions of the exception concerning oral tobacco, namely with paragraph (b) of letter X in Annex XV, which says that the Kingdom of Sweden "shall take all measures necessary to ensure that the product referred to in paragraph (a) is not placed on the market in the Member States for which Directives 89/622/EEC and 92/41/EEC are fully applicable". Those directives are fully applicable in Finland, including the Åland Islands.

tobacco into a competitive advantage, potentially affecting also the number of passengers on Ålandic ferryboats in a negative way. As a consequence and with regard to the slim economic margins due to the fairly harsh competition between the ferry-lines, ship-owners on the Åland Islands operating ferryboats between Finland and Sweden may be compelled to change the flag of their ship from Finnish (and Ålandic) to Swedish. Such a change of flag would, as a further consequence, affect the tax status of the Ålandic employees on the vessels, decreasing the amount of tax that the local government on the islands will be able to collect from those employed on the ferryboats in municipal taxes, and causing ultimately a negative development in public finances in the Åland Islands. It is actually incredible that such a trivial issue as oral tobacco and the exception under EU law concerning the prohibition of its marketing in one EU Member State has the potential to threaten a whole segment of economic activity in the neighboring country and in a very special part of it.[63]

It is not always so that the Åland Islands as an entity are negatively implicated in court proceedings before the ECJ, but Åland may nonetheless have an interest to appear before the court. The Government of the Åland Islands can, under section 59c(3) of the Self-Government Act, present a motivated initiative to the Council of State that Finland should intervene in a pending case before the ECJ. This would be relevant if issues of general importance for autonomies or sub-state entities are dealt with before the ECJ. The Government of the Åland Islands may also, by way of a motivated initiative, request that the Council of State initiate legal action before the ECJ in cases which belong to the legislative competence of Åland, or which may otherwise have particular importance for the islands. The court of first

[63]See the Act of Åland Amending the Act of Åland on Tobacco (SoÅ 4/2007). The Government of the Åland Islands took action on the matter by proposing to the Legislative Assembly a Bill amending the tobacco legislation of the Åland Islands. The Bill contained a provision according to which it is prohibited to sell oral tobacco or carry out business transactions involving oral tobacco. The Bill contains a separate provision according to which the prohibition is applicable also on vessels registered in the province of Åland while they remain in the territorial waters of the Åland Islands and Finland. The Legislative Assembly agreed to this on 25 September 2006 after a specification of the extent of the territorial waters of the Åland Islands. This separate provision seems to imply that vessels registered in the province of Åland may sell oral tobacco while they remain in international waters or in the territorial waters of such a third country in which oral tobacco is allowed, that is, in Swedish territorial waters. The Åland Islands Delegation, which is a joint committee with representatives from the Åland Islands and mainland Finland with the task of controlling as a first instance the compliance of the legislative decision of the Legislative Assembly with the division of competence between the Åland Islands and mainland Finland, concluded on 23 October 2006 that there is no legal obstacle to be found in the Self-Government Act to the entering into force of the piece of law. As a second instance of competence control, the Supreme Court of Finland reviewed the matter on 13 December 2006 and expressed doubts of whether the prohibition is as extensive as the directive and the decision of the ECJ indicate but concluded that the legislative decision did not breach the definition of the legislative competence of the Legislative Assembly as established in the Self-Government Act. With a view to the Opinion of the Supreme Court, the President of Finland decided on 16 January 2007 not to exercise her absolute veto powers in respect of any of the provisions in the legislative decision, which means that the new provisions of the Ålandic tobacco legislation could enter into force on 1 February 2007 after the promulgation of the provisions by the Government of the Åland Islands on 11 January 2007.

instance of the EU, the General Court, may be more accessible for the Åland Islands, because any legal person (including a legal person constituted as a public authority, such as the Åland Islands) may, on the basis of Art. 263(4) of the Treaty on the Functioning of the European Union, institute an action for annulment in order to challenge acts of the Union if the act is of direct and individual concern to it and does not entail implementing measures.[64]

8.6.4 *Pecuniary Liability for Breaches of Treaty Law*

It still remains to be seen how the European Commission reacts to the tobacco legislation enacted in the Åland Islands after the issue reached its judicial peak. If the Commission does not approve the measures undertaken, the next step could be to bring the case again to the ECJ on the basis of Art. 260 of the Treaty on the Functioning of the European Union for the determination of a lump sum and/or a penalty payment, and an imposition of such a sum.[65] The interesting point here is that under EU law, such a sanction is to be paid by the Member State, in this case Finland, and is determined, *inter alia*, in relation to the GDP of the Member State and to the relative weight of its votes in the Council. This means that it is the Republic of Finland that would be fined according to these indicators, not the much smaller sub-state entity of the Åland Islands.

During the first decade of Finnish EU membership, it was unclear what would happen domestically if Finland as a Member State was found to be liable for an Ålandic breach of EU law. In 2004, however, the Self-Government Act was supplemented with section 59d, according to which the Åland Islands is liable for a possible sanction (such as a fixed compensation, a conditional fine, or some other comparable pecuniary sanction) meted out for the State, in so far as the sanction is based on an act or an omission on the part of the Åland Islands. In a corresponding manner, if Finland is under the rules of liability of a Member State liable to refund EU funds to the EU, the Åland Islands is liable for the refund *vis-à-vis* the state, in so far as the administration or supervision of the refunded funds were the responsibility of Åland. Finally, if Finland has been rendered liable in damages to a private party for loss arising from the fact that his or her rights under EU law have been incompletely or incorrectly implemented in a matter falling within the powers of

[64]See Silverström (2008a), p. 269, who also points out that the Åland Islands has so far never availed itself of this opportunity.

[65]It seems that the European Commission has, so far, not taken any particular measures in the matter. However, on 23 October 2007, the European Commission declared in a press-release its intention to ask the ECJ to impose on Finland a lump-sum fine of over 2.029.536 € and if Finland fails to comply before the judgment, a daily penalty payment of 19.828,8 €/day. See press release IP/07/1592. See also Silverström (2008b), p. 47. It seems that the matter has not progressed since 2007, but in principle, the Commission could re-ignite the process.

the Åland Islands, Åland is liable for the damages *vis-à-vis* the state for the corresponding amount. At the outset, it would seem that the entire sum of money would be charged to the Åland Islands. However, because such pecuniary penalties are counted as a ratio based on the size of the Member State, the fines and compensations for which the Åland Islands are liable might greatly exceed their economic resources. Section 59d(4) of the Self-Government Act contains a legal basis for a procedure by which the state and the Åland Islands may seek a settlement regarding the amount of the liability. In case the state and the Åland Islands fail to strike an agreement about sharing the financial burden, the dispute as to the liability can be brought before the Administrative Court of the Åland Islands as an action of administrative litigation.[66]

As a consequence of this, the issue of the internal distribution of the fine between Finland and the Åland Islands under section 59d of the Self-Government Act concerning the liability of Åland could arise,[67] for the first time ever, in the *Oral tobacco* case. If, in such a situation, the Government of the Åland Islands and the state of Finland fail to reach an agreement about the internal distribution of such a fine, the financial burden of the fine imposed by the ECJ would be distributed by the Administrative Court of the Åland Islands in administrative litigation. The EU law in the context of *Spring hunting* and *Oral tobacco* are pointers in the direction that the Legislative Assembly of the Åland Islands has a duty under EU law to implement it and also to enact legislative provisions to that effect. Unless this takes place and Finland is concluded by the ECJ to be in breach of EU law, there is even a pecuniary mechanism to compel Finland in the first instance, but in the second instance through a domestic process, also the Åland Islands to compliance through the fine and the distribution of the fine between Finland and Åland.

There is no corresponding mechanism for pecuniary actions on the part of the Åland Islands that might breach the international commitments of Finland outside of EU law. However, the Åland Islands are under an obligation to fulfill those international obligations that apply to the Åland Islands through the consent mechanism established in section 59 of the Self-Government Act. This became

[66]Nauclér (2005), p. 111 f., is critical of the mechanism, because it is an untested novelty that replaces the regular forum adjudicating economic issues between the Åland Islands and mainland Finland, namely the Åland Delegation (see above, Sect. 4.2.8). Because the procedure of administrative litigation has not been used so far, it is not possible to evaluate whether the new system is good or not. However, as pointed out by Silverström (2008b), p. 44, the mechanism means that the Åland Islands has a right to defence in the proceedings.

[67]Section 59 d, para. 1: "If the Court of Justice of the European Communities has rendered Finland liable to pay a fixed compensation, a conditional fine or some other comparable pecuniary sanction, Åland shall be liable for that sanction *vis-à-vis* the State in so far as it has arisen from an act or omission on the part of Åland." Section 59 d, para. 2: "The State and Åland may seek a settlement regarding the amount of the liability referred to in paragraphs 1–3. A dispute as to the liability may be brought before the Åland Administrative Court as a matter of administrative litigation as provided in chapter 12 of the Act on Administrative Judicial Procedure (SoF 586/1996) and above in this section."

apparent in the case of *Ekholm v. Finland*,[68] which was based on a complaint concerning the refusal of authorities of Åland to apply such decisions by the Administrative Court of the Åland Islands and the Supreme Administrative Court of Finland, which interpreted Ålandic legislation in the area of the environment. The issue in the case dealt with a dog-cage placed close to an adjacent property, and the neighbors requested from the environmental authorities of the Åland Islands that the dog-cage should be moved because of the noise. The authorities refused to make such a decision, and the authorities also refused several times to heed the judgments of the administrative courts, including those of the Supreme Administrative Court of Finland. When the owners of the adjacent property finally complained to the European Court of Human Rights, the Court concluded that the inaction on the part of the authorities of the Åland Islands as regards the court judgments amounted to a violation of the rule of law, in particular the right to a fair hearing, established in Art. 6(1) of the European Convention on Human Rights. As a consequence, the State of Finland was faulted for a breach of the Convention and was also ordered to pay altogether 20,000 euro in compensation to the complainant.[69]

The unclear issue here is the domestic dimension: what can the state of Finland do in relation to the Åland Islands? The authorities of the central government cannot commandeer the administrative authorities of the Åland Islands to make a particular decision, as much as they cannot commandeer the Legislative Assembly to enact a particular piece of law.[70] However, at the same time, it is important to understand that autonomous entities, the Åland Islands included, are not immune to such human rights norms that regulate the behavior of states in relation to their citizens. In most cases, autonomy involves the granting of law-making powers to a territorially circumscribed jurisdiction, and in that capacity, the autonomous entity becomes, for all practical and legal purposes, the State in relation to the individual.

---

[68]ECtHR, Judgment of 24 July 2007.

[69]The dog-cage was ultimately moved, but not so that the problem was completely solved. In the mean time, the SAC has handed down a third judgment in the same matter. Of the total compensation ordered by the European Court of Human Rights, the Åland Islands agreed to pay 15,000 euro and the Ministry of Justice of mainland Finland 5,000 euro (a share that could be attributed to the overlong legal procedures). However, the Åland Islands actually has no duty on the basis of the Self-Government Act to pay its share of such costs that the State is ordered to pay by, for instance, the European Court of Human Rights, because section 54d of the Self-Government Act only applies to costs the EU Court has ordered Finland to pay.

[70]See Silverström (2008a), p. 270, who concludes that in Finland, "the central authorities have no constitutional means for implementing international obligations falling within the competence of Åland".

8.6.5 Bringing in Autonomous Territories in Nordic Cooperation

The dimension of the international relations of the Åland Islands is not exclusively regulated in the Self-Government Act. The so-called Helsinki Agreement, or the 1962 Co-operation Agreement between Denmark, Finland, Iceland, Norway and Sweden, actually creates two international organizations, the Nordic Council and the Nordic Council of Ministers. Originally, the Helsinki Agreement facilitated co-operation between the Nordic States only, but on the basis of amendments in 1970 and 1984 to the Helsinki Agreement, the Nordic Council also incorporates the Nordic self-governing entities, that is the autonomous areas of the Åland Islands, Faeroe Islands, and Greenland.[71] The three self-governing entities participate in the work of the Nordic Council through their respective delegations, although under Finnish national law,[72] the representatives of the Åland Islands to the Nordic Council constitute a separate part of the national delegation of Finland. The Nordic Council is not empowered to make decisions that are binding on the States, and therefore, it was not perceived as very problematic to include self-governing territories amongst the States. After all, the functions of the Nordic Council, to take initiatives and to give recommendations to one or all Nordic States as concerns, *inter alia*, development of law in the Nordic States, would not threaten the position of the home States, even if the self-governing entities were active in these areas. As a consequence, the self-governing areas, the Åland Islands included, have the right to vote in the Nordic Council and to put questions to the members of the State Governments on the basis of the reports given concerning the implementation of the recommendations. A representative of the Åland Islands has held the presidency of the Nordic Council and has also been chairperson of some committees of the Nordic Council, which means that the representatives of Åland are involved in the work of the Nordic Council on an equal footing with the

---

[71]Nauclér (2005), p. 114, is of the opinion that "[t]he three autonomous territories in question are considered as subjects according to international law in the context of the Helsinki Agreement, but not in a European Union context". This position would seem to indicate that subjectivity under international law can be determined according to the context and be functional. Although the rights of the Åland Islands in the context of the Nordic Council would seem to be the same as those of a subject of international law, the responsibilities that follow from such membership are, however, not of the kind that a subject of international law would assume. Instead, the participation of the Åland Islands in the Nordic Council is still carried out within the framework of the Finnish subjectivity of international law. Although permissive, the policy of Finland in this context does not create a subjectivity of international law in the Åland Islands. See also Spiliopoulou Åkermark (1997), p. 275, who concludes that "Åland is a subject of international law. This does not entail that Åland is a sovereign State. It means, however, that Åland should have the right, as well as an effective possibility, to participate effectively in international cooperation."

[72]Act on the Finnish Delegation to the Nordic Council (SoF 170/1960). See also Nauclér (2005), pp. 100–106.

representatives of the State of Finland and other Nordic States and autonomous territories.[73]

The status of the Nordic self-governing territories is different in the Nordic Council of Ministers, which is empowered to make decisions binding on the five States. The self-governing territories have the right to be present in the meetings of the Nordic Council of Ministers,[74] and in practice, they also have the opportunity to express themselves on the various issues, but they do not have the formal right to vote, which is reserved for the five Member States. Although the decisions of the Nordic Council of Ministers are not binding on the self-governing entities, they may commit themselves to the decisions to the extent that the decisions fall within their legislative competence and thus facilitate the domestic implementation of the decisions.[75]

In this Nordic context, it is also not unnatural that the Government of the Åland Islands maintains occasional contacts with Sweden by means of visits at a ministerial level. For instance, the Swedish Ministers of Foreign Affairs, of Finance, and of Social Construction have visited Åland for discussions with the Government of the Åland Islands. It is entirely possible to think that such contacts are interpreted as contacts with third States that constitute foreign relations in the meaning of section 27, para. 4, of the Self-Government Act. Here, the administrative competence would belong to the Government of Finland, but it does not seem to have protested against such contacts, which evidently are to be placed in the category of unofficial discussions and information meetings with Swedish ministers that do not lead to international commitments or obligations for the Åland Islands or Finland in the meaning of sections 58–59 of the Self-Government Act, or in the meaning of *ultra vires* in the *Memel* case.

However, there is a particular area where the situation may be interpreted differently. As of 2010, admission of students from EU Member States other than Sweden makes a separation, *inter alia*, between students from the Åland Islands, on the one hand, and students from mainland Finland, so that students of the Åland Islands are admitted amongst the domestic students, that is, Swedish students, while Finnish and other foreign students are admitted in a separate procedure. It appears that such a system has been proposed by the Government of the Åland

[73]The position that the Åland Islands has acquired in international relations has caused Bring (2007), p. 40, to characterize the Åland Islands as an international subject of a lower dignity than a subject of international law. See also Spiliopoulou Åkermark (1997), pp. 270 f., 275.

[74]As pointed out in Nauclér (2005), p. 104, the Governments of the three autonomous areas can send as many government representatives as they wish to the meetings of the Nordic Council of Ministers. In practice, the Government of the Åland Islands has nominated all its members as its representatives in the Nordic Council of Ministers.

[75]The decisions in the Nordic Council of Ministers are made by consensus between the States, but the mechanism of consent on the part of the autonomous territories enables them to join in into the decision between the States and to commit themselves at least politically to implement the decisions made in the Nordic Council of Ministers. The mechanism of consent is frequently used by the Nordic autonomous territories. See Nauclér (2005), p. 104.

Islands in a letter of 6 November 2008 to the Department of Education of the Government of Sweden, entitled Application of an Ålandic Exception to the New Admission Rules at Swedish Universities from 2010.[76] The Swedish National Agency for Higher Education advised the Government of Sweden on 7 April 2009 that such a system would not be unproblematic.[77] In its report of 29 September 2009, the National Agency for Higher Education clarifies that a preferential treatment of students from the Åland Islands is in breach of, *inter alia*, EU law and the Nordic Convention of 3 September 1996 between Denmark, Finland, Iceland, Norway and Sweden concerning Access to Higher Education, as revised by 22 April 2009.[78] In spite of the complications cited, the Government of Sweden decided against the advice of the National Agency and issued on 10 December 2009 the Decree (2009:1519) amending the Decree on Institutions of Higher Education (1993:100, as amended). The National Agency later on implemented the decree in its rules and regulations.[79] In addition to the likely breaches of EU and international norms, the preferential treatment granted by the Government of Sweden to the students of Åland, after communication from the Government of the Åland Islands, appears to approach the *Memel* situation of *ultra vires* on the part of the Åland Islands.

The PCIJ was of the opinion that the attempt by the Directorate of Memel "to secure an arrangement as to the admission of agricultural produce by negotiations

[76]Brev nr 247 U10 (6.11.2008, Dnr U10/08/1/9) med Anhållan om åländskt undantag från de nya tillträdesreglerna till svensk högskola från 2010. In the letter, reference is made to the particular responsibilities that Sweden has assumed for the maintenance of the Swedish language, culture and traditions from the inception of the Ålandic self-government arrangement. Without doubt, there may, from the point of view of the students of the Åland Islands and the Government of the Åland Islands, exist good reasons to secure access for the Åland Islanders to higher education in the Swedish language, as stated in the communications from the Government of the Åland Islands to the Department of Education in Sweden. However, the responsibilities have been assumed by Finland, not by Sweden, in para. 1 of the Åland Islands Settlement. There is no indication in the correspondence between the Government of the Åland Islands and the Department of Education of Sweden that the Government of Åland would have been authorized by the Government of Finland to act in relation to the Government of Sweden.

[77]See Högskoleverkets Avrapportering (2009), p. 15. Letter to the Government of Sweden with registration number 83-1825-09.

[78]See Högskoleverkets Avrapportering (2009), pp. 19–22. Article 1 of the Nordic Convention creates the obligation to a Nordic State to grant access to students from other Nordic countries to its higher education on the same or equal conditions as the students of the State. The current Swedish rule does this for the students of the Åland Islands, but not anymore for students from other Nordic countries, including mainland Finland. However, a fiscal distinction is made in Art. 8 of the Nordic Convention in that the Nordic countries pay to each other compensation for the students that study in the country each year, but when the compensation quotas are calculated, the self-governing territories of the Nordic countries, the Åland Islands, the Faroe Islands and Greenland, are not included in the calculation.

[79]Föreskrifter om ändring i Högskoleverkets föreskrifter (HSVFS 2009:1) om grundläggande behörighet och urval; beslutade den 21 januari 2010, nr 2010:1. It appears that the problematic decision of the Swedish Government will be revoked as of 2012.

with the officials of the competent departments of the German Government" fell within the sphere of foreign relations, so as to constitute an excess of competence and a violation of the Memel Statute.[80] If this test is applied to the issue of the Ålandic students in Sweden, it could be said that the successful attempt by the Government of the Åland Islands, evidently on the basis of its powers within the area of education, to secure admission of students by negotiations with the officials of the competent department of the Swedish Government that led to the creation of a most preferred status for the Ålandic students could be in excess of the competences of the Åland Islands, because under section 27, para. 4, of the Self-Government Act, relations with foreign powers belong to the competence of the central government of Finland. Of course, the *Memel* case does not create a norm that is applicable in the interpretation of the provision in the Self-Government Act, but the *Memel* test offers a general indication that there might exist a problem in this context, probably the first one ever as concerns the Åland Islands. The determination of the legality of the contacts between the Government of the Åland Islands and the Government of Sweden in this issue could be done by the Supreme Court of Finland, under section 60(2) of the Self-Government Act (see above, Sect. 7.2.4). There is no precedence from the application of this provision in the area of foreign relations,[81] but the Finnish Government or a department thereof could, in principle, request a decision from the Supreme Court on the competence issue.

The Government of the Åland Islands maintains an official information agency in Stockholm, which distributes information in Sweden about the self-government of the islands and about the relationship between them and the EU, and it can also assist, for instance, Swedish business enterprises in establishing contacts with politicians and civil servants in their territory. It seems that state authorities of Finland have not protested against such informational activities, but they have instead co-operated with the Åland Agency in Sweden concerning the arrangements of a seminar in Stockholm.[82]

---

[80]The *Memel* case, p. 35.

[81]From the area of the competence control of legislative enactments on the basis of section 19 of the Self-Government Act where section 27, para. 4, concerning relations to foreign powers have been dealt with, see HDu 2742/28.8.1998 and HDu 2743/28.8.1998. See also Suksi (2005d), p. 265 f.

[82]Suksi (2006), p. 94. Both Sweden and the Russian Federation maintain consulates general in the Åland Islands. The Swedish Consulate General is not established on the basis of any particular treaty provision, but is in principle a regular outpost for administrative matters relevant for Swedish citizens resident in the Åland Islands and for facilitating contacts between Sweden and the Åland Islands. It can nevertheless be presumed that the reports from the Consulate General deal with the demilitarisation and neutralization issues based on the 1921 Convention, to which Sweden is a party, and probably also with the protection of the Swedish language and culture on the basis of the 1921 Åland Islands Settlement, where Sweden may have an interest, although the obligations are on Finland. The Russian Consulate General is based on art. 3 of the 1940 bilateral treaty concerning the Åland Islands, according to which the consulate deals with both regular consular matters and with the supervision of the demilitarization and non-fortification of the Åland Islands.

In spite of the fact that no commitments relevant at the level of public international law can be or have been concluded between the Government of the Åland Islands and third States, there exists at least one agreement of a private law nature between the administrative agencies of the Åland Islands, on the one hand, and administrative agencies outside Finland, on the other. In 1997, the Health Care of Åland signed a framework agreement with the University Hospital of Uppsala in Sweden about the purchase of medical services for patients in need of highly specialized care (a similar agreement of an administrative law nature exists with the University Hospital of Turku/Åbo in mainland Finland).[83] Obviously, health care is a matter that under the Self-Government Act belongs to the legislative competence of the Åland Islands, and on the basis of that competence, there is a health care legislation and also an administrative agency in place for the implementation of that competence. Hence, although the Åland Islands cannot conclude treaties under public international law, it seems possible to enter into contractual relations of a private law nature with public entities abroad for the purchase of services. Because the Åland Islands as a sub-state entity is a legal person, it is possible to conclude contracts governed by private law with legal persons outside of Finland. For instance, the Åland Islands has joined the CALRE, that is, the *Conférence des assemblées legislatives régionales*, which is a meeting of the speakers of legislative assemblies at the sub-state level. The CALRE is probably best understood as a private association, an NGO, that tries to exert influence on the EU.[84]

From the perspective of international relations, the Åland Islands Settlement established in the most unequivocal way that the Åland Islands could not secede from Finland and join Sweden. The peaceful development of the relationships between the Nordic States, in particular between Finland and Sweden, have since made it possible to elevate, *inter alia*, the Åland Islands to the status of a full participant in the Nordic Council and an observer with partial membership rights in the Nordic Council of Ministers. Through the Nordic co-operation, Finland as well as the Åland Islands have grown closer to Sweden by acquiring a share in the joint decision-making structures at the international level. This development is at least to some extent not only replicated but also accentuated within the EU, where the various Member States, including Finland and Sweden, pool together in supranational decision-making and receive a share in decision-making concerning the

[83]Suksi (2005d), p. 364. As concerns the agreement under private law with the hospital in Sweden (owned and maintained by the Region of Uppsala, which is a separate legal person), possible legal problems are ultimately to be resolved, according to para. 19 of the current agreement from 2009, before a Swedish court of law under Swedish law. The choice of law in this procurement of services in Sweden is thus made so that Swedish law is applied, which seems to be in harmony with the analysis of Persson (2005), pp. 252–255, 264–268. As concerns the agreement under administrative law with the mainland Finnish hospital, possible legal problems are to be resolved, according to para. 19 of the current agreement from 2008, before the Administrative Court of Turku/Åbo in a process of administrative litigation.

[84]Suksi (2006), p. 94 f. See also Eriksson (2008). CALRE is a meeting of seventy-four presidents of European regional legislative assemblies. Scotland is a member of CALRE, too.

law applicable in each other's territory. In that way, Sweden is participating in decisions about the common rules that apply not only in Finland but also in the Åland Islands, to the extent that they are not exempted on the basis of Protocol 2 to the Finnish Accession Treaty. The developments in the international role of the Åland Islands are clearly significant against the background of the split that existed between Finland and Sweden from 1917 to 1922 over the Åland Islands issue.

The position of Hong Kong is, however, even further away from the position expressed in the *Memel* case and is an illustration of a completely different point of view into the regulation of sub-state competence in the area of international relations.

8.7 Hong Kong: Competence Granted

8.7.1 Broad Competence in International Relations

Article 3 of the Joint Declaration contains basic provisions concerning the position of Hong Kong within the interface between the sovereignty of China and the various facets of the international community. According to Art. 3(9), the HKSAR may establish mutually beneficial economic relations with the United Kingdom and other countries, whose economic interests in Hong Kong will be given due regard. In addition, as established in Art. 3(10) of the Joint Declaration, the HKSAR may, using the name of "Hong Kong, China", maintain on its own and develop economic and cultural relations and conclude relevant agreements with States, regions and relevant international organizations.

The Chinese declaration attached to the Joint Declaration as Annex I contains a broad range of provisions that specify the basic provisions of the Declaration, *inter alia*, those on the free port and free trade policy, the customs territory and the General Agreement on Tariffs and Trade (GATT), trade missions, air service agreements, other international agreements, establishment of consular missions and other missions in Hong Kong, as well as passport formalities, use of travel documents and immigration controls (including the freedom to leave the SAR and visa abolition agreements).

As a consequence, apart from most other autonomous territories, the HKSAR has own international borders for the purposes of customs and travel, and the latter it manages by maintaining its own passports, visa and immigration regime. Under Art. 154, the Central People's Government shall authorize (and continues to do so) the Government of the HKSAR to issue, in accordance with law, passports of the Hong Kong Special Administrative Region of the People's Republic of China to all Chinese citizens who hold the permanent identity cards of the HKSAR. The same applies to travel documents of the Hong Kong Special Administrative Region of the People's Republic of China, which can be issued to all other persons lawfully residing in the HKSAR. Article 154 recognizes that such passports and documents shall be valid for all States and regions and shall record the holder's right to return to the HKSAR. The issuance of passports and other travel documents is combined with the right of the Government of the HKSAR to apply immigration controls on entry into, stay in and departure from the HKSAR by persons from foreign States and regions, including Mainland China. In addition, as provided for in Art. 155, the Central People's Government shall assist or authorize the Government of the HKSAR to conclude visa abolition agreements with foreign States or regions. In effect, entry to the HKSAR is visa free for citizens of a far greater number of States than to Mainland China.

Annex I of the Joint Declaration is not only about principles, but about the modes of operation of Hong Kong in the international environment, often with a very concrete substance. The area of civil aviation offers examples of how specifically the interface between Chinese sovereignty and the needs of the HKSAR was crafted in terms of the preservation of the previous system of civil aviation management,[85] the air services,[86] and air service agreements.[87] In this area, in particular, China

[85]According to Annex I, "the Hong Kong Special Administrative Region shall maintain the status of Hong Kong as a centre of international and regional aviation. Airlines incorporated and having their principal place of business in Hong Kong and civil aviation related businesses may continue to operate. The Hong Kong Special Administrative Region shall continue the previous system of civil aviation management in Hong Kong, and keep its own aircraft register in accordance with provisions laid down by the Central People's Government concerning nationality marks and registration marks of aircraft. The Hong Kong Special Administrative Region shall be responsible on its own for matters of routine business and technical management of civil aviation, including the management of airports, the provision of air traffic services within he flight information region of the Hong Kong Special Administrative Region, and the discharge of other responsibilities allocated under the regional air navigation procedures of the International Civil Aviation Organisation."

[86]According to Annex I, "the Central People's Government shall, in consultation with the Hong Kong Special Administrative Region Government, make arrangements providing for air services between the Hong Kong Special Administrative Region and other parts of the People's Republic of China for airlines incorporated and having their principal place of business in the Hong Kong Special Administrative Region and other airlines of the People's Republic of China. All Air Service Agreements providing for air services between other parts of the People's Republic of China and other states and regions with stops at the Hong Kong Special Administrative Region and air services between the Hong Kong Special Administrative Region and other states and regions with stops at other parts of the People's Republic of China shall be concluded by the Central People's Government. For this purpose, the Central People's Government shall take account of the special conditions and economic interests of the Hong Kong Special Administrative Region and consult the Hong Kong Special Administrative Region Government. Representatives of the Hong Kong Special Administrative Region Government may participate as members of delegations of the Government of the People's Republic of China in air service consultations with foreign governments concerning arrangements for such services."

[87]According to Annex I, "acting under specific authorisations from the Central People's Government, the Hong Kong Special Administrative Region Government may: renew or amend Air Service Agreements and arrangements previously in force; in principle, all such Agreements and arrangements may be renewed or amended with the rights contained in such previous Agreements and arrangements being as far as possible maintained; negotiate and conclude new Air Service

commits itself in the treaty to a certain behavior in relation to Hong Kong in a manner that can be characterized as liberal in comparison with many other autonomous entities.

8.7.2 Distribution of Powers in the Conclusion and Implementation of Treaties

The Central People's Government is, under Annex I, responsible for foreign affairs, but it shall authorize the HKSAR to conduct on its own those external affairs specified in section XI of the Annex,[88] such as participation by the HKSAR in negotiations at the diplomatic level directly affecting the HKSAR, and maintenance and development of relations and conclusion and implementation of agreements with States, regions and relevant international organizations in the appropriate fields, including the economic, trade, financial and monetary, shipping, communications, touristic, cultural and sporting fields. Representatives of the Government of the HKSAR may participate, as members of delegations of the Government of the People's Republic of China, in international organizations or conferences in appropriate fields limited to States and affecting the HKSAR, or they may attend in such other capacity as may be permitted by the Central People's Government and the organization or conference concerned. In addition, they may express their views in the name of "Hong Kong, China". According to Annex I, the HKSAR may, using the name "Hong Kong, China", participate in international organizations and conferences not limited to States.

The Basic Law specifies most of these commitments to Hong Kong's position in foreign relations and international affairs. According to Art. 13, the Central People's Government shall be responsible for foreign affairs relating to the HKSAR, and the Ministry of Foreign Affairs of China shall establish an office in

---

Agreements providing routes for airlines incorporated and having their principal place of business in the Hong Kong Special Administrative Region and rights for overflights and technical stops; and negotiate and conclude provisional arrangements where no Air Service Agreement with a foreign state or other region is in force. All scheduled air services to, from or through the Hong Kong Special Administrative Region which do not operate to, from or through the Mainland of China shall be regulated by Air Service Agreements or provisional arrangements referred to in this paragraph. The Central People's Government shall give the Hong Kong Special Administrative Region Government the authority to: negotiate and conclude with other authorities all arrangements concerning the implementation of the above Air Service Agreements and provisional arrangements; issue licences to airlines incorporated and having their principal place of business in the Hong Kong Special Administrative Region; designate such airlines under the above Air Service Agreements and provisional arrangements; and issue permits to foreign airlines for services other than those to, from or through the mainland of China."

[88]The distinction between foreign affairs and external affairs is evidently relevant, because the former refers to the functions of a sovereign State in relation to other subjects of international law in the political field, while the latter is limited to more technical matters. See also Ghai (1999), pp. 457–480.

Hong Kong to deal with foreign affairs.[89] The office of the Ministry of Foreign Affairs is evidently a liaison office between Beijing and the HKSAR in relation to those external affairs which Hong Kong can conduct on its own in accordance with the Basic Law and as authorized by the Central People's Government, but also in relation to those external affairs which are conducted by Beijing at the international level and which are relevant for the HKSAR. It seems that the HKSAR is always consulted by the central government when the matter can have a bearing on the HKSAR, such as in the case of contacts with Taiwan.[90]

The direct contacts between the HKSAR and foreign States, regions and international organizations are regulated under Art. 151, according to which the HKSAR may on its own, using the name "Hong Kong, China", maintain and develop relations and conclude and implement agreements with such entities in the appropriate fields, including the economic, trade, financial and monetary, shipping, communications, tourism, cultural and sports fields.[91] It seems, on the basis of the provision, that the HKSAR has acquired a limited international legal personality, although China as a State should be regarded as the party ultimately responsible for the commitments concluded by the HKSAR. As concerns the domestic implementation of international norms that the HKSAR has agreed to by way of treaties, it seems that they need, following the British tradition of dualism, to be incorporated by means of legislative decision by the Legislative Council, while norms of customary international law might be directly applicable.[92] In so far as the international matter does not fall within the categories mentioned in Art. 151, representatives of the Government of the HKSAR may, under Art. 150, as members of delegations of the Government of the People's Republic of China, participate in negotiations conducted by the Central People's Government at the diplomatic level in matters directly affecting the HKSAR.[93]

While old international agreements applicable to Hong Kong, that is, such to which the People's Republic of China is not a party, but which were implemented in Hong Kong, may continue to be implemented in the HKSAR,[94] if needed even with

---

[89]This office is one of the three central government offices in the HKSAR, the other two being thedefence office (that it, the office of the People's Liberation Army) and the liaison office of the Central People's Government.

[90]See also Ghai (1999), p. 480.

[91]As reported in Hong Kong 2008 (2009), p. 13, the HKSAR "concluded 12 agreements with foreign states in 2008 on matters such as telecom co-operation, insurance co-operation and co-operation on wine-related businesses". In addition, according to Hong Kong 2008 (2009), p. 13, "[w]ith the authorisation of the Central People's Government (CPG), the HKSAR also concluded three bilateral agreements with foreign states on mutual legal assistance during the year".

[92]See also Mushkat (1997), pp. 167–177. See also the case of *C v Director of Immigration*, [2008] HKCU 256.

[93]As an example, it can be mentioned that there are members from Hong Kong in the Chinese delegations attending the high level international meetings on the economy, such as G20.

[94]For lists of bilateral and multilateral treaties that apply to Hong Kong after 1 July 1999, see Leung Mei-fun (2006), pp. 414–430. Such multilateral treaties include, *inter alia*, the CCPR.

the authorization or assistance by the Central People's Government, the application in the HKSAR of such international agreements to which the People's Republic of China is or becomes a party is not automatic. In such cases, the matter shall, according to Art. 153 of the Basic Law, be decided by the Central People's Government, in accordance with the circumstances and needs of the HKSAR, and after seeking the views of the Government of the HKSAR.[95] Consequently, as concerns domestic implementation, the Government of Hong Kong must be asked, but it remains unclear what the effect of such a consultation would be. Because the Central People's Republic is under an obligation to obey the Basic Law, it would seem problematic to decide to implement such an international agreement in Hong Kong, which is not in harmony with the Basic Law (or the Joint Declaration, for that matter).[96] As concerns international agreements that are in harmony with the Basic Law, the opinion of the HKSAR should probably be accorded (and has been given)[97] the determining weight on the matter, because the implementation of the agreement has legal consequences for the internal legal order of Hong Kong. In case Hong Kong would decline to accept the treaty, China could file a territorial exception to the treaty.[98]

8.7.3 Relations with States, Inter-governmental Organizations and Non-governmental Organizations

Regularized foreign relations normally take place through exchange between the governments of sovereign States of diplomatic missions of different kinds. In deviation from this pattern, articles 156 and 157 deal with missions of the

[95]As reported in the yearbook Hong Kong 2008 (2009), p. 13, "[p]ursuant to the CPG's decision after seeking the views of the HKSAR Government, six multilateral conventions became applicable to the HKSAR in 2008".

[96]Leung Mei-fun (2006), p. 38, identifies a couple of sensitive points in this respect: "Therefore, the legal conflicts between Mainland China and Hong Kong may be the conflicts between their domestic laws and the other side's applicable international agreements. It may also be the conflicts between their applicable international agreements which include reservation clauses in an international agreement."

[97]See Petersen (2008), p. 623 f., citing the Refugee Convention as a treaty the application of which Hong Kong has successfully resisted with reference to its small size and densely populated area.

[98]See Ghai (1999), p. 478 f. However, as pointed out in Petersen (2008), p. 624 f., China had decided to apply the Convention on the Rights of Persons with Disabilities to Hong Kong already before August 2008, when a report was filed in Hong Kong concerning the implementation measures that the Convention would require, and "in its communication to the Secretary General (effected 1 August 2008), the Chinese government stated that the CRPD would apply to both the Hong Kong and Macao Special Administrative Regions". This seems to indicate that not much consultation took place. At the same time the ratification instrument was deposited, the Chinese Government nonetheless "entered a declaration for Hong Kong, stating that the CRPD would have no impact upon Hong Kong's immigration laws", which amounts to a regional clause.

HKSAR in other countries and missions of other countries in the HKSAR. Such missions are not on an ambassadorial or political level, something which seems to be reserved for the central government, but the HKSAR may, as necessary, establish official or semi-official economic and trade missions in foreign countries, and shall report the establishment of such missions to the Central People's Government for the record. The missions are hence not of a political kind, but related to economy and trade.[99] The situation is somewhat different with regard to foreign missions in the HKSAR. Foreign consular and other official or semi-official missions in the HKSAR may be established with the approval of the Central People's Government.[100] However, as determined in Art. 157(3), States that are not recognized by China may only establish non-governmental institutions in the HKSAR.

According to Art. 152, representatives of the Government of the HKSAR may, as members of delegations of the People's Republic of China, participate in international organizations or conferences in appropriate fields limited to States affecting the HKSAR,[101] or may attend in such other capacity as may be permitted by the Central People's Government and the international organization or conference concerned, and may express their views, using the name "Hong Kong, China". In addition, the HKSAR may, using the name "Hong Kong, China", participate in international organizations and conferences not limited to States.[102] This is the case concerning, *inter alia*, the World Trade Organization (WTO), which Hong Kong joined in 1995 and Mainland China in 2001, and the Asia-Pacific Economic Community (APEC), although both Hong Kong and China joined the APEC at the same time in 1991. This is also the case with the Asian Development Bank,

---

[99]The HKSAR has economic and trade offices in the following countries: Singapore, Australia (Sydney), Japan (Tokyo), Belgium (Brussels), the United Kingdom (London), Switzerland (Geneva), the United States of America (New York, San Francisco and Washington), and Canada (Toronto).

[100]As concerns old consular and official missions that existed in Hong Kong prior to the resumption of Chinese sovereignty and that were of States which have formal diplomatic relations with China, Art. 157 provides that such may be maintained. Such issues were decided on a case-by-case basis concerning States that had no formal diplomatic relations with China: the missions could be permitted either to remain in the HKSAR or they were changed to semi-official missions. As reported in the yearbook Hong Kong 2008 (2009), p. 13, [t]here is a large foreign representation in the HKSAR, including 58 consulates general, 58 honorary consuls and five officially recognised international bodies".

[101]According to Hong Kong 2008 (2009), p. 12, in 2008, representatives of the HKSAR Government, "as members of the PRC delegation, took part in over 140 international conferences limited to states, including those organised by the World Intellectual Property Organisation, the World Health Organisation and the International Civil Aviation Organisation".

[102]According to Hong Kong 2008 (2009), p. 12, the HKSAR also took part in 2008 "in about 760 inter-governmental conferences not limited to states in the capacity of 'Hong Kong, China', including those organised by the World Trade Organisation, Asia-Pacific Economic Co-operation and the World Customs Organisation". Concerning the international organisations in which Hong Kong participated in 1997, see Mushkat (1997), pp. 191–194.

which Hong Kong joined in 1969 and China in 1986, and with the International Maritime Organization (IMO), which Hong Kong joined in 1967 and China in 1973.

Article 152 of the Basic Law contains an obligation for the Central People's Government to take the necessary steps to ensure that the HKSAR shall continue to retain its status in an appropriate capacity in those international organizations of which the People's Republic of China is a member and in which Hong Kong participates in one capacity or another. The same dynamic obligation exists for such international organizations of which China is not a member but of which Hong Kong is. The Central People's Government shall, where necessary, facilitate the continued participation of the HKSAR in an appropriate capacity in such international organizations. Therefore, the State is under an obligation to promote the international presence of one of its sub-state entities.

On the top of official relations between States, the Basic Law regulates in Art. 149 the position of Hong Kong's NGOs in relation to similar organizations abroad and to international organizations.

Non-governmental organizations in fields such as education, science, technology, culture, art, sports, the professions, medicine and health, labor, social welfare and social work, as well as religious organizations in the HKSAR may maintain and develop relations with their counterparts in foreign countries and regions and with relevant international organizations. They may, as required, use the name "Hong Kong, China" in the relevant activities, that is, they may identify themselves as separate from the Mainland Chinese organizations. It should be noted that the fields listed are, at the outset, of a non-political nature, including religious organizations, the mentioning of which in the list of fields may actually have a political dimension from the point of view of the central government. Contacts of Hong Kong political organizations with their foreign counterparts may, however, be sensitive and could trigger penal consequences under the laws of Hong Kong, because Art. 23 of the Basic Law creates an obligation for the HKSAR to prohibit political organizations or bodies of the HKSAR from establishing ties with foreign political organizations or bodies and to prohibit foreign political organizations or bodies from conducting political activities in the HKSAR.

The liberal attitude of the Basic Law to relationships between Hong Kong and the international community both in its formal and less formal appearances does not mean that China as a State is unconcerned about the protection of the State or of its official ideology. It could be expected that a broad category of acts against the state would be criminalized in the legislation of the state and applied over its entire territory. However, Art. 23 of the Basic Law creates a territorial clause and in this respect places the HKSAR under a duty to enact laws on its own to prohibit any act of treason, secession, sedition or subversion against the Central People's Government, or theft of state secrets, to prohibit foreign political organizations or bodies from conducting political activities in the HKSAR, and to prohibit political organizations or bodies of the HKSAR from establishing ties with foreign political organizations or bodies.[103] In Mainland China, such prohibitions are included in the legislation enacted by the law-making body of China, but they do not apply in Hong Kong. At the same time, crimes such as secession, sedition and subversion are unknown to the common law-based legal order of Hong Kong, so there was an inherent unwillingness to deal with the matter. The Government of Hong Kong submitted a bill to the Legislative Council, but suspended its second reading and, ultimately, withdrew it altogether because of unprecedented public protests, such as mass-demonstrations on 1 July 2003, and other forms of political pressure.[104]

8.8 Reflections

The participation of sub-state entities in international relations is generally taking place within a constitutional space that either rules out such participation by reference to the fact that international relations is a competence of the state or its central government, on the one hand, or creates a special competence in the autonomy statute that permits certain international action within the international responsibility of the State, on the other.

Departing from the historical situation in the Memel Territory in our consideration of the possibilities that the sub-state entities have to participate in international relations, it is apparent that in the entities studied here, no such contacts between the sub-state entities and subjects of international law have existed that would imply a direct treaty-making or binding international commitment outside of the legislative powers of the sub-state entity. Zanzibar tried to join the OIC, but was compelled to withdraw after protestation from Tanzania on grounds that the

[103]Because Art. 23 implies a limitation of the powers of the Mainland Chinese authorities, it can be asked under what circumstances would the central government be entitled to take action in the HKSAR. As discussed in Leung Mei-fun (2006), p. 23, there may exist situations in which the central government would want to intervene, such as situations in which Hong Kong's autonomy is in danger, and under such circumstances, the consent of the special administrative region may be needed. A former Chief Executive has reportedly stated that the Chinese troops would not take any action without his orders, but the question is to what extent and under what circumstances is the order of the Chief Executive required? "Obviously, when security of the Mainland is endangered by an action in Hong Kong and the Chief Executive refuses to take any measure to stop it, the central government may order troops to stop such action. Thus, consent of the Chief Executive for the central government's intervention must be rather limited." See also Leung Mei-fun (2006), p. 55, where she considers the implementation of Art. 23 an obligation for the HKSAR, and pp. 218–237, where she considers the abortive attempts to enact legal provisions by the Legislative Council to fulfil the duty under the Basic Law. For a rich treatment of the issues related to the National Security (Legislative Provisions) Bill 2003 under Art. 23 of the Basic Law, withdrawn from the Legislative Council, see Hualing et al. (2005a, b).

[104]See Hualing et al. (2005a, b), p. xv.

matter belonged to the competence of the Union.[105] With a view to the divided implementation of treaties in Tanzania, it might be more important for Zanzibar (and also easier from the point of view of international law) to try to join the IMO.

The various states appear to be keen on either explaining to the sub-state entities that they do not have any powers in the area of international relations or drawing up careful boundaries in autonomy statutes as concerns the extent to which an international capacity is permitted. Both approaches actually fit within the principle followed in the *Memel* case: a sub-state entity does not have any independent power to enter into international commitments with subjects of international law. It is within the powers of the state itself to determine that a sub-state entity is not entitled to participate in international relations, but the state can also make the determination that the sub-state entity can participate in international relations to a lesser or a greater extent.

This determination normally takes place in the autonomy statute, as in the case of Hong Kong, but it should also be possible to authorize the actions of the sub-state entity in other ways, such as individual authorization in a concrete situation by decision of the state. As concerns Puerto Rico, case law from courts makes clear that the entity does not have any international dimension for its actions and that Puerto Rico is in this respect to be compared with the states in the federation. For Aceh, it has apparently been possible to conclude an agreement not involving legal commitments with some states in the US federation, but from the point of view of autonomous territories, the matter could be even more interesting if Aceh would try to conclude such an agreement with, for instance, Puerto Rico.

Against this background, it is possible to distinguish between such international relations where international commitments arise, on the one hand, and such international relations where no international commitments arise, on the other. As concerns the latter category, a State can afford to be more relaxed and permissive. Therefore, contacts between Hong Kong and other States are possible through missions that are established below the ambassadorial level. Contacts between the sub-state entity and corresponding entities abroad that can be perceived as administrative appear to be entirely possible. This may be the explanation for why Aceh could enter into an agreement with three states in the US federation, and an agreement under private law about purchase of public services between the Åland Islands and a hospital in Sweden has probably been perceived as completely uncomplicated from the perspective of the sovereignty of Finland. Because the sub-state entities are legal persons with legal capacity, it should therefore be possible to enter into contractual relationships of a private law nature and, as a consequence, to take up membership in NGOs. However, at least as concerns Aceh,

[105] As pointed out in Silverström (2008a), p. 261, "it is possible to single out two groups of autonomous entities having competences related to treaty-making. An important dividing line can be drawn between autonomous entities given formal competence for treaty-making and entities which are not empowered to conclude international treaties." However, he also concludes that in practice, the distinction between these two groups is more complex.

the right to take up loans abroad is managed via the central government, so even this avenue may be circumscribed under national legislation.

There is also a domestic sub-state dimension to the international relations of the State, namely the conclusion by the State of international commitments that affect the legislative competences of the sub-state entity, on the one hand, and the implementation of such commitments in the domestic legal sphere, on the other.

As concerns the conclusion of international commitments, such as treaties, Puerto Rico and Zanzibar appear to be completely sidelined, while Aceh and Scotland have a position in a context that may involve them in certain preparatory consultations. The position of the Åland Islands is somewhat stronger in this respect, because they could even become involved in the negotiations. However, Hong Kong is clearly equipped with the broadest powers in this area, because the entity can, under certain conditions established in the Basic Law, conclude international treaties of its own within its legislative powers and join various international organizations. In addition, Hong Kong may participate in such treaty negotiations that the national government carries out with foreign powers in case such treaties could affect Hong Kong. Clearly, in granting Hong Kong competences in the area of international relations, the lawmaker has given proof of creative imagination, but the lawmaker has also proven that it is doable, provided that the political will is there. Few other sub-state entities have their own powers to conclude international treaties. What the example of Hong Kong shows is that even within the area of external sovereignty, traditionally reserved for the state and protected in the *Memel* case, there is space for distribution of powers between the central government and a sub-state entity. The exercise of external powers of sovereignty is thus malleable in the same way as the exercise of internal powers of sovereignty. The State may be willing to go at great lengths in using its creative imagination in situations where it feels safe and does not have to worry about secession.

After the conclusion of a treaty, it normally has to be implemented in the domestic legal order(s) in one way or the other. In the case of Hong Kong, domestic implementation is probably not a problem concerning those treaties that Hong Kong has entered into, because it may be assumed that if it has concluded a treaty, it will also execute it in good faith, for instance, by making the necessary adjustments to the legislation of the territory. However, the situation may be complicated in respect to such treaties that the State of China has concluded and that fall within the sphere of competence of Hong Kong. In such situations, the advance opinion of Hong Kong could be secured in order to facilitate a territorial exception in the treaty to be concluded. The situation is often very different concerning the other sub-state entities. Their legal orders may be open to the impact of a treaty concluded by the national government, which is the case with Puerto Rico and also Scotland and Aceh, and should be so with Zanzibar. However, in Zanzibar, it is often argued that the domestic implementation is split between the Union and Zanzibar according to the distribution of powers in the Constitution of the Union. As a consequence, Zanzibar tends to adopt its own implementing legislation, which, if not properly done, may result in a situation where the State of Tanzania is faulted for incorrect implementation of a treaty obligation.

This matter is resolved in the case of the Åland Islands so that domestically, they are requested to give their consent to a treaty that Finland has concluded. As a consequence, the expectation would be that a possible denial of consent will activate a territorial clause at ratification which relieves the State from responsibility under the treaty to that extent. If consent is given, the Åland Islands is under the obligation to implement the treaty in its jurisdiction. One question remains, however: what happens if the sub-state entity is in breach of the international obligations, provided that no territorial clause or other reservation applies? Current public international law holds the entire State responsible for such a breach, and depending on the commitment, such a breach may also result in pecuniary consequences for the State. Our study indicates no general solution to the matter, but as concerns breaches in the application of EU law, there exist certain principles for distribution of the financial consequences for Scotland and the Åland Islands.

The relationship of the sub-state entities to international organizations seems to follow the same pattern as the role of those entities in treaty-making. In cases where the state adopts a strict attitude towards the treaty-making powers of autonomous territories, the state is also likely to be careful in not granting the sub-state entities any degree of freedom as concerns membership in international organizations of a public law nature. The opposite seems to be true as concerns states which involve the sub-state entity in the treaty-making powers, and in these situations, the incorporation of sub-state entities in international co-operation is easier to achieve. The example of the Nordic structures is illuminating in this respect and through those structures, the Åland Islands and the other Nordic autonomous territories are treated almost as quasi-States of some sort. A relaxed attitude may also be facilitated within the EU frame. As a consequence, the conclusion might be warranted that close relationships between two States through participation in joint international structures could promote the position of sub-state entities within those states with respect to various functions that otherwise would not be possible in the area of international relations. This distinction between strict and relaxed attitudes is probably not duplicated in respect of NGOs, but NGOs seldom deal with matters that pose a risk to the interests of the State. Therefore, States can be more permissive towards sub-state involvement in the NGO sphere.

In a European context, the supra-state level constituted by the European Union creates an additional challenge not only to the internal distribution of powers but also to the entire operation of the multi-centric law-making framework. Altogether ten of the 27 EU Member States have sub-state entities either by way of federal organization of the state or through autonomous territories of different kinds. The challenge in this context is how to incorporate the sub-state entities in suitable ways in the co-operation, which in principle only takes place between the Member States. While the EU itself is showing some signs of recognition of sub-state entities as a relevant consideration in addition to Member States, different Member States deal differently with the sub-state level. It is clear on the basis of the examples of Scotland and the Åland Islands that the sub-state entities are increasingly recognized by the individual Member States and incorporated in the various structures of the EU. For instance, the position of the Åland Islands has been improved and will probably be further improved through amendments to the autonomy statute. Although both entities are increasingly involved in EU activities, the implementation is differently organized: the UK Government may intervene in the Scottish jurisdiction for the implementation of EU law, whereas the Finnish Government cannot do so in respect to the Ålandic jurisdiction. This difference can probably be explained by the historical context in which the two sub-state entities became incorporated into the EU. The Åland Islands joined only after its legislative powers had been established, which means that the pre-existing distribution of powers had to be fitted to the EU frame, while Scotland was granted law-making powers only after the UK already was a member, which means that the entire scheme of the distribution of powers could be drawn up against the background of the existing obligations of the UK in relation to the EU.

The extent of the possibility of sub-state entities to participate in international relations varies very much, from no participation at all to an almost State-like position in the international community. In this respect, the sub-state entities appear to have traveled far from the initial position upon which the *Memel* case was based, that the State is the sole actor in the sphere of international relations. However, in those instances where the sub-state entities have a role in international relations, that role is normally carefully defined in the applicable legal norms that distribute competence in the area of international relations to the sub-state entities. As long as the sub-state entity keeps itself within that distribution of competence relevant for international relations, it is within the *Memel* principle. However, if it transgresses the boundaries of the grant of powers in the area of international relations, it is *ultra vires* in a similar manner as the Memel Territory when it entered into a separate trade agreement with Germany.

Chapter 9
Concluding Remarks

9.1 Confirming the Definition of Territorial Autonomy

Territorial jurisdictions raise particular issues and problems, especially within the area of constitutional law. We know this from federations and also from territorial autonomies. The issues and problems are often attached to the powers that the territorial jurisdictions have and to the attempts to manage, use and implement those powers. Without doubt, international law and even domestic administrative law are important in understanding how territorial autonomies work, but the different dimensions of territorial autonomy are mainly dealt with at the level of constitutional law in the states that make possible the existence of such entities.

The number of autonomy arrangements reviewed in this context is limited. Therefore, the conclusions that are drawn below need to be considered with care and against that backdrop. All cases included in our study have an international dimension, and in most cases a stronger or a weaker background in public international law can be identified. Quite often, a relationship of the entities to the principle and/or right of self-determination can be pointed at.

The diversity amongst the cases is manifest. From a more empirical point of view, the entities range, in terms of absolute numbers of population, from very small (the Åland Islands) to relatively large (such as Hong Kong), but what seems to unite them all (except Scotland) is that they represent only a small fraction of the national population, around 1%. This means that the power of these entities to influence the national level could be quite limited, and that the entities could run the risk of being forgotten about when the matters of an entire nation are dealt with at the national level.[1] The formalization of the position of these entities in national constitutional law nonetheless seems to result in at least some political and legal

[1]Following the terminology of Wolff (2010), p. 23, it seems that in most of these cases, the significance of the territorial entity in the national context would be "low" rather than "high" and that territorial self-government of a particular kind could be motivated for that reason.

DOI 10.1007/978-3-642-20048-9_9,

clout, for instance, through procedures attached to the conclusion and implementation of treaties between the State and other subjects of international law. The diversity of the entities reviewed here is also reflected in the modes of establishment of their autonomy. Some of the entities have been established by way of a fragmentation of the jurisdiction from the ordinary state structure (the Åland Islands, Scotland, Aceh), while others have emerged as autonomous territories through integration of some sort into the state (Puerto Rico, Hong Kong, Zanzibar). In this context, the Memel Territory fits well into this pattern, because the territory was integrated into the State of Lithuania by an international convention.

In all of the cases, the point of departure for the definition of the sub-state entity is the territorial definition of the jurisdiction for the purposes of the exercise of public authority. All the cases studied break the unitary (or the federal, as is the case with Puerto Rico in the context of the United States of America) nature of the state through a particular arrangement that is territorially circumscribed. In a number of cases (at least Indonesia and China and perhaps also Tanzania), the creation of the autonomy arrangement is, in fact, conditioned by the strong wish of the state to maintain its defining characteristics so as not to facilitate secession or transformation of the state from a unitary mode of organization into a federation.

The construction of the ideal type of territorial autonomy by way of contrasting the historical example of the Memel Territory and academic opinions about autonomy, on the one hand, with a doctrinary analysis of federalism and federal forms of organization, on the other, allows us to establish a definition of territorial autonomy. Our definition goes on to hold that the core of territorial autonomy involves a singular entity in what otherwise would be a unitary state or a federal state, so that the entity introduces an asymmetrical feature in the state through a transfer of exclusive law-making powers on the basis of provisions, which often are of a special nature and defined in such a manner that the state level remains with the residual powers, while the sub-state level relies on enumerated powers, at the same time as the state level contains no institutional representation of the sub-state entity. This is a relatively stringent definition of a core understanding of territorial autonomy, where the reference to exclusive law-making powers implies the absence of a supremacy doctrine on the part of the legislation of the state, so as not to allow preemption on the part of the national level within the competences of the sub-state entity. Our definition does not require the existence of a separate court system, because it is assumed that the courts, be they state courts or courts of the autonomous entity, act under the principle of independence of the judiciary, which means that the courts would, under any circumstances, be neutral in their decision-making. Therefore, a separate court system is not a necessary component of a definition of autonomy.

This stringent definition could be relaxed in some respects, but even when relaxed, the definition facilitates distinctions between the different sub-state entities of a non-federal nature. Hence, the stringent definition can be used for producing a graded scale of sub-state entities, where some entities clearly constitute territorial autonomies, while others may approach, for instance, administrative self-government. However, another graded scale may be drawn from territorial autonomy towards

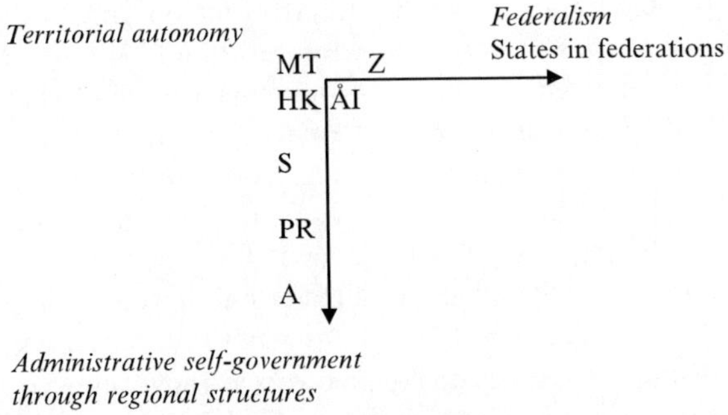

Fig. 9.1 Two dimensions of sub-state organization

federal arrangements, so as to facilitate an analysis of cases also along a second dimension (see Fig. 9.1 above).

Obviously, the Memel Territory fulfills our stringent definition of territorial autonomy, but the entity was, during its existence, more or less constantly subjected to attempts on the part of the state of Lithuania to break into the sphere of competence of Memel. The behavior of the state of Lithuania amounts, in many respects, to attempts to create a supremacy or preemption principle on the part of the legislation established by the Parliament of Lithuania. However, a legal interpretation of the competence lines was produced only at a point when the Memel Territory acted *ultra vires* when agreeing with Germany on a most favored status for agricultural produce from Memel.

Hong Kong and the Åland Islands cluster around the Memel Territory as autonomous territories. Hong Kong follows closely our definition of territorial autonomy with its enumerated law-making powers that are exclusive in relation to the national law-making powers (although democratic centralism could function in a manner which is similar to a supremacy clause, it seems that the position of the central government is very limited in this respect). At the same time, Hong Kong is not institutionally represented in the national decision-making organs. From the institutional point of view, the situation is the same for the Åland Islands, although there is a reserved mandate for an MP from the Åland Islands, but the definition of legislative powers is differently organized through the enumeration of two lists of competence: one for the Åland Islands and another for the national lawmaker. It is also important to notice that the absence of a supremacy clause or a preemption doctrine is confirmed in a number of court cases which, even in the situation of a normative void, deny the applicability of such legislation within the competence of the Åland Islands that has been enacted by the Parliament of Finland.

Zanzibar has been adamant in asserting its autonomy in relation to mainland Tanzania and to the Union Republic, but in terms of our definition of territorial autonomy, Zanzibar seems to exist in the fringes of territorial autonomy because of its over-representation in the institutions of the Union Republic, and because of the federal-like definition of competences, which leave the residual powers to Zanzibar. At the same time, there evidently is an absence of a supremacy clause or a preemption doctrine in relation to Zanzibar. Therefore, Zanzibar is probably best placed amongst territorial autonomies. Zanzibar is also the only sub-state entity that has the formal possibility to affect the enactment of the national constitution and thus the possibility to protect its position. The Åland Islands has that possibility to a limited extent as concerns some material dimensions of the national constitution, but the general picture that emerges is that sub-state entities do not have any such constitution-making roles as the constituent states in at least a classical federation would normally have with regard to amendments to the federal constitution.

Moving from the horizontal dimension of the above figure to the vertical dimension, Scotland can already be viewed as an entity, which is moving from the core of the stringent definition of territorial autonomy towards the fringes of that definition. The law-making powers are not exclusive quite in the same way as in the cases of Hong Kong and the Åland Islands, and the UK Parliament has a superior position in relation to the Scottish Parliament, although the Sewel Convention dictates restraint on the part of the UK Parliament. Institutionally, Scotland is well within our autonomy definition.

Puerto Rico and Aceh could perhaps be seen as a "cluster", too, but at the "weaker" end of the scale. The legislative powers of Puerto Rico are considerable, although completely under the supremacy of federal law or legislation enacted under the plenary powers of the US Congress, which in all instances preempts the legislative space of Puerto Rico. In that context, it is remarkable that Puerto Rico does not even have elected representatives seated in the two houses of the US Congress, but only an advisory representative.

In this comparison, Aceh displays the weakest position amongst the sub-state entities, in particular as concerns its law-making powers. They are subordinated to national law and national standards and premised on negotiations, the result of which is recorded in a presidential decree at the national level. Under these circumstances, it is problematic to claim that there would exist a genuinely exclusive legislative competence in Aceh. Institutionally, however, the position of Aceh is in compliance with our autonomy definition.

9.2 Applying the Elements of Autonomy

The characterization of the sub-state entities involved in this inquiry is a general one, and the profile of the entities may change somewhat if they are studied through the four elements chosen as a comparative platform on the basis of the *Memel* case.

Within the *first* element, the definition of the legislative and administrative powers of the sub-national entity, the distinction made in this inquiry is between the law-making powers proper held by the legislative body, on the one hand, and the administrative or regulatory powers held by the norm-making body on the other. The legislative powers imply the adoption of the law in the formal sense, not in the material sense, and results in legislative enactments of a general application by the sub-state entity. Most of the sub-state entities studied in this context have law-making powers proper. This is certainly the case with Hong Kong, the Åland Islands, and Zanzibar, while the legislative powers of Scotland are in principle subordinated to those of the UK Parliament. Also in Puerto Rico, the normative decisions made by the Legislative Assembly are solid law, but constantly faced with at least the theoretical possibility that the US Congress will set aside the Puerto Rican law by exercising its plenary powers of law-making. While the Scottish law-making powers are protected by the Sewel Convention, which is of a political nature, the Puerto Rican powers have no such protection (except the more practical point of departure that Puerto Rico is normally treated in the same manner as the states in the US federation). Therefore, a distinction can be made between Scotland, on the one hand, and Puerto Rico, on the other. In this respect, Aceh is probably in the weakest position among the sub-state entities included in the study, because the normative enactments of Aceh are in a secondary relationship to national laws and standards.

The material contents of the law-making profile vary greatly. From the point of view of the continental European rough division of law into public law and private law, it is possible to say that Hong Kong, Puerto Rico and Zanzibar, as well as Scotland, control matters over both spheres of the legal order, while the competence of the Åland Islands and also of Aceh is mainly in the public law sphere. The same distribution of sub-state entities applies in the area of criminal law: the former group has more general powers in the area of criminal law, while the latter group is more limited or specialized in its competence to criminalize behavior, but is not lacking that competence altogether. As concerns the judicial review of the competences exercised by the sub-state entities, it seems that in Puerto Rico only, the review of competences is organized in the same way as elsewhere in the state, while in Zanzibar, the Åland Islands, Scotland, Aceh, and even Hong Kong, competence review concerning the powers of the sub-state entities is carried out on the basis of rules and procedures that deviate from the regular pattern in the various states. This feature enhances further the asymmetrical nature of the sub-state arrangements in their respective national settings. In Zanzibar, the constitutional review of competence is completely defunct, while in Hong Kong, the independence of the interpretation system has been called into question.

A dimension of autonomy which is not directly addressed by the elements, but which is present in the context of the distribution of powers is the financial platform of sub-state entities, often boiled down to the right of taxation. All of the sub-state entities reviewed here have powers of taxation, some more complete (Hong Kong, Puerto Rico, Zanzibar), some more limited (the Åland Islands and Scotland, and to some extent even Aceh). Irrespective of the powers of taxation, it seems that at least Zanzibar, the Åland Islands, Scotland and Aceh also receive budgetary transfers over the budget of the central government, which is probably justifiable against the background of the fact that these entities are in charge of public functions that the state otherwise would have to organize through its own organs. The root of the fiscal and budgetary position of the sub-state entities can be found in the fact that the entities are legal persons that have the legal capacity of possessing rights and obligations, but the extent to which each sub-state entity is open to economic scrutiny from the state varies considerably from great independence (Hong Kong, the Åland Islands, Zanzibar, Puerto Rico), to reporting procedures of various kinds

(Scotland, Aceh). The proceeds or part thereof from the use of natural resources is explicitly committed to the sub-state entity in the cases of Aceh and Hong Kong (where the proceeds from the lease of land goes to the budget of Hong Kong), but implicitly, this seems to be the case in Zanzibar too.

The distribution of powers between the national level and the sub-state level is organized in different ways. As pointed out above, in Hong Kong, the enumerated powers are held by the sub-state entity, while the national level actually holds the rest, including foreign affairs and defense, explicitly mentioned in the autonomy statute. For the Åland Islands, both lawmakers have enumerated competences, complemented by a provision that allows for the consideration of a matter in one or the other sphere of competence, depending on which of the power profiles is better suited to handle the matter. In Zanzibar, the national level holds the enumerated powers, while the powers of the sub-state entity are premised on the idea of residual powers. This more "federal" principle of distribution of powers appears to be used in relation to Scotland, too, but because the Scottish powers are not regarded as truly exclusive, the UK Parliament perhaps nonetheless holds the overall residual powers. It is possible to distinguish Puerto Rico and Aceh from this group of four sub-state entities by reference to the fact that in the case of Puerto Rico and Aceh, the national law-making powers are framed in such a manner, in relation to the sub-state powers, that a comprehensive area of overlapping powers is created. In addition, the normative powers of Aceh are of a secondary order, subordinate to national laws and standards. For that reason, although it could be argued that in both cases the ultimate residual powers are held by the national lawmaker in a manner typical for territorial autonomies, the two sub-state entities do not seem to be in the possession of such law-making powers that could qualify them as autonomies proper. This is clearer in the case of Aceh (as a matter of fact, there was a wish during the domestic legislative process not to describe Aceh as an autonomy because specific autonomy experiments from an earlier date had failed), but a greater measure of doubt prevails in the case of Puerto Rico, because the law produced in Puerto Rico is in all respects enforceable in relation to, for instance, individuals without the support of federal law (provided that the federal law does not set aside the Puerto Rican provision) and could result in, for example, a prison sentence.

In this context, the position of Puerto Rico and Aceh in relation to autonomies proper could perhaps be resolved by reference to the possibilities of the national government to exercise veto powers over the normative enactments of the sub-state entities. In Puerto Rico, the national executive has no role in the legislative process of Puerto Rico, while in Aceh, the Governor of Aceh, as a representative of the national government, is party to the legislative process at the same time as the national government may invalidate the bylaws or *qanuns* of Aceh (except when the bylaw implements Islamic law, when only the Supreme Court of Indonesia can invalidate the bylaw), and such drafts of bylaws that deal with the budget of Aceh. For these reasons, Puerto Rico seems more autonomous than Aceh, which gives the impression of being in the possession of normative powers of an administrative or a regulatory kind. It is another matter if the autonomy of Puerto Rico reaches up to the same levels as the other sub-state entities reviewed in this inquiry. It is also important to point out in this context that in the European Union, the sub-state entities with law-making powers are affected by EU norms in a similar manner as the member states: in addition to the transfer of law-making powers from the national and sub-national levels to the EU, the implementation of an EU directive that has been adopted on the basis of the powers transferred to the supra-state level takes place at both the national and sub-state level in a way that actually leaves both the national level and sub-state entities in the possession of normative powers of an administrative or regulatory kind.

The situation is even more marked with EU regulations, which are directly applicable as law and do not even allow implementation measures by autonomies, except if specifically provided. Sub-state entities in the EU display varying degrees of autonomy in relation to their own states, but under the supremacy of EU law, they are not autonomous in relation to the EU. Because the Åland Islands and Scotland are subject to the supremacy doctrine under EU law, which means that EU norms that are enacted preempt the normative powers of these sub-state entities, it is possible to conclude that the Åland Islands and Scotland are not autonomous in relation to the EU, although they are autonomous in relation to the states in which they exist. In relation to the EU, Åland and Scotland assume the same position as Puerto Rico in relation to the US: the EU can exercise its "plenary powers" in any area of law within its competence that under the national law is assigned to the sub-state entity. At the same time, a sub-state entity is not likely to have any real power or influence at the EU level.

It is also important to point out in this context that general international law or human rights law do not contain any norm about the distribution of the legislative powers between the national level and the sub-state level, but some of the international agreements that constitute the foundation of a sub-state arrangement may do so on an *ad hoc* basis. This is the case with Hong Kong and Zanzibar, and this may have been the intention with Aceh, too, although the agreement is not concluded as a treaty under public international law, but is instead an internal resolution of a violent conflict. If the Aceh peace agreement had been concluded as an international treaty, it would probably not have been possible to enact the domestic legislation about the position of Aceh so that the consent mechanism was changed into a consideration mechanism.

As concerns the *second* element, elections to and dissolution of the representative body in the sub-national entity, different forms of participation in the sub-state entities were reviewed. The inquiry reveals similar variation with respect to elections and referendums at the sub-state level that is relatively regularly found in the national political systems. At the same time as the sub-state level presents itself as an important forum for participation, there are competing forums of participation, such as the national political system and local government. In the European context there is, in addition, the supra-state level of participation, which seems in the minds of the inhabitants of the two European sub-state entities included in the study, to be unable to compete for political attention amongst the voters in the sub-state entities. As concerns national participation, there are two sub-state entities that are not featured at the national level through elections to the national legislature, namely

Hong Kong and Puerto Rico. As concerns Hong Kong, the reason is that no national elections are held in China, but in Puerto Rico, the situation amounts to a denial of the right to be represented in the national legislature in a regular manner (although an advisory representative is elected, the situation underlines the unequal relationship between Puerto Rico and the US federation).

From the point of view of participation, the sub-state level studied here may be understood as a mechanism that enhances the mechanisms of participation that the population in the sub-state entities have at their disposal. Therefore, the creation of sub-state autonomies with decision-making bodies directly elected by the voters of those entities can be linked to the right, and also to the opportunity, to participate in public life in the meaning of Art. 25 of the CCPR. In addition to elections, the sub-state entities may also employ other forms of participation. At least to some extent the referendum is used, and in Aceh, Scotland and Hong Kong, draft laws and other public policy documents may be released for advisory processes amongst the population. The referendum is not used very much in this context, but it seems that a certain referendum practice is actually evolving in sub-state entities. This means that the referendum is not completely avoided at the sub-state level, although the fear of secession could dictate a cautious attitude at the state level towards an increased use of the referendum at the sub-state level. After all, the referendum is a mechanism through which the self-determination aspirations of a people may be manifested.[2]

Some potential limitations of the right to participate exist. In some of the sub-state entities (the Åland Islands and Zanzibar), the right to vote in the elections to the legislative assembly is limited to the holders of a particular status of residency in a manner which is exclusive in relation to those persons living in the jurisdiction who do not fulfill the required qualifications. This may be problematic from a human rights point of view, although there could exist justifiable reasons that make this limitation of the right to participation proportional in relation to the result sought. There is one example that goes in the other direction, namely Scotland, where the right to vote is opened up also for such categories of persons who do not have the right to vote in the national elections. As in the Memel Territory, election legislation at the sub-state level is sometimes a matter within the legislative competence of the national lawmaker (Scotland and Aceh), but in most cases, the sub-state entities are themselves in charge of the electoral norms.

The right to participation in elections at the sub-state level implies at the same time the existence of a political environment that is dependent on other human rights, such as parties that make use of the freedom of association and rely on the freedom of expression for political communication. As concerns the parties, the legislation is within the competence of the national lawmaker in the cases of Scotland, Aceh and Zanzibar, and this is the case with the Åland Islands too,

[2]See Suksi (2005a), pp. 209–226, where the cases related to Tatarstan in the Russian Federation, Quebec in the Canadian confederation and Katanga in Zaire are examined both from the point of view of international law and national constitutional law.

although there, political groupings based on the general freedom of association are used instead of parties in the formal sense of the word. Following the example of the Memel Territory, the political systems of sub-state autonomies are often home-grown and they distinguish themselves clearly from the national political systems, except in Scotland and Aceh and also in Zanzibar, where the political parties display an integration with the national political structures. In principle, the political systems of all sub-state entities are based on the political contestation of the mandates in the legislative assemblies, but Hong Kong, with its functional constituencies, is an exception in this respect and continues to present a problem in relation to the right to participate directly through elections under Art. 25 of the CCPR. In addition, there are appointed members in the legislative assemblies of Zanzibar and Puerto Rico, but mainly in a form that does not disturb the results of the elections.

As concerns the electoral systems, both proportional and majoritarian, as well as mixed systems exist in the sub-state entities. Normally, the elections at the sub-state level have functioned well, but in the case of Zanzibar, the pledge of the two-party system of alternation in power has not really been realized after the transition from a one-party rule to a multi-party rule. Instead of opting for proportional election to the legislature, the response to political tensions has been to create a government of national unity. It will remain to be seen how that power-sharing solution works.

Elected assemblies may be dissolved, but in none of the cases is there any independent power granted to the national level to dissolve the parliamentary organ at the sub-state level, although in the Åland Islands, the President of Finland has a formal role in a potential dissolution that has its root cause inside the political system of the sub-state entity itself. Evidently, the untimely dissolution of the parliamentary assemblies of the sub-state entities has not taken place even through their internal mechanisms, which means that the political forces have been able to work within the constitutional frames created by the autonomy statutes. From that perspective, the dissolution that took place in the case of Memel is truly exceptional (as it should be under the illegal forms it was performed) and has remained the only one amongst the sub-state entities reviewed here.

As concerns the *third* element, the executive power within the sub-state entity and the various directions of accountability that this executive power may be embedded in, the normative situation allows a distinction between those where the governmental body is only or mainly connected through mechanisms of horizontal accountability to the legislative assembly of the sub-state entity (the Åland Islands, Puerto Rico and Zanzibar, as well as Scotland and also the Memel Territory from a historical point of view), and those where there is a vertical accountability between the executive body at the sub-state level and the central government at the national level (Hong Kong and Aceh). It may be that an emphasis at the national level of control over the sub-state executive effectively rules out parliamentary accountability inside sub-state entities. However, even in situations of no central government involvement, the choice of the internal accountability mechanisms is not always that of parliamentary accountability, which is the case concerning the Åland Islands and Scotland, but the option of presidential forms of the executive power is also used (Puerto Rico and Zanzibar). In this respect, there exists amongst the sub-state entities reviewed here a distinction between entities where the system of government is based on a separation of powers in a more strict sense, on the one hand, and entities where the legislative branch and the executive branch are joined by means of the political link of parliamentary accountability, on the other.

From this distribution, the conclusion can probably be drawn that sub-state entities tend to follow the model of the state in which they exist, whether they have a genuine choice in doing so in their own internal legislation, as is the case in the Åland Islands and Zanzibar, or if the choice is made in the autonomy statute, which has taken place with respect to Scotland and Puerto Rico. In Aceh and, in particular, Hong Kong, the situation is different, because the executives in those sub-state entities are, at the same time, incorporated in the vertical dimension and framed as the representatives of the central government, although in different ways: in Aceh, the elected Governor is at the same time the representative of the central government in the region, while the philosophy of democratic centralism may create a certain expectation of a vertical alignment of the chief executive of Hong Kong. Of course, Aceh and Hong Kong could also be placed in the group of presidentially organized sub-state entities, although they would constitute a particular case in that category.

If a *Memel* situation of transgression of competences by the head of the executive organ emerged in one of the sub-state entities reviewed here, the responses from the national government would be varied. As concerns Aceh and Hong Kong, the central government could react and cause the dismissal of the head of the executive of these sub-state entities, while in the Åland Islands, Puerto Rico and Zanzibar and also in Scotland, the national executive could not, under the prevailing norms, dismiss the head of the sub-state executive. However, in Scotland, such a matter would probably be dealt with primarily on the basis of contacts between the Scottish Government and the UK Government by way of administrative settlement. It is another matter that the central government could try to achieve the dismissal of the chief executive officer outside of the established norms, which was the reaction in the *Memel* case by the Lithuanian Government. The norms relevant for those currently existing sub-state entities reviewed here do not contain an answer for such situations, except that the national governments could avail themselves of such judicial proceedings that may exist for the determination of competence. In the case of the Åland Islands, the Government of Finland could initiate a particular judicial proceeding in the Supreme Court of Finland for the determination of the administrative competence line, and the Puerto Rican Government could, for instance, be sued by the federal government in a federal court for *ultra vires* actions. In the case of Zanzibar, the mechanism formally provided under the Constitution of Tanzania is defunct.

Generally speaking, the governmental bodies of autonomy arrangements mainly implement legislation that has been adopted by the legislative assembly of the autonomous entity. This means that national legislation is normally not implemented by the executive bodies of the autonomous entities. There are some exceptions to this pattern, such as in Scotland, Zanzibar and the Åland Islands, where national legislation is implemented by the sub-state entities, albeit to a limited extent only and, as in the case of the Åland Islands, subject to a particular agreement. In Aceh as well, the sub-state entity is at least to some extent involved in the implementation of national law. What is an additional feature in relation to the executive power of the sub-state entities is that in Scotland and Aceh, the civil service of sub-state entities is at least formally part of the national civil service. This is a very particular arrangement, which at face value would not seem to promote autonomy, but at least in the case of Scotland, there do not seem to exist doubts about the integrity of the civil service under the Scottish Government.

As concerns the *fourth* element, the international relations of the sub-state entity, it seems that the states are still quite concerned about their sphere of action in that sovereign realm. With the exception of Hong Kong, the autonomy statutes are careful in delineating the competences of the sub-state entities so that international relations are clearly attributed to the state. Even in the case of Hong Kong, the broad grant of a sphere of action for Hong Kong seems ultimately to be defined as the responsibility of China. However, Hong Kong stands out as a very particular sub-state entity with broad possibilities to participate in international relations. The trend that can be discerned from our study indicates that the needs of the sub-state entities to be present at the international level are primarily taken care of by involving the sub-state entities in, for instance, different stages of treaty negotiations.

It is possible to assume in a relatively straight forward manner on the basis of our review and the *Memel* case that whenever a sub-state entity exceeds its competences within the area of international relations, the State becomes active in enforcing its competence. The reason for this is the overall responsibility that the State has over international commitments that the State or a part thereof has assumed. In this respect, the Åland Islands appear to constitute an exception of a certain kind, because the long interaction between the Nordic States has created trust on the part of Finland that tolerates a certain measure of contacts between the Governments of the Åland Islands and Sweden. In addition, the Government of the Åland Islands has been granted the right to maintain direct contacts with the European Commission, but in the context of European co-operation, such contacts do not perhaps anymore take place in the area of international relations, but are instead an expression of more "domestic" European affairs.

Although the State is, under public international law, responsible also for the international commitments of sub-state entities of the state, international law has developed in this respect at least to the extent inter-governmental organizations are concerned. Increasingly, inter-governmental organizations are at least in some cases developing their membership requirements in a more functional direction, allowing as members also entities that are not States in the formal sense. This is significant for sub-state entities, because the inter-governmental organizations are originally created on the basis of the treaty-making powers of States. Thus, if the States agree that sub-state entities could be included as members in organizations that traditionally have been the reserved domain of States, this may perhaps be interpreted as a relaxation of the strict attitude of the States concerning the participation of sub-state entities in international relations relevant also in other contexts of international relations. Reliance on the functional attributes of the sub-state entities so that they can, within the sphere of their competences, act also at the international level may, however, require that rules concerning the distribution of liability are established in the autonomy statute, and that a suitable level of "diplomatic" engagement of sub-state entities is determined in the autonomy statute.

9.3 Conflict-Resolution and Self-Determination

By way of combining the four elements of sub-state governance, it is possible to say that many of the cases included in our study appear in a conflict-resolution context, but from very different angles. Irrespective of the angle of conflict-resolution from which the creation of the solution has been approached, it appears as if the original conflict may have disappeared, although in reality, the original conflict has changed form and content. Sub-state governance through territorial autonomy probably contributes to resolving the original conflict, but sub-state governance does not necessarily extinguish conflict altogether. Instead, sub-state governance through territorial autonomy institutionalizes conflict and indicates such an avenue of action where overall agreement exists on the proper space of the autonomy arrangement. In their position as sub-state entities, these jurisdictional arrangements are in a constant interplay with the national government, and as is known from federal contexts, this relationship is, by its nature, conflict-oriented to a greater or a lesser extent. The art of sub-state governance is about confining the level of conflict to something that is manageable and about providing mechanisms that are capable of handling the difficult issues that will arise.

At least in cases where law-making powers proper are accorded to the sub-state entity, territorial autonomy directs the exercise of sovereign powers, and thus also self-determination into a channel which is internal in nature. Legislative powers are distributed between the state level and the sub-state level and the inhabitants of the sub-state jurisdiction can participate in the exercise of the law-making competences at that level. At the same time, an implementation mechanism for the application of norms established by the sub-state entity is set up in the form of a separate government in a manner which tends to fulfill the attributes of a state in all other respects than the exercise of original treaty-making powers in the international sphere. Consequently, there are internal ways for dividing sovereignty. These ways of distributing sovereignty contribute to the realization of the internal variant of the right of self-determination, at least of the population of the jurisdiction and perhaps also of the people, provided that the inhabitants of the territory qualify as a people. This would be the case concerning Puerto Rico and Zanzibar, and this was claimed also by the population of Aceh, now referred to as a people in the legislation creating the sub-state entity. In the other three cases, the populations cannot be regarded as distinct peoples under public international law.

The creation of particular jurisdictions of the kind reviewed in this inquiry raise questions about the definition of a people or population, which is the beneficiary of the arrangement. Solutions that create distinct categories of persons with regard to their rights in the sub-state jurisdiction are problematic from the point of view of human rights and of non-discrimination, in particular, although there may exist such reasons for the arrangements that are justifiable from the point of view of human rights. It is also important to note that when exercising law-making powers, a sub-state entity is expected to enact the law in compliance with the human rights commitments of the State and, in addition, when those norms of the sub-state entity are implemented in individual cases by the administrative organs (or courts, as the case may be) of the sub-state entity, the implementing decisions have to be made in compliance with the human rights commitments of the State. The point here is that the sub-state entity actually assumes the position of the State when laws are made and implemented, although the primary responsibility before treaty-monitoring bodies lies with the State party to the human rights convention. A particular consideration in this context is that when the sub-state entity is furnished with legislative powers, the law created would normally reflect the opinions of the majority in the territory. From an ethnic, linguistic or religious perspective, the sub-state entity thus assumes the position of the State in relation to other groups of persons determined on the basis of divergent ethnicity, language or religion. When public powers are exercised in such contexts, considerations of "a minority within a minority" arise. This could be the case at least in the Åland Islands and Aceh, where other groups exist than the local linguistic or ethnic majority, while the other entities are not necessarily touched by such considerations. However, in Hong Kong, some particular measures are taken for the benefit of an indigenous group.

The sub-state entities reviewed here display less of a connection to minorities and to the protection of the rights of minorities than might be expected, for instance, against the background of the Memel example. This could, of course, be a coincidence, but minority protection is probably not amongst the most important reasons that led to the creation of many of the sub-state entities. Hong Kong and Zanzibar are not touched by that background consideration, while this appears to be a consideration in the cases of the Åland Islands and Scotland and probably also in the cases of Puerto Rico and Aceh. However, three of the six entities are actually bilingually constructed, namely Puerto Rico, Hong Kong and Zanzibar, although the proportions at which the two languages are used may vary between the three entities. The Åland Islands is the only entity where a particular language is designated as the official language.

In the case of a failure of an autonomy arrangement, the question is whether there are possibilities to address violations of autonomy agreements. There was a mechanism available for the Åland Islands until the Second World War, but it vanished together with the League of Nations. Therefore, there are no explicit mechanisms currently in place through which the sub-state entities could bring problems to particular bodies for resolution. There may exist some general possibilities depending on the case and where it is situated, such as the ICJ for breaches of foundational treaty arrangements in cases where a treaty exist, but the sub-state entities themselves could perhaps not avail themselves of these mechanisms. Instead, they would have to engage an interested State party.

9.4 Various Autonomy Positions

The sub-state arrangement is normally of a constitutional nature, but the range within which the contents of the arrangement are determined by the state or the sub-state entity varies quite considerably. Normally, the sub-state arrangement is established in an autonomy statute of some sort, enacted by the legislature of the state. Zanzibar is the only sub-state entity included in our review where the details of the arrangement are spelled out in the national constitution, while the Åland Islands relies on two general provisions in the national constitution that identify the autonomy statute as the locus of the more specific norms. Even more general is the reference in the Constitution of China to special administrative regions, because the provision does not provide any explicit reference to Hong Kong. Three sub-state arrangements completely lack positive regulation at the level of the national constitution, namely Aceh, Puerto Rico and Scotland, and in these cases, the autonomy statute remains the only norm for laying the foundation of the sub-state entity. In the case of Scotland, this situation is a natural consequence of the lack of a written constitution for Great Britain, although there is a constitutional convention, the so-called Sewel Convention, that offers some measure of constitutional protection for the arrangement, and although the Scottish arrangement is adopted by a referendum and is, for that reason, understood as a particular arrangement under the unwritten constitution of Britain.

The applicability of the national constitution in the jurisdiction of the sub-state entity is related to the issue of the constitutional nature of the arrangement. Leaving aside Scotland because of the unwritten nature of the British constitution (which fact in itself would indicate that the constitution applies in general terms in Scotland, too), the applicability of the national constitution seems complete in Aceh. As concerns Puerto Rico, the matter is much more complex, and what at least seems to apply is the provision on the plenary powers of the US Congress, while the inhabitants of Puerto Rico are not regarded as US citizens under the Constitution, but under the Federal Relations Act. Formally speaking, Puerto Rico is outside the federation and thus outside the US Constitution. The autonomy statutes of the Åland Islands and Hong Kong make very broad exceptions to the respective national constitutions, but whereas Hong Kong has its own constitutional rights on the basis of the autonomy statute, the general constitutional rights of the Finnish Constitution apply on the Åland Islands (unless special provisions in the autonomy statute make exceptions). As concerns Zanzibar, the application of the national constitution seems very patchy and limited, and the impression is created that the Zanzibari arrangement constitutes a large exception to the constitutional provisions of Tanzania. Therefore, generally speaking it seems that sub-state arrangements are to be viewed as exceptions to the national constitution, although a greater or a smaller number of provisions of the national constitutions also apply in the sub-state arrangements. One typical area where national provisions apply is elections to the national parliament, except in the case of Puerto Rico in the USA.

Although the fundamental provisions are laid down in constitutional norms or in other legislative enactments of the state, the sub-state entity may be involved in the enactment or amendment of these fundamental provisions. The strong position of Zanzibar in the parliament of Tanzania should be able to guarantee a say in the adoption of constitutional provisions that affect the position of Zanzibar in the Union Republic. The Åland Islands is expected to give its consent to any amendment of the autonomy statute before it can enter into force. The other sub-state entities do not have similar protection mechanisms for their autonomy statutes. This distinction is also to some extent symptomatic regarding the possibility to exercise organizational powers of a constitutional nature inside the sub-state entity. As concerns Hong Kong, Aceh and Scotland, the autonomy statutes do not leave much space for local variation. Instead, the autonomy statutes establish the organizational and procedural structures of the sub-state entities at a relatively high level of detail. As concerns Zanzibar and the Åland Islands, the internal constitutional space is left much more open for a determination of constitutional issues at the sub-state level. While the Åland Islands has elaborated its governmental structures very much along lines that apply in Finland and in the Nordic countries in general, Zanzibar has established a tradition of going its own way in designing its internal structures. While there may still be some constitutional space in the Åland Islands that can be filled by enactments at the sub-state level, Zanzibar has actually over-utilized the constitutional space that is available for it under the Constitution of Tanzania, and at least partly this over-utilization can probably be attributed to the resentment felt in Zanzibar over the expansion of the powers of the Union Republic at the expense of the powers of Zanzibar. Hence, the governmental structures are generally speaking (but with some notable exceptions) determined in fairly great detail in the autonomy acts enacted by the national lawmaker (or by the parties to the convention, as in the case of the Memel Territory), without the possibility of the autonomous entity to vary the rules very much.

Although the autonomy statutes of the sub-state entities can be studied along different elements and dimensions, it is, against this background, evident that the sub-state constitutional space displays few similarities between each other. They regulate similar matters, organs and processes, but in ways that are quite different, and there is no evidence that there would be any cross-fertilization between the sub-state entities, at least not in the ones reviewed in this study. The models for autonomy statutes do not seem to come from other sub-state entities, but probably more from the national context, where historical examples or other sub-state entities may provide a contrasting vantage point. The above observations about the normative level at which the sub-state arrangements are created may, however, be combined with the nature of the competences that the sub-state entities have been vested with, so as to provide a platform for a general characterization of the different entities in relation to each other along these two dimensions (see below, Fig. 9.2; see also Sect. 1.3 and Fig. 1.1, above, for a discussion of other sub-state entities along the two dimensions).

It is evident that the sub-state entities are quite different from each other. While some of the entities can be referred to as autonomies proper, in particular those in

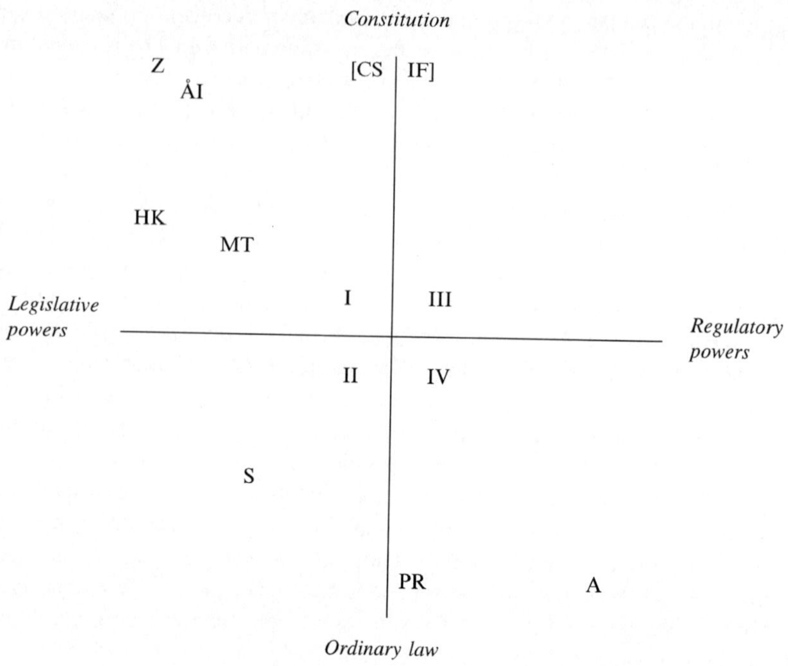

Fig. 9.2 Various autonomy positions II

section I of the table (Zanzibar, the Åland Islands and Hong Kong as well as the Memel Territory as a historical example), it is debatable whether Aceh and Puerto Rico qualify as autonomies. They probably fail according to a more stringent definition, but at least Puerto Rico could, if the conditions for territorial autonomy are relaxed, be regarded a territorial autonomy. In any case, an indication of the position of the federal frame by which Puerto Rico exists would seem to hold that states in the US federation could be placed on the same horizontal position as Puerto Rico as concerns the powers, but at the same vertical level as Zanzibar as concerns the normative level of the sub-state norms, that is, between sections I and III in the upper end of the chart (where the abbreviation CSIF denotes constituent states in classical federations). In comparison with the other sub-state entities, in particular with those in section I, the position of Aceh is clearly much weaker. The position of Scotland is difficult to indicate in the table because there is no written constitution in the UK, but weighing in the effect of the Sewel Convention and the fact that the Scottish devolution was brought about by means of a referendum, it should be possible to argue that there is at least some protection of a constitutional nature for Scotland too, and therefore, the Scottish arrangement involving relatively broad law-making powers is not only dependent on the ordinary legislation of the UK Parliament.

Hong Kong is clearly a strong autonomy in terms of powers, but its position in the Chinese constitutional setting is dependent on a treaty of a temporary nature and on a constitutional provision about special administrative regions. At the moment the time period established in the treaty comes to an end, the position of Hong Kong changes from section I of the chart to the lower part of section II. This will take place unless the Chinese constitution is amended so as to include a more elaborate set of autonomous entities than there already is (the two types of which can be placed in section III). By entrenching the autonomy of Hong Kong in the Chinese constitution in explicit terms, the sub-state arrangement could be guaranteed a continuation also after the fifty-year period has ended. Because the population of Hong Kong cannot be viewed as a distinct people in the meaning of Art. 1 of the CCPR, it would probably not be possible to expect that the provision in the convention would protect Hong Kong against potential dilutions of its autonomous status.

Zanzibar and the Åland Islands stand out as the two sub-state entities accorded the strongest normative position in combination with broad law-making powers, although with respect to the latter, Hong Kong is clearly the most advanced. It seems, in fact, that these three autonomous territories are organized in manners that are to be preferred over the historical example of the Memel Territory, where the autonomy was directly based on an international treaty that did not require any national implementation by the Lithuanian authorities. Although section I illustrates the normative situation which any sub-state entity probably would like to achieve, other positions (sections II and III, and possibly also IV) could be quite sufficient, as well, to fulfill the purpose of the arrangement, provided that the population of the jurisdiction agrees with it. There is no objective way of deciding which of the various types of sub-state governance it is that should be instituted when, for instance, conflicts are being resolved, but the solutions within section I may be those which stop short of secession and contribute to the maintenance of the territorial integrity and sovereignty of the State while allowing a large measure of self-government, even self-determination, to the population of the area.

9.5 Specific Reflections Concerning the Sub-state Entities

9.5.1 Particular Issues in Particular Places

The general issues related to sub-state organization indicate that territorial autonomies form a particular category of public organizations that can be studied from the perspective of certain characteristics that they share. Yet at the same time, within the notion of territorial autonomy, it is necessary to be aware of the fact that the debates, issues and problems vary very much between each of these entities. Some of the entities are more hesitant about their status as territorial autonomies than others, and in some entities, integration in international or supra-state forms of organization pose challenges that require further accommodation of state and sub-state interests.

The various autonomy positions indicated above (see Fig. 9.2 above) are in many ways reflective of and relevant for the current concerns in the sub-state entities. Therefore, some further discussions and interpretations may be presented against the background of those positions.

9.5.2 *Zanzibar*

The identity of Zanzibar as a territorial entity within the United Republic of Tanzania has been much debated during the entire existence of Zanzibar. Amongst the autonomies studied in this context and also generally, the history of Zanzibar is exceptional, because the State of Tanzania was created by a union between two independent States so that the smaller part, the islands of Zanzibar, was made something else than a regular region of the state, which would have been the case if Zanzibar had gone through a complete integration into Tanzania. Instead, a two-government solution was forged in a manner that guaranteed Zanzibar a large measure of internal self-determination on the basis of residual law-making powers. At the same time, the possibility of Zanzibar to take part in the exercise of the external self-determination of Tanzania was almost completely extinguished, leaving the domestic implementation of the international obligations of Tanzania as an arena where Zanzibar may still act within its powers and, potentially, cause problems for the Union.

A number of issues seem to be recurrent in the debate about the position of Zanzibar in relation to the Union in a manner that makes them relevant still today:

> The issues that were raised in both the 1983/84 and 1990/92 debates centred on the following: 1. Whether the 'Articles of Union' of 1964 provided for a federation, that is three governments (one of Tanganyika, the other of Zanzibar, and a third a federal one) or only two governments as presently existing; 2. As the Union government is also the government for the Mainland in non-union matters, does this not give the impression that Mainland is the Union? 3. Does Zanzibar get a fair share in the distribution of benefits coming from the Union? 4. Is Zanzibar well represented in the diplomatic service? 5. Does it get a fair share of foreign aid coming to Tanzania? 6. Since the people of Zanzibar were not consulted at the time of the formation of the Union, should there not be a referendum now to ascertain whether the people wanted the Union or not?[3]

It is very clear on the basis of our analysis that the relationship with the two-government solution in the case of Tanzania and Zanzibar is often discussed with reference to two other options of governmental organization, namely the unitary state and the federation, as if no other options were conceptually possible. The constitutional thinking has been formed along the lines of the one-government solution or the three-government solution, and it seems as if the one-party rule, practiced until the 1990s, had created the *de facto* image of a one-government

[3]Othman (2006), pp. 62–63.

solution that endangered the *de jure* constitutional position of the original two-party solution. There seems to exist two main opinions as to the theoretical description of what Zanzibar should be, that is, either a federal entity in a federation of Tanzania, or an independent unitary state, which implies that Zanzibar should secede from Tanzania and restore its sovereignty.[4] This, and a federation, in particular, has been forcefully advocated.[5] Evidently, it is difficult to understand that an autonomy arrangement could prevail, and it is, by some, understood as a temporary phase only, although the two-government solution is also not without supporters.[6]

As so many other things in Zanzibar, the attitudes towards the autonomy of Zanzibar are politically driven. "Although some opposition parties, especially the CUF in Zanzibar advocates for more Zanzibar autonomy, the party's formal policies usually emphasises the need of having more autonomy of constituent parts through a Federation instead of the present confusing union. No political party openly advocates for the break-up of the Union."[7] Instead, there is often a return to the unclear roots of the Union that makes the point that "[a] careful study of the Articles will show that a TRUE FEDERATION was visualised",[8] while the one-party period propels the opinion that the National Executive Committee of the one party, the CCM, "tried to move towards the creation of a unitary state",[9] which leaves the CCM of today with the legacy of an illegitimate exercise of power. In fact, the argument of Zanzibar being a constituent part of the Union gained more force through the amendment of Art. 2 of the Constitution of Zanzibar in 2010, which now identifies Zanzibar among the two constituent states of the United Republic of Tanzania, without, however, transforming the Union in to a federation.

The original historical intention to create a federation in the former British East Africa may be the reason why the current position of Zanzibar is often analyzed in a binary manner between the unitary state and the federation: "The constitutional structure of the union may be described as a unitary state with federal

[4] Tanzania Human Rights Report (2009), p. 181: "Is Tanzania a federal entity or not? Did the founding fathers of the Union have in mind the present two-government structure as a permanent one or did they see a possibility of a complete Union with one government?" See also Kirkby and Murray (2010), p. 98, who conclude that "the Tanzanian federacy is a unique arrangement with both federal and unitary features".

[5] See, for instance, Dourado (2006), pp. 90, 101–108.

[6] See also Othman (2006), p. 53 f., 61, with reference to full autonomy in Europe, 67 ff. with proposals on what should be done.

[7] Maalim (2006), p. 157 f.

[8] Dourado (2006), p. 80. See also Dourado (2006), p. 86, who gives an account of structural elements of a federation in a list of six points. See also Dourado (2006), p. 92 f.: "Federation can be defined as Constitutional system in which there is a division of legislative and executive powers between a central government and two or more state governments and each government being supreme in matters left to them. The governments are co-ordinate with one another and not subordinate. The essence of a Federation is the supremacy of each government in its own sphere."

[9] Dourado (2006), p. 91.

characteristics. Seen from the vantage point of the Zanzibar Constitution it is more federal than unitary; opposite is the case when seen from the standpoint of the Union Constitution. This means that there are some very fundamental and substantial inconsistencies between the two constitutions. The Eighth Constitutional Amendment to the Zanzibar Constitution further reinforces this hiatus."[10] It is also not unusual to learn in the debate that the principle of distribution of power between two legislatures and two executives is the core of the federal principle underlying the Articles of Union and the basis of Zanzibar's autonomy[11] and that the distribution of power between the Union and Zanzibar is a central feature of any association between states based on a federal principle.[12] The case of *S.M.Z. v. Machano Khamis Ali & 17 Others*[13] nonetheless makes the practical point that "[b]e it as it may, that discussion, though interesting, should not detain us but suffice it is to say that the constitutional set-up of the United Republic is unique. It is a union but with some elements of federalism". This reference to a unique union is important in the context, because it allows us to propose that Zanzibar should be identified as a territorial autonomy, although the arrangement certainly contains dimensions that one would not expect to find in an autonomy. In particular, the distribution of powers between the Union and Zanzibar, based on the enumerated powers of the former and the residual powers of the latter, is of a more federal kind. In addition, the significant over-representation of Zanzibar in the governing structures of Tanzania, in particular in the Union Parliament, points in the direction of a federation, although the Constitution of Tanzania does not contain a regular federal chamber in which the constituent parts would be institutionally represented. It should also be pointed out that the several additions to the list of Union Matters without following the original amendment procedures could be an expression of the existence of an unofficial preemption doctrine of a federal nature in the area of constitutional law (although in this case leading to the direction of a more "unitary" arrangement). It is thus possible to say that the arrangement in which Zanzibar is embedded is bordering on federalism, but that Zanzibar could still, in our analysis, be placed among the autonomies.

The Constitution of Tanzania incorporates many provisions concerning the internal structure of the autonomous entity of Zanzibar, and in its own Constitution, Zanzibar is trying to relate to the structures of the Union, albeit sometimes in ways that underline the particularities of Zanzibar in a manner that may lead to constitutional inconsistencies. The existence of Zanzibari security forces is one example of the autonomous behavior of Zanzibar in the Union, so too the identification of Zanzibar as a state and a constituent state. The Court of Appeal of Tanzania has several times pointed out inconsistencies between the Constitution of Tanzania and

[10] Shivji (2006), p. 185.

[11] Shivji (2008), p. 172.

[12] Shivji (2008), p. 174.

[13] Court of Appeal of Tanzania at Zanzibar, Criminal Application No. 8 of 2000 on 3 April 2000. The decision of the High Court of Zanzibar was overturned.

the Constitution of Zanzibar,[14] but because the Court of Appeal is not empowered to exercise constitutional review over the institutional relationships between the two Governments, the cases involving constitutional dimensions that arise on the basis of individual application of ordinary legislation are not sufficient to establish a proper constitutional interpretation about the position of Zanzibar as a part of the Union. With the limited role of the Court of Appeal and the complicated structure of the Special Constitutional Court, there would seem to exist a great need for a vigorous culture of consultations between the two Governments. However, although there are some institutional forums for contacts between the two Governments, it seems as if the political contacts between the Government of Zanzibar and the Government of the Union would be relatively scarce.

The creation in 2010 of a constitutional basis for a government of national unity in Zanzibar is an internal measure that will certainly change the dynamics of the internal constitutional and political process in Zanzibar. It is too early at this stage to evaluate the impact of the new governmental set-up, but the aim of it seems to be to bring an end to the political division of Zanzibar rooted in its early history and to make possible a new, more issue-based and bi-partisan constitutional and political system. At the same time, however, the system of parliamentary government, which ideally could be of a Westminster kind, is replaced by something else that may (or perhaps may not) be a system of power sharing.

9.5.3 The Åland Islands

With territorial demarcation as a starting point, the autonomy of the Åland Islands has grown ever stronger over the years: a specially guaranteed self-government of a higher order created in 1920 was supplemented, on the basis of the League of Nations conflict solving decisions of 1921, by a set of special features in the so-called Guaranty Act of 1922. Here the position of Ålandic culture based on the Swedish language was entrenched at the same time as specific provisions concerning the right to vote and stand as a candidate in elections and the acquisition and possession of real estate were created. Amendments to this autonomy arrangement in 1951 and 1991 deepened the autonomy and the position of the Islanders by establishing a distinct right of domicile to which a number of features were connected: the right to vote and stand as a candidate in Ålandic and municipal elections, the acquisition and possession of real estate, the right of trade (which was *not* an element of the original Settlement), and exemption from military service (which already was an element of the self-government in 1920). Although this arrangement, which also could be called a "sandwich" of exclusive rights, contains elements of minority protection, one could, nevertheless, conclude that the

[14]See *Seif Sharif Hamad v. S.M.Z.*, *supra* note 162 in Chap. 4, and *S.M.Z. v. Machano Khamis*, *supra* note 151 in Chap. 4.

protection of the territory is a central theme here. It is, at the same time, recalled that the right of domicile and, as one of its dimensions, the right of trade, are not covered by the 1921 decision of the League of Nations, but depend on legislation enacted by the Parliament of Finland.

Formally speaking the Åland Islands arrangement is now regarded an obligation binding on Finland within customary international law, and the possible dilutions of this arrangement would probably propel the Government of Finland to invoke such an argument. This took place, for instance, during the negotiations leading to the Finnish accession to the European Union: the Finnish accession affected the right to vote and to stand as a candidate, the right to acquire real estate, and the right of trade (involving the freedoms of establishment and services). It could indeed be concluded that the special accession arrangements with the Åland Islands in this respect display recognition of the internationally entrenched territorial aspect. With membership in the European Union, a matrix of pluralistic sources of law has evolved, making it more difficult than before to know where legislative sovereignty actually resides. The loss of power to the EU has certainly caused dissatisfaction on the Åland Islands, but nobody knows if the alternative that existed in 1994 (that is, remaining outside of the EU) would have been any better.

In the case of the Åland Islands, the federal criteria are not fulfilled with regard to the institutional part of the theory, although the Åland Islands are one constituency in the elections to the unicameral Parliament of Finland. The Åland Islands have no institutional representative in the Parliament, but the inhabitants of the Åland Islands elect one MP. This is also true with respect to the competence criterion, which accords enumerated powers to the Legislative Assembly, although it does so also with regard to the national lawmaker: the legislative competence of the Åland Islands is based on enumeration, but this is the case also concerning the legislative competences of the Parliament of Finland (or mainland Finland). Therefore, in terms of the two principal dimensions describing the differences between federal and autonomous forms of organization, the Åland Islands are approaching a mid-position, but in such a manner that the characteristics of autonomy remain predominant.

The legislative and administrative powers as well as the possibility of the Åland Islands' involvement in international affairs have been on the increase. Therefore, materially speaking, the autonomy arrangement has grown beyond its original frames as they were laid down at the beginning of the 1920s. More importantly, however, the constitutional position of the Åland Islands has been very strong and has grown even stronger during the 1990s, at least from a very formal point of view, with explicit stipulations in the Finnish Constitution. At the same time as the legislative powers of the Åland Islands have become broader, we may conclude that the entrenchment of the position of the Åland Islands in the Constitution of Finland has given rise to the development of new dimensions. It is not anymore solely a matter of a special and regional entrenchment, but since 1994, there is also a general entrenchment in the Finnish Constitution of the position of the Åland Islands. The current Self-Government Act, enacted in 1991, served to strengthen the self-government of the Åland Islands and restrict the state's supervision, mainly by expanding the legislative competences of Åland and by giving Åland more administrative powers. The cogs of the Self-Government Act are fitted into the cogs of the Constitution in a multitude of ways, making the relationship a very complex issue.

The matters within the legislative and administrative competence of the Åland Islands are mainly in the sphere of public law (as the term 'public law' is understood in continental Europe). The Finnish Parliament is, naturally, competent to pass legislation in these areas, but only to the extent that the law is applied on the mainland. If the Legislative Assembly of the Åland Islands chooses not to pass laws on a certain public law matter, the laws of the mainland are not applicable to those matters in the Åland Islands. However, in so far as the constitutional provisions concerning the rights and liberties of individuals contain references to the law and demand legislative action, then the Legislative Assembly is under a duty to pass legislation that fulfills their prescriptions. The same applies to regulatory demands imposed by the EU by way of directives. The loss of legislative powers to the EU as a consequence of EU membership, and the fact that the distribution of legislative powers between the Legislative Assembly and the Parliament of Finland has been quite static over the years, has resulted in a loss of law-making powers in the Åland Islands. It is possible to argue that legislative competences, *inter alia*, tax powers, should be moved from the enumeration of the Parliament to the enumeration of the Legislative Assembly, so as to increase the powers of the Legislative Assembly. Amendments of this kind to sections 18 and 27 of the Self-Government Act can only be done by way of a rigid formula that combines the requirements of qualified majorities in both the Parliament of Finland and the Legislative Assembly of the Åland Islands. An alternative that would allow at least some flexibility would be to transfer the powers mentioned in section 29, because they can be transferred on the basis of ordinary legislation enacted by the Parliament of Finland.

The model of the Åland Islands is often cited in discussions on territorial autonomy and minority protection. However, solutions of this kind may not be universally relevant and applicable, but are often tied to the particular circumstances surrounding the case in question. Therefore, the Åland Islands are more a laboratory of autonomy than a model. So why is the Ålandic autonomy laboratory so attractive? In the contemporary world, its appeal seems to depend on its close relationship with the international law concepts of self-determination and sovereignty. These concepts have various interrelated dimensions, some of which are relevant for areas which form the parts of a state. After the First World War, the people's right to self-determination was understood as the right of a certain part of the population to choose the State in which it wants to live and the sovereignty under which it wants to be governed. This was a common theme in territorial changes at that time and concerned almost exclusively such areas that were inhabited by a minority population.[15] This quite narrow version of the concept of

[15]Suksi (1993), p. 236.

self-determination (in comparison to the one that emerged after the Second World War) had tremendous appeal on the Åland Islands at the end of 1910s and the beginning of the 1920s, and resulted in the organization of two petition campaigns on the Islands advocating secession from Finland and accession to Sweden. However, the League of Nations did not apply that understanding of self-determination to the Åland Islands. After the consolidation of the position of the Åland Islands as an autonomous part of Finland, the question about their national affiliation has mainly ceased to be contentious.

In the beginning of the 1920s, the entire Åland Islands question turned on the issue of the (external) sovereignty of the State: which State should have sovereignty over the Åland Islands and who should decide the matter, the League of Nations by peaceful means, or Finland and Sweden by war? The matter was resolved peacefully, and autonomy was established on the Åland Islands by way of dividing internal sovereignty and thus also internal self-determination between the Parliament of Finland, on the one hand, and the Legislative Assembly of the Åland Islands, on the other. At the same time, international guarantees established special rights for the Åland Islanders that are exclusive in relation to other citizens of Finland and also in relation to persons who are not citizens. Although the special rights of the Åland Islanders can be defended against challenges from the direction of human rights by reference to their historical position and the understanding that the autonomy arrangement is based on customary international law, it is unlikely that such a set of special rights could be created today for some other autonomy arrangement, with the possible exception of indigenous populations. The complications from the point of view of human rights would probably be too many.

The legislation concerning the autonomy of the Åland Islands created a second lawmaker in Finland, but with competencies only in certain fields within the jurisdiction territorially limited to the Åland Islands. This could nonetheless be described as a delegation of the internal sovereignty of Finland to the Legislative Assembly of the Åland Islands. While it may have been a matter of some debate in the 1920s and 1930s among academics whether acts of Åland should assume a lower position than the acts of the Parliament of Finland, the preparatory materials for the 1920 Self-Government Act are clear about the fact that two spheres of legislation were being established which are exclusive in relation to each other. Since the Second World War, this has been unquestioned, and in the current Constitution, legislative enactments of the Parliament of Finland and those of the Legislative Assembly of the Åland Islands are placed on the same norm-hierarchical level. In fact, over the years, the State of Finland has consented to two different peace projects, which have involved the transfer of law-making power from the national Parliament, namely the self-government of the Åland Islands in the 1920s, and membership of the European Union in 1995. Thus, there exists two different lawmakers in the territory of Finland, but whether either can still be considered as sovereign in the traditional sense of the word after the conclusion of a multitude of treaties of international law and after membership in the European Union is a complicated matter. Although difficult from a legal point of view, the Ålandic loss of legislative competence due to EU membership should perhaps be compensated, at least to some extent and in suitable ways, by agreeing either at the national level or at the EU level, for instance, to the creation of a special Ålandic mandate in the European Parliament or to other structural measures that would strengthen the position of the Åland Islands in the field of EU matters.

9.5.4 Hong Kong

Conceptually, the autonomy of Hong Kong is caught between two fixed points of Mainland Chinese thinking: Hong Kong is not a constituent state in a federation, because China is not a federation but a unitary state, and because China is a unitary state, the overriding powers are exercised by the central government in Beijing, in spite of the fact that under the Constitution of China, a system of regional autonomy for recognized minorities is implemented.[16] Therefore, the concept of territorial autonomy as defined on the basis of the Memel Territory and in our theoretical exploration does not really have any explicit place in the Chinese constitutional framework. As a consequence, Hong Kong has been placed in the category of "special administrative region" with the understanding that its powers are based on a delegation from the central government.[17] However, this is not necessarily the only option for interpretation. On the basis of our study, it is argued that the position of the HKSAR in China could well be defined in terms of territorial autonomy. It is evident that the Basic Law provides the HKSAR not only with a vast share of internal sovereignty and internal self-determination within China, but also a share as established in the Joint Declaration and the Basic Law in the exercise of the external sovereignty of China.

The Basic Law creates a separate legal order in the HKSAR within which the inhabitants of Hong Kong or business enterprises active in the region almost never come under the provisions of the Mainland Chinese legal order, but only under the laws of Hong Kong. Because the allocation of powers to the HKSAR is also developed in the Joint Declaration, and because the recognition of the HKSAR as an autonomous territory would not make China a federal state, there should be no obstacle to arguing that the autonomy of the HKSAR is based on a distribution of legislative powers between Mainland China and the HKSAR, instead of a mere delegation of powers. This distribution seems to be designed as an enumeration both for Mainland China and for the HKSAR, and the sphere of the Mainland Chinese authority is restricted to only very few issues, those of foreign affairs and defense, although the case can be made for residual powers for the state. A territorial autonomy of a similar nature could potentially be used to accommodate

[16]See also Ghai (2000a), p. 96.

[17]See Weiyun (2001), p. 136, writing from a Mainland Chinese point of view: "Therefore, there is direct control and a supervisory relationship between the highest Central Authorities and the HKSAR."

the position of Tibet within China, so that the internal self-determination of Tibet would be developed without consequences for the external self-determination and the territorial integrity of China.

The Basic Law spells out the details of governmental powers and structures in Hong Kong without leaving much space for the regulation of these matters by Hong Kong's internal norms. In this respect, the rules pertaining to the Government of Hong Kong do not only reflect the interests of the central government of China, but may in fact have a root in the British administration of Hong Kong, with a strong governor at the top of the executive branch and a strong vertical line of accountability to the central government in London.[18] Instead of governmental accountability through the principle of parliamentarianism, it seems that there is an attempt, albeit a weak one, to create governmental accountability through checks and balances. As concerns the parties in Hong Kong in relation to the party structure in Mainland China, it is obvious that the multi-party setting in Hong Kong shows no affinity to the one-party system of Mainland China. The functional constituencies used in the elections to the Legislative Assembly introduce certain anomalies to the system of governance of the HKSAR, sustained by the election of the Chief Executive, who is ultimately appointed to his or her office by the CPG. The limitations on suffrage and on the functioning of the Legislative Assembly have not prevented Hong Kong from becoming a vibrant political community. Although universal suffrage is the ultimate aim concerning both organs of governance in the HKSAR, it will remain to be seen how such directly elected institutions will manage their contacts with the central government.

Despite initial concerns that were aggravated, in particular, by the first Interpretation of the NPCSC, the autonomy arrangement seems to have worked reasonably well.[19] Nevertheless, a number of problematic areas prevail, such as the unclear situation with the interpretations by the NPCSC (with the possibility that they overturn decisions of the Hong Kong courts), the unclear situation with the development of universal suffrage, and the tight control of the executive of the HKSAR by the CPG to the extent that it may be possible for the CPG to control the direction of legislative activities in Hong Kong. It has been pointed out that the Basic Law "is primarily about control and not autonomy, as is obvious in the provisions about Beijing's control over the chief executive, senior public servants, and the Legislative Council",[20] a relationship characterized by the absence of real inter-governmental bodies where policies or problems can be negotiated and resolved. "In particular, it lacks institutions with the ability to restrain the Mainland authorities from possible interference in the political and legal systems of Hong Kong."[21] This

[18] See Ghai (1997), pp. 223 f., 242, 259.

[19] See, e.g., Yiu-chung (2004), p. 27, who concludes that "there has been very little overt intervention from Beijing, which has exercised self-restraint".

[20] Ghai (2007b), p. 128.

[21] Hualing et al. (2007), p. 6. See also Yiu-chung (2004), p. 27, who is of the opinion that the arrangement "lacks a constitutional mechanism to limit or demarcate the power of the central

is evident, *inter alia*, in the area of constitutional interpretation, where the interpretations of the NPCSC have the status of a norm of the sovereign, and it is commendable that only three such interpretations have been issued during the first decade of the existence of the HKSAR. Although the Basic Law establishes the common law as one of the main features of the HKSAR, the constitutional jurisdiction exercised on the basis of the Basic Law is arguably different from other areas of law in the HKSAR. Therefore, in spite of the fact that the legal system is based on common law, the court interpretations of the provisions of the Basic Law are probably to be understood as a regular statutory interpretation of a civil law kind, in spite of the fact that interpretation is carried out by common law courts in the style of common law.

9.5.5 Scotland

The Scotland Act is an exhaustive collection of norms that create the Scottish sub-state entity at the same time as it purports to define in detail in which ways the autonomous entity is integrated in the governmental structures of the central government (or, to express the relationship somewhat more accurately from the point of view of the sub-state entity, to define in detail in which ways the central government can be integrated in the governmental processes of the autonomous entity). In fact, from a legal point of view, the integration seems so far-reaching that doubts can be presented if there is much space at all for a genuinely autonomous existence.[22] Although the interaction is in principle very comprehensive already on the basis of the existing norms, a proposal to develop the Scottish devolution scheme further foresees even more interaction (and perhaps integration) between the two governments involved, but instead of developing the executive interaction, the proposal is to create mechanisms of interaction between the legislatures, that is, between the UK Parliament and the Scottish Parliament.[23]

government and Hong Kong", and that the "one country always takes precedence over the two systems, as one senior NPC official publicly claimed": "The Basic Law seems to regulate or restrict Hong Kong but not Beijing."

[22]Trench (2007a), p. 270: "[T]he devolved territories have only minimal scope to alter their own internal constitutions." Scotland may be able to initiate such a process, but all decisions are made at the UK level and require a political majority in the national political system.

[23]Serving Scotland Better (2009), pp. 11–14, 142–146. Such mechanisms actually already exist to some extent. See for instance Scottish Ministerial Code (2008), para. 3.10. See also House of Commons Scottish Affairs Committee, Commission on Scottish Devolution. Third Report of Session 2009–2010. Report together with formal minutes, oral and written evidence. HC 255. London: The Stationery Office Limited, 2010. It is possible that the need to improve the governance of Scotland through the project *Serving Scotland Better* and the separate project of the Scottish Government entitled *Scotland's Future* is based on a feeling that there is not yet good government in the territory of Scotland. Whether enhanced devolution or even independence can improve the performance of the Scottish Government is a matter of debate.

Competences have been devolved to the regional tier of government, but "the powers and the authorities themselves can be legally removed or altered by decision of the centre. Devolution UK style does not carry with it any constitutional entrenchment".[24] The powers of the Secretary of State and the power of the UK Government to make subordinate legislation for Scotland are also potentially very intrusive, because there may have existed a perception by the time of the enactment of the Scotland Act that they are a necessary element in such a system of devolution, where the central government in some circumstances may have to "assert its authority in support of some wider UK interest".[25] Secondary acts of this kind might, however, easily be set aside by Scottish courts, who would not in such cases feel the constraints of the concept of parliamentary sovereignty.

Actual practice, both political and "empirical", builds up another, more nuanced picture; one which can support the conclusion that devolution has resulted in Scotland in the emergence of an autonomous entity. During the first session of the Scottish Parliament (1999–2003), it passed altogether 62 bills on different matters, while during the ten years preceding devolution, the UK Parliament passed 48 Scottish acts[26] and only a couple after devolution, which means that the workload of the UK Parliament in respect of Scotland has been reduced[27] or at least simplified through the Sewel mechanism of consent. During the same period of 1999–2003, it seems that the quantity of UK legislation passed that applies to Scotland was 92.[28] What the reach and depth of Scottish autonomy is may, however, be discussed, because even in the most decentralized of federal systems, the federal government generally has the upper hand. "What is notable in the case of the UK is the extent of this",[29] and as a consequence, "the constraints on the devolved administrations mean that in many ways they are not masters in their own houses".[30] Ultimately, the sovereignty of the UK Parliament remains untouched and the UK Parliament can legislate and, in fact, has legislated "for all

[24]Henig (2006), p. 23. However, there are some court cases of a constitutional order in which it is suggested, at least by way of *obiter dicta* in individual opinions of judges, that a constitutional layer of norms is, in fact, discernible and that the Scotland Act would belong to those acts of a constitutional order together with such norms as the Act of Union (and perhaps also the Wales Act) as well as the Magna Carta and the Human Rights Act. See *Jackson and others (appellants) v. Her Majesty's Attorney General (Respondent)*, [2005] UKHL 56, [2006], at 102 and 106, and *Thoburn v. Sunderland City Council*, [2002] EWHC 195 (Admin), at 62.

[25]Himsworth and O'Neill (2003), p. 263.

[26]Page (2005), p. 10 f.

[27]Hazell (2005b), p. 228 f.

[28]Hazell (2005b), p. 234.

[29]Trench (2007b), p. 61. As a consequence, Trench (2007b), p. 70, concludes that the UK Government has a structural advantage in the conduct of intergovernmental relations.

[30]Trench (2007b), p. 68.

parts of the UK, for devolved as well as non-devolved matters".[31] This has not prevented the Scots from increasingly taking their problems to the Scottish Parliament instead of the UK Parliament,[32] although the latter has remained a surprisingly important source of legislation even in the devolved areas of law.[33]

In principle, the autonomy of Scotland is limited, although the co-operation in intergovernmental relations with the UK Government may have enhanced its position. Scotland has, when using its own competence, also to take into consideration how the UK competence is exercised in the area of England. If those UK competences impact on Scotland, there is no formal veto or other mechanism for adjudicating differences, except more informal ones within intergovernmental relations where the UK Government has an upper hand.[34] "The UK Government has, for its part, proved that it can change rules that affect the devolved administrations, unilaterally, without consultation and sometimes by oversight or at least without considering the implications of its actions for the devolved administrations. On a formal level, the UK can act unilaterally even as regards devolved matters, and may be able to pass legislation without devolved consent in matters that are devolved – but these powers are doubtful on the formal level, would be contrary to convention (of huge importance in the UK context) and if used would surely provoke a political and constitutional crisis."[35]

At the same time, the Scottish Parliament is generally prevented from modifying the Scotland Act (although a few exceptions exist), which means that the Scottish Parliament is not free to adjust the terms of the devolution scheme by its own decision.[36] The constraints on the financial autonomy add another dimension to this characterization, as does the fact that the civil servants remain within a unified UK civil service.[37] "The devolved administrations have meaningful (if constrained) autonomy, are at significant disadvantage in intergovernmental relations, which limit their ability to exercise that autonomy, but despite this have still been able to operate in distinctive ways compared with the UK."[38] The reasons for the existence

---

[31]Trench (2007b), p. 71.

[32]Pilkington (2002), p. 119, Page (2005), p. 11.

[33]Page (2005), p. 33, Winetrobe (2005), p. 39. Winetrobe (2005), p. 233, concludes that post-devolution, "the Westminster Parliament continues to be the most important source of primary legislation for each part of the country, and the UK government continues to be the most important source of secondary legislation". See also Hazell (2005b), p. 250, who concludes that the "difficulty is that England dominates, and Welsh and Scottish concerns tend to be overlooked". However, see Himsworth and O'Neill (2003), p. 151, who make the point that acts of the Scottish Parliament are becoming more and more important as sources of law in Scotland.

[34]Trench (2007a), p. 270.

[35]Trench (2007a), p. 270.

[36]See Himsworth and Munro (2000), p. 168.

[37]Trench (2007a), p. 271 f. For an overview of resource dependency by devolved administrations and UK intergovernmental relations in the areas of constitutional resources, legal and hierarchical resources, financial resources, organisational resources, lobbying resources, and informational resources, see Trench (2007a), pp. 272–273.

[38]Trench (2007a), p. 278.

of an ambit of autonomy for the Scottish jurisdiction are probably to be found in the generally favorable environment, in the methods for containing conflict and in the willingness of the UK Government and Parliament to be constrained by the self-regulation that devolution implies in the UK, not only at the formal legislative level, but also at the intergovernmental level and the daily management of issues.[39] With different parties in power in Scotland and in the UK Government since 2007, the position of the mechanisms, such as the JMC, the Memorandum of Understanding and concordats, may be underlined and enhanced. The SNP could use the intergovernmental forums for its own purposes on the basis of a political instinct of some sort, while the UK Government could start acting more actively through these forums if it would seem likely that UK interests are affected.

9.5.6 Puerto Rico

The potentially permanent status of Puerto Rico as an unincorporated territory, which is an asymmetrical feature in comparison with the symmetrical organization of the states in the US federation in spite of the fact that Puerto Rico is, in many respects, treated as a state, was made clearly more temporal in the de-colonization process that started in the wake of the Second World War. The US Congress has, however, not been able to act on the issue, in spite of the fact that several proposals have been made both inside Congress and by Puerto Rico. In addition to outright independence (which is less likely as an alternative and which probably would involve a close relationship through association), the domestic alternatives at hand are dependent on actions taken by Congress which depart from such options offered on the basis the US Constitution that transport Puerto Rico from the ambit of the territorial clause to some other status alternative. The two domestic alternatives would lead to a permanent sub-state existence, either as a state in the federation, which would institute a symmetrical relationship, or as an entity with some other political status, which would be asymmetrical in nature. However, the latter is procedurally very difficult to produce within the constitutional fabric of the US, because it would necessarily involve an amendment to the US Constitution. In the statehood scenario, the position of Puerto Rico according to our comparative chart would be moved from the lower part to the upper part of the chart and positioned somewhere close to the vertical axis between sections I and III (see Fig. 9.2 above). The option of "any other political status" could in theory be placed in any of the four sections, but proceeding from the assumption that exclusive law-making powers would be granted to Puerto Rico in a manner which withdraws Puerto Rican laws from the ambit of the supremacy clause in Art. VI of the US Constitution, it is possible to envision a categorization of Puerto Rico in section I of the chart, somewhere close to the Åland Islands. However, at the moment, due to the

[39] Trench (2007a), pp. 277–281.

very clear federal supremacy and plenary powers, it is difficult to conclude that Puerto Rico would be a territorial autonomy proper.

In anticipation of a solution to the colonial problem posed by Puerto Rico to the United States, it is possible to say that in terms of the distribution of powers, the problems are more or less as follows:

> United States laws apply to the Puerto Rican people without their consent; United States laws can override provisions of the Commonwealth Constitution; Through the unilateral grant by Congress of diversity jurisdiction, United States courts decide cases involving strictly local matters of law; Congress assumes that it can unilaterally exercise plenary powers over Puerto Rico under the territorial clause of the United States Constitution; Both Congress and the executive branch of the United States government accordingly act as if there were no compact between the United States and Puerto Rico, and some officials even argue that none is legally possible. In spite of statements to the contrary by the Supreme Court of the United States and the Court of Appeals for the First Circuit, both Congress and the executive branch of the United States treat the Commonwealth in practice as if it were no different than any other territory or possession of the United States; Even if the courts eventually hold that there is now a binding compact and that this compact encompasses the Federal Relations Act, the consent extended by the Puerto Rican people in 1950 when accepting Law 600 in a referendum is overbroad. Consent to the unrestricted application to Puerto Rico of all federal laws, past and future, does not thereby erase the colonial nature of such an arrangement. (...) The realization of such a weakness in the Commonwealth structure has been, together with the insistence that Congress is vested with plenary powers over Puerto Rico, what has fueled Puerto Rican attempts in the past forty-odd years to enhance or improve Commonwealth status.[40]

However, one main issue with the distribution of powers is the unclear reference to "not locally inapplicable" as a definition of both federal and Puerto Rican legislative powers, leading up to virtually completely coinciding law-making powers.

As concerns participation in a broad sense of the term, the following problems have been observed: "There is no equality or comparability of rights between United States citizens residing in Puerto Rico and those domiciled in the States; The United States government contends that sovereignty over Puerto Rico resides solely in the United States and not in the people of Puerto Rico; Commonwealth status as it is at present does not meet the decolonization standards established by the United Nations; There is no known noncolonial relationship in the present world where one people exercises such vast, almost unbounded power over the government of another."[41] While the latter statement is very categorical and provocative, actual practice concerning the relationship between Puerto Rico and the United States is probably not quite that reprehensible, although the relationship is problematic. More specifically, the Puerto Ricans residing in Puerto Rico are not allowed to vote in federal elections, which creates an inequality between US citizens and a lack of representative national government for the Puerto Ricans. Finally, in the area of foreign powers, the following has been stated: "Puerto Rico

[40]Trías Monge (1997), pp. 161–163.

[41]Trías Monge (1997), pp. 161–163.

plays no role in the life of the international community, either directly or indirectly as a participant in the decisions taken by the United States; The President of the United States and executive appointees negotiate treaties and take other actions which affect Puerto Rico without consulting it."[42]

Any status solution, freely chosen by the people of Puerto Rico, is likely to remedy all these problems in one way or the other. However, there is a great likelihood that such a status solution will transform Puerto Rico into another kind of sub-state entity, either a regular state in the federation or an autonomous entity with a broad range of exclusive law-making powers.

Evidently, the compact construction is not effective in guaranteeing an exclusive law-making space for Puerto Rico. It may nevertheless be an overstatement to conclude that the compact construction is a complete disappointment, because the US Congress has not very actively enacted federal legislation of relevance for Puerto Rico without Puerto Rican consent or revoked such legislation without consent, although examples of such legislative action exist. But has the compact construction used to create the Commonwealth in 1952 failed so miserably that it could be called a monumental hoax (what it was not said to be in a federal court case)? Not necessarily, at least if the Commonwealth position is developed into a viable alternative under the federal Constitution in a future status referendum. If the Commonwealth position is not further elaborated as a third alternative parallel to statehood and independence, then it can be said that the decades of governance after 1952 were based on the erroneous premise that the compact actually meant something, in particular from the point of view of self-determination. It is, in this context, notable that if Puerto Rico were a part of current Spain, the autonomy granted to it in 1898 would probably have been realized within the current autonomy structure of Spain in a manner that would place the entity in the upper left-hand corner of section I in the figure indicating various autonomy positions (see above, Fig. 9.2).

9.5.7 Aceh

The Indonesian legislation concerning Aceh is very comprehensive and addresses in a variety of ways those elements of governance that are of interest in our inquiry. Almost the entire LoGA is devoted to the four elements that have, in this study, been derived from the historical example of the Memel Territory, that is, distribution of powers, participation, the executive, and foreign affairs. Those elements constituted the core of the MoU, that is, the peace agreement, which maintained the territorial integrity of Indonesia while at the same time recognizing a position for the Acehnese in governing themselves in many substantive fields. Aceh is formally part of a unitary state, but against the background of the Constitution of Indonesia,

[42]Trías Monge (1997), pp. 161–163.

as amended during the past decade, it could also be argued that the entire state may be slowly moving towards a more federal mode of existence.

At the same time as the LoGA implements the commitments to participation for the people of Aceh by creating inclusive electoral procedures, and by allowing local political parties, there are various provisions in the LoGA that require the different governmental bodies of Aceh to act in ways that are in harmony with the *Pancasila* (the five guiding principles), the Constitution of Indonesia and the laws and regulations, that is, the national norms, when the particularities of the arrangement are concretized. In combination with the open-ended distribution of powers between the national government and Aceh, subject to specifications by means of negotiations before the more exact distribution of powers is established in a government regulation, and the supervision over the exercise of Acehnese powers by the Indonesian Government, there is actually very little autonomy in the arrangement. The ideological principles of governance are not limited to the *Pancasila*, but are also present in the statutory references to Islam that establish Islam as a state religion in the territory of Aceh.

Interestingly, in the 2006 gubernatorial elections, the GAM secured governorship with a vote of close to 40% of those casting valid votes, while in the 2009 elections, Partai Aceh, the political party into which the GAM transformed itself, won more or less 46% of the vote. The two figures represent nearly the portion of ethnic Acehnese individuals, but without further studies it is difficult to conclude that the voting behavior would be ethnically determined. It is also interesting to take note of the fact that the relatively profane GAM, which negotiated the peace treaty with the Indonesian Government, is now in charge of the denominationally Muslim province of Aceh and expected to give effect also to the religious provisions of the LoGA. Obviously, there may be different levels of implementation, and it seems as if the current Governor and his support party, the *Partai Aceh* (and its supporters from the former GAM), were less interested in implementation of religious provisions and more interested in promoting substantive issues relevant to the Acehnese,[43] although the Government has been involved in passing a number of *qanuns* with Islamic content. The more substantive and practical emphasis in the implementation by the Government of Aceh has, *inter alia*, led to a limitation of funds over the Acehnese regional budget to the activities of the special police force for the enforcement of the *Syari'yah*.[44]

If the references to the people in the MoU and LoGA are taken as indications of the existence of the internal self-determination of the Acehnese, supported by the references in both documents to the existence of legislative powers, it should be possible to expect that the legislative powers granted to Aceh would be legislative powers proper, exclusive in relation to the legislative powers of the Indonesian

[43]It would probably be difficult to dismantle *qanuns* that created *Sharia*, because the bureaucracy and the budget that already exist have become entrenched.

[44]The Sharia police has actually been merged with the police of the district/municipal government, and at least in 2009, the level of enforcement of Sharia law seems to be relatively low.

parliament. That is, however, not the case, but instead, the normative powers exercised by the DPRA exist at the level of bylaws, subject to national legislation and national standards. The concept of law is therefore not to be understood as law in the formal sense, but as law in the material sense.

In comparison with the other Indonesian provinces at the regional level, Aceh is different for several reasons, three of which could be mentioned here. Firstly, autonomy in Aceh lies at the provincial (and also district) level, but elsewhere it is actually on the district level.[45] In Indonesia, decentralization was deliberately brought to the district level in order to avoid the risk of a Balkanization of the country at the provincial level. Secondly, the Islamic sharia is applied in Aceh, but not in any other region of Indonesia. The Government of Aceh has also been given means to enforce sharia. Thirdly, there are local political parties in Aceh, which give a local flavor to political decision-making. In other parts of Indonesia, local political parties are not allowed.

Even with these features, Aceh has, nonetheless, a relatively limited autonomy that could only be described as an executive or regulatory autonomy through self-government. A point of comparison among other entities of the same kind could be Corsica in France. Its creation was a face-saving measure for both parties, taken when armed struggle was not going anywhere and when both parties were shaken by a natural catastrophe. Autonomy has broadened the opportunity of the former armed opposition to be involved, which, of course, also was the point with the independence that was attempted. The main part of the LoGA is about making a point about powers that are shared at the level of ordinary law, that is, in the LoGA, between Aceh and the Indonesian Government in a confusing way. The details of the distribution of functions are worked out in a government regulation, which Aceh needs to consider and discuss with the Indonesian Government in negotiations.

9.6 General Trends of Sub-state Organization

One observation that may be combined with the above chart concerning different autonomy positions (see above, Fig. 9.2) is that the level of autonomy regulation (whether the main rules are passed in the constitution or just in ordinary law; the vertical dimension) may affect the generosity at which autonomy is organized. It appears, on the basis of our study, that a high normative level of regulation tends to produce rigidity and detail, while a low normative level of regulation tends to allow for flexibility and a more open determination of distribution of powers. Broad

[45] However, it should be taken into account that the LoGA also regulates the district/municipal government in Aceh and that the provisions concerning the sub-provincial level are in most cases similar to those dealing with the structure and powers of the provincial level of Aceh. Therefore, it could be said that the district/municipal level is also a part of the Aceh arrangement.

overlapping spheres of competence may have been opted for in the cases of Puerto Rico and Aceh, perhaps for the reason that all of that can be amended in a simple order by ordinary legislation of the national lawmaker. The same general idea may at least in part exist behind the Scottish arrangement, which is in some respects organized in a "patchy" way. One proposition that could perhaps be made in this context (but that cannot be tested here) is that the lower the normative level of the norms establishing the autonomy, the more flexible the state can be in granting new concessions to the sub-state entity. This would be so because the state could just as flexibly roll back the concessions in the absence of a formal constitutional protection for the permanency of the arrangement. The entrenchment of the sub-state arrangement in the formal possibility of the sub-state entity to affect amendments of the autonomy statute is therefore of high importance. Such an entrenchment exists in relation to the Åland Islands through the consent requirement, and Zanzibar can, of course, utilize its strong representation in the Union Parliament and the formal amendment requirements of qualified majorities to protect its position. However, there is nothing of the sort with regard to Scotland, Puerto Rico, Hong Kong or Aceh, although it should be obvious that Aceh should be consulted and its consideration received and taken into account, and although the position of Scotland is politically entrenched in a way that would make it difficult to rewind the arrangement.

Of the states reviewed here, at least China and Indonesia have, in their respective constitutions, adopted a series of constitutional or political principles that are aimed at steering the country when legislation is adopted and decisions are made. Aceh is governed very much under the explicit expectation that the *Pancasila* or the five leading principles of the Indonesian Constitution shall apply throughout all decision-making. In contrast to Indonesia with respect to Aceh, China has explicitly exempted Hong Kong from its ideological constitution by introducing the principle of "one country, two systems". While the general socialist ideology may proceed from the expectation that the other system will subside at some future point in time and that socialism and even communism as the ultimate aim of social organization will prevail (although not necessarily immediately after the fifty years of autonomy in Hong Kong), such an abandonment of the fundamental principles is exceptional. It could therefore be said that the autonomy of Hong Kong is also supported by the ideological exception, while the sub-state status of Aceh is limited by several degrees by the expectation that governance in Aceh takes place according to the national ideology. On the basis of our review, it is thus not possible to conclude that authoritarian states necessarily have difficulties in recognizing autonomous territories within their borders, in particular if the autonomous territories themselves are less than democratic. This was so with regard to the Memel Territory, when it was a part of Lithuania and when it experienced pressure from the central government, but China does not, at the present time, confirm that proposition, and also Indonesia has been undergoing profound changes in this respect, although the *Pancasila* is still utilized as a set of guiding principles in relation to Aceh. It should also be noted that Zanzibar survived through the ideologically colored one-party era of Tanzania, and today, it remains to be seen how it finds its place in the new constitutional and political setting.

The sub-state arrangements reviewed in our study do not confirm the belief that the prospects of establishing autonomy arrangements are strongest when the state undergoes a regime change,[46] because out of the six cases of current sub-state arrangements, four (Aceh, Hong Kong, Puerto Rico and Scotland) were not created as a result of such extraordinary events in the political and constitutional environment surrounding the soon-to-be sub-state entity that would have amounted to a regime change. Obviously, there was a change of regime in the cases of Hong Kong and Puerto Rico, but the state in which the sub-state entities exist did not undergo a regime change at the moment when the sub-state entity was created. However, in the cases of the Åland Islands and Zanzibar, regime change appears to have played a role. Likewise, our study does not support the notion that autonomy arrangements are likely to be established if the international community becomes involved in conflict resolution. This was so with respect to the Memel Territory and some involvement of the international community may be detected behind the creation of the sub-state arrangements of the Åland Islands and Aceh (although in both cases it is more limited than is commonly thought; in the case of the Åland Islands, the sub-state arrangement was confirmed at the international level after its creation at the national level as a response to an escalating conflict between the interested states parties). However, the international community was not involved in Scotland, Hong Kong, Zanzibar and Puerto Rico (although the Commonwealth construction came into being in a supportive international setting).

Evidence is divided on the suggestion that autonomy arrangements are most likely to succeed in states with established traditions of democracy and the rule of law.[47] This seems to be so with regard to the Åland Islands and Puerto Rico and obviously also Scotland (although the arrangement is only one decade old), but there is no reason to put a failed label on Zanzibar or Hong Kong, on the contrary (and the Aceh arrangement is still too recent for an evaluation on this dimension, but the start has been promising in the new Indonesian style of governance). Autonomy seems indeed to be easier to concede and likely to succeed when there is no dispute about the sovereignty of the state to which the sub-state entity belongs, but sub-state status has been conceded also in situations where the territory has presented claims of secession (the Åland Islands and Aceh). In light of the cases reviewed in our study, autonomy is not more likely to be negotiated and to succeed if there are several ethnic or linguistic groups involved instead of only two, and it also appears that autonomy arrangements which have been negotiated in a democratic and participatory way do not necessarily have a better chance of success than those which are imposed. In addition, it is not confirmed by our study that an independent dispute settlement mechanism is essential to long-term success.

[46]See Ghai (2000b), pp. 14–23, for a series of propositions concerning autonomy.

[47]See Ghai (2000b), pp. 14–23, for a series of propositions concerning autonomy.

However, the sub-state arrangements reviewed here appear to confirm the conclusion that autonomy does not promote secession, but may instead work towards preventing secession, although in several sub-state entities, secession and independence is to some extent a part of the political debate (while weak as a political force). What our inquiry certainly underlines is that the sub-state entities base their functioning on a careful design of institutional structures and therefore, if we qualify all the currently existing entities as successful examples of sub-state governance, we would be in a position to conclude that a careful design of institutional structures, procedures and powers is essential for the success of territorial autonomy.

Appendix

A *constructed* illustration of the allocation of seats after elections to the Scottish Parliament, courtesy of the UK Election Commission, is as follows (see also Sect. 6.4.4 concerning the counting of votes in the AMS electoral system of Scotland).

	Party 1	Party 2	Party 3	Party 4
Regional votes	61,974	63,362	61,189	37,206
Constituency seats	2	4	1	0
1st win party 4	÷3 = 20,658	÷5 = 12,672	÷2 = 30,595	÷1 = *37,206*
2nd win party 3	20,658	12,672	*30,595*	÷2 = 18,603
3rd win party 1	*20,658*	12,672	÷3 = 20,396	18,603
4th win party 3	÷4 = 15,494	12,672	*20,396*	18,603
5th win party 4	15,494	12,672	÷4=15,297	*18,603*
6th win party 1	*15,494*	12,672	15,297	÷3 = 12,402
7th win party 3	÷5 = 12,395	12,672	*15,297*	12,402
Additional seats	2	0	3	2
Total seats in region	4	4	4	2

M. Suksi, *Sub-State Governance through Territorial Autonomy*,
DOI 10.1007/978-3-642-20048-9, © Springer-Verlag Berlin Heidelberg 2011

References

Ahlström C (1997) Demilitarised and neutralised zones in a European perspective. In: Hannikainen L, Horn F (eds) Autonomy and demilitarisation in international law: the Åland Islands in a Changing Europe. Kluwer Law International, London

Álvarez Gonzáles JJ (2001) Law, language, and statehood: the role of English in the great state of Puerto Rico. In: Duffy Burnett C, Marshall B (eds) Foreign in a domestic sense – Puerto Rico, American expansion, and the constitution. Duke University Press, Durham

Alvarez-Gonzalez JJ (1991) Judicial views on the status of Puerto Rico. In: Blaustein AP (ed) Constitutions of dependencies and special sovereignties – United States/Commonwealth of Puerto Rico, Booklet 1. Oceana Publications, Dobbs Ferry

Amoretti U (2011) Italy: increasing decentralization, decreasing asymmetry. In: Requejo F, Nagel K-J (eds) Federalism beyond federations. Asymmetry and processes of resymmetrisation in Europe. Ashgate, Farnham

Anderson RW (1998a) La Ley electoral. In: Anderson RW (ed) Política Electoral en Puerto Rico. Editoral Plaza Mayor, San Juan

Anderson RW (1998b) Las elecciones y la política. In: Anderson RW (ed) Política Electoral en Puerto Rico. Editoral Plaza Mayor, San Juan

Anderson G (2008) Federalism: an introduction. Oxford University Press, Don Mills

Austen J, Butler D, Ranney A (1987) Referendums, 1978–1986. Electoral Stud 6:139–147

Avonius L (2004) Reforming Wetu Telu: Islam, Adat, and the Promises of Regionalism in Post-New Order Lombok. Yliopistopaino, Helsinki

Baogang H (2007) Democratization and federalization in Asia. In: Baogang H, Galligan B, Inoguchi T (eds) Federalism in Asia. Edward Elgar, Cheltenham

Baralt GA (2004) History of the federal court in Puerto Rico: 1899–1999. Publicaciones Puertorriqueñas, Hato Rey

Barbora S (2008) Autonomous districts and/or ethnic homelands: an ethnographic account of the genesis of political violence in Assam (North-East India) against the normative frame of the Indian constitution. Int J Minor Group Rights 15:313–334

Barros J (1968) The Aland Islands question: its settlement by the League of Nations. Yale University Press, New Haven

Bartole S (1998) Regionalism and federalism in the Italian constitutional experience. In: Suksi M (ed) Autonomy: applications and implications. Kluwer Law International, The Hague

Bell D, Christie A (2007) Funding devolution: the power of money. In: Trench A (ed) Devolution and power in the United Kingdom. Manchester University Press, Manchester

Benedikter T (2007) The World's Working Regional Autonomies: an introduction and comparative analysis. Anthem Press, New Delhi

Benedikter T (ed) (2009) Solving ethnic conflict through self-government – a short guide to autonomy in South Asia and Europe. EURAC, Bolzano/Bozen

Bernhard M (2006) Law on the governing of Aceh – a brief review and assessment. http://www.geocities.com/bouviersmith/bin/May-governing_aceh.ppt. Accessed 11 June 2009
Bing L (2007) Subject matter limitation on the NPCSC's power to interpret the basic law. Hong Kong Law J 37(part 2):619–646
Björkholm M, Rosas A (1990) Ålandsöarnas demilitarisering och neutralisering. Åbo Academy Press, Åbo
Blaustein AP (ed) (1991) Constitutions of dependencies and special sovereignties – United States/Commonwealth of Puerto Rico, Booklet 2. Oceana Publications, Dobbs Ferry
Blindenbacher R, Saunders C (2005) A global dialogue on federalism: conceptual framework. In: Kincaid J, Tarr GA (eds) Constitutional origins, structure, and change in federal countries. McGill-Queen's University Press, London
Bogdanor V (1997) Forms of autonomy and protection of minorities. Daedalus 126:65–87
Bogdanor V (1999) Devolution in the United Kingdom. Oxford University Press, Oxford
Bourchier D (2008) Positivism and romanticism in Indonesian legal thought. In: Lindsey T (ed) Indonesia: law and society, 2nd edn. The Federation Press, Singapore
Bring O (2007) Åland som internationellt subject: Idag och i framtiden. In: Jansson H (ed) Vitbok om utveckling av Ålands självbestämmanderätt. Ålands Framtid r.f, Mariehamn
Buchanan A (2006) Uncoupling secession from nationalism and intrastate autonomy from secession. In: Hannum H, Babbitt EF (eds) Negotiating self-determination. Lexington Books, Oxford
Burgess M (1993) Federalism and federation: a reappraisal. In: Burgess M, Gagnon A-G (eds) Comparative federalism and federation – competing traditions and future directions. University of Toronto Press, Toronto
Burgess M, Gagnon A-G (eds) (1993) Comparative federalism and federation – competing traditions and future directions. University of Toronto Press, Toronto
Carr R (1984) Puerto Rico: a colonial experiment. Vintage Books, New York
Chan J (2010) Asymmetry in the face of heavily disproportionate power relations: Hong Kong. In: Weller M, Nobbs K (eds) Asymmetric autonomy and the settlement of ethnic conflicts. University of Pennsylvania Press, Philadelphia
Chan JMM, Fu HL, Ghai Y (2000) Hong Kong's constitutional debate: conflict over interpretation. Hong Kong University Press, Hong Kong
Chang D (2007) The imperatives of one country, two systems: one country before two systems? Hong Kong Law J 37(part 2):351–362
Chen AHY (2004) The constitutional controversy of Spring 2004. Hong Kong Law J 34(part 2):215–225
Chen AHY (2005) The fate of the constitutional reform proposal of October 2005. Hong Kong Law J 35(part 2):537–543
Chen AHY (2008a) A new era in Hong Kong's constitutional history. Hong Kong Law J 38(part 1):1–3
Chen AHY (2008b) The controversial appointment of under secretaries and political assistants in 2008. Hong Kong Law J 38(part 2):325–331
Chen AHY (2009) The theory, constitution and practice of autonomy: the case of Hong Kong. In: Costa Oliveira J, Cardinal P (eds) One country, two systems, three legal orders – perspectives of evolution. Essays on Macau's autonomy after the resumption of sovereignty by China. Springer Verlag, Berlin
Cheung PTY (2007) Toward federalism in China? The experience of the Hong Kong Special Administrative Region. In: Baogang H, Galligan B, Inoguchi T (eds) Federalism in Asia. Edward Elgar, Cheltenham
Choy DW, Hualing F (2007) Small circle, entrenched interest: the electoral anomalies of Hong Kong Deputies to the National People's Congress. Hong Kong Law J 37(part 2):579–604
Chunli X (2009) Autonomous legislative power in regional ethnic autonomy of the People's Republic of China: the law and the reality. In: Costa Oliveira J, Cardinal P (eds) One country, two systems, three legal orders – perspectives of evolution. Essays on Macau's autonomy after the resumption of sovereignty by China. Springer Verlag, Berlin

Cole JSR, Denison WN (1964) Tanganyika – the development of its laws and constitution. Int Comp Law Q 13:1512–1515

Cómision Estatal de Elecciones (2008) Divulgación Resultados Electorales. http://196.42.5.130/staticpub/main/ and http://cee.ceepur.org/escrutinio/principal.aspx?Nivel=VI. Accessed 27 Feb 2009

Condor S, Abell J (2006) Vernacular constructions of 'national identity' in post-devolution Scotland and England. In: Wilson J, Stapleton K (eds) Devolution and identity. Ashgate, Aldershot

Davis SR (1978) The Federal Principle – a journey through time in quest of a meaning. University of California Press, Berkeley

Davis MC (2007) Interpreting constitutionalism and democratization in Hong Kong. In: Hualing F, Harris L, Young SNM (eds) Interpreting Hong Kong's basic law – the struggle for coherence. Palgrave Macmillan, New York

de Geer-Hancock Y (1986) Åländskhet. Nationsbygge på fredens öar. Ålands Tidnings-Tryckeri Ab:s förlag, Mariehamn

Diario de Sesiones de la Convencion Constituyente de Puerto Rico, 1951 y 1952 (2003) Edición Conmemorativa, Julio 25, 2003, Tomos 1–4. El Estado Libre Asociado de Puerto Rico, San Juan

Domínguez García F (2009) Autonomy experiences in Europe – a comparative approach: Portugal, Spain and Italy. In: Costa Oliveira J, Cardinal P (eds) One country, two systems, three legal orders – perspectives of evolution. Essays on Macau's autonomy after the resumption of Sovereignty by China. Springer Verlag, Berlin

Dourado W (2006) The consolidation of the union: a basic re-appraisal. In: Peter CM, Othman H (eds) Zanzibar and the union question. Zanzibar Legal Services Centre, Zanzibar

Dowdle MW (2007) Constitutionalism in the shadow of the common law – the dysfunctional interpretive politics of Article 8 of the Hong Kong Basic Law. In: Hualing F, Harris L, Young SNM (eds) Interpreting Hong Kong's Basic Law – the struggle for coherence. Palgrave Macmillan, New York

Drexler EF (2008) Aceh, Indonesia: securing the insecure state. University of Pennsylvania Press, Philadelphia

Duffy Burnett C (2001) A note on the insular cases. In: Duffy Burnett C, Marshall B (eds) Foreign in a domestic sense – Puerto Rico, American expansion, and the constitution. Duke University Press, Durham

Duffy Burnett C (2005) Untied States: American expansion and territorial deannexation. Univ Chic Law Rev 72:797–879

Duffy Burnett C, Marshall B (2001) Between the foreign and the domestic: the doctrine of territorial incorporation, invented and reinvented. In Duffy Burnett C, Marshall B (eds) Foreign in a domestic sense – Puerto Rico, American expansion, and the constitution. Duke University Press, Durham

Eastern Africa Centre for Constitutional Development (2009) Zanzibar: key historical and constitutional developments. http://www.kituochakatiba.co.ug/zanz%20const.htm. Accessed 5 Feb 2010

Eide A (1998) Cultural autonomy: concept, content, history and role in the world order. In: Suksi M (ed) Autonomy: applications and implications. Kluwer Law International, The Hague

Elazar DJ (1987) Exploring federalism. The University of Alabama Press, Tuscaloosa

Elazar DJ (1994) Federal systems of the world – a handbook of federal, confederal and autonomy arrangements, 2nd edn. Stockton, Harlow

Elazar DJ (1998) Covenant & constitutionalism: the great frontier and the matrix of federal democracy. Transaction Publishers, New Brunswick

Eriksson S (2008) The role of the Åland Parliament in EU matters. In: Spiliopoulou Åkermark S (ed) Constitutions, autonomies and the EU. Åland Islands Peace Institute, Mariehamn

European Union Election Observation Mission (2007) Aceh, Indonesia: Governor and Regent/Mayor Elections, 11 December 2006. Final Report of 4 March 2007

Fagerlund N (1993) Ålands folkrättsliga status och EG. Meddelanden från Ålands högskola, Nr 3. Ålands högskola, Mariehamn

Fagerlund N (1997) The special status of the Åland Islands in the European Union. In: Hannikainen L, Horn F (eds) Autonomy and demilitarisation in international law. Kluwer Law International, The Hague

Feng L, Lo PY (2007) One term, two interpretations. In: Hualing F, Harris L, Young SNM (eds) Interpreting Hong Kong's basic law – the struggle for coherence. Palgrave Macmillan, New York

Fitzpatrick D (2008) Culture, ideology and human rights: the case of Indonesia's code of Criminal Procedure. In: Lindsey T (ed) Indonesia: law and society, 2nd edn. The Federation Press, Singapore

Flores Juberías C (1998) Regionalization and autonomy in Spain: the making of the "Estado de las Autonomías". In: Suksi M (ed) Autonomy: applications and implications. Kluwer Law International, The Hague

Folkomröstningarna om anslutning till Europeiska Unionen. Statistik med kommentarer (1994) Ålands statistik- och utredningsbyrå, Rapport nr 1994:4. Ålands statistik- och utredningsbyrå, Mariehamn

Friedrich CJ (1968) Trends of federalism in theory and practice. Pall Mall Press, London

Galligan B (2007) Federalism in Asia. In: Baogang H, Galligan B, Inoguchi T (eds) Federalism in Asia. Edward Elgar, Cheltenham

Gamper A (2004) Austrian federalism and the protection of minorities. In: Tarr GA, Williams RF, Marko J (eds) Federalism, subnational constitutions, and minority rights. Praeger, Westport

Gayim E (1993) The Eritrean question – the conflict between the right to self-determination and the interests of states. Uppsala University, Uppsala

Gee G (2005) Devolution and the courts. In: Hazell R, Rawlings R (eds) Devolution, law making and the constitution. Imprint Academic, Exeter

Ghai Y (1997) Hong Kong's new constitutional order – the resumption of chinese sovereignty and the basic law, 1st edn. Hong Kong University Press, Hong Kong

Ghai Y (1999) Hong Kong's New constitutional order – the resumption of Chinese Sovereignty and the basic law, 2nd edn. Hong Kong University Press, Hong Kong

Ghai Y (2000a) Autonomy regimes in China: coping with ethnic and economic diversity. In: Ghai Y (ed) Autonomy and ethnicity – negotiating competing claims in multi-ethnic states. Cambridge University Press, Cambridge

Ghai Y (2000b) Ethnicity and autonomy: a framework for analysis. In: Ghai Y (ed) Autonomy and ethnicity: negotiating competing claims in multi-ethnic states. Cambridge University Press, Cambridge

Ghai Y (2004) Putting the cat among the pigeons: the politics of the referendum. Hong Kong Law J 34(part 3):433–450

Ghai Y (2007a) The intersection of Chinese law and the common law in the Hong Kong Special Administrative Region: question of technique or politics. Hong Kong Law J 37(part 2):363–406

Ghai Y (2007b) The political economy of interpretation. In: Hualing F, Harris L, Young SNM (eds) Interpreting Hong Kong's basic law – the struggle for coherence. Palgrave Macmillan, New York

Ghai Y (2009) The intersection of Chinese Law and the common law in the special administrative region of Hong Kong: question of technique or politics. In: Costa Oliveira J, Cardinal P (eds) One country, two systems, three legal orders – perspectives of evolution. Essays on Macau's autonomy after the resumption of Sovereignty by China. Springer Verlag, Berlin

Gloag R, Henderson C et al (eds) (2001) The law of Scotland. W. Green/Sweet & Maxwell, Edinburgh

Greer SL (2007) The fragile divergence machine: citizenship, policy divergence and devolution in health policy. In: Trench A (ed) Devolution and power in the United Kingdom. Manchester University Press, Manchester

Guide to Collective Decision-Making (2008) Scottish Government, Edinburgh

Hall RL (ed) (1979) Ethnic autonomy – comparative dynamics: the Americas, Europe and the developing world. Pergamon Press, New York

Hamad M (2007) The right to participate in elections in Zanzibar. Master's Thesis at the University of Oslo, Oslo (unpublished)

Hannikainen L (1993a) Ahvenanmaan itsehallinnon ja ruotsinkielisyyden kansainoikeudelliset perusteet. Åbo Akademin ihmisoikeusinstituutti, Turku

Hannikainen L (1993b) Cultural, linguistic and educational rights in the Åland Islands. An analysis in international law. Publications of the Advisory Board for International Human Rights Affairs, No. 5. Ministry of Foreign Affairs, Helsinki

Hannikainen L (2004) De folkrättsliga grunderna för Ålands självstyrelse och svenskspråkighet. Institutet för mänskliga rättigheter vid Åbo Akademi, Åbo

Hannikainen L (2007) Åland och rätten till självbestämmande – i går, i dag och i morgon. In: Jansson H (ed) Vitbok för utveckling av Ålands självbestämmanderätt. Ålands Framtid r.f, Mariehamn

Hannum H (1990) Autonomy, sovereignty and self-determination: the accommodation of conflicting rights. University of Pennsylvania Press, Philadelphia

Hannum H (ed) (1993) Documents on autonomy and minority rights. Martinus Nijhoff, Dordrecht

Hannum H (1996) Autonomy, sovereignty, and self-determination – the accommodation of conflicting rights, Revisedth edn. University of Pennsylvania Press, Philadelphia

Hannum H, Babbitt EF (eds) (2006) Negotiating self-determination. Lexington Books, Oxford

Hazell R (2005a) Devolution as a legislative partnership. In: Hazell R, Rawlings R (eds) Devolution, law making and the constitution. Imprint Academic, Exeter

Hazell R (2005b) Westminster as a 'three-in-one' legislature for the UK and its devolved territories. In: Hazell R, Rawlings R (eds) Devolution, law making and the constitution. Imprint Academic, Exeter

Hazell R, Rawlings R (2005) Asymmetrical devolution. In: Hazell R, Rawlings R (eds) Devolution, law making and the constitution. Imprint Academic, Exeter

He B, Galligan B, Inoguchi T (eds) (2007) Federalism in Asia. Edward Elgar, Cheltenham

Henig S (2006) Modernising British government – constitutional challenges and federal solutions. Federal Trust for Education and Research, London

Herbert S, Burnside R, Earle M, Edwards T, Foley T, McIver I (2007) Election 2007. http://www.scottish.parliament.uk/business/research,briefings-07/SB07-21.pdf. Accessed 30 Mar 2010

Himsworth C (2006) The Domesticated Executive of Scotland. In: Craig P, Tomkins A (eds) The Executive and Public Law. Oxford University Press, Oxford

Himsworth C (2007) Analysis: presiding officer statements on the competence of bills. EdinLR 11:397–401

Himsworth C (2009) Scotland: The Constitutional Protection of a Mixed Legal System. In: Costa Oliveira J, Cardinal P (eds) One country, two systems, three legal orders - perspectives of evolution. Essays on Macau's autonomy after the resumption of sovereignty by China. Springer Verlag, Berlin

Himsworth CMG, Munro CR (2000) The Scotland Act 1998, 2nd edn. W.Green/Sweet & Maxwell, Edinburgh

Himsworth CMG, O'Neill CM (2003) Scotland's constitution: law and practice. LexisNexis UK, London

Högman G (1981) Ålänningarna och Ålandsfrågan. Opinioner, påverkan och publicistik 1917–1919. Avhandling pro gradu i Nordisk historia vid Åbo Akademi, historiska institutionen, 1981 (unpublished)

Högskoleverkets Avrapportering (2009) Uppdrag att utreda vissa frågor om urval till högskoleutbildning på grundval av betyg 2009-09-29 (Reg. nr. 121-3561-09). Högskoleverket, Stockholm

Holleman JF, Sonius HWJ (eds) (1981) van Wollenhoven on Indonesian Adat Law. Martinus Nijhoff, The Hague

Hong Kong 2007 (2008) Hong Kong SAR 10th Anniversary Special Edition. Information Services Department of the Hong Kong SAR Government, Hong Kong

Hong Kong 2008 (2009) Hong Kong SAR Yearbook, at http://www.yearbook.gov.hk/2008/en/pdf/E01.pdf (accessed on 18 August 2009)

Horlemann R (2003) Hong Kong's transition to Chinese Rule. RoutledgeCurzon, London

Hsu BFC (2004) Judicial independence under the basic law. Hong Kong Law J 34(part 1):279–302

Hualing F, Choy DW (2007) Of iron or rubber? People's deputies of Hong Kong to the National People's Congress. In: Hualing F, Harris L, Young SNM (eds) Interpreting Hong Kong's basic law – the struggle for coherence. Palgrave Macmillan, New York

Hualing F, Petersen CJ, Young SNM (2005a) Chronology and abbreviations. In: Hualing F, Petersen DJ, Young SNM (eds) National security and fundamental freedoms – Hong Kong's Article 23 under scrutiny. Hong Kong University Press, Hong Kong

Hualing Fu, Petersen CJ, Young SNM (2005b) National security and fundamental freedoms – Hong Kong's Article 23 Under Scrutiny. Hong Kong University Press, Hong Kong

Hualing F, Harris L, Young S (2007) Introduction. In: Hualing F, Harris L, Young SNM (eds) Interpreting Hong Kong's basic law – the struggle for coherence. Palgrave Macmillan, New York

Huang J (2009) Interaction and integration between the legal systems of Hong Kong, Macao and Mainland China 50 years after their return to China. In: Costa Oliveira J, Cardinal P (eds) One country, two systems, three legal orders – perspectives of evolution. Essays on Macau's autonomy after the resumption of Sovereignty by China. Springer Verlag, Berlin

Husain F, Shabab S, Siadari EE (2007) To see the unseen: scenes behind the Aceh Peace Treaty. Health & Hospital Indonesia, Jakarta

International Development Law Organisation (2008) Judicial assessment of political parties' programs in Aceh towards the 2009 General Election. http://www.aceh-eye.org/data_files/english_format/ngo/ngo_idlo/ngo_idlo.asp. Accessed 11 June 2009

International Development Law Organization (2008) A brief account on the Qanun on education in Aceh. http://www.aceh-eye.org/data_files/english_format/ngo/ngo_idlo/ngo_idlo_2008_11_00.pdf. Accessed 11 June 2009

International Development Law Organization (2008) Judicial review of *Al-Qur'an* reading test for candidates for members of the parliament' of 6 September 2008. http://www.aceh-eye.org/data_files/english_format/aceh_politic/aceh_politic_other/aceh_politic_other_2008_09_06.pdf. Accessed 11 June 2009

International Development Law Organization (2008) Review on the revisions being made to the three Qanuns on Jinayah. http://www.aceheye.org/data_files/english_format/issues/issues_women/women_2008_11_01.pdf. Accessed 11 June 2008

Jääskinen N (2003) EU:s behörighet och Åland—Utredningsman Niilo Jääskinens utredning. Statsrådets kanslis publikationsserie 7/2003. Statsrådets Kansli, Helsingfors

Jääskinen N (2006) Selvitys eräistä Ahvenanmaan maakuntalakien valvontaan liittyvistä erityiskysymyksistä – Utredning om vissa specialfrågor som gäller kontrollen av åländska landskapslagar. Oikeusministeriön Julkaisuja 2006:2. Oikeusministeriö, Helsinki

Jeffery C, Palmer R (2007) The European Union, devolution and power. In: Trench A (ed) Devolution and power in the United Kingdom. Manchester University Press, Manchester

Jiménez Polanco J (1998) Referéndums y plebiscitos. In: Anderson RW (ed) Política Electoral en Puerto Rico. Editoral Plaza Mayor, San Juan

Jyränki A (1995) Autonomy of the Åland Islands: a federal element in the constitution of a unitary state? In: Pohjolainen K (ed) Constitutionalism in Finland – reality and perspectives. The Finnish Society of Constitutional Law, Helsinki

Kalijarvi T (1936) The problem of Memel. Am J Int Law 30:204–215

Kalijarvi T (1937) The Memel Statute – its origin, legal nature, and observation to the present day. Robert Hale, London

Khamis Bakary A (2006) The union and the Zanzibar constitutions. In: Peter CM, Othman H (eds) Zanzibar and the union question. Zanzibar Legal Services Centre, Zanzibar

King P (1982) Federalism and federation. Croom Helm, London

King P (1993) Federation and representation. In: Burgess M, Gagnon A-G (eds) Comparative federalism and federation – competing traditions and future directions. University of Toronto Press, Toronto

Kirkby C, Murray C (2010) Elusive autonomy in Sub-Saharan Africa. In: Weller M, Nobbs K (eds) Asymmetric autonomy and the settlement of ethnic conflicts. University of Philadelphia Press, Philadelphia

Koskelo P (2009) The role of the Supreme Court of Finland in issues relating to the division of powers between the Finnish State and Åland. In: Spiliopoulou Åkermark S (ed) The right of domicile on Åland. The Åland Islands Peace Institute & the Åland Parliament, Mariehamn

Kurland PB, Lerner R (eds) (2000) The founders' constitution, vol 1, Chap. 13, Document 7. http://press-pubs.uchicago.edu/founders/documents/v1ch13s7.html. Accessed 18 Nov 2010

Kymlicka W (2007) Multicultural Odysseys – navigating the new international politics of diversity. Oxford University Press, Oxford

Laffin M, Shaw E, Taylor G (2007) The parties and intergovernmental relations. In: Trench A (ed) Devolution and power in the United Kingdom. Manchester University Press, Manchester

Landskapsregeringens berättelse 2009 (2010) Ålands landskapsregering, Mariehamn

Lapidoth R (1997) Autonomy – flexible solutions to ethnic conflicts. United States Institute of Peace Press, Washington

Légaré A (2008) Canada's experiment with aboriginal self-determination in Nunavut: from vision to illusion. Int J Minor Group Rights 15:335–367

Leopold PM (1998) Autonomy and the British constitution. In: Suksi M (ed) Autonomy: applications and implications. Kluwer Law International, Dordrecht

Leung E (1999) The new constitutional order under the basic law of 1 November 1999: "Acting under this Article 160 of the Basic Law, the NPCSC in February 1997 adopted all the laws previously in force in Hong Kong, save for 24 Ordinances which were found (in whole or in part) to contravene the Basic Law." A speech. http://www.doj.gov.hk/eng/archive/doc/sj011199e.rtf. Accessed 14 Jan 2010

Leung Mei-fun P (2006) The Hong Kong basic law: hybrid of common law and Chinese law. LexisNexis, Hong Kong

Lijphart A (1985) Non-majoritarian democracy: a comparison of federal and consociational themes. Publius 15:3–15

Lindbäck P (2009) Reflections and discussion. In: Spiliopoulou Åkermark S (ed) The right of domicile on Åland. The Åland Islands Peace Institute and the Åland Parliament, Mariehamn

Lindh K (1984) Det åländska samhället. Ab Svenska Läromedel, Esbo

Lindsey T (2008) Constitutional reform in Indonesia: muddling towards democracy. In: Lindsey T (ed) Indonesia: law and society, 2nd edn. The Federation Press, Singapore

Lindsey T, Achmad Santosa M (2008) The trajectory of law reform in Indonesia: a short overview of legal systems and change in Indonesia. In: Lindsey T (ed) Indonesia: law and society, 2nd edn. The Federation Press, Singapore

Lo PY (2004) Masters of one's own court. Hong Kong Law J 34(part 1):47–65

Lo PY (2007) Rethinking judicial reference – barricades at the gateway? In: Hualing F, Harris L, Young SNM (eds) Interpreting Hong Kong's basic law – the struggle for coherence. Palgrave Macmillan, New York

Local Government Boundary Commission for Scotland (1995) Scottish Local Authority Areas 1995 onwards. http://www.lgbc-scotland.gov.uk/maps/LAs_Scotland_1995_on.pdf. Accessed 20 Mar 2009

Maalim MJ (2006) The Union between Tanganyika and Zanzibar and the right of secession under international law. In: Peter CM, Othman H (eds) Zanzibar and the union question. Zanzibar Legal Services Centre, Zanzibar

Máiz R, Losada A (2011) The erosion of regional powers in the Spanish 'State of Autonomies'. In: Requejo F, Nagel K-J (eds) Federalism beyond federations. Asymmetry and processes of resymmetrisation in Europe. Ashgate, Farnham

Maliyamkono TL (2000a) What next? In: Maliyamkono TL (ed) The political plight of Zanzibar. TEMA Publishers Company, Dar es Salaam

Maliyamkono TL (ed) (2000b) The political plight of Zanzibar. TEMA Publishers Company, Dar es Salaam

Marko J (1995) Autonomie und integration. Rechtsinstitute des Nationaltätenrechts im funktionalen Vergleich. Böhlau Verlag, Wien

Marsden S (2006) Regional autonomy, judicial criticism and the 2005 interpretation: judicial independence in Hong Kong compromised again? Hong Kong Law J 36(part 1):117–142

Mattern J (1920) The employment of the plebiscite in the determination of sovereignty. Johns Hopkins University Studies in Historical and Political Science, Departments of History, Political Economy, and Political Science. Series XXXVIII, No. 3. The Johns Hopkins Press, Baltimore

McFadden J, Lazarowicz M (2002) The Scottish Parliament – an introduction. LexisNexis UK, London

McGarry J (2010) Asymmetric autonomy in the United Kingdom. In: Weller M, Nobbs K (eds) Asymmetric autonomy and the settlement of ethnic conflicts. University of Pennsylvania Press, Philadelphia

Meléndez E (1998) Partidos y elecciones. In: Anderson RW (ed) Política Electoral en Puerto Rico. Editoral Plaza Mayor, San Juan

Memorandum of Understanding and Supplementary Agreements between the United Kingdom Government Scottish Ministers, the Cabinet of the National Assembly for Wales and the Northern Ireland Executive Committee. Presented to Parliament by the Deputy Prime Minister by Command of Her Majesty, December 2001/CM 5240.

Miller MA (2009) Rebellion and reform in Indonesia – Jakarta's security and autonomy policies in Aceh. Routledge, London

Mitchell J (2007) The United Kingdom as a state of unions: unity of government, equality of political rights and diversity of institutions. In: Trench A (ed) Devolution and power in the United Kingdom. Manchester University Press, Manchester

Modeen T (1973) De folkrättsliga garantierna för bevarandet av Ålandsöarnas nationella karaktär. Meddelanden från Institutet för samhällsforskning upprätthållet av statsvetenskapliga fakulteten vid Åbo Akademi, Ser. A, No. 76. Åbo Akademi, Åbo

Morris RJ (2007) Forcing the dance – interpreting the Hong Kong basic law dialectically. In: Hualing F, Harris L, Young SNM (eds) Interpreting Hong Kong's basic law – the struggle for coherence. Palgrave Macmillan, New York

Mushkat R (1997) One country, two international legal personalities – the case of Hong Kong. Hong Kong University Press, Hong Kong

Myntti K (1996) The protection of persons belonging to national minorities in Finland, 4th edn. Publications of the Advisory Board of International Human Rights Affairs. Ministry of Foreign Affairs, Helsinki

Myntti K, Scheinin M (1997) The right of domicile in the Åland Islands in the light of human rights treaties and the European integration process. In: Hannikainen L, Horn F (eds) Autonomy and demilitarisation in international law: the Åland Islands in a changing Europe. Kluwer Law International, The Hague

Nauclér E (2005) Autonomy and multilevel governance – experiences in Nordic and Continental European cooperation. In: Weller M, Wolff S (eds) Autonomy, self-governance and conflict resolution – innovative approaches to institutional design in divided societies. Routledge, London

Navaratna-Bandara AM (1995) The management of ethnic secessionist conflict – the big neighbour syndrome. Darthmouth, Aldershot

Negash T (1997) Eritrea and Ethiopia – the federal experience. Transaction Publishers, New Brunswick

Neuman GL (2001) Constitutionalism and individual rights. In: Duffy Burnett C, Marshall B (eds) Foreign in a domestic sense – Puerto Rico, American Expansion, and the Constitution. Duke University Press, Durham

Nordquist K-Å (1998) Autonomy as a conflict-solving mechanism – an overview. In: Suksi M (ed) Autonomy: applications and implications. Kluwer Law International, Dordrecht

Okbazghi Y (1991) Eritrea, a pawn in world politics. University of Florida Press, Gainesville

Olivetti M (2009) The special administrative regions of the PRC in comparison with autonomous regions models. In: Costa Oliveira J, Cardinal P (eds) One country, two systems, three legal orders – perspectives of evolution. Essays on Macau's autonomy after the resumption of sovereignty by China. Springer Verlag, Berlin

Oquendo ÁR (2001) Puerto Rican national identity. In: Duffy Burnett C, Marshall B (eds) Foreign in a domestic sense – Puerto Rico, American Expansion, and the Constitution. Duke University Press, Durham

Othman H (2006) Tanzania: the withering away of the union? In: Peter CM, Othman H (eds) Zanzibar and the union question. Zanzibar Legal Services Centre, Zanzibar

Page A (2005) A parliament that is different? In: Hazell R, Rawlings R (eds) Devolution, law making and the constitution. Imprint Academic, Exeter

Palermo F (2004) Asymmetric, "Quasi-Federal" Regionalism and the Protection of Minorities: The Case of Italy. In: Tarr GA, Williams RF, Marko J (eds) Federalism, subnational constitutions, and minority rights. Praeger, Westport

Palmgren S (1995) Landskapet Ålands lagstiftning. Nord Administrativt Tidskr 1(1995):22–32

Palmgren S (1997) The autonomy of the Åland Islands in the constitutional law of Finland. In: Hannikainen L, Horn F (eds) Autonomy and demilitarisation in international law: the Åland Islands in a changing Europe. Kluwer Law International, London

Perea JF (2001) Fulfilling manifest destiny: conquest, race and the *Insular Cases*. In: Duffy Burnett C, Marshall B (eds) Foreign in a domestic sense – Puerto Rico, American Expansion, and the Constitution. Duke University Press, Durham

Persson V (2005) Rättsliga ramar för gränsöverskridande samarbete – Förvaltningsmyndigheters internationella avtalsförhållanden. Juristförlaget, Lund

Peter CM, Sikand I (eds) (2006) The Judiciary in Zanzibar. Zanzibar Legal Services Centre Publication Series, Book No. 2. Zanzibar Legal Services Centre, Zanzibar Town

Petersen CJ (2007) Embracing universal standards? The role of international human rights treaties in Hong Kong's constitutional jurisprudence. In: Hualing F, Harris L, Young SNM (eds) Interpreting Hong Kong's basic law – the struggle for coherence. Palgrave Macmillan, New York

Petersen CJ (2008) China's ratification of the convention on the rights of persons with disabilities: the implications for Hong Kong. Hong Kong Law J 38(part 3):611–644

Pilkington C (2002) Devolution in Britain today. Manchester University Press, Manchester

Plieg E-A (1962) Das Memelland 1920–1939: Deutsche Autonomiebestrebungen im litauischen Gesamtstaat. Holzner-Verlag, Würzburg

Po Jen Y (2007) Constitutional review under the basic law: the rise, retreat and resurgence of judicial power in Hong Kong. Hong Kong Law J 37(part 2):449–474

Protsyk O (2010) Gagauz Autonomy in Moldova: The Real and the Virtual in Post-Soviet State Design. In: Weller M, Nobbs K (eds) Asymmetric Autonomy and the Settlement of Ethnic Conflicts. University of Pennsylvania Press, Philadelphia, Oxford

Puerto Rico Democracy Act of 2007 (2007) Report together with Additional Views [To accompany H.R. 900] of 22 April 2008 by Mr. Rahall, from the Committee on Natural Resources, committed to the Committee of the Whole House on the State of the Union. http://frwebgate.access.gpo.gov/cgi-bin/getdoc.cgi?dbname=110%5Fcong%5Freports&docid=f:hr597.pdf. Accessed 13 Feb 2009

Reid A (2007) Indonesia's post-revolutionary aversion to federalism. In: Baogang H, Galligan B, Inoguchi T (eds) Federalism in Asia. Edward Elgar, Cheltenham

Rivera Ramos E (2001) Deconstructing colonialism: the "unincorporated territory" as a category of domination. In: Duffy Burnett C, Marshall B (eds) Foreign in a domestic sense – Puerto Rico, American Expansion, and the Constitution. Duke University Press, Durham

Rivera Ramos E (2007) American Colonialism in Puerto Rico – the judicial and social legacy. Markus Wiener Publishers, Princeton

Robinson J (1934a) Kommentar der Konvention über das Memelgebiet, Band I. Verlag "Spaudos Fondas", Kaunas

Robinson J (1934b) Kommentar der Konvention über das Memelgebiet, Band II. Verlag "Spaudos Fondas", Kaunas

Rogge A (1928) Die Verfassung des Memelgebiets – Ein Kommentar zur Memelkonvention. Deutsche Rundschau G.m.b.H, Berlin

Rolla G (2009) The development of asymmetric regionalism and the principle of autonomy in the new constitutional systems: a comparative approach. In: Costa Oliveira J, Cardinal P (eds) One country, two systems, three legal orders – perspectives of evolution. Essays on Macau's autonomy after the resumption of sovereignty by China. Springer Verlag, Berlin

Rosas A (1997) The Åland Islands as a demilitarised and neutralised zone. In: Hannikainen L, Horn F (eds) Autonomy and demilitarisation in international law: the Åland Islands in a changing Europe. Kluwer Law International, The Hague

Rosas A, Armati L (2010) EU Constitutional law – an Introduction. Hart Publishing, Oxford

Rosas A, Suksi M (1996) Finnish nationality law. In: Nascimbene B (ed) Nationality laws in the European Union. Butterworths/Giuffrè Editore, Milano

Rosselló P (2005) The unfinished business of American Democracy. Public Policy Institute of the Ana G. Méndez University System, San Juan

Rossum RA, Tarr GA (2007) American Constitutional Law – volume I: the structure of the government. Thomson Wadsworth, Belmont

Rotkirch H (2003) A peace institute on the war-path: the application of the treaty on open skies to the neutralized and demilitarized Åland Islands and the powers of the Åland autonomy. In: Petman J, Klabbers J (eds) Nordic cosmopolitanism – essays in international law for Martti Koskenniemi. Brill Academic Publishers, Leiden

Rotunda RD, Nowak JE (1999) Treatise on constitutional law – substance and procedure, vol 2, 3rd edn. West Group, St. Paul

Rugalabamu CA (2000) Electoral administration during the 1995 general elections in Zanzibar. In: Maliyamkono TL (ed) The political plight of Zanzibar. TEMA Publishers Company, Dar es Salaam

Ruiz Vieytez EJ (2004) Federalism, subnational constitutional arrangements and the protection of minorities in Spain. In: Tarr GA, Williams RF, Marko J (eds) Federalism, subnational constitutions, and minority rights. Praeger, Westport

Salamun M (2005) Democratic Governance in International Territorial Administration – institutional prerequisites for democratic governance in the constitutional documents of territories administered by international organisations. Nomos Verlagsgesellschaft, Baden-Baden

Salim A (2008) Challenging the secular state – the islamization of law in modern Indonesia. University of Hawai'i Press, Honolulu

Salim (2009) Dynamic legal pluralism in Indonesia: the shift in plural legal orders of contemporary Aceh. Working Paper No. 110 of Max Planck Institute for Social Anthropology Working Papers. Max Planck Institute for Social Anthropology, Halle/Saale

Schmit L (2008) Decentralisation and legal reform in Indonesia: the pendulum effect. In: Lindsey T (ed) Indonesia: law and society, 2nd edn. The Federation Press, Singapore

Scotland's Future (2010) Scotland's future: draft referendum (Scotland) bill consultation paper. The Scottish Government, Edinburgh. http://www.scotland.gov.uk/referendum. Accessed 18 Mar 2010

Scottish Elections 2007 (2007) The independent review of the Scottish Parliamentary and local government elections 3 May 2007. Electoral Commission, London

Scottish Ministerial Code (2008) A code of conduct and guidance on procedures for Members of the Scottish Government and Junior Scottish Ministers. Scottish Government, Edinburgh

Serving Scotland Better (2009) Serving Scotland Better: Scotland and the United Kingdom in the 21st Century. Final Report – June 2009 by the Commission on Scottish Devolution. Commission on Scottish Devolution, Edinburgh

Shivji IG (2006) Sovereignty and statehood in Zanzibar in the Union: Critical Comments on *S.M. Z. v. Machano Khamis Ali & 17 Others*. In: Peter CM, Othman H (eds) Zanzibar and the union question. Zanzibar Legal Services Centre, Zanzibar

Shivji IG (2008) Pan-Africanism or Pragmatism? Lessons of the Tanganyika – Zanzibar Union. Mkuki na Nyota Publishers, Dar es Salaam

Silverström S (2008a) The competence of autonomous entities in the international arena – with special reference to the Åland Islands in the European Union. Int J Minor Group Rights 15:259–271

Silverström S (2008b) Implementation of EU legislation in the Åland Islands. In: Spiliopoulou Åkermark S (ed) Constitutions, autonomies and the EU. Åland Islands Peace Institute, Mariehamn

Sisk TD (1997) Power sharing and international mediation in ethnic conflicts. Carnegie Commission on Preventing Deadly Conflict and the United States Institute of Peace, New York

Sjölund A-L (2009) Acquisition of the right of domicile on Åland upon application. In: Spiliopoulou Åkermark S (ed) The right of domicile on Åland. The Åland Islands Peace Institute and the Åland Parliament, Mariehamn

Skurbaty ZA (ed) (2005) Beyond one-dimensional state: an emerging right to autonomy? Martinus Nijhoff, Leiden

Smith RM (2001) The bitter roots of Puerto Rican citizenship. In: Duffy Burnett C, Marshall B (eds) Foreign in a domestic sense – Puerto Rico, American Expansion, and the Constitution. Duke University Press, Durham

Sofyan Gueci R (1999) Verfassungsstaat, traditionelles Recht und Genossenschaftstheorie in Indonesien. Lang, Frankfurt

Spencer JH (1984) Ethiopia at bay – a personal account of the Haile Sellassie years. Reference Publications, Algonac

Spiliopoulou Åkermark S (2007) Ålands demilitarisering och neutralisering: gammal skåpmat eller levande folkrätt? In: Jansson H (ed) Vitbok för utveckling av Ålands självbestämmanderätt. Ålands Framtid r.f, Mariehamn

Spiliopoulou Åkermark A (1997) The Åland Islands in international law and cooperation: the legal capacity of an autonomous region. In: Hannikainen L, Horn F (eds) Autonomy and demilitarisation in international law: the Åland Islands in a changing Europe. Kluwer Law International, The Hague

Spiliopoulou Åkermark A (1998) The procedural position of autonomous regions before international judicial and quasi-judicial organs. In: Markku S (ed) Autonomy: applications and implications. Kluwer Law International, The Hague

Spiliopoulou Åkermark S (2009) The development of the concept of the right of domicile: from the Åland Agreement to the 1951 Autonomy Act – and today? In: Spiliopoulou Åkermark S (ed) The right of domicile on Åland. The Åland Islands Peace Institute and the Åland Parliament, Mariehamn

Suksi M (1993) Bringing in the people – a comparison of constitutional forms and practices of the referendum. Martinus Nijhoff, Dordrecht

Suksi M (ed) (1998a) Autonomy: applications and implications. Kluwer Law International, Dordrecht

Suksi M (1998b) On the entrenchment of autonomy. In: Suksi M (ed) Autonomy: applications and implications. Kluwer Law International, Dordrecht

Suksi M (2002a) Autonomy by international decision: the cases of the Åland Islands and Kosovo. In: Jansson H, Salminen J (eds) The Second Åland Islands question—autonomy or independence. Julius Sundbloms Minnesstiftelse, Mariehamn

Suksi M (2002b) Good governance in the electoral process. In: Sano H-O, Alfredsson G (eds) Human rights and good governance. Kluwer Law International, Dordrecht

Suksi M (2004) On the voluntary re-definition of the status of a sub-state entity: the historical example of Finland and the modern example of Serbia and Montenegro. Faroese Law Rev 4:33–49

Suksi M (2005a) Keeping the lid on the secession kettle – a review of legal interpretations concerning claims of self-determination by minority populations. Int J Minor Group Rights 12:189–226

Suksi M (2005b) Participation in development through "emergence into any other political status": with special reference to Africa. In: Scheinin M, Suksi M (eds) Empowerment, participation, accountability and non-discrimination: operationalising a human rights-based approach to development. Human Rights in Development Yearbook 2002. Martinus Nijhoff, Leiden

Suksi M (2005c) The protection of the rights of minorities by means of autonomy: the cases of the Åland Islands and Kosovo. In: Skurbaty Z (ed) Beyond one-dimensional state: an emerging right to autonomy? Martinus Nijhoff Publishers, Leiden

Suksi M (2005d) Ålands konstitution. Åbo Akademis förlag, Åbo

Suksi M (2006) Ålands ställning – rapport till Nordiska ministerrådets sekretariat med anledning av kartläggning av de självstyrande områdenas ställning i det nordiska samarbetet. In: De självstyrande områdena och det nordiska samarbetet – Generalsekreterarens kartläggning. ANP 2006:743. Nordiska ministerrådet, Köpenhamn

Suksi M (2007) Sub-national issues: local government reform, re-districting administrative jurisdictions, and the Åland Islands in the European union. Eur Public Law 13:379–406

Suksi M (2008a) Functional autonomy: the case of Finland with some notes on the basis of international human rights law and comparisons with other cases. Int J Minor Group Rights 15:195–225

Suksi M (2008b) Land rights and real property in the Nordic countries: a tentative sketch of an argument with some Nordic examples. Eur Ethnica 65:71–81

Suksi M (2008c) Stegvisa förändringar i Ålandsöverenskommelsens innehåll? In: Aarto M, Vartiainen M (eds) Oikeus kansainvälisessä maailmassa – Ilkka Saraviidan juhlakirja. Edita, Helsinki

Suksi M (2009) Governmental accountability in autonomies: Åland Islands in comparison with select autonomies in Europe and elsewhere. In: Bakardjieva Engelbrekt A, Nergelius J (eds) New Directions in Comparative Law. Edward Elgar, Cheltenham, Northampton

Suksi M (2011) Autonomy [April 2010]. In: Wolfrum R (ed) Max Planck encyclopedia of public international law. Oxford University Press, Oxford

Szeftel M (1976) The Russian constitution of April 23, 1906. Political institutions of the Duma Monarchy. Les éditions de la librairie encyclopédique, Bruxelles

Tanzania Human Rights Report (2009) Tanzania Human Rights Report 2008, Incorporating Specific Part on Zanzibar. Legal and Human Rights Centre, Dar es Salaam

Tarr GA (2005) Constitutional origins, structure, and change. In: Kincaid J, Tarr GA (eds) Constitutional origins, structure, and change in federal countries. McGill-Queen's University Press, London

Tarr GA, Williams RF, Marko J (eds) (2004) Federalism, subnational constitutions, and minority rights. Praeger, Westport

The 2004 European Parliament Elections in the United Kingdom (2004) The official report by the Electoral Commission. Electoral Commission, London 2004. http://www.electoralcommission.org.uk/__data/assets/electoral_commission_pdf_file/0018/13167/ECPartElections2004_15438-11422__E__N__S__W__.pdf. Accessed 20 Mar 2009

The Aaland Islands Question (1920) Report of the Committee of Jurists. Official Journal of the League of Nations, Special Supplement No. 3, October 1920

The Aaland Islands Question (1921) Report submitted to the Council of the League of Nations by the Commission of Rapporteurs. Document du Conseil B7, 21/68/106, of 16 April 1921

The Constitution of the United States of America – Analysis of Cases Decided by the Supreme Court of the United States to June 28, 2002 (2004) U.S. Government Printing Office, Washington

Thornburgh R (2001) Puerto Rican separatism and United States Federalism. In Duffy Burnett C, Marshall B (eds) Foreign in a domestic sense – Puerto Rico, American Expansion, and the Constitution. Duke University Press, Durham

Thornburgh D (2007) Puerto Rico's future – a time to decide. Center for Strategic and International Studies, Washington

Töpperwien N (2004) Participation in the decision-making process as a means of group accommodation. In: Tarr GA, Williams RF, Marko J (eds) Federalism, subnational constitutions, and minority rights. Praeger, Westport

Torode N (2008) National cultural autonomy in the Russian Federation: implementation and impact. Int J Minor Group Rights 15:179–193

Torruella JR (2007) The insular cases: the establishment of a regime of political apartheid. Univ Pa J Int Law 2:283–347

Treaties, Conventions, International Acts, Protocols and Agreements between the United States of America and Other Powers 1776–1909, vol. II (1910). Government Printing Office, Washington

Trench A (2007a) Conclusion: devolution and the territorial distribution of power in the UK. In: Trench A (ed) Devolution and power in the United Kingdom. Manchester University Press, Manchester

Trench A (2007b) The framework of devolution: the formal structure of devolved power. In: Trench A (ed) Devolution and power in the United Kingdom. Manchester University Press, Manchester

Trench A (2007c) Introduction: territory, devolution and power in the United Kingdom. In: Trench A (ed) devolution and power in the United Kingdom. Manchester University Press, Manchester

Trench A (2007d) The politics of devolution finance and the power of the treasury. In: Trench A (ed) Devolution and power in the United Kingdom. Manchester University Press, Manchester

Trench A (2007e) Washing dirty linen in private: the processes of intergovernmental relations and the resolution of disputes. In: Trench A (ed) Devolution and power in the United Kingdom. Manchester University Press, Manchester

Trench A, Jarman H (2007) The practical outcomes of devolution: policy-making across the UK. In: Trench A (ed) Devolution and power in the United Kingdom. Manchester University Press, Manchester

Trías Monge J (1997) Puerto Rico – the trials of the oldest colony in the world. Yale University Press, New Haven

Trías Monge J (2001) Injustice According to law. In: Duffy Burnett C, Marshall B (eds) Foreign in a domestic sense – Puerto Rico, American Expansion, and the Constitution. Duke University Press, Durham

Veiter T (1984) Die Entwicklung des Selbstbestimmungsrechts. In: Blumenwitz D, Meissner B (eds) Das Selbstbestimmungsrecht der Völker und die deutsche Frage. Staats- und völkerrechtliche Abhandlungen der Studiengruppe für Politik und Völkerrecht. Band 2. Verlag Wissenschaft und Politik, Köln

von Bonsdorff G (1950) Självstyrelsetanken I finlandssvensk politik åren 1917–1923. Finska vetenskaps-societeten, Helsingfors

von Freytagh-Loringhoven (1935) Das litauische Statutgerichts-Gezetz vom 13. März 1935. Zeitschrift für osteuropäische Recht 10:520–525

Wambaugh S (1933) Plebiscites since the World War, with a collection of official documents, vols 1 and 2. Carnegie Endowment for International Peace, Washington

Watts R (2007) The United Kingdom as a federalised or regionalised union. In: Trench A (ed) Devolution and power in the United Kingdom. Manchester University Press, Manchester

Watts RL (2008) Comparing federal systems. McGill-Queen's University Press, London

Weiss N (2004) The protection of minorities in a federal state: the case of Germany. In: Tarr GA, Williams RF, Marko J (eds) Federalism, subnational constitutions, and minority rights. Praeger, Westport

Weiyun X (2001) One country, two systems – an account of the drafting of the Hong Kong basic law. Peking University Press, Beijing

Weller M (2010a) Introduction. In: Weller M, Nobbs K (eds) Asymmetric Autonomy and the Settlement of Ethnic Conflicts. University of Pennsylvania Press, Philadelphia

Weller M (2010b) Conclusion. In: Weller M, Nobbs K (eds) Asymmetric autonomy and the settlement of ethnic conflicts. University of Pennsylvania Press, Philadelphia

Weller M, Nobbs K (eds) (2010) Asymmetric autonomy and the settlement of ethnic conflicts. University of Pennsylvania Press, Philadelphia

Weller M, Wolff S (eds) (2005) Autonomy, self-governance and conflict resolution – innovative approaches to institutional design in divided societies. Routledge, London

Wesley-Smith P (2004) Judges and judicial power under the Hong Kong basic law. Hong Kong Law J 34(part 1):83–103

Westerlund L (1993) Länsförvaltningen. Förvaltningshistoriekommittén & Tryckericentralen, Helsingfors

Wheare KC (1964) Federal government. Oxford University Press, New York

Williams R (2009) Exclusing to protect: land rights and minority protection in international law. In: Spiliopoulou Åkermark S (ed) The right of domicile on Åland. The Åland Islands Peace Institute and the Åland Parliament, Mariehamn

Williams RF, Tarr GA (2004) Subnational constitutional space: a view from the states, provinces, regions, länder, and cantons. In: Tarr GA, Williams RF, Marko J (eds) Federalism, subnational constitutions, and minority rights. Praeger, Westport

Wilson J, Stapleton K (2006a) Introduction. In: Wilson J, Stapleton K (eds) Devolution and identity. Ashgate, Hampshire

Wilson J, Stapleton S (eds) (2006b) Devolution and identity. Ashgate, Hampshire

Winetrobe BK (2005) A partnership of the parliaments? Scottish law making under the Sewel Convention at Westminster and Holyrood. In: Hazell R, Rawlings R (eds) Devolution, law making and the constitution. Imprint Academic, Exeter

Wolff S (2010) Cases of asymmetrical territorial autonomy. In: Weller M, Nobbs K (eds) Asymmetric autonomy and the settlement of ethnic conflicts. University of Pennsylvania Press, Philadelphia

Xiaoping D (2004) On "One Country, Two Systems". Joint Publishing (H.K.), Hong Kong

Yang X (2008) Legislative interpretations by the standing committee of the National People's Congress in China. Hong Kong Law J 38(part 1):255–286

Yiu-chung W (2004) "One country" and "two systems": where is the line? In: Yiu-chung W (ed) "One country, two systems" in crisis. Lexington Books, Lanham

Yongnian Z (2007) China's de facto federalism. In: Baogang H, Galligan B, Inoguchi T (eds) Federalism in Asia. Edward Elgar, Cheltenham

Young SNM (2004) Restricting basic law rights in Hong Kong. Hong Kong Law J 34(part 1):109–132

Young SNM (2007) Legislative history, original intent, and the interpretation of the basic law. In: Hualing F, Harris L, Young SNM (eds) Interpreting Hong Kong's basic law – the struggle for coherence. Palgrave Macmillan, New York

Young SNM, Law A (2006) Privileged to vote: inequalities and anomalies of the FC-system. In: Loh C, *Civic Exchange* (eds) Functional constituencies – a unique feature of the Hong Kong Legislative Council. Hong Kong University Press, Hong Kong

Zanzibar Referendum (2010) Afr Res Bull Polit Soc Cultural Ser 47:18503

Index

Q

R

S

T